Charles T. Horngren Stanford University

Walter T. Harrison, Jr. Baylor University

W. Morley Lemon University of Waterloo

Peter R. Norwood Langara College

Jo-Ann L. Johnston British Columbia Institute of Technology

CANADIAN SEVENTH EDITION

VOLUME ONE

ACCOUNTING

PEARSON
Prentice Hall

Toronto

Library and Archives Canada Cataloguing in Publication

Accounting / Charles T. Horngren ... [et al.]. — Canadian 7th ed.
Includes index.
Canadian ed. published under title: Accounting / Charles T. Horngren,
   Walter T. Harrison, W. Morley Lemon ; with Carol E. Dilworth
ISBN-13: 978-0-13-201894-4 (v. 1)
ISBN-10: 0-13-201894-2 (v. 1)
ISBN-13: 978-0-13-201895-1 (v. 2)
ISBN-10: 0-13-201895-0 (v. 2)
ISBN-13: 978-0-13-201896-8 (v. 3)
ISBN-10: 0-13-201896-9 (v. 3)
1. Accounting—Textbooks. 2. Managerial accounting—Textbooks.
I. Horngren, Charles T., 1926- . Accounting
HF5635.A366 2007   657'.044   C2006-905919-5

ISBN-10: 0-13-201894-2
ISBN-13: 978-0-13-201894-4

Editor-in-Chief: Gary Bennett
Executive Editor: Samantha Scully
Executive Marketing Manager: Cas Shields
Developmental Editor and Copy Editor: Anita Smale, CA
Production Editor: Mary Ann Field
Production Coordinator: Deborah Starks
Composition: Hermia Chung
Photo and Permissions Research: Sandy Cooke
Art Director: Julia Hall
Cover and Interior Design: Anthony Leung
Cover Image: Jupiterimages

6   11 10
Printed and bound in the United States.

Photo Credits

1 Gerard Warrener/Alamy; **48** Dick Hemingway; **99** Courtesy of WestJet; **156** photo
by Dave Sandford/Getty Images; **212** Courtesy of Dell Inc.; **287** The Forzani Group
Ltd.; **329** Photo by Anthony De Ridder; **387** Jupiter; **435** CP PHOTO/Steve White;
481 Courtesy of WestJet; **483** Logo courtesy of The Forzani Group Ltd.; **531**
Courtesy of GM Canada

B R I E F
Contents

Contents

---

*In each chapter, Assignment Material includes Questions, Starters, Exercises, Beyond the Numbers, an Ethical Issue, and Problems (Group A and B, and Challenge Problems).
**Extending Your Knowledge includes Decision Problems and Financial Statement Cases.

4 Completing the Accounting Cycle   156

5 Merchandising Operations and the Accounting Cycle   212

6 Accounting for Merchandise Inventory   287

7 Accounting Information Systems   329

Part 2   Accounting for Assets and Liabilities   387

8 Internal Control and Cash   387

9 Receivables   435

Capital Assets and Intangibles 481

Current Liabilities and Payroll 531

About the Authors

Charles T. Horngren is the Edmund W. Littlefield Professor of Accounting, Emeritus, at Stanford University. A graduate of Marquette University, he received his M.B.A. from Harvard University and his Ph.D. from the University of Chicago. He is also the recipient of honorary doctorates from Marquette University and DePaul University.

A Certified Public Accountant, Horngren served on the Accounting Principles Board for six years, the Financial Accounting Standards Board Advisory Council for five years, and the Council of the American Institute of Certified Public Accountants for three years. For six years, he served as a trustee of the Financial Accounting Foundation, which oversees the Financial Accounting Standards Board and the Government Accounting Standards Board.

Horngren is a member of the Accounting Hall of Fame.

A member of the American Accounting Association, Horngren has been its President and its Director of Research. He received its first annual Outstanding Accounting Educator Award.

The California Certified Public Accountants Foundation gave Horngren its Faculty Excellence Award and its Distinguished Professor Award. He is the first person to have received both awards.

The American Institute of Certified Public Accountants presented its first Outstanding Educator Award to Horngren.

Horngren was named Accountant of the Year, Education, by the national professional accounting fraternity, Beta Alpha Psi.

Professor Horngren is also a member of the Institute of Management Accountants, from whom he has received its Distinguished Service Award. He was a member of the Institute's Board of Regents, which administers the Certified Management Accountant examinations.

Horngren is the author of other accounting books published by Prentice-Hall: *Cost Accounting: A Managerial Emphasis*, Twelfth Edition, 2006 (with Srikant Datar and George Foster); *Introduction to Financial Accounting*, Ninth Edition, 2006 (with Gary L. Sundem and John A. Elliott); *Introduction to Management Accounting*, Thirteenth Edition, 2005 (with Gary L. Sundem and William Stratton); *Financial Accounting*, Sixth Edition, 2006 (with Walter T. Harrison, Jr.).

Horngren is the Consulting Editor for Prentice-Hall's Charles T. Horngren Series in Accounting.

Walter T. Harrison, Jr. is Professor Emeritus of Accounting at the Hankamer School of Business, Baylor University. He received his B.B.A. degree from Baylor University, his M.S. from Oklahoma State University, and his Ph.D. from Michigan State University.

Professor Harrison, recipient of numerous teaching awards from student groups as well as from university administrators, has also taught at Cleveland State Community College, Michigan State University, the University of Texas, and Stanford University.

A member of the American Accounting Association and the American Institute of Certified Public Accountants, Professor Harrison has served as Chairman of the Financial Accounting Standards Committee of the American Accounting Association, on the Teaching/Curriculum Development Award Committee, on the Program Advisory Committee for Accounting Education and Teaching, and on the Notable Contributions to Accounting Literature Committee.

Professor Harrison has lectured in several foreign countries and published articles in numerous journals, including *The Accounting Review, Journal of Accounting Research, Journal of Accountancy, Journal of Accounting and Public Policy, Economic Consequences of Financial Accounting Standards, Accounting Horizons, Issues in Accounting Education,* and *Journal of Law and Commerce*. He is co-author of *Financial Accounting,* Sixth

Edition, 2006 (with Charles T. Horngren), published by Prentice Hall. Professor Harrison has received scholarships, fellowships, and research grants or awards from PriceWaterhouse Coopers, Deloitte & Touche, the Ernst & Young Foundation, and the KPMG Foundation.

W. Morley Lemon is Professor Emeritus, University of Waterloo, where he was a faculty member for 24 years. He served as Director of the School of Accountancy in 1987–1988 and 1988–2002. He obtained his BA from the University of Western Ontario, his MBA from the University of Toronto, and his PhD from the University of Texas at Austin. Professor Lemon obtained his CA in Ontario. In 1985, he was honoured by that Institute, which elected him a Fellow; in 2003, he received that Institute's ICAO Award of Outstanding Merit. Professor Lemon received his CPA in Texas.

Professor Lemon was awarded the University of Waterloo Distinguished Teacher Award at the 1998 University of Waterloo convocation. In 2004, he was awarded the L.S. Rosen Outstanding Educator award by the Canadian Academic Accounting Association.

Professor Lemon recently has been a Visiting Professor at the University of Texas at Austin and at the University of Auckland, New Zealand. He has been appointed to the boards of Transparency International Canada and Salvation Army Grace Health Centre.

Professor Lemon co-authored six previous Canadian editions of *Auditing and Other Assurance Services*, published by Pearson Education Canada. He is a co-author, with Harrison, Horngren, Carroll, and Lemon of *Financial Accounting*, Second Canadian Edition, published by Pearson Education Canada. He has co-authored all Canadian editions of *Accounting*.

He was a member of the Canadian Institute of Chartered Accountants' Assurance Standards Board. He has also served on the Institute of Chartered Accountants of Ontario Council, as well as a number of committees for both bodies. He has chaired and served on a number of committees of the Canadian Academic Accounting Association. Professor Lemon has served on Council and chaired and served on a number of committees of the American Accounting Association.

Professor Lemon has presented lectures and papers at a number of universities and academic and professional conferences and symposia in Canada, the United States, and China. He has chaired and organized six audit symposia held at the University of Waterloo. He has served on the editorial board of and reviewed papers for a number of academic journals including *The Accounting Review, Contemporary Accounting Research, Journal of Business Ethics, Issues in Accounting Education, Auditing: A Journal of Practice and Theory, Advances in Accounting, Journal of Accounting and Public Policy*, and *CA Magazine*. Professor Lemon has co-authored two monographs and has had papers published in *Contemporary Accounting Research, Research on Accounting Ethics, Journal of Accounting, Auditing and Finance, The Chartered Accountant in Australia*, and *CA Magazine*. He has had a chapter published in R*esearch Opportunities in Internal Auditing* and papers published in the following collections: *Educating the Profession of Accountancy in the Twenty-First Century, Comparative International Accounting Education Standards, Comparative International Auditing Standards*, and *The Impact of Inflation on Accounting: A Global View*. Professor Lemon served as a judge for *CA Magazine's* Walter J. Macdonald Award.

Professor Lemon has received a number of research grants and has served as the Director of the Centre for Accounting Ethics, School of Accountancy, University of Waterloo. He has written a number of ethics cases published by the Centre.

Peter R. Norwood is an instructor in accounting and the assistant chair of the Financial Management Program at Langara College. A graduate of the University of Alberta, he received his MBA from the University of Western Ontario. He is a Chartered Accountant, a Certified Management Accountant, and was recently awarded the designation as a Fellow by the Society of Management Accountants of Canada.

Before entering the academic community, Mr. Norwood worked in public practice and industry for over fifteen years. He is a member of Council for the Institute of Chartered Accountants of British Columbia and a member of the board of the Chartered Accountants School of Business (CASB). He is a past member of the Board of Evaluators of the Canadian Institute of Chartered Accountants and has served on a variety of committees for the British Columbia Institute of Chartered Accountants. In addition to his duties at Langara College, Mr. Norwood lectures in the Diploma Accounting Program at the University of British Columbia. He is a past chair of the Langara College Foundation.

Jo-Ann L. Johnston is an instructor in accounting and the Program Head of the first year of the Financial Management Program at the British Columbia Institute of Technology (BCIT). She obtained her Bachelor in Administrative Studies from British Columbia Open University, her Diploma of Technology in Financial Management from BCIT, and her MBA from Simon Fraser University. She is also a Certified General Accountant.

Prior to entering the field of education, Mrs. Johnston worked in public practice and industry for over 10 years. She is a past member of the Board of Governors of the Certified General Accountants Association of British Columbia and has served on various committees for the Association. She was also a member of the Board of Directors for the BCIT Faculty and Staff Association, and served as Treasurer during that tenure. She currently serves as chair of the CGA Student Advisory Group and is a member of the Strategic Planning Committee for the Certified General Accountants Association of British Columbia.

In addition to teaching duties and committee work for the British Columbia Institute of Technology, Mrs. Johnston is the financial officer for two family-owned businesses and serves as Treasurer for a community sports organization.

A Letter to Students

Welcome to your introductory accounting course! Accounting is the language of business. Whether you intend to be an accountant or not, you owe it to yourself to develop your skills with this language so that you can your give yourself a winning edge in your career.

As instructors, we know that you want to ace your accounting course, and we also know that the volume of material covered in introductory accounting can be overwhelming. To help you develop your skills and understanding of accounting principles—to help you "get it"—we first had to create a really solid textbook, one that covered the material in a way that makes new and possibly intimidating topics easier to understand. To make sure we were on the right track, we created a Student Review Board of first-year accounting students like you. Read more about the Student Review Board on the next page.

We have also created a number of tools and resources to support you, two of which are MyAccountingLab and the Accounting Cycle Tutorials. In intro accounting, sometimes the only way to "get it" is to do it—to practise similar questions many times until the concepts are clear, and MyAccountingLab allows you to do this. Sometimes seeing the basics of accounting presented in a slightly different, interactive way will help you "get it," and the Accounting Cycle Tutorials (on the Student CD-ROM that comes with this text) do this. These tools and the features of the text are described in detail in the tour, Helping You "Get" Accounting, which is presented over the next few pages. And reminders appear in Chapter 1 to describe how each feature in the text can help you to master accounting.

While you work through your course, we'd like to hear from you. Let us know what you like about this book and your ideas for improving it by visiting our web site at **www.pearsoned.ca/horngren** and clicking on the Feedback link within any chapter.

Best of luck with your course, and much success!

Morley Lemon
Peter Norwood
Jo-Ann Johnston

Student Review Board

We would like to acknowledge and thank the members of our **Student Review Board** whose feedback and suggestions helped guide this new edition.

Sherri Bird, Camosun College
Natina DaSilva, Durham College
April Lynn Duffy, Algonquin College
Tracy Dunbar, Camosun College
Deonne Hanson, SIAST
Erin Froese, Douglas College
Kaleena Hogan, SIAST
Mark Hrycenko, SAIT
Paul Karesa, Kwantlen University College
Jurgen Mornard, Dawson College
Rangolie Prasad, BCIT
Sara Reginato, Humber College
Russ Senior, Algonquin College
Jacqueline Smith, Douglas College
Liliana Tuzi, Durham College
Robin Urie, Durham College
Salma Wahid, Durham College

These students took the time to give us feedback on what we have been doing well and what we could improve upon with this new edition. As a result of their feedback, many changes were incorporated into the revision. For example, based on the Board's recommendation, in this new edition you will find check figures in the margins so you can immediately confirm that you are on track. We have moved exhibits to be closer to where they are discussed on the page, to avoid flipping back and forth; we have added journal entries to each inventory costing method in Chapter 6 for improved clarity. Several students asked for a new design with a fresh and open feel, and we have completely redesigned this new edition with this in mind.

Here are some of the comments we received from the Board:

"I found the book did a very good job of explaining and it also used very helpful diagrams." *Deonne Hanson*

"I very much appreciate getting a good feeling for the 'why' of the statement before getting to the nuts and bolts . . . . The income statement example . . . is clear, uncluttered and useful. It is something I would be turning to again and again, doing homework and exam preparation." *Sherri Bird*

"Good detailed explanations. Good examples. I liked the diagrams, they were very clear. . . . Having more examples that are challenging really does help you understand the material better." *Rangolie Prasad*

"The overall layout and explanation of the material is good. I was able to understand and grasp the concept of the material my first time reading it. . . . The Learning Tips and Key Points in the margins I also found particularly helpful. However, the strongest aspect I believe is the Mid-Chapter Summary Problem and the Summary Problem. They really help to bring all the information you have just read together in one problem systematically. The Decision Guidelines and the Stop & Think sections are also good mini summaries and good for note taking." *Jacqueline Smith*

Helping You "Get" Accounting

GUIDING

Each chapter of *Accounting* includes a number of tools designed to guide you through the process of developing your skills and understanding of key accounting concepts. Please read through the next few pages to learn more about these tools and the many ways in which they will help you learn, understand, and apply accounting concepts.

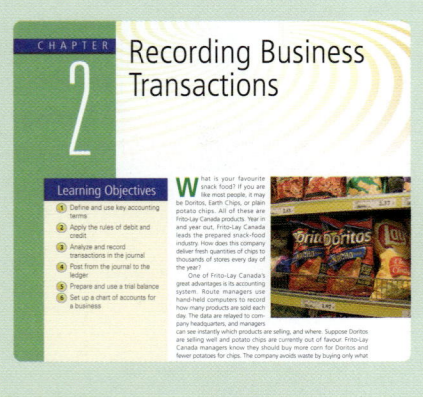

Learning Objectives are listed on the first page of each chapter. This "roadmap" shows you what will be covered and what is especially important. Each Learning Objective is repeated in the margin where the material is first covered. The Learning Objectives are summarized at the end of the chapter.

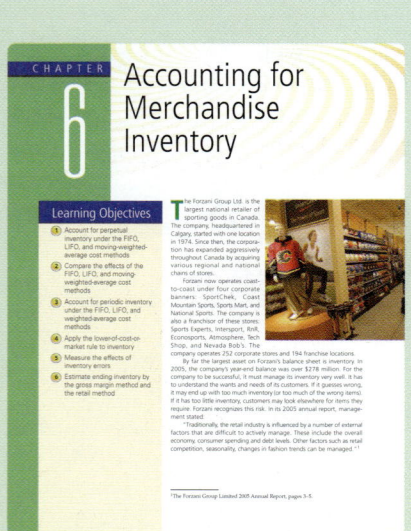

Chapter openers present a story about a real company or a real business situation, and show why the topics in the chapter are important to real companies. Some of the companies you'll read about include WestJet Airlines, Canadian Tire, and The Forzani Group. Students tell us that using real companies makes it easier for them to learn and remember accounting concepts.

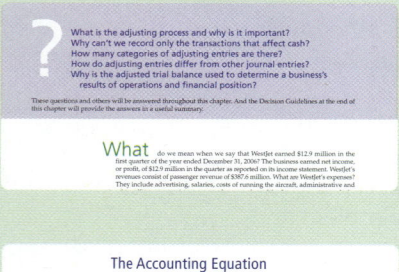

Why Is This Important? boxes appear at the beginning of each chapter to highlight the important issues and questions that will be answered in the chapter. Once you read these questions, they will remain in the back of your mind. As you work through the chapter, you'll discover the answers and see why the chapter topics really are important.

Learning Objectives in the margin visually signal the beginning of the section that covers the objective topic. Look for this feature when you are studying and want to review a particular topic.

Exhibits are provided in full colour to make the concepts easier to understand and easier to remember.

Learning Tips in the margin are suggestions for learning or remembering concepts that you might find difficult.

Key Points in the margin highlight important details from the text. These are good review tools for when you prepare for tests or exams.

Thinking It Over are short questions about concepts just covered in the text. Answers are provided to give you immediate feedback. You can use Thinking It Over questions to check your progress and to prepare for exams.

Real World Examples show how real companies make use of the concepts just discussed in the text. Linking concepts to real companies makes them easier to understand and remember.

Stop and Think boxes are "speed bumps" that allow you to slow down for a moment, review and apply to a decision situation material just covered in the text. These serve as an excellent way to check your progress because the answers are provided in the same box.

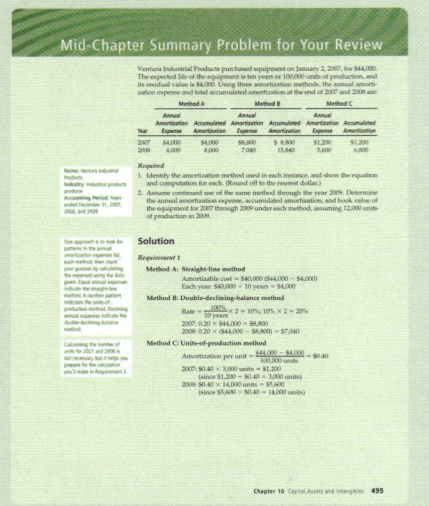

Mid-Chapter Summary Problem for Your Review gives you another chance to review your understanding of the material covered in the first half of the chapter. A full worked solution is provided so you can judge whether you should look at the material again or proceed to the last half of the chapter. Green notes in the margin or in the solution give you hints for how to tackle the solution, reminders of things to watch for, and further explanations about the solutions.

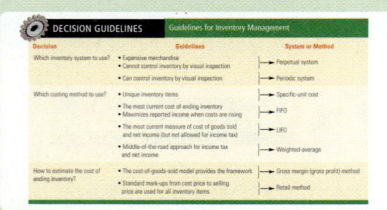

Decision Guidelines show how the accounting concepts covered in the chapter are used by business people to make business decisions. This feature shows why accounting principles and concepts are important in a broader business context, not just to accountants. The Decision Guidelines also serve as an excellent summary of the chapter topics.

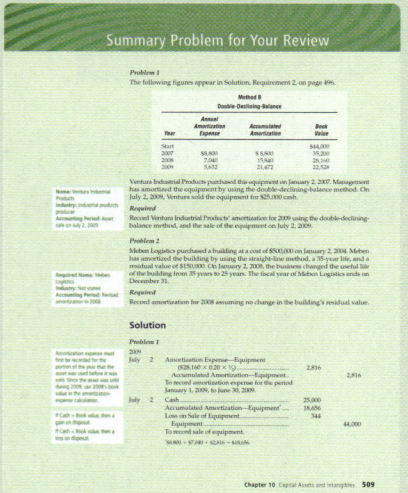

Summary Problem for Your Review pulls together the chapter concepts with an extensive and challenging review problem. Full worked solutions are given so that you can check your progress. Again, green notes in the margin or in the solution give you hints for how to tackle the solution, reminders of things to watch for, and further explanations about the solutions.

MyAccountingLab feature appears before the Summary to remind you to go to MyAccountingLab for extra practice with the new material introduced in the chapter. You can learn more about MyAccountingLab later in this walk-through.

Summary appears at the end of each chapter. It gives a concise description of the material covered in the chapter and is organized by objective. Use this summary as a starting point for organizing your review when studying for a test or exam.

Self-Study Questions are multiple-choice questions that allow you to test your understanding of the chapter on your own. Page references are given so that you can review a section quickly if you miss an answer. The answers are provided after the Similar Accounting Terms (see below) so you can check your progress.

Accounting Vocabulary lists all the terms that were defined and appeared in bold type in the chapter. The page references are given so you can review the meanings of the terms. These terms are also collected and defined in the Glossary at the end of the text.

Similar Accounting Terms link the accounting terms used in the chapter to similar terms you might have heard outside your accounting class, in the media, in other courses, or in day-to-day business dealings. Knowing similar terms should make it easier to remember the accounting terms.

Answers to Self-Study Questions appear after the Similar Accounting Terms.

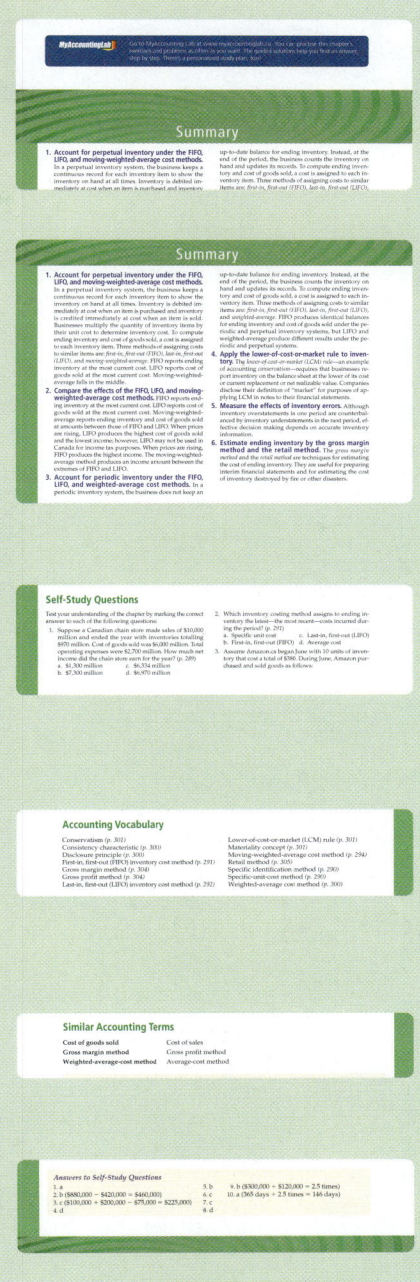

PRACTISING

While practice may not make you perfect, it is still the best way to make sure you grasp new accounting concepts and procedures. Working through the end of chapter exercises and problems will help you confirm your understanding of accounting concepts and develop your accounting skills. These review and practice materials are described in the following pages.

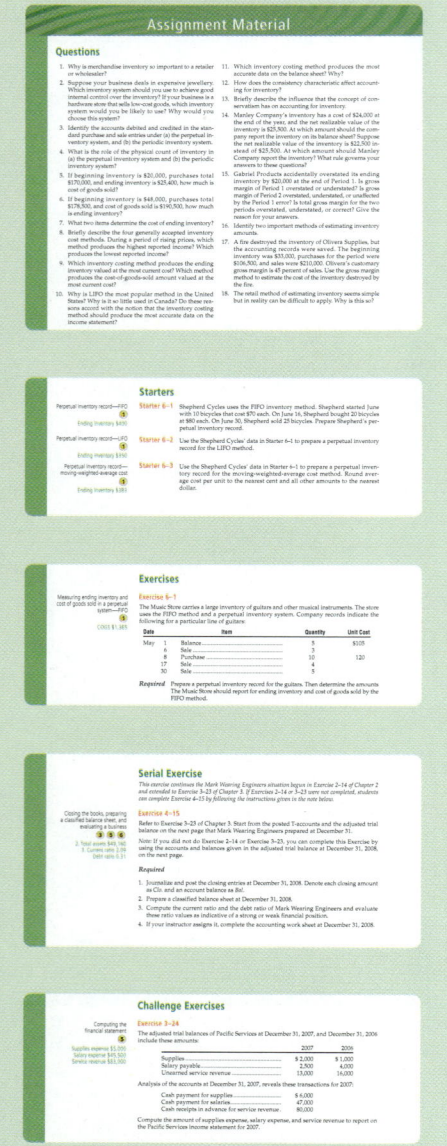

Questions require short, written answers or short calculations, often on a single topic.

Starters serve as warm-ups and confidence builders at the beginning of the assignment material. They address a single topic from the chapter. A brief description, the learning objectives covered, and **Check figures** appear in the margin beside each Starter.

Exercises on a single or a few topics require you to "do the accounting" and, often, to consider the implications of the results in the same way that real companies would.

Serial Exercise in Chapters 2 to 5 follows one company and builds in complexity with each chapter, providing an excellent review of the accounting cycle.

Challenge Exercises provide a challenge for those students who have mastered the Exercises.

Beyond the Numbers exercises require analytical thinking and written responses about the topics presented in the chapter.

Ethical Issues are thought-provoking situations that help you recognize when ethics should affect an accounting decision.

Problems are presented in two groups that mirror each other, "A" and "B." Many instructors work through problems from Group A in class to demonstrate accounting concepts, then assign problems from Group B for homework or extra practice. **Check figures** are included to make sure you're on the right track.

Challenge Problems encourage you to consider the effect of accounting information and apply it to decision situations.

Decision Problems allow you to prepare and interpret accounting information and then make recommendations to a business based on this information.

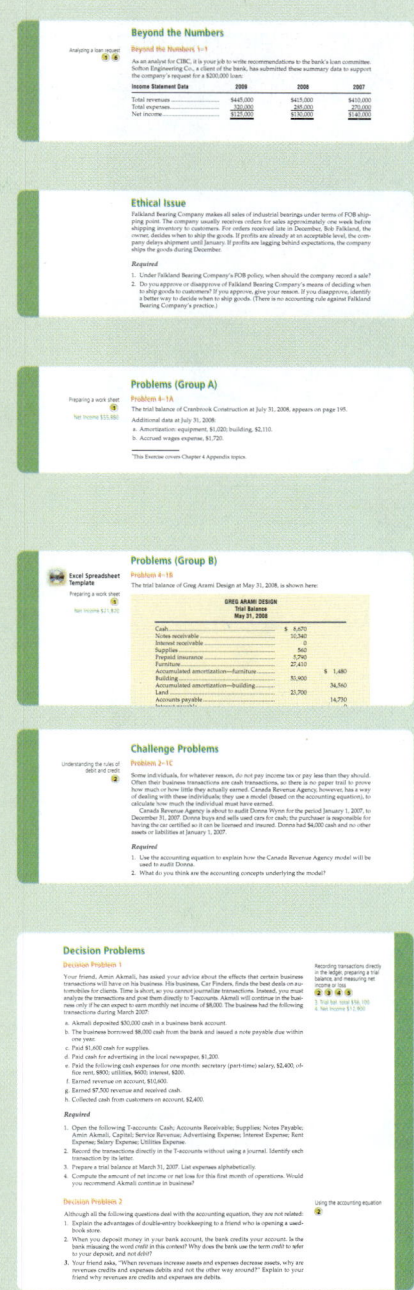

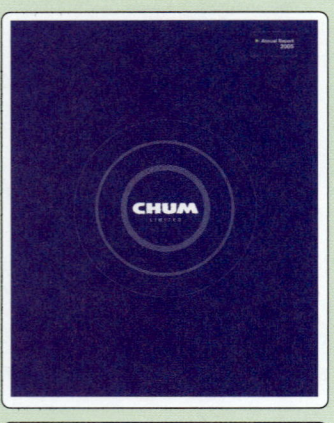

Financial Statement Cases allow you to use real financial information from a service company and a manufacturer/merchandiser. CHUM Limited is one of Canada's leading media companies and content providers. Sun-Rype Products Ltd. is a leading Canadian manufacturer and marketer of juice-based beverages and fruit-based snacks. Selected financial information from each company's 2005 Annual Report appear in Appendix A and Appendix B of Volume I and Volume II of *Accounting*. The full annual reports appear on the Student CD-ROM that comes with this book.

 Excel Spreadsheet Template **Student CD-ROM** icons appear beside selected Exercises and Problems to remind you that Excel spreadsheets have been created to answer these questions. You can find these spreadsheets on the Student CD-ROM packaged with your book. You don't have to use the spreadsheets to answer the questions, but you may find they save you time.

In addition to the features above that appear in each chapter, two additional features appear at the end of each part of Volume I and Volume II.

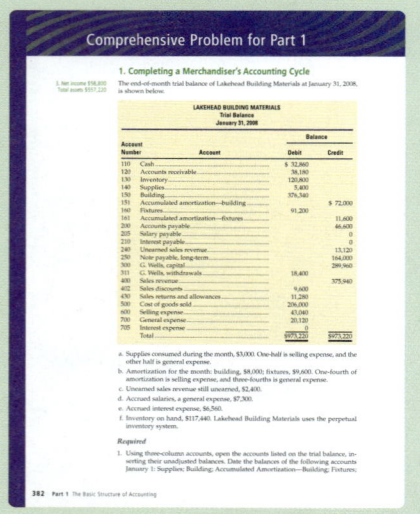

Comprehensive Problem covers the content addressed in the book so far. This is a relatively long problem that provides an excellent review of all of the topics covered in the chapters in that part. See your instructor for the solution to this problem.

CBC **CBC Video Cases** appear at the end of each of the Parts in Volume I and Volume II. Links to the CBC videos that accompany these cases are included on the Student CD-ROM packaged with your text.

The videos demonstrate the importance of accounting concepts to real businesses and real entrepreneurs in a truly interesting way.

REINFORCING

Interactive media and supplements can reinforce the material you learn within the text. We have developed a series of resources to enhance your experience as you build your accounting skills:

The **Student CD-ROM** that accompanies this book contains an array of tools to help you learn accounting concepts and test your understanding.

- A complete Study Guide with chapter reviews, exercises, problems, and solutions
- Links to the CBC videos that accompany the CBC Video Cases in the text
- An Excel tutorial that you can use as a refresher
- Excel spreadsheet templates that accompany selected text Exercises and Problems
- An animated Accounting Cycle Tutorial:

  This interactive tutorial includes six modules that will guide you through every step in the accounting cycle process:

  - Balance Sheet Accounts – Transactions
  - Income Statement Accounts – Transactions
  - The Journal and the Ledger
  - Adjustments
  - Financial Statements
  - Adjusting and Closing Entries

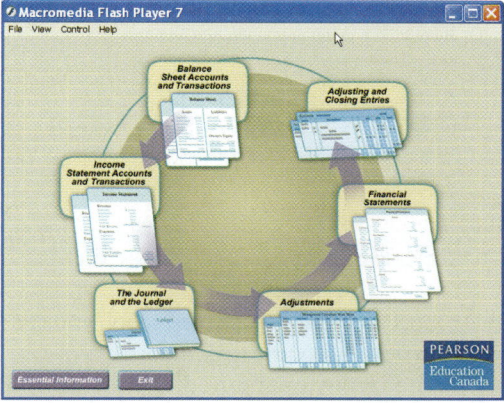

Within each module, you will find three types of valuable content:

TUTORIAL—A detailed walkthrough of concepts, with pop-up definitions for key terms and voice-over narration to provide clarification and additional information

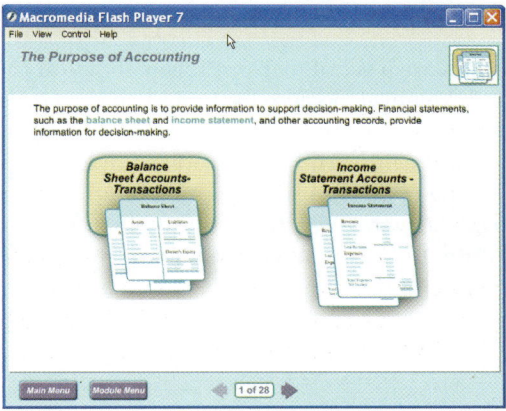

APPLICATION—Five assignments, based on different companies, to help you apply and reinforce the concepts you learned in the tutorial

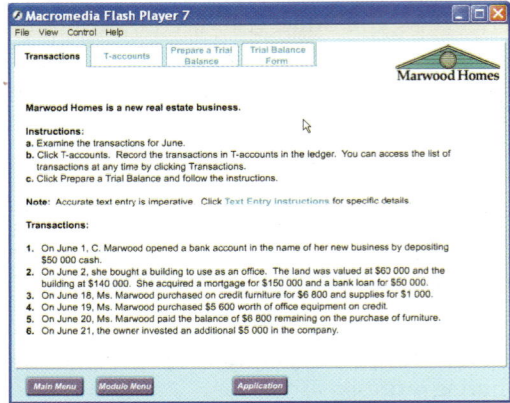

GLOSSARY—A list of terminology covered in the tutorial, with an interactive quiz to help you check your understanding of key terms

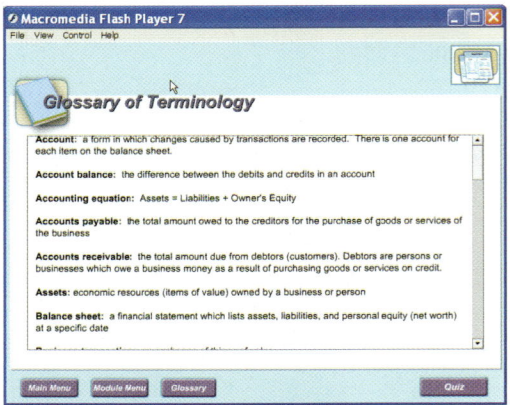

With the help of this robust and easy-to-use study tool, you can master the accounting cycle and achieve success in your accounting course!

The **Companion Website (www.pearsoned.ca/horngren)** provides a wealth of resources for you, including:

- An Online Study Guide with quizzes and immediate feedback
- Links to the CBC videos that accompany the CBC Video Cases in the text
- Links to the websites of companies mentioned in each chapter
- A link to our Accounting Online Tutor, an accounting instructor who will help you work through chapter or problem material that you find particularly challenging

The **Working Papers** are a set of tear-out forms that you can use to solve all the exercises and problems in Volume I. Because the forms you need have already been created, you avoid time-consuming set-up and can focus on the accounting right away.

The *A-1 Photography Practice Set*, Fifth Canadian Edition, gives you the opportunity to complete the accounting cycle for a sole proprietorship service business.

The *Fitness Universe Practice Set*, Second Canadian Edition, provides you with the opportunity to perform the accounting cycle for a sole proprietorship merchandising business.

 Meet the Power of Practice!

MyAccountingLab is an online homework and assessment tool that supports the same theme as the text by providing "I get it!" moments inside and outside of class. It is in MyAccountingLab where "I get it!" moments meet the power of practice.

MyAccountingLab:

- Helps students at their teachable moment, whether that is at 1 p.m. or 1 a.m.
- Includes algorithmically generated versions of the same end-of-chapter material in the text that students are used to doing as homework.
- Features a similar look and feel to the text so that students find it familiar and comfortable to work with.

In MyAccountingLab, instructors can create homework assignments that cover a wide variety of accounting questions.

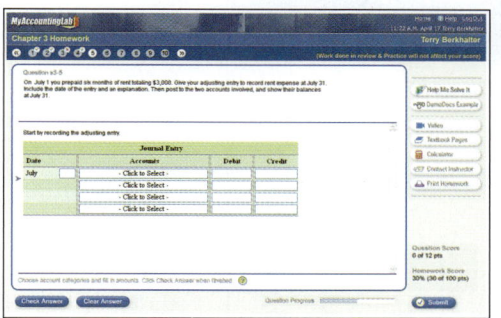 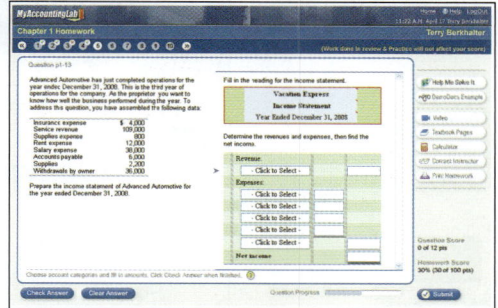

Instructors can copy a sample homework assignment, or create a new assignment from scratch using questions from the textbook.

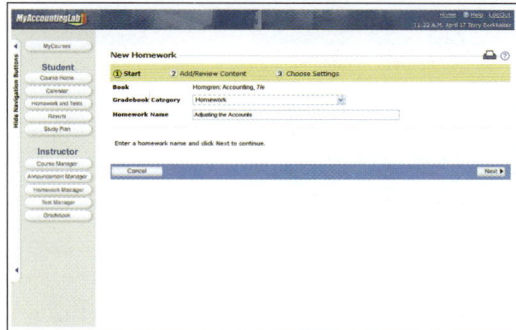

You can select questions from any chapter and objective in *Accounting*.

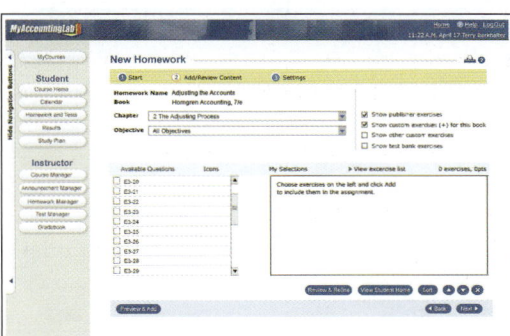

With each assignment, instructors can select start dates, due dates, allow printing, and even allow partial credit.

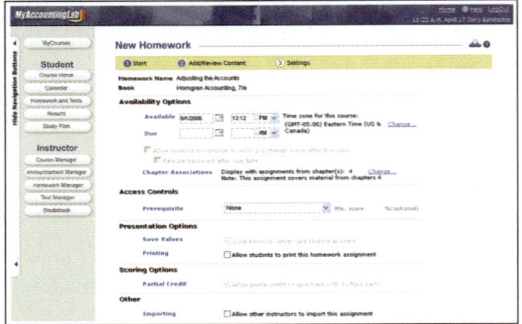

Students access the homework from the Do Homework page.

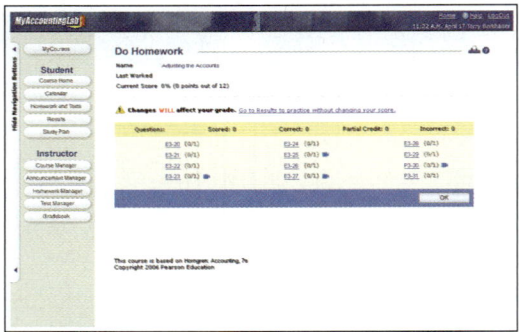

Each homework question begins with a problem statement and any additional instructions.

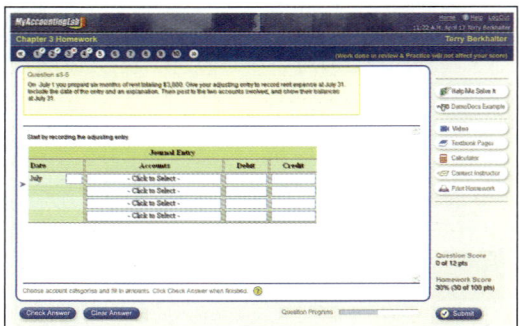

Students enter information in the spaces provided or choose from a list of options.

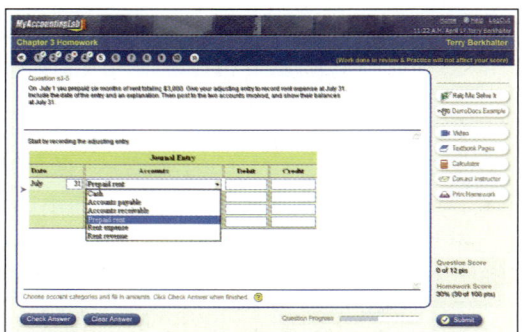

When they have completed answering that part of the question, they click Check Answer to see how they've done.

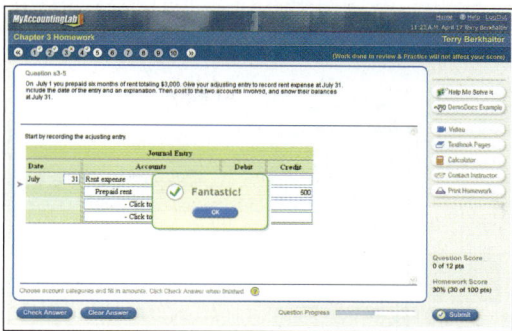

Students will work on additional steps until they have completed the entire question.

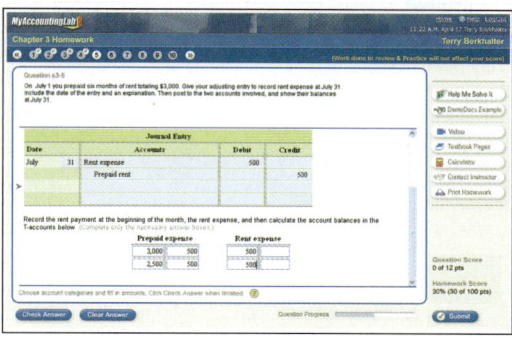

At all times, students have access to a wide variety of learning tools:

Students can create an individualized **Study Plan** by taking a diagnostic test that shows them which topics they have mastered and which ones need additional practice.

DemoDocs are comprehensive worked-through problems to help students when they are trying to solve exercises and problems on their own. The idea is to help students duplicate the classroom experience outside of class. Entire problems that mirror end-of-chapter material are presented in Flash format and narrated in a conversational style, essentially imitating what an instructor might say if standing over a student's shoulder.

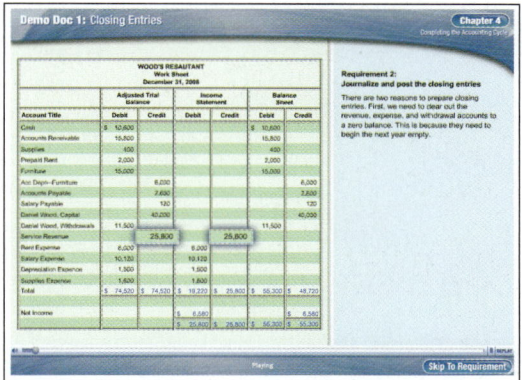

Help Me Solve It is a step-by-step interactive tutoring feature that walks students through the steps required to complete each question. Students can use Help Me Solve It to guide them to the solution for a question, and then regenerate the question with new values so they can practice what they've learned.

Concept Lecture Videos, commissioned specifically to accompany *Accounting*, provide additional reinforcement of core accounting concepts.

A comprehensive flash-based **E-text** links students directly to the relevant chapter content and support materials whenever they need reinforcement or clarification.

Depending on the assignment, students can work on multiple-choice questions, simple starter questions, exercises, and complicated problems. Students can also work on quizzes and even tests that the instructor can decide when and how they access.

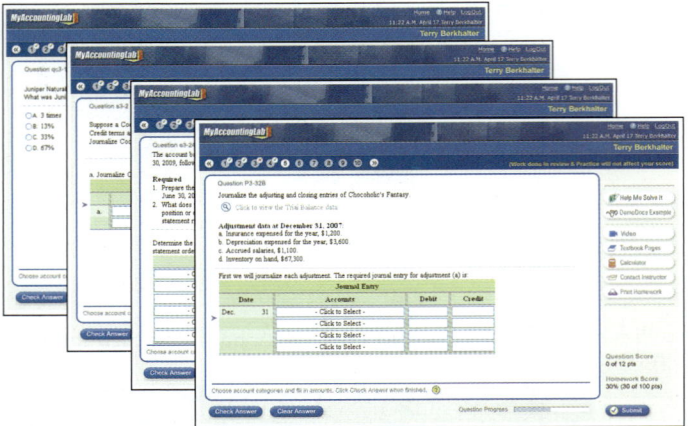

MyAccountingLab is yet another tool in providing students with the help they need to "get it" in accounting!

To the Instructor

Welcome to *Accounting*! Instructors have told us that their greatest challenges are effectively teaching students with very different business and accounting backgrounds, and motivating students to give accounting the study time and attention it deserves. *Accounting*'s approach and features were designed to help you address and overcome these challenges.

A Student-Friendly Textbook

Instructors have told us that if students miss an accounting class, they must be able to keep up by reading the text. An accounting textbook must help students prepare for class or, should they miss a session, catch up without being overwhelmed. To help students do this, here is what we did:

- We **redesigned the book** to be more open and inviting. We added more bulleted points and more art to highlight key ideas and make the layout of explanations less imposing. We reserved the margins for Key Points, Learning Tips, Thinking It Over, and Real World Examples—features that help students when they study. We moved the artwork to reduce page flipping. In all, the new design makes the book easier to use and makes the concepts more clear, and that is encouraging for students.

- We added **highlights in Chapter 1** to describe each feature of the text and explain how the feature can help students study and learn. A feature can't be effective unless students understand it and use it.

- We added **worked solutions** to the Mid-Chapter Summary Problem for Your Review and the Summary Problem for Your Review. In addition to the full solution that we always provided, we added green notes in the margin to give students hints for how to tackle the solution, reminders of things to watch for, and further explanations about the solutions. These should help students overcome the "How do I start?" dilemma, as well as the "Why did they do that?" questions that can arise even when a full solution is given.

- We added **check figures** in the margins so students can make sure they are on track when they are working on their own.

- We continue to include **examples from real Canadian** companies wherever possible. This real-world context enlivens the material, make difficult concepts easier to grasp, and illustrates the role of accounting in business. For that reason, we now include the **annual reports of two Canadian companies** in the text and on the Student CD-ROM—CHUM Limited and Sun-Rype Products Ltd.

  In those situations where "live" data drawn from real companies would complicate the material for introductory students, we illustrate the accounting with realistic examples from generic companies to give students the clearest examples possible.

- We added the **Student CD-ROM icon** in the margins of Chapters 1 to 4 to remind students that the topics just discussed in the chapter are also presented in the Accounting Cycle Tutorials on the Student CD-ROM that comes with each text. Seeing a topic presented in a different, interactive way may help students understand it more fully. The Student CD-ROM also includes a complete Study Guide, Excel Spreadsheet Templates, an Excel tutorial, and links to the CBC Videos.

Accuracy

As instructors, we know that **accuracy in problems and solutions** is every bit as important as clear writing and effective pedagogy. Tremendous effort has been made to ensure that the solutions to problem materials in *Accounting*, Canadian Seventh Edition are correct.

- The **authors** have developed their own problem and solutions materials.
- Our **Developmental Editor**, Anita Smale, CA, reviewed all problems and solutions.
- In this edition, we added a new step—the **Chapter Champion**. Chapter Champions are instructors like you who reviewed each chapter's contents, end-of-chapter material, and solutions in depth to ensure accuracy. We thank our Chapter Champions for their excellent and diligent work in the Acknowledgements section of this book.
- As a final stage, **technical checkers** have reviewed all problems and solutions.

We have made every effort to bring you the most accurate text possible. However, if you discover something that is inaccurate, please let us know so we can fix it as soon as possible.

Features for Instructors

As always, market feedback has been crucial in the development of this new edition. With the Canadian Seventh Edition of *Accounting*, we have continued to build on the improvements to the previous edition with the following changes based directly on reviewer and user feedback:

- We added at least 10 new **Starters** to each chapter. Starters are short, single-topic questions that you can use in class to demonstrate topics or assign to help students gain confidence before they launch into the rest of the end-of-chapter material.
- We have moved chapter appendices forward, from the end of chapters to just before the end-of-chapter material, to better integrate their content, exercises, and problems with those of the text. Questions, Starters, Exercises, and Problems related to the appendix topics are highlighted with an asterisk and a footnote reminder. As a result of this shift, many chapters now have more end-of-chapter material.
- Chapter 2 has been rearranged to be more streamlined. It now flows better and repeated transactions have been eliminated.
- Chapter 6 has been "beefed up," with more exercises and problems added for the periodic inventory system. Chapter 6 also includes a comparison of the perpetual and periodic inventory systems' journal entries in its new Appendix B.
- As always, we have tried to make this text as current as possible. We explained the *Sarbanes-Oxley Act of 2002* a number of times in the book, we used the latest GST and payroll rates in effect at the time of printing, and we incorporated the most current *CICA Handbook* recommendations, especially as they relate to investments (primarily in Chapter 16 in Volume II).

We also recognize the benefits of an extensive and varied supplement package, so we are pleased to offer the following instructor supplements to support your use of Accounting, *Canadian Seventh Edition:*

Instructor's Resource CD-ROM This CD-ROM provides a collection of resources to help you with lecture preparation, presentation, and assessment. It contains the following supplements:

- **Instructor's Solutions Manual** Now provided in both Adobe PDF and MS Word format for ease of use.
- **Instructor's Resource Manual** Also provided in both Adobe PDF and MS Word format, the Instructor's Resource Manual includes Chapter Overviews and Outlines, Assignment Grids, Ten-Minute Quizzes, and other valuable teaching resources. In addition is a new section describing all the supplements that come with *Accounting*, along with suggestions for how and when they can be used, written by an instructor who has used them all!

- **TestGen** This powerful and user-friendly computerized test bank includes well over 100 questions per chapter, ranging from True False, Multiple-Choice, and Matching to Problems and Critical Thinking Exercises.
- **PowerPoint Teaching Transparencies** For flexibility of use, we provide two sets of transparencies: a brief set with six to eight slides per chapter, and a comprehensive set with 40 to 50 slides per chapter.
- **Exhibits** We are pleased to provide the exhibits from the text in GIF format for use in the classroom and easy conversion to acetate format.
- **Adapting Your Lecture Notes** These detailed transition notes, including comparison of tables of content, chapter objectives, and chapter content, will facilitate your course preparation if you make the switch to *Accounting* from another introductory accounting text.

Printed Solutions Acetates In response to instructor feedback, we continue to provide all text solutions printed on acetates for easy classroom use.

CBC/Pearson Canada Video Library We now offer this excellent teaching and learning resource in digitized format for use in technology-enhanced classrooms. However, we also continue to provide these videos in VHS format for those instructors who prefer this delivery method.

Finally, we want to draw your attention to a great service offered by Pearson to further enhance the use of *Accounting* in your course:

Pearson Custom Publishing We know that not every instructor follows the exact order of a course text. Some may not even cover all the material in a given volume. Pearson Custom Publishing provides the flexibility to select the chapters you need, presented in the order you want, to tailor fit your text to your course and your students' needs. Contact your Pearson Education Canada Sales and Editorial Representative to learn more.

Developing high-quality textbooks is an ongoing effort. As you deliver your course, we'd like to hear from you. Let us know what you like about this book and your ideas for improving it by visiting our web site at **www.pearsoned.ca/horngren** and clicking on the Feedback link.

We hope you enjoy *Accounting*!

Morley Lemon
Peter Norwood
Jo-Ann Johnston

Acknowledgements for the Canadian Seventh Edition

We would like to thank Charles Horngren and Tom Harrison for their encouragement and support.

Accuracy in an accounting textbook is of utmost importance. Each new edition of a text is technically checked many times during its creation: during the revision by the authors, during the editing process, during the production process, and then once more before being printed. To help make this text as accurate as possible, we have added a new step to the accuracy-checking process: the Chapter Champion. Chapter Champions are seasoned accounting instructors who agreed to focus on and review one or two chapters in depth, giving us feedback and suggestions for making the chapter material as clear and accurate as possible, and for helping us ensure the end-of-chapter questions and solutions are as accurate as possible. The Chapter Champions' work has further improved the accuracy of a text and solutions that are already subject to an extensive process of accuracy checking. We want to acknowledge their excellent work and thank our Volume I Chapter Champions:

Chapter 1	Penny Parker, Fanshawe College
Chapters 2 and 3	Vanessa Oltmann, Malaspina University College
Chapters 4 and 8	Meredith Delaney, Seneca College
Chapters 5 and 11	Cécile Laurin, Algonquin College
Chapters 6 and 9	Helen Stavaris, Dawson College
Chapter 7	Don Hutton, Durham College
Chapter 10	Elizabeth Hicks, Douglas College

Thanks are due to the following instructors for reviewing the previous edition of this text during the planning stages of this new edition, and for their excellent suggestions and ideas:

Cécile Ashman, Algonquin College
Delano Antoine, Seneca College
Peggy Coady, Memorial University of Newfoundland
Vincent Durant, St. Lawrence College
Dave Fleming, George Brown College
Abbe Nielsen, Langara College
Joe Pidutti, Durham College
David Sale, Kwantlen University College
Patricia Zima, Mohawk College

Special thanks to the following instructors for participating in our two MyAccountingLab focus groups and helping to shape the development of this exciting product:

Delano Antoine, Seneca College
Jerry Aubin, Algonquin College
Sheila Elworthy, Camosun College
Richard Farrar, Conestoga College
Ellen Hamer, Langara College
John Janzen, Sheridan College
Terry Kosowick, Okanagan College
Barb Lee, College of New Caledonia
Darlene Lowe, Grant MacEwan College
Penny Parker, Fanshawe College
Joe Pidutti, Durham College
Glen Stanger, Douglas College
Helen Vallee, Kwantlen University College

Thanks are extended to CHUM Limited and Sun-Rype Products Ltd. for permission to use their annual reports in Volumes I and II of this text. Thanks are extended to JVC Canada Inc. for permission to use its invoice in Chapter 5. We acknowledge the support provided by *The Globe and Mail's Report on Business,* the *Financial Post,* and by the annual reports of a large number of public companies.

The Canadian Institute of Chartered Accountants, as the official promulgator of generally accepted accounting principles in Canada, and the *CICA Handbook,* are vital to the conduct of business and accounting in Canada. We have made every effort to incorporate the most current *Handbook* recommendations in this new edition of *Accounting.*

We would like to acknowledge the people of Pearson Education Canada, in particular President Steve O'Hearn, Editor-in-Chief Gary Bennett, Executive Editor Samantha Scully, and Marketing Manager Cas Shields. Special thanks to Production Editor Mary Ann Field, Production Coordinator Deborah Starks, and their teams for their superior efforts in guiding this edition through the various phases of preparation and production. We would also like to acknowledge the editorial and technical support of Anita Smale, CA.

I would like to thank my wife Sandra for her assistance.

W. Morley Lemon

I would like to thank my wife, Helen, and my family very much for their support, assistance, and encouragement.

Peter R. Norwood

I would like to thank my husband Bill and my family for their encouragement and support.

Jo-Ann L. Johnston

The accounting profession offers exciting career opportunities because every organization uses accounting. The corner grocery store keeps accounting records to measure its success in selling groceries. The largest corporations need accounting to monitor their locations and transactions. And the dot.coms must account for their transactions. Why is accounting so important? Because it helps an organization understand its business in the same way a model helps an architect construct a building. Accounting helps a manager understand the organization as a whole without drowning in its details.

The Work of Accountants

Positions in the field of accounting may be divided into several areas. Two general classifications are *public accounting* and *private accounting*.

In Canada, most accountants, both public and private, belong to one of three accounting bodies, which set the standards for admission of members and deal with matters like the rules of professional conduct followed by their members: The Canadian Institute of Chartered Accountants (CICA), whose members are called *Chartered Accountants (CA)*; the Certified General Accountants Association of Canada (CGAAC), whose members are called *Certified General Accountants (CGA)*; and the Society of Management Accountants of Canada (SMAC), whose members are called *Certified Management Accountants (CMA)*. The role and activities of each of these bodies are discussed below.

Private accountants work for a single business, such as a local department store, the St-Hubert restaurant chain, or McCain Foods Ltd. Charitable organizations, educational institutions, and government agencies also employ private accountants. The chief accounting officer usually has the title of controller, treasurer, or chief financial officer. Whatever the title, this person often carries the status of vice-president.

Public accountants are those who serve the general public and collect professional fees for their work, much as doctors and lawyers do. Their work includes auditing, income tax planning and preparation of returns, management consulting, and various accounting services. These specialized accounting services are discussed in the next section. Public accountants represent about a quarter of all professional accountants.

Some public accountants pool their talents and work together within a single firm. Public accounting firms are called CA firms, CGA firms, or CMA firms, depending on the accounting body from which the partners of the firm come. Public accounting firms vary greatly in size. Some are small businesses, and others are medium-sized partnerships. The largest firms are worldwide partnerships with over 2,000 partners. There are four large, international accounting firms:

Deloitte & Touche LLP	KPMG LLP
Ernst & Young LLP	PricewaterhouseCoopers LLP

Although these firms employ less than 25 percent of the more than 60,000 CAs in Canada, they audit most of the 1,000 largest corporations in Canada. The top partners in large accounting firms earn about the same amount as the top managers of other large businesses.

Exhibit 1 shows the accounting positions within public accounting firms and other organizations. Of special interest in the exhibit is the upward movement of accounting personnel, as the arrows show. In particular, note how accountants may move from positions in public accounting firms to similar or higher positions in industry and government. This is a frequently travelled career path. Because accounting deals with all facets of an organization—such as purchasing, manufacturing, marketing, and distribution—it provides an excellent basis for gaining broad business experience.

EXHIBIT 1 | Accounting Position within Organizations

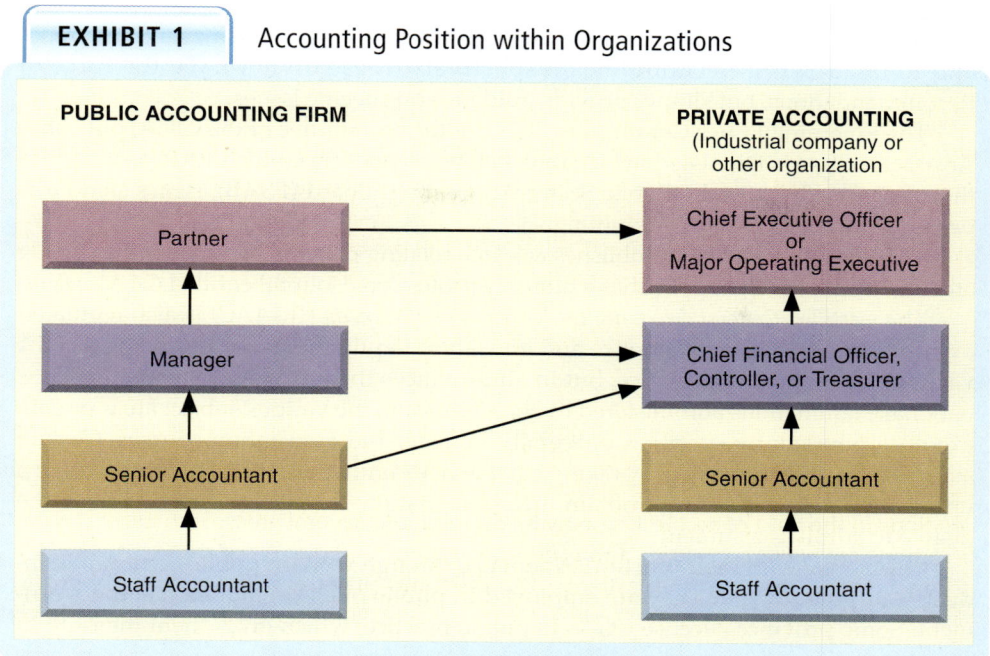

Accounting Organizations and Designations

The position of accounting in today's business world has created the need for control over the professional, educational, and ethical standards of accountants. Through statutes passed by provincial legislatures, the three accounting organizations in Canada have received the authority to set educational requirements and professional standards for their members and to discipline members who fail to adhere to their codes of conduct. The acts make them self-regulating bodies, just as provincial associations of doctors and lawyers are.

The *Canadian Institute of Chartered Accountants (CICA)*, whose members are chartered accountants or CAs, is the oldest accounting organization in Canada. Experience and education requirements for becoming a CA vary among the provinces. Generally, the educational requirement includes a university degree. All the provincial institutes require is that an individual, to qualify as a CA, pass a national three-day uniform examination administered by the CICA and meet articling requirements. The provincial institutes grant the right to use the professional designation CA.

CAs in Canada generally must earn their practical experience by working for a public accounting firm; subsequently, about half the CAs in Canada leave public practice for jobs in industry, government, or education. A small number of CAs meet their experience requirements working for the federal or provincial governments. CAs in public accounting have the right to perform audits and issue opinions on the audited financial statements in all provinces in Canada.

CAs belong to a provincial institute (*Ordre* in Quebec) and through that body to the CICA. The provincial institutes have the responsibility for developing and enforcing the code of professional conduct that guides the actions of the CAs in that province.

The CICA, through the Accounting Standards Board and the Assurance Standards Board respectively, issues accounting standards or GAAP (discussed in Chapter 1) and auditing standards (Generally Accepted Auditing Standards or GAAS). These standards are collected in the *CICA Handbook*. Specific standards are italicized and called *Recommendations*. Accounting Recommendations are the standards or regulations that govern the preparation of financial statements in Canada. The Accounting Standards

Board and the Assurance Standards Board publish Accounting Guidelines and Assurance and Related Services Guidelines respectively; these do not have the force of Recommendations, but simply provide guidance on specific issues.

The Emerging Issues Committee (EIC), another committee of the CICA, publishes Abstracts of Issues Discussed, which rank below Accounting Guidelines in terms of authority. A fourth body, the Public Sector Accounting Board (PSAB), issues standards pertaining to public sector accounting.

The CICA supports and publishes research relating primarily to financial reporting and auditing. The CICA publishes a monthly professional journal entitled *CA Magazine*.

The *Certified General Accountants Association of Canada (CGAAC)* is also regulated by provincial law. The experience and education requirements for becoming a CGA vary from province to province, but in all provinces the individual must either pass national examinations administered by the CGAAC in the various subject areas or gain exemption by taking specified university, college, and association courses. Certain subjects may only be passed by taking a national examination. CGA students require a university degree in order to obtain their designation; they do not need to have the degree to enroll as a student.

CGAs may gain their practical experience through work in public accounting, industry, or government. They are employed in public practice, industry, and government. Some provinces license CGAs in public practice, which gives them the right to conduct audits and issue opinions on financial statements, while some other provinces do not require a licence for them to perform audits.

The association supports research in various areas pertaining to accounting through the Canadian CGA Research Foundation. CGAAC publishes a professional journal entitled *CGA Magazine*.

The *Society of Management Accountants of Canada (SMAC)* administers the Certified Management Accountant program that leads to the Certified Management Accountant (CMA) designation. The use of this designation is similarly controlled by provincial law. Students generally must have a university degree. The SMAC administers an admission or entrance examination that students must pass before embarking on a two-year professional program and completing two years of required work experience. After completing the professional program and the work experience, they write a final examination and make a presentation to a SMAC committee, based on the professional program administered by the SMAC, in order to obtain the CMA designation. The SMAC also administers the professional program and the final examination. CMAs earn their practical experience in industry or government, and are generally employed in industry or government, although some CMAs are in public accounting. The Society issues standards relating to management accounting through the SMAC. The SMAC conducts and publishes research relating primarily to management accounting. The SMAC publishes a professional journal entitled *Cost and Management*.

The *Financial Executives Institute (FEI)* is an organization composed of senior financial executives from many of the large corporations in Canada, who meet on a regular basis with a view to sharing information on how they can better manage their organizations. Most of these executives have one of the three designations just discussed. The FEI supports and publishes research relating to management accounting. The FEI also publishes a journal, the *Financial Executive*.

The *Institute of Internal Auditors (IIA)* is a world-wide organization of internal auditors. It administers the examinations leading to and grants the Certified Internal Auditor (CIA) designation. Internal auditors are employees of an organization whose job is to review the operations, including financial operations, of the organization with a view to making it more economical, efficient, and effective. Many Canadian internal auditors are members of Canadian chapters of the IIA. The IIA supports and publishes research and conducts courses related to internal auditing. The IIA journal is *The Internal Auditor*.

The *Canadian Academic Accounting Association (CAAA)* directs its attention toward the academic and research aspects of accounting. A high percentage of its members are professors. The CAAA publishes a journal devoted to research in accounting and auditing, *Contemporary Accounting Research*.

While it is not an accounting organization or designation, *Canada Revenue Agency (CRA)* enforces the tax laws and collects the revenue needed to finance the federal government.

Specialized Accounting Services

As accounting affects so many people in so many different fields, public accounting and private accounting include specialized services.

Public Accounting

Auditing is one of the accounting profession's most significant services to the public. An audit is the independent examination that ensures the reliability of the reports that management prepares and submits to investors, creditors, and others outside the business. In carrying out an audit, public accountants from outside a business examine the business's financial statements. If the public accountants believe that these documents are a fair presentation of the business's operations, they offer a professional opinion stating that the firm's financial statements have been prepared in accordance with generally accepted accounting principles, or, if generally accepted accounting principles are not applicable, with an appropriate disclosed basis of accounting. Why is the audit so important? Creditors considering loans want assurance that the facts and figures the borrower submits are reliable. Shareholders, who have invested in the business, need to know that the financial picture management shows them is complete. Government agencies need information from businesses. All want information that is unbiased.

Tax accounting has two aims: complying with the tax laws and minimizing taxes to be paid. Because combined federal and provincial income tax rates range as high as 53 percent for individuals and 46 percent for corporations, reducing income tax is an important management consideration. Tax work by accountants consists of preparing tax returns and planning business transactions to minimize taxes. In addition, since the imposition of the Goods and Services Tax (GST), public accountants have been involved in advising their clients how to properly collect and account for GST. Public accountants advise individuals on what types of investments to make, and on how to structure their transactions. Accountants in corporations provide tax planning and preparation services as well.

Management consulting is the term that describes the wide scope of advice public accountants provide to help managers run a business. As they conduct audits, public accountants look deep into a business's operations. With the insight they gain, they often make suggestions for improvements in the business's management structure and accounting systems. The *Sarbanes-Oxley Act of 2002* has created the need for auditors to help their clients ensure the clients have complied with the Act. This includes ensuring that proper and effective internal controls are in place. However, Sarbanes-Oxley has also limited the management consulting services that auditors can supply to their audit clients.

Accounting services is also a catchall term used to describe the wide range of services related to accounting provided by public accountants. These services include bookkeeping and preparation of financial statements on a monthly or annual basis. Some small companies have all their accounting done by a public accounting firm.

Private Accounting

Cost accounting analyzes a business's costs to help managers control expenses or set selling prices. Good cost accounting records guide managers in pricing their products to achieve greater profits. Also, cost accounting information shows management when a product is not profitable and should be dropped from a product line.

Budgeting sets sales and profit goals, and develops detailed plans—called budgets—for achieving those goals. Some of the most successful companies in Canada have been pioneers in the field of budgeting.

Information systems design identifies the organization's information needs, both internal and external. Using flow charts and manuals, designers develop and implement the system to meet those needs.

Internal auditing is performed by a business's own audit staff. Many large organizations, Ontario Power Generation Inc., Hudson's Bay Co., and The Bank of Nova Scotia among them, maintain a staff of internal auditors. These accountants evaluate the firm's own accounting and management systems to improve operating efficiency, and to ensure that employees follow management's policies. Internal auditors also help to ensure that organizations comply with Sarbanes-Oxley by documenting and assessing internal controls, and by implementing checklists of items prescribed by the Act. Organizations are increasingly hiring outside, freelance accountants to help their own accountants ensure compliance with Sarbanes-Oxley.

Exhibit 2 summarizes these accounting specializations.

As you work through Accounting you will learn how to use accounting to make business decisions. With the exciting career opportunities accounting offers, consider a career in accounting.

| EXHIBIT 2 | Specialization in Public and Private Accounting |

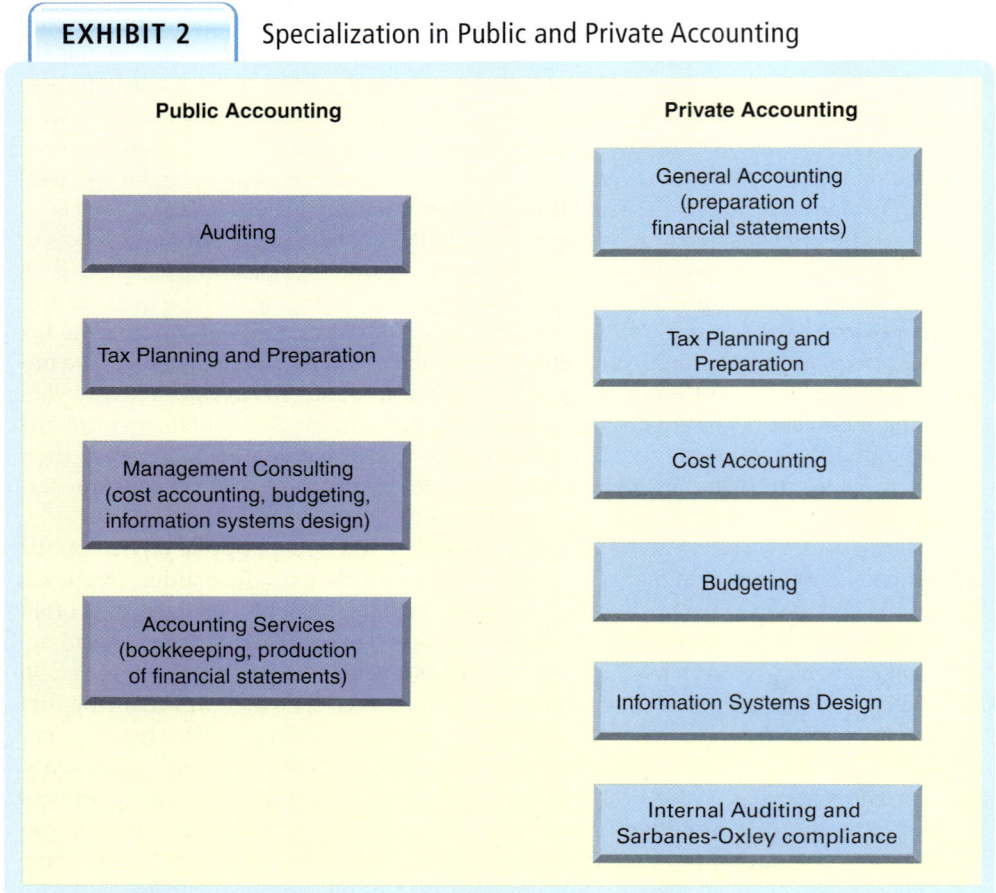

Public Accounting	Private Accounting
Auditing	General Accounting (preparation of financial statements)
Tax Planning and Preparation	Tax Planning and Preparation
Management Consulting (cost accounting, budgeting, information systems design)	Cost Accounting
Accounting Services (bookkeeping, production of financial statements)	Budgeting
	Information Systems Design
	Internal Auditing and Sarbanes-Oxley compliance

Accounting and the Business Environment

Learning Objectives

1. Define accounting, and describe the users of accounting information

2. Explain why ethics and rules of conduct are crucial in accounting and business

3. Describe and discuss the forms of business organizations

4. Explain the development of accounting standards, and describe the concepts and principles

5. Describe and use the accounting equation to analyze business transactions

6. Prepare and evaluate the financial statements

Doug Copely is a college student. After successfully completing his first term in December, Doug started looking for a summer job that would pay him enough to cover his expenses for his second year of school. He noticed an advertisement from College Joe Painters. Doug met with the managers of College Joe Painters and was granted a franchise to operate in Richmond, a suburb of Vancouver. Doug's income would be determined by his ability to successfully operate his own business. Overnight, Doug became an entrepreneur. He had to find customers, hire painters, set up an office, and learn some basic bookkeeping. By the time the second term of school had ended in April, Doug had lined up enough work to keep two crews of painters working full-time for the entire summer.

"I've never worked so hard in my life," Doug confided. "It's been a lot of fun but a lot of work. I had to learn how to bid for jobs, deal with customers, and find painters. My objective is to make enough income to pay for my tuition, books, and room and board next year. I think I've succeeded, but I won't know for sure until I prepare financial statements at the end of the summer. I never knew keeping track of my expenses would be so important!"

Why is accounting and the business environment important?
How do we organize a business?
How much do we record for assets and liabilities?
How do we measure profits and losses?
How do we determine where a business stands financially?

These questions and others will be answered throughout this chapter. And the Decision Guidelines at the end of this chapter will provide the answers in a useful summary.

Each chapter opens with questions about why this chapter is important. The questions are answered throughout the chapter and summarized in the Decision Guidelines at the end of the chapter.

What

role does accounting play in Doug Copely's situation? Doug had to decide how to organize his franchise. He set up his business as a proprietorship—a single-owner company—with Doug Copely as the owner. As the business grows, he may consider joining forces with a fellow franchisee to form a partnership or he could choose to incorporate—that is, to form a corporation. In this chapter, we discuss all three forms of business organization: proprietorships, partnerships, and corporations.

You may already know various accounting terms and relationships, because accounting affects people's behaviour in many ways. This first accounting course will sharpen your focus by explaining how accounting works. As you progress through this course, you will see how accounting helps people like Doug Copely—and you—achieve business goals.

Boldfaced words are new terms that are explained here and defined in the Glossary at the end of the book.

Accounting: The Language of Business

Objective 1
Define accounting, and describe the users of accounting information

Accounting is the information system that measures business financial activities, processes that information into reports, and communicates the results to decision makers. For this reason it is called "the language of business." The better you understand the language, the better your decisions will be, and the better you can manage financial information. A recent survey indicates that business managers believe it is more important for college students to learn accounting than any other business subject. Decisions concerning personal financial planning, education expenses, loans, car payments, income taxes, and investments are based on the *information system* that we call accounting.

Learning Objectives in the margin signal the beginning of the section that covers the learning-objective topic. Look for this when you want to review this topic.

Financial statements are a key product of an accounting system and provide information that helps people make informed business decisions. **Financial statements** report on a business in monetary terms. Is my business making a profit? Should I hire assistants? Am I earning enough money to expand my business? Answering business questions like these requires the financial statements.

Students sometimes mistake bookkeeping for accounting. *Bookkeeping* is a procedural element of accounting, just as arithmetic is a procedural element of mathematics. Increasingly, people are using computers to do detailed bookkeeping—in households, businesses, and organizations of all types. Exhibit 1–1 illustrates the role of accounting in business. The process starts and ends with people making decisions.

EXHIBIT 1–1 The Accounting System: The Flow of Information

People make decisions

Business transactions occur

Businesses prepare reports to show the results of their operations

Exhibits summarize key ideas in a visual way that makes them easier to understand and remember.

Decision Makers: The Users of Accounting Information

Decision makers need information. The more important the decision, the greater the need for information. Virtually all businesses and most individuals keep accounting records to aid decision making. Here are some decision makers who use accounting information.

Individuals People use accounting information in day-to-day affairs to manage bank accounts, evaluate job prospects, make investments, and decide whether to lease or buy a new car.

Businesses Business owners and managers use accounting information to set goals for their organizations. They evaluate their progress toward those goals, and they take corrective action when it is necessary. For example, Doug Copely of College Joe Painters makes decisions, based on accounting information, that include which jobs to accept, how many painters to hire, and how much to charge customers to meet his goal of earning enough to pay for school.

Investors Outside investors often provide the money a business needs to begin operations. To decide whether to invest, potential investors predict the amount of income to be earned on their investment. This evaluation means analyzing the financial statements of the business and keeping up with developments in the business press, for example, *The Financial Post* (a part of *The National Post*) and *Report on Business* published by *The Globe and Mail*.

Creditors Before loaning money, creditors (lenders) such as banks evaluate the borrower's ability to make scheduled payments. This evaluation includes a report of the borrower's financial position and a prediction of future operations, both of which are based on accounting information.

Government Regulatory Agencies Most organizations face government regulation. For example, the provincial securities commissions, such as the Ontario Securities Commission, dictate that businesses that sell their shares to or borrow money from the public disclose certain financial information to the investing public.

Taxing Authorities Provincial and federal governments levy taxes on individuals and businesses. Income tax is calculated using accounting information. Businesses use their accounting records to help them determine their goods and services tax and sales tax.

Nonprofit Organizations Nonprofit organizations such as churches, hospitals, government agencies, and colleges, which operate for purposes other than to earn a profit, use accounting information in much the same way that profit-oriented businesses do.

Other Users Employees and labour unions may make wage demands based on the accounting information that shows their employer's reported income. Consumer groups and the general public are also interested in the amount of income that businesses earn. And newspapers may report "an improved profit picture" of a major company as it emerges from economic difficulties. Such news, based on accounting information, is related to the company's health.

Financial Accounting and Management Accounting

Users of accounting information are a diverse population, but they may be grouped as external users or internal users. This distinction allows us to classify accounting into two fields—financial accounting and management accounting.

Financial accounting provides information to people outside the company. Creditors and outside investors, for example, are not part of the day-to-day management of the company. Likewise, government agencies and the general public are external users of a company's accounting information. Chapters 2 through 18 in Volumes I and II of this book deal primarily with financial accounting.

Management accounting generates information for internal decision makers, such as company executives, department heads, college deans, and hospital administrators. Chapters 19 through 26 in Volume III of this book cover management accounting.

Exhibit 1–2 shows how financial accounting and management accounting are used by Doug Copely's College Joe Painter's internal and external decision makers.

| **EXHIBIT 1–2** | How Financial Accounting and Management Accounting Are Used |

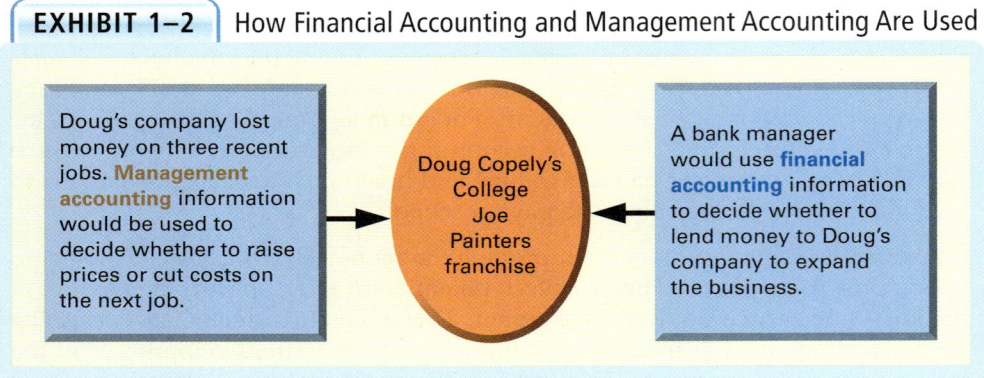

The History and Development of Accounting

Accounting has a long history. Some scholars claim that writing arose in order to record accounting information. Account records date back to the ancient civilizations of China, Babylonia, Greece, and Egypt. The rulers of these civilizations used accounting to keep track of the cost of labour and materials used in building structures like the great pyramids. The need for accounting has existed as long as there has been business activity.

Accounting developed further as a result of the information needs of merchants in the city-states of Italy during the 1400s. In that busy commercial climate, the monk Luca Pacioli, a mathematician and friend of Leonardo da Vinci, published the first known description of double-entry bookkeeping in 1494.

In the Industrial Revolution of the nineteenth century, the growth of corporations spurred the development of accounting. The corporation owners—the shareholders—were no longer necessarily the managers of their business. Managers had to create accounting systems to report to the owners and government how well their businesses were doing. Because managers want their performance to look good, society needs a way to ensure that the business information provided is reliable. To meet this need, generally accepted accounting principles were developed. These will be discussed in more detail shortly.

Like other segments of society, accounting must be practised in an ethical manner. We look next at the ethical dimension of accounting.

Ethical Considerations in Accounting and Business

Ethical considerations affect all areas of accounting and business. Investors, creditors, and regulatory bodies need relevant and reliable information about a company. Naturally, companies want to make themselves look as good as possible to attract investors, so there is a potential for conflict. An **audit** is a financial examination. Audits are conducted by independent accountants who express an opinion on whether or not the financial statements fairly reflect the economic events that occurred during the accounting period. It is vital that companies and their auditors behave in an ethical manner. Exhibit 1–3 illustrates the relationship among accounting and business entities.

Objective 2

Explain why ethics and rules of conduct are crucial in accounting and business

| **EXHIBIT 1–3** | Relationship Among Accounting and Business Entities |

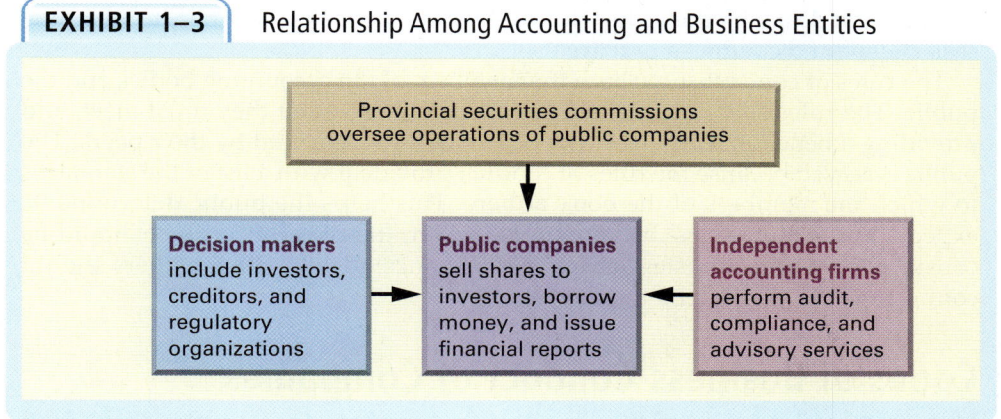

Unfortunately for the accounting profession, accounting scandals involving both public companies and their auditors have made the headlines in recent years. Most of these incidents occurred in the United States. For example, Enron Corporation, which was the seventh-largest company in the United States, allegedly issued misleading financial statements that reported fewer debts than the company really owed. Enron was forced into bankruptcy and its auditors were forced out of business (although on May 31, 2005, the U.S. Supreme Court overturned the Arthur Andersen accounting firm's conviction). The impact of the Enron bankruptcy was felt by many different parties, including Enron shareholders, who saw their investments become worthless, employees who lost their jobs and their pension funds, and the accounting profession, which lost some of its integrity and reputation as gatekeepers and stewards for the investing public. Scandals like this shocked the business community and hurt investor confidence.

In response to the scandals, the *Sarbanes-Oxley Act of 2002* was introduced. It is landmark legislation designed to make U.S. public companies more transparent in their financial reporting and more proactive in sharing material information with other participants in the financial reporting chain, including auditors, audit committees, analysts, and investors. If Canadian companies are registered in the United States, they must follow the rules of the *Sarbanes-Oxley Act*. Nortel Networks Corporation, the Canadian communication-networks company, was forced to comply with these rules and, as a result, restated its December 31, 2004, financial statements.

Rather than move toward U.S. standards, there is a movement in Canada toward the convergence of Canadian standards with International Financial Reporting Standards (IFRSs) over a transition period, expected to be five years.

In this book, we provide several problems that allow you to consider ethical dilemmas. Consider them carefully. The perception that accountants follow the highest standard of professional conduct must also be the reality. In today's business climate, behaving in an ethical manner is crucial.

The Professional Accounting Bodies and Their Standards of Professional Conduct

Chartered Accountants (CAs), Certified General Accountants (CGAs), and Certified Management Accountants (CMAs) are all governed by rules of conduct created by their respective organizations. Many of the rules apply whether the members are public accountants working in public practice or private accountants working in industry or government. These rules concern the confidentiality of information the accountant is privy to, maintenance of the reputation of the profession, the need to perform their work with integrity and due care, competence, refusal to be associated with false or misleading information, and compliance by the accountant with professional standards. Other rules are applicable only to those members in public practice, and deal with things like the need for independence, and how to advertise, seek clients, and conduct a practice.

The rules of conduct serve both the members of the accounting bodies and the public. The rules serve members by setting standards that they must meet, and providing a benchmark against which they will be measured by their peers. The public is served because the rules of conduct provide it with a list of the standards to which the members of the body adhere. This helps the public determine its expectations of members' behaviour. However, the rules of conduct should be considered a minimum standard of performance; ideally, the members should continually strive to exceed them.

Codes of Business Conduct of Companies

Many companies have codes of conduct that apply to their employees in their dealings with each other and with the companies' suppliers and customers. Some of these companies mention their code in the annual report or on their website. For example, Vancouver City Savings Credit Union states on its website:

> **Our Values**
> **Integrity:** We act with courage, consistency and respect to do what is honest, fair and trustworthy.
> **Innovation:** We anticipate and respond to challenges and changing needs with creativity, enthusiasm and determination.
> **Responsibility:** We are accountable to our members, employees, colleagues and communities for the results of our decisions and actions.[1]

The company indicates to its employees and to the general public how management expects employees to behave.

---

[1]From Vancouver City Savings Credit Union's website, **www.vancity.com** (accessed March 16, 2006).

Types of Business Organizations

A business can be organized as a

- Proprietorship
- Partnership
- Corporation

You should understand the differences among the three.

Objective 3
Describe and discuss the forms of business organizations

Proprietorship A **proprietorship** has a single owner, called the proprietor, who often manages the business. Proprietorships tend to be small retail stores and individual professional businesses, such as those of physicians, lawyers, and accountants, but also can be very large. From the accounting viewpoint, each proprietorship is distinct from its owner. Thus the accounting records of the proprietorship do *not* include the proprietor's personal accounting records. However, from a legal perspective, the business *is* the proprietor. In this book, we start with a proprietorship because many students organize their first business that way.

Partnership A **partnership** joins two or more individuals together as co-owners. Each owner is a partner. Many retail stores and professional organizations of physicians, lawyers, and accountants are partnerships. Most partnerships are small and medium-sized, but some are quite large; there are public accounting firms in Canada with more than 500 partners and law firms with more than 100 partners. Accounting treats the partnership as a separate organization distinct from the personal affairs of each partner. But again, from a legal perspective, a partnership *is* the partners in a manner similar to the proprietorship.

Corporation A **corporation** is a business owned by **shareholders**. These are the people or other corporations who own shares of ownership in the business. The corporation is the dominant form of business organization in Canada. Although proprietorships and partnerships are more numerous, corporations engage in more business and are generally larger in terms of total assets, income, and number of employees. In Canada, generally, corporations must have *Ltd.* or *Limited, Inc.* or *Incorporated,* or *Corp.* or *Corporation* in their legal name to indicate that they are incorporated. Corporations need not be large; a business with only a few assets and employees could be organized as a corporation.

From a legal perspective, a corporation is formed when the federal government or a provincial government approves its articles of incorporation. Unlike a proprietorship or partnership, a corporation is a legal entity distinct from its owners. The corporation operates as an "artificial person" that exists apart from its owners and that conducts business in its own name. The corporation has many of the rights that a person has. For example, a corporation may buy, own, and sell property. The corporation may enter into contracts and sue and be sued.

Corporations differ significantly from proprietorships and partnerships in another way. If a proprietorship or partnership cannot pay its debts, lenders can take the owners' personal assets—cash and belongings—to satisfy the business's obligations. But if a corporation goes bankrupt, lenders cannot take the personal assets of the shareholders. This *limited personal liability* of shareholders for corporate debts explains why corporations are so popular compared to proprietorships and partnerships. Exhibit 1–4 shows the formation and ownership of a corporation.

Another factor for corporations is the division of ownership into individual shares. Companies such as BCE Inc., Canadian Imperial Bank of Commerce, and Canadian Tire Corporation, Limited have issued millions of shares of stock and have tens of thousands of shareholders. An investor with no personal relationship either to the corporation or to any other shareholder can become an owner by buying 30, 100, 5,000, or any number of shares of its stock. For most corporations, the investor may sell the shares at any time. It is usually harder to sell one's investment in a proprietorship or a partnership than to sell one's investment in a corporation.

KEY POINT

A proprietorship and a partnership (Ch. 12) are not legal entities separate from their owners, so the income from proprietorships and partnerships is taxable to their owners, not to the business. But in accounting, the owner and the business are considered separate entities, and separate records are kept for each. A corporation (Ch. 13) is a separate legal entity. The corporation is taxed on its income, and the owners are taxed on any income they receive from the corporation.

Key Points highlight important details from the text and are good tools for reviewing concepts.

EXHIBIT 1–4

The Formation and Ownership of a Corporation

Federal or **provincial government** approves Articles of Incorporation

Corporations
Examples include Bombardier Inc. McCain Foods Ltd. Royal Bank of Canada

Shareholders invest in corporations

Limited-Liability Partnership (LLP) and Limited-Liability Company (LLC) A **limited-liability partnership (LLP)** is a partnership in which one partner cannot create a large liability for the other partners. Each partner is liable only for his or her own actions and those actions under his or her control. A proprietorship can be organized as a **limited-liability company (LLC)**, where the company and not the proprietor is liable for the company's debts. Today, most proprietorships and partnerships are organized as LLCs and LLPs. The limited-liability aspect gives these organizations one of the chief advantages of a corporation.

Exhibit 1–5 summarizes the differences between proprietorships, partnerships, and corporations.

EXHIBIT 1–5 Comparison of the Three Forms of Business Organization

	Proprietorship	Partnership	Corporation
1. Owner(s)	Proprietor—one owner	Partners—two or more owners	Shareholders—generally many owners
2. Life of organization	Limited by owner's choice or death	Limited by owners' choices or death	Indefinite
3. Personal liability of owner(s) for business debts	Proprietor is personally liable[*]	Partners are personally liable[**]	Shareholders are not personally liable
4. Legal status	The proprietorship is the proprietor[*]	The partnership is the partners[**]	The corporation is separate from the shareholders (owners)

[*]Unless it is a limited-liability company (LLC)
[**]Unless it is a limited-liability partnership (LLP)

Accounting for corporations includes some unique complexities. For this reason, we initially focus on proprietorships. We cover partnerships in Chapter 12 and begin our discussion of corporations in Chapter 13.

Accounting Concepts

Objective 4

Explain the development of accounting standards, and describe the concepts and principles

Accounting practices follow certain guidelines. The rules that govern how accountants measure, process, and communicate financial information fall under the heading GAAP, which stands for **generally accepted accounting principles**. In Canada, the *Accounting Standards Board (AcSB)* of the Canadian Institute of Chartered Accountants (CICA) is responsible for creating GAAP. The AcSB consists of a maximum of nine members from a variety of backgrounds. Members are chosen so that the AcSB has an appropriate balance of competencies and expertise to set accounting standards. The federal and provincial legislatures through the various companies' acts and the various provincial securities commissions have given the standards or GAAP issued by the AcSB and collected in the *CICA Handbook* their legal status.

Accounting principles draw their authority from their acceptance in the business community. They are generally accepted by those people and organizations who need guidelines in accounting for their financial undertakings.

Currently, GAAP in Canada are based on the *CICA Handbook*, Section 1000, Financial Statement Concepts, and Section 1100, Generally Accepted Accounting Principles. Section 1100 lists the sources of GAAP in Canada, which include accounting sections in the *CICA Handbook* and other guidelines, abstracts, and background information issued by the Accounting Standards Board of the CICA and its committees. Section 1100 states that standards can change over time to reflect changes in economic and social conditions. Section 1100 also states that the *Handbook* cannot (and is not intended to) address every possible financial transaction or situation. When a transaction or situation is not addressed specifically in the *Handbook* or other primary sources of GAAP listed in Section 1100, then accountants should refer to Section 1000 and apply their professional judgment.

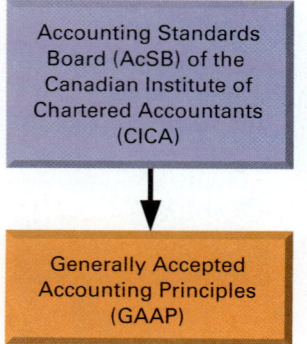

Accounting Standards Board (AcSB) of the Canadian Institute of Chartered Accountants (CICA)

↓

Generally Accepted Accounting Principles (GAAP)

Exhibit 1–6 summarizes the financial statement concepts described in *Handbook Section 1000*. Level 1 in Exhibit 1–6 shows that the primary objective of financial statements is to provide information useful for making resource allocation decisions (helping people decide where to invest their money) and for assessing management's stewardship (judging whether managers are running a company well).

The qualitative characteristics that increase the value of accounting information appear in Level 2 of Exhibit 1–6.

To be useful, information must be *understandable, relevant,* and *reliable,* as well as *comparable.* The information must be *understandable* to users if they are to be able to use it. *Relevant* information influences decisions and is useful for making predictions and for evaluating past performance. *Reliable* information is free from error and the bias of a particular viewpoint; it is in agreement with the underlying events and transactions. *Comparable* information is information that is produced by organizations using the same accounting principles and policies, and that allows comparison between the organizations. Comparability also allows comparisons over time or at two points in time.

There are two constraints to providing information to users that is understandable, relevant, reliable, and comparable. They are shown in Level 4 of Exhibit 1–6. The first constraint is that the benefits of the information produced should exceed the costs of producing the information, as stated in Paragraph 1000.16 in the *CICA Handbook.* The second constraint is *materiality,* as stated in Paragraph 1000.17; a piece of information is material if it would affect a decision maker's decision. Materiality is not defined in the standards but is a matter of the information preparer's judgment. For example, information about inventory is important to users of Canadian Tire's financial statements, since a change in inventory could change a decision maker's decision about investing in Canadian Tire or selling products to Canadian Tire. Thus, such information would be provided to decision makers. However, information about the supplies inventory at Coast Capital Savings Credit Union would not likely change the investment decision of a member of the credit union, so details of such information are not provided.

EXHIBIT 1–6   A Hierarchy of Financial-Statement Concepts

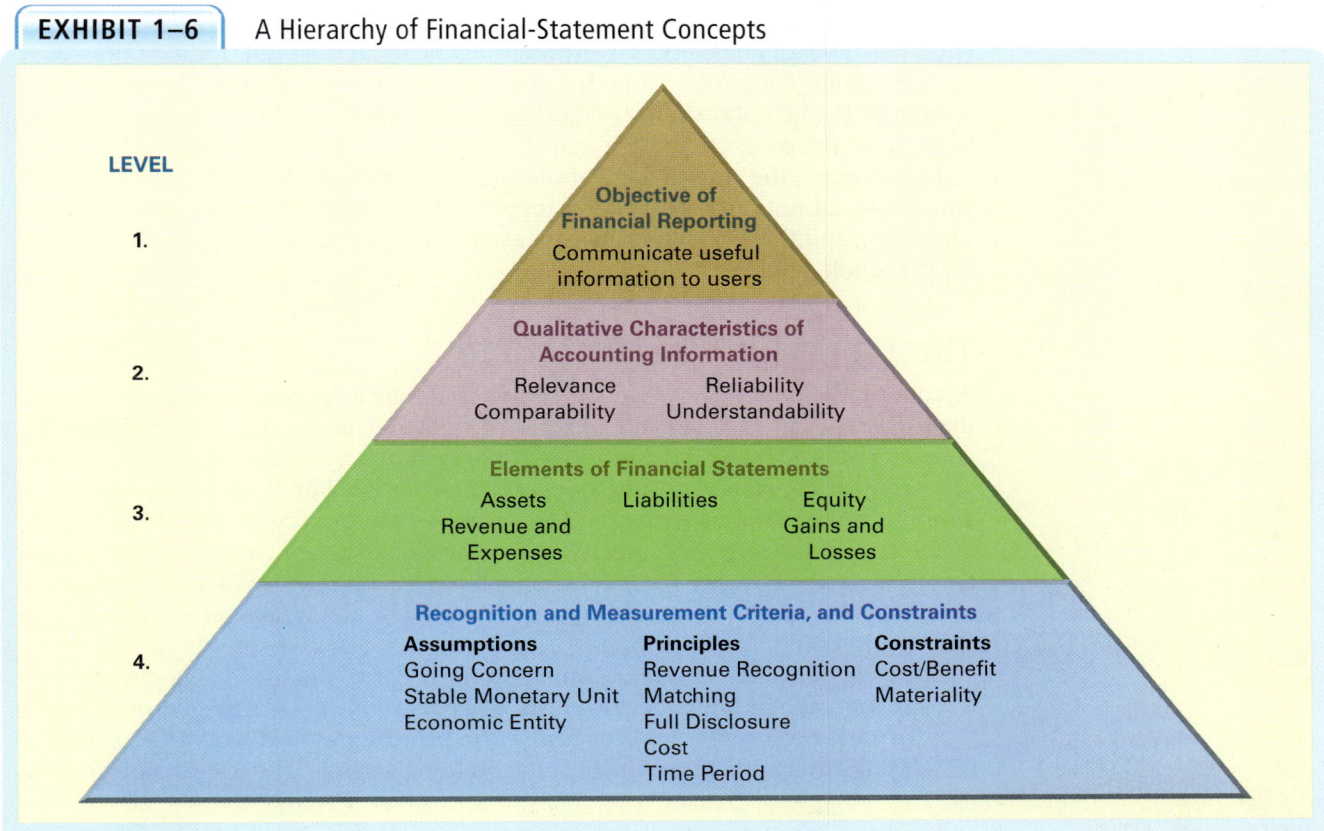

Level 3 in Exhibit 1–6 shows the standard elements of the financial statements. We will learn more about these items later in this chapter. In addition to the constraints described above, Level 4 in Exhibit 1–6 also contains the recognition and measurement criteria that form the basis of GAAP.

Exhibit 1–6 summarizes the key points of *Handbook* Section 1000: For any financial transaction or situation, the GAAP in Level 4 are used as guidelines for classifying the transaction's financial data into the standard financial-statement elements shown in Level 3. If these elements meet the Level-2 qualitative characteristics of accounting information, they are combined into financial statements that meet the Level-1 objective of reporting financial information useful for users.

This course will expose you to the generally accepted methods of accounting. We begin the discussion of GAAP in this section and introduce additional assumptions and principles as needed throughout the book.

Appendix C at the end of Volume I and II summarizes the major elements of generally accepted accounting principles.

The Economic-Entity Assumption

The most basic assumption in accounting is that of the **entity**. An accounting entity is an organization or a section of an organization that stands apart from other organizations and individuals as a separate economic unit. From an accounting perspective, sharp boundaries are drawn around each entity so as not to confuse its affairs with those of other entities.

Suppose you decided to tutor other students, so you started a proprietorship. After the first year, you had $2,000 in your bank account. Suppose only $1,000 of that amount came from your business's operation. The other $1,000 was a gift from your parents. If you follow the entity concept, you will keep separate the money generated by the business—one economic unit—from the money generated by the gift from your family—a second economic unit. This separation makes it possible to view the business's operating result clearly; otherwise, you might be misled into believing that the business produced more cash than it did.

The economic-entity assumption also applies to nonprofit organizations such as churches, synagogues, and government agencies. A hospital, for example, may have an emergency room, a pediatrics unit, and a surgery unit. The accounting system of the hospital should account for each separately to allow the managers to evaluate the progress of each unit.

In summary, the transactions of different entities making up the whole organization should not be accounted for together. Each entity should be accounted for separately, and then later, the results of each entity can be combined to create results for the whole organization.

The Reliability Characteristic

Accounting records and statements are based on the most reliable data available so that they will be as accurate and useful as possible. This guideline is the **reliability characteristic,** also called the **objectivity characteristic.** Reliable data are verifiable. They may be confirmed by any independent observer. For example, a purchase of supplies can be supported by paid invoices. A paid invoice is objective evidence of the cost of the supplies. Ideally, accounting records are based on information that flows from activities that are documented using objective evidence. Without the reliability characteristic, accounting records might be based on whims and opinions and would be subject to dispute.

Suppose you want to open a music store. To have a place for operations, you transfer a small building to the business. You believe the building is worth $200,000. Two real-estate professionals appraise the building at $190,000. Is $200,000 or $190,000 the more reliable estimate of the building's value? The real-estate appraisal

KEY POINT

The economic-entity assumption requires that the transactions of each entity be accounted for separately from the transactions of all other organizations and persons.

of $190,000 is, because it is supported by independent, objective observations. The business should record the building at a cost of $190,000.

The Cost Principle

The **cost principle** states that acquired assets and services should be recorded at their actual cost (also called *historical cost*). Even though the purchaser may believe the price paid is a bargain, the item is recorded at the price actually paid and not at the "expected" cost. Suppose your music store purchased some compact discs from a supplier who was going out of business. Assume you got a good deal on this purchase and paid only $5,000 for merchandise that would have cost you $8,000 elsewhere. The cost principle requires you to record this merchandise at its actual cost of $5,000, not the $8,000 that you believe the compact discs to be worth.

The cost principle also holds that the accounting records should continue reporting the historical cost of an asset for as long as the business holds the asset. Why? Because cost is a reliable measure. Suppose your store holds the compact discs for three months. During that time, compact disc prices increase, and the compact discs can be sold for $9,000. Should their accounting value—the figure "on the books"—be the actual cost of $5,000 or the current market value of $9,000? According to the cost principle, the accounting value of the compact discs remains at actual cost of $5,000. There are some exceptions—investments are discussed in Chapter 16.

The Going-Concern Assumption

Another reason for measuring assets at historical cost is the **going-concern assumption**, which assumes that the entity will remain in operation for the foreseeable future. Most assets—that is, the firm's resources, such as supplies, land, buildings, automobiles, and equipment—are acquired to use rather than to sell. Under the going-concern assumption, accountants assume the business will remain in operation long enough to use existing assets for their intended purpose.

To understand the going-concern assumption, assume a business bought a delivery van for $5,000 and it is now worth $3,000. The going-concern assumption ensures that proper accounting procedures are followed, as if the business is going to continue operating indefinitely. For a going concern, the delivery van is valued at its cost of $5,000 in the accounting records. However, if the business is holding a Going-Out-of-Business Sale, it would want to value the delivery van at $3,000 in the accounting records because that is the amount the business could sell it for today, on its final day of business. Accountants assume a business will operate indefinitely.

The Stable-Monetary-Unit Assumption

We think of the cost of a loaf of bread and a month's apartment rent in terms of their dollar value. In Canada, accountants record transactions in dollars because the dollar is the medium of exchange. French and German transactions are measured in euros. The Japanese record transactions in yen.

Unlike a litre, a kilometre, or a tonne, the value of a dollar or a euro changes over time. A rise in the general level of prices is called *inflation.* During inflation a dollar will purchase less milk, less toothpaste, and less of other goods. When prices are relatively stable—when there is little inflation—the purchasing power of money is also stable.

Accountants assume that the dollar's purchasing power is relatively stable. The **stable-monetary-unit assumption** is the basis for ignoring the effect of inflation in the accounting records. It allows accountants to add and subtract dollar amounts as though each dollar has the same purchasing power as any other dollar at any other time. In certain countries in South America, where inflation rates are often high, accountants make adjustments to report monetary amounts in units of current buying power—a very different concept.

STOP AND THINK

Suppose you are considering the purchase of land for future expansion. The seller is asking $100,000 for land that cost her $70,000. An appraisal shows the land has a value of $94,000. You first offer $80,000. The seller counteroffers with $96,000. Finally, you and the seller agree on a price of $92,000. What dollar amount for this land is reported on your financial statements? Which accounting assumption or principle guides your answer?

Answer: According to the *cost principle*, goods and services should be recorded at their actual cost. You paid $92,000 for the land. Therefore, $92,000 is the cost to report on your financial statements.

The Accounting Equation

Objective 5

Describe and use the accounting equation to analyze business transactions

Financial statements tell us how a business is performing and where it stands. They are the final product of the accounting process. But how do we arrive at the items and amounts that make up the financial statements? The most basic tool of the accountant is the **accounting equation**. It measures the resources of a business and the claims to those resources.

Assets and Liabilities

Assets are economic resources that are expected to benefit the business in the future. Cash, office supplies, merchandise inventory, furniture, land, and buildings are examples of assets.

Claims to those assets come from two sources. **Liabilities** are debts that are payable to outsiders. These *outside* parties are called *creditors*. For example, a creditor who has loaned money to a business has a claim—a legal right—to a part of the assets until the business pays the debt. Many liabilities have the word *payable* in their titles. Examples include Accounts Payable, Notes Payable, and Salaries Payable. *Insider* claims to the business assets are owners' claims called **owner's equity** or **capital**. An owner's claim to some of the entity's assets begins when the owner invests in the business.

The accounting equation in Exhibit 1–7 shows how assets, liabilities, and owner's equity are related. Assets appear on the left side of the equation. The legal and

EXHIBIT 1–7

The Accounting Equation

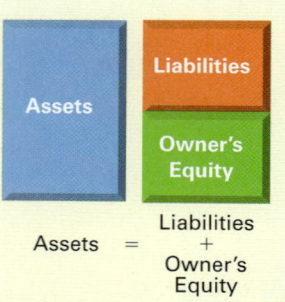

Assets = Liabilities + Owner's Equity

STOP AND THINK

1. If the assets of a business are $10,000 and the liabilities total $2,000, how much is the owner's equity?

2. If the owner's equity in a business is $20,000 and the liabilities are $5,000, how much are the assets?

Answers: To answer both questions, use the accounting equation:

1.
Assets	−	Liabilities	=	Owner's Equity
$10,000	−	$2,000	=	$8,000

2.
Assets	=	Liabilities	+	Owner's Equity
$25,000	=	$5,000	+	$20,000

economic claims against the assets—the liabilities and owner's equity—appear on the right side of the equation. As Exhibit 1–7 shows, *the two sides must be equal*:

Economic Resources		Claims to Economic Resources
(Outsiders)		(Insiders)
ASSETS	**=**	**LIABILITIES + OWNER'S EQUITY**

Owner's Equity

Owner's equity is the amount of an entity's assets that remains after the liabilities are subtracted. For this reason, owner's equity is often referred to as *net assets* and the accounting equation can be written to show this:

$$\textbf{ASSETS} - \textbf{LIABILITIES} = \textbf{OWNER'S EQUITY}$$

The purpose of business is to increase owner's equity through **revenues**, which are amounts earned by delivering goods or services to customers. Revenues increase owner's equity because they increase the business's assets but not its liabilities. As a result, the owner's share of business assets increases. Examples of revenue include sales revenue from selling goods, service revenue from selling services, interest revenue from saving money in a bank, and dividend revenue from investing in shares of stock. Exhibit 1–8 shows that owner investments and revenues increase the owner's equity of the business.

Exhibit 1–8 also shows that owner withdrawals and expenses decrease owner's equity. **Owner withdrawals** are those amounts or resources removed from the business by the owner. Withdrawals are the opposite of owner investments. **Expenses** are decreases in owner's equity that occur from using or consuming assets or increasing liabilities in the course of delivering goods and services to customers. Expenses are the cost of doing business and are the opposite of revenues. Expenses include the cost of office rent, interest payments, salaries of employees, insurance, advertisements, property taxes, utility payments for water, electricity, gas, and so forth.

Increases in cash are not always revenues. Cash also increases when a company borrows money, but borrowing money creates a liability—not a revenue. Revenue results from rendering a service or selling a product, not necessarily from the receipt of cash.

Decreases in cash are not always expenses. Cash decreases when land is purchased, for example, but the purchase also increases the asset Land, which is not an expense. Expenses result from using goods or services in the course of earning revenue, not necessarily from the payment of cash.

EXHIBIT 1–8 Transactions That Increase and Decrease Owner's Equity

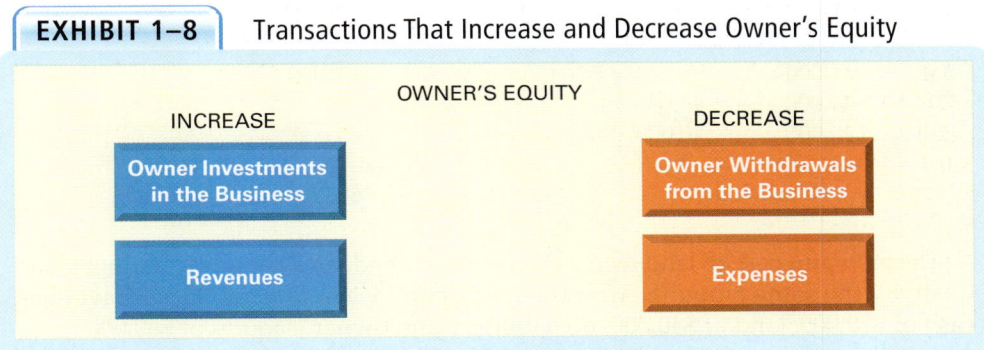

Accounting for Business Transactions

Accounting is based on transactions, not opinions or desires. A **transaction** is any event that affects the financial position of the business entity *and* can be measured reliably. Many events may affect a company, including elections and economic booms. Accountants do not record the effects of these events because they cannot be measured reliably. An accountant records as transactions only events with dollar amounts that can be measured reliably, such as purchases and sales of merchandise inventory, payment of rent, and collection of cash from customers. In Exhibit 1–1 on page 3, transactions are the middle step in the flow of information in an accounting system.

To illustrate accounting for business transactions, let's assume that John Lapp opens a travel agency that he calls SuperTravel. We will now consider 11 events

A transaction is an event that must always satisfy these two conditions:

1. It affects the financial position of a business entity, and
2. It can be reliably recorded in the accounting records.

and analyze each in terms of its effect on the accounting equation of SuperTravel. *Remember that the accounting equation must always remain in balance.* Transaction analysis is the essence of accounting.

Transaction 1: Starting the Business John Lapp invests $60,000 of his money to start the business. Specifically, he deposits $60,000 in a bank account entitled SuperTravel.

The effect of this transaction on the accounting equation of the SuperTravel business entity is

	Assets	=	Liabilities +	Owner's Equity	Types of Owner's Equity Transaction
	Cash			John Lapp, Capital	
(1)	+60,000			+60,000	*owner investment*

For every transaction, the amount on the left side of the equation must equal the amount on the right side. The first transaction increases both the assets (in this case, Cash) and the owner's equity of the business (John Lapp, Capital). The transaction involves no liabilities of the business because it creates no obligation for SuperTravel to pay an outside party. The Assets and Liabilities elements of the accounting equation will be expanded to show the specific accounts affected by a transaction, but Owner's Equity will not be expanded. Therefore, to the right of the transaction, we write "owner investment" to keep track of the reason for the effect on Owner's Equity.

Transaction 2: Purchase of Land SuperTravel purchases land for a future office location, paying cash of $40,000. The effect of this transaction on the accounting equation is

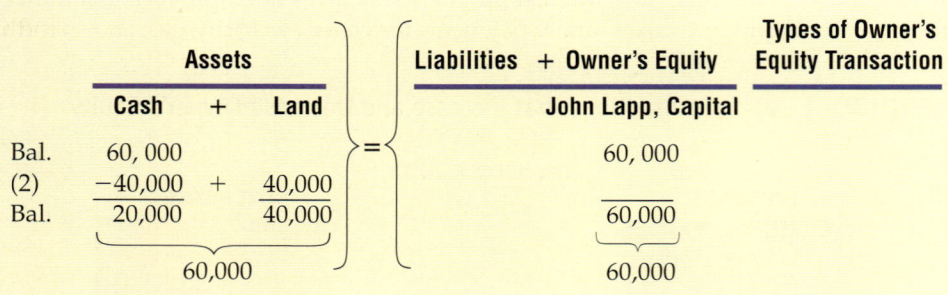

	Assets			=	Liabilities + Owner's Equity	Types of Owner's Equity Transaction
	Cash	+	Land		John Lapp, Capital	
Bal.	60,000				60,000	
(2)	−40,000	+	40,000			
Bal.	20,000		40,000		60,000	
		60,000			60,000	

The cash purchase of land increases one asset, Land, and decreases another asset, Cash, by the same amount. After the transaction is completed, SuperTravel has cash of $20,000, land of $40,000, no liabilities, and owner's equity of $60,000.

STOP AND THINK

The realtor that arranged SuperTravel's land purchase assures the company that the land is worth $75,000. Could the company ethically record the land at $75,000?

Answer: Regardless of the realtor's belief about the true value of the land, it is recorded at $40,000 because of the *cost principle* and the *reliability characteristic*. Actual cost is a reliable measure of an asset.

Transaction 3: Purchase of Office Supplies SuperTravel buys stationery and other office supplies, agreeing to pay $1,000 within 30 days. This transaction increases both the assets and the liabilities of the company, as follows:

	Assets					Liabilities	+	Owner's Equity	
	Cash	+	Office Supplies	+	Land	Accounts Payable	+	John Lapp, Capital	
Bal.	20,000				40,000			60,000	
(3)			+1,000			+1,000			
Bal.	20,000		1,000		40,000	1,000		60,000	
			61,000				61,000		

The asset affected is Office Supplies, and the liability is called an **account payable**. A *payable is always a liability.* Because SuperTravel is obligated to pay $1,000 in the future but signs no formal promissory note, we record the liability as an Account Payable. (If a promissory note had been signed, we would have recorded the liability as a **Note Payable**.)

Transaction 4: Earning of Service Revenue SuperTravel earns service revenue by providing travel arrangement services for clients. Assume the business earns $5,000 and collects this amount in cash. The effect on the accounting equation is an increase in the asset Cash and an increase in John Lapp, Capital, as follows:

	Assets					Liabilities	+	Owner's Equity		Types of Owner's Equity Transaction
	Cash	+	Office Supplies	+	Land	Accounts Payable	+	John Lapp, Capital		
Bal.	20,000		1,000		40,000	1,000		60,000		
(4)	+5,000							5,000		*Service revenue*
Bal.	25,000		1,000		40,000	1,000		65,000		
			66,000				66,000			

A revenue transaction causes the business to grow, as shown by the increase in total assets and in the sum of total liabilities plus owner's equity. A company like Canadian Tire or Zellers that sells goods to customers is a merchandising business. Its revenue is called *sales revenue.* In contrast, SuperTravel performs services for clients. SuperTravel's revenue is called *service revenue.*

STOP AND THINK

SuperTravel has now completed four business transactions. Answer these questions about the business:

1. How much in total assets does SuperTravel have to work with?
2. How much of the total assets does SuperTravel actually own? How much does SuperTravel owe to outsiders?

Answers:

1. SuperTravel owns three assets totalling $66,000, which is the sum of cash ($25,000) + office supplies ($1,000) + land ($40,000).
2. SuperTravel or John Lapp owns $65,000, the amount of owner's equity. The business owes $1,000 (Accounts Payable) to outsiders.

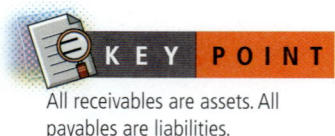

Transaction 5: Earning of Service Revenue on Account SuperTravel performs services for clients who do not pay immediately. In return for the services, SuperTravel issues an invoice and the clients will pay the $6,000 amount within one month. This debt is an asset to SuperTravel, an **account receivable** because the business expects to collect the cash in the future. In accounting, we say that SuperTravel performed this service *on account* and earned the revenue. Performing the service, not collecting the cash, earns the revenue. This $6,000 of service revenue is as real an increase in the wealth of SuperTravel's business as the $5,000 of revenue that was collected immediately in Transaction 4. SuperTravel records an increase in the asset Accounts Receivable and an increase in Service Revenue, which increases John Lapp, Capital, as follows:

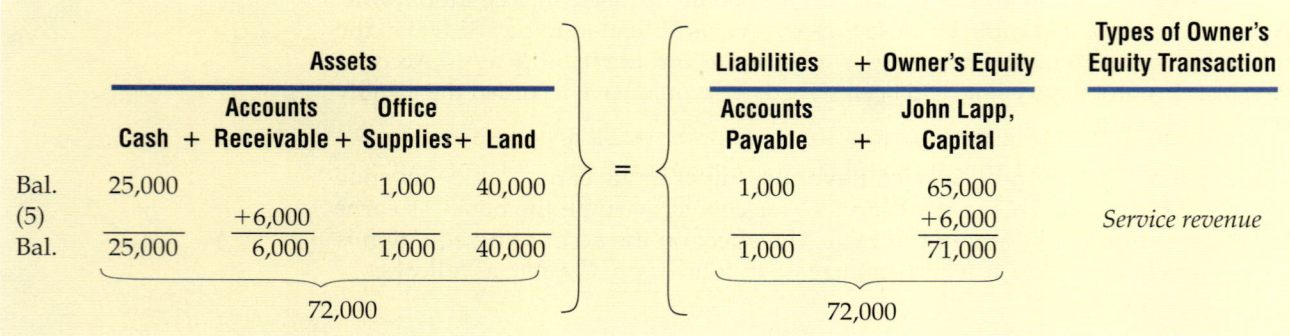

	Assets				=	Liabilities	+ Owner's Equity	Types of Owner's Equity Transaction
	Cash +	Accounts Receivable +	Office Supplies +	Land		Accounts Payable +	John Lapp, Capital	
Bal.	25,000		1,000	40,000		1,000	65,000	
(5)		+6,000					+6,000	*Service revenue*
Bal.	25,000	6,000	1,000	40,000		1,000	71,000	
		72,000					72,000	

Transaction 6: Payment of Expenses During the month, SuperTravel pays $5,200 in cash expenses: office rent, $2,200; employee salary, $2,400 (for a part-time assistant); and total utilities, $600. The effects on the accounting equation are

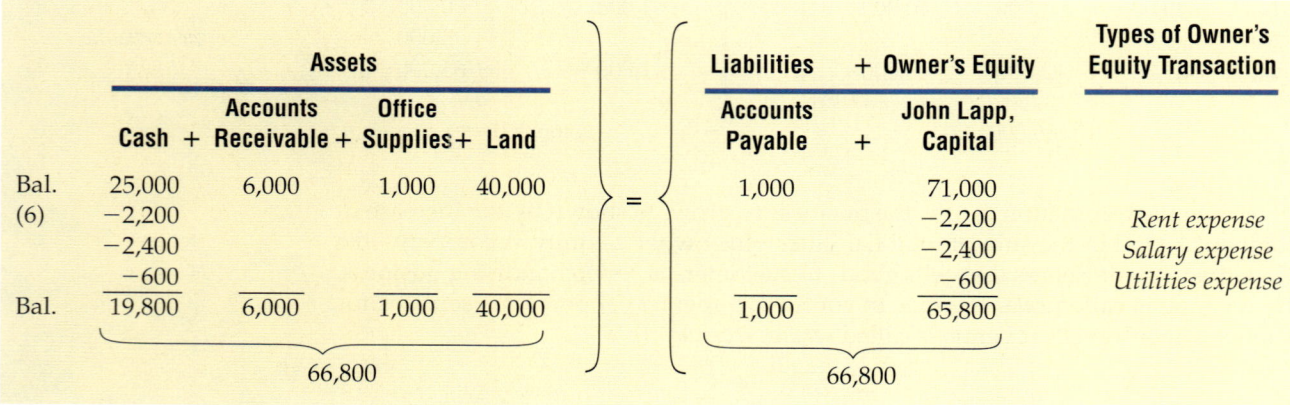

	Assets				=	Liabilities	+ Owner's Equity	Types of Owner's Equity Transaction
	Cash +	Accounts Receivable +	Office Supplies +	Land		Accounts Payable +	John Lapp, Capital	
Bal.	25,000	6,000	1,000	40,000		1,000	71,000	
(6)	−2,200						−2,200	*Rent expense*
	−2,400						−2,400	*Salary expense*
	−600						−600	*Utilities expense*
Bal.	19,800	6,000	1,000	40,000		1,000	65,800	
		66,800					66,800	

Expenses have the opposite effect of revenues. Expenses cause the business to shrink, as shown by the decreased balances of total assets and owner's equity.

Each expense should be recorded in a separate transaction. Here, for simplicity, the expenses are listed together. Alternatively, we could record the cash payment in a single amount for the sum of those three expenses, $5,200 ($2,200 + $2,400 + $600). In either case, the "balance" of the equation holds, as we know it must.

Transaction 7: Payment on Account SuperTravel pays $800 to the store from which it purchased $1,000 worth of office supplies in Transaction 3. In accounting, we say that the business pays $800 *on account*. The effect on the accounting equation is a decrease in the asset Cash and a decrease in the liability Accounts Payable as follows:

	Assets					Liabilities +	Owner's Equity
	Cash +	Accounts Receivable +	Office Supplies +	Land	=	Accounts Payable +	John Lapp, Capital
Bal.	19,800	6,000	1,000	40,000		1,000	65,800
(7)	−800					−800	
Bal.	19,000	6,000	1,000	40,000		200	65,800
	66,000					66,000	

The payment of cash on account has no effect on the asset Office Supplies because the payment does not increase or decrease the supplies available to the business. Likewise, the payment on account does not affect expenses. SuperTravel was paying off a liability, not an expense.

Transaction 8: Personal Transaction John Lapp remodels his home at a cost of $30,000, paying cash from personal funds. This event is *not* a transaction of SuperTravel. It has no effect on SuperTravel's business affairs and therefore is not recorded by the business. It is a transaction of the John Lapp *personal* entity, not the SuperTravel business entity. We are focusing now solely on the *business* entity, and this event does not affect it. This transaction illustrates the *economic-entity assumption*.

Transaction 9: Collection on Account In Transaction 5, SuperTravel performed services for clients on account. The business now collects $2,000 from a client. We say that it collects the cash *on account*. It will record an increase in the asset Cash and a decrease in the asset Accounts Receivable. Should it also record an increase in service revenue? No, because SuperTravel already recorded the revenue when it performed the service in Transaction 5. The effect on the accounting equation is

	Assets					Liabilities +	Owner's Equity
	Cash	+ Receivable +	Office Supplies +	Land	=	Accounts Payable +	John Lapp, Capital
Bal.	19,000	6,000	1,000	40,000		200	65,800
(9)	+2,000	−2,000					
Bal.	21,000	4,000	1,000	40,000		200	65,800
	66,000					66,000	

Total assets are unchanged from the preceding transaction's total. Why? Because SuperTravel merely exchanged one asset for another.

Transaction 10: Sale of Land John Lapp sells a parcel of land owned by SuperTravel. The sale price of $22,000 is equal to SuperTravel's cost of the land. SuperTravel sells the land and receives $22,000 cash, and the effect on the accounting equation is

	Assets					Liabilities +	Owner's Equity
	Cash	+ Receivable +	Office Supplies +	Land	=	Accounts Payable +	John Lapp, Capital
Bal.	21,000	4,000	1,000	40,000		200	65,800
(10)	+22,000			−22,000			
Bal.	43,000	4,000	1,000	18,000		200	65,800
	66,000					66,000	

Transaction 11: Withdrawing of Cash John Lapp withdraws $2,000 cash for his personal use. The effect on the accounting equation is

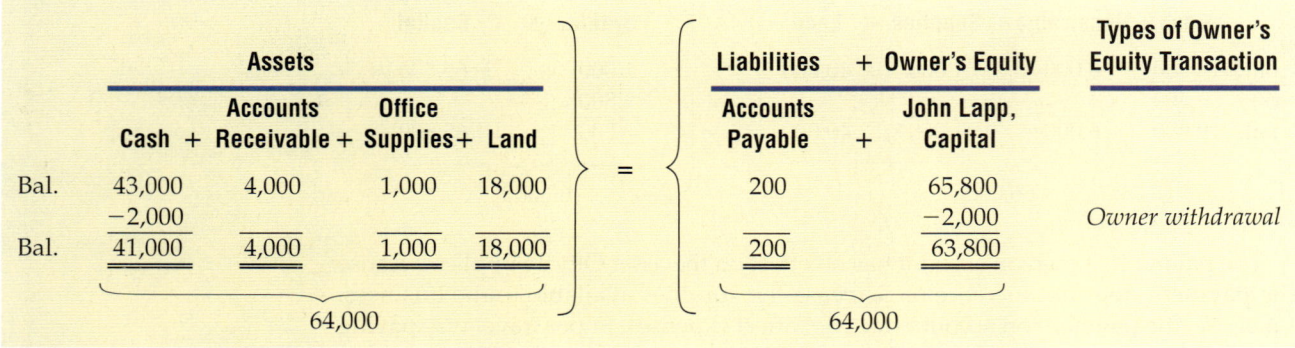

		Assets			=	Liabilities	+ Owner's Equity	Types of Owner's Equity Transaction
	Cash +	Accounts Receivable +	Office Supplies+	Land		Accounts Payable	John Lapp, + Capital	
Bal.	43,000	4,000	1,000	18,000		200	65,800	
	−2,000						−2,000	Owner withdrawal
Bal.	41,000	4,000	1,000	18,000		200	63,800	
			64,000				64,000	

Student CD-ROM

Accounting Cycle Tutorials
1. Balance Sheet Accounts and Transactions pages 1–12
2. Income Statement Accounts and Transactions pages 1–6

These references to the Student CD-ROM are reminders that you can review these topics using the Accounting Cycle Tutorials on the CD-ROM that comes with this book.

John Lapp's withdrawal of $2,000 cash decreases the asset Cash and also the owner's equity of the business.

Owner withdrawals do not represent a business expense because the cash is used for the owner's personal affairs unrelated to the business. We record this decrease in owner's equity as Withdrawals or Drawings. The double underlines below each column indicate a final total after the last transaction.

Evaluating Business Transactions

Exhibit 1–9 summarizes the 11 preceding transactions. Panel A of the exhibit lists the details of the transactions, and Panel B presents the analysis. As you study the exhibit, note that every transaction maintains the equality of the equation

$$\text{ASSETS} = \text{LIABILITIES} + \text{OWNER'S EQUITY}$$

EXHIBIT 1–9 Analysis of Transactions of SuperTravel

PANEL A: DETAILS OF TRANSACTIONS

(1) The business recorded the $60,000 cash investment made by John Lapp.

(2) Paid $40,000 cash for land.

(3) Bought $1,000 of office supplies on account.

(4) Received $5,000 cash from clients for service revenue earned.

(5) Performed services for clients on account, $6,000.

(6) Paid cash expenses: rent, $2,200; employee salary, $2,400; utilities, $600.

(7) Paid $800 on the account payable created in Transaction 3.

(8) Remodelled John Lapp's personal residence. This is *not* a transaction of the business.

(9) Collected $2,000 on the account receivable created in Transaction 5.

(10) Sold land for cash equal to its cost of $22,000.

(11) The business paid $2,000 cash to John Lapp as a withdrawal.

Panel B: Analysis of Transactions

	Assets					Liabilities	+ Owner's Equity	Types of Owner's Equity Transaction
	Cash +	Accounts Receivable +	Office Supplies+	Land		Accounts Payable +	John Lapp, Capital	
(1)	+60,000						+60,000	Owner investment
Bal.	60,000						60,000	
(2)	−40,000			+40,000				
Bal.	20,000			+40,000			60,000	
(3)			+1,000			+1,000		
Bal.	20,000		1,000	40,000		1,000	60,000	
(4)	+5,000						+5,000	Service revenue
Bal.	25,000		1,000	40,000		1,000	65,000	
(5)		+6,000					+6,000	Service revenue
Bal.	25,000	6,000	1,000	40,000	=	1,000	71,000	
(6)	−2,200						−2,200	Rent expense
	−2,400						−2,400	Salary expense
	−600						−600	Utilities expense
Bal.	19,800	6,000	1,000	40,000		1,000	65,800	
(7)	−800					−800		
Bal.	19,000	6,000	1,000	40,000		200	65,800	
(8)	Not a transaction of the business							
(9)	+2,000	− 2,000						
Bal.	21,000	4,000	1,000	40,000		200	65,800	
(10)	+22,000			−22,000				
Bal.	43,000	4,000	1,000	18,000		200	65,800	
(11)	−2,000						−2,000	Owner withdrawal
Bal.	41,000	4,000	1,000	18,000		200	63,800	

64,000   64,000

The Financial Statements

Once the analysis of the transactions is complete, what is the next step in the accounting process? How does a business present the results of the transactions? We now look at the *financial statements,* which are the formal reports of an entity's financial information. The primary financial statements are the:

Objective 6

Prepare and evaluate the financial statements

- Income statement
- Statement of owner's equity
- Balance sheet
- Cash flow statement

Income Statement The **income statement** presents a summary of the *revenues* and *expenses* of an entity for a specific period of time, such as a month or a year. The income statement, also called the **statement of earnings** or **statement of operations**, is like a video of the entity's operations—a moving financial picture of business operations during the period. The income statement holds perhaps the most important single piece of information about a business—its *net income or net loss.* Businesspeople run their businesses with the objective of having more revenues than expenses. An excess of total revenues over total expenses is called **net income, net earnings**, or **net profit**. If total expenses exceed total revenues, the result is called a **net loss**.

Statement of Owner's Equity The **statement of owner's equity** presents a summary of the changes that occurred in the entity's *owner's equity* during a specific period of time, such as a month or a year.

Increases in owner's equity arise from

- Owner investments
- Net income (revenues exceed expenses)

Decreases in owner's equity arise from:

- Owner withdrawals
- Net loss (expenses exceed revenues)

Net income or net loss comes directly from the income statement. Owner investments and withdrawals are capital transactions between the business and its owner, so they do not affect the income statement.

Balance Sheet The **balance sheet** lists all the assets, liabilities, and owner's equity of an entity as of a specific date, usually the end of a month or a year. The balance sheet is like a snapshot of the entity. For this reason, it is also called the **statement of financial position**.

Cash Flow Statement The **cash flow statement** reports the cash coming in (*cash receipts*) and the cash going out (*cash payments* or *disbursements*) during a period. Business activities result in a net cash inflow (receipts greater than payments) or a net cash outflow (payments greater than receipts). The cash flow statement shows the net increase or decrease in cash during the period and the cash balance at the end of the period. We focus on the cash flow statement in Chapter 17.

Computers and software programs have had a significant impact on the preparation of the financial statements. Financial statements can be produced instantaneously after the data from the financial records are entered into the computer. Of course, in manual *and* computerized accounting systems, any errors that occur in the financial records will be passed on to the financial statements. For this reason, the person responsible for analyzing the accounting data is critical to the accuracy of the financial statements.

STOP AND THINK

Why does John Lapp, or anyone else, go into business? If you could identify only one reason, what would it be? What can accounting information tell John Lapp about his business?

Answer: John Lapp went into business to earn a profit—and thereby to make a living. He hopes SuperTravel's accounting revenues exceed its expenses to provide an excess—a net income. Accounting tells John Lapp how much income the business has earned, how much cash and other assets the business has, and how much in liabilities the business owes.

Financial Statement Headings

Each financial statement has a heading, which gives three pieces of data:

- The proper name of the business (in our discussion SuperTravel)
- The full name of the particular statement
- The date or time period covered by the statement

A balance sheet taken at the end of year 2007 would be dated December 31, 2007. A balance sheet prepared at the end of March 2008 is dated March 31, 2008.

An income statement or a statement of owner's equity covering a year ending on December 31, 2007, is dated "For the Year Ended December 31, 2007." A monthly income statement or statement of owner's equity for September 2008 has in its heading "For the Month Ended September 30, 2008" or simply "For the Month of September 2008." Income *must* be identified with a particular time period.

Why does the income statement and statement of owner's equity have to be dated for a particular time period?

Answer: If December 31, 2007, appeared in the heading of these statements, you would not know whether the net income amount was good or bad if you do not know the time period covered by the statements. The net income amount could be good if the time period was one day, but it could be bad if the time period was one year.

Relationships among the Financial Statements

Exhibit 1–10 on page 22 illustrates all four financial statements. Their data come from the transaction analysis in Exhibit 1–9. We are assuming the transactions occurred during the month of April 2007. Study the exhibit carefully, because it shows the relationships among the four financial statements.

Observe the following in Exhibit 1–10:

1. The *income statement* for the month ended April 30, 2007
   a. Reports all *revenues* and all *expenses* during the period. Expenses are often listed alphabetically, but can also be listed in decreasing order of amount, with the largest expense first.
   b. Reports *net income* of the period if total revenues exceed total expenses, as in the case of SuperTravel's operations for April. If total expenses exceed total revenues, a *net loss* is reported instead.

2. The *statement of owner's equity* for the month ended April 30, 2007
   a. Opens with the owner's capital balance at the beginning of the period.
   b. Adds *investment by the owner* and adds *net income* (or subtracts *net loss,* as the case may be). Net income (or net loss) comes directly from the income statement (see arrow ① in Exhibit 1–10).
   c. Subtracts *withdrawals by the owner.* The parentheses around an amount indicate a subtraction.
   d. Ends with the owner's capital balance at the end of the period.

3. The *balance sheet* at April 30, 2007, the end of the period
   a. Reports all *assets,* all *liabilities,* and *owner's equity* of the business at the end of the period.
   b. Reports that total assets equal the sum of total liabilities plus total owner's equity.
   c. Reports the owner's ending capital balance, taken directly from the statement of owner's equity (see arrow ②).

4. The *cash flow statement* for the month ended April 30, 2007
   a. Reports cash flows from three types of business activities (*operating, investing,* and *financing* activities) during the month. Each category of cash-flow activities includes both cash receipts, which are positive amounts, and cash payments, which are negative amounts (denoted by parentheses). Each category results in a net cash inflow or a net cash outflow for the period. We discuss these categories in detail in Chapter 17.
   b. Reports a net increase in cash during the month and ends with the cash balance at April 30, 2007. This is the amount of cash to report on the balance sheet (see arrow ③).

EXHIBIT 1–10 Financial Statements of SuperTravel

SUPERTRAVEL
Income Statement
For the Month Ended April 30, 2007

Revenue:		
Service revenue...		$11,000
Expenses:		
Rent expense	$2,200	
Salary expense	2,400	
Utilities expense	600	
Total expenses..		5,200
Net income...		$ 5,800

SUPERTRAVEL
Statement of Owner's Equity
For the Month Ended April 30, 2007

(1)

John Lapp, capital, April 1, 2007	$ 0
Add: Investment by owner	60,000
Net income for the month	5,800
	65,800
Less: Withdrawals by owner	(2,000)
John Lapp, capital, April 30, 2007	$63,800

SUPERTRAVEL
Balance Sheet
April 30, 2007

(2)

Assets		Liabilities	
Cash.................................	$41,000	Accounts payable	$ 200
Accounts receivable	4,000	**Owner's Equity**	
Office supplies	1,000	John Lapp, capital	63,800
Land	18,000		
		Total liabilities and	
Total assets............................	$64,000	owner's equity..................	$64,000

SUPERTRAVEL
Cash Flow Statement*
For the Month Ended April 30, 2007

(3)

Cash flows from operating activities		
Cash collections from customers**		$ 7,000
Cash payments to suppliers***	$ (3,600)	
Cash payments to employees..	(2,400)	(6,000)
Net cash inflow from operating activities		1,000
Cash flows from investing activities		
Acquisition of land..	$(40,000)	
Proceeds from sale of land..	22,000	
Net cash outflow from investing activities............		(18,000)
Cash flows from financing activities		
Investment by owner..	$ 60,000	
Withdrawal by owner...	(2,000)	
Net cash inflow from financing activities..............		58,000
Net increase in cash...		$41,000
Cash balance, April 1, 2007		0
Cash balance, April 30, 2007		$41,000

* Chapter 17 explains how to prepare this statement.
** $5,000 + $2,000 = $7,000
***$2,200 + $600 + $800 = $3,600

Study Exhibit 1–10, which gives the financial statements for SuperTravel at April 30, 2007, the end of the first month of operations. Answer these questions for SuperTravel to evaluate the business's results.

1. What was the business's result of operations for the month of April—a net income (profit) or a net loss, and how much? Which financial statement provides this information?

2. How much revenue did the business earn during April? What was the business's largest expense? How much were total expenses?

3. Is the income statement dated at the last day of the period or for the entire period? Why?

4. How much owner capital did the company have at the beginning of April? At the end of April? Identify all the items that changed owner capital during the month, along with their amounts. Which financial statement provides this information?

5. How much cash does the company have as it moves into the next month—that is, May 2007? Which financial statement provides this information?

6. How much do clients owe SuperTravel at April 30? Is this an asset or a liability for the business? What does the business call this item?

7. How much does the business owe outsiders at April 30? Is this an asset or a liability for the business? What does the business call this item?

8. How is the balance sheet dated? Why is it dated this way? Why does the balance sheet's date differ from the date on the income statement?

Answers:

1. Net income = $5,800. The income statement provides this information.

2. From the income statement: Total revenue = $11,000. Salary was the largest expense, at $2,400. Total expenses = $5,200.

3. The income statement is dated "For the Month Ended April 30, 2007." The income statement is dated for the entire period because the revenues and the expenses occurred during the month, not at the end of the month. The income statement reports on the business's operations during the whole span of the period.

4. From the statement of owner's equity:

   Beginning owner capital = $0 Ending owner capital = $63,800

   Increases: Investment by owner = $60,000; Net income for the month = $5,800

   Decrease: Withdrawal by owner = $2,000

5. Cash = $41,000. The balance sheet or cash flow statement provides this information.

6. Clients owe the business $4,000, which is an asset called Accounts Receivable.

7. The business owes outsiders $200, which is a liability called Accounts Payable.

8. The balance sheet is dated April 30, 2007, which means at midnight on April 30, 2007. The balance sheet is dated at a single moment in time (in this case, April 30, 2007) to show the amount of assets, liabilities, and owner's equity the business had on that date. The balance sheet is like a snapshot, while the income statement provides a moving picture of the business through time.

As we conclude this chapter, we return to our opening question: Why is accounting and the business environment important? The Decision Guidelines feature below summarizes the chapter by examining examples of business decisions that are made. The chapter-opening questions are answered here. A Decision Guidelines feature appears in each chapter of this book. The Decision Guidelines serve as useful summaries of the decision-making process and its foundation in accounting information.

DECISION GUIDELINES — Major Business Decisions

Decision	Guidelines
How should we organize a business?	If a single owner, but not incorporated—a *proprietorship*. If two or more owners, but not incorporated—a *partnership*. If the business issues shares of stock to shareholders—a *corporation*.
What should we account for?	Account for the business, which is a separate entity apart from its owner (*Economic-entity assumption*). Account for transactions and events that affect the business *and* can be measured objectively. (*Reliability characteristic.*)
How much should we record for assets and liabilities?	Actual historical amount (*Cost principle*).
How to analyze a transaction?	Use accounting equation: $$ASSETS = LIABILITIES + OWNER'S\ EQUITY$$ Note: Owner's equity is called shareholders' equity if the entity is a corporation.
How do we measure profits and losses?	Income statement: $$REVENUES - EXPENSES = NET\ INCOME\ (or\ NET\ LOSS)$$
Did owner's equity increase or decrease?	Statement of owner's equity: Beginning capital + Owner investments + Net income (or − Net loss) − Owner withdrawals = Ending capital
Where does the business stand financially?	Balance sheet (accounting equation): $$ASSETS = LIABILITIES + OWNER'S\ EQUITY$$ Income statement
How did the owner's investment change over the period?	Statement of owner's equity
Where did the business's cash come from? Where did the cash go?	Cash flow statement: *Operating activities:* Net cash inflow (or outflow) + *Investing activities:* Net cash inflow (or outflow) + *Financing activities:* Net cash inflow (or outflow) = Net increase (decrease) in cash

MyAccountingLab Go to MyAccountingLab at www.myaccountinglab.ca. You can practise this chapter's exercises and problems as often as you want. The guided solutions help you find an answer, step by step. There's a personalized study plan, too!

The Summary Problem for Your Review is an extensive, challenging review problem that pulls together the chapter concepts.

Lynn Rani opens an apartment locator business in Edmonton. She is the sole owner of the proprietorship, which she names Fast Apartment Locators. During the first month of operations, July 2007, the following transactions occurred:

a. Rani invests $50,000 of personal funds to start the business.

b. The business purchases, on account, office supplies costing $800.

c. Fast Apartment Locators pays cash of $40,000 to acquire a parcel of land. The business intends to use the land as a future building site for its business office.

d. The business locates apartments for clients and receives cash of $4,000.

e. The business pays $400 on the account payable created in Transaction (b).

f. Lynn Rani pays $3,000 of personal funds for a vacation for her family.

g. The business pays cash expenses for office rent, $1,000, and utilities, $300.

h. The business returns to the supplier office supplies that cost $200. The wrong supplies were shipped.

i. Lynn Rani withdraws $1,500 cash for personal use.

Required

1. Analyze the preceding transactions in terms of their effects on the accounting equation of Fast Apartment Locators. Use Exhibit 1–9 as a guide but show balances only after the last transaction.

2. Prepare the income statement, statement of owner's equity, and balance sheet of Fast Apartment Locators after recording the transactions. Use Exhibit 1–10 as a guide.

Name: Fast Apartment Locators
Industry: Apartment locator proprietorship
Fiscal Period: Month of July 2007

Solution

As you review the details of each transaction, think of the names of the accounts that will be affected.

The worked solution provides a full solution so you can check your progress, as well as reminders and hints for how to find the solution.

1. Panel A: Details of Transactions

a. Rani invested $50,000 cash to start the business.

b. Purchased $800 in office supplies on account.

c. Paid $40,000 to acquire land as a future building site.

d. Earned service revenue and received cash of $4,000.

e. Paid $400 on account.

f. Paid for a personal vacation, which is not a transaction of the business.

g. Paid cash expenses for rent, $1,000, and utilities, $300.

h. Returned office supplies that cost $200.

i. Withdrew $1,500 cash for personal use.

Panel B: Analysis of Transactions

For each transaction, make sure the accounting equation Assets = Liabilities + Owner's Equity balances before going on to the next transaction.

	Assets				=	Liabilities	+	Owner's Equity	Types of Owner's Equity Transaction
	Cash	+	Office Supplies	+ Land		Accounts Payable	+	Lynn Rani, Capital	
(a)	+ 50,000							+ 50,000	Owner investment
(b)			+ 800			+ 800			
(c)	− 40,000			+ 40,000					
(d)	+ 4,000							+ 4,000	Service revenue
(e)	− 400					− 400			
(f)	Not a business transaction								
(g)	− 1,000							− 1,000	Rent expense
	− 300							− 300	Utilities expense
(h)			− 200			− 200			
(i)	− 1,500							− 1,500	Owner withdrawal
Bal.	10,800		600	40,000		200		51,200	

51,400 = 51,400

---

2. Financial Statements of Fast Apartment Locators

The title must include the name of the company, "Income Statement," and the specific period of time covered. It is critical that the time period is defined.

FAST APARTMENT LOCATORS
Income Statement
For the Month Ended July 31, 2007

Revenue:		
Service revenue		$4,000
Expenses:		
Rent expense	$1,000	
Utilities expense..	300	
Total expenses		1,300
Net Income		$2,700

Gather all the revenue and expense account names and amounts from Panel B. They appear in the Lynn Rani, Capital column.
• List the revenue account first.
• List the expense accounts next. Expenses are usually listed in alphabetical order.

FAST APARTMENT LOCATORS
Statement of Owner's Equity
For the Month Ended July 31, 2007

Lynn Rani, capital, July 1, 2007..	$ 0
Add: Investment by owner	50,000
Net income for July	2,700
	52,700
Less: Withdrawal by owner	1,500
Lynn Rani, capital, July 31, 2007..	$51,200

The title must include the name of company, "Statement of Owner's Equity," and the specific period of time covered. It is critical that the time period is defined.
The net income amount (or net loss amount) is transferred from the income statement.
The withdrawal amount is found in Panel B in the Lynn Rani, Capital column.

FAST APARTMENT LOCATORS
Balance Sheet
July 31, 2007

Assets		Liabilities	
Cash..............................	$10,800	Accounts payable	$ 200
Office supplies	600	**Owner's Equity**	
Land	40,000	Lynn Rani, capital	51,200
		Total liabilities and	
Total assets	$51,400	owner's equity..........................	$51,400

The title must include the name of the company, "Balance Sheet," and the date of the balance sheet. It shows the financial position on one specific date.
Gather all the asset and liability accounts and Bal. amounts from Panel B. List assets first, then liabilities. The owner's equity amount is transferred from the statement of owner's equity.
It is vital that total Assets = total Liabilities + Equity

Summary

The Summary gives a concise description of the material covered in the chapter. It is organized by Learning Objective.

1. **Define accounting, and describe the users of accounting information.** Accounting is an information system for measuring, processing, and communicating financial information. As the "language of business," accounting helps a wide range of users make business decisions. Examples of users include individual investors, businesses, government agencies, and lenders.

2. **Explain why ethics and rules of conduct are crucial in accounting and business.** Ethical considerations affect all areas of accounting and business. Users need relevant and reliable information about companies to make decisions. The professional accounting groups in Canada have codes of ethics and rules of conduct to assure society that accountants behave ethically.

3. **Describe and discuss the forms of business organizations.** The three basic forms of business organizations are the proprietorship, the partnership, and the corporation. A summary and comparison of the three forms are given in Exhibit 1–5 on page 8. Limited-liability partnerships (LLPs) and limited-liability companies (LLCs) are special forms of partnerships and proprietorships.

4. **Explain the development of accounting standards, and describe the concepts and principles.** *Generally accepted accounting principles (GAAP)* guide accountants in their work. They are developed by the *Accounting Standards Board (AcSB)* of the CICA and published in the *CICA Handbook.* For example, accountants use the *economic-entity assumption* to keep the business's records

separate from the records of other economic units. Other important guidelines or standards are the *reliability characteristic*, the *cost principle*, the *going-concern assumption,* and the *stable-monetary-unit assumption.*

5. **Describe and use the accounting equation to analyze business transactions.** In its most common form, the accounting equation is

$$\textbf{Assets} = \textbf{Liabilities} = \textbf{Owner's Equity}$$

A transaction is an event that affects the financial position of an entity *and* can be reliably recorded. Transactions affect a business's assets, liabilities, and owner's equity. Therefore, transactions are often analyzed in terms of their effect on the accounting equation.

6. **Prepare and evaluate the financial statements.** The *financial statements* communicate information for decision making by an entity's users, including managers, owners, and creditors. The *income statement* summarizes the entity's operations in terms of revenues earned and expenses incurred during a specific period of time. Total revenues minus total expenses equal net income. The *statement of owner's equity* reports the changes in owner's equity during the period. The *balance sheet* lists the entity's assets, liabilities, and owner's equity at a specific date. The *cash flow statement* reports the changes in cash during the period.

High net income indicates success in business; a net loss indicates a lack of success in business.

Self-Study Questions

Test your understanding with these multiple-choice questions. Page references are given if you need review, and the answers are given after the Similar Accounting Terms.

Test your understanding of the chapter by marking the correct answer for each of the following questions:

1. The organization that formulates generally accepted accounting principles is the (*p. 8*)
   a. Ontario Securities Commission
   b. Public Accountants Council of Canada
   c. Canadian Institute of Chartered Accountants (CICA)
   d. Canada Revenue Agency (CRA)

2. Which of the following forms of business organization is an "artificial person" and must obtain legal approval from the federal government or a province to conduct business? (*p. 7*)
   a. Law firm   c. Partnership
   b. Proprietorship   d. Corporation

3. You have purchased some T-shirts for $1,000 and can sell them immediately for $1,500. What accounting assumption or principle governs the amount at which to record the goods you purchased? (*p. 11*)
   a. Economic-entity assumption
   b. Reliability characteristic
   c. Cost principle
   d. Going-concern assumption

4. The economic resources of a business are called (*p. 12*)
   a. Assets   c. Owner's equity
   b. Liabilities   d. Accounts payable

5. If the assets of a business are $174,300 and the liabilities are $82,000, how much is the owner's equity? (*p. 13*)
   a. $256,300   c. $174,300
   b. $92,300   d. $82,000

6. A business has assets of $60,000 and liabilities of $140,000. How much is its owner's equity? (*p. 13*)
   a. $0   c. $80,000
   b. ($80,000)   d. $200,000

7. If the owner's equity in a business is $22,000 and the liabilities are $36,000, how much are the assets? (*p. 13*)
   a. $22,000   c. $58,000
   b. $14,000   d. $36,000

8. Purchasing office supplies on account will (*p. 14*)
   a. Increase an asset and increase a liability
   b. Increase an asset and increase owner's equity
   c. Increase one asset and decrease another asset
   d. Increase an asset and decrease a liability

9. Performing a service for a customer or client and the immediate receiving of cash will (p. 15)
   a. Increase one asset and decrease another asset
   b. Increase an asset and increase owner's equity
   c. Decrease an asset and decrease a liability
   d. Increase an asset and increase a liability
10. Paying an account payable will (p. 16)
   a. Increase one asset and decrease another asset
   b. Decrease an asset and decrease owner's equity
   c. Decrease an asset and decrease a liability
   d. Increase an asset and increase a liability
11. The financial statement that summarizes assets, liabilities, and owner's equity is called the (p. 20)
   a. Cash flow statement   c. Income statement
   b. Balance sheet   d. Statement of owner's equity
12. The financial statements that are dated for a time period (rather than for a specific point in time) are the (pp. 18–20)
   a. Balance sheet and income statement
   b. Balance sheet and statement of owner's equity
   c. Income statement, statement of owner's equity, and cash flow statement
   d. All financial statements are dated for a time period.

Answers to the Self-Study Questions follow the Similar Accounting Terms.

Accounting Vocabulary

Accounting Vocabulary lists all the new boldfaced terms that were explained in the chapter and are defined in the Glossary. Page references help you to review the terms.

Like many other subjects, accounting has a special vocabulary. It is important that you understand the following terms. They are explained in the chapter and also in the glossary at the end of the book.

account payable   (p. 15)
account receivable   (p. 16)
accounting   (p. 2)
accounting equation   (p. 12)
asset   (p. 12)
audit   (p. 5)
balance sheet   (p. 20)
capital   (p. 12)
cash flow statement   (p. 20)
corporation   (p. 7)
cost principle   (p. 11)
entity   (p. 10)
expense   (p. 13)
financial accounting   (p. 4)
financial statements   (p. 2)
generally accepted accounting principles (GAAP)   (p. 8)
going-concern assumption   (p. 11)
income statement   (p. 19)
liability   (p. 12)

limited-liability company (LLC)   (p. 8)
limited-liability partnership (LLP)   (p. 8)
management accounting   (p. 4)
net earnings   (p. 19)
net income   (p. 19)
net loss   (p. 19)
net profit   (p. 19)
note payable   (p. 15)
objectivity characteristic   (p. 10)
owner's equity   (p. 12)
owner withdrawals   (p. 13)
partnership   (p. 7)
proprietorship   (p. 7)
reliability characteristic   (p. 10)
revenue   (p. 13)
shareholder   (p. 7)
stable-monetary-unit assumption   (p. 11)
statement of earnings   (p. 19)
statement of financial position   (p. 20)
statement of operations   (p. 19)
statement of owner's equity   (p. 19)
transaction   (p. 13)

Similar Accounting Terms

Similar Accounting Terms are a link between the terms used in this book and similar terms you might have heard outside your accounting class in the media or your day-to-day business dealings.

Accounting equation	Assets = Liabilities + Owner's Equity
Balance Sheet	Statement of Financial Position
Income Statement	Statement of Operations; Statement of Earnings
Net income	Net earnings; Net profit

Check how well you answered the Self-Study Questions.

Answers to Self-Study Questions

1. c	3. c	5. b	7. c	9. b	11. b
2. d	4. a	6. b	8. a	10. c	12. c

Assignment Material

Questions

1. Distinguish between accounting and bookkeeping.
2. Identify five users of accounting information and explain how they use it.
3. Name two important historical reasons for the development of accounting.
4. Name three professional designations of accountants. Also give their abbreviations.
5. What organization formulates generally accepted accounting principles? Is this organization a government agency?
6. Identify the owner(s) of a proprietorship, a partnership, and a corporation.
7. Why do ethical standards exist in accounting? Which professional organizations direct their standards more toward independent auditors? Which organizations direct their standards more toward management accountants?
8. Why is the economic-entity assumption so important to accounting?
9. Give four examples of types of accounting entities.
10. Briefly describe the reliability characteristic.
11. What role does the cost principle play in accounting?
12. If assets = liabilities + owner's equity, then how can liabilities be expressed?
13. Explain the difference between an account receivable and an account payable.
14. What role do transactions play in accounting?
15. A company reported monthly revenues of $87,600 and expenses of $91,300. What is the result of operations for the month?
16. Give a more descriptive title for the balance sheet.
17. What feature of the balance sheet gives this financial statement its name?
18. Give another title for the income statement.
19. Which financial statement is like a snapshot of the entity at a specific time? Which financial statement is like a video of the entity's operation during a period of time?
20. What information does the statement of owner's equity report?
21. Give another term for the owner's equity of a proprietorship.
22. What piece of information flows from the income statement to the statement of owner's equity? What information flows from the statement of owner's equity to the balance sheet? What balance sheet item is explained by the cash flow statement?

> A brief description and the objectives covered appear beside each Starter, Exercise, and Problem.

Starters

Starter 1–1 What is accounting, and why is accounting information important?

Explaining accounting

Starter 1–2 Refer to the Student Policies, Bylaws, and Codes of Conduct of your college or university. Why do these policies exist?

Codes of conduct in colleges and universities

Starter 1–3 Alexis Andrews wants to start a business renting kayaks to tourists over the Internet. She is not sure whether she needs to incorporate to begin operations. Advise Alexis on the forms of business organizations that exist, and suggest one that would suit her needs.

Forms of business organizations

Starter 1–4 List the major categories of accounts that appear on the balance sheet, and describe a typical heading for this statement.

Describing the balance sheet

Starter 1–5 List the major categories of accounts that appear on the income statement, and describe a typical heading for this statement.

Describing the income statement

Starter 1–6 What are generally accepted accounting principles?

Generally accepted accounting principles

Describing accounting concepts, principles, and constraints

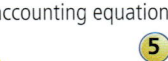

Starter 1–7 Match the assumption, principle, or constraint description with the appropriate term by placing a, b, c, d, e, and f on the appropriate line.

a. Cost principle   _____ Benefits of the information produced by an accounting system must be greater than the costs

b. Going-concern assumption   _____ Amounts may be ignored if the effect on a decision maker's decision is not significant

c. Stable-monetary- unit assumption   _____ Transactions recorded based on cash amount received or paid

d. Economic-entity assumption   _____ Transactions are expressed using units of money

e. Cost/benefit constraint   _____ Assumes that a business is going to continue operations indefinitely

f. Materiality constraint   _____ Business must keep its accounting records separate from its owner's accounting records

Check figures appear in the margin when applicable to help you make sure you are "on track."

Using the accounting equation

Owner's equity $25,000

Starter 1–8 Suppose Alexis Andrews Kayaks purchased a storage building for the kayaks for $100,000, and financed the purchase with a loan of $75,000 and an investment by the owner for the remainder. Use the accounting equation to calculate the owner's equity amount.

Defining transactions

Starter 1–9 A customer in the United States is extremely interested in renting a number of products from Alexis Andrews Kayaks and e-mails his intention to rent kayaks in the summer. Would an accountant consider this event a transaction to be recorded in the accounting records? Explain.

Examples of financial statements

Starter 1–10 What are the four main financial statements that are provided in a company's annual report? Examples of two companies' annual reports are provided in Appendix A and Appendix B at the back of this textbook.

Exercises

Explaining assets, liabilities, owner's equity

Exercise 1–1

Shortly after starting Red River Express Company you realize the company needs a bank loan to purchase office equipment. To prepare for the loan request, you review some basic accounting concepts. In your own words define *assets, liabilities,* and *owner's equity*. What is the *relationship* among assets, liabilities, and owner's equity?

Explaining the income statement and the balance sheet

Exercise 1–2

Raymond and Lupita Rodriguez want to open a Mexican restaurant in Winnipeg. In need of cash, they ask TD Canada Trust for a loan. With little knowledge of finance, Raymond and Lupita don't know how the lending process works. Explain to them the information provided to the bank by the income statement (statement of operations) and the balance sheet (statement of financial position). Indicate why a lender would require this information.

Defining the forms of business organization

Exercise 1–3

Fill in the following table.

	Owners(s)	Life of organization	Personal liability of owner(s) for business debts	Legal status
Proprietorship				
Partnership				
Corporation				

Business transactions

Exercise 1–4

Give an example of a business transaction that has each of the following effects on the accounting equation:

a. Increases an asset and increases a liability.

b. Increases one asset and decreases another asset.

c. Decreases an asset and decreases owner's equity.

d. Decreases an asset and decreases a liability.

e. Increases an asset and increases owner's equity.

Exercise 1–5

Transaction analysis

Chang Enterprises, a business owned by Sophie Chang, experienced the following events. State whether each event (1) increased, (2) decreased, or (3) had no effect on the *total assets* of the business. Identify any specific asset affected.

a. Sophie Chang increased her cash investment in the business.

b. Paid cash on accounts payable.

c. Purchased office equipment; signed a note payable in payment.

d. Performed service for a customer on account.

e. Sophie Chang withdrew cash for personal expenses.

f. Received cash from a customer on account receivable.

g. Sophie Chang used personal funds to purchase a swimming pool for her home.

h. Sold undesirable land for a price equal to the cost of the land; received cash.

i. Borrowed money from the bank.

j. Cash purchase of desirable land for a future building site.

Exercise 1–6

Accounting equation

Business B liabilities $32,000

Compute the missing amount in the accounting equation of each of the following three entities:

	Assets	Liabilities	Owner's Equity
Business A	$?	$60,000	$21,000
Business B	72,000	?	40,000
Business C	100,000	79,000	?

Exercise 1–7

Using the accounting equation

Owner's equity $12,000

Theresa Hanson owns Common Grounds Coffee House, near the campus of Western College. The company has cash of $14,000 and furniture that cost $34,000. Debts include accounts payable of $12,000 and a $24,000 note payable. Write the accounting equation of Common Grounds Coffee House. What is the owner's equity of the company?

Exercise 1–8

Accounting equation

1. Increase in owner's equity $58 million

Diamond Works, a mineral exploration and development company in Vancouver, had total assets of $140 million and total liabilities of $70 million at January 31, 2007. At the company's year end on January 31, 2008, Diamond Works's total assets were $137 million and total liabilities were $9 million.

Required

1. Did the owner's equity of Diamond Works increase during the period February 1, 2007, to January 31, 2008? By how much?

2. Identify two possible reasons for the change in owner's equity of Diamond Works during the period February 1, 2007, to January 31, 2008.

Exercise 1–9

Transaction analysis

Indicate the effects of the following business transactions on the accounting equation of a proprietorship. Transaction *a* is answered as a guide.

a. Received $20,000 cash from the owners.

   Answer: Increase asset (Cash)
            Increase owner's equity (Owner, Capital)

b. Paid the current month's office rent of $2,000.

c. Paid $2,700 cash to purchase office supplies.

d. Performed engineering service for a client on account, $3,000.

e. Purchased on account office furniture at a cost of $2,000.

f. Received cash on account, $2,000.

g. Paid cash on account, $1,000.

h. Sold land for $15,000, which was the business's cost of the land.

i. Performed engineering services for a client and received cash of $2,000.

Excel Spreadsheet Template

Transaction analysis, accounting equation

Total assets $181,000

Exercise 1–10

Doug Mossley, M.D., opens a medical clinic. During his first month of operation, January, the clinic, entitled Austin Heights Clinic, experienced the following events:

Jan.	6	Mossley invested $170,000 in the clinic by opening a bank account in the name of Austin Heights Clinic.
	9	Austin Heights Clinic paid cash for land costing $162,500. There are plans to build a clinic on the land. Until then, the business will rent an office.
	12	The clinic purchased medical supplies for $5,300 on account.
	15	On January 15, Austin Heights Clinic officially opened for business.
	15–31	During the rest of the month, the clinic earned professional fees of $12,000 and received cash immediately.
	15–31	The clinic paid cash expenses: employee salaries, $2,100; office rent, $1,500; utilities, $450.
	28	The clinic sold supplies to another clinic at cost for $750.
	31	The clinic paid $2,250 on account.

Required Analyze the effects of these events on the accounting equation of Austin Heights Clinic. Use a format similar to that of Exhibit 1–9, Panel B, on page 19 with headings for: Cash; Medical Supplies; Land; Accounts Payable; and Doug Mossley, Capital.

Business organization, transactions, and net income

2. Net income $4,075

Exercise 1–11

The analysis of the transactions that Penfild Equipment Rental engaged in during its first month of operations follows. The business buys electronic equipment that it rents out to earn rental revenue. The owner of the business, Steve Penfild, made only one investment to start the business and made no withdrawals from Penfild Equipment Rental.

	Cash	+	Accounts Receivable	+	Rental Equipment	=	Accounts Payable	+	S. Penfild, Capital
a.	+25,000								+25,000
b.	+ 375								+ 375
c.					+60,000		+60,000		
d.			+ 400						+ 400
e.	− 500								− 500
f.	+ 3,800								+ 3,800
g.	+ 75		− 75						
h.	− 6,000						− 6,000		

Required

1. Describe each transaction of Penfild Equipment Rental.

2. If these transactions fully describe the operations of Penfild Equipment Rental during the month, what was the amount of net income or net loss?

Business organization, balance sheet

2. Total assets $119,750

Exercise 1–12

Presented below are the balances of the assets and liabilities of Whitehead Consulting Services as of September 30, 2007. Also included are the revenue and expense account balances of the business for September. Darlene Whitehead, the owner, invested $30,000 when the business was formed.

Consulting service revenue.....	$45,500	Computer equipment................	$77,500
Accounts receivable.................	34,500	Supplies.......................................	4,000
Accounts payable.....................	18,750	Note payable..............................	36,000
Salary expense..........................	10,000	Rent expense.............................	3,500
D. Whitehead, Capital.............	?	Cash...	3,750

Required

1. What type of business entity or organization is Whitehead Consulting Services? How can you tell?

2. Prepare the balance sheet of Whitehead Consulting Services as of September 30, 2007.

3. What does the balance sheet report—financial position or operating results? Which financial statement reports the other information?

Exercise 1–13

Examine Exhibit 1–9 on page 19. The exhibit summarizes the transactions of SuperTravel for the month of April 2007. Suppose the business completed transactions 1 to 7 and needed a bank loan on April 21, 2007. The vice-president of the bank requires financial statements to support all loan requests.

Required Prepare the income statement, statement of owner's equity, and balance sheet that SuperTravel would present to the banker on April 21, 2007, after completing the first seven transactions. Exhibit 1–10, page 22, shows the format of these financial statements.

Exercise 1–14

The assets, liabilities, owner's equity, revenue and expenses of Maclean Company, a proprietorship, have the following balances at December 31, 2007, the end of its first year of business. During the year the proprietor, Nancy Maclean, invested $45,000 in the business.

Note payable.............................	$ 63,000	Office furniture.............................	$ 105,000
Utilities expense.........................	10,400	Rent expense..................................	24,000
Accounts payable.......................	9,900	Cash...	10,800
N. Maclean, capital....................	63,000	Office supplies...............................	14,400
Service revenue...........................	543,600	Salary expense...............................	165,000
Accounts receivable..................	27,000	Salary payable...............................	6,000
Supplies expense........................	24,000	Realty tax expense........................	4,200
Equipment....................................	30,000	N. Maclean, withdrawals............	?

Required

1. Prepare the income statement of Maclean Company for the year ended December 31, 2007. What is Maclean Company's net income or net loss for 2007? (Hint: Ignore balance sheet items.)

2. What was the total amount of Nancy Maclean's withdrawals during the year?

Exercise 1–15

The 2005 annual report of Bombardier Inc. reported revenue of $15,839 million. Total expenses for the year were $15,787 million. Bombardier ended the year with $20,080 million in total assets and $17,782 million in total liabilities.

During 2004, Bombardier earned income from continuing operations (net income) of $311 million. At the end of 2004, Bombardier reported total assets of $19,277 million and total liabilities of $16,827 million.

Required

1. Compute Bombardier's income from continuing operations (net income) for 2005. Did income increase or decrease from 2004 to 2005? By how much?

Preparing the financial statements

Total assets $66,000

This symbol reminds you that an Excel template is available on the Student CD-ROM to help you answer this question.

 Excel Spreadsheet Template

Income statement for a proprietorship

1. Net income $316,000
2. Capital, ending $63,000

Evaluating the performance of a real company

1. Net income $52 mil.
2. Shareholder's equity, ending $2,298 mil.

2. Did Bombardier's shareholders' equity (which is the owner's equity of a corporation) increase or decrease during 2005? By how much?

3. Bombardier's management strives for a steady increase in net income and shareholders' equity. How would you rate Bombardier's performance for 2005—excellent, fair, or poor? Give your reason.

Challenge Exercise

Using the financial statements

Net income:
Yew Co. $120,000
Ash Co. $90,000
Arbutus Co. $100,000

Exercise 1–16

Compute the missing amounts for each of the following businesses.

	Yew Co.	Ash Co.	Arbutus Co.
Beginning:			
Assets	$220,000	$100,000	$180,000
Liabilities	100,000	40,000	120,000
Ending:			
Assets	$320,000	$140,000	$?
Liabilities	140,000	70,000	160,000
Owner's equity:			
Investments by owner	$?	$ 0	$ 20,000
Withdrawals by owner	220,000	80,000	140,000
Income Statement:			
Revenues	$440,000	$210,000	$400,000
Expenses	320,000	?	300,000

Using the accounting equation, and preparing the statement of owner's equity

1. Net loss, $10,000
2. Owner's equity, ending $64,000

Exercise 1–17

Oriole Travel Company's balance sheet data are shown below.

	January 1, 2007	December 31, 2007
Total assets	$150,000	$ 195,000
Total liabilities	109,000	131,000

Required

1. Compute the amount of net income or net loss for the company during the year ended December 31, 2007, if the owner invested $39,000 in the business and withdrew $6,000 during the year. Show all calculations.

2. Prepare the statement of owner's equity for Mary Jones, the owner of Oriole Travel Company, for the year ended December 31, 2007. Use the format shown in Exhibit 1–10 on page 22.

Beyond the Numbers

Analyzing a loan request

Beyond the Numbers 1–1

As an analyst for CIBC, it is your job to write recommendations to the bank's loan committee. Softon Engineering Co., a client of the bank, has submitted these summary data to support the company's request for a $200,000 loan:

Income Statement Data	2009	2008	2007
Total revenues	$445,000	$415,000	$410,000
Total expenses	320,000	285,000	270,000
Net income	$125,000	$130,000	$140,000

Statement of Owner's Equity Data	2009	2008	2007
Beginning capital	$190,000	$200,000	$195,000
Add: Net income..........................	125,000	130,000	140,000
	$315,000	$330,000	$335,000
Less: Withdrawals.........................	(145,000)	(140,000)	(135,000)
Ending capital	$170,000	$190,000	$200,000

Balance Sheet Data	2009	2008	2007
Total assets	$365,000	$360,000	$330,000
Total liabilities	$195,000	$170,000	$130,000
Total owner's equity......................	170,000	190,000	200,000
Total liabilities and owner's equity	$365,000	$360,000	$330,000

Required   Analyze these financial statement data to decide whether the bank should lend $200,000 to Softon Engineering Co. Consider the trends in net income and owner's equity and the change in total liabilities in making your decision. Write a one-paragraph recommendation to the bank's loan committee.

Beyond the Numbers 1–2

Transaction analysis, effects on financial statements

White Pine Camp conducts summer camps for children with physical challenges. Because of the nature of its business, White Pine Camp experiences many unusual transactions. Evaluate each of the following transactions in terms of its effect on White Pine Camp's income statement and balance sheet.

a. A camper suffered a dental injury that was not covered by insurance. White Pine Camp paid $500 for the child's dental care. How does this transaction affect the income statement and the balance sheet?

b. One camper's mother is a physician. White Pine Camp allows this child to attend camp in return for the mother's serving part-time in the camp infirmary for the two-week term. The standard fee for a camp term is $1,000. The physician's salary for this part-time work would be $1,000. How should White Pine Camp account for this arrangement?

c. Lightning during a storm damaged the camp dining hall. The cost to repair the damage will be $5,400 over and above what the insurance company will pay.

Ethical Issues

Ethical Issue 1

The following excerpt was taken from the Chief Executive Officer's message to the shareholders in the Nortel Networks Corporation 2004 Annual Report:

> This was a challenging year for your company. Early in 2004, after concerns were raised regarding the integrity of previously reported financial results, new management examined these statements in depth. That examination led to the restatement of the years ended 2001, 2002, the revision of previously announced results for the year ended 2003, and the restatement of the first three quarters of 2003, which have all now been filed. The company has now completed its financial statements for 2004.

Required

1. Why is it important that this type of information be disclosed?

2. Suppose you are the chief financial officer (CFO) responsible for the financial statements of Nortel. What ethical issues would you face as you consider what to report in the Nortel 2004 Annual Report?

3. What are the negative consequences to Nortel of not telling the truth? What are the negative consequences to Nortel of telling the truth?

Ethical Issue 2

The board of directors of Cloutier Inc. is meeting to discuss the past year's results before releasing financial statements to the public. The discussion includes this exchange:

> Sue Cloutier, company president: "Well, this has not been a good year! Revenue is down and expenses are up—way up. If we don't do some fancy stepping, we'll report a loss for the third year in a row. I can temporarily transfer some land that I own into the company's name, and that will beef up our balance sheet. Rob, can you shave $500,000 from expenses? Then we can probably get the bank loan that we need."

> Rob Samuels, company chief accountant: "Sue, you are asking too much. Generally accepted accounting principles are designed to keep this sort of thing from happening."

Required

1. What is the fundamental ethical issue in this situation?
2. Discuss how Sue Cloutier's proposals violate generally accepted accounting principles. Identify the specific concept(s) or principle(s) involved.

Problems (Group A)

Entity concept, transaction analysis, accounting equation

2. Total assets $17,700

Problem 1–1A

Gail Bradley was a civil engineer and partner in a large firm, a partnership, for five years after graduating from university. Recently she resigned her position to open her own consultancy practice, which she operates as a proprietorship. The name of the new company is Bradley Consultants.

Bradley recorded the following events during the organizing phase of her new business and its first month of operations. Some of the events were personal and did not affect the consultancy practice. Others were business transactions and should be accounted for by the business.

July	4	Bradley received $60,000 cash from her former partners in the firm from which she resigned.
	5	Bradley invested $10,500 cash in her business, Bradley Consultants.
	5	The business paid office rent expense for the month of July, $1,800.
	6	The business paid $450 cash for letterhead stationery for the office.
	7	The business purchased office furniture for the office and will pay the account payable, $3,000, within six months.
	10	Bradley sold 750 shares of Dofasco stock, which she had owned for several years, receiving $27,000 cash from her stockbroker.
	11	Bradley deposited the $27,000 cash from sale of the Dofasco stock in her personal bank account.
	12	A representative of a large construction company telephoned Bradley and told her of the company's intention to transfer its consulting business to Bradley Consultants.
	29	The business finished an assessment for a client and submitted the bill for services, $7,500. The business expected to collect from this client within two weeks.
	31	Bradley withdrew $1,500 cash from the business.

Required

1. Classify each of the preceding events as one of the following (list each date, then choose a, b, or c):
   a. A business transaction to be accounted for by the business, Bradley Consultants.
   b. A business-related event but not a transaction to be accounted for by Bradley Consultants.
   c. A personal transaction not to be accounted for by Bradley Consultants.
2. Analyze the effects of the above events on the accounting equation of Bradley Consultants. Use a format similar to Exhibit 1–9, Panel B, on page 19.

Problem 1–2A

Paul Keeler is a realtor. He buys and sells properties on his own, and he also earns commission revenue as a real estate agent. He organized his business as a sole proprietorship on November 24, 2007. Consider the following facts as of November 30, 2007:

a. Keeler owed $16,500 on a note payable for some undeveloped land. This land had been acquired by the business for a total price of $30,000.

b. Keeler's business had spent $7,500 for a Re/Max Ltd. real estate franchise, which entitled him to represent himself as a Re/Max agent. Re/Max is a national affiliation of independent real estate agents. This franchise is a business asset.

c. Keeler owed $240,000 on a personal mortgage on his personal residence, which he acquired in 2001 for a total price of $510,000.

d. Keeler had $30,000 in his personal bank account and $5,100 in his business bank account.

e. Keeler owed $1,800 on a personal charge account with The Bay.

f. The business acquired business furniture for $5,100 on November 25. Of this amount, the company owed $1,800 on account at November 30.

g. The real estate office had $300 worth of office supplies on hand on November 30.

Required

1. Prepare the balance sheet of the real estate business of Paul Keeler, Realtor, at November 30, 2007.

2. Identify the personal items given in the preceding facts that would not be reported on the balance sheet of the business.

Balance sheet for a sole proprietorship, entity concept

1. Total assets $48,000

Problem 1–3A

Port Hardey Suppliers was recently formed. The balance of each item in the business's accounting equation is shown below for June 21 and for each of the nine following business days.

Business transactions and analysis

		Cash	Accounts Receivable	Supplies	Land	Accounts Payable	Owner's Equity
June	21	$12,000	$ 6,000	$1,500	$12,000	$6,000	$25,500
	22	19,500	6,000	1,500	12,000	6,000	33,000
	23	9,000	6,000	1,500	22,500	6,000	33,000
	24	9,000	6,000	6,000	22,500	10,500	33,000
	25	7,500	6,000	6,000	22,500	9,000	33,000
	26	10,500	3,000	6,000	22,500	9,000	33,000
	27	21,000	3,000	6,000	22,500	9,000	43,500
	28	16,500	3,000	6,000	22,500	4,500	43,500
	29	13,500	3,000	9,000	22,500	4,500	43,500
	30	3,000	3,000	9,000	22,500	4,500	33,000

Required Assuming that a single transaction took place on each day, describe briefly the transaction that was most likely to have occurred. Begin with June 22 and complete up to June 30. Indicate which accounts were affected and by what amount. No revenue or expense transactions occurred on these dates.

Problem 1–4A

Presented below are the amounts of (a) the assets and liabilities of Premium Sounds as of December 31, 2008, and (b) the revenues and expenses of the company for the year ended December 31, 2008. The items are listed in alphabetical order.

Excel Spreadsheet Template

Income statement, statement of owner's equity, balance sheet

1. Net income $70,000
2. S. Chai, capital, Dec. 31, 2008 $165,000
3. Total assets $335,000

Accounts payable	$ 36,000	Insurance expense	$ 2,000
Accounts receivable	22,000	Interest expense	9,000
Advertising expense	13,000	Note payable	125,000
Building	170,000	Rent expense	23,000
Cash	10,000	Salary expense	120,000
Consultant expense	18,000	Salary payable	9,000
Electronic equipment	110,000	Service revenue	255,000
Furniture	20,000	Supplies	3,000

The opening balance of owner's equity was $150,000. At year end, after the calculation of net income, the owner, Shiraz Chai, withdrew $55,000.

Required

1. Prepare the business's income statement for the year ended December 31, 2008.
2. Prepare the statement of owner's equity of the business for the year ended December 31, 2008.
3. Prepare the balance sheet of the business at December 31, 2008.
4. Answer these questions about the business:
   a. Was the result of operations for the year a profit or a loss? How much was it?
   b. Did the business's owner's equity increase or decrease during the year? How would this affect the business's ability to borrow money from a bank in the future?
   c. How much in total economic resources does the business have at December 31, 2008, as it moves into the new year? How much does the business owe? What is the dollar amount of the owner's portion of the business at December 31, 2008?

Balance sheet for a proprietorship

1. Total assets $220,000

Problem 1–5A

The bookkeeper of Kirkham Services Co., a proprietorship, prepared the balance sheet of the company while the accountant was ill. The balance sheet is not correct. The bookkeeper knew that the balance sheet should balance, so he plugged in the owner's equity amount needed to achieve this balance. The owner's equity amount, however, is not correct. All other amounts are accurate.

KIRKHAM SERVICES CO.
Balance Sheet
For the Month Ended July 31, 2007

Assets		Liabilities	
Cash	$ 44,000	Service revenue	$144,000
Office supplies	2,000	Note payable	32,000
Land	88,000	Accounts payable	36,000
Advertising expense	5,000		
Office furniture	40,000	**Owner's Equity**	
Accounts receivable	46,000	J. Kirkham, capital	29,000
Rent expense	16,000	Total liabilities and	
Total assets	$241,000	owner's equity	$241,000

Required

1. Prepare the correct balance sheet, and date it correctly. Compute total assets, total liabilities, and owner's equity.
2. Identify the accounts listed above that should *not* be presented on the balance sheet and state why you excluded them from the correct balance sheet you prepared for Requirement 1.

Transaction analysis, accounting equation, financial statements

2. Net income $31,600
3. Phyllis Fauburn, capital, Sept. 30, 2007, $148,600
4. Total assets $152,600

Problem 1–6A

Phyllis Fauburn is the proprietor of a career counselling and employee search business, Fauburn Personnel Services. The following amounts summarize the financial position of the business on August 31, 2007:

	Assets			=	Liabilities	+	Owner's Equity
		Accounts		Furniture and		Accounts	P. Fauburn,
	Cash +	Receivable +	Supplies +	Computers =	Payable	+	Capital
Bal.	15,000	16,000		48,000	26,000		53,000

During September 2007, the following company transactions occurred:

a. Phyllis Fauburn deposited $80,000 cash in the business bank account.

b. Performed services for a client and received cash of $3,600.

c. Paid off the August 31, 2007, balance of accounts payable.

d. Purchased supplies on account, $4,000.

e. Collected cash from a customer on account, $4,000.

f. Consulted on a large downsizing by a major corporation and billed the client for services rendered, $32,000.

g. Recorded the following business expenses for the month:
   (1) Paid office rent for September 2007—$3,600.
   (2) Paid advertising—$400.

h. Sold supplies to another business for $600 cash, which was the cost of the supplies.

i. Phyllis Fauburn withdrew $16,000 cash.

Required

1. Analyze the effects of the above transactions on the accounting equation of Fauburn Personnel Services. Adapt the format of Exhibit 1–9, Panel B on page 19.

2. Prepare the income statement of Fauburn Personnel Services for the month ended September 30, 2007. List expenses in decreasing order by amount.

3. Prepare the business's statement of owner's equity for the month ended September 30, 2007.

4. Prepare the balance sheet of Fauburn Personnel Services at September 30, 2007.

Problem 1–7A

Accounting concepts/principles

Michael Chung had been operating his law practice in Mississauga under the name Michael Chung, Lawyer, for two years and had the following business assets and liabilities (at their historical costs) on April 30, 2007:

Cash...	$ 9,000
Accounts receivable	4,500
Supplies.......................................	600
Furniture and computers	21,000
Accounts payable	3,000

The following business transactions took place during the month of May 2007:

May   1   Chung deposited $30,000 cash into the business bank account.

            3   Chung completed legal work for a home builder. He charged the builder $1,500, not the $2,700 the work was worth, in order to promote business from the builder.

            5   The business bought furniture from Arthur Frame for $6,000, paying $1,500 cash and promising to pay $750 a month at the beginning of each month starting June 1, 2007, for six months. Chung would like to expense the entire amount to reduce net income for tax reasons.

         10   The company signed a lease to rent additional space at a cost of $1,350 per month. Michael Chung will occupy the premises effective June 1, 2007.

         18   Determining that the business would need more cash in June, Chung went to the bank and borrowed $1,500 on a personal loan and transferred the money to the company.

         25   Chung purchased a painting for his home from one of his clients. He paid for the $450 purchase with his personal credit card.

         28   Chung withdrew $4,500 from the business. He used $1,500 of the money to repay a portion of the loan arranged on May 18.

         31   The business did legal work with a value of $6,000 for Apex Computers Ltd. Apex paid for the work by giving the company computer equipment with a selling price of $12,000.

Required
Identify the accounting characteristic, assumption, or principle that would be applicable to each of the transactions and discuss the effects it would have on the financial statements of Michael Chung, Lawyer.

Accounting concepts/principles, transaction analysis, accounting equation, financial statements, evaluation

 4 5 6

3. Net income $100,000
4. Jason Elliot, capital, Dec. 31, 2008, $250,000
5. Total assets $256,000

Problem 1–8A

Herley City was started on December 31, 2007, by Jason Elliott with an investment of $30,000 cash. It has been operating for one year. Elliott has made additional investments of $20,000 but he has not withdrawn any funds. The company rents out snowboards and related gear from a small store. The balance sheet accounts at November 30, 2008, are as follows:

Cash	$ 2,000
Accounts receivable	18,000
Rental gear..................................	36,000
Rental snowboards...................	68,000
Store equipment........................	26,000
Accounts payable	24,000

The following transactions took place during the month of December 2008:

Dec.	1	Elliott borrowed $30,000 from his family and invested $24,000 in the business. The other $6,000 was intended for Elliott's living expenses.
	1	The business paid $6,000 for the month's rent on the store space.
	4	The business signed a one-year lease for the rental of additional store space at a cost of $4,000 per month. The lease is effective January 1. The business will pay the first month's rent in January.
	6	Rental fees for the week were: Gear, $12,000; Boards, $28,000. Half the fees were paid in cash and half on account.
	10	The business paid the accounts payable from November 30, 2008.
	12	The business purchased gear for $18,000 and boards for $32,000, all on account.
	13	Rental fees for the week were: Gear, $6,000; Boards, $12,000. All the fees were paid in cash.
	15	The company received payment for the accounts receivable owing at November 30, 2008.
	18	The company purchased store equipment for $8,000 by paying $2,000 cash with the balance due in 60 days.
	20	Rental fees for the week were: Gear, $8,000; Boards, $20,000. Half the fees were paid in cash and half on account.
	24	The company paid the balance owing for the purchases made on December 12.
	27	Rental fees for the week were: Gear, $4,000; Boards, $16,000. All the fees were paid in cash.
	27	The company received payment for rental fees on account from December 6.

Required

1. What is the total net income earned by the business over the period of December 31, 2007 to November 30, 2008?
2. Analyze the effects of the December 2008 transactions on the accounting equation of Herley City. Include the account balances from November 30, 2008.
3. Prepare the income statement for Herley City for the month ended December 31, 2008.
4. Prepare the statement of owner's equity for Herley City for the month ended December 31, 2008.
5. Prepare the balance sheet for Herley City at December 31, 2008.
6. Elliott has expressed concern that although the business seems to be profitable and growing, he constantly seems to be investing additional money into it and has been unable to make any withdrawals for the work he has put into it. Prepare a reply to his concerns.

Problems (Group B)

Problem 1–1B

Entity concept, transaction analysis, accounting equation

4 5

2. Total assets $21,920

Sam Shipley is an architect and was a partner with a large firm, a partnership, for 10 years after graduating from university. Recently he resigned his position to open his own architecture office, which he operates as a proprietorship. The name of the new entity is Shipley Design.

Shipley recorded the following events during the organizing phase of his new business and its first month of operations. Some of the events were personal and did not affect the practice of architecture. Others were business transactions and should be accounted for by the business.

July	1	Sam Shipley sold 2,000 shares of Royal Bank stock, which he had owned for several years, receiving $11,000 cash from his stockbroker.
	2	Sam Shipley deposited the $11,000 cash from sale of the Royal Bank stock in his personal bank account.
	3	Sam Shipley received $30,000 cash from his former partners in the architecture firm from which he resigned.
	5	Sam Shipley deposited $20,000 into a bank account in the name of Shipley Design.
	5	Shipley Design paid office rent for the month of July, $1,380.
	6	A representative of a large real estate company telephoned Sam Shipley and told him of the company's intention to transfer its design business to his business, Shipley Design.
	7	Shipley Design paid $110 cash for letterhead stationery.
	9	Shipley Design purchased office furniture for the office, on account, for $1,900, promising to pay in three months.
	23	Shipley Design finished design work for a client and submitted the bill for design services, $2,600. It expects to collect from this client within one month.
	31	Sam Shipley withdrew $1,200 for personal use.

Required

1. Classify each of the preceding events as one of the following (list each date and then choose a, b, or c):
   a. A business transaction to be accounted for by the business, Shipley Design.
   b. A business-related event but not a transaction to be accounted for by Shipley Design.
   c. A personal transaction not to be accounted for by Shipley Design.
2. Analyze the effects of the above events on the accounting equation of Shipley Design. Use a format similar to Exhibit 1–9, Panel B, on page 19.

Problem 1–2B

Balance sheet, entity concept

1. Total assets $265,000

Luella Hyde is a realtor. She buys and sells properties on her own, and she also earns commission revenue as a real estate agent. She invested $60,000 on March 10, 2007, in the business, Luella Hyde Realty. Consider the following facts as of March 31, 2007:

a. Hyde had $15,000 in her personal bank account and $74,000 in the business bank account.

b. The real estate office had $11,500 of office supplies on hand on March 31, 2007.

c. Luella Hyde Realty had spent $22,500 for a Realty World Canada franchise, which entitled the company to represent itself as a Realty World Canada member firm. This franchise is a business asset.

d. The company owed $105,500 on a note payable for some undeveloped land that had been acquired by the company for a total price of $116,000.

e. Hyde owed $165,000 on a personal mortgage on her personal residence, which she acquired in 2001 for a total price of $360,000.

f. Hyde owed $1,500 on a personal charge account with The Bay.

g. The company acquired business furniture for $41,000 on March 26. Of this amount, Luella Hyde Realty owed $32,000 on account at March 31, 2007.

Required

1. Prepare the balance sheet of the real estate business of Luella Hyde Realty at March 31, 2007.
2. Identify the personal items given in the preceding facts that would not be reported on the balance sheet of the business.

Problem 1–3B

Business transactions and analysis

Recently, Carole Gallagher formed a management accounting practice as a proprietorship. The balance of each item in the proprietorship accounting equation follows for November 2 and for each of the eight following business days.

	Cash	Accounts Receivable	Office Supplies	Land	Accounts Payable	Owner's Equity
Nov. 2	$ 900	$2,100	$240	$3,300	$1,140	$5,400
9	1,800	1,200	240	3,300	1,140	5,400
14	1,200	1,200	240	3,300	540	5,400
17	1,200	1,200	330	3,300	630	5,400
19	1,800	1,200	330	3,300	630	6,000
20	1,470	1,200	330	3,300	300	6,000
22	3,270	1,200	330	1,500	300	6,000
26	3,210	1,200	390	1,500	300	6,000
30	1,980	1,200	390	1,500	300	4,770

Required Assuming that a single transaction took place on each day, describe briefly the transaction that was most likely to have occurred. Begin with November 9 and complete up to November 30. Indicate which accounts were affected and by what amount. No revenue or expense transactions occurred on these dates.

Excel Spreadsheet Template

Income statement, statement of owner's equity, balance sheet

1. Net income $200,000
2. Jill Jiffey, capital, Dec. 31, 2007, $360,000
3. Total assets $630,000

Problem 1–4B

The amounts of (a) the assets and liabilities of Jiffey Office Cleaning as of December 31, 2007, and (b) the revenues and expenses of the company for the year ended on December 31, 2007, appear below. The items are listed in alphabetical order.

Accounts payable	$ 85,000	Land	$140,000
Accounts receivable	15,000	Notes payable	180,000
Building	255,000	Property tax expense	10,000
Cash	5,000	Repairs expense	60,000
Equipment	105,000	Salary expense	210,000
Interest expense	25,000	Service revenue	520,000
Interest payable	5,000	Supplies	110,000
		Utilities expense	15,000

The beginning amount of owner's equity was $305,000. During the year, the owner, Jill Jiffey, withdrew $145,000.

Required

1. Prepare the income statement of Jiffey Office Cleaning for the year ended December 31, 2007.

2. Prepare the statement of owner's equity of the business for the year ended December 31, 2007.

3. Prepare the balance sheet of the business at December 31, 2007.

4. Answer these questions about Jiffey Office Cleaning.
   a. Was the result of operations for the year a profit or a loss? How much was it?
   b. Did the business's owner's equity increase or decrease during the year? How would this affect the business's ability to borrow money from a bank in the future?
   c. How much in total economic resources does the company have at December 31, 2007, as it moves into the new year? How much does the company owe? What is the dollar amount of the owner's portion of the business at December 31, 2007?

Balance sheet

1. Total assets $73,600

Problem 1–5B

The bookkeeper of Shamanski Insurance Agency prepared the balance sheet of the company while the accountant was ill. The balance sheet contains errors. In particular, the bookkeeper knew that the balance sheet should balance, so she "plugged in" the owner's equity amount needed to achieve this balance. The owner's equity amount, however, is not correct. All other amounts are accurate.

SHAMANSKI INSURANCE AGENCY
Balance Sheet
For the Month Ended October 31, 2007

Assets		Liabilities	
Cash..............................	$11,700	Premium revenue.......................	$56,500
Insurance expense	150	Accounts payable.......................	21,500
Land....................................	10,750	Note payable...............................	20,000
Salary expense...........................	1,650		
Office furniture	22,850		
Accounts receivable	16,300	**Owner's Equity**	
Utilities expense.......................	1,050	C. Shamanski, capital	(21,550)
Notes receivable.......................	12,000	Total liabilities and	
Total assets................................	$76,450	owner's equity.......................	$76,450

Required

1. Prepare the correct balance sheet, and date it correctly. Compute total assets, total liabilities, and owner's equity.

2. Identify the accounts listed above that should *not* be presented on the balance sheet and state why you excluded them from the correct balance sheet you prepared for Requirement 1.

Problem 1–6B

Terry Thibert operates an interior design studio called Thibert Design Studio. The following amounts summarize the financial position of the business on April 30, 2007:

Transaction analysis, accounting equation, financial statements

2. Net income $10,480
3. T. Thibert, capital, May 31, 2007, $91,000
4. Total assets $92,440

	Assets			=	Liabilities	+	Owner's Equity
	Accounts				**Accounts**		**T. Thibert,**
Cash +	**Receivable + Supplies +**		**Land**	**=**	**Payable**	**+**	**Capital**
Bal. 13,440	14,480		48,200		20,800		55,320

During May 2007 the company did the following:

a. Thibert received $28,000 as a gift and deposited the cash in the business bank account.

b. Paid the beginning balance of accounts payable.

c. Performed services for a client and received cash of $2,200.

d. Collected cash from a customer on account, $1,800.

e. Purchased supplies on account, $1,440.

f. Consulted on the interior design of a major office building and billed the client for services rendered, $12,000.

g. Recorded the following business expenses for the month:
   (1) Paid office rent for May 2007—$2,400.
   (2) Paid advertising—$1,320.

h. Sold supplies to another interior designer for $160 cash, which was the cost of the supplies.

i. Terry Thibert withdrew $2,800 cash for personal use.

Required

1. Analyze the effects of the above transactions on the accounting equation of Thibert Design Studio. Adapt the format of Exhibit 1–9, Panel B, on page 19.

2. Prepare the income statement of Thibert Design Studio for the month ended May 31, 2007. List expenses in decreasing order by amount.

3. Prepare the statement of owner's equity of Thibert Design Studio for the month ended May 31, 2007.

4. Prepare the balance sheet of Thibert Design Studio at May 31, 2007.

Problem 1–7B

Jesse Burgess has been operating a plumbing business as a proprietorship (Jesse Burgess Plumbing) for four years and had the following business assets and liabilities (at their historical costs) on May 31, 2007:

Cash...	$30,000
Accounts receivable	15,000
Shop supplies..............................	6,000
Shop equipment..........................	45,000
Accounts payable	15,000

The following events took place during the month of June 2007:

June 1 Jesse's brother, John, had been in a similar business in the same city and moved to England. He sold Jesse his equipment for $27,000. The equipment had cost $51,000 and had a replacement cost of $33,000.

3 The business did some plumbing repairs for Sheldon Kantor, a customer. The business would normally have charged $600 for the work, but had agreed to do it for $450 cash in order to promote more business from the client.

10 The business signed a lease to rent additional shop space for the business at a cost of $2,400 per month. The business will occupy the premises effective July 1, 2007.

18 Finding he was low on cash, Jesse Burgess went to the bank and borrowed $4,500 on a personal loan.

22 Inflation has caused the value of the shop equipment to double to $90,000. Jesse does not understand why accountants ignore the effect of inflation in the accounting records.

28 Jesse Burgess withdrew $6,000 from the business and used $4,500 to repay the personal bank loan of June 18.

Required Identify the accounting assumption, principle, or constraint that would be applicable to each of the events, and discuss the effects it would have on the financial statements of Jesse Burgess Plumbing.

Problem 1–8B

Select Computer Concepts, a proprietorship owned by Melanie Rindt, was started on January 1, 2005, by Melanie Rindt with an investment of $20,000 cash. It has been operating for three years. Rindt has made additional investments of $44,000 but has not made any withdrawals. The company prepares marketing plans for clients and has seen business grow from a small business using rented equipment and having only a few customers to one with the following balances as of December 31, 2007:

Cash...	$ 8,000
Accounts receivable	16,000
Software	12,000
Office furniture	48,000
Computer equipment	72,000
Accounts payable	26,000
Owner's equity	130,000

The following transactions took place during the month of January 2008:

Jan. 2 Rindt invested $30,000 in the business.

2 The business paid $4,000 for the month's rent on the office space.

4 The business signed a lease for the rental of additional office space at a cost of $2,000 per month. The lease is effective February 1. The business will pay the first month's rent in February.

6 The business developed a systems design for Fleming Ltd. and received $18,000 now plus additional $10,000 payments to be received on the 15th of the month for the next three months.

10 The business paid $1,000 to a courier service.

12 Rindt signed an agreement to provide design work to Smith Inc. for $50,000 to be paid upon completion of the work.

14 The company purchased $10,000 of software that will be required for the Smith assignment. The company paid $6,000 and promised to pay the balance by the end of the month.

Jan.	15	The company received $10,000 as the monthly payment from Fleming Ltd. of January 6.
	18	The company purchased computer equipment for $40,000 by paying $8,000 cash with the balance due in 60 days.
	23	The company completed a network design for Wong Ltd., which promised to pay $15,000 by the end of the month.
	29	The company paid the balance owing for the software purchased on January 14.

Required

1. What is the total net income earned by the business over the period of January 1, 2005, to December 31, 2007?

2. Analyze the effects of the January 2008 transactions on the accounting equation of Select Computer Concepts. Be sure to include the account balances from December 31, 2007.

3. Prepare the income statement for Select Computer Concepts for the month ended January 31, 2008.

4. Prepare the statement of owner's equity for Select Computer Concepts for the month ended January 31, 2008.

5. Prepare the balance sheet for Select Computer Concepts at January 31, 2008.

6. Rindt has expressed concern that although the business seems to be profitable and growing, she constantly seems to be investing additional money into it and has been unable to make any withdrawals for the work she has put into it. Prepare a reply to her concerns.

Challenge Problems

Problem 1–1C

Understanding the going-concern assumption

The going-concern assumption is becoming an increasing source of concern for users of financial statements. There are instances of companies filing for bankruptcy several months after issuing their annual audited financial statements. The question is: why didn't the financial statements predict the problem?

A friend has just arrived on your doorstep; you realize she is very angry. After calming her down, you ask what the problem is. She tells you that she had inherited $25,000 from an uncle and invested the money in the common shares of Always Good Yogurt Corp. She had carefully examined Always Good Yogurt's financial statements for the year ended six months previously and concluded that the company was financially sound. This morning, she had read in the local paper that the company had gone bankrupt and her investment was worthless. She asks you why the financial statements valued the assets at values that are in excess of those the Trustee in Bankruptcy expects to realize from liquidating the assets. Why have the assets suddenly lost so much of the value they had six months ago?

Required Explain to your friend why assets are valued on a going-concern basis in the financial statements and why they are usually worth less when the company goes out of business. Use inventory and accounts receivable as examples.

Problem 1–2C

Accounting for business transactions

You and three friends have decided to go into the lawn care business for the summer to earn money to pay for your schooling in the fall. Your first step was to sign up customers to satisfy yourselves that the business had the potential to be profitable. Next, you planned to go to the bank to borrow money to buy the equipment you would need.

After considerable effort, your group obtained contracts from customers for 200 lawns for the summer. One of your partners wants to prepare a balance sheet showing the value of the contracts as an asset. She is sure that you will have no trouble with borrowing the necessary funds from the bank on the basis of the proposed balance sheet.

Required Explain to your friend why the commitments (signed contracts) from customers cannot be recognized as assets. What suggestions do you have that might assist your group in borrowing the necessary funds?

Decision Problems

Using financial statements to evaluate a request for a loan

Decision Problem 1

Two businesses, Tyler's Bicycle Centre and Ryan's Catering, have sought business loans from you. To decide whether to make the loans, you have requested their balance sheets.

TYLER'S BICYCLE CENTRE
Balance Sheet
December 31, 2007

Assets		Liabilities	
Cash..	$ 13,500	Accounts payable	$ 18,000
Accounts receivable	21,000	Notes payable	177,000
Merchandise inventory............	127,500	Total liabilities..............................	195,000
Store supplies	750		
Furniture and fixtures..............	13,500	**Owner's Equity**	
Building	123,000	T. Jones, capital	125,250
Land...	21,000	Total liabilities and	
Total assets................................	$320,250	owner's equity	$320,250

RYAN'S CATERING
Balance Sheet
December 31, 2007

Assets		Liabilities	
Cash..	$ 15,000	Accounts payable	$ 4,500
Accounts receivable	6,000	Note payable.........................	102,000
Office supplies	3,000	Total liabilities.............................	106,500
Inventory	30,000		
Office furniture	7,500	**Owner's Equity**	
Investments*	300,000	R. Smith, capital...........................	255,000
		Total liabilities and	
Total assets................................	$361,500	owner's equity	$361,500

*The investments of $300,000 can be sold today for $380,000.

Required

1. Based solely on these balance sheets, which entity would you be more comfortable loaning money to? Explain fully, citing specific items and amounts from the balance sheets.

2. In addition to the balance sheet data, what other financial statement information would you require? Be specific.

Using accounting information

Decision Problem 2

A friend learns that you are taking an accounting course. Knowing that you do not plan a career in accounting, the friend asks why you are "wasting your time." Explain to the friend:

1. Why you are taking the course.

2. How accounting information is used or will be used:
   a. In your personal life.
   b. In the business life of your friend, who plans to be a farmer.
   c. In the business life of another friend, who plans a career in sales.

Financial Statement Cases

These and similar problems in later chapters focus on the financial statements of two real Canadian companies—CHUM Limited and Sun-Rype Products Ltd. CHUM Limited is one of Canada's leading media companies and content providers, which owns and operates 33 radio stations, 12 local television stations, and 21 specialty channels, as well as an environmental music distribution division. (On August 31, 2006, Bell Globemedia Inc. was successful in its offer to acquire CHUM Limited. As a result, Bell Globemedia will de-list CHUM Limited's common shares and Class B Shares on the Toronto Stock Exchange.) Sun-Rype Products Ltd. is a leading manufacturer and marketer of juice-based beverages and fruit-based snacks located in the fruit-growing district of British Columbia but with sales across Canada. As you study each financial statement problem using these two companies, you will gradually build the confidence that you can understand and use actual financial statements.

Financial Statement Case 1

Refer to the CHUM Limited financial statements located in Appendix A at the end of this book. Notice that the amounts reported in CHUM's financial statements are in thousands of dollars.

Identifying items from a company's financial statements

5. Aug. 31, 2005, net income $41,365,000

Required

1. How much cash and short-term deposits did CHUM Limited have at August 31, 2005?

2. What were total assets at August 31, 2005? At August 31, 2004?

3. Write the company's accounting equation at August 31, 2005, by filling in the dollar amounts:

ASSETS = LIABILITIES + SHAREHOLDERS' EQUITY

4. Identify total revenue for the year ended August 31, 2005. Do the same for the year ended August 31, 2004. Did revenue increase or decrease in fiscal 2005?

5. How much net income or net loss did CHUM Limited experience for the year ended August 31, 2005? Was 2005 a good year or bad year compared to 2004?

Financial Statement Case 2

Refer to the Sun-Rype Products Ltd. financial statements located in Appendix B at the end of this book. Notice that the amounts reported in Sun-Rype's financial statements are in thousands of dollars.

Identifying items from a company's financial statements

6. Dec. 31, 2005, net income $6,524,000

Required

1. During 2006, Sun-Rype announced a special dividend declaration. Use the Internet to summarize the details of the March 3, 2006, press release and your interpretation of this announcement. Sun-Rype's website is accessible at www.sun-rype.com; you can also find financial information and press releases at www.sedar.com.

2. How much cash and cash equivalents did Sun-Rype have at December 31, 2005?

3. What were total assets at December 31, 2005? At December 31, 2004?

4. Write the company's accounting equation at December 31, 2005, by filling in the dollar amounts:

ASSETS = LIABILITIES + SHAREHOLDERS' EQUITY

5. Identify total sales revenue for the year ended December 31, 2005, and the year ended December 31, 2004. Did revenue increase or decrease during 2005?

6. How much net income or net loss did Sun-Rype experience for the year ended December 31, 2005? Was 2005 a good year or bad year compared to 2004?

Recording Business Transactions

What is your favourite snack food? If you are like most people, it may be Doritos, Earth Chips, or plain potato chips. All of these are Frito-Lay Canada products. Year in and year out, Frito-Lay Canada leads the prepared snack-food industry. How does this company deliver fresh quantities of chips to thousands of stores every day of the year?

One of Frito-Lay Canada's great advantages is its accounting system. Route managers use hand-held computers to record how many products are sold each day. The data are relayed to company headquarters, and managers can see instantly which products are selling, and where. Suppose Doritos are selling well and potato chips are currently out of favour. Frito-Lay Canada managers know they should buy more corn for Doritos and fewer potatoes for chips. The company avoids waste by buying only what it needs to meet consumer demand.

The result? Frito-Lay Canada is very profitable. Th s chapter shows how Frito-Lay Canada and other companies record their business transactions. The procedures outlined in this chapter are followed by entities ranging from giants like Frito-Lay Canada to a local travel agency such as SuperTravel.

Why is recording business transactions important?

How do we know if a transaction has occurred?

If a transaction has occurred, where do we record it and what amount do we record?

How do we record the increases and decreases in various types of accounts?

How do we report a business's results of operations and financial position?

These questions and others will be answered throughout this chapter. And the Decision Guidelines at the end of this chapter will provide the answers in a useful summary.

Chapter 1 introduced transaction analysis and the financial statements.
That chapter showed simple financial statements but not how they are prepared. Chapters 2, 3, and 4 cover the accounting process that results in the financial statements. The following diagram summarizes the accounting process—steps 2, 3, and 4 are covered in this chapter.

1. Identify and analyze transactions

2. Record transactions in a journal

3. Post (copy) from the journal to the accounts in the ledger

4. Prepare the trial balance

5. Journalize and post adjusting entries

6. Prepare the financial statements

7. Close the books
(closing entries, postclosing trial balance)

By learning how accounting information is processed, you will understand where the facts and figures reported in the financial statements come from. This knowledge will increase your confidence and ability to understand and analyze financial information.

Accounting begins and ends with accounts.

The Account, the Ledger, and the Journal

The basic summary device of accounting is the **account,** which is the detailed record of the changes that have occurred in a particular asset, liability, or item of owner's equity during a period of time. As we saw in Chapter 1, business transactions cause the changes.

Accountants record transactions first in a **journal,** which is the chronological record of transactions. Accountants then copy (post) the data to the book (or

Objective 1

Define and use key accounting terms

printout) of all the accounts called the **ledger**. In the phrase "keeping the books," *books* refers to the ledger. A list of all the ledger accounts and their balances is called a **trial balance**.

Accounts are grouped in three broad categories, according to the accounting equation:

ASSETS = LIABILITIES + OWNER'S EQUITY

Recall that in Chapter 1, page 12, we learned that the accounting equation is the basic tool of accounting. It measures assets and claims to those assets.

Exhibit 2–1 shows how asset, liability, and owner's equity accounts can be grouped into the ledger.

EXHIBIT 2–1 The Ledger (Asset, Liability, and Owner's Equity Accounts)

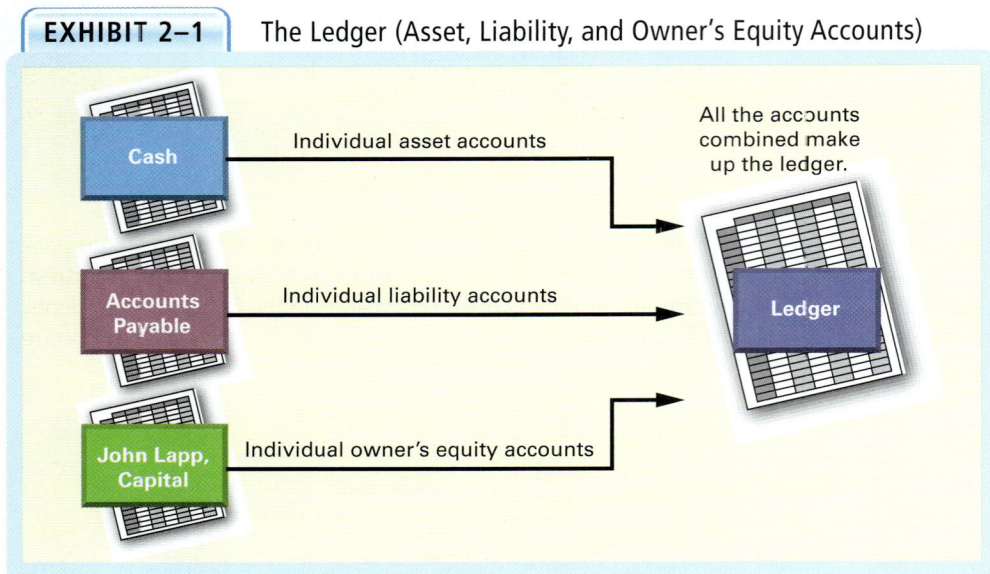

Assets

Assets are economic resources that will benefit the business in the future. Most firms use the following asset accounts.

Cash The Cash account shows the changes in cash from a business's transactions. Cash means money and any medium of exchange that a bank accepts at face value, such as bank account balances, paper currency, coins, certificates of deposit, and cheques. Successful companies such as Frito-Lay Canada usually have plenty of cash. Most business failures result from a shortage of cash.

Accounts Receivable A business may sell its goods or services in exchange for an oral or implied promise of future cash receipts. Such sales are made on credit ("on account") to customers that buy a business's products or services. The Accounts Receivable account contains these amounts.

Notes Receivable A business may sell its goods or services in exchange for a *promissory note*, which is a written pledge that the customer will pay the business a fixed amount of money by a certain date. The Notes Receivable account is a record of the promissory notes that the business expects to collect in cash. A **note receivable** offers more security for collection than an account receivable does and it can require the customer to pay interest on the amount the customer owes.

Prepaid Expenses A business often pays certain expenses in advance. A *prepaid expense* is an asset because it provides future benefits to the business. The business avoids having to pay cash in the future for the specified expense. The ledger holds a separate asset account for each prepaid expense. Prepaid Rent, Prepaid Insurance, and Office Supplies are accounted for as prepaid expenses.

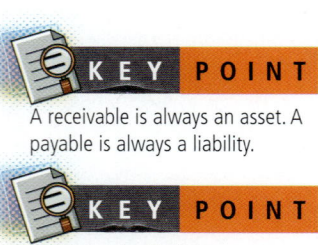

KEY POINT

A receivable is always an asset. A payable is always a liability.

KEY POINT

Notes Receivable, Interest Receivable, and Rent Receivable are *not* the same as Accounts Receivable.

Land The Land account is a record of the cost of land a business owns and uses in its operations. Land held for sale is accounted for separately—in an investment account.

Building The cost of a business's buildings—office, warehouse, garage, and the like—appear in the Building account. Buildings held for sale are separate assets accounted for as investments. Intrawest Corporation is a Canadian developer and operator of ski and golf resorts. Intrawest's Whistler ski lodge would appear in its Buildings account. However, the condominiums that Intrawest builds at its resorts and sells would *not* be included in the Building account; they would be a part of inventory, discussed in Chapter 5.

Equipment, Furniture, and Fixtures A business has a separate asset account for each type of equipment—Computer Equipment, Office Equipment, and Store Equipment, for example. The Furniture and Fixtures account shows the costs of furniture and fixtures such as lights and signs.

We will discuss other asset categories and accounts as needed. For example, many businesses have investment accounts for their investments in the shares and bonds of other companies.

Liabilities

Recall that a *liability* is a debt. A business generally has fewer liability accounts than asset accounts because a business's liabilities can be summarized under relatively few categories.

Bank Indebtedness This account shows the amount of money a business owes to its bank that it expects to repay within one year.

Accounts Payable This account is the opposite of the Accounts Receivable account. The oral or implied promise to pay off debts arising from credit purchases appears in the Accounts Payable account. Such purchases are said to be made on account and are usually amounts owed to a business's suppliers for goods or services purchased. All companies, including Frito-Lay Canada, have accounts payable.

Notes Payable The Notes Payable account is the opposite of the Notes Receivable account. Notes Payable represents the amounts that the business must pay because it signed a promissory note to borrow money to purchase goods or services.

Accrued Liabilities Liability categories and accounts are added as needed. Taxes Payable, Interest Payable, and Salaries Payable are accrued liability accounts used by most companies.

Owner's Equity

The owner's claims to the assets of a business are called *owner's equity*. In a proprietorship, like that of Doug Copely or John Lapp, described in Chapter 1, or a partnership, owner's equity is split into separate accounts for the owner's capital balance and for the owner's withdrawals. In a partnership, each partner would have a separate capital account and a separate withdrawals account.

Capital The Capital account shows the owner's claim to the assets of the business, whether it is Doug Copely or John Lapp of SuperTravel. Amounts received from the owner's investment in the business are recorded directly in the Capital account. The Capital balance equals the owner's investments in the business plus net income minus net losses and owner withdrawals over the life of the business.

Withdrawals When John Lapp withdraws cash or other assets from SuperTravel for personal use, the business's assets and owner's equity decrease. The amounts taken out of the business appear in a separate account entitled John Lapp, Withdrawals, or John Lapp, Drawings. If withdrawals were recorded directly in the Capital account, the amount of owner withdrawals would *not* be highlighted and decision making would be more difficult.

THINKING IT OVER

Suppose you bought a Honda Civic for $28,000 and had to borrow $18,000 to pay for the car. Write your personal accounting equation for this transaction.

A:
Assets = Liabilities + Owner's Equity
$28,000 = $18,000 + $10,000

Revenues The increase in owner's equity created by delivering goods or services to customers or clients is called *revenue*. The ledger contains as many revenue accounts as needed. SuperTravel would have a Service Revenue account for amounts earned by providing services for clients. If a business lends money to an outsider, it will need an Interest Revenue account for the interest earned on the loan. If the business rents a building to a tenant, it will need a Rent Revenue account.

Expenses Expenses use up assets or create liabilities in the course of operating a business. Expenses have the opposite effect of revenues; they decrease owner's equity. A business needs a separate account for each type of expense, such as Salaries Expense, Rent Expense, Advertising Expense, and Utilities Expense. Businesses strive to minimize their expenses in order to maximize net income whether they are Doug Copely, SuperTravel, or Frito-Lay Canada.

Exhibit 2–2 shows the effect on the Capital account of the owner's equity items described above.

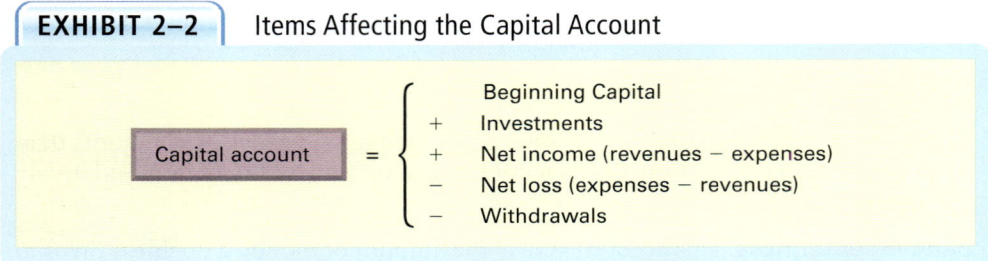

EXHIBIT 2–2   Items Affecting the Capital Account

$$\text{Capital account} \; = \; \begin{cases} & \text{Beginning Capital} \\ + & \text{Investments} \\ + & \text{Net income (revenues} - \text{expenses)} \\ - & \text{Net loss (expenses} - \text{revenues)} \\ - & \text{Withdrawals} \end{cases}$$

Double-Entry Accounting

Each business transaction has dual effects:

- The receiving side
- The giving side

For example, in the $60,000 cash receipt by SuperTravel, the business

- Received cash of $60,000
- Gave John Lapp $60,000 of owner's equity in the business.

Accounting uses the *double-entry system*, which means that we record the dual effects of each transaction. As a result, *every transaction affects at least two accounts*. It would be incomplete to record only the giving side, or only the receiving side, of a transaction.

Consider a cash purchase of supplies. What are the dual effects of this transaction? A cash purchase of supplies

1. Increases supplies (the business *received* supplies)
2. Decreases cash (the business *gave* cash)

A credit purchase of equipment (a purchase on account)

1. Increases equipment (the business *received* equipment)
2. Increases accounts payable (the business *gave* a promise to pay in the future)

As you can see, all transactions have at least two effects on the accounts of an entity.

KEY POINT

A T-account is a quick way to show the effect of transactions on a particular account—a useful shortcut or tool used in accounting.

The T-Account

How do we record transactions? The form of account used for most illustrations in this book is called the *T-account* because it takes the form of the capital letter "T."

The vertical line divides the account into its left and right sides, with the account title at the top. For example, the Cash account appears in the following T-account format:

Cash

(Left side)	(Right side)
Debit	*Credit*

The left side of the account is called the **debit** side, and the right side is called the **credit** side. The words *debit* and *credit* can be confusing because they are new. To become comfortable using them, simply remember this:

Debit = Left	Credit = Right

Even though *left side* and *right side* may be more convenient, *debit* and *credit* are deeply entrenched in business.[1] Debit and credit are abbreviated as follows:

Dr = Debit	Cr = Credit

 **KEY POINT**

The accounting equation must balance after every transaction. But verifying that total assets = total liabilities + owner's equity is no longer necessary after every transaction. The equation will balance as long as the debits in each transaction equal the credits in the transaction.

Increases and Decreases in the Accounts

Objective ②

Apply the rules of debit and credit

In everyday conversation, we may praise someone by saying, "She deserves credit for her good work." In your study of accounting, forget this general usage because accounting uses this term in a specialized way. Remember that *debit means left side* and *credit means right side*.

The type of an account (asset, liability, equity) determines how we record increases and decreases. For any given account, all increases are recorded on one side, and all decreases are recorded on the other side. Increases in *assets* are recorded in the left (debit) side of the account. Decreases in assets are recorded in the right (credit) side of the account. Conversely, increases in *liabilities* and *owner's equity* are recorded by *credits*. Decreases in liabilities and owner's equity are recorded by *debits*. These are the *rules of debit and credit*, and can be summarized as follows:

Assets		**Liabilities and Owner's Equity**	
Increase = Debit	Decrease = Credit	Decrease = Debit	Increase = Credit

STOP AND THINK

Indicate on which side of these accounts—debit (Dr) or credit (Cr)—you record an increase.

	Accounts Receivable		Salary Payable
_____	Accounts Receivable	_____	Salary Payable
_____	Accounts Payable	_____	Building
_____	Equipment	_____	Supplies
_____	John Lapp, Capital	_____	Interest Payable
_____	Notes Payable	_____	Furniture

Answer:

Dr	Accounts Receivable	Cr	Salary Payable
Cr	Accounts Payable	Dr	Building
Dr	Equipment	Dr	Supplies
Cr	John Lapp, Capital	Cr	Interest Payable
Cr	Notes Payable	Dr	Furniture

---

[1] The words *debit* and *credit* abbreviate the Latin terms *debitum* and *creditum*. Luca Pacioli, the Italian monk who wrote about accounting in the fifteenth century, used these terms.

This pattern of recording debits and credits is based on the accounting equation:

ASSETS = LIABILITIES + OWNER'S EQUITY
DEBITS = CREDITS

Assets are on the opposite side of the accounting equation from liabilities and owner's equity. Therefore, increases and decreases in assets are recorded in the opposite manner from increases and decreases in liabilities and owner's equity. Liabilities and owner's equity are on the same side of the equal sign, so they are treated in the same way. Exhibit 2–3 shows the relationship between the accounting equation and the rules of debit and credit.

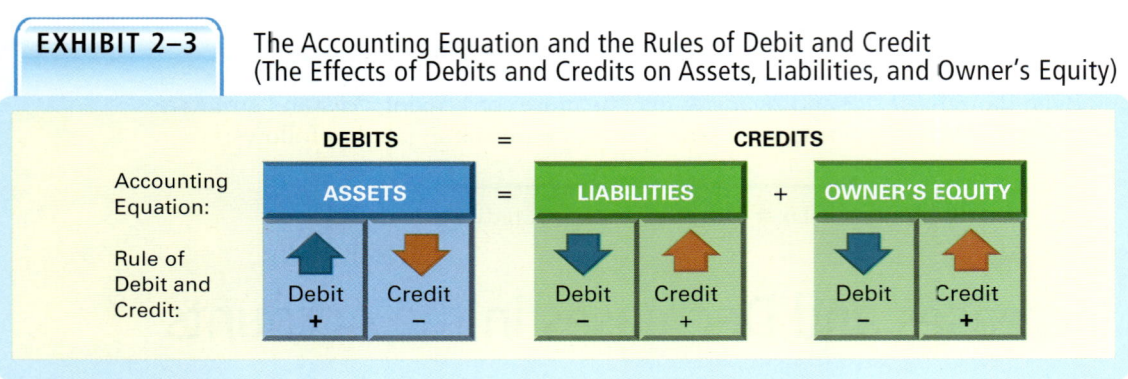

EXHIBIT 2–3 The Accounting Equation and the Rules of Debit and Credit (The Effects of Debits and Credits on Assets, Liabilities, and Owner's Equity)

To illustrate the ideas diagrammed in Exhibit 2–3, reconsider Transaction 1 from Chapter 1. John Lapp invested $60,000 cash to begin the travel agency. The company received $60,000 cash from John Lapp and gave him the owner's equity. We are accounting for the business entity, SuperTravel. What accounts of SuperTravel are affected? By what amounts? On what side (debit or credit)? The answer is that Assets and Capital would increase by $60,000, as the following T-accounts show:

ASSETS   =   LIABILITIES   +   OWNER'S EQUITY

Cash   John Lapp, Capital

Debit for   Credit for
increase,   increase,
60,000   60,000

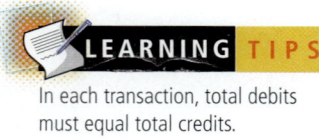
The amount remaining in an account is called its *balance*. Transaction 1 gives Cash a $60,000 debit balance, and John Lapp, Capital a $60,000 credit balance. Notice that Assets = Liabilities + Owner's Equity *and* that total debit amounts = total credit amounts. Exhibit 2–4 illustrates the accounting equation and SuperTravel's first two transactions.

Transaction 2 is a $40,000 cash purchase of land. This transaction affects two assets: Cash and Land. It decreases (credits) Cash and increases (debits) Land, as shown in the T-accounts:

ASSETS   =   LIABILITIES   +   OWNER'S EQUITY

Cash   John Lapp, Capital

Balance 60,000   Credit for   Balance 60,000
                   decrease,
                   40,000

Balance 20,000

Land

Debit for
increase,
40,000

Balance 40,000

After this transaction, Cash has a $20,000 debit balance ($60,000 debit balance reduced by the $40,000 credit amount), Land has a debit balance of $40,000, and John Lapp, Capital has a $60,000 credit balance as shown in the section of Exhibit 2–4 labelled Transaction 2.

EXHIBIT 2–4 The Accounting Equation after the First Two Transactions of SuperTravel

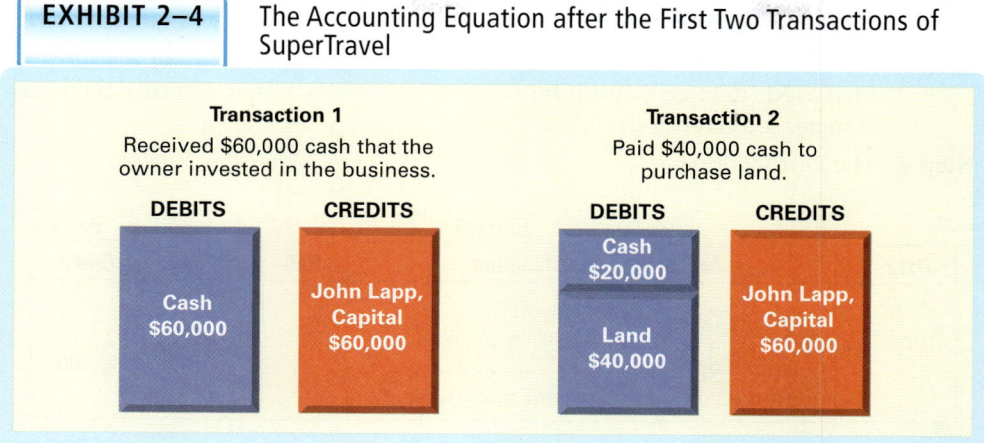

We create accounts as they are needed. The process of creating a new account in preparation for recording a transaction is called *opening the account.* For Transaction 1, we opened the Cash account and the John Lapp, Capital account. For Transaction 2, we opened the Land account.

We could record all transactions directly in the accounts as we have shown for the first two transactions. However, that way of accounting does not leave a clear record of each transaction. You may have to search through all the accounts to find both sides of a particular transaction. To save time, accountants first keep a record of each transaction in a *journal* and then transfer this information from the journal into the accounts.

Recording Transactions in the Journal

In practice, accountants record transactions in a *journal*, the chronological record of the entity's transactions. The journalizing process follows four steps:

Objective 3

Analyze and record transactions in the journal

1. Identify the transactions from source documents, such as bank deposit slips, sales invoices, or cheque stubs.
2. Identify each account affected by the transaction and its type (asset, liability, or owner's equity).
3. Determine whether each account is increased or decreased by the transaction. Using the rules of debit and credit, determine whether to debit or credit the account to record its increase or decrease.
4. Record the transaction in the journal, including a brief explanation for the journal entry. The debit side of the entry is entered first and the credit side last. Total debits must always equal total credits. This step is also called "making the journal entry" or "journalizing the transaction."

These four steps are completed in a computerized accounting system as well as in a manual system. In step 4, however, the computerized journal entry is generally entered into the computer by account number, and the account name then appears automatically. Most computer programs replace the explanation in the journal entry with some other means of tracing the entry back to its source documents.

Let's apply the four steps to journalize Transaction 1 of SuperTravel—the business's receipt of John Lapp's $60,000 cash investment in the business.

Step 1. The source documents are SuperTravel's bank deposit slip and the $60,000 cheque, which is deposited in the business bank account.

Step 2. The accounts affected by the transaction are Cash and John Lapp, Capital. Cash is an asset account, and John Lapp, Capital is an owner's equity account.

Step 3. Both accounts increase by $60,000. Therefore, Cash, the asset account, is increased (debited), and John Lapp, Capital, the owner's equity account, is increased (credited).

Step 4. The journal entry is

	Journal				Page 1
Date	Accounts and Explanation	Ref.	Debit	Credit
2007 Apr. 2[a]	Cash[b]		60,000[b]	
	John Lapp, Capital[c]			60,000[c]
	Received initial investment from owner.[d]			

The journal entry includes the

a. date of the transaction

b. title of the account debited (placed flush left), along with the dollar amount

c. title of the account credited (indented slightly), along with the dollar amount

d. short explanation of the transaction.

Dollar signs are omitted in the money columns because it is understood that the amounts are in dollars.

The journal offers detailed information that the ledger accounts do not provide. Each journal entry shows the complete effect of a business transaction. Consider John Lapp's initial investment. The Cash account shows the $60,000 debit. We know that every transaction has a credit, so the corresponding $60,000 credit is in the Capital account. But imagine the difficulties you would face trying to link debits and credits for hundreds of daily transactions—without a separate record of each transaction. The journal solves this problem and presents the full story for each transaction. Exhibit 2–5 shows how Journal page 1 looks after the first transaction is recorded.

Regardless of the accounting system in use, an accountant must analyze every business transaction in the manner we are presenting in these opening chapters. Once the transaction has been analyzed, a computerized accounting package performs the same actions as accountants do in a manual system. For example, when a sales clerk keys in your transaction and runs your VISA card through the credit card reader, the underlying accounting system records the store's sales revenue and receivable from VISA. The computer automatically records the transaction as a journal entry, but an accountant had to program the computer to do so. A computer's ability to perform routine tasks and mathematical operations quickly and without error frees accountants for decision making.

Student CD-ROM

Accounting Cycle Tutorials
3. The Journal and the Ledger
pages 1–6

EXHIBIT 2–5 The Journal

	Journal				Page 1
Date	Accounts and Explanation	Ref.	Debit	Credit
2007 Apr. 2	Cash		60,000	
	John Lapp, Capital			60,000
	Received initial investment from owner.			

Posting (Transferring Information) from the Journal to the Ledger

Objective 4

Post from the journal to the ledger

Journalizing a transaction records the data only in the journal—but not in the ledger. To appear in the ledger, the data must be copied or transferred to the ledger. The process of transferring data from the journal to the ledger is called **posting**. We *post* from the journal to the ledger.

Debits in the journal are posted as debits in the ledger, and credits in the journal as credits in the ledger—there are no exceptions. The first transaction of SuperTravel is posted to the ledger as shown in Exhibit 2–6. Computers perform this tedious task quickly and without error.

| EXHIBIT 2–6 | Making a Journal Entry and Posting to the Ledger |

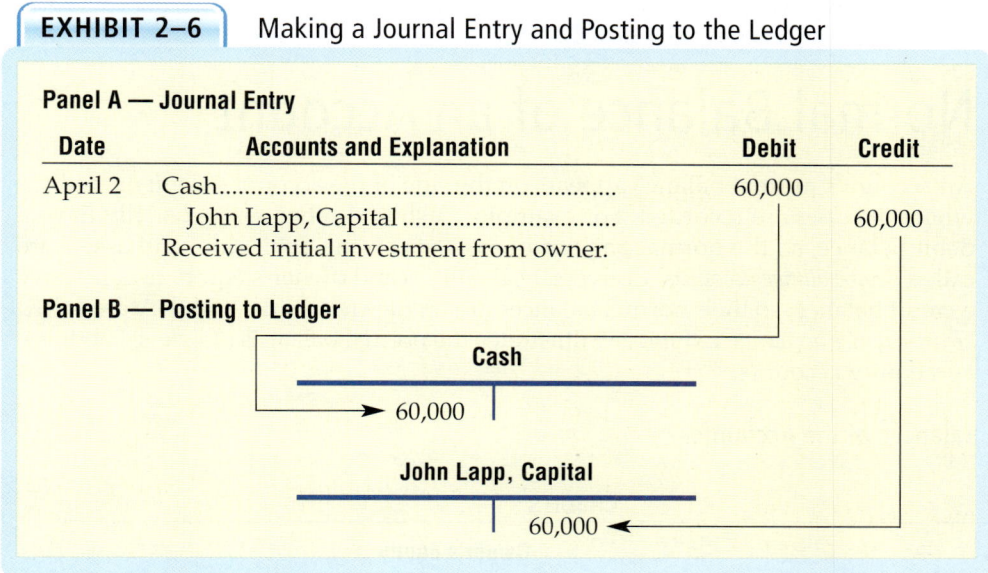

Panel A — Journal Entry

Date	Accounts and Explanation	Debit	Credit
April 2	Cash..	60,000	
	John Lapp, Capital		60,000
	Received initial investment from owner.		

Panel B — Posting to Ledger

Cash

60,000

John Lapp, Capital

60,000

Expanding the Rules of Debit and Credit: Revenues and Expenses

Owner's equity includes Revenues and Expenses because revenues and expenses make up net income or net loss, which flows into owner's equity. As we have discussed, *revenues* are increases in owner's equity from providing goods and services to customers. *Expenses* are decreases in owner's equity from using assets or increasing liabilities in the course of operating the business. Therefore, we must expand the accounting equation. Exhibit 2–7 shows revenues and expenses under equity because they directly affect owner's equity.

| EXHIBIT 2-7 | Expansion of the Accounting Equation to Include Revenues and Expenses |

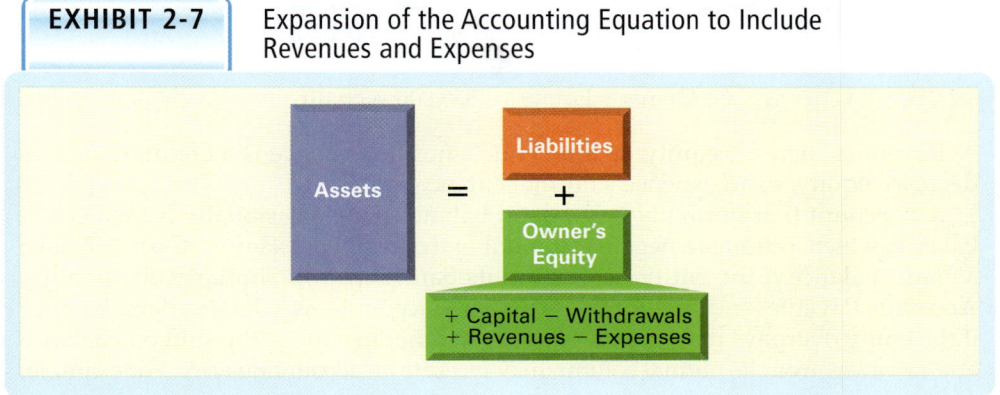

Assets = Liabilities + Owner's Equity

+ Capital − Withdrawals
+ Revenues − Expenses

EXHIBIT 2-8 | Final Rules of Debit and Credit

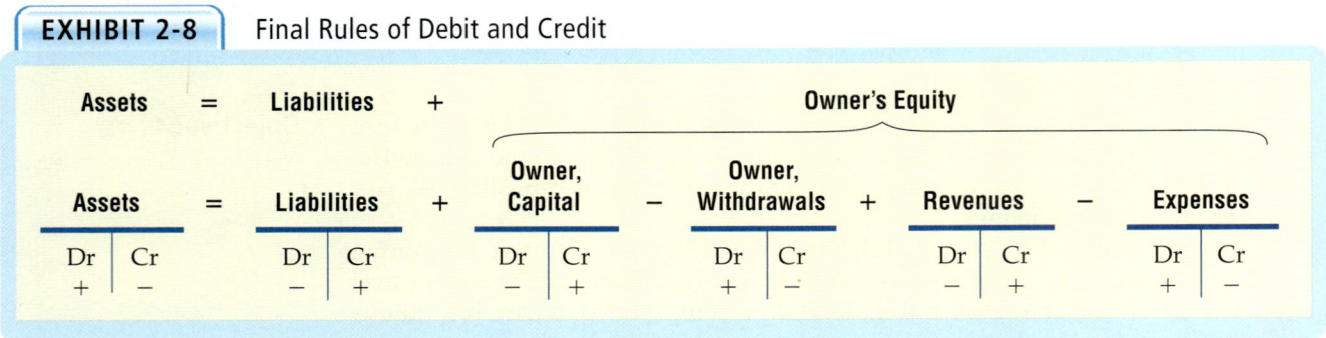

Assets	=	Liabilities	+			Owner's Equity				

Assets	=	Liabilities	+	Owner, Capital	−	Owner, Withdrawals	+	Revenues	−	Expenses
Dr | Cr		Dr | Cr		Dr | Cr		Dr | Cr		Dr | Cr		Dr | Cr
+ | −		− | +		− | +		+ | −		− | +		+ | −

We can now express the rules of debit and credit in final form as shown in Exhibit 2–8.

Normal Balance of an Account

KEY POINT

The normal balance of an account is the side on which increases are recorded.

An account's **normal balance** appears on the side of the account—debit or credit—where *increases* are recorded. For example, Cash and other assets usually have a debit balance, so the normal balance of assets is on the debit side, and assets are called *debit-balance accounts*. Conversely, liabilities and owner's equity usually have a credit balance, so their normal balances are on the credit side, and they are called *credit-balance accounts*. Exhibit 2–9 illustrates the normal balances of assets, liabilities, and equity accounts.

EXHIBIT 2–9 | Normal Balances of the Accounts

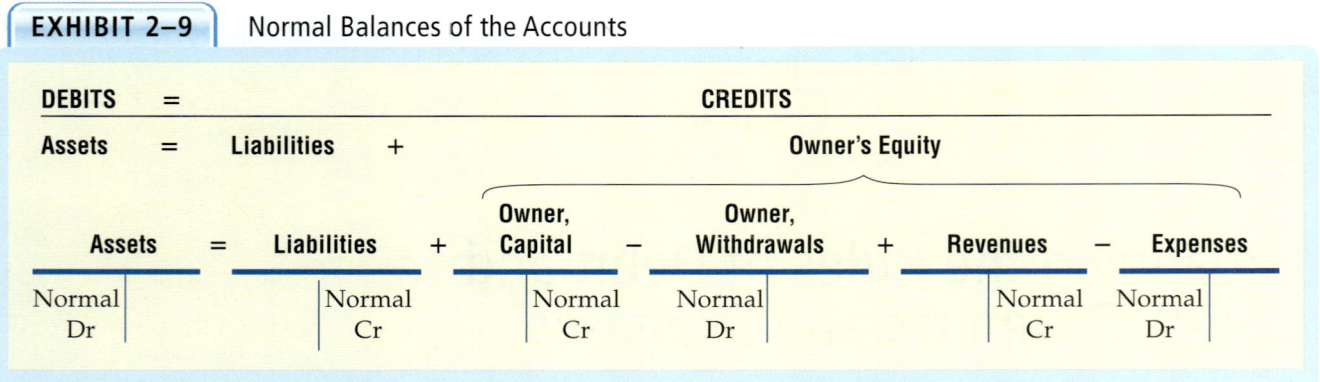

DEBITS	=					CREDITS				
Assets	=	Liabilities	+			Owner's Equity				

Assets	=	Liabilities	+	Owner, Capital	−	Owner, Withdrawals	+	Revenues	−	Expenses
Normal Dr		Normal Cr		Normal Cr		Normal Dr		Normal Cr		Normal Dr

As we have seen, owner's equity includes

John Lapp, Capital—a credit-balance account
John Lapp, Withdrawals—a debit-balance account

The sum of these two accounts should be a credit, for example,

John Lapp, Capital	John Lapp, Withdrawals
| 60,000	2,000 |

Owner's Equity = $58,000, a credit

Revenues increase equity, so a revenue's normal balance is a credit. Expenses decrease equity, so an expense's normal balance is a debit.

An account that normally has a debit balance may occasionally have a credit balance, which indicates a negative amount of the item. For example, Cash will have a credit balance if the entity overdraws its bank account. Similarly, the liability Accounts Payable—normally a credit-balance account—will have a debit balance if the entity overpays its accounts payable. In other instances, the shift of a balance amount away from its normal column may indicate an accounting error. For example, a credit balance in Office Supplies, Furniture, or Buildings is an error because negative amounts of these assets cannot exist.

The Flow of Accounting Data

Exhibit 2–10 summarizes the flow of accounting data from the business transaction all the way through the accounting system to the ledger. In the pages that follow, we record SuperTravel's early transactions. Keep in mind that we are accounting for the business entity, SuperTravel. We are *not* accounting for John Lapp's *personal* transactions. We temporarily ignore the date of each transaction in order to focus on the accounts and their dollar amounts.

| EXHIBIT 2–10 | Flow of Accounting Data |

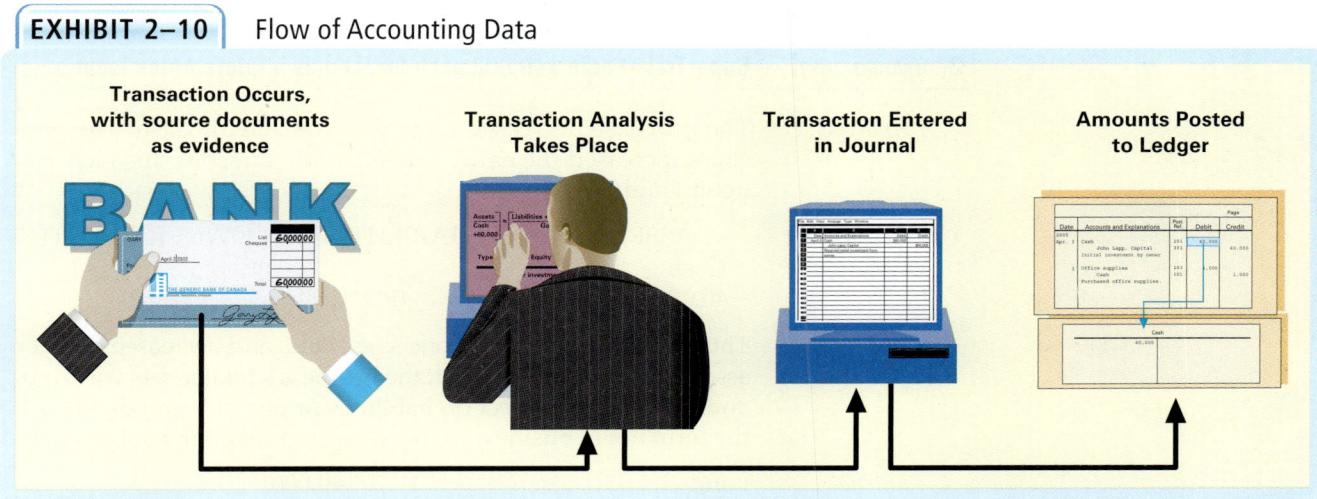

| Transaction Occurs, with source documents as evidence | Transaction Analysis Takes Place | Transaction Entered in Journal | Amounts Posted to Ledger |

Transaction Analysis, Journalizing, and Posting to the Ledger

1. Transaction: **John Lapp invested $60,000 cash to begin his travel business, SuperTravel.**

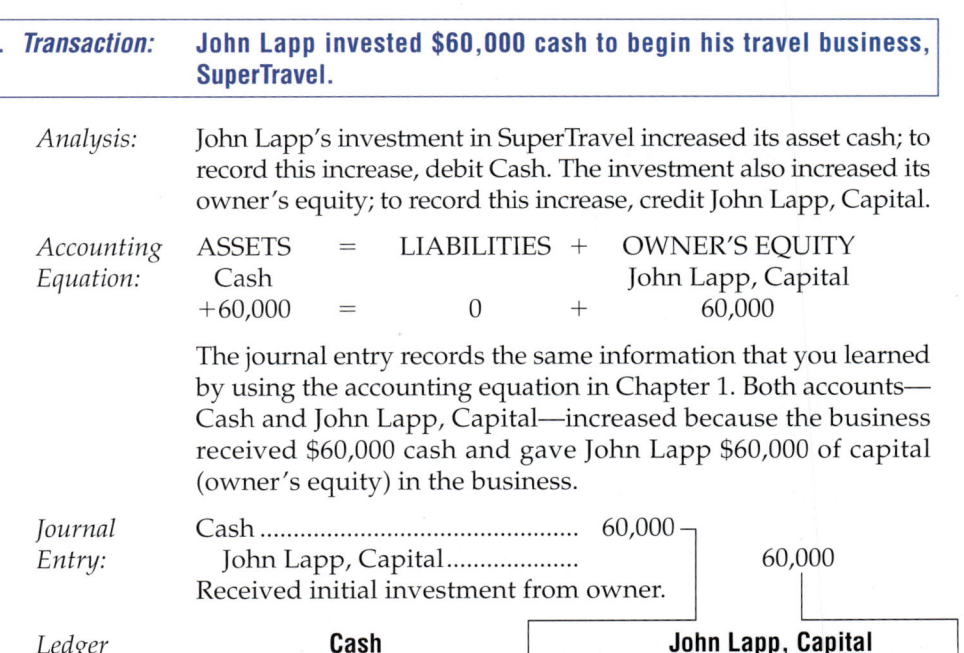

Analysis: John Lapp's investment in SuperTravel increased its asset cash; to record this increase, debit Cash. The investment also increased its owner's equity; to record this increase, credit John Lapp, Capital.

Accounting Equation:

ASSETS	=	LIABILITIES	+	OWNER'S EQUITY
Cash				John Lapp, Capital
+60,000	=	0	+	60,000

The journal entry records the same information that you learned by using the accounting equation in Chapter 1. Both accounts—Cash and John Lapp, Capital—increased because the business received $60,000 cash and gave John Lapp $60,000 of capital (owner's equity) in the business.

Journal Entry:

Cash 60,000
    John Lapp, Capital....................   60,000
Received initial investment from owner.

Ledger Accounts:

Cash	John Lapp, Capital
(1) 60,000	(1) 60,000

2. Transaction: **SuperTravel paid $40,000 cash for land as a future office location.**

Analysis: The purchase decreased cash; therefore, credit Cash. The purchase increased the entity's asset, land; to record this increase, debit Land.

Accounting Equation:

ASSETS		=	LIABILITIES	+	OWNER'S EQUITY
Cash	Land				
−40,000	+40,000	=	0	+	0

This transaction increased one asset, land, and decreased another asset, cash. The net effect on the business's total assets was zero, and there was no effect on liabilities or owner's equity. We use the term net in business to mean an amount after a subtraction.

Journal Entry:

Land 40,000
      Cash 40,000
Paid cash for land.

Ledger Accounts:

Cash			Land	
(1) 60,000	(2) 40,000		(2) 40,000	

3. Transaction: **The business purchased office supplies for $1,000 on account.**

Analysis: The credit purchase of office supplies increased this asset, so we debit Office Supplies. The purchase also increased a liability; to record this increase, credit Accounts Payable.

Accounting Equation:

ASSETS	=	LIABILITIES	+	OWNER'S EQUITY
Office Supplies		Accounts Payable		
+1,000	=	+1,000	+	0

Journal Entry:

Office Supplies 1,000
      Accounts Payable...................... 1,000
Purchased office supplies on account.

Ledger Accounts:

Office Supplies		Accounts Payable	
(3) 1,000			(3) 1,000

4. Transaction: **The business provided travel services for clients and received $5,000 cash.**

Analysis: The asset, cash, is increased; therefore, debit Cash. The revenue account, service revenue, is increased; credit Service Revenue.

Accounting Equation:

ASSETS = LIABILITIES + OWNER'S EQUITY
+ REVENUES

Cash   Service Revenue
+5,000 =   0   +   5,000

Journal Entry:

Cash 5,000
    Service Revenue   5,000
Performed service and received cash.

Ledger Accounts:

Cash		**Service Revenue**	
(1) 60,000	(2) 40,000		(4) 5,000
(4) **5,000**			

---

5. Transaction: **The business provided travel services of $6,000 to clients who will pay for the services within one month.**

Analysis: The asset, accounts receivable, is increased; therefore, debit Accounts Receivable. Service revenue is increased; credit Service Revenue.

Accounting Equation:

ASSETS = LIABILITIES + OWNER'S EQUITY
+ REVENUES

Accounts   Service
Receivable   Revenue
+6,000 =   0   +   6,000

Journal Entry:

Accounts Receivable 6,000
    Service Revenue   6,000
Performed service on account.

Ledger Accounts:

Accounts Receivable		**Service Revenue**	
(5) 6,000			(4) 5,000
			(5) 6,000

---

6. Transaction: **The business paid the following cash expenses: office rent, $2,200; employee salary, $2,400; and utilities, $600.**

Analysis: The asset cash is decreased; therefore, credit Cash for each of the three expense amounts. The following expenses are increased: Rent Expense, Salary Expense, and Utilities Expense. Each should be debited for the appropriate amount.

Accounting Equation:

ASSETS = LIABILITIES + OWNER'S EQUITY
− EXPENSES

                          Rent   Salary   Utilities
Cash   Expense Expense Expense
−5,200 =   0   −2,200   −2,400   −600

Journal Entry:	Rent Expense	2,200	
	Salary Expense	2,400	
	Utilities Expense	600	
	Cash		5,200
	Issued three cheques to pay cash for expenses.		

Ledger Accounts:

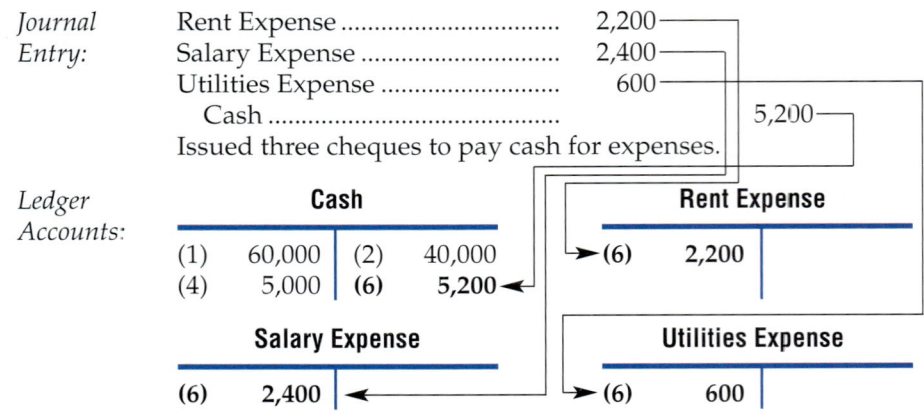

| *Note:* | In practice, the business would record these three transactions separately since they are all paid with separate cheques. To save space, we can record them together to illustrate a compound journal entry. No matter how many accounts a compound entry affects—there may be any number—total debits must equal total credits. |

7. Transaction: The business paid $800 on the account payable created in Transaction 3.

Analysis: The payment decreased the asset cash; therefore, credit Cash. The payment also decreased the liability accounts payable, so we debit Accounts Payable.

Accounting Equation:

ASSETS	=	LIABILITIES	+	OWNER'S EQUITY
Cash		Accounts Payable		
−800	=	−800	+	0

Journal Entry:

Accounts Payable	800	
Cash		800
Paid cash on account.		

Ledger Accounts:

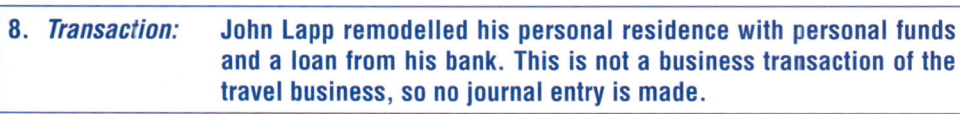

8. Transaction: John Lapp remodelled his personal residence with personal funds and a loan from his bank. This is not a business transaction of the travel business, so no journal entry is made.

9. Transaction: The business received $2,000 cash from one of the clients discussed in Transaction 5.

Analysis: The asset cash is increased; therefore, debit Cash. The asset accounts receivable is decreased; therefore, credit Accounts Receivable.

Accounting Equation:

	ASSETS		=	LIABILITIES	+	OWNER'S EQUITY
		Accounts				
	Cash	Receivable				
	+2,000	−2,000	=	0	+	0

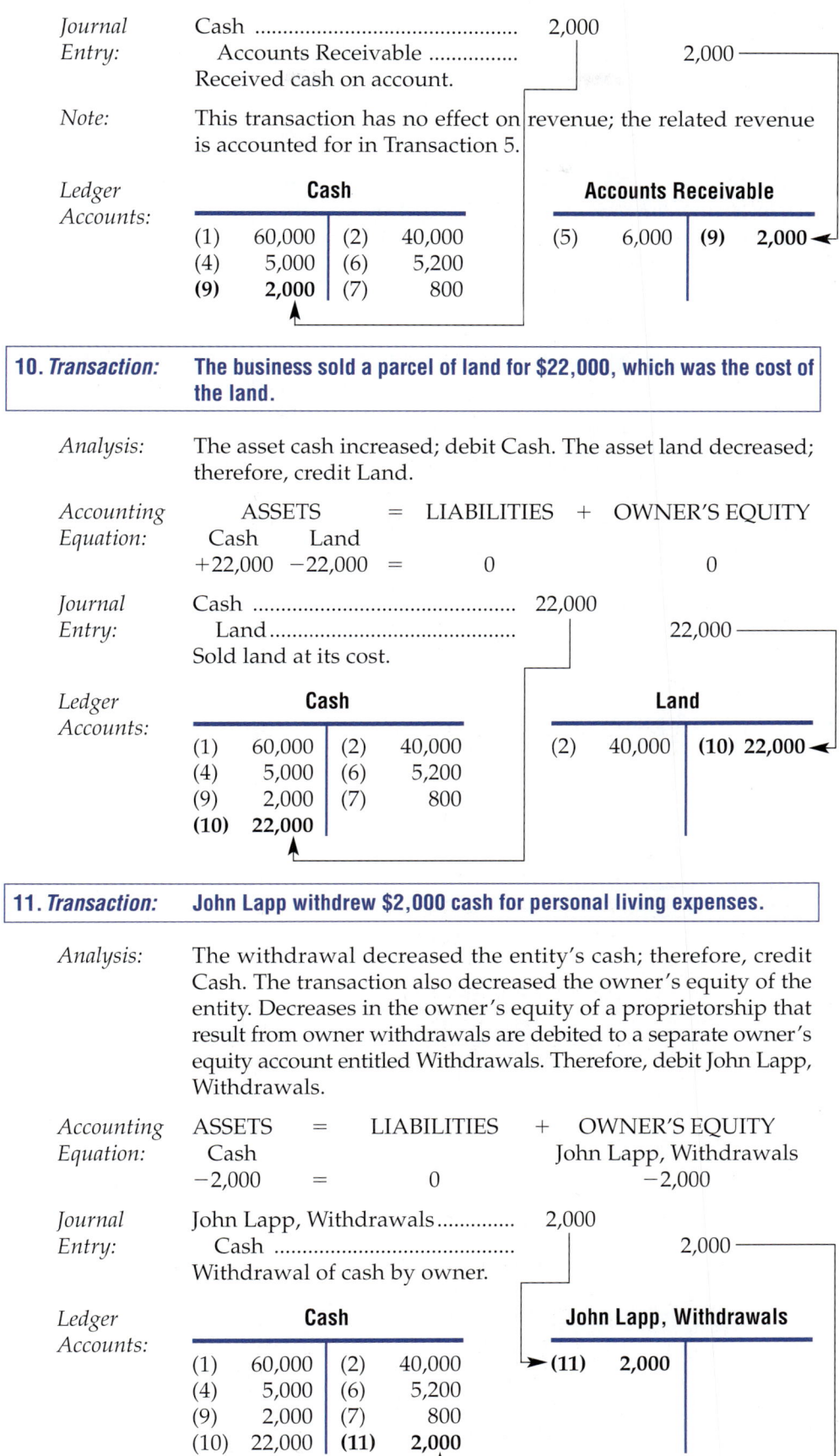

Journal	Cash 2,000	
Entry:	Accounts Receivable	2,000
	Received cash on account.	

Note: This transaction has no effect on revenue; the related revenue is accounted for in Transaction 5.

Ledger Accounts:

Cash			**Accounts Receivable**	
(1) 60,000	(2) 40,000		(5) 6,000	(9) 2,000
(4) 5,000	(6) 5,200			
(9) 2,000	(7) 800			

---

10. Transaction: **The business sold a parcel of land for $22,000, which was the cost of the land.**

Analysis: The asset cash increased; debit Cash. The asset land decreased; therefore, credit Land.

Accounting Equation:

ASSETS		=	LIABILITIES	+	OWNER'S EQUITY
Cash	Land				
+22,000	−22,000	=	0		0

Journal	Cash 22,000	
Entry:	Land..	22,000
	Sold land at its cost.	

Ledger Accounts:

Cash			**Land**	
(1) 60,000	(2) 40,000		(2) 40,000	(10) 22,000
(4) 5,000	(6) 5,200			
(9) 2,000	(7) 800			
(10) 22,000				

---

11. Transaction: **John Lapp withdrew $2,000 cash for personal living expenses.**

Analysis: The withdrawal decreased the entity's cash; therefore, credit Cash. The transaction also decreased the owner's equity of the entity. Decreases in the owner's equity of a proprietorship that result from owner withdrawals are debited to a separate owner's equity account entitled Withdrawals. Therefore, debit John Lapp, Withdrawals.

Accounting Equation:

ASSETS	=	LIABILITIES	+	OWNER'S EQUITY
Cash				John Lapp, Withdrawals
−2,000	=	0		−2,000

Journal	John Lapp, Withdrawals.............. 2,000	
Entry:	Cash	2,000
	Withdrawal of cash by owner.	

Ledger Accounts:

Cash			**John Lapp, Withdrawals**	
(1) 60,000	(2) 40,000		(11) 2,000	
(4) 5,000	(6) 5,200			
(9) 2,000	(7) 800			
(10) 22,000	**(11) 2,000**			

Each journal entry posted to the ledger is identified by date or by transaction number. In this way any transaction can be traced from the journal to the ledger, and, if need be, back to the journal. This helps to locate efficiently any information you may need.

The Ledger Accounts after Posting

We next show the accounts of SuperTravel after posting. The accounts are grouped under the accounting equation's headings in Exhibit 2–11.

EXHIBIT 2-11 SuperTravel's Ledger Accounts after Posting

ASSETS	=	LIABILITIES	+	OWNER'S EQUITY

Cash

(1) 60,000	(2) 40,000
(4) 5,000	(6) 5,200
(9) 2,000	(7) 800
(10) 22,000	(11) 2,000
Bal. 41,000	

Accounts Payable

(7) 800	(3) 1,000
	Bal. 200

John Lapp, Capital

	(1) 60,000
	Bal. 60,000

Accounts Receivable

(5) 6,000	(9) 2,000
Bal. 4,000	

John Lapp, Withdrawals

(11) 2,000	
Bal. 2,000	

Office Supplies

(3) 1,000	
Bal. 1,000	

REVENUE

Service Revenue

	(4) 5,000
	(5) 6,000
	Bal. 11,000

Land

(2) 40,000	(10) 22,000
Bal. 18,000	

EXPENSES

Rent Expense

(6) 2,200	
Bal. 2,200	

Salary Expense

(6) 2,400	
Bal. 2,400	

Utilities Expense

(6) 600	
Bal. 600	

Each account has a balance, denoted as *Bal.* This amount is the difference between the account's total debits and its total credits. For example, the $41,000 balance in the Cash account is the difference between

- Total debits, $89,000 ($60,000 + $5,000 + $2,000 + $22,000)
- Total credits, $48,000 ($40,000 + $5,200 + $800 + $2,000)

We set a balance apart by a horizontal line. The final figure in an account below the horizontal line is the balance of the account after the transactions have been posted.

If the sum of an account's debits is greater than the sum of its credits, that account has a debit balance, as the Cash account does here. If the sum of its credits is greater, that account has a credit balance, as Accounts Payable does.

STOP AND THINK

Compute the missing amount in each account:

(1)	Cash		(2)	Accounts Payable		(3)	S. Scully, Capital	
Bal. 10,000	13,000		X	Bal. 12,800		22,000	Bal.	X
20,000				45,600				56,000
Bal. X				Bal. 23,500				15,000
							Bal.	73,000

Answers:

(1) The ending balance (X) for Cash is
    X = $10,000 + 20,000 − $13,000
    X = $17,000

(2) We given the beginning and ending balances. We can compute the debit entry as follows:
    $12,800 + $45,600 − X = $23,500
    $12,800 + $45,600 − $23,500 = X
    X = $34,900

(3) The Capital account has an ending credit balance of $73,000. We can calculate the beginning credit balance as follows:
    X + $56,000 + $15,000 − $22,000 = $73,000
    X = $73,000 − $56,000 − $15,000 + $22,000
    X = $24,000

The Trial Balance

A *trial balance* summarizes the ledger by listing all accounts with their balances—assets first, followed by liabilities and then owner's equity. Before computers, the trial balance provided an accuracy check by showing whether the total debits equalled the total credits. The trial balance is still useful as a summary of all the accounts and their balances. A trial balance may be taken at any time the postings are up to date. The most common time is at the end of the accounting period. Exhibit 2–12 on page 66 is the trial balance of SuperTravel at April 30, 2007, the end of the first month of operations.

Note: Do not confuse the trial balance with the balance sheet. A trial balance is an internal document seen only by the company's owners, managers, and accountants. The company reports its financial position—both inside the business and to the public—on the balance sheet, a formal financial statement. And remember that the financial statements are the focal point of the accounting process. The trial balance is merely a step in the preparation of the financial statements.

Accounting Cycle Tutorials

3. The Journal and the Ledger pages 7–11

Objective 5

Prepare and use a trial balance

Details of Journals and Ledgers

In practice, the journal and the ledger provide additional details that create a "trail" through the accounting records for future reference. For example, suppose a supplier bills us twice for the same item we purchased on account. To prove we have already

EXHIBIT 2–12 | Trial Balance

SUPERTRAVEL
Trial Balance
April 30, 2007

Account Titles	Balance	
	Debit	Credit
Cash..	$41,000	
Accounts receivable	4,000	
Office supplies	1,000	
Land	18,000	
Accounts payable		$ 200
John Lapp, Capital		60,000
John Lapp, Withdrawals	2,000	
Service revenue		11,000
Rent expense	2,200	
Salary expense	2,400	
Utilities expense	600	
Total..	$71,200	$71,200

paid the bill, we must prove that we made our payment. To do this, we must use the journal and the ledger.

Details in the Journal Exhibit 2–13, Panel A, describes two transactions and Panel B presents a widely used journal format. The journal page number appears in the upper-right corner. As the column headings indicate, the *journal* displays the following information:

1. The *date,* which indicates when the transaction occurred. The year appears directly under the Date heading at the top of each journal page or when the year has changed. The date of the transaction is recorded for every transaction
2. The *account titles* and *explanations* of the transaction, as in Exhibit 2–5
3. The *posting reference,* abbreviated Post. Ref. (or sometimes PR). How this column helps the accountant becomes clear when we discuss the details of posting
4. The *debit* column, which shows the amount debited
5. The *credit* column, which shows the amount credited

Details in the Ledger Exhibit 2–13, Panel C, presents the *ledger* in the three-column format. The first two amount columns are for the debit and credit amounts posted from the journal. The third amount column is for the account's balance. This three-column format keeps a running balance in the account. The balance can be followed by the letters Dr or Cr (indicating a debit or credit respectively); however, this is not always required. Each account has its own record in the illustrative ledger. Our example shows SuperTravel's Cash account, Office Supplies account, and John Lapp, Capital account. Each account in the ledger has its own identification number.

The column headings identify the ledger account's features:

1. The date
2. The item column. This space is used for any special notation. An example is "Beginning balance"
3. The journal reference column, abbreviated Jrnl. Ref. (or sometimes JR). The importance of this column becomes clear when we discuss the mechanics of posting

EXHIBIT 2–13 | Details of Journalizing and Posting

Panel A: Two of SuperTravel's Transactions

Date	Transaction
Apr. 2, 2007	John Lapp invested $60,000 in travel agency. The business received cash and gave Lapp owner's equity in the business.
Apr. 3, 2007	Paid $40,000 cash for land.

Panel B: The Journal

Page 1

Date	Account Titles and Explanations	Post. Ref.	Debit	Credit
2007				
Apr. 2	Cash	1100	60,000	
	John Lapp, Capital	3000		60,000
	Received initial investment from owner.			
3	Land	1900	40,000	
	Cash	1100		40,000
	Purchased land.			

① ② ③ ④

Panel C: The Ledger

Account: **Cash**   Account No. **1100**

Date	Item	Jrnl. Ref.	Debit	Credit	Balance
2007					
Apr. 2		J1	60,000		60,000 Dr
Apr. 3		J1		40,000	20,000 Dr

1 Transfer the date of the transaction from the journal to the ledger.

2 Transfer the page number from the journal to the journal reference column of the ledger. "J1" signifies Journal Page 1.

3 Post the debit figure from the journal as a debit figure in the ledger account.

4 Enter the account number in the posting reference column of the journal once the figure has been posted to the ledger.

Account: **Land**   Account No. **1900**

Date	Item	Jrnl. Ref.	Debit	Credit	Balance
2007					
Apr. 3		J1	40,000		40,000 Dr

Account: **John Lapp, Capital**   Account No. **3000**

Date	Item	Jrnl. Ref.	Debit	Credit	Balance
2007					
Apr. 2		J1		60,000	60,000 Cr

4. The debit column, with the amount debited

5. The credit column, with the amount credited

6. The balance column, with the debit or credit running balance

Posting from the Journal to the Ledger

We know that posting means transferring information from the journal to the ledger accounts. But how do we handle the additional details that appear in the journal and the ledger formats that we have just seen? Exhibit 2–13 illustrates the steps in full detail. Panel A lists the first two transactions of the business entity SuperTravel; Panel B presents the journal; and Panel C shows the ledger. The posting process includes four steps:

After recording the transaction in the journal:

Arrow ① —Post the transaction date from the journal to the ledger.

Arrow ② —Post the journal page number from the journal to the ledger. We use several abbreviations:
Jrnl. Ref. means Journal Reference. J1 refers to Journal page 1.
This step indicates where the information in the ledger came from: Journal page 1.

Arrow ③ —Post the dollar amount of the debit ($60,000) from the journal as a debit to the same account (Cash) in the ledger. Likewise, post the dollar amount of the credit (also $60,000) from the journal to the appropriate account in the ledger. Now the ledger accounts have their correct amounts.

Arrow ④ —Copy (post) the account number (1100) from the ledger back to the journal. This step indicates that the $60,000 debit to Cash has been posted to the Cash account in the ledger. Also, copy the account number (3000) for John Lapp, Capital back to the journal to show that the $60,000 amount of the credit has been posted to the ledger.
Post. Ref. is the abbreviation for Posting Reference.

After posting, you should prepare the trial balance, as we discussed earlier.

Chart of Accounts in the Ledger

Objective 6

Set up a chart of accounts for a business

The ledger contains the business's accounts grouped under these headings:

1. Balance Sheet Accounts: Assets, Liabilities, and Owner's Equity
2. Income Statement Accounts: Revenues and Expenses.

Exhibit 2–13 presented ledger accounts in a three-column format. To keep track of their accounts, organizations have a **chart of accounts**, which lists all the accounts in the ledger and their account numbers. These account numbers are used as posting references, as illustrated by Arrow 4 in Exhibit 2–13. This numbering system makes it easy to locate individual accounts in the ledger.

Accounts are identified by account numbers with two or more digits. Assets are often numbered beginning with 1, liabilities with 2, owner's equity with 3, revenues with 4, and expenses with 5. The second, third, and higher digits in an account number indicate the position of the individual account within the category. For example, Cash might be account number 1001, which is the first asset account. Accounts Receivable may be account number 1101, the second asset account. Accounts Payable may be number 2001, the first liability account. All accounts are numbered by this system. Many numbers remain between 1001 and 1101 in case new accounts with new account numbers are added later.

EXHIBIT 2–14 Partial Chart of Accounts—Law Practice of Brown and Hansell

Account Number	Account Name
11001	Petty Cash
11100	Cash in Bank
12001	Accounts Receivable
13000	Office Supplies
16001	Office Furniture
17001	Computers
22001	Accounts Payable
22500	Notes Payable
23000	Employee Withholdings Payable
30000	H. Brown, Capital
30001	B. Hansell, Capital
31000	H. Brown, Withdrawals
31001	B. Hansell, Withdrawals
40000	Fee Revenue
50001	Rent Expense
51001	Supplies Expense
54001	Wages Expense

The chart of accounts of Brown and Hansell, a law partnership, in Exhibit 2–14, uses a five-digit account number. The assignment material reflects the variety of digits used in account numbers found in practice.

The chart of accounts for SuperTravel appears in Exhibit 2–15. Notice the gap in account numbers between 1200 and 1400. John Lapp realizes that at some later date the business may need to add another category of receivables—for example, Notes Receivable—to be numbered 1210.

Appendix D at the end of Volume I and Volume II gives three expanded charts of accounts that you will find helpful as you work through this course. The first chart lists the typical accounts of a large *service* proprietorship, along with those of a service partnership. The second chart is for a *merchandising* corporation, one that sells a product rather than a service. The third chart lists some accounts a *manufacturing* company uses. These accounts will be used in connection with Chapters 19–26.

EXHIBIT 2–15 Chart of Accounts—SuperTravel

Accounts:

Assets		Liabilities		Owner's Equity	
1100	Cash	2100	Accounts Payable	3000	John Lapp, Capital
1200	Accounts Receivable	2300	Notes Payable	3100	John Lapp,
1400	Office Supplies				Withdrawals
1500	Office Furniture				
1900	Land				

**Income Statement Accounts
(part of Owner's Equity)**

Revenues		Expenses	
4000	Service	5100	Rent Expense
	Revenue	5200	Salary Expense
		5300	Utilities Expense

Study the service proprietorship chart of accounts now, and refer to the other charts of accounts as needed later.

The expense accounts are listed in alphabetical order throughout this chapter. Many businesses follow such a scheme for their records and financial statements since computer programs often list accounts alphabetically. The other system of ordering is by balance or size, with the accounts with the largest balances listed first. The service, merchandising, and manufacturing accounts shown in Appendix D are taken from the financial statements of real companies and are listed in the order used by those companies.

Correcting Trial Balance Errors

Throughout the accounting process, total debits should always equal total credits. If they are not equal, then accounting errors exist. Computerized accounting systems eliminate many errors because most software will not let you make a journal entry that doesn't balance. But computers cannot *eliminate* all errors because humans sometimes input the wrong data or input data to the wrong accounts.

Some errors can be detected by computing the difference between total debits and total credits on the trial balance. Then perform one or more of the following actions:

1. Search the trial balance for a missing account. For example, suppose the accountant omitted John Lapp, Withdrawals from the trial balance in Exhibit 2–12 on page 66. Total debits would then be $69,200 ($71,200 – $2,000) and total credits would be $71,200, a difference of 2,000. Trace each account and its balance from the ledger to the trial balance, and you will locate the missing account.

2. Search the journal for the amount of the difference. For example, suppose the total credits on SuperTravel's trial balance equal $71,200 and total debits equal $69,000. A $2,200 transaction may have been posted incorrectly to the ledger by omitting the debit entry. Search the journal for a $2,200 transaction and check its posting to the ledger.

3. Divide the difference between total debits and total credits by 2. A debit treated as a credit, or vice versa, doubles the amount of error. Suppose the accountant paid $600 cash to pay the utilities expenses. This transaction was recorded correctly in the journal, but was posted as a debit to Cash and a debit to Utilities Expense. Thus, $1,200 appears on the debit side of the trial balance, and there is nothing on the credit side relating to this transaction. The out-of-balance amount is $1,200, and dividing by 2 reveals that the relevant transaction may have had a value of $600. Search the journal for a $600 transaction and check the posting to the ledger.

4. Divide the out-of-balance amount by 9. If the result is evenly divisible by 9, the error may be a *slide*, which is adding or deleting one or several zeroes in a figure (example: writing $61 as $610), or a *transposition* (example: treating $61 as $16). Suppose the accountant listed the $2,000 balance in John Lapp, Withdrawals as $20,000 on the trial balance—a slide-type error. Total debits would differ from total credits by $18,000 (i.e., $20,000 − $2,000 = $18,000). Dividing $18,000 by 9 yields $2,000, the correct amount of the withdrawals. Trace this amount through the ledger until you reach the John Lapp, Withdrawals account with a balance of $2,000. Dividing by 9 can give the correct transaction amount for a slide, but not for a transposition.

As we conclude this chapter, we return to our opening question: Why is recording business transactions important? By recording business transactions, posting to the ledger accounts, and preparing a trial balance, we have the process we need to assess the results of operations and financial condition. The Decision Guidelines feature summarizes all our chapter-opening questions.

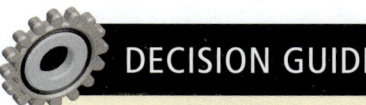

DECISION GUIDELINES | Analyzing and Recording Transactions

Decision	Guidelines
Has a transaction occurred?	If the event affects the entity's financial position *and* can be reliably recorded—*Yes* If either condition is absent—*No*
Where do we record the transaction?	In the *journal*, the chronological record of transactions
What do we record for each transaction?	Increases and/or decreases in all the accounts affected by the transaction (at the business's cost)

How do we record an increase/decrease in a(n)

Rules of debit and credit:

	Increase	Decrease
Asset?	Debit	Credit
Liability?	Credit	Debit
Owner's equity?	Credit	Debit
Revenue?	Credit	Debit
Expense?	Debit	Credit

Decision	Guidelines
Where do we store all the information for each account?	In the *ledger*, the book of accounts and their balances
Where do we list all the accounts and their balances?	In the *trial balance*
Where do we report the results of operations?	In the income statement (Revenues − Expenses = Net income, or Expenses − Revenues = Net loss)
Where do we report the financial position?	In the balance sheet (Assets = Liabilities + Owner's equity)

Summary Problem for Your Review

The trial balance of Damir Service Centre on March 1, 2008, lists the company's assets, liabilities, and owner's equity on that date.

Account Titles	Balance Debit	Balance Credit
Cash	$26,000	
Accounts receivable	4,500	
Accounts payable		$ 2,000
Jim Damir, Capital..		28,500
Total	$30,500	$30,500

During March the business engaged in the following transactions:

a. Borrowed $45,000 from the bank and signed a note payable in the name of the business.

b. Paid cash of $40,000 to a real estate company to acquire land.

c. Performed service for a customer and received cash of $5,000.

d. Purchased supplies on account, $300.

e. Performed customer service and earned revenue on account, $2,600.

f. Paid $1,200 of the Accounts Payable from the March 1, 2008, trial balance.

g. Paid the following cash expenses: salaries, $3,000; rent, $1,500; and interest, $400.

h. Received $3,100 of the Accounts Receivable balance from the March 1, 2008, trial balance.

i. Received a $200 utility bill that will be paid next week.

j. Damir withdrew $1,800 for personal use.

Name: Damir Service Centre
Industry: Services proprietorship
Fiscal Period: Month of March 2008
Key Fact: An existing, ongoing business

Required

1. Open the following accounts, with the balances indicated, in the ledger of Damir Service Centre. Use the T-account format.

    Assets: Cash, $26,000; Accounts Receivable, $4,500; Supplies, no balance; Land, no balance

    Liabilities: Accounts Payable, $2,000; Notes Payable, no balance

    Owner's Equity: Jim Damir, Capital, $28,500; Jim Damir, Withdrawals, no balance

    Revenues: Service Revenue, no balance

    Expenses: Salaries Expense, Rent Expense, Utilities Expense, Interest Expense (none have balances)

Prepare a T-account for each account name. Place the opening balance in the T-account, remembering that the normal balance in an asset account is a debit, in a liability or equity account is a credit, in a revenue account is a credit, and in an expense account is a debit.

For each transaction, ensure that the Assets = Liabilities + Owner's equity.

Refer to the rules of debit and credit shown in Exhibit 2–7 on page 57.

2. Journalize the preceding transactions. Identify journal entries by their transaction letter.

3. Post to the ledger.

4. Prepare the trial balance of Damir Service Centre at March 31, 2008.

5. Compute the net income or net loss of the entity during the month of March by producing an income statement. List expenses in alphabetical order.

Solution

To make sure all the account balances have been entered correctly, trace each T-account's balance back to the March 1, 2008, trial balance given on the previous page.

Requirement 1

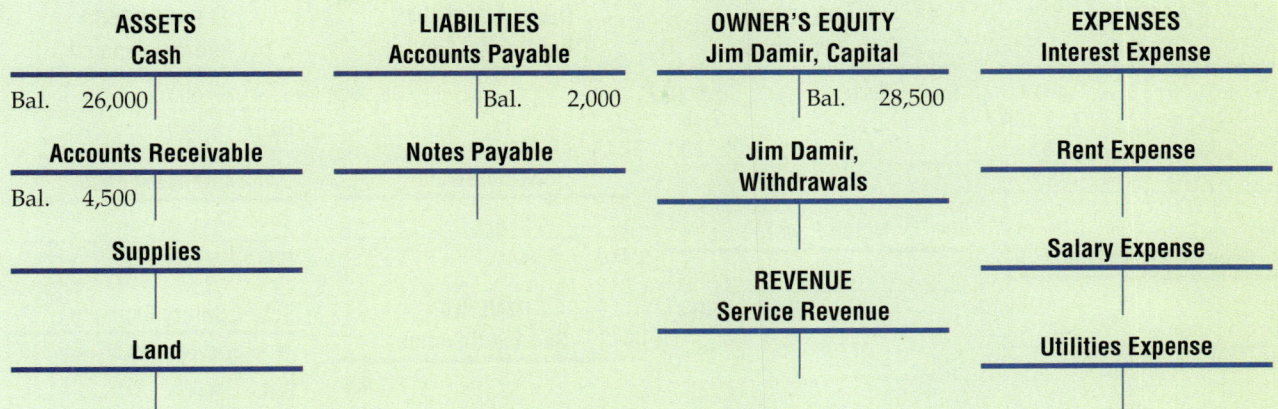

ASSETS	LIABILITIES	OWNER'S EQUITY	EXPENSES
Cash	**Accounts Payable**	**Jim Damir, Capital**	**Interest Expense**
Bal. 26,000	Bal. 2,000	Bal. 28,500	
Accounts Receivable	**Notes Payable**	**Jim Damir, Withdrawals**	**Rent Expense**
Bal. 4,500			**Salary Expense**
Supplies		**REVENUE**	
		Service Revenue	
Land			**Utilities Expense**

Ensure total debits equal total credits in each journal entry. Selected journal entries are explained more fully.

Requirement 2

When a transaction involves cash, always first decide whether cash increased or decreased. An increase is a debit to Cash. A decrease is a credit to Cash. Then decide which other accounts are affected.

"On account" means no cash was used in the transaction. Therefore, use Accounts Payable or Accounts Receivable since cash will be paid or collected in the future.

"Paid" means a cheque was written, so Cash is credited.

This transaction could also have been recorded with three journal entries, with a debit to the expense and a credit to Cash for each of the expenses.

Receiving a bill indicates an amount is owed for goods or services received. Increase the liability Accounts Payable, since cash will be paid for the utility bill in the future.

	Account Titles and Explanations	Debit	Credit
a.	Cash	45,000	
	Notes Payable		45,000
	Borrowed cash on note payable.		
b.	Land	40,000	
	Cash		40,000
	Purchased land for cash.		
c.	Cash	5,000	
	Service Revenue		5,000
	Performed service and received cash.		
d.	Supplies	300	
	Accounts Payable		300
	Purchased supplies on account.		
e.	Accounts Receivable	2,600	
	Service Revenue		2,600
	Performed service on account.		
f.	Accounts Payable	1,200	
	Cash		1,200
	Paid cash to reduce accounts payable.		
g.	Salary Expense	3,000	
	Rent Expense	1,500	
	Interest Expense	400	
	Cash		4,900
	Issued three cheques to pay cash expenses.		
h.	Cash	3,100	
	Accounts Receivable		3,100
	Received cash on account.		
i.	Utilities Expense	200	
	Accounts Payable		200
	Received utility bill.		
j.	Jim Damir, Withdrawals	1,800	
	Cash		1,800
	Withdrew cash for personal use.		

Transfer amounts from the journal entries in Requirement 2 into the T-accounts here. Write the letter of each transaction beside the amount in the T-account.

Requirement 3

ASSETS				LIABILITIES				OWNER'S EQUITY			EXPENSES		
Cash				**Accounts Payable**				**Jim Damir, Capital**			**Interest Expense**		

Cash

Bal.	26,000	b.	40,000
a.	45,000	f.	1,200
c.	5,000	g.	4,900
h.	3,100	j.	1,800
Bal.	31,200		

Accounts Receivable

Bal.	4,500	h.	3,100
e.	2,600		
Bal.	4,000		

Supplies

d.	300	
Bal.*	300	

Land

b.	40,000	
Bal.*	40,000	

LIABILITIES

Accounts Payable

f.	1,200	Bal.	2,000
		d.	300
		i.	200
		Bal.	1,300

Notes Payable

		a.	45,000
		Bal.*	45,000

OWNER'S EQUITY

Jim Damir, Capital

		Bal.	28,500

Jim Damir, Withdrawals

j.	1,800	
Bal.*	1,800	

REVENUE

Service Revenue

		c.	5,000
		e.	2,600
		Bal.	7,600

EXPENSES

Interest Expense

g.	400	
Bal.*	400	

Rent Expense

g.	1,500	
Bal.*	1,500	

Salary Expense

g.	3,000	
Bal.*	3,000	

Utilities Expense

i.	200	
Bal.*	200	

Make sure each transaction is posted to the proper T-account, and make sure no transactions were missed. Make sure that Assets = Liabilities + Owner's Equity for each transaction before going to the next transaction.

* For consistency, we have totalled this account and labelled its balance, but you do not have to if there was only one transaction.

The title must include the name of the company, "Trial Balance," and the date of the trial balance. It shows the account balances on one specific date.

List all the accounts that have a balance in their T-accounts. Accounts with a zero balance typically are not listed on the trial balance. Write the "Bal." amount for each account from Requirement 3 into the debit or credit column of the trial balance. Make sure that the total of the Debit column equals the total of the Credit column. Double underline the totals to show that the columns have been added and the totals are final.

Requirement 4

DAMIR SERVICE CENTRE
Trial Balance
March 31, 2008

Account Title	Balance	
	Debit	Credit
Cash	$31,200	
Accounts receivable	4,000	
Supplies	300	
Land	40,000	
Accounts payable		$ 1,300
Notes payable		45,000
Jim Damir, capital		28,500
Jim Damir, withdrawals	1,800	
Service revenue		7,600
Interest expense	400	
Rent expense	1,500	
Salary expense	3,000	
Utilities expense	200	
Total	$82,400	$82,400

The title must include the name of the company, "Income Statement," and the specific period of time covered. It is critical that the time period is defined.

Prepare the income statement by listing the revenue accounts first, then the expense account names in alphabetical order from the trial balance. Then transfer the amounts from the trial balance to the income statement, and calculate net income or net loss.

Requirement 5

DAMIR SERVICE CENTRE
Income Statement
For the Month Ended March 31, 2008

Revenues		
Service revenue		$7,600
Expenses:		
Interest expense	$ 400	
Rent expense	1,500	
Salary expense	3,000	
Utilities expense	200	
Total expenses		5,100
Net income		$2,500

Summary

1. **Define and use key accounting terms:** *Accounts* can be viewed either in the form of the letter "T" or in the three-column format shown in Exhibit 2–13. The left side of each T-account is its *debit* side. The right side is its *credit* side. The first amount column in a three-column ledger account is the *debit* column, and the second is the credit column. The *ledger*, which contains a record for each account, groups and numbers accounts by category in the following order: assets, liabilities, and owner's equity (and its subparts, revenues and expenses).

2. **Apply the rules of debit and credit.** *Assets* and *expenses* are increased by debits and decreased by credits. *Liabilities, owner's equity*, and *revenues* are increased by credits and decreased by debits. An account's *normal balance* is the side of the account—debit or credit—in which increases are recorded. Thus, the normal balance of assets and expenses is a debit, and the normal balance of liabilities, owner's equity, and revenues is a credit. The Withdrawals account, which decreases owner's equity, normally has a debit balance. *Revenues*, which are increases in owner's equity, have a normal credit balance. *Expenses*, which are decreases in owner's equity, have a normal debit balance.

3. **Analyze and record transactions in the journal.** The accountant begins the recording process by analyzing the transaction and entering the transaction's information in the *journal*, a chronological list of all the entity's transactions.

4. **Post from the journal to the ledger.** Posting means transferring to the *ledger* accounts. Posting references are used to trace amounts back and forth between the journal and the ledger.

5. **Prepare and use a trial balance.** The *trial balance* is a summary of all the non-zero account balances in the ledger. When *double-entry accounting* has been done correctly, the total debits and the total credits in the trial balance are equal.

6. **Set up a chart of accounts for a business.** A *chart of accounts* lists all the accounts in the ledger and their account numbers.

We can now trace the flow of accounting information through these steps:

Business Transaction generates → Source Documents → Journal Entry → Posting to Ledger Accounts → Trial Balance

Self-Study Questions

Test your understanding of the chapter by marking the correct answer for each of the following questions:

1. A T-account has two sides called the *(p. 53)*
   a. Debit and credit
   b. Asset and liability
   c. Revenue and expense
   d. Journal and ledger

2. Increases in liabilities are recorded by *(p. 53)*
   a. Debits
   b. Credits

3. Why do accountants record transactions in the journal? *(p. 55)*
   a. To ensure that all transactions are posted to the ledger
   b. To ensure that total debits equal total credits
   c. To have a chronological record of all transactions
   d. To help prepare the financial statements

4. Posting is the process of transferring information from the *(p. 57)*
   a. Journal to the trial balance
   b. Ledger to the trial balance
   c. Ledger to the financial statements
   d. Journal to the ledger

5. The purchase of land for cash is recorded by a *(p. 60)*
   a. Debit to Cash and a credit to Land
   b. Debit to Cash and a debit to Land
   c. Debit to Land and a credit to Cash
   d. Credit to Cash and a credit to Land

6. The purpose of the trial balance is to *(p. 64)*
   a. List all accounts with their balances
   b. Ensure that all transactions have been recorded
   c. Speed the collection of cash receipts from customers
   d. Increase assets and owner's equity

7. What is the normal balance of the Accounts Receivable, Office Supplies, and Rent Expense accounts? *(p. 58)*
   a. Debit
   b. Credit

8. A business has Cash of $3,000, Notes Payable of $2,500, Accounts Payable of $4,300, Service Revenue of $7,000 and Rent Expense of $2,400. Based on these data, how much are its total liabilities? *(p. 58)*
   a. $4,600
   b. $6,800
   c. $9,800
   d. $13,800

9. Smale Transport earned revenue on account. The earning of revenue on account is recorded by a *(p. 61)*
   a. Debit to Cash and a credit to Revenue
   b. Debit to Accounts Receivable and a credit to Revenue
   c. Debit to Accounts Payable and a credit to Revenue
   d. Debit to Revenue and a credit to Accounts Receivable

10. The account credited for a receipt of cash on account is *(p. 63)*
    a. Cash
    b. Accounts Payable
    c. Service Revenue
    d. Accounts Receivable

Answers to the Self-Study Questions follow the Similar Accounting Terms.

Accounting Vocabulary

Account *(p. 49)*
Chart of accounts *(p. 68)*
Credit *(p. 53)*
Debit *(p. 53)*
Journal *(p. 49)*

Ledger *(p. 50)*
Normal balance *(p. 58)*
Note receivable *(p. 50)*
Posting *(p. 57)*
Trial balance *(p. 50)*

Similar Accounting Terms

Cr	Credit; right
Dr	Debit; left
The Journal	A general journal; book of original entry
The Ledger	The Books; the General Ledger
Entering the transaction in a journal	Making the journal entry; journalizing the transaction
Withdrawals by owner(s)	In a proprietorship or partnership, distributions from a company to its owner(s)
Open the accounts	Set up the accounts; create the ledger accounts

Answers to Self-Study Questions

1. a	3. c	5. c	7. a	9. b
2. b	4. d	6. a	8. b ($6,800 = $2,500 + $4,300)	10. d

Questions

1. Name the basic shortcut device or tool used in accounting. What letter of the alphabet does it resemble? Name its two sides.

2. Is the following statement true or false? Debit means decrease and credit means increase. Explain your answer.

3. Write two sentences that use the term *debit* differently.

4. What are the three *basic* types of accounts? Name two additional types of accounts. To which one of the three basic types are these two additional types of accounts most closely related?

5. Suppose you are the accountant for Smith Courier Service. Keeping in mind double-entry bookkeeping, identify the *dual effects* of Mary Smith's investment of $10,000 cash in her business.

6. Briefly describe the flow of accounting information using the accounting cycle.

7. To what does the *normal balance* of an account refer?

8. Indicate the normal balance of the five types of accounts.

Account Type	Normal Balance
Assets	
Liabilities	
Owner's equity	
Revenues	
Expenses	

9. What does posting accomplish? Why is it important? Does it come before or after journalizing?

10. Label each of the following transactions as increasing owner's equity (+), decreasing owner's equity (−), or as having no effect on owner's equity (0). Write the appropriate symbol in the space provided.

____ Investment by owner
____ Invoice customer for services
____ Purchase of supplies on credit
____ Pay expenses
____ Cash payment on account
____ Withdrawal by owner
____ Borrowing money on a note payable
____ Sale of services on account

11. What four steps does posting include? Which step is the fundamental purpose of posting?

12. Rearrange the following accounts in their logical sequence in the chart of accounts:

Note Payable	Cash
Accounts Receivable	Jane East, Capital
Sales Revenue	Salary Expense

13. What is the meaning of the statement, Accounts Payable has a credit balance of $1,700?

14. Campus Cleaners launders the shirts of customer Bobby Baylor, who has a charge account at the cleaners. When Bobby picks up his clothes and is short of cash, he charges it. Later, when he receives his monthly statement from the cleaners, Bobby writes a cheque on his bank account and mails the cheque to the cleaners. Identify the two business transactions described here. Which transaction increases the business's owner's equity? Which transaction increases Campus Cleaners' cash?

15. Explain the difference between the ledger and the chart of accounts.

16. Why do accountants prepare a trial balance?

17. What is a compound journal entry?

18. The accountant for Bower Construction mistakenly recorded a $500 purchase of supplies on account as $5,000. He debited Supplies and credited Accounts Payable for $5,000. Does this error cause the trial balance to be out of balance? Explain your answer.

19. What is the effect on total assets of collecting cash on account from customers?

20. Briefly summarize the similarities and differences between manual and computer-based accounting systems in terms of journalizing, posting, and preparing a trial balance.

Starters

Using accounting terms
(1)

Starter 2–1 Review basic accounting definitions by completing the following crossword puzzle.

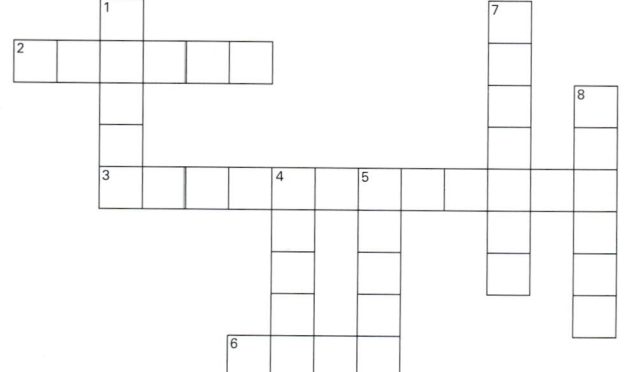

Down:
1. Left side of an account
4. Book of accounts
5. An economic resource
7. Record of transactions
8. Normal balance of a revenue

Across:
2. Records an increase in a liability
3. List of accounts with their balances
6. Another word for liability

Starter 2–2 Fill in the blanks to review some key definitions.

Using accounting terms
1

Lynn Bratton is describing the accounting process for a friend who is a philosophy major. Lynn states, "The basic summary device in accounting is the _____. The left side is called the _____ side, and the right side is called the _____ side. We record transactions first in a _____. Then we post (copy the data) to the _____. It is helpful to list all the accounts with their balances on a _____."

Starter 2–3 Accounting has its own vocabulary and basic relationships. Match the accounting terms at left with the corresponding definitions at right.

Using accounting terms
1

_____	1. Posting	A. Record of transactions
_____	2. Normal balance	B. Always an asset
_____	3. Payable	C. Left side of an account
_____	4. Journal	D. Side of an account where increases are recorded
_____	5. Receivable	E. Copying data from the journal to the ledger
_____	6. Capital	F. Using up assets in the course of operating a business
_____	7. Debit	G. Always a liability
_____	8. Expense	H. Revenues − Expenses
_____	9. Net income	I. Grouping of accounts
_____	10. Ledger	J. Owner's equity in the business

Starter 2–4 Art Sudan is tutoring Nick Mull, who is taking introductory accounting. Art explains to Nick that *debits* are used to record increases in accounts and *credits* record decreases. Nick is confused and seeks your advice.

Explaining the rules of debit and credit
2

- When are credits increases? When are credits decreases?
- When are debits increases? When are debits decreases?

Exhibit 2–8, page 58, gives the rules of debit and credit.

Starter 2–5 The accounting records of all businesses include three basic categories of accounts: assets, liabilities, and owner's equity. In turn, owner's equity holds the following categories: capital, withdrawals, revenues, and expenses. Identify which categories of all the accounts—including the subparts of owner's equity—have a normal debit balance and which categories have a normal credit balance.

Normal account balances
2

Starter 2–6 Liana Garcia opened a veterinary practice. Record the following transactions in the journal of Liana Garcia, Veterinarian. Include an explanation with each journal entry.

Recording transactions
3

September	1	Garcia invested $30,000 cash in a business bank account to start her practice. The business received the cash and gave Garcia owner's equity in the business.
	2	Purchased medical supplies on account, $10,000.
	2	Paid monthly office rent of $4,000.
	3	Recorded $5,000 revenue for service rendered to patients on account.

Starter 2–7 After operating for a month, Liana Garcia, Veterinarian, completed the following transactions during the latter part of October:

Recording transactions
3

October	22	Performed service for patients on account, $3,600.
	30	Received cash on account from patients, $2,000.
	31	Received a utility bill, $2,000, which will be paid during November.
	31	Paid monthly salary to nurse, $3,000
	31	Paid advertising expense of $900.

Journalize the transactions of Liana Garcia, Veterinarian. Include an explanation with each journal entry.

Starter 2–8 Stuart Deng Computer Services bought supplies on account for $5,000. Two weeks later, the company paid half on account.

1. Journalize the two transactions for Stuart Deng Computer Services. Include an explanation for each transaction.
2. Open the Accounts Payable T-account and post to Accounts Payable. Compute the balance, and denote it as *Bal.*

Starter 2–9 Lance Alworth performed legal services for a client who could not pay immediately. Alworth expected to collect the $6,000 the following month. Later, he received $3,500 cash from the client.

1. Record the two transactions for Lance Alworth, Lawyer. Include an explanation for each transaction.
2. Open these accounts: Cash; Accounts Receivable; Service Revenue. Post to all three accounts. Compute each account's balance, and denote as *Bal.*
3. Answer these questions based on your analysis:
   a. How much did Alworth earn? Which account shows this amount?
   b. How much in total assets did Alworth acquire as a result of the two transactions? Identify each asset and show its amount.

Note: Starter 2–10 should be used in connection with Starter 2–6.

Starter 2–10 Use the September transaction data for Liana Garcia, Veterinarian, given in Starter 2–6.

1. Open the following T-accounts: Cash; Accounts Receivable; Medical Supplies; Accounts Payable; Liana Garcia, Capital; Service Revenue, Rent Expense.
2. After making the journal entries in Starter 2–6, post to the ledger. No dates or posting references are required. Compute the balance of each account, and denote it as *Bal.*
3. Prepare the trial balance, complete with a proper heading, at September 3, 2008. Use the trial balance on page 66 as a guide.

Starter 2–11 Redbird Flooring reported the following summarized data at December 31, 2008. Accounts appear in no particular order.

Revenue	$29,000	Other Liabilities	$19,000
Equipment	40,000	Cash	12,000
Accounts payable	1,000	Expenses	22,000
Capital	25,000		

Prepare the trial balance of Redbird Flooring at December 31, 2008. List the accounts in proper order, as on page 66.

Starter 2–12 SuperTravel prepared its trial balance on page 66. Suppose John Lapp made an error: He erroneously listed his capital balance of $60,000 as a debit rather than a credit.

Compute the incorrect trial balance totals for debits and credits. Then refer to the discussion of correcting errors on page 70 and show how to correct this error.

Starter 2–13 Return to SuperTravel's trial balance on page 66. Assume that John Lapp accidentally listed his withdrawals as $200 instead of the correct amount of $2,000. Compute the incorrect trial balance totals for debits and credits. Then show how to correct this error, which is called a *slide.*

Exercises

Exercise 2–1

Your employer, Prairie Tours, has just hired an office manager who does not understand accounting. The Prairie Tours trial balance lists Cash of $57,800. Write a short memo to the office manager, explaining the accounting process that produced this listing on the trial balance. Mention *debits, credits, journal, ledger, posting,* and *trial balance.*

Exercise 2-2

Refer to the Summary Problem for Your Review, specifically the trial balance on page 74.

Refer to the Summary Problem for Your Review, specifically the trial balance on page 74.

Required

1. Write the company's accounting equation, and label each element as a debit amount or a credit amount. If you use $28,500 for the owner's equity, why is the accounting equation out of balance?

2. Write the equation to compute Damir Service Centre's net income or net loss for March 2008. Indicate which element is a debit amount and which element is a credit amount. Does net income represent a net debit or a net credit? Does net loss represent a net debit or a net credit?

3. How much did the owner, Jim Damir, withdraw during March 2008? Did the withdrawal represent a debit amount or a credit amount?

4. Considering both the net income (or net loss) and withdrawal for March 2008, by how much did the company's owner's equity increase or decrease? Was the change in owner's equity a debit amount or a credit amount?

Exercise 2-3

Analyze the following transactions of Ryan Peterson Engineering in the manner shown for the December 1 transaction. Also, record each transaction in the journal.

Dec.   1   Paid monthly utilities expense of $140.
(Analysis: The expense, utilities expense, is increased; therefore, debit Utilities Expense. The asset, cash, is decreased; therefore, credit Cash.)

1	Utilities Expense 140	
	Cash	140

    4   Borrowed $10,000 cash, signing a note payable.
    8   Performed service on account for a customer, $3,000.
  12   Purchased equipment on account, $2,000.
  19   Sold for $14,000 land that had cost this same amount.
  24   Purchased supplies for $600 and paid cash.
  27   Paid the liability created on December 12.

Exercise 2-4

Refer to Exercise 2-3 for the transactions of Ryan Peterson Engineering.

Required

1. Open the following T-accounts with their December 1 balances: Cash, debit balance $3,000; Accounts Receivable $0; Supplies, $0; Equipment $0; Land, debit balance $29,000; Accounts Payable $0; Notes Payable $0; R. Peterson, Capital, credit balance $32,000; Service Revenue $0; Utilities Expense $0.

2. Record the transactions of Exercise 2-3 directly in the T-accounts affected. Use dates as posting references in the T-accounts. Start with December 1. Journal entries are not required.

3. Compute the December 31 balance for each account, and prove that total debits equal total credits.

Exercise 2-5

Yula's Yoga engaged in the following transactions during March 2007, its first month of operations:

March 1   The business received $90,000 cash investment from Yula Gregore to start Yula's Yoga.
     2   Purchased studio supplies for $2,000 on account.
     4   Paid $80,000 cash for building to use as a studio.
     6   Presented a wellness seminar for a corporate customer and received cash, $2,500.
     9   Paid $500 on accounts payable.
  17   Taught yoga classes for customers on account, $400.
  23   Received $160 cash from a customer on account.
  31   Paid the following expenses: utilities, $240; cell phone, $100.

Using debits and credits with the accounting equation

2. Net income $2,500
4. Net increase in owner's equity $700

Analyzing and journalizing transactions

Applying the rules of debit and credit

2

3. Total debits $45,000

 Excel Spreadsheet Template

Journalizing transactions

Required Record the preceding transactions in the journal of Yula's Yoga. Identify transactions by their date and include an explanation for each entry, as illustrated in the chapter. Use the following accounts: Cash; Accounts Receivable; Studio Supplies; Building; Accounts Payable; Yula Gregore, Capital; Service Revenue; Utilities Expense; Cellphone Expense.

Posting to the ledger and preparing a trial balance

④ ⑤

2. Trial bal. total $94,400

Exercise 2–6

Refer to Exercise 2–5 for the transactions of Yula's Yoga.

Required

1. After journalizing the transactions of Exercise 2–5, post the entries to the ledger, using T-account format. Identify transactions by their date. Date the ending balance of each account Mar. 31.
2. Prepare the trial balance of Yula's Yoga at March 31, 2007.

Describing transactions and posting

③ ④

4. Trial bal. total $5,284

Exercise 2–7

The journal of Alert Defensive Driving for October 2008 is below.

Required

1. Describe each transaction.
2. Set up T-accounts using the following account numbers: Cash, 1000; Accounts Receivable, 1200; Supplies, 1400; Accounts Payable, 2000; Tom Marshall, Capital, 3000; Service Revenue, 4000; Advertising Expense, 5100; Rent Expense, 5600; Fuel Expense, 5800.
3. Post to the ledger accounts. Identify each transaction by date. You may write the account numbers as posting references directly in the journal in your book unless directed otherwise by your instructor. Compute the balance in each account after posting.
4. Prepare Alert Defensive Driving's trial balance at October 31, 2008.

Journal				Page 5
Date 2008	Account Titles and Explanations	Post Ref.	Debit	Credit
Oct. 2	Cash		3,600	
	Tom Marshall, Capital			3,600
9	Supplies...		54	
	Accounts Payable			54
11	Accounts Receivable		1,620	
	Service Revenue			1,620
14	Rent Expense.....................................		400	
	Cash...			400
22	Cash		280	
	Accounts Receivable....................			280
25	Advertising Expense.........................		70	
	Cash...			70
27	Accounts Payable		54	
	Cash...			54
31	Fuel Expense		64	
	Accounts Payable			64

Journalizing transactions

③

Exercise 2–8

The first five transactions of Dale Carter Hockey School have been posted to the company's accounts as shown on the next page:

Cash				Supplies		Hockey Equipment	
(1)	7,500	(3)	5,250	(2)	75	(5)	750
(4)	1,375	(5)	750				

Land		Accounts Payable		Note Payable	
(3)	5,250		(2)	75	(4)	1,375

D. Carter, Capital	
	(1)	7,500

Required Prepare the journal entries that served as the sources for posting the five trans-actions. Date each entry April 30, 2007, and include an explanation for each entry as illustrated in the chapter.

Exercise 2–9

Prepare the trial balance of Dale Carter Hockey School at April 30, 2007, using the account data from Exercise 2–8.

Preparing a trial balance

Trial bal. total $8,950

Exercise 2–10

The accounts of Pioneer Consulting are listed below with their normal balances at October 31, 2007. The accounts are listed in no particular order.

Excel Spreadsheet Template

Preparing a trial balance

Trial bal. total $756,600

Required Prepare the company's trial balance at October 31, 2007, listing accounts in the sequence illustrated in the chapter. Supplies comes before Building and Land. List the expenses alphabetically.

Account	Balance
T. Pioneer, Capital	$292,800
Advertising expense	9,900
Accounts payable	31,800
Services revenue	162,000
Land	174,000
Notes payable	270,000
Cash	30,000
Salary expense	36,000
Building	390,000
Computer rental expense	42,000
T. Pioneer, withdrawals	36,000
Utilities expense	2,400
Accounts receivable	33,000
Supplies expense	1,800
Supplies	1,500

Exercise 2–11

Open the following three-column ledger accounts for Yoon Strategic Consulting at May 1, 2007: Cash; Accounts Receivable; Office Supplies; Office Furniture; Accounts Payable; Florence Yoon, Capital; Florence Yoon, Withdrawals; Consulting Revenue; Rent Expense; Salary Expense.

Journalize the following May transactions and then post to the ledger accounts. Use the dates to identify the transactions.

Journalizing and posting transactions

May	2	Florence Yoon opened a strategic consulting firm by investing $37,200 cash and office furniture valued at $16,200.
	2	Paid monthly rent of $4,500.
	2	Purchased office supplies on account, $1,800.
	15	Paid employee salary, $3,000.
	17	Paid $1,200 of the account payable from May 2.
	19	Performed consulting service on account, $69,000.
	30	Withdrew $6,000 for personal use.

Exercise 2–12

After recording the transactions in Exercise 2–11, prepare the trial balance of Yoon Strategic Consulting at May 31, 2007.

Exercise 2–13

The trial balance of Zoom Travel at February 28, 2008, does not balance.

Cash	$ 8,400	
Accounts receivable	5,800	
Supplies	1,200	
Land	130,000	
Accounts payable		$ 44,000
D. Tudin, capital		83,200
Service revenue		21,400
Rent expense	1,600	
Salary expense	3,600	
Utilities expense	600	
Total	$151,200	$148,600

Investigation of the accounting records reveals that the bookkeeper

a. Recorded a $800 cash revenue transaction by debiting Accounts Receivable. The credit entry was correct.

b. Posted a $2,000 credit to Accounts Payable as $200.

c. Did not record utilities expense or the related account payable in the amount of $400.

d. Understated D. Tudin, Capital by $800.

Required Prepare the correct trial balance at February 28, 2008, complete with a heading. Journal entries are not required.

Serial Exercise

Exercise 2–14 begins an accounting cycle that is completed in Chapter 5.

Exercise 2–14

Mark Wearing Engineers completed these transactions during early December 2008:

Dec. 2 Received $28,000 cash from Mark Wearing. The business gave owner's equity in the business to Wearing.

2 Paid monthly office rent, $2,000.

3 Paid cash for Dell computers, $7,000. The computers are expected to remain in service for five years.

4 Purchased office furniture on account, $11,200. The furniture should last for five years.

5 Purchased supplies on account, $600.

9 Performed consulting services for a client and received cash for the full amount of $4,000.

12 Paid utility expenses, $400.

18 Performed consulting services for a client on account, $6,400.

Required

1. Open T-accounts in the ledger: Cash; Accounts Receivable; Supplies; Equipment; Furniture; Accounts Payable; Mark Wearing, Capital; Mark Wearing, Withdrawals; Service Revenue; Rent Expense; Salaries Expense; and Utilities Expense. (Some of these T-accounts will be used in later chapters.)

2. Journalize the transactions. Explanations are not required.

3. Post to the T-accounts. Identify all items by date, and label an account balance as *Bal.* Formal posting references are not required.

4. Prepare a trial balance at December 18, 2008. (In the Serial Exercise of Chapter 3, we will add transactions for the remainder of December and will require a trial balance at December 31, 2008.)

Challenge Exercises

Exercise 2–15

Computing financial statement amounts

b. Cash paid $10,880
c. Cash collected $9,840

The owner of Wilkinson Technical Services is an architect with little understanding of accounting. She needs to compute the following summary information from the accounting records:

a. Net income for the month of March

b. Total cash paid during March

c. Cash collections from customers during March

d. Payments on account during March

The quickest way to compute these amounts is to analyze the following accounts:

	Balance		Additional Information for the Month of March
Account	Feb. 28	Mar. 31	
a. B. Wilkinson, Capital	$1,440	$2,400	Withdrawals, $640
b. Cash	800	640	Cash receipts, $10,720
c. Accounts Receivable	3,840	4,160	Sales on account, $10,160
d. Accounts Payable	2,080	2,560	Purchases on account, $1,008

The net income for March can be computed as follows:

B. Wilkinson, Capital

March Withdrawals	640	Feb. 28 Bal.	1,440	
		March Net Income	x	= $1,600
		March 31 Bal.	2,400	

Use a similar approach to compute the other three items.

Exercise 2–16

Analyzing accounting errors

Carol has trouble keeping her debits and credits equal. During a recent month she made the following errors:

a. In journalizing a cash receipt, Carol debited Cash for $10,000 instead of the correct amount of $19,000. She credited Service Revenue for $10,000, the incorrect amount.

b. Carol posted a $7,000 utility expense as $700. The credit posting to Cash was the correct amount of $7,000.

c. In preparing the trial balance, Carol omitted an $80,000 note payable.

d. Carol recorded a $1,200 purchase of supplies on account by debiting Supplies and crediting Accounts Payable for $2,100.

e. In recording a $7,000 payment on account, Carol debited Supplies instead of Accounts Payable.

Required

1. For each of these errors, state whether the total debits equal total credits on the trial balance.

2. Identify any accounts with misstated balances, and indicate the amount and direction of the error (account balance too high or too low).

Beyond the Numbers

Beyond the Numbers 2–1

Jim Gallager asks your advice in setting up the accounting records for his new business, Jim's Photo Shoppe. The business will be a photography studio and will operate in a rented building. Jim's Photo Shoppe will need office equipment and cameras. The business will borrow money using a note payable to buy the needed equipment. Jim's Photo Shoppe will purchase on account photographic supplies and office supplies. Each asset has a related expense account, some of which have not yet been discussed. For example, equipment wears out (amortizes) and thus needs an amortization account. As supplies are used up, the business must record a supplies expense.

The business will need an office manager. This person will be paid a weekly salary of $1,800. Other expenses will include advertising and insurance. Since Jim's Photo Shoppe will want to know which aspects of the business generate the most and the least revenue, it will use separate service revenue accounts for portraits, school pictures, and weddings. Jim's Photo Shoppe's better customers will be allowed to open accounts receivable with the business.

Required   List all the accounts Jim's Photo Shoppe will need, starting with the assets and ending with the expenses. Indicate which accounts will be reported on the balance sheet and which accounts will appear on the income statement.

Ethical Issue

Associated Charities Inc., a charitable organization in Brandon, Manitoba, has a standing agreement with Prairie Trust. The agreement allows Associated Charities Inc. to overdraw its cash balance at the bank when donations are running low. In the past, Associated Charities Inc. managed funds wisely and rarely used this privilege. Greg Osadchuk has recently become the president of Associated Charities Inc. To expand operations, Osadchuk is acquiring office equipment and spending large amounts for fund-raising. During his presidency, Associated Charities Inc. has maintained a negative bank balance (a credit Cash balance) of approximately $14,000.

Required   What is the ethical issue in this situation? State why you approve or disapprove of Osadchuk's management of Associated Charities Inc.'s funds.

Problems (Group A)

Analyzing a trial balance

①

Net income $55,000

Problem 2–1A

The owner of Olerud Communications, Nancy Olerud, is selling the business. She offers the trial balance shown below to prospective buyers.

OLERUD COMMUNICATIONS Trial Balance December 31, 2008		
Cash	$ 18,000	
Accounts receivable	40,500	
Prepaid expenses	6,000	
Land for future expansion	64,000	
Accounts payable		$ 52,500
Note payable		48,000
N. Olerud, Capital		45,000
N. Olerud, Withdrawals	72,000	
Service revenue		151,000
Advertising expense	4,500	
Rent expense	39,000	
Supplies expense	10,500	
Wages expense	42,000	
Totals	$296,500	$296,500

Your best friend is considering buying Olerud Communications. He seeks your advice in interpreting this information. Specifically, he asks whether this trial balance is the same as a balance sheet and an income statement. He also wonders whether Olerud Communications is a sound company because all the accounts are in balance.

Required Write a short note to answer your friend's questions. To aid his decision, state how he can use the information on the trial balance to compute Olerud Communications' net income or net loss for the current period. State the amount of net income or net loss in your note.

Problem 2–2A

Analyzing and journalizing transactions

Eastside Theatres owns movie theatres in the shopping centres of a major metropolitan area. The business engaged in the following transactions in 2007:

Feb.	1	Received cash of $200,000 from the owner Tony Fonesca.
	1	Paid February rent on a theatre building, $4,000.
	2	Paid $100,000 cash to purchase land for a theatre site.
	5	Borrowed $220,000 from the bank to finance the first phase of construction of the new theatre. The business signed a note payable to the bank.
	7	Received $40,000 cash from ticket sales and deposited this amount in the bank. (Label the revenue as Sales Revenue.)
	10	Purchased theatre supplies on account, $6,800.
	15	Paid theatre employee salaries, $5,600.
	15	Paid property tax expense on a theatre building, $6,400.
	16	Paid $3,200 on account.
	17	The owner withdrew $13,000 for personal expenses.

Eastside Theatres uses the following accounts: Cash; Supplies; Land; Accounts Payable; Notes Payable; Tony Fonesca, Capital; Tony Fonesca, Withdrawals; Sales Revenue; Property Tax Expense; Rent Expense; Salary Expense.

Required

1. Prepare an analysis of each business transaction of Eastside Theatres as shown for the February 1 transaction:

   Feb. 1   The asset Cash is increased. Increases in assets are recorded by debits; therefore, debit Cash. The owner's equity of the entity is increased. Increases in owner's equity are recorded by credits; therefore, credit Tony Fonesca, Capital.

2. Record each transaction in the journal, using the account titles given. Identify each transaction by its date. Explanations are not required.

Problem 2–3A

Journalizing transactions, posting to T-accounts, and preparing a trial balance

3. Trial bal. total $86,125

Harry Lawson opened a renovation business called Lawson Renovations on September 3, 2008. During the first month of operations, the business completed the following transactions:

Sept.	3	Harry Lawson deposited his cheque for $61,250 into the business bank account to start the business.
	4	Purchased supplies, $350, and furniture, $3,150, on account.
	5	Paid September rent expense, $875.
	6	Performed design services for a client and received $17,000 cash.
	7	Paid $45,000 cash to acquire land for a future office site.
	10	Designed a bathroom for a client, billed the client, and received her promise to pay the $1,750 within one week.
	14	Paid for the furniture purchased September 4 on account.
	15	Paid assistant's salary, $2,050.
	17	Received cash on account, $875.
	20	Prepared a recreation room design for a client on account, $3,150.
	28	Received $2,625 cash from a client for renovation of a cottage.
	30	Paid assistant's salary, $2,050.
	30	H. Lawson withdrew $3,000 for personal use.

Required

Open the following T-accounts: Cash; Accounts Receivable; Supplies; Furniture; Land; Accounts Payable; H. Lawson, Capital; H. Lawson, Withdrawals; Service Revenue; Rent Expense; Salary Expense.

1. Record each transaction in the journal, using the account titles given. Identify each transaction by date. Explanations are not required.

2. Post the transactions to the T-accounts, using transaction dates as posting references in the T-accounts. Label the balance of each account *Bal.*, as shown in the chapter.

3. Prepare the trial balance of Lawson Renovations at September 30, 2008.

Journalizing transactions, posting to ledger accounts, and preparing a trial balance

3. Trial bal. total $71,400

Problem 2–4A

The trial balance of Cambridge Engineering is dated February 28, 2007. During March, Cambridge Engineering completed the following transactions:

March		
	4	Collected $600 cash from a client on account.
	8	Designed a system for a client on account, $580.
	13	Paid for items purchased on account, $320.
	18	Purchased supplies on account, $120.
	20	R. Cambridge withdrew $200 for personal use.
	21	Received a verbal promise of a $2,000 contract.
	22	Received cash of $620 for consulting work just completed.
	31	Paid employees' salaries, $1,300.

CAMBRIDGE ENGINEERING
Trial Balance
February 28, 2007

Account Number	Account	Debit	Credit
1100	Cash	$ 4,000	
1200	Accounts receivable	16,000	
1300	Supplies	1,600	
1600	Automobile	37,200	
2000	Accounts payable		$ 6,000
3000	R. Cambridge, Capital		50,000
3100	R. Cambridge, Withdrawals	2,400	
5000	Service revenue		14,400
6100	Rent expense	2,000	
6200	Salary expense	7,200	
	Total	$70,400	$70,400

Required

1. Record the March transactions in *Page 3* of the journal. Include an explanation for each entry.

2. Open three-column ledger accounts for the accounts listed in the trial balance, together with their balances at February 28. Enter *Bal.* (for previous balance) in the Item column, and place a check mark (✓) in the journal reference column for the February 28 balance in each account.

   Post the transactions to the ledger, using dates, account numbers, journal references, and posting references.

3. Prepare the trial balance of Cambridge Engineering at March 31, 2007.

Recording transactions; using three-column ledger accounts; preparing a trial balance

4. Trial bal. total $191,000

Problem 2–5A

Jane Frideris started an investment counselling business, Frideris Consulting, in Montreal on June 1, 2008. During the first month of operations, the business completed the following selected transactions:

a. Frideris began the business with an investment of $40,000 cash, land valued at $40,000, and a building valued at $80,000. The business gave Frideris owner's equity in the business for the value of the cash, land, and building.

b. Purchased office supplies on account, $5,200.

c. Paid $30,000 for office furniture.

d. Paid employee salary, $4,400.

e. Performed consulting service on account for client, $12,200.

f. Paid $1,600 of the account payable created in transaction b.

g. Received a $4,000 bill for advertising expense that will be paid in the near future.

h. Performed consulting services for customers and received cash, $11,200.

i. Received cash on account, $4,800.

j. Paid the following cash expenses:
   (1) Rent of photocopier, $2,400.
   (2) Utilities, $800.

k. Jane Frideris withdrew $5,000 for personal use.

Required

1. Record each transaction in the journal. Use the letters to identify the transactions.

2. Open the following three-column ledger accounts: Cash; Accounts Receivable; Office Supplies; Office Furniture; Building; Land; Accounts Payable; Jane Frideris, Capital; Jane Frideris, Withdrawals; Service Revenue; Advertising Expense; Equipment Rental Expense; Salary Expense; Utilities Expense.

3. Post to the accounts and keep a running balance for each account.

4. Prepare the trial balance of Frideris Consulting at June 30, 2008.

Problem 2–6A

Refer to Problem 2–5A. After completing the trial balance in Problem 2–5A, prepare the following financial statements for Frideris Consulting:

1. Income statement for the month ended June 30, 2008.

2. Statement of owner's equity for the month ended June 30, 2008.

3. Balance sheet at June 30, 2008.

Draw arrows linking the financial statements. If needed, use Exhibit 1–10, page 22, as a guide for preparing the financial statements.

Preparing the financial statements

1. Net income $11,800
2. Jane Frideris, capital, June 30, 2008, $166,800
3. Total assets $174,400

Problem 2–7A

The following trial balance does not balance:

Correcting errors in a trial balance

Trial bal. total $35,000

MINTER LANDSCAPE CONSULTING Trial Balance June 30, 2007		
Cash...	$ 800	
Accounts receivable	5,000	
Supplies	450	
Office furniture...	1,800	
Land for future expansion	23,300	
Accounts payable...		$ 1,900
Notes payable		11,500
R. Minter, Capital		15,800
R. Minter, Withdrawals	1,000	
Consulting service revenue		3,650
Advertising expense	200	
Rent expense...	500	
Salary expense	1,050	
Utilities expense	205	
Total..	$34,305	$32,850

The following errors were detected:

a. The cash balance is understated by $650.

b. The cost of the land was $22,300, not $23,300.

c. A $200 purchase of supplies on account was neither journalized nor posted.

d. A $1,500 credit to Consulting Service Revenue was not posted.

e. Rent Expense of $100 was posted as a credit rather than a debit.

f. The balance of Advertising Expense is $300, but it was listed as $200 on the trial balance.

g. A $150 debit to Accounts Receivable was posted as $15. The credit to Consulting Service Revenue was correct.

h. The balance of Utilities Expense is overstated by $40.

i. A $450 debit to the R. Minter, Withdrawals account was posted as a debit to R. Minter, Capital.

Required Prepare the correct trial balance at June 30, 2007. Journal entries are not required.

Applying the rules of debit and credit, and recording transactions in the journal

Problem 2–8A

Ken Suzuki operates a fishing charter business, Pacific Charters. The business had the following transactions in September 2007:

Sept.		
	1	Suzuki invested $30,000 cash and his 10-metre power boat in the charter business. The business gave Suzuki owner's equity in the business. The boat had originally cost him $120,000, but had a fair market value of $75,000 on September 1, 2007.
	3	Purchased a new boat by paying $21,000 cash and promising to pay another $52,000 in one week. Suzuki felt that this was an excellent bargain as the boat had a catalogue price of $90,000 and he knew it was worth at least $75,000.
	4	Paid moorage fees of $2,400 for the month of September. These fees covered two moorage slips—one for each charter boat.
	5	Hired a deckhand at a rate of $1,000 per week.
	9	Took clients out on a charter for $3,900. They paid $2,000 and promised to pay the balance in 30 days.
	10	Paid $4,000 of the amount owing on the boat purchased on September 3. Signed a promissory note for the balance, as the company was unable to pay the full amount that day.
	15	Purchased $4,000 of equipment from a supplier. To pay for the equipment, Pacific Charters took the supplier and her employees out on a day charter and also paid the supplier $1,000 cash.
	20	Received $1,900 from the clients of September 9 as payment on the charter.
	26	Paid the deckhand for three weeks' work.
	29	A client chartered the two boats for two days for $12,000. In payment, the client, the owner of a service station, provided Pacific Charters with $6,000 of repair parts that can be used on the boats, and cash.
	30	Used $1,600 of repair parts on one boat of $6,000 (a boat operating expense).

Required Record each transaction in the journal. Identify each transaction by date. Explanations are not required.

Applying the rules of debit and credit, and recording transactions

Problem 2–9A

CrossCountry Movers had the following account balances, in random order, on December 15, 2007 (all accounts have their "normal" balances):

Moving fees earned	$130,800	Cash	$ 3,600
Accounts receivable	8,700	Storage fees earned	28,950
Rent expense	23,550	Notes receivable	22,500
H. Martinez, Capital	75,000	Utilities expense	1,200
Office supplies expense	1,050	Office supplies	4,800
Mortgage payable	19,500	Accounts payable	16,500
Salaries expense	80,550	Office equipment	6,150
Insurance expense	3,150	Moving equipment	116,100

The following events took place during the final days of the year:

Dec.   16   The accountant discovered that an error had been made in posting an entry to the Moving Fees Earned account. The entry was correctly journalized but $1,200 was accidentally posted as $2,100 in the account.

17   Moved a customer's goods to CrossCountry's rented warehouse for storage. The moving fees were $2,000. Storage fees are $300 per month. The customer was billed for one month's storage and the moving fees.

18   Collected a $7,500 note owed to CrossCountry Movers and collected interest of $900.

19   Used a company cheque to pay for H. Martinez's hydro bill in the amount of $200.

21   Purchased storage racks for $6,000. Paid $1,800, provided moving services for $750, and promised to pay the balance in 60 days.

23   Collected $1,500; $1,300 of this was for moving goods on December 15 (recorded as an accounts receivable at that time) and the balance was for storage fees for the period of December 16 to 23.

24   CrossCountry Movers paid $9,000 owing on the mortgage.

27   Henry Martinez withdrew $2,500 for personal use.

29   Provided moving services to a lawyer for $1,200. The lawyer paid CrossCountry Movers $750 and provided legal work for the balance.

31   Henry Martinez, the owner of CrossCountry Movers, sold 1,000 shares he held in Brandon Haulage Inc. for $6,000.

Required   Where appropriate, record each transaction from December 16 to 31 in the journal. Explanations are not required.

Problems (Group B)

Problem 2–1B

Joan Simpson, the owner of Simpson Designs, is selling the business. She offers the trial balance below to prospective buyers.

Your best friend is considering buying Simpson Designs. She seeks your advice in interpreting this information. Specifically, she asks whether this trial balance is the same as a balance sheet and an income statement. She also wonders whether Simpson Designs is a sound company. She thinks it must be because the accounts are in balance.

Analyzing a trial balance

Net loss $34,000

Required   Write a short note to answer your friend's questions. To aid her decision, state how she can use the information on the trial balance to compute the Simpson Designs net income or net loss for the current period. State the amount of net income or net loss in your note.

SIMPSON DESIGNS Trial Balance December 31, 2008		
Cash	$ 26,000	
Accounts receivable	10,000	
Prepaid expenses	4,000	
Land for future expansion	68,000	
Accounts payable		$ 62,000
Note payable		44,000
Joan Simpson, Capital		66,000
Joan Simpson, Withdrawals	30,000	
Service revenue		120,000
Advertising expense	16,000	
Rent expense	24,000	
Supplies expense	18,000	
Wage expense	96,000	
Total	$292,000	$292,000

Problem 2–2B

Angela Chong practises civil engineering under the business title Angela Chong Consulting. During April 2008 the company engaged in the following transactions:

April	1	Chong deposited $30,000 cash in the business bank account. The business gave Chong owner's equity in the business.
	5	Paid monthly rent on drafting equipment, $200.
	9	Paid $25,000 cash to purchase land for an office site.
	10	Purchased supplies on account, $300.
	19	Paid $100 on account for supplies purchased on April 10.
	22	Borrowed $10,000 from the bank for business use. Chong signed a note payable to the bank in the name of the business.
	30	Revenues earned during the month included $1,300 cash and $2,400 on account.
	30	Paid employee salaries of $2,000, office rent of $900, and utilities of $180.
	30	Angela Chong withdrew $1,200 from the business for personal use.

Angela Chong Consulting uses the following accounts: Cash; Accounts Receivable; Supplies; Land; Accounts Payable; Notes Payable; A. Chong, Capital; A. Chong, Withdrawals; Service Revenue; Rent Expense; Salaries Expense; Utilities Expense.

Required

1. Prepare an analysis of each business transaction of Angela Chong Consulting, as shown for the April 1 transaction:

    > Apr. 1   The asset cash is increased. Increases in assets are recorded by debits; therefore, debit Cash. The owner's equity is increased. Increases in owner's equity are recorded by credits; therefore, credit A. Chong, Capital.

2. Record each transaction in the journal, using the dates and account titles given. Explanations are not required.

Problem 2–3B

Journalizing transactions, posting
to T-accounts, and preparing a
trial balance

3. Trial bal. total $48,250

Scott Jameson opened a translation business on January 2, 2007. During the first month of operations, the business completed the following transactions:

Jan.	2	The business received $40,000 cash from Scott Jameson, which was deposited in a business bank account entitled Jameson Translation Service.
	3	Purchased supplies, $750, and furniture, $2,800, on account.
	3	Paid January rent expense, $1,100.
	4	Performed translation services for a client and received cash, $2,250.
	7	Paid $28,000 cash to acquire land for a future office site.
	11	Translated a brochure for a client and billed the client $1,200.
	15	Paid secretary salary, $975.
	16	Paid for the furniture purchased January 3 on account.
	18	Received partial payment from client on account, $600.
	19	Translated legal documents for a client on account, $1,350.
	22	Paid the water and electricity bills, $300.
	29	Received $2,700 cash for translation for a client in an overseas business transaction.
	31	Paid secretary salary, $975.
	31	Scott Jameson withdrew $2,000 for personal use.

Required

Open the following T-accounts: Cash; Accounts Receivable; Supplies; Furniture; Land; Accounts Payable; Scott Jameson, Capital; Scott Jameson, Withdrawals; Translation Revenue; Rent Expense; Salary Expense; Utilities Expense.

1. Record each transaction in the journal, using the account titles given. Key each transaction by date. Explanations are not required.

2. Post the transactions to the ledger using T-accounts, using transaction dates in the ledger. Label the balance of each account *Bal.* as shown in the chapter.

3. Prepare the trial balance of Jameson Translation Service at January 31, 2007.

4. How will what you have learned in this problem help you manage a business?

Problem 2–4B

The trial balance of the desktop publishing business of Doug Foster at November 15, 2008, is shown below.

Journalizing transactions, posting to three-column ledger accounts, and preparing a trial balance

 2 3 4 5

3. Trial bal. total $105,400

FOSTER PUBLISHING
Trial Balance
November 15, 2008

Account Number	Account	Debit	Credit
1100	Cash	$ 6,000	
1200	Accounts receivable	16,000	
1300	Supplies	1,200	
1900	Equipment	70,000	
2100	Accounts payable		$ 9,200
4000	D. Foster, Capital		80,000
4100	D. Foster, Withdrawals	4,600	
5000	Service revenue		14,200
6000	Rent expense	2,000	
6100	Salaries expense	3,600	
	Total	$103,400	$103,400

During the remainder of November, the business completed the following transactions:

Nov.   16   Collected $4,000 cash from a client on account.
17   Performed publishing services for a client on account, $2,100.
21   Paid on account, $2,600.
22   Purchased supplies on account, $600.
23   Doug Foster withdrew $2,100 for personal use.
24   Was advised that Desk Top Inc. was prepared to buy all of Foster Publishing for $60,000.
26   Received $1,900 cash for design work just completed.
30   Paid employees' salaries, $2,400.

Required

1. Record the transactions that occurred during November 16 through 30 in *Page 6* of the journal. Include an explanation for each entry.

2. Post the transactions to three-column accounts in the ledger, using dates, account numbers, journal references and posting references. Open the ledger accounts listed in the trial balance together with their balances at November 15. Enter *Bal.* (for previous balance) in the Item column, and place a check mark (✓) in the journal reference column for the November 15 balance of each account.

3. Prepare the trial balance of Foster Publishing at November 30, 2008.

Problem 2–5B

Bill Ronalds started a catering service called Blue Ribbon Catering. During the first month of operations, January 2007, the business completed the following selected transactions:

Recording transactions; using three-column ledger accounts; preparing a trial balance

 2 3 4 5

4. Trial bal. total $73,000

a. Bill Ronalds began the company with an investment of $30,000 cash and a van (automobile) valued at $26,000. The business gave Bill owner's equity in the business.

b. Paid $8,000 for food service equipment.

c. Purchased supplies on account, $4,800.

d. Paid employee salary, $2,600.

e. Received $4,000 for a catering job.

f. Performed services at a wedding on account, $8,600.

g. Paid $2,000 of the account payable created in transaction c.

h. Received a $1,600 bill for advertising expense that will be paid in the near future.

i. Received cash on account, $2,200.

j. Paid the following cash expenses:
   (1) Rent, $3,000.
   (2) Insurance, $1,600.

k. Bill Ronalds withdrew $2,000 for personal use.

Required

1. Record the transactions in the journal. Use the letters to identify the transactions.
2. Open the following three-column ledger accounts: Cash; Accounts Receivable; Supplies; Food Service Equipment; Automobile; Accounts Payable; B. Ronalds, Capital; B. Ronalds, Withdrawals; Service Revenue; Advertising Expense; Insurance Expense; Rent Expense; Salary Expense.
3. Post to the accounts and keep a running balance for each account.
4. Prepare the trial balance of Blue Ribbon Catering at January 31, 2007.

Preparing the financial statements

1. Net income $3,800
2. Bill Ronalds, Capital, Jan. 31, 2007, $57,800
3. Total assets $62,200

Problem 2–6B

Refer to Problem 2–5B. After completing the trial balance in Problem 2–5B, prepare the following financial statements for Blue Ribbon Catering.

1. Income statement for the month ended January 31, 2007.
2. Statement of owner's equity for the month ended January 31, 2007.
3. Balance sheet at January 31, 2007.

Draw arrows linking the financial statements. If needed, use Exhibit 1–10, page 22, as a guide for preparing the financial statements.

Correcting errors in a trial balance

Trial bal. total $928,500

Problem 2–7B

The trial balance for Carlisle Fitness, shown below, does not balance. The following errors were detected:

a. The cash balance is overstated by $6,000.

b. Rent expense of $3,000 was posted as a credit rather than a debit.

c. The balance of Advertising Expense is $4,500, but it is listed as $6,000 on the trial balance.

d. A $9,000 debit to Accounts Receivable was posted as $900.

e. The balance of Utilities Expense is understated by $900.

f. A $19,500 debit to the J. Carlisle, Withdrawals account was posted as a debit to J. Carlisle, Capital.

g. A $1,500 purchase of supplies on account was neither journalized nor posted.

h. An $87,000 credit to Service Revenue was not posted.

i. Office furniture should be listed in the amount of $19,500.

CARLISLE FITNESS
Trial Balance
October 31, 2007

Cash	$ 57,000	
Accounts receivable	30,000	
Supplies	7,500	
Office furniture	34,500	
Fitness equipment	690,000	
Accounts payable		$ 30,000
Notes payable		274,500
J. Carlisle, Capital		442,500
J. Carlisle, Withdrawals	55,500	
Service revenue		73,500
Salary expense	22,500	
Rent expense	9,000	
Advertising expense	6,000	
Utilities expense	3,000	
Total	$915,000	$820,500

Required Prepare the correct trial balance at October 31, 2007. Journal entries are not required.

Problem 2–8B

Ryan Kessler operates a heavy equipment transport company, Kessler Transport. The company had the following transactions for the month of August 2007:

Applying the rules of debit and credit, recording transactions in the journal

Aug. 1 Kessler Transport received $10,000 cash and a truck and trailer from Kessler. The truck had originally cost Kessler $300,000, but had a fair market value of $230,000 on August 1. The trailer had a fair market value of $30,000.

3 Purchased a new trailer by paying $5,000 cash and promising to pay another $20,000 in one week. The trailer had a list price of $35,000 and Kessler knew it was worth at least $30,000.

4 Paid parking space rental fees of $400 for the month of August. These fees covered three spaces—two for the trailers and one for the truck.

5 Hired an assistant at a rate of $750 per week.

9 Transported equipment for clients for $3,200. They paid $1,600 and promised to pay the balance in 30 days.

10 Paid $3,000 of the amount owing on the trailer purchase on August 3. Signed a promissory note for the balance, as the company was unable to pay the full amount that day.

15 Paid Ryan Kessler's personal telephone bill for $110. Treat this as a withdrawal.

20 Received $1,600 from the clients of August 9 as payment on the haulage.

26 Paid the assistant for three weeks' work.

29 Billed a client $3,000 for hauling equipment from Prince Albert to Saskatoon. The client, who was the owner of a service station, paid the bill by providing the company with $3,000 of repair parts that can be used on the truck.

30 Used $60 of repair parts on the truck (a truck operating expense).

Required Record each transaction in the journal. Identify each transaction by its date. Explanations are not required.

Problem 2–9B

Maquina Lodge, owned by Bob Palmiter, had the following account balances, in random order, on December 15, 2007 (all accounts have their "normal" balances):

Applying the rules of debit and credit, and recording transactions

Guest revenue	$209,000	Furniture	$57,800
Accounts receivable	8,800	Cash	3,800
Equipment rental expense	11,800	Notes receivable	26,000
B. Palmiter, Capital	93,800	Utilities expense	1,000
Supplies expense	2,800	Supplies inventory	5,800
Mortgage payable	30,000	Accounts payable	12,000
Salaries expense	81,000	Office equipment	10,200
Insurance expense	6,800	Boating equipment	96,800

The following events also took place during the final days of the year:

Dec. 16 The accountant discovered that an error had been made in posting an entry to the Guest Revenue account. The entry was correctly journalized but $4,200 was accidentally posted as $2,400 in the account.

17 Signed an agreement to let a retired professor move in, in the off season for a long stay, beginning today. The monthly rate is $3,200 payable in advance.

18 Collected a $18,000 note owed to Maquina and collected interest of $1,200.

21 Purchased boating equipment for $14,000 from Boats Unlimited. Maquina Lodge paid $5,000, provided room rentals for $1,600 to Boats Unlimited, and promised to pay the balance in 60 days.

23 Collected $2,800 for rooms for a conference held from December 16 to 23.

24 Maquina Lodge paid $4,000 owing on the mortgage.

27 Bob Palmiter withdrew $7,000 for personal use.

29 Provided meeting rooms to a lawyer for $2,000. The lawyer paid Maquina Lodge $1,100 and provided legal work for the balance.

Required Where appropriate, record each transaction from December 16 to 29 in the journal. Explanations are not required.

Challenge Problems

Understanding the rules of debit and credit

Problem 2–1C

Some individuals, for whatever reason, do not pay income tax or pay less than they should. Often their business transactions are cash transactions, so there is no paper trail to prove how much or how little they actually earned. Canada Revenue Agency, however, has a way of dealing with these individuals; they use a model (based on the accounting equation), to calculate how much the individual must have earned.

Canada Revenue Agency is about to audit Donna Wynn for the period January 1, 2007, to December 31, 2007. Donna buys and sells used cars for cash; the purchaser is responsible for having the car certified so it can be licensed and insured. Donna had $4,000 cash and no other assets or liabilities at January 1, 2007.

Required

1. Use the accounting equation to explain how the Canada Revenue Agency model will be used to audit Donna.

2. What do you think are the accounting concepts underlying the model?

Using a formal accounting system.

Problem 2–2C

Over the years you have become friendly with a farmer, Jack Russell, who raises crops, which he sells, and has small herds of beef cattle and sheep. Jack maintains his basic herds and markets the calves and lambs each fall. His accounting system is quite simple; all his transactions are in cash. Jack pays tax each year on his income, which he estimates. He indicated to you once that he must be doing it right because Canada Revenue Agency audited him recently and assessed no additional tax.

You are taking your first accounting course and are quite impressed with the information one can gain from a formal accounting system.

Required
Explain to Jack Russell why it would be to his advantage to have a more formal accounting system with accounts, ledgers, and journals.

The rules of debit and credit; preparing a trial balance

Trial bal. total $14,881

Problem 2–3C

Cash	$2,840	Notes payable	$1,200
Accounts receivable	3,331	Fees earned	2,380
Supplies	800	Salary expense	3,400
Equipment	3,000	Office expense	910
Accounts payable	2,666		

Each of the above accounts has a normal balance in the ledger of Thomas Services at December 31, 2008. An examination of the ledger and journal reveals the following errors:

a. Cash received from a customer on account was debited for $570 and Accounts Receivable was credited for the same amount. The actual collection was for $750.

b. The purchase of a computer monitor on account for $340 was recorded as a debit to Supplies for $340 and a credit to Accounts Payable for $340.

c. Services were performed on account for a client for $890. Accounts Receivable was debited for $890 and Fees Earned was credited for $89.

d. A debit posting to Salaries Expense of $600 was omitted.

e. A payment on account for $206 was credited to Cash for $206 and credited to Accounts Payable for $260.

f. The withdrawal of $400 cash for Pete Thomas's personal use was debited to Salaries Expense for $400 and credited to Cash for $400.

Required

1. For each item above, describe how a correction would be made, either by giving a correcting journal entry or by describing how a posting error would be corrected in the ledger.

2. Prepare the trial balance for Thomas Services after the corrections are made.

Decision Problems

Decision Problem 1

Your friend, Amin Akmali, has asked your advice about the effects that certain business transactions will have on his business. His business, Car Finders, finds the best deals on automobiles for clients. Time is short, so you cannot journalize transactions. Instead, you must analyze the transactions and post them directly to T-accounts. Akmali will continue in the business only if he can expect to earn monthly net income of $8,000. The business had the following transactions during March 2007:

a. Akmali deposited $30,000 cash in a business bank account.

b. The business borrowed $8,000 cash from the bank and issued a note payable due within one year.

c. Paid $1,600 cash for supplies.

d. Paid cash for advertising in the local newspaper, $1,200.

e. Paid the following cash expenses for one month: secretary (part-time) salary, $2,400; office rent, $800; utilities, $600; interest, $200.

f. Earned revenue on account, $10,600.

g. Earned $7,500 revenue and received cash.

h. Collected cash from customers on account, $2,400.

Required

1. Open the following T-accounts: Cash; Accounts Receivable; Supplies; Notes Payable; Amin Akmali, Capital; Service Revenue; Advertising Expense; Interest Expense; Rent Expense; Salary Expense; Utilities Expense.

2. Record the transactions directly in the T-accounts without using a journal. Identify each transaction by its letter.

3. Prepare a trial balance at March 31, 2007. List expenses alphabetically.

4. Compute the amount of net income or net loss for this first month of operations. Would you recommend Akmali continue in business?

Recording transactions directly in the ledger, preparing a trial balance, and measuring net income or loss

3. Trial bal. total $56,100
4. Net income $12,900

Decision Problem 2

Although all the following questions deal with the accounting equation, they are not related:

1. Explain the advantages of double-entry bookkeeping to a friend who is opening a used-book store.

2. When you deposit money in your bank account, the bank credits your account. Is the bank misusing the word *credit* in this context? Why does the bank use the term *credit* to refer to your deposit, and not *debit*?

3. Your friend asks, "When revenues increase assets and expenses decrease assets, why are revenues credits and expenses debits and not the other way around?" Explain to your friend why revenues are credits and expenses are debits.

Using the accounting equation

Financial Statement Cases

Financial Statement Case 1

This problem helps to develop journalizing skills by using an actual company's account titles. Refer to the CHUM Limited financial statements in Appendix A. Assume CHUM Limited completed the following selected transactions during November 2007:

Journalizing transactions

Nov. 5 Earned advertising revenues on account, $6,000,000 (revenue).
  9 Borrowed $8,000,000 by signing a note payable (long-term debt).
  12 Purchased equipment on account, $9,000,000 (property, plant, and equipment section).
  17 Paid $1,200,000, which represents payment of $1,000,000 on long-term debt plus interest expense.
  19 Earned advertising revenues and immediately received cash of $500,000.
  22 Collected the cash on account that was earned on November 5.
  29 Received an electricity bill for $10,000 for the CHUM studio and offices in Toronto.
  29 Paid half the account payable created on November 12.

Required Journalize these transactions using the following account titles taken from the financial statements of CHUM Limited: Cash; Accounts Receivable; Equipment; Accounts Payable; Long-Term Debt; Revenue; Operations Expense; Interest Expense. Explanations are not required.

Journalizing transactions

Financial Statement Case 2

Refer to the Sun-Rype Products Ltd. financial statements in Appendix B at the back of the book. Assume Sun-Rype completed the following selected transactions during December 2005. All amounts are in thousands of dollars.

a. Made sales on account, $4,435.

b. Paid cash for advertising (selling, general, and administrative expenses), $15,330.

c. Paid income tax expense of $3,502.

d. Collected accounts receivable of $7,567.

e. Paid cash for inventory, $3,330.

f. Purchased equipment on account for $5,000.

g. Paid cash for annual rent (selling, general, and administrative expenses), $15,440.

Required

1. Set up T-accounts for Cash (debit balance of $50,000); Accounts Receivable (debit balance of $15,000); Inventory (debit balance of $10,001); Property, Plant, and Equipment (debit balance of $17,312); Accounts Payable (credit balance $11,211); Sales Revenue (credit balance of $120,976); Selling, General, and Administrative Expenses ($0 balance); Income Tax Expense ($0 balance).

2. Journalize Sun-Rype's transactions a to g. Explanations are not required.

3. Post to the T-accounts and compute the balance for each account. Identify each posting by its transaction letter.

4. For each of the accounts, compare your balances to Sun-Rype's actual balances as shown on the December 31, 2005, balance sheet and income statement in Appendix B. All of your amounts should agree with the actual figures rounded to the nearest thousand.

   Cash
   Accounts receivable
   Inventories
   Property, plant and equipment
   Accounts payable and accrued liabilities
   Net sales
   Selling, general and administrative expenses
   Income tax

5. Balance sheet and income statement accounts listed are really categories representing summarized account balances. List three accounts that would be reflected in the following categories:

   a) Property, plant, and equipment,
   b) Accounts payable and accrued liabilities, and
   c) Selling, general, and administrative expenses.

Measuring Business Income: The Adjusting Process

Learning Objectives

1. Distinguish accrual-basis accounting from cash-basis accounting
2. Apply the revenue-recognition and matching principles
3. Make adjusting entries
4. Prepare an adjusted trial balance
5. Prepare the financial statements from the adjusted trial balance

Chapter 3 Appendix

A1. Account for a prepaid expense recorded initially as an expense
A2. Account for an unearned (deferred) revenue recorded initially as a revenue

WestJet Airlines Ltd. is a Canadian success story. The company was started in 1996 by four Calgary entrepreneurs who saw an opportunity to provide low-fare air travel across western Canada. The company followed the format for success used by Southwest Airlines and Morris Air, two similar and successful operations. WestJet began with 220 employees and three aircraft. Its initial routes were solely in Western Canada, stretching from Vancouver to Winnipeg.

The airline industry in Canada changed significantly in 1999 when Canadian Airlines was acquired by Air Canada. The merger provided WestJet with an opportunity to add routes to several Eastern-Canadian cities. Since that time, the company has continued to expand its operations and maintain its profitability. In a press release, WestJet reported that the quarterly profit for the period January to March 2006 was $12.9 million, up from the $9.6 million loss experienced in the same period of the previous year. Operating revenue rose by 31.6% to $387.6 million from $294.6 million in the same quarter of the previous year.

In the press release, Clive Beddoe, WestJet's President and CEO, commented, "Our quarterly results for the first three months of 2006 mark the most successful first quarter in our history."

He also stated that "our fuel expense was 11.9% higher in the first quarter of 2006 versus the same period in 2005. We managed to mitigate this expense with the early retirement of our less fuel-efficient 200-series aircraft. With an average age of 2.1 years, our fleet of Next-Generation aircraft is the youngest fleet in North America. These aircraft are 30% more fuel efficient than the 200-series and are vital to our continued success as a low-cost carrier."

Source: April 27, 2006 press release filed online at SEDAR.com; accessed on April 28, 2006.

? What is the adjusting process and why is it important?
Why can't we record only the transactions that affect cash?
How many categories of adjusting entries are there?
How do adjusting entries differ from other journal entries?
Why is the adjusted trial balance used to determine a business's results of operations and financial position?

These questions and others will be answered throughout this chapter. And the Decision Guidelines at the end of this chapter will provide the answers in a useful summary.

THINKING IT OVER

All parts of the financial statements are important in describing the financial condition of a business. Which financial statement would be most helpful to WestJet's management in evaluating the company's performance for the January–March 2006 quarter?

A: The income statement, because it reports how profitable the company has been for that period.

1. Identify and analyze transactions

2. Record transactions in a journal

3. Post (copy) from the journal to the accounts in the ledger

4. Prepare the trial balance

5. Journalize and post adjusting entries

6. Prepare the financial statements

7. Close the books (closing entries, postclosing trial balance)

What

do we mean when we say that WestJet earned $12.9 million in the first quarter of the year ended December 31, 2006? The business earned net income, or profit, of $12.9 million in the quarter as reported on its income statement. WestJet's revenues consist of passenger revenue of $387.6 million. What are WestJet's expenses? They include advertising, salaries, costs of running the aircraft, administrative and other office costs, maintenance, and many others. WestJet operates in much the same way, except on a much larger scale, as SuperTravel, the travel business we studied in Chapters 1 and 2.

Whether the business is WestJet Airlines Ltd. or SuperTravel, the profit motive increases the owners' drive to carry on the business. As you study this chapter, consider how important net income is to a business.

At the end of each accounting period, the entity prepares its financial statements. The period may be a month, three months, six months, or a full year. WestJet is typical. The company reports on a quarterly basis—at the end of every three months—with audited financial statements at the end of its year.

Whatever the length of the period, the end accounting product is the set of financial statements. And one of the most important single amounts in these statements is the net income or net loss for the period. Net income or net loss captures much information: total revenues minus total expenses for the period. A business that consistently earns net income adds value to its owners, its employees, its customers, and society.

An important step in financial statement preparation is the trial balance. The trial balance, introduced in Chapter 2 on page 64, lists the ledger accounts and their balances. The account balances in the trial balance include the effects of the transactions that occurred during the period—cash collections, purchases of assets, payments of bills, sales of assets, and so on. To measure its income, however, a business must do some additional accounting at the end of the period to bring the records up to date before preparing the financial statements. This process is called *adjusting the books* and it consists of making special entries called *adjusting entries*. This chapter focuses on these adjusting entries to show how to measure business income. This is Step 5 of the accounting cycle shown in the margin.

The accounting profession has concepts and principles to guide the measurement of business income. Chief among these are

- Accrual-basis accounting versus cash-basis accounting
- The accounting period
- The revenue-recognition principle
- The matching principle

In this chapter, we apply these (and other) concepts and principles to measure the income and prepare the financial statements of SuperTravel for the month of April. All other companies follow the same principles.

Accrual-Basis Accounting versus Cash-Basis Accounting

There are two ways to do accounting:

Objective 1
Distinguish accrual-basis accounting from cash-basis accounting

- **Accrual-basis accounting,** frequently called simply *accrual accounting,* records the effect of every business transaction as it occurs, no matter when cash receipts and cash payments occur. Most businesses use the accrual basis, and that is the method covered in this book. The Canada Revenue Agency (CRA) requires accrual accounting for income tax purposes except in special cases.
- **Cash-basis accounting** records transactions only when cash receipts and cash payments occur. It ignores receivables, payables, and amortization. Only very small businesses tend to use cash-basis accounting.

Suppose SuperTravel purchased $2,000 of supplies on account. On the accrual basis, SuperTravel records the asset Supplies and the liability Accounts Payable as follows:

Supplies..	2,000	
Accounts Payable		2,000
Purchased supplies on account.		

Under the accrual basis, SuperTravel's balance sheet reports the asset Supplies and the liability Accounts Payable.

In contrast, cash-basis accounting ignores this transaction because SuperTravel paid no cash. The cash basis records only cash receipts and cash payments.

- Most cash receipts are treated as revenues.
- Most cash payments are handled as expenses.

Therefore, under the cash basis, SuperTravel would record the transaction only when the cash is paid for the supplies, and the $2,000 cash payment is recorded as an expense rather than as an asset. This is faulty accounting: SuperTravel acquired supplies, which are assets.

Now let's see how differently the accrual basis and the cash basis account for a revenue. Suppose SuperTravel performed service and earned revenue but collected no cash. Under the accrual basis, SuperTravel records $10,000 of revenue on account as follows:

Accounts Receivable......................................	10,000	
Service Revenue..		10,000
Earned revenue on account.		

The balance sheet then reports the asset Accounts Receivable, and the income statement reports Service Revenue. We have a complete picture of the transaction.

Under the cash basis, SuperTravel would record no revenue because there is no cash receipt. Instead, it would wait until cash is received and then record the cash as revenue. As a result, cash-basis accounting never reports accounts receivable from customers. Cash-basis accounting shows the revenue in the wrong accounting period if cash is *received* in a different period than it is *earned.* Revenue should be recorded when it is earned, and that is how the accrual basis operates.

Exhibit 3–1 illustrates the difference between the accrual basis and the cash basis for a flower shop. Keep in mind that the accrual basis is the correct way to do accounting.

As we saw in Exhibit 1–6 on page 9, the objective of financial statements is to communicate information that is useful to users. Clearly, accrual-basis accounting provides more complete information than does cash-basis accounting. This difference is important because the more complete the data, the better equipped decision makers are to reach accurate conclusions about the firm's financial health and

EXHIBIT 3–1 | Accrual-Basis Accounting versus Cash-Basis Accounting

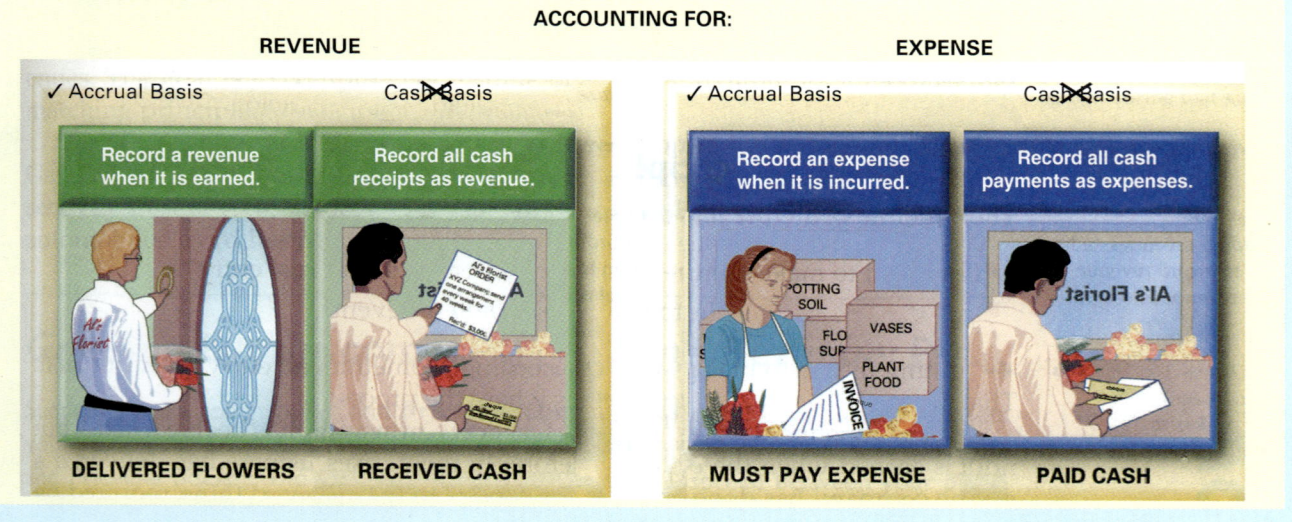

future prospects. Four concepts used in accrual accounting are the accounting period, the revenue-recognition principle, the matching principle, and the time-period principle.

The Accounting Period

SuperTravel will know for certain how well it has operated only after it sells all its assets, pays the liabilities, and returns any leftover cash to the owner. This process, called *liquidation*, is the same as going out of business. Obviously, it is not practical for accountants to measure business income in this manner because businesses

LEARNING TIPS

You can distinguish cash-basis and accrual accounting this way:

Cash basis: Record revenue when you receive cash, regardless of when the service was performed or the sale made. Record expenses when you pay cash, regardless of when the expense was incurred or the item used. There are no accounts receivable and no accounts payable.

Accrual basis: Forget cash flow. Record revenue when you make a sale or perform a service. Record expenses when the business uses goods or services. Revenues and expenses may not coincide with cash flows.

STOP AND THINK

Suppose SuperTravel collects $3,000 from customers on January 1. The company will earn the $3,000 evenly during January, February, and March. How much service revenue will SuperTravel report each month under (a) accrual-basis accounting and (b) cash-basis accounting?

Answer:

		Jan.	Feb.	Mar.
(a) *Accrual-basis accounting:*	Service revenue	$1,000	$1,000	$1,000
(b) *Cash-basis accounting:*	Service revenue	$3,000		

Under accrual-basis accounting, SuperTravel records the revenue when the company earns it. This is the correct way to do the accounting.

Now suppose SuperTravel prepays $600 for TV advertising on October 1. The ads will run during October, November and December. How much advertising expense will SuperTravel report each month under the two methods of accounting?

Answer:

		Oct.	Nov.	Dec.
(a) *Accrual-basis accounting:*	Advertising expense......	$200	$200	$200
(b) *Cash-basis accounting:*	Advertising expense......	$600		

The accrual basis is the correct way to do the accounting.

need periodic reports on their progress. Accountants slice time into small segments and prepare financial statements for specific periods.

The most basic accounting period is one year, and virtually all businesses prepare annual financial statements. For most companies, the annual accounting period is the calendar year from January 1 through December 31. Other companies use a *fiscal year* ending on some date other than December 31. The year-end date is usually the low point in business activity for the year. Retailers are a notable example. Traditionally, their fiscal year ends on January 31, because the low point in their business activity has followed the after-Christmas sales in January; the Forzani Group and the Hudson's Bay Co. are two examples.

Managers and investors cannot wait until the end of the year to gauge a company's progress. Companies therefore prepare financial statements for *interim* periods, which are less than a year. Managers want financial information more often, so monthly financial statements are common. A series of monthly statements can be combined for quarterly and semiannual periods. Most of the discussions in this book are based on an annual accounting period, but the procedures and statements can be applied to interim periods as well.

Revenue-Recognition Principle

The **revenue-recognition principle** tells accountants

Objective 2

Apply the revenue-recognition and matching principles

- *When* to record revenue—that is, when to make a journal entry for a revenue.
- The *amount* of revenue to record.

Revenue, defined in Chapter 1, page 13, is the increase in owner's equity from delivering goods and services to customers in the course of operating a business. When we speak of "recording" something in accounting, we mean to make an entry in the journal. That is where the accounting process starts.

When to Record Revenue The revenue-recognition principle states that revenue should be recorded when it has been earned—but not before. In *most* cases, revenue is earned when the business has delivered a completed good or service to the customer. The business has done everything required by the agreement, including transferring the item to the customer.

Exhibit 3–2 shows two situations that provide guidance on when to record revenue. The first situation illustrates when *not* to record revenue, because the client merely states her plans. Situation 2 illustrates when revenue should be recorded—after SuperTravel has performed the service for the client.

| EXHIBIT 3–2 | Recording Revenue: The Revenue-Recognition Principle |

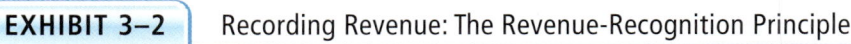

The Amount of Revenue to Record   The general principle is to record revenue equal to the cash value of the goods or the service transferred to the customer. Suppose that, in order to obtain a new client, SuperTravel performs travel service for the price of $1,000. Ordinarily, the business would have charged $1,200 for this service. How much revenue should the business record? The answer is $1,000 because that was the cash value of the transaction. SuperTravel will not receive the full value of $1,200, so that is not the amount of revenue to record. The business will receive only $1,000 cash, and that pinpoints the amount of revenue earned.

The Matching Principle

The **matching principle** is the basis for recording expenses. Recall that expenses—such as rent, utilities, and advertising—are the costs of assets and services that are consumed in the earning of revenue. The matching principle directs accountants to

1. Identify all expenses incurred during the accounting period.
2. Measure the expenses.
3. Match the expenses against the revenues earned during that period.

To match expenses against revenues means to subtract the related expenses from the revenues in order to compute net income or net loss. Exhibit 3–3 illustrates the matching principle.

There is a natural link between some expenses and revenues. Accountants follow the matching principle by first identifying the revenues of a period and then the expenses that can be linked to particular revenues. For example, a business that pays sales commissions to its sales persons will have commission expense if the employees make sales. If they make no sales, the business has no commission expense.

Other expenses are not so easy to link with particular sales. SuperTravel's monthly rent expense occurs, for example, regardless of the revenues earned during the period. The matching principle directs accountants to identify these types of expenses with a particular time period, such as a month or a year. If SuperTravel employs a secretary at a monthly salary of $2,300, the business will record salary expense of $2,300 each month.

How does SuperTravel bring its accounts up to date for preparing the financial statements? To address this question, accountants use the time period principle.

EXHIBIT 3–3   Recording Expenses: The Matching Principle

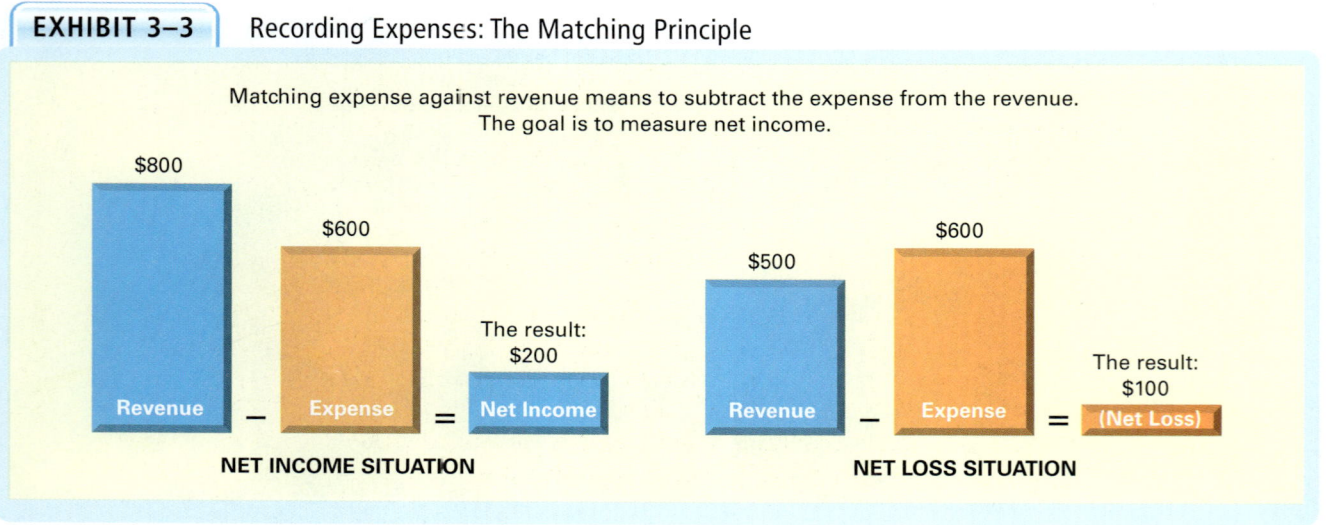

Time Period Principle

Managers, investors, and creditors make decisions daily and need periodic readings on the business's progress. Therefore, accountants prepare financial statements at regular intervals.

The **time period principle** ensures that accounting information is reported at regular intervals. It interacts with the accounting period, revenue-recognition principle, and matching principle to underlie the use of accruals. To measure income accurately, companies update the revenue and expense accounts immediately prior to the end of the period. The Royal Bank provides a real example of an expense accrual. The Royal Bank has an October 31 year end. When October 31 falls during a pay period—say on a Tuesday—and the Royal Bank pays its employees bi-weekly on Fridays, the company must record the employee compensation owed to the workers for unpaid services performed up to and including October 31. Assume weekly salary and wages expense for the Royal Bank's B.C. Division is $4,600,000; the entry to accrue the expense would be ($\frac{2}{5} \times \$4,600,000 = \$1,840,000$):

Oct. 31	Salary and Wages Expense..............................	1,840,000	
	Salary and Wages Payable...........................		1,840,000
	Accrued salary and wages expense for October 30 and 31.		

This entry serves two purposes. First, it assigns the expense to the proper period. Without the accrual entry at October 31, total expenses for the year would be understated, and, as a result, net income would be overstated. Incorrectly, the expense would fall in the following fiscal year when the Royal Bank makes the next payroll disbursement. Second, the accrual entry also records the liability for reporting on the balance sheet at October 31. Without the accrual entry, total liabilities would be understated.

At the end of the accounting period, companies also accrue revenues that have been earned but not collected. The remainder of the chapter discusses how to make the adjusting entries to bring the accounts up to date.

Adjusting the Accounts

Objective 3

Make adjusting entries

At the end of the period, the accountant prepares the financial statements. This end-of-the-period process begins with the trial balance that lists the accounts and their balances after the period's transactions have been recorded in the journal and posted to the accounts in the ledger. We prepared trial balances in Chapter 2.

Exhibit 3–4 is the trial balance of SuperTravel at April 30, 2008. (Accounts and balances differ from those in Chapter 2. Assume the company has been in business for one year.) This *unadjusted trial balance* includes some new accounts that will be explained here. It lists most, but not all, of the revenue accounts and the expenses of the travel agency for the month of April. These trial balance amounts are incomplete because they omit certain revenue and expense transactions that affect more than one accounting period. That is why the trial balance is *unadjusted*. In most cases, however, we refer to it simply as the trial balance, without the label "unadjusted."

Accrual-basis accounting requires adjusting entries at the end of the period in order to produce correct balances for the financial statements. To see why, consider the Supplies account in Exhibit 3–4.

SuperTravel uses supplies (an asset) in providing travel services for clients during the month. This use reduces the supplies on hand and creates an expense, just like salary expense or rent expense. It is not worth the effort to record supplies expense each time supplies are used. But by the end of the month, the Supplies balance of $1,400 on the unadjusted trial balance (Exhibit 3–4) is not correct. So how does the business account for supplies expense? SuperTravel must adjust the accounts at April 30.

When an asset is used up, it becomes an expense.

EXHIBIT 3–4 Unadjusted Trial Balance

SUPERTRAVEL
Unadjusted Trial Balance
April 30, 2008

Cash	$ 49,600	
Accounts receivable	4,500	
Supplies	1,400	
Prepaid insurance	4,200	
Furniture	36,000	
Accounts payable		$ 26,000
Unearned service revenue		900
John Lapp, capital		65,200
John Lapp, withdrawals	5,900	
Service revenue		14,000
Rent expense	1,800	
Salary expense	1,900	
Utilities expense	800	
Total	$106,100	$106,100

Adjusting entries assign revenues to the period in which they are earned and expenses to the period in which they are incurred. Adjusting entries also update the asset and liability accounts. They are needed to

1. Measure properly the period's income on the income statement.
2. Bring related asset and liability accounts to correct balances for the balance sheet.

The end-of-period process of updating the accounts is called *adjusting the accounts,* *making the adjusting entries,* or *adjusting the books.* This chapter shows the adjusting process as it moves from the trial balance to the adjusted trial balance.

Prepaids (Deferrals) and Accruals

Two basic types of adjustments are *prepaids* and *accruals.* In a *prepaid*-type adjustment, the cash transaction occurs before the related expense or revenue is recorded. Prepaids are also called *deferrals* because the recording of the expense or the revenue is deferred to periods after cash is paid or received. *Accrual*-type adjustments are the opposite of prepaids. For accruals we record the expense or revenue before the related cash is paid or received.

Adjusting entries can be further divided into five categories:

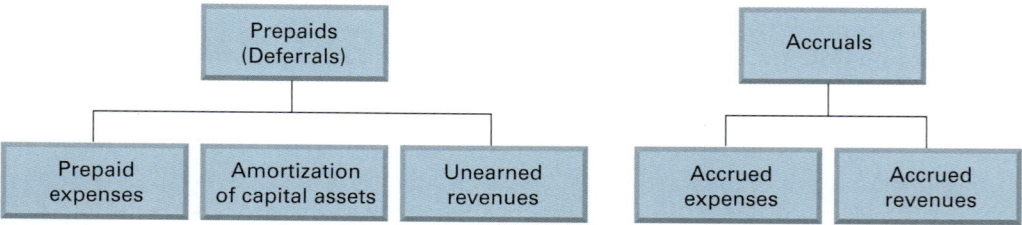

The core of this chapter is the discussion of these five types of adjusting entries on pages 107–116. Study this material carefully because it is the most challenging topic in all of introductory accounting.

Prepaid Expenses

Prepaid expenses are advance payments of expense. The category includes miscellaneous assets that typically expire or are used up in the near future. Prepaid rent and prepaid insurance are examples of prepaid expenses. They are called "prepaid" expenses because they are expenses that are paid in advance. Salary expense and utilities expense, among others, are typically *not* prepaid expenses because they are not paid in advance. All companies, large and small, must make adjustments regarding prepaid expenses. For example, Swiss Chalet makes prepayments for rents, packaging supplies, and insurance. Prepaid expenses are assets, not expenses.

Prepaid Insurance Automobile insurance is usually paid in advance. This prepayment creates an asset for the policyholder, because that person has purchased the future benefit of insurance protection. Suppose SuperTravel purchases insurance on April 1, 2008, for two automobiles. The cost of the insurance is $4,200. The entry to record the payment is a debit to the asset account, Prepaid Insurance, as follows:

Apr. 1	Prepaid Insurance..	4,200	
	Cash..		4,200
	Paid annual premium for automobile insurance.		

After posting, Prepaid Insurance appears as follows:

ASSETS
Prepaid Insurance

Apr. 1	4,200

The trial balance at April 30, 2008, lists Prepaid Insurance as an asset with a debit balance of $4,200. Throughout April, the Prepaid Insurance account maintains this beginning balance, as shown in Exhibit 3–4 (page 106). But $4,200 is *not* the amount of Prepaid Insurance for SuperTravel's balance sheet at April 30. Why?

At April 30, Prepaid Insurance should be adjusted to remove from its balance the amount of insurance that has been used up, which is one month's worth of the prepayment. By definition, the amount of an asset that has been used, or has expired, is an *expense*. The adjusting entry transfers one-twelfth, or $350 ($4,200 × $\frac{1}{12}$), of the debit balance from Prepaid Insurance to Insurance Expense. The debit side of the entry records an increase in Insurance Expense and the credit records a decrease in the asset Prepaid Insurance.

Apr. 30	Insurance Expense..	350	
	Prepaid Insurance		350
	To record insurance expense ($4,200 × $\frac{1}{12}$).		

After posting, Prepaid Insurance and Insurance Expense show correct ending balances as follows:

ASSETS					**EXPENSES**			
Prepaid Insurance					**Insurance Expense**			
Apr. 1	4,200	Apr. 30	350		Apr. 30	350		
Bal.	3,850				Bal.	350		

Correct asset amount, $3,850 → **Total accounted for, $4,200** ← Correct expense amount, $350

The full $4,200 has been accounted for. Eleven-twelfths measures the asset, and one-twelfth measures the expense. Recording this expense illustrates the matching principle.

The same analysis applies to a prepayment of twelve months' rent. The only difference is in the account titles, which would be Prepaid Rent and Rent Expense instead of Prepaid Insurance and Insurance Expense. In a computerized system, the adjusting entry crediting the prepaid account and debiting the expense account could be established to recur automatically in each subsequent accounting period until the prepaid account has a zero balance.

The chapter appendix shows an alternative treatment of prepaid expenses. The end result on the financial statements is the same as that for the method given here.

Supplies Supplies are accounted for the same way as prepaid expenses. On April 2, SuperTravel paid cash of $1,400 for office supplies.

Apr. 2	Supplies	1,400	
	Cash		1,400
	Paid cash for supplies.		

Assume that the business purchased no additional supplies during April. The April 30 trial balance, therefore, lists Supplies with a $1,400 debit balance as shown in Exhibit 3–4. But SuperTravel's April 30 balance sheet should *not* report supplies of $1,400. Why?

During April, SuperTravel used supplies in performing services for clients. The cost of the supplies used is the measure of *supplies expense* for the month. To measure SuperTravel's supplies expense during April, John Lapp counts the supplies on hand at the end of the month. This is the amount of the asset still available to the business. Assume the count indicates that supplies costing $800 remain. Subtracting the entity's $800 of supplies on hand at the end of April from the cost of supplies available during April ($1,400) measures supplies expense during the month ($600).

Cost of asset available during the period	−	Cost of asset on hand at the end of the period	=	Cost of asset used (expense) during the period
$1,400	−	$800	=	$600

The April 30 adjusting entry updates the Supplies account and records the supplies expense for April as follows:

Apr. 30	Supplies Expense...	600	
	Supplies		600
	To record supplies expense ($1,400 − $800).		

After posting, the Supplies and Supplies Expense accounts hold correct ending balances:

ASSETS		EXPENSES	
Supplies		**Supplies Expense**	
Apr. 2 1,400	Apr. 30 600 ⟶	Apr. 30 600	
Bal. 800		Bal. 600	

Correct asset amount, $800	→	Total accounted for, $1,400	←	Correct expense amount, $600

The Supplies account enters the month of May with an $800 balance, and the adjustment process is repeated each month.

Amortization of Capital Assets

The logic of the accrual basis of accounting is best illustrated by how businesses account for capital assets. **Capital assets** include long-lived *tangible* assets, such as land, buildings, furniture, machinery, and equipment, as well as long-lived *intangible* assets, such as patents and trademarks. All capital assets but land decline in usefulness as they age. This decline is an *expense* to the business. Accountants systematically spread the cost of each capital asset, except land, over the years of its useful life. The *CICA Handbook* calls this process of allocating the cost of a long-lived or capital asset to an expense account over its life **amortization**. (Another term for amortization in common usage is *depreciation*.) Land is the exception. We record no amortization for land.

LEARNING TIPS

An expense is recorded whenever a good or service is used. As capital assets are used, the portion of the cost that is used during the period is an expense called *amortization*.

Similarity to Prepaid Expenses The concept of accounting for capital assets and amortization expense is the same as for prepaid expenses. In a sense, capital assets are large prepaid expenses that expire over a number of periods. For both prepaid expenses and capital assets, the business purchases an asset that wears out or is used up. As the asset is used, more and more of its cost is transferred from the asset account to the expense account. The major difference between prepaid expenses and capital assets is the length of time it takes for the asset to lose its usefulness (or expire). Prepaid expenses usually expire within a year, whereas most capital assets remain useful for a number of years.

Consider SuperTravel's operations. Suppose that, on April 3, the business purchased furniture for $36,000 and made this journal entry:

Apr. 3   Furniture... 36,000
             Cash... 36,000
         Purchased office furniture.

After posting, the Furniture account appears as follows:

ASSETS
Furniture

Apr. 3   36,000

In accrual-basis accounting, an asset is recorded when the furniture is acquired. Then, a portion of the asset's cost is transferred from the asset account to Amortization Expense each period that the asset is used. This method matches the asset's expense to the revenue of the period, which is an application of the matching principle. In many computerized systems, the adjusting entry for amortization is programmed to occur automatically each month for the duration of the asset's life.

John Lapp believes the furniture will remain useful for five years and be virtually worthless at the end of its life. One way to compute the amount of amortization for each year is to divide the cost of the asset ($36,000 in our example) by its useful life (5 years). This procedure—called the straight-line method—gives annual amortization of $7,200 ($36,000/5 years = $7,200 per year). Amortization for the month of April is $600 ($7,200/12 months = $600 per month). Amortization expense for April is recorded by the following entry:

Apr. 30	Amortization Expense—Furniture	600	
	Accumulated Amortization—Furniture		600
	To record monthly amortization expense on furniture.		

The Accumulated Amortization Account   Accumulated Amortization is credited—not Furniture—because the original cost of the tangible capital asset should remain in the asset account as long as the business uses the asset. Accountants and managers may refer to the Furniture account to see how much the asset cost. This information is useful in a decision about whether to replace the furniture and the amount to pay. Accountants use the **Accumulated Amortization** account to show the cumulative sum of all amortization expense from the date of acquiring the tangible capital asset. Therefore, the balance in this account increases over the life of the asset—the account balance continues to "accumulate" over the life of the asset.

Accumulated Amortization is a *contra asset* account, which means an asset account with a normal credit balance. (Recall from Chapter 2, page 58, that the normal balance on an account marks the side of the account where increases are recorded.) A **contra account** has two main characteristics:

- A contra account has a companion account.
- A contra account's normal balance (debit or credit) is the opposite of the companion account's normal balance.

In this case, Accumulated Amortization—Furniture is the contra account that accompanies Furniture. It appears in the ledger directly after Furniture. Furniture has a debit balance, and therefore Accumulated Amortization—Furniture, a contra asset, has a credit balance. *All contra asset accounts have credit balances.*

A business carries an accumulated amortization or depreciation account for each depreciable tangible asset. If a business has a building and a machine, for example, it will carry the accounts Accumulated Amortization—Building, and Accumulated Amortization—Machine.

After posting the amortization, the Furniture, Accumulated Amortization—Furniture, and Amortization Expense accounts of SuperTravel are

ASSETS Furniture	CONTRA ASSET Accumulated Amortization— Furniture	EXPENSES Amortization Expense— Furniture
Apr. 3 36,000	Apr. 30 600	Apr. 30 600
Bal. 36,000	Bal. 600	Bal. 600

Carrying Value   The balance sheet reports both Furniture and Accumulated Amortization—Furniture. Because it is a contra account, the balance of Accumulated Amortization—Furniture is subtracted from the balance of Furniture. This net amount (cost minus accumulated amortization) of a capital asset is called its **carrying value,** or *net carrying value,* or *book value,* as shown on the next page for Furniture:

Furniture	$36,000	
Less: Accumulated Amortization—Furniture	600	
Carrying value..	$35,400	

Suppose SuperTravel owns a building that cost $96,000, on which annual amortization is $4,800. The amount of amortization for one month would be $400 ($4,800/12), and the following entry records amortization for April.

Apr. 30	Amortization Expense—Building.........................	400	
	Accumulated Amortization—Building...........		400
	To record monthly amortization on building.		

The balance sheet at April 30 would report SuperTravel's property, plant, and equipment (the general category for tangible capital assets) as shown in Exhibit 3–5.

EXHIBIT 3–5   Capital Assets on the Balance Sheet of SuperTravel (April 30)

Property, Plant, and Equipment

Furniture..	$36,000	
Less: Accumulated Amortization—Furniture..............	600	$ 35,400
Building	96,000	
Less: Accumulated Amortization—Building	400	95,600
Property, Plant, and Equipment, Net		$131,000

Exhibit 3–6 shows information about Sun-Rype Products Ltd., the company whose financial statements are in Appendix B of this text. In its 2005 financial statements, the balance sheet reports Property, Plant and Equipment of $22,312,000, and Note 4 of the financial statements shows the details. The first column shows the cost, the middle column shows the accumulated amortization, and the third column shows the net book value (carrying value) for each type of capital asset.

EXHIBIT 3–6   Sun-Rype Products Ltd. Reporting of Property, Plant, and Equipment (Amounts in Thousands)

From Note 4 of the financial statements:

	Cost	Accumulated Amortization	Net Book Value
Land	$ 170	$ –	$ 170
Building	16,475	11,487	4,988
Processing equipment	38,659	24,038	14,621
Other equipment	7,850	5,317	2,533
Total	$63,154	$40,842	$22,312

Let's now return to SuperTravel's situation.

Accrued Expenses

Businesses incur many expenses before they pay cash. Payment is not due until later. Consider an employee's salary. The employer's salary expense and salary payable grow as the employee works, so the liability is said to *accrue*. Another example is interest expense on a note payable. Interest accrues as time passes. The term **accrued expense** refers to an expense that the business has incurred but has not yet recorded. An accrued expense always creates a liability. Therefore, accrued expenses can be viewed as the opposite of prepaid expenses.

KEY POINT

A prepaid expense is paid first and expensed later. An accrued expense is expensed first and paid later. Prepaids and accruals are opposites.

It is time-consuming to make hourly, daily, or even weekly journal entries to accrue expenses. Consequently, the accountant waits until the end of the period. Then an adjusting entry brings each expense (and related liability) up to date just before the financial statements are prepared.

Accruing Salary Expense Most companies pay their employees at predetermined times. Suppose SuperTravel pays its employee a monthly salary of $3,800, half on the 15th and half on the last day of the month. Here is a calendar for April with the two paydays circled:

			APRIL			
S	M	T	W	T	F	S
					1	2
3	4	5	6	7	8	9
10	11	12	13	14	(15)	16
17	18	19	20	21	22	23
24	25	26	27	28	29	(30)

Assume that, if either payday falls on a weekend, SuperTravel pays the employee on the following Monday. During April, the travel agency paid its employee's first half-month salary of $1,900 on Friday, April 15, and recorded the following entry:

Apr. 15	Salary Expense	1,900	
	Cash...		1,900
	To pay salary.		

After posting, the Salary Expense account is

EXPENSES
Salary Expense

Apr. 15	1,900	

The trial balance at April 30 (Exhibit 3–4, page 106) includes Salary Expense, with its debit balance of $1,900. Because April 30, the second payday of the month, falls on a Saturday, the second half-month amount of $1,900 will be paid on Monday, May 2. Without an adjusting entry, this second $1,900 amount is not included in the April 30 trial balance amount for Salary Expense. Therefore, at April 30, the business adjusts for additional *salary expense* and *salary payable* of $1,900 by recording an increase in each of these accounts as follows:

Apr. 30	Salary Expense	1,900	
	Salary Payable		1,900
	To accrue salary expense.		

After posting, the Salary Expense and Salary Payable accounts are updated to April 30:

EXPENSES			**LIABILITIES**		
Salary Expense			**Salary Payable**		
Apr.15	1,900			Apr. 30	1,900
Apr. 30	1,900			Bal.	1,900
Bal.	3,800				

The accounts at April 30 now contain the complete salary information for the month of April. The expense account has a full month's salary, and the liability account shows the portion that the business still owes at April 30. SuperTravel will record the payment of this liability on Monday, May 2.

This payment entry does not affect April or May expenses because the April expense was recorded on April 15 and April 30. May expense will be recorded in a like manner, starting on May 15. All accrued expenses are recorded with similar entries—a debit to the appropriate expense account and a credit to the related liability account.

(In reality, most companies pay their employees on the last business day *before* the end of the period, to allow employees to make rent and other payments due at the beginning of the month. In such a situation, no accrual for Salary Expense would be made.)

STOP AND THINK

Weekly salaries for a five-day workweek total $3,500, payable on a Friday. This year November 30 falls on a Tuesday.

1. Which accounts require adjustment at November 30?
2. Make the adjusting entry.

Answers:

1. Salary Expense and Salary Payable require adjustment.
2. Salary Expense 1,400
       Salary Payable   1,400
     To accrue salary expense ($3,500 $\times$ $^2/_5$).

Accrued Revenues

As we have just seen, expenses can occur before the cash payment, and that creates an accrued expense. Likewise, businesses often earn revenue before they collect the cash. Collection occurs later. A revenue that has been earned but not yet collected is called an **accrued revenue.**

Assume SuperTravel is hired on April 15 by Rutledge Tours Co. to make travel arrangements on a monthly basis. Under this agreement, Rutledge will pay SuperTravel $1,000 monthly, with the first payment on May 15. During April, SuperTravel will earn half a month's fee, $500, for work performed April 15 through April 30. On April 30, SuperTravel makes the following adjusting entry to record an increase in Accounts Receivable and Service Revenue:

Apr. 30   Accounts Receivable   500
              Service Revenue...   500
        To accrue service revenue ($1,000 $\times$ $^1/_2$).

We see from the unadjusted trial balance in Exhibit 3–4 (page 106) that Accounts Receivable has an unadjusted balance of $4,500. The Service Revenue unadjusted balance is $14,000. Posting the April 30 adjustment has the following effects on these two accounts:

ASSETS Accounts Receivable				REVENUES Service Revenue	
	4,500				14,000
Apr. 30	500			Apr. 30	500
Bal.	5,000			Bal.	14,500

This adjusting entry illustrates the revenue principle. Without the adjustment, the travel agency's financial statements would be misleading—they would understate Accounts Receivable and Service Revenue by $500 each. All accrued revenues are accounted for similarly: Debit a receivable and credit a revenue.

We now turn to a different category of adjusting entries.

Unearned Revenues

KEY POINT

An unearned revenue is a liability, not a revenue. With all unearned revenue, cash is received before the work is performed or the goods are delivered.

Some businesses collect cash from customers in advance of doing work for them. Receiving cash in advance creates a liability called **unearned revenue** or **deferred revenue.** The company owes a product or service to the customer. Only when the job is completed will the business have earned the revenue.

Suppose a law firm engages SuperTravel to provide services, agreeing to pay the travel agency $900 monthly in advance beginning immediately. Suppose SuperTravel receives in advance the first payment on April 20. SuperTravel records the cash receipt and the related increase in the business's liabilities as follows:

Apr. 20   Cash..   900
          Unearned Service Revenue   900
       Received revenue in advance.

After posting, the liability account appears as follows:

LIABILITIES
Unearned Service Revenue

	Apr. 20 900

THINKING IT OVER

In which, if any, of the five categories of adjusting entries would the following transactions fall?

(1) Paid one year's insurance in advance.
(2) Recorded part of a building's cost as an expense for the current period.
(3) Recorded revenue from renting a building before receiving cash.
(4) Paid a bill for maintenance of company automobiles.

A: (1) Prepaid expense
    (2) Amortization
    (3) Accrued revenue
    (4) No adjusting entry necessary

Unearned Service Revenue is a liability because it represents SuperTravel's obligation to perform service for the client. The April 30 unadjusted trial balance (Exhibit 3–4) lists Unearned Service Revenue with a $900 credit balance prior to the adjusting entries. During the last 10 days of the month—April 21 through April 30—the travel agency will have *earned* one-third (10 days divided by April's total 30 days) of the $900, or $300. Therefore, the accountant makes the following adjustment to decrease the liability, Unearned Service Revenue, and to record an increase in Service Revenue as follows:

Apr. 30   Unearned Service Revenue   300
          Service Revenue...   300
       To record service revenue that was collected in advance ($900 × $\frac{1}{3}$).

This adjusting entry shifts $300 of the total amount of unearned service revenue from the liability account to the revenue account. After posting, the balance of Service Revenue is increased by $300 and the balance of Unearned Service Revenue has been reduced by $300 to $600. Now, both accounts have their correct balances at April 30, as follows:

What is the result on the financial statements of omitting the adjusting entry for unearned service revenue?

A: Liabilities are overstated by $300; revenues, net income, and owner's equity are understated by $300.

LIABILITIES				REVENUES	
Unearned Service Revenue				**Service Revenue**	
Apr. 30	**300**	Apr. 20	900		14,000
		Bal.	600	Apr. 30	500
				Apr. 30	**300**
				Bal.	14,800

Correct liability amount, $600 → **Total accounted for, $900** ← **Correct revenue amount, $300**

All types of revenues that are collected in advance are accounted for similarly. Remember, an unearned revenue is a liability, not a revenue.

An unearned revenue to one company is a prepaid expense to the company that made the payment. Consider the law firm in the preceding example. The law firm had prepaid travel expense—an asset. SuperTravel had unearned service revenue—a liability.

STOP AND THINK

Consider the tuition you pay. Assume that one semester's tuition costs $2,000 and that you make a single payment at the start of the term. Journalize the tuition transaction on your own books and on the books of your college or university.

Answer:

Start of semester:

Your Entries			**Your College's Entries**		
Prepaid Tuition	2,000		Cash	2,000	
Cash		2,000	Unearned Tuition		
Paid semester tuition.			Revenue		2,000
			Received revenue in advance.		

End of semester:

Tuition Expense	2,000		Unearned Tuition Revenue	2,000	
Prepaid Tuition		2,000	Tuition Revenue		2,000
To record tuition expense.			To record unearned tuition revenue that has been earned.		

Exhibit 3–7 on page 116 diagrams the timing of prepaid-type and accrual-type adjusting entries. The chapter appendix shows an alternate treatment of unearned revenues and prepaid expenses.

Summary of the Adjusting Process

The adjusting process has two purposes:

1. Measure accurately net income or net loss on the *income statement*. Every adjusting entry affects either a *Revenue* or an *Expense*.

2. Update the *balance sheet*. Every adjusting entry affects either an *Asset* or a *Liability*.

No adjusting entry debits or credits Cash because the cash transactions are recorded at other times. (The exception to this rule is when an adjusting entry is made to correct an error involving Cash.)

PREPAIDS—The cash transaction occurs initially. (The expense is incurred or the revenue is earned later.)

	Initially		Later

Prepaid expenses	Pay expense in advance and record an asset:
	Prepaid Expense (e.g. Insurance).. 4,200
	    Cash 4,200
		→	Record the expense later and decrease the asset:
			Expense (e.g. Insurance).................... 350
			    Prepaid Expense (e.g. Insurance) .. 350

Unearned revenues	Receive cash in advance and record unearned revenue (a liability):
	Cash.. 900
	    Unearned Revenue (e.g. Travel) 900
		→	Record the revenue later and decrease unearned revenue:
			Unearned Revenue (eg. Travel)....... 300
			    Revenue (e.g. Travel Service)....... 300

ACCRUALS—The cash transaction occurs later. (The expense is incurred or the revenue is earned first.)

	Initially		Later

Accrued expenses	Record (accrue) an expense first and the related payable:
	Expense (e.g. Salary)....................... 1,900
	    Payable (e.g. Salary) 1,900
		→	Pay the liability later.
			
			Payable (e.g. Salary).......................... 1,900
			    Cash (e.g. Salary).......................... 1,900

Accrued revenues	Record (accrue) a revenue first and the related receivable:
	Receivable (e.g. from customer).... 500
	    Revenue (e.g. Travel service).... 500
		→	Collect cash later:
			
			Cash.. 500
			    Receivable (e.g. from customer) ... 500

The authors thank Darrel Davis and Alfonso Oddo for suggesting this exhibit.
*See the Appendix of this chapter for an alternative treatment of accounting for prepaids and accruals.

Exhibit 3–8 summarizes the adjusting entries. Exhibit 3–9 on page 117 summarizes the adjusting entries of SuperTravel at April 30. The adjustments are identified by their letter.

- Panel A of the exhibit briefly describes the data for each adjustment.
- Panel B gives the adjusting entries.
- Panel C shows the accounts after they have been posted.

EXHIBIT 3–8 | Summary of Adjusting Entries

	Type of Account	
Category of Adjusting Entry	**Debited**	**Credited**
Prepaid expense	Expense	Asset
Amortization	Expense	Contra asset
Accrued expense	Expense	Liability
Accrued revenue	Asset	Revenue
Unearned revenue	Liability	Revenue

Adapted from material provided by Beverly Terry.

The Adjusted Trial Balance

Objective 4

Prepare an adjusted trial balance

This chapter began with the trial balance before any adjusting entries—the unadjusted trial balance (Exhibit 3–4). After the adjustments are journalized and posted, the accounts appear as shown in Exhibit 3–9, Panel C. A useful step in

PANEL A: Information for Adjustments at April 30, 2008

a. Prepaid insurance expired during April, $350.
b. Supplies remaining on hand at April 30, 2008, $800.
c. Amortization on furniture for the month of April, $600.
d. Accrued salary expense, $1,900.
e. Accrued service revenue, $500.
f. Amount of unearned service revenue that was earned during April, $300.

PANEL B: Adjusting Entries

a.	Insurance Expense	350	
	Prepaid Insurance		350
	To record insurance expense.		
b.	Supplies Expense	600	
	Supplies		600
	To record supplies used.		
c.	Amortization Expense—Furniture	600	
	Accumulated Amortization—Furniture		600
	To record amortization on furniture.		
d.	Salary Expense	1,900	
	Salary Payable		1,900
	To accrue salary expense.		
e.	Accounts Receivable	500	
	Service Revenue		500
	To accrue service revenue.		
f.	Unearned Service Revenue...	300	
	Service Revenue		300
	To record unearned revenue that has been earned.		

PANEL C: Ledger Accounts

ASSETS

Cash

Bal. 49,600	

Accounts Receivable

Bal. 4,500	
(e) 500	
Bal. 5,000	

Supplies

Bal. 1,400	(b) 600
Bal. 800	

Prepaid Insurance

Bal. 4,200	(a) 350
Bal. 3,850	

Furniture

Bal. 36,000	

Accumulated Amortization— Furniture

	(c) 600
	Bal. 600

LIABILITIES

Accounts Payable

	Bal. 26,000

Salary Payable

	(d) 1,900
	Bal. 1,900

Unearned Service Revenue

(f) 300	Bal. 900
	Bal. 600

OWNER'S EQUITY

John Lapp, Capital

	Bal. 65,200

John Lapp, Withdrawals

Bal. 5,900	

REVENUES

Service Revenue

	Bal. 14,000
	(e) 500
	(f) 300
	Bal. 14,800

EXPENSES

Amortization Expense— Furniture

(c) 600	
Bal. 600	

Insurance Expense

(a) 350	
Bal. 350	

Rent Expense

Bal. 1,800	

Salary Expense

Bal. 1,900	
(d) 1,900	
Bal. 3,800	

Supplies Expense

(b) 600	
Bal. 600	

Utilities Expense

Bal. 800	

preparing the financial statements is to list the accounts, along with their adjusted balances, on an **adjusted trial balance.** This document has the advantage of listing all the accounts and their adjusted balances in a single place. Exhibit 3–10 shows the preparation of the adjusted trial balance.

Exhibit 3–10 shows the first six columns of a *work sheet.* We will consider the complete work sheet in Chapter 4. For now, simply note how clearly this format presents the data. The information in the Account Title column and in the Trial Balance columns is drawn directly from the ledger. The two Adjustments columns list the debit and credit adjustments directly across from the appropriate account title. Each adjusting debit and credit is identified by a letter in parentheses that refers to the adjusting entry in Exhibit 3–9. For example, the debit labelled (a) on the work sheet refers to the debit adjusting entry of $350 to Insurance Expense in Panel B of Exhibit 3–9. The corresponding credit—labelled (a)—refers to the $350 credit to Prepaid Insurance.

The Adjusted Trial Balance columns give the adjusted account balances. Each amount on the adjusted trial balance of Exhibit 3–10 is computed by combining the amounts from the unadjusted trial balance plus or minus the adjustments. For example, Accounts Receivable starts with a debit balance of $4,500. Adding the $500 debit amount from adjusting entry (e) gives Accounts Receivable an adjusted balance of $5,000. Supplies begins with a debit balance of $1,400. After the $600 credit adjustment, its adjusted balance is $800. More than one entry may affect a single account, as is the case for Service Revenue. If an account is unaffected by the adjustments, it will show the same amount on both the adjusted and unadjusted trial balances. This is true for the Cash, Furniture, Accounts Payable, and John Lapp, Withdrawals accounts, to name a few.

EXHIBIT 3–10 | Preparation of Adjusted Trial Balance

SUPERTRAVEL
Preparation of Adjusted Trial Balance
April 30, 2008

Account Title	Trial Balance Debit	Trial Balance Credit	Adjustments Debit	Adjustments Credit	Adjusted Trial Balance Debit	Adjusted Trial Balance Credit	
Cash	49,600				49,600		Balance Sheet (Exhibit 3-13)
Accounts receivable	4,500		(e) 500		5,000		
Supplies	1,400			(b) 600	800		
Prepaid insurance	4,200			(a) 350	3,850		
Furniture	36,000				36,000		
Accumulated amortization		0		(c) 600		600	
Accounts payable		26,000				26,000	
Salary payable		0		(d) 1,900		1,900	
Unearned service revenue		900	(f) 300			600	
John Lapp, capital		65,200				65,200	Statement of Owner's Equity (Exhibit 3-12)
John Lapp, withdrawals	5,900				5,900		
Service revenue		14,000		(e) 500		14,800	
				(f) 300			
Amortization expense	0		(c) 600		600		Income Statement (Exhibit 3-11)
Insurance expense	0		(a) 350		350		
Rent expense	1,800				1,800		
Salary expense	1,900		(d) 1,900		3,800		
Supplies expense	0		(b) 600		600		
Utilities expense	800				800		
	106,100	106,100	4,250	4,250	109,100	109,100	

A large company would use accounting software to print out a trial balance. For example, at Nexen Inc., a multidivisional company that locates, produces, and transports oil and natural gas, each division has its own accounting software that prints a monthly trial balance. The accountants then analyze the amounts on the trial balance. This analysis results in the adjusting entries. Nexen posts the adjusting entries to update its ledger accounts. The trial balance has now become the company's *adjusted* trial balance. At Nexen, the adjusted trial balances from all divisions are consolidated, or grouped.

Preparing the Financial Statements from the Adjusted Trial Balance

The April financial statements of SuperTravel can be prepared from the adjusted trial balance in Exhibit 3–10. The right margin shows how the accounts are distributed from the adjusted trial balance to three of the four main financial statements.

Objective 5

Prepare the financial statements from the adjusted trial balance

- The income statement (Exhibit 3–11) comes from the revenue and expense accounts.
- The statement of owner's equity (Exhibit 3–12) shows the reasons for the change in the owner's capital account during the period.
- The balance sheet (Exhibit 3–13) reports the assets, liabilities, and owner's equity.

The financial statements are best prepared in the order shown: the income statement first, followed by the statement of owner's equity, and then the balance sheet. The essential features of all financial statements are:

Heading:
- Name of the entity
- Title of the statement
- Date of the statement, or period covered by the statement

Body of the statement

Many large companies list expenses in descending order by amount, as shown in Exhibit 3–11; many small and medium-sized companies list expenses in alphabetical order. However, Miscellaneous Expense, a catch-all account for expenses that do not fit another category, is usually reported last. Miscellaneous Expense should be a relatively low dollar amount. If it is not, new expense accounts should be created.

Relationships among the Three Financial Statements

The arrows in Exhibits 3–11, 3–12, and 3–13 illustrate the relationship among the income statement, the statement of owner's equity, and the balance sheet. (The relationships among the financial statements were introduced in Chapter 1, page 21.) Consider why the income statement is prepared first and the balance sheet last.

 Student CD-ROM

Accounting Cycle Tutorials
5. Financial Statements pages
  1–10

1. The income statement reports net income or net loss, calculated by subtracting expenses from revenues. Because revenues and expenses are owner's equity accounts, their net figure is then transferred to the statement of owner's equity. Note that net income in Exhibit 3–11, $6,850, increases owner's equity in Exhibit 3–12. A net loss would decrease owner's equity.

2. Capital is a balance sheet account, so the ending balance in the statement of owner's equity is transferred to the balance sheet. This amount is the final balancing element of the balance sheet. To solidify your understanding of this relationship, trace the $66,150 figure from Exhibit 3–12 to Exhibit 3–13.

EXHIBIT 3–11 Income Statement

SUPERTRAVEL
Income Statement
For the Month Ended April 30, 2008

Revenue:		
Service revenue		$14,800
Expenses:		
Salary expense..	$3,800	
Rent expense...	1,800	
Utilities expense...	800	
Supplies expense..	600	
Amortization expense...................................	600	
Insurance expense	350	
Total expenses		7,950
Net income		$ 6,850

EXHIBIT 3–12 Statement of Owner's Equity

①

SUPERTRAVEL
Statement of Owner's Equity
For the Month Ended April 30, 2008

John Lapp, capital, April 1, 2008	$65,200
Add: Net income	6,850
	72,050
Less: Withdrawals	5,900
John Lapp, capital, April 30, 2008	$66,150

EXHIBIT 3–13 Balance Sheet

②

SUPERTRAVEL
Balance Sheet
April 30, 2008

Assets			Liabilities		
Cash		$49,600	Accounts payable		$26,000
Accounts receivable ...		5,000	Salary payable...................		1,900
Supplies........................		800	Unearned service		
Prepaid insurance.......		3,850	revenue		600
Furniture	$36,000		Total liabilities		28,500
Less: Accumulated					
amortization.............	600	35,400	**Owner's Equity**		
			John Lapp, capital.............		66,150
			Total liabilities and		
Total assets...................		$94,650	owner's equity................		$94,650

You may be wondering why the total assets on the balance sheet ($94,650 in Exhibit 3–13) do not equal the total debits on the adjusted trial balance ($109,100 in Exhibit 3–10). Likewise, the total liabilities and owner's equity do not equal the total credits on the adjusted trial balance ($109,100 in Exhibit 3–10). One reason for these differences is that Accumulated Amortization and John Lapp, Withdrawals are contra accounts. Recall that contra accounts are *subtracted* from their companion accounts on the balance sheet. However, on the adjusted trial balance, contra accounts are *added* as a debit or credit in their respective columns.

STOP AND THINK

Examine SuperTravel's adjusted trial balance in Exhibit 3–10. Suppose the accountant forgot to record the $1,900 accrual of salary expense at April 30. What net income would the travel agency have reported for April? What total assets, total liabilities, and total owner's equity would the balance sheet have reported at April 30?

Answer: Omission of the salary accrual would produce these effects:

1. Net income on the income statement (Exhibit 3–11) would have been $8,750 ($6,850 + $1,900).

2. Total assets would have been unaffected by the error—$94,650, as reported on the balance sheet (Exhibit 3–13).

3. Total liabilities on the balance sheet (Exhibit 3–13) would have been $26,600 ($28,500 − $1,900).

4. Owner's equity on the balance sheet (Exhibit 3–13) would have been $68,050 ($66,150 + $1,900).

Ethical Issues in Accrual Accounting

Like most other aspects of life, accounting poses ethical challenges. At the most basic level, accountants must be honest in their work. Only with honest and complete information, including accounting data, can people expect to make wise decisions. An example will illustrate the importance of ethics in accrual accounting.

SuperTravel has been quite successful and so John Lapp decides to open a second SuperTravel office. He needs to borrow $50,000. Suppose SuperTravel understated expenses purposely in order to inflate net income as reported on the company's income statement. A banker could be tricked into lending money to SuperTravel. Then if SuperTravel could not repay the loan, the bank would lose money—all because the banker relied on incorrect accounting information.

Accrual accounting provides several opportunities for unethical accounting. Recall from earlier in this chapter that amortization expense is an estimated figure. No business can foresee exactly how long its buildings and equipment will last, so accountants must estimate these assets' useful lives. Accountants then record amortization on capital assets over their *estimated* useful lives. A dishonest proprietor could buy a five-year asset and amortize it over 10 years. For each of the first five years, the company will report less amortization expense, and more net income, than it should. Or a dishonest business owner could overlook amortization expense altogether. Failing to record amortization would overstate net income. In both these situations, people who rely on the company's financial statements, such as bank lenders, can be deceived into doing business with the company. Accounting information must be honest and complete—completely ethical—to serve its intended purpose. As you progress through introductory accounting, you will see other situations that challenge the ethics of accountants.

The cash basis of accounting poses fewer ethical challenges because cash is not an estimated figure. Either the company has the cash, or it does not. Therefore, the amount of cash a company reports is rarely disputed. By contrast, adjusting entries for accrued expenses, accrued revenues, and amortization often must be estimated. Whenever there is an estimate, the accountant must often deal with pressure from managers or owners of the business to use the adjusting process to make the company look different from its true condition. The rules of conduct of the various professional accounting associations (discussed in Chapter 1) prohibit accountants from being associated with false or misleading financial information. Even with added ethical challenges, the accrual basis provides more complete accounting information than the cash basis. That is why accounting rests on the accrual basis.

As we conclude this chapter, we return to our opening question: What is the adjusting process and why is it important? It all comes down to the advantages of accrual-basis accounting over cash-basis accounting. The Decision Guidelines feature summarizes all of our chapter-opening questions and provides a map of the adjusting process that leads up to the adjusted trial balance.

DECISION GUIDELINES — Measuring Business Income: The Adjusting Process

Decision	Guidelines
Which basis of accounting better measures income (revenues 2 expenses)?	*Accrual basis*, because it provides more complete reports of operating performance
How do you measure Revenues? Expenses?	Revenue-recognition principle Matching principle
Where do you start when you want to measure income at the end of the period?	Unadjusted trial balance, usually referred to simply as the *trial balance*
How do you update the accounts for preparation of the financial statements?	*Adjusting entries* at the end of the accounting period
What are the categories of adjusting entries?	Prepaid expenses Amortization of capital assets Accrued expenses Accrued revenues Unearned revenues

How do the adjusting entries differ from other journal entries?	1. Adjusting entries are usually made at the end of the accounting period.
	2. Adjusting entries never affect cash (except to correct errors).
	3. All adjusting entries debit or credit
	  • At least one *income statement* account (a **Revenue** or an **Expense**)
	    and
	  • At least one *balance sheet* account (an **Asset** or a **Liability**)

Which statements summarizes the accounts with their adjusted balances?	*Adjusted trial balance*, which becomes the basis for preparing the financial statements

The trial balance of Clay Employment Services pertains to December 31, 2008, which is the end of its year-long accounting period.

CLAY EMPLOYMENT SERVICES
Trial Balance
December 31, 2008

Cash	$ 6,900	
Accounts receivable	5,000	
Supplies	1,000	
Furniture	10,000	
Accumulated amortization—furniture		$ 4,000
Building	50,000	
Accumulated amortization—building		30,000
Land	22,000	
Accounts payable		2,000
Salary payable		0
Unearned service revenue		8,000
Jay Clay, capital		32,000
Jay Clay, withdrawals	25,000	
Service revenue		60,000
Salary expense	16,000	
Supplies expense	0	
Amortization expense—furniture	0	
Amortization expense—building	0	
Miscellaneous expense	100	
Total	$136,000	$136,000

Data needed for the adjusting entries include:

a. A count of supplies shows $200 of unused supplies on hand on December 31.

b. Amortization for the year on furniture, $2,000

c. Amortization for the year on building, $1,000

d. Salary owed but not yet paid, $500

e. Accrued service revenue, $1,300

f. Of the $8,000 balance of unearned service revenue, $3,000 was earned during the year.

Required

1. Open the ledger accounts with their unadjusted balances using T-account format.

2. Journalize Clay Employment Services' adjusting entries at December 31, 2008. Identify entries by their letter as in Exhibit 3–9 (page 117).

3. Write the trial balance on a work sheet, enter the adjusting entries, and prepare an adjusted trial balance, as shown in Exhibit 3–10 (page 118).

4. Prepare the income statement, the statement of owner's equity, and the balance sheet. Draw the arrows linking these three statements.

5. Post the adjusting entries into the T-accounts.

Name: Clay Employment Services
Industry: Service proprietorship
Fiscal Period: Year ended December 31, 2008
Key Fact: Existing, ongoing business

Solution

Requirements 1 and 5

For Requirement 1, create a T-account for each account name listed in the December 31, 2008, trial balance on the previous page. Insert the opening balances into the T-accounts from the trial balance, ensuring debit and credit balances on the trial balance are debit and credit balances in the T-accounts. To make sure all the account balances have been entered correctly, trace each T-account's balance back to the December 31, 2008, trial balance.

For Requirement 5, make sure each transaction is posted to the proper T-account, and make sure no transactions were missed.

ASSETS

Cash

Bal. 6,900	

Accounts Receivable

Bal. 5,000	
(e) 1,300	
Bal. 6,300	

Supplies

Bal. 1,000	(a) 800
Bal. 200	

Furniture

Bal. 10,000	

Accumulated Amortization—Furniture

	Bal. 4,000
	(b) 2,000
	Bal. 6,000

Building

Bal. 50,000	

Accumulated Amortization—Building

	Bal. 30,000
	(c) 1,000
	Bal. 31,000

Land

Bal. 22,000	

LIABILITIES

Accounts Payable

	Bal. 2,000

Salary Payable

	(d) 500
	Bal. 500

Unearned Service Revenue

(f) 3,000	Bal. 8,000
	Bal. 5,000

OWNER'S EQUITY

Jay Clay, Capital

	Bal. 32,000

Jay Clay, Withdrawals

Bal. 25,000	

REVENUE

Service Revenue

	Bal. 60,000
	(e) 1,300
	(f) 3,000
	Bal. 64,300

EXPENSES

Salary Expense

Bal. 16,000	
(d) 500	
Bal. 16,500	

Supplies Expense

(a) 800	
Bal. 800	

Amortization Expense—Furniture

(b) 2,000	
Bal. 2,000	

Amortization Expense—Building

(c) 1,000	
Bal. 1,000	

Miscellaneous Expense

Bal. 100	

Refer to the rules of debit and credit shown in Chapter 2, Exhibit 2–8 on page 58.

Make sure that Assets = Liabilities + Owner's Equity for each transaction before going to the next transaction.

Selected transactions are explained more fully:

a. On the December 31, 2008, trial balance, Supplies has a balance of $1,000. If the supplies on hand at year end are $200, then make an adjusting entry for the $800 of supplies that were used ($1,000 − $200). Increase Supplies Expense (expense) and decrease Supplies (assets).

The remaining transactions do not require further calculations to determine the amounts of the adjustments.

Requirement 2

2008

a. Dec. 31	Supplies Expense		800	
	Supplies			800
	To record supplies used ($1,000 − $200).			
b. Dec. 31	Amortization Expense—Furniture		2,000	
	Accumulated Amortization—Furniture			2,000
	To record amortization expense on furniture.			
c. Dec. 31	Amortization Expense—Building		1,000	
	Accumulated Amortization—Building			1,000
	To record amortization expense on building.			
d. Dec. 31	Salary Expense		500	
	Salary Payable			500
	To accrue salary expense.			
e. Dec. 31	Accounts Receivable		1,300	
	Service Revenue			1,300
	To accrue service revenue.			
f. Dec. 31	Unearned Service Revenue		3,000	
	Service Revenue			3,000
	To record unearned service revenue that has been earned.			

Requirement 3

Write the account balances from the December 31, 2008, trial balance in the first two columns (the Trial Balance columns). Write the adjustment amounts from Requirement 2 in the next two columns. For each account name, add across (or subtract) the amounts in the first four columns to fill in the Adjusted Trial Balance columns. Ensure total debits equal total credits for each pair of columns, then double underline the totals to show they are final.

CLAY EMPLOYMENT SERVICES
Preparation of Adjusted Trial Balance
December 31, 2008

Account Title	Trial Balance Debit	Trial Balance Credit	Adjustments Debit	Adjustments Credit	Adjusted Trial Balance Debit	Adjusted Trial Balance Credit
Cash	6,900				6,900	
Accounts receivable	5,000		(e) 1,300		6,300	
Supplies	1,000			(a) 800	200	
Furniture	10,000				10,000	
Accumulated amortization —furniture		4,000		(b) 2,000		6,000
Building	50,000				50,000	
Accumulated amortization —building		30,000		(c) 1,000		31,000
Land	22,000				22,000	
Accounts payable		2,000				2,000
Salary payable		0		(d) 500		500
Unearned service revenue		8,000	(f) 3,000			5,000
Jay Clay, capital		32,000				32,000
Jay Clay, withdrawals	25,000				25,000	
Service revenue		60,000		(e) 1,300		64,300
				(f) 3,000		
Salary expense	16,000		(d) 500		16,500	
Supplies expense	0		(a) 800		800	
Amortization expense —furniture	0		(b) 2,000		2,000	
Amortization expense —building	0		(c) 1,000		1,000	
Miscellaneous expense	100				100	
	136,000	136,000	8,600	8,600	140,800	140,800

The title must include the name of the company, "Income Statement," and the specific period of time covered. It is critical that the time period is defined.

Gather all the revenue and expense account names and amounts from the Debit and Credit Adjusted Trial Balance columns of the worksheet.

Expenses are listed here from highest to lowest dollar amount, with Miscellaneous Expense always listed as the final expense item. They could be also be listed alphabetically.

CLAY EMPLOYMENT SERVICES
Income Statement
For the Year Ended December 31, 2008

Revenues:		
Service revenue..		$64,300
Expenses:		
Salary expense...	$16,500	
Amortization expense—furniture.............................	2,000	
Amortization expense—building..............................	1,000	
Supplies expense	800	
Miscellaneous expense	100	
Total expenses		20,400
Net income		$43,900

The title must include the name of company, "Statement of Owner's Equity," and the specific period of time covered. It is critical that the time period is defined.

CLAY EMPLOYMENT SERVICES
Statement of Owner's Equity
For the Year Ended December 31, 2008

J. Clay, capital, January 1, 2008	$32,000
Add: Net income...	43,900
	75,900
Less: Withdrawals...	25,000
J. Clay, capital, December 31, 2008	$50,900

Beginning owner's equity and withdrawals are from the Adjusted Trial Balance columns of the worksheet.

The net income amount is transferred from the income statement.

The title must include the name of the company, "Balance Sheet," and the date of the balance sheet. It shows the financial position on one specific date.

CLAY EMPLOYMENT SERVICES
Balance Sheet
December 31, 2008

Assets			Liabilities		
Cash...........................		$ 6,900	Accounts payable		$ 2,000
Accounts			Salary payable.........................		500
receivable................		6,300	Unearned service revenue.....		5,000
Supplies		200	Total liabilities.....................		7,500
Furniture....................	$10,000				
Less: Accumulated			**Owner's Equity**		
amortization	6,000	4,000	J. Clay, capital.........................		50,900
Building	$50,000				
Less: Accumulated					
amortization	31,000	19,000			
Land		22,000			
			Total liabilities and		
Total assets...............		$58,400	owner's equity.....................		$ 58,400

Gather all the asset and liability accounts and amounts from the Adjusted Trial Balance columns of the worksheet. The owner's equity amount is transferred from the statement of owner's equity.

It is vital that Total assets = Total liabilities + Owner's equity.

Summary

1. **Distinguish accrual-basis accounting from cash-basis accounting.** In *accrual accounting*, business events are recorded as they occur. In *cash-basis accounting*, only those events that affect cash are recorded. The cash basis omits important events such as purchases and sales of assets on account. It also distorts the financial statements by labelling as expenses those cash payments that have long-term effects, such as the purchases of buildings and equipment. The generally accepted method of accounting is the accrual basis.

2. **Apply the revenue-recognition and matching principles.** Businesses divide time into definite periods—such as a month, a quarter, and a year—to report the entity's financial statements. The year is the basic *accounting period*, but companies prepare financial statements as often as they need the information. Accountants have developed the *revenue-recognition principle* to determine when to record revenue and the amount of revenue to record. The *matching principle* guides the accounting for expenses. It directs accountants to match expenses against the revenues earned during a particular period of time.

3. **Make adjusting entries.** *Adjusting entries* are a result of the accrual basis of accounting. Made at the end of the period, these entries update the accounts for preparation of the financial statements. Adjusting entries can be divided into five categories: *prepaid expenses, amortization, accrued expenses, accrued revenues,* and *unearned revenues.*

4. **Prepare an adjusted trial balance.** To prepare the *adjusted trial balance* using a worksheet, enter the adjusting entries next to the *unadjusted trial balance* and compute each account's balance by adding or subtracting horizontally.

5. **Prepare the financial statements from the adjusted trial balance.** The adjusted trial balance can be used to prepare the financial statements. The three financial statements are related as follows: Income, shown on the *income statement*, increases the owner's capital, which also appears on the *statement of owner's equity*. The ending balance of capital is the last amount reported on the *balance sheet*.

Chapter 3 Appendix

Alternative Treatment of Accounting for Prepaid Expenses and Unearned Revenues

Objective A1

Account for a prepaid expense recorded initially as an expense

Chapters 1 through 3 illustrate the most popular way to account for prepaid expenses and unearned revenues. This appendix illustrates an alternative—and equally appropriate—approach to handling prepaid expenses and unearned revenues.

Prepaid Expenses

Prepaid expenses are advance payments of expenses. Prepaid Insurance, Prepaid Rent, Prepaid Advertising, and Prepaid Legal Cost are prepaid expenses. Supplies that will be used up in the current period or within one year are also accounted for as prepaid expenses.

When a business prepays an expense—insurance, for example—it can debit an *asset* account (Prepaid Insurance) as illustrated on page 107 as follows:

Aug. 1	Prepaid Insurance	4,200	
	Cash		4,200

Alternatively, it can debit an *expense* account in the entry to record this cash payment:

Aug. 1	Insurance Expense	4,200	
	Cash		4,200

Regardless of the account debited, the business must adjust the accounts at the end of the period to report the correct amounts of the expense and the asset.

Prepaid Expense Recorded Initially as an Expense

Prepaying an expense creates an asset, as explained under the "Prepaid Insurance" heading on page 107. However, the asset may be so short-lived that it will expire in the current accounting period—within one year or less. Thus the accountant may decide to debit the prepayment to an expense account at the time of payment. A $4,200 cash payment for an advertising contract (for one year, in advance) on August 1, 2008, may be debited to Advertising Expense:

2008			
Aug. 1	Advertising Expense................................	4,200	
	Cash		4,200

At December 31, 2008, only five months' prepayment has expired, leaving seven months' advertising still prepaid. In this case, the accountant must transfer $7/_{12}$ of the original prepayment of $4,200, or $2,450, to Prepaid Advertising. At December 31, 2008, the business still has the benefit of the prepayment for January through July of 2009. The December 31, 2008, adjusting entry is

Adjusting Entries

2008			
Dec. 31	Prepaid Advertising................................	2,450	
	Advertising Expense		2,450
	Prepaid advertising is $2,450 ($4,200 × $7/_{12}$).		

After posting, the two accounts appear as follows:

ASSETS Prepaid Advertising		EXPENSES Advertising Expense	
2008		2008	2008
Dec. 31 Adj. 2,450		Aug. 1 Payment 4,200	Dec. 31 Adj. 2,450
Dec. 31 Bal. 2,450		Dec. 31 Bal. 1,750	
7 months remaining		5 months expired	

The balance sheet for 2008 reports Prepaid Advertising of $2,450, and the income statement for 2008 reports Advertising Expense of $1,750, regardless of whether the business initially debits the prepayment to an asset account or to an expense account.

Unearned (Deferred) Revenues

Unearned (deferred) revenues arise when a business collects cash in advance of earning the revenue. The recognition of revenue is *deferred* until later when it is earned. Unearned revenues are liabilities because the business that receives cash owes the other party goods or services to be delivered later.

Unearned (Deferred) Revenue Recorded Initially as a Revenue

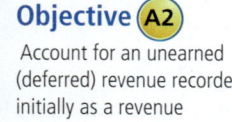

Objective A2

Account for an unearned (deferred) revenue recorded initially as a revenue

Receipt of cash in advance of earning the revenue creates a liability, as discussed on page 114. Another way to account for the initial receipt of cash is to credit a *revenue* account when the business receives the cash. If the business then earns all the revenue within the period during which it received the cash, no adjusting entry is needed at the end of the period. However, if the business earns only a part of the revenue during the period, it must make adjusting entries.

Suppose on October 1, 2009, a consulting firm records as consulting revenue the receipt of $9,000 cash for revenue to be earned over nine months. The cash receipt entry is

2009			
Oct. 1	Cash	9,000	
	Consulting Revenue............................		9,000

At December 31 the firm has earned only $3/9$ of the $9,000, or $3,000. Accordingly, the firm makes an adjusting entry, to transfer the unearned portion ($6/9$ of $9,000, or $6,000) from the revenue account to a liability account as follows:

Adjusting Entries

2009			
Dec. 31	Consulting Revenue	6,000	
	Unearned Consulting Revenue		6,000
	Consulting revenue earned in advance.		

The adjusting entry moves the unearned portion ($6/9$, or $6,000) of the original amount into the liability account because the consulting firm still owes consulting service to the client during January through June of 2010. After posting, the total amount ($9,000) is properly divided between the liability account ($6,000) and the revenue account ($3,000), as follows:

LIABILITIES
Unearned Consulting Revenue

	2009	
	Dec. 31	Adj. 6,000
	Dec. 31	Bal. 6,000

REVENUE
Consulting Revenue

2009		2009	
Dec. 31 Adj. 6,000		Oct. 1 Receipt 9,000	
		Dec. 31 Bal. 3,000	

$2/3$ **of the balance is still unearned** $1/3$ **of the balance is earned**

The firm's 2009 income statement reports consulting revenue of $3,000, and the balance sheet at December 31, 2009, reports as a liability the unearned consulting revenue of $6,000, regardless of whether the business initially credits a liability account or a revenue account.

THINKING IT OVER

The required adjusting entry depends on the way the transaction was originally recorded.
(1) If the receipt of cash is recorded as a liability before it is earned, what adjusting entry is required?
(2) If the receipt of cash is originally recorded as revenue, what adjusting entry is required?

A:
(1)
Unearned Revenue   XX
   Revenue   XX
(2)
Revenue   XX
   Unearned Revenue   XX
These entries are not interchangeable.

Self-Study Questions

Test your understanding of the chapter by marking the correct answer for each of the following questions:

1. Accrual accounting (pp. 101–102)
    a. Results in higher income than cash-basis accounting
    b. Leads to the reporting of more complete information than does cash-basis accounting
    c. Is not acceptable under GAAP
    d. Omits adjusting entries at the end of the period

2. Under the revenue-recognition principle, revenue is recorded (pp. 103-104)
    a. At the earliest acceptable time
    b. At the latest acceptable time
    c. After it has been earned, but not before
    d. At the end of the accounting period

3. The matching principle provides guidance in accounting for (pp. 104–105)
    a. Expenses   c. Assets
    b. Owner's equity   d. Liabilities

4. Adjusting entries (p. 106)
    a. Assign revenues to the period in which they are earned
    b. Help to properly measure the period's net income or net loss
    c. Bring asset and liability accounts to correct balances
    d. All of the above

5. A building-cleaning firm began November with supplies of $210. During the month, the firm purchased supplies of $290. At November 30, supplies on hand total $160. Supplies expense for the period is (p. 108)
    a. $160   c. $290
    b. $340   d. $500

6. A building that cost $120,000 has accumulated amortization of $70,000. The carrying value of the building is (pp. 110–111)
    a. $70,000   c. $120,000
    b. $50,000   d. $190,000

7. The adjusting entry to accrue salary expense (*pp. 112–113*)
   a. Debits Salary Expense and credits Cash
   b. Debits Salaries Payable and credits Salary Expense
   c. Debits Salaries Payable and credits Cash
   d. Debits Salary Expense and credits Salaries Payable

8. A business received cash of $3,000 in advance for service that will be provided later. The cash receipt entry debited Cash and credited Unearned Revenue for $3,000. At the end of the period, $1,100 is still unearned. The adjusting entry for this situation will (*pp. 114–115*)
   a. Debit Unearned Revenue and credit Revenue for $1,900
   b. Debit Unearned Revenue and credit Revenue for $1,100
   c. Debit Revenue and credit Unearned Revenue for $1,900
   d. Debit Revenue and credit Unearned Revenue for $1,100

9. The links among the financial statements are (*pp. 119–121*)
   a. Net income from the income statement to the statement of owner's equity
   b. Ending capital from the statement of owner's equity to the balance sheet
   c. Net income from the balance sheet to the income statement.
   d. Both a and b above

10. Accumulated Amortization is reported on the (*p. 120*)
   a. Balance sheet
   b. Income statement
   c. Statement of owner's equity
   d. Both a and b

Answers to the Self-Study Questions follow the Similar Accounting Terms.

Accounting Vocabulary

Accrual-basis accounting   (*p. 101*)
Accrued expense   (*p. 111*)
Accrued revenue   (*p. 113*)
Accumulated amortization   (*p. 110*)
Adjusted trial balance   (*p. 118*)
Adjusting entry   (*p. 106*)
Amortization   (*p. 109*)
Capital asset   (*p. 109*)
Carrying value (of a capital asset)   (*p. 110*)

Cash-basis accounting   (*p. 101*)
Contra account   (*p. 110*)
Deferred revenue   (*p. 114*)
Matching principle   (*p. 104*)
Prepaid expense   (*p. 107*)
Revenue-recognition principle   (*p. 103*)
Time period principle   (*p. 105*)
Unearned revenue   (*p. 114*)

Similar Accounting Terms

Accrual accounting	Accrual-basis accounting
Adjusting the accounts	Making the adjusting entries; adjusting the books
Amortization	Depreciation; depletion
Carrying value	Book value
Deferred	Unearned
Tangible capital asset	Property, plant, and equipment; plant asset; fixed asset

Assignment Material

Questions

1. Distinguish accrual accounting from cash-basis accounting.

2. How long is the basic accounting period? What is a fiscal year? What is an interim period?

3. What two questions does the revenue principle help answer?

4. Briefly explain the matching principle.

5. What is the purpose of making adjusting entries?

6. Why are adjusting entries usually made at the end of the accounting period, not during the period?

7. Name five categories of adjusting entries and give an example of each.

8. Do all adjusting entries affect the net income or net loss of the period? Include the definition of an adjusting entry.

9. Why must the balance of Supplies be adjusted at the end of the period?

10. Manning Supply Company pays $3,600 for an insurance policy that covers three years. At the end of the first year, the balance of its Prepaid Insurance account contains two elements. What are the two elements, and what is the correct amount of each?

11. The title Prepaid Expense suggests that this type of account is an expense. If it is, explain why. If it is not, what type of account is it?

12. What is a contra account? Identify the contra account introduced in this chapter, along with the account's normal balance.

13. The manager of Quickie-Pickie, a convenience store, presents the company's balance sheet to a banker to obtain a loan. The balance sheet reports that the company's tangible capital assets have a carrying value of $135,000 and accumulated amortization of $65,000. What does *carrying value* of a capital asset mean? What was the cost of the tangible capital assets?

14. Give the entry to record accrued interest revenue of $500.

15. Why is an unearned revenue a liability? Give an example.

16. Identify the types of accounts (assets, liabilities, and so on) debited and credited for each of the five types of adjusting entries.

17. What purposes does the adjusted trial balance serve?

18. Explain the relationship among the income statement, the statement of owner's equity, and the balance sheet.

19. Bellevue Company failed to record the following adjusting entries at December 31, the end of its fiscal year: (a) accrued expenses, $1,000; (b) accrued revenues, $1,700; and (c) amortization, $2,000. Did these omissions cause net income for the year to be understated or overstated and by what overall amount?

*20. A company pays $6,000 on February 1 to rent its office for February, March, and April. Make journal entries dated February 1 to illustrate the two ways this company can record its prepayment of rent.

*21. *Swim World Magazine* received $3,000 for magazine subscriptions in advance and recorded the cash receipt as Subscription Revenue. At the end of the year, only $1,400 of this revenue has been earned. What is the required year-end adjusting entry?

Starters

Starter 3–1 Suppose you work summers mowing lawns. Most of your customers pay you immediately after you cut their grass. A few ask you to send them a bill at the end of each month. It is now June 30 and you have collected $900 from cash-paying customers. Your remaining customers owe you $300. How much service revenue would you have under the (a) cash basis and (b) accrual basis? Which method of accounting provides more information about your lawn-service business? Explain your answer.

Comparing accrual-basis accounting and cash-basis accounting

Service revenue:
Cash basis $900
Accrual basis $1,200

Starter 3–2 Smith Barnes Chartered Accountants uses a client database. Suppose the company paid $3,000 for a Dell computer. Describe how the company would account for the $3,000 expenditure under (a) the cash basis and (b) the accrual basis. State in your own words why the accrual basis is more realistic for this situation.

Accrual-basis accounting versus cash-basis accounting for expenses

Starter 3–3 *Sports Unlimited* sells annual subscriptions for the 12 monthly magazines mailed to customers each year. The company collects cash in advance and then mails out the magazines to subscribers each month. Suppose the company collected $60,000 for subscriptions for January to December.

Applying the revenue-recognition principle

2. Revenue $15,000

*These Questions cover Chapter 3 Appendix topics.

Apply the revenue-recognition principle to determine (1) when the company should record revenue for this situation and (2) the amount of revenue the company should record for the January through March mailings.

Adjusting prepaid expenses

Prepaid Rent bal. $2,500
Rent Expense bal. $500

Starter 3–4 On April 1, 2008, you prepaid six months of rent, for a total of $3,000. Give your adjusting entry to record rent expense at April 30, 2008. Include the date of the entry and an explanation. Then using T-accounts, post to the two accounts involved, and show their balances at April 30, 2008.

Recording amortization

(b) Amort. Expense $1,000

Starter 3–5 On May 1, your company paid cash of $36,000 for computers that are expected to remain useful for three years. At the end of three years, the value of the computers is expected to be zero.

Make journal entries to record (a) purchase of the computers on May 1 and (b) amortization on May 31. Include dates and explanations, and use the following accounts: Computer Equipment; Accumulated Amortization—Computer Equipment; and Amortization Expense—Computer Equipment.

Recording amortization

2. Carrying value $35,000

Starter 3–6 Refer to the data in Starter 3–5.
1. Using T-accounts, post to the accounts listed in Starter 3–5, and show their balances at May 31.
2. What is the computer equipment's carrying value at May 31?

Accruing and paying interest expense

2. Interest Payable at Dec. 31 $300

Starter 3–7 Suppose SuperTravel borrowed $50,000 on October 1 by signing a note payable to Royal Bank. SuperTravel's interest expense for the remainder of the year (October through December) is $300.
1. Make SuperTravel's adjusting entry to accrue interest expense at December 31. Date the entry and include its explanation.
2. Using T-accounts, post to the two accounts affected by the adjustment.

Accounting for unearned revenues

Starter 3–8 *The Big Clipper Magazine* collects cash from subscribers in advance and then mails the magazines to subscribers over a one-year period. Give the adjusting entry that the company makes to record the earning of $8,000 of Subscription Revenue that was collected in advance. Include an explanation for the entry, as illustrated in the chapter.

Preparing an adjusted trial balance

4

Adjusted trial bal. total $23,300

Starter 3–9 Scissors Hair Stylists has begun the preparation of its adjusted trial balance as follows:

SCISSORS HAIR STYLISTS
Preparation of Adjusted Trial Balance
December 31, 2007

Account Title	Trial Balance Debit	Trial Balance Credit	Adjustments Debit	Adjustments Credit	Adjusted Trial Balance Debit	Adjusted Trial Balance Credit
Cash	400					
Supplies	700					
Equipment	17,000					
Accumulated amortization		1,000				
Accounts payable		200				
Interest payable		0				
Note payable		3,000				
Suzanne Byrd, capital		6,000				
Service revenue		12,000				
Rent expense	4,000					
Supplies expense	0					
Amortization expense	0					
Interest expense	100					
	22,200	22,200				

Year-end data:

a. Supplies remaining on hand, $200
b. Amortization, $1,000
c. Accrued interest expense, $100

Complete the company's adjusted trial balance. Identify each adjustment by its letter. To save time, you may write your answer in the spaces provided on the adjusted trial balance.

Note: Starters 3–10 and 3–11 should be used only after completing Starter 3–9.

Starter 3–10 Refer to the data in Starter 3–9. Compute Scissors Hair Stylists' net income for the year ended December 31, 2007.

Computing net income
(5)
Net income $6,300

Starter 3–11 Refer to the data in Starter 3–9. Compute Scissors Hair Stylists' total assets at December 31, 2007. Remember that Accumulated Amortization is a contra asset.

Computing total assets
(5)
Total assets $15,600

Exercises

Exercise 3–1

Accrual-basis accounting

(1)

Sorento Lodge had the following selected transactions during January:

Jan. 1 Paid cash for rent for January, February, and March, $3,900.
      5 Paid electricity expenses, $600.
      9 Received cash for the day's room rentals, $2,100.
      14 Paid cash for six television sets, $4,500. They will last three years.
      23 Served a banquet on account, $1,800.
      31 Made an adjusting entry for January's rent (from January 1).
      31 Accrued salary expense, $1,350.

Show how each transaction would be handled using the accrual basis of accounting. Give the amount of revenue or expense for January. Journal entries are not required. Use the following format for your answer, and show your computations:

Sorento Lodge—Amount of Revenue or Expense for January		
Date	**Revenue (Expense)**	**Accrual-Basis Amount**

Exercise 3–2

Applying accounting assumptions and principles
(2)

Identify the accounting assumption or principle that gives the most direction on how to account for each of the following situations:

a. The owner of a business desires monthly financial statements to measure the financial progress of the entity on an ongoing basis.

b. Expenses of the period total $5,500. This amount should be subtracted from revenue to compute the period's income.

c. Expenses of $3,000 must be accrued at the end of the period to measure income properly.

d. A customer states her intention to switch travel agencies. Should the new travel agency record revenue based on this intention? Give the reason for your answer.

Exercise 3–3

Applying the revenue-recognition and matching principles; accrual basis versus cash basis
(1) (2)
1. Net income $9.6 mil.

National Storage operates approximately 300 miniwarehouses across Canada. The company's headquarters are in Lethbridge, Alberta. During 2008, National earned rental revenue of $24.0 million and collected cash of $22.6 million from customers. Total expenses for 2008 were $14.4 million, of which National paid $13.9 million.

Required

1. Apply the revenue-recognition principle and the matching principle to compute National Storage's net income for 2008.

2. Identify the information that you did not use to compute National Storage's net income. Give the reason for not using the information.

Exercise 3–4

Write a memo to your supervisor explaining in your own words the concept of amortization as it is used in accounting. Use the following format:

Date:	(fill in)
To:	Supervisor
From:	(Student Name)
Subject:	The concept of amortization

Excel Spreadsheet Template

Allocating prepaid expense to the asset and expense

A. Insurance Expense $8,000
B. Total to account for $13,200

Exercise 3–5

Compute the amounts indicated by question marks for each of the following Prepaid Insurance situations. For situations A and B, make the needed journal entry. Consider each situation separately.

	Situation			
	A	B	C	D
Beginning Prepaid Insurance	$ 3,600	$6,000	$10,800	$ 7,200
Payments for Prepaid Insurance during the year	16,800	?	13,200	?
Total amount to account for	?	?	24,000	15,600
Ending Prepaid Insurance	12,400	4,800	?	6,000
Insurance Expense	$?	$8,400	$16,800	$ 9,600

Journalizing adjusting entries

Exercise 3–6

Journalize the entries for the following adjustments at January 31, the end of the accounting period:

a. Amortization, $4,800.

b. Prepaid insurance expired, $600.

c. Interest expense accrued, $400.

d. Employee salaries owed for Monday through Thursday of a five-day workweek; weekly payroll, $15,000.

e. Unearned service revenue that becomes earned, $1,600.

Analyzing the effects of adjustments on net income

Overall, net income is overstated by $16,200

Exercise 3–7

Suppose the adjustments required in Exercise 3–6 were not made. Compute the overall over-statement or understatement of net income as a result of the omission of these adjustments.

Journalizing adjusting entries

Exercise 3–8

Journalize the adjusting entry needed at December 31 for each of the following independent situations.

a. On July 1, when we collected $36,000 rent in advance, we debited Cash and credited Unearned Rent Revenue. The tenant was paying for one year's rent in advance. At December 31, we must account for the amount of rent we have earned.

b. The business owes interest expense of $5,400 that it will pay early in the next period.

c. Interest revenue of $4,200 has been earned but not yet received on a $60,000 note receivable held by the business.

d. Salary expense is $6,000 per day—Monday through Friday—and the business pays employees each Friday. This year December 31 falls on a Wednesday.

e. The unadjusted balance of the Supplies account is $13,500. The total cost of supplies remaining on hand on December 31 is $4,500.

f. Equipment was purchased last year at a cost of $150,000. The equipment's useful life is four years. It will have no value after four years. Record the year's amortization.

g. On September 1, when we paid $5,400 for a one-year insurance policy, we debited Prepaid Insurance and credited Cash.

Exercise 3–9

Recording adjustments in T-accounts

The accounting records of Event Planners include the following unadjusted balances at March 31: Accounts Receivable, $3,600; Supplies, $1,800; Salary Payable, $0; Unearned Service Revenue, $1,600; Service Revenue, $58,800; Salary Expense, $4,800; and Supplies Expense, $0.

Service Revenue bal. $60,650

The company's accountant develops the following data for the March 31 adjusting entries:

a. Service revenue accrued, $1,050

b. Unearned service revenue that has been earned, $800

c. Supplies on hand, $600

d. Salary owed to employee, $1,800

Open T-accounts as needed and record the adjustments directly in the accounts, identifying each adjustment amount by its letter. Show each account's adjusted balance. Journal entries are not required.

Exercise 3–10

Explaining unearned revenues

Write a paragraph to explain why unearned revenues are liabilities rather than revenues. In your explanation use the following actual example: *Maclean's Magazine* collects cash from subscribers in advance and later mails the magazines to subscribers over a one-year period. Explain what happens to the unearned subscription revenue over the course of a year as the magazines are mailed to subscribers. Into what other account does the unearned subscription revenue go? Give the adjusting entry that *Maclean's Magazine* would make to record the earning of $75,000 of subscription revenue. Include an explanation for the entry.

Exercise 3–11

Preparing an adjusted trial balance

Happy Cleaners, a cleaning service, started the preparation of its adjusted trial balance as follows:

Adjusted trial balance total $36,500

Account Title	Trial Balance Debit	Trial Balance Credit	Adjustments Debit	Adjustments Credit	Adjusted Trial Balance Debit	Adjusted Trial Balance Credit
Cash	800					
Supplies	2,000					
Prepaid insurance	900					
Equipment	20,000					
Accumulated amortization		3,000				
Accounts payable		2,100				
Salary payable		0				
Unearned service revenue		600				
Lou Smith, capital		8,000				
Lou Smith, Withdrawals	4,000					
Service revenue		22,000				
Salary expense	8,000					
Supplies expense	0					
Amortization expense	0					
Insurance expense	0					
	35,700	35,700				

HAPPY CLEANERS
Preparation of Adjusted Trial Balance
June 30, 2007

During the six months ended June 30, 2007, Happy Cleaners

a. Used supplies of $1,500.

b. Used up prepaid insurance of $600.

c. Used up $500 of the equipment through amortization.

d. Accrued salary expense of $300 that still must be paid.

e. Earned $400 of the unearned service revenue.

Complete the adjusted trial balance. Identify each adjustment by its letter. To save time, you may write your answers directly in the spaces provided.

Using an adjusted trial balance

Exercise 3–12

Refer to the data in Exercise 3–11. Journalize the five adjustments, all dated June 30, 2007. Explanations are not required.

Note: Exercise 3–13 should be used only in conjunction with Exercise 3–11.

Computing net income

a. Net income $11,500

Exercise 3–13

Refer to the data in Exercise 3–11.

a. Compute Happy Cleaners' net income for the period ended June 30, 2007.

b. Compute Happy Cleaners' total assets at June 30, 2007.

Excel Spreadsheet Template

Adjusting the accounts

Adjustments total $17,860

Exercise 3–14

The adjusted trial balance below of Swindon Consulting is incomplete. Enter the adjustment amounts directly in the adjustment columns of the text. Service Revenue is the only account affected by more than one adjustment.

	SWINDON CONSULTING Preparation of Adjusted Trial Balance May 31, 2008						
	Trial Balance		Adjustments		Adjusted Trial Balance	
Account Title	Debit	Credit	Debit	Credit	Debit	Credit
Cash	18,000				18,000	
Accounts receivable	39,000				44,600	
Supplies	6,240				4,800	
Office furniture	193,800				193,800	
Accumulated amortization		84,240				86,400
Salary payable		0				7,400
Unearned revenue		5,400				4,140
T. Swindon, capital		158,160				158,160
T. Swindon, withdrawals	36,000				36,000	
Service revenue		69,780				76,640
Salary expense	16,140				23,540	
Rent expense	8,400				8,400	
Amortization expense	0				2,160	
Supplies expense	0				1,440	
	317,580	317,580			332,740	332,740

Journalizing adjustments

Exercise 3–15

Make journal entries for the adjustments that would complete the preparation of the adjusted trial balance in Exercise 3–14. Date the entries and include explanations.

Explaining the adjusted trial balance

Exercise 3–16

Write a business memorandum to your supervisor explaining the difference between the unadjusted amounts and the adjusted amounts in Exhibit 3–10, page 118. Use Accounts Receivable in your explanation. If necessary, refer back to the discussion of Accrued Revenues that begins on page 113.

Business memos are formatted as follows:

Date:	(fill in)
To:	Supervisor
From:	(Student Name)
Subject:	Difference between the *unadjusted* and the *adjusted* amounts on an adjusted trial balance.

Exercise 3–17

Refer to the adjusted trial balance in Exercise 3–14. Prepare Swindon Consulting's income statement and statement of owner's equity for the month ended May 31, 2008, and its balance sheet on that date. Draw the arrows linking the three statements.

Excel Spreadsheet Template

Preparing the financial statements

⑤

Net income $41,100;
Total assets $174,800

Exercise 3–18

The accountant for Sandra Rubin's business, Rubin Technologies has posted adjusting entries (a) through (e) to the accounts at December 31, 2008. Selected balance sheet accounts and all the revenues and expenses of the entity follow in T-account form:

Preparing the financial statements

1. Net income $469,250

Accounts Receivable

103,500	
(e) 29,250	

Supplies

18,000	(a) 4,500

Accumulated Amortization— Furniture

	22,500
	(b) 9,000

Accumulated Amortization— Electronic Equipment

	148,500
	(c) 22,500

Salary Payable

	(d) 6,750

Service Revenue

	607,500
	(e) 40,500

Salary Expense

126,000	
(d) 6,750	

Supplies Expense

(a) 4,500	

Amortization Expense— Furniture

(b) 19,000	

Amortization Expense— Electronic Equipment

(c) 22,500	

Required

1. Prepare the income statement of Rubin Technologies for the year ended December 31, 2008. List expenses in order from the largest to the smallest.

2. Were the company's 2008 operations successful? Give the reason for your answer.

Exercise 3–19

Gibbens Consulting began the year on January 1, 2008, with capital of $52,500. On July 12, 2008, Eric Gibbens (the owner) invested $12,000 cash in the business. On September 26, 2008, he transferred to the company land valued at $35,000. The income statement for the year ended December 31, 2008, reported a net loss of $14,000. During this fiscal year, Gibbens withdrew $1,000 monthly for personal use.

Preparing the statement of owner's equity

1. Owner's equity, Dec. 31, 2008 $73,500

Required

1. Prepare the company's statement of owner's equity for the year ended December 31, 2008.

2. Did the owner's equity of the business increase or decrease during the year? What caused this change?

*Exercise 3–20

At the beginning of the year, supplies of $3,380 were on hand. During the year, the business paid $10,800 for more supplies. At the end of the year, the count of supplies indicates supplies of $2,720 on hand.

Recording supplies transactions two ways

Supplies bal. $2,720

Required

1. Assume that the business records supplies by initially debiting an asset account. Therefore, place the beginning balance in the Supplies T-account, and record the above entries directly in the accounts without using a journal.

2. Assume that the business records supplies by initially debiting an *expense* account. Therefore, place the beginning balance in the Supplies Expense T-account, and record the above entries directly in the accounts without using a journal.

3. Compare the ending account balances under both approaches. Are they the same? Explain.

Recording unearned revenues
two ways

Unearned Service
Revenue bal. $7,400

*Exercise 3–21

At the beginning of the year, a business owed customers $5,500 for unearned service revenue collected in advance. During the year, the business received advance cash receipts of $20,000. At year end, the company still owed customers $7,400 for unearned service revenue collected in advance.

Required

1. Assume that the company records unearned revenues by initially crediting a *liability* account. Open T-accounts for Unearned Service Revenue and Service Revenue, and place the beginning balance in Unearned Service Revenue. Journalize the cash collection and adjusting entries, and post their dollar amounts. As references in the T-accounts, label the balance, the cash receipt, and the adjustment.

2. Assume that the company records unearned revenues by initially crediting a *revenue* account. Open T-accounts for Unearned Service Revenue and Service Revenue, and place the beginning balance in Service Revenue. Journalize the cash collection and adjusting entries, and post their dollar amounts. As references in the T-accounts, label the balance, the cash receipt, and the adjustment.

3. Compare the ending balances in the two accounts. Explain why they are the same or different.

Recording prepaids as expenses
and unearned revenues as
revenues; adjusting entries

Supplies Expense Cr $700

*Exercise 3–22

Aberfoyle Services initially records all prepaid expenses as expenses and all unearned revenues as revenues. Given the following information, prepare the necessary adjusting entries at December 31, 2008, the company's year end.

a. On January 3, 2008, the company's first day of operations, $3,500 of supplies were purchased. A physical count revealed $700 of supplies still on hand at December 31, 2008.

b. On January 4, 2008, a $21,000 payment for insurance was made to an insurance agency for a 30-month policy.

c. On June 30, 2008, Aberfoyle Services received nine months' rent totalling $8,100 in advance from a tenant.

Serial Exercise

Exercise 3–23 continues the Mark Wearing Engineers situation begun in Exercise 2–14 of Chapter 2. If Exercise 2–14 was not completed, students can complete Exercise 3–23 by following the instructions in the note below.

Adjusting the accounts, preparing
an adjusted trial balance, and
preparing the financial statements

6. Adjusted trial balance total
$57,440
7. Net income $9,360
Total assets $49,160

Exercise 3–23

Refer to Exercise 2–14 of Chapter 2. Start from the trial balance and the posted T-accounts that Mark Wearing Engineers prepared for this engineering practice at December 18. Make sure the account balances in your trial balance and T-accounts match those in the trial balance at December 18, 2008, shown on the next page.

---

*These Exercises cover Chapter 3 Appendix topics.

Note: If you did not do Exercise 2–14, you can complete this Exercise by creating T-accounts for the accounts and balances given in the trial balance at December 18, 2008, shown below.

MARK WEARING ENGINEERS
Trial Balance
December 18, 2008

Cash	$22,600	
Accounts receivable	6,400	
Supplies	600	
Equipment	7,000	
Furniture	11,200	
Accounts payable		$11,800
Mark Wearing, capital		28,000
Mark Wearing, withdrawals	0	
Service revenue		10,400
Rent expense	2,000	
Utilities expense	400	
Salaries expense	0	
Total	$50,200	$50,200

Later in December, the business completed these transactions:

Dec. 21   Received $3,600 in advance for engineering work to be performed evenly over the next 30 days.

       21   Hired a secretary to be paid $4,200 salary on the 20th day of each month. The secretary begins work immediately.

       26   Paid $600 for the supplies purchased on December 5.

       28   Collected $1,200 from the consulting client of December 18.

       30   Mark Wearing withdrew $3,200 cash for personal use.

Required

1. Open these T-accounts: Accumulated Amortization—Equipment; Accumulated Amortization—Furniture; Salaries Payable; Unearned Service Revenue; Amortization Expense—Equipment; Amortization Expense—Furniture; Supplies Expense.

2. Journalize the transactions of December 21 through 30.

3. Post to the T-accounts, identifying all items by date.

4. Prepare a trial balance at December 31. Also set up columns for the adjustments and for the adjusted trial balance, as illustrated in Exhibit 3–10 on page 118.

5. At December 31, the company gathers the following information for the adjusting entries:
   a. Accrued service revenue, $2,400
   b. Earned a portion of the service revenue collected in advance on December 21.
   c. Supplies remaining on hand at December 31, $200
   d. Amortization expense—equipment, $200; furniture, $240
   e. Accrued $1,400 expense for the secretary's salary

   Make these adjustments directly in the adjustments columns, and complete the adjusted trial balance at December 31.

6. Journalize and post the adjusting entries. Label each adjusting amount as *Adj.* and an account balance as *Bal.*

7. Prepare the income statement and statement of owner's equity of Mark Wearing Engineers for the month ended December 31, 2008, and prepare the balance sheet at that date.

Challenge Exercises

Computing the
financial statement

Supplies expense $5,000
Salary expense $45,500
Service revenue $83,000

Exercise 3–24

The adjusted trial balances of Pacific Services at December 31, 2007, and December 31, 2006 include these amounts:

	2007	2006
Supplies	$ 2,000	$ 1,000
Salary payable..	2,500	4,000
Unearned service revenue	13,000	16,000

Analysis of the accounts at December 31, 2007, reveals these transactions for 2007:

Cash payment for supplies...............................	$ 6,000
Cash payment for salaries................................	47,000
Cash receipts in advance for service revenue .	80,000

Compute the amount of supplies expense, salary expense, and service revenue to report on the Pacific Services income statement for 2007.

Beyond the Numbers

Beyond the Numbers 3–1

Suppose a new management team is in charge of Alpine Waters Inc., a micro-brewery. Assume Alpine Waters Inc.'s new top executives rose through the company ranks in the sales and marketing departments and have little appreciation for the details of accounting. Consider the following conversation between two executives:

John Ramsay, President: "I want to avoid the hassle of adjusting the books every time we need financial statements. Sooner or later we receive cash for all our revenues, and we pay cash for all our expenses. I can understand cash transactions, but all these accruals confuse me. If I cannot understand *our own* accounting, I'm fairly certain the average person who invests in our company cannot understand it either. Let's start recording only our cash transactions. I bet it won't make any difference to anyone."

Kate McNamara, Chief Financial Officer: "Sounds good to me. This will save me lots of headaches. I'll implement the new policy immediately."

Write a business memo to the company president giving your response to the new policy. Identify at least five individual items (such as specific accounts) in the financial statements that will be reported incorrectly. Will outside investors care? Use the format of a business memo given with Exercise 3–16 on page 137.

Ethical Issue

The net income of Corcorran's, a specialty store, decreased sharply during 2007. Mary Corcorran, owner of the store, anticipates the need for a bank loan in 2008. Late in 2007, she instructs the accountant to record a $24,600 sale of furniture to the Corcorran family, even though the goods will not be shipped from the manufacturer until January 2008. Corcorran also tells the accountant not to make the following December 31, 2007 adjusting entries:

Salaries owed to employees...............................	$27,000
Prepaid insurance that has expired	1,200

Required

1. Compute the overall effect of these transactions on the store's reported income for 2007.
2. Why did Corcorran take this action? Is this action ethical? Give your reason, identifying the parties helped and the parties harmed by Corcorran's action.
3. As a personal friend, what advice would you give *the accountant*?

Problems (Group A)

Problem 3–1A

Applying accounting principles
2 **3**

As the controller of Chow Security Systems, you have hired a new bookkeeper, whom you must train. She objects to making an adjusting entry for accrued salaries at the end of the period. She reasons, "We will pay the salaries soon. Why not wait until payment to record the expense? In the end, the result will be the same." Write a business memo to explain to the bookkeeper why the adjusting entry for accrued salary expense is needed.

This is the format of the business memo:

Date:	(fill in)
To:	New Bookkeeper
From:	(Student Name)
Subject:	Why the adjusting entry for salary expense is needed.

Problem 3–2A

Cash-basis versus accrual-basis accounting
1 **2**

2. Net income $1,000

Thompson Office Design had the following transactions during January:

Jan.	1	Paid for insurance for January through March, $3,600.
	4	Performed design service on account, $6,000.
	5	Purchased office furniture on account, $900.
	8	Paid advertising expense, $1,800.
	11	Purchased office equipment for cash, $4,800.
	19	Performed design services and received cash, $4,200.
	24	Collected $2,400 on account for the January 4 service.
	26	Paid account payable from January 5.
	29	Paid salary expense, $6,200.
	31	Recorded adjusting entry for January insurance expense (see January 1).

Required

1. Show how each transaction would be accounted for using the accrual basis of accounting. Use the format below for your answer, and show your computations. Give the amount of revenue or expense for January. Journal entries are not required.

Amount of Revenue or Expense for January

Date	Revenue/Expense	Accrual-Basis Amount

2. Compute January net income or net loss under the accrual basis of accounting.
3. State why the accrual basis of accounting is preferable to the cash basis.

Problem 3–3A

Journalizing adjusting entries
3

c. Supplies Expense $10,000

Journalize the adjusting entry needed on December 31, the company's year end, for each of the following independent cases affecting MDC Telecommunications:

a. Each Friday the company pays its employees for the current week's work. The amount of the payroll is $9,000 for a five-day workweek. The current accounting period ends on Tuesday.

b. MDC Telecommunications has received notes receivable from some clients for professional services. During the current year, MDC Telecommunications has earned interest revenue of $610, which will be received next year.

c. The beginning balance of Supplies was $5,400. During the year the company purchased supplies costing $7,590, and at December 31 the inventory of supplies remaining on hand is $2,990.

d. The company is developing a wireless communication system for a large company, and the client paid MDC $108,000 at the start of the project. MDC recorded this amount as Unearned Consulting Revenue. The development will take several months to complete. MDC executives estimate that the company has earned three-fourths of the total fee during the current year.

e. Amortization for the current year includes: Office Furniture, $16,500, and Design Equipment, $19,080. Make a compound entry.

f. Details of Prepaid Insurance are shown in the account:

Prepaid Insurance

Jan. 2 Bal. 3,000	

MDC Telecommunications prepays a full year's insurance on January 2. Record insurance expense for the year ended December 31.

Journalizing and posting adjustments to T-accounts; preparing and using the adjusted trial balance

3. Adjusted trial bal. total $50,310

Problem 3–4A

The trial balance of Bella Printing at December 31, 2008, appears below. The data needed for the month-end adjustments follow the trial balance.

BELLA PRINTING
Trial Balance
December 31, 2008

Cash..	$ 5,325	
Accounts receivable	17,835	
Prepaid rent...	1,815	
Supplies	885	
Furniture and equipment................................	14,800	
Accumulated amortization—		
furniture and equipment.............................		$ 2,720
Accounts payable..		2,480
Salary payable...		0
Unearned printing revenue		2,100
S. Bella, capital...		29,630
S. Bella, withdrawals	4,000	
Printing revenue...		11,780
Salary expense	2,850	
Rent expense	0	
Amortization expense—		
furniture and equipment.............................	0	
Advertising expense	1,200	
Supplies expense	0	
Total...	$48,710	$48,710

Adjustment data:

a. Unearned printing revenue still remaining to be earned at December 31, $1,000.

b. Prepaid rent still available at December 31, $815.

c. Supplies used during the month, $585.

d. Amortization for the month, $300.

e. Accrued advertising expense at December 31, $900. (Credit Accounts Payable.)

f. Accrued salary expense at December 31, $400.

Required

1. Open T-accounts for the accounts listed in the trial balance, inserting their December 31 unadjusted balances.

2. Journalize the adjusting entries on December 31, and post them to the T-accounts. Identify the journal entries and posted amounts by their letter.

3. Prepare the adjusted trial balance.

4. How will the company use the adjusted trial balance?

Problem 3–5A

Felix Consulting's unadjusted and adjusted trial balances at December 31, 2009, follow:

Analyzing and journalizing adjustments

Consulting Revenue
$5,830 + $680
Supplies Expense $810
Salary Expense $1,960

FELIX CONSULTING
Adjusted Trial Balance
December 31, 2009

Account Title	Trial Balance Debit	Trial Balance Credit	Adjusted Trial Balance Debit	Adjusted Trial Balance Credit
Cash	10,990		10,990	
Accounts receivable	8,260		14,090	
Supplies	1,090		280	
Prepaid insurance	3,600		2,330	
Office furniture	21,630		21,630	
Accumulated amortization— office furniture		9,220		12,500
Accounts payable		6,310		6,310
Salary payable		0		1,960
Interest payable		0		480
Note payable		12,000		12,000
Unearned consulting revenue		1,840		1,160
Ava Felix, capital		13,510		13,510
Ava Felix, withdrawals	22,500		22,500	
Consulting revenue		69,890		76,400
Amortization expense—furniture	0		3,280	
Supplies expense	0		810	
Utilities expense	4,960		4,960	
Salary expense	26,660		28,620	
Rent expense	12,200		12,200	
Interest expense	880		1,360	
Insurance expense	0		1,270	
	112,770	112,770	124,320	124,320

Required Journalize the adjusting entries that account for the differences between the two trial balances.

Problem 3–6A

The adjusted trial balance of Renaud Antique Auctioneers at the end of its year, December 31, 2009, is shown on the next page.

Required

1. Prepare Renaud Antique Auctioneer's 2009 income statement, statement of owner's equity, and balance sheet. List expenses in decreasing-balance order on the income statement and show total liabilities on the balance sheet. If your three financial statements appear on one page, draw the arrows linking the three financial statements. If they are on separate pages, write a short paragraph describing how the three financial statements are linked. How will what you have learned in this problem help you manage a business?

2. a. Which financial statement reports Renaud's results of operations? Were 2009 operations successful? Cite specifics from the financial statements to support your evaluation.
   b. Which statement reports the company's financial position? Does Renaud's financial position look strong or weak? Give the reason for your evaluation.

Excel Spreadsheet Template

Preparing the financial statements from an adjusted trial balance

1. Net income $287,880;
Total assets $480,120

RENAUD ANTIQUE AUCTIONEERS
Adjusted Trial Balance
December 31, 2009

Cash..	$ 9,360	
Accounts receivable	165,960	
Prepaid rent..	5,400	
Supplies	3,880	
Equipment..	302,760	
Accumulated amortization—equipment.........		$ 88,960
Office furniture	96,400	
Accumulated amortization—office furniture...		14,680
Accounts payable..		54,400
Unearned service revenue		8,080
Interest payable		8,520
Salary payable...		3,720
Notes payable		180,000
A. Renaud, capital...		129,520
A. Renaud, withdrawals	192,000	
Service revenue...		783,160
Amortization expense—equipment	45,200	
Amortization expense—office furniture..........	7,640	
Salary expense	351,200	
Rent expense...	48,000	
Interest expense..	12,800	
Utilities expense	15,080	
Insurance expense..	12,600	
Supplies expense	2,760	
Total..	$1,271,040	$1,271,040

Preparing an adjusted trial balance
and the financial statements

2. Net income $16,312;
Total assets $107,312

Problem 3–7A

Consider the unadjusted trial balance of Hutton Landscaping at October 31, 2008, and the related month-end adjustment data.

HUTTON LANDSCAPING
Trial Balance
October 31, 2008

Cash...	$ 24,175	
Accounts receivable	18,000	
Prepaid rent..	9,000	
Supplies	1,350	
Equipment..	60,750	
Accumulated amortization—equipment.........		$ 6,750
Accounts payable		6,300
Salary payable..		0
T. Hutton, capital...		91,000
T. Hutton, withdrawals	8,100	
Landscaping design revenue............................		21,150
Salary expense	3,150	
Rent expense...	0	
Utilities expense	675	
Amortization expense—equipment	0	
Supplies expense	0	
Total..	$125,200	$125,200

Adjustment data:

a. Accrued landscaping design revenue at October 31, $4,500.

b. Some of the prepaid rent had expired during the month. The unadjusted prepaid balance of $9,000 relates to the period October 1, 2008, through January 31, 2009.

c. Supplies remaining on hand at October 31, $900.

d. Amortization on equipment for the month. The equipment's expected useful life is five years; it will have no value at the end of its useful life, and the straight-line method of amortization is used.

e. Accrued salary expense at October 31 should be for one day only. The five-day weekly payroll is $9,000.

Required

1. Recopy the trial balance using the format in Exhibit 3–10 (page 118), and prepare the adjusted trial balance of Hutton Landscaping at October 31, 2008. Identify each adjusting entry by its letter.

2. Prepare the income statement and the statement of owner's equity for the month ended October 31, 2008, and the balance sheet at October 31, 2008. Draw the arrows linking the three financial statements, or write a short description of how they are linked.

Problem 3–8A

Success Employment Counsellors provides counselling services to employees of companies that are downsizing. On December 31, 2008, the end of its first year of operations, the business had the following account balances (in alphabetical order):

Applying the revenue and matching principles; making adjusting entries; preparing an adjusted trial balance and income statement

2. Adjusted trial bal. total $721,200
3. Net income $128,000

Accounts payable	$78,000
Accounts receivable	16,800
Accumulated amortization—building	0
Accumulated amortization—computer equipment	0
Building	240,000
Cash	7,200
Computer equipment	57,600
Counselling revenue	306,000
K. Vineberg, capital	276,000
K. Vineberg, withdrawals	66,000
Land	120,000
Prepaid advertising	9,600
Salaries expense	100,800
Supplies	4,200
Supplies expense	20,400
Utilities expense	17,400

The following information was available on December 31, 2008:

a. A physical count shows $6,800 of supplies remaining on hand on December 31.

b. The building has an expected useful life of 8 years, with no expected value after 8 years. The building was purchased on January 2, and the straight-line method of amortization is used.

c. The computer equipment, purchased on January 2, is expected to be used for four years with no expected value after four years. The straight-line method of amortization is used.

d. On November 1, the company hired a marketing consultant and agreed to pay her $2,400 per month. The company paid her for four months' advertising, in advance.

e. The company's Managing Director, who earns $800 per day, worked the last six days of the year and will be paid on January 4, 2009.

f. On December 29, the company provided counselling services to a customer for $12,000, to be paid in 30 days.

Required

1. Journalize the adjusting entries required on December 31, 2008.

2. Prepare, with accounts in the correct sequence, an adjusted trial balance on December 31, 2008.

3. Prepare an income statement for the year ended December 31, 2008.

Recording prepaid rent and service revenue collected in advance two ways

A1 **A2**

Rent Expense bal. $4,000

*Problem 3–9A

Johal Sales and Service completed the following transactions during 2008:

Aug. 31   Paid $6,000 store rent covering the six-month period ending February 28, 2009.
Dec.   1   Collected $6,400 cash in advance from customers. The service revenue will be earned $1,600 each month over the four-month period ending March 31, 2009.

Required

1. Journalize these entries by debiting an asset account for Prepaid Rent and by crediting a liability account for Unearned Service Revenue. Explanations are not required.

2. Journalize the related adjustments at December 31, 2008.

3. Post the entries to T-accounts, and show their balances at December 31, 2008. Posting references are not required.

4. Repeat Requirements 1 through 3. This time debit Rent Expense for the rent payment and credit Service Revenue for the collection of revenue in advance.

5. Compare the account balances in Requirements 3 and 4. They should be equal.

Applying the revenue and matching principles, making adjusting entries, accounting for prepaid expenses recorded initially as an expense, accounting for unearned revenue recorded initially as a revenue

1. Insurance Expense
   adj. $4,200 Cr
3. Total effects:
   a. −$10,300
   b. +$1,300

*Problem 3–10A

Jasmine Consulting develops custom software for clients in the construction business. Jasmine Consulting had the following information available at the close of its first year of business, June 30, 2008:

1. Insurance payments during the year were debited to Insurance Expense. An examination of the policies showed the following:
   • Policy 1: a two-year policy purchased on March 31, 2008, for $4,800.
   • Policy 2: a one-year policy purchased on July 2, 2007, for $1,800.

2. On July 2, 2007, the company purchased $1,000 of supplies and recorded the purchase as a debit to Supplies Expense. Throughout the year the company purchased additional supplies for $2,400, recording the purchase the same way. An inventory count on June 30, 2008, showed that $1,600 of supplies remained on hand.

3. Computer equipment was purchased on January 2, 2008 for $36,000. The equipment was expected to be used for four years and then discarded.

4. The six employees each earn an average of $600 per day for a five-day week and are paid each Thursday. June 30, 2008, was a Friday.

5. An examination of the contracts signed with clients showed the following:
   • Customer A signed a contract on September 1, 2007 and paid $48,000 to Jasmine Consulting. The contract was for software that was to be completed in twelve months from the date of signing.
   • Customer B signed a contract on October 30, 2007, and was to make progress payments of $2,000 each month commencing November 1. The contract was for 30 months. Revenue was recognized on a monthly basis.

All money received to date on the two contracts was credited to Development Fees Earned. Any change to the contract amount will be made at the end of the contract.

Required

1. Journalize the adjusting entries on June 30, 2008.

2. Give the journal entry required to record the payment of wages on July 6, 2008. Since all employees are paid for the July 1 holiday, each was paid for five working days on July 6.

3. Calculate the *total effects* of the adjusting entries (parts 1 to 5) on each of the:
   a. Income statement
   b. Balance sheet

---

*These Problems cover Chapter 3 Appendix topics.

Problems (Group B)

Problem 3–1B

Applying accounting principles

Write a business memo to a new bookkeeper to explain the difference between the cash basis of accounting and the accrual basis. Mention the roles of the revenue-recognition principle and the matching principle in accrual-basis accounting.

This is the format of a business memo:

Date:	(fill in)
To:	New Bookkeeper
From:	(Student Name)
Subject:	Difference between cash-basis and accrual-basis accounting.

Problem 3–2B

Accrual-basis accounting
2. Net income $600

Highlands Speech and Hearing Clinic experienced the following selected transactions during October:

Oct.		
	1	Paid for insurance for October through December, $5,400.
	4	Paid gas bill, $2,400.
	5	Performed services on account, $6,000.
	9	Purchased office equipment for cash, $8,400.
	12	Received cash for services performed, $5,400.
	14	Purchased office equipment on account, $1,800.
	28	Collected $3,000 on account from October 5.
	31	Paid salary expense, $6,600.
	31	Paid account payable from March 14.
	31	Recorded adjusting entry for October insurance expense (see October 1).

Required

1. Show how each transaction would be accounted for using the accrual basis of accounting. Use the format below for your answer, and show your computations. Give the amount of revenue or expense for October. Journal entries are not required.

Amount of Revenue or Expense for October

Date	Revenue (Expense)	Accrual-Basis Amount

2. Compute October net income or net loss under the accrual basis of accounting.
3. Why is the accrual basis of accounting preferable to the cash basis?

Problem 3–3B

Journalizing adjusting entries
a. Rent Expense $12,000
d. Supplies Expense $18,120

Journalize the adjusting entry needed on December 31, the company's year end, for each of the following independent cases affecting West Coast Contractors:

a. Details of Prepaid Rent are shown in the account:

Prepaid Rent

Jan.	1	Bal.	3,000
Mar.	31		6,000
Sept.	30		6,000

West Coast Contractors pays office rent semiannually on March 31 and September 30. At December 31, part of the last payment is still available to cover January to March of the next year. No rent expense was recorded during the year.

b. West Coast Contractors pays its employees each Friday. The amount of the weekly payroll is $12,000 for a five-day workweek, and the daily salary amounts are equal. The current accounting period ends on Wednesday.

c. West Coast Contractors has lent money to help employees find housing, receiving notes receivable in return. During the current year the entity has earned interest revenue of $2,250 from employees' loans, which it will receive next year.

d. The beginning balance of Supplies was $6,030. During the year the company purchased supplies costing $18,540, and at December 31 the inventory of supplies remaining on hand is $6,450.

e. West Coast Contractors is installing cable in a large building, and the owner of the building paid West Coast Contractors $37,500 as the annual service fee. West Coast Contractors recorded this amount as Unearned Service Revenue. Robin Zweig, the general manager, estimates that the company has earned one-fourth of the total fee during the current year.

f. Amortization for the current year includes: Equipment, $11,550; and Trucks, $30,960. Make a compound entry.

Problem 3–4B

Journalizing and posting adjustments to T-accounts; preparing the adjusted trial balance

3. Adjusted trial bal. total $151,230

The trial balance of Sefton Realty at December 31, 2009, appears below. The data needed for the month-end adjustments follow the trial balance.

SEFTON REALTY Trial Balance December 31, 2009		
Cash	$ 13,300	
Accounts receivable	44,250	
Prepaid rent	9,300	
Supplies	2,340	
Furniture	68,130	
Accumulated amortization—furniture		$ 34,920
Accounts payable		5,820
Salary payable		0
Unearned commission revenue		6,870
I. Jarvis, capital		75,180
I. Jarvis, withdrawals	2,000	
Commission revenue		25,200
Salary expense	6,480	
Rent expense	0	
Amortization expense—furniture	0	
Advertising expense	2,190	
Supplies expense	0	
Total	$147,990	$147,990

Adjustment data at December 31:

a. Prepaid rent still available at December 31, $2,400.

b. Supplies used during the month, $1,920.

c. Amortization on furniture for the month, $2,700.

d. Accrued salary expense at December 31, $540.

e. Unearned commission revenue still remaining to be earned at December 31, $3,000.

Required

1. Open T-accounts for the accounts listed in the trial balance, inserting their December 31 unadjusted balances.

2. Journalize the adjusting entries and post them to the T-accounts. Key the journal entries and the posted amounts by letter. Show the ending balance of each account.

3. Prepare the adjusted trial balance.

4. How will the company use the adjusted trial balance?

Problem 3–5B

Perry Construction's unadjusted and adjusted trial balances at April 30, 2008, are shown below.

Analyzing and journalizing adjustments

Supplies Expense $3,760; Wages Expense $2,280

PERRY CONSTRUCTION
Adjusted Trial Balance
April 30, 2008

Account Title	Trial Balance		Adjusted Trial Balance	
	Debit	Credit	Debit	Credit
Cash	24,720		24,720	
Accounts receivable	25,440		26,800	
Supplies	4,920		1,160	
Prepaid rent	9,920		2,880	
Equipment	265,800		265,800	
Accumulated amortization—equipment		65,040		71,160
Accounts payable		27,680		27,680
Wages payable		0		2,280
Unearned service revenue		2,680		440
H. Owner, capital		217,280		217,280
H. Owner, withdrawals	14,400		14,400	
Service revenue		39,760		43,360
Wages expense	6,400		8,680	
Rent expense	0		7,040	
Amortization expense—equipment	0		6,120	
Supplies expense	0		3,760	
Utilities expense	840		840	
	352,440	352,440	362,200	362,200

Required Journalize the adjusting entries that account for the differences between the two trial balances.

Problem 3–6B

The adjusted trial balance of Belford Systems at December 31, 2008, is shown on the next page.

Excel Spreadsheet Template

Preparing the financial statements from an adjusted trial balance

1. Net income $128,090; Total assets $188,430

Required

1. Prepare Belford Systems' 2008 income statement, statement of owner's equity, and balance sheet. List expenses in decreasing-balance order on the income statement and show total liabilities on the balance sheet. If your three financial statements appear on one page, draw the arrows linking the three financial statements. If they are on separate pages, write a short paragraph describing how the three financial statements are linked. How will what you have learned in this problem help you manage a business?

2. a. Which financial statement reports Belford Systems' results of operations? Were operations successful during 2008? Cite specifics from the financial statements to support your evaluation.

   b. Which statement reports the company's financial position? Does Belford Systems' financial position look strong or weak? Give the reason for your evaluation.

BELFORD SYSTEMS
Adjusted Trial Balance
December 31, 2008

Cash	$ 3,960	
Accounts receivable	26,760	
Supplies	6,900	
Prepaid rent	4,800	
Equipment	60,540	
Accumulated amortization—equipment		$ 13,050
Office furniture	113,130	
Accumulated amortization—office furniture		14,610
Accounts payable		14,220
Interest payable		2,490
Unearned service revenue		11,860
Notes payable		40,500
J. Belford, capital		78,270
J. Belford, withdrawals	87,000	
Service revenue		374,730
Amortization expense—equipment	20,040	
Amortization expense—office furniture	9,110	
Salary expense	119,700	
Rent expense	52,200	
Interest expense	13,300	
Utilities expense	8,010	
Insurance expense	11,430	
Supplies expense	12,850	
Total	$549,730	$549,730

Preparing an adjusted trial balance and the financial statements

2. Net income $21,600; Total assets $147,100

Problem 3–7B

The unadjusted trial balance of Quest Data at July 31, 2009, and the related month-end adjustment data appear below:

QUEST DATA
Trial Balance
July 31, 2009

Cash	$ 26,800	
Accounts receivable	34,800	
Prepaid rent	10,800	
Supplies	2,400	
Furniture	86,400	
Accumulated amortization—furniture		$ 10,500
Accounts payable		10,350
Salary payable		0
N. Wong, capital		125,950
N. Wong, withdrawals	12,000	
Consulting revenue		35,250
Salary expense	7,200	
Rent expense	0	
Utilities expense	1,650	
Amortization expense—furniture	0	
Supplies expense	0	
Total	$182,050	$182,050

Adjustment data:

a. Accrued consulting revenue at July 31, $2,700.

b. Prepaid rent had expired during the month. The unadjusted prepaid balance of $10,800 relates to the period July through October 2009.

c. Supplies remaining on hand at July 31, $600.

d. Amortization on furniture for the month. The estimated useful life of the furniture is four years, it will have no value at the end of the four years, and the straight-line method of amortization is used.

e. Accrued salary expense at July 31 for one day only. The five-day weekly payroll is $6,000.

Required

1. Using Exhibit 3–10 (page 118) as an example, recopy the trial balance and prepare the adjusted trial balance of Quest Data at July 31, 2009. Key each adjusting entry by letter.

2. Prepare the income statement and the statement of owner's equity for the month ended July 31, 2009, and the balance sheet at July 31, 2009. Draw the arrows linking the three financial statements, or write a short description of how they are linked.

Problem 3–8B

Tasktel provides telecommunications consulting services. On December 31, 2009, the end of its first year of operations, the business had the following account balances (in alphabetical order):

Accounts payable	$12,000
Accounts receivable	11,400
Accumulated amortization—equipment	0
Accumulated amortization—furniture	0
Cash	6,000
Computer equipment	36,000
Consulting revenue	213,000
Furniture	120,000
G. Tasker, capital	96,000
G. Tasker, withdrawals	45,000
Prepaid advertising	7,500
Salaries expense	54,900
Supplies	2,700
Supplies expense	11,700
Travel expense	25,800

Applying the revenue-recognition and matching principles; making adjusting entries; preparing an adjusted trial balance and income statement

2. Adjusted trial bal. total $351,000
3. Net income $92,700

The following information was available on December 31, 2009:

a. A physical count shows $3,300 of supplies remaining on hand on December 31.

b. The computer equipment has an expected useful life of four years, with no expected value after four years. The computers were purchased on January 2, and the straight-line method of amortization is used.

c. The furniture, purchased on January 2, is expected to be used for eight years, with no expected value after eight years. The straight-line method of amortization is used.

d. On October 1, Tasktel hired an advertising firm to prepare a marketing plan and agreed to pay the firm $1,500 per month. The business paid for five months' work in advance and has made no adjusting entries for this during 2009.

e. The company's office manager, who earns $600 per day, worked the last five days of the year and will be paid on January 5, 2010.

f. On December 30, Tasktel provided consulting for a client for $3,000 to be paid in 30 days.

Required

1. Journalize the adjusting entries required on December 31, 2009. Identify the journal entries by their letter.

2. Prepare, with accounts in the correct sequence, an adjusted trial balance on December 31, 2009.

3. Prepare an income statement for the year ended December 31, 2009. List expenses in alphabetical order.

Recording prepaid advertising and flight travel revenue collected in advance two ways

Advertising Expense bal. $7,500

*Problem 3-9B

Allegience Airways completed the following transactions during 2008:

Oct.   15   Paid $12,000 for advertising and promotional material covering the four-month period ending February 15, 2009.

Nov   1   Received $13,200 payment in advance for a series of charter flights. Revenue of $2,200 will be earned each month over the six-month period ending April 30, 2009.

Required

1. Open T-accounts for Advertising Expense, Prepaid Advertising, Unearned Flight Revenue, and Flight Revenue.

2. Journalize these entries by debiting an asset account for Prepaid Advertising and by crediting a liability account for Unearned Flight Revenue. Explanations are not required.

3. Journalize the related adjustments at December 31, 2008.

4. Post the entries to the T-accounts, and show their balances at December 31, 2008. Posting references are not required.

5. Repeat requirements 1 through 3. This time debit Advertising Expense instead of Prepaid Advertising, and credit Flight Revenue instead of Unearned Flight Revenue.

6. Compare the account balances in requirements 4 and 5. They should be equal.

Applying the revenue and matching principles, making adjusting entries, accounting for prepaid expenses recorded initially as an expense, accounting for unearned revenue recorded initially as a revenue

1. Wages payable $21,600
3. Total effects
   a. −$4,400
   b. +$29,200

*Problem 3–10B

Magistrale Construction specializes in industrial and commercial renovations. Magistrale had the following information available at the close of its first year of business, March 31, 2008:

1. On April 1, 2007, the company purchased $2,000 of supplies and recorded the purchase as a debit to Supplies Expense. Throughout the year, the company purchased additional supplies for $4,800, recording the purchase the same way. An inventory count on March 31, 2008, showed that $3,200 of supplies remained on hand.

2. The 12 employees each earn an average of $600 per day for a five-day week and are paid each Friday. March 31 was a Wednesday.

3. An examination of the contracts signed with clients showed the following:
    *   Customer A signed a contract on September 1, 2007, and paid $96,000 to Magistrale Construction. The contract was for a building renovation that was to be completed in eight months from the date of signing.
    *   Customer B signed a contract on July 31, 2007, and was to make progress payments of $4,000 each month commencing August 1. The contract was for 60 months. The company has received three payments.

    All money received to date on the two contracts was credited to Construction Revenue. Any change to the contract amount will be made at the end of the contract.

4. Equipment was purchased on October 1, 2007, for $64,000. The equipment was expected to be used for eight years and then discarded.

5. Insurance payments during the year were debited to Insurance Expense. An examination of the policies showed the following:
    *   Policy 1: a two-year policy purchased on December 31, 2007, for $9,600.
    *   Policy 2: a three-year policy purchased on April 2, 2007, for $2,400.

Required

1. Journalize the adjusting entries on March 31, 2008.

2. Give the journal entry required to record the payment of wages on April 2, 2008.

3. Calculate the total effects of the adjusting entries (parts 1 to 5) on each of the
    a. Income statement
    b. Balance sheet

---

*These Problems cover Chapter 3 Appendix topics.

Challenge Problems

Problem 3–1C

The basic accounting period is one year and all organizations report on an annual basis. It is common for large companies to report on a semiannual basis, and some even report monthly. Interim reporting has a cost, however.

   You are working part-time as an accounting clerk for Paradise Corp. The company was private and prepared only annual financial statements for its shareholders. Paradise has gone public and now must report quarterly. Samantha Fleming, your supervisor in the accounting department, is concerned about all the additional work that will be required to produce the quarterly statements.

Required   What does Samantha mean when she talks about "additional work"?

Understanding accrual-basis accounting

Problem 3–2C

The matching principle is well established as a basis for recording expenses.

Required

1. New accountants sometimes state the principle as matching revenues against expenses. Explain to a new accountant why matching revenues against expenses is incorrect.

2. It has been suggested that not-for-profit organizations, such as churches and hospitals, should flip their income statements and show revenues as a deduction from expenses. Why do you think that the suggestion has been made?

Application of the matching principle

Decision Problems

Valuing a business on the basis of its net income

Decision Problem 1

Cameron Masson has owned and operated Alberta Biotech, a management consulting firm, since its beginning 10 years ago. From all appearances the business has prospered. Masson lives in the fast lane—flashy car, home located in an expensive suburb, frequent trips abroad, and other signs of wealth. In the past few years, you have become friends with him through weekly rounds of golf at the country club. Recently, he mentioned that he has lost his zest for the business and would consider selling it for the right price. He claims that his clientele is firmly established, and that the business "runs on its own." According to Masson, the consulting procedures are fairly simple, and anyone could perform the work.

Assume you are interested in buying this business. You obtain its most recent monthly trial balance, which follows. Assume that revenues and expenses vary little from month to month and April is a typical month.

Your investigation reveals that the trial balance does not include the effects of monthly revenues of $3,300 and expenses totalling $6,300. If you were to buy Alberta Biotech, you would hire a manager so you could devote your time to other duties. Assume that this person would require a monthly salary of $6,000.

ALBERTA BIOTECH
Trial Balance
April 30, 2009

Cash	$ 29,100	
Accounts receivable	44,700	
Prepaid expenses	7,800	
Property, plant, and equipment	723,900	
Accumulated amortization		$568,800
Land for future expansion	144,000	
Accounts payable		41,400
Salaries payable		0
Unearned consulting revenue		170,100
C. Masson, capital		172,200
C. Masson, withdrawals	27,000	
Consulting revenue		36,900
Salary expense	10,200	
Rent expense	0	
Utilities expense	2,700	
Amortization expense	0	
Supplies expense	0	
Total	$989,400	$989,400

Required

1. Is this an unadjusted or adjusted trial balance? How can you tell?

2. Assume that the most you would pay for the business is 40 times the monthly net income you could expect to earn from it. Compute this possible price.

3. Masson states that the lowest price he will accept for the business is $450,000 plus the balance in owner's equity on April 30. Compute this amount.

4. Under these conditions, how much should you offer Masson? Give your reasons.

Decision Problem 2

Understanding the concepts underlying the accrual basis of accounting

The following independent questions relate to the accrual basis of accounting:

1. It has been said that the only time a company's financial position is known for certain is when the company is wound up and its only asset is cash. Why is this statement true?

2. A friend suggests that the purpose of adjusting entries is to correct errors in the accounts. Is your friend's statement true? What is the purpose of adjusting entries if the statement is wrong?

3. The text suggested that furniture (and each other capital asset that is amortized) is a form of prepaid expense. Do you agree? Why do you think some accountants view capital assets this way?

Financial Statement Cases

Financial Statement Case 1

Journalizing and posting transactions

CHUM Limited—like all other businesses—makes adjusting entries prior to year end in order to measure assets, liabilities, revenues, and expenses properly.

Examine CHUM's balance sheet in Appendix A at the back of this book.

Required

1. Open T-accounts for: Accounts Receivable; Prepaid Expenses and Other; Accounts Payable and Accrued Liabilities; Revenue—Less Agency Commissions; and Operations Expenses. Insert CHUM Limited's balances (in thousands) at August 31, 2004.

2. Journalize the following for the current year ended August 31, 2005. Identify entries by their letter. Explanations are not required.

   Cash transactions (amounts in thousands of dollars):
   a. Paid prepaid expenses, $2,000.
   b. Paid the August 31, 2004, accounts payable, $27,956.
   c. Collected $34,111 of receivables.

   Adjustments at August 31, 2005 (amounts in thousands of dollars):
   d. Prepaid expenses expired, $2,235. (Debit Operations Expenses.)
   e. Accrue rent expense of $41,561. (Debit Operations Expense.)
   f. Earned revenue of $67,600 on account.

Financial Statement Case 2

Explaining the effects of accruals and deferrals on the financial statements

During the year ended December 31, 2005, Sun-Rype Products Ltd. experienced numerous accruals and deferrals. As a long-term employee of Sun-Rype's accounting and financial staff, it is your job to explain the effects of accruals and deferrals on Sun-Rype's 2005 financial statements. (Sun-Rype's 2005 financial statements appear in Appendix B.) The following questions were raised at the shareholders' meeting in February 2006 (all amounts are in thousands of dollars):

1. "Prepaid expenses" in the amount of $515 are listed on the December 31, 2005, balance sheet. What items would be included in this balance, and why is this account listed as a balance-sheet account instead of an expense account?

2. The balance sheet lists an account called Deferred Expenses in the amount of $41 at December 31, 2004. What do you think this account represents?

3. Accounts payable and accrued liabilities is shown on the balance sheet in the amount of $ 16,211. Define an accrued liability.

4. What is amortization, and how much amortization would have been recorded for the year ended December 31, 2005?

Completing the Accounting Cycle

Learning Objectives

1. Prepare an accounting work sheet
2. Use the work sheet to complete the accounting cycle
3. Close the revenue, expense, and withdrawal accounts
4. Correct typical accounting errors
5. Classify assets and liabilities as current or long-term, and prepare a classified balance sheet
6. Use the current ratio and debt ratio to evaluate a company

Chapter 4 Appendix

A1. Describe and prepare reversing entries.

It's a beautiful day in late spring in Vancouver, but you are still immersed in hockey as you watch the Vancouver Canucks play the Toronto Maple Leafs in the sixth game of the Stanley Cup Championship. The teams are playing a best-of-seven series and the Leafs lead the series three games to two. The Canucks need to win this game or Toronto will win the Stanley Cup.

The game is close. After the first period, the score is tied at 1–1. There is no scoring in the second, but Toronto scores early in the third period to take a 2–1 lead. The Canucks fight back and score the tying goal with two minutes to go. There is no more scoring in regulation time and the final result will be decided in overtime.

The game goes back and forth in overtime, before the Canucks finally score to force a seventh game back in Toronto.

When the teams return to Toronto to play the seventh game, what will the scoreboard say at the start of the game? Will it be 3–2 to carry over the score from the previous game? Or will the scoreboard be set back to zero? The answer is obvious: After a game is completed, the scoreboard is always set back to zero.

In the same way, the accounting process sets the scoreboard back to zero at the end of each fiscal period. The process is called "closing the books," and that is the main topic in this chapter. The logic behind the closing process in accounting is the same as setting the scoreboard back to zero after a game. The final step in the process is preparing the financial statements.

**How do you complete the accounting cycle, and why is it important?
What are closing entries?
How do closing entries differ from other journal entries?
Why are some types of accounts closed and other types of accounts
     not closed?
How do decision makers evaluate a company?**

These questions and others will be answered throughout this chapter. And the Decision Guidelines at the end of this chapter will provide the answers in a useful summary.

Thus far, we have prepared the financial statements from an adjusted

trial balance. That approach works well for quick decision making, but organizations of all sizes take the accounting process a step further. Whether it's General Motors or SuperTravel, the closing process follows the basic pattern outlined in this chapter. It marks the end of the *accounting cycle* for a given period, as shown in the margin.

The accounting process often uses a document known as the accountant's *work sheet*. Work sheets are useful because they summarize a lot of data and aid decision making.

The Accounting Cycle

The **accounting cycle** is the process by which companies produce their financial statements for a specific period of time. For a new business, the cycle begins with setting up (opening) the ledger accounts. John Lapp started SuperTravel on April 2, 2007, so the first step in the cycle was to plan and open the accounts. After a business has operated for one period, however, the account balances carry over from period to period. Therefore, the accounting cycle usually starts with the account balances at the beginning of the period. Exhibit 4–1 outlines the complete accounting cycle, and shows examples of data and documents you see at each step. The boldface items in Panel A indicate the new steps that we will be discussing in this chapter.

The accounting cycle includes work performed at two different times:

- During the period—Journalizing transactions
                Posting to the ledger
- End of the period—Adjusting the accounts
                Preparing the financial statements
                Closing the accounts

The end-of-period work also readies the accounts for the next period. In Chapters 3 and 4, we cover the end-of-period accounting for a service business such as SuperTravel. Chapter 5 will show how a merchandising entity adjusts and closes its books.

Companies prepare financial statements on a monthly or a quarterly basis, and steps 1 to 6a in Exhibit 4–1 are adequate for statement preparation. Steps 6b through 7 can be performed monthly or quarterly but are necessary only at the end of the year.

---

1. Identify and analyze transactions

2. Record transactions in a journal

3. Post (copy) from the journal to the accounts in the ledger

4. Prepare the trial balance

5. Journalize and post adjusting entries

6. Prepare the financial statements

7. Close the books (closing entries, postclosing trial balance)

KEY POINT

The accounting cycle is repeated each accounting period. The goal of the cycle is the financial statements.

EXHIBIT 4-1 | The Accounting Cycle

PANEL A

During the Period

1. Start with the account balances in the ledger at the beginning of the period.
2. Analyze and journalize transactions as they occur.
3. Post journal entries to the ledger accounts.

End of the Period

4. Compute the unadjusted balance in each account at the end of the period.
5. Determine adjustments and create the adjusted trial balance. **Steps 4 and 5 can be completed using a work sheet. (Optional)**
6. Using the adjusted trial balance or the full work sheet as a guide,
   a. Prepare the financial statements.
   b. Journalize and post the adjusting entries.
   c. Journalize and post the closing entries.
7. **Prepare the postclosing trial balance. This trial balance becomes Step 1 for the next period.**

PANEL B

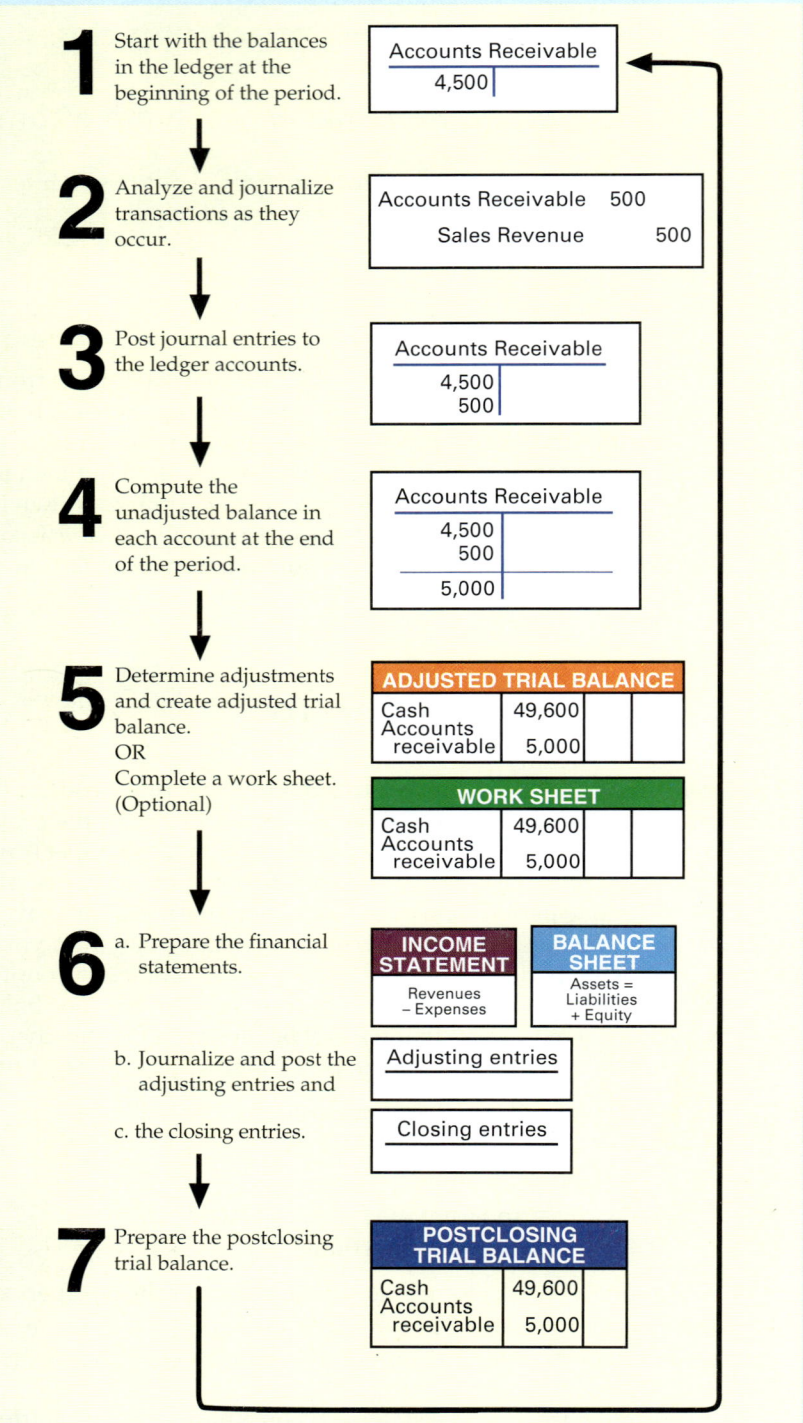

The Work Sheet

Accountants often use a **work sheet,** a document with many columns, to help summarize data for the financial statements. Listing all the accounts and their unadjusted balances helps identify the accounts that need adjustment. The work sheet aids the closing process by listing the ending adjusted balances of all the accounts.

The work sheet is not part of the journal or the ledger, nor is it a financial statement. Therefore, it is not part of the formal accounting system. Instead, it is a summary device that exists for the accountant's convenience. An Excel spreadsheet works well for an accounting work sheet.

Exhibits 4–2 through 4–6 illustrate the development of a typical work sheet for SuperTravel. The heading at the top, displays the

- Name of the business (SuperTravel)
- Title of the document (Accounting Work Sheet.)
- Period covered by the work sheet (For the Month Ended April 30, 2008)

A step-by-step description of its preparation follows, with all amounts given in Exhibits 4–2 through 4–6. Simply turn the acetate pages to follow from exhibit to exhibit.

Exhibit 4–2 *1. Print the account titles and their unadjusted ending balances in the Trial Balance columns of the work sheet, and total the amounts.* The account titles and balances come directly from the ledger accounts before any adjusting entries are prepared. Accounts are grouped on the work sheet by category (assets, liabilities, owner's equity, revenues, expenses) and are usually listed in the order in which they appear in the ledger (Cash first, Accounts Receivable second, and so on). Total debits must equal total credits.

Accounts may have zero balances (for example, Amortization Expense). All accounts are listed on the trial balance because they appear in the ledger. Electronically prepared work sheets list all the accounts, not just those with a balance.

Exhibit 4–3 *2. Enter the adjusting entries in the Adjustments columns, and total the amounts.* Exhibit 4–3 includes the April adjusting entries that we made in Chapter 3 to prepare the adjusted trial balance.

We can identify the accounts that need to be adjusted by scanning the trial balance. Cash needs no adjustment because all cash transactions are recorded as they occur during the period. Consequently, Cash's balance is up to date.

Accounts Receivable is listed next. Has SuperTravel earned revenue that it has not yet recorded? The answer is yes. At April 30, the business has earned $500, which must be accrued because the cash will be received during May. SuperTravel debits Accounts Receivable and credits Service Revenue on the work sheet in Exhibit 4–3. A letter is used to link the debit and the credit of each adjusting entry ("(e)" in this case).

By moving down the trial balance, the accountant identifies other accounts that need adjustment, such as Supplies. The business has used supplies during April, so it debits Supplies Expense and credits Supplies. The other adjustments are analyzed and entered on the work sheet as you learned in Chapter 3. After the adjustments are entered on the work sheet, the amount columns are totalled. Total debits equal total credits.

Listing all the accounts in their proper sequence aids the process of identifying accounts that need to be adjusted. But suppose that one or more accounts are omitted from the trial balance. This account can always be written below the first column totals—$106,100. Assume that Supplies Expense was accidentally omitted and thus did not appear on the trial balance. When the accountant identifies the need to update the Supplies account, he or she knows that the debit in the adjusting entry is to Supplies Expense. In this case, the accountant can write Supplies Expense on the line beneath the amount totals and enter the debit adjustment—$600—on the Supplies Expense line. Keep in mind that the work sheet is not the finished version of the financial statements, so the order of the accounts on the work sheet is not critical. Supplies Expense should preferably be listed in its proper sequence on the income statement.

Objective ①

Prepare an accounting work sheet

KEY POINT

Cash needs no adjusting entry unless there is an error that needs to be corrected. An error in cash is a rare occurrence.

EXHIBIT 4–2 | Trial Balance

SUPERTRAVEL
Accounting Work Sheet
For the Month Ended April 30, 2008

Account Title	Trial Balance		Adjustments		Adjusted Trial Balance		Income Statement		Balance Sheet	
	Dr.	Cr.	Dr.	Cr.	Dr.	Cr.	Dr.	Cr.	Dr.	Cr.
Cash	49,600									
Accounts receivable	4,500									
Supplies	1,400									
Prepaid insurance	4,200									
Furniture	36,000									
Accumulated amortization		0								
Accounts payable		26,000								
Salary payable		0								
Unearned service revenue		900								
John Lapp, capital		65,200								
John Lapp, withdrawals	5,900									
Service revenue		14,000								
Insurance expense	0									
Rent expense	1,800									
Salary expense	1,900									
Supplies expense	0									
Amortization expense	0									
Utilities expense	800									
	106,100	106,100								
Net income										

Print the account titles and their unadjusted ending balances in the Trial Balance columns of the work sheet. Total the amounts.

Exhibit 4–4 *3. Compute each account's adjusted balance by combining the trial balance and adjustment figures. Enter the adjusted amounts in the Adjusted Trial Balance columns.* Exhibit 4–4 shows the work sheet with the adjusted trial balance columns completed. Accountants perform this step as illustrated in Chapter 3. For example, Cash is up to date, so it receives no adjustment. Accounts Receivable's adjusted balance of $5,000 is computed by adding the $500 debit adjustment to the trial balance debit amount of $4,500. Supplies' adjusted balance of $800 is determined by subtracting the $600 credit adjustment from the unadjusted debit balance of $1,400. An account may receive more than one adjustment, as does Service Revenue. In the adjusted trial balance columns, total debits equal total credits.

Steps 1, 2, and 3 were introduced in Chapter 3 to prepare the adjusted trial balance. Steps 4 and 5 are introduced in this chapter.

Exhibit 4–5 *4. Extend (that is, transfer) the asset, liability, and owner's equity amounts from the Adjusted Trial Balance to the Balance Sheet columns. Extend the revenue and expense amounts to the Income Statement columns. Total the statement columns.* Every account is either a balance sheet account or an income statement account. The asset, liability, and owner's equity accounts go to the balance sheet, and the revenues and expenses go to the income statement. Debits on the adjusted trial balance remain debits in the statement columns, and credits remain credits. Generally, each account's adjusted balance should appear in only one statement column, as shown in Exhibit 4–5.

Total the *income statement* columns first, as follows:

Income Statement

- Debits (Dr.) Total expenses = $7,950 ⎫
- Credits (Cr.) Total revenues = $14,800 ⎬ Difference = $6,850, a net income because revenues exceed expenses

Then total the *balance sheet* columns:

Balance Sheet

- Debits (Dr.) Total assets and withdrawals = $101,150 ⎫
- Credits (Cr.) Total accumulated amortization, liabilities and owner's equity = $ 94,300 ⎬ Difference = $6,850, a net income because total debits are greater

Exhibit 4–6 *5. On the income statement, compute net income or net loss as the difference between total revenues and total expenses. Enter net income as a debit balancing amount on the income statement. Also add net income as a credit balancing amount on the balance sheet. Then total the financial statement columns.* Exhibit 4–6 presents the completed accounting work sheet, which shows net income of $6,850, computed as follows:

Revenue (total *credits* on the income statement)	$14,800
Expenses (total *debits* on the income statement)	7,950
Net income	$ 6,850

Net Income Net income of $6,850 is entered as a "plug figure" in the debit column of the income statement. This brings total debits up to total credits on the income statement. Net income is also entered as a "plug figure" in the credit column of the balance sheet because an excess of revenues over expenses increases capital, and increases in capital are recorded by a credit. In the closing process, net income will find its way into the Capital account, as we shall soon see. After completion, total debits equal total credits in the Income Statement columns and in the Balance Sheet columns. The balance sheet columns are totalled at $101,150. This process is shown on the next page:

THINKING IT OVER

Where is each account extended—Income Statement, debit column; Income Statement, credit column; Balance Sheet, debit column; or Balance Sheet, credit column?

1. Cash.
   A: Balance Sheet, debit

2. Supplies.
   A: Balance Sheet, debit

3. Supplies Expense.
   A: Income Statement, debit

4. Unearned Revenue.
   A: Balance Sheet, credit

5. Service Revenue.
   A: Income Statement, credit

6. Owner's Equity.
   A: Balance Sheet, credit

KEY POINT

Net income is the difference between the debit and credit Income Statement columns.

SUPERTRAVEL
Accounting Work Sheet
For the Month Ended April 30, 2008

	Trial Balance		Adjustments		Adjusted Trial Balance		Income Statement		Balance Sheet	
	Dr.	Cr.	Dr.	Cr.	Dr.	Cr.	Dr.	Cr.	Dr.	Cr.
Cash	49,600				49,600				49,600	
Accounts Receivable	4,500		(e) 500		5,000				5,000	
Amortization expense	0		(c) 600		600		600			
Utilities expense	800				800		800			
	106,100	106,100	4,250	4,250	109,100	109,100	7,950	14,800	101,150	94,300
Net income							6,850			6,850
							14,800	14,800	101,150	101,150

Net Loss If expenses exceed revenues, the result is a net loss. In that event, *Net loss* is printed on the work sheet. The net loss amount should be entered in the *credit* column of the income statement (to balance out) and in the *debit* column of the balance sheet (to balance out). This is because an excess of expenses over revenue decreases capital, and decreases in capital are recorded by a debit. After completion, total debits equal total credits in the Income Statement columns and in the Balance Sheet columns, as shown here (amounts are assumed):

SUPERTRAVEL
Accounting Work Sheet
For the Month Ended April 30, 2008

	Trial Balance		Adjustments		Adjusted Trial Balance		Income Statement		Balance Sheet	
	Dr.	Cr.	Dr.	Cr.	Dr.	Cr.	Dr.	Cr.	Dr.	Cr.
Cash	49,600				49,600				49,600	
Accounts Receivable	4,500		(e) 500		5,000				5,000	
Amortization expense	0		(c) 600		600		600			
Utilities expense	800				800		800			
	186,100	186,100	4,250	4,250	189,100	189,100	25,000	15,000	170,000	180,000
Net Loss								10,000	10,000	
							25,000	25,000	180,000	180,000

The trial balance of Curry's Service Company at December 31, 2008, the end of its fiscal year, is presented below:

CURRY'S SERVICE COMPANY
Trial Balance
December 31, 2008

Cash	$ 6,000	
Accounts receivable	5,000	
Supplies	1,000	
Furniture	10,000	
Accumulated amortization—furniture		$ 4,000
Building	60,000	
Accumulated amortization—building		30,000
Land	20,000	
Accounts payable		2,000
Salary payable		0
Unearned service revenue		8,000
Bill Curry, capital		40,000
Bill Curry, withdrawals	25,000	
Service revenues		60,000
Salary expense	16,000	
Supplies expense	0	
Amortization expense—furniture	0	
Amortization expense—building	0	
Miscellaneous expense	1,000	
Total	$144,000	$144,000

Name: Curry's Service Company
Industry: Service proprietorship
Fiscal Period: Year ended December 31, 2008
Key Fact: Existing, ongoing business

Data needed for the adjusting entries include:

a. Supplies remaining on hand at year end, $200

b. Amortization on furniture, $2,000

c. Amortization on building, $1,000

d. Salary owed but not yet paid, $500

e. Service revenues to be accrued, $1,300

f. Of the $8,000 balance of Unearned Service Revenue, $3,000 was earned during 2008.

To plan your work sheet, check the adjusting entries data to see if the same account is affected more than once. If it is, leave 1 or 2 blank lines under the account name. Do this for Service Revenues on the work sheet.

Required Prepare the work sheet of Curry's Service Company for the year ended December 31, 2008. Identify each adjusting entry by the letter corresponding to the data given.

Solution

CURRY'S SERVICE COMPANY
Work Sheet
For the Year Ended December 31, 2008

Account Title	Trial Balance Debit	Trial Balance Credit	Adjustments Debit	Adjustments Credit	Adjusted Trial Balance Debit	Adjusted Trial Balance Credit	Income Statement Debit	Income Statement Credit	Balance Sheet Debit	Balance Sheet Credit
Cash	6,000				6,000				6,000	
Accounts receivable	5,000		(e) 1,300		6,300				6,300	
Supplies	1,000			(a) 800	200				200	
Furniture	10,000				10,000				10,000	
Accumulated amortization —furniture		4,000		(b) 2,000		6,000				6,000
Building	60,000				60,000				60,000	
Accumulated amortization —building		30,000		(c) 1,000		31,000				31,000
Land	20,000				20,000				20,000	
Accounts payable		2,000				2,000				2,000
Salary payable		0		(d) 500		500				500
Unearned service revenue		8,000	(f) 3,000			5,000				5,000
Bill Curry, capital		40,000				40,000				40,000
Bill Curry, withdrawals	25,000				25,000				25,000	
Service revenue		60,000		(e) 1,300 (f) 3,000		64,300		64,300		
Salary expense	16,000		(d) 500		16,500		16,500			
Supplies expense	0		(a) 800		800		800			
Amortization expense —furniture	0		(b) 2,000		2,000		2,000			
Amortization expense—building	0		(c) 1,000		1,000		1,000			
Miscellaneous expense	1,000				1,000		1,000			
	144,000	144,000	8,600	8,600	148,800	148,800	21,300	64,300	127,500	84,500
Net income							43,000			43,000
							64,300	64,300	127,500	127,500

Selected adjusting entries are explained further:
(a) Supplies on hand ($1,000) – Supplies still on hand ($200) = $800 adjustment
(e) $1,300 of service revenues were earned but not yet recorded as an account receivable.
(f) Unearned Service Revenue ($8,000) – Service revenue earned ($3,000) = $5,000 of service revenue still to be earned, which is a liability.

Completing the Accounting Cycle

The work sheet helps organize accounting data and compute the net income or net loss for the period. It also helps accountants prepare the financial statements, record the adjusting entries, and close the accounts.

Objective 2
Use the work sheet to complete the accounting cycle

Preparing the Financial Statements

The work sheet shows the amount of net income or net loss for the period, but it is still necessary to prepare the financial statements. (The financial statements can be prepared directly from the adjusted trial balance; see page 118. This is why completion of the work sheet is optional.) The sorting of accounts to the balance sheet and income statement eases the preparation of the statements. The work sheet also provides the data for the statement of owner's equity. Exhibit 4–7 presents the April financial statements for SuperTravel (based on the data from the work sheet in Exhibit 4–6). We can prepare SuperTravel's financial statements immediately after completing the work sheet.

Recording the Adjusting Entries

The adjusting entries are a key element of accrual-basis accounting. The work sheet helps identify the accounts that need adjustments. But, actual adjustment of the accounts requires journal entries that are posted to the ledger accounts. Panel A of Exhibit 4–8 repeats SuperTravel's adjusting entries that we journalized in Chapter 3. Panel B shows the postings to the accounts, with "Adj." denoting an amount posted from an adjusting entry. Only the revenue and expense accounts are presented in the exhibit in order to focus on the closing process, which is discussed in the next section.

The adjusting entries can be recorded in the journal as they are entered on the work sheet, but it is not necessary to journalize them at the same time. Most accountants prepare the financial statements immediately after completing the work sheet. They can wait to journalize and post the adjusting entries before they make the closing entries.

KEY POINT

Adjusting entries must be journalized and posted prior to closing the accounts.

Delaying the journalizing and posting of the adjusting entries illustrates another use of the work sheet. Many companies journalize and post the adjusting entries—as in Exhibit 4–8—only at the end of the year. The need for monthly and quarterly financial statements, however, requires a tool like the work sheet. The entity can use the work sheet to aid in preparing interim statements without journalizing and posting the adjusting entries.

If a work sheet is not used, it is common practice to record the adjusting entries and then prepare the financial statements.

We are now ready to move to the last step—closing the accounts.

Closing the Accounts

Closing the accounts occurs at the end of the period. Closing prepares the accounts for recording the transactions of the next period and consists of journalizing and posting the closing entries. Closing results in the balances of the revenue and expense accounts becoming zero in order to clearly measure the net income of each period separately from all other periods. The example regarding the hockey play-off game discussed at the beginning of this chapter illustrates this concept.

Recall that the income statement reports net income for a specific period. For example, net income for Molson Breweries for the year ended March 31, 2007, relates exclusively to the twelve months ended on that date. At March 31, 2007, Molson accountants close the company's revenue and expense accounts for that year. Because these accounts' balances relate to a particular accounting period (2007 in this case)

Objective 3
Close the revenue, expense, and withdrawal accounts

EXHIBIT 4–7 April 2008 Financial Statements of SuperTravel

SUPERTRAVEL
Income Statement
For the Month Ended April 30, 2008

Revenues:

Service revenue		$14,800

Expenses:

Salary expense	$3,800	
Rent expense	1,800	
Utilities expense	800	
Supplies expense	600	
Amortization expense—furniture	600	
Insurance expense	350	
Total expenses		7,950
Net income		$ 6,850

SUPERTRAVEL
Statement of Owner's Equity
For the Month Ended April 30, 2008

John Lapp, capital, April 1, 2008	$65,200
Add: Net income	6,850
	72,050
Less: Withdrawals	5,900
John Lapp, capital, April 30, 2008	$66,150

SUPERTRAVEL
Balance Sheet
April 30, 2008

Assets			Liabilities		
Cash		$49,600	Accounts payable		$26,000
Accounts receivable		5,000	Salary payable		1,900
Supplies		800	Unearned service revenue		600
Prepaid insurance		3,850	Total liabilities		28,500
Furniture	$36,000				
Less: Accumulated			**Owner's Equity**		
amortization	600	35,400	John Lapp, capital		66,150
			Total liabilities and		
Total assets		$94,650	owner's equity		$94,650

and are therefore closed at the end of the period (March 31, 2007), the revenue and expense accounts are called **temporary (nominal) accounts**. For example, assume SuperTravel's year end is April 30, 2008. The balance of Service Revenue at April 30, 2008, is $14,800. This balance relates exclusively to the month of April and must be zeroed out before SuperTravel records revenue for May.

The Withdrawals account—although not a revenue or an expense—is also a temporary account, because it measures withdrawals taken during a specific period. The Withdrawals account is also closed at the end of the period. The closing process applies only to temporary accounts.

To better understand the closing process, contrast the nature of the temporary accounts with the nature of the **permanent (real) accounts**—the assets, liabilities, and owner's capital. The asset, liability, and owner's capital accounts are *not* closed at the

EXHIBIT 4–8   Journalizing and Posting the Adjusting Entries

Panel A: Journalizing   **Page 4**
Adjusting Entries

Apr. 30	Insurance Expense	350	
	Prepaid Insurance		350
30	Supplies Expense...	600	
	Supplies		600
30	Amortization Expense—Furniture	600	
	Accumulated Amortization—Furniture		600
30	Salary Expense...	1,900	
	Salaries Payable..		1,900
30	Accounts Receivable	500	
	Service Revenue		500
30	Unearned Service Revenue..................................	300	
	Service Revenue		300

Panel B: Posting the Adjustments to the Revenue and Expense Accounts

REVENUE   **EXPENSES**

Service Revenue   **Rent Expense**   **Salary Expense**

	14,000	1,800		1,900	
Adj. 500		Bal. 1,800		Adj. 1,900	
Adj. 300				Bal. 3,800	
	Bal. 14,800				

Amortization Expense—
Furniture   **Utilities Expense**

Adj.	600		800	
Bal.	600	Bal.	800	

Supplies Expense   **Insurance Expense**

Adj.	600	Adj.	350	
Bal.	600	Bal.	350	

Adj. = Amount posted from an adjusting entry
Bal. = Balance

end of the period because their balances are not used to measure income. Consider Cash, Accounts Receivable, Supplies, Buildings, Accounts Payable, Notes Payable, and John Lapp, Capital. These accounts do not represent *business activity* for a single period, as do revenues and expenses, which relate exclusively to one accounting period. Instead, the permanent accounts represent assets, liabilities, and capital that are on hand at a specific time. This is why their balances at the end of one accounting period carry over to become the beginning balances of the next period. For example, the Cash balance at December 31, 2007 is also the beginning balance for 2008.

Closing entries transfer the revenue, expense, and withdrawal balances from their respective accounts to the Capital account. Recall that

REVENUES	*increase*	owner's equity
EXPENSES and WITHDRAWALS	*decrease*	owner's equity

It is when we post the closing entries that the Capital account absorbs the impact of the balances in the temporary accounts.

As an intermediate step, however, the revenues and the expenses are transferred first to an account entitled **Income Summary**. This temporary account collects in one place the sum of all the expenses (a debit) and the sum of all the revenues (a credit). The Income Summary account is like a temporary "holding tank" that is used only in the closing process. The balance of Income Summary is then transferred to the Capital account. Exhibit 4–9 summarizes the closing process. Start with Revenues at the far right and Expenses at the left. Work toward the middle and then down. Owner, Capital is the final account in the closing process.

EXHIBIT 4–9 The Closing Process

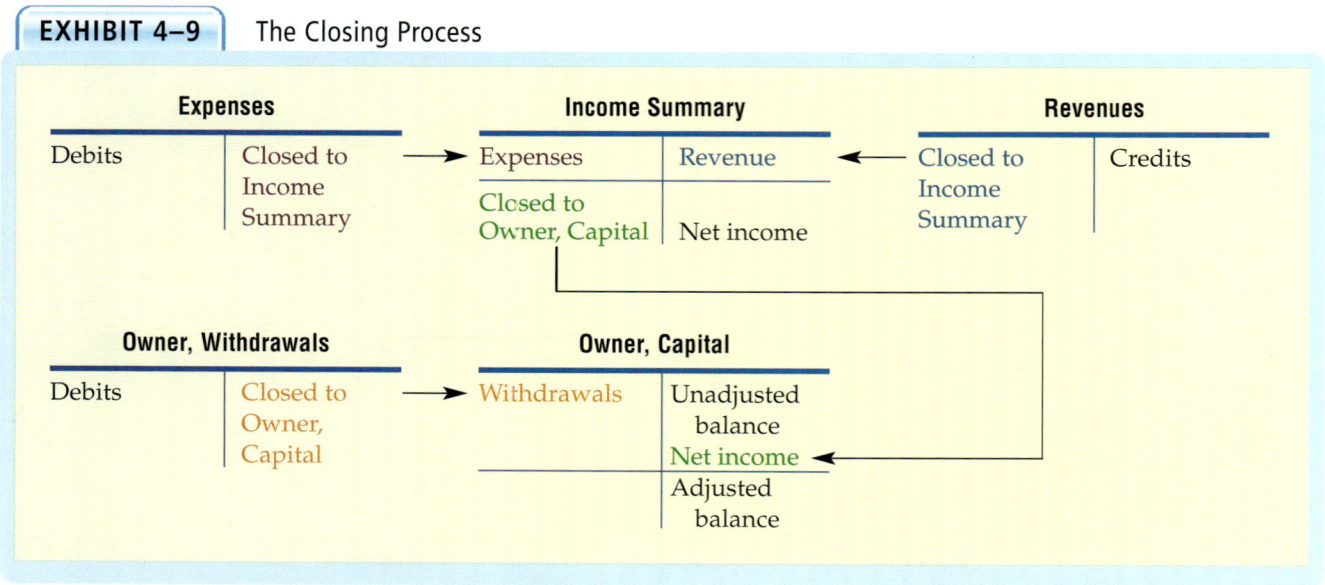

Closing a Net Income The steps in closing the accounts of a company like SuperTravel that has a net income are as follows (the circled numbers are keyed to Exhibit 4–10 on page 167):

① Debit each *revenue* account for the amount of its credit balance. Credit Income Summary for the sum of the revenues. This closing entry transfers the sum of the revenues to the *credit* side of the Income Summary.

② Credit each *expense* account for the amount of its debit balance. Debit Income Summary for the sum of the expenses. This closing entry transfers the sum of the expenses to the *debit* side of the Income Summary. It is not necessary to make a separate closing entry for each expense. In one closing entry, record one debit to Income Summary and a separate credit to each expense account.

③ The Income Summary account now holds the net income of the period, but only for a moment. To close net income, debit Income Summary for the amount of its *credit balance* (*net income* equals revenues minus expenses) and credit the Capital account. This closing entry transfers the net income from Income Summary to the Capital account.

④ Credit the *Withdrawals* account for the amount of its debit balance. Debit the Capital account. This entry transfers the Withdrawals amount to the *debit* side of the Capital account. Withdrawals are not expenses and do not affect net income or net loss.

These steps are best illustrated with an example. Suppose SuperTravel closes the books at the end of April. Exhibit 4–10 presents the complete closing process for the business. Panel A gives the closing journal entries, and Panel B shows the accounts after the closing entries have been posted.

EXHIBIT 4–10 Journalizing and Posting the Closing Entries

Panel A: Journalizing

Closing Entries   Page 5

① Apr. 30	Service Revenue	14,800	
	Income Summary..		14,800
	To close the revenue account and create the		
	Income Summary account.		
② 30	Income Summary	7,950	
	Insurance Expense...		350
	Rent Expense		1,800
	Salary Expense		3,800
	Supplies Expense...		600
	Amortization Expense		600
	Utilities Expense		800
	To close the expense accounts.		
③ 30	Income Summary..	6,850	
	John Lapp, Capital..		6,850
	To close the Income Summary account and		
	transfer net income to the Capital account.		
	(Income Summary balance = $14,800 − $7,950).		
30	John Lapp, Capital	5,900	
④	John Lapp, Withdrawals.................................		5,900
	To close the Withdrawals account and transfer		
	the Withdrawals amount to the Capital account.		

Panel B: Posting

Insurance Expense

Adj.	350		
Bal.	350	Clo.	350

Rent Expense

Adj.	1,800		
Bal.	1,800	Clo.	1,800

Salary Expense

	1,900		
Adj.	1,900		
Bal.	3,800	Clo.	3,800

Supplies Expense

Adj.	600		
Bal.	600	Clo.	600

Amortization Expense

Adj.	600		
Bal.	600	Clo.	600

Utilities Expense

	800		
Bal.	800	Clo.	800

② ③ ④ ①

Income Summary

Clo.	7,950	Clo.	14,800
Clo.	6,850	Bal.	6,850

Service Revenue

			14,000
		Adj.	500
		Adj.	300
Clo.	14,800	Bal.	14,800

John Lapp, Withdrawals

Bal.	5,900	Clo.	5,900

John Lapp, Capital

Clo.	5,900		65,200
		Clo.	6,850
		Bal.	66,150

Adj. = Amount posted from an adjusting entry   Clo. = Amount posted from a closing entry   Bal. = Balance

The amount in the debit side of each expense account is its adjusted balance. For example, Insurance Expense has a $350 debit balance. Also note that Service Revenue has a credit balance of $14,800 before closing. These amounts come directly from the adjusted balances in Exhibit 4–8, Panel B.

- Closing entry ① , denoted in the Service Revenue account by *Clo.*, transfers Service Revenue's balance to the Income Summary account. This entry zeroes out Service Revenue for April and places the revenue on the credit side of Income Summary.
- Closing entry ② zeroes out the expenses and moves their total ($7,950) to the debit side of Income Summary. At this point, Income Summary contains the impact of April's revenues and expenses; hence Income Summary's balance is the month's net income ($6,850).
- Closing entry ③ closes the Income Summary account by transferring net income to the credit side of John Lapp, Capital.[1]
- The last closing entry, ④ , moves the owner withdrawals to the debit side of John Lapp, Capital, leaving a zero balance in the John Lapp, Withdrawals account.

The closing entries set all the revenues, the expenses, and the Withdrawals account back to zero. Now the Capital account includes the full effects of the April revenues, expenses, and withdrawals. These amounts, combined with the beginning Capital's balance, give John Lapp, Capital an ending balance of $66,150. Trace this ending Capital balance to the statement of owner's equity and also to the balance sheet in Exhibit 4–7 on page 164.

Closing a Net Loss   What would the closing entries be if SuperTravel had suffered a net *loss* during April? Suppose April expenses totalled $15,400 and all other factors were unchanged. Only closing entries ② and ③ would change. Closing entry ② would transfer expenses of $15,400 to Income Summary, as follows:

Income Summary

Clo.	15,400	Clo.	14,800
Bal.	600		

Closing entry ③ would then credit Income Summary to close its debit balance and to transfer the net loss to John Lapp, Capital:

③ Apr. 30   John Lapp, Capital...   600
                       Income Summary   600

After posting, these two accounts would appear as follows:

Income Summary					**John Lapp, Capital**		
Clo.	15,400	Clo.	14,800		Clo.	600	65,200
Bal.	600	Clo.	600				

Finally, the Withdrawals balance would be closed to Capital, as before. The double line in a T-account means that the account has a zero balance; nothing more will be posted to it in the current period.

The closing process is fundamentally mechanical and is completely automated in a computerized system. Accounts are identified as either temporary or permanent. The temporary accounts are closed automatically by selecting that option from the software's menu. Posting also occurs automatically.

---

[1]The Income Summary account is a convenience for combining the effects of the revenues and expenses prior to transferring their income effect to Capital. It is not necessary to use the Income Summary account in the closing process. Another way of closing the revenues and expenses makes no use of this account. In this alternative procedure, the revenues and expenses are closed directly to Capital.

THINKING IT OVER

(1) Would the Income Summary have a debit or a credit balance if the company suffers a net loss?

(2) In the event of a loss, how is Income Summary closed?

A: (1) Expenses would exceed revenues, and Income Summary would have a debit balance. (2) Income Summary is credited, and Capital is debited.

KEY POINT

The double line in a T-account means that the account has a zero balance; nothing more will be posted to it in the current period. The double line is drawn immediately after the closing entry is posted. In the general ledger, the account has a zero balance.

Postclosing Trial Balance

The accounting cycle can end with the **postclosing trial balance** (Exhibit 4–11). The postclosing trial balance is the final check on the accuracy of journalizing and posting the adjusting and closing entries. It lists the ledger's accounts and their adjusted balances after closing. This step shows where the business stands as it moves into the next accounting period. The postclosing trial balance is dated as of the end of the period for which the statements have been prepared.

The postclosing trial balance resembles the balance sheet. It contains the ending balances of the permanent accounts—the balance sheet accounts: the assets, liabilities, and owner's equity. No temporary accounts—revenues, expenses, or withdrawal accounts—are included because their balances have been closed. The ledger is up to date and ready for the next period's transactions.

Accounting Cycle Tutorials

6. Adjusting and Closing Entries pages 1–13

EXHIBIT 4–11	Postclosing Trial Balance

SUPERTRAVEL
Postclosing Trial Balance
April 30, 2008

Cash	$49,600	
Accounts receivable	5,000	
Supplies	800	
Prepaid insurance	3,850	
Furniture	36,000	
Accumulated amortization—Furniture		$ 600
Accounts payable		26,000
Salary payable		1,900
Unearned service revenue		600
John Lapp, Capital		66,150
Total	$95,250	$95,250

Correcting Journal Entries

In Chapter 2 we discussed errors that affect the trial balance: treating a debit as a credit and vice versa; transpositions; and slides. Here we show how to correct errors in journal entries.

When a journal entry contains an error and the error is detected before posting, the entry can be corrected.

If the error is detected after posting, the accountant makes a *correcting entry*. Suppose SuperTravel paid $10,000 cash for furniture and erroneously debited Supplies as follows:

Objective 4

Correct typical accounting errors

Incorrect Entry

May 13	Supplies	10,000	
	Cash		10,000
	Bought supplies.		

The debit to Supplies is incorrect, so it is necessary to make the following correcting entry:

Correcting Entry

May 15	Furniture	10,000	
	Supplies		10,000
	To correct May 13 entry. Furniture was purchased.		

The credit to Supplies in the second entry offsets the incorrect debit of the first entry. The debit to Furniture in the correcting entry places the furniture's cost in the correct account. Now both Supplies and Furniture are correct. Cash was unaffected by the error because Cash was credited correctly in the entry on May 13.

Classifying Assets and Liabilities

Objective 5

Classify assets and liabilities as current or long-term, and prepare a classified balance sheet

On the balance sheet, assets and liabilities are classified as either *current* or *long-term* to show their relative liquidity. **Liquidity** is a measure of how quickly an item can be converted to cash. Cash is the most liquid asset. Accounts receivable is a relatively liquid asset because the business expects to collect the amount in cash in the near future. Supplies are less liquid than accounts receivable, and furniture and buildings are even less so.

Users of financial statements are interested in liquidity because business difficulties often arise from a shortage of cash. How quickly can the business convert an asset to cash and pay a debt? How soon must a liability be paid? These are questions of liquidity. A classified balance sheet lists assets and liabilities in the order of their relative liquidity.

Assets

Current Assets **Current assets** are assets that are expected to be converted to cash, sold, or consumed during the next 12 months or within the business's normal operating cycle if longer than a year. The **operating cycle** is the time span during which

1. Cash is used to acquire goods and services.
2. Those goods and services are sold to customers.
3. The business collects cash from those customers.

For most businesses, the operating cycle is a few months. A few types of business have operating cycles longer than a year. Cash, Accounts Receivable, Notes Receivable due within a year or less, Supplies, and Prepaid Expenses are current assets. Merchandising entities such as The Bay and Canadian Tire and manufacturing entities such as Magna International Inc. and Bombardier Inc. have an additional current asset, Inventory. This account shows the cost of goods that are held for sale to customers.

Long-Term (Capital) Assets **Long-term assets**, defined as **capital assets** in Section 3061 of the *CICA Handbook*, are all assets other than goodwill and current assets. One category of capital assets is **property, plant, and equipment**, and this category includes the accounts Land, Buildings, Furniture and Fixtures, and Equipment. Of these, SuperTravel has only Furniture.

Other categories of long-term assets include Long-Term Investments and Other Assets (a catchall category for assets that are not classified more precisely). We discuss these categories in more detail in later chapters.

Liabilities

Financial statement users (such as creditors) are interested in the due dates of an entity's liabilities. Liabilities that must be paid the soonest create the greatest strain on cash. Therefore, the balance sheet lists liabilities in the order they are due to be paid. Balance sheets usually have at least two liability classifications, *current liabilities* and *long-term liabilities*. Knowing how many of a business's liabilities are current and how many are long-term helps creditors assess the likelihood of collecting from the entity.

Current Liabilities **Current liabilities** are debts that are due to be paid with cash or with goods and services within one year or one of the entity's operating cycles if the cycle is longer than a year. Accounts Payable, Notes Payable due within one year, Salaries Payable, Goods and Services Tax Payable, Interest Payable, and Unearned Revenue are current liabilities.

Long-Term Liabilities All liabilities that are not current are classified as **long-term liabilities**. Many notes payable are long-term—payable after the longer of one year or the entity's operating cycle. Some notes are paid in installments, with the first installment due within one year, the second installment due the second year, and so on. The first installment would be a current liability and the remainder long-term liabilities. For example, a $100,000 note payable to be paid $10,000 per year over ten years would include:

- A current liability of $10,000 for next year's payment, and
- A long-term liability of $90,000.

The Classified Balance Sheet

Thus far in this book we have presented the *unclassified* balance sheet of SuperTravel. Our purpose was to focus on the main points of assets, liabilities, and owner's equity without the details of *current* assets, *current* liabilities, and so on. Exhibit 4–12 presents SuperTravel's classified balance sheet. (Notice that SuperTravel has no long-term liabilities. Suppose the company had incurred a debt for its furniture and the debt would not be repaid during the coming year. This debt would have appeared as a long-term liability on the balance sheet.)

EXHIBIT 4–12   Classified Balance Sheet of SuperTravel in Account Format

SUPERTRAVEL
Balance Sheet
April 30, 2008

Assets			Liabilities		
Current assets:			Current liabilities:		
Cash		$49,600	Accounts payable		$26,000
Accounts receivable		5,000	Salary payable		1,900
Supplies		800	Unearned service revenue		600
Prepaid insurance		3,850	Total current liabilities		28,500
Total current assets		59,250			
			Owner's Equity		
Property, plant, and equipment:					
Furniture	$36,000		John Lapp, capital		66,150
Less: Accumulated					
amortization	600				
Total capital assets		35,400	Total liabilities and		
Total assets		$94,650	owner's equity		$94,650

Compare SuperTravel's *classified* balance sheet in Exhibit 4–12 with the *unclassified* balance sheet in Exhibit 4–7. The classified balance sheet reports totals for current assets and current liabilities, which do not appear on the unclassified balance sheet. Also, SuperTravel has no long-term liabilities, so there are none to report on either balance sheet.

The classified balance sheet of Ivaco Products Company, a fictitious company, is shown in Exhibit 4–13. It shows how a company with many different accounts could present its data on a classified balance sheet.

EXHIBIT 4–13 | Classified Balance Sheet of Ivaco Products Company

IVACO PRODUCTS COMPANY
Balance Sheet
June 30, 2009

Assets

Current assets:

Cash	$ 26,400	
Held-for-trading investments	57,000	
Accounts receivable	235,000	
Interest receivable	26,800	
Current portion of note receivable	51,600	
Inventory	847,800	
Supplies	5,200	
Prepaid insurance	24,600	
Prepaid rent	27,000	
Total current assets		$1,301,400

Other assets:

Note receivable	100,000	
Less: Current portion of note receivable	51,600	
Total other assets		48,400

Property, plant, and equipment:

Equipment	$ 60,000		
Less: accumulated amortization	18,000	42,000	
Furniture and fixtures	70,000		
Less: accumulated amortization	30,000	40,000	
Buildings	240,000		
Less: accumulated amortization	160,000	80,000	
Land		70,000	
Total property, plant, and equipment			232,000
Total assets			$1,581,800

Liabilities

Current liabilities:

Accounts payable	$357,000	
Salaries and wages payable	22,400	
Interest payable	24,600	
Current portion of notes payable	60,000	
Goods and services tax payable	64,600	
Current portion of mortgage payable	72,200	
Other current liabilities	23,600	
Total current liabilities		$ 624,400

Long-term liabilities:

Notes payable	$340,000		
Less current portion of notes payable	60,000	280,000	
Mortgage payable	220,000		
Less current portion of mortgage payable	72,200	147,800	
Total long-term liabilities			427,800
Total liabilities			1,052,200

Owner's Equity

Ivan Hanley, capital		529,600
Total liabilities and owner's equity		$1,581,800

Formats of Balance Sheets

The balance sheets of Ivaco Products Company shown in Exhibit 4–13 and of SuperTravel shown in Exhibit 4–14 list the assets at the top, with the liabilities and owner's equity below. This is the *report format*. SuperTravel's balance sheet in Exhibit 4–7 lists the assets at the left, with the liabilities and the owner's equity at the right. That is the *account format*.

Either format is acceptable. The report format is more extensively used by Canadian companies.

Accounting Cycle Tutorials

5. Financial Statements
pages 12–14

EXHIBIT 4–14 Classified Balance Sheet of SuperTravel in Report Format

SUPERTRAVEL
Balance Sheet
April 30, 2008

Assets

Current assets:

Cash		$49,600
Accounts receivable		5,000
Supplies		800
Prepaid insurance		3,850
Total current assets		59,250

Property, plant, and equipment:

Furniture	$36,000	
Less: Accumulated amortization	600	35,400
Total assets		$94,650

Liabilities

Current liabilities:

Accounts payable		$26,000
Salary payable		1,900
Unearned service revenue		600
Total current liabilities		28,500

Owner's Equity

John Lapp, capital		66,150
Total liabilities and owner's equity		$94,650

Accounting Ratios

Objective 6

Use the current ratio and debt ratio to evaluate a company

The purpose of accounting is to provide information for decision making. Chief users of accounting information include managers, investors, and creditors. A creditor considering lending money must predict whether the borrower can repay the loan. If the borrower already has a large amount of debt, the probability of repayment is lower than if the borrower has a small amount of liabilities. To assess financial position, decision makers use ratios they compute from a company's financial statements. Two of the most widely used decision aids in business are the current ratio and the debt ratio.

Current Ratio

One of the most common ratios is the **current ratio,** which is the ratio of an entity's current assets to its current liabilities:

$$\text{Current Ratio} = \frac{\text{Total current assets}}{\text{Total current liabilities}}$$

THINKING IT OVER

A company has current assets of $100,000 and current liabilities of $50,000. How will the payment of a $10,000 account payable affect the current ratio?

A: The payment of an account payable would cause both cash and accounts payable to decrease and thus would increase the current ratio from 2.00 to 2.25. In other words, payment of the liability would make the company look better.

The current ratio measures the ability to pay current liabilities with current assets. A company prefers a high current ratio, which means the business has sufficient current assets to pay current liabilities when they come due, plus a cushion of additional current assets. An increasing current ratio from period to period generally indicates improvement in ability to pay current debts.

A rule of thumb: A strong current ratio would be in the range of 2.00, which indicates that the company has approximately $2.00 in current assets for every $1.00 in current liabilities. A company with a current ratio of 2.00 would probably have little trouble paying its current liabilities. Most successful businesses operate with current ratios between 1.30 and 2.00. A current ratio of 1.00 is considered quite low. Lenders and investors would view a company with a current ratio of 1.50 to 2.00 as substantially less risky. Such a company could probably borrow money on better terms and also attract more investors.

STOP AND THINK

Compute SuperTravel's current ratio. Use the company's balance sheet in Exhibit 4–14.

Answer:

$$\text{Current ratio} = \frac{\text{Total current assets}}{\text{Total current liabilities}} = \frac{\$59,250}{\$28,500} = 2.08$$

How much in current assets does SuperTravel have for every dollar the company owes in current liabilities?

Answer:

$2.08

Is SuperTravel's current ratio high or low? Is this ratio value risky?

Answer:

SuperTravel's current ratio is very high, which is not risky and makes the business look safe.

Debt Ratio

A second aid to decision making is the **debt ratio,** which is the ratio of total liabilities to total assets:

$$\text{Debt Ratio} = \frac{\text{Total liabilities}}{\text{Total assets}}$$

The debt ratio indicates the proportion of a company's assets that are financed with debt, as opposed to the proportion financed by the owner(s) of the company. This ratio measures a company's ability to pay both current and long-term debts—total liabilities.

A *low* debt ratio is safer than a high debt ratio. Why? Because a company with low liabilities has low required payments. Such a company is unlikely to get into financial difficulty. A rule of thumb: A debt ratio below 0.60, or 60%, is considered safe for most businesses. A debt ratio above 0.80, or 80%, borders on high risk. Most companies have debt ratios in the range of 0.60 to 0.80.

STOP AND THINK

Compute SuperTravel's debt ratio from the company's balance sheet in Exhibit 4–14.

Answer:

$$\text{Debt ratio} = \frac{\text{Total liabilities}}{\text{Total assets}} = \frac{\$28,500}{\$94,650} = 0.30, \text{ or } 30\%$$

What percentage of SuperTravel's total assets is financed with debt?

Answer:

0.30, or 30%

If you owed $0.30 for every dollar of your total assets, would you worry about your ability to pay your debts?

Answer:

No, a debt ratio of 30% looks safe.

Managing Both the Current Ratio and the Debt Ratio In general, a *high* current ratio is preferred over a low current ratio. *Increases* in the current ratio indicate improving financial position. By contrast, a *low* debt ratio is preferred over a high debt ratio. Improvement is indicated by a *decrease* in the debt ratio.

Financial ratios are an important aid to decision makers. However, it is unwise to place too much confidence in a single ratio or group of ratios. For example, a company may have a high current ratio, which indicates financial strength. It may also have a high debt ratio, which suggests weakness. Which ratio gives the more reliable signal about the company? Experienced managers, lenders, and investors evaluate a company by examining a large number of ratios over several years to spot trends and turning points. These people also consider other facts, such as the company's cash position and its trend in net income. No single ratio gives the whole picture about a company.

As you progress through the study of accounting, we will introduce key ratios used for decision making. Chapter 18 (in Volume II) then summarizes all the ratios discussed in this book and provides a good overview of ratios used in decision making.

As we conclude this chapter, we return to our opening questions: How do you complete the accounting cycle and why is it important? What are closing entries? Closing the books is a necessary process so that the accounting cycle can begin anew in the next accounting period, ensuring the results of the next accounting period will be measured accurately. The Decision Guidelines feature summarizes all of our chapter-opening questions, highlighting the final step in the accounting cycle and the topics covered in this chapter.

DECISION GUIDELINES — Completing the Accounting Cycle

Decision

What document summarizes the effects of all the company's transactions and adjustments throughout the period?

Guidelines

Accountant's *work sheet* with columns for:
- Trial balance
- Adjustments
- Adjusted trial balance
- Income statement
- Balance sheet

Decision

What is the last *major* step in the accounting cycle?

Guidelines

Closing entries for the *temporary accounts*:

Revenues
Expenses } Income statement accounts
Owner's withdrawals

Decision

Why close revenues, expenses, and owner's withdrawals?

Guidelines

Because the *temporary accounts* have balances that relate only to one accounting period (fiscal year) and do *not* carry over to the next accounting period (fiscal year).

Decision

Which accounts do not get closed?

Guidelines

Permanent (balance sheet) accounts:
- Assets
- Liabilities
- Owner's capital

The balances of these accounts *do* carry over to the next accounting period.

Decision

How do businesses classify their assets and liabilities for reporting on the balance sheet?

Guidelines

Current (within one year or the company's operating cycle if longer than a year)

or

Long-term (not current). Long-term assets are capital assets and goodwill.

Decision

How do decision makers evaluate a company?

Guidelines

There are many ways, such as the company's net income or net loss on the income statement, and the trend of net income from year to year.

Another way to evaluate a company is based on the company's *financial ratios*. Two key ratios:

$$\text{Current ratio} = \frac{\text{Total current assets}}{\text{Total current liabilities}}$$

The current ratio measures the ability to pay current liabilities with current assets.

$$\text{Debt ratio} = \frac{\text{Total liabilities}}{\text{Total assets}}$$

The debt ratio measures the overall ability to pay liabilities. The debt ratio shows the proportion of the entity's assets that are financed with debt.

Refer to the data in the Mid-Chapter Summary Problem for Your Review, presented on pages 161–162.

Required

1. Journalize and post the adjusting entries. (Before posting to the T-accounts, enter into each T-account its balance as shown in the trial balance. For example, enter the $5,000 balance in the Accounts Receivable account before posting its adjusting entry.) Identify adjusting entries by *letter,* as shown in the work sheet solution to the mid-chapter review problem. You can take the adjusting entries straight from the work sheet on p. 162. Explanations are not required. Find the ending balances of the permanent accounts.

2. Journalize and post the closing entries. (Each T-account should carry its balance as shown in the adjusted trial balance.) Provide explanations. To distinguish closing entries from adjusting entries, identify the closing entries by *number.* Draw the arrows to illustrate the flow of data, as shown in Exhibit 4–10, page 167. Indicate the balance of the Capital account after the closing entries are posted.

3. Prepare the income statement for the year ended December 31, 2008. List Miscellaneous Expense last among the expenses, a common practice.

4. Prepare the statement of owner's equity for the year ended December 31, 2008. Draw the arrow that links the income statement to the statement of owner's equity, if both statements are on the same page. Otherwise, explain how they are linked.

5. Prepare the classified balance sheet at December 31, 2008. Use the report format. All liabilities are current. Draw the arrow that links the statement of owner's equity to the balance sheet, if both statements are on the same page. Otherwise, explain how they are linked.

Name: Curry's Service Company
Industry: Service proprietorship
Fiscal Period: Year ended December 31, 2008
Key Fact: Existing, ongoing business

Solution

Requirement 1

Refer to the work sheet on page 162. Refer to the Adjustments columns of the work sheet. Make journal entries for all the transactions in the Adjustments columns.

a. Dec. 31	Supplies Expense		800	
	Supplies			800
b. Dec. 31	Amortization Expense—Furniture		2,000	
	Accumulated Amortization—Furniture			2,000
c. Dec. 31	Amortization Expense—Building		1,000	
	Accumulated Amortization—Building			1,000
d. Dec. 31	Salary Expense		500	
	Salary Payable			500
e. Dec. 31	Accounts Receivable		1,300	
	Service Revenue			1,300
f. Dec. 31	Unearned Service Revenue		3,000	
	Service Revenue			3,000

Create T-accounts only for the accounts affected by the adjusting entries.

Remember that the beginning balance in each of these T-accounts is the amount from the Trial Balance columns of the work sheet on page 162.

When you post the adjusting entries, use the letters a to f to identify each adjustment.

Find the balance of each T-account.

Accounts Receivable

	5,000	
(e)	1,300	
Bal.	6,300	

Supplies

	1,000	(a)	800
Bal.	200		

Accumulated Amortization—Furniture

		4,000
	(b)	2,000
	Bal.	6,000

Accumulated Amortization—Building

		30,000
	(c)	1,000
	Bal.	31,000

Salary Payable

	(d)	500
	Bal.	500

Unearned Service Revenue

(f)	3,000		8,000
		Bal.	5,000

Service Revenue

		60,000
	(e)	1,300
	(f)	3,000
	Bal.	64,300

Salary Expense

	16,000	
(d)	500	
Bal.	16,500	

Supplies Expense

(a)	800	
Bal.	800	

Amortization Expense—Furniture

(b)	2,000	
Bal.	2,000	

Amortization Expense—Building

(c)	1,000	
Bal.	1,000	

Requirement 2

1. Dec. 31	Service Revenue..	64,300	
	Income Summary		64,300
	To close the revenue account and create the Income Summary account.		
2. Dec. 31	Income Summary	21,300	
	Salary Expense...		16,500
	Supplies Expense...		800
	Amortization Expense—Furniture		2,000
	Amortization Expense—Building..............		1,000
	Miscellaneous Expense................................		1,000
	To close the expense accounts.		
3. Dec. 31	Income Summary	43,000	
	Bill Curry, Capital		43,000
	To close the Income Summary account. (Income Summary balance = \$64,300 − \$21,300).		
4. Dec. 31	Bill Curry, Capital	25,000	
	Bill Curry, Withdrawals..............................		25,000
	To close the Withdrawals account and transfer the Withdrawals amount to the Capital account.		

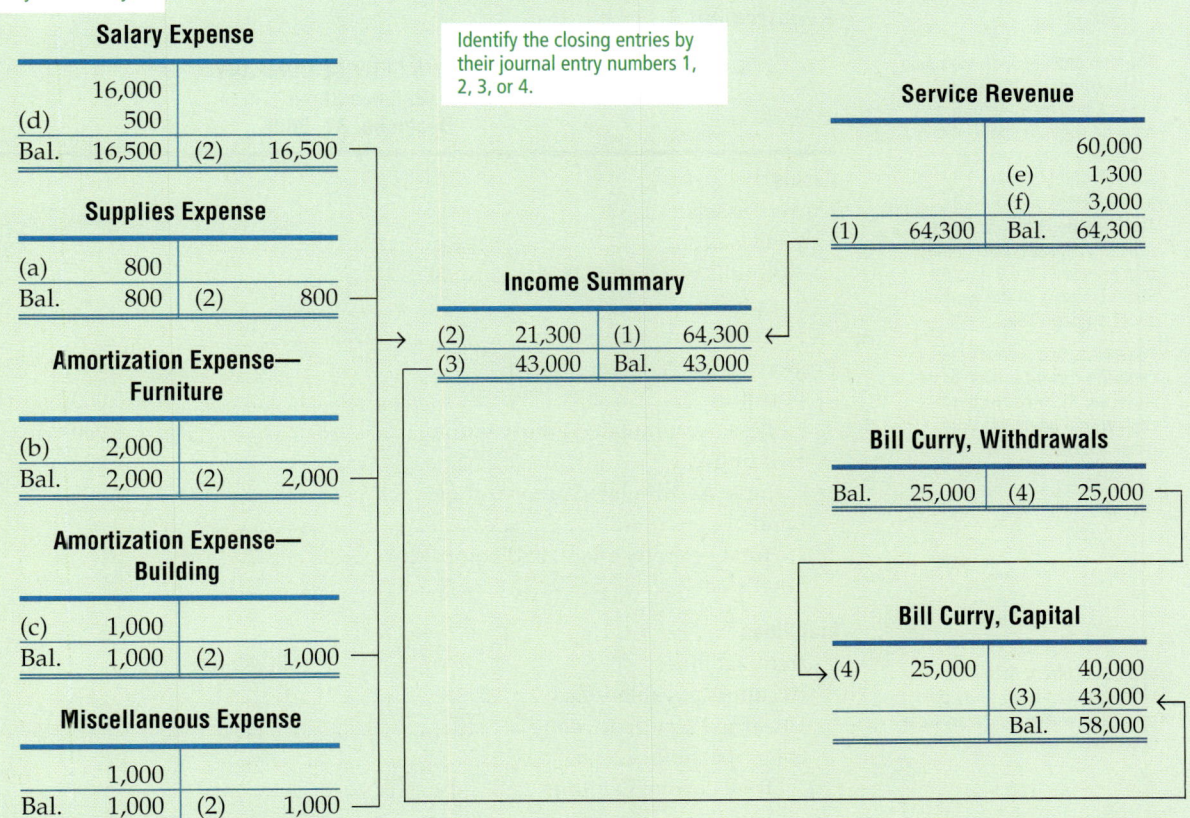

Requirement 3

CURRY'S SERVICE COMPANY
Income Statement
For the Year Ended December 31, 2008

Revenues:		
Service revenue		$64,300
Expenses:		
Salary expense	$16,500	
Amortization expense—furniture	2,000	
Amortization expense—building	1,000	
Supplies expense	800	
Miscellaneous expense	1,000	
Total expenses		21,300
Net income		$43,000

Requirement 4

CURRY'S SERVICE COMPANY
Statement of Owner's Equity
For the Year Ended December 31, 2008

Bill Curry, Capital, January 1, 2008	$40,000
Add: Net income	43,000
	83,000
Less: Withdrawals	25,000
Bill Curry, Capital, December 31, 2008	$58,000

Requirement 5

CURRY'S SERVICE COMPANY
Balance Sheet
December 31, 2008

Assets

Current assets:		
Cash		$ 6,000
Accounts receivable		6,300
Supplies		200
Total current assets		12,500
Property, plant, and equipment:		
Furniture	$10,000	
Less: Accumulated amortization	6,000	4,000
Building	60,000	
Less: Accumulated amortization	31,000	29,000
Land		20,000
Total property, plant, and equipment		53,000
Total assets		$65,500

Liabilities

Current liabilities:	
Accounts payable	$2,000
Unearned service revenue	5,000
Salary payable	500
Total current liabilities	7,500

Owner's Equity

Bill Curry, capital	58,000
Total liabilities and owner's equity	$65,500

Summary

1. **Prepare an accounting work sheet.** The *accounting cycle* is the process by which accountants produce the financial statements for a specific period of time. The cycle starts with the beginning account balances. During the period, the business journalizes transactions and posts them to the ledger accounts. At the end of the period, the trial balance is prepared, and the accounts are adjusted in order to measure the period's net income or net loss. Completion of the accounting cycle is aided by use of a *work sheet*. This multicolumned document summarizes the effects of all the period's activity.

2. **Use the work sheet to complete the accounting cycle.** The work sheet is neither a journal nor a ledger but merely a convenient device for completing the accounting cycle. It has columns for the trial balance, the adjustments, the adjusted trial balance, the income statement, and the balance sheet. It aids the adjusting process, and it is the place where the period's net income or net loss is first computed. The work sheet also provides the data for the financial statements and the *closing entries*. It is not, however, a necessity. The accounting cycle can be completed from the less elaborate adjusted trial balance.

3. **Close the revenue, expense, and withdrawal accounts.** Revenues, expenses, and owner withdrawals represent increases and decreases in the capital account for a specific period. At the end of the period, their balances are closed out to zero, and, for this reason, they are called *temporary accounts*. Assets, liabilities, and capital accounts are not closed out to zero because they are the *permanent accounts*. Their balances at the end of one period become the beginning balances of the next period. The final accuracy check of the period is the *postclosing trial balance*.

4. **Correct typical accounting errors.** Accountants correct errors by making correcting journal entries.

5. **Classify assets and liabilities as current or long-term, and prepare a classified balance sheet.** The balance sheet reports *current* and *long-term* (or *capital*) *assets* and *current* and *long-term liabilities*. It can be presented in *report format* or *account format*.

6. **Use the current ratio and debt ratio to evaluate a company.** Two decision-making aids are the *current ratio* (total current assets divided by total current liabilities) and the *debt ratio* (total liabilities divided by total assets).

Chapter 4 Appendix

Reversing Entries: An Optional Step

Reversing entries are special types of entries that ease the burden of accounting after adjusting and closing entries have been made at the end of a period. Reversing entries are used most often in conjunction with accrual-type adjustments such as an accrued salary expense and accrued service revenue. Reversing entries are *not* used for adjustments to record amortization and prepayments. *GAAP do not require reversing entries. They are used only for convenience and to save time.*

Objective
Describe and prepare reversing entries

Accounting for Accrued Expenses To see how reversing entries work, return to SuperTravel's unadjusted trial balance at April 30, 2008 (Exhibit 4–2, page 158b).

Salary Expense has a debit balance of $1,900 from salaries paid during April. At April 30, the company owes employees an additional $1,900 for the last part of the month.

Assume for this illustration that on May 5, the next payroll date, SuperTravel will pay $1,900 of accrued salary plus $200 in salary that the employee has earned in the first few days of May. SuperTravel's next payroll payment will be $2,100 ($1,900 + $200). But SuperTravel must include the $1,900 in salary expense for April. To do so, SuperTravel makes the following adjusting entry on April 30:

Adjusting Entries

April 30	Salary Expense..	1,900	
	Salary Payable..		1,900

After posting, the Salary Payable and Salary Expense accounts appear as follows:

Salary Payable

		Apr. 30 Adj.[1]	1,900
		Apr. 30 Bal.	1,900

Salary Expense

Paid during		
April CP	1,900	
Apr. 30 Adj.	1,900	
Apr. 30 Bal.	3,800	

After the adjusting entry,

- The April income statement reports salary expense of $3,800.
- The April 30 balance sheet reports salary payable of $1,900.

The $3,800 debit balance of Salary Expense is eliminated by this closing entry at April 30, 2008, as follows:

Closing Entries

April 30	Income Summary	3,800	
	Salary Expense		3,800

After posting, Salary Expense has a zero balance as follows:

Salary Expense

Paid during				
April CP	1,900			
Apr. 30 Adj.	1,900			
Apr. 30 Bal.	3,800	Apr. 30 Clo.	3,800

Accounting without a Reversing Entry   On May 5, the next payday, SuperTravel pays the payroll of $2,100 and makes this journal entry:

May 5	Salary Payable	1,900	
	Salary Expense	200	
	Cash		2,100

This method of recording the cash payment is correct. However, it wastes time because the company's accountant must refer to the adjusting entries of April 30. Otherwise, SuperTravel does not know the amount of the debit to Salary Payable (in this example, $1,900). Searching the preceding period's adjusting entries takes time and, in business, time is money. To save time, accountants use reversing entries.

---

[1] Entry explanations used throughout this discussion are

Adj. = Adjusting entry	CP = Cash payment entry—includes a credit to Cash
Bal. = Balance	CR = Cash receipt entry—includes a debit to Cash
Clo. = Closing entry	Rev. = Reversing entry

Making a Reversing Entry   A **reversing entry** switches the debit and the credit of a previous adjusting entry. *A reversing entry, then, is the exact opposite of a prior adjusting entry.* The reversing entry is dated the first day of the period following the adjusting entry.

To illustrate reversing entries, recall that on April 30, 2008, SuperTravel made the following adjusting entry to accrue Salary Payable:

Adjusting Entries

Apr. 30	Salary Expense	1,900	
	Salary Payable		1,900

The reversing entry simply reverses the position of the debit and the credit:

Reversing Entries

May 1	Salary Payable..	1,900	
	Salary Expense		1,900

Observe that the reversing entry is dated the first day of the new period. It is the exact opposite of the April 30 adjusting entry. Ordinarily, the accountant who makes the adjusting entry also prepares the reversing entry at the same time. SuperTravel dates the reversing entry as of the first day of the next period, however, so that it affects only the new period. Note how the accounts appear after the company posts the reversing entry:

Salary Payable

May 1 Rev.	1,900	Apr. 30 Bal.	1,900

Zero balance

Salary Expense

Apr. 30 Bal.	3,800	Apr. 30 Clo.	3,800

Zero balance

	May 1 **Rev.**	1,900 ←

The arrow shows the transfer of the $1,900 credit balance from Salary Payable to Salary Expense. This credit balance in Salary Expense does not mean that the entity has negative salary expense, as you might think. Instead, the odd credit balance is merely a temporary result of the reversing entry. The credit balance is eliminated on May 5 when the $2,100 cash payment for salaries is debited to Salary Expense in the customary manner:

May 5	Salary Expense..	2,100	
	Cash		2,100

Then this cash payment entry is posted as follows:

Salary Expense

May 5 CP	2,100	May 1 Rev.	1,900
May 5 Bal.	200		

Now Salary Expense has its correct debit balance of $200, which is the amount of salary expense incurred thus far in May. The $2,100 cash disbursement also pays the liability for Salary Payable so that Salary Payable has a zero balance, which is correct.

Exhibit 4–A1 shows these transactions side-by-side to highlight the differences and show that the results are the same whether or not reversing entries are used.

Accounting for Accrued Revenues   While most reversing entries are made to accrue expenses, reversing entries may be made to accrue revenues. For example, if SuperTravel had completed some consulting work for a client, an entry would be

Accounting Cycle Tutorials

6. Adjusting and Closing Entries pages 16–17

made to debit Accounts Receivable and credit Fee Revenue at April 30, 2008. Fee Revenue would be closed to the Income Summary in the usual way. A reversing entry on May 1, 2008, would reduce the Accounts Receivable and temporarily create a debit balance in the Fee Revenue account. When the payment is received, the accountant would debit Cash and credit Fee Revenue.

EXHIBIT 4–A1   Reversing Entries for Accrued Expenses

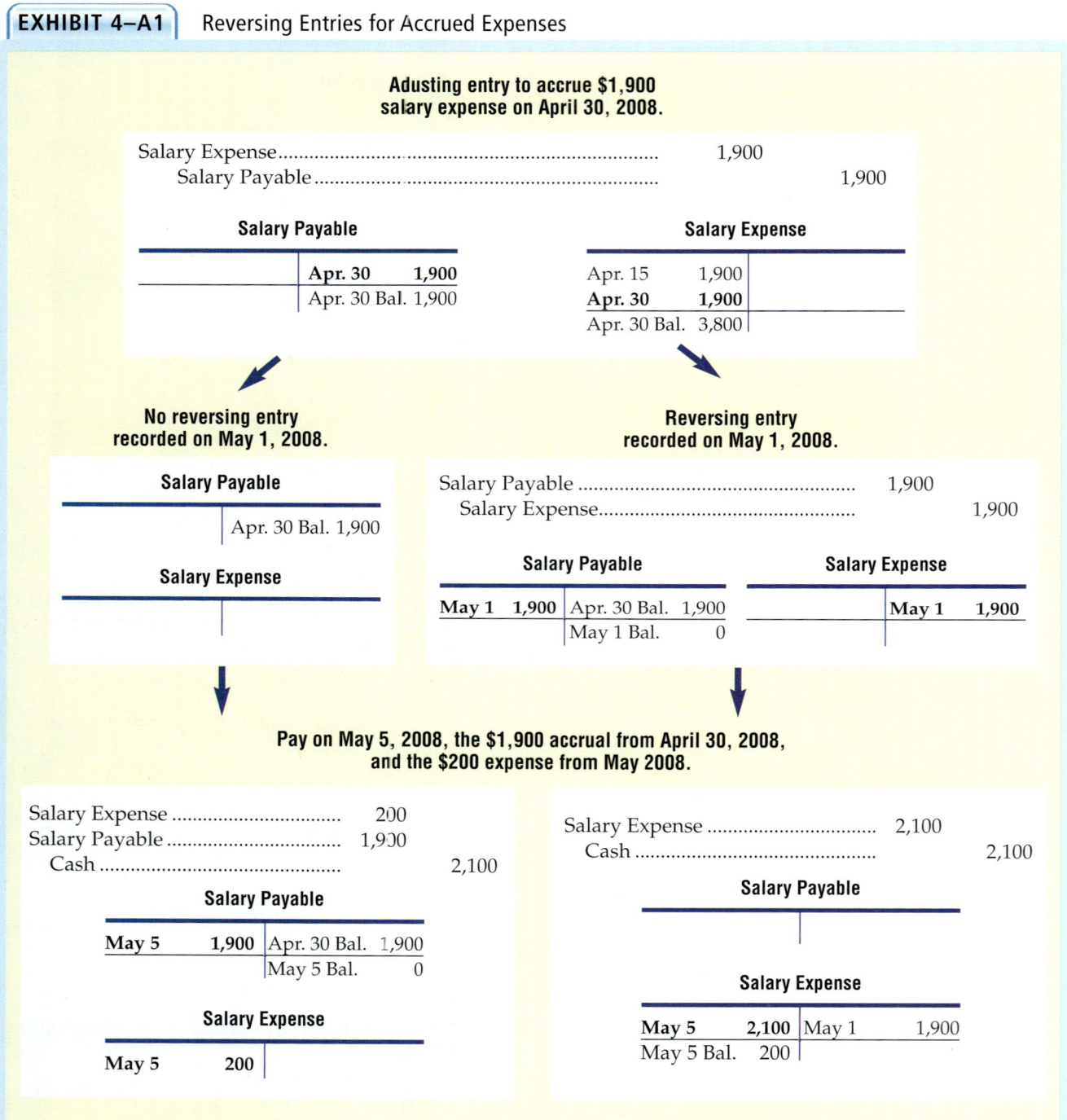

Without and with adjusting entries, Salary Payable and Salary Expense have the same May 5, 2008, balances after the May 5 payment of salary.

Self-Study Questions

Test your understanding of the chapter by marking the correct answer to each of the following questions:

1. The focal point of the accounting cycle is the (p. 157)
   a. Financial statements   c. Adjusted trial balance
   b. Trial balance   d. Work sheet

2. Arrange the following accounting cycle steps in their proper order assuming a work sheet is used (p. 158)
   a. Complete the work sheet
   b. Journalize and post adjusting entries
   c. Prepare the postclosing trial balance
   d. Journalize and post cash transactions
   e. Prepare the financial statements
   f. Journalize and post closing entries

3. The work sheet is a (p. 158a)
   a. Journal
   b. Ledger
   c. Financial statement
   d. Convenient device for completing the accounting cycle

4. The usefulness of the work sheet is (pp. 158–158a)
   a. Identifying the accounts that need to be adjusted
   b. Summarizing the effects of all the transactions of the period
   c. Aiding the preparation of the financial statements
   d. All of the above

5. Which of the following accounts is not closed? (pp. 163–165)
   a. Supplies Expense
   b. Prepaid Insurance
   c. Interest Revenue
   d. Withdrawals

6. The closing entry for Salary Expense, with a balance of $322,000, is (pp. 163–165)

   a. Salary Expense   322,000
         Income Summary   322,000
   b. Salary Expense   322,000
         Salary Payable   322,000
   c. Income Summary   322,000
         Salary Expense   322,000
   d. Salary Payable   322,000
         Salary Expense   322,000

7. The purpose of the postclosing trial balance is to (p. 169)
   a. Provide the account balances for preparation of the balance sheet
   b. Ensure that the ledger is in balance for the start of the next period
   c. Aid the journalizing and posting of the closing entries
   d. Ensure that the ledger is in balance for completion of the work sheet

8. A $500 payment on account was recorded by debiting Supplies and crediting Cash. This entry was posted. The correcting entry is (pp. 169–170)

   a. Accounts Payable   500
         Supplies   500
   b. Supplies   500
         Accounts Payable   500
   c. Cash   500
         Accounts Payable   500
   d. Cash   500
         Supplies   500

9. The classification of assets and liabilities as current or long-term depends on (pp. 170–172)
   a. Their order of listing in the ledger
   b. Whether they appear on the balance sheet or the income statement
   c. The relative liquidity of the item
   d. The format of the balance sheet—account format or report format

10. Suppose in 2008, SuperTravel debited Amortization Expense for the cost of a computer used in the business. For 2008, this error (pp. 169–170)
    a. Overstated net income
    b. Understated net income
    c. Either a or b, depending on the circumstances
    d. Had no effect on net income

Answers to the Self-Study Questions follow the Similar Accounting Terms.

Accounting Vocabulary

Accounting cycle   (p. 157)
Capital asset   (p. 170)
Closing entries   (p. 165)
Closing the accounts   (p. 163)
Current asset   (p. 170)
Current liability   (p. 171)
Current ratio   (p. 174)
Debt ratio   (p. 175)
Income Summary   (p. 166)
Liquidity   (p. 170)
Long-term asset   (p. 170)

Long-term liability   (p. 171)
Nominal account   (p. 164)
Operating cycle   (p. 170)
Permanent account   (p. 164)
Postclosing trial balance   (p. 169)
Property, plant, and equipment   (p. 170)
Real account   (p. 164)
Reversing entry   (p. 183)
Temporary account   (p. 164)
Work sheet   (p. 158a)

Similar Accounting Terms

Capital assets	Long-term assets except goodwill
Property, plant, and equipment	Fixed assets; Plant and equipment; Plant assets
Current ratio	Working capital ratio
Permanent account	Real account
Temporary account	Nominal account

Answers to Self-Study Questions

1. a	3. d	5. b	7. b	9. c
2. d, a, e, b, f, c	4. d	6. c	8. a	10. b

Assignment Material

Questions

1. Identify the steps in the accounting cycle; distinguish those that occur during the period from those that are performed at the end of the period.

2. Why is the work sheet a valuable accounting tool?

3. Name two advantages the work sheet has over the adjusted trial balance.

4. Why must the adjusting entries be journalized and posted if they have already been entered on the work sheet?

5. Why should the adjusting entries be journalized and posted before the closing entries are made?

6. Which types of accounts are closed?

7. What purpose is served by closing the accounts?

8. State how the work sheet helps with recording the closing entries.

9. Distinguish between permanent accounts and temporary accounts; indicate which type is closed at the end of the period. Give five examples of each type of account.

10. Is Income Summary a permanent account or a temporary account? When and how is it used?

11. Is net income a permanent account, a temporary account, or something else? Explain.

12. Give the closing entries for the following accounts (balances in parentheses): Service Revenue ($4,700), Salary Expense ($1,100), Income Summary (credit balance of $2,000), Withdrawals ($2,300).

13. Why are assets classified as current or long-term? On what basis are they classified? Where do the classified amounts appear?

14. Indicate which of the following accounts are current assets, which are capital assets, and which are other assets: Prepaid Rent, Building, Furniture, Accounts Receivable, Merchandise Inventory, Cash, Note Receivable (due within one year), Note Receivable (due after one year).

15. In what order are assets and liabilities listed on the balance sheet?

16. Name an outside party that is interested in whether a liability is current or long-term. Why would this party be interested in this information?

17. A friend tells you that the difference between a current liability and a long-term liability is that they are payable to different types of creditors. Is your friend correct? Include in your answer the definitions of these two categories of liabilities.

18. Show how to compute the current ratio and the debt ratio. Indicate what ability each ratio measures, and state whether a high value or a low value is safer for each.

19. Capp Company purchased supplies of $120 on account. The accountant debited Inventory and credited Accounts Payable for $120. A week later, after this entry has been posted to the ledger, the accountant discovers the error. How should he correct the error?

*20. Why are reversing entries used?

---

*This Question covers Chapter 4 Appendix topics.

Starters

Starter 4–1 Explain why the following accounts must be adjusted:

  a. Salary payable   d. Prepaid rent
  b. Unearned service revenue   e. Accumulated amortization
  c. Supplies

Explaining items on the work sheet

Starter 4–2 Explain what the following items mean:

  a. Accounts receivable   f. Accounts payable
  b. Supplies   g. Unearned service revenue
  c. Prepaid rent   h. Service revenue
  d. Furniture   i. Rent expense
  e. Accumulated amortization

Explaining items on the work sheet

Starter 4–3 Answer the following questions:

  1. What type of balance does the Owner's Capital account have—debit or credit?
  2. Which income statement account has the same type of balance as the Capital account?
  3. Which type of income statement account has the opposite type of balance as the Capital account?
  4. What do we call the difference between total debits and total credits on the income statement? Into what account is the difference figure closed at the end of the period?

Using the work sheet

Starter 4–4 It is December 31, 2008, and time to close the books. Journalize the following closing entries for Kaufman Services:

  a. Service revenue, $22,000
  b. Make a compound closing entry for all the expenses: Salaries, $7,000; Rent, $4,000; Advertising, $3,000.
  c. Income Summary
  d. Owner's withdrawals, $6,000. Brett Kaufman is the owner.

Making closing entries

Starter 4–5 This exercise should be used in conjunction with Starter 4–4.

  1. Set up all the T-accounts in Starter 4–4 and insert their adjusted balances (denote as *Bal.*) at December 31, 2008. Also set up a T-account for Brett Kaufman, Capital, $25,000, and for Income Summary. Post the closing entries to the accounts, denoting posted amounts as *Clo.*
  2. Compute the ending balance of Brett Kaufman, Capital.

Analyzing the overall effect of the closing entries on the owner's capital account

2. B. Kaufman, Capital $27,000

Starter 4–6 Mega Insurance Agency reported the following items at May 31:

Sales and marketing expense ...	$2,622,000	Cash	$1,786,000
Other assets................................	477,000	Service revenue	5,139,000
Interest expense..........................	21,000	Accounts payable.......	284,000
Long-term liabilities	382,000	Accounts receivable...	2,238,000

Make Mega's closing entries, as needed, for these accounts.

Making closing entries

Starter 4–7 This exercise should be used in conjunction with Starter 4–6. Use the data in Starter 4–6 to set up T-accounts for those accounts that Mega Insurance Agency closed on May 31. Insert their account balances prior to closing, post the closing entries to these accounts, and show each account's ending balance after closing. Also show the Income Summary T-account. Label a balance as *Bal.* and a closing entry amount as *Clo.*

Posting closing entries

Income Summary Credit bal. $2,496,000

Starter 4–8 After closing its accounts at March 31, 2009, Lakehead Home Services had the following account balances:

Long-term liabilities............	$ 500	Equipment	$4,000
Other assets..........................	800	Cash	300
Accounts receivable	2,000	Service revenue	0
Total expenses	0	Will Hueske, capital	4,400
Accounts payable	900	Supplies.......................................	100
Unearned service revenue .	400	Accumulated amortization	1,000

Preparing a postclosing trial balance

Trial bal. total $7,200

Prepare Lakehead Home Services' postclosing trial balance at March 31, 2009. List accounts in proper order, as shown in Exhibit 4–11 on page 169.

(List accounts in proper order, as shown in Exhibit 4–11 on page 169.)

Identifying errors

Starter 4–9 Assume that there is only one transposition error in the following trial balance. Identify the incorrect amount, and correct the trial balance.

ABC SERVICES
Trial Balance
December 31, 2008

Cash...	$ 5,000	
Accounts receivable	8,300	
Supplies	750	
Accounts payable		$ 7,700
R. Ackerman, capital.............................		750
R. Ackerman, withdrawals	1,000	
Service fees earned...............................		10,000
Insurance expense.................................	950	
Salaries expense.....................................	3,100	
Utilities expense	1,150	
Total	$20,250	$18,450

Classifying assets and liabilities as current or long-term

Starter 4–10 Ink Jet Printing reported the following (amounts in thousands):

Sales revenue	$1,300	Land and building....................	$ 4,000
Cash...	200	Accounts payable	400
Accounts receivable	500	Total expenses	1,050
Interest expense....................	90	Accumulated amortization	2,800
Equipment.............................	800	Accrued liabilities (such as	
Prepaid expenses.................	100	Salaries payable)...................	300

1. Identify the assets (including contra assets) and liabilities.
2. Classify each asset as current or capital and each liability as current or long-term.

Computing the current ratio and the debt ratio

Current ratio 2.00
Debt ratio 0.63

Starter 4–11 Belleville Services has these account balances at December 31, 2009:

Accounts payable................	$ 4,000	Note payable, long-term..........	$ 9,000
Accounts receivable	6,000	Prepaid rent...............................	2,000
Cash..	3,000	Salary payable...........................	2,000
Amortization expense	4,000	Service revenue.........................	31,000
Equipment.............................	12,000	Supplies......................................	1,000

Compute Belleville Services' current ratio and debt ratio.

Computing and using the current ratio and the debt ratio

1. $2.00
2. 63%

Starter 4–12 This exercise should be used in conjunction with Starter 4–11.
1. How much in *current* assets does Belleville Services have for every dollar of *current* liabilities that it owes? What ratio measures this relationship?
2. What percentage of Belleville Services total assets are financed with debt? What is the name of this ratio?
3. What percentage of Belleville Services total assets does the owner of the company actually own?

Exercises

Excel Spreadsheet Template

Preparing a work sheet

Net income $12,280

Exercise 4–1

The trial balance of Brighter Testing Services appears at the top of the following page.

Additional information at September 30, 2009:
a. Accrued service revenue, $420.
b. Amortization, $80.
c. Accrued salary expense, $2,000.
d. Prepaid rent expired, $1,200.
e. Supplies used, $3,300.

BRIGHTER TESTING SERVICES
Trial Balance
September 30, 2009

Cash	$ 7,120	
Accounts receivable	11,880	
Prepaid rent	2,400	
Supplies	6,780	
Equipment	65,200	
Accumulated amortization		$ 5,680
Accounts payable		3,200
Salary payable		0
J. Brighter, capital		72,060
J. Brighter, withdrawals	6,000	
Service revenue		23,600
Amortization expense	0	
Salary expense	3,600	
Rent expense	0	
Utilities expense	1,560	
Supplies expense	0	
Total	$104,540	$104,540

Required Complete the Brighter Testing Services work sheet for September 2009. What was net income for the month ended September 30, 2009?

Exercise 4–2

Journalize the adjusting and closing entries for the company in Exercise 4–1.

Journalizing adjusting and closing entries

Exercise 4–3

Set up T-accounts for those accounts affected by the adjusting and closing entries in Exercise 4–1. Post the adjusting and closing entries to the accounts, identifying adjustment amounts as *Adj.*, closing amounts as *Clo.*, and balances as *Bal.* Double underline the accounts with zero balances after you close them and show the ending balance in each account.

Posting adjusting and closing entries

J. Brighter, capital bal. $78,340

Exercise 4–4

After completing Exercises 4–2 and 4–3, prepare the postclosing trial balance for the company in Exercise 4–1.

Preparing a postclosing trial balance

Trial bal. total $89,300

Exercise 4–5

Bombardier Inc., the transporation, aerospace, and capital company, reported the following items adapted from a recent financial report (amounts in millions of U.S. dollars):

Identifying and journalizing closing entries

Cash and term deposits	$ 2,917	Amortization expense	$ 545	
Revenues	14,726	Other assets	843	
Accounts payable	6,866	Interest expense	363	
Accounts receivable	1,684	Long-term liabilities	5,666	

Prepare Bombardier Inc.'s closing entries for the above accounts.

Exercise 4–6

Viera Printers reported the following selected accounts in its June 30, 2008, annual financial statements. Prepare the company's closing entries.

Identifying and journalizing closing entries

Dan Viera, capital bal. $205,600

Dan Viera, Capital	$118,400	Interest expense	$ 8,800
Service revenue	336,400	Accounts receivable	56,000
Unearned revenues	5,400	Salaries payable	3,400
Salary expense	50,000	Amortization expense	40,800
Accumulated amortization	140,000	Rent expense	23,600
Supplies expense	11,800	Dan Viera, Withdrawals	120,000
Interest revenue	5,800	Supplies	5,600

Prepare a T-account for Dan Viera, Capital. What is the ending capital balance at June 30, 2008?

Exercise 4–7

The accountant for Decker Environmental Consulting has posted adjusting entries (a) through (e) to the accounts at December 31, 2009. All the revenue, expense, and owner's equity accounts of the entity are listed here in T-account form.

Accounts Receivable		Supplies		Accumulated Amortization—Furniture	
39,000		6,000	(b) 3,000		9,000
(a) 7,250					(c) 1,650

Accumulated Amortization—Building		Salaries Payable		B. Decker, Capital	
	49,500		(e) 1,050		78,600
	(d) 9,000				

B. Decker, Withdrawals		Service Revenue		Salary Expense	
92,100			166,500	36,000	
			(a) 7,250	(e) 1,050	

Supplies Expense		Amortization Expense—Furniture		Amortization Expense—Building	
(b) 3,000		(c) 1,650		(d) 9,000	

Required

1. Journalize Decker Environmental Consulting's closing entries at December 31, 2009.
2. Determine Decker Environmental Consulting's ending capital balance at December 31, 2009.

Exercise 4–8

From the following accounts of Howser Consulting, prepare the entity's statement of owner's equity for the year ended December 31, 2009.

J. Howser, Capital				J. Howser, Withdrawals			
Dec. 31	8,000	Jan. 1	9,000	Mar. 31	2,250	Dec. 31	8,000
		Dec. 31	10,750	Jun. 30	1,750		
				Sept. 30	2,250		
				Dec. 31	1,750		

Income Summary			
Dec. 31	21,250	Dec. 31	32,000
Dec. 31	10,750		

Exercise 4–9

The adjusted trial balance and income statement amounts from the March work sheet of O'Neill Systems follow:

Account Title	Adjusted Trial Balance		Income Statement	
Cash	$ 17,600			
Supplies	7,000			
Prepaid rent	3,600			
Office equipment	200,400			
Accumulated amortization		$ 26,000		
Accounts payable		18,400		
Salaries payable		3,200		
Unearned service revenue		17,600		
P. O'Neill, capital		143,200		
P. O'Neill, withdrawals	4,000			
Service revenue		52,000		$52,000
Salary expense	15,200		$15,200	
Rent expense	5,600		5,600	
Amortization expense	1,200		1,200	
Supplies expense	2,600		2,600	
Utilities expense	3,200		3,200	
	$260,400	$260,400	$27,800	$52,000
Net income			?	
			$52,000	$52,000

Required

1. Journalize the closing entries of O'Neill Systems at March 31.
2. How much net income or net loss did O'Neill Systems earn for March? How can you tell?

Exercise 4–10

Refer to Exercise 4–9.

Preparing a classified balance sheet

1. Total assets $202,600
2. Current ratio at Mar. 31, 2009 0.72

Required

1. After solving Exercise 4–9, use the data in that exercise to prepare O'Neill Systems' classified balance sheet at March 31, 2009. Use the report format. You must compute the ending balance of P. O'Neill, Capital.

2. Compute O'Neill Systems' current ratio and debt ratio at March 31, 2009. One year ago, the current ratio was 1.20 and the debt ratio was 0.30. Indicate whether O'Neill Systems' ability to pay its debts has improved or deteriorated during the current year.

Exercise 4–11

Making correcting entries

1. Suppose SuperTravel paid an account payable of $1,200 and erroneously debited Supplies. Make the journal entry to correct this error.

2. Suppose SuperTravel made the following adjusting entry to record amortization at April 30:
   Amortization Expense—Furniture........... 2,000
      Furniture....... 2,000
   Make the journal entry to correct this error.

3. Suppose, in closing the books to a profitable year, SuperTravel made this closing entry:
   Income Summary... 29,600
      Service Revenue...................................... 29,600
   Make the journal entry to correct this error.

Exercise 4–12

Correcting accounting errors

Prepare a correcting entry for each of the following accounting errors:

a. Debited Supplies and credited Accounts Payable for a $4,500 purchase of office equipment on account.

b. Accrued interest revenue of $1,500 by a debit to Accounts Receivable and a credit to Interest Revenue.

c. Adjusted prepaid rent by debiting Prepaid Rent and crediting Rent Expense for $2,000. This adjusting entry should have debited Rent Expense and credited Prepaid Rent for $2,000.

d. Debited Salary Expense and credited Accounts Payable to accrue salary expense of $6,000.

e. Recorded the earning of $3,900 service revenue collected in advance by debiting Accounts Receivable and crediting Service Revenue.

Classifying assets and liabilities as current or long-term

Exercise 4–13

Wu Appraisal Services' financial statements reported the following at December 31, 2008, the end of the company's fiscal year:

Sales revenue	$180,000	Prepaid expenses	$ 3,000
Long-term debt	20,000	Land and buildings	160,000
Receivables	12,000	Accounts payable	17,000
Interest expense	2,000	Operating expenses	50,000
Equipment	60,000	Accumulated amortization	15,000
Cash	7,000	Accrued liabilities (such as Salaries payable)	14,000

Required

1. Identify the assets (including contra assets) and liabilities.

2. Classify each asset as current or capital and each liability as current or long-term.

Journalizing reversing entries

*Exercise 4–14

On December 31, 2008, Tristar Industries recorded an adjusting entry for $5,000 of accrued interest revenue. On January 15, 2009, the company received interest payments in the amount of $11,000. Assuming Tristar Industries uses reversing entries, prepare the 2008 and 2009 journal entries for these interest transactions.

Serial Exercise

This exercise continues the Mark Wearing Engineers situation begun in Exercise 2–14 of Chapter 2 and extended to Exercise 3–23 of Chapter 3. If Exercises 2–14 or 3–23 were not completed, students can complete Exercise 4–15 by following the instructions given in the note below.

Closing the books, preparing a classified balance sheet, and evaluating a business

2. Total assets $49,160
3. Current ratio 2.09
Debt ratio 0.31

Exercise 4–15

Refer to Exercise 3–23 of Chapter 3. Start from the posted T-accounts and the adjusted trial balance on the next page that Mark Wearing Engineers prepared at December 31.

Note: If you did not do Exercise 2–14 or Exercise 3–23, you can complete this Exercise by using the accounts and balances given in the adjusted trial balance at December 31, 2008, on the next page.

Required

1. Journalize and post the closing entries at December 31, 2008. Denote each closing amount as *Clo.* and an account balance as *Bal.*

2. Prepare a classified balance sheet at December 31, 2008.

3. Compute the current ratio and the debt ratio of Mark Wearing Engineers and evaluate these ratio values as indicative of a strong or weak financial position.

4. If your instructor assigns it, complete the accounting work sheet at December 31, 2008.

---

*This Exercise covers Chapter 4 Appendix topics.

MARK WEARING ENGINEERS
Adjusted Trial Balance
December 31, 2008

Cash	$23,600	
Accounts receivable	7,600	
Supplies	200	
Equipment	7,000	
Accumulated amortization—equipment		$ 200
Furniture	11,200	
Accumulated amortization—furniture		240
Accounts payable		11,200
Salaries payable		1,400
Unearned service revenue		2,400
Mark Wearing, capital		28,000
Mark Wearing, withdrawals	3,200	
Service revenue		14,000
Rent expense	2,000	
Utilities expense	400	
Salary expense	1,400	
Amortization expense—equipment	200	
Amortization expense—furniture	240	
Supplies expense	400	
Total	$57,440	$57,440

Challenge Exercise

Exercise 4–16

The unadjusted account balances of Stinson Consulting follow:

Cash	$ 1,900	Unearned service revenue	$ 5,300
Accounts receivable	7,200	Scott Stinson, capital	90,200
Supplies	1,100	Scott Stinson, withdrawals	46,200
Prepaid Insurance	3,200	Service revenue	90,600
Furniture	8,400	Salary expense	32,700
Accumulated amortization—		Amortization expense—	
furniture	1,300	furniture	0
Building	53,800	Amortization expense—	
Accumulated amortization—		building	0
building	14,900	Supplies expense	0
Land	51,200	Insurance expense	0
Accounts payable	6,100	Utilities expense	2,700
Salaries payable	0		

Adjusting data at the end of the year included the following:

a. Unearned service revenue that has been earned, $3,600.

b. Accrued service revenue, $1,700.

c. Supplies used in operations, $900.

d. Accrued salary expense, $1,400.

e. Insurance expense, $1,800.

f. Amortization expense—furniture, $1,300; building, $2,100.

Scott Stinson, the proprietor of Stinson Consulting, has received an offer to sell his company. He needs to know the following information as soon as possible:

1. Net income for the year covered by these data.

2. Total assets.

3. Total liabilities.

Computing financial statement amounts

1. Net income $53,000
2. Total assets $106,200
3. Total liabilities $9,200

4. Total owner's equity.

5. Proof that total assets equal total liabilities plus total owner's equity after all items are updated.

Required   Without opening any accounts, making any journal entries, or using a work sheet, provide Scott Stinson with the requested information. Show all computations.

Reversing entries

*Exercise 4–17

Refer to Exercise 4–16. Which adjusting entries (a, b, c, d, e, f) can be reversed with reversing journal entries?

Correcting accounting errors

Exercise 4–18

The Adjusted Trial Balance columns on the work sheet have total debits of $55,000 and total credits of $64,000. Show how the following errors would create this imbalance. How would you correct each error?

a. A $3,000 debit adjustment to Prepaid Insurance was incorrectly subtracted on the work sheet and appears as a $3,000 credit. The Prepaid Insurance account balance after the error is $4,000.

b. A 1,000 credit (accrual) to Fees Earned was subtracted from the Fees Earned credit balance. The Fees Earned account balance after the error is $3,000.

c. A $2,500 debit adjustment to Wages Expense was subtracted from Wages Expense debit balance. Wages Expense had a zero balance after the error.

Ethical Issue

Discount Hardware wishes to expand its business and has borrowed $200,000 from TD Canada Trust. As a condition for making this loan, the bank required Discount Hardware to maintain a current ratio of at least 1.50 and a debt ratio of no more than 0.50, and to submit annual financial statements to the bank.

Business during the third year has been good but not great. Expansion costs have brought the current ratio down to 1.40 and the debt ratio up to 0.51 at December 15. The managers of Discount Hardware are considering the implication of reporting this current ratio to TD Canada Trust. One course of action that the managers are considering is to record in December of the third year some revenue on account that Discount Hardware will earn in January of next year. The contract for this job has been signed, and Discount Hardware will deliver the materials during January.

Required

1. Journalize the revenue transaction using your own numbers, and indicate how recording this revenue in December would affect the current ratio and the debt ratio.

2. State whether it is ethical to record the revenue transaction in December. Identify the accounting principle relevant to this situation.

3. Propose an ethical course of action for Discount Hardware.

Problems (Group A)

Preparing a work sheet

Net income $55,880

Problem 4–1A

The trial balance of Cranbrook Construction at July 31, 2008, appears on page 195.

Additional data at July 31, 2008:

a. Amortization: equipment, $1,020; building, $2,110.

b. Accrued wages expense, $1,720.

---

*This Exercise covers Chapter 4 Appendix topics.

CRANBROOK CONSTRUCTION
Trial Balance
July 31, 2008

Cash..	$ 63,600	
Accounts receivable	113,460	
Supplies	52,980	
Prepaid insurance	11,900	
Equipment...	98,070	
Accumulated amortization—equipment.........		$ 78,720
Building	128,670	
Accumulated amortization—building.............		31,500
Land	89,900	
Accounts payable..		68,070
Interest payable		0
Wages payable		0
Unearned service revenue		31,680
Notes payable, long-term...............................		67,200
T. Jackson, capital..		237,390
T. Jackson, withdrawals	12,600	
Service revenue...		70,570
Amortization expense—equipment	0	
Amortization expense—building	0	
Wages expense..	9,600	
Insurance expense...	0	
Interest expense..	0	
Utilities expense	3,330	
Advertising expense	1,020	
Supplies expense	0	
Total...	$585,130	$585,130

c. A count of supplies showed that unused supplies amounted to $44,220.

d. During July, $3,500 of prepaid insurance coverage expired.

e. Accrued interest expense, $540.

f. Of the $31,680 balance of Unearned Service Revenue, $14,910 was earned during July.

g. Accrued advertising expense, $1,300. (Credit Accounts Payable.)

h. Accrued service revenue, $3,300.

Required   Complete Cranbrook Construction's work sheet for July. Identify each adjusting entry by its letter.

Problem 4–2A

The *adjusted* trial balance of Alan Wood Design at June 30, 2007, the end of the company's fiscal year, appears on the following page.

Adjusting data at June 30, 2007, which *have been incorporated* into the trial balance figures on page 196, consist of:

a. Amortization for the year: equipment, $8,760; building, $4,764.

b. Supplies used during the year, $4,296.

c. During the year, $3,920 of prepaid insurance coverage expired.

d. Accrued interest expense, $2,828.

e. Accrued service revenue, $1,128.

f. Of the balance of Unearned Service Revenue at the beginning of the year, $9,348 was earned during the year.

g. Accrued wages expense, $2,924.

Preparing financial statements from an adjusted trial balance; journalizing adjusting and closing entries; evaluating a business

2. Net income $97,556
Total assets $299,216
3. Current ratio 1.65
Debt ratio 0.59

ALAN WOOD DESIGN
Adjusted Trial Balance
June 30, 2007

Cash	$ 25,220	
Accounts receivable	31,764	
Supplies	37,548	
Prepaid insurance	3,840	
Equipment	66,960	
Accumulated amortization—equipment		$ 19,776
Building	137,880	
Accumulated amortization—building		20,220
Land	36,000	
Accounts payable		50,080
Interest payable		3,788
Wages payable		2,924
Unearned service revenue		2,760
Notes payable, long-term		116,400
Alan Wood, capital		82,068
Alan Wood, withdrawals	56,360	
Service revenue		167,832
Amortization expense—equipment	8,760	
Amortization expense—building	4,764	
Wages expense	27,764	
Insurance expense	3,720	
Interest expense	15,812	
Utilities expense	5,160	
Supplies expense	4,296	
Total	$465,848	$465,848

Required

1. Journalize the adjusting entries that would lead to the adjusted trial balance shown above. Also journalize the closing entries.

2. Prepare the income statement and statement of owner's equity for the year ended June 30, 2007, and the classified balance sheet on that date. Use the account format for the balance sheet.

3. Compute Alan Wood Design's current ratio and debt ratio at June 30, 2007. One year ago, the current ratio stood at 1.01, and the debt ratio was 0.71. Did Alan Wood Design's ability to pay debts improve or deteriorate during the fiscal year?

Taking the accounting cycle
through the closing entries

2. Net income $174,000
Total assets $300,000

Problem 4–3A

The unadjusted T-accounts of Sanford Systems at December 31, 2009, appear on the next page and the related year-end adjustment data are given below.

Adjustment data at December 31, 2009, include:

a. Of the $15,000 balance of Unearned Service Revenue at the beginning of the year, all of it was earned during the year.

b. Supplies still unused at year end, $6,000.

c. Amortization for the year, $27,000.

d. Accrued salary expense, $6,000.

e. Accrued service revenue, $9,000.

Required

1. Write the account data in the Trial Balance columns of a work sheet, and complete the work sheet. Identify each adjusting entry by the letter corresponding to the data given.

2. Prepare the income statement, the statement of owner's equity, and the classified balance sheet in account format.

Cash					Accounts Receivable					Supplies	
Bal.	15,000			Bal.	108,000			Bal.	27,000		

Equipment					Accumulated Amortization					Accounts Payable	
Bal.	297,000					Bal.	108,000			Bal.	18,000

Salary Payable					Unearned Service Revenue					Note Payable, Long-Term	
			0			Bal.	15,000			Bal.	180,000

T. Sanford, Capital					T. Sanford, Withdrawals					Service Revenue	
		Bal.	108,000	Bal.	186,000					Bal.	447,000

Salary Expense					Supplies Expense					Rent Expense	
Bal.	159,000				0			Bal.	45,000		

Amortization Expense					Interest Expense					Insurance Expense	
	0			Bal.	18,000			Bal.	21,000		

3. Journalize the adjusting and closing entries.

4. Did Sanford Systems have a profitable year or a bad year during 2009? Give the reason for your answer.

Problem 4–4A

This problem should be used only in conjunction with Problem 4–3A. It completes the accounting cycle by posting to T-accounts and preparing the postclosing trial balance.

Required

1. Using the Problem 4–3A data, post the adjusting and closing entries to the T-accounts, identifying adjusting amounts as *Adj.*, closing amounts as *Clo.*, and account balances as *Bal.*, as shown in Exhibit 4–10 (page 167). Double underline all accounts with a zero ending balance.

2. Prepare the postclosing trial balance.

Problem 4–5A

The trial balance of Breitman Insurance Agency at August 31, 2009, appears on page 198. The data needed for the month-end adjustments follow.

Adjustment data:

a. Commission revenue received in advance that had not been earned at August 31, $20,250.

b. Rent still prepaid at August 31, $1,150.

c. Supplies used during the month, $1,020.

d. Amortization on furniture for the month, $1,110.

e. Amortization on building for the month, $1,390.

f. Accrued salary expense at August 31, $1,380.

Required

1. Open ledger accounts for the accounts listed in the trial balance and insert their August 31 unadjusted balances. Also open the Income Summary account. Date the balances of the following accounts as of August 1: Prepaid Rent, Supplies, Furniture, Accumulated Amortization—Furniture, Building, Accumulated Amortization—Building, Unearned Commission Revenue, and O. Breitman, Capital.

Completing the accounting cycle

 2 3

2. Trial bal. total $435,000

Excel Spreadsheet Template

Completing the accounting cycle

 2 3 5

3. Net income $74,250
Total assets $304,960
5. Trial bal. total $426,660

BREITMAN INSURANCE AGENCY
Trial Balance
August 31, 2009

Account Title	Debit	Credit
Cash	$ 71,400	
Accounts receivable	41,680	
Prepaid rent	3,870	
Supplies	2,700	
Furniture	46,050	
Accumulated amortization—furniture		$ 38,400
Building	224,700	
Accumulated amortization—building		80,800
Land	40,000	
Accounts payable		12,720
Salaries payable		0
Unearned commission revenue		26,700
O. Breitman, capital		210,760
O. Breitman, withdrawals	14,400	
Commission revenue		81,900
Salary expense	3,300	
Rent expense	0	
Utilities expense	1,230	
Amortization expense—furniture	0	
Amortization expense—building	0	
Advertising expense	1,950	
Supplies expense	0	
Total	$451,280	$451,280

2. Write the trial balance on a work sheet and complete the work sheet of Breitman Insurance Agency for the month ended August 31, 2009.

3. Using the completed work sheet, prepare the income statement, the statement of owner's equity, and the classified balance sheet in account format.

4. Using the work sheet data, journalize and post the adjusting and closing entries. Use dates and posting references. Use page 7 as the number of the journal page.

5. Prepare a postclosing trial balance.

Problem 4–6A

Preparing a classified balance sheet in report format; evaluating a business

1. Total assets $787,800
2. Current ratio 1.19
   Debt ratio 0.38

The accounts of Beaton Travel at December 31, 2008, are listed in alphabetical order:

Accounts payable	$ 30,600	Interest payable	$ 8,600
Accounts receivable	39,600	Interest receivable	1,200
Accumulated amortization		Land	125,000
—building	226,800	Notes payable, long-term	176,800
Accumulated amortization		Notes receivable, long-term	24,000
—furniture	69,600	Other assets	26,600
Advertising expense	13,200	Other current liabilities	28,200
Amortization expense	7,800	Prepaid insurance	6,600
Building	626,400	Prepaid rent	39,600
Cash	44,000	Salary expense	147,600
Commission revenue	561,000	Salary payable	23,400
E. Beaton, capital	418,800	Supplies	15,000
E. Beaton, withdrawals	284,400	Supplies expense	34,200
Furniture	136,200	Unearned commission	
Insurance expense	4,800	revenue	32,400

Required

1. *All adjustments have been journalized and posted, but the closing entries have not yet been made.* Prepare the company's classified balance sheet in report format at December 31, 2008.

2. Compute Beaton Travel's current ratio and debt ratio at December 31, 2008. At December 31, 2007, the current ratio was 1.52 and the debt ratio was 0.37. Did Beaton Travel's ability to pay both current and total debts improve or deteriorate during 2008?

Problem 4–7A

Analyzing and journalizing corrections, adjustments, and closing entries

d. Net income overstated by $2,190

Accountants for Mainland Catering Service encountered the following situations while adjusting and closing the books at December 31. Consider each situation independently.

a. The company bookkeeper made the following entry to record a $2,250 credit purchase of office equipment:

| Nov. 12 | Office Supplies............................... | 2,250 | |
| | Accounts Payable .... | | 2,250 |

Prepare the correcting entry, dated December 31.

b. A $4,500 credit to Accounts Receivable was posted as a debit.
   (1) At what stage of the accounting cycle will this error be detected?
   (2) Describe the technique for identifying the amount of the error.

c. The $88,500 balance of Equipment was entered as $8,850 on the trial balance.
   (1) What is the name of this type of error?
   (2) Assume this is the only error in the trial balance. Which will be greater, the total debits or the total credits, and by how much?
   (3) How can this type of error be identified?

d. The accountant failed to make the following adjusting entries at December 31:
   (1) Accrued property tax expense, $1,200.
   (2) Supplies expense, $6,540.
   (3) Accrued interest revenue on a note receivable, $3,900.
   (4) Amortization of equipment, $6,000.
   (5) Earned service revenue that had been collected in advance, $7,650.

   Compute the overall net income effect of these omissions.

e. Record each of the adjusting entries identified in item d.

f. The revenue and expense accounts, *after* the adjusting entries had been posted, were Service Revenue, $57,600; Interest Revenue, $4,500; Salary Expense, $12,690; Rent Expense, $3,825; and Amortization Expense, $6,160. Two balances prior to closing were S. Jones, Capital, $36,450, and S. Jones, Withdrawals, $22,500. Journalize the closing entries.

Problem 4–8A

Preparing a work sheet, journalizing the adjustments, closing the accounts

4. Trial bal. total $714,000

Slee Truck Services performs overhauls and repairs to trucks. The company's trial balance for the year ended March 31, 2008, is shown on the next page.

Additional information:

a. On March 31, repair supplies costing $7,800 were still on hand.

b. An examination of the insurance policies showed $6,300 of insurance coverage had expired during the year ended March 31, 2008.

c. An examination of the equipment and the building showed the following:

	Equipment	Building
Estimated useful life	5 years	10 years
Estimated value at the end of the useful life	$0	$0

Amortization is calculated on a straight-line basis over the asset's life.

d. The company had performed $2,400 of services for a client who had paid $4,500 in advance.

e. Accrued interest on the mortgage at March 31, $3,600.

f. Accrued wages at March 31 for 10 employees for one day. Each employee earned $27 per hour and worked a 10-hour day.

SLEE TRUCK SERVICES
Trial Balance
March 31, 2008

Cash	$ 10,200	
Accounts receivable	43,600	
Repair supplies	26,700	
Prepaid insurance	11,700	
Equipment	210,000	
Accumulated amortization—equipment		$ 84,000
Building	242,000	
Accumulated amortization—building		56,400
Land	195,000	
Accounts payable		21,600
Unearned repair revenues		4,500
Employee withholdings payable		6,000
Notes payable, long-term		24,000
Mortgage payable		140,000
J. Slee, capital		267,100
J. Slee, withdrawals	27,000	
Repair fees earned		242,900
Wages expense	54,200	
Utilities expense	3,300	
Travel expenses	22,800	
Total	$846,500	$846,500

Required

1. Complete a work sheet for the year ended March 31, 2008.
2. Journalize the adjusting entries required on March 31, 2008.
3. Journalize the closing entries that would be required on March 31, 2008.
4. Prepare a postclosing trial balance at March 31, 2008.

Preparing a work sheet, closing the accounts, classifying the assets and liabilities, evaluating the current and debt ratios

1 3 4 5 6

3. Total assets $411,200
4. Current ratio 2.31
   Debt ratio 0.46

Problem 4–9A

Shawn Venne, the accountant for Lancaster Consulting, prepared the work sheet shown on the next page on a computer spreadsheet but has lost much of the data. The only particular item Venne can recall is that there was an adjustment made to correct an error made where $1,200 of supplies, purchased on credit, had been incorrectly recorded as $1,200 of equipment.

Required

1. Complete the work sheet by filling in the missing data.
2. Journalize the closing entries that would be required on December 31, 2009.
3. Prepare the company's classified balance sheet at December 31, 2009.
4. Compute Lancaster Consulting's current ratio and debt ratio for December 31, 2009. On December 31, 2008, the current ratio was 2.14 and the debt ratio was 0.47. Comment on the changes in the ratios.

Using reversing entries

A1

*Problem 4–10A

Refer to the data in Problem 4–5A, pages 197–198.

Required

1. Open ledger accounts for Salaries Payable and Salary Expense. Insert their unadjusted balances at August 31, 2009.
2. Journalize adjusting entry *f* and the closing entry for Salary Expense at August 31. Post to the accounts.
3. On September 5, Breitman Insurance Agency paid the next payroll amount of $1,740. Journalize this cash payment, and post to the accounts. Show the balance in each account.

---

*This Problem covers Chapter 4 Appendix topics.

LANCASTER CONSULTING
Accounting Work Sheet
For the Year Ended December 31, 2009

Account Title	Trial Balance Debit	Trial Balance Credit	Adjustments Debit	Adjustments Credit	Adjusted Trial Balance Debit	Adjusted Trial Balance Credit	Income Statement Debit	Income Statement Credit	Balance Sheet Debit	Balance Sheet Credit
Cash	38,000								38,000	
Accounts receivable	40,800				41,400					
Supplies	5,700			(b) 2,400						
Prepaid insurance	6,000				4,800					
Equipment	82,500				81,300					
Accumulated amortization—equipment		7,200				10,800				
Building	180,000				180,000					
Accumulated amortization—building		12,000		(e) 6,000						
Land	90,000				90,000					
Accounts payable		15,000								
Interest payable		9,000								
Wages payable		3,600		(f) 1,800						
Unearned consulting fees		10,500	(g) 1,500							
Mortgage payable		150,000								150,000
L. Lancaster, capital		123,000								123,000
L. Lancaster, withdrawals	18,000				18,000				18,000	
Consulting fees earned		254,900						257,000		
Wages expense	100,500				102,300					
Insurance expense	13,200									
Interest expense	9,000									
Utilities expense	1,500				1,500					
Totals	585,200	585,200								
Supplies expense			(b) 2,400				2,400			
Amortization expense—equipment			(d) 3,600				3,600			
Amortization expense—building										
Totals										

4. Repeat Requirements 1 through 3 using a reversing entry. Compare the balances of Salaries Payable and Salary Expense computed by using a reversing entry with those balances computed without using a reversing entry (as they appear in your answer to Requirement 3).

Problems (Group B)

Problem 4–1B

Excel Spreadsheet Template

Preparing a work sheet

Net income $21,820

The trial balance of Greg Arami Design at May 31, 2008, is shown here:

GREG ARAMI DESIGN
Trial Balance
May 31, 2008

Cash	$ 8,670	
Notes receivable	10,340	
Interest receivable	0	
Supplies	560	
Prepaid insurance	5,790	
Furniture	27,410	
Accumulated amortization—furniture		$ 1,480
Building	53,900	
Accumulated amortization—building		34,560
Land	23,700	
Accounts payable		14,730
Interest payable		0
Salary payable		0
Unearned design services revenue		8,800
Notes payable, long-term		18,700
Greg Arami, capital		34,290
Greg Arami, withdrawals	3,800	
Design services revenue		26,970
Interest revenue		0
Amortization expense—furniture	0	
Amortization expense—building	0	
Salary expense	3,170	
Insurance expense	0	
Interest expense	0	
Utilities expense	1,130	
Advertising expense	1,060	
Supplies expense	0	
Total	$139,530	$139,530

Additional data at May 31, 2008:

a. Amortization: furniture, $480; building, $460.

b. Accrued salary expense, $600.

c. A count of supplies showed that unused supplies amounted to $410.

d. During May, $1,390 of prepaid insurance coverage expired.

e. Accrued interest expense, $220.

f. Of the $8,800 balance of Unearned Revenue, $4,400 was earned during May.

g. Accrued advertising expense, $1,060. (Credit Accounts Payable.)

h. Accrued interest revenue, $170.

Required Complete Greg Arami Design's work sheet for May 2008. Identify each adjusting entry by its letter.

Problem 4–2B

The adjusted trial balance of Musquem Golf School at April 30, 2009, the end of the company's fiscal year, is shown here.

Preparing financial statements from an adjusted trial balance; journalizing adjusting and closing entries; evaluating a business

2. Net income $114,960
Total assets $652,640
3. Current ratio 1.82

MUSQUEM GOLF SCHOOL
Adjusted Trial Balance
April 30, 2009

Cash	$ 7,480	
Accounts receivable	174,960	
Supplies	14,760	
Prepaid insurance	9,160	
Equipment	255,720	
Accumulated amortization—equipment		$ 113,720
Building	297,320	
Accumulated amortization—building		73,040
Land	80,000	
Accounts payable		82,200
Interest payable		11,120
Wages payable		5,320
Unearned teaching revenue		14,640
Notes payable, long-term		279,600
J. Wilson, capital		256,800
J. Wilson, withdrawals	112,000	
Teaching revenue		394,200
Amortization expense—equipment	27,600	
Amortization expense—building	14,840	
Wages expense	133,240	
Insurance expense	21,480	
Interest expense	34,680	
Utilities expense	19,880	
Supplies expense	27,520	
Total	$1,230,640	$1,230,640

Adjusting data at April 30, 2009, which have all been incorporated into the trial balance figures, consist of:

a. Of the balance of Unearned Teaching Revenue at the beginning of the year, $16,720 was earned during the year.

b. Supplies used during the year, $23,520.

c. During the year, $21,480 of prepaid insurance coverage expired.

d. Accrued interest expense, $7,120.

e. Accrued teaching revenue, $8,800.

f. Amortization for the year: equipment, $27,600; building, $14,840.

g. Accrued wages expense, $5,320.

Required

1. Journalize the adjusting entries that would lead to the adjusted trial balance shown here. Also journalize the closing entries.

2. Prepare Musquem Golf School's income statement and statement of owner's equity for the year ended April 30, 2009, and the classified balance sheet on that date. Use the account format for the balance sheet.

3. Compute Musquem Golf School's current ratio and debt ratio at April 30, 2009. One year ago, the current ratio stood at 1.21, and the debt ratio was 0.82. Did Musquem Golf School's ability to pay debts improve or deteriorate during 2009?

Problem 4–3B

Taking the accounting cycle through the closing entries

  3

2. Net income $220,000
Total assets $365,000

The unadjusted T-accounts of World Media at December 31, 2008 follow on the next page. The related year-end adjustment data appear below them.

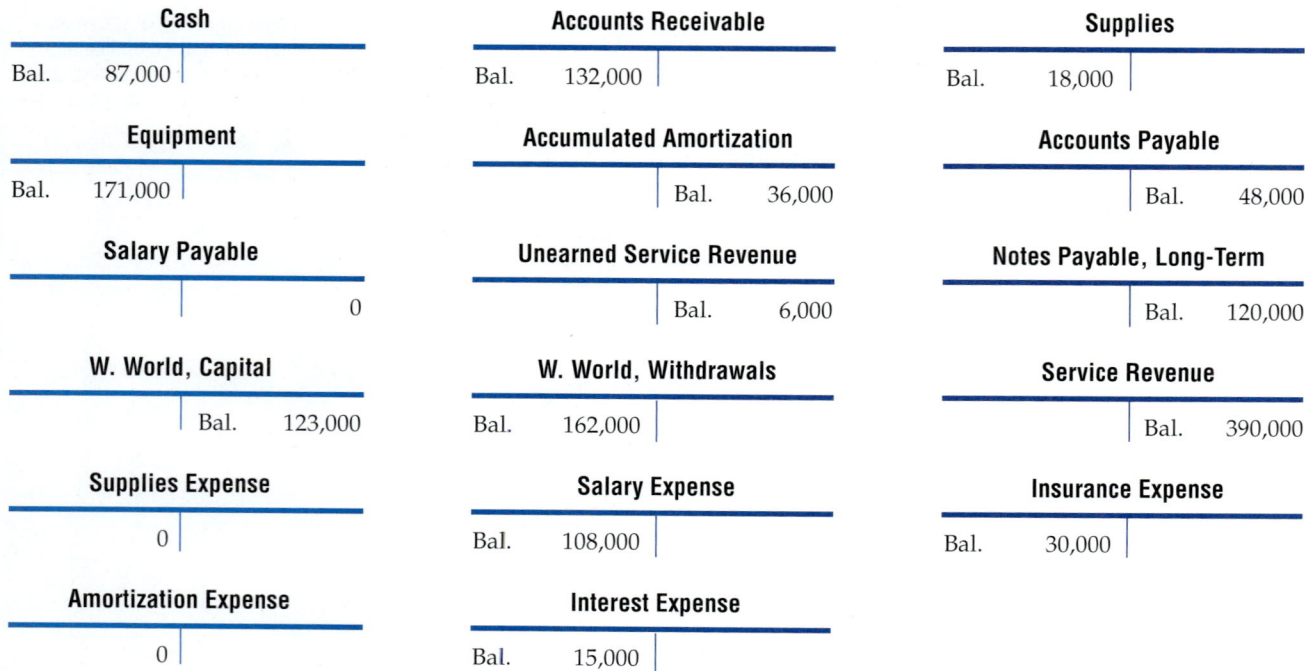

Cash			Accounts Receivable			Supplies	
Bal.	87,000		Bal.	132,000		Bal.	18,000

Equipment			Accumulated Amortization			Accounts Payable	
Bal.	171,000			Bal.	36,000		Bal.	48,000

Salary Payable			Unearned Service Revenue			Notes Payable, Long-Term	
		0		Bal.	6,000		Bal.	120,000

W. World, Capital			W. World, Withdrawals			Service Revenue	
	Bal.	123,000	Bal.	162,000			Bal.	390,000

Supplies Expense		Salary Expense			Insurance Expense	
0		Bal.	108,000		Bal.	30,000

Amortization Expense		Interest Expense	
0		Bal.	15,000

Adjustment data at December 31, 2008, include:

a. Amortization for the year, $15,000.

b. Supplies still unused at the year end, $2,000.

c. Accrued service revenue, $24,000.

d. Of the $6,000 balance of Unearned Service Revenue at the beginning of the year, the entire amount was earned during the year.

e. Accrued salary expense, $16,000.

Required

1. Write the account data in the Trial Balance columns of a work sheet and complete the work sheet. Identify each adjusting entry by the letter corresponding to the data given.

2. Prepare the income statement, the statement of owner's equity, and the classified balance sheet in account format.

3. Journalize the adjusting and closing entries.

4. Did World Media have a profitable year or a bad year during 2008? Give the reason for your answer.

Completing the accounting cycle

2. Trial bal. total $416,000

Problem 4–4B

This problem should be used only in conjunction with Problem 4–3B. It completes the accounting cycle by posting to T-accounts and preparing the postclosing trial balance.

Required

1. Using the Problem 4–3B data, post the adjusting and closing entries to the T-accounts, identifying adjusting amounts as *Adj.,* closing amounts as *Clo.,* and account balances as *Bal.,* as shown in Exhibit 4–10 (page 167). Double underline all accounts with a zero ending balance.

2. Prepare the postclosing trial balance.

Completing the accounting cycle

3. Net income $34,955
Total assets $529,860
5. Trial bal. total $597,345

Problem 4–5B

The trial balance of Featherstone Environmental Services at October 31, 2009, and the data needed for the month-end adjustments, are shown on the next page.

FEATHERSTONE ENVIRONMENTAL SERVICES
Trial Balance
October 31, 2009

Account Title	Debit	Credit
Cash..	$ 22,050	
Accounts receivable	63,895	
Prepaid rent...	9,900	
Supplies	3,780	
Furniture..	120,735	
Accumulated amortization—furniture...........		$ 15,300
Building	307,350	
Accumulated amortization—building.............		49,450
Land	76,000	
Accounts payable..		32,805
Salary payable..		0
Unearned consulting revenue		23,850
K. Featherstone, capital		456,205
K. Featherstone, withdrawals..........................	17,550	
Consulting revenue...		56,520
Salary expense	8,280	
Rent expense...	0	
Utilities expense	4,590	
Amortization expense—furniture	0	
Amortization expense—building	0	
Supplies expense...	0	
Total...	$634,130	$634,130

The data needed for the month-end adjustments are as follows:

a. Unearned consulting revenue that still had not been earned at October 31, $22,050.

b. Rent still prepaid at October 31, $7,000.

c. Supplies used during the month, $3,465.

d. Amortization on furniture for the month, $1,125.

e. Amortization on building for the month, $1,610.

f. Accrued salary expense at October 31, $1,395.

Required

1. Open ledgers for the accounts listed in the trial balance, inserting their October 31 unadjusted balances. Also open the Income Summary account. Date the balances of the following accounts October 1: Prepaid Rent, Supplies, Furniture, Accumulated Amortization—Furniture, Building, Accumulated Amortization—Building, Unearned Consulting Revenue, and K. Featherstone, Capital.

2. Write the trial balance on a work sheet and complete the work sheet of Featherstone Environmental Services for the month ended October 31, 2009.

3. Using the completed work sheet, prepare the income statement, the statement of owner's equity, and the classified balance sheet in account format.

4. Using the work sheet data, journalize and post the adjusting and closing entries. Use dates and posting references. Use 12 as the number of the journal page.

5. Prepare a postclosing trial balance.

Problem 4–6B

The accounts of Kingsgate Financial Services at March 31, 2008, are listed in alphabetical order at the top of the next page.

Preparing a classified balance sheet in report format; evaluating a business

1. Total assets $85,560			
2. Current ratio 1.18			
Debt ratio 0.39			

Accounts payable $11,760
Accounts receivable 9,200
Accumulated amortization—
  building................................. 37,840
Accumulated amortization—
  furniture.............................. 6,160
Advertising expense 720
Amortization expense............. 1,520
A. Kingsgate, capital 40,560
A. Kingsgate, withdrawals...... 24,960
Building 44,720
Cash... 7,720
Furniture.................................... 34,560
Insurance expense 480
Interest payable........................ 5,240

Interest receivable.................... $ 720
Land.. 13,000
Notes payable, long-term........ 12,560
Notes receivable, long-term.... 5,520
Other assets 6,840
Other current liabilities............ 880
Prepaid insurance.................... 480
Prepaid rent.............................. 3,760
Salary expense........................... 14,240
Salaries payable 1,920
Service revenue......................... 56,880
Supplies....................................... 3,040
Supplies expense 3,680
Unearned service revenue....... 1,360

Required

1. *All adjustments have been journalized and posted, but the closing entries have not yet been made.* Prepare the company's classified balance sheet in report format at March 31, 2008. Use captions for total assets, total liabilities, and total liabilities and owner's equity.

2. Compute Kingsgate Financial Services' current ratio and debt ratio at March 31, 2008. At March 31, 2007, the current ratio was 1.28, and the debt ratio was 0.32. Did Kingsgate Financial Services' ability to pay both current and total debts improve or deteriorate during fiscal 2008?

Analyzing and journalizing corrections, adjustments, and closing entries
d. Net income overstated by $5,880

Problem 4–7B

The auditors of Cohen Logistics encountered the following situations while adjusting and closing the books at February 28. Consider each situation independently.

a. The company bookkeeper made the following entry to record a $1,240 credit purchase of supplies:

Feb. 26   Equipment 1,240
                   Accounts Payable   1,240

Prepare the correcting entry, dated February 28.

b. A $540 debit to Accounts Receivable was posted as $450.
   (1) At what stage of the accounting cycle will this error be detected?
   (2) Describe the technique for identifying the amount of the error.

c. The $3,480 balance of Utilities Expense was entered as $34,800 on the trial balance.
   (1) What is the name of this type of error?
   (2) Assume this is the only error in the trial balance. Which will be greater, the total debits or the total credits, and by how much?
   (3) How can this type of error be identified?

d. The accountant failed to make the following adjusting entries at February 28:
   (1) Accrued service revenue, $5,400.
   (2) Insurance expense that had been prepaid, $2,160.
   (3) Accrued interest expense on a note payable, $3,120.
   (4) Amortization of equipment, $22,200.
   (5) Earned service revenue that had been collected in advance, $16,200.

   Compute the overall net income effect of these five omissions.

e. Record each of the adjusting entries identified in item d.

f. The revenue and expense accounts *after* the adjusting entries had been posted were Service Revenue, $179,995; Wages Expense, $78,325; Amortization Expense, $30,540; and Insurance Expense, $1,860. Two balances prior to closing were N. Cohen, Capital, $137,725, and N. Cohen, Withdrawals, $91,000. Journalize the closing entries.

Problem 4–8B

Glen Eagle Marina performs overhauls and repairs to boats and motors at the marina and at the customer's location. The company's trial balance for the year ended June 30, 2009, follows.

Prepare a work sheet, journalizing the adjustments, closing the accounts

4. Trial bal. total $502,500

GLEN EAGLE MARINA
Trial Balance
June 30, 2009

Cash	$ 6,900	
Accounts receivable	36,600	
Repair supplies	59,400	
Prepaid insurance	14,100	
Equipment	18,000	
Accumulated amortization—equipment		$ 12,000
Building	264,000	
Accumulated amortization—building		52,800
Land	165,000	
Accounts payable		19,500
Unearned repair revenues		6,000
Property taxes payable		3,000
Notes payable, long-term		27,000
Mortgage payable		128,000
J. Alexander, capital		172,800
J. Alexander, withdrawals	41,000	
Repair fees earned		367,500
Wages expense	133,800	
Utilities expense	2,400	
Travel expenses	47,400	
Total	$788,600	$788,600

Additional information:

a. On June 30, repair supplies costing $6,600 were still on hand.

b. An examination of the insurance policies showed $8,700 of insurance coverage had expired in the year ended June 30, 2009.

c. An examination of the equipment and the building showed the following:

	Equipment	Building
Estimated useful life	5 years	10 years
Estimated value at the end of the useful life	$0	$0

Amortization is calculated on a straight-line basis over the asset's life.

d. The company had performed $3,000 of services for a client who had paid $6,000 in advance.

e. Accrued interest on the mortgage at June 30, $4,800.

f. Accrued wages at June 30 were for 60 employees for one day at a rate of $60 per day.

Required

1. Complete a work sheet for the year ended June 30, 2009.
2. Journalize the adjusting entries required on June 30, 2009.
3. Journalize the closing entries that would be required on June 30, 2009.
4. Prepare a postclosing trial balance for June 30, 2009.

Problem 4–9B

Preparing a work sheet, closing the accounts, classifying the assets and liabilities, evaluating the current and debt ratios

Mark Hanson, the accountant for Botwin Graphics, had prepared the work sheet shown on the next page on a computer spreadsheet but has lost much of the data. The only particular item the accountant can recall is that there was an adjustment made to correct an error made where $900 of supplies, purchased on credit, had been incorrectly recorded as $9,000 of equipment.

BOTWIN GRAPHICS
Accounting Work Sheet
For the Year Ended December 31, 2008

Account Title	Trial Balance Debit	Trial Balance Credit	Adjustments Debit	Adjustments Credit	Adjusted Trial Balance Debit	Adjusted Trial Balance Credit	Income Statement Debit	Income Statement Credit	Balance Sheet Debit	Balance Sheet Credit
Cash	8,000								8,000	
Accounts receivable	34,050				34,200					
Supplies	2,100			(b) 1,050						
Prepaid insurance	2,400				2,100					
Equipment	39,000				30,000					
Accumulated amortization—equipment		4,500				6,750				
Building	129,000				129,000					
Accumulated amortization—building		36,900		(e) 3,450						
Land	36,000				36,000					
Accounts payable		24,000								
Wages payable		1,350								
Interest payable		3,000		(f) 600						
Unearned revenues		4,050	(g) 600							
Mortgage payable		60,000								60,000
W. Botwin, capital		88,500								88,500
W. Botwin, withdrawals	27,000				27,000				27,000	
Graphics fees earned		147,650						148,400		
Wages expense	85,050				85,650					
Insurance expense	3,300									
Interest expense	3,000									
Utilities expense	1,050				1,050					
Supplies expense			(b) 1,050				1,050			
Amortization expense—equipment			(d) 2,250				2,250			
Amortization expense—building										
Totals	369,950	369,950								

Required

1. Complete the work sheet by filling in the missing data.
2. Journalize the closing entries that would be required on December 31, 2008.
3. Prepare the company's classified balance sheet as of December 31, 2008.
4. Compute Botwin Graphics' current ratio and debt ratio for December 31, 2008. On December 31, 2007, the current ratio was 2.25 and the debt ratio was 0.41. Comment on the changes in the ratios.

3. Total assets $194,150
4. Current ratio 1.90
Debit ratio 0.43

*Problem 4–10B

Using reversing entries

Refer to the data in Problem 4–3B on pages 203–204.

Required

1. Open ledger accounts for Accounts Receivable and Service Revenue. Insert their unadjusted balances at December 31, 2008.
2. Journalize the adjusting entry *c* only and the resulting closing entry for Service Revenue at December 31, 2008. Post to the accounts.
3. On January 10, 2009, World Media received a payment of $24,000 in settlement of this invoice. Journalize this cash receipt, and post to the accounts. Show the balance in each account.
4. Repeat Requirements 1 through 3 using a reversing entry. Compare the balances of Accounts Receivable and Service Revenue computed by using a reversing entry with those balances computed without using a reversing entry (as they appear in your answer to Requirement 3).

Challenge Problems

Problem 4–1C

Identifying and correcting errors

The following errors were made by Classy Catering's new bookkeeper:

a. A debit of $3,000 was recorded as an account receivable instead of a note receivable.
b. A salary expense accrual in the amount of $5,000 was overlooked when the work sheet was prepared.
c. A catering service revenue accrual of $10,000 was not recorded.

How would you correct these errors if the error occurred

1. After completing the work sheet, but before the financial statements were prepared (the accounts have not yet been closed)?
2. After closing entries were completed?

Problem 4–2C

Understanding the current ratio

It is July 15, 2008. A friend, who works in the office of a local company that has four fast-food restaurants, has come to you with a question. He knows you are studying accounting and asks if you could help him sort something out. He acknowledges that although he has worked for the company for three years as a general clerk, he really does not understand the accounting work he is doing.

The company has a large bank loan and, as your friend understands it, the company has agreed with the bank to maintain a current ratio (he thinks that is what it is called) of 1.8 to 1 (1.8:1). The company's year end is June 30. The owner came to him on July 7, 2008, and asked him to issue a batch of cheques to suppliers but to date them June 30. Your friend recognizes that the cheques will have an effect on the June 30, 2008, financial statements but doesn't think the effect will be too serious.

Required   Explain to your friend what the effect of paying invoices after June 30 but dating the cheques prior to June 30 has on the current ratio. Provide an example to illustrate your explanation.

---

*This Problem covers Chapter 4 Appendix topics.

Decision Problems

Completing the accounting cycle to develop the information for a bank loan

4 6

Net income $80,310
Ending owner's equity $52,680

Decision Problem 1

One year ago, your friend Don Jenner founded Jenner Consulting Services. The business has prospered. Jenner, who remembers that you took an accounting course while in college, comes to you for advice. He wishes to know how much net income his business earned during the past year. He also wants to know what the entity's total assets, liabilities, and owner's equity are. The accounting records consist of the T-accounts of the company's ledger, which were prepared by a bookkeeper who moved to another city. The ledger at December 31 of the fiscal year appears as follows:

Cash		Accounts Receivable		Prepaid Rent	
Dec. 31 8,745		Dec. 31 18,540		Jan. 2 4,200	

Supplies		Computer Equipment		Accumulated Amortization	
Jan. 2 3,900		Jan. 2 65,400			0

Accounts Payable		Unearned Service Revenue		Salaries Payable	
	Dec. 31 27,810		Dec. 31 6,195		0

D. Jenner, Capital		D. Jenner, Withdrawals		Service Revenue	
	Jan. 2 37,500	Dec. 31 65,130			Dec. 31 121,110

Amortization Expense		Salary Expense		Supplies Expense	
0		Dec. 31 25,500		0	

Rent Expense		Utilities Expense	
0		Dec. 31 1,200	

    Jenner indicates that at the year's end customers owe the company $2,400 accrued service revenue, which he expects to collect early next year. These revenues have not been recorded. During the year, the company collected $6,195 service revenue in advance from customers, but the company earned only $900 of that amount. Rent expense for the year was $3,600, and the company used up $3,150 in supplies. Jenner estimates that amortization on the equipment was $8,850 for the year. At December 31, Jenner Consulting owes an employee $1,800 accrued salary.

    Jenner expresses concern that his withdrawals during the year might have exceeded the business's net income. To get a loan to expand the business, Jenner must show the bank that Jenner Consulting's owner's equity has grown from its original $37,500 balance. Has it? You and Jenner agree that you will meet again in one week. You perform the analysis and prepare the financial statements to answer his questions.

Finding an error in the work sheets

1 4

Decision Problem 2

You are preparing the financial statements for the year ended October 31, 2008, for Cusik Publishing Company, a weekly newspaper. You began with the trial balance of the ledger, which balanced, and then made the required adjusting entries. To save time, you omitted preparing an adjusted trial balance. After making the adjustments on the work sheet, you extended the balances from the trial balance, adjusted for the adjusting entries, and computed amounts for the income statement and balance sheet columns.

a. When you added the debits and credits in the income statement columns, you found that the credits exceeded the debits by $30,000. According to your finding, did Cusik Publishing Company have a profit or a loss?

b. You took the balancing amount from the income statement columns to the debit column of the balance sheet and found that the total debits exceeded the total credits in the balance sheet. The difference between the total debits and the total credits on the balance sheet is $60,000, which is two times the amount of the difference you calculated for the income statement columns. What is the cause of this difference? (Except for these errors, everything else is correct.)

Financial Statement Cases

Financial Statement Case 1

This case, based on CHUM Limited's balance sheet in Appendix A, will familiarize you with some of the assets and liabilities of this actual company. Answer these questions, using CHUM's balance sheet.

Using an actual balance sheet

6. Aug. 31, 2005 current ratio 1.38
7. Aug. 31, 2005 debt ratio 0.52

Required

1. Compare CHUM's balance sheet to the balance sheet in Exhibit 4–13. What differences in style do you notice between these two balance sheets? Describe these differences.

2. What is CHUM's largest current asset in 2005? In 2004?

3. What is the company's largest current liability in 2005? In 2004?

4. What were total current assets in 2005? In 2004?

5. What were total current liabilities in 2005? In 2004?

6. Compute CHUM's current ratio at August 31, 2005, and at August 31, 2004. Did the ratio values improve or deteriorate during fiscal 2005?

7. Compute CHUM's debt ratio at August 31, 2005, and at August 31, 2004. Did the ratio values improve or deteriorate during fiscal 2005?

8. Many items on the balance sheet refer to notes that accompany the financial statements. Refer to the property, plant and equipment Note 5, and calculate the total cost of the assets, the accumulated amortization (depreciation), and the book value at August 31, 2005.

9. What is the main purpose of the notes to the financial statements?

Financial Statement Case 2

This case, based on Sun-Rype Products Ltd.'s balance sheet in Appendix B, will familiarize you with some of the assets and liabilities of this actual company. Answer these questions, using Sun-Rype's balance sheet.

Using an actual balance sheet

6. Dec. 31, 2005 current ratio 2.58
7. Dec. 31, 2005 debt ratio 0.29

Required

1. Compare Sun-Rype's balance sheet to the balance sheet in Exhibit 4–13. What differences in style do you notice between these two balance sheets? Describe these differences.

2. What is Sun-Rype's largest current asset in 2005? In 2004?

3. What is the company's largest current liability in 2005? In 2004?

4. What were total current assets in 2005? In 2004?

5. What were total current liabilities in 2005? In 2004?

6. Compute Sun-Rype's current ratio at December 31, 2005, and at December 31, 2004. Did the ratio values improve or deteriorate during the year?

7. Compute Sun-Rype's debt ratio at December 31, 2005, and at December 31, 2004. Did the ratio values improve or deteriorate during the year?

8. Many items on the balance sheet refer to notes that accompany the financial statements. Refer to the property, plant and equipment Note 4, and calculate the total cost of the assets, the accumulated amortization (depreciation), and the book value at December 31, 2005.

9. What is the main purpose of the notes to the financial statements?

Merchandising Operations and the Accounting Cycle

Learning Objectives

1. Use sales and gross margin to evaluate a company

2. Account for the purchase and sale of inventory under the perpetual inventory system

3. Adjust and close the accounts of a merchandising business under the perpetual inventory system

4. Prepare a merchandiser's financial statements under the perpetual inventory system

5. Use the gross margin percentage and the inventory turnover ratio to evaluate a business

Chapter 5 Appendix A

6. Account for the purchase and sale of inventory under the periodic inventory system

7. Compute the cost of goods sold under the periodic inventory system

8. Adjust and close the accounts of a merchandising business under the periodic inventory system

9. Prepare a merchandiser's financial statements under the periodic inventory system

Chapter 5 Appendix B

10. Compare the perpetual and periodic inventory systems

Dell Inc., founded by Michael Dell in 1984, makes and sells Dell computers. In 2005, the company's sales were estimated to be $52 billion, placing it at position 28 on the Fortune 500 list of the world's largest companies. Dell is famous for its strategy of making computers to order and selling directly to its customers, eliminating the need for retail stores. Dell's strategy allows the company to be in direct contact with its customers and to offer high-value products at a lower price than its competitors. With an average growth rate of over 35 per cent, its outlook is very optimistic.

"Part of Dell's success has been its drive to work in real time. Today, Dell's suppliers are updated on an hourly basis about order status. While Dell assembles more than 90,000 computers a day, it maintains only two hours of inventory in its factories and three days of inventory across its entire organization. Given that computer components fall in value on average by one per cent per week, Dell benefits from an immediate cost advantage over indirect sellers (retailers) who have weeks of inventory on hand."[1]

---

[1] Harris, Jim. "Analyze This: Knowledge is Not Enough," *Backbone Magazine*, November/December 2005, page 70.

How do merchandising operations differ from service operations, and why is it important?

What are inventory and cost of goods sold?

What types of inventory systems are there?

How do decision makers evaluate a company's inventory operations?

These questions and others will be answered throughout this chapter. And the Decision Guidelines at the end of this chapter will provide the answers in a useful summary.

What comes to mind when you think of *merchandising?* You probably think of the clothing that you purchase from a department store, the bread you buy at the grocery store, or the gas you purchase at your local service station. In addition to Dell Inc., merchandisers include Zellers, The Bay, Canadian Tire, Petro-Canada, and Shoppers Drug Mart.

How do the operations of Dell Inc. and other merchandisers differ from those of the businesses we have studied so far? In the first four chapters, SuperTravel provided an illustration of a business that earns revenue by selling its services. Service enterprises include Fairmont Hotels, WestJet, physicians, lawyers, public accountants, the Toronto Maple Leafs hockey club, and the twelve-year-old who cuts lawns in your neighbourhood. A *merchandising entity* earns its revenue by selling products, called *merchandise inventory* or, simply, *inventory*.

This chapter demonstrates the central role of inventory in a business that sells merchandise, such as Dell. **Inventory** includes all goods that the company owns and expects to sell to customers in the normal course of operations. Some businesses, such as Wal-Mart department stores, Esso gas stations, and Safeway grocery stores, buy their inventory in finished form ready for sale to customers. Others, such as Big Rock Breweries and Dell Inc., manufacture their own products. Both groups sell products rather than services.

Chapter 5 introduces merchandising. We show how to account for the purchase and sale of inventory. We feature a small electronics store, and we use an actual business document to illustrate transactions.

Before launching into merchandising, let's compare service entities, with which you are familiar, with merchandising companies. Exhibit 5–1 shows how a service entity (on the left) differs from a merchandiser (on the right).

What Are Merchandising Operations?

Merchandising consists of buying and selling products rather than services. Merchandisers have some new balance sheet and income statement items.

Objective ❶

Use sales and gross margin to evaluate a company

Balance Sheet

- Inventory, an asset

Income Statement

- Sales revenue
- Cost of goods sold, an expense

These items are highlighted in Exhibit 5–1 for Merchandising Co. and explained further here.

The selling price of merchandise sold by a business is called **sales revenue**, often abbreviated as **sales**. (**Net sales** equals sales revenue minus any sales returns and sales discounts.) The major revenue of a merchandising entity, sales revenue, results in an increase in capital from delivering inventory to customers.

SERVICE CO.* Income Statement For the Year Ended June 30, 2008			MERCHANDISING CO.** Income Statement For the Year Ended June 30, 2008	
Service revenue		$XXX	Sales revenue	$XXX
Expenses			Cost of goods sold	X
Salary expense	X		Gross margin	XX
Amortization expense	X		Operating expenses	
Net income		$ X	Salary expense	X
			Amortization expense	X
			Rent expense	X
			Net income	$ X

SERVICE CO. Balance Sheet June 30, 2008		MERCHANDISING CO. Balance Sheet June 30, 2008	
Assets		**Assets**	
Current assets:		Current assets:	
Cash	$X	Cash	$X
Held-for-trading investments...	X	Held-for-trading investments...	X
Accounts receivable, net	X	Accounts receivable, net	X
Prepaid expenses	X	**Inventory**	X
		Prepaid expenses	X

*Such as SuperTravel

**Such as Austin Sound Centre, a music store in Kingston, Ontario.

The major expense of a merchandiser is **cost of goods sold**, also called **cost of sales**. It represents the entity's cost of the goods (the inventory) it sold to customers. While inventory is held by a business, it is an asset because the goods are an economic resource with future value to the company. When the inventory is sold, however, its cost becomes an expense to the seller because the goods are no longer available.

Net sales minus cost of goods sold is called **gross margin** or **gross profit**.

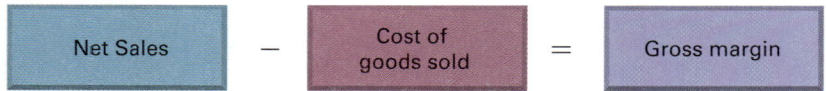

Gross margin is a measure of business success. A sufficiently high gross margin is vital to a merchandiser, since all other expenses of the company are deducted from this gross margin.

The following example will clarify the nature of gross margin. Consider Danier Leather Inc., the company that sells leather clothing and accessories across Canada. Suppose Danier Leather's cost for a certain jacket is $150 and Danier sells the jacket to a customer in Winnipeg for $250. Danier's gross margin on the jacket is $100 ($250 − $150). The gross margin reported on Danier's year-end income statement is the sum of the gross margins on all the products the company sold during its fiscal year.

What Goes into Inventory Cost?

The cost of inventory on a merchandiser's balance sheet represents all the costs incurred to bring the merchandise to the point of sale. Suppose Danier Leather Inc.

purchases purses from a manufacturer in Asia. Danier's cost of a purse would include

- Cost of the purse—say $50.00 per purse.
- Customs duties paid to the Canadian government in order to import the purses—say $5.00, added to the cost of each purse.
- Shipping cost from the manufacturer in Asia to one of Danier's stores. This cost is called *freight* or *freight in*. Assume freight adds $2.50 of cost to each purse.
- Insurance on the purses while in transit—say $1.50 per purse.

In total, Danier Leather's cost of this purse totals $59.00 ($50.00 + $5.00 + $2.50 + $1.50). The cost principle applies to all assets, as follows:

The cost of any asset is the sum of all the costs incurred to bring the asset to its intended use.

For merchandise inventory, the intended use is readiness for sale. After the goods are ready for sale, then other costs, such as advertising, display, and sales commissions, are expensed. Thus these costs are *not* included as the cost of inventory.

The Operating Cycle for a Merchandising Business

Some merchandising entities buy inventory, sell the inventory to their customers, and use the cash to purchase more inventory to repeat the cycle. Other merchandisers, like Mission Hills Winery or the Ford Motor Company, manufacture their products and sell them to customers. The balance of this chapter considers the first group of merchandisers that buy products and resell them. Exhibit 5–2 diagrams the operating cycle for *cash sales* and for *sales on account*. For a cash sale—Panel A—the cycle is from cash to inventory, which is purchased for resale, and back to cash. For a sale on account—Panel B—the cycle is from cash to inventory to accounts receivable and back to cash. In all lines of business, managers strive to shorten the cycle in order to keep assets active. The faster the sale of inventory and the collection of cash, the higher the profits, assuming cost and selling price stay the same.

EXHIBIT 5–2 Operating Cycle of a Merchandiser

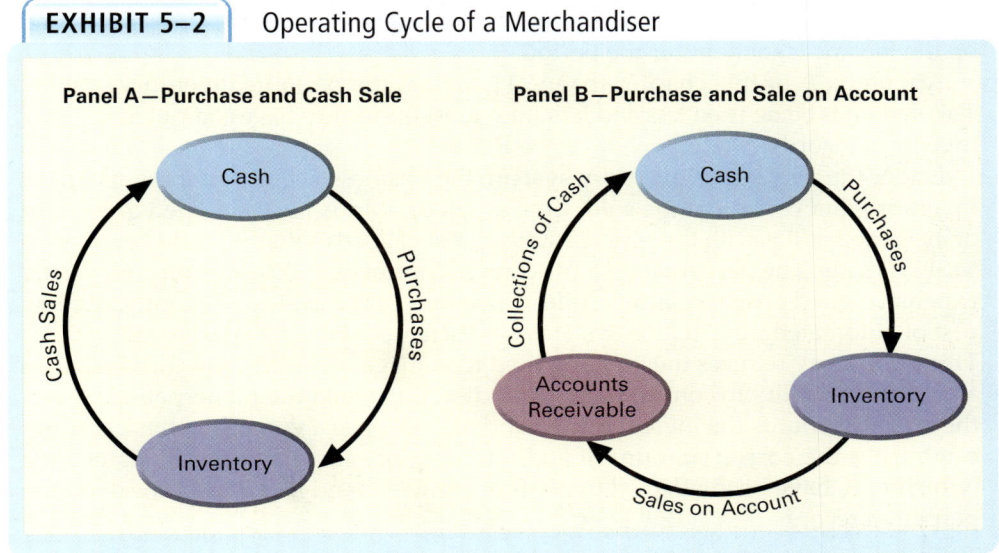

Now let's see how companies account for their inventory. We begin with journal entries, post to the ledger accounts, and prepare the financial statements.

Inventory Systems: Perpetual and Periodic

There are two main types of inventory accounting systems:

- Periodic system
- Perpetual system

The **periodic inventory system** is used by businesses that sell relatively inexpensive goods. A very small grocery store without an optical-scanning cash register to read UPC codes does not keep a daily running record of every loaf of bread and litre of milk that it buys and sells. The cost of record keeping would be overwhelming. Instead, it counts its inventory periodically—at least once a year—to determine the quantities on hand. The inventory amounts are used to prepare the annual financial statements. Businesses such as restaurants and small retail stores also use the periodic inventory system.

Once the cost of the goods remaining in inventory at the end of the period (ending inventory) is determined by the inventory count, then we can calculate the cost of the inventory sold during the period. To do this, follow these steps:

1. Determine the cost of the goods that were in inventory at the beginning of the period, which is beginning inventory. This is the same amount as the prior period's ending inventory.
2. Add the cost of goods purchased during the period. Adding beginning inventory and purchases will give the cost of the goods available for sale during the period.
3. Subtract the cost of the goods on hand at the end of the period (ending inventory, based on the inventory count).

The formula for cost of goods sold is:

The resulting cost of goods sold amount, a merchandiser's major expense, is included on the income statement for the period.

Appendix A of this chapter (page 244) covers the periodic inventory system. This system is being used less and less since most businesses have computerized their inventory records.

Under the **perpetual inventory system**, the business keeps a running record of inventory and cost of goods sold. Cost of goods sold is *not* calculated at the end of the period as it is with the periodic system; cost of goods sold is recorded every time a sale is made. The perpetual system achieves control over the inventory, especially expensive goods such as automobiles, jewellery, and furniture. Recently, the low cost of automated information systems has increased the use of perpetual systems. This technology reduces the time required to manage inventory and thus increases a company's ability to control its merchandise. But even under a perpetual system the business counts the inventory on hand at least once a year. The physical count establishes the correct amount of ending inventory for the financial statements (which may have been affected by theft or spoilage) and serves as a check on the perpetual records.

The following chart compares the perpetual and periodic systems:

Perpetual Inventory System	Periodic Inventory System
• Keeps a running record of all inventory as it is bought and sold (units and price)	• Does *not* keep a running record of all goods bought and sold
• Inventory counted at least once a year	• Inventory counted at least once a year

Automated Perpetual Inventory Systems

A modern automated perpetual inventory system records

• Units purchased

• Units sold

• The quantity of inventory on hand.

Inventory systems are often integrated with accounts receivable and sales. The computer can keep up-to-the-minute records, so managers can call up current inventory information at any time. For example, in a perpetual system the "cash register" at IKEA or Home Depot is a computer terminal that records sales and also updates the inventory records. Bar codes, such as the one shown here, are scanned by a laser. The lines of the bar code represent inventory and cost data that keep track of each item. Most businesses use bar codes, so we focus our inventory discussions on the perpetual system.

Bar code

Accounting for Inventory in the Perpetual Inventory System

The cycle of a merchandising entity begins with the purchase of inventory, as Exhibit 5–2 shows. For example, a menswear store records the purchase of sweaters, shirts, and other items of inventory acquired for resale by debiting the Inventory account. A $20,000 purchase on account is recorded as follows:

May 14	Inventory...	20,000	
	Accounts Payable		20,000
	Purchased inventory on account.		

The Inventory account should be used only for purchases of merchandise for resale. Purchases of any other assets are recorded in a different asset account. For example, the purchase of supplies is debited to Supplies, not to Inventory. Inventory is an asset until it is sold.

The Purchase Invoice: A Basic Business Document

Business documents are the tangible evidence of transactions. In this section, we trace the steps that Austin Sound Centre, a small electronics store in Kingston, Ontario, takes to order, receive, and pay for inventory. Many companies buy and sell their goods electronically—with no invoices, no cheques, and so on. Here we use actual documents to illustrate what takes place behind the scenes.

1. Suppose Austin Sound Centre wants to stock JVC brand CD players, DVD players, and speakers. Austin prepares a *purchase order* and transmits it to JVC Canada Inc.

Objective 2

Account for the purchase and sale of inventory under the perpetual inventory system

2. On receipt of the purchase order, JVC searches its warehouse for the inventory that Austin Sound Centre ordered. JVC ships the equipment and sends the invoice to Austin Sound on the same day. The **invoice** is the seller's request for payment from the purchaser. It is also called the *bill*.

3. Often the purchaser receives the invoice before the inventory arrives. Austin Sound does not pay immediately. Instead, Austin Sound waits until the inventory arrives in order to ensure that it is the correct type and quantity ordered, and that it arrives in good condition. After the inventory is inspected and approved, Austin Sound pays JVC the invoice amount according to the terms of payment previously negotiated.

Exhibit 5–3 is a copy of an invoice from JVC Canada Inc. to Austin Sound Centre.

EXHIBIT 5–3 Purchase Invoice

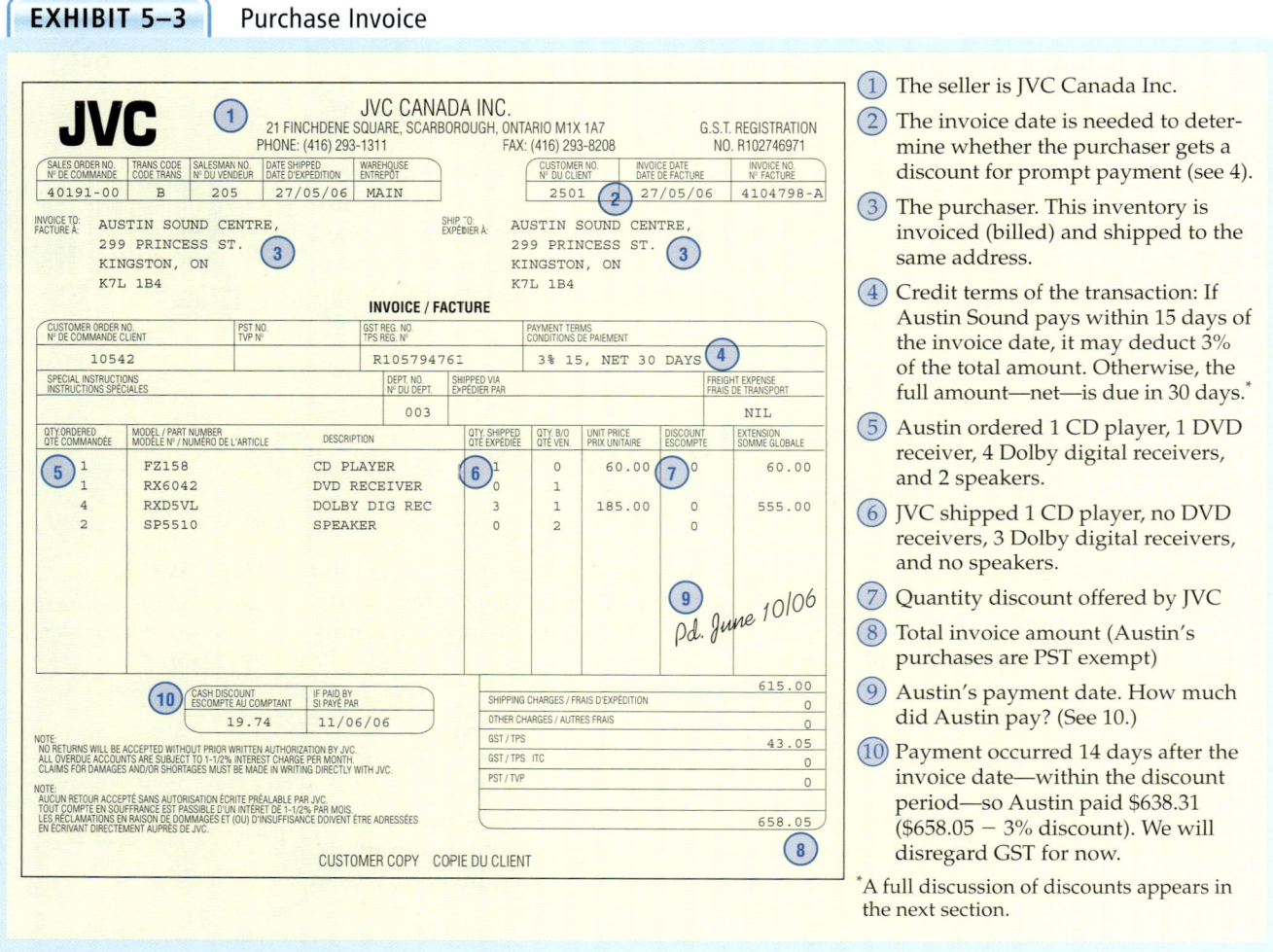

1. The seller is JVC Canada Inc.
2. The invoice date is needed to determine whether the purchaser gets a discount for prompt payment (see 4).
3. The purchaser. This inventory is invoiced (billed) and shipped to the same address.
4. Credit terms of the transaction: If Austin Sound pays within 15 days of the invoice date, it may deduct 3% of the total amount. Otherwise, the full amount—net—is due in 30 days.*
5. Austin ordered 1 CD player, 1 DVD receiver, 4 Dolby digital receivers, and 2 speakers.
6. JVC shipped 1 CD player, no DVD receivers, 3 Dolby digital receivers, and no speakers.
7. Quantity discount offered by JVC
8. Total invoice amount (Austin's purchases are PST exempt)
9. Austin's payment date. How much did Austin pay? (See 10.)
10. Payment occurred 14 days after the invoice date—within the discount period—so Austin paid $638.31 ($658.05 − 3% discount). We will disregard GST for now.

*A full discussion of discounts appears in the next section.

Discounts from Purchase Prices

There are two major types of discounts from purchase prices: quantity discounts and cash discounts (called *purchase discounts*).

Quantity Discounts A *quantity discount* works this way: The larger the quantity purchased, the lower the price per item. For example, JVC may offer no quantity discount for the purchase of only one or two CD players, and charge the *list* price—

the full price—of $100 per unit. However, JVC may offer the following quantity discount terms in order to persuade customers to buy more CD players:

Quantity	Quantity Discount	Net Price per Unit
Buy minimum quantity, 3 CD players	5%	$95 [$100 – 0.05($100)]
Buy 4–9 CD players	10%	$90 [$100 – 0.10($100)]
Buy more than 9 CD players	20%	$80 [$100 – 0.20($100)]

Suppose Austin Sound Centre purchases five CD players from JVC. The cost of each CD player is, therefore, $90. Purchase of five units on account would be recorded by debiting Inventory and crediting Accounts Payable for the total price of $450 ($90 per unit × 5 items purchased).

There is no Quantity Discount account and no special accounting entry for a quantity discount. Instead, all accounting entries are based on the net price of a purchase after the quantity discount has been subtracted, as shown on the invoice.

Purchase Discounts Many businesses also offer purchase discounts to their customers. A purchase discount is totally different from a quantity or volume discount. A *purchase discount* (also referred to as a *cash discount*) is a reward for prompt payment. If a quantity discount is also offered, the purchase discount is computed on the net purchase amount after the quantity discount has been subtracted, further reducing the cost of the inventory to the purchaser.

JVC's credit terms of "3% 15, NET 30 DAYS" can also be expressed as "3/15, n/30." This means that Austin Sound Centre may deduct 3 percent of the total amount due if Austin pays within 15 days of the invoice date. Otherwise, the full amount—NET—is due in 30 days.

Terms of "n/30" indicate that no discount is offered, and payment is due 30 days after the invoice date. Terms of *eom* mean that payment is due by the end of the current month. However, a purchase after the 25th of the current month on terms of *eom* can be paid at the end of the next month.

A computerized accounting system is typically programmed to flag invoices as the date for taking the discount approaches so the business can take advantage of the purchase discount.

Let's use the Exhibit 5–3 transaction to illustrate accounting for a purchase discount. For the moment, disregard GST and use the invoice total of $658.05 when recording purchases and purchase discounts. GST is discussed on page 226. Austin Sound Centre records the purchase on account as follows:

May 27	Inventory..	658.05	
	Accounts Payable		658.05
	Purchased inventory on account.		

Austin paid within the discount period of 15 days, so its cash payment entry is

June 10	Accounts Payable	658.05	
	Cash		638.31
	Inventory...		19.74
	Paid on account within discount period.		
	The discount is $19.74 ($658.05 × 0.03).		

The discount is credited to Inventory. After Austin Sound has taken its discount, Austin Sound must adjust the Inventory account to reflect its true cost of the goods. In effect, this inventory cost Austin Sound $638.31 ($658.05 minus the purchase discount of $19.74) as shown in the following Inventory account:

Inventory

May 27	658.05	June 10	19.74
Bal.	638.31		

However, if Austin Sound pays this invoice after the discount period, it must pay the full invoice amount. In this case, the payment entry is

```
June  29   Accounts Payable ......................................   658.05
                 Cash .......................................................         658.05
                 Paid on account after discount period.
```

Without the discount, Austin Sound's cost of the inventory is the full amount of $658.05, as shown in the following T-account:

Inventory

May 27 658.05	

Purchase Returns and Allowances

Most businesses allow their customers to *return* merchandise that is defective, damaged in shipment, or otherwise unsuitable. Or, if the buyer chooses to keep damaged goods, the seller may deduct an *allowance* from the amount the buyer owes. Both purchase returns and purchase allowances decrease the amount that the buyer must pay the seller.

Suppose the $60.00 CD player (model FZ158) purchased by Austin Sound Centre (in Exhibit 5–3) was not the CD player ordered. Austin Sound returns the merchandise to the seller and records the purchase return as follows:

```
June   3   Accounts Payable ......................................   60.00
                 Inventory.................................................         60.00
                 Returned inventory to seller.
```

Now assume that one of the JVC Dolby digital receivers was damaged in shipment to Austin Sound Centre. The damage is minor, and Austin decides to keep the receiver in exchange for a $15.00 allowance from JVC. To record this purchase allowance, Austin Sound Centre makes this entry:

```
June   4   Accounts Payable ......................................   15.00
                 Inventory.................................................         15.00
                 Received a purchase allowance.
```

The return and the allowance had two effects:

(1) They decreased Austin Sound's liability, which is why we debit Accounts Payable.

(2) They decreased the net cost of the inventory, which is why we credit Inventory.

Assume that Austin Sound has not yet paid its liability to JVC. After these return ($60.00) and allowance ($15.00) transactions are posted, Austin Sound's accounts will show these balances:

Inventory				Accounts Payable			
May 27 658.05	June 3	60.00		June 3	60.00	May 27	658.05
	June 4	15.00		June 4	15.00		
Bal. 583.05						Bal.	583.05

Austin Sound's cost of *inventory* is $583.05, and Austin Sound owes JVC $583.05 on *account payable*. If Austin Sound pays within the discount period, 3 percent will be deducted from the $583.05 balance.

Transportation Costs: Who Pays?

The transportation cost of moving inventory from seller to buyer can be significant. Someone must pay this cost. The purchase agreement specifies FOB (*free on board*) terms to indicate who pays the shipping charges. FOB governs

(1) when legal title passes from the seller to buyer, and

(2) who pays the freight.

- Under FOB *shipping point* terms, title passes when the inventory leaves the seller's place of business—the shipping point. The buyer owns the goods while they are in transit, and therefore the buyer pays the transportation cost, or freight.

- Under FOB *destination* terms, title passes when the goods reach the destination, so the seller pays the freight.

Exhibit 5-4 on page 222 summarizes FOB.

Freight costs are either Freight in or Freight out.

- *Freight in* is the transportation cost on *purchased goods.*
- *Freight out* is the transportation cost on *goods sold.*

Freight In FOB shipping point terms are the most common. The buyer owns the goods while they are in transit, so the buyer pays the freight. In accounting, the cost of an asset includes all costs incurred to bring the asset to its intended use. For inventory, cost therefore includes the

- *Net cost* after all discounts, returns, and allowances have been subtracted, plus
- *Freight in*

To record the payment for freight in, the buyer debits Inventory and credits Cash or Accounts Payable for the amount. Suppose Austin Sound receives an $80.00

EXHIBIT 5–4 | FOB Terms Determine Who Pays the Freight

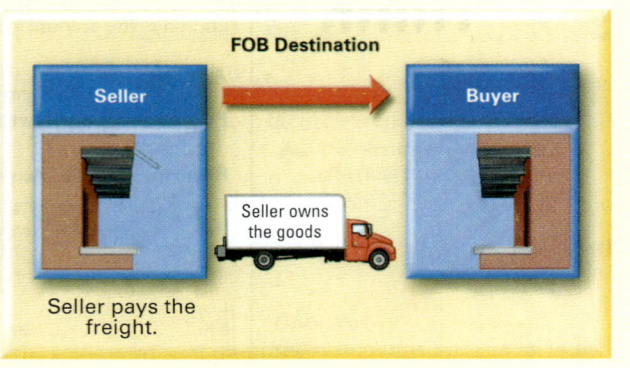

shipping bill directly from the freight company. Austin's entry to record payment of the freight charge is:

June	1	Inventory	80.00	
		Cash		80.00
		Paid a freight bill.		

The freight charge increases the cost of the inventory to $663.05 as follows:

Inventory

(Purchase)	May 27	658.05	June 3	60.00	(Return)
(Freight)	June 1	80.00	June 4	15.00	(Allowance)
(Net cost)	Bal.	663.05			

Any discounts would be computed only on the account payable to the seller, not on the transportation costs, because the discount was offered by the seller, not the freight company. The freight company usually offers no discount.

Under FOB shipping point, the seller sometimes prepays the transportation cost as a convenience and adds this cost on the invoice. The buyer can debit Inventory for the combined cost of the inventory and the shipping cost because both costs apply to the merchandise. A $10,000 purchase of goods, coupled with a related freight charge of $800, would be recorded as follows:

March 12	Inventory	10,800	
	Accounts Payable		10,800
	Purchased inventory on account, including		
	freight of $800.		

If the buyer pays within the discount period, the discount will be computed on the $10,000 merchandise cost, not on the $10,800. No discount is offered on transportation cost.

STOP AND THINK

This Stop and Think example is exactly like the preceding one, but with freight in. On September 15, Austin Sound Centre purchased $1,000 of merchandise, with *$80 freight added*, for an invoice total of $1,080. Austin returns $100 of the goods for credit on September 20 and pays the account payable in full on September 25. Journalize these transactions.

Answer continued on the next page

Freight Out The seller may pay freight charges to ship goods to customers. This is called *freight out*. Freight out is a delivery expense. Delivery expense is a selling expense, an operating expense for the seller. It is debited to the Delivery Expense account.

Summary of Purchase Returns and Allowances, Discounts, and Transportation Costs Suppose Austin Sound Centre buys $35,000 of audio/video inventory, takes a discount, and returns some of the goods. Austin Sound also pays some freight in. The following summary shows Austin Sound's net purchases of this inventory. All amounts are assumed for this illustration.

Purchases of Inventory		Purchase Returns and Allowances		Purchase Discounts		Freight in		Net Purchases of Inventory
Inventory	−	and Allowances	−	Discounts	+	Freight in	=	Inventory
$35,000	−	$700	−	$800	+	$2,100	=	$35,600

Inventory

Purchases of inventory 35,000	Purchase ret. & allow. 700
Freight in 2,100	Purchase discount 800
Balance 35,600	

Selling Inventory and Recording Cost of Goods Sold

After a company buys inventory, the next step in the operating cycle is to sell the goods. We shift now to the selling side and follow Austin Sound Centre through a sequence of selling transactions. A sale earns a reward, Sales Revenue. A sale also requires a sacrifice in the form of an expense, Cost of Goods Sold, as the seller gives up the asset Inventory.

After making a sale on account, Austin Sound Centre may experience any of the following:

- A sales return: The customer may return goods to Austin Sound.
- A sales allowance: For one reason or another, Austin Sound may grant a sales allowance to reduce the amount of cash to be collected from the customer.
- A sales discount: If the customer pays within the discount period—under terms such as 2/10, n/30—Austin Sound collects the discounted (reduced) amount.
- Freight out: Austin Sound may have to pay Delivery Expense to transport the goods to the buyer's location.

The sale of inventory may be for cash or on account, as Exhibit 5–2 shows. Let's begin with a cash sale.

Cash Sale Sales by retailers, such as Austin Sound Centre, grocery stores, and restaurants, are often for cash. Cash sales of $7,000 would be recorded by debiting Cash and crediting Sales Revenue as follows:

Jan.	9	Cash	7,000	
		Sales Revenue..		7,000
		Cash sale.		

To update the inventory records for the goods sold, the business also must decrease the Inventory balance. Suppose these goods cost the seller $4,200. An accompanying entry is needed to transfer the $4,200 cost of the goods—*not their selling price of $7,000*—from the Inventory account to the Cost of Goods Sold account as follows:

Jan.	9	Cost of Goods Sold	4,200
		Inventory...		4,200
		Recorded the cost of goods sold.	

KEY POINT

The recording of cost of goods sold along with sales revenue is an example of the matching principle (Chapter 3, page 104)—matching expense against revenue to measure net income.

Cost of goods sold (also called cost of sales) is the largest single expense of most businesses that sell merchandise, such as Best Buy, JVC, and Austin Sound Centre. It is the cost of the inventory that the business has sold to customers. The Cost of Goods Sold account keeps a current balance as transactions are journalized and posted.

After posting, the Cost of Goods Sold account holds the cost of the merchandise sold ($4,200 in this case):

Inventory				Cost of Goods Sold		
Purchases 60,000 (amount assumed)		Jan. 9	4,200	Jan. 9	4,200	

The computer automatically records the cost of goods sold entry. The cashier scans the bar code on the product and the computer performs this task.

Sale on Account Most sales in Canada are made on account (on credit), using either the seller's credit facility or a credit card such as Visa or MasterCard. To simplify the discussion, we will assume the seller records the receivable as a regular account receivable rather than a special receivable from the credit card company. A $10,000 sale on account is recorded by a debit to Accounts Receivable and a credit to Sales Revenue, as follows:

Jan.	11	Accounts Receivable	10,000
		Sales Revenue...		10,000
		Sale on account.	

If we assume that these goods cost the seller $5,200, the accompanying cost of goods sold and inventory entry is

Jan.	11	Cost of Goods Sold	5,200
		Inventory...		5,200
		Recorded the cost of goods sold.	

When the cash is received, the seller records the cash receipt on account as follows:

Jan.	19	Cash	10,000
		Accounts Receivable		10,000
		Collection on account.	

STOP AND THINK

Why is there no January 19 entry to Sales Revenue, Cost of Goods Sold, or Inventory?

Answer: On January 19 the seller merely receives one asset—Cash—in place of another asset—Accounts Receivable. The sales revenue, the related cost of goods sold, and the decrease in inventory for the goods sold were recorded on January 11. Examine the two entries on January 11.

Offering Sales Discounts and Sales Returns and Allowances

We saw that purchase discounts and purchase returns and allowances decrease the cost of inventory purchases. In the same way, **sales discounts** and **sales returns and allowances** decrease the revenue earned on sales. Sales Discounts and Sales Returns and Allowances are contra accounts to Sales Revenue.

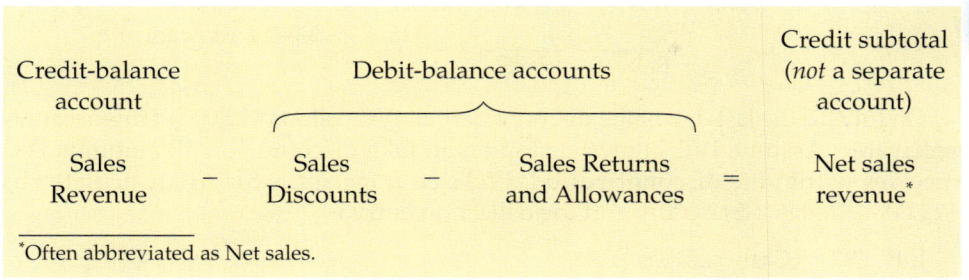

Credit-balance account		Debit-balance accounts				Credit subtotal (*not* a separate account)
Sales Revenue	−	Sales Discounts	−	Sales Returns and Allowances	=	Net sales revenue*

*Often abbreviated as Net sales.

This equation calculates net sales. Sales discounts can be given on both goods and services.

Companies keep close watch on their customers' paying habits and on their own sales of defective and unsuitable merchandise. They maintain separate accounts for Sales Discounts and Sales Returns and Allowances. Let's examine a sequence of JVC sale transactions. Assume JVC is selling to Austin Sound Centre.

On July 7, JVC sells stereo components for $21,600 on credit terms of 3/15, n/30. These goods cost JVC $14,100. JVC's entries to record this credit sale and the related cost of goods sold are:

July	7	Accounts Receivable	21,600	
		Sales Revenue...		21,600
		Sale on account.		

July	7	Cost of Goods Sold	14,100	
		Inventory..		14,100
		Recorded the cost of goods sold.		

Sales Returns Assume the buyer, Austin Sound Centre, returns goods that were sold by JVC for $1,800. These goods are not damaged and can be resold. JVC, the seller, records the sales return and the related decrease in Accounts Receivable as follows:

July	12	Sales Returns and Allowances................	1,800	
		Accounts Receivable		1,800
		Received returned goods.		

JVC receives the returned merchandise and updates the inventory records. JVC must also decrease cost of goods sold as follows (the returned goods cost JVC $1,200):

July	12	Inventory...	1,200	
		Cost of Goods Sold		1,200
		Returned goods to inventory.		

Sales Allowances Suppose JVC grants to the buyer a $300 sales allowance for damaged goods. Austin Sound then subtracts $300 from the amount it will pay JVC. JVC journalizes this transaction by debiting Sales Returns and Allowances and crediting Accounts Receivable as follows:

July	15	Sales Returns and Allowances................	300	
		Accounts Receivable		300
		Granted a sales allowance for damaged goods.		

No inventory entry is needed for a sales allowance transaction because the seller, JVC, receives no returned goods from the customer. Instead, JVC will simply receive less cash from the customer.

After the preceding entries are posted, all the accounts have up-to-date balances. JVC's Accounts Receivable has a $19,500 debit balance, as follows:

Accounts Receivable

(Sale)	July 7	21,600	July 12	1,800	(Return)
			15	300	(Allowance)
	Bal.	19,500			

On July 22, the last day of the discount period, JVC collects $12,000 of this accounts receivable. Assume JVC allows customers to take discounts on all amounts JVC receives within the discount period. JVC's cash receipt is $11,640 [calculated as $12,000 − (0.03 × $12,000)], and the collection entry is

July	22	Cash	11,640	
		Sales Discounts	360	
		Accounts Receivable		12,000
		Cash collection within the discount period.		
		Sales discount is $360 (0.03 × $12,000).		

Suppose JVC collects the remaining amount outstanding of $7,500 on July 28. That date is after the discount period, so there is no sales discount. To record this collection on account, JVC debits Cash and credits Accounts Receivable for the same amount, as follows:

July 28		Cash..	7,500	
		Accounts Receivable..		7,500
		Cash collection after the discount period.		

Now, JVC's Accounts Receivable balance is zero:

Accounts Receivable

(Sale)	July 7	21,600	July 12	1,800	(Return)
			15	300	(Allowance)
			22	12,000	(collection)
			28	7,500	(collection)
	Bal.	0			

Goods and Services Tax

This topic is introduced here to make you aware of the goods and services tax because most goods and services sold today in Canada have the Goods and Services Tax (GST) levied on them by the federal government at the time of sale. However, it was decided to omit consideration of the GST from the discussion and examples in the early chapters to avoid making the material overly complicated. The following discussion provides a brief introduction to the topic; GST is dealt with more fully in Chapter 11.

The manufacturer, wholesaler, and retailer pay the GST on the cost of their purchases, and then pass it on to the next link in the economic chain by charging and collecting it on their respective sales. The consumer, the last link in the chain, pays the final tax. Each entity that collects the GST remits the net tax collected to the Receiver General at the Canada Revenue Agency (CRA).

The GST is designed to be a consumption tax and, as was suggested above, the entity ultimately paying the tax is the final purchaser of the product or service. Earlier links in the chain (for example, the retailer) pay tax on their purchases, but are then allowed to deduct (or recover) that tax from the tax they themselves collect on their sales. Therefore the GST paid on purchases does not really affect the cost of the purchase. For example, Austin Sound Centre paid the GST of 7 percent (the GST rate in effect on May 27, 2006), or $4.20 ($60 × 0.07), on the FZ158 purchased in Exhibit 5–3. The entry to record the purchase of the single CD player would have been:

May 27	Inventory	60.00	
	GST Recoverable	4.20	
	Accounts Payable		64.20
	Purchased JVC FZ158 CD player on account.		

Assume Austin Sound sold the JVC FZ158 CD player for $100.00 to a customer; the GST on the sale would be $7.00 ($100.00 × 0.07). The entry to record the sale would be

June 10	Cash	107.00	
	GST Payable		7.00
	Sales		100.00
	Sold JVC FZ158 CD player for cash.		

Subsequently, Austin Sound would have to remit to the Receiver General at the CRA the difference between the GST paid and the GST collected, the net GST. The entry would be

July 31	GST Payable	7.00	
	GST Recoverable...................................		4.20
	Cash		2.80
	Payment of GST collected net of GST paid		
	(recoverable) on purchases ($7.00 – $4.20).		

The discussion of GST above is greatly simplified for the purposes of this text. The actual GST is more complicated than as presented for two major reasons:

1. Supplies and services are divided into three classes and each class is taxed differently. The three classes are (1) Taxable supplies and services; (2) Zero-rated supplies and services; (3) Exempt supplies and services.
2. Some provinces (Quebec, Nova Scotia, New Brunswick, and Newfoundland and Labrador) have harmonized, or combined, their provincial sales tax with the GST to some degree.

As well, the GST rate of 7 percent was in effect until July 1, 2006, when it changed to 6 percent. The rate may change again in the future. Discussion of the GST beyond the level above is beyond the scope of this chapter.

Name: Oak Sales Company
Industry: Merchandising
Fiscal Period: Month ended September 30, 2008
Key Fact: Existing, ongoing business

Oak Sales Company engaged in the following transactions during September 2008.

Sept.		
	3	Purchased inventory on credit terms of 1/10, net eom, $6,440.
	9	Returned 40 percent of the inventory purchased on September 3. It was defective.
	12	Sold goods for cash, $3,680 (cost, $2,200).
	15	Purchased goods of $20,400, less a $400 quantity discount. Credit terms were 3/15, n/30.
	16	Paid a $1,040 freight bill on goods purchased.
	18	Sold inventory for $8,000 on credit terms of 2/10, n/30 (cost, $4,720).
	22	Received merchandise returned from the customer from the September 18 sale, $3,200 (cost, $1,920). Merchandise was the wrong size.
	24	Borrowed exactly enough money from the bank to pay for the September 15 purchase in time to take advantage of the discount offered. Signed a note payable to the bank for the net amount, $19,400.
	24	Paid supplier for goods purchased on September 15, less all returns and discounts.
	28	Received cash in full settlement of the account from the customer who purchased inventory on September 18, less the return on September 22 and less the discount.
	29	Paid the amount owed on account from the purchase of September 3, less the September 9 return.
	30	Purchased inventory for cash, $3,600, less a quantity discount of $140.

Required

1. Journalize the transactions above. Explanations are not required.

2. Set up T-accounts and post the journal entries to show the ending balances in the Inventory and Cost of Goods Sold accounts.

3. Assume that the note payable signed on September 24 requires the payment of $380 interest expense. Was the decision to borrow funds to take advantage of the cash discount wise or unwise?

Solution

Requirement 1

Note: To save space, calculations have been included in the journal entries. Normally, they would be included in the explanations and space would be left between each journal entry.

Ensure total debits equal total credits for each transaction, especially those with more than two accounts. Selected transactions are explained more fully:

Sept. 3 and 15: Whenever goods are purchased and credit terms are given, the purchase is on account.

Sept. 12 and 18: All inventory sales (for cash or on account) require two journal entries:
1. Record the sale (at selling price)
2. Record the cost of the goods sold (at cost)

Sept. 15: There is *not* an account for quantity discounts. They reduce inventory's cost.

Sept. 16: This is freight in—a cost of inventory, *not* a selling expense.

Sept. 22: If goods are not damaged, they can be returned to inventory.

Sept. 24 and 29: When payments are made for goods purchased on account, check the original purchase date and payment date to see if a purchase discount can be taken.

Sept. 28: Always subtract returns from the original sales amount before calculating sales discounts.

Date		Account	Debit	Credit
Sept.	3	Inventory	6,440	
		Accounts Payable		6,440
	9	Accounts Payable ($6,440 × 0.40)	2,576	
		Inventory		2,576
	12	Cash	3,680	
		Sales Revenue		3,680
	12	Cost of Goods Sold	2,200	
		Inventory		2,200
	15	Inventory ($20,400 − $400)	20,000	
		Accounts Payable		20,000
Sept	16	Inventory	1,040	
		Cash		1,040
	18	Accounts Receivable	8,000	
		Sales Revenue		8,000
	18	Cost of Goods Sold	4,720	
		Inventory		4,720
	22	Sales Returns and Allowances	3,200	
		Accounts Receivable		3,200
	22	Inventory	1,920	
		Cost of Goods Sold		1,920
	24	Cash [$20,000 − 0.03($20,000)]	19,400	
		Note Payable		19,400
	24	Accounts Payable	20,000	
		Inventory ($20,000 × 0.03)		600
		Cash ($20,000 × 0.97)		19,400
	28	Cash [($8,000 − $3,200) × 0.98]	4,704	
		Sales Discounts [($8,000 − $3,200) × 0.02]	96	
		Accounts Receivable ($8,000 − $3,200)		4,800
	29	Accounts Payable ($6,440 − $2,576)	3,864	
		Cash		3,864
	30	Inventory ($3,600 − $140)	3,460	
		Cash		3,460

Requirement 2

Check each journal entry one by one in order of date for amounts that affect only the Inventory and Cost of Goods Sold accounts. Record these transactions in the T-accounts.

Inventory

Sept. 3	6,440	Sept. 9	2,576
15	20,000	12	2,200
16	1,040	18	4,720
22	1,920	24	600
30	3,460		
Bal.	22,764		

Cost of Goods Sold

Sept. 12	2,200	Sept. 22	1,920
18	4,720		
Bal.	5,000		

Requirement 3

Compare the amount of the purchase discount with the interest paid on the note.

The decision to borrow funds was wise, because the discount ($600) exceeded the interest paid on the amount borrowed ($380). Thus the entity was $220 better off as a result of its decision.

Adjusting and Closing the Accounts of a Merchandising Business

Objective 3

Adjust and close the accounts of a merchandising business under the perpetual inventory system

A merchandising business adjusts and closes the accounts the same way a service entity does. If a work sheet is used, the trial balance is entered and the work sheet is completed to determine net income or net loss. The work sheet provides the data for journalizing the adjusting and closing entries, and for preparing the financial statements.

Adjusting Inventory Based on a Physical Count

In theory, the Inventory account remains up to date at all times. However, the actual amount of inventory on hand may differ from what the books show. Losses due to theft and damage can be significant. Also, accounting errors can cause Inventory's balance to need adjustment either upwards or, more often, downwards. For this reason virtually all merechandising businesses take a physical count of inventory at least once each year. The most common time for a business to count its inventory is at the end of the fiscal year, before the financial statements are prepared. The business then adjusts the Inventory account to the correct amount based on the physical count.

At year end, Austin Sound Centre's inventory account shows an unadjusted balance of $162,000.

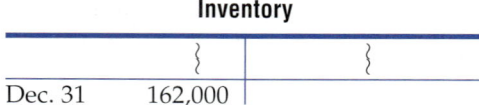

Inventory

Dec. 31	162,000	

With no shrinkage—due to theft or error—the business should have on hand inventory costing $162,000. But on December 31, Steve Austin, the owner of Austin Sound, counts the merchandise in the store, and the total cost of the goods on hand comes to only $160,800.

KEY POINT

If book inventory exceeds physical inventory, book inventory would be adjusted downwards. As a result of this inventory adjustment, cost of goods sold is higher and gross margin is lower. The cost associated with buying these missing units is not accompanied by the revenue from a sale. Therefore gross margin shrinks by this amount (cost).

Inventory Balance Before Adjustment	−	Actual Inventory on Hand	=	Adjusting Entry to Inventory
$162,000	−	$160,800	=	Credit of $1,200

Austin Sound would record the inventory shrinkage of $1,200 (which is $162,000 − $160,800) with this adjusting entry:

Dec. 31	Cost of Goods Sold..	1,200	
	Inventory		1,200
	Adjustment for inventory shrinkage.		

This entry brings Inventory to its correct balance.[1]

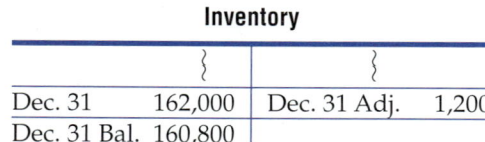

Inventory

Dec. 31	162,000	Dec. 31 Adj.	1,200
Dec. 31 Bal.	160,800		

The physical count can indicate that more inventory is present than the books show. A search of the records may reveal that Austin Sound received inventory but did not record the corresponding purchase entry. This would be entered the standard

---

[1] Some companies record the inventory shrinkage of $1,200 with this adjusting entry:

Dec. 31	Loss on Inventory	1,200	
	Inventory...		1,200

This is done to highlight the shrinkage so it can be monitored and to identify it as a loss.

way: debit Inventory and credit Cash or Accounts Payable. If the reason for the excess inventory could not be identified, the business adjusts the accounts by debiting Inventory and crediting Cost of Goods Sold.

Closing the Accounts of a Merchandising Business

Exhibit 5–5 presents Austin Sound Centre's Closing entries, which are similar to those you have seen previously, except for the new accounts highlighted with bold text.

The first closing entry

- Debits the revenue accounts for their credit balances.
- Credits Income Summary for total revenues ($677,400).

The second closing entry

- Debits Income Summary for total expenses plus the contra revenues ($473,500).
- Credits the contra revenues (Sales Discounts and Sales Returns and Allowances) and all the expenses, including Cost of Goods Sold, for their debit balances.

The last two closing entries

- Close net income from Income Summary to the Capital account.
- Close the owner withdrawals into the Capital account.

LEARNING TIPS

The closing entries here are very similar to those discussed in Chapter 4, pages 163–169. The closing entries also clear the Cost of Goods Sold expense account for accumulating costs in the next period.

EXHIBIT 5–5 Closing Entries for a Merchandiser

Journal

Closing Entries

1. Dec. 31	**Sales Revenue**		674,600	
	Interest Revenue		2,800	
	Income Summary			677,400
2. Dec. 31	Income Summary		473,500	
	Cost of Goods Sold			**363,200**
	Sales Discounts			**5,600**
	Sales Returns and Allowances			**8,000**
	Wages Expense			71,200
	Rent Expense			16,800
	Amortization Expense			2,400
	Insurance Expense			2,000
	Supplies Expense			900
	Interest Expense			3,400
3. Dec. 31	Income Summary ($677,400 − $473,500)		203,900	
	Steve Austin, Capital			203,900
4. Dec. 31	Steve Austin, Capital		58,200	
	Steve Austin, Withdrawals			58,200

Income Summary

Closing	473,500	Closing	677,400
Closing	203,900	Balance	203,900

Steve Austin, Withdrawals

Bal.	58,200	Closing	58,200

Steve Austin, Capital

Closing	58,200	Balance (assumed)	51,800
		Closing	203,900
		Balance	197,500

Preparing a Merchandiser's Financial Statements

Objective ④

Prepare a merchandiser's financial statements under the perpetual inventory system

Exhibit 5–6 presents Austin Sound Centre's financial statements.

Income Statement The income statement reports **operating expenses**, which are those expenses other than cost of goods sold incurred in the entity's major line of business—merchandising. Austin Sound's operating expenses include wages expense, rent, insurance, amortization of furniture and fixtures, and supplies expense.

Many companies report their operating expenses in two categories:

- *Selling expenses* are those expenses related to marketing the company's products—sales salaries; sales commissions; advertising; amortization, rent, utilities, and property taxes on store buildings; amortization on store furniture; delivery expense; and so on.

- *General expenses* include office expenses, such as the salaries of the executives and office employees; amortization, rent, utilities, property taxes on the home office building; and office supplies.

Gross margin minus operating expenses equals **income from operations**, or **operating income**. Many people view operating income as an important indicator of a business's performance because it measures the results of the entity's major ongoing activities.

The last section of Austin Sound's income statement is **other revenue and expense**. This category reports revenues and expenses that are outside the main operations of the business. Examples include gains and losses on the sale of capital assets like property, plant, and equipment (not inventory), and gains and losses on lawsuits. Accountants have traditionally viewed Interest Revenue and Interest Expense as "other" items, because they arise from loaning money and borrowing money. These are financing activities that are outside the operating scope of selling merchandise.

The bottom line of the income statement is net income:

$$\text{Net income} = \text{Total revenues and gains} - \text{Total expenses and losses}$$

We often hear the term *bottom line* used to refer to a final result. *Bottom line* originated from the position of net income on the income statement.

Statement of Owner's Equity A merchandiser's statement of owner's equity looks exactly like that of a service business. In fact, you cannot determine whether the entity sells merchandise or services from looking at the statement of owner's equity.

Balance Sheet If the business is a merchandiser, the balance sheet shows inventory as a current asset. In contrast, service businesses usually have no inventory at all or minor amounts of inventory.

An adjusting entry for inventory shrinkage is unique to merchandisers, who have inventory. All other adjusting entries are the same for service entities and merchandisers, and they were described in Chapter 4.

Work Sheet for a Merchandising Business

The work sheet of a merchandiser is similar to the work sheet for a service business. The main new account is the Inventory account, which must be adjusted based on a physical count, as discussed on page 230. Also, the merchandiser's work sheet carries the other new merchandising accounts (Sales Revenue, Cost of Goods Sold, and so on).

EXHIBIT 5–6 Financial Statements of Austin Sound Centre

AUSTIN SOUND CENTRE
Income Statement
For the Year Ended December 31, 2006

Sales revenue		$674,600
Less: Sales discounts	$ 5,600	
Sales returns and allowances	8,000	13,600
Net sales revenue		661,000
Cost of goods sold		363,200
Gross margin		297,800
Operating expenses:		
Wages expense	71,200	
Rent expense	16,800	
Insurance expense	2,000	
Amortization expense	2,400	
Supplies expense	900	93,300
Income from operations		204,500
Other revenue and (expense):		
Interest revenue	2,800	
Interest expense	(3,400)	(600)
Net income		$203,900

AUSTIN SOUND CENTRE
Statement of Owner's Equity
For the Year Ended December 31, 2006

Steve Austin, capital, January 1, 2006	$ 51,800
Add: Net income	203,900
	255,700
Less: Withdrawals	58,200
Steve Austin, capital, December 31, 2006	$197,500

AUSTIN SOUND CENTRE
Balance Sheet
December 31, 2006

Assets

Current assets:

Cash	$ 5,700	
Accounts receivable	18,400	
Note receivable	32,000	
Interest receivable	1,600	
Inventory	160,800	
Prepaid insurance	400	
Supplies	400	
Total current assets	219,300	

Property, plant, and equipment:

Furniture and fixtures	$202,400	
Less: Accumulated amortization	7,200	195,200
Total assets		$414,500

Liabilities

Current liabilities:

Accounts payable	$188,000	
Unearned sales revenue	1,400	
Wages payable	1,600	
Interest payable	800	
Total current liabilities	191,800	

Long-term liability:

Note payable	25,200	
Total liabilities	217,000	

Owner's Equity

S. Austin, capital	197,500
Total liabilities and owner's equity	$414,500

Austin Sound Centre's work sheet for the year ended December 31, 2006, appears in Exhibit 5–7. The year-end adjustments reflected on the worksheet are:

a. Interest revenue earned but not yet collected, $1,600
b. Inventory on hand based on a physical count of inventory, $160,800
c. Supplies on hand, $400
d. Prepaid insurance expired during the year, $2,000.
e. Amortization, $2,400
f. Unearned sales revenue earned during the year, $2,600
g. Accrued wages expense, $1,600
h. Accrued interest expense, $800

The Exhibit 5–7 work sheet is similar to the work sheets we have seen so far, but there are a few differences. This work sheet does not include adjusted trial balance columns. In most accounting systems, a single operation combines trial balance amounts with the adjustments and extends the adjusted balances directly to the income statement and balance sheet columns. Therefore, to reduce clutter, the adjusted trial balance columns are omitted so that the work sheet contains four pairs of columns, not five.

Account Title Column The trial balance lists a number of accounts without balances. Ordinarily, these accounts are affected by the adjusting process. Examples include Interest Receivable, Wages Payable, and Amortization Expense. The accounts are listed in order by account number, the order in which they appear in the ledger. If additional accounts are needed, they can be written in at the bottom of the work sheet above the net income amount.

Trial Balance Columns Examine the Inventory account in the Trial Balance. Inventory has a balance of $162,000 before the physical count at the end of the year. Cost of Goods Sold's balance is $362,000 before any adjustment based on the physical count. We shall assume that any difference between the Inventory amount on the trial balance ($162,000) and the correct amount based on the physical count ($160,800) is unexplained and should be debited or credited directly to Cost of Goods Sold.

KEY POINT

If you were preparing a work sheet, you could omit the adjusted trial balance columns. Once you understand the mechanics of the work sheet, you can take a trial balance amount, add or subtract the adjustments, and extend the new amount to either the income statement or balance sheet columns.

Adjustments Columns The adjustments are similar to those discussed in Chapters 3 and 4. They may be entered in any order desired. The debit amount of each entry should equal the credit amount, and total debits should equal total credits. You should review the adjusting data in Exhibit 5–7 to reassure yourself that the adjustments are correct.

Income Statement Columns The income statement columns contain adjusted amounts for the revenues and expenses. Sales Revenue, for example, has an adjusted balance of $674,600.

The *income statement* column subtotals indicate whether the business had a net income or a net loss.

- Net income: Total credits > Total debits
- Net loss: Total debits > Total credits

Austin Sound's total credits of $677,400 exceed the total debits of $473,500, so the company earned a net income.

Insert the net *income* amount in the debit column to bring total debits into agreement with total credits. Insert a net *loss* amount in the credit column to equalize total debits and total credits. Net income or net loss is then extended to the opposite column of the balance sheet, so that total debits equal total credits.

234 **Part 1** The Basic Structure of Accounting

EXHIBIT 5–7 Work Sheet for a Merchandiser

AUSTIN SOUND CENTRE
Accounting Work Sheet
For the Year Ended December 31, 2006

Account Title	Trial Balance		Adjustments		Income Statement		Balance Sheet	
	Debit	Credit	Debit	Credit	Debit	Credit	Debit	Credit
Cash	5,700						5,700	
Accounts receivable	18,400						18,400	
Note receivable, current	32,000						32,000	
Interest receivable	0		(a) 1,600				1,600	
Inventory	**162,000**			**(b) 1,200**			**160,800**	
Supplies	1,300			(c) 900			400	
Prepaid insurance	2,400			(d) 2,000			400	
Furniture and fixtures	202,400						202,400	
Accumulated amortization		4,800		(e) 2,400				7,200
Accounts payable		188,000						188,000
Unearned sales revenue		4,000	(f) 2,600					1,400
Wages payable		0		(g) 1,600				1,600
Interest payable		0		(h) 800				800
Note payable, long-term		25,200						25,200
Steve Austin, capital		51,800						51,800
Steve Austin, withdrawals	58,200						58,200	
Sales revenue		**672,000**		(f) 2,600		674,600		
Sales discounts	**5,600**				5,600			
Sales returns and allowances	**8,000**				8,000			
Interest revenue		1,200		(a) 1,600		2,800		
Cost of goods sold	**362,000**		**(b) 1,200**		**363,200**			
Wages expense	69,600		(g) 1,600		71,200			
Rent expense	16,800				16,800			
Amortization expense	0		(e) 2,400		2,400			
Insurance expense	0		(d) 2,000		2,000			
Supplies expense	0		(c) 900		900			
Interest expense	2,600		(h) 800		3,400			
	947,000	947,000	13,100	13,100	473,500	677,400	479,900	276,000
Net income					203,900			203,900
					677,400	677,400	479,900	479,900

Balance Sheet Columns The only new item on the balance sheet, compared to previous chapters, is Inventory. The balance listed in Exhibit 5–7 is the ending amount of $160,800, as determined by the physical count of goods on hand at the end of the period.

Income Statement Formats: Multi-Step and Single-Step

As we saw in Chapter 4, the balance sheet appears in two formats:

For a review of balance sheet formats, see Chapter 4, page 173.

- The report format (assets on top, owner's equity at the bottom)
- The account format (assets at left, liabilities and owner's equity at right).

There are also two basic formats for the income statement:

- The multi-step format
- The single-step format

The multi-step format is the most popular.

Multi-Step Income Statement

A **multi-step income statement** shows subtotals to highlight significant relationships. In addition to net income, it also presents gross margin and operating income, or income from operations. This format communicates a merchandiser's results of operations especially well, because gross margin and income from operations are two key measures of operating performance. The income statements presented thus far in this chapter have been multi-step income statements. Austin Sound Centre's multi-step income statement appears in Exhibit 5–6 on page 233.

Single-Step Income Statement

The **single-step format** groups all revenues together, and then lists and deducts all expenses together without drawing any subtotals. Maple Leaf Foods Inc. uses this format. The single-step format has the advantage of listing all revenues together and all expenses together. Thus it clearly distinguishes revenues from expenses. The income statements in Chapters 1 through 4 were single-step. This format works well for service entities, because they have no gross margin to report, and for companies that have several types of revenues. Exhibit 5–8 shows a single-step income statement for Austin Sound Centre.

| **EXHIBIT 5–8** | Single-Step Income Statement |

AUSTIN SOUND CENTRE
Income Statement
For the Year Ended December 31, 2006

Revenues:		
Sales revenue		$674,600
Less: Sales discounts	$5,600	
Sales returns and allowances	8,000	13,600
Net sales revenue		661,000
Interest revenue		2,800
Total revenues		663,800
Expenses:		
Cost of goods sold		$363,200
Wages expense		71,200
Rent expense		16,800
Interest expense		3,400
Amortization expense		2,400
Insurance expense		2,000
Supplies expense		900
Total expenses		459,900
Net income		$203,900

Most published financial statements are highly condensed. Appendix A at the end of the book gives the income statements for CHUM Limited, and Appendix B gives the income statement for Sun-Rype Products Ltd. Of course, condensed statements can be supplemented with desired details in the notes to the financial statements.

Two Ratios for Decision Making

Inventory is the most important asset to a merchandising business because it captures the essence of the entity. To manage the business, owners and managers focus on the best way to sell the inventory. They use several ratios to evaluate operations, among them *gross margin percentage* and *rate of inventory turnover*.

Objective 5

Use the gross margin percentage and the inventory turnover ratio to evaluate a business

The Gross Margin Percentage

Gross margin (gross profit) is net sales minus cost of goods sold. Merchandisers strive to increase the **gross margin percentage**, which is computed as follows:

For Austin Sound Centre
(Exhibit 5–6)

$$\text{Gross margin percentage} = \frac{\text{Gross margin}}{\text{Net sales revenue}} = \frac{\$297,800}{\$661,000} = 0.451 = 45.1\%$$

A 45-percent gross margin means that each dollar of sales generates 45 cents of gross profit. On average, the goods cost the seller 55 cents. The gross margin percentage (also called the *gross profit percentage*) is one of the most carefully watched measures of profitability. A small increase in the gross margin percentage may signal an important rise in income, and vice versa for a decrease.

Exhibit 5–9 compares Austin Sound Centre's gross margin to Wal-Mart's gross margin.

EXHIBIT 5–9

Gross Margin on $1.00 of Sales for Two Merchandisers

The Rate of Inventory Turnover

Owners and managers strive to sell inventory as quickly as possible. This is because there is a cost to carrying inventory. If a company purchases inventory on credit (creating an account payable), there is a risk it may buy too much inventory and be unable to sell it before having to pay for the inventory. If this happens, the company either has to borrow funds to pay for the inventory and incur interest expense, or use cash that could have been in a bank earning interest. The chapter-opening story highlighted this issue. Dell carries only *two hours* of parts inventory. Why? Prices of parts are continually declining, and Dell does not want to have any more inventory on hand than is absolutely necessary.

Dell is in a unique position in that it sells directly to customers and does not have to keep an inventory of computers on hand. Most retailers, such as Austin Sound Centre, must keep inventory on hand for customers. Successful merchandisers purchase carefully to keep goods moving through the business at a rapid pace. **Inventory turnover**, the ratio of cost of goods sold to average inventory, indicates how rapidly inventory is sold. Its computation follows:

For Austin Sound Centre
(Exhibit 5–6)

$$\frac{\text{Inventory}}{\text{turnover}} = \frac{\text{Cost of goods sold}}{\text{Average inventory}} = \frac{\text{Cost of goods sold}}{(\text{Beginning inventory}^* + \text{ending inventory})/2} = \frac{\$363,200}{(\$154,400 + \$160,800)/2}$$

$$= 2.3 \text{ times per year (about every 159 days}^{**})$$

*Taken from the balance sheet at the end of the preceding period.
**Calculation: 365 days ÷ 2.3 times = app. 159 days

Inventory turnover is usually computed for an annual period, and the relevant cost-of-goods sold figure is the amount from the entire year. Average inventory is computed from the beginning and ending balances of the annual period. Austin

Sound Centre's beginning inventory would be taken from the business's balance sheet at the end of the preceding year. The resulting inventory turnover statistic shows how many times the average level of inventory was sold during the year. A high rate of turnover is preferable to a low turnover rate. An increase in turnover rate usually means higher profits, but may sometimes lead to a shortage of inventory to sell.

Inventory turnover varies from industry to industry. Grocery stores, for example, turn their goods over faster than automobile dealers do. Drug stores have a higher turnover than furniture stores do. Retailers of electronic products, such as Austin Sound Centre, have an average turnover of 3.6 times per year. Exhibit 5–10 compares the inventory turnover rate of Austin Sound and Wal-Mart Stores, Inc.

EXHIBIT 5–10   Rate of Inventory Turnover for Two Merchandisers

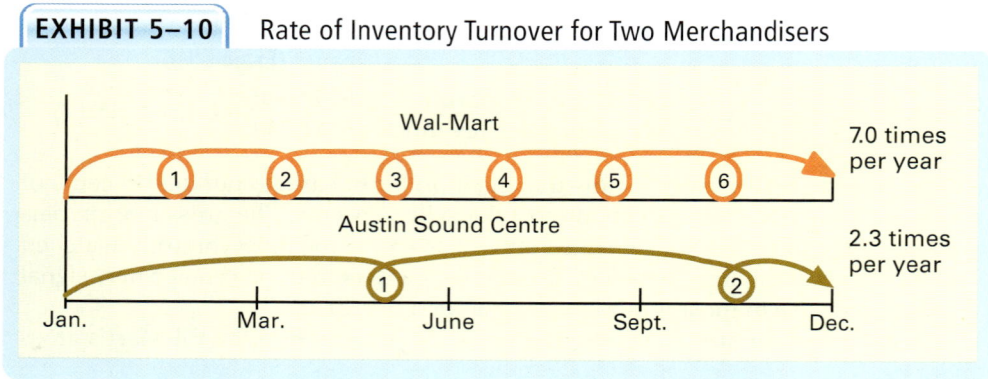

Exhibits 5–9 and 5–10 tell an interesting story. Wal-Mart sells lots of inventory at a relatively low gross profit margin. Wal-Mart earns its profits by turning its inventory over rapidly—7.0 times during the year. Austin Sound Centre, a small business, prices inventory to earn a higher gross margin on each dollar of sales and only turns over its inventory 2.3 times during the year.

Gross margin percentage and rate of inventory turnover do not provide enough information to yield an overall conclusion about a merchandiser, but this example shows how owners and managers may use accounting information to evaluate a company.

As we conclude this chapter, we return to our opening questions: How do merchandising operations differ from service operations, and why is it important? What are inventory and cost of goods sold? What types of inventory systems are there? How do decision makers evaluate a company's inventory operations? The Decision Guidelines feature summarizes all of our chapter-opening questions and highlights inventory, the item that makes merchandisers different from service entities.

Decision	Guidelines
How do merchandising operations differ from service operations?	• Merchandisers, such as Austin Sound Centre, buy and sell *merchandise inventory* (often called inventory, or goods). • Service entities, such as SuperTravel, perform a *service*.

How do a merchandiser's financial statements differ from the financial statements of a service business?

Balance sheet:

Decision	Guidelines
Merchandiser has *Inventory*, an asset.	Service business has no inventory.

Income statement (assumed amounts):

Merchandiser

Sales revenue	$1,000
− Cost of goods sold	500
= Gross margin	$ 500
− Operating expenses	300
= Net income	$ 200

Service Business

Service revenue	$1,000
− Operating expenses	700
= Net income	$ 300

Decision	Guidelines
Statements of owner's equity:	No difference

Decision	Guidelines
What types of inventory systems are there?	• *Perpetual system* shows the amount of inventory on hand (the asset) and the cost of goods sold (the expense) at all times. • *Periodic system* shows the correct balances of inventory and cost of goods sold only after a count of the inventory and adjustment of the books to reflect that count, which occurs at least once each year.

Use the *cost of goods sold formula* for the periodic system (assumed amounts):

Beginning inventory	$100
+ Net purchases and freight in	800
= Cost of goods available	900
− Ending inventory	200
= Cost of goods sold	$700

Cost of goods sold is computed continuously in the perpetual inventory system.

Decision	Guidelines
How do the adjusting and closing processes of merchandisers and service entities differ?	Very little. The merchandiser • Adjusts Inventory for shrinkage • Closes Cost of Goods Sold and the contra revenue accounts

How can you format the merchandiser's income statement?

Multi-step format (assumed amounts)

Sales revenue	$1,000
− Cost of goods sold	500
= Gross margin	$ 500
− Operating expenses	300
= Income from operations	$ 200
+ Other revenues	30
− Other expenses	(50)
= Net income	$ 180

Single-step format (assumed amounts)

Revenues:

Sales revenue	$1,000
Other revenues	30
Total revenues	$1,030

Expenses:

Cost of goods sold	500
Operating expenses	300
Other expenses	50
Total expenses	$ 850
Net income	$ 180

Decision	Guidelines
How can you evaluate merchandising operations?	Two ratios:

$$\text{Gross margin percentage}^* = \frac{\text{Gross margin}}{\text{Net sales revenue}} \qquad \text{Inventory turnover}^* = \frac{\text{Cost of goods sold}}{\text{Average inventory}}$$

*In most cases—the higher, the better

Summary Problem for Your Review

The following trial balance and additional data are related to Sierra Distributing Company for the year ended December 31, 2008.

SIERRA DISTRIBUTING COMPANY
Trial Balance
December 31, 2008

Cash	$ 17,010	
Accounts receivable	111,300	
Inventory	181,500	
Supplies	11,790	
Prepaid rent	18,000	
Furniture	79,500	
Accumulated amortization—furniture		$ 63,600
Accounts payable		139,020
Salaries payable		0
Interest payable		0
Unearned sales revenue		10,500
Notes payable, long-term		105,000
Susan Sierra, capital		71,040
Susan Sierra, withdrawals	144,000	
Sales revenue		1,040,100
Sales discounts	30,900	
Sales returns and allowances	24,600	
Cost of goods sold	515,310	
Salaries expense	248,250	
Rent expense	21,000	
Amortization expense—furniture	0	
Utilities expense	17,400	
Supplies expense	0	
Interest expense	8,700	
Total	$1,429,260	$1,429,260

Additional data at December 31, 2008:

a. Supplies used during the year, $7,740.

b. Prepaid rent remaining in force, $3,000.

c. Unearned sales revenue still not earned, $7,200. The company expects to earn this amount during the next few months.

d. Amortization. The furniture's estimated useful life is ten years, and it is expected to have no value when it is retired from service.

e. Accrued salaries, $3,900.

f. Accrued interest expense, $1,800.

g. Inventory still remaining on hand, $179,200.

Required

1. Enter the trial balance on a work sheet and complete the work sheet.

2. Journalize the adjusting and closing entries at December 31, 2008. Post to the Income Summary account as an accuracy check on the entries affecting that account. The credit balance closed out of Income Summary should equal net income computed on the work sheet.

Name: Sierra Distributing Company
Industry: Merchandising
Fiscal Period: Year ended December 31, 2008
Key Fact: Merchandiser uses the perpetual inventory system

3. Prepare the company's multi-step income statement, statement of owner's equity, and balance sheet in account format. Draw arrows connecting the statements, or state how the statements are linked.

4. Compute the inventory turnover for 2008. Inventory at December 31, 2007, was $168,400. Turnover for 2007 was 2.1 times. Would you expect Sierra Distributing Company to be more or less profitable in 2008 than in 2007? Give your reason.

Solution

Requirement 1

> Notice that this work sheet has eliminated the two Adjusted Trial Balance columns, as shown in the chapter.
> Adjustments a. through f. are similar to the adjustments you made in Chapter 4. For adjustment g., the only new adjustment, compare the amount of inventory remaining on hand with the Inventory amount on the trial balance. If inventory on hand is lower, record inventory shrinkage. If inventory on hand is higher, record a correction to increase the Inventory account.

SIERRA DISTRIBUTING COMPANY
Work Sheet
For the Year Ended December 31, 2008

Account Title	Trial Balance Debit	Trial Balance Credit	Adjustments Debit	Adjustments Credit	Income Statement Debit	Income Statement Credit	Balance Sheet Debit	Balance Sheet Credit
Cash	17,010						17,010	
Accounts receivable	111,300						111,300	
Inventory	181,500			(g) 2,300			179,200	
Supplies	11,790			(a) 7,740			4,050	
Prepaid rent	18,000			(b) 15,000			3,000	
Furniture	79,500						79,500	
Accum. amort.—furniture		63,600		(d) 7,950				71,550
Accounts payable		139,020						139,020
Salaries payable		0		(e) 3,900				3,900
Interest payable		0		(f) 1,800				1,800
Unearned sales revenue		10,500	(c) 3,300					7,200
Notes payable, long-term		105,000						105,000
Susan Sierra, capital		71,040						71,040
Susan Sierra, withdrawals	144,000						144,000	
Sales revenue		1,040,100		(c) 3,300		1,043,400		
Sales discounts	30,900				30,900			
Sales returns and allowances	24,600				24,600			
Cost of goods sold	515,310		(g) 2,300		517,610			
Salaries expense	248,250		(e) 3,900		252,150			
Rent expense	21,000		(b) 15,000		36,000			
Amort. exp.—furniture	0		(d) 7,950		7,950			
Utilities expense	17,400				17,400			
Supplies expense	0		(a) 7,740		7,740			
Interest expense	8,700		(f) 1,800		10,500			
	1,429,260	1,429,260	41,990	41,990	904,850	1,043,400	538,060	399,510
Net income					138,550			138,550
					1,043,400	1,043,400	538,060	538,060

Requirement 2

Adjusting entries

2008

a. Dec. 31	Supplies Expense...	7,740	
	Supplies...		7,740
b. Dec. 31	Rent Expense...	15,000	
	Prepaid Rent..		15,000
c. Dec. 31	Unearned Sales Revenue ($10,500 − $7,200).....	3,300	
	Sales Revenue..		3,300
d. Dec. 31	Amortization Expense—furniture ($79,500/10)	7,950	
	Accumulated Amortization—furniture.........		7,950
e. Dec. 31	Salaries Expense..	3,900	
	Salaries Payable		3,900
f. Dec. 31	Interest Expense..	1,800	
	Interest Payable..		1,800
g. Dec. 31	Cost of Goods Sold ($181,500 − $179,200).........	2,300*	
	Inventory...		2,300

> **Adjustment g.** The amount of inventory remaining on hand is lower than the Inventory amount on the trial balance. This indicates shrinkage, so reduce the Inventory account balance.

Closing entries

2008

Dec. 31	Sales Revenue...	1,043,400	
	Income Summary		1,043,400
Dec. 31	Income Summary...	904,850	
	Cost of Goods Sold......................................		517,610
	Sales Discounts		30,900
	Sales Returns and Allowances...................		24,600
	Salaries Expense		252,150
	Rent Expense..		36,000
	Amortization Expense—Furniture		7,950
	Utilities Expense		17,400
	Supplies Expense...		7,740
	Interest Expense..		10,500
Dec. 31	Income Summary ($1,043,000 − $904,850).....	138,550	
	Susan Sierra, Capital		138,550
Dec. 31	Susan Sierra, Capital	144,000	
	Susan Sierra, Withdrawals		144,000

> The merchandiser's accounts Cost of Goods Sold, Sales Discounts, and Sales Returns and Allowances are all expenses. They are temporary accounts that are closed just like other expense accounts.
>   All other closing entries are the same for service entities and for merchandisers that use the perpetual inventory system.

Income Summary

Clo.	904,850	Clo.	1,043,400
Clo.	138,550	Bal.	138,550

> The T-account balance of $138,550 matches the net income amount on the work sheet.

---

*Adjustment of inventory to reflect physical count. This adjustment brings Inventory to its correct balance.

Requirement 3

The title must include the name of the company, "Income Statement," and the specific period of time covered. It is critical that the time period is defined.

Present the calculation of net sales revenue on a merchandiser's multi-step income statement.

SIERRA DISTRIBUTING COMPANY
Income Statement
For the Year Ended December 31, 2008

Sales revenue..		$1,043,400
Less: Sales discounts..	$ 30,900	
Sales returns and allowances...	24,600	55,500
Net sales revenue...		987,900
Cost of goods sold		517,610
Gross margin..		470,290
Operating expenses:		
Salaries expense	252,150	
Rent expense...	36,000	
Utilities expense...	17,400	
Amortization expense...	7,950	
Supplies expense..	7,740	321,240
Income from operations		149,050
Other expense:		
Interest expense..		10,500
Net income		$ 138,550

The title must include the name of company, "Statement of Owner's Equity," and the specific period of time covered. It is critical that the time period is defined.

The statement of owner's equity is the same for service entities and merchandisers.

SIERRA DISTRIBUTING COMPANY
Statement of Owner's Equity
For the Year Ended December 31, 2008

Susan Sierra, capital, January 1, 2008...	$ 71,040
Add: Net income..	138,550
	209,590
Less: Withdrawals..	144,000
Susan Sierra, capital, December 31, 2008..	$ 65,590

The title must include the name of the company, "Balance Sheet," and the date of the balance sheet. It shows the financial position on one specific date.

This is a classified balance sheet with Inventory listed among the current assets.

The Inventory balance is the cost of the inventory on hand based on the inventory count.

SIERRA DISTRIBUTING COMPANY
Balance Sheet
December 31, 2008

Assets			Liabilities		
Current assets:			Current liabilities:		
Cash................................	$ 17,010		Accounts payable................	$139,020	
Accounts receivable.....	111,300		Salaries payable...................	3,900	
Inventory......................	179,200		Interest payable	1,800	
Supplies	4,050		Unearned sales revenue	7,200	
Prepaid rent	3,000		Total current liabilities....	151,920	
Total current assets....		314,560	Long-term liabilities		
Property, plant, and			Notes payable	105,000	
equipment:			Total liabilities..................	256,920	
Furniture......................	$79,500				
Less: Accumulated			**Owner's Equity**		
amortization...............	71,550	7,950	Susan Sierra, capital	65,590	
			Total liabilities and		
Total assets		$322,510	owner's equity	$322,510	

Requirement 4

Refer to page 237 for the inventory turnover formula. Generally, the higher the inventory turnover, the better.

$$\text{Inventory turnover} = \frac{\text{Cost of goods sold}}{\text{Average inventory}} = \frac{\$517,610}{(\$168,400 + \$179,200)/2} = 2.98 \text{ times}$$

The increase in the rate of inventory turnover from 2.1 to 2.98 *suggests* higher profits in 2008 than in 2007. However, gross margin and expenses for both years must be checked to verify this suggestion.

Chapter 5 Appendix A

Accounting for Merchandise in a Periodic Inventory System

Purchasing Merchandise in the Periodic Inventory System

Objective 6

Account for the purchase and sale of inventory under the periodic inventory system

Some businesses find it too expensive to invest in a computerized (perpetual) inventory system that keeps up-to-the-minute records of merchandise on hand and cost of goods sold. Sometimes the nature of the inventory makes the perpetual inventory system impractical. These businesses use the periodic inventory system.

Recording Purchases of Inventory

All inventory systems use the Inventory account. But in a periodic inventory system, purchases, purchase discounts, purchase returns and allowances, and transportation costs are recorded in separate expense accounts bearing these titles. Let's account for Austin Sound Centre's purchase of the JVC goods shown in Exhibit 5–3 on page 218. For the moment, disregard GST and use the invoice total of $658.05 when recording purchases and purchase discounts. GST is discussed on page 226. The following entries record the purchase and payment on account within the discount period:

May	27	Purchases..	658.05	
		Accounts Payable.................................		658.05
		Purchased inventory on account.		
June	10	Accounts Payable.......................................	658.05	
		Cash...		638.31
		Purchase Discounts..............................		19.74
		Paid for inventory on account within discount period.		
		The discount is $19.74 [$658.05 × 0.03].		

Recording Purchase Returns and Allowances

KEY POINT

A contra account always has a companion account with the opposite balance. Thus, both Purchase Discounts and Purchase Returns and Allowances (credit balances) are reported with Purchases (debit balance) on the income statement

Suppose instead that prior to payment, Austin Sound returned to JVC goods costing $60.00 and also received from JVC a purchase allowance of $15.00. Austin Sound would record these transactions as follows:

June	3	Accounts Payable.......................................	60.00	
		Purchase Returns and Allowances ...		60.00
		Returned inventory to seller.		
June	4	Accounts Payable.......................................	15.00	
		Purchase Returns and Allowances ...		15.00
		Received a purchase allowance.		

During the period, the business records the cost of all inventory bought in the Purchases account. The balance of Purchases is a *gross* amount because it does not include subtractions for purchase discounts, returns, or allowances. **Net purchases** is the remainder computed by subtracting the contra accounts from Purchases:

Purchase (*debit* balance account)
− **Purchase Discounts** (*credit* balance account)
− **Purchase Returns and Allowances** (*credit* balance account)
= **Net purchases** (a *debit* subtotal, not a separate account)

Recording Transportation Costs

Under the periodic system, costs to transport purchased inventory from seller to buyer are debited to a separate expense account, as shown for payment of an $80.00 freight bill:

June	1	Freight In	80.00	
		Cash...		80.00
		Paid a freight bill.		

Recording Sales of Inventory

Recording sales is streamlined in the periodic system. With no running record of inventory to maintain, we can record a $5,000 sale as follows:

June	5	Accounts Receivable...............................	5,000	
		Sales Revenue		5,000
		Sale on account.		

No accompanying entry to Inventory and Cost of Goods Sold is required in the periodic system.

Accounting for sales discounts, and sales returns and allowances is the same as in the perpetual inventory system (page 225) except that there are no entries to Inventory and Cost of Goods Sold.

Cost of Goods Sold

Cost of goods sold (also called **cost of sales**) is the largest single expense of most businesses that sell merchandise, such as Dell Inc. and Austin Sound Centre. It is the cost of the inventory that the business has sold to customers. In a periodic system, cost of goods sold must be computed as shown in Exhibit 5A–1 and is *not* a ledger account. It is the residual left when we subtract ending inventory from the cost of goods available for sale. Exhibit 5A–1 is an expansion of the cost of goods sold formula introduced on page 216.

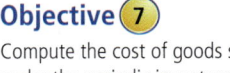

Objective 7
Compute the cost of goods sold under the periodic inventory system

EXHIBIT 5A–1 | Measuring Cost of Goods Sold in the Periodic Inventory System

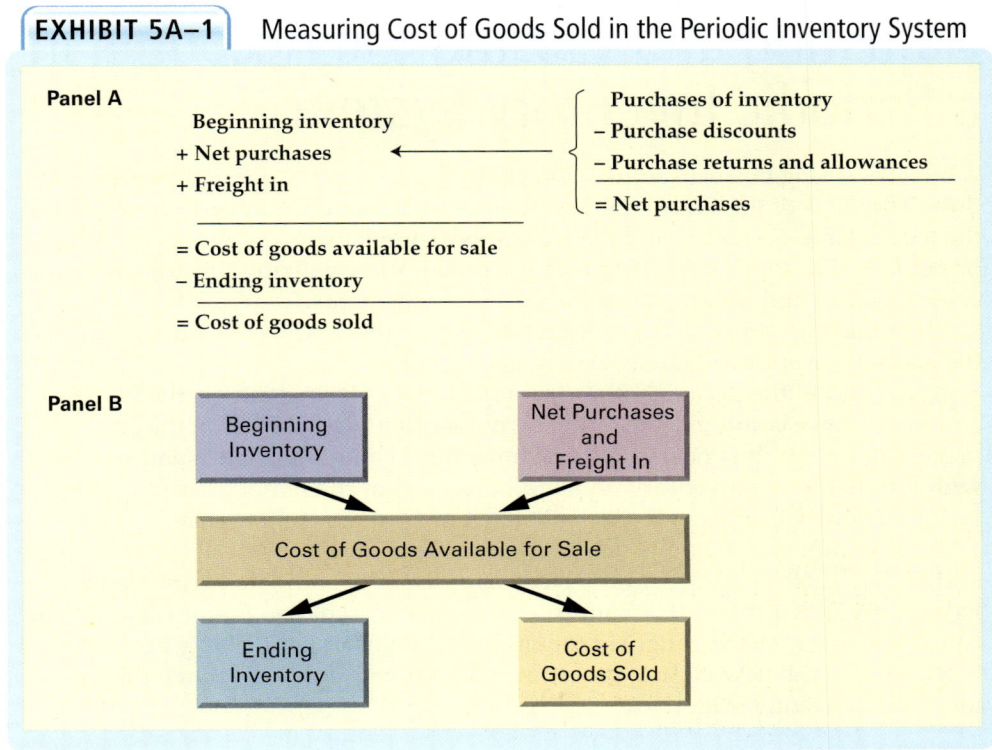

AUSTIN SOUND CENTRE
Income Statement
For the Year Ended December 31, 2006

PANEL A—Detailed Gross Margin Section—Often Required by Management

Sales revenue			$674,600
Less: Sales discounts		$ 5,600	
Sales returns and allowances		8,000	13,600
Net sales			661,000
Cost of goods sold:			
Beginning inventory		154,400	
Purchases	$365,600		
Less: Purchase discounts	12,000		
Purchase returns and allowances	4,800		
Net purchases		348,800	
Freight in		20,800	
Cost of goods available for sale		524,000	
Less: Ending inventory		160,800	
Cost of goods sold			363,200
Gross margin			$297,800

PANEL B—Summary Gross Margin Section—Most Common in Annual Reports to Outsiders

Net sales	$661,800
Cost of goods sold	363,200
Gross margin	$297,800

Exhibit 5A–2 shows Austin Sound's net sales revenue, cost of goods sold—including net purchases and freight in—and gross margin on the income statement for the periodic system. (All amounts are assumed.)

Adjusting and Closing the Accounts in a Periodic Inventory System

Objective 8

Adjust and close the accounts of a merchandising business under the periodic inventory system

KEY POINT

Recall that Purchases (not Inventory) was debited for merchandise purchased. In the periodic system, no entries are made to the Inventory account for purchases or sales. Beginning inventory remains on the books and on the trial balance until ending inventory replaces it at the end of the period.

A merchandising business adjusts and closes the accounts much as a service entity does. The steps of this end-of-period process are the same: If a work sheet is used, the trial balance is entered and the work sheet completed to determine net income or net loss. The work sheet provides the data for journalizing the adjusting and closing entries and for preparing the financial statements.

The adjusting entries are the same for service entities and merchandisers that use the periodic inventory system. These adjusting entries were described in Chapter 4.

At the end of the period, before any adjusting or closing entries, the Inventory account balance is still the cost of the inventory that was on hand at the end of the preceding period. It is necessary to remove this beginning balance and replace it with the cost of the inventory on hand at the end of the period, based on the inventory count. Closing entries bring the inventory records up to date.

To illustrate a merchandiser's closing process under the periodic inventory system, let's use Austin Sound's December 31, 2006, adjusted trial balance in Exhibit 5A–3. All the new accounts—Inventory, Purchases, Freight In, and the contra accounts—are highlighted for emphasis. Inventory is the only account that is affected by the new closing procedures. The physical count of inventory gives the ending inventory figure of $160,800.

AUSTIN SOUND CENTRE
Trial Balance
December 31, 2006

Cash	$ 5,700	
Accounts receivable	18,400	
Note receivable, current	32,000	
Interest receivable	1,600	
Inventory	**154,400**	
Supplies	400	
Prepaid insurance	400	
Furniture and fixtures	202,400	
Accumulated amortization		$ 7,200
Accounts payable		188,000
Unearned sales revenue		1,400
Wages payable		1,600
Interest payable		800
Note payable, long-term		25,200
Steve Austin, capital		51,800
Steve Austin, withdrawals	58,200	
Sales revenue		674,600
Sales discounts	5,600	
Sales returns and allowances	8,000	
Interest revenue		2,800
Purchases	**365,600**	
Purchase discounts		**12,000**
Purchase returns and allowances		**4,800**
Freight in	**20,800**	
Wages expense	71,200	
Rent expense	16,800	
Amortization expense	2,400	
Insurance expense	2,000	
Supplies expense	900	
Interest expense	3,400	
Total	$970,200	$970,200

Journalizing the Closing Entries in the Periodic Inventory System

Exhibit 5A–4 gives Austin Sound's closing entries.
   The first closing entry

- Debits the revenue accounts and the contra expenses (Purchase Discounts, and Purchase Returns and Allowances) for their credit balances
- Credits Income Summary for the total revenues plus the contra expenses ($694,200)

   The second closing entry

- Debits Income Summary for total expenses ($496,700)
- Credits the contra revenues (Sales Discounts, and Sales Returns and Allowances) and all the expenses, including Purchases and Freight In, for their debit balances.

   Closing entries 3 and 4 are new. Closing entry 3

- Debits Income Summary for the amount of the beginning balance of the Inventory account ($154,400)
- Credits Inventory for its debit balance.

KEY POINT

Closing entries for a merchandising company accomplish the same tasks as in Chapter 4 and also replace beginning inventory with the ending inventory balance. The debit and credit to Income Summary match the income statement column totals from the work sheet.

Journal

Closing Entries

1.	Dec. 31	Sales Revenue	674,600	
		Interest Revenue	2,800	
		Purchase Discounts	12,000	
		Purchase Returns and Allowances......................	4,800	
		Income Summary		694,200
2.	Dec. 31	Income Summary..	496,700	
		Sales Discounts		5,600
		Sales Returns and Allowances........................		8,000
		Purchases..		365,600
		Freight In		20,800
		Wages Expense		71,200
		Rent Expense...		16,800
		Amortization Expense		2,400
		Insurance Expense..		2,000
		Supplies Expense...		900
		Interest Expense..		3,400
3.	Dec. 31	Income Summary..	154,400	
		Inventory (beginning balance)		154,400
4.	Dec. 31	Inventory (ending balance)	160,800	
		Income Summary..		160,800
5.	Dec. 31	Income Summary ($694,200 − $496,700 −		
		$154,400 + $160,800)	203,900	
		Steve Austin, Capital......................................		203,900
6.	Dec. 31	Steve Austin, Capital	58,200	
		Steve Austin, Withdrawals.............................		58,200

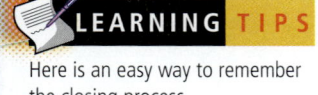

LEARNING TIPS

Here is an easy way to remember the closing process.

1. Debit all income statement accounts that have a credit balance. Credit Income Summary for the sum of all these debits.

2. Credit all income statement accounts that have a debit balance. Debit Income Summary for the sum of all these credits.

3. Credit the inventory account for the amount of opening inventory and debit inventory for the amount of ending inventory obtained from the year-end physical count.

4. Calculate the balance in the Income Summary account. If the account has a debit balance, there is a net loss; credit Income Summary for that amount, and debit Capital. If Income Summary has a credit balance, there is a net income for the period; debit Income Summary for that amount, and credit Capital.

5. Look at the debit balance of Withdrawals in the balance-sheet column. Credit Withdrawals for its balance, and debit Capital for the same amount.

Closing entry 4

- Debits Inventory for its ending balance, which was determined by the count of inventory at the end of the period ($160,800)
- Credits Income Summary for the amount of the ending balance of the Inventory account.

The last two closing entries

- Close net income from Income Summary to the Capital account.
- Close the owner withdrawals into the Capital account.

Now Inventory has its correct ending balance as shown below.

Inventory

Jan. 1	Bal. 154,400	Dec. 31	Clo. 154,400
Dec. 31	Clo. 160,800		
Dec. 31	Bal. 160,800		

The entries to the Inventory account deserve additional explanation. Recall that before the closing process Inventory still has the period's beginning balance. At the end of the period, this balance is one year old and must be replaced with the ending balance in order to prepare the financial statements at December 31, 2006. The closing entries give Inventory its correct ending balance of $160,800.

Preparing the Financial Statements of a Merchandiser

Objective 9

Prepare a merchandiser's financial statements under the periodic inventory system

Exhibit 5A–5 presents Austin Sound's financial statements. The *income statement* through gross margin repeats Exhibit 5A–2. This information is followed by the **operating expenses**, expenses other than cost of goods sold that are incurred in the entity's major line of business—merchandising. Wages expense is Austin Sound's cost of employing workers. Rent is the cost of obtaining store space. Insurance helps to protect the inventory. Store furniture and fixtures wear out; the expense is amortization. Supplies expense is the cost of stationery, mailing, and the like, used in operations.

Many companies report their operating expenses in two categories.

- *Selling expenses* are those expenses related to marketing the company's products—sales salaries; sales commissions; advertising; amortization, rent, utilities, and property taxes on store buildings; amortization on store furniture; delivery expense; and so on.
- *General expenses* include office expenses, such as the salaries of office employees; and amortization, rent, utilities, and property taxes on the head office building.

Gross margin minus operating expenses and plus any other operating revenues equals **operating income**, or **income from operations**. Many business people view operating income as the most reliable indicator of a business's success because it measures the entity's major ongoing activities.

The last section of Austin Sound's income statement is **other revenue and expenses**, which is handled the same way in both inventory systems. This category reports revenues and expenses that are outside the company's main line of business.

Net sales, cost of goods sold, operating income, and net income are unaffected by the choice of inventory system. You can prove this by comparing Austin Sound's financial statements given in Exhibit 5A–5 with the corresponding statements in Exhibit 5–6 on page 233. The only differences appear in the cost-of-goods-sold section of the income statement, and those differences are unimportant. In fact, virtually all companies report cost of goods sold in streamlined fashion, as shown for Austin Sound in Exhibit 5–6.

Preparing and Using the Work Sheet in a Periodic Inventory System

The Exhibit 5A–6 work sheet on page 251 is similar to the work sheets we have seen so far, but a few differences appear. This work sheet is slightly different from the one you saw in Chapter 4; it does not include adjusted trial balance columns. In most accounting systems, a single operation combines trial balance amounts with the adjustments and extends the adjusted balances directly to the income statement and balance sheet columns. Therefore, to reduce clutter, the adjusted trial balance columns are omitted so that the work sheet contains four pairs of columns, not five. The differences from the merchandiser's work sheet for the perpetual inventory system (page 235) are highlighted here.

Trial Balance Columns Examine the Inventory account, $154,400 in the trial balance. This $154,400 is the cost of the beginning inventory. The work sheet is designed to replace this outdated amount with the new ending balance, which in our example is $160,800 [additional data item (h)]. As we saw, this task is accomplished in the columns for the income statement and the balance sheet during the closing process.

Income Statement Columns The income statement columns contain adjusted amounts for the revenues and the expenses. Recall why the two inventory amounts appear in the income statement columns. The reason is that both beginning inventory and ending inventory enter the computation of cost of goods sold. *Placement of beginning inventory ($154,400) in the work sheet's income statement debit column has the effect of adding beginning inventory in computing cost of goods sold. Placing ending inventory ($160,800) in the credit column decreases cost of goods sold.*

Purchases and Freight In appear in the debit column because they are added in computing cost of goods sold. Purchase Discounts and Purchase Returns and Allowances appear as credits because they are subtracted in computing cost of goods sold.

KEY POINT

If you were preparing a work sheet, you could omit the adjusted trial balance columns. Once you understand the mechanics of the work sheet, you can take a trial balance amount, add or subtract the adjustments, and extend the new amount to either the income statement or balance sheet column.

AUSTIN SOUND CENTRE
Income Statement
For the Year Ended December 31, 2006

Sales revenue			$674,600
Less: Sales discounts		$ 5,600	
Sales returns and allowances		8,000	13,600
Net sales revenue			661,000
Cost of goods sold:			
Beginning inventory		154,400	
Purchases	$365,600		
Less: Purchase discounts	12,000		
Purchase returns and allowances	4,800		
Net purchases		348,800	
Freight in		20,800	
Cost of goods available for sale		524,000	
Less: Ending inventory		160,800	
Cost of goods sold			363,200
Gross margin			297,800
Operating expenses:			
Wages expense		71,200	
Rent expense		16,800	
Insurance expense		2,000	
Amortization expense		2,400	
Supplies expense		900	93,300
Income from operations			204,500
Other revenue and (expense):			
Interest revenue		2,800	
Interest expense		(3,400)	(600)
Net income			$203,900

AUSTIN SOUND CENTRE
Statement of Owner's Equity
For the Year Ended December 31, 2006

Steve Austin, capital, January 1, 2006	$ 51,800
Add: Net income	203,900
	255,700
Less: Withdrawals	58,200
Steve Austin, capital, December 31, 2006	$197,500

AUSTIN SOUND CENTRE
Balance Sheet
December 31, 2006

Assets

Current assets:		
Cash	$ 5,700	
Accounts receivable	18,400	
Note receivable	32,000	
Interest receivable	1,600	
Inventory	160,800	
Prepaid insurance	400	
Supplies	400	
Total current assets	219,300	
Property, plant and equipment:		
Furniture and fixtures	$202,400	
Less: Accumulated amortization	7,200	195,200
Total assets		$414,500

Liabilities

Current liabilities:		
Accounts payable		$188,000
Unearned sales revenue		1,400
Wages payable		1,600
Interest payable		800
Total current liabilities		191,800
Long-term liability:		
Note payable		25,200
Total liabilities		217,000

Owner's Equity

S. Austin, capital		197,500
Total liabilities and owner's equity		$414,500

AUSTIN SOUND CENTRE
Accounting Work Sheet
For the Year Ended December 31, 2006

Account Title	Trial Balance Debit	Trial Balance Credit	Adjustments Debit	Adjustments Credit	Income Statement Debit	Income Statement Credit	Balance Sheet Debit	Balance Sheet Credit
Cash	5,700						5,700	
Accounts receivable	18,400						18,400	
Note receivable, current	32,000						32,000	
Interest receivable	0		(a) 1,600				1,600	
Inventory	**154,400**				154,400	160,800	160,800	
Supplies	1,300			(b) 900			400	
Prepaid insurance	2,400			(c) 2,000			400	
Furniture and fixtures	202,400						202,400	
Accumulated amortization		4,800		(d) 2,400				7,200
Accounts payable		188,000						188,000
Unearned sales revenue		4,000	(e) 2,600					1,400
Wages payable		0		(f) 1,600				1,600
Interest payable		0		(g) 800				800
Note payable, long-term		25,200						25,200
Steve Austin, capital		51,800						51,800
Steve Austin, withdrawals	58,200						58,200	
Sales revenue		672,000		(e) 2,600		674,600		
Sales discounts	5,600				5,600			
Sales returns and allowances	8,000				8,000			
Interest revenue		1,200		(a) 1,600		2,800		
Purchases	**365,600**				365,600			
Purchase discounts		**12,000**				12,000		
Purchase returns and allowances		**4,800**				4,800		
Freight in	**20,800**				20,800			
Wages expense	69,600		(f) 1,600		71,200			
Rent expense	16,800				16,800			
Amortization expense	0		(d) 2,400		2,400			
Insurance expense	0		(c) 2,000		2,000			
Supplies expense	0		(b) 900		900			
Interest expense	2,600		(g) 800		3,400			
	963,800	963,800	11,900	11,900	651,100	855,000	479,900	276,000
Net income					203,900			203,900
					855,000	855,000	479,900	479,900

Additional data at December 31, 2006:

a. Interest revenue earned but not yet collected, $1,600.
b. Supplies on hand, $400.
c. Prepaid insurance expired during the year, $2,000.
d. Amortization for the year, $2,400.
e. Unearned sales revenue earned during the year, $2,600.
f. Accrued wage expense, $1,600.
g. Accrued interest expense, $800.
h. Inventory on hand based on inventory count, $160,800.

The income statement column subtotals on the work sheet indicate whether the business earned net income or incurred a net loss. If total credits are greater, the result is net income, as shown in Exhibit 5A–6. If total debits are greater, a net loss has occurred.

Balance Sheet Columns The only new item on the balance sheet is inventory. The balance listed is the ending amount of $160,800, which is determined by a physical count of inventory on hand at the end of the period.

The following trial balance pertains to Sierra Distributing Company.

The Summary Problem for Your Review on pages 240–243 was for a merchandiser using the perpetual inventory system. This Summary Problem uses the same data for the same company, but this time the company uses the periodic inventory system. The only differences are that this problem includes purchase discounts, and purchase returns and allowances.

SIERRA DISTRIBUTING COMPANY
Trial Balance
December 31, 2008

Account	Debit	Credit
Cash	$ 17,010	
Accounts receivable	111,300	
Inventory	168,400	
Supplies	11,790	
Prepaid rent	18,000	
Furniture	79,500	
Accumulated amortization—furniture		$ 63,600
Accounts payable		139,020
Salaries payable		0
Interest payable		0
Unearned sales revenue		10,500
Notes payable, long-term		105,000
Susan Sierra, capital		71,040
Susan Sierra, withdrawals	144,000	
Sales revenue		1,040,100
Sales discounts	30,900	
Sales returns and allowances	24,600	
Purchases	540,800	
Purchase discounts		18,000
Purchase returns and allowances		22,290
Freight in	27,900	
Salaries expense	248,250	
Rent expense	21,000	
Amortization expense—furniture	0	
Utilities expense	17,400	
Supplies expense	0	
Interest expense	8,700	
Total	$1,469,550	$1,469,550

Additional data at December 31, 2008:

a. Supplies used during the year, $7,740.

b. Prepaid rent remaining in force, $3,000.

c. Unearned sales revenue still not earned, $7,200. The company expects to earn this amount during the next few months.

d. Amortization. The furniture's estimated useful life is ten years, and it is expected to have no value when it is retired from service.

e. Accrued salaries, $3,900.

f. Accrued interest expense, $1,800.

g. Inventory on hand based on an inventory count, $179,200.

Name: Sierra Distributing Company
Industry: Merchandising
Fiscal Period: Year ended December 31, 2008
Key Fact: Merchandiser uses the periodic inventory system

Required

1. Enter the trial balance on a work sheet and complete the work sheet.

2. Journalize the adjusting and closing entries at December 31, 2008. Post to the Income Summary account as an accuracy check on the entries affecting that

account. The credit balance closed out of Income Summary should equal net income computed on the work sheet.

3. Prepare the company's multi-step income statement, statement of owner's equity, and balance sheet in account format. Draw arrows connecting the statements, or state how the statements are linked.

4. Compute the inventory turnover for 2008. Turnover for 2007 was 2.1 times. Would you expect Sierra Distributing Company to be more or less profitable in 2008 than in 2007? Give your reason.

Solution

Requirement 1

Notice that this work sheet has eliminated the two Adjusted Trial Balance columns, as shown in the chapter. Adjustments a. through f. are similar to the adjustments you made on page 241. Use additional data item g. when you create the closing entries.

SIERRA DISTRIBUTING COMPANY
Work Sheet
For the Year Ended December 31, 2008

Account Title	Trial Balance Debit	Trial Balance Credit	Adjustments Debit	Adjustments Credit	Income Statement Debit	Income Statement Credit	Balance Sheet Debit	Balance Sheet Credit
Cash	17,010						17,010	
Accounts receivable	111,300						111,300	
Inventory	168,400				168,400	179,200	179,200	
Supplies	11,790			(a) 7,740			4,050	
Prepaid rent	18,000			(b) 15,000			3,000	
Furniture	79,500						79,500	
Accum. amort.—furniture		63,600		(d) 7,950				71,550
Accounts payable		139,020						139,020
Salaries payable		0		(e) 3,900				3,900
Interest payable		0		(f) 1,800				1,800
Unearned sales revenue		10,500	(c) 3,300					7,200
Notes payable, long-term		105,000						105,000
Susan Sierra, capital		71,040						71,040
Susan Sierra, withdrawals	144,000						144,000	
Sales revenue		1,040,100		(c) 3,300		1,043,400		
Sales discounts	30,900				30,900			
Sales returns and allowances	24,600				24,600			
Purchases	540,800				540,800			
Purchase discounts		18,000				18,000		
Purchase returns and allowances		22,290				22,290		
Freight in	27,900				27,900			
Salaries expense	248,250		(e) 3,900		252,150			
Rent expense	21,000		(b)15,000		36,000			
Amort. exp.—furniture	0		(d) 7,950		7,950			
Utilities expense	17,400				17,400			
Supplies expense	0		(a) 7,740		7,740			
Interest expense	8,700		(f) 1,800		10,500			
	1,469,550	1,469,550	39,690	39,690	1,124,340	1,262,890	538,060	399,510
Net income					138,550			138,550
					1,262,890	1,262,890	538,060	538,060

Requirement 2

Adjusting Entries

These adjusting entries are the same as adjusting entries a. to f. on page 242.

2008

a.	Dec. 31	Supplies Expense	7,740	
		Supplies		7,740
b.	Dec. 31	Rent Expense	15,000	
		Prepaid Rent		15,000
c.	Dec. 31	Unearned Sales Revenue ($10,500 − $7,200)	3,300	
		Sales Revenue		3,300
d.	Dec. 31	Amortization Expense—furniture ($79,500/10)	7,950	
		Accumulated Amortization—furniture		7,950
e.	Dec. 31	Salaries Expense	3,900	
		Salaries Payable		3,900
f.	Dec. 31	Interest Expense	1,800	
		Interest Payable		1,800

Closing Entries

The contra accounts Purchase Discounts, and Purchase Returns and Allowances are temporary accounts closed at the same time as the revenue accounts.

The Sales Discounts, Sales Returns and Allowances, Purchases, and Freight In are all expenses. They are temporary accounts that are closed just like other expense accounts.

The beginning balance of Inventory is first closed to Income Summary, then the ending balance of Inventory is debited and Income Summary is credited.

All other closing entries are the same for service entities and for merchandisers that use the periodic or the perpetual inventory system.

2008

Dec. 31	Sales Revenue	1,043,400	
	Purchase Discounts	18,000	
	Purchase Returns and Allowances	22,290	
	Income Summary		1,083,690
Dec. 31	Income Summary	955,940	
	Sales Discounts		30,900
	Sales Returns and Allowances		24,600
	Purchases		540,800
	Freight-in		27,900
	Salaries Expense		252,150
	Rent Expense		36,000
	Amortization Expense—furniture		7,950
	Utilities Expense		17,400
	Supplies Expense		7,740
	Interest Expense		10,500
Dec. 31	Income Summary	168,400	
	Inventory (beginning balance)		168,400
Dec. 31	Inventory (ending balance)	179,200	
	Income Summary		179,200
Dec. 31	Income Summary ($1,083,690 − $955,940 − $168,400 + $179,200)	138,550	
	Susan Sierra, Capital		138,550
Dec. 31	Susan Sierra, Capital	144,000	
	Susan Sierra, Withdrawals		144,000

The T-account balance of $138,550 matches the net income amount on the work sheet.

Income Summary

Clo.	955,940	Clo.	1,083,690
Clo.	168,400	Clo.	179,200
Clo.	138,550	Bal.	138,550

Requirement 3

The title must include the name of the company, "Income Statement," and the specific period of time covered. It is critical that the time period is defined.

Cost of goods sold is a *calculation* on the income statement under the periodic inventory system. (It is an *account balance* under the perpetual inventory system.) If the income statement is prepared for a company's external users, only the final cost of goods sold balance is typically presented, and then the income statement is the same regardless of the inventory system used.

SIERRA DISTRIBUTING COMPANY
Income Statement
For the Year Ended December 31, 2008

Sales revenue			$1,043,400
Less: Sales discounts		$ 30,900	
Sales returns and allowances		24,600	55,500
Net sales revenue			987,900
Cost of goods sold:			
Beginning inventory		168,400	
Purchases	$540,800		
Less: Purchase discounts	18,000		
Purchase returns and allowances	22,290		
Net purchases		500,510	
Freight-in		27,900	
Cost of goods available for sale		696,810	
Less: Ending inventory		179,200	
Cost of goods sold			517,610
Gross margin			470,290
Operating expenses:			
Salaries expense		252,150	
Rent expense		36,000	
Utilities expense		17,400	
Amortization expense		7,950	
Supplies expense		7,740	321,240
Income from operations			149,050
Other expense:			
Interest expense			10,500
Net income			$ 138,550

The title must include the name of company, "Statement of Owner's Equity," and the specific period of time covered. It is critical that the time period is defined.

The statement of owner's equity is the same for service entities and merchandisers using either of the inventory systems.

SIERRA DISTRIBUTING COMPANY
Statement of Owner's Equity
For the Year Ended December 31, 2008

Susan Sierra, capital, January 1, 2008	$ 71,040
Add: Net income	138,550
	209,590
Less: Withdrawals	144,000
Susan Sierra, capital, December 31, 2008	$ 65,590

The title must include the name of the company, "Balance Sheet," and the date of the balance sheet. It shows the financial position on one specific date.

This is a classified balance sheet with Inventory listed among the current assets.

The Inventory balance is the cost of the inventory on hand based on the inventory count, and it is the same regardless of the inventory system used.

SIERRA DISTRIBUTING COMPANY
Balance Sheet
December 31, 2008

Assets			Liabilities		
Current assets:			Current liabilities:		
Cash	$ 17,010		Accounts payable	$139,020	
Accounts receivable	111,300		Salaries payable	3,900	
Inventory	179,200		Interest payable	1,800	
Supplies	4,050		Unearned sales revenue	7,200	
Prepaid rent	3,000		Total current liabilities	151,920	
Total current assets		314,560	Long-term notes payable	105,000	
Property, plant, and equipment:			Total liabilities		256,920
Furniture	$79,500				
Less: Accumulated			**Owner's Equity**		
amortization	71,550	7,950	Susan Sierra, capital		65,590
Total assets		$322,510	Total liabilities and owner's equity		$322,510

Refer to page 237 for the inventory turnover formula. Generally, the higher the inventory turnover, the better.

$$\frac{\text{Inventory}}{\text{turnover}} = \frac{\text{Cost of goods sold}}{\text{Average inventory}} = \frac{\$517,610}{(\$168,400 + \$179,200)/2} = 2.98 \text{ times}$$

The increase in the rate of inventory turnover from 2.1 to 2.98 times *suggests* higher profits in 2008 than in 2007. However, gross margin and expenses for both years must be checked to verify this suggestion.

Chapter 5 Appendix B

Comparing the Perpetual and Periodic Inventory Systems

Objective 10

Compare the perpetual and periodic inventory systems

Exhibit 5B-1 provides a side-by-side comparison of the two inventory accounting systems. It gives the journal entries, the T-accounts, and all financial-statement effects of both inventory systems.

In the periodic system, the purchase of inventory is *not* recorded in the Inventory account. Instead, purchases are recorded in the Purchases account, which is an expense (see transaction 1 in the exhibit, right column). A sale transaction includes *no* cost of goods sold entry (transaction 2). How, then, does the business record inventory and cost of goods sold?

Transactions 3a and 3b give the end-of-period entries to update the Inventory account. Transaction 3c closes the Purchases account into Income Summary to complete the periodic process.

Panel B of the exhibit shows the financial statements under both systems.

Panel A—Recording in the Journal and Posting to the Accounts

Perpetual System	Periodic System

1. Credit purchases of $600,000:

Perpetual			Periodic		
Inventory	600,000		Purchases	600,000	
Accounts Payable....................		600,000	Accounts Payable.......................		600,000

2. Credit sales of $1,000,000 (cost $550,000): *(Perpetual)*
2. Credit sales of $1,000,000: *(Periodic)*

Perpetual			Periodic		
Accounts Receivable	1,000,000		Accounts Receivable......................	1,000,000	
Sales Revenue		1,000,000	Sales Revenue............................		1,000,000
Cost of Goods Sold.......................	550,000				
Inventory		550,000			

3. End-of-period entries: *(Perpetual)*
No entries required. Both Inventory and
Cost of Goods Sold are up-to-date.

3. End-of-period entries to update Inventory: *(Periodic)*

a. Transfer the cost of beginning inventory ($100,000) to Income Summary:

Income Summary............................	100,000	
Inventory (beginning balance)...		100,000

b. Record the cost of ending inventory ($150,000) based on a physical count:

Inventory (ending balance)	150,000	
Income Summary......................		150,000

c. Transfer the cost of purchases to Income Summary:

Income Summary............................	600,000	
Purchases		600,000

INVENTORY AND COST OF GOODS SOLD ACCOUNTS (Perpetual)

INVENTORY AND INCOME SUMMARY ACCOUNTS (Periodic)

Perpetual:

Inventory		Cost of Goods Sold	
100,000*	550,000	550,000	
600,000			
150,000			

*Beginning inventory was $100,000.

Periodic:

Inventory		Income Summary	
100,000**	100,000	100,000	150,000
150,000		600,000	
150,000		550,000	

**Beginning inventory was $100,000.

Panel B—Reporting in the Financial Statements

Perpetual System	Periodic System

Income Statement (partial)

Perpetual System:

Sales revenue	$1,000,000
Cost of goods sold........................	550,000
Gross margin................................	$ 450,000

Periodic System:

Sales revenue		$1,000,000
Cost of goods sold:		
Beginning inventory	$100,000	
Purchases	600,000	
Cost of goods available for sale	700,000	
Less: Ending inventory............	(150,000)	
Cost of goods sold		550,000
Gross margin		$ 450,000

Balance Sheet (partial)

Perpetual System:

Current assets:		
Cash...	$	XXX
Accounts receivable		XXX
Inventories.................................		150,000

Periodic System:

Current assets:		
Cash...	$	XXX
Accounts receivable		XXX
Inventories.................................		150,000

Summary

1. **Use sales and gross margin to evaluate a company.** The major revenue of a merchandising business is *sales revenue*, or *net sales*. The major expense is *cost of goods sold*. Net sales minus cost of goods sold is called *gross margin*, or *gross profit*. This amount measures the business's success or failure in selling its products at a higher price than it paid for them. The cost of goods sold formula is: Beginning inventory + Purchases − Ending inventory = Cost of goods sold.

2. **Account for the purchase and sale of inventory under the perpetual inventory system.** The merchandiser's major asset is *inventory*. In a merchandising entity the accounting cycle is from cash to inventory as the inventory is purchased for resale, and back to cash as the inventory is sold. The *invoice* is the business document generated by a purchase or sale transaction. Most merchandising entities offer *purchase returns* to their customers to allow them to return unsuitable merchandise. They also grant *allowances* for damaged goods that the buyer chooses to keep. Sales Discounts and Sales Returns and Allowances are contra accounts to Sales Revenue. Some suppliers offer merchandising entities (their customers) *purchase discounts* to encourage them to pay their invoice promptly within the discount period.

3. **Adjust and close the accounts of a merchandising business under the perpetual inventory system.** The end-of-period adjusting and closing process of a merchandising business is similar to that of a service business. In addition, a merchandiser adjusts inventory for theft losses, damage, and accounting errors.

4. **Prepare a merchandiser's financial statements under the perpetual inventory system.** The income statement may appear in the *single-step format* or the *multi-step format*. A single-step income statement has only two sections—one for revenues and the other for expenses—and a single income amount for net income. A multi-step income statement has subtotals for gross margin and income from operations. The multi-step format is the most widely used format.

5. **Use the gross margin percentage and the inventory turnover ratio to evaluate a business.** Two key decision aids for a merchandiser are the *gross margin percentage* (gross margin ÷ net sales revenue) and the *rate of inventory turnover* (cost of goods sold ÷ average inventory). Increases in these measures usually signal an increase in profits.

6. **Account for the purchase and sale of inventory under the periodic inventory system.** Under the periodic system, purchases of inventory are recorded in the Purchases account, and purchase discounts, and purchase returns and allowances are recorded in separate contra accounts. The Inventory account is *not* used to record inventory purchases. Sales are recorded in the normal way but no entry is made to record the cost of the goods sold (as is done under the perpetual system).

7. **Compute the cost of goods sold under the periodic inventory system.** Cost of goods sold is computed at the end of the period using an expansion of the cost of goods sold formula. The physical inventory count gives the amount of ending inventory that is required by the cost of goods sold formula. There is *no* cost of goods sold account in the chart of accounts, as there is under the perpetual inventory system.

8. **Adjust and close the accounts of a merchandising business under the periodic inventory system.** The closing entries for the periodic system are more complicated than the corresponding entries for the perpetual system. The purchases, purchase returns and allowances, and freight-in accounts are all closed to the income summary. As well, the opening inventory is closed to the income summary and replaced by the ending inventory balance, which is credited to the income summary. The result of these income summary transactions related to inventory is the cost of the goods sold amount appearing on the income statement.

9. **Prepare a merchandiser's financial statements under the periodic inventory system.** The financial statements report the same results regardless of whether the merchandiser uses the periodic inventory system or the perpetual inventory system. The only difference is on the income statement, where the cost of goods sold amount is a calculation under the periodic system as compared to an account balance under the perpetual system.

10. **Compare the perpetual and periodic inventory systems.** In the perpetual system, inventory purchases are recorded in the Inventory account; in the periodic system, they are recorded in the Purchases account, an expense. In the perpetual system, each sale is accompanied by a transaction that records the cost of the sale and reduces inventory, giving the current amount of inventory on hand. In the periodic system, only the sale is recorded; the cost of goods sold is calculated at the end of the period. Both inventory systems require a physical count of inventory at least once per year, usually at the end of the period. Both inventory systems report the same financial results at the end of the period since both adjust inventory to match the amount based on the physical count.

Self-Study Questions

Test your understanding of the chapter by marking the correct answer for each of the following questions:

1. The major expense of a merchandising business is (*p. 214*)
   a. Cost of goods sold
   b. Amortization
   c. Rent
   d. Interest

2. Sales total $880,000, cost of goods sold is $420,000, and operating expenses are $320,000. How much is gross margin? (*p. 214*)
   a. $880,000
   b. $460,000
   c. $420,000
   d. $140,000

3. If a merchandiser's beginning inventory was $100,000, it purchased $200,000 during the period and a count shows $75,000 of inventory on hand at the end of the period, what was the cost of the goods sold? (*p. 216*)
   a. $250,000
   b. $300,000
   c. $225,000
   d. $275,000

4. A purchase discount results from (*p. 219*)
   a. Returning goods to the seller
   b. Receiving a purchase allowance from the seller
   c. Buying a large enough quantity of merchandise to get the discount
   d. Paying within the discount period

5. Which of the following is *not* an account? (*p. 213*)
   a. Sales revenue
   b. Net sales
   c. Inventory
   d. Supplies expense

6. Which account causes the main difference between a merchandiser's adjusting and closing process and that of a service business? (*pp. 230–231*)
   a. Advertising expense
   b. Interest revenue
   c. Cost of goods sold
   d. Accounts receivable

7. The closing entry for Sales Discounts includes (*pp. 230–231*)
   a. Sales Discounts
        Income Summary
   b. Sales Discounts
        Sales Revenue
   c. Income Summary
        Sales Discounts
   d. Not used: Sales Discounts is a permanent account, which is not closed.

8. Which income statement format reports income from operations? (*p. 236*)
   a. Account format
   b. Report format
   c. Single-step format
   d. Multi-step format

9. A company has sales of $500,000, cost of goods sold of $300,000, average inventory during the year of $120,000, and ending inventory of $100,000. The company's inventory turnover for the year is (*p. 237*)
   a. 4.17 times
   b. 2.5 times
   c. 3 times
   d. 2 times

10. Refer to Self-Study Question 9. About how many days does it take the inventory to turn over? (*p. 237*)
    a. 146
    b. 88
    c. 122
    d. 250

Answers to the Self-Study Questions follow the Similar Accounting Terms.

Accounting Vocabulary

Cost of goods sold   (*pp. 214, 245*)
Cost of sales   (*pp. 214, 245*)
Gross margin   (*p. 214*)
Gross margin percentage   (*p. 237*)
Gross profit   (*p. 214*)
Income from operations   (*pp. 232, 250*)
Inventory   (*p. 213*)
Inventory turnover   (*p. 237*)
Invoice   (*p. 218*)
Multi-step income statement   (*p. 236*)
Net purchases   (*p. 244*)
Net sales   (*p. 213*)

Operating expense   (*pp. 232, 248*)
Operating income   (*pp. 232, 250*)
Other expense   (*pp. 232, 250*)
Other revenue   (*pp. 232, 250*)
Periodic inventory system   (*p. 216*)
Perpetual inventory system   (*p. 216*)
Sales   (*p. 213*)
Sales discounts   (*p. 225*)
Sales returns and allowances   (*p. 225*)
Sales revenue   (*p. 213*)
Single-step income statement   (*p. 236*)

Similar Accounting Terms

Freight in   Freight; Transportation-in; Transportation costs
Gross margin   Gross profit
Income from operations   Operating income

Invoice	Bill
List price	Full price; Price with no discounts deducted
Purchase discount	Cash discount; Discount given to reward prompt payment
Quantity discount	Volume discount; Discount given to reward purchase of more than one of a particular item
Sales revenue	Sales
Cost of goods sold	Cost of sales

Answers to Self-Study Questions

1. a
2. b ($880,000 − $420,000 = $460,000)
3. c ($100,000 + $200,000 − $75,000 = $225,000)
4. d
5. b
6. c
7. c
8. d
9. b ($300,000 ÷ $120,000 = 2.5 times)
10. a (365 days ÷ 2.5 times = 146 days)

Assignment Material

Questions

1. Gross margin is often mentioned in the business press as an important measure of success. What does gross margin measure, and why is it important?

2. Describe the operating cycle for (a) the purchase and cash sale of inventory, and (b) the purchase and sale of inventory on account.

3. Identify ten items of information on an invoice.

4. Indicate which accounts are debited and credited under the perpetual inventory system for (a) a credit purchase of inventory and the subsequent cash payment, and (b) a credit sale of inventory and the subsequent cash collection. Assume no discounts, returns, allowances, or freight.

5. Inventory costing $2,000 is purchased and invoiced on July 28 under terms of 3/10, n/30. Compute the payment amount on August 6. How much would the payment be on August 9? What explains the difference? What is the latest acceptable payment date under the terms of sale?

6. Inventory listed at $70,000 is sold subject to a quantity discount of $6,000 and under payment terms of 2/15, n/45. What is the net sales revenue on this sale if the customer pays within 15 days?

7. Name the new contra accounts introduced in this chapter.

8. Briefly discuss the similarity in computing supplies expense and computing cost of goods sold under the periodic inventory system using the formula shown on page 216.

9. Why is the title of Cost of Goods Sold especially descriptive? What type of account is Cost of Goods Sold?

10. Beginning inventory is $7,500, net purchases total $45,000, and freight in is $1,500. If ending inventory is $12,000, what is cost of goods sold?

11. You are evaluating two companies as possible investments. One entity sells its services; the other entity is a merchandiser. How can you identify the merchandiser by examining the two entities' balance sheets and income statements?

12. You are beginning the adjusting and closing process at the end of your company's fiscal year. Does the trial balance carry the final ending amount of inventory if your company uses the perpetual inventory system? Why or why not?

13. Give the adjusting entry for inventory if shrinkage is $10,200.

14. What is the identifying characteristic of the "other" category of revenues and expenses? Give an example of each.

15. Name and describe two formats for the income statement, and identify the type of business to which each format best applies.

16. List eight different operating expenses.

17. Which financial statement reports sales discounts and sales returns and allowances? Show how they are reported, using any reasonable amounts in your illustration.

18. Does a merchandiser prefer a high or low rate of inventory turnover? Explain.

19. In general, what does a decreasing gross margin percentage, coupled with an increasing rate of inventory turnover, suggest about a business's pricing strategy?

*20. In the periodic inventory system, what is meant by the term "cost of goods available for sale"?

*21. In a periodic inventory system, why must inventory be physically counted to determine cost of goods sold?

*22. Why do accountants use a Purchases account when inventory items are acquired in a periodic inventory system?

*23. How are purchase discounts accounted for in a periodic inventory system?

*24. Suppose you are starting a new retail business. What factors would you consider in determining whether to implement a periodic or perpetual inventory system?

Starters

Starter 5–1 Ending inventory of the previous period was $400,000, and net purchases this period were $1,000,000. If ending inventory this period is $200,000, what is cost of goods sold?

Using the cost of goods sold formula

COGS $1,200,000

Starter 5–2 You may have shopped at a Gap store. Suppose Gap purchased T-shirts on account for $10,000. Credit terms are 2/10, n/30. Gap paid within the discount period. Journalize the following transactions for Gap:

a. Purchase of inventory.
b. Payment on account.

Recording purchase and cash payment transactions—perpetual

b. Cash credit $9,800

Starter 5–3 Suppose Toys Unlimited buys $100,000 of Lego toys on credit terms of 3/15, n/45. Some of the goods are damaged in shipment, so Toys Unlimited returns $10,000 of the merchandise to Lego. How much must Toys Unlimited pay Lego

a. After the discount period?
b. Within the discount period?

Accounting for the purchase of inventory, purchase discount—perpetual

b. $87,300

Starter 5–4 Refer to the Toys Unlimited situation in Starter 5–3 and journalize the following transactions on the books of Toys Unlimited. Explanations are not required.

a. Purchase of the goods.
b. Return of the damaged goods.
c. Payment within the discount period. Before journalizing this transaction, it is helpful to post the first two transactions to the Accounts Payable T-account.
d. In the end, how much did the inventory cost Toys Unlimited?

Recording purchase, purchase return, and cash payment transactions—perpetual

c. Cash credit $87,300

Starter 5–5 Suppose The Bay purchases $60,000 of women's sportswear on account from Liz Claiborne, Inc. Credit terms are 2/10, net 30. The Bay pays electronically, and Liz Claiborne receives the money on the tenth day.

Journalize The Bay's (a) purchase and (b) payment transactions. What was The Bay's net cost of this inventory?

Note: Starter 5–6 covers this same situation for the seller.

Recording purchase transactions—perpetual

(b) Net inventory cost $58,800

Starter 5–6 Liz Claiborne, Inc. sells $60,000 of women's sportswear to The Bay under credit terms of 2/10, net 30. Liz Claiborne's cost of the goods is $32,000 and Claiborne receives the appropriate amount of cash from The Bay on the tenth day.

Journalize Liz Claiborne's (a) sale, (b) cost of goods sold, and (c) cash receipt.

Note: Starter 5–5 covers the same situation for the buyer.

Recording sales, cost of goods sold, and cash collections—perpetual

(c) Cash receipt $58,800

Starter 5–7 Suppose Pearson Education, the publisher, sells 1,000 books on account for $50 each (cost of these books is $40,000). One hundred of these books (cost, $4,000) were the wrong edition, so Pearson later received these books as sales returns. Then the customer paid the balance within the discount period. Credit terms were 2/15, net 30.

Journalize Pearson's (a) sale, (b) sale return, and (c) cash collection transactions.

Recording sales, sales return, and collection entries—perpetual

(c) Cash receipt $44,100

Starter 5–8 Use the data in Starter 5–7 to compute Pearson Education's

a. Net sales revenue
b. Gross margin

Computing net sales and gross margin—perpetual

b. Gross margin $8,100

---

*This Question covers Chapter 5 Appendix A or B topics.

Adjusting inventory for
shrinkage—perpetual

3

Debit COGS $1,100

Starter 5–9 Patio Furniture's Inventory account at year end showed a debit balance of $65,000. A physical count of inventory showed goods on hand of $63,900. Journalize the adjusting entry.

Making closing entries—
perpetual

3

c. Income Summary debit
$276,000

Starter 5–10 Hayes RV Centre accounting records include the following accounts at December 31:

Cost of goods sold	$385,000	Accumulated amortization	$ 38,000
Accounts payable	16,000	Cash	40,000
Rent expense	20,000	Sales revenue	700,000
Building	110,000	Amortization expense	10,000
J. Hayes, capital	140,000	J. Hayes, withdrawals	60,000
Inventory	260,000	Sales discounts	9,000

Journalize closing entries for Hayes RV Centre's

a. Revenues
b. Expenses
c. Income Summary account
d. Withdrawals

Preparing a merchandiser's
income statement—perpetual

4

Net income $1,500

Starter 5–11 Suppose Northern Communications reported these figures in its December 31, 2008, financial statements:

Cash	$ 3,800
Total operating expenses	3,500
Accounts payable	4,000
Owner capital	4,200
Long-term notes payable	900
Inventory	400
Cost of goods sold	20,000
Equipment, net	3,700
Accrued liabilities	1,600
Net sales revenue	25,000
Accounts receivable	2,800

Prepare Northern Communications' multi-step income statement for the year ended December 31, 2008.

Preparing a merchandiser's
balance sheet—perpetual

4

Total assets $10,700

Starter 5–12 Use the data in Starter 5–11 to prepare Northern Communications' classified balance sheet at December 31, 2008. Use the report format with all headings.

Computing the gross margin
percentage and the rate of
inventory turnover

5

Gross margin 20%

Starter 5–13 Refer to the Northern Communications' situation in Starters 5–11 and 5–12. Compute the gross margin percentage and rate of inventory turnover for 2008. One year earlier, at December 31, 2007, Northern's inventory balance was $300.

Recording purchase and
cash payment transactions—
periodic system

6

b. $87,300

*Starter 5–14 Suppose Toys Unlimited buys $100,000 of Lego toys on credit terms of 3/15, n/45. Some of the goods are damaged in shipment, so Toys Unlimited returns $10,000 of the merchandise to Lego. Assuming Toys Unlimited uses a periodic inventory system, how much must Toys Unlimited pay Lego

a. After the discount period?
b. Within the discount period?
c. Journalize the purchase of the goods. An explanation is not required.
d. Journalize the return of the damaged goods. An explanation is not required.

Recording sales and cash
collections—periodic system

6

c. Cash receipt $58,800

*Starter 5–15 Liz Claiborne, Inc. sells $60,000 of women's sportswear to The Bay under credit terms of 2/10, net 30. Liz Claiborne's cost of goods sold is $32,000, and Liz Claiborne receives the appropriate amount of cash from The Bay on the tenth day. Assume Liz Claiborne uses a periodic inventory system.

Journalize Liz Claiborne's (a) sale, (b) cost of goods sold, and (c) cash receipt.

*This Starter covers Chapter 5 Appendix A or B topics.

Exercises

Exercise 5–1

The Electronics Store reported the information shown below.

Evaluating a company's revenues, gross margin, operating income, and net income

2. Gross margin 2009 $2,250 thou.

THE ELECTRONICS STORE
Income Statement
(Dollars in thousands)

	Fiscal Year Ended	
	January 31, 2009	January 31, 2008
Net sales	$7,500	$7,125
Costs and expenses:		
Cost of goods sold	5,250	5,025
Selling, advertising, general, and administrative	1,525	1,425
Amortization	155	144
Other charges	45	297
Interest expense	75	78
Other income (expenses)	(14)	(14)
	7,036	6,955
Net earnings	$ 464	$ 170

THE ELECTRONICS STORE
Balance Sheet (partial)
(Dollars in thousands)

	January 31, 2009	January 31, 2008
Assets		
Current assets:		
Cash	$ 575	$ 155
Accounts and other receivables	108	173
Inventory	1,660	1,500
Prepaid expenses and other current assets	33	66
Total current assets	$2,376	$1,894

Required

1. Is The Electronics Store a merchandising entity, a service business, or both? How can you tell? List the items in The Electronics Store financial statements that influence your answer.

2. Compute The Electronics Store's gross margin for fiscal years 2009 and 2008. Did the gross margin increase or decrease in 2009? Is this a good sign or a bad sign about the company?

3. Write a brief memo to the owner advising her of The Electronics Store's trend of sales, gross margin, and net income. Indicate whether the outlook for The Electronics Store is favourable or unfavourable, based on this trend. Use the following memo format:

> Date: _____
>
> To: The Owner
> From: Student Name
> Subject: Trend of sales, gross margin, and net income for The Electronics Store

Exercise 5–2

Using the cost of goods sold formula in a periodic inventory system

COGS $82,000

T Wholesale Company began the year with inventory of $8,000. During the year, the company purchased $91,000 of goods and returned $6,000 due to damage. At year end, the inventory balance was $11,000. T Wholesale Company uses the periodic inventory system.

Compute T Wholesale Company's cost of goods sold for the year.

Exercise 5–3

Computing inventory purchases

Purchase $671 mil.

Suppose SportChek reported Cost of Goods Sold totalling $651 million. Ending inventory was $279 million, and beginning inventory was $259 million. How much inventory did SportChek purchase during the year?

Recording purchase
transactions under the
perpetual inventory system

b. Net inventory cost $490,000

Exercise 5–4

Suppose The Bay purchases $500,000 of sporting goods on account from Nike. Credit terms are 2/10, net 30. The Bay pays electronically, and Nike receives the money on the tenth day.

Journalize The Bay's (a) purchase and (b) cash payment transactions. What was The Bay's net cost of this inventory?

Note: Exercise 5–5 covers this same situation for the seller.

Recording sales, cost of goods
sold, and cash collections under
the perpetual inventory system

c. Gross margin $140,000

Exercise 5–5

Nike sells $500,000 of sporting goods to The Bay under credit terms of 2/10, net 30. Nike's cost of the goods is $350,000, and it receives the appropriate amount of cash from The Bay on the tenth day.

Journalize Nike's (a) sale, (b) cost of goods sold, and (c) cash receipt. How much gross margin did Nike earn on this sale?

Note: Exercise 5–4 covers the same situation for the buyer.

Journalizing purchase and sale
transactions under the perpetual
inventory system

June 23 cash receipt $5,880

Exercise 5–6

Journalize, without explanations, the following transactions of Serendipity Fashions during the month of June 2008:

June 3 Purchased $4,200 of inventory under terms of 2/10, n/eom and FOB shipping point.
  7 Returned $1,800 of defective merchandise purchased on June 3.
  9 Paid freight bill of $660 on June 3 purchase.
  10 Sold inventory for $13,200, collecting cash of $2,400. Payment terms on the remainder were 2/15, n/30. The goods cost Serendipity Fashions $7,800.
  12 Paid amount owed on credit purchase of June 3, less the discount and the return.
  16 Granted a sales allowance of $4,800 on the portion of the June 10 sale that was on account.
  23 Received cash from June 10 customer in full settlement of her debt, less the allowance and the discount.

Journalizing transactions from a
purchase invoice under the
perpetual inventory system

3. Net cash paid $2,175.60

Exercise 5–7

As the proprietor of Arbutus Auto Service, you receive the invoice below from a supplier (GST has been disregarded).

Required

1. Record the May 14 purchase on account.

ABC AUTO PARTS WHOLESALE DISTRIBUTORS
2600 Victoria Avenue
Saskatoon, Saskatchewan S4P 1B3

Invoice date: May 14, 2008   **Payment terms:** 2/10, n/30

Sold to: Arbutus Auto Service
4219 Cumberland Avenue
Prince Albert, SK S7M 1X3

Quantity Ordered	Description	Quantity Shipped	Price	Amount
6	P135-X4 Radials.........	6	$90.00	$540.00
8	L912 Belted-bias........	8	100.00	800.00
14	R39 Truck tires.........	14	120.00	1,680.00
	Total..			$3,020.00

Due date:	Amount:
May 24, 2008	$2,959.60
May 25 through June 13, 2008	$3,020.00

Paid:

---

2. The L912 Belted-bias tires were ordered by mistake and therefore were returned to ABC. Journalize the return on May 19.

3. Record the May 22 payment of the net amount owed.

Exercise 5–8

On April 30, Sooke Jewellers purchased inventory of $30,000 on account from Northern Gems Ltd., a jewellery importer. Terms were 3/15, n/45. On receiving the goods Sooke checked the order and found $4,800 worth of items that were not ordered. Therefore, Sooke returned this amount of merchandise to Northern on May 4. On May 14, Sooke paid Northern.

Required Record the indicated transactions in the journal of Sooke Jewellers. Explanations are not required.

Journalizing purchase transactions under the perpetual inventory system

May 14 cash paid $24,444

Exercise 5–9

Refer to the business situation in Exercise 5–8. Journalize the transactions of Northern Gems Ltd. Northern's gross margin is 45 percent, so cost of goods sold is 55 percent of sales. Explanations are not required.

Journalizing sale transactions under the perpetual inventory system

May 14 cash receipt $24,444

Exercise 5–10

Supply the missing income statement amounts in each of the following situations:

Sales	Sales Discounts	Net Sales	Cost of Goods Sold	Gross Margin
$91,500	$1,800	$89,700	$59,400	(a)
98,300	(b)	92,800	(c)	$33,000
62,400	2,100	(d)	44,100	(e)
(f)	3,000	(g)	72,500	39,600

Computing inventory and cost of goods sold amounts

f. $115,100 g. $112,100

Exercise 5–11

Ferguson Hardware Store's accounting records (partial) carried the following accounts at January 31, 2008:

Accounts receivable..............	$ 39,120	Selling expense........................	$ 334,080
Interest revenue	2,400	Sales revenue...........................	1,856,400
Accounts payable	99,000	Interest expense	480
Other expense	61,920	Inventory.................................	261,600
Cost of goods sold	1,342,200	General and administrative	
J. Ferguson, withdrawals	81,600	expense...............................	32,280

Making closing entries under a perpetual inventory system

2. J. Ferguson, Capital bal. $46,840

Required

Note: For simplicity, all operating expenses have been summarized in the accounts Selling Expense and General and Administrative Expenses.

1. Journalize all of this company's closing entries at January 31, 2008.

2. Set up T-accounts for the Income Summary account and the J. Ferguson, Capital account. Post to these accounts and calculate their ending balances. One year earlier, at January 31, 2007, the Capital balance was $40,600.

Exercise 5–12

Candy Creations' accounts at June 30 included these unadjusted balances:

Inventory...	$ 5,600
Cost of goods sold	41,200
Sales revenue	86,900
Sales discounts	900
Sales returns and allowances	1,400

The physical count of inventory showed $5,400 of inventory on hand. This is the only adjustment needed.

Adjusting and closing entries under the perpetual inventory system; computing gross margin

c. Gross margin $43,200

Required

a. Journalize the adjustment for inventory shrinkage. Include an explanation.

b. Journalize the closing entries for the appropriate accounts.

c. Compute the gross margin.

Exercise 5–13

The trial balance and adjustments columns of the work sheet of Terrace Decorating Centre include the accounts and balances at March 31, 2009.

Account Title	Trial Balance Debit	Trial Balance Credit	Adjustments Debit	Adjustments Credit
Cash	$ 900			
Accounts receivable	7,650		(a) 2,790	
Inventory	33,390			(b) 1,053
Supplies	11,700			(c) 8,640
Store fixtures	38,223			
Accumulated amortization		$ 10,125		(d) 2,025
Accounts payable		7,470		
Salary payable		0		(e) 1,080
Note payable, long-term		6,750		
G. Terrace, capital		30,528		
G. Terrace, withdrawals	40,500			
Sales revenue		210,600		(a) 2,790
Sales discounts	1,800			
Cost of goods sold	100,440		(b) 1,053	
Selling expenses	18,945		(c) 5,130	
			(e) 1,080	
General expenses	9,450		(c) 3,510	
			(d) 2,025	
Interest expense	2,475			
Total	$265,473	$265,473	$15,588	$15,588

Required Compute the adjusted balance for each account that must be closed. Then journalize Terrace Decorating Centre's closing entries at March 31, 2009. How much was Terrace Decorating Centre's net income or net loss?

Exercise 5–14

Use the data in Exercise 5–13 to prepare the multi-step income statement of Terrace Decorating Centre for the year ended March 31, 2009.

Exercise 5–15

Refer to Exercise 5–14. After completing Terrace Decorating Centre's income statement for the year ended March 31, 2009, compute these ratios to evaluate Terrace Decorating Centre's performance:

- Gross margin percentage
- Inventory turnover (Ending inventory one year earlier, at March 31, 2008, was $27,450.)

Compare your figures with the 2008 gross margin percentage of 49 percent and the inventory turnover rate of 3.16 times. Does the two-year trend suggest that Terrace Decorating Centre's profits are increasing or decreasing?

Exercise 5–16

Selected accounts of Galloway Video Sales are listed in alphabetical order, with their balances at December 31, 2009.

Accounts receivable	$ 22,680	B. Galloway, capital	$176,498
Accumulated amortization	26,180	Sales discounts	12,600
Cost of goods sold	127,820	Sales returns	6,440
General expenses	32,900	Sales revenue	281,400
Interest revenue	2,100	Selling expense	52,920
Inventory, Dec. 31, 2008	29,400	Unearned sales revenue	9,750
Inventory, Dec. 31, 2009	27,160		

Required

1. Prepare the business's multi-step income statement for the year ended December 31, 2009.

2. Compute the rate of inventory turnover for the year. Last year the turnover was 3.8 times. Does this two-year trend suggest improvement or deterioration in inventory turnover?

Exercise 5–17

Prepare Galloway Video Sales' single-step income statement for 2009, using the data from Exercise 5–16. Compute the gross margin percentage, and compare it with last year's value of 58 percent for Galloway Video. Does this two-year trend suggest better or worse profitability during the current year?

Exercise 5–18

Networking Systems earned sales revenue of $65 million in 2009. Cost of goods sold was $33 million, and net income reached $8 million, Networking's highest ever. Total current assets included inventory of $3 million at December 31, 2009. Last year's ending inventory was $4 million. The managers of Networking Systems need to know the company's gross margin percentage and rate of inventory turnover for 2009. Compute these amounts.

*Exercise 5–19

Journalize, without explanations, the following transactions of Now Fashions during the month of June 2009:

June	3	Purchased $8,400 of inventory under terms of 2/10, n/eom (end of month) and FOB shipping point.
	7	Returned $3,600 of defective merchandise purchased on June 3.
	9	Paid freight bill of $660 on June 3 purchase.
	10	Sold inventory for $26,400, collecting cash of $4,800. Payment terms on the remainder were 2/15, n/30.
	12	Paid amount owed on credit purchase of June 3, less the discount and the return.
	16	Granted a sales allowance of $3,200 on the June 10 sale.
	23	Received cash from June 10 customer in full settlement of her debt, less the allowance and the discount.

*Exercise 5–20

As the proprietor of OK Auto Repair, you receive this invoice from a supplier (GST has been disregarded).

ABC AUTO PARTS WHOLESALE DISTRIBUTORS
2600 Victoria Avenue
Saskatoon, Saskatchewan S4P 1B3

Invoice date: May 14, 2008   **Payment terms:** 2/10, n/30

Sold to: Arbutus Auto Service
4219 Cumberland Avenue
Prince Albert, SK S7M 1X3

Quantity Ordered	Description	Quantity Shipped	Price	Amount
6	P135-X4 Radials.........	6	$90.00	$540.00
8	L912 Belted-bias........	8	100.00	800.00
14	R39 Truck tires.........	14	120.00	1,680.00
	Total..$3,020.00			

Due date:		Amount:
May 24, 2008		$2,959.60
May 25 through June 13, 2008		$3,020.00
Paid:		

---

*This Exercise covers Chapter 5 Appendix A topics.

Excel Spreadsheet Template

Preparing a single-step income statement for a merchandising business under the perpetual inventory system

4 **5**

Net income $50,820

Computing gross margin percentage and inventory turnover

5

Gross margin 49.2%

Journalizing purchase and sale transactions under the periodic inventory system

6

June 23 cash receipt $18,032

Journalizing transactions from a purchase invoice under the periodic inventory system

6

3. May 22 payment $2,175.10

Required

1. Record the May 14 purchase on account.
2. The L912 Belted-bias tires were ordered by mistake and therefore were returned to ABC. Journalize the return on May 19.
3. Record the May 22 payment of the amount owed.

Journalizing purchase transactions under the periodic inventory system

May 14 cash paid $24,444

*Exercise 5–21

On April 30, Sooke Jewellers purchased inventory of $30,000 on account from Northern Gems Ltd., a jewellery importer. Terms were 3/15, net 45. On receiving the goods, Sooke checked the order and found $4,800 of unsuitable merchandise. Therefore, Sooke returned the merchandise to Northern on May 4.

On May 14, Sooke Jewellers paid the net amount owed from April 30, less the return.

Required Record the required transactions in the journal of Sooke Jewellers. Use the periodic inventory system. Explanations are not required.

Journalizing sale transactions under the periodic inventory system

May 14 cash received $24,444

*Exercise 5–22

Refer to the business situation in Exercise 5–21. Journalize the transactions of Northern Gems Ltd., which uses the periodic inventory system. Explanations are not required.

Computing cost of goods sold in a periodic inventory system

COGS $127,820

*Exercise 5–23

The periodic inventory records of Galloway Video Sales include these accounts at December 31, 2009:

Purchases of inventory	$126,840
Purchase discounts	4,200
Purchase returns and allowances	2,800
Freight in	5,740
Inventory, December 31, 2008	29,400

At December 31, 2009, Galloway Video's inventory balance stood at $27,160.

Required Compute Galloway Video's cost of goods sold for 2009. (Note: Your answer should be the same as the amount given in Exercise 5–16.)

Computing inventory and cost of goods sold under the periodic inventory system

a. $700 f. $9,275 j. $20,010

*Exercise 5–24

Supply the missing income statement amounts in each of the following situations:

Sales	Sales Discounts	Net Sales	Beginning Inventory	Net Purchases	Ending Inventory	Cost of Goods Sold	Gross Margin
$24,075	(a)	$23,375	$8,875	$16,675	$9,850	(b)	$7,675
20,600	$525	(c)	6,440	10,750	(d)	$11,025	(e)
23,375	450	22,925	(f)	11,225	5,650	14,850	(g)
(h)	750	(i)	10,175	(j)	12,060	18,125	9,650

Computing cost of goods sold under the periodic inventory system

Net purchases $289,000

*Exercise 5–25

For the year ended December 31, 2008, Home Distributors, a retailer of home-related products, reported net sales of $659,000 and cost of goods sold of $300,000. The company's balance sheet at December 31, 2007 and 2008 reported inventories of $346,000 and $335,000, respectively. What were Home Distributors' net purchases during 2008?

Cost of goods sold in a periodic inventory system

c. Gross margin $78,000

*Exercise 5–26

Baker Electric Co. uses the periodic inventory system. Baker reported these amounts at May 31, 2007:

Inventory, May 31, 2006	$19,000		Freight in	$ 4,000
Inventory, May 31, 2007	21,000		Sales revenue	170,000
Purchases (of inventory)	82,000		Sales discounts	3,000
Purchase discounts	2,000		Sales returns	15,000
Purchase returns	8,000			

*This Exercise covers Chapter 5 Appendix A topics.

Compute Baker Electric Co.'s

a. Net sales revenue

b. Cost of goods sold

c. Gross margin

Serial Exercise

This exercise completes the Mark Wearing Engineers situation begun in Exercise 2–14 of Chapter 2 and extended to Exercise 3–23 of Chapter 3 and Exercise 4–15 of Chapter 4. If Exercises 2–14 or 3–23 or 4–15 were not completed, students can still complete Exercise 5–27 as it is presented.

Exercise 5–27

The engineering practice of Mark Wearing now includes a great deal of systems consulting business. In conjunction with the consulting, the business has begun selling design software. During January 2009, the business completed these transactions:

Accounting for both merchandising and service transactions under the perpetual inventory system

4. Net income $9,700

Jan.	2	Completed a consulting engagement and received cash of $17,400.
	2	Prepaid three months' office rent, $6,000.
	7	Purchased design software on account for merchandise inventory, $11,700, plus freight in, $300.
	16	Paid employee salary, $4,200.
	18	Sold design software on account, $3,300 (cost $2,100).
	19	Consulted with a client for a fee of $2,700 on account.
	21	Paid on account, $6,000.
	24	Paid utilities, $900.
	28	Sold design software for cash, $1,800 (cost $1,200).
	31	Recorded these adjusting entries:
		Accrued salary expense, $4,200.
		Prepaid rent expired, $2,000.
		Amortization of office furniture, $600.
		Physical count of inventory, $8,400

Required

1. Open the following T-accounts in the ledger: Cash, Accounts Receivable, Design Software Inventory, Prepaid Rent, Accumulated Amortization—Office Furniture, Accounts Payable, Salaries Payable, Mark Wearing, Capital, Income Summary, Service Revenue, Sales Revenue, Cost of Goods Sold, Salaries Expense, Rent Expense, Utilities Expense, and Amortization Expense—Office Furniture.

2. Journalize and post the January transactions. Key all items by date. Compute each account balance, and denote the balance as *Bal.*

3. Journalize and post the closing entries. Denote each closing amount as *Clo.* After posting, prove the equality of debits and credits in the ledger.

4. Prepare the January 2009 income statement of Mark Wearing Engineers. Use the single-step format.

Beyond the Numbers

Beyond the Numbers 5–1

Hopkin's Distributors is a provider of automotive products. The company recently reported the figures on the following page.

Evaluating a company's profitability

Gross margin in 2009 27%

Required Evaluate Hopkin's Distributors' operations during 2009 in comparison with 2008. Consider sales, gross margin, operating income, and net income. Track the gross margin percentage and inventory turnover in both years. Hopkin's Distributors' inventories at December 31, 2009, 2008, and 2007 were $46,200, $72,960 and $61,080 in thousands, respectively. In the annual report management describes the restructuring charges in 2009, the costs of down-sizing the company, as a one-time event. How does this additional information affect your evaluation?

HOPKIN'S DISTRIBUTORS
Consolidated Statements of Operations (Adapted)
For the Years Ended July 31, 2009 and 2008

	2009	2008
Sales..	$660,000	$492,000
Cost of sales	480,000	366,000
Gross margin..	180,000	126,000
Cost and expenses:		
Selling, general, and administrative............	132,000	102,000
Amortization..	12,000	5,400
Restructuring charges.................................	42,000	—
	186,000	107,400
Operating income (loss)	(6,000)	18,600
Other items (summarized).............................	(3,600)	(7,800)
Net income (loss)...	$ (9,600)	$ 10,800

Ethical Issue

Falkland Bearing Company makes all sales of industrial bearings under terms of FOB shipping point. The company usually receives orders for sales approximately one week before shipping inventory to customers. For orders received late in December, Bob Falkland, the owner, decides when to ship the goods. If profits are already at an acceptable level, the company delays shipment until January. If profits are lagging behind expectations, the company ships the goods during December.

Required

1. Under Falkland Bearing Company's FOB policy, when should the company record a sale?
2. Do you approve or disapprove of Falkland Bearing Company's means of deciding when to ship goods to customers? If you approve, give your reason. If you disapprove, identify a better way to decide when to ship goods. (There is no accounting rule against Falkland Bearing Company's practice.)

Problems (Group A)

Explaining the perpetual inventory system

Problem 5–1A

Canadian Tire is one of the largest retailers in Canada. The hardware department of Canadian Tire purchases tools from many well-known manufacturers. Canadian Tire uses a sophisticated perpetual inventory system.

Required

You are the manager of a Canadian Tire store in Edmonton. Write a memo to a new employee in the hardware department that explains how the company accounts for the purchase and sale of merchandise inventory.

Use the following heading for your memo:

Date:	_____
To:	New Employee
From:	Store Manager
Subject:	Canadian Tire's accounting system for inventories

Problem 5–2A

The following transactions occurred between BioTech Pharmaceuticals and Morrison Drug Store during February of the current year.

Feb. 6   Morrison purchased $50,000 of merchandise from BioTech on credit terms of 2/10, n/30, FOB shipping point. Separately, Morrison paid a $2,000 bill for freight in. BioTech invoiced Morrison for $50,000 (these goods cost BioTech $33,000).

      10   Morrison returned $7,000 of the merchandise purchased on February 6. BioTech issued a credit memo for this amount and returned the goods to inventory (cost, $4,800).

      15   Morrison paid $24,000 of the invoice amount owed to BioTech for the February 6 purchase. This payment included none of the freight charge.

      27   Morrison paid the remaining amount owed to BioTech for the February 6 purchase.

Required   Journalize these transactions, first on the books of Morrison Drug Store and second on the books of Biotech Pharmaceuticals.

Problem 5–3A

Wong Distributing Company engaged in the following transactions during May of the current year:

May 3   Purchased office supplies for cash, $5,400.

      7   Purchased inventory on credit terms of 3/10, net eom, $36,000.

      8   Returned half the inventory purchased on May 7. It was not the inventory ordered.

      10   Sold goods for cash, $8,100 (cost, $4,500).

      13   Sold inventory on credit terms of 2/15, n/45, for $70,200, less $10,800 quantity discount offered to customers who purchased in large quantities (cost, $32,400).

      16   Paid the amount owed on account from the purchase of May 7, less the discount and the return.

      17   Received wrong-sized inventory as a sales return from May 13 sale, $16,200, which is the net amount after the quantity discount. Wong's cost of the inventory received was $10,800.

      18   Purchased inventory of $72,000 on account. Payment terms were 2/10, net 30.

      26   Paid supplier for goods purchased on May 18, less the discount.

      28   Received cash in full settlement of the account from the customer who purchased inventory on May 13, less the discount and the return.

      29   Purchased inventory for cash, $36,000, less a quantity discount of $7,200, plus freight charges of $2,880.

Required   Journalize the preceding transactions on the books of Wong Distributing Company.

Problem 5–4A

The trial balance of Cameron's Fine Gems's pertains to December 31, 2008 and is shown on the top of the next page.

Additional data at December 31, 2008:

a. Rent expense for the year, $24,000.

b. Jewellery-making equipment has an estimated useful life of ten years and is expected to have no value when it is retired from service.

c. Accrued salaries at December 31, $3,240.

d. Accrued interest expense at December 31, $1,296.

e. Inventory based on the inventory count on December 31, $175,680.

Required   Complete Cameron's Fine Gems' work sheet for the year ended December 31, 2008.

Accounting for the purchase and sale of inventory under the perpetual inventory system

(2)

Feb. 27 Cash amount $19,000

Journalizing purchase and sale transactions under the perpetual inventory system

(2)

May 29 Cash Payment $31,680

Excel Spreadsheet Template

Preparing a merchandiser's work sheet under the perpetual inventory system

(3)

Net income $119,904

CAMERON'S FINE GEMS
Trial Balance
December 31, 2008

Cash	$ 3,048	
Accounts receivable	10,632	
Inventory	177,360	
Prepaid rent	10,560	
Jewellery-making equipment	53,040	
Accumulated amortization—equipment		$ 20,112
Accounts payable		15,096
Salary payable		0
Interest payable		0
Note payable, long-term		43,200
M. Cameron, capital		134,208
M. Cameron, withdrawals	94,920	
Sales revenue		408,360
Cost of goods sold	162,888	
Salary expense	59,280	
Rent expense	18,480	
Advertising expense	10,824	
Utilities expense	9,312	
Amortization expense—equipment	0	
Insurance expense	6,648	
Interest expense	3,984	
Total	$620,976	$620,976

Journalizing the adjusting and closing entries of a merchandising business under the perpetual inventory system

2. Dec. 31, 2008 Capital bal. $159,192

Excel Spreadsheet Template

Preparing a multi-step income statement and a classified balance sheet under the perpetual inventory system

1. Net income $260,610

Problem 5–5A

Refer to the data in Problem 5–4A.

Required

1. Journalize the adjusting and closing entries.
2. Determine the December 31, 2008, balance of Capital for Cameron's Fine Gems.

Problem 5–6A

Items from the accounts of High River Distributors at May 31, 2009, follow, listed in alphabetical order. The General Expenses account summarizes all operating expenses.

Accounts payable	$ 51,000	Interest revenue	$ 510
Accounts receivable	127,500	Inventory: May 31, 2009	167,025
Accumulated amortization —equipment	96,900	Notes payable, long-term	114,750
		Salaries payable	7,140
C. Rivers, capital	146,625	Sales discounts	26,520
C. Rivers, withdrawals	46,840	Sales returns and allowances	45,900
Cash	19,890	Sales revenue	1,991,550
Cost of goods sold	986,850	Selling expenses	357,000
Equipment	340,760	Supplies	13,005
General expenses	306,000	Unearned sales revenue	35,190
Interest expense	9,180		
Interest payable	2,805		

Required

1. Prepare the business's multi-step income statement for the year ended May 31, 2009.
2. Prepare High River Distributors' classified balance sheet in *report format* at May 31, 2009. Show your computation of the May 31, 2009, balance of Capital.

Problem 5–7A

1. Use the data of Problem 5–6A to prepare High River Distributors' *single-step* income statement for the year ended May 31, 2009.
2. Prepare High River Distributors' classified balance sheet in report format at May 31, 2009. Show your computation of the May 31 balance of Capital.

Preparing a single-step income statement and a balance sheet under the perpetual inventory system

2. Total assets $571,280

Problem 5–8A

The adjusted trial balance of Grande Prairie Products at November 30, 2008, is shown below.

Required

1. Journalize Grande Prairie Products' closing entries.
2. Compute the gross margin percentage and the rate of inventory turnover for 2008. Inventory on hand one year ago was $12,600. For 2007, Grande Prairie Products' gross margin percentage was 50 percent, and inventory turnover was 4.9 times during the year. Does the two-year trend in these ratios suggest improvement or deterioration in profitability?

Making closing entries; computing gross margin percentage and inventory turnover under the perpetual inventory system

2. Gross margin % for 2008 53.9%

Account Title	Adjusted Trial Balance	
	Debit	Credit
Cash	4,000	
Accounts receivable	38,500	
Inventory	17,400	
Supplies	400	
Furniture	39,600	
Accumulated amortization—furniture		8,700
Accounts payable		13,600
Salary payable		900
Unearned sales revenue		6,800
Note payable, long-term		15,000
A. Curtis, capital		36,400
A. Curtis, withdrawals	42,000	
Sales revenue		185,000
Sales returns	7,000	
Cost of goods sold	82,000	
Selling expenses	19,000	
General expenses	15,000	
Interest expense	1,500	
Total	266,400	266,400

Problem 5–9A

Dryden Distributors uses the perpetual inventory method in tracking its inventory purchases and sales. All sales that result in a return, allowance, or discount are tracked in separate accounts in order to give management the proper information to control operations. The following information is available for the month of April 2009:

Under the perpetual inventory system, accounting for the purchase and sale of inventory, computing cost of goods sold and gross margin, using the gross margin percentage to evaluate a business

3. Gross margin $59,440

April	1	Inventory on hand at the beginning of the month was $110,400.
	2	Purchased $40,000 of merchandise from Smith Ltd., terms 2/10, n/30. The goods were expected to be resold for $88,000.
	4	Sold merchandise for $56,000 to Coast Ltd., terms 2/10, n/60. The goods had a cost of $32,000 to Dryden Distributors.
	6	Dryden Distributors returned $16,000 of defective merchandise purchased from Smith Ltd. on April 2.
	8	Sold merchandise for $64,000 on account; the goods had a cost of $48,000.
	9	Purchased $72,000 of merchandise from Goodwin Inc., terms 2/10, n/30.
	10	Dryden Distributors paid the balance owing to Smith Ltd.
	12	Dryden Distributors accepted the return of half of the merchandise sold on April 8 as it was not compatible with the customer's needs. The goods were returned to inventory and a cash refund paid.
	18	Paid the balance owing to Goodwin Inc. from the purchase of April 9.
	20	Sold merchandise for $32,000 to Prairie Ltd., terms 2/10, n/60. The goods had cost $24,000.

April 22   Prairie Ltd. complained about the quality of goods it received, and Dryden Distributors gave an allowance of $4,000.

      25   Purchased $48,000 of merchandise for cash and paid $4,000 for freight.

      29   Dryden Distributors sold merchandise for $48,000 to Atlantic Inc., terms 2/10, n/30. The goods had cost $24,000. The terms of the sale were FOB shipping point, but, as a convenience, Dryden prepaid $3,200 of freight for Atlantic Inc.

      30   Collected the balance owing from Prairie Ltd.

Required

1. Record any journal entries required for the above transactions.

2. What is the inventory balance on April 30, 2009?

3. Prepare a multi-step income statement, to the point of gross margin, for the month of April 2009.

4. The average gross margin percentage for the industry is 50 percent; how does Dryden Distributors compare with the industry?

Problem 5–10A

Under the perpetual inventory system, computing cost of goods sold and gross margin, adjusting and closing the accounts of a merchandising company, preparing a merchandiser's financial statements

3 4 5

2. Net loss $60,350

Outdoor Adventures has the following account balances (in alphabetical order) on July 31, 2008:

Accounts payable	$ 10,875
Accounts receivable	11,625
Accumulated amortization—equipment	32,250
Cash	3,750
Cost of goods sold	342,375
E. Correa, capital	181,875
E. Correa, withdrawals	7,500
Equipment	90,000
Interest earned	3,000
Inventory	70,125
Operating expenses	180,750
Sales discounts	4,125
Sales returns and allowances	28,500
Sales revenues	517,500
Supplies	14,250
Unearned sales revenue	7,500

Note: For simplicity, all operating expenses have been summarized in the account Operating Expenses.

Additional data at July 31, 2008:

a. A physical count of items showed $1,500 of supplies on hand.

b. An inventory count showed inventory on hand at July 31, 2008, $66,400.

c. The equipment has an estimated useful life of eight years and is expected to have no value at the end of its life.

d. Unearned sales revenues of $2,625 were earned by July 31, 2008.

Required

1. Record all adjustments and closing entries that would be required on July 31, 2008.

2. Prepare the financial statements of Outdoor Adventures for the year ended July 31, 2008.

*Problem 5–11A

Accounting for the purchase and sale of inventory under the periodic system

6

The following transactions occurred between BioTech Pharmaceuticals and Morrison Drug Store during February of the current year.

Feb. 6   Morrison purchased $50,000 of merchandise from BioTech on credit terms 2/10, n/30, FOB shipping point. Separately, Morrison paid a $2,000 bill for freight in. BioTech invoiced Morrison for $50,000.

      10   Morrison returned $7,000 of the merchandise purchased on February 6. BioTech issued a credit memo for this amount.

---

*This Problem covers Chapter 5 Appendix A topics.

Feb 15   Morrison paid $24,000 of the invoice amount owed to BioTech for the February 6 purchase. This payment included none of the freight charge.

27   Morrison paid the remaining amount owed to BioTech for the February 6 purchase.

Required   Journalize these transactions, first on the books of Morrison Drug Store and second on the books of BioTech Pharmaceuticals.

*Problem 5–12A

Wong Distributing Company engaged in the following transactions during May of the current year:

Journalizing purchase and sale transactions under the periodic inventory system

May   3   Purchased office supplies for cash, $5,400.

7   Purchased inventory on credit terms of 3/10, net eom, $36,000.

8   Returned half the inventory purchased on May 7. It was not the inventory ordered.

10   Sold goods for cash, $8,100.

13   Sold inventory on credit terms of 2/15, n/45 for $70,200, less $10,800 quantity discount offered to customers who purchased in large quantities.

16   Paid the amount owed on account from the purchase of May 7, less the discount and the return.

17   Received wrong-sized inventory returned from May 13 sale, $16,200, which is the net amount after the quantity discount.

18   Purchased inventory of $72,000 on account. Payment terms were 2/10, net 30.

26   Paid supplier for goods purchased on May 18, less the discount.

28   Received cash in full settlement of the account from the customer who purchased inventory on May 13, less the discount and the return.

29   Purchased inventory for cash, $36,000, less a quantity discount of $7,200, plus freight charges of $2,880.

Required   Journalize the preceding transactions on the books of Wong Distributing Company.

*Problem 5–13A

The trial balance of Cameron's Fine Gems pertains to December 31, 2008 and is shown here.

Preparing a merchandiser's work sheet under the periodic inventory system

Net income $119,904

CAMERON'S FINE GEMS
Trial Balance
December 31, 2008

Cash	$ 3,048	
Accounts receivable	10,632	
Inventory	168,400	
Prepaid rent	10,560	
Jewellery-making equipment	53,040	
Accumulated amortization—equipment		$ 20,112
Accounts payable		15,096
Salary payable		0
Interest payable		0
Note payable, long-term		43,200
M. Cameron, capital		134,208
M. Cameron, withdrawals	94,920	
Sales revenue		408,360
Purchases	171,848	
Salary expense	59,280	
Rent expense	18,480	
Advertising expense	10,824	
Utilities expense	9,312	
Amortization expense—equipment	0	
Insurance expense	6,648	
Interest expense	3,984	
Total	$620,976	$620,976

*This Problem covers Chapter 5 Appendix A topics.

Additional data at December 31, 2008:

a. Rent expense for the year, $24,000.

b. Jewellery-making equipment has an estimated useful life of ten years and is expected to have no value when it is retired from service.

c. Accrued salaries at December 31, $3,240.

d. Accrued interest expense at December 31, $1,296.

e. Inventory based on the inventory count on December 31, $175,680.

Required   Complete Cameron's Fine Gems work sheet for the year ended December 31, 2008.

*Problem 5–14A

Refer to the data in Problem 5–13A.

Required

1. Journalize the adjusting and closing entries.

2. Determine the December 31, 2009, balance of Capital for Cameron's Fine Gems.

*Problem 5–15A

Items from the accounts of High River Distributors at May 31, 2009, follow, listed in alphabetical order. The General Expenses account summarizes all operating expenses.

Accounts payable	$ 51,000	Interest revenue	$	510
Accounts receivable	127,500	Inventory: May 31, 2008		152,500
Accumulated amortization		Notes payable, long-term		114,750
—equipment	96,900	Purchases		1,001,375
C. Rivers, capital	146,625	Salaries payable		7,140
C. Rivers, withdrawals	46,840	Sales discounts		26,520
Cash	19,890	Sales returns and allowances		45,900
Equipment	340,760	Sales revenue		1,991,550
General expenses	306,000	Selling expenses		357,000
Interest expense	9,180	Supplies		13,005
Interest payable	2,805	Unearned sales revenue		35,190

Required

1. Prepare the business's multi-step income statement for the year ended May 31, 2009. A physical count of inventory on May 31, 2009 valued it at $167,025.

2. Prepare High River Distributors' classified balance sheet in *report format* at May 31, 2009. Show your computation of the May 31, 2009, balance of Capital.

*Problem 5–16A

1. Use the data of Problem 5–15A to prepare High River Distributors' *single-step* income statement for the year ended May 31, 2009.

2. Prepare High River Distributors' classified balance sheet in report format at May 31, 2009. Show your computation of the May 31 balance of Capital.

*Problem 5–17A

Selected accounts from the accounting records of Ozel Security had the balances shown below at November 30, 2008.

Purchases of inventory	$120,000
Selling expenses	8,000
Furniture and fixtures	34,000
Purchase returns and allowances	900
Salaries payable	300

*This Problem covers Chapter 5 Appendix A topics.

Journalizing the adjusting and closing entries of a merchandising business under the periodic inventory system

 3

Dec. 31, 2009 Capital bal. $159,192

Preparing a multi-step income statement and a classified balance sheet under the periodic inventory system

 9

1. Net income $260,610

Preparing a single-step income statement and a balance sheet under the periodic inventory system

 9

2. Total assets $571,280

Computing cost of goods sold and gross margin in a periodic inventory system; evaluating the business

 1 5 9

1. Gross margin $51,300

N. Ozel, capital	$ 27,900
Sales revenue	177,000
Sales returns and allowances	2,900
Inventory: November 30, 2007	38,000
November 30, 2008	37,000
Accounts payable	8,600
Cash	3,400
Freight in	1,400
Accumulated amortization—furniture and fixtures	12,300
Purchase discounts	600
Sales discounts	1,900
General expenses	18,000

Required

1. Show the computation of Ozel Security's net sales, cost of goods sold, and gross margin for the year ended November 30, 2008.

2. Nancy Ozel, the proprietor of Ozel Security, strives to earn a gross margin percentage of 25 percent. Did she achieve this goal?

3. Did the rate of inventory turnover reach the industry average of 3.4 times per year?

Problems (Group B)

Problem 5–1B

Explaining the perpetual inventory system

Jarvis Optical is a regional chain of optical shops in Manitoba. The company offers a large selection of eyeglass frames, and Jarvis Optical stores provide while-you-wait service. Jarvis Optical has launched a vigorous advertising campaign promoting its two-for-the-price-of-one frame sale.

Required

Jarvis Optical expects to grow rapidly and increase its level of inventory. As chief accountant of the company, you wish to install a perpetual inventory system. Write a memo to the company president to explain how the system would work.

Use the following heading for your memo:

```
Date: _____

To:      Company President

From:   Chief Accountant

Subject: How a perpetual inventory system works
```

Problem 5–2B

Accounting for the purchase and sale of inventory under the perpetual inventory system

June 26 cash entry $6,900

The following transactions occurred between Martin Pharmaceuticals and Jones Drug Stores during June of the current year.

June   8   Jones purchased $14,700 of merchandise from Martin on credit terms 2/10, n/30, FOB shipping point. Separately, Jones paid freight in of $300. Martin invoiced Jones for $14,700. These goods cost Martin $6,300.

      11   Jones returned $1,800 of the merchandise purchased on June 8. Martin issued a credit memo for this amount and returned the goods, in excellent condition, to inventory (cost $750).

      17   Jones paid $6,000 of the invoice amount owed to Martin for the June 8 purchase. This payment included none of the freight charge. Jones took the purchase discount on the partial payment.

      26   Jones paid the remaining amount owed to Martin for the June 8 purchase.

Required   Journalize these transactions, first on the books of Jones Drug Stores, and second on the books of Martin Pharmaceuticals.

Journalizing purchase and
sale transactions under the
perpetual inventory system

July 21 cash payment $15,470

Problem 5–3B

Sznadel Furniture Company engaged in the following transactions during July of the current year:

July	2	Purchased inventory for cash, $4,800, less a quantity discount of $900.
	5	Purchased store supplies on credit terms of net eom, $2,700.
	8	Purchased inventory of $18,000 less a quantity discount of 10%, plus freight charges of $920. Credit terms are 3/15, n/30.
	9	Sold goods for cash, $7,200. Sznadel's cost of these goods was $4,200.
	11	Returned $1,200 (net amount after the quantity discount) of the inventory purchased on July 8. It was damaged in shipment.
	12	Purchased inventory on credit terms of 3/10, n/30, $20,000.
	14	Sold inventory on credit terms of 2/10, n/30, for $57,600, less a $3,600 quantity discount (cost, $30,000).
	16	Received and paid the electricity bill, $1,600.
	20	Received returned inventory from the July 14 sale, $2,400 (net amount after the quantity discount). Sznadel shipped the wrong goods by mistake. Sznadel's cost of the inventory received was $1,500.
	21	Paid supplier for goods purchased on July 8 less the discount and the return.
	23	Received $41,160 cash in partial settlement of the account from the customer who purchased inventory on July 14. Granted the customer a 2% discount and credited his account receivable for $42,000.
	30	Paid for the store supplies purchased on July 5.

Required Journalize the preceding transactions on the books of Sznadel Furniture Company.

Excel Spreadsheet Template

Preparing a merchandiser's work
sheet under the perpetual
inventory system

Net income $163,230

Problem 5–4B

Brooke Produce Company's trial balance below pertains to December 31, 2008.

BROOKE PRODUCE COMPANY
Trial Balance
December 31, 2008

Cash	$ 13,095	
Accounts receivable	29,520	
Inventory	457,920	
Store supplies	8,955	
Prepaid insurance	14,400	
Store fixtures	287,550	
Accumulated amortization—fixtures		$ 169,380
Accounts payable		133,965
Salaries payable		0
Interest payable		0
Notes payable, long-term		167,400
F. Brooke, capital		284,040
F. Brooke, withdrawals	163,350	
Sales revenue		1,288,665
Cost of goods sold	724,905	
Salaries expense	209,610	
Rent expense	65,835	
Utilities expense	30,510	
Amortization expense—fixtures	0	
Insurance expense	23,850	
Store supplies expense	0	
Interest expense	13,950	
Total	$2,043,450	$2,043,450

Additional data at December 31, 2008:

a. Insurance expense for the year should total $27,255.

b. Store fixtures have an estimated useful life of ten years and are expected to have no value when they are retired from service.

c. Accrued salaries at December 31, $5,670.

d. Accrued interest expense at December 31, $3,915.

e. Store supplies on hand at December 31, $3,420.

f. Inventory based on the inventory count on December 31, $448,425.

Required Complete Brooke Produce Company's work sheet for the year ended December 31, 2008. Key adjustments by letter.

Problem 5–5B

Refer to the data in Problem 5–4B.

Required

1. Journalize the adjusting and closing entries of Brooke Produce Company.
2. Determine the December 31, 2008 balance in the Capital account.

Journalizing the adjusting and closing entries of a merchandising business under the perpetual inventory system

2. Dec. 31, 2008 Capital bal. $283,920

Problem 5–6B

For simplicity, all operating expenses are summarized in the accounts Selling Expenses and General Expenses. Selected accounts of Edwards Sheds, at July 31, 2009, are listed in alphabetical order below.

Excel Spreadsheet Template

Preparing a multi-step income statement and a classified balance sheet under the perpetual inventory system

1. Net loss $31,500

Accounts payable	$238,688	Inventory: July 31, 2009	$351,180
Accounts receivable	58,500	Notes payable, long-term	300,000
Accumulated amortization		Salaries payable	11,450
—store equipment	30,750	Sales discounts	15,560
B. Edwards, capital	125,800	Sales returns and	
B. Edwards, withdrawals	21,213	allowances	33,575
Cash	23,060	Sales revenue	996,750
Cost of goods sold	676,690	Selling expenses	158,625
General expenses	142,125	Store equipment	236,250
Interest expense	2,250	Supplies	8,050
Interest payable	5,625	Unearned sales revenue	17,440
Interest revenue	575		

Required

1. Prepare the entity's multi-step income statement for the year ended July 31, 2009.
2. Prepare Edwards Sheds' classified balance sheet in *report format* at July 31, 2009. Show separately your computation of the July 31, 2009, balance of B. Edwards, Capital.

Problem 5–7B

1. Use the data of Problem 5–6B to prepare Edwards Sheds' *single-step* income statement for the year ended July 31, 2009.
2. Prepare Edwards Sheds' classified balance sheet in *report format* at July 31, 2009. Show your computation of the July 31 balance of B. Edwards, Capital.

Preparing a single-step income statement and a classified balance sheet under the perpetual inventory system

2. Total assets $646,290

Problem 5–8B

The adjusted trial balance of Bonds Trading Company at September 30, 2008, appears on the next page.

Required

1. Journalize Bonds Trading Company's closing entries.
2. Compute the gross margin percentage and the rate of inventory turnover for 2008. Inventory on hand at September 30, 2007, was $40,000. For 2007, Bonds Trading Company's gross

Making closing entries; computing gross margin percentage and inventory turnover under the perpetual inventory system

2. Gross margin % in 2008 46.1%

margin percentage was 50 percent and the inventory turnover rate was 3.0 times. Does the two-year trend in these ratios suggest improvement or deterioration in profitability?

Account Title	Adjusted Trial Balance	
	Debit	Credit
Cash	7,000	
Accounts receivable..	4,500	
Inventory...	42,000	
Supplies...	1,500	
Building..	140,000	
Accumulated depreciation—building		29,000
Accounts payable...		11,000
Salary payable		200
Unearned sales revenue...................................		1,600
Note payable, long-term		30,000
B. Bonds, capital..		111,600
B. Bonds, withdrawals	45,000	
Sales revenue		201,400
Sales returns..	14,000	
Cost of goods sold	101,000	
Selling expenses	17,900	
General expenses	9,900	
Interest expense...	2,000	
Total	384,800	384,800

Under the perpetual inventory system, accounting for the purchase and sale of inventory, computing cost of goods sold and gross margin, using the gross margin percentage to evaluate a business

3. Gross margin $32,904

Problem 5–9B

Hartley Distributors uses the perpetual inventory method in tracking its inventory purchases and sales. All sales that result in a return, allowance, or discount are tracked in separate accounts in order to give management the proper information to control operations. The following information is available for the month of April 2008:

April 1   The balance of inventory on hand at the beginning of the month was $159,750.

2   Purchased $18,000 of merchandise from Grier Corp., terms 2/10, n/30. The goods were expected to be resold for $40,500.

4   Sold merchandise for $27,000 to Armstrong Ltd., terms 2/10, n/60. The goods had a cost of $13,500 to Hartley.

6   Hartley returned $4,500 of defective merchandise purchased from Grier Corp. on April 2.

8   Sold merchandise for $40,500 cash; the goods had a cost of $27,000.

9   Purchased $36,000 of merchandise from Robson Corp., terms 2/10, n/30.

10   Hartley paid the balance owing to Grier Corp.

12   Hartley accepted the return of half of the merchandise sold on April 8 as it was not compatible with the customer's needs. The goods were returned to stock and a cash refund paid.

18   Paid the balance owing to Robson Corp. for the purchase of April 9.

20   Sold merchandise for $22,500 to Clearbrook Ltd., terms 2/10, n/60. The goods had cost $15,750.

22   Clearbrook Ltd. complained about the quality of goods it received, and Hartley gave an allowance of $2,700.

25   Purchased $31,500 of merchandise for cash and paid $1,500 for freight.

29   Hartley sold merchandise for $22,500 to Golden Ltd., terms 2/10, n/30. The goods had cost $13,500. The terms of the sale were FOB shipping point, but, as a convenience, Hartley prepaid $1,350 of freight for Golden Ltd. and included the charge on its invoice.

30   Collected the balance owing from Clearbrook Ltd.

Required

1. Record any journal entries required for the above transactions.

2. What is the inventory balance on April 30, 2008?

3. Prepare a multi-step income statement, to the point of gross margin, for the month of April 2008.

4. The average gross margin percentage for the industry is 48 percent; how does Hartley Distributors compare to the industry?

Problem 5–10B

Park Sports Products has the following account balances (in alphabetical order) on August 31, 2009:

Accounts payable	$ 41,760
Accounts receivable	44,640
Accumulated amortization—equipment	123,840
Cash	14,400
C. Park, capital	453,600
C. Park, withdrawals	28,800
Cost of goods sold	796,320
Equipment	309,600
Interest earned	11,520
Inventory	269,280
Operating expenses	564,480
Sales discounts	15,840
Sales returns and allowances	109,440
Sales revenues	1,548,000
Supplies	54,720
Unearned sales revenue	28,800

Note: For simplicity, all operating expenses have been summarized in the account Operating Expenses.

Additional data at August 31, 2009:

a. A physical count of items showed $936 of supplies were on hand.

b. An inventory count showed inventory on hand at August 31, 2009, $259,200.

c. The equipment is expected to last five years and have no value at the end of five years.

d. Unearned sales of $7,200 were earned by August 31, 2009.

Required

1. Record all adjustments and closing entries that would be required on August 31, 2009.

2. Prepare the financial statements of Park Sports Products for the year ended August 31, 2009.

*Problem 5–11B

The following transactions occurred between Martin Pharmaceuticals and Jones Drug Stores during June of the current year.

June	6	Jones purchased $14,700 of merchandise from Martin on credit terms 2/10, n/30, FOB shipping point. Separately, Jones paid freight in of $300. Martin invoiced Jones for $14,700.
	10	Jones returned $1,800 of the merchandise purchased on February 6. Martin issued a credit memo for this amount.
	15	Jones paid $6,000 of the invoice amount owed to Martin for the February 6 purchase. This payment included none of the freight charge.
	27	Jones paid the remaining amount owed to Martin for the February 6 purchase.

Required Journalize these transactions, first on the books of Jones Drug Stores and second on the books of Martin Pharmaceuticals.

*Problem 5–12B

Sznadel Furniture Company engaged in the following transactions during July of the current year:

July	2	Purchased inventory for cash, $4,800, less a quantity discount of $900.
	5	Purchased store supplies on credit terms of net eom, $2,700.
	8	Purchased inventory of $18,000, less a quantity discount of 10%, plus freight charges of $920. Credit terms are 3/15, n/30.

*This Problem covers Chapter 5 Appendix A topics.

Under the perpetual inventory system, computing cost of goods sold and gross margin, adjusting and closing the accounts of a merchandising company, preparing a merchandiser's financial statements

2. Net loss $45,144

Accounting for the purchase and sale of inventory under the periodic system

June 27 cash amount $6,900

Journalizing purchase and sale transactions under the periodic inventory system

July 21 cash payment $15,470

July   9   Sold goods for cash, $7,200.
       11   Returned $1,200 (net amount after the quantity discount) of the inventory purchased on July 8. It was damaged in shipment.
       12   Purchased inventory on credit terms of 3/10, n/30, $20,000.
       14   Sold inventory on credit terms of 2/10, n/30, for $57,600, less a $3,600 quantity discount.
       16   Received and paid the electricity bill, $1,600.
       20   Received returned inventory from the July 14 sale, $2,400 (net amount after the quantity discount). Sznadel shipped the wrong goods by mistake.
       21   Paid supplier for goods purchased on July 8 less the discount and the return.
       23   Received $41,160 cash in partial settlement of the account from the customer who purchased inventory on July 14. Granted the customer a 2% discount and credited his account receivable for $42,000.
       30   Paid for the store supplies purchased on July 5.

Required   Journalize the preceding transactions on the books of Sznadel Furniture Company.

Preparing a merchandiser's work sheet under the periodic inventory system

Net income $163,230

*Problem 5–13B

Brooke Produce Company's trial balance below pertains to December 31, 2008.

BROOKE PRODUCE COMPANY Trial Balance December 31, 2008		
Cash	$ 13,095	
Accounts receivable	29,520	
Inventory	415,155	
Store supplies	8,955	
Prepaid insurance	14,400	
Store fixtures	287,550	
Accumulated amortization—fixtures		$ 169,380
Accounts payable		133,965
Salaries payable		0
Interest payable		0
Notes payable, long-term		167,400
F. Brooke, capital		284,040
F. Brooke, withdrawals	163,350	
Sales revenue		1,288,665
Purchases	767,670	
Salaries expense	209,610	
Rent expense	65,835	
Utilities expense	30,510	
Amortization expense—fixtures	0	
Insurance expense	23,850	
Store supplies expense	0	
Interest expense	13,950	
Total	$2,043,450	$2,043,450

Additional data at December 31, 2008:

a. Insurance expense for the year should total $27,255.

b. Store fixtures have an estimated useful life of ten years and are expected to have no value when they are retired from service.

c. Accrued salaries at December 31, $5,670.

d. Accrued interest expense at December 31, $3,915.

e. Store supplies on hand at December 31, $3,420.

f. Inventory based on the inventory count on December 31, $448,425.

Required   Complete Brooke Produce Company's work sheet for the year ended December 31, 2008. Key adjustments by letter.

*This Problem covers Chapter 5 Appendix A topics.

*Problem 5–14B

Refer to the data in Problem 5–13B.

Required

1. Journalize the adjusting and closing entries of Brooke Produce Company.
2. Determine the December 31, 2008 balance in the Capital account.

*Problem 5–15B

For simplicity, all operating expenses are summarized in the accounts Selling Expenses and General Expenses. Selected accounts of Edwards Sheds, at July 31, 2009, are listed in alphabetical order below.

Accounts payable	$238,688	Inventory: July 31, 2008	$365,000
Accounts receivable	58,500	Inventory: July 31, 2009	351,180
Accumulated amortization		Notes payable, long-term	300,000
—store equipment	30,750	Purchases	662,870
B. Edwards, capital	125,800	Salaries payable	11,450
B. Edwards, withdrawals	21,213	Sales discounts	15,560
Cash	23,060	Sales returns and allowances	33,575
Equipment	236,250	Sales revenue	996,750
General expenses	142,125	Selling expenses	158,625
Interest expense	2,250	Supplies	8,050
Interest payable	5,625	Unearned sales revenue	17,440
Interest revenue	575		

Required

1. Prepare the entity's multi-step income statement for the year ended July 31, 2009.
2. Prepare Edwards Sheds' classified balance sheet in *report format* at July 31, 2009. Show separately your computation of the July 31, 2009, balance of B. Edwards, Capital.

*Problem 5–16B

1. Use the data of Problem 5–15B to prepare Edwards Sheds' *single-step* income statement for the year ended July 31, 2009.
2. Prepare Edwards Sheds' classified balance sheet in *report format* at July 31, 2009. Show your computation of the July 31 balance of B. Edwards, Capital.

*Problem 5–17B

Selected accounts from the accounting records of Schwartz Imports at June 30, 2009, are shown below.

Cash	$ 14,280
Purchases of inventory	103,005
Freight in	4,515
Sales revenue	188,055
Purchases returns and allowances	1,470
Salaries payable	1,890
Glen Schwartz, capital	33,390
Sales returns and allowances	12,705
Inventory: June 30, 2008	24,990
June 30, 2009	29,925
Selling expense	31,290
Equipment	46,935
Purchase discounts	1,365
Accumulated amortization—equipment	7,245
Sales discounts	3,570
General expenses	17,115
Accounts payable	24,990

---

*This Problem covers Chapter 5 Appendix A topics.

Journalizing the adjusting and closing entries of a merchandising business under the periodic inventory system

2. Dec. 31, 2008 Capital bal. $283,920

Preparing a multi-step income statement and a classified balance sheet under the periodic inventory system

1.Net loss $31,500

Preparing a single-step income statement and a classified balance sheet under the periodic inventory system

2. Total assets $646,290

Computing cost of goods sold and gross margin in a periodic system; evaluating the business

1. Gross margin $72,030

Required

1. Show the computation of Schwartz Imports' net sales, cost of goods sold, and gross margin for the year ended June 30, 2009.
2. Glen Schwartz, owner of Schwartz Imports, strives to earn a gross margin percentage of 40 percent. Did he achieve this goal?
3. Did the rate of inventory turnover reach the industry average of 3.4 times per year?

Challenge Problems

Understanding purchasing and gross margin

Problem 5–1C

You have been recently hired as an accountant by Best Cellular, a small chain of stores that sells wireless products. One of your first activities is to review the accounting system for Best Cellular.

In your review, you discover that the company determines selling prices by adding a standard markup on cost of 10 percent (i.e., cost plus 10 percent of cost) to the cost of all products. The company uses a perpetual inventory system. You also discover that your predecessor, a bookkeeper, had set up the accounting system so that all purchase discounts and purchase returns and allowances were accumulated in an account that was treated as "other income" for financial statement purposes because he believed that they were financing items and not related to operations.

Megan Flowers, owner of Best Cellular, uses modern decision-making techniques in running Best Cellular. Two ratios she particularly favours are the gross margin percentage and inventory turnover ratio.

Required

1. What is a possible effect of the accounting system described on the pricing of products and thus operations of Best Cellular stores?
2. What is the effect of the accounting system instituted by your predecessor on the two ratios Ms. Flowers favours?

Using an inventory system for control

Problem 5–2C

David Chan is concerned about theft by shoplifters in his chain of three discount stores and has come to your public accounting firm for advice. Specifically, he has several questions he would like you to answer.

a. He wonders if there is any inventory system he can use that will allow him to keep track of products that leave his stores as legitimate sales and will also allow him to determine if inventory has been lost or stolen.

b. He realizes that carrying inventory is expensive. He wants to know if you have any suggestions as to how he can keep close tabs on his inventory at the three stores so he can be sure that the stores don't run out of product or have too much on hand.

c. The space in the stores is limited. David wants to install an inventory system that will tell him when a product is slow-moving or obsolete so he can clear it out and replace it with a potentially faster-moving product.

Required Indicate whether a perpetual inventory system or a periodic inventory system will provide David with answers to the three questions he has asked. Explain how the inventory system indicated will provide the specific information he has requested.

Extending Your Knowledge

Decision Problems

Decision Problem 1

Using financial statements to decide on a business expansion

④ ⑤

Net income $125,100

John Dyer owns the Meadowvale Drug Store, which has prospered during its second year of operation. To help Dyer decide whether to open another pharmacy in the area, his book-keeper has prepared the current income statement of the business.

MEADOWVALE DRUG STORE
Income Statement
For the Year Ended December 31, 2008

Sales revenue		$540,000
Interest revenue		20,000
Total revenue		560,000
Cost of goods sold		261,000
Gross margin		299,000
Operating expenses:		
Salary expense	80,000	
Rent expense	24,000	
Interest expense	8,000	
Amortization expense	18,900	
Utilities expense	5,000	
Supplies expense	3,000	
Total operating expenses		138,700
Income from operations		160,100
Other revenues:		
Sales discounts ($11,000) and returns ($24,000)		35,000
Net income		$195,100

John Dyer recently read in an industry trade journal that a successful two-year-old pharmacy meets these criteria:

a. Gross margin is at least 50%.

b. Net income is at least $150,000.

Basing his opinion on the entity's income statement data, John Dyer believes the business meets both criteria. He plans to go ahead with the expansion plan, and asks your advice on preparing the pharmacy's income statement in accordance with generally accepted accounting principles. When you point out that the income statement includes errors, John assures you that all amounts are correct.

Required Prepare a correct multi-step income statement and make a recommendation about whether to undertake the expansion at this time.

Decision Problem 2

Understanding the operating cycle of a merchandiser

① ③

Calvin Wong has come to you for advice. Earlier this year, he opened a music store in a plaza near the university he had attended. The store sells compact discs at very low prices and on special credit for students. Many of the students at the university are co-op students who alternate school and work terms. Calvin allows co-op students to buy on credit while they are on a school term, with the understanding that they will pay their account shortly after starting a work term.

Business has been very good. Calvin is sure it is because of his competitive prices and the unique credit terms he offers. His problem is that he is short of cash, and his loan with the bank has grown significantly. The bank manager has indicated that he wishes to reduce Wong's line of credit because he is worried that Calvin will get into financial difficulties.

Required

1. Explain to Wong why he, in your opinion, is short of cash.
2. Wong has asked you to explain his problem to the bank manager and to assist in asking for more credit. What might you say to the bank manager to assist Wong?

Correcting an inventory error

Decision Problem 3

The employees of Orford Furniture Company made an error when they performed the periodic inventory count at year end, October 31, 2008. Part of one warehouse was not counted and therefore was not included in inventory.

Required

1. Indicate the effect of the inventory error on cost of goods sold, gross margin, and net income for the year ended October 31, 2008.
2. Will the error affect cost of goods sold, gross margin, and net income in 2009? If so, what will be the effect?

Financial Statement Problem

Closing entries for a corporation that sells merchandise; evaluating ratio data

3. 2005 Inventory $13,331,000

This problem uses both the income statement (statement of earnings) and the balance sheet of Sun-Rype Products Ltd. in Appendix B. It will aid your understanding of the closing process of a business.

1. Journalize Sun-Rype's closing entries for the year ended December 31, 2005. You will be unfamiliar with certain revenues and expenses, but you should treat them all similarly. Make "Loss (gain) on capital dispositions" the final expense you close. Instead of closing to a Capital account, close to the Retained Earnings account (since Sun-Rype is a corporation, not a proprietorship).
2. What amount was closed to Retained Earnings? What were dividends in 2005?
3. Sun-Rype Products Ltd. is a manufacturer and distributor of juice-based beverages and fruit-based snacks. On the balance sheet, the company reports an inventory figure and the detail is provided in the notes to the financial statements. What amount is shown on the balance sheet for the inventory account for December 31, 2005, and December 31, 2004? Of these amounts, how much is raw materials in 2004 and 2005? How much is finished goods in 2004 and 2005?

Accounting for Merchandise Inventory

The Forzani Group Ltd. is the largest national retailer of sporting goods in Canada. The company, headquartered in Calgary, started with one location in 1974. Since then, the corporation has expanded aggressively throughout Canada by acquiring various regional and national chains of stores.

Forzani now operates coast-to-coast under four corporate banners: SportChek, Coast Mountain Sports, Sports Mart, and National Sports. The company is also a franchisor of these stores: Sports Experts, Intersport, RnR, Econosports, Atmosphere, Tech Shop, and Nevada Bob's. The

company operates 252 corporate stores and 194 franchise locations.

By far the largest asset on Forzani's balance sheet is inventory. In 2005, the company's year-end balance was over $278 million. For the company to be successful, it must manage its inventory very well. It has to understand the wants and needs of its customers. If it guesses wrong, it may end up with too much inventory (or too much of the wrong items). If it has too little inventory, customers may look elsewhere for items they require. Forzani recognizes this risk. In its 2005 annual report, management stated:

"Traditionally, the retail industry is influenced by a number of external factors that are difficult to actively manage. These include the overall economy, consumer spending and debt levels. Other factors such as retail competition, seasonality, changes in fashion trends can be managed."[1]

---

[1] The Forzani Group Limited 2005 Annual Report, pages 3–5.

?

Which inventory system should a merchandiser use, and
why is it important?

What are the different inventory costing methods?

How do they differ?

Which methods can and cannot be used for income-tax purposes?

Which inventory costing method should a merchandiser choose?

How can merchandisers estimate the cost of inventory destroyed in a
fire or other disaster?

These questions and others will be answered throughout this chapter. And the Decision Guidelines at the end of
this chapter will provide the answers in a useful summary.

Chapter 5 introduced the accounting for merchandise inventory.

It showed how Austin Sound Centre, a music store, recorded the purchase and
sale of its inventory. Amazon.com, Wal-Mart, and The Forzani Group Ltd. are other
merchandising companies. This chapter completes the accounting for merchandise
inventory.

SportChek, one of The Forzani Group Ltd.'s chain of stores, sells running shoes
(among many other items) for men, women, and children. SportChek, like all other
companies, may select from several different methods of accounting for its inventory.
Inventory is the first area in which a company must pick the accounting method it
will use and it is a key decision for a merchandiser. SportChek is the company we
will use to illustrate the different inventory accounting methods.

This chapter will introduce a new vocabulary, including the terms FIFO and LIFO.
By the end of this chapter, you will also be prepared to decide which accounting
method is most appropriate if you ever start your own business.

First let's review the balance sheet and the income statement, because the
financial statements show how merchandise inventory affects a company. Exhibit
6–1 gives the merchandising section of The Forzani Group Ltd.'s balance sheet and

EXHIBIT 6–1 The Forzani Group Ltd. Merchandising Section of the
Financial Statements

THE FORZANI GROUP LTD.
Balance Sheet (partial; adapted)
January 29, 2006

Assets:	(thousands)
Current assets:	
Cash	$ 19,266
Accounts receivable	68,927
Inventories	278,002 (A)
Prepaid expenses	2,647

THE FORZANI GROUP LTD.
Income Statement (partial; adapted)
For the Year Ended January 29, 2006

	(thousands)
Net sales	$1,129,404
Cost of goods sold	746,313 (B)
Gross margin	383,091 (C)

income statement. Inventories, cost of goods sold, and gross margin are labelled A, B, and C, respectively, to indicate that, throughout the chapter, we will be computing them using various accounting methods.

As you can see in Exhibit 6–1, inventory is the most significant current asset for The Forzani Group Ltd., as it is for most retail companies. Companies like Forzani want to make sure that they carry enough inventory to meet customer demand. At the same time, if companies carry too much inventory, they risk "tying up" too much of the company's assets in inventory.

The remainder of the chapter explores how to compute these amounts:

- Ending inventory on the balance sheet
- Cost of goods sold and gross margin on the income statement

We turn now to the different inventory costing methods.

Inventory Costing Methods

As we saw in Chapter 5,

$$\text{Ending inventory} = \text{Number of units } \textit{on hand} \times \text{Unit cost}$$
$$\text{Cost of goods sold} = \text{Number of units } \textit{sold} \times \text{Unit cost}$$

Companies determine the number of units from perpetual inventory records that are verified by a physical count. The cost of each unit of inventory is

$$\text{Unit cost} = \text{Purchase price} - \text{Purchase discounts} - \text{Quantity discounts}$$
$$+ \text{ Any costs necessary to put the unit in a saleable condition, such as freight in, customs duties, and insurance}$$

Exhibit 6–2 gives the inventory data for a line of running shoes carried by SportChek.

| EXHIBIT 6–2 | Perpetual Inventory Record—Quantities Only |

Item: Running Shoes, Model XL

Date	Quantity Purchased	Quantity Sold	Quantity on Hand
Nov. 1			10
5	60		70
15		40	30
26	70		100
30		80	20
Totals	130	120	20

In this illustration, SportChek began November with 10 pairs of running shoes on hand. After buying and selling, SportChek had 20 pairs at the end of the month.

Assume that SportChek's unit cost of each pair is $60. In this case,

$$\text{Ending inventory} = \textbf{Number of units } \textit{\textbf{on hand}} \textbf{ (Exhibit 6–2)} \times \textbf{Unit cost}$$
$$= \quad\quad\quad 20 \quad\quad\quad\quad\quad \times \quad \$60$$
$$= \$1,200$$

$$\text{Cost of goods sold} = \textbf{Number of units } \textit{\textbf{sold}} \textbf{ (Exhibit 6–2)} \quad \times \textbf{Unit cost}$$
$$= \quad\quad\quad 120 \quad\quad\quad\quad\quad \times \quad \$60$$
$$= \$7,200$$

What would SportChek's ending inventory and cost of goods sold be if the cost of these running shoes increased from $60 to $65 or $70 during the period? Companies face price increases like these all the time. To determine inventory costs, the accounting profession has developed several costing methods.

Measuring inventory cost is easy when prices are constant. However, in reality, the unit cost often changes. A pair of running shoes that cost SportChek $60 in January may cost $65 in April. Suppose SportChek sells 10,000 pairs of these running shoes in November. How many of the shoes cost $60? How many cost $65? To compute ending inventory and cost of goods sold, SportChek must assign a unit cost to each item. The four costing methods GAAP allow are

1. Specific-unit cost
2. Weighted-average cost
3. First-in, first-out (FIFO) cost
4. Last-in, first-out (LIFO) cost

A company can use any of these methods to account for its inventory.

The **specific-unit-cost method** is also called the **specific identification method**. This method uses the specific cost of each unit of inventory for items that have a distinctive identity. Some businesses deal in items that differ from unit to unit, such as automobiles, jewels, and real estate. For instance, a Toyota dealer may have two vehicles—a model with serial number 010 that costs $21,000 and a model with serial number 020 that costs $27,000. If the dealer sells the model with serial number 020, cost of goods sold is $27,000, the cost of the specific unit. Suppose the model with serial number 010 is the only unit left in inventory at the end of the period; ending inventory is $21,000, the dealer's cost of that particular car.

Amazon.ca uses the specific-unit-cost method to account for its inventory. But very few other companies use this method, and so we shift to the more popular inventory costing methods. These methods are *cost-flow assumptions* that do not have to match the actual flow of inventory costs. Exhibit 6–3 illustrates how each method works.

- Under the first-in, first-out (FIFO) method, the cost of goods sold is based on the oldest purchases. This is illustrated by the cost of goods sold coming from the *bottom* of the container.
- Under the last-in, first-out (LIFO) method, the cost of goods sold is based on the most recent purchase. This is illustrated by the cost of goods sold coming from the *top* of the container.
- Under the weighted-average method, the cost of goods sold is based on an average cost for the period. This is illustrated by the cost of goods sold coming from the *middle* of the container.

Now let's see how to compute inventory amounts under the FIFO, LIFO, and weighted-average cost method. We use the following transaction data for all the illustrations:

Running Shoes, Model XL	Number of Units	UnitCost
Nov. 1 Beginning inventory	10	$60
5 Purchase	60	65
15 Sale	40	
26 Purchase	70	70
30 Sale	80	

We begin with inventory costing in a perpetual system.

KEY POINT

The four inventory costing methods affect the cost of inventory and, consequently, cost of goods sold. The method used does *not* have to match the physical flow of goods.

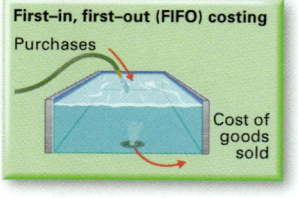
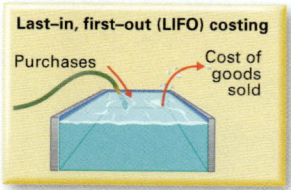
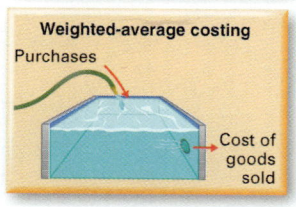

EXHIBIT 6–3

Cost Flows for the Three Most Popular Inventory Methods

First–in, first–out (FIFO) costing
Purchases
Cost of goods sold

Last–in, first–out (LIFO) costing
Purchases
Cost of goods sold

Weighted-average costing
Purchases
Cost of goods sold

KEY POINT

Remember that the terms *FIFO* and *LIFO* describe which goods are sold, *not* which goods are left. FIFO assumes that goods in first are sold first; therefore, the last goods purchased are left in ending inventory. LIFO assumes that the last goods in are sold first; therefore, the first goods purchased are left in ending inventory.

Inventory Costing in a Perpetual System

The inventory costing methods produce different amounts for:

- Ending inventory
- Cost of goods sold

Objective 1

Account for perpetual inventory under the FIFO, LIFO, and moving-weighted-average cost methods

First-in, First-out (FIFO) Method

Many companies use the **first-in, first-out (FIFO) method** to account for their inventory. FIFO costing is consistent with the physical movement of inventory for most companies. That is, they sell their oldest inventory first.

Under FIFO, the first costs incurred by SportChek each period are the first costs assigned to cost of goods sold. FIFO leaves in ending inventory the last—the most recent—costs incurred during the period. This is illustrated in the FIFO perpetual inventory record in Exhibit 6–4.

EXHIBIT 6–4 Perpetual Inventory Record—FIFO Cost for SportChek

Running Shoes, Model XL

Date	Purchases Qty.	Purchases Unit Cost	Purchases Total Cost	Cost of Goods Sold Qty.	Cost of Goods Sold Unit Cost	Cost of Goods Sold Total Cost	Inventory on Hand Qty.	Inventory on Hand Unit Cost	Inventory on Hand Total Cost
Nov. 1							10	$60	$ 600
5	60	$65	$3,900				10	60	600
							60	65	3,900
15				10	$60	$ 600			
				30	65	1,950	30	65	1,950
26	70	70	4,900				30	65	1,950
							70	70	4,900
30				30	65	1,950			
				50	70	3,500	20	70	1,400
30	130		$8,800	120		$8,000	20		$1,400

SportChek began November with 10 pairs of running shoes that cost $60. After the November 5 purchase, the inventory on hand consists of 70 units.

$$70 \text{ units on hand} \begin{cases} 10 @ \$60 = \$\ 600 \\ 60 @ \$65 = \underline{3,900} \end{cases}$$
$$\text{Inventory on hand} = \underline{\underline{\$4,500}}$$

On November 15, SportChek sold 40 units. Under FIFO, the first 10 units sold are costed at the oldest cost ($60 per unit). The next 30 units sold come from the group that cost $65 per unit. That leaves 30 units in inventory on hand, and those units cost $65 each. The remainder of the inventory record follows that same pattern.

The FIFO monthly summary at November 30 is

- Cost of goods sold: 120 units that cost a total of $8,000
- Ending inventory: 20 units that cost a total of $1,400

If SportChek used the FIFO method, it would measure cost of goods sold and inventory in this manner to prepare its financial statements.

Journal Entries Under FIFO

The journal entries under FIFO follow the data in Exhibit 6–4. For example, on November 5, SportChek purchased $3,900 of inventory and made the first journal entry. On November 15, SportChek sold 40 pairs of running shoes for the sale price of $100 each. SportChek recorded the sale ($4,000) and the cost of goods sold ($2,550). The remaining journal entries (November 26 and 30) follow the inventory data in Exhibit 6–4.

FIFO Journal Entries: (All purchases and sales on account. The sale price of a pair of running shoes is $100 per unit.)

Nov.	5	Inventory...	3,900	
		Accounts Payable..		3,900
		Purchased inventory on account (60 × $65 = $3,900).		
	15	Accounts Receivable..	4,000	
		Sales Revenue..		4,000
		Sale on account (40 × $100 = $4,000).		
	15	Cost of Goods Sold	2,550	
		Inventory..		2,550
		Cost of goods sold ($600 + $1,950 = $2,550).		
	26	Inventory...	4,900	
		Accounts Payable..		4,900
		Purchased inventory on account (70 × $70 = $4,900).		
	30	Accounts Receivable..	8,000	
		Sales Revenue..		8,000
		Sale on account (80 × $100 = $8,000).		
	30	Cost of Goods Sold	5,450	
		Inventory..		5,450
		Cost of goods sold ($1,950 + $3,500 = $5,450).		

Last-in, First-out (LIFO) Method

Under the **last-in, first-out (LIFO) method,** cost of goods sold comes from the newest—the most recent—purchases. Ending inventory's cost comes from the oldest costs of the period. LIFO costing does not follow the physical movement of goods for most companies. Canada Revenue Agency does not allow the use of LIFO to determine taxable income because it often results in the highest cost of goods sold and the lowest net income (and, therefore, a lower amount of taxes payable). Although LIFO is acceptable for accounting purposes in Canada, most Canadian companies do not want to incur the cost of maintaining two sets of inventory records. Exhibit 6–5 gives a perpetual inventory record for the LIFO method.

Again, SportChek had 10 pairs of running shoes that cost $60 per pair at the beginning of November. After the purchase on November 5, SportChek holds 70 units of inventory (10 at $60 plus 60 at $65). On November 15, SportChek sells 40 units. Under LIFO, the cost of goods sold always comes from the newest purchase. That leaves 30 pairs in inventory on November 15.

30 units on hand	10 @ $60	=	$ 600
	20 @ $65	=	1,300
Inventory on hand		=	$1,900

The purchase of 70 units on November 26 adds $70 running shoes to inventory. Now Inventory holds 100 units.

EXHIBIT 6–5 Perpetual Inventory Record— LIFO Cost for SportChek

Running Shoes, Model XL

Date	Purchases Qty.	Unit Cost	Total Cost	Cost of Goods Sold Qty.	Unit Cost	Total Cost	Inventory on Hand Qty.	Unit Cost	Total Cost
Nov. 1							10	$60	$ 600
5	60	$65	$3,900				10	60	600
							60	65	3,900
15				40	$65	$2,600	10	60	600
							20	65	1,300
26	70	70	4,900				10	60	600
							20	65	1,300
							70	70	4,900
30				70	70	4,900			
				10	65	650	10	60	600
							10	65	650
30	130		$8,800	120		$8,150	20		$1,250

$$
\begin{array}{rl}
& 10\ @\ \$60\ =\ \$\ \ 600 \\
100 \text{ units on hand} \to & 20\ @\ \$65\ =\ \ 1{,}300 \\
& 70\ @\ \$70\ =\ \ \underline{4{,}900} \\
\text{Inventory on hand} & =\ \underline{\$6{,}800}
\end{array}
$$

Then the sale of 80 units on November 30 reduces units in LIFO order. The LIFO monthly summary at November 30 is

- Cost of goods sold: 120 units that cost a total of $8,150
- Ending inventory: 20 units that cost a total of $1,250

If SportChek used the LIFO method, it would measure cost of goods sold and inventory in this manner to prepare its financial statements.

STOP AND THINK

Examine Exhibit 6–4 (FIFO) and Exhibit 6–5 (LIFO). Focus on the sale of goods on November 15. Why is cost of goods sold different between first-in, first-out (FIFO) costing and last-in, first-out (LIFO) costing? Explain.

Answer: Cost of goods is very different under FIFO and LIFO. The two methods make opposite assumptions about when costs leave inventory (an asset) and move into cost of goods sold (an expense).

- Under FIFO, the first costs into inventory are the first costs out to cost of goods sold. Under FIFO, the oldest costs are expensed first.
- Under LIFO, the last costs into inventory are the first costs out to cost of goods sold. The newest costs are expensed first.

FIFO and LIFO are opposites!

Journal Entries Under LIFO

The journal entries under LIFO follow the data in Exhibit 6–5. On November 5, SportChek purchased inventory for $3,900. The November 15 sale brought in sales revenue of $4,000 and had cost of goods sold of $2,600. The November 26 and 30 entries also come from the data in Exhibit 6–5.

LIFO Journal Entries: (All purchases and sales on account. The sale price of a pair of running shoes is $100 per unit.)

Nov.	5	Inventory...	3,900	
		Accounts Payable...		3,900
		Purchased inventory on account (60 × $65 = $3,900).		
	15	Accounts Receivable..	4,000	
		Sales Revenue..		4,000
		Sale on account (40 × $100 = $4,000).		
	15	Cost of Goods Sold	2,600	
		Inventory..		2,600
		Cost of goods sold (40 × $65 = $2,600).		
	26	Inventory...	4,900	
		Accounts Payable...		4,900
		Purchased inventory on account (70 × $70 = $4,900).		
	30	Accounts Receivable..	8,000	
		Sales Revenue..		8,000
		Sale on account (80 × $100 = $8,000).		
	30	Cost of Goods Sold	5,550	
		Inventory..		5,550
		Cost of goods sold ($4,900 + $650 = $5,550).		

Moving-Weighted-Average Method

Suppose SportChek uses the **moving-weighted-average cost method** to account for its inventory of running shoes. With this method, the business computes a new weighted-average cost per unit after each purchase. Ending inventory and cost of goods sold are then based on the same most-recent weighted-average cost per unit. Exhibit 6–6 shows a perpetual inventory record for the moving-weighted-average cost method. We round average unit cost to the nearest cent and total cost to the nearest dollar.

EXHIBIT 6–6   Perpetual Inventory Record— Moving-Weighted-Average Cost for SportChek

Running Shoes Model XL

	Purchases			Cost of Goods Sold			Inventory on Hand		
Date	Qty.	Unit Cost	Total Cost	Qty.	Unit Cost	Total Cost	Qty.	Unit Cost	Total Cost
Nov. 1							10	$60.00	$ 600
5	60	$65	$3,900				70	64.29	4,500
15				40	$64.29	$2,572	30	64.29	1,928
26	70	70	4,900				100	68.28	6,828
30				80	68.28	5,462	20	68.28	1,366
30	130		$8,800	120		$8,034	20		$1,366

After each purchase, SportChek computes a new average cost per unit. For example, on November 5, the new weighted-average unit cost is:

Total cost of inventory on hand		Number of units on hand		Average cost per unit
Nov. 5	$600 + $3,900 = $4,500	÷	70 units	=	$64.29

The goods sold on November 15 are then costed at $64.29 per unit. SportChek computes a new average cost after the November 26 purchase, which is why it is called a "moving" weighted-average cost.

The moving-weighted-average cost summary at November 30 is

- Cost of goods sold: 120 units that cost a total of $8,034
- Ending inventory: 20 units that cost a total of $1,366

If SportChek used the moving-weighted-average method, it would measure cost of goods sold and inventory in this manner to prepare its financial statements.

Journal Entries Under Moving-Weighted-Average Costing

The journal entries under moving-weighted-average costing follow the data in Exhibit 6–6. On November 5, SportChek purchased $3,900 of inventory and made the first journal entry. On November 15, SportChek sold 40 pairs of running shoes for $100 each. SportChek recorded the sale ($4,000) and the cost of goods sold ($2,572). The remaining journal entries (November 26 and 30) follow the data in Exhibit 6–6.

Moving-Weighted-Average-Cost Journal Entries: (All purchases and sales on account. The sale price of a pair of running shoes is $100 per unit.)

Nov.	5	Inventory...	3,900	
		Accounts Payable...		3,900
		Purchased inventory on account (60 × $65 = $3,900).		
	15	Accounts Receivable...	4,000	
		Sales Revenue..		4,000
		Sale on account (40 × $100 = $4,000).		
	15	Cost of Goods Sold	2,572	
		Inventory..		2,572
		Cost of goods sold (40 × $64.29 = $2,572).		
	26	Inventory...	4,900	
		Accounts Payable...		4,900
		Purchased inventory on account (70 × $70 = $4,900).		
	30	Accounts Receivable...	8,000	
		Sales Revenue..		8,000
		Sale on account (80 × $100 = $8,000).		
	30	Cost of Goods Sold	5,462	
		Inventory..		5,462
		Cost of goods sold, calculated as:		
		Cost of inventory on hand: $1,928 + $4,900 = $6,828		
		Moving-weighted-average cost per unit: $6,828 ÷ 100 = $68.28		
		Cost of goods sold = 80 × $68.28 = $5,462		

Comparing FIFO, LIFO, and Moving-Weighted-Average Cost

What leads SportChek to select the moving-weighted-average cost method, and Celestica Inc. to use FIFO? The different methods have different benefits.

Objective  ②

Compare the effects of the FIFO, LIFO, and moving-weighted-average cost methods

EXHIBIT 6–7

EXHIBIT 6–7 Comparative Results for FIFO, LIFO, and Moving-Weighted-Average Cost

	FIFO	LIFO	Moving-Weighted-Average
Sales revenue (assumed)	$12,000	$12,000	$12,000
Cost of goods sold	8,000	8,150	8,034
Gross margin	$ 4,000	$ 3,850	$ 3,966
	(from Exhibit 6–4)	(from Exhibit 6–5)	(from Exhibit 6–6)

Exhibit 6–7 summarizes the results for the three inventory methods for SportChek. It shows sales revenue (assumed), cost of goods sold, and gross margin for FIFO, LIFO, and moving-weighted-average cost. All data come from Exhibits 6–4, 6–5, and 6–6.

Exhibit 6–7 also shows that FIFO produces the lowest cost of goods sold and the highest gross margin. Net income is also the highest under FIFO when inventory costs are rising. Many companies prefer high income to attract investors and borrow money on favourable terms. FIFO offers this benefit.

LIFO results in the highest cost of goods sold and the lowest gross margin. This leads to the lowest net income when inventory costs are rising. In Canada, this LIFO costing method is not allowed for income tax purposes, so very few companies use this method.

The moving-weighted-average cost method generates gross margin and net income amounts that fall between the extremes of FIFO and LIFO. Companies that seek a "middle-ground" solution, therefore, use the moving-weighted-average cost method for inventory.

Mid-Chapter Summary Problem for Your Review

Name: The Watch Shop
Industry: Retailer
Fiscal Period: Month of June
Key Fact: Perpetual inventory system

The Watch Shop carries only watches. Assume The Watch Shop began June with an inventory of 20 wristwatches that cost $60 each. The Watch Shop sells those watches for $100 each. During June, The Watch Shop bought and sold inventory as follows:

June	3	Sold 16 units for $100 each.
	16	Purchased 20 units at $65 each.
	23	Sold 16 units for $100 each.

Required

1. Prepare a perpetual inventory record for The Watch Shop under each method.
   - FIFO
   - LIFO
   - Moving-weighted-average cost
2. Journalize all of The Watch Shop's inventory transactions for June for each of these cost methods.

3. Show the computation of gross margin for each method.

4. Which method maximizes net income? Which method allowed in Canada (FIFO or moving-weighted-average) minimizes income taxes?

Solution

Requirement 1

Perpetual inventory records:

FIFO

The June 3 items are sold from the opening batch of inventory, which all cost the same amount.

The June 23 items are sold from two batches of inventory that have different costs. Remember, under FIFO, items from the oldest batch are assumed to be sold first.

Wristwatches									
	Purchases			Cost of Goods Sold			Inventory on Hand		
Date	Qty.	Unit Cost	Total Cost	Qty.	Unit Cost	Total Cost	Qty.	Unit Cost	Total Cost
June 1							20	$60	$1,200
3				16	$60	$ 960	4	60	240
16	20	$65	$1,300				4	60	240
							20	65	1,300
23				4	60	240			
				12	65	780	8	65	520
30	20		$1,300	32		$1,980	8		$ 520

LIFO

The June 3 items are sold from the opening batch of inventory, which all cost the same amount.

The June 23 items are sold from the June 16 purchase entirely. Remember, under LIFO, items from the newest batch are assumed to be sold first.

Wristwatches									
	Purchases			Cost of Goods Sold			Inventory on Hand		
Date	Qty.	Unit Cost	Total Cost	Qty.	Unit Cost	Total Cost	Qty.	Unit Cost	Total Cost
June 1							20	$60	$1,200
3				16	$60	$ 960	4	60	240
16	20	$65	$1,300				4	60	240
							20	65	1,300
23				16	65	1,040	4	60	240
							4	65	260
30	20		$1,300	32		$2,000	8		$ 500

Moving-Weighted-Average

The June 3 items are sold from the opening batch of inventory, which all cost the same amount.

The June 23 items are sold from two batches of inventory that have different costs. The moving-weighted-average cost calculation is given at the end of the Requirement 2 solutions. Under the moving-weighted-average method, both cost of goods sold and ending inventory amounts are calculated using the same moving-weighed-average unit cost.

Wristwatches									
	Purchases			Cost of Goods Sold			Inventory on Hand		
Date	Qty.	Unit Cost	Total Cost	Qty.	Unit Cost	Total Cost	Qty.	Unit Cost	Total Cost
June 1							20	$60	$1,200
3				16	$60	$ 960	4	60	240
16	20	$65	$1,300				24	64.17	1,540
23				16	64.17	1,027	8	64.17	513
30	20		$1,300	32		$1,987	8		$ 513

Requirement 2

Journal Entries:

			FIFO		LIFO		Moving-Weighted-Average	
June	3	Accounts Receivable	1,600		1,600		1,600	
		Sales Revenue		1,600		1,600		1,600
	3	Cost of Goods Sold	960		960		960	
		Inventory		960		960		960
	16	Inventory	1,300		1,300		1,300	
		Accounts Payable		1,300		1,300		1,300
	23	Accounts Receivable	1,600		1,600		1,600	
		Sales Revenue		1,600		1,600		1,600
	23	Cost of Goods Sold	1,020*		1,040**		1,027***	
		Inventory		1,020		1,040		1,027

*(4 units × $60) + (12 units × $65) = $1,020
** 16 units × $65 = $1,040
*** (4 units × $60) + (20 units × $65) = $1,540; $1,540 ÷ 24 units = $64.17 per unit
  16 units × $64.17 = $1,027 (rounded)

Requirement 3

		FIFO	LIFO	Moving-Weighted-Average
Sales revenue	($1,600 + $1,600)	$3,200	$3,200	$3,200
Cost of goods sold	($960 + $1,020)	1,980		
	($960 + $1,040)		2,000	
	($960 + $1,027)			1,987
Gross margin		$1,220	$1,200	$1,213

Requirement 4

FIFO maximizes net income.
   Even though LIFO gives the lowest gross margin, LIFO is not allowed for income-tax purposes in Canada. Therefore, of the methods allowed in Canada, moving-weighted-average minimizes income taxes.

Margin notes:

June 3 and 23 sales entries are the same among the three inventory costing methods because the selling price is $100 per unit.

June 3 COGS entries are the same because the sale was from beginning inventory.

June 16 purchase is recorded as a normal inventory purchase, no matter which inventory-costing system is used.

Only the June 23 COGS entries differ. Refer to the calculations provided.

The sales and COGS amounts are gathered from the journal entries in Requirement 2.

Gross margin =
   Sales revenue − COGS

The method with
• The greatest gross margin will maximize net income.
• The lowest gross margin will minimize income taxes.

Inventory Costing in a Periodic System

Objective 3

Account for periodic inventory under the FIFO, LIFO and weighted-average cost methods

We described the periodic inventory system in Chapter 5. Accounting is simpler in a periodic system because the company keeps no daily running record of inventory on hand. The only way to determine the ending inventory and cost of goods sold in a periodic system is to count the goods—usually at the end of the year. The periodic system works well for a small business where the owner can control inventory by visual inspection. Appendix A in Chapter 5 illustrates how the periodic system works.

   Cost of goods sold in a periodic inventory system is computed by the following formula (using assumed amounts for this illustration):

Beginning inventory (the inventory on hand at the end of the preceding period)	$ 5,000
Net purchases (often abbreviated as Purchases)	20,000*
Cost of goods available for sale	25,000

(continued)

Less: Ending inventory
   (the inventory on hand at the end of the current period) ....   (7,000)
Cost of goods sold $18,000

*Net purchases is determined as follows (all amounts assumed):
   Purchases $21,000
      Less: Purchase discounts ....   (2,000)
         Purchase returns and allowances ....   (5,000)
      Add: Freight in...   6,000
         Net purchases.. $20,000

The application of the various costing methods (FIFO, LIFO, and weighted-average) in a periodic inventory system follows the pattern illustrated earlier for the perpetual system. To show how the periodic inventory system works, we use the same SportChek data that we used for the perpetual system, as follows:

Running Shoes, Model XL	Number of Units	Unit Cost
Nov. 1 Beginning inventory	10	$60
5 Purchase	60	$65
15 Sale	40	
26 Purchase	70	$70
30 Sale	80	

First-in, First-out (FIFO) Method

SportChek could use the FIFO costing method with a periodic inventory system. The FIFO computations follow:

Beginning inventory (10 units at $60) .... $ 600
Purchases (60 units at $65 + 70 units at $70)   8,800
Cost of goods available for sale (140 units)...............................   9,400
Less: Ending inventory (20 units at $70)...................................   (1,400)
Cost of goods sold (120 units) $8,000

The cost of goods available is always the sum of beginning inventory plus purchases. Under FIFO, the ending inventory comes from the latest—the most recent—purchases, which cost $70 per unit. Ending inventory is therefore $1,400, and cost of goods sold is $8,000. These amounts will always be the same as the amounts calculated under the perpetual system.

There are fewer journal entries in the periodic system because SportChek would record a sale with only a single entry. For example, SportChek's sale of four pairs of running shoes for $100 each is recorded as follows:

Nov. 15   Accounts Receivable (4 × $100)..............................   400
               Sales Revenue..   400.

There is no cost-of-goods-sold entry in the periodic system.

Last-in, First-out (LIFO) Method

The LIFO method fits well with a periodic inventory system. SportChek's LIFO computations follow:

Beginning inventory (10 units at $60) .... $ 600
Purchases (60 units at $65 + 70 units at $70)   8,800
Cost of goods available for sale (140 units)...............................   9,400
Less: Ending inventory (10 units at $60 + 10 units at $65) .....   (1,250)
Cost of goods sold (120 units) $8,150

Under LIFO, the ending inventory comes from the earliest units obtained—the 10 units in beginning inventory that cost $60 plus 10 of the units purchased for $65. Ending inventory is therefore $1,250, and cost of goods sold is $8,150. These amounts are the same as we saw for the perpetual system in Exhibit 6–5. In most cases, the LIFO amounts will differ between the perpetual and the periodic systems.

Weighted-Average Cost Method

In the **weighted-average cost method**, we compute a single weighted-average cost per unit for the entire period as follows:

Cost of goods available for sale		Number of units available for sale		Average cost per unit for the entire period
$9,400	÷	140 units	=	$67.14

This average cost per unit is then used to compute the ending inventory and cost of goods sold as follows:

Beginning inventory (10 units at $60)	$ 600
Purchases (60 units at $65 + 70 units at $70)	8,800
Cost of goods available for sale	
(140 units at weighted-average cost of $67.14)	9,400
Less: Ending inventory (20 units at $67.14)................................	(1,343)
Cost of goods sold (120 units at $67.14).....................................	$8,057

Using the weighted-average cost method, ending inventory and cost of goods sold under the periodic system differ from the amounts in a perpetual system. Why? Because under the perpetual system, a new average cost is computed after each purchase (it is a "moving" weighted-average cost). But the periodic system uses a single average cost that is determined at the end of the period.

Accounting Principles and Inventories

Several accounting concepts have special relevance to inventories. Among them are consistency, disclosure, materiality, and accounting conservatism.

Consistency

The characteristic of **consistency** states that businesses should use the same accounting methods and procedures from period to period. Consistency helps investors compare a company's financial statements from one period to the next.

Suppose you are analyzing a company's net income pattern over a two-year period. The company switched from LIFO to FIFO during that time. Its net income increased dramatically, but only as a result of the change in inventory method. If you did not know of the change, you might believe that the company's income increased because of improved operations. Therefore, companies must report any changes in the accounting methods they use. Investors need this information in order to make wise decisions about the company.

Disclosure Principle

The **disclosure principle** holds that a company's financial statements should report enough information for outsiders to make knowledgeable decisions about the company. In short, the company should report *relevant*, *reliable*, and *comparable* information about itself. This means disclosing the method or methods used to value inventories. Suppose a banker is comparing two companies—one using LIFO and the other FIFO. The FIFO company reports higher net income, but only because it uses the FIFO inventory method. Without knowledge of these accounting methods, the banker could loan money to the wrong business. In addition, different categories of inventory should be disclosed, such as raw materials, work-in-process, and finished goods categories.

Materiality Concept

The **materiality concept** states that a company must perform strictly proper accounting *only* for items that are significant to the business's financial statements. Information is significant—or, in accounting terminology, *material*—when its presentation in the financial statements would cause someone to change a decision. The materiality concept frees accountants from having to report every item in strict accordance with GAAP. For inventory, this means immaterial items can be expensed rather than included in inventory. For example, if freight for an inventory item is immaterial, then it could be expensed immediately, even if the inventory item is sold in a later period.

Accounting Conservatism

Conservatism in accounting means reporting items in the financial statements at amounts that lead to the most cautious immediate results. Conservatism appears in accounting guidelines such as

- "Anticipate no gains, but provide for all probable losses."
- "If in doubt, record an asset at the lowest reasonable amount and a liability at the highest reasonable amount."
- "When there's a question, record an expense rather than an asset."

The goal is for financial statements to report realistic figures. However, do not deliberately understate assets, revenues, and gains, nor deliberately overstate liabilities, expenses, and losses.

Other Inventory Issues

In addition to the FIFO, LIFO and weighted-average inventory costing methods, accountants face other inventory issues. This section covers

- The lower-of-cost-or-market rule
- Effects of inventory errors
- Ethical issues
- Estimating ending inventory

Lower-of-Cost-or-Market Rule

The **lower-of-cost-or-market rule** (abbreviated as **LCM**) shows accounting conservatism in action. LCM requires that inventory be reported in the financial statements at whichever is lower:

Objective 4

Apply the lower-of-cost-or-market rule to inventory

- The historical cost of the inventory
- The net realizable value (market value) of the inventory.

For inventories, *net realizable value* generally means the expected selling price (that is, the amount the business could get if it sold the inventory less the costs of selling it).

If the net realizable value of inventory falls below its historical cost, the business must write down the value of its goods. On the balance sheet, the business reports ending inventory at its LCM value.

Suppose SportChek paid $6,000 for inventory on September 26. By December 31, the inventory can only be sold for $4,800, and the decline in value appears permanent. Net realizable value is below FIFO cost, and the entry to write down the inventory to LCM follows:

Costs of Goods Sold..	1,200	
Inventory		1,200

To write down inventory to net realizable value.
(cost, $6,000 − market, $4,800)

In this case, The Forzani Group Ltd.'s balance sheet would report this inventory as follows:

Balance Sheet
Current assets:
Inventory, at market $4,800
(which is lower than $6,000 cost)

Companies often disclose LCM in notes to their financial statements, as shown here for The Forzani Group Ltd., SportChek's parent company:

NOTE 2: STATEMENT OF SIGIFICANT ACCOUNTING POLICES
Inventories
Inventories are carried at the lower of laid-down cost or net realizable value. Cost is determined using the average cost method.

Effects of Inventory Errors

Objective 5

Measure the effects of inventory errors

Businesses count their inventories at the end of the period. For the financial statements to be accurate, it is important to get a correct count of ending inventory. This can be difficult for a company with inventory in many locations.

An error in ending inventory creates a whole string of errors. To illustrate, suppose SportChek accidentally counted too much ending inventory. Therefore, ending inventory is overstated on the balance sheet. The following diagram shows how an overstatement of ending inventory affects cost of goods sold, gross margin, and net income:

	Ending Inventory Overstated
Sales revenue	Correct
Cost of goods sold:	
Beginning inventory	Correct
Net purchases	Correct
Cost of goods available for sale	Correct
Ending inventory	**ERROR: Overstated**
Cost of goods sold..	**Understated**
Gross margin...	**Overstated**
Operating expenses	Correct
Net income...	**Overstated**

Understating the ending inventory—reporting the inventory too low—has the opposite effect, as shown here:

	Ending Inventory Understated
Sales revenue	Correct
Cost of goods sold:	
Beginning inventory	Correct
Net purchases	Correct
Cost of goods available for sale	Correct
Ending inventory	**ERROR: Understated**
Cost of goods sold.......................................	**Overstated**
Gross margin..	**Understated**
Operating expenses	Correct
Net income...	**Understated**

Recall that one period's ending inventory is the next period's beginning inventory. Thus, an error in ending inventory carries over into the next period. Exhibit 6–8 illustrates the effect of an inventory error. Period 1's ending inventory is overstated by $10,000. The error carries over to Period 2. Period 3 is correct. In fact, both Period 1 and Period 2 should look like Period 3.

EXHIBIT 6–8   Inventory Errors: An Example

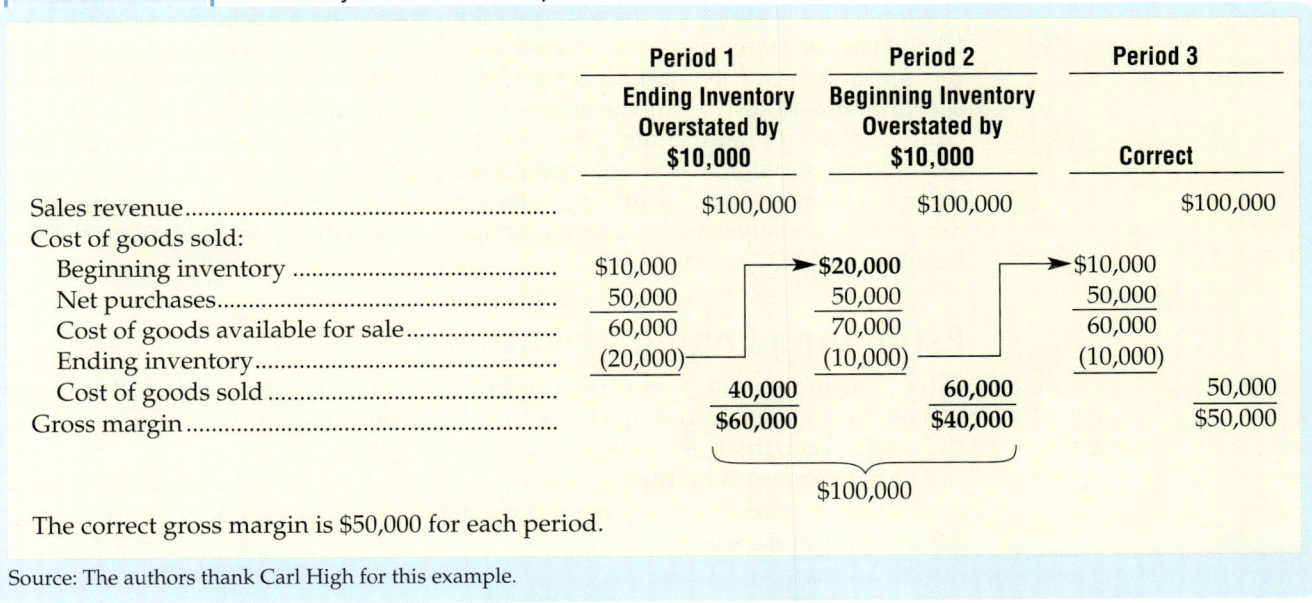

The correct gross margin is $50,000 for each period.

Source: The authors thank Carl High for this example.

Ending inventory is *subtracted* in computing cost of goods sold in one period and the same amount is *added* as beginning inventory the next period. Therefore, an inventory error cancels out after two periods. The overstatement of cost of goods sold in Period 2 counterbalances the understatement for Period 1. Thus, the total gross margin for the two periods combined is correct. These effects are summarized in Exhibit 6–9 on page 304.

Ethical Issues

No area of accounting has a deeper ethical dimension than inventory. Companies whose profits do not meet expectations can be tempted to "cook the books" to increase reported income. The increase in reported income will make the business look more successful than it really is.

KEY POINT

Recognize that a dollar change in ending inventory means a dollar change in income. This is one reason auditors examine the ending inventory so carefully. An income statement may be manipulated by altering the amount of ending inventory.

EXHIBIT 6–9 Effects of Inventory Errors

Inventory Error	Period 1		Period 2	
	Cost of Goods Sold	Gross Margin and Net Income	Cost of Goods Sold	Gross Margin and Net Income
Period 1 ending inventory *overstated*	Understated	Overstated	Overstated	Understated
Period 1 ending inventory *understated*	Overstated	Understated	Understated	Overstated

There are two main schemes for using inventory to increase reported income. The easier, and the more obvious, is to overstate ending inventory. In Exhibit 6–9, we see how an error in ending inventory affects net income.

The second way of using inventory to increase reported income involves sales. Sales schemes are more complex than simple inventory overstatements. Datapoint Corporation and MiniScribe, both computer-related companies, were charged with creating fictitious sales to boost reported profits.

Datapoint is alleged to have hired drivers to transport its inventory around the city so that the goods could *not* be counted. Datapoint's plan was to create the impression that the inventory must have been sold. This scheme broke down when the trucks returned the goods to the warehouse. The sales returns were much too high to be realistic, and the sales proved to be phony.

MiniScribe is alleged to have "cooked its books" by shipping boxes of bricks labelled as computer parts to its distributors right before year end. The distributors refused to accept the goods and returned them to MiniScribe—but in the next accounting period. The scheme affected MiniScribe's reported year-end assets and equity: sales and net income were overstated and inventories were understated by millions of dollars—but only temporarily. The offsetting effect of the scheme occurred in the next accounting period when MiniScribe had to record the sales returns. In virtually every area, accounting imposes a discipline that brings out the facts sooner or later.

Estimating Ending Inventory

Objective 6

Estimate ending inventory by the gross margin method and the retail method

Often a business must *estimate* the value of its ending inventory. Suppose the company suffers a fire loss and must estimate the value of the inventory destroyed. Or suppose a company needs monthly financial statements.

The **gross margin method** (also known as the **gross profit method**) provides a way to estimate inventory using the cost of goods sold model (amounts are assumed for illustration):

Beginning inventory	$ 20
+ Net purchases	100
= Cost of goods available for sale	120
− **Ending inventory**	(40)
= **Cost of goods sold**	$ 80

Rearranging *ending inventory* and *cost of goods sold* makes the model useful for estimating ending inventory (amounts are assumed for illustration):

Beginning inventory	$ 20
+ Purchases	100
= Cost of goods available for sale	120
− **Cost of goods sold**	(80)
= **Ending inventory**	$ 40

Beginning inventory		$14,000
Purchases..		66,000
Cost of goods available for sale		80,000
Estimate cost of goods sold:		
Sales revenue	$100,000	
Less: Estimated gross margin of 40%......................	(40,000)	
Estimated cost of goods sold.......................................		(60,000)
Estimated cost of *ending inventory*		$20,000

Suppose a fire destroys your inventory. To collect insurance, you must estimate the cost of the ending inventory. Using your normal *gross margin percent* (that is, gross margin divided by net sales revenue), you can estimate cost of goods sold. Then subtract cost of goods sold from cost of goods available to estimate ending inventory. Exhibit 6–10 illustrates the gross margin method using assumed amounts.

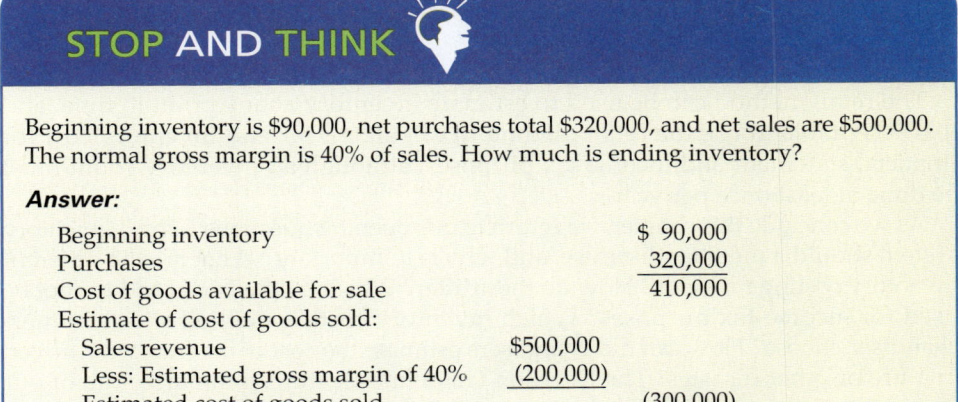

STOP AND THINK

Beginning inventory is $90,000, net purchases total $320,000, and net sales are $500,000. The normal gross margin is 40% of sales. How much is ending inventory?

Answer:

Beginning inventory		$ 90,000
Purchases		320,000
Cost of goods available for sale		410,000
Estimate of cost of goods sold:		
Sales revenue	$500,000	
Less: Estimated gross margin of 40%	(200,000)	
Estimated cost of goods sold		(300,000)
Estimated cost of *ending inventory*		$110,000

LEARNING TIPS

Remember that the gross margin % + the cost of goods sold % = 100%. If gross margin is 35% of sales, then cost of goods sold is 65% of sales.

Retail Method The **retail method** of estimating the cost of ending inventory is often used by retail establishments that use the periodic system. This is because it is often easier for retail establishments to calculate the selling price, or retail price, of a wide range of items rather than to look at all the individual invoices to find the costs of each of those items.

Like the gross margin method, the retail method is based on the familiar cost of goods sold model, rearranged to calculate ending inventory:

Beginning inventory
+ Net purchases
= Cost of goods available for sale
− Cost of goods sold
= Ending inventory

However, to use the retail method, a business must know both the total cost and the total selling price of its opening inventory, as well as both the total cost and total selling price of its net purchases. Total selling price is determined by counting each item of inventory and multiplying it by the item's retail selling price (the price given on the price tag). By summing the costs and selling prices of beginning inventory and net purchases, the business knows the cost and retail selling price of the goods it has available for sale.

REAL WORLD EXAMPLE

The gross margin and retail methods are also used to estimate inventory for interim periods when it is impractical to take a physical inventory.

The business can calculate the selling price of its sales because this is the sum of the amounts recorded on the cash register when sales are made. The total of sales at retail is deducted from the total selling price of the goods available for sale to give the total selling price of ending inventory. To convert ending inventory at selling price to ending inventory at cost, the business multiplies the ending inventory at selling price by the *retail ratio*. The retail ratio is the ratio of cost of goods available for sale at *cost* to the cost of goods available for sale at *selling price*. It is usually expressed as a percent. Exhibit 6–11 illustrates the retail method.

EXHIBIT 6–11	Retail Method of Estimating Inventory (amounts assumed)	

	Cost	Selling Price
Beginning inventory	$151,200	$216,000
Purchases	504,000	720,000
Goods available for sale	655,200	936,000
Net sales, at selling price (retail)		696,000
Ending inventory, at selling price (retail)		$240,000
Ending inventory, at cost ($240,000 × *70%)	$168,000	

*Retail ratio = ($655,200 ÷ 936,000) × 100 = 70%

The retail method can be used to estimate inventory at any point in time, and it is acceptable to use the retail method to calculate year-end inventory cost for financial statement and income tax purposes, although an inventory count must be done at least once per year.

As we conclude this chapter, we return to our opening questions: Which inventory system should a merchandiser use, and why is it important? What are the different inventory costing methods? How do they differ? Which methods can and cannot be used for income-tax purposes? Which inventory costing method should a merchandiser choose? How can merchandisers estimate the cost of inventory destroyed in a fire or other disaster? The Decision Guidelines feature summarizes all of our chapter-opening questions and gives guidelines that are helpful for managing a business's inventory operations.

DECISION GUIDELINES — Guidelines for Inventory Management

Decision	Guidelines	System or Method
Which inventory system to use?	• Expensive merchandise • Cannot control inventory by visual inspection	→ Perpetual system
	• Can control inventory by visual inspection	→ Periodic system
Which costing method to use?	• Unique inventory items	→ Specific-unit cost
	• The most current cost of ending inventory • Maximizes reported income when costs are rising	→ FIFO
	• The most current measure of cost of goods sold and net income (but not allowed for income tax)	→ LIFO
	• Middle-of-the-road approach for income tax and net income	→ Weighted-average
How to estimate the cost of ending inventory?	• The cost-of-goods-sold model provides the framework	→ Gross margin (gross profit) method
	• Standard mark-ups from cost price to selling price are used for all inventory items	→ Retail method

Summary Problem for Your Review

Name: Computer Parts Division, Total Computer Sales
Industry: Retailer
Fiscal Period: Month of January 2009
Key Fact: Periodic inventory system

Suppose a division of Total Computer Sales that handles computer parts uses the periodic inventory system and has these inventory records for January 2009.

Date		Item	Quantity	Unit Cost	Sale Price
Jan.	1	Beginning inventory...................	100 units	$ 8	
	10	Purchase..	60 units	9	
	15	Sale..	70 units		$20
	21	Purchase..	100 units	10	
	30	Sale..	90 units		25

Company accounting records reveal that operating expenses for January were $2,000.

Required

Prepare the January income statement in multi-step format. Show amounts for FIFO, LIFO, and weighted-average cost. Label the bottom line "Operating income." (Round the average cost per unit to three decimal places and all other figures to whole-dollar amounts.) Show your computations, and use the periodic inventory model from pages 298–299 to compute cost of goods sold.

Solution

The best approach to this solution is an organized one. One approach is to complete one income statement line before going to the next, until "Ending inventory." Notice that the amounts for sales revenue, beginning inventory, net purchases, and operating expenses are the same for all three inventory costing methods.

TOTAL COMPUTER SALES
Income Statement for Computer Parts Division
For the Month Ended January 31, 2009

	FIFO	LIFO	Weighted-Average
Sales revenue	$3,650	$3,650	$3,650
Cost of goods sold:			
Beginning inventory	$ 800	$ 800	$ 800
Net purchases..	1,540	1,540	1,540
Cost of goods			
available for sale	2,340	2,340	2,340
Ending inventory..	(1,000)	(800)	(900)
Cost of goods sold	1,340	1,540	1,440
Gross margin	2,310	2,110	2,210
Operating expenses	2,000	2,000	2,000
Operating income	$ 310	$ 110	$ 210

Computations
Sales revenue:	$(70 \times \$20) + (90 \times \$25)$	=	$3,650
Beginning inventory:	$100 \times \$8$	=	$800
Purchases:	$(60 \times \$9) + (100 \times \$10)$	=	$1,540
Ending inventory			
FIFO	$100^* \times \$10$	=	$1,000
LIFO	$100^* \times \$8$	=	$800
Average cost:	$100^* \times \$9^{**}$	=	$900

* Number of units in ending inventory = $100 + 60 - 70 + 100 - 90 = 100$.
** Average cost per unit = $\$2,340/260^{\dagger}$ units = $9.
† Number of units available = $100 + 60 + 100 = 260$.

Summary

1. Account for perpetual inventory under the FIFO, LIFO, and moving-weighted-average cost methods.

In a perpetual inventory system, the business keeps a continuous record for each inventory item to show the inventory on hand at all times. Inventory is debited immediately at cost when an item is purchased and inventory is credited immediately at cost when an item is sold. Businesses multiply the quantity of inventory items by their unit cost to determine inventory cost. To compute ending inventory and cost of goods sold, a cost is assigned to each inventory item. Three methods of assigning costs to similar items are: *first-in, first-out (FIFO), last-in, first-out (LIFO)*, and *moving-weighted-average*. FIFO reports ending inventory at the most current cost. LIFO reports cost of goods sold at the most current cost. Moving-weighted-average falls in the middle.

2. Compare the effects of the FIFO, LIFO, and moving-weighted-average cost methods.

FIFO reports ending inventory at the most current cost. LIFO reports cost of goods sold at the most current cost. Moving-weighted-average reports ending inventory and cost of goods sold at amounts between those of FIFO and LIFO. When prices are rising, LIFO produces the highest cost of goods sold and the lowest income; however, LIFO may not be used in Canada for income tax purposes. When prices are rising, FIFO produces the highest income. The moving-weighted-average method produces an income amount between the extremes of FIFO and LIFO.

3. Account for periodic inventory under the FIFO, LIFO, and weighted-average cost methods.

In a periodic inventory system, the business does not keep an up-to-date balance for ending inventory. Instead, at the end of the period, the business counts the inventory on hand and updates its records. To compute ending inventory and cost of goods sold, a cost is assigned to each inventory item. Three methods of assigning costs to similar items are: *first-in, first-out (FIFO), last-in, first-out (LIFO)*, and *weighted-average*. FIFO produces identical balances for ending inventory and cost of goods sold under the periodic and perpetual inventory systems, but LIFO and weighted-average produce different results under the periodic and perpetual systems.

4. Apply the lower-of-cost-or-market rule to inventory.

The *lower-of-cost-or-market (LCM) rule*—an example of accounting *conservatism*—requires that businesses report inventory on the balance sheet at the lower of its cost or current replacement or net realizable value. Companies disclose their definition of "market" for purposes of applying LCM in notes to their financial statements.

5. Measure the effects of inventory errors.

Although inventory overstatements in one period are counterbalanced by inventory understatements in the next period, effective decision making depends on accurate inventory information.

6. Estimate ending inventory by the gross margin method and the retail method.

The *gross margin method* and the *retail method* are techniques for estimating the cost of ending inventory. They are useful for preparing interim financial statements and for estimating the cost of inventory destroyed by fire or other disasters.

Self-Study Questions

Test your understanding of the chapter by marking the correct answer to each of the following questions:

1. Suppose a Canadian chain store made sales of $10,000 million and ended the year with inventories totalling $970 million. Cost of goods sold was $6,000 million. Total operating expenses were $2,700 million. How much net income did the chain store earn for the year? (*p. 289*)
   a. $1,300 million   c. $6,334 million
   b. $7,300 million   d. $6,970 million

2. Which inventory costing method assigns to ending inventory the latest—the most recent—costs incurred during the period? (*p. 291*)
   a. Specific unit cost   c. Last-in, first-out (LIFO)
   b. First-in, first-out (FIFO)   d. Average cost

3. Assume Amazon.ca began June with 10 units of inventory that cost a total of $380. During June, Amazon purchased and sold goods as follows:

June	8	Purchase	30 units at $40
	14	Sale	25 units at $80
	22	Purchase	20 units at $44
	27	Sale	30 units at $80

Assume Amazon uses the FIFO inventory method and the perpetual inventory system. How much is Amazon's cost of goods sold for the transaction on June 14? (p. 291)

a. $1,580   c. $1,000
b. $2,000   d. $980

4. After the purchase on June 22 in question 3, what is Amazon's cost of the inventory on hand? (p. 291)

a. $600   c. $1,480
b. $880   d. $1,440

5. Amazon's journal entry (entries) on June 14 is (are) (p. 291)

a. Accounts Receivable   980
     Inventory   980
b. Accounts Receivable 2,000
     Sales Revenue.................   2,000
c. Cost of Goods Sold...........   980
     Inventory   980
d. Both b and c

6. Which inventory costing method results in the lowest net income during a period of rising inventory costs? (p. 296)

a. Specific unit cost   c. Last-in, first-out (LIFO)
b. First-in, first out (FIFO)   d. Average cost

7. Suppose Amazon.ca used the weighted-average cost method and the periodic inventory system. Use the Amazon data in question 3 to compute the cost of the

company's inventory on hand at June 30. Round unit cost to the nearest cent. (p. 300)

a. $205.00   c. $410.00
b. $210.40   d. $420.80

8. Which of the following is most closely linked to accounting conservatism? (p. 301)

a. Consistency principle
b. Disclosure principle
c. Materiality concept
d. Lower-of-cost-or-market rule.

9. At December 31, 2008, McAdam Company overstated ending inventory by $40,000. How does this error affect cost of goods sold and net income for 2008? (p. 302)

a. Overstates cost of goods sold, understates income
b. Understates cost of goods sold, overstates net income
c. Overstates both cost of goods sold and net income
d. Leaves both cost of goods sold and net income correct because the errors cancel each other

10. Suppose a SportChek location suffered a fire loss and needs to estimate the cost of the goods destroyed. Beginning inventory was $100,000, net purchases totalled $600,000, and sales came to $1,000,000. SportChek's normal gross margin percentage is 45%. Use the gross margin method to estimate the cost of the inventory lost in the fire. (p. 305)

a. $300,000   c. $150,000
b. $250,000   d. $350,000

Answers to the Self-Study Questions follow the Similar Accounting Terms.

Accounting Vocabulary

Conservatism *(p. 301)*
Consistency characteristic *(p. 300)*
Disclosure principle *(p. 300)*
First-in, first-out (FIFO) inventory cost method *(p. 291)*
Gross margin method *(p. 304)*
Gross profit method *(p. 304)*
Last-in, first-out (LIFO) inventory cost method *(p. 292)*

Lower-of-cost-or-market (LCM) rule *(p. 301)*
Materiality concept *(p. 301)*
Moving-weighted-average cost method *(p. 294)*
Retail method *(p. 305)*
Specific identification method *(p. 290)*
Specific-unit-cost method *(p. 290)*
Weighted-average cost method *(p. 300)*

Similar Accounting Terms

Cost of goods sold	Cost of sales
Gross margin method	Gross profit method
Weighted-average-cost method	Average-cost method

Answers to Self-Study Questions

1. a ($10,000 − $6,000 − $2,700 = $1,300, all in millions)   2. b
3. d (10 × $38) + (15 × $40) = $980   4. c (15 × $40) + (20 × $44) = $1,480
5. d   6. c
7. a Cost of goods available = $380 + $1,200 + $880 = $2,460
    Number of units available = 10 + 30 + 20 = 60
    $2,460/60 units = $41.00; $41.00 × 5 = $205.00
8. d   9. b
10. c $100,000 + $600,000 = $700,000
    $1,000,000 − (0.45 × $1,000,000) = $550,000
    $700,000 − $550,000 = $150,000

Assignment Material

Questions

1. Why is merchandise inventory so important to a retailer or wholesaler?

2. Suppose your business deals in expensive jewellery. Which inventory system should you use to achieve good internal control over the inventory? If your business is a hardware store that sells low-cost goods, which inventory system would you be likely to use? Why would you choose this system?

3. Identify the accounts debited and credited in the standard purchase and sale entries under (a) the perpetual inventory system, and (b) the periodic inventory system.

4. What is the role of the physical count of inventory in (a) the perpetual inventory system and (b) the periodic inventory system?

5. If beginning inventory is $20,000, purchases total $170,000, and ending inventory is $25,400, how much is cost of goods sold?

6. If beginning inventory is $48,000, purchases total $178,500, and cost of goods sold is $190,500, how much is ending inventory?

7. What two items determine the cost of ending inventory?

8. Briefly describe the four generally accepted inventory cost methods. During a period of rising prices, which method produces the highest reported income? Which produces the lowest reported income?

9. Which inventory costing method produces the ending inventory valued at the most current cost? Which method produces the cost-of-goods-sold amount valued at the most current cost?

10. Why is LIFO the most popular method in the United States? Why is it so little used in Canada? Do these reasons accord with the notion that the inventory costing method should produce the most accurate data on the income statement?

11. Which inventory costing method produces the most accurate data on the balance sheet? Why?

12. How does the consistency characteristic affect accounting for inventory?

13. Briefly describe the influence that the concept of conservatism has on accounting for inventory.

14. Manley Company's inventory has a cost of $24,000 at the end of the year, and the net realizable value of the inventory is $25,500. At which amount should the company report the inventory on its balance sheet? Suppose the net realizable value of the inventory is $22,500 instead of $25,500. At which amount should Manley Company report the inventory? What rule governs your answers to these questions?

15. Gabriel Products accidentally overstated its ending inventory by $20,000 at the end of Period 1. Is gross margin of Period 1 overstated or understated? Is gross margin of Period 2 overstated, understated, or unaffected by the Period 1 error? Is total gross margin for the two periods overstated, understated, or correct? Give the reason for your answers.

16. Identify two important methods of estimating inventory amounts.

17. A fire destroyed the inventory of Olivera Supplies, but the accounting records were saved. The beginning inventory was $33,000, purchases for the period were $106,500, and sales were $210,000. Olivera's customary gross margin is 45 percent of sales. Use the gross margin method to estimate the cost of the inventory destroyed by the fire.

18. The retail method of estimating inventory seems simple but in reality can be difficult to apply. Why is this so?

Starters

Perpetual inventory record—FIFO

①

Ending inventory $400

Starter 6–1 Shepherd Cycles uses the FIFO inventory method. Shepherd started June with 10 bicycles that cost $70 each. On June 16, Shepherd bought 20 bicycles at $80 each. On June 30, Shepherd sold 25 bicycles. Prepare Shepherd's perpetual inventory record.

Perpetual inventory record—LIFO

①

Ending inventory $350

Starter 6–2 Use the Shepherd Cycles' data in Starter 6–1 to prepare a perpetual inventory record for the LIFO method.

Perpetual inventory record—moving-weighted-average cost

①

Ending inventory $383

Starter 6–3 Use the Shepherd Cycles' data in Starter 6–1 to prepare a perpetual inventory record for the moving-weighted-average cost method. Round average cost per unit to the nearest cent and all other amounts to the nearest dollar.

Starter 6-4 Use the Shepherd Cycles data in Starter 6–1 to journalize

a. The June 16 purchase of inventory on account.
b. The June 30 sale of inventory on account. Shepherd sold each bicycle for $140.
c. Cost of goods sold under FIFO.

Recording inventory transactions—FIFO

c. COGS $1,900

Starter 6-5 Answer these questions in your own words:

1. Why does FIFO produce the lowest cost of goods sold during a period of rising prices?
2. Why does LIFO produce the highest cost of goods sold during a period of rising prices?

Comparing cost of goods sold under FIFO and LIFO

Starter 6-6 Explain in your own words which inventory method results in the highest, and the lowest, cost of ending inventory. Prices are rising. Exhibits 6–4 and 6–5, on pages 291 and 293, provide the needed information.

Comparing ending inventory under FIFO and LIFO

Starter 6-7 Louis Dry Goods uses a periodic inventory system. Louis completed the following inventory transactions during April:

April	1	Purchased 10 shirts at $40 each
	7	Sold 6 shirts for $70 each
	13	Sold 2 shirts for $80 each
	21	Purchased 3 shirts at $50 each

Compute Louis's ending inventory and cost of goods sold under both LIFO and FIFO. Compute gross margin under both methods. Which method results in more gross margin?

Computing FIFO and LIFO amounts in a periodic system

Gross margin FIFO $260; LIFO $230

Starter 6-8 Louis Dry Goods uses a periodic inventory system. Use the Louis Dry Goods data in Starter 6–7 to compute ending inventory and cost of goods sold under the weighted-average-cost method. Round average unit cost to the nearest cent.

Computing weighted-average-cost amounts in a periodic system

COGS $338

Starter 6-9 Van Dyke Cycles' inventory data for the year ended December 31, 2008, follow.

Sales revenue	$50,000
Cost of goods sold:	
Beginning inventory	4,200
Net purchases	27,400
Cost of goods available for sale	31,600
Less: Ending inventory	(4,600)
Cost of goods sold	27,000
Gross margin	$23,000

Assume that the ending inventory was accidentally overstated by $1,000. What are the correct amounts of cost of goods sold and gross margin?

Effect of an inventory error— one year only

COGS $28,000

Starter 6-10 Refer back to the Van Dyke Cycles' inventory data in Starter 6–9. How would the inventory error affect Van Dyke's cost of goods sold and gross margin for the year ended December 31, 2009?

Next year's effect of an inventory error

COGS overstated by $1,000

Starter 6-11 Carpetmaster began the year with inventory of $350,000. Inventory purchases for the year total $1,600,000, and cost of goods sold will be $1,750,000. How much is Carpetmaster's estimated cost of ending inventory? Use the gross margin method.

Estimating ending inventory by the gross margin method

Ending inventory $200,000

Starter 6-12 Leather Goods Ltd. began the year with inventory of $50,000 and purchased $250,000 of goods during the year. Sales for the year are $500,000, and Leather Goods' gross margin percentage is 55% of sales. Compute the estimated cost of ending inventory by the gross margin method.

Estimating ending inventory by the gross margin method

Est. cost of ending inventory $75,000

Exercises

Measuring ending inventory and cost of goods sold in a perpetual system—FIFO

COGS $1,365

Exercise 6–1

The Music Store carries a large inventory of guitars and other musical instruments. The store uses the FIFO method and a perpetual inventory system. Company records indicate the following for a particular line of guitars:

Date		Item	Quantity	Unit Cost
May	1	Balance...	5	$105
	6	Sale	3	
	8	Purchase	10	120
	17	Sale	4	
	30	Sale	5	

Required Prepare a perpetual inventory record for the guitars. Then determine the amounts The Music Store should report for ending inventory and cost of goods sold by the FIFO method.

Recording perpetual inventory transactions

Exercise 6–2

After preparing the FIFO perpetual inventory record in Exercise 6–1, journalize The Music Store's May 8 purchase of inventory on account and cash sale on May 17 (sale price of each guitar was $210).

Measuring ending inventory and cost of goods sold in a perpetual system—LIFO

COGS $1,395

Exercise 6–3

Refer to The Music Store inventory data in Exercise 6–1. Assume that The Music Store uses the LIFO cost method. Prepare the store's perpetual inventory record for the guitars on the LIFO basis. Then identify the cost of ending inventory and cost of goods sold for the month.

Applying the moving-weighted-average-cost method in a perpetual inventory system

COGS $1,373

Exercise 6–4

Refer to The Music Store inventory data in Exercise 6–1. Assume that the store uses the moving-weighted-average cost method. Prepare The Music Store's perpetual inventory record for the guitars on the moving-weighted-average cost basis. Round average cost per unit to the nearest cent and all other amounts to the nearest dollar.

Recording perpetual inventory transactions

2. Gross margin $34,000

Exercise 6–5

Richmond Tackle Shop's accounting records yield the following data for the year ended December 31, 2008.

Inventory, January 1, 2008......................................	$ 8,000
Purchases of inventory (on account)....................	49,000
Sales of inventory—80 percent on account;	
20 percent for cash (cost $41,000)......................	75,000
Inventory at FIFO cost December 31, 2008..........	?

Required

1. Journalize Richmond Tackle Shop's inventory transactions for the year in the perpetual system.

2. Report ending inventory, sales, cost of goods sold, and gross margin on the appropriate financial statement.

Recording periodic inventory transactions

2. Gross margin $34,000

Exercise 6–6

Refer to the Richmond Tackle Shop data in Exercise 6–5. Inventory on hand at December 31, 2008, was $16,000, based on the physical count.

Required

1. Journalize Richmond Tackle Shop's inventory transactions for the year in the periodic system.

2. Report ending inventory, sales, cost of goods sold, and gross margin on the appropriate financial statement. How do these amounts compare to the same amounts in the perpetual inventory system calculated in Exercise 6–5, requirement 2?

Exercise 6–7

Truro Office Products markets the ink used in laser printers. Truro started the year with 100 containers of ink (weighted-average cost of $9.00 each; FIFO cost of $8 each; LIFO cost of $10 each). During the year, Truro purchased 800 containers of ink at $11 and sold 700 units for $23 each, with all transactions on account. Truro paid operating expenses throughout the year, a total of $5,000.

Journalize Truro's purchases, sales, and operating expense transactions under the following format. Truro uses the perpetual inventory system to account for laser-printer ink.

	DEBIT/CREDIT AMOUNTS		
Accounts	Moving-Weighted-Average*	FIFO	LIFO

*Round moving-weighted-average unit cost to the nearest cent.

Applying the moving-weighted-average, FIFO, and LIFO methods in a perpetual inventory system

1

COGS:
Moving-weighted-average $7,544
FIFO $7,400
LIFO $7,700

Exercise 6–8

Kirby Electrical's inventory records for industrial switches indicate the following at November 30, 2009:

Nov.	1	Beginning inventory	7 units at	$120
	8	Purchase	4 units at	$120
	15	Purchase	11 units at	$130
	26	Purchase	5 units at	$135

The physical count of inventory at November 30, 2009 indicates that six units remain in ending inventory, and the company owns them.

Required

Compute ending inventory and cost of goods sold using each of the following methods, assuming the periodic inventory system:

1. Specific unit cost, assuming three $130 units and three $120 units are on hand on November 30, 2009.
2. Weighted-average cost
3. First-in, first-out
4. Last-in, first-out

Excel Spreadsheet Template

Computing ending inventory by applying four inventory costing methods in a periodic inventory system

3

4. LIFO COGS $2,705

Exercise 6–9

1. Supply the missing income statement amounts for each of the following companies for the year ended December 31, 2008:

Company	Net Sales	Beginning Inventory	Net Purchases	Ending Inventory	Cost of Goods Sold	Gross Margin
Arc Co.	$92,800	$12,500	$62,700	$19,400	(a)	$37,000
Bell Co.	(b)	27,450	93,000	(c)	$94,100	51,200
Court Co.	94,000	(d)	54,900	22,600	59,400	(e)
Dormer Co.	101,400	10,700	(f)	8,200	(g) 54,300	47,100

2. Prepare the income statement for Dormer Co., which uses the periodic inventory system. Dormer's operating expenses for the year were $32,100.

Determining amounts for the income statement: periodic system

3

(a) $55,800 (c) $26,350
(d) $27,100 (f) $51,800

Exercise 6–10

This exercise tests your understanding of the four inventory methods. In the space provided, write the name of the inventory method that best fits the description. Assume that the cost of inventory is rising.

_____ a. Matches the most current cost of goods sold against sales revenue.

_____ b. Results in an older measure of the cost of ending inventory.

_____ c. Results in a cost of ending inventory that is close to the current cost of replacing the inventory.

Identifying income and other effects of the inventory methods

2

_____ d. Maximizes reported income.

_____ e. Enables a company to buy high-cost inventory at year end and thereby decrease reported income.

_____ f. Used to account for automobiles, jewellery, and art objects.

_____ g. Provides a middle-ground measure of ending inventory and cost of goods sold.

Applying the lower-of-cost-or-market rule to inventories: perpetual system

Exercise 6–11

Princeton Garden Supplies, which uses a perpetual inventory system and the FIFO method, has these account balances at December 31, 2009, prior to releasing the financial statements for the year:

Inventory	Cost of Goods Sold	Sales Revenue
Beg. bal. 25,000		
End. bal. 42,000	Bal. 250,000	Bal. 470,000

The company has determined that the net realizable value of the December 31, 2009 ending inventory is $35,000.

Required

Prepare Princeton Garden Supplies' balance sheet at December 31, 2009 to show how Princeton would apply the lower-of-cost-or-market rule to inventories. Include a complete heading for the statement.

Excel Spreadsheet Template

Applying the lower-of-cost-or-market rule to inventories: periodic system

Gross margin $65,700

Exercise 6–12

Signal Tool Company's income statement for the month ended August 31, 2008, reported the following data:

Income Statement

Sales revenue		$267,000
Cost of goods sold:		
Beginning inventory	$ 51,600	
Net purchases	203,100	
Cost of goods available for sale	254,700	
Ending inventory	71,400	
Cost of goods sold		183,300
Gross margin		$ 83,700

Before the financial statements were released, it was discovered that the current net realizable value of ending inventory was $53,400. Adjust the preceding income statement to apply the lower-of-cost-or-market rule to Signal Tool Company's inventory. Also, show the relevant portion of Signal Tool Company's balance sheet. The net realizable value of the beginning inventory was $55,800.

Measuring the effect of an inventory error

b. Gross margin $19,000

Exercise 6–13

Paris Bakery reported sales revenue of $28,000 and cost of goods sold of $12,000. Compute Paris Bakery's correct gross margin if the company made each of the following accounting errors. Show your work.

a. Ending inventory is overstated by $3,000.

b. Ending inventory is understated by $3,000.

Correcting an inventory error

Net income before taxes 2008 $34,560

Exercise 6–14

Myrtle Bay Marine Supply reported the comparative income statement for the years ended September 30, 2009 and 2008 shown on the next page.

MYRTLE BAY MARINE SUPPLY
Income Statements
For the Years Ended September 30, 2009 and 2008

	2009		2008	
Sales revenue		$164,760		$146,040
Cost of goods sold:				
Beginning inventory	$ 16,800		$ 15,360	
Net purchases	91,200		78,000	
Cost of goods available	108,000		93,360	
Ending inventory	23,520		16,800	
Cost of goods sold...................		84,480		76,560
Gross margin................................		80,280		69,480
Operating expenses.....................		36,360		31,320
Net income before taxes.............		$ 43,920		$ 38,160

During 2009, accountants for the company discovered that ending 2008 inventory was overstated by $3,600. Prepare the corrected comparative income statement for the two-year period, complete with a heading for the statement. What was the effect of the error on net income for the two years combined? Explain your answer.

Exercise 6–15

Assessing the effect of an inventory error on two years' statements

Janet Crawford, accountant of Prairie Electronics Ltd., learned that Prairie Electronics' $12 million cost of inventory at the end of last year was overstated by $3.6 million. She notified the company president of the accounting error and the need to alert the company's lenders that last year's reported net income was incorrect. Eric Brewer, president of Prairie Electronics Ltd., explained to Crawford that there is no need to report the error to lenders because the error will counterbalance this year. This year's error will affect this year's net income in the opposite direction of last year's error. Even with no correction, Brewer reasons, net income for both years combined will be the same whether or not Prairie Electronics Ltd. corrects its errors.

Required

1. Was last year's reported net income of $24.0 million overstated, understated, or correct? What was the correct amount of net income last year?

2. Is this year's net income of $27 million overstated, understated, or correct? What is the correct amount of net income for the current year?

3. Whose perspective is better, Crawford's or Brewer's? Give your reason. Consider the trend of reported net income both without the correction and with the correction.

Exercise 6–16

Ethical implications of inventory actions

Determine whether each of the following actions in buying, selling, and accounting for inventories is ethical or unethical. Give your reason for each answer.

1. Spartan Corporation consciously overstated purchases to produce a high figure for cost of goods sold (low amount of net income). The real reason was to decrease the company's income tax payments to the government.

2. In applying the lower-of-cost-or-market rule to inventories, Pierstone Industries recorded an excessively low market value for ending inventory. This allowed the company to pay no income tax for the year.

3. Eagle Distributors purchased lots of inventory shortly before year end to increase the LIFO cost of goods sold and decrease reported income for the year.

4. Vimy Electrical Products delayed the purchase of inventory until after December 31, 2008, in order to keep 2008's cost of goods sold from growing too large. The delay in purchasing inventory helped net income of 2008 to reach the level of profit demanded by the company's investors.

5. Stetler Sales Company deliberately overstated ending inventory in order to report higher profits (net income).

Estimating inventory by the
gross margin method

Est. inventory cost $208,000

Exercise 6–17

Dundas Company began April with inventory of $100,000. The business made net purchases of $300,000 and had net sales of $320,000 before a fire destroyed the company's inventory. For the past several years, Dundas Company's gross margin on sales has been 40 percent. Estimate the cost of the inventory destroyed by the fire. Identify another reason owners and managers use the gross margin method to estimate inventory on a regular basis.

Estimating inventory by the
retail method

Est. ending inventory cost,
Teenage line $70,000

Exercise 6–18

Mandy's Designs has three lines of women's sportswear: Teenage, Young Woman, and Mature. The selling price of each item is double its cost price. On May 18, 2009, Mandy's Designs had a fire that destroyed all the inventory. Sales for the period January 1 to May 18 were: Teenage, $440,000; Young Woman, $540,000; and Mature, $720,000. Inventory at January 1, 2009, was: Teenage, $90,000; Young Woman, $120,000; and Mature, $150,000. Purchases made from January 1 to May 18, at cost, were: Teenage, $200,000; Young Woman, $200,000; and Mature, $300,000.

Required   Use the retail method to calculate the cost of the inventory lost in the fire.

Challenge Exercises

Inventory policy decisions

Exercise 6–19

For each of the following situations, identify the inventory method that you are using or would prefer to use, or, given the use of a particular method, state the strategy that you would follow to accomplish your goal.

a. Inventory costs are increasing. Your business uses LIFO and is having an unexpectedly good year. It is near year end, and you need to keep net income from increasing too much.

b. Inventory costs have been stable for several years, and you expect costs to remain stable for the indefinite future. (Give your reason for your choice of method.)

c. Inventory costs are decreasing, and you want to maximize income.

d. Company management prefers a middle-of-the-road inventory policy that avoids extremes.

e. Your inventory turns over very rapidly, and the business uses a perpetual inventory system. Inventory costs are increasing, and the business prefers to report high income.

Evaluating a company's
profitability

Exercise 6–20

Western Glass Products Ltd. is a leading provider of bottles for the brewing industry. Suppose the company recently reported these figures.

WESTERN GLASS PRODUCTS LTD.
Income Statement
For the Years Ended July 31, 2009 and 2008 (amounts in thousands)

	2009	2008
Sales	$135,000	$103,160
Cost of sales	97,200	77,666
Gross margin	37,800	25,494
Cost and expenses		
Selling, general and administrative	27,765	21,111
Amortization	2,762	1,169
Restructuring charges	9,039	—
	39,566	22,280
Operating income (loss)	(1,766)	3,214
Other items (summarized)	(808)	(1,675)
Net income (loss)	$ (2,574)	$ 1,539

Required   Evaluate Western Glass's operations during 2009 in comparison with 2008. Consider sales, gross margin, operating income, and net income. In the annual report, Western Glass's management describes the restructuring charges in 2009 as a one-time event that is not expected to recur. How does this additional information affect your evaluation?

Beyond the Numbers

The inventory costing method chosen by a company can affect the financial statements and thus the decisions of the users of those statements.

Assessing the impact of the inventory costing method on the financial statements

 2 4

Required

1. A leading accounting researcher stated that one inventory costing method reports the most recent costs in the income statement, while another method reports the most recent costs in the balance sheet. In this person's opinion, this results in one or the other of the statements being "inaccurate" when prices are rising. What did the researcher mean?

2. Conservatism is an accepted accounting concept. Would you want management to be conservative in accounting for inventory if you were (a) a shareholder, and (b) a prospective shareholder? Give your reason.

3. Goldeneye's Cycle Shoppe follows conservative accounting and writes the value of its inventory of bicycles down to market, which has declined below cost. The following year, an unexpected cycling craze results in a demand for bicycles that far exceeds supply, and the market price increases well above the previous cost. What effect will conservatism have on the income of Goldeneye's Cycle Shoppe over the two years?

Ethical Issue

During 2008, Simpson Electronics changed to the LIFO method of accounting for inventory. Suppose that during 2009, Simpson Electronics changes back to the FIFO method, and in the following year switches back to LIFO again.

Required

1. What would you think of a company's ethics if it changed accounting methods every year?

2. What accounting principle would changing methods every year violate?

3. Who can be harmed when a company changes its accounting methods too often? How?

Problems (Group A)

Problem 6–1A

A Danier Leather Inc. outlet store, which uses the FIFO method, began August with 50 units of an inventory item that cost $40 each. During August, the store completed these inventory transactions:

Using the perpetual inventory system—FIFO

 1

2. COGS $4,640
3. Gross margin $3,410

			Units	Unit Cost	Unit Sale Price
Aug.	3	Sale	40		$70
	8	Purchase	80	$44	
	21	Sale	70		$75
	30	Purchase	10	$48	

Required

1. Prepare a perpetual inventory record for this item.
2. Determine the store's cost of goods sold for August.
3. Compute gross margin for August.

Problem 6–2A

Acme Distributors purchases inventory in crates of merchandise.

Assume the company began January with an inventory of 20 units that cost $3,000 each. During the month, the company purchased and sold merchandise on account as shown on the top of the next page.

Accounting for inventory using the perpetual system—LIFO

 1

1. COGS $386,000

| Purchase 1 | 30 units at $3,200 | Purchase 2 | 70 units at $3,500 |
| Sale 1 | 40 units at $6,000 | Sale 2 | 75 units at $7,000 |

Assume Acme Distributors uses the LIFO cost method.

Cash payments on account totalled $200,000. Company operating expenses for the month were $150,000. The department paid two-thirds in cash, with the rest accrued as Accounts Payable.

Required

1. Prepare a perpetual inventory record, at LIFO cost, for this merchandise.
2. Make journal entries to record the company's transactions.

Accounting for inventory in a perpetual system—moving-weighted-average cost

Problem 6–3A

1. COGS $383,738

Refer to the Acme Distributors situation in Problem 6–2A. Keep all the data unchanged, except assume that Acme uses the moving-weighted-average cost method.

Required

1. Prepared a perpetual inventory record at moving-weighted-average cost. Round average unit cost to the nearest cent and all other amounts to the nearest dollar.
2. Prepare a multistep income statement for Acme Distributors for the month of January.

Accounting for inventory in a perpetual system—FIFO

Problem 6–4A

3. Gross margin $18,050

Western Hardware operates a store in Red Deer, Alberta. Assume the company's fiscal year end is January 31. Also assume the company began fiscal year 2009 with an inventory of 50 power drills that cost $3,000 in total. During the year, the company purchased merchandise on account as follows:

March (60 units at $65)	$ 3,900
August (40 units at $70)	2,800
October (180 units at $75)	13,500
Total purchases	$20,200

Cash payments on account during the year totalled $18,000.

During fiscal year 2009, the company sold 300 drills for $39,000, of which $26,000 was for cash and the balance was on account. Western uses the FIFO method for inventories.

Required

1. Make summary journal entries to record the department's transactions for the year ended January 31, 2009. The company uses a perpetual inventory system.
2. Determine the FIFO cost of the company's ending inventory at January 31, 2009. Use a T-account.
3. Calculate Western Hardware's gross margin for the year ended January 31, 2009.

Computing inventory by three methods—periodic system

Problem 6–5A

2. Gross margin:
Weighted-avg. $10,141
FIFO $10,377
LIFO $9,779

Simcoe Framing Co. began March with 73 units of inventory that cost $30 each. During the month, Simcoe made the following purchases:

March 4		113 at $35
12		81 at $38
19		167 at $40
25		44 at $42

The company uses the periodic inventory system, and the physical count at March 31 includes 51 units of inventory on hand.

Required

1. Determine the ending inventory and cost-of-goods-sold amounts for the March financial statements under (a) average cost, (b) FIFO cost, and (c) LIFO cost. Round average cost per unit to the nearest cent and all other amounts to the nearest dollar.

2. Sales revenue for March totalled $26,000. Compute Simcoe's gross margin for March under each method.

3. Which method will result in the lowest income taxes for Simcoe? Why?

4. Which method will result in the highest net income for Simcoe? Why?

Problem 6–6A

Using the periodic inventory system—LIFO

2. COGS $305,000

Renfrew Baseball Products, which uses a periodic inventory system, began 2008 with 6,000 units of inventory that cost a total of $60,000. During 2008, Renfrew purchased merchandise on account as follows:

Purchase 1 (10,000 units costing $12.50 per unit)	$125,000
Purchase 2 (20,000 units costing $14.00 per unit)	280,000

At year end, the physical count indicated 14,000 units of inventory on hand.

Required

1. How many units did Renfrew sell during the year? The sale price per unit was $25. Determine Renfrew's sales revenue for the year.

2. Compute cost of goods sold by the LIFO method. Then determine gross margin for the year.

Problem 6–7A

Using the perpetual and periodic inventory systems

3. Gross margin $4,100

Timmins Performance Tire began June with 50 units of inventory that cost $122 each. The sale price of each was $190. During June, Timmins Performance Tire completed these inventory transactions:

			Unit	Unit Cost	Unit Selling Price
June	2	Purchase	12	$125	$175
	8	Sale	27	122	170
	13	Sale	23	122	170
		Sale	3	125	175
	17	Purchase	24	125	175
	22	Sale	31	125	175
	29	Purchase	24	130	180

Required

1. The above data are taken from Timmins Performance Tire's perpetual inventory records. Which cost method does Timmins Performance Tire use?

2. Compute Timmins Performance Tire's cost of goods sold for June under the
   a. Perpetual inventory system
   b. Periodic inventory system

3. Compute gross margin for June.

Problem 6–8A

Applying the lower-of-cost-or-market rule to inventories

COGS $69,700,000

Jennings Home Furniture has recently been plagued with lacklustre sales. The rate of inventory turnover has dropped, and some of the business's merchandise is gathering dust. At the same time, competition has forced the business to lower the selling prices of its inventory. It is now December 31, 2008. Assume the net realizable value of a Jennings Home Furniture store's ending inventory is $1,500,000 below what Jennings Home Furniture paid for the goods, which was $12,300,000. Before any adjustments at the end of the period, assume the store's Cost of Goods Sold account has a balance of $68,200,000.

What action should Jennings Home Furniture take in this situation, if any? Give any journal entry required. At what amount should Jennings Home Furniture report Inventory on the balance sheet? At what amount should the business report Cost of Goods Sold on the income statement? Discuss the accounting principle or concept that is most relevant to this situation.

Correcting inventory errors
over a three-year period

5

1. Net income 2009 $58 thou.

Problem 6–9A

The accounting records of Best Music Stores show these data (in thousands):

	2009	2008	2007
Net sales revenue	$456	$396	$408
Cost of goods sold:			
Beginning inventory	$ 36	$ 60	$ 96
Net purchases	276	240	216
Cost of goods available	312	300	312
Less ending inventory	72	36	60
Cost of goods sold	240	264	252
Gross margin	216	132	156
Operating expenses	148	92	110
Net income	$ 68	$ 40	$ 46

In early 2010, a team of auditors discovered that the ending inventory of 2007 had been understated by $8 thousand. Also, the ending inventory for 2009 had been overstated by $10 thousand. The ending inventory at December 31, 2008 was correct.

Required

1. Show corrected comparative income statements for the three years.

2. State whether each year's net income as reported here and the related owner's equity amounts are understated or overstated. For each incorrect figure, indicate the amount of the understatement or overstatement.

**Excel Spreadsheet
Template**

Estimating inventory by the
gross margin method; preparing
the income statement

 6

2. Gross margin $2,805,000

Problem 6–10A

Assume Park Stores estimates its inventory by the gross margin method when preparing monthly financial statements (assume Park Stores uses the periodic method otherwise). For the past two years, gross margin has averaged 30 percent of net sales. Assume further that the business's inventory records for its stores reveal the following data:

Inventory, July 1, 2008	$ 200,000
Transactions during July:	
Purchases	6,575,000
Purchases returns	25,000
Sales	9,375,000
Sales returns	25,000

Required

1. Estimate the July 31, 2008 inventory using the gross margin method.

2. Prepare the July 2008 income statement through gross margin for Park Stores.

Accounting for inventory by the
periodic system; estimating
inventory by the
gross margin method

 3 6

1. Est. inventory, Aug. 31, 2009
$103,750

Problem 6–11A

The Lynden Shoe Company has a periodic inventory system and uses the gross margin method of estimating inventories for interim financial statements. The company had the following account balances for the fiscal year ended August 31, 2009:

Inventory—Sept. 1, 2008	$ 150,000
Purchases	890,000
Purchases returns and allowances	29,000
Freight in	6,000
Sales	1,450,000
Sales returns and allowances	45,000

Required

1. Use the gross margin method to estimate the cost of the business's ending inventory, assuming the business has an average gross margin rate of 35 percent.

2. The business has done a physical count of the inventory on hand on August 31, 2009. For convenience, this inventory was calculated using the retail selling prices marked on the

goods, which amounted to $175,000. Use the information from Requirement 1 to calculate the cost of the inventory counted.

3. What is the cost of the business's estimated inventory overage?

4. Give the summary journal entries required at August 31, 2009. Also record any shortage or overage.

Problem 6–12A

Computing ending inventory by applying three inventory costing methods in a periodic inventory system

Balic Office Supplies distributes office furniture from its location in Kitchener, Ontario. The company's fiscal year ends on January 31, 2008. One department in the company had 20 office suites that cost $1,500 each. During the quarter, the department purchased merchandise on account as follows:

2. Gross margin (a) $165,300 (b) $164,500 (c) $163,500

	Units	Unit cost	Total
November 2007	60	$1,600	$96,000
December 2007	40	1,650	66,000
January 2008	30	1,550	46,500

Sales for each month in the quarter were as follows:

	Units	Selling price	Total
November 2007	50	$3,000	$150,000
December 2007	20	2,700	54,000
January 2008	60	2,800	168,000

Operating expenses in the quarter were $100,000.

Required

1. Determine the cost of the department's ending inventory at January 31, 2008, under (a) weighted average, (b) FIFO, and (c) LIFO. Assume the company uses the periodic inventory system and determines cost of goods sold at the end of each quarter.

2. Prepare the department's income statement for the quarter ended January 31, 2008, under each method described in Requirement 1. Show gross margin and operating income.

Problem 6–13A

Computing ending inventory by applying three inventory costing methods in a perpetual inventory system

Refer to the information in Problem 6–12A. Assume that the company uses a perpetual inventory system. Also assume that monthly purchases of inventory occur on the first day of each month.

2. Gross margin (a) $165,348 (b) $164,500 (c) $163,500

Required

1. Determine the cost of the department's ending inventory at January 31, 2008, under (a) moving-weighted-average, (b) FIFO, and (c) LIFO.

2. Prepare the department's income statement for the quarter ended January 31, 2008, under each method described in Requirement 1. Show gross margin and operating income.

Problem 6–14A

Accounting for inventory by the perpetual inventory system; applying the LIFO and FIFO costing methods; estimating inventory by the gross margin method.

Andrew's Auto Parts uses the perpetual inventory system for the purchase and sale of inventory and had the following information available on April 30, 2009:

1. COGS (a) LIFO $346,500; (b) FIFO $340,200

Purchases and Sales		Number of Units	Cost or Selling Price per Unit
April	1 Balance of inventory	3,900	$10
	7 Purchased	6,000	$14
	8 Sold	4,500	$19
	12 Purchased	7,500	$13
	16 Sold	9,000	$21
	21 Purchased	4,500	$13
	25 Purchased	10,500	$12
	29 Sold	13,500	$21

Required

1. Calculate the cost of goods sold and the cost of the ending inventory for May under each of the following inventory costing methods: (a) LIFO, (b) FIFO.

2. Prepare the journal entries required to record the transactions using the perpetual inventory system with FIFO costing.

3. An internal audit has discovered that a new employee—an accounting clerk—had been stealing merchandise and covering up the shortage by changing the inventory records. For example, if 120 units were purchased at $10 per unit, he would record it as 100 units purchased at $12 per unit and then steal the other 20 units.

    The external auditors examined the accounting records prior to the employment of the individual and noted that the company has an average gross margin rate of 40 percent. They estimate that 95 percent of the incorrectly costed units have been sold.

    Use the gross margin method to estimate the cost of the inventory shortage (under the FIFO costing method) and give the journal entry required to correct it.

4. What would be the effect on the net income for the year ending April 30, 2009, if the inventory shortage had not been discovered? For the year ending April 30, 2010?

Problems (Group B)

Using the perpetual inventory system—FIFO

2. COGS $3,140
3. Gross margin $7,580

Problem 6–1B

Atkinson Lawn Supply, which uses the FIFO method, began March with 100 units of inventory that cost $20 each. During March, Atkinson completed these inventory transactions:

		Units	Unit Cost	Unit Sale Price
March 2	Purchase	24	$25	
8	Sale	80		$72
17	Purchase	48	$30	
22	Sale	62		$80

Required

1. Prepare a perpetual inventory record for the lawn supply merchandise.
2. Determine Atkinson's cost of goods sold for March.
3. Compute gross margin for March.

Accounting for inventory in a perpetual system—FIFO

1. COGS $6,000

Problem 6–2B

Aspen Imports is a furniture distributor in Winnipeg. The following information is for one item of inventory, kitchen chairs, for the month of February. The store purchased and sold merchandise on account as follows:

Feb.	1	Opening inventory	50 chairs at $30
	3	Purchase 1	60 chairs at $35
	10	Sale 1	100 chairs at $60
	22	Purchase 2	90 chairs at $40
	24	Sale 2	70 chairs at $70

Assume that Aspen Imports uses the FIFO cost method. All sales were made on account. Operating expenses were $4,800 with two-thirds paid in cash and the rest accrued as Accounts Payable.

Required

1. Prepare a perpetual inventory record, at FIFO cost, for this merchandise.
2. Make journal entries to record the company's transactions.

Accounting for inventory in a perpetual system—moving-weighted-average cost

1. COGS $6,022

Problem 6–3B

Refer to the Aspen Imports situation in Problem 6–2B. Keep all the data unchanged, except that Aspen uses the moving-weighted-average cost method.

Required

1. Prepare a perpetual inventory record at moving-weighted-average cost. Round average unit cost to the nearest cent and all other amounts to the nearest dollar.

2. Prepare a multistep income statement for Aspen Imports for the month of February.

Problem 6–4B

Accounting for inventory in a perpetual system—LIFO

3. Net income $10,400

Suppose Rona purchases inventory in crates of merchandise, so each unit of inventory is a crate of tools or building supplies. Assume you are dealing with a single department in a Rona store in Regina. The fiscal year of Rona ends each January 31.

Assume the department began fiscal year 2008 with an inventory of 40 units that cost a total of $4,000. During the year, the department purchased merchandise on account as follows:

April (60 units at $110)..	$ 6,600
August (100 units at $110)..	11,000
November (200 units at $120)...	24,000
Total purchases	$41,600

Cash payments on account during the year totalled $38,000.

During fiscal year 2008, the department sold 380 units of merchandise for $76,000, of which $12,000 was for cash and the balance was on account. Assume Rona uses the LIFO method for inventories. Department operating expenses for the year were $22,000. The department paid two-thirds of the operating expenses in cash and accrued the rest.

Required

1. Make summary journal entries to record the department transactions for the year ended January 31, 2008. Rona uses a perpetual inventory system.

2. Determine the LIFO cost of the store's ending inventory at January 31, 2008. Use a T-account.

3. Prepare the department's income statement for the year ended January 31, 2008. Include a complete heading, and show totals for the gross margin and net income.

Problem 6–5B

Computing inventory by three methods—periodic system

2. Gross margin:
Weighted-avg. $68,262
FIFO $70,534
LIFO $65,928

Modern Appliances began December with 140 units of inventory that cost $150 each. During December, the store made the following purchases:

Dec.	3	....	217 at $160
	12	....	95 at $164
	18	....	210 at $166
	24	....	248 at $174

The store uses the periodic inventory system, and the physical count at December 31 indicates that 229 units of inventory are on hand.

Required

1. Determine the ending inventory and cost-of-goods-sold amounts for the December financial statements under the weighted-average cost, FIFO, and LIFO methods. Round average cost per unit to the nearest cent and all other amounts to the nearest dollar.

2. Sales revenue for December totalled $180,000. Compute Modern Appliances' gross margin for December under each method.

3. Which method will result in the lowest income taxes for Modern Appliances? Why? Which method will result in the highest net income for Modern Appliances? Why?

Problem 6–6B

Using the periodic inventory system—FIFO and weighted average

2. COGS:
FIFO $292,500
Weighted-Avg. $296,980

Kingston Hardware Company, which uses a periodic inventory system, began 2008 with 6,000 units of inventory that cost a total of $45,000. During 2008, Kingston purchased merchandise on account as follows:

Purchase 1 (10,000 units)...	$ 90,000
Purchase 2 (20,000 units)...	210,000

At year end, the physical count indicated 5,000 units of inventory on hand.

Required

1. How many units did Kingston sell during the year? The sale price per unit was $15. Determine Kingston's sales revenue for the year.

2. Compute cost of goods sold by both the FIFO and the weighted-average method. Then determine gross margin for the year under each method.

Using the perpetual and periodic inventory systems

3. Gross margin $5,100

Problem 6–7B

The Canvas Company (TCC) began May 2009 with 50 units of inventory that cost $70 each. The sale price of each of those units was $120. During May, TCC completed these inventory transactions:

			Units	Unit Cost	Units Sales Price
May	3	Sale	16	$70	$120
	8	Purchase	80	72	124
	11	Sale	34	70	120
	19	Sale	9	72	124
	24	Sale	35	72	124
	30	Purchase	18	74	126
	31	Sale	6	72	124

Required

1. The above data are taken from TCC's perpetual inventory records. Which cost method does the company use?

2. Compute TCC's cost of goods sold for May under the
   a. Perpetual inventory system
   b. Periodic inventory system

3. Compute gross margin for May.

Applying the lower-of-cost-or-market rule to inventories

COGS $61,360,000

Problem 6–8B

Ace Building Supplies has recently been plagued with declining sales. The rate of inventory turnover has dropped, and some of the company's merchandise is gathering dust. At the same time, competition has forced Ace Building Supplies to lower the selling prices of its inventory. It is now December 31, 2008, and the net realizable value of Ace Building Supplies' ending inventory is $1,456,000 below what the business actually paid for the goods, which was $10,192,000. Before any adjustments at the end of the period, Ace Building Supplies' Cost of Goods Sold account has a balance of $59,904,000.

What action should Ace Building Supplies take in this situation, if any? Give any journal entry required. At what amount should Ace Building Supplies report Inventory on the balance sheet? At what amount should the company report Cost of Goods Sold on the income statement? Discuss the accounting principle or concept that is most relevant to this situation.

Correcting inventory errors over a three-year period

1. Net income 2009 $57 thou.

Problem 6–9B

The books of Cape Breton Windows and Siding show these data (in thousands):

	2009		2008		2007	
Net sales revenue		$360		$275		$240
Cost of goods sold:						
Beginning inventory	$ 65		$ 55		$ 70	
Net purchases	195		135		130	
Cost of goods available	260		190		200	
Less ending inventory	70		65		55	
Cost of goods sold		190		125		145
Gross margin		170		150		95
Operating expenses		119		109		72
Net income		$ 51		$ 41		$ 23

In early 2010, a team of Canada Revenue Agency auditors discovered that the ending inventory of 2007 had been overstated by $12 thousand. Also, the ending inventory for 2009 had been understated by $6 thousand. The ending inventory at December 31, 2008 was correct.

Required

1. Show corrected comparative income statements for the three years.
2. State whether each year's net income as reported here and the related owner's equity amounts are understated or overstated. For each incorrect figure, indicate the amount of the understatement or overstatement.

Problem 6–10B

Assume Enderby Linen Stores estimates its inventory by the gross margin method when preparing monthly financial statements (it uses the periodic method otherwise). For the past two years, the gross margin has averaged 40 percent of net sales. Assume further that the company's inventory records for stores in Western Canada reveal the following data:

Inventory, June 1, 2008..	$ 954,000
Transactions during June:	
Purchases..	9,851,000
Sales...	$16,718,000

Required

1. Estimate the June 30, 2008 inventory using the gross margin method.
2. Prepare the June income statement through gross margin for the Enderby Linen Stores locations in the Western Canada region.

Problem 6–11B

Trail Company has a periodic inventory system and uses the gross margin method of estimating inventories for interim financial statements. The business had the following account balances for the fiscal year ended August 31, 2009:

Inventory—Sept. 1, 2008...	$ 57,000
Purchases..	490,500
Purchases returns and allowances...	70,500
Freight in...	3,600
Sales...	663,000
Sales returns and allowances..	12,000

Required

1. Use the gross margin method to estimate the cost of the business's ending inventory, assuming the business has an average gross margin rate of 40 percent.
2. The business has done a physical count of the inventory on hand on August 31, 2009. For convenience, this inventory was calculated using the retail selling prices marked on the goods, which amounted to $121,950. Use the information from Requirement 1 to calculate the cost of the inventory counted.
3. What is the cost of the business's estimated inventory shortage?
4. Give the summary journal entries required at August 31, 2009 and the adjustment required for the shortage.
5. Of what other use would the information in Requirement 4 be to the business?

Problem 6–12B

Pinn's Industrial Supplies distributes industrial equipment from its location in Brandon, Manitoba. The company's fiscal year ends on January 31, 2008. One department in the company had 40 items that cost $600 each on hand at October 31, 2007. During the quarter, the department purchased merchandise on account as shown at the top of the next page.

Excel Spreadsheet Template

Estimating ending inventory by the gross margin method; preparing the income statement

2. Gross margin $6,687,200

Accounting for inventory by the periodic system; estimating inventory by the gross margin method

1. Est. inventory, Aug. 31, 2009 $90,000

Computing ending inventory by applying three inventory costing methods in a periodic inventory system

2. Gross margin (a) $105,550 (b) $103,000 (c) $106,000

	Units	Unit cost	Total
November 2007	100	$650	$65,000
December 2007	20	400	8,000
January 2008	40	500	20,000

Sales for each month in the quarter were as follows:

	Units	Selling price	Total
November 2007	30	$1,400	$ 42,000
December 2007	90	1,200	108,000
January 2008	50	1,100	55,000

Operating expenses in the quarter were $60,000.

Required

1. Determine the cost of the department's ending inventory at January 31, 2008, under (a) weighted average, (b) FIFO, and (c) LIFO. Assume the company uses the periodic inventory system and determines cost of goods sold at the end of each quarter.

2. Prepare the department's income statement for the quarter ended January 31, 2008, under each method described in Requirement 1. Show totals for gross margin and operating income.

Computing ending inventory by applying three inventory costing methods in a perpetual inventory system

2. Gross margin (a) $103,000
(b) $104,492 (c) $106,000

Problem 6–13B

Refer to the information in Problem 6–12B. Assume that the company uses a perpetual inventory system. Also assume that monthly purchases of inventory occur on the first day of each month.

Required

1. Determine the cost of the department's ending inventory at January 31, 2008, under (a) moving-weighted-average, (b) FIFO, and (c) LIFO.

2. Prepare the department's income statement for the quarter ended January 31, 2008, under each method described in 1. Show totals for gross margin and operating income.

Accounting for inventory by the perpetual inventory system, applying the LIFO and FIFO costing methods; estimating inventory by the gross margin method

1. COGS (a) LIFO $145,000
(b) FIFO $142,000

Problem 6–14B

Cochrane Sales uses the perpetual inventory system for the purchase and sale of inventory and had the following information available on August 31, 2008:

Purchases and Sales		Number of Units	Cost or Selling Price per Unit
Aug.	1 Balance of inventory	900	$15
	7 Purchased	2,500	$14
	8 Sold	2,000	$25
	12 Purchased	1,750	$15
	16 Sold	2,900	$26
	21 Purchased	2,000	$17
	25 Purchased	3,000	$19
	29 Sold	4,000	$27

Required

1. Calculate the cost of goods sold and the cost of the ending inventory for August under each of the following inventory costing methods: (a) LIFO, (b) FIFO.

2. Prepare the journal entries required to record the August transactions using the perpetual inventory system with FIFO costing.

3. An internal audit has discovered that two new employees—an accounting clerk and an employee from the purchasing department—had been stealing merchandise and covering up the shortage by changing the inventory records. For example, if 130 units were purchased at $10 per unit, they would record it as 100 units purchased at $13 per unit and then steal the other 30 units.

The external auditors examined the accounting records prior to the employment of the two individuals and noted that the company had an average gross margin rate of 50 percent. They estimate that 90 percent of the incorrectly costed units have been sold.

Use the gross margin method to estimate the cost of the inventory shortage (under the FIFO costing method) and give the journal entry required to correct it.

4. What would be the effect on the net income for the year ending August 31, 2008, if the inventory shortage had not been discovered? For the year ending August 31, 2009?

Challenge Problems

Problem 6–1C

An anonymous source advised Canada Revenue Agency (CRA) that Jim Williams, owner of Williams Grocery Store, has been filing fraudulent tax returns for the past several years. You, a tax auditor with CRA, are in the process of auditing Williams Grocery Store for the year ended December 31, 2008. The tax returns for the past five years show a decreasing value for ending inventory from 2003, when Williams bought the business, to 2007; the return for 2008 shows the same sort of decrease. You have performed a quick survey of the large store and the attached warehouse and observed that both seemed very well stocked.

Required Does the information set forth above suggest anything to you that might confirm the anonymous tip? What would you do to confirm or deny your suspicions?

Inventory measurement and income

Problem 6–2C

It is Monday morning. You heard on the morning news that a client of your public accounting firm, Midland Electronics, had a fire the previous Friday night that destroyed its office and warehouse, and you concluded that inventory records as well as inventory probably perished in the fire. Since you had been at Midland Electronics on the previous Friday preparing the monthly income statement for the previous month that ended on Thursday, you realize you probably have the only current financial information available for Midland Electronics.

Upon arrival at your firm's office, you meet your partner who confirms your suspicions. Midland Electronics lost all its inventory and its records. She tells you that the company wants your firm to prepare information for a fire loss claim for Midland Electronics' insurance company for the inventory.

You know the audit file for the fiscal year that ended three months earlier contains a complete section dealing with inventory and the four product lines Midland Electronics carried, including the most recent gross margin rate for each line. The file will show total inventory and how much inventory there was by product line at the year end. You also recall that the file contains an analysis of sales by product line for the past several years and that Midland Electronics used a periodic inventory system.

Required Explain how you would use the information available to you to calculate the fire loss by product line.

Estimating inventory from incomplete records

Extending Your Knowledge

Decision Problem

Assessing the impact of a year-end purchase of inventory—periodic system

3

1. Without purchase:
FIFO Gross margin $116,250
LIFO Gross margin $108,000

BackCountry Camping Supplies is nearing the end of its first year of operations. The company uses the periodic inventory method and made inventory purchases of $135,750 during the year as follows:

January	150	units at $125	=	$ 18,750
July	600	units at 150	=	90,000
November	150	units at 180	=	27,000
Totals	900			$135,750

Sales for the year will be 750 units for $225,000 revenue. Expenses other than cost of goods sold will be $50,000. The owner of the company is undecided about whether to adopt FIFO or LIFO.

The company has storage capacity for 600 additional units of inventory. Inventory prices are expected to stay at $180 per unit for the next few months. The president is considering purchasing 150 additional units of inventory at $180 each before the end of the year. He wishes to know how the purchase would affect net income before taxes under both FIFO and LIFO.

Required

1. To help the owner make the decision, prepare income statements under FIFO and under LIFO, both without and with the year-end purchase of 150 units of inventory at $160 per unit.

2. Compare net income before taxes under FIFO without and with the year-end purchase. Make the same comparison under LIFO. Under which method does the year-end purchase have the greater effect on net income before taxes?

3. Under which method can a year-end purchase be made in order to manipulate net income before taxes? Can this method be used for income-tax purposes in Canada?

Financial Statement Case

Inventories

1 **4**

The notes are an important part of a company's financial statements, giving valuable details that would clutter the tabular data presented in the statements. This problem will help you learn to use a company's inventory notes. Refer to the Sun-Rype Products Ltd. financial statements and the related notes in Appendix B. Answer the following questions:

1. What types of inventory does Sun-Rype have? What was the value of each category at December 31, 2005? At December 31, 2004?

2. What valuation method does Sun-Rype use for valuing each category of inventory? Hint: Refer to the significant accounting policies in Note 1.

3. What costs are included in the calculation of finished goods inventory?

Accounting Information Systems

Bruce Dunn is a chartered accountant in Vancouver. Bruce has been a sole practitioner for several years and his business has slowly evolved into one that specializes in accounting for small- and medium-size businesses. Bruce's company provides services such as bookkeeping, financial statement preparation, and income tax planning. As well, Bruce files income tax returns with the Canada Revenue Agency for his clients. Bruce has always relied on a computerized accounting package, such as Simply Accounting®, to manage his clients' (and his own) business affairs.

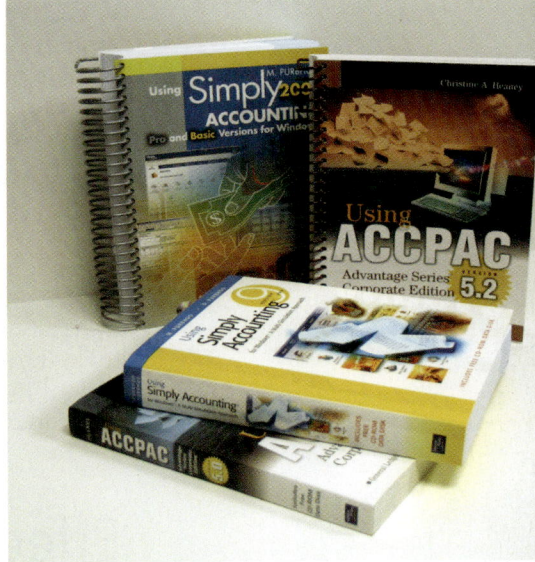

"The computerized accounting packages have become very sophisticated," Bruce observed recently. "Most of my clients can use these packages without extensive training in the fundamentals of accounting. The program will help them manage accounts receivable and accounts payable, and will provide the company with preliminary financial statements. I can then review the statements and make the adjustments necessary to finalize them. It is a real value-added approach. It allows the clients to do their own data entry, and they only pay me for my accounting knowledge, rather than my bookkeeping skills. I can concentrate on analyzing their businesses, and advising them on significant accounting and tax issues. It's a win-win situation for both the client and me. I am so happy with the computerized accounting package I use that I will often buy a copy for a client and install it on their computer for them. It makes my job so much simpler and more rewarding."

? What is an accounting information system, and why is it important?

Are there differences between manual and computerized accounting systems?

How can spreadsheets be used in accounting?

How can special journals be used to combine similar transactions and speed the accounting process?

How can control accounts be used for accounts receivable and accounts payable?

These questions and others will be answered throughout this chapter. And the Decision Guidelines at the end of this chapter will provide the answers in a useful summary.

Every organization needs an accounting system. An **accounting information system** is the combination of personnel, records, and procedures that a business uses to meet its needs for financial data. The system collects information, processes it, and produces reports that meet users' needs. We have already been using an accounting information system in this text. It consists of two basic components:

- A general journal
- A general ledger

Every accounting system has these components, but this simple system can efficiently handle only a few transactions per accounting period. Businesses cope with heavy transaction loads in two ways: computerization and specialization. We *computerize* to do the accounting faster and more reliably. *Specialization* combines similar transactions to speed the process. The second half of this chapter covers special journals that can be used for repetitive transactions.

Effective Accounting Information Systems

**Objective ① **
Describe an effective accounting information system

Good personnel are critical to success. Employees must be both competent and honest. Good design features also make an accounting system run smoothly. An effective system—whether computerized or manual—provides

- Control
- Compatibility
- Flexibility
- A favourable cost/benefit relationship

Features

Control Owners and managers must *control* the business. *Internal controls* safeguard assets and eliminate waste. They are the methods and procedures used to authorize transactions, to ensure adherence to management policy, to safeguard assets and records, to prevent and detect error and fraud, to provide security by limiting access to assets and records, and to ensure that information produced is relevant, accurate, and timely.

For example, in companies such as Sun-Rype Products Ltd. and Nortel Networks Corp., managers control cash payments to avoid theft through unauthorized payments. VISA, MasterCard, American Express, and other credit-card companies keep accurate records of their accounts receivable to ensure that customers are billed and collections are received on time.

Compatibility A *compatible* system is one that works smoothly with the business's operations, personnel, and organizational structure. An example is The Bank of Nova Scotia, which is organized as a network of branch offices. The bank's top managers want to know how much revenue was generated in each region where the bank does business. They also want to analyze the bank's loans in different geographic regions. If revenues and loans in Alberta or Nova Scotia are lagging, the managers can concentrate their collection efforts in that region. They may relocate some branch offices, open new branches, or hire new personnel to increase their revenues and net income. A compatible accounting *information* system conforms to the particular needs of the business.

Flexibility Organizations evolve. They develop new products, sell off unprofitable operations and acquire new ones, adjust employee pay scales and decide to "go green." Changes in the business often call for changes in the accounting system. A well-designed system is *flexible* if it accommodates changes without needing a complete overhaul. Consider Bombardier's acquisition of Canadair, the aircraft manufacturer. Bombardier's accounting system had the flexibility to fold Canadair's financial statements into those of Bombardier Inc., the parent company.

Good Cost/Benefit Relationship Achieving control, compatibility, and flexibility costs money. Managers strive for a system that offers maximum benefits at a minimum cost—that is, a favourable *cost/benefit relationship*. Most small companies, such as Steveston Marine and Hardware, an independent hardware store near Vancouver, use off-the-shelf computerized accounting packages. Such packages include ACCPAC®, Simply Accounting®, and QuickBooks®. Less-expensive accounting software may have limited flexibility and limited capabilities. The very smallest businesses might not computerize at all. But large companies, such as the brokerage firm ScotiaMcLeod, have specialized needs for information. For them, customized programming is a must because the benefits—in terms of information tailored to the company's needs—far outweigh the cost of the system. The result? Better decisions.

All these features are needed whether the accounting system is computerized or manual. Let's begin with a computerized system.

Components of a Computerized Accounting System

A computerized accounting system has two basic components.

- Hardware
- Software

Hardware is the electronic equipment that includes computers, monitors, printers, and the network that connects them. Most systems require a **network** to link computers. In a networked system, a **server** stores the program and the data. With its network, a KPMG auditor in Calgary can access the data of a client located in Tokyo, Japan. The result is a speedier audit for the client, often at lower cost than if the auditor had to perform all the work on site in Tokyo.

Software is the set of programs that drives the computer. Accounting software reads, edits, and stores transaction data. It also generates the reports you can use to run the business. Many software packages are flexible. For example, a company that is only partly computerized may use the computer to account for employee payrolls, and sales and accounts receivable. The other parts of the accounting system may be manual.

THINKING IT OVER

How might a business, such as Zellers, save money with a computerized information system?

A: Personnel time saved from collecting sales data manually and stocking excess inventories; revenue saved from avoiding deep discounts on slow-moving goods; costs saved by avoiding errors.

For large enterprises, such as Molson Canada and the Royal Bank of Canada, the accounting software is integrated into the company **database**, or computerized storehouse of information. Many business databases, or *management information systems*, include both accounting and nonaccounting data. For example, VIA Rail, in negotiating a union contract, often needs to examine the relationship between the employment history and salary levels of company employees. VIA's database provides the data that managers need to negotiate effectively with their labour unions. During negotiations, both parties carry laptops so that they can access the database and analyze data on the spot.

Personnel who operate the system must be properly trained. Properly trained staff are critical to the success of any accounting information system. Modern accounting systems give nonaccounting personnel access to parts (but not all) of the system. For example, a Frito-Lay Canada marketing manager (a nonaccountant) may use a computer and regional sales data (accounting information) to identify the territory that needs a promotional campaign. Management of a computerized accounting system requires careful consideration of data security and screening of the people in the organization who will have access to the data. Security is usually achieved with *passwords,* codes that restrict access to computerized records.

How Computerized and Manual Accounting Systems Work

Computerized accounting systems have replaced manual systems in many organizations—even small businesses such as Steveston Marine and Hardware. As we discuss the stages of data processing, observe the differences between a computerized system and a manual system. The relationship among the three stages of data processing—inputs, processing, outputs—is shown in Exhibit 7–1.

EXHIBIT 7–1   The Three Stages of Data Processing

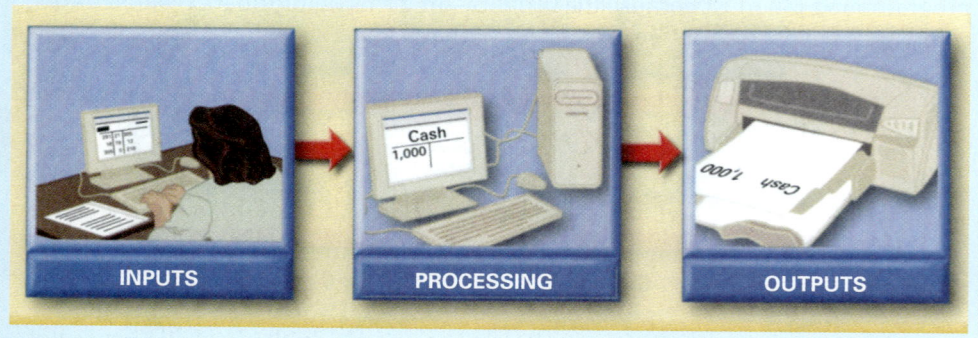

INPUTS | PROCESSING | OUTPUTS

Inputs Inputs come from source documents, such as orders received from customers, sales receipts, and bank deposit slips. Inputs are usually grouped by type. For example, a firm would enter cash sales separately from credit sales and purchases.

Processing In a manual system, *processing* includes journalizing transactions, posting to the accounts, and preparing the financial statements. A computerized system also processes transactions, but without the intermediate steps (journal, ledger, and trial balance). The initial data entered will be posted automatically to the ledger and then processed into reports and financial statements.

Outputs *Outputs* are the reports used for decision making, including the financial statements. Business owners can make better decisions with the reports produced by a good accounting system. In a computerized accounting system, a trial balance is a report (an output). But a manual system would treat the trial balance as a *processing* step leading to the preparation of financial statements. Exhibit 7–2 is an overview of a computerized accounting system. Start with data inputs in the lower left corner.

EXHIBIT 7–2   Overview of a Computerized Accounting System

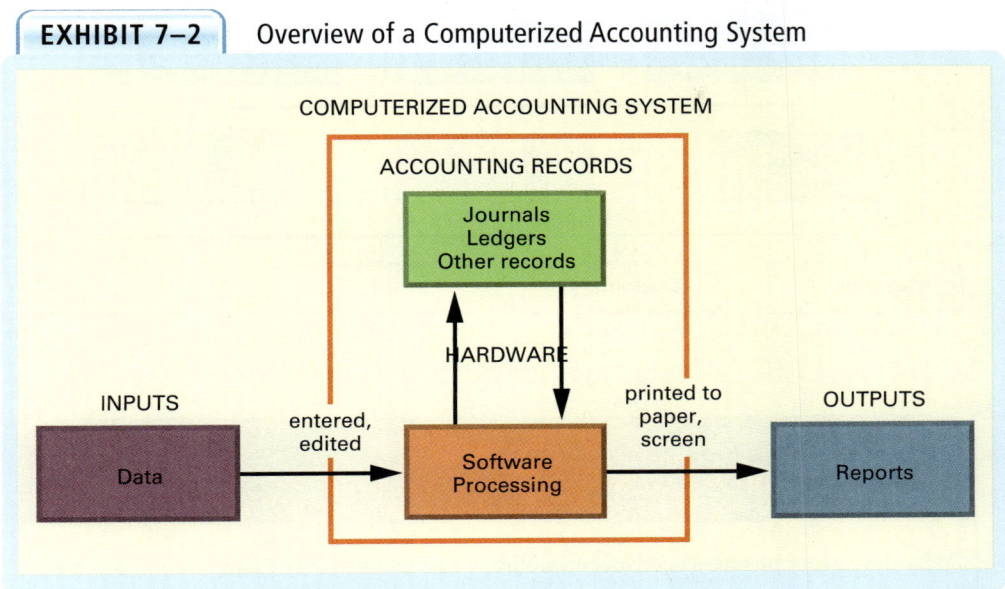

Designing an Accounting System: The Chart of Accounts

An accounting system begins with the chart of accounts. Recall from Chapter 2, page 68, that the chart of accounts lists all accounts in the general ledger and their account numbers. In the accounting system of most companies, the account *numbers* take on added importance. It is efficient to represent a complex account title, such as Accumulated Amortization—Photographic Equipment, with a concise account number (for example, 16570).

Recall the asset accounts generally begin with the digit 1, liabilities with the digit 2, owner's equity accounts with the digit 3, revenues with 4, and expenses with 5. Exhibit 7–3 diagrams one structure for computerized accounts. Assets in this case are divided into current assets, property, plant, and equipment, and other assets. Among the current assets we illustrate only three general ledger accounts: Cash (Account No. 111), Accounts Receivable (No. 115), and Inventory (No. 120). Accounts Receivable holds the *total* dollar amount receivable from all customers.

The account numbers in Exhibit 7–3 get longer and more detailed as you move from top to bottom. For example, Customer A's account number is 1150001, in which 115 represents Accounts Receivable and 0001 refers to Customer A.

The importance of a well-structured chart of accounts cannot be over-emphasized. This is because the reporting component of a computerized accounting system relies on *account number ranges* to translate accounts and their balances into properly organized financial statements and other reports. For example, the accounts numbered 101–399 (assets, liabilities, and owner's equity) are sorted to the balance sheet, and the accounts numbered 401–599 (revenues and expenses) go to the income statement. As another example, reports can be generated based on account numbers if the account numbers are detailed enough to include departments, locations, or divisions of the company. It is crucial to leave room for future accounts and account numbers when designing a chart of accounts.

REAL WORLD EXAMPLE

Businesses use account numbers to input transactions. The account numbers can be chosen to provide additional data. For example, account numbers for the housewares department might end with the digit 2. Thus, a departmental income statement could easily be prepared for the housewares department by selecting all revenue and expense accounts that end in "2".

EXHIBIT 7–3 | Structure for Computerized Accounts

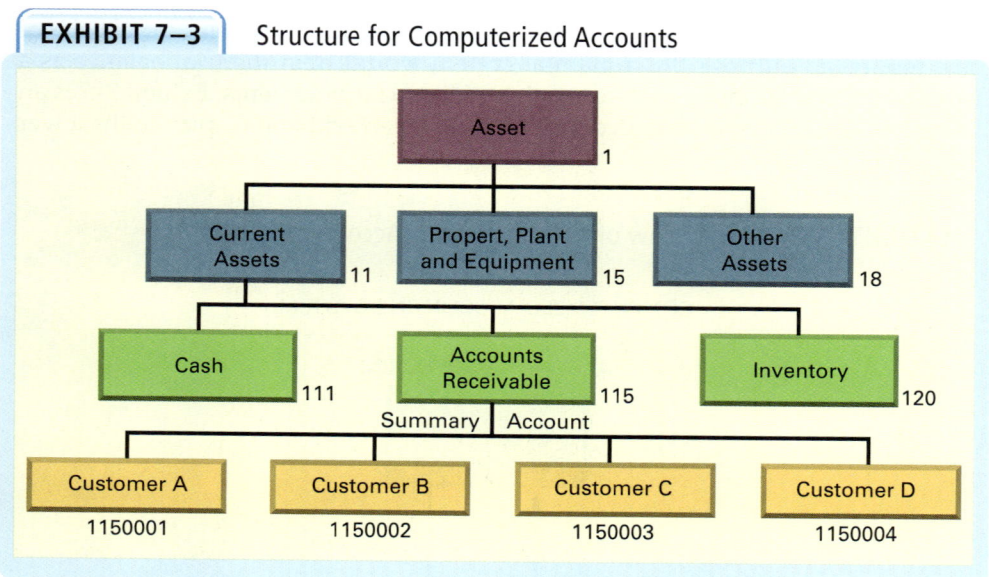

STOP AND THINK

Why does every business need an accounting information system? Give several reasons.

Answer: Owners and managers of businesses must make decisions, and they need information to run the organization. The business's accounting system provides much of this information. Likewise, lenders and outside investors use accounting information in their lending and investment decisions. Most businesses are subject to some form of taxation. An accounting system provides tax information as well.

Processing Transactions: Manual and Menu-Driven Accounting Systems

KEY POINT

The general journal will have the fewest entries. Most transactions fall into one of these four categories: credit sales, cash receipts, credit purchases, or cash payments.

Recording transactions in an actual accounting system requires an additional step that we have skipped thus far. A business of any size *classifies* transactions by type for efficient handling. In a manual system, credit sales, purchases on account, cash receipts, and cash payments are treated as four separate categories. Each category of transactions has its own special journal. (We discuss these journals in detail later in this chapter.) For example:

Sales Journal	Cash Receipts Journal	Purchases Journal	Cash Payments Journal	General Journal
For recording credit sales	For recording cash receipts	For recording credit purchases	For recording cash payments	For transactions *not* in special journals

Payroll payments are another category of transactions and are recorded in the *payroll journal*.

Transactions that do not fit any of the special journals, such as the adjusting and closing entries at the end of the period, are recorded in the *general journal*, which serves as the "journal of last resort."

Computerized systems are organized by function, or task. You can select a function, such as recording sales on account, from a menu. A **menu** is a list of options for choosing computer functions. In such a *menu-driven* system, you first access the *main menu*. You then choose from a submenu until you reach the function you want.

Exhibit 7–4 illustrates one type of menu structure. The menu bar at the top gives the main menu. In the diagram, the computer operator (or accountant) had chosen the Ledger option, as shown by the highlighting. This action opened a submenu of four items—Transactions, Posting, Account Maintenance, and Closing. The Transactions option was then chosen (highlighted by the cursor).

EXHIBIT 7–4 Main Menu of a Computerized Accounting System

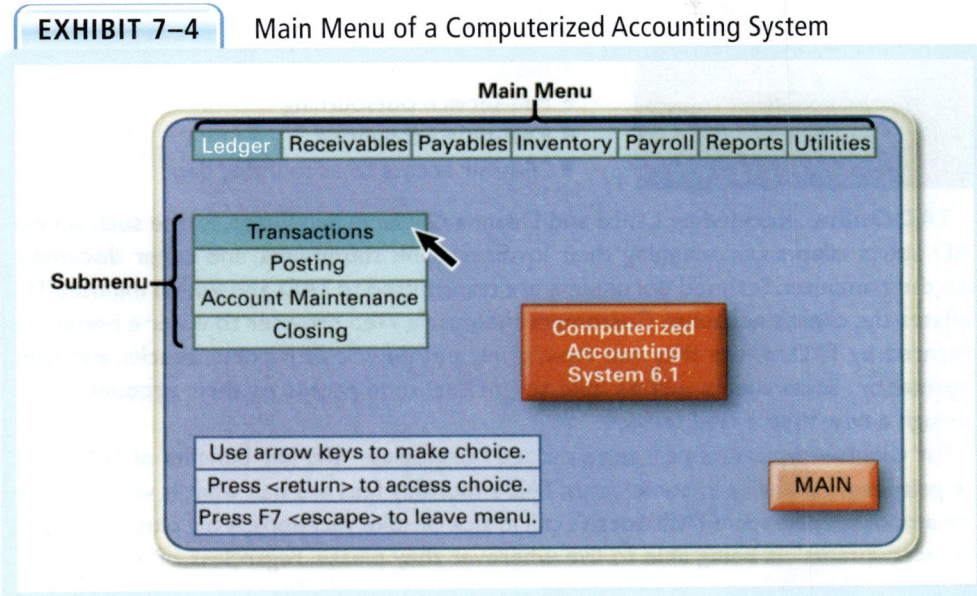

Posting in a computerized system can be performed continuously (**online** or **real-time processing**) or later for a group of similar transactions (**batch processing**). The posting then updates the account balances automatically. Outputs—accounting reports—are the final stage of data processing. In a computerized system, the financial statements can be printed automatically.

Exhibit 7–5 summarizes the accounting cycle in a computerized system and in a manual system. As you study the exhibit, compare and contrast the two types of systems.

Enterprise Resource Planning (ERP) Systems

Many small businesses use QuickBooks® or Simply Accounting®. But larger companies like Nova Scotia Power and Eastlink Telephone are using **enterprise resource planning (ERP)** systems to manage their data. ERP systems such as SAP®, Oracle®, and PeopleSoft® (now owned by Oracle) can integrate all company data into a single data warehouse. ERP feeds the data into software for all company activities— from purchasing to production and customer service.

Advantages of ERP systems include:

- A centralized ERP system can save lots of money in the long run by allowing integration of data and systems.

- ERP helps companies adjust to changes. A change in sales ripples through the purchasing, shipping, and accounting systems.

- An ERP system can replace separate software systems, such as sales and payroll systems.

ERP is expensive in the short run. Major installations can cost millions of dollars. Implementation also requires a large commitment of time and people. For example,

You may think a computer skips steps when data are entered because the computer performs some of the steps internally. However, a computerized system performs all the steps a manual system does, except for the work sheet. Even if you never keep a manual set of books, you still need to understand the entire accounting system.

EXHIBIT 7–5 Comparison of the Accounting Cycle in a Computerized and a Manual System

1	Start with the account balances in the ledger at the beginning of the period.

COMPUTERIZED SYSTEM	**MANUAL SYSTEM**
2 Analyze and classify business transactions by type. Access appropriate menus for data entry.	**2** Analyze and classify business transactions by type. Journalize transactions in special journals or the general journal.
3 Computer automatically posts transactions as a batch or when entered online.	**3** Post journal entries to the ledger accounts.
4 The unadjusted balances are generated immediately after each posting.	**4** Compute the unadjusted balance in each account at the end of the period.
5 The trial balance, if needed, can be accessed as a report.	**5** Enter the trial balance on the work sheet, and complete. (optional)
6 Enter and post adjusting entries. Print the financial statements. Run automatic closing procedures after backing up the period's accounting records.	**6** Prepare the financial statements. Journalize and post the adjusting entries. Journalize and post the closing entries.
7 The next period's opening balances are created automatically as a result of closing.	**7** Prepare the postclosing trial balance. This trial balance becomes Step 1 for the next period.

Hershey Foods Corporation tried to shrink a four-year ERP project into two-and-a-half years. The result? The software did not map into Hershey's operations, and the resulting disrupted deliveries decreased profits in the critical Halloween candy-buying season.

Integrated Accounting Software and Spreadsheets

Objective 3

Understand how spreadsheets are used in accounting

Computerized accounting packages are organized by **modules**, which are integrated units that are compatible and that function together. Changes affecting one module will affect others. For example, entering and posting a credit-sale transaction will update two modules: Accounts Receivable/Sales and Inventory/Cost of Goods Sold. Accounting packages, such as Simply Accounting and QuickBooks, come as a complete set of accounting modules to form an integrated system. However, ACCPAC and Microsoft Business Solutions—Great Plains™ can only be purchased as separate modules.

Spreadsheets are computer programs that link data by means of formulas and functions. Spreadsheets are organized by *cells,* each defined by a column and a row. A cell can contain

- Words (labels), such as Assets, Current assets, or Sales revenue, to identify an item.
- Numbers, such as 10,000 for the balance of Cash or Accounts receivable. Use a *number* if its amount will not change.
- Formulas, where you need to compute an amount that may change. Examples of formulas include
  a. Current assets + Capital assets = Total assets
  b. Revenues − Expenses = Net income
  c. Current assets/Current liabilities = Current ratio

The *cursor,* or electronic highlighter, indicates which cell is active, and it can be moved around the spreadsheet. When the cursor is clicked on a cell, information can be entered there for processing.

Exhibit 7–6 shows an income statement on a spreadsheet screen. The labels were entered in cells A1 through A4. The dollar amount of revenues was entered in cell B2 and expenses in cell B3. A formula was placed in B4 as follows: = B2-B3. This formula subtracts expenses from revenues to compute net income in cell B4. If revenues in cell B2 increase to $200,000, net income in B4 automatically increases to $110,000. No other cells will change.

EXHIBIT 7–6 A Spreadsheet Screen

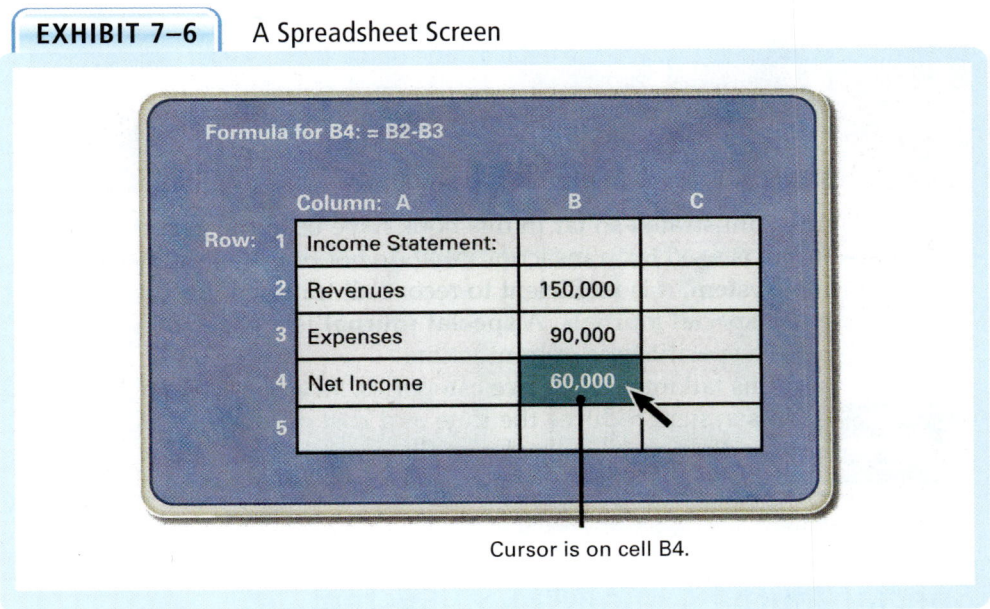

Cursor is on cell B4.

We can add or delete whole rows and columns of data and move blocks of numbers and words on a spreadsheet. The power and versatility of spreadsheets are apparent when enormous amounts of data are entered on the spreadsheet with formula relationships. Change only one number, and you can save hours of manual recalculation. Exhibit 7–7 shows the basic arithmetic operations in Excel spreadsheets.

EXHIBIT 7–7 Basic Arithmetic Operations in Excel Spreadsheets

Operation	Symbol
Addition	+
Subtraction	−
Multiplication	*
Division..	/
Addition of a range of cells	= SUM(beginning cell:ending cell)
Examples:	
Add the contents of cells A2 through A9	= SUM(A2:A9)
Divide the contents of cell C2 by the	
contents of cell D1	= C2/D1

Special Journals

Exhibit 7–8 diagrams a typical accounting system for a merchandising business. The remainder of this chapter describes how this system works.

EXHIBIT 7–8 Overview of an Accounting System with Special Journals for a Merchandising Business

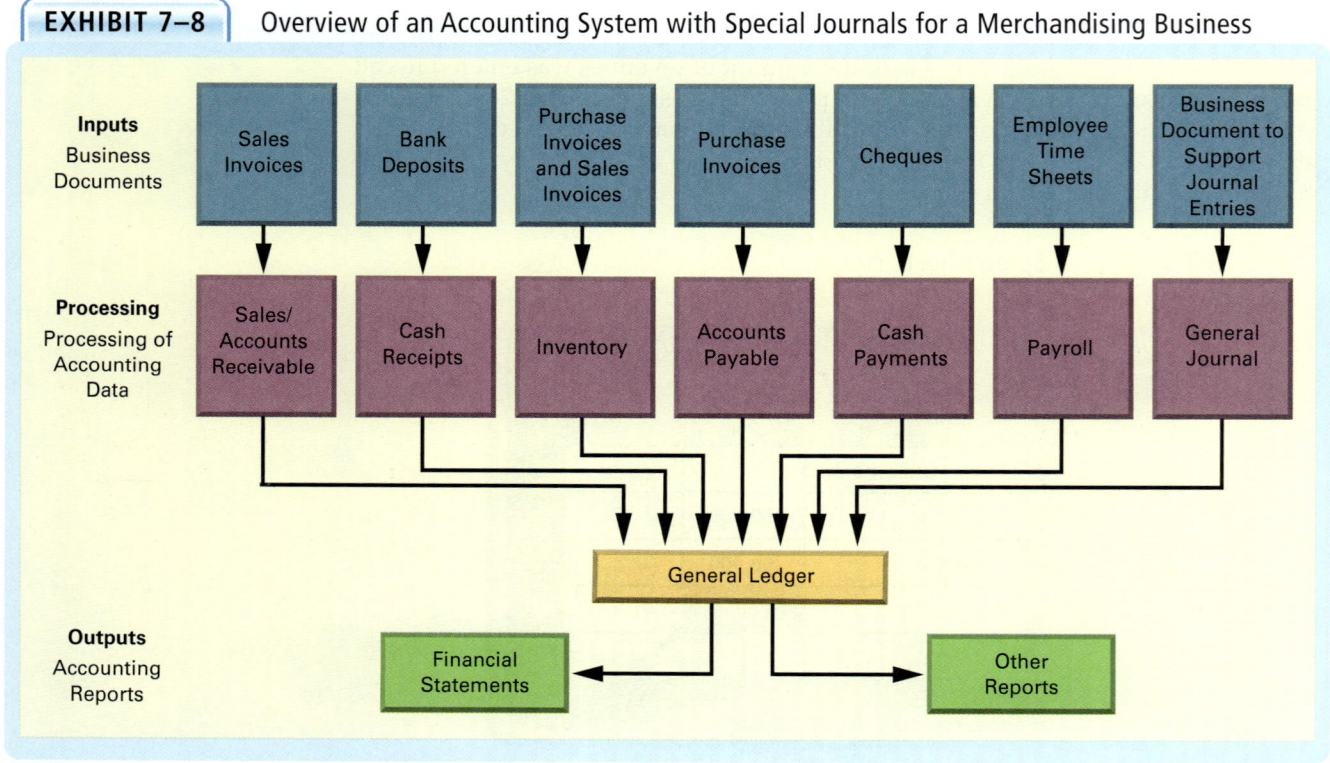

Special Journals in a Manual System

The journal entries illustrated so far have been made in the **general journal**. It is not efficient to record all transactions in the general journal, so we use special journals. A **special journal** is an accounting journal designed to record one specific type of transaction.

Most transactions fall into one of five categories, so accountants use five different journals. This system saves time and money, as we will see. The five types of transactions, the special journals, and the posting abbreviations are as follows:

Transaction	Special Journal	Posting Abbreviation
1. Sale of merchandise on account	Sales journal	S
2. Cash receipt	Cash receipts journal	CR
3. Purchase on account	Purchases journal	P
4. Cash payment*	Cash payments journal	CP
5. All others	General journal	J

*Some companies also use a Payroll Journal for payroll transactions, which is a part of the companies' payroll system. Payroll systems are covered in Chapter 11.

Transactions are recorded in either the general journal or a special journal, but not in both.

You may be wondering why we cover manual accounting systems, since many businesses have computerized accounting systems. There are four main reasons:

1. Learning a manual system will equip you to work with both manual and electronic systems. The accounting is the same regardless of the system.

2. Few small businesses have computerized all their accounting. Even companies that use QuickBooks or Simply Accounting keep some manual accounting records. For businesses that use manual systems, they follow the principles and procedures that we illustrate in this chapter.

3. Learning a manual system will help you master accounting. One of the authors of this book has a friend who uses QuickBooks for his business. This man knows only which keys to punch. If he knew the accounting, he could better manage his business.

4. Learning a manual system will help you recognize a computer system that is not set up properly or is not working as intended.

The Sales Journal

Most merchandisers sell inventory on account. These *credit sales* are recorded in the **sales journal**. Credit sales of assets other than inventory—for example, buildings—occur infrequently and may be recorded in the general journal.

Exhibit 7–9 illustrates a sales journal (Panel A) and the related posting to the ledgers (Panel B) of Austin Sound Centre, the stereo shop we introduced in Chapter 5. Each entry in the Accounts Receivable Dr./Sales Revenue Cr. column of the sales journal in Exhibit 7–9 is a debit (Dr.) to Accounts Receivable and a credit (Cr.) to Sales Revenue, as the heading above this column indicates. For each transaction, the accountant enters the

- Date
- Invoice number
- Customer name and number
- Transaction amount

This streamlined way of recording sales on account saves a vast amount of time that, in a manual system, would be spent entering account titles and dollar amounts in the general journal.

In recording credit sales in the previous chapters, we did not record the names of credit-sale customers. In practice, the business must know the amount receivable from each customer. How else can the company identify who owes it money, when payment is due, and how much?

Consider the first transaction in Panel A. On November 2, Austin Sound sold stereo equipment on account to Claudette Cabot for $935. The invoice number is 422. All this information appears on a single line in the sales journal. No explanation is necessary. The transaction's presence in the sales journal means that it is a credit

Objective 4

Journalize and post transactions using the sales journal, the cash receipts journal, and the accounts receivable subsidiary ledger

KEY POINT

Transactions are recorded in either the general journal or a special journal, but not in both.

KEY POINT

Only credit sales of merchandise are recorded in the sales journal.

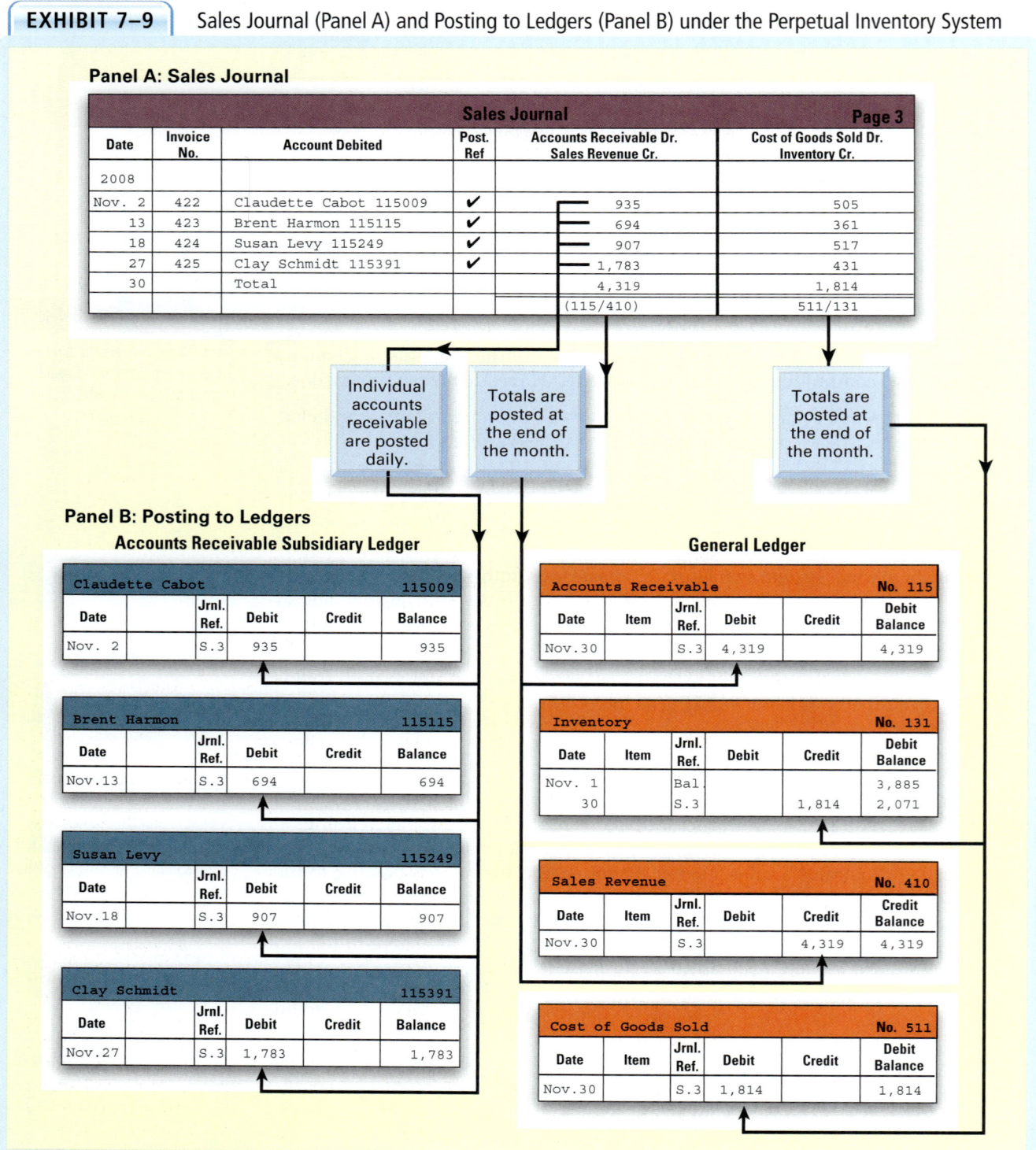

Panel A: Sales Journal

Sales Journal — Page 3

Date	Invoice No.	Account Debited	Post. Ref	Accounts Receivable Dr. Sales Revenue Cr.	Cost of Goods Sold Dr. Inventory Cr.
2008					
Nov. 2	422	Claudette Cabot 115009	✔	935	505
13	423	Brent Harmon 115115	✔	694	361
18	424	Susan Levy 115249	✔	907	517
27	425	Clay Schmidt 115391	✔	1,783	431
30		Total		4,319	1,814
				(115/410)	511/131

Individual accounts receivable are posted daily.

Totals are posted at the end of the month.

Totals are posted at the end of the month.

Panel B: Posting to Ledgers

Accounts Receivable Subsidiary Ledger

Claudette Cabot — 115009

Date		Jrnl. Ref.	Debit	Credit	Balance
Nov. 2		S.3	935		935

Brent Harmon — 115115

Date		Jrnl. Ref.	Debit	Credit	Balance
Nov. 13		S.3	694		694

Susan Levy — 115249

Date		Jrnl. Ref.	Debit	Credit	Balance
Nov. 18		S.3	907		907

Clay Schmidt — 115391

Date		Jrnl. Ref.	Debit	Credit	Balance
Nov. 27		S.3	1,783		1,783

General Ledger

Accounts Receivable — No. 115

Date	Item	Jrnl. Ref.	Debit	Credit	Debit Balance
Nov. 30		S.3	4,319		4,319

Inventory — No. 131

Date	Item	Jrnl. Ref.	Debit	Credit	Debit Balance
Nov. 1		Bal.			3,885
30		S.3		1,814	2,071

Sales Revenue — No. 410

Date	Item	Jrnl. Ref.	Debit	Credit	Credit Balance
Nov. 30		S.3		4,319	4,319

Cost of Goods Sold — No. 511

Date	Item	Jrnl. Ref.	Debit	Credit	Debit Balance
Nov. 30		S.3	1,814		1,814

sale, debited to Accounts Receivable—Claudette Cabot and credited to Sales Revenue. To gain any additional information about the transaction, we would look at the actual invoice.

Recall from Chapter 5 that Austin Sound uses a *perpetual* inventory system. When recording the sale, Austin Sound also records the cost of goods sold and the decrease in inventory.

Computerized accounting systems can read both the sales amount and the cost of goods sold from the bar code on the package of the item sold. The far-right column of the sales journal records the cost of goods sold and inventory amount—$505 for the goods sold to Claudette Cabot. If Austin Sound used a *periodic* inventory system, it would not record cost of goods sold or the decrease in inventory at the time of sale. The sales journal would need only one column to debit Accounts Receivable and to credit Sales Revenue for the amount of the sale.

Additional data can be recorded in the sales journal. For example, a company may add a column to record sale terms, such as 2/10, n/30. The design of the journal depends on the managers' needs for information. Special journals are flexible—they can be tailored to meet any special needs of a business.

Posting to the General Ledger The only ledger we have used so far is the **general ledger**, which holds the accounts reported in the financial statements. We will soon introduce other ledgers.

Posting from the sales journal to the general ledger can be done at any time, but for efficiency, most companies post only once each month. In Exhibit 7–9 (Panel A), November's credit sales total $4,319. This column has two headings, Accounts Receivable and Sales Revenue. In a manual system, when the $4,319 is posted to Accounts Receivable and Sales Revenue in the general ledger, you can print their account numbers beneath the total in the sales journal. In Panel B of Exhibit 7–9, the account number for Accounts Receivable is 115 and the account number for Sales Revenue is 410. Printing these account numbers beneath the credit sales total in the sales journal shows that the $4,319 has been posted to the two accounts.

The debit to Cost of Goods Sold and the credit to Inventory for the monthly total of $1,814 is normally posted at the end of the month. After posting, these account numbers are written beneath the total to show that Cost of Goods Sold and Inventory have been updated. No such posting would be necessary if Austin Sound used a periodic inventory system.

Posting to the Accounts Receivable Subsidiary Ledger The $4,319 debit to Accounts Receivable does not identify the amount receivable from any specific customer. A business may have many customers. For example, *Maclean's Magazine* has a customer account for each of its thousands of subscribers.

Businesses must create an account for each customer in a subsidiary ledger called the Accounts Receivable Subsidiary ledger. A <mark>subsidiary ledger</mark> is a book or file of the individual accounts that make up a total for a general ledger account. The customer accounts in the subsidiary ledger usually are arranged in alphabetical order and often have a customer number.

Amounts in the sales journal are posted to the subsidiary ledger *daily* to keep a current record of the amount receivable from each customer. The amounts are debits. Daily posting allows the business to answer customer inquiries promptly. Suppose Claudette Cabot telephones Austin Sound on November 11 to ask how much money she owes. The subsidiary ledger readily provides that information, $935 in Exhibit 7–9, Panel B.

When each transaction amount is posted to the subsidiary ledger in a manual system, a check mark or some other notation is printed in the posting reference column of the sales journal (see Exhibit 7–9, Panel A). This is because subsidiary ledger accounts are not part of the general ledger, and, thus, have no general ledger account numbers.

Journal References in the Ledgers As you post to the ledgers, print the journal page number in the account to identify the source of the data. All transaction data in Exhibit 7–9 originated on page 3 of the sales journal, so all posting references in the ledger accounts are S.3. "S" indicates sales journal.

Trace all the postings in Exhibit 7–9. The way to learn about accounting systems and special journals is to study the flow of data.

Balancing the Ledgers The arrows in Exhibit 7–9 indicate the direction of the information. The arrows show the links between the individual customer accounts

KEY POINT

The accounts debited and credited are the same whether or not the accounting system uses special journals. However, the debits and credits are grouped together and totalled in a special journal system.

KEY POINT

The purpose of a subsidiary ledger account is to provide detail of a customer's account to facilitate billing and collection. The subsidiary ledger should show all sales to, and collections from, the customer—the customer's credit history.

KEY POINT

You may think that posting to the subsidiary ledger and to the general ledger is double posting. However, the subsidiary ledger is *not* part of the general ledger and the subsidiary accounts will *not* appear on the trial balance. Posting to both the subsidiary ledger and the general ledger is necessary to keep the two in balance.

in the subsidiary ledger and the Accounts Receivable account. (The arrows are for illustration only—they do not appear in the accounting records.) The Accounts Receivable debit balance in the general ledger should equal the sum of the individual customer balances in the subsidiary ledger, as follows. This is called balancing the ledgers.

Accounts Receivable debit balance in the general ledger:

Accounts Receivable... $4,319

Data from the Accounts Receivable Subsidiary Ledger

AUSTIN SOUND CENTRE
Schedule of Accounts Receivable
November 30, 2008

115009 Claudette Cabot..	$ 935
115115 Brent Harmon	694
115249 Susan Levy	907
115391 Clay Schmidt	1,783
Total accounts receivable....................................	$4,319

Accounts Receivable in the general ledger is an example of a **control account**. A control account's balance equals the sum of the balances of a group of related accounts in a subsidiary ledger. The individual customer accounts are subsidiary accounts. They are said to be "controlled" by the Accounts Receivable account in the general ledger.

STOP AND THINK

Suppose Austin Sound Centre had 400 credit sales for the month. How many postings to the general ledger would be made from the sales journal? (Ignore Cost of Goods Sold and Inventory.) How many postings would there be if all sales transactions were routed through the general journal?

Answer: There are only two postings from the sales journal to the general ledger: one to Accounts Receivable and one to Sales Revenue. There would be 800 postings from the general journal: 400 to Accounts Receivable and 400 to Sales Revenue. This difference clearly shows the benefit of a sales journal.

The Cash Receipts Journal

Cash transactions are common in most businesses because cash receipts from customers are the lifeblood of business. To record a large number of cash receipt transactions, accountants use the **cash receipts journal**.

Exhibit 7–10, Panel A, illustrates the cash receipts journal. The related posting to the ledgers is shown in Panel B. The exhibit illustrates November transactions for Austin Sound Centre.

Every transaction recorded in this journal is a cash receipt, so the first column is for debits to the Cash account. The next column is for debits to Sales Discounts on collections from customers. In a typical merchandising business, the main sources of cash are collections on account, and cash sales.

The cash receipts journal has credit columns for Accounts Receivable, Sales Revenue, and Other Accounts. The Other Accounts columns list sources of cash

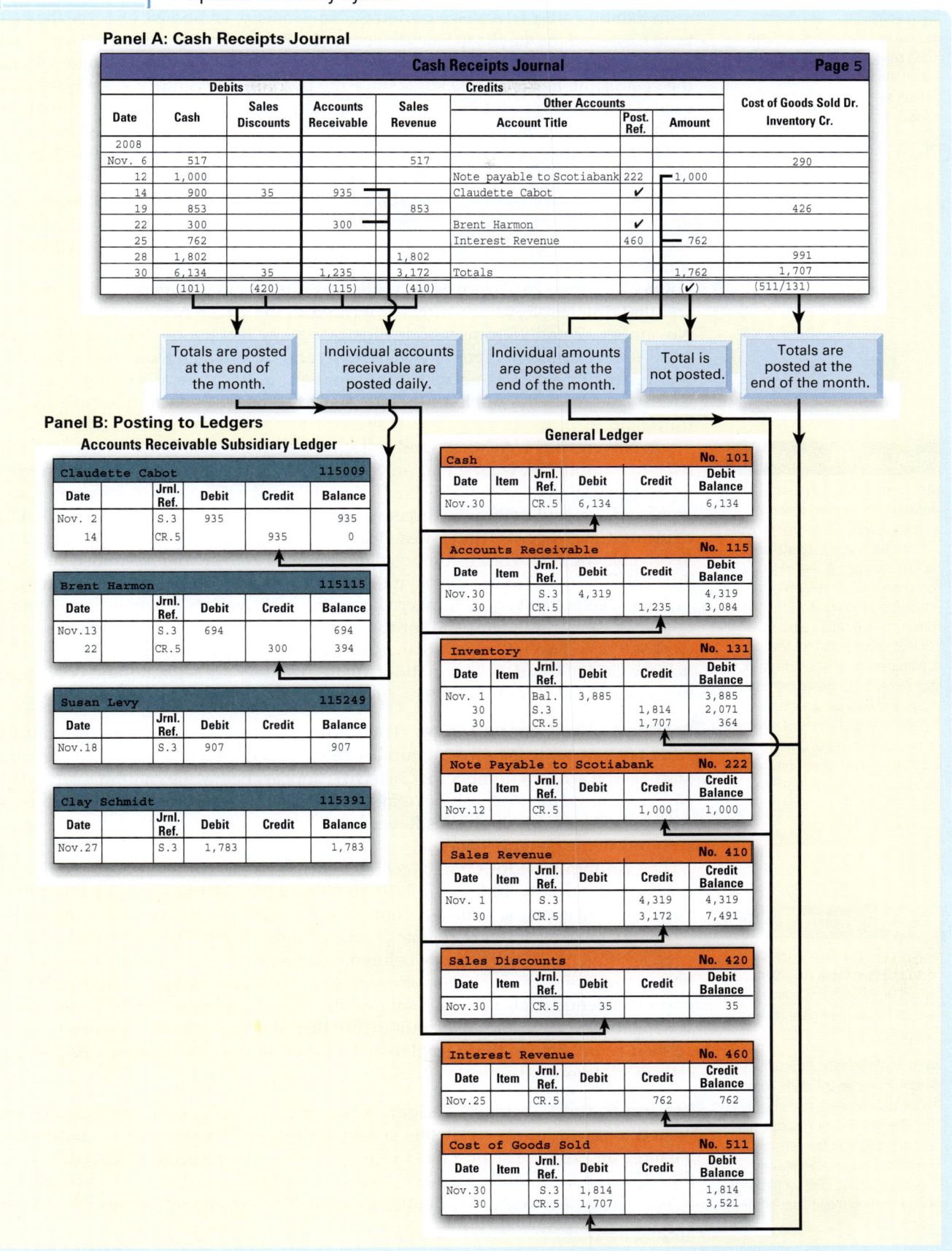

Panel A: Cash Receipts Journal

					Cash Receipts Journal			Page 5
	Debits		**Credits**					
Date	Cash	Sales Discounts	Accounts Receivable	Sales Revenue	Other Accounts — Account Title	Post. Ref.	Amount	Cost of Goods Sold Dr. Inventory Cr.
2008								
Nov. 6	517			517				290
12	1,000				Note payable to Scotiabank	222	1,000	
14	900	35	935		Claudette Cabot	✔		
19	853			853				426
22	300		300		Brent Harmon	✔		
25	762				Interest Revenue	460	762	
28	1,802			1,802				991
30	6,134	35	1,235	3,172	Totals		1,762	1,707
	(101)	(420)	(115)	(410)			(✔)	(511/131)

Totals are posted at the end of the month.

Individual accounts receivable are posted daily.

Individual amounts are posted at the end of the month.

Total is not posted.

Totals are posted at the end of the month.

Panel B: Posting to Ledgers

Accounts Receivable Subsidiary Ledger

Claudette Cabot   115009

Date	Jrnl. Ref.	Debit	Credit	Balance
Nov. 2	S.3	935		935
14	CR.5		935	0

Brent Harmon   115115

Date	Jrnl. Ref.	Debit	Credit	Balance
Nov.13	S.3	694		694
22	CR.5		300	394

Susan Levy   115249

Date	Jrnl. Ref.	Debit	Credit	Balance
Nov.18	S.3	907		907

Clay Schmidt   115391

Date	Jrnl. Ref.	Debit	Credit	Balance
Nov.27	S.3	1,783		1,783

General Ledger

Cash   No. 101

Date	Item	Jrnl. Ref.	Debit	Credit	Debit Balance
Nov.30		CR.5	6,134		6,134

Accounts Receivable   No. 115

Date	Item	Jrnl. Ref.	Debit	Credit	Debit Balance
Nov.30		S.3	4,319		4,319
30		CR.5		1,235	3,084

Inventory   No. 131

Date	Item	Jrnl. Ref.	Debit	Credit	Debit Balance
Nov. 1		Bal.	3,885		3,885
30		S.3		1,814	2,071
30		CR.5		1,707	364

Note Payable to Scotiabank   No. 222

Date	Item	Jrnl. Ref.	Debit	Credit	Credit Balance
Nov.12		CR.5		1,000	1,000

Sales Revenue   No. 410

Date	Item	Jrnl. Ref.	Debit	Credit	Credit Balance
Nov. 1		S.3		4,319	4,319
30		CR.5		3,172	7,491

Sales Discounts   No. 420

Date	Item	Jrnl. Ref.	Debit	Credit	Debit Balance
Nov.30		CR.5	35		35

Interest Revenue   No. 460

Date	Item	Jrnl. Ref.	Debit	Credit	Credit Balance
Nov.25		CR.5		762	762

Cost of Goods Sold   No. 511

Date	Item	Jrnl. Ref.	Debit	Credit	Debit Balance
Nov.30		S.3	1,814		1,814
30		CR.5	1,707		3,521

REAL WORLD EXAMPLE

Accountants call the process of totalling the columns *footing* (adding down). *Cross-foot* means to add debits and subtract credits across the page. A special journal or spreadsheet that foots and cross-foots has numbers that add down correctly and adds across so that debits equal credits. Computers do most of this work, but computer programs can contain bugs, and data can be entered erroneously and generate incorrect amounts. Users must always evaluate the reasonableness of amounts or they may make bad decisions.

THINKING IT OVER

If Austin Sound did not use an accounts receivable subsidiary ledger and Claudette Cabot asked you for her account balance, could you answer her?

A: It would be difficult! A subsidiary ledger is needed for ready access to the data for each customer. The alternative is to look through all transactions in the general journal for the ones involving Claudette Cabot. (This would be a very inefficient and error-prone alternative.)

other than cash sales and collections on account, and are also used to record the names of customers from whom cash is received on account.

In Exhibit 7–10, cash sales occurred on November 6, 19, and 28. Observe the debits to Cash and the credits to Sales Revenue ($517, $853, and $1,802). Each sale entry is accompanied by an entry that debits Cost of Goods Sold and credits Inventory for the cost of the merchandise sold, since the perpetual inventory system is being used. The column for this entry is at the far right side of the cash receipts journal. No such entry would be made if Austin Sound used a periodic inventory system.

On November 12, Austin Sound borrowed $1,000 from Scotiabank. Cash is debited, and Note Payable to Scotiabank is credited in the Other Accounts column because it is a rare transaction and no specific credit column is set up to account for borrowings. For this transaction, we enter the account title, Note Payable to Scotiabank, in the Other Accounts/Account Title column. This entry records the source of cash.

On November 25, Austin Sound collected $762 of interest revenue. The account credited, Interest Revenue, must be written in the Other Accounts column. The November 12 and 25 transactions illustrate a key fact about business. Different entities have different types of transactions, and they design their special journals to meet their particular needs for information. In this case, the Other Accounts Credit column is the catch-all that is used to record all nonroutine cash receipt transactions.

On November 14, Austin Sound collected $900 from Claudette Cabot. Referring back to Exhibit 7–9, we see that on November 2 Austin Sound sold merchandise for $935 to Claudette Cabot. The terms of sale allowed a $35 discount for prompt payment and she paid within the discount period. Austin's cash receipt is recorded by debiting Cash for $900 and Sales Discounts for $35 and by crediting Accounts Receivable for $935. The customer's name appears in the Other Accounts/Account Title column to make sure the payment received is posted to the subsidiary ledger.

Total debits must equal total credits in the cash receipts journal. This equality holds for each transaction and for the monthly totals. For the month, total debits ($6,134 + $35 = $6,169) equal total credits ($1,235 + $3,172 + $1,762 = $6,169). The debit to Cost of Goods Sold and the credit to Inventory are separate, and only apply to the perpetual inventory system.

Posting to the General Ledger The column totals are usually posted monthly. After posting, write the account number below the column total in the cash receipts journal. The account number for Cash (101) appears below the column total $6,134, and likewise for the other column totals posted to the general ledger (Sales Discounts, Accounts Receivable, and Sales Revenue). Trace the posting to Cash and the other accounts in the general ledger.

The column total for Other Accounts is *not* posted. Instead, these credits are posted individually. In Exhibit 7–10, the November 12 transaction reads "Note Payable to Scotiabank." This account's number (222) in the Post. Ref. column indicates that the transaction amount was posted individually. The check mark, instead of an account number, below the column total means that the column total was not posted because individual items above were posted. The November 25 collection of interest revenue is also posted individually. These amounts can be posted to the general ledger at the end of the month. But their date in the ledger accounts should be their actual date in the journal to make it easy to trace each amount back to the cash receipts journal.

Posting to the Subsidiary Ledger Amounts from the cash receipts journal are posted to the accounts receivable subsidiary ledger daily to keep the individual balances up to date. The postings to the accounts receivable ledger are credits. Trace the $935 credit to Claudette Cabot's account. It reduces the balance in her account to zero. The $300 receipt from Brent Harmon reduces his accounts receivable balance to $394.

Balancing the Ledgers After posting, the sum of the individual balances that remain in the accounts receivable subsidiary ledger equals the general ledger balance in Accounts Receivable.

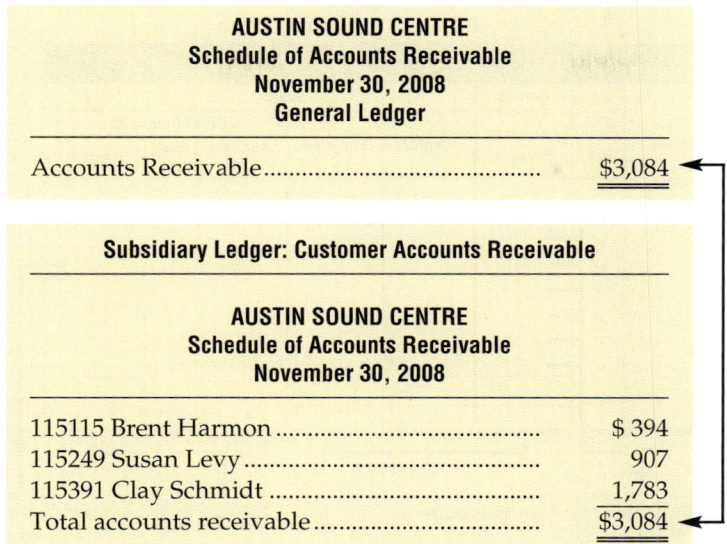

Austin Sound's list of account balances from the subsidiary ledger helps it follow up on slow-paying customers. Good accounts receivable records help a business manage its cash.

The Purchases Journal

A merchandising business such as Austin Sound Centre purchases inventory and supplies frequently. Such purchases are usually made on account. The **purchases journal** is designed to account for all purchases of inventory, supplies, and other assets *on account*. It can also be used to record expenses incurred *on account*. Cash purchases are recorded in the cash payments journal.

Exhibit 7–11 illustrates Austin Sound's purchases journal (Panel A) and posting to the ledgers (Panel B).[1] The purchases journal in Exhibit 7–11 has amount columns for

- Credits to Accounts Payable
- Debits to Inventory, Supplies, and Other Accounts.

A periodic inventory system would replace the Inventory column with a column entitled "Purchases." The Other Accounts columns record purchases of assets other than inventory and supplies. Each business designs its purchases journal to meet its own needs for information and efficiency. Accounts Payable is credited for all transactions recorded in the purchases journal.

On November 2, Austin Sound purchased stereo inventory costing $700 from JVC Canada Inc. The supplier's name (JVC Canada Inc.) is entered in the Account Credited column. The purchase terms of 3/15, n/30 are also entered to help identify the due date and the discount available. Accounts Payable is credited and Inventory is debited for the transaction amount. On November 19, a purchase of supplies on account is entered as a debit to Supplies and a credit to Accounts Payable.

Note the November 9 purchase of equipment from City Office Supply Co. The purchases journal contains no column for equipment, so the Other Accounts debit column is used. Because this was a credit purchase, the accountant enters the supplier

Objective 5

Journalize and post transactions using the purchases journal, the cash payments journal, and the accounts payable subsidiary ledger

KEY POINT

The source document for entries in the purchases journal is the supplier's (creditor's) invoice or bill.

KEY POINT

Every transaction in the purchases journal will include a credit to Accounts Payable.

REAL WORLD EXAMPLE

Companies design journals to meet their special needs. A repair service might not use a Supplies column but might need a Small Tools column for frequent purchases of tools.

---

[1] This is the only special journal that we illustrate with the credit column usually placed to the left and the debit columns to the right. This arrangement of columns focuses on Accounts Payable, which is credited for each entry to this journal, and on the individual supplier to be paid.

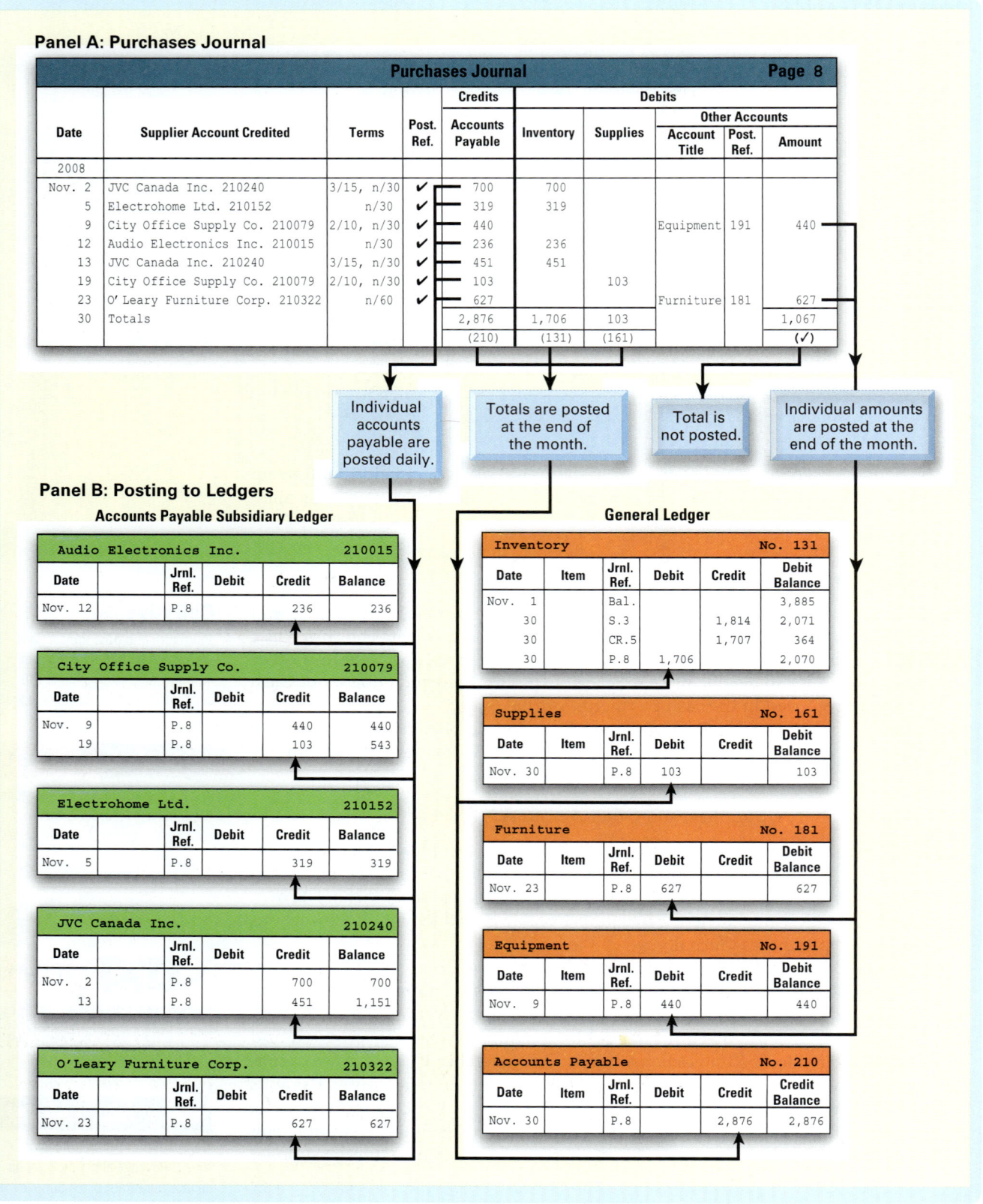

Panel A: Purchases Journal

				Credits	Debits				
							Other Accounts		
Date	Supplier Account Credited	Terms	Post. Ref.	Accounts Payable	Inventory	Supplies	Account Title	Post. Ref.	Amount
2008									
Nov. 2	JVC Canada Inc. 210240	3/15, n/30	✔	700	700				
5	Electrohome Ltd. 210152	n/30	✔	319	319				
9	City Office Supply Co. 210079	2/10, n/30	✔	440			Equipment	191	440
12	Audio Electronics Inc. 210015	n/30	✔	236	236				
13	JVC Canada Inc. 210240	3/15, n/30	✔	451	451				
19	City Office Supply Co. 210079	2/10, n/30	✔	103		103			
23	O'Leary Furniture Corp. 210322	n/60	✔	627			Furniture	181	627
30	Totals			2,876	1,706	103			1,067
				(210)	(131)	(161)			(✔)

Purchases Journal — Page 8

Individual accounts payable are posted daily.

Totals are posted at the end of the month.

Total is not posted.

Individual amounts are posted at the end of the month.

Panel B: Posting to Ledgers

Accounts Payable Subsidiary Ledger

Audio Electronics Inc. 210015

Date		Jrnl. Ref.	Debit	Credit	Balance
Nov. 12		P.8		236	236

City Office Supply Co. 210079

Date		Jrnl. Ref.	Debit	Credit	Balance
Nov. 9		P.8		440	440
19		P.8		103	543

Electrohome Ltd. 210152

Date		Jrnl. Ref.	Debit	Credit	Balance
Nov. 5		P.8		319	319

JVC Canada Inc. 210240

Date		Jrnl. Ref.	Debit	Credit	Balance
Nov. 2		P.8		700	700
13		P.8		451	1,151

O'Leary Furniture Corp. 210322

Date		Jrnl. Ref.	Debit	Credit	Balance
Nov. 23		P.8		627	627

General Ledger

Inventory No. 131

Date	Item	Jrnl. Ref.	Debit	Credit	Debit Balance
Nov. 1		Bal.			3,885
30		S.3		1,814	2,071
30		CR.5		1,707	364
30		P.8	1,706		2,070

Supplies No. 161

Date	Item	Jrnl. Ref.	Debit	Credit	Debit Balance
Nov. 30		P.8	103		103

Furniture No. 181

Date	Item	Jrnl. Ref.	Debit	Credit	Debit Balance
Nov. 23		P.8	627		627

Equipment No. 191

Date	Item	Jrnl. Ref.	Debit	Credit	Debit Balance
Nov. 9		P.8	440		440

Accounts Payable No. 210

Date	Item	Jrnl. Ref.	Debit	Credit	Credit Balance
Nov. 30		P.8		2,876	2,876

name (City Office Supply Co.) in the Account Credited column and writes "Equipment" in the Other Accounts / Account Title column.

The total credits in the purchases journal ($2,876) must equal the total debits ($1,706 + $103 + $1,067 = $2,876). This equality proves the accuracy of the entries in the purchases journal.

Accounts Payable Subsidiary Ledger To pay debts on time, a company must know how much it owes each supplier. The Accounts Payable account in the general ledger shows only a single total for the amount owed on account. It does not indicate the amount owed to each supplier. Companies keep an accounts payable subsidiary ledger that is similar to the accounts receivable subsidiary ledger.

The accounts payable subsidiary ledger lists suppliers in alphabetical order, often by account number, along with the amounts owed to them. Exhibit 7–11, Panel B, shows Austin Sound's accounts payable subsidiary ledger, which includes accounts for Audio Electronics Inc., City Office Supply Co., and others. After the daily and period-end postings are done, the total of the individual balances in the subsidiary ledger equals the balance in the Accounts Payable control account in the general ledger.

Posting from the Purchases Journal Posting from the purchases journal is similar to posting from the sales journal and the cash receipts journal. Exhibit 7–11, Panel B, illustrates the posting process.

Individual accounts payable in the purchases journal are posted daily to the *accounts payable subsidiary ledger*, and column totals and other amounts are usually posted to the *general ledger* at the end of the month. The column total for *Other Accounts* is not posted. Each account's number in the Post. Ref. column indicates the transaction amount was posted individually. The check mark below the column total indicates the column total was *not* posted because individual items in the column were posted. In the ledger accounts, in the Jrnl. Ref. (journal reference) column, P.8 indicates the source of the posted amounts—that is, page 8 of the purchases journal.

STOP AND THINK

Contrast the number of *general ledger* postings from the purchases journal in Exhibit 7–11 with the number that would be required if the general journal were used to record the same seven transactions.

Answer: Use of the purchases journal requires only five general ledger postings—$2,876 to Accounts Payable, $1,706 to Inventory, $103 to Supplies, $440 to Equipment, and $627 to Furniture. Without the purchases journal, there would have been 14 postings, two for each of the seven transactions.

The Cash Payments Journal

Businesses make most cash payments by cheque, and all payments by cheque are recorded in the **cash payments journal**. This special journal is also called the *cheque register* and the *cash disbursements journal*. Like the other special journals, it has multiple columns for recording cash payments that occur frequently.

Exhibit 7–12, Panel A, illustrates the cash payments journal, and Panel B shows the postings to the ledgers of Austin Sound. This cash payments journal has two debit columns—for Other Accounts and Accounts Payable. It has two credit columns—one for purchase discounts, which are credited to the Inventory account in a perpetual inventory system, and one for Cash. This special journal also has columns for the date, cheque number, and payee of each cash payment.

REAL WORLD EXAMPLE

Businesses make most cash payments by cheque to control their cash. Imagine the confusion and the opportunity for theft if all employees could take cash from the cash register to pay for purchases.

EXHIBIT 7–12

Cash Payments Journal (Panel A) and Posting to the Ledgers (Panel B) under the Perpetual Inventory System

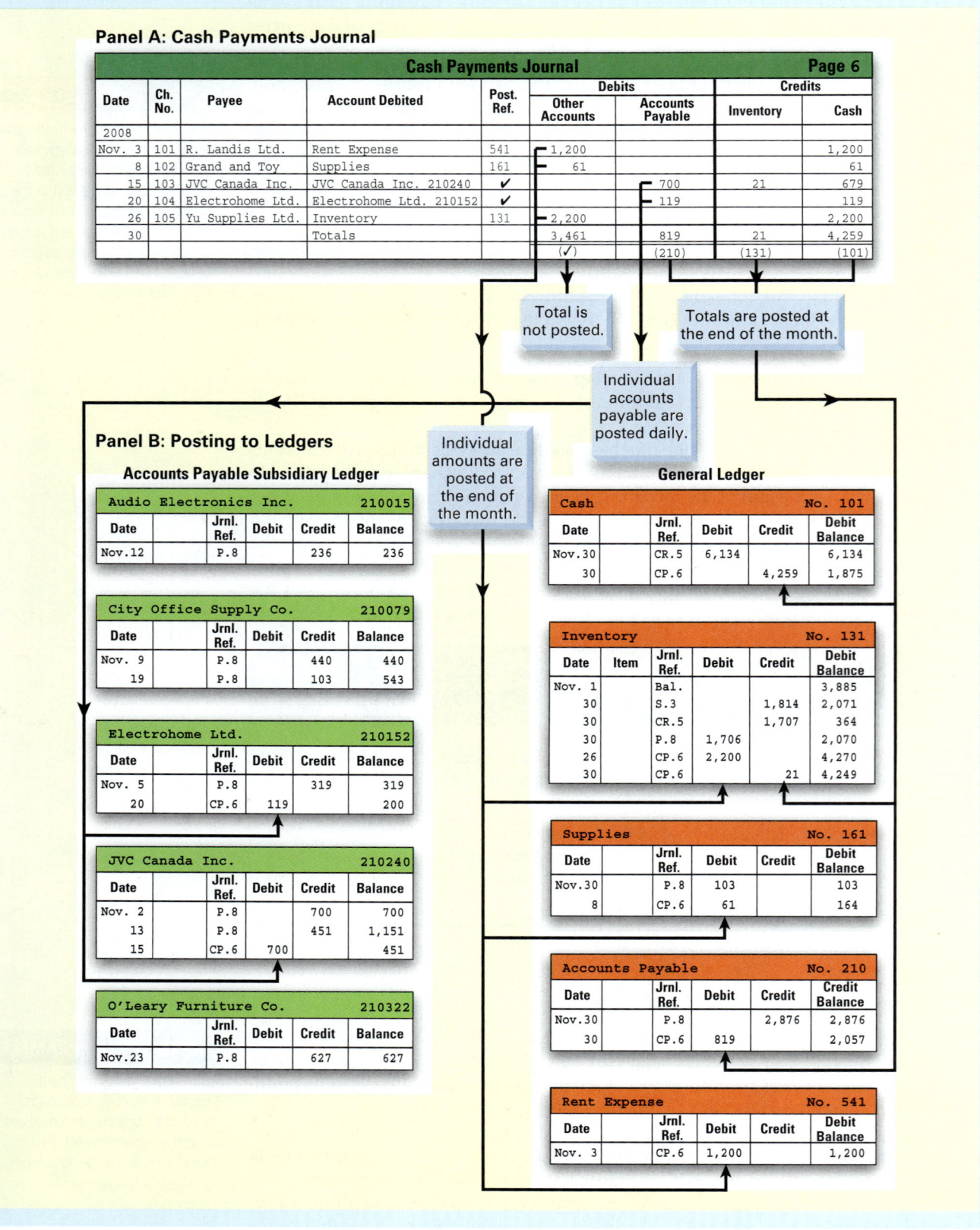

Panel A: Cash Payments Journal

Date	Ch. No.	Payee	Account Debited	Post. Ref.	Other Accounts (Debits)	Accounts Payable (Debits)	Inventory (Credits)	Cash (Credits)
2008								
Nov. 3	101	R. Landis Ltd.	Rent Expense	541	1,200			1,200
8	102	Grand and Toy	Supplies	161	61			61
15	103	JVC Canada Inc.	JVC Canada Inc. 210240	✔		700	21	679
20	104	Electrohome Ltd.	Electrohome Ltd. 210152	✔		119		119
26	105	Yu Supplies Ltd.	Inventory	131	2,200			2,200
30			Totals		3,461	819	21	4,259
					(✔)	(210)	(131)	(101)

Total is not posted.

Totals are posted at the end of the month.

Individual accounts payable are posted daily.

Panel B: Posting to Ledgers

Individual amounts are posted at the end of the month.

Accounts Payable Subsidiary Ledger

Audio Electronics Inc. 210015

Date	Jrnl. Ref.	Debit	Credit	Balance
Nov.12	P.8		236	236

City Office Supply Co. 210079

Date	Jrnl. Ref.	Debit	Credit	Balance
Nov. 9	P.8		440	440
19	P.8		103	543

Electrohome Ltd. 210152

Date	Jrnl. Ref.	Debit	Credit	Balance
Nov. 5	P.8		319	319
20	CP.6	119		200

JVC Canada Inc. 210240

Date	Jrnl. Ref.	Debit	Credit	Balance
Nov. 2	P.8		700	700
13	P.8		451	1,151
15	CP.6	700		451

O'Leary Furniture Co. 210322

Date	Jrnl. Ref.	Debit	Credit	Balance
Nov.23	P.8		627	627

General Ledger

Cash No. 101

Date	Jrnl. Ref.	Debit	Credit	Debit Balance
Nov.30	CR.5	6,134		6,134
30	CP.6		4,259	1,875

Inventory No. 131

Date	Item	Jrnl. Ref.	Debit	Credit	Debit Balance
Nov. 1		Bal.			3,885
30		S.3		1,814	2,071
30		CR.5		1,707	364
30		P.8	1,706		2,070
26		CP.6	2,200		4,270
30		CP.6		21	4,249

Supplies No. 161

Date	Jrnl. Ref.	Debit	Credit	Debit Balance
Nov.30	P.8	103		103
8	CP.6	61		164

Accounts Payable No. 210

Date	Jrnl. Ref.	Debit	Credit	Credit Balance
Nov.30	P.8		2,876	2,876
30	CP.6	819		2,057

Rent Expense No. 541

Date	Jrnl. Ref.	Debit	Credit	Debit Balance
Nov. 3	CP.6	1,200		1,200

The cash payments journal for a company using a periodic inventory system would have the same two debit columns as those shown in Exhibit 7–12, Panel A—Other Accounts and Accounts Payable—and two credit columns—for Purchase Discounts and Cash.

Suppose a business makes numerous cash purchases of inventory and uses the perpetual inventory system. What additional column would its cash payments journal need to be most useful? A Debit column for Inventory would be added.

All entries in the cash payments journal include a credit to Cash. Payments on account are debits to Accounts Payable. On November 15, Austin Sound paid JVC Canada Inc. on account, with credit terms of 3/15, n/30 (for details, see the first transaction in Exhibit 7–11). Therefore, Austin took the 3 percent discount and paid $679 ($700 less the $21 discount). The discount is credited to the Inventory account.

The Other Accounts column is used to record debits to accounts for which no special column exists. For example, on November 3, Austin Sound paid rent expense of $1,200.

As with all the other journals, the total debits ($3,461 + $819 = $4,280) must equal the total credits ($21 + $4,259 = $4,280).

Posting from the Cash Payments Journal Posting from the cash payments journal is similar to posting from the cash receipts journal. Individual creditor amounts are posted daily. Column totals and Other Accounts are usually posted at the end of the month. Exhibit 7–12, Panel B, illustrates the posting process.

Observe the effect of posting to the Accounts Payable account in the general ledger. The first posted amount in the Accounts Payable account (credit $2,876) originated in the purchases journal, page 8 (P.8). The second posted amount (debit $819) came from the cash payments journal, page 6 (CP.6). The resulting credit balance in Accounts Payable is $2,057. Also, see the Cash account. After posting, its debit balance is $1,875.

Amounts in the Other Accounts column are posted individually (for example, Rent Expense—debit $1,200). When each Other Accounts amount is posted to the general ledger, the account number is written in the Post. Ref. column of the journal. The check mark below the column total signifies that the total is *not* posted.

To review their accounts payable, companies list the individual supplier balances in the accounts payable subsidiary ledger:

General Ledger

Accounts Payable (control account)................. $2,057

From the Accounts Payable Subsidiary Ledger:
AUSTIN SOUND CENTRE
Schedule of Accounts Payable
November 30, 2006

210015 Audio Electronics Inc.	$ 236
210079 City Office Supply Co.............................	543
210152 Electrohome Ltd....................................	200
210240 JVC Canada Inc.	451
210322 O'Leary Furniture Co.	627
Total accounts payable......................................	$2,057

This total agrees with the Accounts Payable balance in Exhibit 7–12. Agreement of the two amounts indicates that the resulting account balances are correct.

The payroll register is a special form of cash payments journal and is discussed in Chapter 11.

The Role of the General Journal

Special journals save much time in recording repetitive transactions and posting to the ledgers. But some transactions do not fit into any of the special journals. Examples include the amortization of buildings and equipment, the expiration of prepaid insurance, and the accrual of salary payable at the end of the period.

> Even the most sophisticated accounting system needs a general journal. The adjusting entries and the closing entries that we illustrated in Chapters 3 through 5 are recorded in the general journal, along with other non-routine transactions.

Many companies also use the general journal for sales returns and allowances and purchase returns and allowances. Let's turn now to sales returns and allowances, and the related business document, the *credit memo*.

The Credit Memo—The Document for Recording Sales Returns and Allowances

KEY POINT

Receipt of a "credit" memo does not indicate that you should "credit" Accounts Receivable. The originator of the credit memo is "crediting" Accounts Receivable. The receiver of the credit memo debits Accounts Payable.

As we saw in Chapter 5, customers sometimes return merchandise to the seller, and sellers grant sales allowances to customers because of product defects and for other reasons. The effect of sales returns and sales allowances is the same—they decrease net sales and accounts receivable in the same way a sales discount does. The document issued by the seller for a credit to the customer's Account Receivable is called a **credit memo**, because the company gives the customer credit for the returned merchandise. When a company issues a credit memo, it debits Sales Returns and Allowances and credits Accounts Receivable.

On November 27, Austin Sound sold four stereo speakers for $1,783 on account to Clay Schmidt. Later, Schmidt discovered a defect and returned the speakers. Austin Sound then issued to Schmidt a credit memo like the one in Exhibit 7–13.

EXHIBIT 7–13   Credit Memo

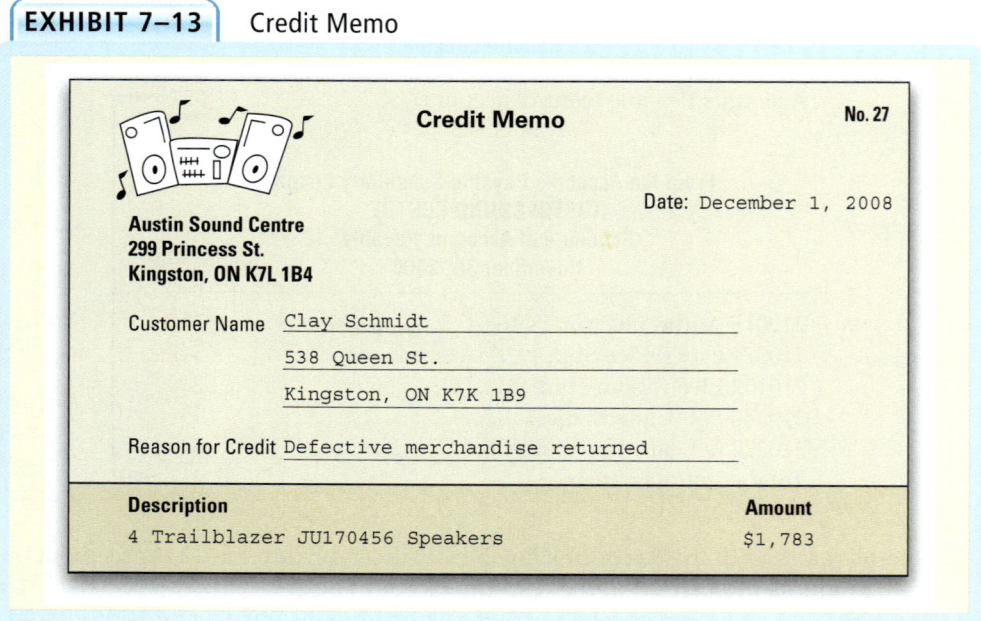

To record the *sale return* and receipt of the defective speakers from customer Clay Schmidt, Austin Sound would make the following entries in the general journal:

General Journal				Page 9
Date 2008	Accounts	Post Ref.	Debit	Credit
Dec. 1	Sales Returns and Allowances...	430	1,783	
	Accounts Receivable—Clay Schmidt 115391	115/✓		1,783
	Credit memo no. 27.			
Dec. 1	Inventory	131	431	
	Cost of Goods Sold...	511		431
	Received defective goods from customer.			

Focus on the first entry. The debit side of the entry is posted to Sales Returns and Allowances. After posting, its account number (430) is written in the posting reference column. The credit side of the entry requires two $1,783 postings, one to Accounts Receivable, the *control account* in the general ledger (account number 115), and the other to Clay Schmidt's *individual account* in the accounts receivable subsidiary ledger, account number 115391. These credit postings explain why the document is called a *credit memo*.

Observe that the posting reference of the credit includes two notations. The account number (115) denotes the posting to Accounts Receivable in the general ledger. The check mark (✓) denotes the posting to Schmidt's account in the subsidiary ledger. It doesn't have specially designed columns, so it is necessary to write both posting references on the same line.

A business with a high volume of sales returns, such as a department store chain, may use a special journal for sales returns and allowances.

The second general-journal entry records Austin Sound's receipt of the defective inventory from the customer. The speakers cost Austin Sound $431, and Austin Sound, like all other merchandisers, records its inventory at cost. Now let's see how Austin Sound records the return of the defective speakers to JVC, from which Austin Sound purchased them.

The Debit Memo—The Business Document for Recording Purchase Returns and Allowances

Purchase returns occur when a business returns goods to the seller. The procedures for handling purchase returns are similar to those dealing with sales returns. The purchaser gives the merchandise back to the seller and receives either a cash refund or replacement goods.

When a business returns merchandise to the seller, it may also send a business document known as a **debit memo.** This document states that the buyer no longer owes the seller for the amount of the returned purchases. The buyer debits the Accounts Payable to the seller and credits Inventory for the cost of the goods returned to the seller.

Many businesses record their purchase returns in the general journal. Austin Sound would record its return of defective speakers to JVC as follows:

General Journal				Page 9
Date	Accounts	Post Ref.	Debit	Credit
Dec. 2	Accounts Payable—JVC Corp. 210240	210/✓	431	
	Inventory	131		431
	Debit memo no. 16.			

When you first learn about special journals, it may be confusing to remember which special journal to use for a transaction. Exhibit 7–14 summarizes a process you can follow to choose the special journal to use for a transaction.

KEY POINT

Two posting are needed for Accounts Receivable because the control account and customer must both be updated. This is noted in the general journal on the same line.

THINKING IT OVER

Suppose Brown Sales Co. returned $700 of goods to the supplier from whom the goods were originally purchased. What account is credited and why?

A: When using a perpetual inventory system, Inventory must be kept up to date for all such transactions. Therefore, Inventory is credited, because the items are no longer on hand. When using a periodic inventory system, the Purchase Returns and Allowances account would be credited so that cost of goods sold can be calculated properly.

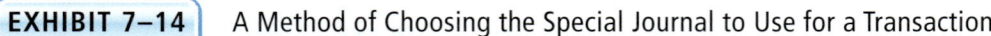

EXHIBIT 7–14 A Method of Choosing the Special Journal to Use for a Transaction

Does the transaction involve cash?
Yes
Is cash received?
Yes
Use the **Cash Receipts Journal**
No
Is cash paid?
Yes
Use the **Cash Payments Journal**
No
Does the transaction involve a credit sale?
Yes
Use the **Sales Journal**
No
Does the transaction involve a credit purchase?
Yes
Use the **Purchases Journal**
No
Use the **General Journal**

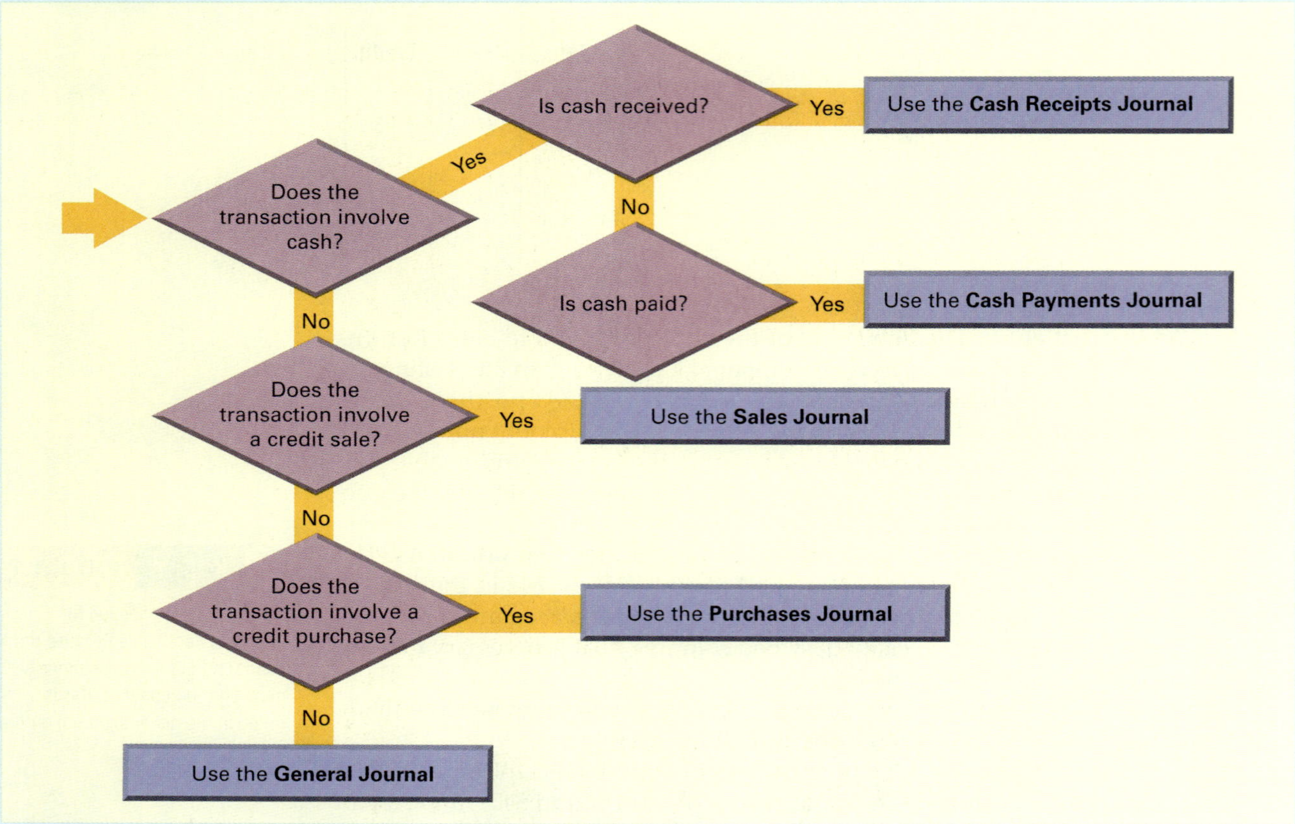

The authors would like to thank Sharon Hatten for suggesting this flowchart.

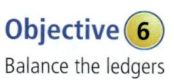

Objective 6
Balance the ledgers

Balancing the Ledgers

At the end of the period, after all postings have been made, equality should exist as follows:

1. *General ledger:*

   Total debits = Total credits

   A trial balance would prove that total debits equal total credits.

2. *General ledger and Accounts receivable subsidiary ledger:*

Balance of the Accounts Receivable control account	=	Sum of all the customer balances in the Accounts Receivable Subsidiary Ledger

   Page 342 illustrates this objective. The comparison shows that the general ledger control account balance equals the total of the Schedule of Accounts Receivable.

3. *General ledger and Accounts payable subsidiary ledger:*

Balance of the Accounts Payable control account	=	Sum of all the creditor balances in the Accounts Payable Subsidiary Ledger

   Page 345 illustrates this objective. The general ledger control account balance equals the total of the Schedule of Accounts Payable.

This process of ensuring that these equalities exist is called *balancing the ledgers, reconciling the ledgers,* or *proving the ledgers*. It is an important control procedure because it helps ensure the accuracy of the accounting records.

Special Journals and Sales Taxes

In Chapter 5, the federal Goods and Services Tax (GST) was discussed; recall that the GST is collected at each level of transaction right down to the consumer, the final level. The discussion that follows relates to consumption or sales taxes levied by all the provinces except Alberta. The Yukon, the Northwest Territories, and Nunavut also do not have a sales tax. Sellers must add the tax to the sale amount, then pay or remit the tax to the provincial government. In most jurisdictions, sales tax is levied only on final consumers, so retail businesses usually do not pay sales tax on the goods they purchase for resale. For example, Austin Sound Centre would not pay sales tax on a purchase of equipment from JVC Canada Inc., a wholesaler. However, when retailers like Austin Sound Centre make sales, they must collect sales tax from the consumer. In effect, retailers serve as collecting agents for the taxing authorities. The amount of tax depends on the total sales and the provincial tax rate.

Retailers set up procedures to collect the sales tax, account for it, and pay it on time. Invoices may be preprinted with a place for entering the sales tax amount, and the general ledger has a liability account entitled Sales Tax Payable. Special journals may include a special column for sales tax, such as those illustrated in Exhibit 7–15. The sales tax rate in the exhibit is 7 percent, the rate of sales tax in Manitoba and British Columbia, and the GST rate is 6 percent, the rate in effect at the time of printing.

In the sales journal in Exhibit 7–15, note that the amount debited to Accounts Receivable ($3,750.47) is the sum of the credits to Sales Tax Payable ($232.33), GST Payable ($199.14), and Sales Revenue ($3,319.00). This is so because the customers' payments, the Accounts Receivable figures, are partly for the purchase of merchandise (Sales Revenue) and partly for taxes charged on the sale. The check marks in the Posting Reference column show that individual amounts have been posted to the customer accounts. The absence of account numbers under the column totals shows that the total amounts have not yet been posted.

Objective 7

Use special journals to record and post transactions with sales taxes

| **EXHIBIT 7–15** | Special Journals Designed to Account for Sales Tax |

Sales Journal Page 4

Date	Inv. No.	Account Debited	Post. Ref.	Accounts Receivable Dr.	Sales Tax Payable Cr.	GST Payable Cr.	Sales Revenue Cr.	Cost of Goods Sold Dr. Inventory Cr.
2008								
Nov. 2	422	Anne Fortin	✔	1,056.55	65.45	56.10	935.00	600.00
13	423	Brent Mooney	✔	784.22	48.58	41.64	694.00	380.00
18	424	Debby Levy	✔	1,024.91	63.49	54.42	907.00	550.00
27	425	Dan Girardi	✔	884.79	54.81	46.98	783.00	500.00
30		Totals		3,750.47	232.33	199.14	3,319.00	2,030.00

Cash Receipts Journal Page 5

	Debits			Credits				Other Accounts			Cost of Goods Sold Dr.
Date	Cash	Sales Discounts	Accounts Receivable	Sales Revenue	PST Payable	GST Payable	Account Title	Post. Ref.	Amount	Inventory Cr.
2008										
Nov. 6	565			500	35	30				290
12	1,000						Note payable to Scotiabank	222	1,000	
29	1,130			1,000	70	60				750
30	2,695			1,500					1,000	1,040

(to be continued)

Purchases Journal   Page 2

Date	Account Credited	Terms	Post. Ref.	Accounts Payable	Inventory	GST Recoverable	Account Title	Post. Ref.	Amount
				Credits			**Debits** — Other Accounts		
2008									
Nov. 2	JVC Canada Inc. 210240	3/15, n/30	✔	742	700	42			
5	Electrohome Ltd. 210152	n/30	✔	318	300	18			
9	City Office Supply Co. 210079	2/10, n/30	✔	477		27	Fixtures	191	450
30	Totals			1,537	1,000	87			450

Cash Payments Journal   Page 4

Date	Ch. No.	Payee	Accounts Debited	Post. Ref.	Other Accounts	Accounts Payable	GST Recoverable	Inventory	Cash
					Debits			**Credits**	
2008									
Nov. 3	101	R. Landis Ltd.	Inventory	131	1,200		72		1,272
8	102	Grand and Toy	Supplies	161	100		6		106
26	130	JVC Canada Inc.	JVC Canada Inc. 210240	✔		742		21	721
30					1,300	742		21	2,099

Most companies that use point-of-sale cash registers have them programmed to calculate separate totals, as sales are being rung in, of taxable items and nontaxable items; the register then calculates the relevant taxes—sales tax, if applicable, and GST—and computes the total owing. Provincial sales tax and the federal GST are not applicable to all items. (For example, food and prescription medicines are excluded from both; reading material is excluded from most sales taxes but not from the GST, except textbooks.) Most businesses calculate sales tax and GST at the time of sale.

Sales tax and GST are also discussed in Chapter 11.

Blending Computers and Special Journals in an Accounting Information System

Computerizing special journals to create accounting modules requires no drastic change in the accounting system's design. Systems designers create a special screen for each accounting application (module)—credit sales, cash receipts, purchases on account, payroll, and cash payments. The special screen for credit sales would prompt the operator entering the data, for example, on a terminal or a cash register, to type in the following information:

- Date
- Customer number
- Customer name
- Invoice number
- Dollar amount of the sale
- Cost of the goods sold

These data can generate the sales journal and monthly statements for customers that show activity and ending balances.

As we conclude this chapter, we return to our opening questions: What is an accounting information system, and why is it important? Are there differences between manual and computerized accounting systems? How can spreadsheets be used in accounting? How can special journals be used to combine similar transactions and speed the accounting process? How can control accounts be used for accounts receivable and accounts payable? These questions were answered throughout this chapter. And the Decision Guidelines end this chapter with a summary that provides guidelines for some of the major decisions accountants must make as they use an information system.

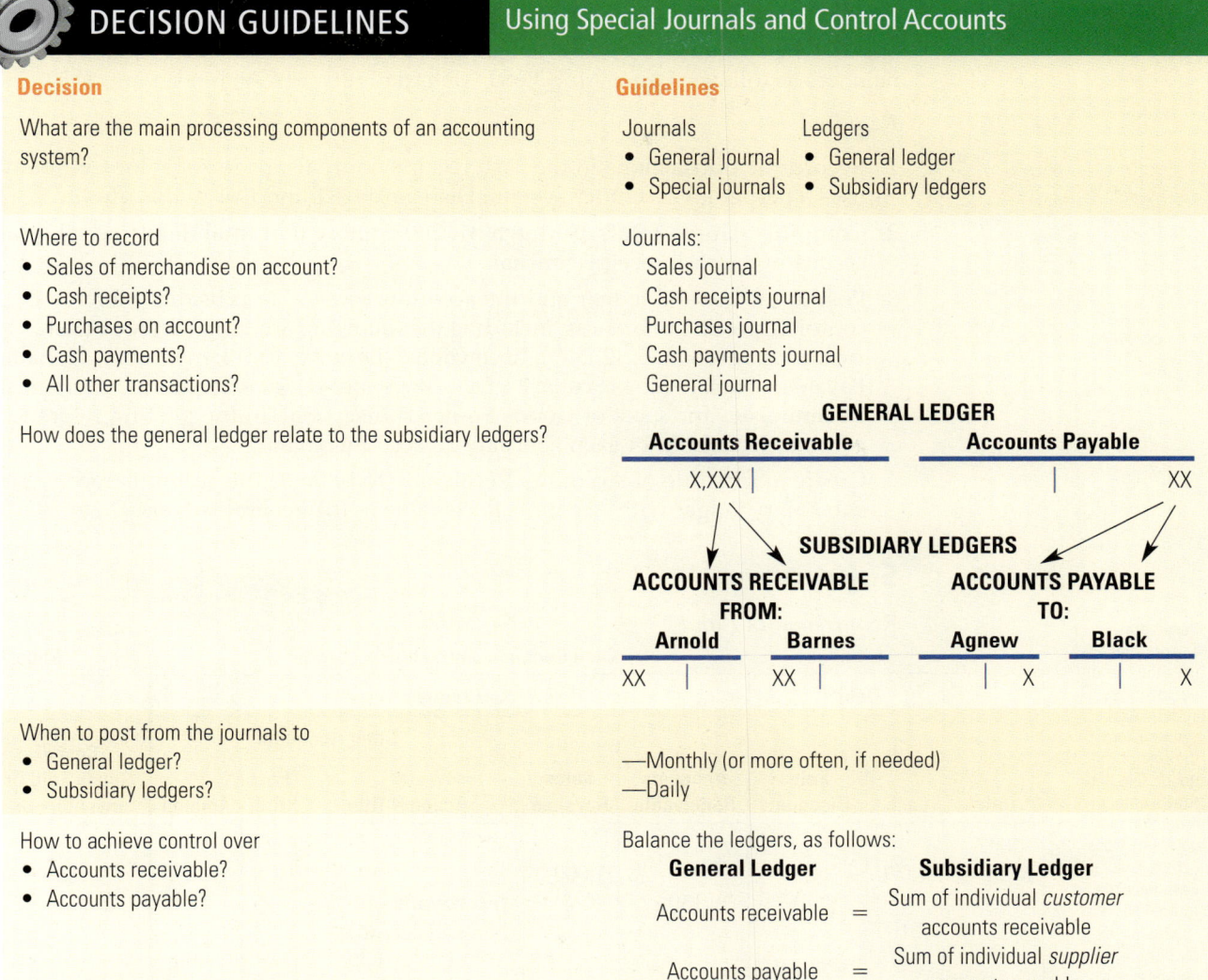

DECISION GUIDELINES — Using Special Journals and Control Accounts

Decision	Guidelines
What are the main processing components of an accounting system?	Journals Ledgers • General journal • General ledger • Special journals • Subsidiary ledgers

Where to record
• Sales of merchandise on account?
• Cash receipts?
• Purchases on account?
• Cash payments?
• All other transactions?
	Journals:
	  Sales journal
	  Cash receipts journal
	  Purchases journal
	  Cash payments journal
	  General journal

When to post from the journals to • General ledger? • Subsidiary ledgers?	—Monthly (or more often, if needed) —Daily

How does the general ledger relate to the subsidiary ledgers?

GENERAL LEDGER

Accounts Receivable	Accounts Payable
X,XXX |	| XX

SUBSIDIARY LEDGERS

ACCOUNTS RECEIVABLE FROM:

Arnold	Barnes
XX |	XX |

ACCOUNTS PAYABLE TO:

Agnew	Black
| X	| X

How to achieve control over
• Accounts receivable?
• Accounts payable?

Balance the ledgers, as follows:

General Ledger		Subsidiary Ledger
Accounts receivable	=	Sum of individual *customer* accounts receivable
Accounts payable	=	Sum of individual *supplier* accounts payable

Summary Problem for Your Review

Name: Taylor Company
Accounting Period: Month of March 2007
Key Fact: Merchandiser using perpetual inventory system

Taylor Company completed the following selected transactions during March 2007:

Mar. 4   Received $1,000 from a cash sale to a customer (cost $638).

6   Received $120 on account from Jim Bryant. The full invoice amount was $130, but Bryant paid within the discount period to earn the $10 discount.

9   Received $2,160 on a note receivable from Lesley Cliff. This amount includes the $2,000 note receivable plus $160 of interest revenue.

15   Received $1,600 from a cash sale to a customer (cost $1,044).

24 Borrowed $4,400 by signing a note payable to the Bank of Nova Scotia.
27 Received $2,400 on account from Lance Au. Payment was received after the discount period lapsed.

The general ledger showed the following balances at February 28, 2007: Cash, $2,234; Accounts Receivable, $5,580; Note Receivable—Lesley Cliff, $2,000; Inventory, $3,638. The accounts receivable subsidiary ledger at February 28 contained debit balances as follows: Lance Au, $3,680; Melinda Fultz, $1,770; Jim Bryant, $130.

Required

1. Record the transactions in the cash receipts journals, page 7. Taylor Company uses a perpetual inventory system. Disregard GST and PST in this question.

2. Compute column totals at March 31, 2007. Show that total debits equal total credits in the cash receipts journal.

3. Post to the general ledger and the accounts receivable subsidiary ledger. Use complete posting references, including the following account numbers: Cash, 11; Accounts Receivable, 12; Note Receivable—Lesley Cliff, 13; Inventory, 14; Note Payable—Bank of Nova Scotia, 22; Sales Revenue, 41; Sales Discounts, 42; Interest Revenue, 46; and Cost of Goods Sold, 51. Insert Bal. in the posting reference column (Jrnl. Ref.) for each February 28 account balance.

4. Create a Schedule of Accounts Receivable to balance the accounts receivable subsidiary ledger with Accounts Receivable in the general ledger.

Solution

Requirements 1 and 2

Recall that Taylor Company uses the perpetual inventory system. As a result, record the cost of the goods sold and the inventory reduction for each sale transaction. Taylor's Cash Receipts Journal has a column at the far right for this purpose.

Items recorded in the Other Accounts columns must be listed and posted individually.

For each transaction, make sure all amounts in the Debits columns equal all amounts in the Credits columns.

Cash Receipts Journal — Page 7

Date	Cash (Debits)	Sales Discounts (Debits)	Accounts Receivable (Credits)	Sales Revenue (Credits)	Account Title (Other Accounts)	Post. Ref.	Amount	Cost of Goods Sold Dr. Inventory Cr.
2007								
Mar. 4	1,000			1,000				638
6	120	10	130		Jim Bryant	✔		
9	2,160				Note Receivable			
					— Lesley Cliff	13	2,000	
					Interest Revenue	46	160	
15	1,600			1,600				1,044
24	4,400				Note Payable—			
					Bank of			
					Nova Scotia	22	4,400	
27	2,400		2,400		Lance Au	✔		
31	11,680	10	2,530	2,600	Total		6,560	1,682
	(11)	(42)	(12)	(41)			(✔)	(51/14)

Total Dr. = 11,690   Total Cr. = 11,690

Selected transactions are explained more fully:

Mar. 4 and 15: For each of these sales transactions, the cost of goods sold and inventory reduction is also recorded.

Mar. 6: The debit columns include the $120 cash received (invoice amount less the discount) and the $10 discount. Accounts Receivable is credited for $130, and Jim Bryant is entered in the Other Accounts column so that his Accounts Receivable subsidiary ledger account balance is reduced by $130.

Mar. 9: This is an example of a compound entry with infrequently used accounts. Therefore, the Note Receivable—Lesley Cliff and Interest Revenue accounts are listed in the Other Accounts columns.

For Requirements 2 and 3:

In the Other Accounts columns above,
• the check mark in the Post. Ref. column indicates credits were individually posted to the Accounts Receivable subsidiary ledger
• the check mark under the Amount total indicates posting was completed for all items in the column

Requirement 3

Accounts Receivable Subsidiary Ledger

Lance Au

Date 2007	Item	Jrnl. Ref.	Debit	Credit	Balance
Feb. 28		Bal.			3,680
Mar. 27		CR. 7		2,400	1,280

Jim Bryant

Date 2007	Item	Jrnl. Ref.	Debit	Credit	Balance
Feb. 28		Bal.			130
Mar. 6		CR. 7		130	0

Melinda Fultz

Date 2007	Item	Jrnl. Ref.	Debit	Credit	Balance
Feb. 28		Bal.			1,770

Recall that subsidiary ledger postings occur on the date of the transaction. General ledger postings occur at the end of the month. Both types of posting use CR.7 to indicate the Cash Receipts Journal as the source of the entry.

General Ledger

Cash   No. 11

Date 2007	Item	Jrnl. Ref.	Debit	Credit	Debit Balance
Feb. 28		Bal.			2,234
Mar. 31		CR. 7	11,680		13,914

Accounts Receivable   No. 12

Date 2007	Item	Jrnl. Ref.	Debit	Credit	Debit Balance
Feb. 28		Bal.			5,580
Mar. 31		CR. 7		2,530	3,050

Note Receivable—Lesley Cliff   No. 13

Date 2007	Item	Jrnl. Ref.	Debit	Credit	Debit Balance
Feb. 28		Bal.			2,000
Mar. 9		CR. 7		2,000	0

Inventory   No. 14

Date 2007	Item	Jrnl. Ref.	Debit	Credit	Debit Balance
Feb. 28		Bal.			3,638
Mar. 31		CR.7		1,682	1,956

Note Payable—Bank of Nova Scotia   No. 22

Date 2007	Item	Jrnl. Ref.	Debit	Credit	Credit Balance
Mar. 24		CR. 7		4,400	4,400

Sales Revenue   No. 41

Date 2007	Item	Jrnl. Ref.	Debit	Credit	Credit Balance
Mar. 31		CR. 7		2,600	2,600

Sales Discounts   No. 42

Date 2007	Item	Jrnl. Ref.	Debit	Credit	Debit Balance
Mar. 31		CR. 7	10		10

Interest Revenue   No. 46

Date 2007	Item	Jrnl. Ref.	Debit	Credit	Credit Balance
Mar. 9		CR. 7		160	160

Cost of Goods Sold   No. 51

Date 2007	Item	Jrnl. Ref.	Debit	Credit	Debit Balance
Mar. 31		CR. 7	1,682		1,682

At month end, customer account balances from the Accounts Receivable subsidiary ledger are listed and compared to the general ledger control account.

Requirement 4

General Ledger	
Accounts Receivable	$3,050

Using the Accounts Receivable Subsidiary Ledger:

TAYLOR COMPANY
Schedule of Accounts Receivable

Lance Au	$1,280
Melinda Fultz	1,770
Total accounts receivable	$3,050

Note: If Taylor Company had used the periodic inventory system, account No. 51, Cost of Goods Sold, would not exist, so there would be no Cost of Goods Sold column in the cash receipts journal. As well, there would be no $1,682 credit posting to Inventory.

Summary

1. **Describe an effective accounting information system.** An effective *accounting information system* captures and summarizes transactions to provide timely, accurate information to users and decision makers. The four major aspects of a good accounting system are (1) control over operations, (2) compatibility with the particular features of the business, (3) flexibility in response to changes in the business, (4) a favourable cost/benefit relationship, with benefits outweighing costs.

2. **Understand the elements of computerized and manual accounting systems.** Computerized accounting systems process inputs faster than do manual systems and can generate more types of reports. The key components of a computerized accounting system are hardware, software, and company personnel. Account numbers play a bigger role in the operation of computerized systems than they do in manual systems, because computers classify accounts by account numbers. Both computerized and manual accounting systems require transactions to be classified by type.

Computerized systems use a *menu* structure to organize accounting functions. The system can be designed so that data are entered and the computer does the rest. Posting, trial balances, financial statements, and closing procedures are easily completed in a computerized accounting system. Computerized accounting systems are integrated so that the different *modules* of the system are updated automatically. While computers cannot fix data entry errors, programs can reduce the chance of data errors by highlighting unbalanced or unusual journal entries.

3. **Understand how spreadsheets are used in accounting.** *Spreadsheets* are electronic work sheets whose grid points, or cells, are linked by means of formulas. The numerical relationships in the spreadsheet are maintained whenever changes are made to the spreadsheet. Spreadsheets are ideally suited to detailed computations, as in budgeting. Spreadsheets are usually used along with a computerized accounting system, not as a substitute for a computerized accounting system.

4. **Journalize and post transactions using the sales journal, the cash receipts journal, and the accounts receivable subsidiary ledger.** Many accounting systems use *special journals* to record transactions by category. Credit sales are recorded in a *sales journal*, and cash receipts in a *cash receipts journal*. Posting from these journals is both to the *general ledger* and to the *accounts receivable subsidiary ledger*, which lists each customer and the amount receivable from that customer. The accounts receivable subsidiary ledger is the main device for ensuring that the company collects from customers.

5. **Journalize and post transactions using the purchases journal, the cash payments journal, and the accounts payable subsidiary ledger.** Credit purchases are recorded in a *purchases journal*, and cash payments in a *cash payments journal*. Posting from these journals is to the *general ledger* and to the *accounts payable subsidiary ledger*. The accounts payable subsidiary ledger helps the company stay current in payments to suppliers and take advantage of purchase discounts.

6. **Balance the ledgers.** At the end of the period, general ledger account balances are summarized on a trial balance to ensure total debits equal total credits. Accounts receivable subsidiary ledger customer account balances are totalled and compared to the Accounts Receivable control account in the general ledger. The same comparison is done for the accounts payable subsidiary ledger supplier account balances and the Accounts Payable control account in the general ledger. Balancing the ledgers helps to ensure the accounting records are accurate.

7. **Use special journals to record and post transactions with sales taxes.** In those provinces with provincial sales taxes, sellers must add and collect sales tax on the goods they sell to consumers, and remit the tax to the provincial government. They must do the same for the Goods and Services Tax (GST). Sellers must also pay GST on the goods and services they purchase but can recover this tax from the federal government. Special journals can include columns for PST Payable, GST Payable, and GST Recoverable, as applicable, to streamline accounting for these amounts.

Self-Study Questions

Test your understanding of the chapter by marking the correct answer for each of the following questions:

1. Why does a jewellery store need an accounting system different from that which a physician uses? (*p. 331*)
   a. They have different kinds of employees.
   b. They have different kinds of journals and ledgers.
   c. They have different kinds of business transactions.
   d. They work different hours.

2. Which feature of an effective information system is most concerned with safeguarding assets? (*p. 330*)
   a. Control
   c. Flexibility
   b. Compatibility
   d. Favourable cost/benefit relationship

3. The account number 211031 most likely refers to (*p. 333*)
   a. Liabilities
   c. Accounts payable
   b. Current liabilities
   d. An individual supplier

4. If the amount of total revenues is in cell E7 of a spreadsheet and the amount for total expenses is in cell E20, then net income would be computed by the formula (*pp. 337–338*)
   a. =E7+E20
   b. =E7–E20
   c. =E20–E7
   d. None of the above formulas will work

5. Special journals help most by (*p. 339*)
   a. Limiting the number of transactions that have to be recorded
   b. Reducing the cost of operating the accounting system
   c. Improving accuracy in posting to subsidiary ledgers
   d. Easing the preparation of the financial statements

6. Centex Sound Systems purchased inventory costing $8,000 from Sony on account. Where should Centex record this transaction, and what account is credited? (*p. 345*)
   a. Cash payments journal; credit Cash
   b. Sales journal; credit Sales Revenue
   c. Purchases journal; credit Accounts Payable
   d. General journal; credit Inventory

7. Every transaction recorded in the cash receipts journal includes a (*p. 342*)
   a. Credit to Cash
   b. Debit to Accounts Receivable
   c. Debit to Sales Discounts
   d. Debit to Cash

8. Entries in the purchases journal are posted to the (*p. 345*)
   a. General ledger only
   b. General ledger and the accounts payable subsidiary ledger
   c. General ledger and the accounts receivable subsidiary ledger
   d. Accounts receivable subsidiary ledger and the accounts payable subsidiary ledger

9. Every transaction recorded in the cash payments journal includes a (*p. 347*)
   a. Debit to Accounts Payable
   b. Debit to an Other Account
   c. Credit to Inventory
   d. Credit to Cash

10. The individual accounts in the accounts receivable subsidiary ledger identify (*p. 341*)
   a. Payees
   c. Amounts to be paid
   b. Debtors
   d. Suppliers

Answers to the Self-Study Questions follow the Similar Accounting Terms.

Accounting Vocabulary

Accounting information system   (p. 330)
Batch processing   (p. 335)
Cash payments journal   (p. 347)
Cash receipts journal   (p. 342)
Control account   (p. 342)
Credit memo   (p. 350)
Database   (p. 332)
Debit memo   (p. 351)
Enterprise resource planning (ERP) system   (p. 335)
General journal   (p. 338)
General ledger   (p. 341)
Hardware   (p. 331)

Menu   (p. 334)
Module   (p. 336)
Network   (p. 331)
Online processing   (p. 335)
Purchases journal   (p. 345)
Real-time processing   (p. 335)
Sales journal   (p. 339)
Server   (p. 331)
Software   (p. 331)
Special journal   (p. 338)
Spreadsheet   (p. 337)
Subsidiary ledger   (p. 341)

Similar Accounting Terms

Accounts payable subsidiary ledger	Accounts payable ledger, accounts payable subledger
Accounts receivable subsidiary ledger	Accounts receivable ledger, accounts receivable subledger
Balancing the ledgers	Proving the ledgers, reconciling the ledgers, reconciling receivables and payables
Cash payments journal	Cash disbursements journal, cheque register
Credit memo	Credit memorandum
Database	Management information system
Debit memo	Debit memorandum
Online processing	Real-time processing

Answers to Self-Study Questions

1. c	3. d	5. b	7. d	9. d
2. a	4. b	6. c	8. b	10. b

Assignment Material

Questions

1. Describe the four criteria of an effective accounting system.
2. Distinguish batch computer processing from online computer processing.
3. What accounting categories correspond to the account numbers 1, 2, 3, 4, and 5 in the chart of accounts in a typical computerized accounting system?
4. Why might the number 112 be assigned to Accounts Receivable and the number 1120708 to Carl Erickson, a customer?
5. Describe the function of menus in a computerized accounting system.
6. How do formulas in spreadsheets speed the process of budget preparation and revision?
7. Name four special journals used in accounting systems. For what type of transaction is each designed?
8. Describe the two advantages that special journals have over recording all transactions in the general journal.
9. What is a control account, and how is it related to a subsidiary ledger? Name two common control accounts.
10. Graff Company's sales journal has one amount column headed Accounts Receivable Dr. and Sales Revenue Cr. In this journal, 86 transactions are recorded. How many posting references or (✓) appear in the journal? State what each posting reference represents.
11. The accountant for Bannister Co. posted all amounts correctly from the cash receipts journal to the general ledger. However, she failed to post three credits to customer accounts in the accounts receivable subsidiary ledger. How would this error be detected?
12. At what two times is posting done from a special journal? What items are posted at each time?
13. Describe how to use the sales journal to account for sales tax collected from customers.
14. What is the purpose of balancing, or reconciling, the ledgers?
15. Posting from the journals of McKedrick Realty is complete. But the total of the individual balances in the accounts payable subsidiary ledger does not equal the balance in the Accounts Payable control account in the general ledger. Does this necessarily indicate that the trial balance is out of balance? Explain.
16. Assume that posting is completed. The trial balance shows no errors, but the sum of the individual accounts payable does not equal the Accounts Payable control balance in the general ledger. What two errors could cause this problem?

Starters

Starter 7–1 Suppose you have invested your life savings in a company that prints rubberized logos on T-shirts. The business is growing fast, and you need a better accounting information system. Consider the features of an effective system, as discussed on pages 330–331. Which do you regard as most important? Why? Which feature must you consider if your financial resources are limited?

Features of an effective information system

Starter 7–2 Identify each of the following items as an element of a computerized accounting system (c) or a manual accounting system (m) or both (b).

1. The trial balance is transferred to or entered on the work sheet.
2. Automatic posting to the general ledger.
3. The use of UPC codes for inventory.
4. Printing financial statements.
5. Closing the accounts by debiting Income Summary and crediting expenses.
6. Start the cycle with account balances in the general ledger.

Identify the elements of computerized and manual accounting systems

Starter 7–3 Complete the crossword puzzle that follows.

Down:
1. Managers need _____ over operations in order to authorize transactions and safeguard assets
3. Programs that drive a computer
4. Electronic computer equipment
5. A _____ ible information system accommodates changes as the organization evolves
6. The opposite of debits

Across:
2. Electronic linkage that allows different computers to share the same information
3. Main computer in a networked system
7. Cost-_____ relationship must be favourable

Starter 7–4 Assign account numbers (from the list that follows) to the accounts of LP Gas Co. Identify the headings, which are *not* accounts and would not be assigned an account number.

Assets	LP, Capital
Current Assets	LP, Withdrawals
Inventory	Revenues
Accounts Payable	Selling Expenses

Number from which to choose:

151	301
191	311
201	411
281	531

Starter 7–5 Refer to the spreadsheet screen in Exhibit 7–6 page 337. Suppose cells B2 through B4 are your business's actual income statement for the current year. You wish to develop your financial plan for the coming year. Revenues should increase by 10% and expenses by 17%. Write the formulas in cells C2 through C4 to compute expected revenues, expenses, and net income for the coming year.

Starter 7–6 Use the following abbreviations to indicate the journal in which you would record transactions a through n.

J	=	General journal	P =	Purchases journal
S	=	Sales journal	CP =	Cash payments journal
CR	=	Cash receipts journal		

Transactions:

a. _____ Cash sale of inventory

b. _____ Payment of rent

c. _____ Amortization of computer equipment

d. _____ Purchases of inventory on account

e. _____ Collection of accounts receivable

f. _____ Expiration of prepaid insurance

g. _____ Sale on account

h. _____ Payment on account

i. _____ Cash purchase of inventory

j. _____ Collection of dividend revenue earned on an investment

k. _____ Prepayment of insurance

l. _____ Borrowing money on a long-term note payable

m. _____ Purchase of equipment on account

n. _____ Cost of goods sold along with a credit sale

o. _____ Return of merchandise

Starter 7–7 Use the sales journal and the related ledger accounts in Exhibit 7–9, page 340, to answer these questions about Austin Sound Centre.

Using the sales journal and the related ledgers

1. How much inventory did Austin Sound have on hand at the end of November? Where can you get this information?

2. What amount did Austin Sound post to the Sales Revenue account? When did Austin Sound post to the Sales Revenue account? Assume a manual accounting system.

3. After these transactions, how much does Susan Levy owe Austin Sound? Where do you obtain this information? Be specific.

4. If there were no discounts, how much would Austin Sound hope to collect from all its customers? Where is this amount stored in a single figure?

Starter 7–8

Using accounts receivable records and balancing the ledgers

1. A business that sells on account must have good accounts receivable records to ensure collection from customers. What is the name of the detailed record of amounts collectible from individual customers?

2. Where does the total amount receivable from all the customers appear? Be specific.

3. A key control feature of Austin Sound Centre's accounting system lies in the agreement between the detailed customer receivable records and the summary total in the general ledger. Use the data in Exhibit 7–9, page 340, to reconcile Austin Sound's accounts receivable records at November 30, 2008.

Starter 7–9 The cash receipts journal of Austin Sound Centre appears in Exhibit 7–10, page 343, along with the company's various ledger accounts. Use the data in Exhibit 7–10 to answer the following questions raised by Steve Austin, owner of the business.

Using cash receipts data

1. How much were total cash receipts during November?

2. How much cash did Austin Sound collect on account from customers? How much in total discounts did customers earn by paying quickly? How much did Austin Sound's accounts receivable decrease because of collections from customers during November?

3. How much were cash sales during November?

4. How much did Austin Sound borrow during November? Where else could you look to determine whether Austin Sound has paid off part of the loan?

Starter 7–10 Use Austin Sound's purchases journal (Exhibit 7–11, page 346) to address these questions faced by Steve Austin, owner of the business.

Using the purchases journal

1. How much were Austin Sound's total purchases of inventory during November?

2. Suppose it is December 1 and Austin wishes to pay the full amount that Austin Sound owes on account. Examine only the purchases journal. Then make a general journal entry to record payment of the correct amount on December 1. Include an explanation.

Starter 7–11 Refer to Austin Sound Centre's purchases journal (Exhibit 7–11, page 346) and cash payments journal (Exhibit 7–12, page 348). Steve Austin, the owner, has raised the following questions about the business.

Using the purchases journal and the cash payments journal

1. Increase in Accounts Payable $2,876

1. How much did total credit purchases of inventory, supplies, equipment, and furniture increase Austin Sound's accounts payable during November?

2. How much of the accounts payable balance did Austin Sound pay off during November?

3. At November 30, after all purchases and all cash payments, how much does Austin Sound owe JVC Canada Inc.? How much in total does Austin Sound owe on account?

Using all the journals

2. Net sales revenue $7,456

Starter 7–12 Answer the following questions about the November transactions of Austin Sound Centre. You will need to refer to Exhibits 7–9 through 7–12, which begin on page 340.

1. How much cash does Austin Sound have on hand at November 30?

2. Determine Austin Sound's gross sales revenue and net sales revenue for November.

3. How did Austin Sound purchase furniture—for cash or on account? Indicate the basis for your answer.

4. From whom did Austin Sound purchase supplies on account? How much in total does Austin Sound owe this company on November 30?

Effects of taxes and the periodic inventory system on special journals

Starter 7–13 Answer the following questions about Austin Sound Centre's special journals.

1. Refer to Austin Sound Centre's sales journal in Exhibit 7–9 on page 340. How would it look different if Austin Sound used the periodic inventory system and all credit sales transactions are subject to PST and GST? Give the headings for all new columns.

2. Refer to Austin Sound Centre's cash receipts journal in Exhibit 7–10 on page 343. How would it look different if Austin Sound used the periodic inventory system and all cash sales transactions are subject to PST and GST? Give the headings for all new columns.

3. Refer to Austin Sound Centre's purchases journal in Exhibit 7–11 on page 346. How would it look different if Austin Sound used the periodic inventory system and all purchases on account are subject to GST? Give the headings for all new columns.

4. Refer to Austin Sound Centre's cash payments journal in Exhibit 7–12 on page 348. How would it look different if Austin Sound used the periodic inventory system and most cash payments are subject to GST? Give the headings for all new columns.

Exercises

Features of an effective accounting information system

Exercise 7–1

The head office of Global Circuits wants to "go green" and reduce paper use and unnecessary reports. Which features of an effective accounting information system will allow for this initiative? Discuss.

Setting up a chart of accounts

Exercise 7–2

It is very important to set up a properly numbered chart of accounts, especially in a computerized accounting system. Use account numbers 101 through 106, 201, 221, 301, 321, 401, 501, and 521 to correspond to the following selected accounts from the general ledger of Casteel Map Company. List the accounts and their account numbers in proper order, starting with the most liquid current asset.

Randy Casteel, capital	Amortization expense	Accounts receivable
Cost of goods sold	Cash	Note payable, long-term
Accounts payable	Randy Casteel, withdrawals	Computer equipment
Inventory	Supplies	
Sales revenue	Accumulated amortization	

Elements of computerized and manual accounting systems

Exercise 7–3

Refer to Exhibit 7–5 on page 336. Which steps are automatic in a computerized accounting system compared to a manual accounting system?

Exercise 7–4

The following accounts and sums of accounts in the computerized accounting system of Drayton Supplies show some of the company's adjusted balances before closing:

Total assets	?
Current assets	16,800
Long-term assets	40,200
Total liabilities	?
Sam Drayton, Capital	40,800
Sam Drayton, Withdrawals	15,000
Total revenues	54,000
Total expenses	33,000

Compute the missing amounts.

Using a trial balance

Total assets $57,000

Exercise 7–5

A building listed on a spreadsheet has a cost of $180,000; this amount is located in cell E7. The number of years of the asset's useful life (20) is found in cell E9. Write the spreadsheet formula to express annual amortization expense for this asset. Assume the value at the end of the useful life will be zero. How much is annual amortization?

Using a spreadsheet to compute amortization

Exercise 7–6

Suppose the values of the following items appear in the cells of Joe's Photos Co.'s spreadsheet:

Computing financial statement amounts with a spreadsheet

Item	Cell
Total assets	B22
Current assets	B8
Long-term assets	B11
Total liabilities	C11
Current liabilities	C6
Long-term liabilities	C10

Write the spreadsheet formula to calculate the store's:

a. Current ratio
b. Total owner's equity
c. Debt ratio

Exercise 7–7

The sales and cash receipts journals of Northern Electronics include the following entries:

Using the sales and cash receipts journals (perpetual inventory system)

4

Total debits to Cash $530

Sales Journal

Date	Invoice No.	Account Debited	Post. Ref.	Accounts Receivable Dr. Sales Revenue Cr.	Cost of Goods Sold Dr. Inventory Cr.
May. 7	671	I. Woods	✔	110	36
10	672	W. Singh	✔	60	29
10	673	F. Weir	✔	60	25
12	674	J. Leggatt	✔	120	60
31		Total		350	150

Cash Receipts Journal

	Debits		Credits					
					Other Accounts			
Date	Cash	Sales Discounts	Accounts Receivable	Sales Revenue	Account Title	Post. Ref.	Amount	Cost of Goods Sold Dr. Inventory Cr.
May. 16					I. Woods	✔		
19					F. Weir	✔		
24	300			300				190
30					W. Singh	✔		

Complete the cash receipts journal for those transactions indicated. There are no sales discounts. Also, total the journal and show that total debits equal total credits.

Classifying postings from the cash receipts journal ④

Exercise 7–8

The cash receipts journal of Campbell Sports follows:

Cash Receipts Journal   Page 7

	Debits		Credits				
					Other Accounts		
Date	Cash	Sales Discounts	Accounts Receivable	Sales Revenue	Account Title	Post. Ref.	Amount
Jan. 2	790	20	810		Magna Corp.	(a)	
9	490		490		Kamm, Inc.	(b)	
19	4,480				Note Receivable	(c)	4,000
					Interest Revenue	(d)	480
30	310	10	320		J. T. Kazarian	(e)	
31	4,230			4,230			
31	10,300	30	1,620	4,230	Totals		4,480
	(f)	(g)	(h)	(i)			(j)

Campbell Sports' chart of accounts (general ledger) includes the following selected accounts, along with their account numbers:

Number	Account	Number	Account
110	Cash	510	Sales revenue
120	Accounts receivable	512	Sales discounts
125	Note receivable	515	Sales returns
140	Land	520	Interest revenue

Required

Indicate whether each posting reference (a) through (j) should be a

- Check mark (✔) for a posting to a customer account in the accounts receivable subsidiary ledger.
- Account number for a posting to an account in the general ledger. If so, give the account number.
- Letter (x) for an amount not posted.

Exercise 7-9

Identifying transactions from postings to the accounts receivable subsidiary ledger

A customer account in the accounts receivable subsidiary ledger of Kettle Office Supplies follows:

Beaver Valley Lumber Inc.   112590

Date		Jrnl. Ref.	Dr.	Cr.	Debit Balance
Nov. 1	....				400
9	....	S.5	1,180		1,580
18	....	J.8		190	1,390
30	....	CR.9		700	690

Required   Describe the three posted transactions.

Exercise 7-10

Recording purchase transactions in the general journal and purchases journal

Purchases journal: Total credit to Accounts Payable $8,110

During June, Durant Dairy completed the following credit purchase transactions:

April	5	Purchased supplies, $400, from Central Co.
	11	Purchased inventory, $1,200, from McDonald Ltd. Durant Dairy uses a perpetual inventory system.
	19	Purchased equipment, $4,300, from Baker Corp.
	22	Purchased inventory, $2,210, from Khalil Inc.

Record these transactions first in the general journal—with explanations—and then in the purchases journal. Omit credit terms and posting references. After setting up the purchase journal form, which procedure for recording transactions is quicker? Why?

Exercise 7-11

Posting from the purchases journal; balancing the ledgers

3. Total accounts payable $3,270

The purchases journal of Lightning Snowboards follows:

Purchases Journal   Page 7

							Other Accounts Dr.		
Date	Account Credited	Terms	Post. Ref.	Accounts Payable Cr.	Inventory Dr.	Supplies Dr.	Acct. Title	Post. Ref.	Amt. Dr.
Sept. 2	Brotherton Inc.	n/30		800	800				
5	Rolf Office Supply	n/30		170		170			
13	Brotherton Inc.	2/10, n/30		1,400	1,400				
26	Marks Equipment Company	n/30		900			Equipment		900
30	Totals			3,270	2,200	170			900

Required

1. Open three-column general ledger accounts for Inventory, Supplies, Equipment, and Accounts Payable. Post to these accounts from the purchases journal. Use dates and posting references in the ledger accounts.

2. Open accounts in the accounts payable subsidiary ledger for Brotherton Inc., Rolf Office Supply, and Marks Equipment Company. Post from the purchases journal. Use dates and journal references in the ledger accounts.

3. Balance the Accounts Payable control account in the general ledger with the total of the balances in the accounts payable subsidiary ledger.

4. Does Lightning Snowboards use a perpetual or a periodic inventory system?

Using the cash payments journal

3. Total credit to Cash $37,790

Exercise 7–12

During February, Dean Products had the following transactions:

Feb.		
3	Paid $490 on account to Marquis Corp. net of a $10 discount for an earlier purchase of inventory.
6	Purchased inventory for cash, $3,800.
11	Paid $300 for supplies.
15	Purchased inventory on account from Monroe Corporation, $1,548.
16	Paid $24,100 on account to LaGrange Ltd.; there was no discount.
21	Purchased furniture for cash, $2,800.
26	Paid $3,900 on account to Graff Software Ltd. for an earlier $4,000 purchase of inventory. The purchase discount was $100.
28	Made a semiannual interest payment of $2,400 on a long-term note payable. The entire payment was for interest. (Assume none of the interest had been accrued previously.)

Required

1. Prepare a cash payments journal similar to the one illustrated in this chapter. Omit the payee column.

2. Record the transactions in the cash payments journal. Which transaction should not be recorded in the cash payments journal? In what journal does it belong?

3. Total the amount columns of the cash payments journal. Determine that the total debits equal the total credits.

Using business documents to record purchases, sales, and returns

Eddie's: Credit Cash for $1,835

Exercise 7–13

The following documents describe two business transactions:

Invoice		
Date: March 14, 2006		
Sold to: Eddie's Bicycle Shop		
Sold by: Schwinn Company		
Terms: 2/10, n/30		
Items Purchased Bicycles		
Quantity	**Price**	**Total**
8	$152	$1,216
2	112	224
10	96	960
Total $2,400		

Debit Memo		
Date: March 20, 2006		
Issued to: Schwinn Company		
Issued by: Eddie's Bicycle Shop		
Items Returneed Bicycles		
Quantity	**Price**	**Total**
2	$152	$304
2	112	224
Total $528		
Reason: Damaged in shipment		

Required

1. Use the general journal to record these transactions and Eddie's Bicycle Shop's cash payment on March 21. Record the transactions first on the books of Eddie's Bicycle Shop and, second, on the books of Schwinn Company, which makes and sells bicycles. Both Eddie's Bicycle Shop and Schwinn Company use a perpetual inventory system as illustrated in Chapter 5. Schwinn Company's cost of the bicycles sold to Eddie's Bicycle Shop was $1,280. Schwinn Company's cost of the returned merchandise was $256. Round to the nearest dollar. Explanations are not required. Using the perpetual system of inventory, set up your answer in the following format:

Date	Eddie's Bicycle Shop Journal Entries	Schwinn Journal Entries

2. How would your answer be different if both of these companies used the periodic inventory system?

Exercise 7–14

Special journals using PST and GST (perpetual inventory system)

Total debit to Cash from cash receipts journal $4,520

Brights Patio Shop sells garden and patio furniture. All of its sales and purchases are subject to 6% GST, and its sales are also subject to 7% PST. Record all of the following transactions in the appropriate special journals, using the special journal formats shown in Exhibit 7–15.

May	1	Sold $1,300 of patio furniture to Jen Williams, terms n/30, invoice 310 (cost, $850).
	3	Purchased inventory on credit terms of 1/10, n/60 from Sunshine Corp., $4,000.
	5	Sold inventory for cash, $200 (cost, $110).
	10	Purchased patio lanterns from an artisan, $300, issuing cheque no. 401.
	15	Sold $2,500 of outdoor seating to Pat's Restaurant, terms n/30, invoice 311 (cost, $1,700)
	22	Received payment from Jen Williams (May 1).
	26	Received payment from Pat's Restaurant (May 15).
	29	Paid Sunshine Corp. for the purchase made on May 3, cheque no. 402.

Challenge Exercise

Exercise 7–15

Using the special journals

1. Gross margin $3,935

1. Austin Sound Centre's special journals in Exhibits 7–9 through 7–12 (pages 340–348) provide the manager with much of the data needed for preparation of the financial statements. Austin Sound uses the *perpetual* inventory system, so the amount of cost of goods sold is simply the ending balance in that account. The manager needs to know the business's gross margin for November. Compute the gross margin.

2. Suppose Austin Sound used the *periodic* inventory system. In that case, the business must compute cost of goods sold by the formula:

Cost of goods sold:	
Beginning inventory	$ 3,885
+ Net purchases	XXX
= Cost of goods available for sale	X,XXX
− Ending inventory	(4,249)
= Cost of goods sold	$ XX

Perform this calculation of cost of goods sold for Austin Sound. Does this computation of cost of goods sold agree with your answer to requirement 1?

Beyond the Numbers

Beyond the Numbers 7–1

Designing a special journal

King Technology Associates creates and sells cutting-edge network software. King's quality control officer estimates that 20 percent of the company's sales and purchases of inventory are returned for additional debugging. King needs special journals for

- Sales returns and allowances
- Purchase returns and allowances

Required

1. Design on paper or on a computer the two special journals. For each journal, include a column for the appropriate business document.

2. Enter one transaction in each journal, using the Austin Sound transaction data illustrated on pages 350 and 351. Show all posting references, including those for column totals. In the purchase returns and allowances journal, assume debit memo number 14.

Ethical Issue

On a recent trip to Brazil, Carlo Degas, sales manager of Cyber Systems, took his wife along for a vacation and included her airfare and meals on his expense report, which he submitted for reimbursement. Chelsea Brindley, vice-president of sales and Degas' boss, thought his total travel and entertainment expenses seemed excessive. However, Brindley approved the reimbursement because she owed Degas a favour. Brindley, well aware that the company president routinely reviewed all expenses recorded in the cash payments journal, had the accountant record the expenses of Degas' wife in the general journal as follows:

Sales Promotion Expense	7,500	
Cash		7,500

Required

1. Does recording the transaction in the general journal rather than in the cash payments journal affect the amounts of cash and total expenses reported in the financial statements?
2. Why did Ms. Brindley want this transaction recorded in the general journal?
3. What is the ethical issue in this situation? What role does accounting play in the ethical issue?

Problems (Group A)

Excel Spreadsheet Template

Using a spreadsheet to prepare an income statement

Problem 7–1A

The following spreadsheet shows the income statement of McBride Wholesalers.

	A	B
3	Revenues:	
4	Service revenue	number
5	Rent revenue	number
6		————
7	Total revenue	
8		————
9	Expenses:	
10	Salary expense	number
11	Supplies expense	number
12	Rent expense	number
13	Amortization expense	number
14		————
15	Total expenses	
16		————
17	Net income	
18		═══════

Required Write the appropriate formula in each cell that will need a formula. Symbols from which to choose are:

+	add	/	divide
−	subtract		=SUM(beginning cell:ending cell)
*	multiply		

Problem 7–2A

The general ledger of Cannin Distributors includes the following selected accounts, along with their account numbers:

Cash	11	Land	18
Accounts Receivable	12	Sales Revenue	41
Inventory	13	Sales Discounts	42
Notes Receivable	15	Sales Returns and Allowances	43
Supplies	16	Cost of Goods Sold	51

Using the sales, cash receipts, and general journals (with the perpetual inventory system)

1. Cash receipts journal: Total debit to Cash $142,872

All credit sales are on the company's standard terms of 2/10, n/30. Transactions in July that affected sales and cash receipts were as follows:

July		
	2	Sold inventory on credit to Fortin Inc., $2,800. Cannin's cost of these goods was $1,600.
	4	As a favour to a competitor, sold supplies at cost, $3,400, receiving cash.
	7	Cash sales of merchandise for the week totalled $7,560 (cost, $6,560).
	9	Sold merchandise on account to A. L. Price, $29,280 (cost, $20,440).
	10	Sold land that cost $50,000 for cash of $50,000.
	11	Sold goods on account to Sloan Forge Ltd., $20,416 (cost, $14,080).
	12	Received cash from Fortin Inc. in full settlement of its account receivable from July 2.
	14	Cash sales of merchandise for the week were $8,424 (cost, $6,120).
	15	Sold inventory on credit to the partnership of Wilkie & Blinn, $14,600 (cost, $9,040).
	18	Received inventory sold on July 9 to A. L. Price for $2,400. The goods shipped were the wrong size. These goods cost Cannin $1,760.
	20	Sold merchandise on account to Sloan Forge Ltd., $2,516 (cost, $1,800).
	21	Cash sales of merchandise for the week were $3,960 (cost, $2,760).
	22	Received $8,000 cash from A. L. Price in partial settlement of his account receivable.
	25	Received cash from Wilkie & Blinn for its account receivable from July 15.
	25	Sold goods on account to Olsen Inc., $6,080 (cost, $4,200).
	27	Collected $10,500 on a note receivable.
	28	Cash sales of merchandise for the week were $15,096 (cost, $9,840).
	29	Sold inventory on account to R. O. Bankston Inc., $968 (cost, $680).
	30	Received goods sold on July 25 to Olsen Inc. for $160. The wrong items were shipped. The cost of the goods was $100.
	31	Received $18,880 cash on account from A. L. Price.

Required

1. Use the appropriate journal to record the above transactions: a sales journal (omit the Invoice No. column), a cash receipts journal, or a general journal. Cannin Distributors records sales returns and allowances in the general journal.

2. Total each column of the sales journal and the cash receipts journal. Show that the total debits equal the total credits.

3. Show how postings would be made from the journals by writing the account numbers and check marks in the appropriate places in the journals.

Problem 7–3A

The cash receipts journal at the top of the next page contains five entries. All five entries are for legitimate cash receipt transactions, but the journal contains some errors in recording the transactions. In fact, only one entry is correct, and each of the other four entries contains one error.

Correcting errors in the cash receipts journal (perpetual inventory system)

Corrected cash receipts journal: Total debit to Cash $83,000

Cash Receipts Journal — Page 22

Date	Cash	Sales Discounts	Accounts Receivable	Sales Revenue	Account Title	Post. Ref.	Amount	Cost of Goods Sold Dr. Inventory Cr.
Debits			**Credits**		**Other Accounts**			
Jan. 4		4,200		4,200				2,030
7	6,000	220			Marc Fortin	✔	6,220	
13	57,400				Note Receivable	13	53,900	
					Interest Revenue	45	3,500	
20				4,620				2,100
30	15,400		10,780					
31	78,800	4,420	10,780	8,820	Totals		63,620	4,130
	(11)	(42)	(12)	(41)			(✔)	51/13

Total Dr. = $83,220   Total Cr. = $83,220

Required

1. Identify the correct entry in the cash receipts journal above.
2. Identify the error in each of the other four entries.
3. Using the following format, prepare a corrected cash receipts journal.

Cash Receipts Journal — Page 22

Date	Cash	Sales Discounts	Accounts Receivable	Sales Revenue	Account Title	Post. Ref.	Amount	Cost of Goods Sold Dr. Inventory Cr.
Debits			**Credits**		**Other Accounts**			
Jan. 4								
7					Marc Fortin	✔		
13					Note Receivable	13		
					Interest Revenue	45		
20								
30								
31	83,000	220	17,000	8,820	Totals		57,400	
	(11)	(42)	(12)	(41)			(✔)	

Total Dr. = $83,220   Total Cr. = $83,220

Using the purchases, cash payments, and general journals

1. Cash payments journal: Total credit to Cash $19,981

Problem 7–4A

The general ledger of Katie's Supplies includes the following accounts:

Cash	111	Furniture	187
Inventory	131	Accounts Payable	211
Prepaid Insurance	161	Rent Expense	564
Supplies	171	Utilities Expense	583

Transactions in August that affected purchases and cash payments were as follows:

Aug. 1   Purchased inventory on credit from Worth Corp., $6,900. Terms were 2/10, n/30.

1   Paid monthly rent, debiting Rent Expense for $2,000.

Aug.	5	Purchased supplies on credit terms of 2/10, n/30 from Ross Supply Ltd., $450.
	8	Paid electricity bill, $600.
	9	Purchased furniture on account from Rite Office Supply, $9,100. Payment terms were net 30.
	10	Returned the furniture to Rite Office Supply. It was the wrong colour.
	11	Paid Worth Corp. the amount owed on the purchase of August 1.
	12	Purchased inventory on account from Wynne Inc., $4,400. Terms were 3/10, n/30.
	13	Purchased inventory for cash, $650.
	14	Paid a semiannual insurance premium, debiting Prepaid Insurance, $1,200.
	15	Paid the account payable to Ross Supply Ltd., from August 5.
	18	Paid gas and water bills, $100.
	21	Purchased inventory on credit terms of 1/10, n/45 from Cyber Software Ltd., $5,200.
	21	Paid account payable to Wynne Inc., from August 12.
	22	Purchased supplies on account from Favron Sales, $2,740. Terms were net 30.
	25	Returned $1,200 of the inventory purchased on August 21 to Cyber Software Ltd.
	31	Paid Cyber Software Ltd. the net amount owed from August 21.

Required

1. Katie's Supplies records purchase returns in the general journal. Use the appropriate journal to record the above transactions: a purchases journal, a cash payments journal (omit the Cheque No. column), or a general journal.

2. Total each column of the special journals. Show that the total debits equal the total credits in each special journal.

3. Show how postings would be made from the journals by writing the account numbers and check marks in the appropriate places in the journals.

Problem 7–5A

Foxey Distributors had the following transactions for the month of April 2007:

April	1	Sold $1,500 of merchandise to James Moss, terms n/30. Inventory had a cost of $670. The sale was subject to 7% PST and 6% GST.
	3	Purchased $14,250 of merchandise from MNO Suppliers Ltd., terms net 30, subject to 6% GST.
	6	Paid for the purchase of April 3 (MNO Suppliers Ltd.), cheque #12.
	7	Paid $3,250 wages to employee, cheque #13.
	9	Owner withdrew $7,500 for personal use, cheque #14.
	11	Collected the amount owed by James Moss (April 1).
	13	Purchased equipment from MB Machinery Ltd., $14,250 plus 6% GST, terms n/30.
	14	Issued a debit memo to MB Machinery Ltd. (April 13) for $750 plus 6% GST of equipment returned as defective.
	15	Sold $2,000 of merchandise to St. Boniface School. Inventory cost was $1,250. The sale was subject to 7% PST and 6% GST.
	16	Paid the account owing to MB Machinery Ltd., cheque #15.
	17	Purchased $18,750 plus 6% GST of equipment from Dearing Equipment Inc., terms net 60.
	22	Paid a $4,500 note due to the Commercial Bank, plus interest of $450, cheque #16.
	24	Sold $1,100 of merchandise for cash; inventory cost was $750. The sale was subject to 7% PST and 6% GST.
	25	Paid $750 to Canada Revenue Agency for income taxes owing from December 31, 2006, cheque #17.
	26	Returned $4,250 plus 6% GST of the merchandise purchased from MNO Suppliers Ltd.
	28	Purchased inventory for $3,000 plus 6% GST from Artois Ltd., promising to pay in 30 days.
	30	Recorded the adjusting journal entries for the month of April.

Understanding how manual accounting systems are used; using the cash receipts journal and the cash payments journal with GST and PST (perpetual inventory system)

2. Cash receipts journal: Total debit to Cash $5,198

Required

1. For each date, indicate which journal would be used to record the transaction assuming Foxey Distributors uses a general journal, a sales journal, a cash receipts journal, a purchases journal, and a cash payments journal.

2. Record the appropriate transactions in the cash receipts journal and the cash payments journal, using the special journal formats shown in Exhibit 7–15.

Problem 7–6A

Using all the journals, posting, and balancing the ledgers

6. Total accounts receivable $1,488; total accounts payable $13,076

McMillan Distributors, which uses the perpetual inventory system and makes all credit sales on terms of 2/10, n/30, completed the following transactions during July:

July	2	Issued invoice no. 913 for sale on account to Teranishi Inc., $12,300. McMillan's cost of this inventory was $5,400.
	3	Purchased inventory on credit terms of 3/10, n/60 from Chicosky Corp., $7,401.
	5	Sold inventory for cash, $3,231 (cost, $1,440).
	5	Issued cheque no. 532 to purchase furniture for cash, $6,555.
	8	Collected interest revenue of $3,325.
	9	Issued invoice no. 914 for sale on account to Bell Ltd., $16,650 (cost, $6,930).
	10	Purchased inventory for cash, $3,429, issuing cheque no. 533.
	12	Received cash from Teranishi Inc. in full settlement of its account receivable from the sale on July 2.
	13	Issued cheque no. 534 to pay Chicosky Corp. the net amount owed from July 3. (Round to the nearest dollar.)
	13	Purchased supplies on account from Manley Inc., $4,323. Terms were net end of month.
	15	Sold inventory on account to M. O. Brown, issuing invoice no. 915 for $1,995 (cost, $720).
	17	Issued credit memo to M. O. Brown for $1,995 for merchandise sent in error and returned by Brown. Also accounted for receipt of the inventory.
	18	Issued invoice no. 916 for credit sale to Teranishi Inc., $1,071 (cost, $381).
	19	Received $16,317 from Bell Ltd. in full settlement of its account receivable from July 9.
	20	Purchased inventory on credit terms of net 30 from Burgess Distributing Ltd., $6,141.
	22	Purchased furniture on credit terms of 3/10, n/60 from Chicosky Corp., $1,935.
	22	Issued cheque no. 535 to pay for insurance coverage, debiting Prepaid Insurance for $3,000.
	24	Sold supplies to an employee for cash of $162, which was the cost of the supplies.
	25	Issued cheque no. 536 to pay utilities, $3,359.
	28	Purchased inventory on credit terms of 2/10, n/30 from Manley Inc., $4,025.
	29	Returned damaged inventory to Manley Inc., issuing a debit memo for $2,025.
	29	Sold goods on account to Bell Ltd., issuing invoice no. 917 for $1,488 (cost, $660).
	30	Issued cheque no. 537 to pay Manley Inc. $1,323.
	31	Received cash in full on account from Teranishi Inc.
	31	Issued cheque no. 538 to pay monthly salaries of $7,041.

Required

1. Open the following three-column general ledger accounts using the account numbers given:

Cash	111	Sales Revenue	411
Accounts Receivable	112	Sales Discounts	412
Supplies	116	Sales Returns and Allowances	413
Prepaid Insurance	117	Interest Revenue	419
Inventory	118	Cost of Goods Sold	511
Furniture	151	Salaries Expense	531
Accounts Payable	211	Utilities Expense	541

2. Open these accounts in the subsidiary ledgers: Accounts receivable subsidiary ledger—Bell Ltd., M. O. Brown, and Teranishi Inc.; accounts payable subsidiary ledger—Chicosky Corp., Manley Inc., and Burgess Distributing Ltd.

3. Enter the transactions in a sales journal (page 7), a cash receipts journal (page 5), a purchases journal (page 10), a cash payments journal (page 8), and a general journal (page 6), as appropriate.

4. Post daily to the accounts receivable subsidiary ledger and to the accounts payable subsidiary ledger. On July 31, post to the general ledger.

5 Total each column of the special journals. Show that the total debits equal the total credits in each special journal.

6. Balance the total of the customer account balances in the accounts receivable subsidiary ledger against Accounts Receivable in the general ledger. Do the same for the accounts payable subsidiary ledger and Accounts Payable in the general ledger.

Problems (Group B)

Problem 7–1B

Excel Spreadsheet Template

Using a spreadsheet to prepare a partial balance sheet

The spreadsheet below shows the assets section of the TCP Products balance sheet:

	A	B
3	Assets:	
4	Current assets	
5	Cash	number
6	Receivables	number
7	Inventory	number
8		
9	Total current assets	
10		
11	Equipment	number
12	Accumulated amortization	number
13		
14	Equipment, net	
15		
16	Total assets	
17		

Required Write the appropriate formula in each cell that will need a formula. Symbols from which to choose are:

+	add	/	divide
−	subtract		=SUM(beginning cell:ending cell)
*	multiply		

Problem 7–2B

Using the sales, cash receipts, and general journals (with the perpetual inventory system)

2. Cash receipts journal: Total debit to Cash $115,986

The general ledger of Beauchamp Supply includes the following accounts:

Cash	111	Land	142
Accounts Receivable	112	Sales Revenue	411
Notes Receivable	115	Sales Discounts	412
Inventory	131	Sales Returns and Allowances	413
Equipment	141	Cost of Goods Sold	511

All credit sales are on the company's standard terms of 2/10, n/30. Transactions in November that affected sales and cash receipts were as follows:

Nov. 1 Sold inventory on credit to Ijiri Ltd., $4,000. Beauchamp Supply's cost of these goods was $2,228.

Nov.	5	As a favour to another company, sold new equipment for its cost of $13,080, receiving cash in this amount.

Nov. 5   As a favour to another company, sold new equipment for its cost of $13,080, receiving cash in this amount.

6   Cash sales of merchandise for the week totalled $8,400 (cost, $5,400).

8   Sold merchandise on account to McNair Ltd., $11,320 (cost, $7,156).

9   Sold land that cost $44,000 for cash of $44,000.

11   Sold goods on account to Nickerson Builders Inc., $12,198 (cost, $7,706).

11   Received cash from Ijiri Ltd. in full settlement of its account receivable from November 1.

13   Cash sales of merchandise for the week were $7,980 (cost, $5,144).

15   Sold inventory on credit to Montez and Montez, a partnership, $3,200 (cost, $2,068).

18   Received inventory sold on November 8 to McNair Ltd. for $480. The goods shipped were the wrong colour. These goods cost Beauchamp Supply $292.

19   Sold merchandise on account to Nickerson Builders, $10,400 (cost, $7,854).

20   Cash sales of merchandise for the week were $9,320 (cost, $6,296).

21   Received $6,400 cash from McNair Ltd. in partial settlement of its account receivable. There was no discount.

22   Received payment in full from Montez and Montez for its account receivable from November 15.

22   Sold goods on account to Diamond Inc., $8,088 (cost, $5,300).

25   Collected $6,400 on a note receivable.

27   Cash sales of merchandise for the week totalled $8,910 (cost, $5,808).

27   Sold inventory on account to Littleton Corporation, $4,580 (cost, $2,868).

28   Received goods sold on November 22 to Diamond Inc. for $2,720. The goods were shipped in error, so were returned to inventory. The cost of these goods was $1,920.

28   Received $4,440 cash on account from McNair Ltd.

Required

1. Use the appropriate journal to record the above transactions: a sales journal (omit the Invoice No. column), a cash receipts journal, and a general journal. Beauchamp Supply records sales returns and allowances in the general journal.

2. Total each column of the sales journal and the cash receipts journal. Determine that the total debits equal the total credits.

3. Show how postings would be made from the journals by writing the account numbers and check marks in the appropriate places in the journals.

Correcting errors in the cash receipts journal (perpetual inventory system)

3. Corrected cash receipts journal: Total debit to Cash $131,900

Problem 7–3B

The following cash receipts journal contains five entries. All five entries are for legitimate cash receipt transactions, but the journal contains some errors in recording the transactions. In fact, only one entry is correct, and each of the other four entries contains one error.

Cash Receipts Journal

Page 16

| | Debits | | Credits | | | | | Cost of Goods |
| | | | | | Other Accounts | | | |
Date	Cash	Sales Discounts	Accounts Receivable	Sales Revenue	Account Title	Post. Ref.	Amount	Sold Dr. Inventory Cr.
May. 3	7,110	340	7,450		Alcon Labs Ltd.	✔		
9			3,460	3,460	Carl Ryther	✔		
10	110,000			110,000	Land	19		
19	730							440
30	10,600			11,330				6,310
31	128,440	340	10,910	124,790	Totals			6,750
	(11)	(42)	(12)	(41)			(✔)	(51/13)

Total Dr. = $128,780   Total Cr. = $135,700

Required

1. Identify the correct entry in the cash receipts journal on the previous page.
2. Identify the error in each of the other four entries.
3. Using the following format, prepare a corrected cash receipts journal. All column totals are correct in the cash receipts journal that follows.

Cash Receipts Journal

Page 16

	Debits				Credits			
						Other Accounts		
Date	Cash	Sales Discounts	Accounts Receivable	Sales Revenue	Account Title	Post. Ref.	Amount	Cost of Goods Sold Dr. Inventory Cr.
May. 3					Alcon Labs Ltd.	✔		
9					Carl Ryther	✔		
10					Land	19		
19								
30								
31	131,900	340	10,910	11,330	Totals		110,000	6,750
	(11)	(42)	(12)	(41)			(✔)	(51/13)

Total Dr. = $132,240   Total Cr. = $132,240

Problem 7–4B

The general ledger of Samson Supply Company includes the following accounts:

Cash	111	Equipment	189
Inventory	131	Accounts Payable	211
Prepaid Insurance	161	Rent Expense	562
Supplies	171	Utilities Expense	565

Transactions in November that affected purchases and cash payments were as follows:

Nov.
1 Paid monthly rent, debiting Rent Expense for $13,500.
3 Purchased inventory on credit from Sylvania Ltd., $2,000. Terms were 2/15, n/45.
4 Purchased supplies on credit terms of 2/10, n/30 from Harmon Sales Ltd., $800.
7 Paid utility bills, $406.
10 Purchased equipment on account from Lancer Corp., $6,100. Payment terms were 2/10, n/30.
11 Returned the equipment to Lancer Corp. It was defective.
12 Paid Sylvania Ltd. the amount owed on the purchase of November 3.
12 Purchased inventory on account from Lancer Corp., $11,000. Terms were 2/10, n/30.
14 Purchased inventory for cash, $1,600.
15 Paid an insurance premium, debiting Prepaid Insurance, $2,416.
16 Paid the account payable to Harmon Sales Ltd. from November 4.
17 Paid electricity bill, $200.
20 Paid the November 12 account payable to Lancer Corp., less the purchase discount.
21 Purchased supplies on account from Master Supply Ltd., $7,540, terms net 30.
22 Purchased inventory on credit terms of 1/10, n/30 from Linz Brothers Inc., $3,400.
26 Returned $500 of inventory purchased on November 22 to Linz Brothers Inc.
30 Paid Linz Brothers Inc. the net amount owed.

Required

1. Use the appropriate journal to record the above transactions: a purchases journal, a cash payments journal (do not use the Cheque No. column), or a general journal. Sampson Supply Company records purchase returns in the general journal.

Using the purchases, cash payments, and general journals

1. Cash payments journal: Total credit to Cash $34,533

2. Total each column of the special journals. Show that the total debits equal the total credits in each special journal.

3. Show how postings would be made from the journals by writing the account numbers and check marks in the appropriate places in the journals.

Understanding how manual accounting systems are used; using the cash receipts journal and the cash payments journal with GST and PST (perpetual inventory system)

2. Cash receipts journal: Total debit to Cash $9,519

Problem 7–5B

Carey Home Products had the following transactions for the month of June 2007:

June	1	Sold $2,000 of merchandise to Thomas Chase, terms n/30. Inventory had a cost of $1,124. The sale was subject to 8% PST and 6% GST.
	3	Purchased $4,500 of merchandise from STU Suppliers Inc., terms net 30, subject to 6% GST.
	6	Paid for the purchase of June 3 (STU Suppliers Inc.), cheque #12.
	7	Paid $4,250 wages to employee, cheque #13.
	9	Owner withdrew $11,250 for personal use, cheque #14.
	11	Collected the amount owed by Thomas Chase (June 1).
	13	Purchased equipment from DE Machinery Inc. for $12,500 plus 6% GST, terms n/30.
	14	Issued a debit memo to DE Machinery Inc. (June 13) for $1,500 plus 6% GST of equipment returned as defective.
	15	Sold $3,750 plus 8% PST and 6% GST of merchandise to DePloy Construction Ltd. Inventory had a cost of $2,250.
	16	Paid the account owing to DE Machinery Inc. (June 13, 14), cheque #15.
	17	Purchased $10,500 plus 6% GST of equipment from Alfreds Equipment Inc., terms net 60.
	22	Paid a $7,500 note due to the Commercial Bank, plus interest of $750, cheque #16.
	24	Sold $2,600 of merchandise for cash; inventory cost was $1,500. The sale was subject to 8% PST and 6% GST.
	25	Paid $1,125 to Canada Revenue Agency for income taxes owing for the year 2006, cheque #17.
	26	Returned $750 plus 6% GST of the merchandise purchased from STU Suppliers Inc.
	28	Purchased inventory for $4,500 plus 6% GST from Damon Ltd., promising to pay in 30 days.
	30	Recorded the adjusting journal entries for the month of June.

Required

1. For each date, indicate which journal would be used to record the transaction assuming Carey Home Products uses a general journal, a sales journal, a cash receipts journal, a purchases journal, and a cash payments journal.

2. Record the appropriate transactions in the cash receipts journal and the cash payments journal, using the special journal formats shown in Exhibit 7–15.

Using all the journals, posting, and balancing the ledgers (perpetual inventory system)

6. Total accounts receivable $2,268; total accounts payable $8,700

Problem 7–6B

Whitley Sales Company, which uses the perpetual inventory system and makes all credit sales with terms 2/10, n/30, had these transactions during January:

Jan.	2	Issued invoice no. 191 for sale on account to Wooten Design Ltd., $9,400. Whitley's cost of this inventory was $5,560.
	3	Purchased inventory on credit terms of 3/10, n/60 from Delwood Co., $23,600.
	4	Sold inventory for cash, $3,232 (cost, $2,040).
	5	Issued cheque no. 473 to purchase furniture for cash, $4,348.
	8	Collected interest revenue of $10,760.
	9	Issued invoice no. 192 for sale on account to Vachon Inc., $25,000 (cost, $13,200).
	10	Purchased inventory for cash, $3,104, issuing cheque no. 474.
	12	Received $9,212 cash from Wooten Design Ltd. in full settlement of its account receivable.
	13	Issued cheque no. 475 to pay Delwood Co. net amount owed from January 3.
	13	Purchased supplies on account from Lehigh Corp., $5,756. Terms were net end of month.

Jan.	15	Sold inventory on account to Franklin Ltd., issuing invoice no. 193 for $2,972 (cost, $1,640).
	17	Issued credit memo to Franklin Ltd. for $2,972 for merchandise sent in error and returned to Whitley by Franklin. Also accounted for receipt of the inventory.
	18	Issued invoice no. 194 for credit sale to Wooten Design Ltd., $7,300 (cost, $3,880).
	19	Received $24,500 from Vachon Inc. in full settlement of its account receivable from January 9.
	20	Purchased inventory on credit terms of net 30 from Jasper Sales Ltd., $5,600.
	22	Purchased furniture on credit terms of 3/10, n/60 from Delwood Co., $3,100.
	22	Issued cheque no. 476 to pay for insurance coverage, debiting Prepaid Insurance for $5,380.
	24	Sold supplies to an employee for cash of $344, which was the cost of the supplies.
	25	Issued cheque no. 477 to pay utilities, $5,552.
	28	Purchased inventory on credit terms of 2/10, n/30 from Lehigh Corp., $1,684.
	29	Returned damaged inventory to Lehigh Corp., issuing a debit memo for $1,684.
	29	Sold goods on account to Vachon Inc., issuing invoice no. 195 for $2,268 (cost, $1,256).
	30	Issued cheque no. 478 to pay Lehigh Corp. on account from January 13.
	31	Received cash in full on account from Wooten Design Ltd. for credit sale of January 18. There was no discount.
	31	Issued cheque no. 479 to pay monthly salaries of $7,400.

Required

1. For Whitley Sales Company, open the following three-column general ledger accounts using the account numbers given:

Cash	111	Sales Revenue	411
Accounts Receivable	112	Sales Discounts	412
Supplies	116	Sales Returns and Allowances	413
Prepaid Insurance	117	Interest Revenue	419
Inventory	118	Cost of Goods Sold	511
Furniture	151	Salaries Expense	531
Accounts Payable	211	Utilities Expense	541

2. Open these accounts in the subsidiary ledgers: Accounts receivable subsidiary ledger— Vachon Inc., Franklin Ltd., and Wooten Design Ltd.; accounts payable subsidiary ledger— Delwood Co., Lehigh Corp., and Jasper Sales Ltd.

3. Enter the transactions in a sales journal (page 8), a cash receipts journal (page 3), a purchases journal (page 6), a cash payments journal (page 9), and a general journal (page 4), as appropriate. Disregard PST and GST in this question.

4. Post daily to the accounts receivable subsidiary ledger and to the accounts payable subsidiary ledger. On January 31, post to the general ledger.

5. Total each column of the special journals. Show that the total debits equal the total credits in each special journal.

6. Balance the total of the customer account balances in the accounts receivable subsidiary ledger against Accounts Receivable in the general ledger. Do the same for the accounts payable subsidiary ledger and Accounts Payable in the general ledger.

Challenge Problems

Problem 7–1C

Advantage of an effective accounting system

An accounting information system that provides timely, accurate information to management is an important asset of any organization. This is especially true as organizations become larger and move into different parts of the world. The integration of computers into many organizations' information systems has enhanced their usefulness to the organization.

Providing advice about a
computerized accounting system

Required Assume your older sister is a pharmacist. She regards an information system as simply an accounting system that keeps track of her company's revenues and expenses. Explain to her how an effective accounting information system can make her a more effective pharmacist.

Problem 7–2C

Information technology is increasingly sophisticated and everyone wants the latest technology. Your brother has asked you about installing this "wonderful" computer system in his car dealership and auto repair business. The salesperson has promised your brother that the system "will do everything you want and then some." Your brother has come to you for advice about acquiring this new computerized accounting information system. At present he uses a manual accounting system.

Required Provide the advice your brother wants, focusing on the costs of the new computerized accounting information system; your brother has been told all the positive aspects of purchasing the system.

Extending Your Knowledge

Decision Problems

Reconstructing transactions from
amounts posted to the accounts
receivable subsidiary ledger

Cash receipts journal: Total debit
to Cash $15,816

Decision Problem 1

A fire destroyed some accounting records of Red River Company. The owner, Jennifer Chu, asks for your help in reconstructing the records. *She needs to know the beginning and ending balances of Accounts Receivable and the credit sales and cash receipts on account from customers during March.* All Red River Company sales are on credit, with payment terms of 2/10, n/30. All cash receipts on account reached Red River Company within the 10-day discount period, except as noted. The only accounting record preserved from the fire is the accounts receivable subsidiary ledger, which follows:

Adam Chi

Date		Jrnl. Ref.	Debit	Credit	Balance
Mar. 1	Balance				0
8		S.6	7,500		7,500
16		S.6	1,500		9,000
18		CR.8		7,500	1,500
19		J.5		300	1,200
27		CR.8		1,200	0

Anna Fowler

Date		Jrnl. Ref.	Debit	Credit	Balance
Mar. 1	Balance				1,650
5		CR.8		1,650	0
11		S.6	600		600
21		CR.8		600	0
24		S.6	6,000		6,000

Norris Associates Ltd.

Date		Jrnl. Ref.	Debit	Credit	Balance
Mar. 1	Balance				4,500
15		S.6	4,500		9,000
29		CR.8		4,350*	4,650

*Cash receipt did not occur within the discount period.

Robertson Inc.

Date		Jrnl. Ref.	Debit	Credit	Balance
Mar. 1	Balance				750
3		CR.8		750	0
25		S.6	6,000		6,000
29		S.6	1,800		7,800

Decision Problem 2

Understanding an accounting system

The external auditor must ensure that the amounts shown on the balance sheet for Accounts Receivable represent actual amounts that customers owe the company. Each customer account in the accounts receivable subsidiary ledger must represent an actual credit sale to the person or company indicated, and the customer's balance must not have been collected. This auditing concept is called *validity*, or *validating* the existence of the accounts receivable.

The auditor must also ensure that all amounts that the company owes are included in Accounts Payable and other liability accounts. For example, all credit purchases of inventory made by the company (and not yet paid) should be included in the balance of the Accounts Payable account. This auditing concept is called *completeness*.

Required Suggest how an auditor might test a customer's account receivable balance for validity. Indicate how the auditor might test the balance of the Accounts Payable account for completeness.

Comprehensive Problem for Part 1

1. Completing a Merchandiser's Accounting Cycle

3. Net income $58,800
Total assets $557,220

The end-of-month trial balance of Lakehead Building Materials at January 31, 2008, is shown below.

LAKEHEAD BUILDING MATERIALS
Trial Balance
January 31, 2008

Account Number	Account	Balance Debit	Balance Credit
110	Cash	$ 32,860	
120	Accounts receivable	38,180	
130	Inventory	120,800	
140	Supplies	5,400	
150	Building	376,340	
151	Accumulated amortization—building		$ 72,000
160	Fixtures	91,200	
161	Accumulated amortization—fixtures		11,600
200	Accounts payable		46,600
205	Salary payable		0
210	Interest payable		0
240	Unearned sales revenue		13,120
250	Note payable, long-term		164,000
300	G. Wells, capital		289,960
311	G. Wells, withdrawals	18,400	
400	Sales revenue		375,940
402	Sales discounts	9,600	
430	Sales returns and allowances	11,280	
500	Cost of goods sold	206,000	
600	Selling expense	43,040	
700	General expense	20,120	
705	Interest expense	0	
	Total	$973,220	$973,220

a. Supplies consumed during the month, $3,000. One-half is selling expense, and the other half is general expense.

b. Amortization for the month: building, $8,000; fixtures, $9,600. One-fourth of amortization is selling expense, and three-fourths is general expense.

c. Unearned sales revenue still unearned, $2,400.

d. Accrued salaries, a general expense, $7,300.

e. Accrued interest expense, $6,560.

f. Inventory on hand, $117,440. Lakehead Building Materials uses the perpetual inventory system.

Required

1. Using three-column accounts, open the accounts listed on the trial balance, inserting their unadjusted balances. Date the balances of the following accounts January 1: Supplies; Building; Accumulated Amortization—Building; Fixtures;

Accumulated Amortization—Fixtures; Unearned Sales Revenue; and G. Wells, Capital. Date the balance of G. Wells, Withdrawals, January 31.

2. Enter the trial balance on an accounting work sheet, and complete the work sheet for the month ended January 31, 2008. Lakehead Building Materials groups all operating expenses under two accounts, Selling Expense and General Expense. Leave two blank lines under Selling Expense and three blank lines under General Expense.

3. Prepare the company's multi-step income statement and statement of owner's equity for the month ended January 31, 2008. Also prepare the balance sheet at that date in report form.

4. Journalize the adjusting and closing entries at January 31, 2008, using page 3 of the general journal.

5. Post the adjusting and closing entries, using dates and posting references.

6. Compute Lakehead Building Materials' current ratio and debt ratio at January 31, 2008, and compare these values with the industry averages of 1.9 for the current ratio and 0.57 for the debt ratio. Compute the gross margin percentage and the rate of inventory turnover for the month (the inventory balance at the end of December 2007, was $133,000) and compare these ratio values with the industry averages of 0.36 for the gross margin ratio and 1.7 times for inventory turnover. Does Lakehead Building Materials appear to be stronger or weaker than the average company in the building materials industry?

2. Completing the Accounting Cycle for a Merchandising Entity

Note: This problem can be solved with or without special journals. See Requirement 2. Yellowknife Distributors closes its books and prepares financial statements at the end of each month. Yellowknife uses the perpetual inventory system. The company completed the following transactions during August 2009.

5. Net loss $1,057
Total assets $59,293

Aug.	1	Issued cheque no. 682 for August office rent $1,000. (Debit Rent Expense.)
	2	Issued cheque no. 683 to pay salaries of $1,620 which includes salary payable of $465 from July 31. Yellowknife does *not* use reversing entries.
	2	Issued invoice no. 503 for sale on account to R. T. Loeb, $300. Yellowknife's cost of this merchandise was $95.*
	3	Purchased inventory on credit terms of 1/15, n/60 from Grant Ltd., $700.
	4	Received net amount of cash on account from Fullam Corp., $2,058, within the discount period.
	4	Sold inventory for cash, $1,165 (cost, $552).
	5	Received from Park-Hee Inc. merchandise that had been sold earlier for $275 (cost, $87). The wrong merchandise had been sent.
	5	Issued cheque no. 684 to purchase supplies for cash, $390.
	6	Collected interest revenue of $550.
	7	Issued invoice no. 504 for sale on account to K. D. Skipper Inc., $1,200 (cost, $380).
	8	Issued cheque no. 685 to pay Fayda Corp. $1,300 of the amount owed at July 31. This payment occurred after the end of the discount period.
	11	Issued cheque no. 686 to pay Grant Ltd. the net amount owed from August 3.
	12	Received cash from R. T. Loeb in full settlement of her account receivable from August 2.

---

* On August 2, Yellowknife Distributors sold inventory to R. T. Loeb and collected in full on August 12. Upon learning that the shipment to Loeb was incomplete, Yellowknife plans to ship the goods to her during September. At August 31, $225 of unearned sales revenue needs to be recorded and the cost of this merchandise ($71) needs to be removed from Cost of Goods Sold and returned to Inventory.

Aug. 16   Issued cheque no. 687 to pay salary expense of $620.

19   Purchased inventory for cash, $425, issuing cheque no. 688.

22   Purchased furniture on credit terms of 3/15, n/60 from Beaver Corporation, $255.

23   Sold inventory on account to Fullam Corp., issuing invoice no. 505 for $4,983 (cost, $1,576).

24   Received half the July 31 amount receivable from K. D. Skipper Inc.—after the end of the discount period.

25   Issued cheque no. 689 to pay utilities, $1,216.

26   Purchased supplies on credit terms of 2/10, n/30 from Fayda Corp., $90.

30   Returned damaged inventory to company from whom Yellowknife made the cash purchase on August 19, receiving cash of $425.

30   Granted a sales allowance of $88 to K. D. Skipper Inc.

31   Purchased inventory on credit terms of 1/10, n/30 from Suncrest Supply Ltd., $5,165.

31   Issued cheque no. 690 to Jack West, owner of Yellowknife, for $850.

Required

1. Open the following accounts with their account numbers and July 31 balances in the ledgers indicated.

General Ledger:

101	Cash	$ 2,245
102	Accounts Receivable	12,280
104	Interest Receivable	0
105	Inventory	20,900
109	Supplies	670
117	Prepaid Insurance	1,100
140	Note Receivable, Long-term	5,500
160	Furniture	18,635
161	Accumulated Amortization—Furniture	5,275
201	Accounts Payable	5,300
204	Salary Payable	465
207	Interest Payable	2,160
208	Unearned Sales Revenue	0
220	Note Payable, Long-term	21,000
301	Jack West, Capital	27,130
303	Jack West, Withdrawals	0
400	Income Summary	0
401	Sales Revenue	0
402	Sales Discounts	0
403	Sales Returns and Allowances	0
410	Interest Revenue	0
501	Cost of Goods Sold	0
510	Salary Expense	0
513	Rent Expense	0
514	Amortization Expense—Furniture	0
516	Insurance Expense	0
517	Utilities Expense	0
519	Supplies Expense	0
523	Interest Expense	0

Accounts Receivable Subsidiary Ledger: Fullam Corp., $2,100; R. T. Loeb; Park-Hee Inc., $5,795; K. D. Skipper Inc., $4,385.

Accounts Payable Subsidiary Ledger: Beaver Corporation; Fayda Corp., $5,300; Grant Ltd.; Suncrest Supply Ltd.

2. Ask your professor for directions. Journalize the August transactions either in the general journal (page 9; explanations not required) or, as illustrated in Chapter 7, in a series of special journals: a sales journal (page 4), a cash receipts journal (page 11), a purchases journal (page 8), a cash payments journal (page 5), and a general journal (page 9). Yellowknife makes all credit sales on terms of 2/10, n/30.

3. Post daily to the accounts receivable subsidiary ledger and the accounts payable subsidiary ledger. On August 31, 2009, post to the general ledger.

4. Prepare a trial balance in the Trial Balance columns of a work sheet, and use the following information to complete the work sheet for the month ended August 31, 2009.

a. Accrued interest revenue, $500.	e. Accrued salary expense, $515.
b. Supplies on hand, $495.	f. Accrued interest expense, $660.
c. Prepaid insurance expired, $275.	g. Unearned sales revenue, $225.*
d. Amortization expense, $115.	h. Inventory on hand, $23,850.

5. Prepare Yellowknife's multi-step income statement and statement of owner's equity for August 2009. Prepare the balance sheet at August 31, 2009.

6. Journalize and post the adjusting and closing entries.

7. Prepare a postclosing trial balance at August 31, 2009. Also, balance the total of the customer accounts in the accounts receivable subsidiary ledger against the Accounts Receivable balance in the general ledger. Do the same for the accounts payable subsidiary ledger and Accounts Payable in the general ledger.

EARTH BUDDY TO SPIN MASTER AND BEYOND: THE ROLE OF ACCOUNTING IN A NEW BUSINESS

Many young people dream of owning their own business. Four entrepreneurs started their own business after graduating from university in 1993. The product they produced and sold was a head-shaped object that sprouted hair (grass) when watered. The concept was very simple: a nylon stocking was filled with sawdust and some grass seed; the head was shaped and a face was painted on it; then, the head was placed in a printed box ready for shipping.

The company was successful with orders from Canadian Tire and Zellers. It then landed an order from KMart U.S. for 500,000 Earth Buddies.

The partners were good at marketing and production. They were able to get the large order and produce the needed Earth Buddies. But successful companies need more than a product, marketing, and production skills. They also need accounting skills.

The four partners learned early on that to be successful they needed to be as concerned about accounting as they were about marketing. It was this attention to all of the details—marketing, purchasing, production, and accounting—that enabled Spin Master to be successful.

Epilogue

When we first met the partners, they were enthusiastic but inexperienced, but over the 10 years since they began producing Earth Buddy, the partners have become business professionals.

From 1993 to 2003, Earth Buddy morphed into Spin Master with an increasing range of products such as Air Hogs, Shrinky Dinks, Catch-A-Bubble, AquaDoodle and the newest hit products, Mighty Beanz in 2003 and Bella Dancerella in 2004. Each product raised the company to new heights. Customers include Wal-Mart, Toys Я Us, and McDonald's. By building alliances with third parties including inventors and brokers, the company has become North America's ninth-largest toy company with more than 100 employees and annual sales between $200 to $300 million.

CASE QUESTIONS

1. Initially, the four partners were able to make and sell the Earth Buddy but lacked the accounting skills to be successful. "Accounting skills" are important to any organization, but especially important to a new company. Why are "accounting skills" so important to a company such as Earth Buddy?

2. In Earth Buddy's early days the partners were vitally concerned with sales and production and not so concerned with records and record-keeping. The company's accountant stated that the partners "were too busy making money to keep track of it." What do you think the accountant meant? Was he right?

3. Why do you think customers such as Wal-Mart might be interested in Spin Master Ltd.'s financial statements?

4. What have you learned about accounting from these video cases?

Sources: CBC *Venture,* "Earthbuddies" (1994), "Earthbuddies—The Sequel" (2000); "Earthbuddies—Spinmaster Update (2002); Won, Shirley, "Toy maker plays a different game," *The Globe and Mail Report on Business,* January 5, 2004, pp. B1 and B4; Horowitz, Bruce, "McDonald's ventures beyond burgers to duds, toys," *USA Today,* November 14–16, 2003; Pereira, Joseph, "Sales of Mighty Beanz are jumping ahead of the holidays," *The Wall Street Journal,* October 6, 2003, page B1; Strauss, Marina, "Mighty Beanz set to be this year's hot toy," *The Globe and Mail,* September 19, 2003; Grnak, Anthony, John Hughes, and Douglas Hunter, "Lessons from the Sandbox," *National Post,* January 28, 2006, page FW2.

Internal Control and Cash

Learning Objectives

1. Define internal control
2. Describe good internal control procedures
3. Prepare a bank reconciliation and the related journal entries
4. Apply internal controls to cash receipts
5. Apply internal controls to cash payments
6. Make ethical business judgments

John Surrey* worked for ten years at a British Columbia company that provides repair and overhaul services for helicopters, eventually rising to the position of Chief Financial Officer. There was never a hint of a problem until employees noticed that some of the company's account balances were "out of whack." John explained the discrepancies and assured managers the issues would be remedied by the end of the month. When the accounts were not reconciled as promised, further investigation revealed that large sums of money had been wired to bank accounts in Switzerland, Tunisia, Scotland, China, and Spain. John could not explain the transactions and eventually admitted to stealing the money.

During the summer, John invested about $4.6 million of the company's money in an Internet-based investment scheme that promised high returns but was really a fraud. When he tried to extract himself from the scheme, he received threats to him and his family. When confronted, John admitted his embezzlement to the company president and the RCMP. Since the money proved impossible to trace and retrieve, the company expensed the entire amount embezzled.

After news of the embezzlement became public, John, who had been a CGA since 1999, resigned from the Certified General Accountants Association of British Columbia and can no longer refer to himself as a CGA.

---

* The name has been changed.

Source: David Baines, "Embezzler Quits Accountants' Association," *Vancouver Sun*, April 5, 2005, p. D2.

What are internal controls, and why are they important?

Do internal controls affect more than cash?

What is Sarbanes-Oxley and why is it important to some Canadian companies?

How can companies use bank accounts to control cash?

Is there an approach to use when facing an ethical issue?

These questions and others will be answered throughout this chapter. And the Decision Guidelines at the end of this chapter will provide a framework for making ethical judgments.

Every company, and especially expanding companies, faces similar challenges:

- How will the company safeguard its assets?
- How will the company make sure its managers and employees follow policies that are best for the company?

This chapter discusses *internal control*—the organizational plan that companies use to protect their assets and records. The chapter applies internal control techniques mainly to cash, because cash is the most liquid asset. The chapter also provides a framework for making ethical judgments in business. The material covered in this chapter is some of the most important in all of business. Unfortunately, it is sometimes overlooked, as in the actual case of the chief financial officer in the chapter-opening story.

Cash

Cash—including cash on hand in funds such as *petty cash funds*, cash on deposit in banks and trust companies, and cash equivalents, such as Treasury Bills—is the most liquid asset an organization has. Accordingly, it is usually the first item under the heading "Current Assets" on the balance sheet.

Cash's liquidity is a virtue because it is easily exchangeable for other assets. However, cash's liquidity is also a disadvantage because it is the most easily stolen asset. The next section will explain how organizations strive to protect their cash by using internal controls.

Internal Control

Objective 1
Define internal control

One of a business owner's key responsibilities is to control operations. The owners set goals, they hire managers to lead the way, and employees carry out the plan.

Both in Canada, in the *CICA Handbook*, and internationally, **internal control** consists of the policies and procedures that management establishes and maintains to govern an organization and minimize risks. Internal control is the organizational plan and all related measures adopted by an entity to meet management's internal control objectives. The *Handbook* indicates that management's internal control objectives are:

1. Optimizing the use of resources by providing reliable information for decision making, and monitoring the implementation and compliance with management's business policies.

2. Preventing and detecting error and fraud.
3. Safeguarding assets and records.
4. Maintaining reliable control systems to provide reliable information for decision making.

One of the auditor's first steps in auditing a business is to understand and evaluate its internal controls. If a company has good controls, then misstatements are minimized and are usually corrected before the financial statements are prepared. If the control system is weak, then misstatements can go undetected. The auditor increases the tests of the accounting records if the company's internal control system is weak.

Companies cannot afford to waste resources. In the chapter-opening story, the Chief Financial Officer took money from his employer and attempted to make personal gains from an Internet-based investment scheme. He stole company resources. A company must safeguard its assets and prevent errors, or it could experience the type of fraud illustrated in this story and waste its resources.

Accurate, reliable records are essential. Without reliable records, a manager cannot tell what investments to make or how much to charge for products, and banks cannot determine whether to make a loan.

How critical are internal controls? They are so important that the United States Congress passed a law that requires public companies—those that sell their shares of stock to the public—to maintain a system of internal controls.

The Sarbanes-Oxley Act (SOX)

The Enron and WorldCom accounting scandals rocked the United States. Enron overstated profits and went out of business almost overnight. WorldCom (now MCI) reported expenses as assets, and overstated both profits and assets. The company is just now emerging from bankruptcy. Sadly, the same accounting firm, Arthur Andersen, had audited both companies' financial statements. Arthur Andersen then closed its doors.

As the scandals unfolded, many people asked, "How can these things happen? Where were the auditors?" To address public concern, Congress passed the *Sarbanes-Oxley Act of 2002*, abbreviated as SOX. SOX revamped corporate governance in the United States and affected the accounting profession. Here are some of the SOX provisions:

1. Public companies must issue an internal control report, and the outside auditor must evaluate the client's internal controls.
2. A new body, the Public Company Accounting Oversight Board, oversees the work of auditors of public companies.
3. Accounting firms may not both audit a public client and also provide certain consulting services for the same client.
4. Stiff penalties await violators—25 years in prison for securities fraud; 20 years for an executive making false sworn statements.

Recently, the former chief executive officer of WorldCom was convicted of securities fraud and sentenced to 25 years in prison. Litigation against the executives of Enron is pending. You can see that internal controls and related matters can have serious consequences.

SOX is having an impact on Canadian companies in two ways:

1. Canadian companies, such as the Bank of Montreal and EnCana Corporation, are listed on the New York Stock Exchange and, therefore, must abide by Sarbanes–Oxley.
2. Canadian regulators, such as the Ontario Securities Commission, are implementing some of the requirements of Sarbanes–Oxley.

SOX ensures that managers give careful attention to internal controls in their companies.

Exhibit 8–1 shows the shield that internal controls provide for an organization. Internal controls enable people to do business securely and effectively. How does a business achieve good internal control? The next section identifies the components of internal control.

EXHIBIT 8–1 The Shield of Internal Control

The Components of Internal Control

A business can achieve its internal control objectives by applying five components:

- Control environment
- Risk assessment
- Control procedures
- Monitoring of controls
- Information system

Control Environment The control environment is the "tone at the top" of the business. It starts with the owner and the top managers. They must behave honourably to set a good example for company employees. The owner must demonstrate the importance of internal controls if he or she expects the employees to take the controls seriously.

Risk Assessment A company must identify its risks. For example, a food producer faces the risk that its food products may harm people. An airline faces the risk of bad weather that could cause accidents, and all companies face the risk of bankruptcy. Companies facing difficulties are tempted to falsify the financial statements to make themselves look better than they really are.

Control Procedures These are the procedures designed to ensure that the business's goals are achieved. Examples include assigning responsibilities, separating duties, and using security devices to protect assets. The next section discusses internal control procedures.

Monitoring of Controls Companies hire auditors to monitor their controls. Internal auditors monitor company controls to safeguard assets, and external auditors monitor the controls to ensure that the accounting records are accurate.

Information System As we have seen, the information system is critical. The owner of a business needs accurate information to keep track of assets, and measure profits and losses.

Exhibit 8–2 at the top of the next page diagrams the components of internal control.

Internal control is a management priority, not merely a part of the accounting system. Thus it is a responsibility not only of accountants but also of managers in all the functional areas throughout the organization. Internal controls are most effective when employees at all levels and in all areas adopt the organization's goals and ethical standards.

In Sun-Rype Products Ltd.'s 2005 Annual Report (in Appendix B), Sun-Rype's top managers take responsibility for the financial statements and the related system of

EXHIBIT 8–2 The Components of Internal Control

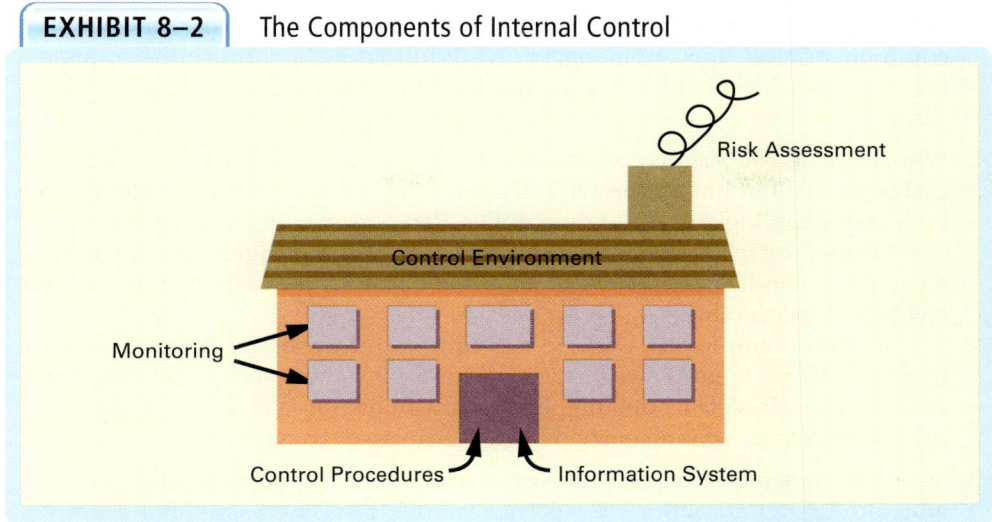

internal control. Management states "[Sun-Rype] maintains appropriate systems of internal control, policies, and procedures that provide management with reasonable assurance that assets are safeguarded and that financial records are reliable and form a proper basis for the preparation of the financial statements."

Let's examine in detail how businesses create an effective system of internal control.

Internal Control Procedures

Whether the business is Sun-Rype Products Ltd. or a local department store, an effective system of internal controls has these characteristics.

Competent, Reliable, and Ethical Personnel Employees should be *competent*, *reliable*, and *ethical*. Paying good salaries will attract high-quality employees. Companies must also train employees to do their job and must supervise their work. This will help to build a competent staff.

Assignment of Responsibilities In a business with good internal controls, no important duty is overlooked. Each employee has certain responsibilities. For example, two important duties are writing cheques and doing the accounting. In a large company, the **treasurer** is responsible for cash management. The **controller** is the chief accounting officer. The controller approves invoices (bills) for payment and the treasurer signs the cheques. With clearly assigned responsibilities, all duties are carried out.

Proper Authorization An organization generally has written rules that outline approved procedures. Any deviation from policy requires *proper authorization*. For example, managers or assistant managers of retail stores must approve customer cheques for amounts above the store's usual limit. Likewise, deans or heads of departments of colleges and universities must give the authorization for a first- or second-year student to enroll in courses that are restricted to upper-year students.

Separation of Duties Smart management divides the responsibilities for transactions between two or more people or departments. *Separation of duties* (also called segregation of duties) limits the chances for fraud and promotes the accuracy of accounting records by dividing up the three tasks of authorization, recording, and custody. Separation of duties can be divided into three parts:

1. *Separate operations from accounting.* Accounting should be completely separate from operating departments, such as production and sales. What would happen

Objective 2

Describe good internal control procedures

 REAL WORLD EXAMPLE

In a small business (or a small office of a large company), the owner/manager can ensure that assets are protected. In a larger business, internal controls can help protect assets by ensuring that policies are in place and are followed.

REAL WORLD EXAMPLE

Most banks and retail businesses assign each cashier a money tray and hold the cashier responsible if that fund is short at the end of the shift. This internal control device clearly assigns responsibility to each employee. Shortages or discrepancies can be traced to the person responsible.

What problems can result when a sales clerk can also grant credit approval and record the sales in addition to handling the cash?

A: The clerk could grant credit approval to friends and others who do not meet the credit standards, steal merchandise and hide the theft in the accounting records. The clerk could also fail to do all three jobs well and make mistakes, or forget to perform a task when the sales floor is busy.

if sales personnel recorded the company's revenue transactions? Sales figures could be inflated, and top managers wouldn't know how much the company actually sold. This is why companies should separate accounting and sales duties.

2. *Separate the custody of assets from accounting.* Accountants must not handle cash, and cashiers must not have access to the accounting records. If one employee had both cash-handling and accounting duties, that person could steal cash and conceal the theft by making a fictitious entry in the general ledger. The treasurer of a company handles cash and the controller accounts for cash. Neither person has both responsibilities.

   Warehouse employees with no accounting duties should have custody of inventory. If they were allowed to account for the inventory, they could steal it and write it off as obsolete by debiting Loss on Inventory Obsolescence and crediting Inventory. A *write-off* is an entry that credits an asset account.

3. *Separation of the authorization of transactions from the custody of related assets.* Persons who authorize transactions should not handle the related asset. For example, the same individual should not authorize the payment of a supplier's invoice and also sign the cheque to pay the invoice.

   Even small businesses should have internal controls and some separation of duties. For example, if the bookkeeper writes all cheques and keeps the general ledger records, the owner should sign all cheques and reconcile the monthly bank statement.

Internal and External Audits To demonstrate to users and to satisfy management that the financial statements fairly present the financial position of an organization and the results of its operations, most companies have an audit. An **audit** is an examination of the organization's financial statements and the accounting systems, controls, and records that produced them. To evaluate the company's accounting system, auditors examine the system of internal controls.

Audits can be internal or external. *Internal auditors* are employees of the organization. They ensure that employees are following company policies and that operations are running efficiently. Internal auditors also determine whether the company is following legal requirements.

External auditors are completely independent of the organization. They are hired to determine that the organization's financial statements are prepared in accordance with generally accepted accounting principles. Both internal and external auditors should be independent of the operations they examine, and both should suggest improvements that can help the business run efficiently.

REAL WORLD EXAMPLE

In some audits of financial institutions, the first day of the audit may occur as a surprise to the employees so that they cannot cover up fraud and/or weaknesses in the system.

Documents and Records Business *documents and records* provide the details of business transactions. Such documents include sales invoices and purchase orders and records include journals and ledgers. Documents should be pre-numbered because a gap in the numbered sequence draws attention to a possible missing document.

In a bowling alley, for example, a key document is the score sheet. The manager can check on cashiers by comparing the number of games scored with the amount of cash received. By multiplying the number of games by the price per game to estimate the revenue and comparing this amount with each day's cash receipts, the manager can see whether the business is collecting all its revenues.

REAL WORLD EXAMPLE

If a clerk in a retail store makes a mistake on the sales receipt, the receipt is not destroyed but is marked VOID. Most businesses use pre-numbered sales receipts, so a missing receipt would be noted.

Electronic Devices and Computer Controls Businesses use electronic devices to protect assets. For example, retailers such as Winners control their inventories by attaching an *electronic sensor* to merchandise. The cashier removes the sensor at checkout. If a customer tries to remove from the store an item with the sensor attached, an alarm sounds. According to Checkpoint Systems, which manufactures electronic sensors, these devices reduce loss due to theft by as much as 50 percent.

Other Controls Businesses of all types keep cash and important documents in *fireproof vaults*. *Burglar alarms* protect buildings and security cameras protect other property. *Loss-prevention specialists* train employees to spot suspicious activity.

Retailers receive most of their cash from customers on the spot. To safeguard cash, they use *point-of-sale terminals* that serve as a cash register and also record each transaction. Several times each day a supervisor removes the cash for deposit in the bank.

Employees who handle cash are in a tempting position. Many businesses purchase *fidelity bonds* on cashiers. The bond is an insurance policy that reimburses the company for any losses due to the employee's theft. Before issuing a fidelity bond, the insurance company investigates the employee's record.

Mandatory vacations and *job rotation* improve internal controls. General Electric Canada, for example, moves employees from job to job. This improves morale by giving employees a broad view of the business. Also, knowing that someone else will be doing that job next month keeps an employee honest.

STOP AND THINK

Geoff works the late movie shift at Classic Theatre. Occasionally Geoff must sell tickets *and* take the tickets as customers enter the theatre. Standard procedure requires that Geoff tear the tickets, give one-half to the customer, and keep the other half. To control cash receipts, the manager compares each night's cash receipts with the number of ticket stubs on hand.

1. How could Geoff take money from the theatre's cash receipts and hide the theft? What additional steps should the manager take to strengthen the internal control over cash receipts?

2. What is the internal control weakness in this situation? Explain the weakness.

Answers:

1. Geoff could	Management could
• Issue no ticket and keep the customer's cash.	• Physically count the number of people watching a movie and compare that number with the number of ticket stubs retained.
• Destroy some tickets and keep the customer's cash.	• Account for all ticket stubs by serial number. Missing serial numbers raise questions.

2. The internal control weakness is lack of separation of duties. Geoff receives cash and also controls the tickets, so he could destroy tickets to cover a theft of cash.

Internal Controls for E-Commerce

E-commerce creates its own risks. Hackers may gain access to confidential information such as account numbers and passwords that would normally be unavailable in face-to-face transactions. Confidentiality is a significant challenge for "dot.com" companies. Pitfalls include stolen credit-card numbers, computer viruses and Trojans, and impersonation of companies and identify theft. To convince people to buy online, companies must ensure security of customer data.

Pitfalls E-commerce pitfalls include:

- Stolen credit-card numbers
- Computer viruses and Trojans
- Phishing expeditions

Ch#8 Notes

Stolen credit-card numbers. Suppose you buy several CDs online from Future Shop. To make the purchase, your credit-card number must travel through cyberspace.

Wireless networks (Wi-Fi) are creating new security hazards. In the U.S., amateur hacker Carlos Salgado Jr. used his home computer to steal 100,000 credit-card numbers from an internet service provider. The cards represented a combined credit limit exceeding $1 billion. Salgado was caught when he tried to sell the credit-card numbers to an undercover FBI agent.

Computer viruses and Trojans. A **computer virus** is a malicious program that (a) enters program code without consent, and (b) performs destructive actions. A **Trojan** hides inside a legitimate program and works like a virus. Viruses can destroy or alter data, make bogus calculations, and infect files. Most firms have found a virus somewhere in their organization.

Phishing expeditions. Thieves phish by creating bogus websites, such as AOL4Free.com. This neat-sounding website attracts lots of visitors and the thieves obtain account numbers and passwords from unsuspecting visitors. They use the data for illicit purposes.

Security Measures To address the risks posed by e-commerce, companies have devised a number of security measures, including

- Encryption
- Firewalls

Encryption. The server holding confidential information may not be secure. One technique for protecting customer data is encryption. **Encryption** rearranges messages by a mathematical process. The encrypted message cannot be read by anyone who does not know the process. An accounting example uses check-sum digits for account numbers. Each account number has its last digit equal to the sum of the previous digits, for example, for Customer Number 2237, where 2 + 2 + 3 = 7. Any account number that fails this test triggers an error message.

Firewalls. **Firewalls** limit access to a local network. Network members can access the network but non-members cannot. Usually several firewalls are built into the system. Think of a fortress with multiple walls protecting the queen's chamber at the centre. At the point of entry, passwords, personal identification numbers (PINs), and signatures are used to restrict entry. More sophisticated firewalls are used deeper in the network.

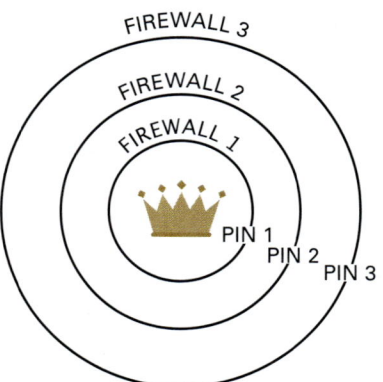

The Limitations of Internal Control— Costs and Benefits

Unfortunately, most internal controls can be circumvented or overcome. Collusion— where two or more people work as a team—can beat internal controls. Consider the Classic Theatre. Geoff and Lana can design a scheme in which Geoff sells the tickets and pockets the cash from 10 customers. Lana, the ticket taker, admits 10 customers without tickets. Geoff and Lana then split the cash. To prevent this situation, the manager must take additional steps, such as counting the people in the theatre and matching that figure against the number of ticket stubs retained. But that takes time away from other duties.

The stricter the internal control system, the more it costs. A complex system of internal control may strangle the business with red tape. How tight should the controls be? Internal controls must be judged in the light of the costs and benefits. An example of a good cost/benefit relationship: a security guard at a store costs about $28,000 a year. On average, each guard prevents about $50,000 of theft. The net benefit to the store is $22,000.

The Bank Account as a Control Device

Cash is the most liquid asset because it is the medium of exchange. Increasingly, cash consists of electronic impulses in a bank's accounting system with no paper cheques or deposit slips. Cash is easy to conceal, easy to move, and relatively easy to steal. As a result, most businesses create specific controls for cash.

Keeping cash in a *bank account* helps because banks have established practices for safeguarding customers' money. Banks also provide customers with detailed records of their transactions. To take full advantage of these control features, a business should deposit all cash receipts in the bank and make all cash payments through the bank. An exception is a petty cash transaction, which we look at later.

The documents used to control a bank account include the

- signature card
- deposit ticket
- cheque
- bank statement
- bank reconciliation

Signature Card Banks require each person authorized to transact business through an account to sign a *signature card*. The bank issues a signature card to protect against forgery.

Deposit Ticket Banks supply standard forms such as *deposit tickets* or *deposit slips*. The customer fills in the dollar amount of each deposit. As proof of the transaction, the customer keeps a deposit receipt.

Cheque To pay cash from an account, the depositor writes a **cheque**, which is the document that tells the bank to pay the designated party a specified amount of money. There are three parties to a cheque:

- The *maker*, who signs the cheque
- The *payee*, to whom the cheque is paid
- The *bank* on which the cheque is drawn.

Exhibit 8–3 shows a cheque drawn on the bank account of Business Research Inc., the maker. The cheque has two parts: the cheque itself and the *remittance advice*, an optional attachment that tells the payee the reason for payment.

Bank Statement Banks send monthly statements to their customers. A **bank statement** reports what the bank did with the customer's cash. The statement shows the account's beginning and ending balances for the period, and lists cash receipts and payments transacted through the bank. Included with the statement are the maker's *cancelled cheques*, the cheques that have been cashed by the payee. The statement also lists deposits and other changes in the account. Exhibit 8–4 on page 397 is the bank statement of Business Research Inc. for the month ended January 31, 2008. The total deposits and total withdrawals are shown at the bottom of the bank statement. Details of the transactions follow.

Electronic funds transfer (EFT) moves cash by electronic communications rather than by paper documents. It is much cheaper for a company to pay employees by EFT (direct deposit) than by issuing hundreds of payroll cheques. Also, many

EXHIBIT 8–3 | Cheque with Remittance Advice

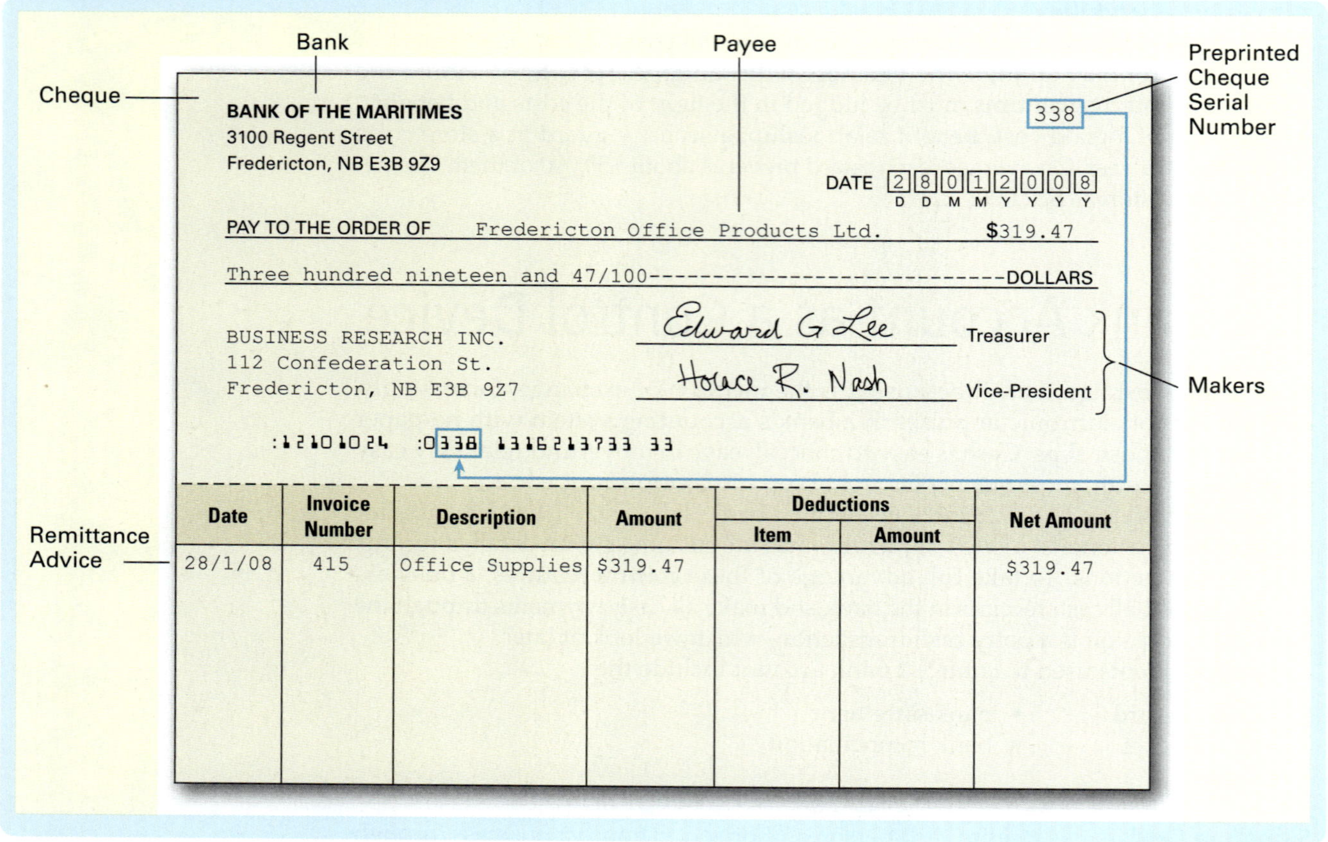

Cheque ———

Bank

BANK OF THE MARITIMES
3100 Regent Street
Fredericton, NB E3B 9Z9

Preprinted Cheque Serial Number

338

DATE 2 8 0 1 2 0 0 8
      D D M M Y Y Y Y

Payee

PAY TO THE ORDER OF   Fredericton Office Products Ltd. $319.47

Three hundred nineteen and 47/100----------------------------DOLLARS

BUSINESS RESEARCH INC.
112 Confederation St.
Fredericton, NB E3B 9Z7

Edward G Lee   Treasurer

Horace R. Nash   Vice-President

Makers

:12101024 :0338 1316213733 33

Date	Invoice Number	Description	Amount	Deductions		Net Amount
				Item	Amount	
28/1/08	415	Office Supplies	$319.47			$319.47

Remittance Advice ———

people make mortgage, rent, insurance, credit-card, and other payments either by prior arrangement with their bank or by means of electronic banking; they never write cheques for those payments. The bank statement lists EFT deposits and payments.

One method of transferring funds electronically is through the use of a *debit card*. When you make a purchase from a store and pay with a debit card, you authorize your bank to immediately withdraw the money for the purchase from your bank account and deposit it into the store's bank account. You will see the amount of the withdrawal on your monthly bank statement or passbook, and the store will see the amount of the deposit on its monthly bank statement. Debit cards, or bank cards, will be discussed more fully in Chapter 9.

The Bank Reconciliation

Objective 3

Prepare a bank reconciliation and the related journal entries

There are two records of the business's cash:

1. The Cash account in the company's general ledger. Exhibit 8–5 on page 399 shows that Business Research Inc.'s ending cash balance is $3,294.21.

2. The bank statement, which shows the cash receipts and payments transacted through the bank. In Exhibit 8–4, the bank shows an ending balance of $5,902.48 for Business Research Inc.

The books and the bank statement usually show different cash balances. Differences arise because of a time lag in recording transactions. When you write a cheque, you immediately deduct the amount of the cheque from the balance in your cheque book. But the bank does not subtract this amount from your account until the bank pays it. That may take days, even weeks, if the payee waits to cash the cheque. Likewise, you immediately add the amount of the cash receipt for each

EXHIBIT 8–4 | Bank Statement

BUSINESS ACCOUNT

Bank of the Maritimes
3100 REGENT STREET
FREDERICTON, NEW BRUNSWICK
E3B 9Z9

1024/ 0/ 5

BUSINESS RESEARCH INC.
112 CONFEDERATION ST.
FREDERICTON, NB

E3B 9Z7

For Current Interest Rates:
CALL OUR INFOLINE
1-800-386-2093
QUEBEC 1-800-386-1600
TORONTO 416-987-7735

Statement of Account	
Branch No.	Account No.
1024	1316213733

Statement From – To	
JAN 01/08	JAN 31/08
Page 1 **of** 1	

DESCRIPTION	WITHDRAWALS	DEPOSITS	DATE	BALANCE
BALANCE FORWARD			Jan01	6,556.12
DEPOSIT		1,112.00	Jan04	
NSF CHEQUE	52.00		Jan04	
NSF CHARGE	25.00		Jan04	7,591.12
CHQ#00256	100.00		Jan06	
CHQ#00334	100.00		Jan06	7,391.12
DEPOSIT		194.60	Jan08	7,585.72
CHQ#00335	100.00		Jan08	7,485.72
CHQ#00332	3,000.00		Jan12	
CHQ#00333	150.00		Jan12	4,335.72
EFT RENT COLLECTION		900.00	Jan17	5,235.72
EFT INSURANCE	361.00		Jan20	4,874.72
BANK COLLECTION		2,114.00	Jan26	6,988.72
CHQ#00336	1,100.00		Jan31	
SERVICE CHARGES	14.25		Jan31	
INTEREST CREDIT		28.01	Jan31	5,902.48
	5,002.25	4,348.61		

deposit you make to your account. But it may take a day or more for the bank to add deposits to your balance. Any EFT payments and cash receipts are recorded by the bank before you learn of them later.

To ensure accurate cash records, you need to update your cheque book—either online or after you receive your bank statement. All businesses do the same. The result of this updating process is a document called the **bank reconciliation**, which is prepared by the company (not the bank). The bank reconciliation explains the differences between the company's cash records and the bank balance. It ensures that all cash transactions have been accounted for. It also establishes that bank and book records of cash are correct. The person who prepares the bank reconciliation should have no other cash duties. Otherwise, he or she could steal cash and manipulate the bank reconciliation to hide the theft.

Debits and Credits in Accounting and Banking

In this introductory accounting course, you have learned that

- Debit means the **left** side of an account
- Credit means the **right** side of an account

In banking

- Debits are bad (for you)
- Credits are good (for you)

Both perspectives are correct. To illustrate, let's consider two transactions: (1) your receipt of $1,000 cash, which you deposit in the bank, and (2) your payment of cash by writing a $600 cheque. Record these transactions, first on your own books, and then on the bank's books. You will understand debits and credits much better.

On *your* books, journalize (1) receipt of $1,000 cash for service revenue (you immediately deposit the cash in your bank account), and (2) payment of $600 cash to purchase supplies (you write a cheque to an office supply store).

Answer: *Journal Entries on Your Books:*

Cash	1,000	
Service Revenue		1,000
Received cash for revenue earned.		
Supplies	600	
Cash		600
Purchased supplies.		

In these journal entries you correctly debit the Cash account for a receipt, and you credit Cash for a payment. Now let's see how the bank accounts for your cash.

When you deposit cash in your account, the amount of cash in the bank increases. Then, when you write a cheque, the bank pays cash from your account. As a result, the amount of cash in the bank decreases. The critical thing to remember is this: *The bank owes your money to you because you can withdraw it or write cheques on it at any time. The bank thus has a Deposit Payable, a liability, for your cash on deposit.*

On the bank's books, journalize the same two transactions: (1) receipt of $1,000 cash from you (when you deposit cash in your account), and (2) payment of $600 cash for you.

Answer: *Journal Entries on the Bank's Books:*

Cash	1,000	
Deposit Payable		1,000
Received cash from deposit customer.		
Deposit Payable	600	
Cash		600
Paid cash for deposit customer.		

In the first entry the bank debits Cash when it receives your deposit. The bank also credits Deposit Payable, a liability, to indicate that it owes you $1,000 whenever you wish to withdraw the money or write a cheque. This explains why a credit is "good" for you in a banking relationship. The bank has a liability for the amount of your money it has on deposit.

Now let's examine the bank's journal entry for the cash payment. The bank credits Cash when it pays your cheque. The bank debits Deposit Payable (to you) because the bank paid the $600 cheque that you wrote. As a result, the bank no longer owes you the $600. This explains why a debit is "bad" for you in a banking relationship: The bank has less liability to you.

The confusion about debits and credits in banking arises because many people view their own cash from the perspective of the bank. This is backwards, because:

- To the bank, your deposit account is a liability (a credit-balance account).
- To you, your cash is an asset (a debit-balance account).

All the information you receive from the bank, such as statement and credit memos, are *always* from the bank's point of view.

EXHIBIT 8–5 Cash Records of Business Research Inc.

General Ledger:

ACCOUNT Cash   **No. 1100**

Date	Item	Jrn. Ref.	Debit	Credit	Balance
2008					
Jan. 1	Balance	✔			6,556.12 Dr
2	Cash receipt	CR. 9	1,112.00		7,668.12 Dr
7	Cash receipt	CR. 9	194.60		7,862.72 Dr
31	Cash payments	CP. 17		6,160.14	1,702.58 Dr
31	Cash receipt	CR. 10	1,591.63		3,294.21 Dr

Cash Payments:

Cheque No.	Amount
332	$3,000.00
333	510.00
334	100.00
335	100.00
336	1,100.00
337	286.00
338	319.47
339	83.00
340	203.14
341	458.53
Total	$6,160.14

Items on the Bank Reconciliation Here are the items that appear on a bank reconciliation. They all cause differences between the bank balance and the book balance. (We refer to the company's cash records as the "Book" records.)

1. Items to show on the Bank side of the bank reconciliation:
   a. **Deposits in transit** (outstanding deposits). The company has recorded these deposits, but the bank has not. *Add* deposits in transit.
   b. **Outstanding cheques**. These cheques have been issued by the company and recorded on its books but the bank has not yet paid them. *Subtract* outstanding cheques.
   c. **Bank errors.** Correct all bank errors on the Bank side of the reconciliation.

2. Items recorded on the Book side of the bank reconciliation:
   a. **Bank collections**. Bank collections are cash receipts. Many businesses have their customers pay directly to the company bank account. This is called a *lock-box system,* and it reduces theft and circulates cash faster than if the cash had to be collected and deposited by company personnel. An example is a bank's collecting a note receivable for the company. *Add* bank collections.
   b. **Electronic funds transfers.** The bank may receive or pay cash on behalf of the depositor. An EFT may be a cash receipt or a cash payment.
   c. **Service charge.** This cash payment is the bank's fee for processing the depositor's transactions. *Subtract* services charges.
   d. **Interest revenue on chequing account**. Depositors earn interest if they keep a specified amount of cash in their accounts. This is sometimes true of business chequing accounts. The bank statement identifies this cash receipt. *Add* interest revenue.

LEARNING TIPS

These are the journal entries for NSF cheques. This journal entry was made by EeZee Transit when J. Doe paid his account by cheque:

Cash	XX
Accounts Rec. —J. Doe	XX

The entry to record the receipt of cash is made when the cheque is received, even though the bank will soon add the cash to EeZee Transit's account. However, J. Doe did not have enough cash in his chequing account to cover the cheque, so the bank removed the cash from EeZee Transit's account. EeZee Transit must reverse the original entry as follows:

Accounts Rec. —J. Doe	XX
Cash	XX

Since very few cheques received will be NSF, it is much more efficient to record the cash when the cheque is received than to wait until the cheque clears the maker's bank.

e. **Nonsufficient funds cheques (NSF).** These are cash receipts that turn out to be worthless. NSF cheques (sometimes called *bounced cheques* or *hot cheques*) are cash payments on a bank reconciliation. *Subtract* NSF cheques.

f. **The cost of printed cheques**. This cash payment is handled like a service charge. *Subtract* this cost.

g. **Book errors**. Correct all book errors on the Book side of the reconciliation.

Preparing the Bank Reconciliation

The steps in preparing the bank reconciliation are as follows:

1. Start with two figures, the balance in the business's Cash account in the general ledger (*balance per books*) and the balance shown on the bank statement (*balance per bank*). These two amounts will probably disagree because of the timing differences discussed earlier.

2. Add to, or subtract from, the *bank* balance those items that appear correctly on the books but not on the bank statement.

   a. Add *deposits in transit* to the bank balance. Deposits in transit are identified by comparing the deposits listed on the bank statement to the business's list of cash receipts. They appear as cash receipts on the books but not as deposits on the bank statement.

   b. Subtract *outstanding cheques* from the bank balance. Outstanding cheques are identified by comparing the cancelled cheques returned with the bank statement to the business's list of cheques written for cash payment. Outstanding cheques appear as cash payments on the books but not as paid cheques on the bank statement. If cheques were outstanding on the bank reconciliation for the preceding month and have still not been cashed, add them to the list of outstanding cheques on this month's bank reconciliation. Outstanding cheques are usually the most numerous item on a bank reconciliation.

3. Add to, or subtract from, the *book* balance those items that appear on the bank statement but not on the company books.

   a. Add to the book balance (1) *bank collections*, (2) *EFT cash receipts,* and (3) *interest revenue* earned on the money in the bank. These items are identified by comparing the deposits listed on the bank statement with the business's list of cash receipts. They show up as cash receipts on the bank statement but not on the books.

   b. Subtract from the book balance (1) *EFT cash payments*, (2) *service charges*, (3) *cost of printed cheques*, and (4) *other bank charges* (for example, charges for NSF or stale-date cheques). These items are identified by comparing the other charges listed on the bank statement to the cash payments recorded on the business's books. They appear as subtractions on the bank statement but not as cash payments on the books.

4. Compute the *adjusted bank balance* and *adjusted book balance*. The two adjusted balances should be equal.

5. Journalize each item in step 3, that is, each item listed on the book portion of the bank reconciliation. These items must be recorded on the business's books because they affect cash.

6. Correct all book errors, and notify the bank of any errors it has made.

Bank Reconciliation Illustrated The bank statement in Exhibit 8–4 (page 397) indicates that the January 31, 2008, bank balance of Business Research Inc. is $5,902.48. However, the company's Cash account has a balance of $3,294.21, as shown in Exhibit 8–5. This situation calls for a bank reconciliation. Exhibit 8–6, Panel A, lists the reconciling items for your easy reference, and Panel B shows the completed reconciliation.

KEY POINT

Errors can be made by the bank or on the books. The balance that is adjusted for the error depends on where the error occurred. If the bank makes the error, the bank statement balance is adjusted. If the error is on the books, the book balance is adjusted.

STOP AND THINK

Why does the company *not* need to record the reconciling items on the bank side of the reconciliation?

Answer: Those items have already been recorded on the company books.

EXHIBIT 8–6 | Bank Reconciliation

PANEL A: Reconciling Items

1. Deposit in transit, $1,591.63.
2. Bank error: The bank deducted $100 for a cheque written by another company. Add $100 to bank balance.
3. Outstanding cheques: no. 337, $286.00; no. 338, $319.47; no. 339, $83.00; no. 340, $203.14; no. 341, $458.53.
4. EFT receipt of rent revenue, $900.00.

5. Bank collection of note receivable, $2,114, including interest revenue of $114.00.
6. Interest earned on bank balance, $28.01.
7. Book error: cheque no. 333 for $150.00 paid to Brown Corp. on account was recorded as $510.00.
8. Bank service charges, $39.25 ($25.00 + $14.25).
9. NSF cheque from L. Ross, $52.00.
10. EFT payment of insurance expense, $361.00.

PANEL B: Bank Reconciliation

BUSINESS RESEARCH INC.
Bank Reconciliation
January 31, 2008

Bank			Books		
Balance, January 31, 2008		$5,902.48	**Balance, January 31, 2008**		$3,294.21
Add:			Add:		
1. Deposit of January 31 in transit		1,591.63	4. EFT receipt of rent revenue		900.00
2. Correction of bank error —Business Research Associates cheque erroneously charged against company account		100.00	5. Bank collection of note receivable, including interest revenue of $114.		2,114.00
		$7,594.11	6. Interest revenue earned on bank balance		28.01
			7. Correction of book error—Overstated amount of cheque no. 333		360.00
					6,696.22
3. Less: outstanding cheques			Less:		
No. 337	$286.00		8. Service charges	$39.25	
338	319.47		9. NSF cheque	52.00	
339	83.00		10. EFT payment of insurance expense	361.00	(452.25)
340	203.14				
341	458.53	(1,350.14)			
Adjusted bank balance		**$6,243.97**	**Adjusted book balance**		**$6,243.97**

Amounts should agree

Each reconciling item is treated in the same way in every situation. Here is a summary of how to treat the various reconciling items:

BANK BALANCE—ALWAYS
- *Add* deposits in transit.
- *Subtract* outstanding cheques.
- *Add* or *subtract* corrections of bank errors.

BOOK BALANCE—ALWAYS
- *Add* bank collections, interest revenue, and EFT receipts.
- *Subtract* service charges, NSF cheques, and EFT payments.
- *Add* or *subtract* corrections of book errors.

Journalizing Transactions from the Reconciliation The bank reconciliation is an accountant's tool that is separate from the company's journals and ledgers. It explains the effects of all cash receipts and all cash payments through the bank. But it does *not* account for transactions in the journals. To get the transactions into the accounts, we must make journal entries and post to the ledger. Each item on the Book side of the bank reconciliation requires a journal entry and affects the Cash account.

The bank reconciliation in Exhibit 8–6 requires Business Research Inc. to make the following journal entries, dated January 31, to bring the Cash account up to date. The numbers in parentheses correspond to the reconciling items listed in Exhibit 8–6, Panel A.

(4) Jan. 31	Cash		900.00	
	Rent Revenue			900.00
	Receipt of monthly rent.			
(5) Jan. 31	Cash		2,114.00	
	Notes Receivable			2,000.00
	Interest Revenue			114.00
	Note Receivable collected by bank.			
(6) Jan. 31	Cash		28.01	
	Interest Revenue			28.01
	Interest earned on bank balance.			
(7) Jan. 31	Cash		360.00	
	Accounts Payable—Brown Corp.			360.00
	Correction of cheque no. 333.			
(8) Jan. 31	Bank Charges Expense		39.25	
	Cash			39.25
	Bank service charges. ($25.00 NSF + $14.25)			
(9) Jan. 31	Accounts Receivable—L. Ross		52.00	
	Cash			52.00
	NSF cheque returned by bank.			
(10) Jan. 31	Insurance Expense		361.00	
	Cash			361.00
	Payment of monthly insurance.			

These entries update the company's books.

The entry for the NSF cheque (entry 9) needs explanation. Upon learning that L. Ross's $52 cheque to Business Research Inc. was not good, Business Research Inc. credits Cash to update the Cash account. Since Business Research Inc. still has a receivable from L. Ross, it must debit Accounts Receivable—L. Ross to reinstate the receivable from L. Ross and pursue collection from him.

STOP AND THINK

The bank statement balance is $9,000 and shows a service charge of $30, interest earned of $10, and an NSF cheque for $600. Deposits in transit total $2,400 and outstanding cheques are $1,150. The bookkeeper incorrectly recorded as $152 a cheque of $125 in payment of an account payable.

(1) What is the book balance before adjustments for bank statement items?

(2) Prepare the journal entries needed to update the company's books.

Answers:

(1) $10,250 ($9,000 + $2,400 - $1,150)

(2) Journal entries on the books:

Bank Charges Expense	30		Accounts Receivable	600	
Cash		30	Cash		600
Cash	10		Cash ($152 – $125)	27	
Interest Revenue		10	Accounts Payable		27

Online and Telephone Banking Canadian banks now permit online and telephone banking, where customers use their computers or telephones to effect transactions such as paying bills, transferring money from one account to another, and arranging a loan. With online banking, customers use a computer and an internet connection to effect transactions. The bank supplies a confirmation number on the customer's computer screen to show the transaction has occurred, and the transaction is confirmed by its appearance in the passbook or on a subsequent bank statement. There is no other "paper trail" as evidence of the transaction.

Since bank statements are usually received monthly, a bank reconciliation is often performed only once a month. However, with online access to bank account information, you are able to print your bank account history at any time. The account history—like a bank statement—lists deposits, cheques, EFT receipts and payments, automated teller machine (ATM) deposits and withdrawals, and interest earned on the bank balance. The account history looks very similar to the bank statement. Thus, companies and individuals could prepare bank reconciliations more frequently than once a month.

How Owners and Managers Use the Bank Reconciliation

The bank reconciliation can be a powerful control device as the following example illustrates.

Randy Vaughn is a CA in Regina, Saskatchewan. Vaughn owns several apartment complexes that are managed by his cousin Alexis Vaughn. His accounting practice keeps him busy, so he has little time to devote to the properties. Vaughn's cousin approves tenants, collects the monthly rent cheques, arranges custodial and maintenance work, hires and fires employees, writes the cheques, and performs the bank reconciliation. This concentration of duties in one person is terrible from an internal control standpoint. Vaughn's cousin could be stealing from him. As a CA, he is aware of this possibility.

Vaughn exercises some internal controls over his cousin's activities. Periodically he drops by his properties to see whether the apartments are in good condition.

To control cash, Vaughn uses a bank reconciliation. On an irregular basis, he examines the bank reconciliations as prepared by his cousin. He matches every cheque that cleared the bank to the journal entry on the books. Vaughn would know immediately if his cousin were writing cheques to herself. Vaughn sometimes prepares his own bank reconciliation to see whether it agrees with his cousin's work. To keep his cousin on her toes, Vaughn lets her know that he periodically checks her work.

Vaughn has a simple method for controlling cash receipts. He knows the occupancy level of his apartments. He also knows the monthly rent he charges. He multiplies the number of apartments—say 100—by the monthly rent (which averages $500 per unit) to arrive at expected monthly rent revenue of $50,000. By tracing the $50,000 revenue to the bank statement, Vaughn can tell that his rent money went into his bank account.

Control activities such as these (often referred to as "executive controls") are critical in small businesses. With only a few employees, a separation of duties may not be feasible. The owner must oversee the operations of the business, or the assets may disappear.

The Cash account of Cambridge Dental Associates at February 28, 2007, follows:

Cash

Feb.	1 Balance	7,990	Feb.	3	800
	6	1,600		12	6,200
	15	3,600		19	2,200
	23	2,200		25	1,000
	28	4,800		27	1,800
	28 Balance	8,190			

Cambridge Dental Associates receives this bank statement data in the first week of March 2007 (negative amounts appear in parentheses):

Bank Statement for February 2007

Beginning balance		$7,990
Deposits:		
Feb. 7	$1,600	
15	3,600	
24	2,200	7,400
Cheques (total per day):		
Feb. 8	$ 800	
16	6,200	
23	2,200	(9,200)
Other items:		
Service charge		(20)
NSF cheque from M. E. Crown		(1,400)
Bank collection of note receivable for the company...		2,000*
EFT—monthly rent expense		(660)
Interest on account balance		5
Ending balance		$6,115

*Includes principal of $1,762 plus interest of $238.

Name: Cambridge Dental Associates
Accounting Period: Month of February 2007
Key Fact: Existing, ongoing business

Additional data: Cambridge Dental Associates deposits all cash receipts in the bank and makes all cash payments by cheque.

Required

1. Prepare the bank reconciliation of Cambridge Dental Associates at February 28, 2007.

2. Journalize the entries based on the bank reconciliation.

Solution

Before creating the bank reconciliation, compare the Cash account and the bank statement. Cross out all items that appear in both places. The items that remain are the reconciling items.

Begin with the ending balance on the bank statement.
• Add deposits (debits) from the Cash account not on the bank statement.
• Deduct cheques (credits) from the Cash account not on the bank statement.

Begin with the ending balance in the Cash general ledger account.
• Add money received by the bank on behalf of the company (increases to the bank statement balance).
• Deduct bank charges, NSF cheques, or pre-authorized payments (decreases to the bank statement balance).

Requirement 1

CAMBRIDGE DENTAL ASSOCIATES
Bank Reconciliation
February 28, 2007

Bank

Balance, February 28, 2007		$6,115
Add: Deposit of February 28 in transit		4,800
		10,915
Less: Outstanding cheques issued on Feb. 25 ($1,000) and Feb. 27 ($1,800)		(2,800)
Adjusted bank balance, February 28, 2007		$8,115

Books

Balance, February 28, 2007		$8,190
Add: Bank collection of note receivable, including interest of $238		2,000
Add: Interest earned on bank balance		5
		10,195
Less: Service charge	$ 20	
NSF cheque	1,400	
EFT—Rent expense	660	(2,080)
Adjusted book balance, February 28, 2007		$8,115

Requirement 2

Prepare journal entries for all reconciling items from the "Books" section of the bank reconciliation.

Feb.	28	Cash	2,000	
		Note Receivable		1,762
		Interest Revenue		238
		Note receivable collected by bank ($2,000 − $232).		
Feb.	28	Cash	5	
		Interest Revenue		5
		Interest earned on bank balance.		
Feb.	28	Bank Charges Expense	20	
		Cash		20
		Bank service charge.		
Feb.	28	Accounts Receivable—M. E. Crown	1,400	
		Cash		1,400
		NSF cheque returned by bank.		
Feb.	28	Rent Expense	660	
		Cash		660
		Monthly rent expense.		

Internal Control over Cash Receipts

Objective 4

Apply internal controls to cash receipts

Internal control over cash receipts (the term includes cash, cheques, credit card charges, and debit card payments) ensures that all cash receipts are deposited quickly for safekeeping in the bank. Companies receive cash over the counter and through the mail. Each source of cash has its own security measures.

EXHIBIT 8–7

Cash Receipts over the Counter

Cash Receipts over the Counter Exhibit 8–7 illustrates a cash receipt made over the counter in a department store. The point-of-sale terminal (cash register) provides control over cash receipts. Consider a Canadian Tire store. The terminal is positioned so that customers can see the amounts the cashier scans into the terminal. No person willingly pays more than the marked price for an item, so the customer helps prevent the sales clerk from overcharging. For each transaction, Canadian Tire issues a receipt to ensure that each sale is recorded.

The cash drawer opens only when the clerk enters a transaction and the machine records it. At the end of the day, a manager proves the cash by comparing the cash in the drawer against the machine's record of sales. This step helps prevent theft by the clerk.

At the end of the day—or several times a day if business is brisk—the cashier or other employee with cash-handling duties deposits the cash in the bank. The machine tape then goes to the accounting department as the basis for the journal entry to record sales revenue. These security measures, coupled with oversight by a manager, discourage theft.

Cash Receipts by Mail Many companies receive payments (cheques and credit card authorizations) by mail. Exhibit 8-8 shows how companies control payments received by mail. All incoming mail is opened by a mailroom employee.

EXHIBIT 8–8   Cash Receipts by Mail

REAL WORLD EXAMPLE

It is important to deposit all cash receipts *intact* daily. Neither managers nor employees should use cash received to make purchases or other cash payments. The deposit then can be an additional record of business transactions. In some rare circumstances where records are destroyed or missing, the bank statement can be used to reconstruct transactions.

The mailroom then sends all customer payments to the treasurer, who has the cashier deposit the money in the bank. The remittance advices go to the accounting department for the journal entries to Cash and customers' accounts. As a final step, the controller compares the records of the day's cash receipts:

1. Bank deposit amount from the treasurer
2. Debit to Cash from the accounting department.

The debit to Cash should equal the amount deposited in the bank. All cash receipts are safe in the bank, and the company books are up to date.

What keeps the mailroom employee from pocketing a customer cheque and destroying the remittance advice?

Answer: If a customer gets a statement listing the invoice and amount a second time, the customer can show the paid cheque to prove he/she already paid. That would indicate the company has a dishonest employee.

Many companies use a lock-box system. Customers send their cheques directly to the company's bank account. Internal control is tight because company personnel never touch incoming cash. The lock-box system improves efficiency because cash is added to the bank account and can be used by the company immediately.

Cash Short and Over A difference may exist between actual cash receipts and the day's record of cash received. Usually the difference is small and results from honest errors. When the recorded cash balance exceeds cash on hand, we have a *cash short* situation. When the actual cash exceeds the recorded cash balance, we have a *cash over* situation. Suppose the tapes from a cash register at Little Short Stop convenience store indicated sales revenue of $15,000, but the cash received was $14,980. To record the day's sales for that register, the store would make this entry:

Cash	14,980	
Cash Short and Over	20	
Sales Revenue		15,000
Daily cash sales.		

As the entry shows, Cash Short and Over, an expense account, is debited when sales revenue exceeds cash receipts. This account is credited when cash receipts exceed sales. A debit balance in Cash Short and Over appears on the income statement as Miscellaneous Expense; a credit balance may be shown as Other Revenue.

The Cash Short and Over account's balance should be small. The debits and credits for cash shorts and overs collected over an accounting period tend to cancel each other out. A large balance signals the accountant to investigate. For example, too large a debit balance may mean an employee is stealing. Cash Short and Over, then, acts as an internal control device.

Exhibit 8–9 summarizes the internal controls over cash receipts.

Internal Control over Cash Payments

Cash payments are as important as cash receipts. It is therefore critical to control cash payments. Companies make most payments by cheque. They also pay small amounts from a petty cash fund. Let's begin with cash payments by cheque.

Objective 5

Apply internal controls to cash payments

Controls over Payment by Cheque

As we have seen, companies need a good separation of duties between operations and writing cheques for cash payments.

Payment by cheque is an important internal control.

- The cheque provides a record of the payment.
- The cheque must be signed by an authorized official.
- Before signing the cheque, the official should study the evidence supporting the payment.

EXHIBIT 8–9   Internal Controls over Cash Receipts

Element of Internal Control	Internal Controls Over Cash Receipts
Competent, reliable, ethical personnel	Companies carefully screen employees for undesirable personality traits. They commit time and effort to training programs.
Assignment of responsibilities	Specific employees are designated as cashiers, supervisors of cashiers, or accountants for cash receipts.
Proper authorization	Only designated employees, such as department managers, can grant exceptions for customers, approve cheque receipts above a certain amount, allow customers to purchase on credit, and void sales.
Separation of duties	Cashiers and mailroom employees who handle cash do not have access to the accounting records. Accountants who record cash receipts have no opportunity to handle cash.
Internal and external audits	Internal auditors examine company transactions for agreement with management policies. External auditors examine the internal controls over cash receipts to determine whether the accounting system produces accurate amounts for revenues, receivables, and other items related to cash receipts.
Documents and records	Customers receive receipts as transaction records. Bank statement lists cash receipts for deposit. Customers who pay by mail include a remittance advice showing the amount of cash they sent to the company.
Electronic devices and computer control	Cash registers serve as transaction records. Each day's receipts are matched with customer remittance advices and with the day's deposit ticket with the bank.
Other controls	Cashiers are bonded. Cash is stored in vaults and banks. Employees are rotated among jobs and are required to take vacations.

THINKING IT OVER

Two officers' signatures are required for cheques over $1,000. One officer is going on vacation and pre-signs several cheques so that the cheques will be available if needed while she is gone. The cheques are locked in the vault. What is the internal control feature in this scenario?

A: Proper authorization. Two signatures are required to ensure that no unauthorized expenditures are made. Pre-signing the cheques defeats the control and should be discouraged.

Controls over Purchase and Payment. To illustrate the internal control over cash payments, let's suppose the business is paying for merchandise inventory. The purchasing and payment process follows these steps, as outlined in Exhibit 8–10:

1. The company sends a *purchase order* to the supplier.
2. The supplier ships the merchandise and mails the *invoice,* or bill. (We introduced the invoice in Chapter 5.)
3. The company receives the goods. The receiving department checks the goods for damage and prepares a list of the goods received on a *receiving report*.

EXHIBIT 8–10   Cash Payments by Cheque

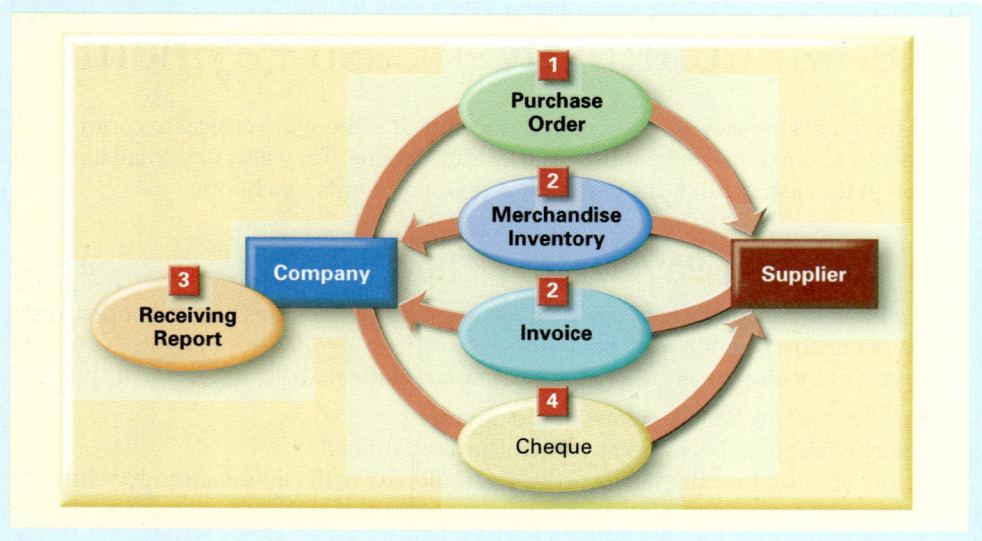

4. After the accounting department checks and agrees all the foregoing documents, the company sends a cheque to the supplier.

EXHIBIT 8–11

Payment Packet

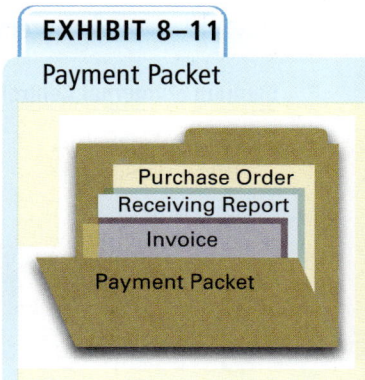

For good internal control, the purchasing agent should neither receive the goods nor approve the payment. If these duties are not separated, a purchasing agent could buy goods and have them shipped to his home. Or the purchasing agent could increase the price of purchases, approve the payment, and then split the price increase with the supplier.

Exhibit 8–11 shows the company's payment packet of documents. Before signing the cheque for payment, the controller or the treasurer should examine the packet to prove that all the documents agree. Only then does the company know that:

1. It received the goods ordered—proved by the receiving report.

2. It is paying only for the goods received—proved by the purchase order and receiving report.

After payment, the cheque signer should punch a hole through the payment packet or otherwise mark the packet and its contents. These actions alert the company that it has paid the bill. Dishonest employees have been known to present a bill for cash payment two or more times.

Some companies include a voucher in their payment packet. This document summarizes the payment details and has spaces for the signatures of officials who can approve the payment. Other companies may stamp the invoice and fill in the blanks with this same information.

Streamlined Procedures Technology is streamlining payment procedures. Evaluated Receipts Settlement (ERS) compresses the approval process into a single step: comparing the receiving report with the purchase order. If the two documents match, that proves that the company received the merchandise it ordered. Then the company pays the supplier.

An even more streamlined process bypasses people and documents altogether. In Electronic Data Interchange (EDI), Canadian Tire's computers can communicate directly with the computers of suppliers like General Tire, Rubbermaid, and Procter & Gamble. When Canadian Tire's automobile tires reach a certain (low) level, the computer sends a purchase order to General Tire. General Tire ships the tires and invoices Canadian Tire electronically. Then an electronic fund transfer (EFT) sends the payment from Canadian Tire to General Tire.

Exhibit 8–12 summarizes the internal controls over cash payments.

Controlling Petty Cash Payments

It is wasteful to write a cheque for an employee's taxi fare (while on company business), or the delivery of a package across town. To meet these needs, companies keep cash on hand to pay small amounts. This fund is called **petty cash**.

Even though petty cash payments are small, the business needs internal controls, such as the following:

1. Designate a custodian of the petty cash fund.

2. Keep a specific amount of cash on hand.

3. Support all fund payments with a petty cash ticket.

Creating the Petty Cash Fund The petty cash fund is opened when a cheque is written for the designated amount. The cheque is made payable to Petty Cash. Assume that on February 28 the business creates a petty cash fund of $400. The custodian cashes a $400 cheque and places the money in the fund. Starting the fund is recorded as follows:

Feb. 28	Petty Cash	400	
	Cash...		400
	To open the petty cash fund.		

EXHIBIT 8–12 | Internal Controls over Cash Payments

Element of Internal Control	Internal Controls over Cash Payments
Competent, reliable, ethical personnel	Cash payments are entrusted to high-level employees, with larger amounts paid by the treasurer or assistant treasurer.
Assignment of responsibility	Specific employees approve purchase documents for payment. Executives examine approvals, then sign cheques.
Proper authorization	Large expenditures must be authorized by the company owner or board of directors to ensure agreement with organizational goals.
Separation of duties	Computer operators and other employees who handle cheques have no access to the accounting records. Accountants who record cash payments have no opportunity to handle cash.
Internal and external audits	Internal auditors examine company transactions for agreement with management policies. External auditors examine the internal controls over cash payments to determine whether the accounting system produces accurate amounts for expenses, assets, and other items related to cash payments.
Documents and records	Suppliers issue invoices that document the need to pay cash. Bank statements list cash payments (cheques and EFT payments) for reconciliation with company records. Cheques are prenumbered and used in sequence to account for payments.
Electronic devices, computer controls, and other controls	Blank cheques are stored in a vault and controlled by a responsible official with no accounting duties. Machines stamp the amount on a cheque in indelible ink. Paid invoices are punched or otherwise mutilated to avoid duplicate payment.

For each petty cash payment, the custodian prepares a *petty cash ticket* like the one illustrated in Exhibit 8–13.

Signatures (or initials) identify the recipient of the cash (Lewis Wright) and the fund custodian (MAR). Requiring both signatures reduces fraudulent payments. The custodian keeps all the pre-numbered petty cash tickets in the fund. The sum of the cash plus the total of the ticket amounts should equal the opening balance ($400) at all times. Also, the Petty Cash account keeps its $400 balance at all times. As the use of company debit cards increases, the use of petty cash accounts is decreasing.

Maintaining the Petty Cash account at its designated balance is the nature of an **imprest system**. This system clearly identifies the amount of cash for which the fund custodian is responsible and is the system's main internal control feature. Imprest systems are also used for branch-office funds, not just petty cash. Payments reduce the cash in the fund, so periodically the fund must be replenished.

KEY POINT

No journal entries are made for petty cash payments until the fund is replenished. At that time, all petty cash payments will be recorded in a summary entry. This procedure avoids the need to journalize many payments for small amounts.

EXHIBIT 8–13 | Petty Cash Ticket

```
                    PETTY CASH TICKET

Date    Mar. 25, 2008                        No.  45

Amount     $34.00

For   Payment for delivery of contract.

Debit   Delivery Expense, Acct. No. 545

Received by   Lewis Wright      Fund Custodian   MAR
```

Replenishing the Petty Cash Fund. On March 31, the petty cash fund holds

- $230 in petty cash
- $164 in petty cash tickets

We can see that $6 is missing:

Fund balance...	$400
Cash on hand	$230
Petty cash tickets	164
Total accounted for	$394
Amount of cash missing.........................	$ 6

To replenish the petty cash fund, we need to bring the cash on hand up to $400. The company writes a cheque, payable to Petty Cash, for $170 ($400 − $230). The fund custodian cashes this cheque and puts $170 back in the fund. Now the fund holds $400 cash as it should.

The petty cash tickets identify the accounts to debit, as shown in the entry to replenish the fund (items assumed for this illustration):

Mar. 31	Office Supplies	46	
	Delivery Expense	34	
	Cash Short and Over	6	
	Selling Expense	84	
	Cash		170
	To replenish the petty cash fund.		

KEY POINT

Attached to the petty cash ticket is a cash register receipt, invoice, or other documentation to support the payment.

The cash payments appear to have exceeded the sum of the tickets, since the fund was short $6, so Cash Short and Over was debited for the missing amount ($6). If the sum of the tickets exceeds the payment, Cash Short and Over would be credited. Replenishing the fund does *not* affect the Petty Cash account. Petty Cash keeps its $400 balance at all times.

The petty cash fund *must* be replenished on the balance sheet date. Otherwise, the income statement will understate the expenses listed on the tickets.

The Petty Cash account in the General Ledger is debited only when the fund is started (see the February 28 entry) or when its amount is changed. In our illustration, suppose the business decides to raise the fund amount from $400 to $500 because of increased demand for petty cash. This step would require a $100 debit to the Petty Cash account and a $100 credit to the Cash account.

Reporting Cash on the Balance Sheet

Cash is the first asset listed on the balance sheet because it is the most liquid asset. Businesses often have several bank accounts and several petty cash funds, but they combine all cash amounts into a single total called "Cash and Cash Equivalents" for reporting on the balance sheet.

Cash equivalents include liquid assets such as time deposits and certificates of deposit. These interest-bearing accounts can be withdrawn with no penalty after a short period of time. These assets are sufficiently similar to be reported along with cash. For example, the December 31, 2005, balance sheet of Nortel Networks Corporation reported U.S. $2,951 million of cash and equivalents and U.S. $77 million of restricted cash and equivalents.

Nortel's cash and equivalents balance means that $2,951 million is available for use as needed. Cash that is restricted and unavailable for immediate use should not be reported as a current asset if the company does not expect to spend the cash within a year or within the company's operating cycle, if longer than a year. For example, some banks require their depositors to maintain a *compensating balance* on deposit in the bank in order to borrow from the bank. The compensating balance is not included in the cash amount on the balance sheet because it is not available for immediate use. Nortel reported restricted cash and equivalents of $77 million as a current asset.

Ethics and Accounting

Objective 6
Make ethical business judgments

Robert Schad, President and CEO of Husky Injection Molding Systems Ltd. in Bolton, Ontario, said, "Ethical practice is, quite simply, good business." Schad has been in business long enough to see the danger in unethical behaviour. Sooner or later unethical conduct comes to light, as was true in our chapter-opening story on page 387. Moreover, ethical behaviour wins out in the end because it is the right thing to do.

Corporate and Professional Codes of Ethics

Most companies have a code of ethics to encourage employees to behave ethically. But codes of ethics are not enough by themselves. Owners and managers must set a high ethical tone. They must make it clear that the company will not tolerate unethical conduct.

REAL WORLD EXAMPLE

In a survey, 81 percent of companies had a corporate code of conduct. Another 7 percent planned to establish such a code.

Accountants have additional incentives to behave ethically. As professionals, they are expected to maintain higher standards than society in general. Their ability to attract business depends entirely on their reputation.

As you learned in Chapter 1, there are three bodies of professional accountants in Canada: the CAs, the CGAs, and the CMAs. Members of each of the bodies must adhere to the rules of professional conduct of their respective organizations. These documents set minimum standards of conduct for members. Unacceptable actions can result in expulsion from the organization, which makes it impossible for the person to remain a professional accountant.

Ethical Issues in Accounting

In many situations the ethical choice is easy. For example, stealing cash, as in the chapter-opening story, is illegal and unethical. In other cases, the choices are more difficult. But, in every instance, ethical judgments are a personal decision. What should I do in a given situation? Let's consider two ethical issues in accounting.

Situation 1 Sonja Kleberg is preparing the income tax return of a client who earned more income than expected. On January 2, the client pays for advertising to run in late January and asks Sonja to backdate the expense to the preceding year. Backdating would decrease taxable income of the earlier year and postpone a few dollars in tax payments. After all, there is a difference of only two days between January 2 and December 31. This client is important to Kleberg. What should she do?

> **She should refuse the request because the transaction took place in January of the new year.**

What internal control device could prove that Kleberg behaved unethically if she backdated the transaction in the accounting records? A Canada Revenue Agency audit could prove that the expense occurred in January rather than in December. Falsifying tax returns is both illegal and unethical.

Situation 2 David Duncan, the lead auditor for Enron Corporation, thinks Enron may be understating the liabilities on its balance sheet. Enron's transactions are very complex, and outsiders may never figure this out. Duncan asks his firm's Standards Committee how he should handle the situation. They reply, "Require Enron to report all its liabilities." Enron is Duncan's most important client, and Enron is pressuring Duncan to certify the liabilities. Duncan can rationalize that Enron's reported amounts are okay. What should Duncan do? To make his decision,

Duncan could follow the framework outlined in the Decision Guidelines feature that follows.

As we conclude this chapter, we return to our opening questions: What are internal controls, and why are they important? Do internal controls affect more than cash? What is the *Sarbanes-Oxley Act of 2002* and why is it important to some Canadian companies? How can companies use bank accounts to control cash? These questions were answered throughout this chapter. And the Decision Guidelines end this chapter with a framework for making ethical judgments, both in business and personal situations.

DECISION GUIDELINES — Framework for Making Ethical Judgments

Weighing tough ethical judgments requires a decision framework. Consider these six questions as general guidelines; they will guide you through answering tough ethical questions.

Let's apply these guidelines to David Duncan.

Decision	Guidelines
1. What are the facts?	1. *Determine the facts*.
2. What is the ethical issue, if any?	2. *Identify the ethical issues*. The root word of ethical is *ethics*, which Webster's dictionary defines as "the discipline dealing with what is good and bad and with moral duty and obligation." Duncan's ethical dilemma is to decide what he should do with the information he has uncovered.
3. What are the alternatives?	3. *Specify the alternatives*. For David Duncan, the alternatives include: (a) go along with Enron's liabilities as reported (i.e., do nothing) or (b) force Enron's management to report liabilities at more correct amounts.
4. Who is involved in the situation?	4. *Identify the stakeholders, the people involved*. Individuals who could be affected include Duncan, the partners and staff of his auditing firm, the management and employees of Enron, Enron's investors, Enron's creditors, the U.S. federal and various state governments.
5. What are the possible consequences of each alternative in question 3?	5. *Assess the possible outcomes of each alternative*. (a) If Duncan certifies Enron's present level of liabilities—and if no one ever objects—Duncan will keep this valuable client. But if Enron's actual liabilities turn out to be higher than reported, Enron's investors and creditors may lose money and take Duncan to court. That would damage his reputation as an auditor and hurt his firm. (b) If Duncan follows the policy suggestion of his company, he must force Enron to increase its reported liabilities. That will anger Enron, and Enron may fire Duncan and his firm as its auditor. In this case Duncan will save his reputation, but it will cost him and his firm business in the short run.
6. What should Duncan do?	6. *Make a decision*. In the end Duncan went along with Enron and certified Enron's liabilities. He went directly against his firm's policies. Enron later admitted understating its liabilities, Duncan had to retract his audit opinion, and Duncan's firm, Arthur Andersen, collapsed soon after. Duncan should have followed company policy. Rarely is one person smarter than a team of experts. Not following company policy cost him and many others dearly.

Summary Problem for Your Review

Leitch Design Studios established a $300 petty cash fund. James C. Brown (JCB) is the fund custodian. At the end of the first week, the petty cash fund contains the following:

1. Cash: $163
2. Petty cash tickets:

No.	Amount	Issued to	Signed by	Account Debited
1	$14	B. Jarvis	B. Jarvis and JCB	Office Supplies
2	39	S. Bell	S. Bell	Delivery Expense
4	43	R. Tate	R. Tate and JCB	—
5	33	G. Blair	G. Blair and JCB	Travel Expense

Required

1. Identify three internal control weaknesses revealed in the given data.
2. Prepare the general journal entries to record
   a. Establishment of the petty cash fund.
   b. Replenishment of the fund. Assume petty cash ticket no. 4 was issued for the purchase of office supplies.
3. What is the balance in the Petty Cash account immediately before replenishment? Immediately after replenishment?

Solution

Requirement 1

The three internal control weaknesses are

1. Petty cash ticket no. 3 is missing. There is no indication of what happened to this ticket. The company should investigate.
2. The petty cash custodian (JCB) did not sign petty cash ticket no. 2. This omission may have been an oversight on his part. However, it raises the question of whether he authorized the payment. Both the fund custodian and recipient of cash should sign the ticket.
3. Petty cash ticket no. 4 does not indicate which account to debit and presumably has no receipt attached. What did Tate do with the money, and what account should be debited? At worst, the funds have been stolen. At best, asking the custodian to reconstruct the transaction from memory is haphazard. Since we are instructed to assume petty cash ticket no. 4 was issued for the purchase of office supplies, debit Office Supplies.

Requirement 2

Petty cash journal entries

a. Entry to establish the petty cash fund

Petty Cash	300	
Cash		300
To open the petty cash fund.		

- Ensure cash in the fund ($163) + the total of all petty cash ticket amounts ($129) = the opening balance of the petty cash fund ($300). If the total is less than $300, the fund is short. If the total is greater than $300, the fund is over.
- Sort the tickets by expense, then record the total for each expense.
- The credit to Cash plus the cash remaining in the fund must *always* equal the petty cash fund total ($300).

The Petty Cash account is only affected when the petty cash fund is created or when the petty cash fund balance is later increased or decreased.

b. Entry to replenish the fund

Office Supplies ($14 + $43)	57	
Delivery Expense	39	
Travel Expense	33	
Cash Short and Over	8	
Cash		137
To replenish the petty cash fund.		

Requirement 3

The balance in Petty Cash is *always* its specified balance, in this case $300, as shown by posting the above entries to the account.

Petty Cash

(a)	300	

Summary

1. **Define internal control.** *Internal control* is the organizational plan and all related measures adopted by an entity to meet management's objectives of discharging statutory responsibilities, profitability, prevention and detection of fraud and error, safeguarding of assets, reliability of accounting records, and timely preparation of reliable financial information.

2. **Describe good internal control procedures.** An effective internal control system includes these features: *competent, reliable and ethical personnel; clear assignment of responsibilities; proper authorization; separation of duties; internal and external audits; documents and records;* and *electronic devices and computer controls.* Many companies also make use of fireproof vaults, point-of-sale terminals, fidelity bonds, mandatory vacations, and job rotation. Effective computerized internal control systems must meet the same basic standards that good manual systems do.

3. **Prepare a bank reconciliation and the related journal entries.** The *bank account* helps to control and safeguard cash. Businesses use the *bank statement* and the *bank reconciliation* to account for banking transactions.

4. **Apply internal controls to cash receipts.** To control cash receipts over the counter, companies use point-of-sale terminals that customers can see, and require that cashiers provide customers with receipts. A duplicate tape inside the machine or a link to a central computer records each sale and cash transaction. Pricing with uneven amounts means that cashiers must open the drawer to make change, which requires the transaction to be recorded on tape. To control cash receipts by mail, a mail-room employee should be assigned the responsibility for opening the mail, comparing the enclosed amount with the remittance advice, and preparing a control tape. This is an essential separation of duties—the accounting

deparment should not open the mail. At the end of the day, the controller compares the three records of the day's cash receipts: the control tape total from the mailroom, the bank deposit amount from the cashier, and the debit to Cash from the accounting department.

5. **Apply internal controls to cash payments.** To control payments by cheque, cheques should be issued and signed only when a *payment packet* including the purchase order, invoice (bill), and receiving report (all with appropriate signatures) has been prepared. To control petty cash payments, the custodian of the fund should require a completed petty cash ticket for all payments.

6. **Make ethical business judgments.** To make ethical decisions, people should proceed in six steps: (1) Determine the facts. (2) Identify the ethical issues. (3) Specify the alternatives. (4) Identify the stakeholders, the people involved. (5) Assess the possible outcomes of each alternative. (6) Make the decision.

Self-Study Questions

Test your understanding of the chapter by marking the correct answer for each of the following questions:

1. Which of the following is an objective of internal control? (pp. 388–389)
   a. Safeguarding assets
   b. Maintaining reliable control systems
   c. Optimizing the use of resources
   d. Preventing and detecting fraud and error
   e. All the above are objectives of internal control.

2. Janice Gould receives cash from customers. Her other assigned job is to post the collections to customer accounts receivable. Her company has weak (p. 391)
   a. Ethics
   b. Assignment of responsibilities
   c. Computer controls
   d. Separation of duties

3. What control function is performed by auditors? (p. 392)
   a. Objective opinion on the fair presentation of the financial statements
   b. Assurance that all transactions are accounted for correctly
   c. Communication of the results of the audit to regulatory agencies
   d. Guarantee that company employees have behaved ethically

4. Encryption (v. 394)
   a. Creates firewalls to protect data
   b. Cannot be broken by hackers
   c. Avoids the need for separation of duties
   d. Rearranges messages by a special process

5. The bank account serves as a control device over (p. 395)
   a. Cash receipts
   b. Cash payments
   c. Both of the above
   d. None of the above

6. Which of the following items appears on the Bank side of a bank reconciliation? (p. 399)
   a. Book error
   b. Outstanding cheque
   c. NSF cheque
   d. Interest revenue earned on bank balance

7. Which of the following items appear on the Book side of a bank reconciliaton? (p. 399)
   a. Outstanding cheques   c. Both a and b
   b. Deposits in transit   d. None of the above

8. Which of the following reconciling items requires a journal entry on the books of the company? (p. 400)
   a. Book error
   b. Outstanding cheque
   c. NSF cheque
   d. Interest revenue earned on bank balance
   e. All of the above, except (b)
   f. None of the above

9. The internal control feature that is specific to petty cash is (p. 410)
   a. Separation of duties
   b. Assignment of responsibility
   c. Proper authorization
   d. The imprest system

10. Ethical judgments in accounting and business (p. 412)
    a. Require employees to break laws to get ahead
    b. Force decision makers to think about what is good and bad
    c. Always hurt someone
    d. Are affected by internal controls but not by external controls

Answers to the Self-Study Questions follow the Similar Accounting Terms.

Accounting Vocabulary

Audit   *(p. 392)*
Bank collection   *(p. 399)*
Bank reconciliation   *(p. 397)*
Bank statement   *(p. 395)*
Cheque   *(p. 395)*
Computer virus   *(p. 394)*
Controller   *(p. 391)*
Deposit in transit   *(p. 399)*
Electronic funds transfer (EFT)   *(p. 395)*

Encryption   *(p. 394)*
Firewall   *(p. 394)*
Imprest system   *(p. 410)*
Internal control   *(p. 388)*
Nonsufficient funds (NSF) cheque   *(p. 400)*
Outstanding cheque   *(p. 399)*
Petty cash   *(p. 409)*
Treasurer   *(p. 391)*
Trojan   *(p. 394)*

Similar Accounting Terms

Cash receipts	Cash, cheques, and other negotiable instruments received
Separation of duties	Segregation of duties, division of duties
Invoice	Bill

Assignment Material

Questions

1. Which of the features of effective internal control is the most fundamental? Why?

2. Which company employees bear primary responsibility for a company's financial statements and for maintaining the company's system of internal control? How do these persons carry out this responsibility?

3. Identify at least seven features of an effective system of internal control.

4. Separation of duties may be divided into three parts. What are they?

5. What is an audit? Identify the two types of audit and the differences between them.

6. Why are documents and records a feature of internal control systems?

7. How has an accounting system's reliance on electronic devices altered internal control?

8. Why should the same employee not write the computer programs for cash payments, sign cheques, and mail the cheques to payees?

9. Briefly state how each of the following serves as an internal control measure over cash: bank account, signature card, deposit ticket, and bank statement.

10. Are internal control systems designed to be foolproof and perfect? What is a fundamental constraint in planning and maintaining systems?

11. How can internal control systems be circumvented?

12. Each of the items in the following list must be accounted for in the bank reconciliation. Next to each item, enter the appropriate letter from the following possible treatments: (a) bank side of reconciliation—add the item; (b) bank side of reconciliation—subtract the item; (c) book side of reconciliation—add the item; and (d) book side of reconciliation—subtract the item.

   _____ Outstanding cheque

   _____ NSF cheque

   _____ Bank service charge

   _____ Cost of printed cheques

   _____ EFT receipt

   _____ Bank error that decreased bank balance

   _____ Deposit in transit

   _____ Bank collection

   _____ EFT payment

   _____ Customer's cheque returned because of unauthorized signature

   _____ Book error that increased balance of Cash account

13. What purpose does a bank reconciliation serve?

14. What role does a cash register play in an internal control system?

15. Describe internal control procedures for cash received by mail.

16. What documents make up the payment packet? Describe three procedures that use the payment packet to ensure that each payment is appropriate.

17. What balance does the Petty Cash account have at all times? Does this balance always equal the amount of cash in the fund? When are the two amounts equal? When are they unequal?

18. Suppose a company has six bank accounts, two petty cash funds, and three certificates of deposit that can be withdrawn on demand. How many cash amounts would this company likely report separately on its balance sheet?

19. Why should accountants adhere to a higher standard of ethical conduct than many other members of society do?

20. "Our managers know that they are expected to meet budgeted profit figures. We don't want excuses. We want results." Discuss the ethical implications of this policy.

Starters

Starter 8–1 Internal controls are designed to safeguard assets, encourage employees to follow company policies, promote operational efficiency, and ensure accurate records. Which objective must the internal controls accomplish for the business to survive? Give your reason.

Starter 8–2 How does the *Sarbanes-Oxley Act of 2002* relate to internal controls? Be specific.

Starter 8–3 Explain in your own words why separation of duties is often described as the cornerstone of internal control for safeguarding assets. Describe what can happen if the same person has custody of an asset and also accounts for the asset.

Starter 8–4 How do external auditors differ from internal auditors? How does an external audit differ from an internal audit? How are the two types of audits similar?

Starter 8–5 Answer the following questions about the bank reconciliation:

1. Is the bank reconciliation a journal, a ledger, an account, or a financial statement? If none of these, what is it?
2. What is the difference between a bank statement and a bank reconciliation?

Starter 8–6 The Cash account of Ranger Security Systems reported a balance of $2,480 at May 31, 2007. There were outstanding cheques totaling $900 and a May 31 deposit in transit of $200. The bank statement, which came from Royal Bank, listed a May 31 balance of $3,800. Included in the bank balance was a collection of $630 on account from Kelly Brooks, a Ranger customer who pays the bank directly. The bank statement also shows a $20 service charge and $10 of interest revenue that Ranger earned on its bank balance. Prepare Ranger's bank reconciliation at May 31, 2007.

Starter 8–7 After preparing Ranger Security Systems' bank reconciliation in Starter 8–6, journalize the company's transactions that arise from the bank reconciliation. Date each transaction May 31, 2007 and include an explanation with each entry.

Starter 8–8 Diedre Chevis sells furniture for DuBois Furniture Company. Chevis is having financial problems and takes $500 that she received from a customer. She recorded the sale through the cash register. What will alert Betsy DuBois, the owner, that something is wrong?

Starter 8–9 Review the internal controls over cash receipts by mail. Exactly what is accomplished by the final step in the process, performed by the controller?

Starter 8–10 A purchasing agent for Westgate Wireless receives the goods that he purchases and also approves payment for the goods. How could this purchasing agent cheat his company? How could Westgate avoid this internal control weakness?

Starter 8–11 Record the following petty-cash transactions of Lexite Laminated Surfaces in general journal form (explanations are not required):

April	1	Established a petty cash fund with a $200 balance.
	30	The petty cash fund has $19 in cash and $187 in petty cash tickets that were issued to pay for Office Supplies ($117) and Entertainment Expense ($70). Replenished the fund with $181 of cash and recorded the expenses.

Starter 8–12 Gwen O'Malley, an accountant for Ireland Limited, discovers that her supervisor, Barney Stone, made several errors last year. Overall, the errors overstated the company's net income by 20%. It is not clear whether the errors were deliberate or accidental. What should O'Malley do?

Exercises

Exercise 8–1

Identifying and correcting an internal control weakness

Lane & Goble Bookstore has a liberal return policy. A customer can return any product for a full refund within 30 days of purchase. When a customer returns merchandise, Lane & Goble policy specifies:

- Store clerk issues a prenumbered return slip and refunds cash from the cash register. Keep a copy of the return slip for review by the manager.
- Store clerk places the returned goods back on the shelf as soon as possible. Lane & Goble uses a periodic inventory system.

1. How can a dishonest store clerk steal from Lane & Goble? What part of company policy enables the store clerk to steal without getting caught?

2. How can Lane & Goble improve its internal controls to prevent this theft?

Exercise 8–2

Correcting an internal control weakness

Trader Nick Leeson worked for Baring Securities (Singapore) Limited (BSS) as the general manager and head trader. Due to his experience in operations, he also acted as head of the "back office" that does the record keeping and tracks who owes what to whom. Leeson appeared to be making huge profits by speculating on Japan's Nikkei stock market—until he fled Singapore, leaving behind a £827,000,000 loss hidden in an unused error account on the Barings balance sheet. As a result of this situation, Britain's Barings Bank collapsed.

What internal control weaknesses at BSS allowed this loss to grow so large? How could Barings have avoided and/or limited the size of the loss?

Exercise 8–3

Identifying internal control strengths and weaknesses

The following situations suggest either a strength or weakness in internal control. Identify each as a *strength* or *weakness* and give the reason for each answer.

a. Top managers delegate all internal control procedures to the accounting department.

b. The accounting department orders merchandise and approves invoices for payment.

c. Cash received over the counter is controlled by the clerk, who rings up the sale and places the cash in the register. The clerk matches the total recorded by the register to each day's cash sales.

d. The vice-president who signs cheques assumes the accounting department has matched the invoice with other supporting documents and therefore does not examine the payment packet.

Exercise 8–4

Identifying internal controls

Identify the missing internal control procedure in the following situations:

a. In the course of auditing the records of a company, you find that the same employee orders merchandise and approves invoices for payment.

b. Business is slow at the Ridge Theatre on Tuesday, Wednesday, and Thursday nights. To reduce expenses, the owner decides not to use a ticket taker on those nights. The ticket seller (cashier) is told to keep the tickets as a record of the number sold.

c. The same trusted employee has served as cashier for ten years.

d. When business is brisk, One-Stop Convenience Store deposits cash in the bank several times during the day. The manager at the convenience store wants to reduce the time employees spend delivering cash to the bank, so he starts a new policy. Cash will build up over weekends, and the total will be deposited on Monday.

e. Grocery stores such as No-Frills and Big Box Groceries purchase large quantities of their merchandise from a few suppliers. At one grocery store, the manager decides to reduce paperwork. He eliminates the requirement that a receiving department employee prepare a receiving report, which lists the quantities of items received from the supplier.

Exercise 8–5

Explaining the role of internal control

The following questions pertain to internal control. Consider each situation separately.

1. Wong Company requires that all documents supporting a cheque be cancelled (stamped Paid) by the person who signs the cheque. Why do you think this practice is required? What might happen if it were not?

2. Separation of duties is an important consideration if a system of internal control is to be effective. Why is this so?

3. Cash may be a relatively small item on the financial statements. Nevertheless, internal control over cash is very important. Why is this true?

4. Many managers think that safeguarding assets is the most important objective of internal control systems, while auditors emphasize internal control's role in ensuring reliable accounting data. Explain why managers are more concerned about safeguarding assets and auditors are more concerned about the quality of the accounting records.

Classifying bank reconciliation items

3

Exercise 8–6

The following items could appear on a bank reconciliation:

a. Outstanding cheques

b. Deposits in transit

c. NSF cheque

d. Bank collection of a note receivable on our behalf

e. Interest earned on bank balance

f. Service charge

g. Book error: We credited Cash for $100. The correct credit was $1,000

h. Bank error: The bank decreased our account for a cheque written by another customer

Classify each item as (1) an addition to the book balance, (2) a subtraction from the book balance, (3) an addition to the bank balance, or (4) a subtraction from the bank balance.

Preparing a bank reconciliation
3
Adjusted balance $16,140

Exercise 8–7

Adams Enterprises began operations on January 2, 2008, depositing $10,000 in the bank. During this first month of business, the following transactions occurred that affected the cash account in the general ledger:

Date	Description	Dr	Cr
January			
2	Deposit	$10,000	
5	Payment, cheque 001		$ 3,000
8	Payment, cheque 002		4,000
9	Cash sales	4,000	
15	Payment, cheque 003		2,500
18	Cash sales	3,000	
20	Bank loan	25,000	
26	Equipment purchase, cheque 004		18,500
30	Payment on account, cheque 005		4,250
31	Cash sales	6,400	

Shortly after the end of January, the company received its first bank statement:

Description	Withdrawals	Deposits	Date	Balance
Balance Forward			Jan01	0
Deposit		10,000	Jan02	10,000
Chq#001	3,000		Jan07	7,000
Deposit		4,000	Jan09	11,000
Chq#002	4,000		Jan13	7,000
Deposit		3,000	Jan18	10,000
Bank Loan		25,000	Jan20	35,000
Chq#004	18,500		Jan28	16,500
Service Charge	12		Jan31	16,488
Interest		2	Jan31	16,490
	25,512	42,002		

Required Prepare Adams Enterprises' bank reconciliation at January 31, 2008.

Exercise 8–8

Marshland Travel's general ledger cash account showed the following transactions during October 2007:

Preparing a bank reconciliation

Adjusted balance $9,667

Date	Description	Dr	Cr	Balance
October				
1	Opening balance			$ 6,400
2	Deposit	$5,000		11,400
5	Payment, cheque 233		$3,000	8,400
8	Payment, cheque 234		4,000	4,400
9	Deposit	4,000		8,400
15	Payment, cheque 235		2,500	5,900
18	Deposit	2,600		8,500
26	Payment, cheque 236		1,650	6,850
30	Payment, cheque 237		2,375	4,475
31	Deposit	5,250		9,725

The bank statement for the month ending October 31, 2007, shows:

DESCRIPTION	WITHDRAWALS	DEPOSITS	DATE	BALANCE
Balance Forward			Oct01	6,400
Deposit		5,000	Oct02	11,400
Chq#00233	3,000		Oct07	8,400
Depost		4,000	Oct09	12,400
Chq#00234	4,000		Oct10	8,400
Deposit		2,600	Oct18	11,000
Chq#00235	2,500		Oct18	8,500
Service Charge	60		Oct31	8,440
Interest		2	Oct31	8,442
	9,560	11,602		

Required Prepare Marshland Travel's bank reconciliation at October 31, 2007.

Exercise 8–9

Preparing a bank reconciliation

Adjusted balance $4,339

Judi Hayer's cheque book lists the entries shown on the next page. Hayer's July bank statement shows:

Balance		$967
Add: Deposits		100
Deduct cheques: No.	Amount	
622	$52	
623	76	
624	79*	
625	67	(274)
Other charges		
Printed cheques.................................	$13	
Service charge....................................	8	(21)
Balance..		$772

*This is the correct amount of cheque number 624

Required

Prepare Judi Hayer's bank reconciliation at July 31, 2008. How much cash does Hayer actually have on July 31?

Date	Cheque No.	Item	Cheque	Deposit	Balance
July					
1					$ 967
4	622	Hobby Store	$ 52		915
9		Dividends received		$ 100	1,015
13	623	TELUS	76		939
14	624	Esso	69		870
18	625	Cash	67		803
26	626	Canadian Cancer Society	33		770
28	627	Park Lane Apartments	733		37
31		Paycheque		4,333	4,370

Preparing a bank reconciliation

Adjusted balance $15,392

Exercise 8–10

Bob Nichols operates two gas stations. He has just received the monthly bank statement at May 31 from the Royal Bank, and the statement shows an ending balance of $11,720. Listed on the statement are an EFT rent collection of $800, a service charge of $30, two NSF cheques totalling $190, and a $50 charge for printed cheques. In reviewing his cash records, Nichols identifies outstanding cheques totalling $858 and a May 31 deposit in transit of $4,530. During May, he recorded a $720 cheque for the salary of a part-time employee by debiting Salary Expense and crediting Cash for $72. Nichols' cash account shows a May 31 cash balance of $15,510. Prepare the bank reconciliation at May 31, 2008.

Making journal entries from a bank reconciliation

Exercise 8–11

Using the data from Exercise 8–10, record the entries that Nichols should make in the general journal on May 31, 2008. Include an explanation for each of the entries.

Applying internal controls to the bank reconciliation

Exercise 8–12

A jury convicted the treasurer of GTX Company of stealing cash from the company. Over a three-year period, the treasurer allegedly took almost $100,000 and attempted to cover the theft by manipulating the bank reconciliation.

Required   What is a likely way that a person would manipulate a bank reconciliation to cover a theft? Be specific. What internal control arrangement could have avoided this theft?

Evaluating internal control over cash receipts

Exercise 8–13

When you pay for goods at Luigi's Discount Store, the cash register displays the amount of the sale, the cash received, and any change returned to you. Suppose the register also produces a customer receipt but keeps no record of the sales transactions. At the end of the day, the clerk counts the cash in the register and gives it to the cashier for deposit in the company bank account.

Required   Write a memo to Luigi Verone, the owner. Identify the internal control weakness over cash receipts, and explain how the weakness gives an employee the opportunity to steal cash. State how to prevent such a theft.

Petty cash, cash short and over

Exercise 8–14

Record the following selected transactions of Kelly's Fine Foods in general journal format (explanations are not required):

2007
June   1   Established a petty cash fund with a $700 balance.
       2   Journalized the day's cash sales. Cash register tapes show a $4,875 total, but the cash in the register is $4,890.
      10   The petty cash fund has $213 in cash and $468 in petty cash tickets issued to pay for Office Supplies ($242), Delivery Expense ($139) and Entertainment Expense ($87). Replenished the fund.

Exercise 8–15

1. Explain how an *imprest* petty cash system works.

2. Atlantic Press maintains an imprest petty cash fund of $100, which is under the control of Brenda Montague. At November 30, the fund holds $20 cash and petty cash tickets for office supplies, $60; and delivery expense, $25.

   Journalize (a) establishment of the petty cash fund on November 1 and (b) replenishment of the fund on November 30.

3. Prepare a T-account for Petty Cash, and post to the account. What is Petty Cash's balance at all times?

Control over petty cash

3. Petty Cash balance $100

Exercise 8–16

Maritime Distributors created a $800 imprest petty cash fund. During the first month of use, the fund custodian authorized and signed petty cash tickets as shown below.

Accounting for petty cash

Ticket No.	Item	Account Debited	Amount
1	Delivery of pledge cards to donors	Delivery Expense	$128.80
2	Stamp purchase	Postage Expense	105.98
3	Newsletter	Supplies Expense	340.40
4	Key to closet	Miscellaneous Expense	9.52
5	Staples	Supplies Expense	14.72

Required Make general journal entries to (a) create the petty cash fund and (b) record its replenishment. Cash in the fund totals $197.58, so $3.00 is missing. Include explanations.

Exercise 8–17

You have a part-time job in a local delicatessen, which is part of a chain of delicatessens. You received the job through your parent's friendship with Samantha Stevens, the deli manager. The job is going well, but you are puzzled by the actions of Samantha and her husband, Fred. Each day, one or both of them fills takeout orders and takes them to Samantha's office. Later you notice Fred and Samantha enjoying the takeout orders, sometimes with friends. You know the orders were not rung through the checkout counter. When you ask a co-worker about the practice, you are told that Samantha is the boss and can do as she wishes, and besides, many employees help themselves to meals.

Evaluating the ethics of conduct by a manager

Required You have been given the assignment in a business ethics course to comment on the issue. Apply the decision guidelines for ethical judgments outlined in the Decision Guidelines feature on page 413 to decide whether a manager of a deli should help herself or himself to meals on a regular basis and not pay for what she or he takes.

Beyond the Numbers

Beyond the Numbers 8–1

This case is based on a situation experienced by one of the authors. Alpha Construction Company, headquartered in Chattanooga, Tennessee, built a Roadway Inn Motel in Cleveland, 35 kilometres east of Chattanooga. The construction foreman, whose name was Slim, moved into Cleveland in March to hire the 40 workers needed to complete the project. Slim hired the construction workers, had them fill out the necessary tax forms, and sent the employment documents to the home office, which opened a payroll file for each employee.

Correcting an internal control weakness

Work on the motel began on April 1 and ended September 1. Each Thursday evening, Slim filled out a time card that listed the hours worked by each employee during the five-day workweek ended at 5 p.m. on Thursday. Slim faxed the time sheets to the home office, which prepared the payroll cheques on Friday morning. Slim drove to the home office after lunch on Friday, picked up the payroll cheques, and returned to the construction site. At 5 p.m. on Friday, Slim distributed the payroll cheques to the workers.

a. Describe in detail the internal control weakness in this situation. Specify what negative result(s) could occur because of the internal control weakness.

b. Describe what you would do to correct the internal control weakness.

Ethical Issue

John Sullivan owns apartment buildings in Nova Scotia, New Brunswick, and Quebec. Each property has a manager who collects rent, arranges for repairs, and runs advertisements in the local newspaper. The property managers transfer cash to Sullivan monthly and prepare their own bank reconciliations.

The manager in New Brunswick has been stealing large sums of money. To cover the theft, she understates the amount of outstanding cheques on the monthly bank reconciliation. As a result, each monthly bank reconciliation appears to balance. However, the balance sheet reports more cash than Sullivan actually has in the bank. In negotiating the sale of the New Brunswick property, Sullivan is showing the balance sheet to prospective investors.

Required

1. Identify two parties other than Sullivan who can be harmed by this theft. In what ways can they be harmed?
2. Discuss the role accounting plays in this situation.

Problems (Group A)

 Identifying the characteristics of an effective internal control system

Problem 8–1A

An employee of Bonneville Marketing recently stole thousands of dollars of the company's cash. The company has decided to install a new system of internal controls.

Required   As controller of Bonneville Marketing, write a memo to the owner, Elizabeth Bean, explaining how a separation of duties helps to safeguard assets.

Identifying internal control weaknesses

Problem 8–2A

Each of the following situations has an internal control weakness:

a. Waterloo Software Associates sells accounting software. Recently, the development of a new software program stopped while the programmers redesigned Waterloo Software Associates' accounting system. Waterloo Software Associates' own accountants could have performed this task.

b. Judy Sloan has been your trusted employee for 30 years. She performs all cash handling and accounting duties. She has just purchased a new Lexus and a new home in an expensive suburb. As the owner of the company, you wonder how she can afford these luxuries because you pay her $35,000 per year and she has no sources of outside income.

c. Sanchez Hardwoods Ltd., a private corporation, falsified sales and inventory figures to get a large loan. The company received the loan but later went bankrupt and couldn't repay the loan.

d. The office supply company from which The Family Shoe Store purchases sales receipts recently notified Family that the last shipped receipts were not prenumbered. Louise Bourseault, the owner, replied that she never uses the receipt numbers, so the omission is not important.

e. Discount stores such as Wal-Mart make most of their sales for cash, with the remainder in debit card and credit card sales. To reduce expenses, one store manager ceases purchasing fidelity bonds on the cashiers.

Required

1. Identify the missing internal control characteristic in each situation.
2. Identify the business's possible problem caused by each control weakness.
3. Propose a solution to each internal-control problem.

 **Excel Spreadsheet Template**

Using the bank reconciliation as a control device

Problem 8–3A

The cash receipts and the cash payments of River Estates Development for November 2007 are as follows:

Cash Receipts (Posting reference is CR)			Cash Payments (Posting reference is CP)	
Date	**Cash Debit**		**Cheque No.**	**Cash Credit**
Nov. 5	$ 3,436		1221	$ 1,819
7	470		1222	1,144
13	1,723		1223	429
15	1,065		1224	111
19	441		1225	816
24	875		1226	109
30	2,598		1227	4,468
Total	$10,608		1228	998
			1229	330
			1230	2,724
			Total	$12,948

The Cash account of River Estates shows a balance of $15,883 on November 30, 2007. On December 3, 2007, River Estates received this bank statement:

Bank Statement for November 2007

DESCRIPTION	WITHDRAWALS	DEPOSITS	DATE	BALANCE
Balance Forward			Nov01	18,223
EFT Rent Collection *Pos*		880	Nov01	19,103
Deposit		3,436	Nov06	22,539
NSF Cheque *Neg*	433		Nov08	22,106
Chq#001221	1,819		Nov09	20,278
Deposit		470	Nov10	20,757
Chq#001222	1,144		Nov13	19,613
Chq#001223	429		Nov14	19,184
Deposit		1,723	Nov14	20,907
Chq#001224	111		Nov15	20,796
Deposit		1,065	Nov15	21,861
EFT Insurance *Neg payment*	275		Nov19	21,586
Deposit		441	Nov20	22,027
Chq#001225	816		Nov22	21,211
Deposit		875	Nov25	22,086
Chq#001226	109		Nov29	21,977
Chq#001227	4,968 *500 Book*		Nov30	17,009
Bank Collection *Includes $100 Interest*		1,430	Nov30	18,439
Service Charge	25		Nov30	18,414
	10,129	10,320		

Explanations: EFT—electronic funds transfer, NSF—nonsufficient funds

Additional data for the bank reconciliation:

a. The EFT deposit was a receipt of monthly rent. The EFT debit was payment of monthly insurance.

b. The NSF cheque was received late in October from a customer.

c. The $1,430 bank collection of a note receivable on November 30 included $100 interest revenue.

d. The correct amount of cheque number 1227, a payment on account, is $4,968. (The River Estates Development accountant mistakenly recorded the cheque for $4,468.)

500

Required

1. Prepare the bank reconciliation of River Estates Development at November 30, 2007.

2. Describe how a bank account and the bank reconciliation help River Estates managers control the business's cash.

Problem 8–4A

The October 31, 2008, bank statement of RCI Distributors has just arrived. To prepare RCI Distributors' bank reconciliation, you gather the following data:

a. The October 31 bank balance is $19,106.

b. The bank statement includes two charges for NSF cheques from customers. One was for $69 and the other was for $185.

c. The following RCI Distributors cheques are outstanding at October 31:

Cheque No.	Amount
712	$549
922	43
934	57
939	556
940	208
941	447

d. A few customers pay their accounts by EFT. The October bank statement lists a $6,366 deposit against customer accounts.

e. The bank statement includes two special deposits: $898, which is the amount of dividend revenue the bank collected on behalf of RCI Distributors; and $15, the interest revenue RCI earned on its bank balance during October.

f. The bank statement lists a $31 subtraction for the bank service charge.

g. On October 31, the company deposited $466, but this deposit does not appear on the bank statement.

h. The bank statement includes a $409 deduction for a cheque drawn by RCI Communications. RCI promptly notified the bank of its error.

i. RCI's Cash account shows a balance of $11,127 on October 31.

Required

1. Prepare the bank reconciliation for RCI Distributors at October 31, 2008.

2. Record in general journal form the entries necessary to bring the book balance of Cash into agreement with the adjusted book balance on the reconciliation. Include an explanation for each entry.

Problem 8–5A

Calibre Interiors makes all sales on credit. Cash receipts arrive by mail, usually within 30 days of sale. Sarah Romano opens envelopes and separates the cheques from the accompanying remittance advices. Romano forwards the cheques to another employee, who makes the daily bank deposit but has no access to the accounting records. Romano sends the remittance advices, which show the amount of cash received, to the accounting department for entry in the accounts. Her only other duty is to grant sales allowances to customers. (Recall that a *sales allowance* decreases the amount that the customer must pay.) When she receives a customer cheque for less than the full amount of the invoice, she records the sales allowance and forwards the document to the accounting department.

Required   You are a new management employee of Calibre Interiors. Write a memo to the company president, Ron Bunnett, identifying the internal control weakness in this situation. State how to correct the weakness.

Problem 8–6A

A-1 Machines is located in Saskatoon, Saskatchewan, with a sales territory covering the province.

The company has established a large petty cash fund to handle small cash payments and cash advances to the salespeople to cover frequent sales trips.

The controller, Tara Goldsmith, has decided that two people (Anne Bloom and Tom Hurry) should be in charge of the fund as money is often needed when one person may be out for coffee or lunch. Goldsmith also feels this will increase internal control, as the work of one person will serve as a check on that of the other.

Regular small cash payments are handled by either Bloom or Hurry, who make the payment and have the person receiving the money sign a sheet of paper listing the date and reason for the payment. Whenever a salesperson requires an advance for a trip, he or she simply signs a receipt for the money received. The salespeople later submit receipts for the cost of the trip to either Bloom or Hurry to offset the cash advance.

Goldsmith is puzzled that the fund is almost always out of balance and either over or short.

Required Comment on the internal control procedures of A-1 Machines. Suggest changes that you think would improve the system.

Problem 8–7A

Accounting for
petty cash transactions

2. Fund should hold $323.50.

Suppose that, on June 1, Wembury Design creates a petty cash fund with an imprest balance of $800. During June, Lucie Ducharme, the fund custodian, signs the following petty cash tickets:

Ticket No.	Item	Amount
101	Office supplies	$ 126.64
102	Cab fare for executive	60.00
103	Delivery of package across town	29.33
104	Dinner money for sales manager entertaining a customer	133.33
105	Office supplies	127.20

On June 30, prior to replenishment, the fund contains these tickets plus $334.39. The accounts affected by petty cash payments are Office Supplies Expense, Travel Expense, Delivery Expense, and Entertainment Expense.

Required

1. Explain the characteristics and internal control features of an imprest fund.
2. On June 30, how much cash should the petty cash fund hold before it is replenished?
3. Make general journal entries to (a) create the fund and (b) replenish it. Include explanations.
4. Make the July 1 entry to increase the fund balance to $1,000. Include an explanation, and briefly describe what the custodian does.

Problem 8–8A

Preparing a bank reconciliation
and related journal entries

1. Adjusted balance $3,832.00

Truro Electronics had a computer failure on March 1, 2008, which resulted in the loss of data, including the balance of its cash account and its bank reconciliation from February 29, 2008. The accountant, Matt Vincent, has been able to obtain the following information from the records of the company and its bank:

a. An examination showed that two cheques (#244 for $172.50 and #266 for $316.25) had not been cashed as of March 1. Vincent recalled that there was only one deposit in transit on the February 29 bank reconciliation, but was unable to recall the amount.

b. The cash receipts and cash payments journal contained the following entries for March 2008:

Cash Receipts:		Cash Payments:	
Amounts		Cheque #	Amount
$ 454.25		275	$ 155.25
874.00		276	224.25
1,863.00		277	233.45
977.50		278	405.95
368.00		279	288.65
$4,536.75		280	1,958.45
		281	void
		282	224.25
		283	529.00
			$4,019.25

c. The company's bank provided the following statement as of March 31, 2008:

Date	Cheques and Other Debits		Deposits and Other Credits		Balance
Mar. 1	#276	224.25		1,173.00	3,260.25
2	#266	316.25			2,944.00
5	#277	233.45			2,710.55
8				454.25	3,164.80
14	#275	155.25		598.00	3,607.55
17	EFT	264.50			3,343.05
19			EFT	207.00	3,550.05
22	#279	288.65		874.00	4,135.05
22	#280	1,988.45	EFT	598.00	2,744.95
24			EFT	235.75	2,980.70
27	NSF	402.50		1,863.00	4,441.20
28	SC	25.00			4,416.20
31	#283	529.00		977.50	4,864.70

Handwritten annotations: "+550 Interest" (near Mar. 14), "Neg payment" (near Mar. 17), "Pos collection" (near Mar. 19), "30¢ diff" (near #280).

d. The deposit made on March 14 was for the collection of a note receivable ($550) plus interest.

e. The electronic funds transfers (EFTs) had not yet been recorded by Truro Electronics as the bank statement was the first notification of them.

  • The March 17 EFT was for the monthly payment on an insurance policy for Truro Electronics.

  • The March 19 and 24 EFTs were collections on accounts receivable.

  • The March 22 EFT was in error—the transfer should have been to Truro Auto Parts.

f. The NSF cheque on March 27 was received from a customer as payment for electronics purchased for $402.50.

g. Cheque #280 was correctly written for $1,988.45 for the purchase of office supplies, but incorrectly recorded by the cash payments clerk.

Required

1. Prepare a bank reconciliation as of March 31, 2008, including the calculation of the book balance of March 31, 2008.

2. Prepare all journal entries that would be required by the bank reconciliation.

Making an ethical judgement

Problem 8–9A

North Venture Capital in Sudbury, Ontario, has received a request for investment funds from Different View Products. The funds are for the production of a new product that will dramatically enhance communications on mining sites. Stewart Donolo, an account manager at North Venture, is assigned to research the application.

  With unlimited access to Different View's records, Donolo learns that one of the potential major customers for this product is Goldore, a local mining company. North Venture Capital has invested in Goldore. Donolo has access to confidential information about Goldore— operations will be on hold pending further investigation of identified deposits. The future of Goldore will be strong, but in the short term, Goldore will not be making large operational purchases.

  Donolo believes there will be a market for the Different Views product. He has a strong motivation to have Different Views succeed and North Venture Capital to share in this success.

Required Apply the ethical judgment framework outlined in the Decision Guidelines feature on page 413 to help Stewart Donolo plan his next action.

Problems (Group B)

Identifying the characteristics of an effective internal control system

Problem 8–1B

White River Real Estate prospered during the recent economic expansion. Business was so good that the company bothered with few internal controls. A decline in the local real estate market, however, has caused White River to experience a shortage of cash. Carol Stuart, the company owner, is looking for ways to save money.

Required As controller of the company, write a memorandum to convince Carol Stuart of the company's need for a system of internal control. Be specific in telling her how an internal control system could possibly lead to saving money. Include the definition of internal control, and briefly discuss each characteristic beginning with competent, reliable, and ethical personnel.

Problem 8–2B

Identifying internal control weaknesses

Each of the following situations has an internal control weakness:

a. Public accounting firms, law firms, and other professional organizations use paraprofessional employees to do some of their routine tasks. For example, a draftsman might prepare drawings to assist an architect. In the architecture firm of Bradshaw and Bos, Nancy Bos, the senior partner, turns over some of her high-level design work to less-qualified draftsmen.

b. Mike Strickland owns a firm that performs interior design services. His staff consists of twelve professional designers, and he manages the office. Often his work requires him to travel to meet with clients. During the past six months, he has observed that when he returns from a business trip, the design jobs in the office have not progressed satisfactorily. He learns that when he is away several of his senior employees take over office management and neglect their design duties. One employee could manage the office.

c. Alison Wong has been an employee of Your Kitchen Store for many years. Because the business is relatively small, Alison performs all accounting duties, including opening the mail, preparing the bank deposit, and preparing the bank reconciliation.

d. Most large companies have internal audit staffs that continuously evaluate the business's internal control. Part of the internal auditor's job is to evaluate how efficiently the company is running. For example, is the company purchasing inventory from the least expensive wholesaler? After a particularly bad year, Eagle Distributors eliminates its internal audit department to reduce expenses.

e. In evaluating the internal control over cash payments, an auditor learns that the purchasing agent is responsible for purchasing materials for use in the company's manufacturing process, approving the invoices for payment, and signing the cheques. No supervisor reviews the purchasing agent's work.

Required

1. Identify the missing internal control characteristic in each situation.
2. Identify the problem that could be caused by each control weakness.
3. Propose a solution to each internal control problem.

Problem 8–3B

Excel Spreadsheet Template

Preparing and using the bank reconciliation as a control device

1. Adjusted balance $24,294

The cash receipts and the cash payments of Kitimat Hardware for January 2008 are as follows:

Cash Receipts (Posting reference is CR)		**Cash Payments** (Posting reference is CP)	
Date	**Cash Debit**	**Cheque No.**	**Cash Credit**
Jan. 3	$10,494	311	$ 1,836
8	740	312	834
10	990	313	6,281
16	3,744	314	1,292
22	10,368	315	4,294
29	1,202	316	1,800
31	864	317	652
Total	$28,402	318	3,134
		319	400
		320	6,482
		Total	$27,005

The Cash account of Kitimat Hardware shows a balance of $19,739 at January 31, 2008.

Kitimat Hardware received the bank statement shown below on January 31, 2008.

Bank Statement for January 2008

DESCRIPTION	WITHDRAWALS	DEPOSITS	DATE	BALANCE
Balance Forward			Jan01	18,342
EFT Rent Collection		526	Jan01	18,868
Deposit		10,494	Jan04	29,362
Chq#00311	1,836		Jan07	27,526
Deposit		740	Jan09	28,266
Deposit		990	Jan12	29,256
Chq#00313	6,218		Jan13	23,038
NSF Chque	1,678		Jan14	21,360
Chq#00312	834		Jan15	20,526
Deposit		3,744	Jan17	24,270
Chq#00314	1,292		Jan18	22,978
EFT Insurance	658		Jan21	22,320
Bank Collection		6,372	Jan22	28,692
Deposit		10,368	Jan23	39,060
Chq#00315	4,294		Jan26	34,766
Chq#00316	1,800		Jan30	32,966
Service Charge	70		Jan31	32,896
	18,680	33,234		

Additional data for the bank reconciliation:

a. The EFT deposit was a receipt of monthly rent. The EFT debit was payment of monthly insurance.

b. The NSF cheque was received from A. N. Garner.

c. The $6,372 bank collection of a note receivable on January 22 included $250 interest revenue.

d. The correct amount of cheque number 313, a payment on account, is $6,218. (Kitimat Hardware's accountant mistakenly recorded the cheque for $6,281.)

Required

1. Prepare the Kitimat Hardware bank reconciliation at January 31, 2008.

2. Describe how a bank account and the bank reconciliation help the Kitimat Hardware's owner control the business's cash.

Excel Spreadsheet Template

Preparing a bank reconciliation and the related journal entries

③

1. Adjusted balance $19,275

Problem 8–4B

The July 31, 2008, bank statement of Red Star Shoes has just arrived from the Royal Bank. To prepare the Red Star Shoes bank reconciliation, you gather the following data:

a. The Red Star Shoes Cash account shows a balance of $19,759 on July 31.

b. The bank statement includes two charges for returned cheques from customers. One is a $1,779 cheque received from St. Mary's Collegiate and deposited on July 20, returned by St. Mary's bank with the imprint "Unauthorized Signature." The other is an NSF cheque in the amount of $494 received from Mavis Jones. This cheque had been deposited on July 17.

c. Red Star Shoes pays rent ($2,925) and insurance ($960) each month by EFT.

d. The following Red Star Shoes cheques are outstanding at July 31:

Cheque No.	Amount
291	$ 153
322	537
327	2,356
329	41
330	1,548
331	16
332	930

e. The bank statement includes a deposit of $5,733, collected by the bank on behalf of Red Star Shoes. Of the total, $5,504 is collection of a note receivable, and the remainder is interest revenue.

f. The bank statement shows that Red Star Shoes earned $13 in interest on its bank balance during July. This amount was added to the Red Star Shoes account by the bank.

g. The bank statement lists a $72 subtraction for the bank service charge.

h. On July 31, the Red Star Shoes accountant deposited $1,689, but this deposit does not appear on the bank statement.

i. The bank statement includes a $2,100 deposit that Red Star Shoes did not make. The bank had erroneously credited the Red Star Shoes account for another bank customer's deposit.

j. The July 31 bank balance is $25,267.

Required

1. Prepare the bank reconciliation for Red Star Shoes at July 31, 2008.
2. Record in general journal form the entries that bring the book balance of Cash into agreement with the adjusted book balance on the reconciliation. Include an explanation for each entry.

Problem 8–5B

Identifying internal control weaknesses in cash receipts
4

Truly Fresh Bakery makes all sales of its bread to retailers on account. Cash receipts arrive by mail, usually within 30 days of the sale. Gary Donell opens envelopes and separates the cheques from the accompanying remittance advices. Donell forwards the cheques to another employee, who makes the daily bank deposit but has no access to the accounting records. Donell sends the remittance advices, which show the amount of cash received, to the accounting department for entry in the accounts. Donell's only other duty is to grant sales allowances to customers. (Recall that a *sales allowance* decreases the amount that the customer must pay.) When he receives a customer cheque for less than the full amount of the invoice, he records the sales allowance and forwards the document to the accounting department.

Required   You are the new controller of Truly Fresh Bakery. Write a memo to the company president, John Fresh, identifying the internal control weakness in this situation. State how to correct the weakness.

Problem 8–6B

Applying internal controls to cash payments, including petty cash transactions
5

MEI Distributors is located in Moncton, New Brunswick, with a sales territory covering the Maritime provinces and Newfoundland. Employees live in New Brunswick and all report to work at the company's offices in Moncton.

The company has established a large petty cash fund to handle cash payments and cash advances to its salespeople to cover trips to and from New Brunswick on sales calls.

The controller, Shelly Frum, has decided that two people (Sarah Wong and Martha Davis) should be in charge of the petty cash fund, as money is often needed when one person is out of the office. Frum also feels this will increase internal control, as the work of one person will serve as a check on that of the other.

Regular small cash payments are handled by either Wong or Davis, who make the payment and have the person receiving the money sign a sheet of paper giving the date and reason for the payment. Whenever a salesperson requires an advance for a sales trip, that person simply signs a receipt for the money received. The salespeople later submit receipts for their costs to either Wong or Davis to offset the cash advance.

Frum, a family friend as well as the controller, doesn't think the system is working and, knowing you are studying accounting, has asked for your advice.

Required   Write a memo to Shelly Frum commenting on the internal control procedures of MEI. Suggest changes that you think would improve the system.

Problem 8–7B

Accounting for petty cash transactions
5
2. Fund should hold $332.52.

Suppose that on September 1, Twain Motors opens a new showroom in Timmins, Ontario, and creates a petty cash fund with an imprest balance of $1,000. During September, Lisa Manfield, the fund custodian, signs the petty cash tickets shown on the next page.

On September 30, prior to replenishment, the fund contains these tickets plus $322.68. The accounts affected by petty cash payments are Office Supplies Expense, Entertainment Expense, and Delivery Expense.

Ticket No.	Item	Amount
1	Courier for package received	$ 39.33
2	Refreshments for showroom opening	282.00
3	Computer disks	96.15
4	Office supplies	75.00
5	Dinner money for sales manager entertaining a customer	175.00

Required

1. Explain the characteristics and the internal control features of an imprest fund.

2. On September 30, how much cash should this petty cash fund hold before it is replenished?

3. Make the general journal entries to (a) create the fund and (b) replenish it. Include explanations.

4. Make the entry on October 1 to increase the fund balance to $1,200. Include an explanation and briefly describe what the custodian does.

Preparing a bank reconciliation and related journal entries

1. Adjusted balance $1,544.50

Problem 8–8B

Excel Communications had a computer failure on February 1, 2007, which resulted in the loss of data, including the balance of its cash account and its bank reconciliation from January 31, 2007. The accountant, Brad Eyers, has been able to obtain the following information from the records of the company and its bank:

a. An examination showed that two cheques (#461 for $172.50 and #492 for $262.50) had not been cashed as of February 1. Barker recalled that there was only one deposit in transit on the January 31 bank reconciliation, but was unable to recall the amount.

b. The cash receipts and cash payments journal contained the following entries for February 2007:

Cash Receipts: Amounts	Cash Payments: Cheque #	Amount
$ 438.00	499	$ 339.00
615.00	500	325.50
622.50	501	1,139.25
456.00	502	423.00
1,230.00	503	163.50
$3,361.50	504	410.00
	505	void
	506	157.00
	507	421.50
		$3,378.75

c. The bank provided the following statement as of February 28, 2007:

Date	Cheques and Other Debits		Deposits and Other Credits		Balance
Feb. 1	#500	325.50		660.00	1,789.50
3	#492	262.50			1,527.00
5	#501	1,139.25			387.75
8				438.00	825.75
16	#499	339.00		292.50	779.25
17	EFT	221.25			558.00
19			EFT	360.00	918.00
21	#503	163.50		615.00	1,369.50
22	#504	430.00	EFT	168.25	1,107.75
24			EFT	235.50	1,343.25
26	NSF	746.25		622.50	1,219.50
27	SC	18.75			1,200.75
27	#507	421.50		456.00	1,235.25

d. The deposit made on February 16 was for the collection of a note receivable ($280.00) plus interest.

e. The electronic funds transfers (EFTs) had not yet been recorded by Excel Communications as the bank statement was the first notification of them.

- The February 17 EFT was for the monthly payment on an insurance policy for Excel Communications.
- The February 19 and 24 EFTs were collections on accounts receivable.
- The February 22 EFT was in error—the transfer should have been to Accel Communications.

f. The NSF cheque on February 26 was received from a customer as payment of $746.25 for installation of a satellite purchased from Excel for $746.25.

g. Cheque #504 was correctly written for $430.00 for the purchase of office supplies, but incorrectly recorded by the cash payments clerk.

Required

1. Prepare a bank reconciliation as of February 28, 2007, including the calculation of the book balance of February 28, 2007.
2. Prepare all journal entries that would be required by the bank reconciliation.

Problem 8–9B

Making an ethical judgment

Hans Skinner is a vice-president of the Laurentian Bank in Markham, Ontario. Active in community affairs, Skinner serves on the board of directors of Orson Tool & Dye. Orson is expanding rapidly and is considering relocating its factory. At a recent meeting, board members decided to try to buy 20 hectares of land on the edge of town. The owner of the property is Sherri Alkiore, a customer of the Laurentian Bank. Alkiore is a recent widow. Skinner knows that Alkiore is eager to sell her local property. In view of Alkiore's anguished condition, Skinner believes she would accept almost any offer for the land. Realtors have appraised the property at $4 million.

Required   Apply the ethical judgment framework outlined in the Decision Guidelines feature on page 413 to help Skinner decide what his role should be in Orson's attempt to buy the land from Sherri Alkiore.

Challenge Problems

Problem 8–1C

Management's role in internal control

"Effective internal control must begin with top management." "The 'tone at the top' is a necessary condition if an organization is to have an effective system of internal control."

These statements are becoming a more important part of internal control literature and thought.

The chapter lists a number of characteristics that are important for an effective system of internal control. Many of these characteristics have been part of the internal control literature for years.

Required   Explain why you think a commitment to good internal control by top management is fundamental to an effective system of internal control.

Problem 8–2C

Applying internal controls to cash transactions

Many companies require some person other than the person preparing the bank reconciliation to review the reconciliation. Organizations routinely require cheques over a certain amount to be signed by two signing officers. The purchasing department orders goods but the receiving department receives the goods.

Required   All of the above situations have a common thread. What is that common thread and why is it important?

Extending Your Knowledge

Decision Problem

Using the bank reconciliation to detect a theft

Adjusted bank balance $6,100

Surrey Tech Solutions has poor internal control over cash. Recently Shikha Ghandi, the owner, has suspected the cashier of stealing. Details of the business's cash position at April 30, 2008 follow:

a. The Cash account in the ledger shows a balance of $6,450.

b. The April 30 bank statement shows a balance of $4,300. The bank statement lists a $200 credit for a bank collection, a $10 debit for the service charge, and a $40 debit for an NSF cheque. C. J. Ellis, the Surrey Tech Solutions accountant, has not recorded any of these items on the books.

c. At April 30 the following cheques are outstanding:

Cheque No.	Amount	Cheque No.	Amount
402	$100	531	600
527	300	561	200

d. There is a $3,000 deposit in transit at April 30, 2008.

e. Arlo Bing, the cashier, handles all incoming cash and makes bank deposits. He also writes cheques and reconciles the monthly bank statement.

Ghandi asks you to determine whether Bing has stolen cash from the business and, if so, how much. Perform a bank reconciliation, using the format illustrated on page 401. There are no bank or book errors. Ghandi also asks you to evaluate the internal controls and recommend any changes needed to improve them.

Financial Statement Cases

Financial Statement Case 1

Audit opinion, management responsibility, internal controls and cash

5. $17,910,000 decrease

Study Management's Report and the auditors' report on CHUM Limited's 2005 financial statements, given in Appendix A. Answer the following questions about CHUM Limited's internal controls and cash position:

1. What is the name of CHUM Limited's outside auditing firm? What office of this firm signed the auditor's report? How long after CHUM Limited's year end did the auditors issue their opinion?

2. Who bears primary responsibility for the financial statements? How can you tell?

3. Which of the two reports indicates who bears primary responsibility for internal controls?

4. What standard of auditing did the outside auditors use in examining CHUM Limited's financial statements? By what accounting standards were the statements evaluated?

5. By how much did CHUM Limited's cash position change during fiscal 2005?

6. The cash flow statement (discussed in detail in Chapter 17) tells why the change in cash position occurred. Which type of activity—operating, investing, or financing—contributed most to this change?

Financial Statement Case 2

Audit opinion, management responsibility, internal controls and cash

5. $10,825,000 increase

For Sun-Rype Products Ltd., study the auditor's report that is given in Appendix B and the Management's Discussion & Analysis given on the Student CD-ROM that accompanies this text. Answer the following questions about Sun-Rype's internal controls and cash position:

1. What is the name of Sun-Rype's outside auditing firm? What office of this firm signed the auditor's report? How long after Sun-Rype's year end did the auditors issue their opinion?

2. Who bears responsibility for the financial statements? How can you tell?

3. Where in the annual report does it indicate who bears primary responsibility for internal controls?

4. What standard of auditing did the outside auditors use in examining Sun-Rype's financial statements? By what accounting standards were the statements evaluated?

5. By how much did Sun-Rype's cash position change during 2005?

6. The cash flow statement, discussed in detail in Chapter 17, tells why the change in cash position occurred. Which type of activity—operating, investing, or financing—contributed most to this change?

CHAPTER

9

Receivables

Canadian Tire Corporation, Limited is a successful Canadian retailer. In 2005, its sales revenue was over $7.5 billion and its net earnings were approximately $330 million. As a major retailer intent on increasing its market share, Canadian Tire is providing services customers may not expect. The company provides Canadian Tire credit cards for customers, and is entering into other personal financial service segments including personal loans and even mortgages!

Issuing Canadian Tire credit cards to customers has two distinct advantages for a company like Canadian Tire. First, it increases sales immediately as customers use the credit card to make purchases. Second, it provides an additional source of income from the interest charged monthly on outstanding credit-card balances. Although Canadian Tire has to manage a credit department, it avoids the fees charged by other credit-card companies for processing the transactions.

Has the policy been successful for Canadian Tire? "We have been rewarded with significant growth in the average balance per account of our credit card customers, which has increased an average of 22% annually over the past three years to reach almost $1,700 at the end of 2005. We also continue to see very high customer acceptance of new credit cards, insurance, and personal loan products. Financial services will continue to grow as our credit card customers increase the balances they carry on their accounts—to the industry average of $2,500—and as we increase the number of cardholders and personal loans granted."[1]

---

[1] Canadian Tire Corporation, Limited 2005 Annual Report, page 30.

?

What are accounts receivable, and why are they important?
Why are accounts receivable recorded at net realizable value?
What are notes receivable, and how is interest computed on notes
    receivable?
How are receivables reported on the balance sheet?
Which ratios use receivables to evaluate a company's financial position?

These questions and others will be answered throughout this chapter. And the Decision Guidelines at the beginning and end of this chapter will provide the answers in a useful summary.

As Canadian Tire's financial services business grows, so do its revenues and receivables. This chapter shows how to account for receivables. The chapter also covers notes receivable, a more formal type of receivable that includes a written promise to pay and a stated interest rate.

A *receivable* arises when a business (or person) sells goods or services to another party on credit. The receivable is the seller's claim for the amount of the transaction. A receivable also arises when one person lends money to another. Each credit transaction involves two parties:

- The **creditor** who sells something and obtains a receivable, which is an asset.
- The **debtor** who makes the purchase and has a payable, which is a liability.

A receivable is an asset, just as cash is. But the receivable is slightly different: It's very close to cash, but it's not cash yet. This chapter focuses on accounting for receivables by the seller (the creditor).

Receivables: An Introduction

Types of Receivables

Receivables are monetary claims against others. The two major types of receivables are

- Accounts receivable
- Notes receivable

Accounts receivable, also called *trade receivables,* are amounts to be collected from customers. Accounts receivable are *current assets*. The Accounts Receivable account in the general ledger serves as a *control account* because it summarizes the total of the receivables from all customers. As we saw in Chapter 7, companies also keep a *subsidiary ledger* of the receivable from each customer. This is illustrated as follows:

KEY POINT

The major advantages of selling on credit are more sales, because it is easier for customers to buy and, therefore, net income will be higher. The major disadvantages of selling on credit are some customers will pay late or not at all; also, credit sales are more costly because the company must maintain a credit department and a billing department.

KEY POINT

Trade Accounts Receivable do not include amounts due from employees or officers (these are called Receivables from Employees or from Officers). Trade Accounts Receivable arise from selling goods or services to customers.

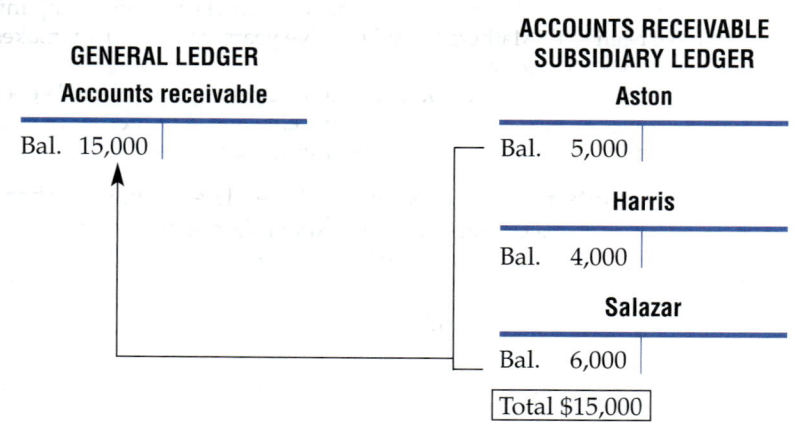

GENERAL LEDGER

Accounts receivable

Bal. 15,000

ACCOUNTS RECEIVABLE
SUBSIDIARY LEDGER

Aston

Bal. 5,000

Harris

Bal. 4,000

Salazar

Bal. 6,000

Total $15,000

Notes receivable are more formal than accounts receivable. The debtor promises in writing to pay the creditor a definite sum at a definite future date—the *maturity* date. A written document known as a *promissory note* serves as the evidence of the receivable. Notes receivable due within one year, or one operating cycle if longer than one year, are current assets. Notes due beyond one year are *long-term*.

Other receivables is a miscellaneous category that may include loans to employees. Usually these are long-term receivables, but they are current assets if receivable within one year or less. Receivables can be reported as shown in Exhibit 9–1. Receivables are highlighted for emphasis.

EXHIBIT 9–1 Receivables on the Balance Sheet

EXAMPLE COMPANY
Assets
Date

Assets		
Current assets:		
Cash		$X,XXX
Accounts receivable	**X,XXX**	
Less: Allowance for uncollectible accounts	(XXX)	X,XXX
Notes receivable, short-term		**X,XXX**
Inventories		X,XXX
Prepaid expenses		X,XXX
Total current assets		X,XXX
Investments and long-term receivables:		
Available-for-sale investments		X,XXX
Notes receivable, long-term		**X,XXX**
Other receivables		**X,XXX**
Total non-current assets		X,XXX
Property, plant, and equipment		
(net of amortization)		X,XXX
Total assets		$X,XXX

Establishing Internal Control over the Collection of Receivables

Businesses that sell on credit receive most cash receipts by mail. Therefore, internal control over collections is very important. A critical element of internal control (introduced in Chapter 8) is the separation of cash-handling and cash-accounting duties. Consider the following case:

> Mathers Supply Co. is family-owned and has loyal workers. Most company employees have been with Mathers for at least five years. The company makes 90 percent of its sales on account.
>
> The office staff consists of a bookkeeper and a supervisor. The bookkeeper maintains the general ledger and the accounts receivable subsidiary ledger. He also makes the daily bank deposit. The supervisor manages the office.

Can you identify the internal control weakness here? The bookkeeper has access to the general ledger and the accounts receivable subsidiary ledger, and also handles the cash. The bookkeeper could steal a customer's cheque and write off the customer's account as uncollectible.[2] Unless someone reviews the bookkeeper's work regularly, the theft may go undetected.

---

[2]The bookkeeper would need to forge the endorsements of the cheques and deposit them in a bank account that he controls.

Objective 1

Design internal controls for receivables

REAL WORLD EXAMPLE

Credit-card companies conduct extensive research on credit risks. They research an applicant's job history, credit history, salary, home rental or ownership, length of time at current address, and other credit transactions.

How can Mathers Supply correct this control weakness? *The bookkeeper should not be allowed to handle cash.* The supervisor should make all bank deposits.

Using a bank lock box can achieve the same result. Customers send their payments directly to Mathers Supply Co.'s bank, which deposits the customer's payment into the company's bank account. We examined the lock-box system in detail in Chapter 8, page 399.

Managing the Collection of Receivables: The Credit Department

Most companies have a credit department to evaluate customers. The extension of credit requires a balancing act. The company does not want to lose sales to good customers, but it also wants to avoid uncollectible receivables.

For good internal control over cash collections of receivables, the credit department should have no access to cash. For example, if a credit employee handles cash, he or she could pocket the money received from a customer. He or she could also then label the customer's account as uncollectible, and the company would write off the account receivable as discussed in the next section. The company would stop billing that customer, and the employee would have covered up the theft. For this reason, a sharp separation of duties is important.

The Decision Guidelines feature below identifies the main issues in controlling and managing receivables. These guidelines serve as a framework for the remainder of the chapter.

DECISION GUILDELINES — Controlling, Managing, and Accounting for Receivables

The main issues in *controlling* and *managing* the collection of receivables, plus a plan of action, are as follows:

Issue	Action
Extend credit only to customers most likely to pay.	Run a credit check on prospective customers.
Separate cash-handling (custody), credit (authorization), and accounting duties (recording) to keep employees from stealing cash collected from customers.	Design the internal control system to separate the duties of custody, authorization, and recording.
Pursue collection from customers to maximize cash flow.	Keep a close eye on collections from customers.

The main issues in *accounting* for receivables, and the related plans of action, are as follows:

Issue	Action
Report receivables at their *net realizable value,* which is the amount we expect to collect.	Estimate the amount of uncollectible receivables.
	The *balance sheet* reports receivables at net realizable value (accounts receivable—allowance for uncollectible accounts).
Report the expense associated with failure to collect receivables. This expense is called *uncollectible-account expense.*	The *income statement* reports the expense of failing to collect from customers.

Accounting for Uncollectible Accounts (Bad Debts)

Selling on credit (on account) creates an account receivable. The revenue—service revenue for a service company or sales revenue for a merchandiser—is recorded as follows (amounts assumed):

Accounts Receivable.......................................	6,000	
Service Revenue		6,000
Performed service on account.		
Accounts Receivable.......................................	10,000	
Sales Revenue		10,000
Sold goods on account.		

The business collects cash for most accounts receivable and makes this entry, which is the same for both service and merchandising companies (amount assumed):

Cash	10,000	
Accounts Receivable....................................		10,000
Collected cash on account.		

Selling on credit provides both a benefit and a cost to the selling company.

- *The benefit:* The business increases sales revenues and profits by making sales to a wide range of customers. Customers can buy now but pay later.
- *The cost:* The company will be unable to collect from some customers, and that creates an expense. The expense is called **bad-debt expense, uncollectible-account expense,** or **doubtful-account expense.**

Bad-debt expense varies from company to company. The older the receivable, the less valuable it is because of the decreasing likelihood of collection. At Alma Ladder Ltd., a $25 million construction-equipment and supply firm, 85 percent of company sales are on account. Each $1.00 of accounts receivable is worth $0.98 because of bad debts. Bad-debt expense is an operating expense, in the same way as salary expense and amortization expense are.

How do companies account for these uncollectible accounts? They use the allowance method or, in certain limited cases, the direct write-off method. We begin with the allowance method because it represents GAAP.

The Allowance Method Most companies use the **allowance method** to measure bad debts. The key concept is to record bad-debt expense in the same period as the sales revenue, which is an application of the *matching principle*. The business doesn't wait to see which customers will not pay. Instead, it records bad-debt expense on the basis of estimates developed from past experience.

The business records Bad-Debt Expense for the estimated amount, and sets up **Allowance for Doubtful Accounts** (or **Allowance for Uncollectible Accounts**), a contra account to Accounts Receivable. The allowance is the amount of receivables that the business expects *not* to collect. Subtracting the allowance from Accounts Receivable yields the net amount that the company does expect to collect, as shown in the following partial balance sheet (using assumed numbers):

Accounts receivable..	$10,000
Less: Allowance for doubtful accounts........	(900)
Accounts receivable, net	$ 9,100

Customers owe this company $10,000, of which the business expects to collect $9,100. The company estimates that it will not collect $900 of its accounts receivable.

Many Canadian companies do not provide information on their gross receivables and allowance for doubtful accounts, but rather simply report the net receivable. For

KEY POINT

Selling on credit enables a company to generate more sales revenue. But there is a cost associated with selling on credit; bad-debt expense arises as a result of not collecting from some customers.

KEY POINT

The longer an account is outstanding, the less chance there is of collection. But even if a past-due account is collected in full, there is a cost associated with collecting an account late. Also, when an account is past due, the seller is essentially giving an interest-free loan to the buyer because the seller does not have the cash to use in the business. This increases the seller's cost of doing business.

example, Hudson's Bay Company (HBC), in its annual report for the year ended January 31, 2006, reported as follows (amounts in thousands):

Credit card receivables.................................... $331,066

Its income statement reports Bad-Debt Expense, included in operating expenses, as follows:

Income statement (partial):

Expenses:

Bad-debt expense... $65,503

In the sections that follow, we show how to arrive at these amounts.

Estimating Uncollectibles

How are bad debts estimated? Companies base estimates on their past experience. There are two ways to estimate uncollectibles:

- *Percent-of-sales method*
- *Aging-of-accounts-receivable method*

Both approaches work under the allowance method, and both normally require an adjusting entry at the end of the period.

Percent-of-Sales Method The **percent-of-sales method** computes bad-debt expense as a percent of net credit sales. This method is also called the **income-statement approach** because it focuses on the amount of expense. Assume it is December 31, 2008, and the accounts have these balances *before the year-end adjustments*:

Accounts Receivable		Allowance for Doubtful Accounts	
100,000			1,000

Accounts Receivable reports the amount that customers owe the company. If it were to collect from all customers, the company would receive $100,000. Allowance for Doubtful Accounts should report the amount of the receivables that the company expects *not* to collect.

Suppose it becomes clear to the company that it will *fail to collect* more than $1,000 of the receivables. The allowance is too low, so the company needs to bring it up to a more realistic credit balance. That requires an adjusting entry at the end of the period.

How the Percent-of-Sales Method Works Based on prior experience, the company's bad-debt expense is 2 percent of net credit sales, which were $500,000 in 2008. The adjusting entry to record bad-debt expense for 2008 and to update the allowance is:

2008

Dec. 31	Bad-Debt Expense		10,000	
	Allowance for Doubtful Accounts			10,000
	To record bad-debt expense for the year ($500,000 × 0.02).			

After posting, the accounts are ready for reporting on the 2008 balance sheet.

Accounts Receivable		Allowance for Doubtful Accounts	
100,000			1,000
			Adj. 10,000
			11,000

Net accounts receivable, $89,000

KEY POINT

The amount of bad-debt expense depends on the volume of credit sales, the effectiveness of the credit department, and the diligence of the collection department.

Objective 2

Use the allowance method to account for uncollectibles, and estimate uncollectibles by the percent-of-sales and the aging-of-accounts-receivable methods

KEY POINT

Owners have to make a number of estimates of expenses when they calculate net income. In this case, estimating bad-debt expense actually makes net income more correct than if it were omitted. This is because reality is better reflected when bad-debt expense is included, based on past experience.

KEY POINT

The percent-of-sales approach is often referred to as the income-statement approach to estimating bad-debt expense because the entry is based on credit sales for the period (an income-statement figure).

Now the allowance for doubtful accounts is realistic. The balance sheet will report accounts receivable at the net amount of $89,000 ($100,000 − $11,000). The income statement will report bad-debt expense of $10,000, along with other operating expenses for the period.

Aging-of-Accounts-Receivable Method The other method for estimating uncollectible accounts is the **aging-of-accounts-receivable method.** This method is also called the **balance-sheet approach** because it focuses on accounts receivable. Assume it is December 31, 2008, and the accounts have these balances *before the year-end adjustment:*

Accounts Receivable	Allowance for Doubtful Accounts
100,000	1,000

Again, the allowance balance is too low. In the aging-of accounts-receivable method, the company groups each customer account (Baring Tools Co., etc.) according to how long amounts due have been outstanding. The computer can sort customer accounts by age. Exhibit 9–2 shows how the company groups its accounts receivable. This is called an aging schedule.

EXHIBIT 9–2 Aging the Accounts Receivable at December 31, 2008 Using an Aging Schedule

	Aging Schedule				
	Age of Account				
Customer Name	1–30 Days	31–60 Days	61–90 Days	Over 90 Days	Total Balance
Baring Tools Co.	$20,000				$ 20,000
Calgary Pneumatic Parts Ltd.	10,000				10,000
Red Deer Pipe Corp.......		$3,000	$ 5,000		8,000
Seal Coatings, Inc.			9,000	$1,000	10,000
Other accounts*	30,000	2,000	12,000	8,000	52,000
Totals................,.................	$60,000	$5,000	$26,000	$9,000	$100,000
Estimated percent uncollectible...............	× 1%	× 2%	× 5%	× 90%	
Allowance for Uncollectible Accounts	$ 600	$ 100	$ 1,300	$8,100	$ 10,100

*Each of the "Other accounts" would appear individually.

Customers owe the company $100,000, but the company expects *not* to collect $10,100 of this amount. These amounts appear in the lower right corner of the aging schedule. Notice that the percentage uncollectible increases as a customer account gets older.

How the Aging-of-Accounts-Receivable Method Works The aging-of-accounts-receivable method tells the company what the credit balance of the allowance account needs to be—$10,100 in this case. The aging-of-accounts-receivable method works like this:

Allowance for Doubtful Accounts:	
Credit balance needed	$10,100
Unadjusted balance already in the allowance...	1,000
Adjusting entry for this amount.........................	$ 9,100

To adjust the allowance, the company makes this adjusting entry at the end of the period:

2008			
Dec. 31	Bad-Debt Expense	9,100	
	Allowance for Doubtful Accounts		9,100
	To record expense for the year ($10,100 − $1,000).		

KEY POINT

It is a common mistake to forget to include the unadjusted balance in the Allowance account when computing bad-debt expense under the aging approach. The unadjusted balance of the Allowance account represents current accounts receivable that have previously been expensed as uncollectible accounts but have not yet been written off. These doubtful accounts should *not* be included in the bad-debt expense for the current period.

After posting, the accounts are ready for reporting on the balance sheet.

Accounts Receivable		Allowance for Doubtful Accounts	
100,000			1,000
			Adj. 9,100
			10,100

Net accounts receivable, $89,900

As with the percent-of-sales method, the income statement reports the bad-debt expense.

Report accounts receivable at net realizable value ($89,900) because that is the amount the company expects to collect in cash.

Using the Percent-of-Sales and the Aging-of-Accounts-Receivable Methods Together In practice, many companies use the percent-of-sales and the aging-of-accounts-receivable methods together.

- For *interim statements* (monthly or quarterly), companies use the percent-of-sales method because it is easier to apply. The percent-of-sales method focuses on the amount of bad-debt *expense*. The adjusting entry is for the amount generated *by* the percent-of-sales method.
- At the end of the year, these companies use the aging-of-accounts-receivable method to ensure that Accounts Receivable is reported at *expected realizable value*. The aging method focuses on the amount of the receivables—the *asset*—that is uncollectible. The adjusting entry is for the amount required to bring the Allowance for Doubtful Accounts *to* the amount generated by the aging-of-accounts-receivable method.
- Using the two methods together provides good measures of both the expense and the asset. Exhibit 9–3 summarizes and compares the two methods.

EXHIBIT 9–3 Comparing the Percent-of-Sales and the Aging-of-Accounts-Receivable Methods for Estimating Uncollectibles

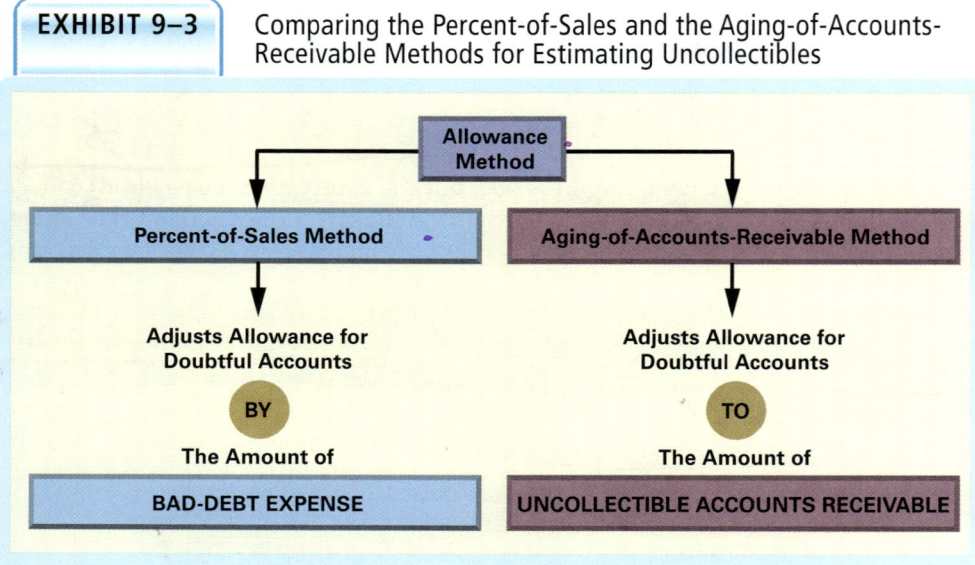

Writing Off Uncollectible Accounts

During early 2009, the company collects on most of its $100,000 accounts receivable and records the cash receipts as follows:

2009		
Jan–Mar.	Cash	80,000
	Accounts Receivable ...	80,000
	To record collections on account.	

Suppose that, after repeated attempts to collect, the company's credit department determines that it cannot collect a total of $1,200 from customers Auger ($900) and Kirsh ($300). The company then writes off the receivables of these customers:

2009			
Mar. 31	Allowance for Doubtful Accounts	1,200	
	Accounts Receivable—Auger		900
	Accounts Receivable—Kirsh.....................................		300
	To write off uncollectible accounts.		

Since Allowance for Doubtful Accounts is a contra-asset account, the write-off of uncollectible accounts has no effect on total assets, liabilities, or equity.

Assets	=	Liabilities	+	Owner's Equity
+1,200	=	0	+	0
−1,200				

The Direct Write-Off Method

As previously mentioned, there is another way to account for uncollectible receivables that is not appropriate for most companies, called the **direct write-off method.** Under the direct write-off method, the company would wait until it decides that a customer's account receivable is uncollectible. Then the company would write off the customer's account receivable by debiting Bad-Debt Expense and crediting the customer's Account Receivable, as follows (using assumed data):

2009			
Jan. 2	Bad-Debt Expense	2,000	
	Accounts Receivable—Kwan......................................		2,000
	Wrote off an uncollectible account.		

The direct write-off method is defective for two reasons:

1. It does not set up an allowance for doubtful accounts. As a result, the direct write-off method always reports the receivables at their full amount. Assets are then overstated on the balance sheet, since the business does not expect to collect the full amount of accounts receivable.

2. It does not match the bad-debt expense against revenue very well. In this example, the company made the sale to Kwan in 2008 and should have recorded the bad-debt expense during 2008. That is the only way to measure net income properly. By recording the bad-debt expense in 2009, the company overstates net income in 2008 and understates net income in 2009. Both years' net income amounts are incorrect.

The direct write-off method is acceptable only when uncollectible receivables are very low. It works for retailers, such as Roots and Wal-Mart, because those companies carry almost no receivables.

KEY POINT

The direct write-off method is easier to use, but it fails to match expenses and revenues properly. It is acceptable only if uncollectibles are immaterial in amount or if the difference between using an allowance method and the direct write-off method is immaterial.

STOP AND THINK

1. How accurately does the direct write-off method measure income?

Answer: Following generally accepted accounting principles (GAAP) means matching each period's expenses against its revenues. The direct write-off method fails this test: In our example above, the full amount of sales revenue appears for 2008, but the uncollectible-account expense incurred to generate this revenue appears in 2009. Consequently, this method gives misleading income figures for both years. The $2,000 bad-debt expense should be matched against the sales revenue for 2008.

2. How accurately does the direct write-off method value accounts receivable?

Answer: The 2008 balance sheet shows accounts receivable at the full figure, say $100,000. But any businessperson knows that uncollectible accounts are unavoidable when selling on credit. There are always a few customers who will fail to pay the amount they owe. Is $100,000, then, the expected realizable value of the accounts? No, showing the full $100,000 in the balance sheet falsely implies that the $100,000 will be collected completely.

Recovery of Accounts Previously Written Off

When an account receivable is written off as uncollectible, the customer still owes the money. However, the company may stop pursuing collection and write off the account as uncollectible.

Some companies turn delinquent receivables over to a lawyer or collection agency to help recover some of the cash. This is called *recovery of a bad account*. Let's see how to record the recovery of an account that we wrote off earlier. Recall that on March 31, 2009, the company wrote off the $900 receivable from customer Auger (see page 443). Suppose it is now October 4, 2009, and the company unexpectedly receives

$900 from Auger. To account for this recovery, the company makes two journal entries to (1) reverse the earlier write-off and (2) record the cash collection, as follows:

2009				
(1) Oct. 4	Accounts Receivable—Auger		900	
	Allowance for Doubtful Accounts			900
	Reinstated Auger's account receivable.			
2009				
(2) Oct. 4	Cash		900	
	Accounts Receivable—Auger			900
	Collected on account.			

KEY POINT

Follow through the entries to Auger's subsidiary ledger account: first the credit sale, then the write-off, then the reversal of the write-off, and finally the credit to the account when Auger pays in full. The customer's subsidiary account shows the complete credit history—an important feature of the subsidiary ledger system.

Accounts Receivable—Auger

Sale	900	900	Write-off
Reinstate	900	900	Collection

Credit-Card and Debit-Card Sales

Credit-Card Sales

Objective 4

Account for credit-card and debit-card sales

Credit-card sales are common in both traditional and online retailing. American Express, Diners Club enRoute, VISA[3] and MasterCard[4] are popular. The customer presents the credit card to pay for purchases. The credit-card company pays the seller and then bills the customer, who pays the credit-card company.

Credit cards offer the convenience of buying without having to pay the cash immediately. A VISA customer receives a monthly statement from VISA, detailing each of the customer's credit-card transactions. The customer can write one cheque to cover the total of these credit-card purchases.

Retailers also benefit from credit-card sales. They do not have to check each customer's credit rating since the credit-card company has already done so. Retailers do not have to keep accounts receivable records, and they do not have to collect cash from customers.

These benefits to the seller do not come free. The seller pays a fee to the credit-card company and, therefore, receives less than the full amount of the sale. The credit-card company takes a fee of 1 to 5 percent[5] on the sale. Suppose you and your family have lunch at The Keg. You pay the bill—$100—with a VISA card. The Keg's entry to record the $100 VISA card sale, subject to the credit-card company's (assumed) 2-percent discount, which is an *expense* to The Keg for a credit-card transaction, is

2008			
Mar. 2	Accounts Receivable—VISA	98	
	Credit-Card Discount Expense	2	
	Sales Revenue..		100
	Recorded credit-card sales.		

On collection of the cash, the Keg records the following:

2008			
Mar. 15	Cash	98	
	Accounts Receivable—VISA		98
	Collected from VISA.		

In this example, the customer pays VISA the $100 after later receiving the VISA statement, the Keg Restaurant receives $98 from VISA, and VISA keeps $2 for this transaction.

REAL WORLD EXAMPLE

Retailers offer credit-card sales to increase revenue. Not only are credit cards more convenient for the customer, but research shows that customers purchase more with credit cards than with cash only. After a credit-card sale is made, the retailer receives the amount of a sale less a fee, usually within a few days. This transaction is essentially a sale of the receivable to the credit-card company. The credit-card company usually assumes the risk of uncollectible accounts.

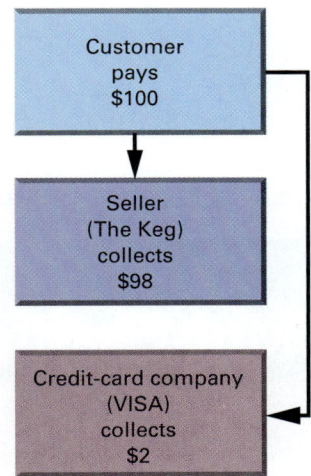

Debit-Card Sales

Debit cards are fundamentally different from credit cards. Using a *debit card* is like paying with cash, except that you don't have to carry cash or write a cheque. All

---

[3, 4]VISA and MasterCard are also known as *bank cards*.
[5]The rate varies among companies and over time.

banks issue debit cards. When a business makes a sale, the customer "swipes" her debit card through an Interac card reader and enters her personal identification number (PIN). The bank deducts the cost of the purchase from the customer's account immediately and transfers the purchase amount, less a debit-card service fee for allowing the transaction, into the business's account. For example, suppose you buy groceries at a grocery store for a total cost of $56.35. You swipe your debit card, enter your PIN, and the grocery store records the sale as follows:

Cash...	55.85	
Debit Card Service Fee...	0.50	
Sales Revenue...		56.35
To record a debit-card sale.		

Credit-Card and Debit-Card Risk Both credit cards and debit cards bear a risk for the cardholder, the issuer, and the business accepting the card. The cards can be lost, and stolen cards can be used to make purchases for which the card-issuer will not receive payment. All parties should recognize this risk when they use, issue, and accept credit and debit cards.

Credit Balances in Accounts Receivable

Occasionally, customers overpay their accounts or return merchandise for which they have already paid. The result is a credit balance in the customer's account receivable. For example, Leather and Stuff's subsidiary ledger contains 213 accounts, with balances as shown:

210	accounts with *debit* balances totalling	$185,000
3	accounts with *credit* balances totalling	2,800
	Net total of all balances...	$182,200

Leather and Stuff should not report the asset Accounts Receivable at the net amount—$182,200. Why not? The credit balance—$2,800—is a liability, even though most customers will apply an overpayment to their next purchase. Like any other liability, customer credit balances are debts of the business. A balance sheet that did not indicate this liability would be misleading. Therefore, Leather and Stuff would report on its balance sheet:

Assets		Liabilities	
Current:		Current:	
Accounts receivable	$185,000	Credit balances in	
		customer accounts	$2,800

Many companies would include this $2,800 with Other Accounts Payable.

Mid-Chapter Summary Problem for Your Review

Acadia Building Supplies is a chain of hardware and building supply stores concentrated in the Maritimes. The company's year-end balance sheet for 2008 reported:

Accounts receivable	$4,000,000
Allowance for doubtful accounts.......................................	(175,000)

Required

1. How much of the December 31, 2008, balance of accounts receivable did Acadia Building Supplies expect to collect? Stated differently, what was the expected realizable value of these receivables?

2. Journalize, without explanations, year 2009 entries for Acadia Building Supplies:

   a. Estimated Bad-Debt Expense was $140,000 for the first three quarters of the year, based on the percent-of-sales method.

   b. Write-offs of accounts receivable totalled $160,000.

   c. December 31, 2009, aging of receivables indicates that $192,000 of total receivables is uncollectible.

   Prepare a T-account for Allowance for Doubtful Accounts, as follows:

   Allowance for Doubtful Accounts

2009 Write-offs	Dec. 31, 2008 Bal. 175,000
	2009 Expense
	Bal. before Adj.
	Dec. 31, 2009 Adj.
	Dec. 31, 2009 Bal. 192,000

   Post all three transactions to the allowance account.

3. Report Acadia Building Supplies' receivables and related allowance on the December 31, 2009, balance sheet. Accounts receivable total $4,155,000.

4. What is the expected realizable value of receivables at December 31, 2009? How much is bad-debt expense for 2009?

Solution

Requirements

1. Acadia Building Supplies expected to collect $3,825,000 (i.e., $4,000,000 − $175,000).

2. a. Bad-Debt Expense 140,000
          Allowance for Doubtful Accounts 140,000

   b. Allowance for Doubtful Accounts.................................... 160,000
          Accounts Receivable 160,000

   c. Bad-Debt Expense ($192,000 − $155,000) 37,000
          Allowance for Doubtful Accounts 37,000

   Allowance for Doubtful Accounts

2009 Write-offs	160,000	Dec. 31, 2008, Bal.	175,000
		2009 Expense	140,000
		Bal. before Adj.	155,000
		Dec. 31, 2009, Adj.	37,000
		Dec. 31, 2009, Bal.	192,000

Name: Acadia Building Supplies
Industry: Building supplies retailer
Accounting Period: Years ended December 31, 2008 and 2009

The expected realizable value of receivables is the full value less the allowance for doubtful accounts.

The estimate increases both the expense and the allowance for doubtful accounts.

Write-offs reduce the allowance for doubtful accounts and accounts receivable. They do *not* affect the bad-debt expense.

First, determine the balance in Allowance for Doubtful Accounts by filling in this T-account. Add the expense amount from 2 a. and deduct the write-offs from 2 b.

The final balance in Allowance for Doubtful Accounts must be $192,000 (given in 2 c.). The balance in the T-account before the adjustment is already $155,000 (calculated above). Therefore, Bad-Debt Expense and Allowance for Doubtful Accounts must be increased by the difference of $37,000.

3. Accounts receivable $4,155,000
   Less: Allowance for doubtful accounts 192,000

4. Expected realizable value of receivables at
   December 31, 2009 ($4,155,000 – $192,000) $3,963,000
   Bad-debt expense for 2009 ($140,000 + $37,000) 177,000

Notes Receivable: An Overview

Notes receivable are more formal than accounts receivable. The debtor signs a promissory note accepting the conditions of borrowing. The note also serves as evidence of the transaction. Let's define the special terms used for notes receivable:

- **Promissory note.** A written promise to pay a specified sum of money at a particular future date.
- **Maker** of the note (**debtor**). The entity that signs the note and promises to pay the required amount; the maker of the note is the *debtor.*
- **Payee** of the note (**creditor**). The entity to whom the maker promises future payment; the payee of the note is the *creditor.*
- **Principal.** The amount lent by the payee and borrowed by the maker of the note.
- **Interest.** The revenue to the payee for lending money; interest is an expense to the debtor.
- **Interest period.** The period of time during which interest is to be computed. It extends from the original date of the note to the maturity date. Also called the **note term,** or simply the **time period.**
- **Interest rate.** The percentage rate of interest specified by the note. Interest rates are always stated for a period of one year. Therefore, a 6-percent note means that the amount of interest for *one year* is 6 percent of the note's principal amount.
- **Maturity date** (also called **due date**). The date on which final payment of the note is due.
- **Maturity value.** The sum of the principal plus interest due at maturity.

Exhibit 9–4 illustrates a promissory note. Study it carefully.

Identifying the Maturity Date of a Note

Some notes specify the maturity date, as shown in Exhibit 9–4. Other notes state the period of the note, in days or months. When the period is given in months, the note matures on the same day of the month as the date the note was issued. A six-month note dated February 16 matures on August 16.

A 120-day note dated September 14, 2008, matures on January 12, 2009, as shown below:

Month		Number of Days	Cumulative Total
Sept.	2008	16*	16
Oct.	2008	31	47
Nov.	2008	30	77
Dec.	2008	31	108
Jan.	2009	12	120

*30 − 14 = 16

EXHIBIT 9–4   A Promissory Note

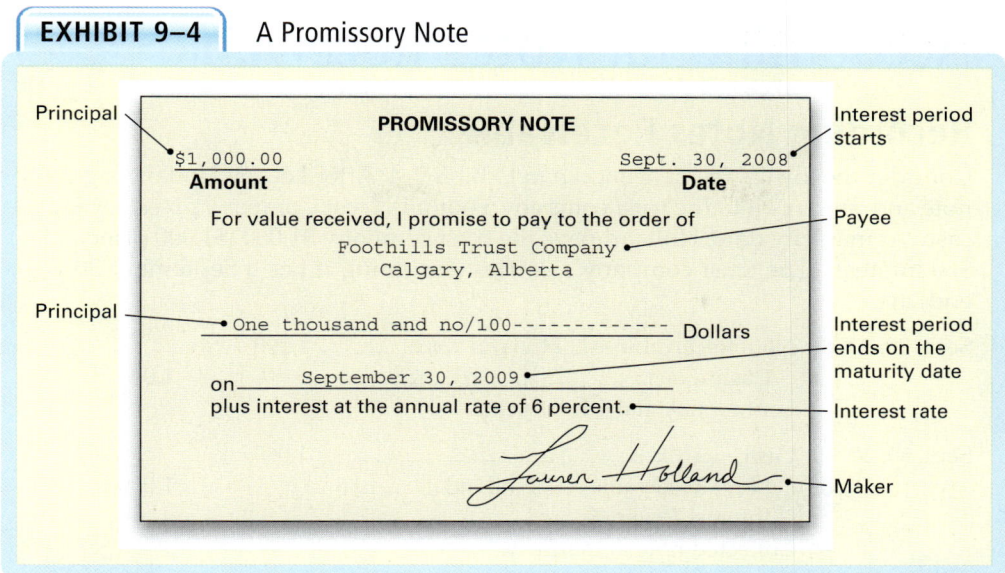

When the period is given in days, the maturity date is determined by counting the days from date of issue. The 120-day note dated September 14, 2008, would have to be *repaid* by January 12, 2009. In counting the days remaining for a note, remember to

- count the maturity date
- omit the date the note was issued

Computing Interest on a Note

The formula for computing interest is:

Here rate means interest rate and time means interest period.

Amount of Interest = Principal × Interest Rate × Time

Using the data in Exhibit 9–4, Foothills Trust Company computes its interest revenue for one year on its note receivable as:

Amount of Interest		Principal		Interest Rate		Time
$60	=	$1,000	×	0.06	×	1 (year)

The maturity value of the note is $1,060 ($1,000 principal + $60 interest). The time element is one (1) because the note's term is one year.

When the term of a note is stated in months, we compute the interest based on the 12-month year. Interest on a $2,000 note at 10 percent for three months is computed as:

Amount of Interest		Principal		Interest Rate		Time
$50	=	$2,000	×	0.10	×	$3/12$

When the interest period of a note is stated in days, we usually compute interest based on a 365-day year. The interest on a $5,000 note at 12 percent for 60 days is computed as:

Amount of Interest		Principal		Interest Rate		Time
$98.63	=	$5,000	×	0.12	×	$60/365$

Keep in mind that interest rates are stated as an annual rate. Therefore, the time in the interest formula should also be expressed in terms of a year.

Accounting for Notes Receivable

Recording Notes Receivable

Objective 5

Account for notes receivable

Consider the loan agreement shown in Exhibit 9–4. After Lauren Holland signs the note and presents it to the trust company, Foothills Trust Company gives her $1,000 cash. At maturity date, Holland pays the trust company $1,060 ($1,000 principal + $60 interest). The trust company's entries (assuming it has a September 30 year end) are

Sept. 30, 2008	Note Receivable—L. Holland	1,000	
	Cash		1,000
	Lent money at 6% for 1 year.		
Sept. 30, 2009	Cash	1,060	
	Note Receivable—L. Holland		1,000
	Interest Revenue		60
	Collected note at maturity.		
	(Interest revenue = $1,000 \times 0.06 \times 1$)		

Some companies sell merchandise in exchange for notes receivable. This arrangement occurs often when the payment term extends beyond the customary accounts receivable period, which generally ranges from 30 to 60 days as indicated by the company's credit terms of 2/10, net 30 or net 60.

Suppose that on October 20, 2008, Midland Distributors sells plumbing supplies for $15,000 to Western Builders. Western signs a 90-day promissory note at 10 percent interest. Midland's entries to record the sale and collection from Western (Midland's year end is June 30) are

REAL WORLD EXAMPLE

The journal entries for October 20, 2008, and January 18, 2009, resemble general journal entries to Accounts Receivable control and the subsidiary ledger. Very often a company will set up a subsidiary ledger for Notes Receivable in the same manner. The subsidiary ledger is especially helpful if the business has many notes receivable.

Oct. 20, 2008	Note Receivable—Western Builders	15,000	
	Sales Revenue...		15,000
	To record sale. Note at 10% for 90 days.		
Jan. 18, 2009	Cash	15,369.86	
	Note Receivable—Western Builders ..		15,000
	Interest Revenue		369.86
	To record collection at maturity.		
	($15,000 \times 0.10 \times {}^{90}/_{365}$)		

A company may accept a note receivable from a trade customer who fails to pay an account receivable. The customer signs a promissory note and gives it to the creditor.

Suppose Clifford Sales sees that it will not be able to pay off its account payable to Slingsby Supply, which is due in 15 days. Slingsby Supply may accept a 12-month, $6,000 note receivable, with 9 percent interest, from Clifford Sales on October 1, 2008. Slingsby Supply's entry is

Oct. 1, 2008	Note Receivable—Clifford Sales	6,000	
	Accounts Receivable—Clifford Sales ..		6,000
	Received a note at 9% for 12 months.		

Accruing Interest Revenue

A note receivable may be outstanding at the end of the accounting period. The interest revenue earned on the note up to the year end is part of that year's earnings. Recall that interest revenue is earned over time, not just when cash is received. We saw in Chapter 3 on page 113 that accrued revenue creates an asset for the amount that has been earned but not received.

Let's continue with the Slingsby Supply note receivable from Clifford Sales. Slingsby Supply's accounting period ends December 31.

- How much of the total interest revenue does Slingsby Supply earn in 2008 (for October, November, and December)?

$$\$6{,}000 \times 0.09 \times {}^{3}/_{12} = \$135$$

Slingsby Supply makes this adjusting entry to accrue interest revenue at December 31, 2008:

Dec. 31, 2008	Interest Receivable....................................	135	
	Interest Revenue		135
	To accrue interest revenue earned in 2008 but not yet received ($6,000 × 0.09 × ³/₁₂).		

- How much interest revenue does Slingsby Supply earn in 2009 (for January through September)?

$$\$6{,}000 \times 0.09 \times {}^{9}/_{12} = \$405$$

On the note's maturity date, Slingsby Supply makes this entry:

Sept. 30, 2009	Cash	6,540	
	Note Receivable—Clifford Sales		6,000
	Interest Receivable...............................		135
	Interest Revenue		405
	To collect note receivable on which interest has been accrued previously. Interest receivable is $135 ($6,000 × 0.09 × ³/₁₂) and interest revenue is $405 ($6,000 × 0.09 × ⁹/₁₂).		

The entries for accrued interest at December 31, 2008 and for collection in 2009 assign the correct amount of interest to each year.

A company holding a note may need cash before the note matures. A procedure for selling the note, called discounting a note receivable, appears in the Chapter 9 Appendix beginning on page 457.

Dishonoured Notes Receivable

If the maker of a note does not pay a note receivable at maturity, the maker **dishonours** or **defaults** on the note. Because the note has expired, it is no longer in force. But the debtor still owes the payee. The payee can transfer the note receivable amount to Accounts Receivable.

Suppose Whitehorse Hardware has a six-month, 10-percent note receivable for $5,000 from Northern Cabinets. On the February 3 maturity date, Northern Cabinets defaults. Whitehorse Hardware would record the default as follows:

Feb. 3	Accounts Receivable—Northern Cabinets	5,250	
	Note Receivable—Northern Cabinets		5,000
	Interest Revenue		250
	To record default on a note receivable. Accounts receivable is $5,250 [$5,000 + ($5,000 × 0.10 × ⁶/₁₂)] and interest revenue is $250 ($5,000 × 0.10 × ⁶/₁₂).		

Whitehorse Hardware would pursue collection from Northern Cabinets for this account receivable and would account for the receivable in the normal way.

Reporting Receivables on the Balance Sheet: Actual Company Reports

Let's look at how some companies report their receivables on the balance sheet. Terminology and set-up vary.

Objective **6**

Report receivables on the balance sheet

Paragraph 3020.01 in the *CICA Handbook* indicates that it is not necessary to present the allowance for doubtful accounts in the financial statements because it is assumed that an adequate allowance for doubtful accounts has been made. *Financial Reporting in Canada*, published by the CICA, indicates that only 24 percent of the 200 companies surveyed made reference, on the balance sheet or in the notes, to the allowance in 2004.[6]

One Canadian company that did provide information was Canadian National Railway Company (CN). In its 2005 annual report, CN reported the following (amounts in millions):

	December 31	
	2005	**2004**
Current assets		
Accounts receivable (note 4)	$623	$793
Notes to the Consolidated Financial Statements		
4. Accounts receivable	703	863
Provision for doubtful accounts	(80)	(70)
	$623	$793

STOP AND THINK

1. How much did customers owe CN at December 31, 2005?
2. How much did CN expect to collect at December 31, 2005?
3. How much did CN expect not to collect at December 31, 2005?

Answers:

1. $703 million ($623 million net + $80 million provision for doubtful accounts)
2. $623 million
3. $80 million

While some companies, like CN, provide information about the allowance for doubtful accounts, as was suggested above, many companies in Canada, such as Enbridge Inc., the Calgary-based energy company, and Sobey's, the food retailer, tend to show only net accounts receivable. They do not show the allowance.

Using Accounting Information for Decision Making

The balance sheet lists assets in their order of relative liquidity (closeness to cash):

- Cash comes first because it *is* the most liquid asset.
- Short-term investments (covered in a later chapter) come next because they are almost as liquid as cash. They can be sold for cash whenever the owner wishes.
- Current receivables are less liquid than short-term investments because the company must collect the receivables.
- Merchandise inventory is less liquid than receivables because the goods must first be sold.

A partial balance sheet of Winpak Ltd., the packaging company whose head office is in Winnipeg, provides an example in Exhibit 9–5.

---

[6]Byrd, C., I. Chen, and J. Smith, *Financial Reporting in Canada 2004.* Thirtieth edition (Toronto: Canadian Institute of Chartered Accountants, 2004), online edition, Chapter 19—Accounts and Notes Receivable—Analysis and Discussion.

EXHIBIT 9–5   Winpak Ltd.'s Partial Balance Sheet

WINPAK LTD.
Consolidated Balance Sheet (adapted)
As at January 1, 2006 and December 31, 2004

(thousands of U.S. dollars)	2005	2004
CURRENT ASSETS		
Cash and cash equivalents...	$ 4,942	$ 11,654
Accounts receivable	50,018	51,841
Inventories	69,889	63,802
Prepaid expenses..	1,707	1,935
Future income taxes...	3,239	2,234
	$129,795	$131,466
CURRENT LIABILITIES		
Accounts payable and accrued liabilities	$ 35,424	$ 36,348
Current portion of long-term debt	15,000	
	$ 50,424	$ 36,348

Balance-sheet data become more useful by showing the relationships among assets, liabilities, and revenues. Let's examine two important ratios.

Acid-Test (or Quick) Ratio

Owners and managers use ratios for decision making. In Chapter 4, for example, we discussed the current ratio, which indicates the ability to pay current liabilities with current assets. A more stringent measure of the ability to pay current liabilities is the **acid-test** (or **quick**) **ratio**. The acid-test ratio tells whether the entity could pay all its current liabilities if they came due immediately.

Objective 7

Use the acid-test ratio and days' sales in receivables to evaluate a company

 REAL WORLD EXAMPLE

The average acid-test ratio in the computer industry is 1.20. For auto dealers, the average is 0.20, and for restaurants, 0.40.

$$\text{Acid-test ratio} = \frac{\text{Cash + Held-for-trading investments + Net current receivables}}{\text{Total current liabilities}}$$

For Winpak Ltd. (Exhibit 9–5) (Dollar amounts in thousands)

$$\frac{\$4,942 + \$0 + 50,018}{\$50,424} = 1.09$$

The higher the acid-test ratio, the better able the business is to pay its current liabilities. Winpak's ratio was 1.09, showing good liquidity.

What is an acceptable acid-test ratio value? In general, an acid-test ratio of 1.00 is considered safe. However, the answer depends on the industry. Automobile dealers can operate smoothly with an acid-test ratio of 0.20. Several things make this possible: Car dealers have almost no current receivables. The acid-test ratio for most department stores clusters about 0.80, while travel agencies average 1.10.

STOP AND THINK

Use the data in Exhibit 9–5 to compute Winpak Ltd.'s current ratio at December 31, 2005. Then compare Winpak Ltd.'s current ratio and acid-test ratio. Why is the current ratio higher?

Answers: Current ratio $= \dfrac{\text{Total current assets}}{\text{Total current liabilities}}$

= $129,795/$50,424

= 2.57

Acid-test ratio = 1.09

The current ratio is higher because it includes all the current assets and not just cash, held-for-trading investments, and receivables.

Days' Sales in Receivables

After a business makes a credit sale, the next critical event in the business cycle is collection of the receivable. Several financial ratios centre on receivables. **Days' sales in receivables**, also called the **collection period,** indicates how many days it takes to collect the average level of receivables. The shorter the collection period, the more quickly the organization has cash to use for operations. The longer the collection period, the less cash is available to pay bills and expand. Days' sales in receivables can be computed in two steps, as follows:

1. $\text{One day's sales} = \dfrac{\text{Net sales}}{\text{365 days}}$

2. $\text{Days' sales in average accounts receivable} = \dfrac{\text{Average net accounts receivable}}{\text{One day's sales}} = \dfrac{\text{(Beginning net receivables} + \text{Ending net receivables)/2}}{\text{One day's sales}}$

For Winpak Ltd. (Exhibit 9–5) (Dollar amounts in thousands):

1. $\text{One day's sales} = \dfrac{\$436,709^{*}}{365} = \$1,196 \text{ per day}$

2. $\text{Days' sales in average accounts receivable} = \dfrac{(\$51,841 + \$50,018)/2}{\$1,196} = 43 \text{ days}$

*Taken from Winpak's 2005 income statement, not reproduced here.

On average, it takes Winpak Ltd. 43 days to collect its accounts receivable. The length of the collection period depends on the credit terms of the sale. For example, sales on net 30 terms should be collected within approximately 30 days. When there is a discount, such as 2/10, net 30, the collection period may be shorter. Terms of net 45 result in a longer collection period.

A company should watch its collection period closely. Whenever the collection period lengthens, the business must find other sources of financing, such as borrowing. During recessions, customers pay more slowly, and a longer collection period may be unavoidable.

STOP AND THINK

Can days' sales in receivables be computed in one step instead of two?

Answer: Yes. It can be calculated as: $\dfrac{\text{Average net accounts receivable}}{\text{Net sales}} \times 365$

Investors and creditors do not evaluate a company on the basis of one or two ratios. Instead they analyze all the information available. They then stand back and ask, "What is our overall impression of this company?"

As we conclude this chapter, we return to our opening questions: What are accounts receivable, and why are they important? Why are accounts receivable recorded at net realizable value? What are notes receivable, and how is interest computed on notes receivable? How are receivables reported on the balance sheet? Which ratios use receivables to evaluate a company's financial position? These questions were answered throughout this chapter. And the Decision Guidelines end this chapter with a summary that shows that accounting for receivables is the same for your own start-up business as it is for Winpak and Canadian Tire.

Decision

Guidelines

Accounts Receivable

How much of our receivables will we collect?

Less than the full amount of the receivables because we cannot collect from some customers.

How do we report receivables at their net realizable value?

1. Use the *allowance method* to account for uncollectible receivables. Set up the Allowance for Doubtful Accounts.
2. Estimate uncollectibles by the
   a. *Percent-of-sales method* (income-statement approach) (page 440)
   b. *Aging-of-accounts-receivable method* (balance-sheet approach) (page 441)
3. Write off uncollectible receivables as they prove uncollectible.
4. Net accounts receivable = Accounts Receivable − Allowance for Doubtful Accounts

Is there a simple way to account for uncollectible receivables?

Yes, but it is unacceptable for most companies. The *direct write-off method* uses no Allowance for Doubtful Accounts and thus reports receivables at their full amount. Under this method, simply debit Bad-Debt Expense and credit the customer's account. This method is acceptable only when uncollectibles are insignificant.

Notes Receivable

What two other accounts are related to notes receivable?

Notes receivable are related to:
- *Interest Revenue*
- *Interest Receivable* (interest revenue earned but not collected)

How do we compute the interest on a note receivable?

Amount of Interest = Principal × Interest Rate × Time

Receivables in General

How can we use receivables to evaluate a company's financial position?

- Acid-test ratio = $\dfrac{\text{Cash} + \dfrac{\text{Held-for-trading}}{\text{investments}} + \dfrac{\text{Net current}}{\text{receivables}}}{\text{Total current liabilities}}$

- $\dfrac{\text{Days' sales in average}}{\text{accounts receivable}} = \dfrac{\text{Average net accounts receivable}}{\text{One day's sales}}$

How do we report receivables on the balance sheet?

Accounts (or Notes) receivable	$XXX
Less: Allowance for doubtful accounts	(X)
Accounts (or notes) receivable, net	$ XX

Summary Problem for Your Review

Suppose Kroeker Distributors engaged in the following transactions:

2008

Apr.	1	Lent $20,000 to Blatchford Agencies. Received a six-month, 10-percent note.
Oct.	1	Collected the Blatchford Agencies note at maturity.
Nov.	30	Lent $15,000 to Fane Industries on a three-month, 12-percent note.
Dec.	31	Accrued interest revenue on the Fane Industries note.

2009

Feb.	28	Collected the Fane Industries note at maturity.

Kroeker Distributors' accounting period ends on December 31.

Required

Explanations are not needed.

1. Record the 2008 transactions on April 1, October 1, and November 30 on Kroecker Distributors' books.
2. Make the adjusting entry needed on December 31, 2008.
3. Record the February 28, 2009, collection of the Fane Industries note.

Name: Kroeker Distributors
Industry: Retailer
Accounting Period: Years ended December 31, 2008 and 2009

Solution

Requirement 1

The Blatchford Agencies' note receivable is for six *months*, so calculate interest based on 12 months in a year (not 365 days in a year).

2008

Apr.	1	Note Receivable—Blatchford Agencies	20,000	
		Cash..		20,000
Oct.	1	Cash..	21,000	
		Note Receivable—Blatchford Agencies		20,000
		Interest Revenue ($20,000 × 0.10 × $^6/_{12}$)....		1,000
Nov.	30	Note Receivable—Fane Industries	15,000	
		Cash..		15,000

Requirement 2

The Fane Industries' note receivable is for three *months*, so calculate accrued interest on December 31, 2008, based on 12 months in a year.

Adjusting Entry

2008

Dec.	31	Interest Receivable	150	
		Interest Revenue...		150
		Interest receivable is $150 ($15,000 × 0.12 × $^1/_{12}$).		

Requirement 3

Calculate interest based on 12 *months* in a year (not 365 days in a year)

2009

Feb.	28	Cash	15,450	
		Note Receivable—Fane Industries		15,000
		Interest Receivable		150
		Interest Revenue		300
		Interest revenue is $300 ($15,000 × 0.12 × $^2/_{12}$).		
		Cash is $15,450 [$15,000 + ($15,000 × 0.12 × $^3/_{12}$)].		

Chapter 9 Appendix

Discounting (Selling) a Note Receivable

A payee of a note receivable may need cash before the maturity date of the note. When this occurs, the payee may sell the note, a practice called **discounting a note receivable.** The price to be received for the note is determined by present-value concepts. We discuss these concepts in detail in Chapter 15. But the transaction between the seller and the buyer of the note can take any form agreeable to the two parties. Here we illustrate one procedure used for discounting short-term notes receivable. To receive cash immediately, the seller is willing to accept a lower price than the note's maturity value.

To illustrate discounting a note receivable, suppose EMCO Ltd. lent $15,000 to Dartmouth Builders on October 20, 2008. The maturity date of the 90-day, 10 percent Dartmouth note is January 18, 2009. Suppose EMCO discounts the Dartmouth Builders note at the National Bank on December 9, 2008, when the note is 50 days old. The bank applies a 12 percent annual interest rate in computing the discounted value of the note. The bank will use a discount rate that is higher than the interest rate on the note in order to earn some interest on the transaction. EMCO may be willing to accept this higher rate in order to get cash quickly. The discounted value, called the *proceeds,* is the amount EMCO receives from the bank. The proceeds can be computed in five steps, as shown in Exhibit 9–1A. At maturity the bank collects $15,370 from the maker of the note and earns $202 interest revenue from holding the note.

EMCO Ltd.'s entry to record discounting (selling) the note on December 9, 2008, is

Dec. 9, 2008	Cash..	15,168	
	Note Receivable—Dartmouth Builders		15,000
	Interest Revenue		168
	To record discounting a note receivable.		

When the proceeds from discounting a note receivable are less than the principal amount of the note, the payee records a debit to Interest Expense for the amount of the difference. For example, EMCO could discount the note receivable for cash proceeds of $14,980. The entry to record this transaction would be

Dec. 9, 2008	Cash..	14,980	
	Interest Expense	20	
	Note Receivable—Dartmouth Builders.		15,000

In the discounting of the note receivable just described, interest revenue accrued from the original date of the note (October 20, 2008) to the date of discounting (December 9, 2008). Since the amount is not material, we will recognize this fact but disregard the interest revenue in the rest of this Appendix.

Objective 8
Discount a note receivable

LEARNING TIPS

A payee who discounts a note receivable will usually have to accept less than the maturity value of the note.

REAL WORLD EXAMPLE

Just as a company can sell a note receivable, a company can also sell accounts receivable for less than full value to receive cash right away. Also, accounts receivable can be pledged as security for a loan, and this fact must be disclosed in the financial statements.

KEY POINT

The bank's discount period is the length of the note minus the days held prior to discounting.

Step	Computation	
1. Compute the original amount of interest of the note receivable.	$15,000 × 0.10 × 90/365	= $ 370
2. Maturity value of note = principal + interest	$15,000 + $370	= $15,370
3. Determine the period (number of days, months, or years) the bank will hold the note (the discount period).	Dec. 9, 2008, to Jan. 18, 2009	= 40 days
4. Compute the bank's discount on the note. This is the bank's interest revenue from holding the note.	$15,370 × 0.12 × 40/365	= $ 202
5. Seller's proceeds from discounting the note receivable* = maturity value of note − bank's discount on the note	$15,370 − $202	= $15,168

*(Buyer's cost of purchasing)
The authors thank Doug Hamilton for suggesting this exhibit.

STOP AND THINK

If a 60-day note dated April 16 is discounted on May 2, what is the discount period?

Answer: 44 days. Method: Compute the number of days the note was held prior to discounting (April 16 to May 2 is 16 days). Subtract the days held from the length of the note (60 − 16 = 44). This method eliminates the necessity of determining the maturity date and then having to count from the discount date to the maturity date.

Summary

1. **Design internal controls for receivables.** Companies that sell on credit receive most customer collections in the mail. Good *internal control* over mailed-in cash receipts means separating cash-handling duties from cash-accounting duties.

2. **Use the allowance method to account for uncollectibles, and estimate uncollectibles by the percent-of-sales and the aging-of-accounts-receivable methods.** Uncollectible receivables are accounted for by the allowance method or the direct write-off method. The *allowance method* matches expenses to sales revenue and also results in a more realistic measure of net accounts receivable. The *percent-of-sales method* and the *aging-of-accounts-receivable method* are the two main approaches to estimating bad debts under the allowance method.

3. **Explain the direct write-off method to account for uncollectibles.** The *direct write-off method* is easy to apply, but it fails to match the bad-debt expense to the corresponding sales revenue. Also, Accounts Receivable are reported at their full amount, which is misleading because it suggests that the company expects to collect all of its accounts receivable.

4. **Account for credit-card and debit-card sales.** When customers pay for their purchases using a *credit card* such as MasterCard, the credit-card company pays the vendor and collects from the customer. When a customer pays with a *debit card*, the issuer (usually a financial institution) removes the amount of the purchase from the customer's bank account and puts it into the vendor's account.

5. **Account for notes receivable.** *Notes receivable* are formal credit agreements. Interest earned by the creditor is com-

puted by multiplying the note's principal amount by the interest rate times the length of the interest period.

6. **Report receivables on the balance sheet.** All accounts receivable, notes receivable, and allowance accounts appear in the balance sheet. However, companies use various formats and terms to report these assets.

7. **Use the acid-test ratio and days' sales in receivables to evaluate a company.** The *acid-test ratio* mea-sures ability to pay current liabilities from the most liquid current assets. *Days' sales in receivables* indicates how long it takes to collect the average level of receivables.

8. **Discount a note receivable.** The payee of a note receivable will sometimes discount, or sell, the note to a bank or other third party before the maturity date of the note. One method of calculating the proceeds appears in Exhibit 9–1A on page 458.

Self-Study Questions

Test your understanding of the chapter by marking the correct answer for each of the following questions:

1. The party that holds a receivable is called the (*p. 436*)
   - a. Creditor
   - b. Debtor
   - c. Maker
   - d. Security holder

2. The function of the credit department is to (*p. 438*)
   - a. Collect accounts receivable from customers
   - b. Report bad credit risks to other companies
   - c. Evaluate customers who apply for credit
   - d. Write off uncollectible accounts receivable

3. Keady Marina made the following general journal entry related to uncollectibles:

   Bad-Debt Expense 700
      Allowance for Doubtful Accounts 700

   The purpose of this entry is to (*pp. 439–443*)
   - a. Write off uncollectibles
   - b. Close the expense account
   - c. Age the accounts receivable
   - d. Record bad-debt expense

4. Keady Marina also made this general journal entry:

   Allowance for Doubtful Accounts 1,800
      Accounts Receivable (detailed) 1,800

   The purpose of this entry is to (*p. 443*)
   - a. Write off uncollectibles
   - b. Close the expense account
   - c. Age the accounts receivable
   - d. Record bad-debt expense

5. Keady Marina also made this general journal entry:

   Accounts Receivable (detailed) 640
      Allowance for Doubtful Accounts 640

   The purpose of this entry is to (*p. 445*)
   - a. Write off uncollectibles
   - b. Close the expense account

   - c. Reverse the write-off of receivables
   - d. Record bad-debt expense

6. The credit balance in Allowance for Doubtful Accounts is $12,600 prior to the adjusting entries at the end of the period. The aging of the accounts indicates that an allowance of $81,200 is needed. The amount of expense to record is (*pp. 441–442*)
   - a. $12,600
   - b. $68,600
   - c. $81,200
   - d. $93,800

7. A critical element of internal control over cash receipts is (*p. 437*)
   - a. Assigning an honest employee the responsibility for handling cash
   - b. Separating the cash-handling and cash-accounting duties
   - c. Ensuring that cash is deposited in the bank daily
   - d. Centralizing the opening of incoming mail in a single location

8. A six-month, $40,000 note specifies interest of 8 percent. The full amount of interest on this note will be (*pp. 448–449*)
   - a. $400
   - b. $800
   - c. $1,600
   - d. $3,200

9. The note in Self-Study Question 8 was issued on August 31, and the company's accounting year ends on December 31. The year-end balance sheet will report interest receivable of (*pp. 450–451*)
   - a. $533
   - b. $1,067
   - c. $1,600
   - d. $3,200

10. The best acid-test ratio among the following is (*p. 453*)
    - a. 0.10
    - b. 0.80
    - c. 1.0
    - d. 1.2

Answers to the Self-Study Questions follow the Similar Accounting Terms.

Accounting Vocabulary

Acid-test ratio   *(p. 453)*
Aging-of-accounts-receivable method   *(p. 441)*
Allowance for Doubtful Accounts   *(p. 439)*
Allowance for Uncollectible Accounts   *(p. 439)*
Allowance method   *(p. 439)*
Bad-debt expense   *(p. 439)*
Balance-sheet approach   *(p. 441)*

Collection period   *(p. 454)*
Creditor   *(pp. 436, 448)*
Days' sales in receivables   *(p. 454)*
Debtor   *(pp. 436, 448)*
Default on a note   *(p. 451)*
Direct write-off method   *(p. 444)*
Discounting a note receivable   *(p. 457)*

Dishonour a note   (p. 451)
Doubtful-account expense   (p. 439)
Due date   (p. 448)
Income-statement approach   (p. 440)
Interest   (p. 448)
Interest period   (p. 448)
Interest rate   (p. 448)
Maker of a note   (p. 448)
Maturity date   (p. 448)
Maturity value   (p. 448)

Note term   (p. 448)
Payee of a note   (p. 448)
Percent-of-sales method   (p. 440)
Principal   (p. 448)
Promissory note   (p. 448)
Quick ratio   (p. 453)
Receivable   (p. 436)
Time period   (p. 448)
Uncollectible-account expense   (p. 439)

Similar Accounting Terms

Acid-test ratio	Quick ratio
Aging-of-accounts-receivable method (of estimating uncollectibles)	Balance-sheet approach (of estimating uncollectibles)
Allowance for Doubtful Accounts	Allowance for Uncollectible Accounts; Allowance for Bad Debts
Bad-debt expense	Uncollectible-account expense; Doubtful-account expense
Days' sales in receivables	Collection period
Dishonour a note	Default on a note
Interest period	Note period; Note term; Time
Maturity date	Due date
Percent-of-Sales Method (of estimating uncollectibles)	Income-statement approach (of estimating uncollectibles)

Answers to Self-Study Questions

1. a	4. a	7. b	10. d
2. c	5. c	8. c ($40,000 \times 0.08 \times {}^{6}/_{12} = \$1,600$)	
3. d	6. b ($81,200 - \$12,600 = \$68,600$)	9. b ($40,000 \times 0.08 \times {}^{4}/_{12} = \$1,067$)	

Assignment Material

Questions

1. Name the two parties to a receivable/payable transaction. Which party has the receivable? Which has the payable? The asset? The liability?

2. List three categories of receivables. State how each category is classified for reporting on the balance sheet.

3. Many businesses receive most of their cash on credit sales through the mail. Suppose you own a business so large that you must hire employees to handle cash receipts and perform the related accounting duties. What internal control feature should you use to ensure that cash received from customers is not taken by a dishonest employee?

4. What duty must be withheld from a company's credit department in order to safeguard cash? If the credit

department does this job, what can a dishonest credit department employee do?

5. Name the two methods of accounting for uncollectible receivables. Which method is easier to apply? Which method is consistent with generally accepted accounting principles?

6. Which of the two methods of accounting for uncollectible accounts—the allowance method or the direct write-off method—is preferable? Why?

7. Identify the accounts debited and credited to account for uncollectibles under (a) the allowance method, and (b) the direct write-off method.

8. What is another term for Allowance for Doubtful Accounts? What are two other terms for Bad-Debt Expense?

9. Which entry decreases net income under the allowance method of accounting for uncollectibles: the entry to record bad-debt expense, or the entry to write off an uncollectible account receivable?

10. Identify and briefly describe the two ways to estimate bad-debt expense and uncollectible accounts.

11. Briefly describe how a company may use both the percent-of-sales method and aging-of-accounts-receivable method to account for uncollectibles.

12. How does a credit balance arise in a customer's account receivable? How does the company report this credit balance on its balance sheet?

13. Show three ways to report Accounts Receivable of $100,000 and Allowance for Doubtful Accounts of $2,800 on the balance sheet or in the related notes.

14. What are the benefits of credit-card sales to a retailer? What is the cost to the retailer? How is the cost of a credit-card sale recorded?

15. Use the terms *maker, payee, principal, maturity date, promissory note,* and *interest* in an appropriate sentence or two describing a note receivable.

16. Name three situations in which a company might receive a note receivable. For each situation, show the account debited and the account credited to record receipt of the note.

17. For each of the following notes receivable, compute the amount of interest revenue earned during 2008:

	Principal	Interest Rate	Interest Period	Maturity Date
a. Note 1	$ 10,000	3%	60 days	Nov. 30, 2008
b. Note 2	50,000	7%	3 months	Sept. 30, 2008
c. Note 3	100,000	5%	½ year	Dec. 31, 2008
d. Note 4	15,000	9%	90 days	Jan. 15, 2009

18. When the maker of a note dishonours the note at maturity, what accounts does the payee debit and credit?

19. Why does the payee of a note receivable usually need to make adjusting entries for interest at the end of the accounting period?

20. Why is the acid-test ratio a more stringent measure of the ability to pay current liabilities than is the current ratio?

21. Which measure of days' sales in receivables is preferable, 30 or 40? Give your reason.

*22. Why would a payee sell a note receivable before its maturity date?

Starters

Starter 9–1 During its first year of operations, Spring Break Travel earned revenue of $350,000 on account. Industry experience suggests that Spring Break's bad debts will amount to 2 percent of revenues. At December 31, 2008, accounts receivable total $40,000. The company uses the allowance method to account for uncollectibles.

1. Journalize Spring Break Travel's bad-debt expense using the percent-of-sales method.
2. Show how Spring Break should report accounts receivable on its balance sheet at December 31, 2008.

Applying the allowance method (percent-of-sales) to account for uncollectibles

2. Accounts receivable, net $33,000

Starter 9–2 This exercise continues the situation of Starter 9–1, in which Spring Break Travel ended 2008 with accounts receivable of $40,000 and an allowance for doubtful accounts of $7,000.

During 2009, Spring Break Travel completed these transactions:

1. Service revenue on account, $400,000 (assume no cost of goods sold).
2. Collections on account, $420,000.
3. Write-offs of uncollectibles, $6,000.
4. Bad-debt expense, 2 percent of service revenue.

Journalize Spring Break Travel's 2009 transactions.

Applying the allowance method (percent-of-sales) to account for uncollectibles

4. Bad-debt expense, $8,000

*This Question covers Chapter 9 Appendix topics.

<table>
<tr><td>

Applying the allowance method (aging-of-accounts) to account for uncollectibles

Bad-debt expense, $200

</td><td>

Starter 9–3

</td><td>

Marble Importers Inc. had the following balances at December 31, 2008, before the year-end adjustments:

</td></tr>
</table>

Accounts Receivable		Allowance for Doubtful Accounts
74,000		2,000

The aging of accounts receivable yields these data:

	Age of Accounts Receivable		
	0–60 Days	Over 60 Days	Total Receivables
Accounts receivable	$70,000	$4,000	$74,000
Percent uncollectible	× 2%	× 20%	

1. Journalize Marble Importers Inc.'s entry to adjust the allowance account to its correct balance at December 31, 2008.

2. Prepare the T-account for Allowance for Doubtful Accounts.

<table>
<tr><td>

Applying the direct write-off method to account for uncollectibles

1. Bad-debt expense, $2,000

</td><td>

Starter 9–4

</td><td>

Diane Libbey is a lawyer in Vancouver. She uses the direct write-off method to account for uncollectible receivables.

At May 31, Libbey's accounts receivable totalled $14,000. During June, she earned revenue of $20,000 on account and collected $19,000 on account. She also wrote off uncollectible receivables of $2,000. Use the direct write-off method to

1. Journalize Libbey's write-off of the uncollectible receivables.

2. What is Libbey's balance of Accounts Receivable at June 30? Does she expect to collect all of this amount? Explain.

</td></tr>
</table>

<table>
<tr><td>

Collecting a receivable previously written off

</td><td>

Starter 9–5

</td><td>

University Cycle Shop had trouble collecting its account receivable from Lance Emmert. On January 19, University finally wrote off Emmert's $600 account receivable. University turned the account over to a lawyer, who pursued Emmert for payment for the rest of the year. On December 31, Emmert sent a $600 cheque to University Cycle Shop with a note that said, "Here's your money. Please call off your bloodhound!"

Journalize for University Cycle Shop:

Jan. 19   Write-off of Emmert's account against Allowance for Doubtful Accounts.

Dec. 31   Reinstatement of Emmert's account.

31   Collection of cash from Emmert.

</td></tr>
</table>

<table>
<tr><td>

Recording credit-card and debit-card sales

Debit cards, Cash, $7,880

</td><td>

Starter 9–6

</td><td>

Gas stations do a large volume of business by customer credit cards and debit cards. Suppose a Petro-Canada station had these transactions on a Saturday in July:

</td></tr>
</table>

VISA credit-card sales...	$10,000
Debit-card sales	8,000

Suppose VISA charges merchants 2 percent and the debit card transactions charge 1.5 percent. Record these sale transactions for the Petro-Canada station.

<table>
<tr><td>

Computing interest amounts on notes receivable

Note 1 $4,000
Note 2 $370

</td><td>

Starter 9–7

</td><td>

For each of the following notes receivable, compute the amount of interest revenue earned during 2009. Use a 365-day year where applicable, and round to the nearest dollar.

</td></tr>
</table>

	Principal	Interest Rate	Interest Period During 2009
Note 1	$100,000	8%	6 months
Note 2	15,000	12%	75 days
Note 3	10,000	9%	60 days
Note 4	50,000	10%	3 months

Starter 9–8 Royal Bank lent $100,000 to Johann Schroeder on a 90-day, 8% note. Record the following transactions for Royal Bank (explanations are not required):

a. Lending the money on May 6.
b. Collecting the principal and interest at maturity. Specify the date. For the computation of interest, use a 365-day year.

Accounting for a note receivable

b. Debit Cash $101,973

Starter 9–9 Vision Equipment, which makes VCRs, reported the following items at February 28, 2009 (amounts in thousands, with last year's—2008—amounts also given as needed):

Accounts payable	$ 449	Accounts receivable, net:	
Cash	215	February 28, 2009	$ 220
Inventories:		February 29, 2008	150
February 28, 2009	190	Cost of goods sold	1,200
February 29, 2008	160	Held-for-trading investments...	165
Net sales revenue	1,930	Other current assets	90
Long-term assets	410	Other current liabilities	145
Long-term liabilities	10		

Compute Vision Equipment's (a) acid-test ratio and (b) days' sales in average receivables for 2009. Evaluate each ratio value as strong or weak. Assume Vision Equipment sells on terms of net 30.

Using the acid-test ratio and days' sales in receivables to evaluate a company
(7)
a. 1.01
b. 35 days

Starter 9–10 Use the data in Starter 9–9 to compute the following 2009 ratios for Vision Equipment:

a. Current ratio
b. Debt ratio
c. Gross margin percentage
d. Rate of inventory turnover

Computing key ratios for a company
(7)
a. 1.48
d. 6.9 times

Exercises

Exercise 9–1

Suppose McCain Foods, the Canadian food products company, is opening a district office in Fredericton, New Brunswick. Sylvester Heath, the office manager, is designing the internal control system for the office. Heath proposes the following procedures for credit checks on new customers, sales on account, cash collections, and write-offs of uncollectible receivables:

- The credit department will run a credit check on all customers who apply for credit.

- Sales on account are the responsibility of the McCain's salespersons. Credit sales above $50,000 (which is a reasonable limit) require the approval of the sales manager.

- Cash receipts come into the credit department, which separates the cash received from the customer remittance slips. The credit department lists all cash receipts by name of customer and the amount of cash received. The cash goes to the treasurer for deposit in the bank. The remittance slips go to the accounting department for posting to individual customer accounts in the accounts receivable subsidiary ledger. Each day's listing of cash receipts goes to the controller for her end-of-day comparison with the daily deposit slip and the day's listing of the total dollar amount posted to customer accounts from the accounting department. The three amounts must agree.

- The credit department reviews customer accounts receivable monthly. Late-paying customers are notified that their accounts are past due. After 90 days, the credit department turns over past-due accounts to a lawyer or collection agency for collection. After 180 days, the credit department writes off a customer account as uncollectible.

Identify the internal control weakness in this situation, and propose a way to strengthen the controls.

Identifying and correcting an internal control weakness

Exercise 9–2

On February 28, Big Mountain Ski Equipment had a $51,000 debit balance in Accounts Receivable. During March, the company had sales of $131,000, which included $116,000 in credit sales. March collections were $106,000, and write-offs of uncollectible receivables totalled $2,500. Other data include:

a. February 28 credit balance in Allowance for Doubtful Accounts, $2,600.
b. Bad-debt expense, estimated as 2 percent of credit sales.

Using the allowance method (percent of sales) for bad debts

2. Net accounts receivable, $56,080

Required

1. Prepare journal entries to record sales, collections, bad-debt expense by the allowance method (using the percent-of-sales method), and write-offs of uncollectibles during March.
2. Prepare T-accounts to show the ending balances in Accounts Receivable and Allowance for Doubtful Accounts. Compute *net* accounts receivable at March 31. How much does Big Mountain expect to collect?

Excel Spreadsheet Template

Using the aging approach to estimate bad debts and reporting receivables on the balance sheet

2. Net accounts receivable, $288,500

Exercise 9–3

At December 31, 2008, the accounts receivable balance of Stenner's Electronics is $300,000. The allowance for doubtful accounts has a $8,900 credit balance. Accountants for Stenner's Electronics prepare the following aging schedule for its accounts receivable:

	Age of Accounts			
Accounts Receivable	**1–30 Days**	**31–60 Days**	**61–90 Days**	**Over 90 Days**
$300,000	$140,000	$80,000	$70,000	$10,000
Estimated percent uncollectible	0.5%	2.0%	6.0%	50.0%
	700	1600	4200	5000 = 11500

Required

1. Journalize the adjusting entry for doubtful accounts based on the aging schedule. Show the T-account for the allowance at December 31, 2008.
2. Show how Stenner's Electronics will report Accounts Receivable on its December 31, 2008, balance sheet.

Using the allowance method to account for uncollectibles

5. Accounts receivable, net $20,130

Exercise 9–4

Green Landscaping Services started the year 2008 with an accounts receivable balance of $19,250 and an allowance for doubtful accounts balance of $1,155. During the year, $2,145 of accounts receivable were identified as uncollectible. Sales revenue for 2008 was $214,500, including credit sales of $211,200. Cash collections on account were $206,800 during the year.

The aging of accounts receivable yields these data:

	Age of Accounts				
	0–30 Days	**31–60 Days**	**61–90 Days**	**Over 90 Days**	**Total Receivables**
Amount of receivable	$13,200	$3,300	$2,750	$2,255	$21,505
Percent uncollectible	× 1%	× 1%	× 3%	× 50%	

You're the accountant preparing the December 31, 2008, year-end entries.

Required

1. Journalize Green's (a) credit sales, (b) cash collections on account, (c) the write-off of the accounts receivable identified as uncollectible, and (d) the bad-debt expense based on 1 percent of credit sales.
2. Prepare a T-account for the Accounts Receivable and Allowance for Doubtful Accounts accounts.
3. Calculate the balance in the Allowance for Doubtful Accounts based on the aging-of-accounts-receivable method.
4. Make any adjustment required to the Allowance for Doubtful Accounts based on your calculation in Requirement 3.
5. Show how Green Landscaping Services should report accounts receivable on the balance sheet.

Sales, write-offs, and bad-debt recovery

Exercise 9–5

High Performance Cell Phones sold $20,000 of merchandise to Avery Trucking Company on account. Avery paid only $14,000 of the account receivable. After repeated attempts to collect,

High Performance finally wrote off its accounts receivable from Avery. Six months later, High Performance received Avery's cheque for $6,000 with a note apologizing for the late payment.

Journalize for High Performance Cell Phones:

a. Sale on account, $20,000. (Ignore cost of goods sold.)

b. Collection of $14,000 on account.

c. Write-off of the remaining portion of the Avery account receivable. High Performance uses the allowance method for uncollectibles.

d. Reinstatement of Avery's account receivable.

e. Collection in full from Avery, $6,000.

Exercise 9–6

Refer to the situation of Exercise 9–2.

Required

1. Record bad-debt expense for February by the direct write-off method.

2. What amount of net accounts receivable would Big Mountain Ski Equipment report on its February 28 balance sheet under the direct write-off method? Does Big Mountain Ski Equipment expect to collect this much of the receivable? Give your reason.

Using the direct write-off method for bad debts

2. Accounts receivable, ending bal. $58,500

Exercise 9–7

Return to the example of accounting for uncollectibles that begins under the heading "Writing Off Uncollectible Accounts" on page 443. Suppose past experience indicates that the company will fail to collect 2 percent of net credit sales, which totalled $150,000 during the three-month period January through March of 2009.

Record bad-debt expense for the three-month period January through March under

a. The allowance method

b. The direct write-off method (You need not identify individual customer accounts. Use the data given for Auger and Kirsh on page 443.)

Which method of accounting for uncollectibles is better? What makes this preferred method better? Mention accounting principles in your answer.

Contrasting the allowance method and the direct write-off method to account for uncollectibles

a. Bad-debt expense, $3,000

Exercise 9–8

Record the following transactions in the journal of Seaview Properties, which ends its accounting year on November 30:

Oct.	1	Lent $88,000 cash to Joe Lazarus on a one-year, 2-percent note.
Nov.	3	Sold goods to Highwater Inc., receiving a 100-day, 4-percent note for $6,325.
	16	Received a $4,400, six-month, 4-percent note on account from STM Inc.
	30	Accrued interest revenue on all notes receivable.

Recording notes receivable and accruing interest revenue

Nov. 30 Interest Revenue, $314.79

Exercise 9–9

Record the following transactions in the general journal of Joe's Plumbing Store. Assume Scotiabank charges merchants 2 percent and VISA charges 3 percent of sales as service fees.

2007		
Mar.	31	Recorded Scotiabank debit-card sales of $11,000.
	31	Recorded VISA credit-card sales of $16,500.
Apr.	1	Lent $5,500 to Sam Brown on a one-year, 4-percent note.
Dec.	31	Accrued interest revenue on the Brown note.

2008		
Apr.	1	Received the maturity value of the note from Brown.

Accounting for debit-card sales and notes receivables

Apr. 1, 2008 Cash $5,720

Exercise 9–10

Franklin Ltd., a gift store, reported the amounts on the next page in its 2008 financial statements. The 2007 figures are given for comparison.

Evaluating ratio data

1. 2008, 0.76

	2008		2007	
Current assets:				
Cash...		$ 3,000		$ 10,000
Held-for-trading investments.....		23,000		11,000
Accounts receivable	$60,000		$74,000	
Less: Allowance for uncollectibles.........................	7,000	53,000	6,000	68,000
Inventory		192,000		189,000
Prepaid insurance.........................		2,000		2,000
Total current assets...................		$273,000		$280,000
Total current liabilities		$104,000		$107,000
Net sales...		$730,000		$732,000

Required

1. Determine whether Franklin Ltd.'s acid-test ratio improved or deteriorated from 2007 to 2008. How does Franklin Ltd.'s acid-test ratio compare with the industry average of 0.90?

2. Compare the days' sales in receivables measure for 2008 with the company's credit terms of net 30. What action, if any, should Franklin Ltd. take?

Collection period for receivables

1. 25 days

Exercise 9–11

Swift Media Sign Company sells on account. Recently, Swift reported these figures:

	2009	2008
Net sales	$600,060	$570,000
Receivables at year end	42,800	38,200

Required

1. Compute Swift Media Sign Company's days' sales in average receivables for 2009.

2. Suppose Swift's normal credit terms for a sale on account are "2/10, net 30." How well does Swift's collection period compare to the company's credit terms? Is this good or bad for Swift? Explain.

Discounting a note receivable

Cash proceeds $797,071

*Exercise 9–12

Major Corporation installs switching systems and receives its pay in the form of notes receivable. It installed a system for the city of Brandon, Manitoba, receiving a nine-month, 10 percent, $800,000 note receivable on May 31, 2008. To obtain cash quickly, Major discounted the note with HSBC on June 30, 2008. The bank charged a discount rate of 11 percent.

Compute Major Corporation's cash proceeds from discounting the note. Follow the five-step procedure outlined in Exhibit 9–1A. Round to the nearest dollar.

Accounting for notes receivable, including a discounted note

June 30 Debit to Cash $797,071

*Exercise 9–13

Use your answers to Exercise 9–12 to journalize Major Corporation's transactions as follows:

May	31	Sold a telecommunications system, receiving a 9-month, 10 percent, $800,000 note from the city of Brandon. Major Corporation's cost of the system was $525,000.
June	30	Received cash for interest revenue for one month.
	30	Discounted the note to HSBC at a discount rate of 11 percent.

Accounting for notes receivable, including a discounted note

Sept. 1, 2007, Debit to Cash $1,860

*Exercise 9–14

Gander Outdoors Store sells on account. When a customer account becomes three months old, Gander Outdoors Store converts the account to a note receivable and immediately discounts the note to a bank. During 2007, Gander Outdoors Store completed these transactions:

May	29	Sold goods on account to Raj Sivak, $2,400.
Sept.	1	Received a $2,000, 60-day, 8 percent note and cash of $400 from Raj Sivak in satisfaction of his past-due account receivable.
	1	Sold the Sivak note by discounting it to a bank for proceeds of $1,860.

Required   Record the transactions in Gander Outdoors Store's journal.

*This Exercise covers Chapter 9 Appendix topics.

Challenge Exercise

Exercise 9–15

Current Fashions provides store credit and manages its own receivables. Average experience for the past three years has been:

	Cash	Credit	Total
Sales	$1,040,000	$700,000	$1,740,000
Cost of goods sold	624,000	420,000	1,044,000
Bad-debt expense	—	28,000	28,000
Other expenses	145,600	126,000	271,600

Helen Tran, the owner, is considering whether to accept debit cards (using the Interac system). Typically, the availability of debit cards increases credit sales by 15 percent. But the Interac system charges approximately 2 percent of debit-card sales. If Tran switches to debit cards, she can save $5,000 on accounting and other expenses. She figures that cash customers will continue buying in the same volume regardless of the type of credit the store offers.

Required Should Current Fashions start offering debit-card service using the Interac system? Show the computations of net income under the present plan and under the debit-card plan.

Evaluating debit-card sales for profitability

(4)

Net income with debit cards, $427,300

Beyond the Numbers

Beyond the Numbers 9–1

Pemberton Communications' cash flow statement reported the following *cash* receipts and *cash* payments (the amounts in brackets) for the year ended August 31, 2008:

Reporting receivables on the balance sheet

(6)

Accounts Receivable at Aug. 31, 2008, $505,000

PEMBERTON COMMUNICATIONS
Cash Flow Statement
For the Year Ended August 31, 2008

Cash flows from operating activities:	
Cash receipts from customers..	$3,310,000
Interest received	9,200
Cash flows from investing activities:	
Loans made on notes receivable...	(55,000)
Collection of loans on notes receivable...	110,000

Pemberton's balance sheet one year earlier—at August 31, 2007—reported Accounts Receivable of $375,000 and Notes Receivable of $83,000. Credit sales for the year ended August 31, 2008, totalled $3,440,000, and the company collects all of its accounts receivable because uncollectibles rarely occur.

Pemberton Communications needs a loan and the manager is preparing the company's balance sheet at August 31, 2008. To complete the balance sheet, the owner needs to know the balances of Accounts Receivable and Notes Receivable at August 31, 2008. Supply the needed information; T-accounts are helpful.

Ethical Issue

Easy Ed's auto showroom sells cars. Easy Ed's bank requires the company to submit quarterly financial statements in order to keep its line of credit. Notes Receivable and Accounts Receivable are 50 percent of current assets. Therefore, Bad-Debt Expense and Allowance for Doubtful Accounts are important accounts.

Easy Ed's president, Ed Edwards, likes net income to increase in a smooth pattern rather than to increase in some periods and decrease in other periods. To report smoothly increasing net income, Edwards underestimates bad-debt expense in some accounting periods. In other accounting periods, Edwards overestimates the expense. He reasons that the income overstatements roughly offset the income understatements over time.

Required Is Easy Ed's practice of smoothing income ethical? Give your reasons, mentioning any accounting principles that might be violated.

Problems (Group A)

Designing internal controls for receivables

Problem 9–1A

Lincoln Hockey distributes merchandise to sporting goods stores and hockey shops. All sales are on credit, so virtually all cash receipts arrive in the mail. Business has tripled in the last year, and the owner, Frank Lincoln, has hired an accountant to manage the financial aspect of the business. Lincoln has requested that strong internal controls over cash receipts and receivables be the first priority.

Required Assume you are Paul Bean, the new accountant. Write a memo to Frank Lincoln outlining the internal controls you intend to establish for Lincoln Hockey. Assume also that you have two employees in the accounting department and a receptionist who report to you. Use this format for your memo:

Date: _____
To: Frank Lincoln
From: Paul Bean, Accountant
RE: Proposed internal controls over cash receipts and receivables

Accounting for uncollectibles by the direct write-off and allowance methods

4. Net Accounts Receivable, allowance method $361,300

Problem 9–2A

On March 31, 2009, Summit Manufacturing had a $290,000 debit balance in Accounts Receivable. During April, the business had sales revenue of $1,050,000, which included $990,000 in credit sales. Other data for April include

a. Collections on accounts receivable, $910,000.

b. Write-offs of uncollectible receivables, $4,500.

Required

1. Record bad-debt expense for April by the direct write-off method. Use T-accounts to show all April activity in Accounts Receivable and Bad-Debt Expense.

2. Record bad-debt expense and write-offs of customer accounts for April by the allowance method. Use T-accounts to show all April activity in Accounts Receivable, Allowance for Doubtful Accounts, and Bad-Debt Expense. The March 31 unadjusted balance in Allowance for Doubtful Accounts was $1,200 (debit). Bad-debt expense was estimated at 1 percent of credit sales.

3. What amount of bad-debt expense would Summit report on its April income statement under the two methods? Which amount better matches expense with revenue? Give your reason.

4. What amount of *net* accounts receivable would Summit report on its April 30 balance sheet under the two methods? Which amount is more realistic? Give your reason.

Use the percent-of-sales and aging-of-accounts-receivable methods for uncollectibles

3. Accounts Receivable, net, 2008, $635,322

Problem 9–3A

The September 30, 2008, balance sheet of Kaslo Products reports the following:

Accounts Receivable..	$620,000
Allowance for Doubtful Accounts (credit balance)	18,000

During the last quarter of 2008, Kaslo Products completed the following selected transactions:

Dec. 30 Wrote off the following accounts receivable as uncollectible: Bert Almond, $5,000; Blocked Inc., $4,400; and Small Mall, $2,200.

31 Recorded bad-debt expense based on the aging of accounts receivable, as follows:

	Age of Accounts			
Accounts Receivable	**1–30 Days**	**31–60 Days**	**61–90 Days**	**Over 90 Days**
$657,000	$358,000	$190,000	$75,000	$34,000
Estimated percent uncollectible	0.1%	0.3%	5.0%	50.0%

358 + 570 + 3750 + 17000

= 21678

Required

1. Record the transactions in the general journal.

2. Open the Allowance for Doubtful Accounts, and post entries affecting that account. Keep a running balance.

3. Most companies report two-year comparative financial statements. If Kaslo Products' Accounts Receivable balance was $620,000 and the Allowance for Doubtful Accounts stood at $20,000 at December 31, 2007, show how the company will report its accounts receivable in a comparative balance sheet for 2008 and 2007.

Problem 9–4A

Rosehill Co. completed the following transactions during 2007 and 2008:

Using the percent-of-sales and aging-of-accounts-receivable approaches for uncollectibles

3. Accounts Receivable, net, $276,065

2007

Dec. 31 Estimated that bad-debt expense for the year was 2 percent of credit sales of $770,000 and recorded that amount as expense. *15 400*

31 Made the closing entry for bad-debt expense.

2008

Mar. 26 Sold inventory to Mabel Arnold, $12,375, on credit terms of 2/10, n/30. Ignore cost of goods sold.

Sept. 15 Wrote off Mabel Arnold's account as uncollectible after repeated efforts to collect from her.

Nov. 10 Received $3,300 from Mabel Arnold, along with a letter stating her intention to pay her debt in full within 30 days. Reinstated her account in full.

Dec. 5 Received the balance due from Mabel Arnold.

31 Made a compound entry to write off the following accounts as uncollectible: Curt Major, $4,400; Bernadette Lalonde, $1,925; Ellen Smart, $2,940.

31 Estimated that bad-debt expense for the year was 1 percent of credit sales of $980,000 and recorded the expense. *9800*

31 Made the closing entry for bad-debt expense.

Required

1. Open general ledger accounts for Allowance for Doubtful Accounts and Bad-Debt Expense. Keep running balances.

2. Record the transactions in the general journal and post to the two ledger accounts.

3. The December 31, 2008, balance of Accounts Receivable is $292,000. Show how Accounts Receivable would be reported at that date.

4. Assume that Rosehill Co. begins aging accounts receivable on December 31, 2008. The balance in Accounts Receivable is $292,000, the credit balance in Allowance for Doubtful Accounts is $15,935 (use your calculations from Requirement #3), and the company estimates that $19,800 of its accounts receivable will prove uncollectible.
   a. Make the adjusting entry for uncollectibles.
   b. Show how Accounts Receivable will be reported on the December 31, 2008, balance sheet after this adjusting entry.

Problem 9–5A

A company received the following notes during 2006:

Accounting for notes receivable, including accruing interest revenue

1. Note (a) $9,181.48
   Note (b) $24,118.36
   Note (c) $31,500.00
   Note (d) $44,800.00

Note	Date	Principal Amount	Interest Rate	Term
(a)	September 30	$18,000	4%	3 months
(b)	November 19	24,000	3%	60 days
(c)	December 1	30,000	5%	1 year
(d)	December 15	40,000	6%	2 years

Required

1. Determine the due date and maturity value of each note. Compute the interest for each note using a 365-day year. Round all interest amounts to the nearest cent.

2. Journalize a single adjusting entry at December 31, 2006, to record accrued interest revenue on the notes. An explanation is not required.

3. Journalize the collection of principal and interest on note (b). Explanations are not required.

4. Show how these notes will be reported on December 31, 2006.

Accounting for credit-card sales, notes receivable, dishonoured notes, and accrued interest revenue

Jan. 20, 2008 Debit
Cash for $9,059.18

Problem 9–6A

Record the following selected transactions in the general journal of Fraser Paper Products. Explanations are not required.

2007

Nov.	21	Received a $9,000, 60-day, 4 percent note from Mary Fisher on account.
	30	Recorded VISA credit card sales of $13,000. VISA charges 2.5 percent of sales.
Dec.	31	Made an adjusting entry to accrue interest on the Mary Fisher note.
	31	Made an adjusting entry to record bad-debt expense based on 2 percent of credit sales of $975,000.
	31	Made a compound closing entry for interest revenue and bad-debt expense (ignore credit-card sales and charges).

2008

Jan.	20	Collected the maturity value of the Mary Fisher note.
Mar.	14	Lent $5,000 cash to Morgan Supplies, receiving a six-month, 5 percent note.
	30	Received a $2,800, 30-day, 10 percent note from Marv Leech on his past-due account receivable.
May	29	Marv Leech dishonoured (failed to pay) his note at maturity; wrote off the account as uncollectible.
Sept.	14	Collected the maturity value of the Morgan Supplies note.
	30	Wrote off as uncollectible the accounts receivable of Sue Parsons, $1,625 and Mac Gally, $2,600.

Journalizing uncollectible notes receivable and accrued interest revenue

Dec. 31, 2007 Debit
Bad-Debt Expense $8,700.00

Problem 9–7A

Assume that Ponoka Tire, a large tire distributor, completed the following selected transactions:

2007

Dec.	1	Sold tires to Select Movers Inc., receiving a $40,000, six-month, 5 percent note. Ignore cost of goods sold.
	31	Made an adjusting entry to accrue interest on the Select Movers note.
	31	Made an adjusting entry to record bad-debt expense based on an aging of accounts receivable. The aging analysis indicates that $56,200 of accounts receivable will not be collected. Prior to this adjustment, the credit balance in Allowance for Doubtful Accounts is $47,500.

2008

June	1	Collected the maturity value of the Select Movers note.
	30	Sold tires for $16,000 on MasterCard. MasterCard charges 1.75 percent.
July	21	Sold merchandise to Marco Donolo, receiving a 45-day, 3 percent note for $11,200. Ignore cost of goods sold.
Sept.	4	Marco Donolo dishonoured (failed to pay) its note at maturity; converted the maturity value of the note to an account receivable.
Nov.	11	Sold merchandise to Solomon Tractor for $9,600, receiving a 120-day, 5 percent note. Ignore cost of goods sold.
Dec.	2	Collected in full from Marco Donolo.
	31	Accrued the interest on the Solomon Tractor note.

Required Record the transactions in the general journal. Explanations are not required. Round interest amounts to the nearest cent.

Problem 9–8A

The comparative financial statements of Crane River Company for 2008, 2007, and 2006 included the following selected data:

Excel Spreadsheet Template

Using ratio data to evaluate a company's financial position

(7)

For 2008:
a. 1.52
b. 0.58
c. 24 days

	2008	2007	2006
	(In thousands)		
Balance Sheet			
Current assets:			
Cash	$ 20	$ 20	$ 10
Held-for-trading investments	70	100	60
Receivables, net	190	150	120
Inventories	420	380	340
Prepaid expenses	30	30	20
Total current assets	$730	$680	$550
Total current liabilities	$480	$410	$380
Income Statement			
Sales revenue	$2,600	$2,500	$1,900

Required

1. Compute these ratios for 2008 and 2007:
   a. Current ratio
   b. Acid-test ratio
   c. Days' sales in receivables

2. Write a memo explaining to Tony Crane, owner of Crane River Company, which ratio values showed improvement from 2007 to 2008 and which ratio values deteriorated. Discuss whether this trend is favourable or unfavourable for the company.

Problem 9–9A

Temporary Personnel started business on January 1, 2007. The company produced monthly financial statements and had total sales of $250,000 (of which $200,000 was on credit) during the first four months.

On April 30, the Accounts Receivable account had a balance of $118,200 (no accounts have been written off to date), which was made up of the following accounts aged according to the date of the sale:

Using the allowance method of accounting for uncollectibles, estimating uncollectibles using the aging-of-accounts method, and reporting receivables on the balance sheet

(2) (6)

2. a. Accounts Receivable, net, May 31, $129,937

Customer:	Month of Sale:			
	January	February	March	April
Target Distributors	$ 1,800	$ 500	$ 1,000	$ 900
PG Courier	500	600	1,700	1,200
Parsons Transport	2,500	7,000	4,000	2,000
Nixon & Nixon	1,000	3,700	4,060	14,200
Other Accounts Receivable	11,880	8,180	26,740	24,740
	$17,680	$19,980	$37,500	$43,040

The following accounts receivable transactions took place in May 2007:

May	12	Decided the PG Courier account was uncollectible and wrote it off.
	15	Collected $3,300 from Target Distributors for sales made in the first three months.
	21	Decided the Parsons Transport account was uncollectible and wrote it off.
	24	Collected $1,000 from Nixon & Nixon for sales made in the month of January.
	26	Received a cheque from Parsons Transport for $9,100 plus four cheques of $1,600 each, post-dated to June 26, July 26, August 26, and September 26.
	31	Total sales in the month were $190,000; 90 percent of these were on credit, and 75 percent of the credit sales were collected in the month.

Required

1. Temporary Personnel has heard that other companies in the industry use the allowance method of accounting for uncollectibles, with many of these estimating the uncollectibles through an aging of accounts receivable. a. Journalize the adjustments that would have to be made on April 30 (for the months of January through April). b. Journalize the transactions of May 2007. c. Journalize the month-end adjustment, assuming the following estimates of uncollectibles:

Age of Accounts Receivable:	Percent Estimated to be Uncollectible:
From current month's sales..	3%
From prior month's sales..	5%
From two months prior	7%
From three months prior	20%
From four months prior...	45%
(Round your total estimate to the nearest whole dollar.)	

2. For the method of accounting for the uncollectibles used above, show
   a. The balance sheet presentation of the accounts receivable.
   b. The overall effect of the credit sales and uncollectibles on the income statement for the month of May 2007.

Problem 9–10A

Using the allowance method of accounting for uncollectibles, estimating uncollectibles by the percent-of-sales and the aging-of-accounts-receivable methods, and accounting for notes receivable

2. Debit Bad-Debt Expense, $48,960

Eastern Supply uses the allowance method in accounting for uncollectible accounts with the estimate based on the aging-of-accounts-receivable method. The company had the following account balances on August 31, 2008:

Accounts Receivable...	$687,000
Allowance for Doubtful Accounts (credit balance)	72,600

The following transactions took place during September 2008:

Sept.	2	Elbow Inc., which owes $48,000, is unable to pay on time and has given a 25-day, 8 percent note in settlement of the account.
	6	Determined the account receivable from Irma Good ($12,600) was uncollectible and wrote it off.
	9	Received notice that a customer (Tony Goad) has filed for bankruptcy. Goad owes $19,200. The courts will confirm the amount recoverable at a later date.
	11	Determined the account receivable from Kay Walsh ($9,120) was uncollectible and wrote it off.
	15	Irma Good, whose account was written off on September 6, has paid $9,000 on the account and promises to pay the balance in 30 days.
	18	Received a cheque from the courts in the amount of $15,000 as final settlement of Tony Goad's account.
	27	Elbow Inc. paid the note received on September 2.
	27	Determined the account receivable for Dave Campbell ($5,040) was uncollectible and wrote it off.
	30	Sales for the month totalled $720,000 (of which 85 percent were on credit) and collections on account totalled $601,200.
	30	Eastern Supply did an aging of accounts receivable that indicated that $75,000 is expected to be uncollectible. The company recorded the appropriate adjustment.

Required

1. Record the above transactions in the general journal.
2. What would be the adjusting entry required on September 30 if the company used the percent-of-sales method with an estimate of uncollectibles equal to 8 percent of credit sales?
3. Which of the two methods of estimating uncollectible accounts would normally be more accurate? Why?

*Problem 9–11A

A company received the following notes during 2008. The notes were discounted on the dates and at the rates indicated.

Note	Date	Principal Amount	Interest Rate	Term	Date Discounted	Discount Rate
(a)	June 15	$20,000	8%	3 months	July 15	12%
(b)	Aug. 1	9,000	10%	90 days	Aug. 27	12%
(c)	Nov. 21	12,000	15%	90 days	Dec. 4	15%

Required

Identify each note by letter, compute interest using a 365-day year for all notes, round all interest amounts to the nearest cent, and present entries in general journal form. Explanations are not required.

1. Determine the due date and maturity value of each note.
2. Determine the discount and proceeds from the sale (discounting) of each note.
3. Journalize the discounting of notes (a) and (b).

Problems (Group B)

Problem 9–1B

North York Laboratories provides laboratory testing for samples that veterinarians send in. All work is performed on account, with regular monthly billing to participating veterinarians. Pete Wilson, accountant for North York Laboratories, receives and opens the mail. Company procedure requires him to separate customer cheques from the remittance slips, which list the amounts he posts as credits to customer accounts receivable in the subsidiary ledger. Wilson deposits the cheques in the bank. He computes each day's total amount posted to customer accounts and makes sure that this total agrees with the bank deposit slip. This is intended to ensure that all receipts are deposited in the bank. Wilson does all customer credit checks, authorizes customer credit limits, and deals with all customer inquiries.

Required As the auditor of North York Laboratories, write a memo to the owners evaluating the company's internal controls over accounts receivable. If the system is effective, identify its strong features. If the system has flaws, propose a way to strengthen the controls.

Problem 9–2B

On June 30, 2007, Alberta Wireless had a $1,013,100 debit balance in Accounts Receivable. During July, the company had sales revenue of $1,430,000, which included $1,415,700 in credit sales. Other data for July include:

a. Collections of accounts receivable, $1,099,945.
b. Write-offs of uncollectible receivables, $23,815.

Required

1. Record bad-debt expense for July by the direct write-off method. Use T-accounts to show all July activity in Accounts Receivable and Bad-Debt Expense.
2. Record bad-debt expense and write-offs of customer accounts for July by the allowance method. Use T-accounts to show all July activity in Accounts Receivable, Allowance for Doubtful Accounts, and Bad-Debt Expense. The June 30 unadjusted balance in Allowance for Doubtful Accounts was $15,950 (credit). Bad-debt expense was estimated at 1 percent of credit sales.
3. What amount of bad-debt expense would Alberta Wireless report on its July income statement under the two methods? Which amount better matches expense with revenue? Give your reason.
4. What amount of *net* accounts receivable would Alberta Wireless report on its July 31 balance sheet under the two methods? Which amount is more realistic? Give your reason.

---

*This Problem covers Chapter 9 Appendix topics.

Using the percent-of-sales and
aging-of-accounts-receivable
methods for uncollectibles

3. Accounts Receivable, net,
2008, $326,720

Problem 9–3B

The November 30, 2008, balance sheet of Sage Company reports the following:

Accounts Receivable...	$358,000
Allowance for Doubtful Accounts (credit balance)	7,700

At the end of each quarter, Sage estimates bad-debt expense to be 2 percent of credit sales. At the end of the year, the company ages its accounts receivable and adjusts the balance in Allowance for Doubtful Accounts to correspond to the aging schedule. During the last month of 2008, Sage completes the following selected transactions:

Dec. 9   Made a compound entry to write off the following uncollectible accounts: M. Yang, $710; Tory Ltd., $315; and S. Roberts, $1,050.

      18   Wrote off as uncollectible the $1,360 account receivable from Acme Ltd. and the $790 account receivable from Data Services.

      31   Recorded bad-debt expense based on credit sales of $420,000.

      31   Recorded bad-debt expense based on the following summary of the aging of accounts receivable.

	Age of Accounts			
Accounts Receivable	**1–30 Days**	**31–60 Days**	**61–90 Days**	**Over 90 Days**
$341,900	$188,400	$78,500	$40,500	$34,500
Estimated percent uncollectible	0.15%	0.5%	6.0%	35.0%

Required

1. Record the transactions in the general journal.

2. Open the Allowance for Doubtful Accounts, and post entries affecting that account. Keep a running balance.

3. Most companies report two-year comparative financial statements. If Sage Company's Accounts Receivable balance was $299,500 and the Allowance for Doubtful Accounts stood at $9,975 on December 31, 2007, show how the company will report its accounts receivable on a comparative balance sheet for 2008 and 2007.

Using the percent-of-sales and
aging-of-accounts methods for
uncollectibles

3. Accounts Receivable, net,
$491,185

Problem 9–4B

Select Clothing completed the following selected transactions during 2007 and 2008:

2007

Dec. 31   Estimated that bad-debt expense for the year was 1 percent of credit sales of $748,000 and recorded that amount as expense.

      31   Made the closing entry for bad-debt expense.

2008

Feb. 17   Sold inventory to Bruce Jones, $1,412, on credit terms of 2/10, n/30. Ignore the cost of goods sold.

July 29   Wrote off Bruce Jones' account as uncollectible after repeated efforts to collect from the customer.

Sep. 6   Received $1,150 from Bruce Jones, along with a letter stating his intention to pay his debt in full within 45 days. Reinstated the account in full.

Oct. 21   Received the balance due from Bruce Jones.

Dec. 31   Made a compound entry to write off the following accounts as uncollectible: Sean Rooney, $1,610; Sargent Ltd., $3,075; and Linda Lod, $1,580.

      31   Estimated that bad-debt expense for the year was 1 percent of credit sales of $860,000 and recorded the expense.

      31   Made the closing entry for bad-debt expense.

Required

1. Open general ledger accounts for Allowance for Doubtful Accounts and Bad-Debt Expense. Keep running balances.

2. Record the transactions in the general journal and post to the two ledger accounts.

3. The December 31, 2008, balance of Accounts Receivable is $501,000. Show how Accounts Receivable would be reported at that date.

4. Assume that Select Clothing begins aging its accounts on December 31, 2008. The balance in Accounts Receivable is $501,000; the credit balance in Allowance for Doubtful Accounts is $9,815; and the company estimates that $16,100 of its accounts receivable will prove uncollectible.
   a. Make the adjusting entry for uncollectibles.
   b. Show how Accounts Receivable will be reported on the December 31, 2008, balance sheet.

Problem 9–5B

Accounting for notes receivable, including accruing interest revenue

Instaloan issued the following notes during 2008.

Note	Date	Principal Amount	Interest Rate	Term
(a)	October 31	$33,000	6%	6 months
(b)	November 10	12,000	4%	60 days
(c)	December 5	30,000	7%	1 year

1. Note (a) $33,987.29;
   Note (b) $12,078.40;
   Note (c) $32,100.00

Required

1. Determine the due date and maturity value of each note. Compute the interest for each note using a 365-day year. Round all interest amounts to the nearest cent.

2. Journalize a single adjusting entry at December 31, 2008, to record accrued interest revenue on all three notes. An explanation is not required.

3. Journalize the collection of principal and interest on note (b). Explanations are not required.

4. Show how these notes will be reported on December 31, 2008.

Problem 9–6B

Accounting for debit-card sales, notes receivable, dishonoured notes, and accrued interest revenue

Record the following selected transactions in the general journal of Quick Couriers. Explanations are not required.

2008
Dec. 12   Received a $5,775, 90-day, 8 percent note from Jacques Alard to settle his $5,775 account receivable balance.

      31   Made an adjusting entry to accrue interest on the Alard note. 114

      31   Made an adjusting entry to record bad-debt expense in the amount of 2.5 percent of credit sales of $288,200.

      31   Recorded $88,000 of debit-card sales. The Royal Bank debit-card service fee is 1.75 percent.

      31   Made a compound closing entry for sales revenue, interest revenue, bad-debt expense, and debit-card service fees.

Mar 12, 2009 Debit Cash for $5,888.92

2009
Mar. 12   Collected the maturity value of the Alard note.
June 1   Lent $16,500 cash to Mercury Inc., receiving a six-month, 7 percent note.
Oct. 31   Received a $3,025, 60-day, 8 percent note from Jim Keller on his past-due account receivable.
Dec. 1   Collected the maturity value of the Mercury Inc. note.
      30   Jim Keller dishonoured (failed to pay) his note at maturity; wrote off the receivable as uncollectible, debiting Allowance for Doubtful Accounts.
      31   Wrote off as uncollectible the account receivable of Art Pierce, $853 and John Grey, $623.

Problem 9–7B

Journalizing credit-card sales, uncollectibles, notes receivable, and accrued interest revenue

Mercury Food Products completed the following selected transactions:

2007
Nov. 1   Sold goods to Buy Low Foods, receiving a $300,000, six-month, 5 percent note. Ignore cost of goods sold.
Dec. 5   Recorded VISA credit-card sale of $30,000. VISA charges a 2.5 percent fee.
      31   Made an adjusting entry to accrue interest on the Buy Low note.
      31   Made an adjusting entry to record bad-debt expense based on an aging of accounts receivable. The aging analysis indicates that $174,000 of accounts receivable will not be collected. Prior to this adjustment, the credit balance in Allowance for Doubtful Accounts is $150,000.

Dec. 31, 2007 Debit Bad-Debt Expense $24,000.00

2008
May	1	Collected the maturity value of the Buy Low note.
	15	Received a 60-day, 8 percent, $7,200 note from Sherwood Market on account.
June	23	Sold merchandise to Delta Foods, receiving a 30-day, 7 percent note for $18,000. Ignore cost of goods sold.
July	14	Collected the maturity value of the Sherwood Market note.
	23	Delta Foods dishonoured (failed to pay) its note at maturity; converted the maturity value of the note to an account receivable.
Nov.	16	Lent $15,600 cash to Urban Provisions, receiving a 120-day, 9 percent note.
Dec.	5	Collected in full from Delta Foods.
	31	Accrued the interest on the Urban Provisions note.

Required   Record the transactions in the general journal. Explanations are not required.

Excel Spreadsheet Template

Using ratio data to evaluate a company's financial position

(7)

1. For 2008:
   a. 1.59
   b. 0.88
   c. 17 days

Problem 9–8B

The comparative financial statements of West Heights for 2008, 2007, and 2006 included the selected data shown below.

	2008	2007	2006
	(In millions)		
Balance Sheet			
Current assets:			
Cash	$ 90	$ 80	$ 60
Held-for-trading investments	140	170	126
Receivables, net	280	260	244
Inventories	360	340	300
Prepaid expenses	50	20	40
Total current assets	$920	$870	$770
Total current liabilities	$580	$600	$660
Income statement			
Sales revenue	$5,840	$5,110	$4,200

Required

1. Compute these ratios for 2008 and 2007:
   a. Current ratio
   b. Acid-test ratio
   c. Days' sales in receivables

2. Write a memo explaining to Jack Dodds, owner of West Heights, which ratio values showed improvement from 2007 to 2008, and which ratio values showed deterioration. Discuss whether this factor conveys a favourable or an unfavourable impression about the company.

Using the allowance method of accounting for uncollectibles, estimating uncollectibles using the aging-of-accounts-receivable method, and reporting receivables on the balance sheet

2. a. Accounts Receivable, net, July 31, 2007, $221,624

Problem 9–9B

Airdrie Services Inc. started business on March 1, 2007. The company produces monthly financial statements and had total sales of $600,000 (of which $570,000 were on credit) during the first four months.

On June 30, the Accounts Receivable account had a balance of $210,000 (no accounts have been written off to date), which was made up of the following accounts aged according to the date of the provision of services:

	Month of Service:			
Customer	March	April	May	June
Torrance Trucks	$ 2,520	$ 1,200	$ 1,800	$ 1,440
Milloy Ltd.	1,500	1,140	1,632	4,344
Marsha Wayne	6,876	4,464	9,168	7,908
Mort Black	6,408	3,468	12,624	15,912
Other Accounts Receivable	14,760	23,916	31,380	57,540
	$32,064	$34,188	$56,604	$87,144

The following accounts receivable transactions took place in July 2007:

July	12	Determined the account of Milloy Ltd. was uncollectible and wrote it off.
	15	Collected $4,200 from Torrance Trucks for services in the first three months.
	21	Decided the account of Marsha Wayne was uncollectible and wrote it off.
	24	Collected $6,408 from Mort Black for services in the month of March.
	26	Received a cheque from Marsha Wayne for $9,600 plus two cheques, of $9,408 each, post-dated to September 10 and November 10.
	31	Total sales of service in the month were $162,000; 90 percent of these were on credit and 60 percent of the credit sales were collected in the month.

Required

1. Airdrie Services Inc. has heard that other companies in the industry use the allowance method of accounting for uncollectibles, with many of these estimating the uncollectibles through an aging of accounts receivable. a. Journalize the adjustments that would have to be made on June 30 (for the months of March through June). b. Journalize the transactions of July 2007. c. Journalize the month-end adjustment, assuming the following estimates of uncollectibles:

Age of Accounts Receivable	Estimated Percent to Be Uncollectible
From current month's sales of service	1%
From prior month's sales of service	3%
From two months prior	7%
From three months prior..	20%
From four months prior	35%
(Round your total estimate to the nearest whole dollar.)	

2. For the method of accounting for the uncollectibles used above, show
   a. the balance sheet presentation of the accounts receivable.
   b. the overall effect of the credit sales and uncollectibles on the income statement for July 2007.

Problem 9–10B

Barrie Supplies uses the allowance method in accounting for uncollectible accounts with the estimate based on an aging of accounts receivable. The company had the following account balances on September 30, 2008:

Accounts Receivable..	$498,000
Allowance for Doubtful Accounts (credit balance)	56,000

The following transactions took place during the month of October 2008:

Oct.	2	Albert Morrison, who owes $51,000, is unable to pay on time and has given a 20-day, 8 percent note in settlement of the account.
	6	Determined the account receivable for Donald Timble ($16,500) was uncollectible and wrote it off.
	9	Received notice that a customer (Will Wong) has filed for bankruptcy. Wong owes $35,000. The courts will confirm the amount recoverable at a later date.
	11	Determined the account receivable for Susan Knight ($7,200) was uncollectible and wrote it off.
	15	Donald Timble, whose account was written off on October 6, paid $11,000 on his account and promises to pay the balance in 60 days.
	18	Received a cheque from the courts in the amount of $23,000 as final settlement of Will Wong's account.
	22	Albert Morrison paid the note received on October 2.
	25	Determined the account receivable for Donald Purcell ($8,200) was uncollectible and wrote it off.
	31	Sales for the month totalled $743,000 (of which 95 percent were on credit) and collections on account totalled $520,000.
	31	Barrie Supplies did an aging of accounts receivable that indicated that $60,000 is expected to be uncollectible. The company recorded the appropriate adjustment.

Using the allowance method of accounting for uncollectibles, estimating uncollectibles by the percent-of-sales and the aging-of-accounts-receivable methods, and accounting for notes receivable

2. Debit Bad-Debt Expense $14,117

Required

1. Record the above transactions in the general journal.

2. What would be the adjusting entry required on October 31 if the company used the percent-of-sales method with an estimate of uncollectibles equal to 2 percent of credit sales?

3. Which of the two methods of estimating uncollectible accounts would normally be more accurate? Why?

Discounting notes receivable

2. Proceeds from discounting:
   Note (a) $10,208.68
   Note (b) $8,982.40
   Note (c) $8,041.72

*Problem 9–11B

A company received the following notes during 2008. The notes were discounted on the dates and at the rates indicated.

Note	Date	Principal Amount	Interest Rate	Term	Date Discounted	Discount Rate
(a)	Aug. 18	$10,000	11%	6 months	Nov. 18	13%
(b)	July 15	9,000	10%	90 days	July 26	12%
(c)	Sept. 1	8,000	10%	180 days	Nov. 2	13%

Required

Identify each note by letter, compute interest using a 365-day year for each note, round all interest amounts to the nearest cent, and present entries in general journal form. Explanations are not required.

1. Determine the due date and maturity value of each note.

2. Determine the discount and proceeds from the sale (discounting) of each note.

3. Journalize the discounting of notes (a) and (b).

Challenge Problems

Understanding accounts receivable management

Problem 9–1C

Kitchener Builders Supply is a six-store chain of retail stores selling home renovation materials and supplies mainly on credit; the company has its own credit card and does not accept other cards. Kitchener Builders Supply had a tendency to institute policies that conflicted with each other. Management rarely became aware of these conflicts until they became serious.

Recently, the owner, Angela Kim, who has been reading all the latest management texts, has instituted a new bonus plan. All managers are to be paid bonuses based on the success of their department. For example, for George Tatulis, the sales manager, his bonus is based on how much he can increase sales. For Sonia Petrov, the credit manager, her bonus is based on reducing the bad-debt expense.

Required Describe the conflict that the bonus plan has created for the sales manager and the credit manager. How might the conflict be resolved?

Explaining days' sales in accounts receivable

Problem 9–2C

Days' sales in receivables is a good measure of a company's ability to collect the amounts owing to it. You have owned shares in Locking Office Equipment Ltd. for some years and follow the company's progress by reading the annual report. You noticed the most recent report indicated that the days' sales in receivables had increased over the previous year, and you are concerned.

Required Suggest reasons that may have resulted in the increase in the number of days' sales in receivables.

---

*This Problem covers Chapter 9 Appendix topics.

Extending Your Knowledge

Decision Problems

Decision Problem 1

Otto Jacina Advertising has always used the direct write-off method to account for uncol-lectibles. The company's revenues, bad-debt write-offs, and year-end receivables for the most recent year follow.

Year	Revenues	Write-Offs	Receivables at Year End
2008	$187,000	$3,300	$44,000

Otto Jacina is applying for a bank loan, and the loan officer requires figures based on the allowance method of accounting for bad debts. Jacina estimates that bad debts run about 4 percent of revenues each year.

Required

Otto Jacina must give the banker the following information:

1. How much more or less would net income be for 2008 if Jacina were to use the allowance method for bad debts?
2. How much of the receivables balance at the end of 2008 does Jacina expect to collect?

Compute these amounts, and then explain for Otto Jacina why net income is more or less for 2008 using the allowance method versus the direct write-off method for uncollectibles.

Comparing allowance and direct write-off methods for uncollectibles

2. $36,520

Decision Problem 2

Garneau Camping Products sells its products either for cash or on notes receivable that earn interest. The business uses the direct write-off method to account for uncollectible accounts. Rae Garneau, the owner, has prepared Garneau Camping Products' financial statements. The most recent comparative income statements, for 2008 and 2007, are as follows:

	2008	2007
Total revenue	$528,000	$468,000
Total expenses	282,600	252,000
Net income	$245,400	$216,000

Based on the increase in net income, Garneau seeks to expand her operations. She asks you to invest $60,000 in the business. You and Garneau have several meetings, at which you learn that notes receivable from customers were $120,000 at the end of 2007, and $540,000 at the end of 2008. Also, total revenues for 2008 and 2007 include interest at 12 percent on the year's ending notes receivable balance. Total expenses include bad-debt expense of $7,200 each year, based on the direct write-off basis. Garneau estimates that bad-debt expense would be 4 percent of sales revenue if the allowance method were used.

Uncollectible accounts and evaluating a business

1. 2008 net income $234,072

Required

1. Prepare for Garneau Camping Products a comparative single-step income statement that identifies sales revenue, interest revenue, bad-debt expense, and other expenses, all com-puted in accordance with generally accepted accounting principles.
2. Is Garneau Camping Products' future as promising as Garneau's income statement makes it appear? Give the reason for your answer.

Financial Statement Cases

Accounts receivable and related uncollectibles

2. 2005, 74.8 days

Financial Statement Case 1

Answer the following questions using the financial statements for CHUM Limited in Appendix A at the end of this book.

1. Analyze the Accounts Receivable account at August 31, 2005. What is the total receivable? What was the total receivable at August 31, 2004?

2. Calculate the days' sales in ending accounts receivable at August 31, 2005 and 2004. Comment on the results.

3. Companies sometimes pledge accounts as security when they borrow money. Did CHUM Limited use its receivables in this way?

Accounts receivable and related uncollectibles

2. 2005, 38.6 days

Financial Statement Case 2

Answer the following questions using the financial statements for Sun-Rype Products Ltd. in Appendix B at the end of this book.

1. Analyze the Accounts Receivable accounts at December 31, 2005. What is the total receivable? What was the total receivable at December 31, 2004?

2. How many days' sales are in Accounts Receivable at December 31, 2005? How does this compare to the number of days' sales of the previous year?

3. What factors would cause a change in the numbers of days' sales that you calculated in question 2?

Capital Assets and Intangibles

Have you ever taken a flight on a commercial airline—Air Canada, WestJet, or CanJet? These companies have some of the most interesting assets in the world—airplanes.

How long can a commercial airplane keep flying safely and efficiently? Some airlines like to use a Boeing 737 for a long time, sometimes 20 years, because that delays spending cash to buy new planes. WestJet's fleet of Next Generation aircraft have an average age of 2.1 years and are 30% more fuel efficient than its previous 200-series aircraft.[1] Top managers of the airlines try to strike a balance between getting the most use from a plane and using one that consumes less fuel.

How do the airlines account for the use of an airplane? They record amortization over the plane's useful life. Managers also have to consider how much they can sell a plane for when it's taken out of service. The airlines don't amortize this residual value because they get it back when they sell a plane.

This chapter covers these and other matters about capital assets. **Capital assets** include the long-term tangible assets that a business uses to operate, such as airplanes for WestJet, copy equipment for Kinko's and automobiles for Discount Car Rental. Capital assets also include **intangibles**, those assets with no physical form, such as trademarks and copyrights. The chapter also shows how to account for natural resources such as oil and timber.

---

[1] WestJet April 21, 2006, press release filed online at SEDAR.com, accessed April 28, 2006.

What are capital assets, and why are they important?
Should you capitalize or expense costs associated with a new asset and with an existing asset?
What is amortization, and how can amortization expense be calculated?
How is amortization reported on the income statement and the balance sheet?
Can a company use different amortization methods for accounting and income-tax purposes?

These questions and others will be answered throughout this chapter. And the Decision Guidelines at the end of this chapter will provide the answers in a useful summary.

Capital assets have some special characteristics. For example, you hold them for uses in the business—not to sell as inventory. Also,

- Capital assets are relatively expensive, and their cost can be a challenge to determine.
- Capital assets last a long time—usually for several years. If capital assets wear out or become obsolete, you need to amortize them.
- Capital assets may be sold or traded in. Accounting for the disposal of a capital asset is more complicated than selling inventory.

Capital assets pose some accounting challenges. This chapter addresses these issues and shows how to account for

1. Tangible capital assets, which are useful because of their physical characteristics
2. Intangible assets, which have no physical form.

Chapter 10 concludes our coverage of assets, except for long-term investments. After completing this chapter, you should understand the various assets of a business and how to account for them.

Capital assets have their own terminology. Exhibit 10–1 shows which expense or loss applies to each category of capital asset.

Measuring the Cost of a Tangible Capital Asset (Property, Plant, and Equipment)

Objective ①

Measure the cost of a tangible capital asset

KEY POINT

Long-lived assets are classified as capital assets. They are often called property, plant, and equipment, or long-term assets.

The *cost principle* directs a business to carry an asset on the balance sheet at its cost— the amount paid for the asset, or the market value if the asset is transferred into the business. The general rule for measuring cost (repeated from Chapter 6) is

$$\text{The cost of an asset} = \frac{\text{The sum of all the costs incurred to bring the}}{\text{asset to its intended purpose, net of all discounts}}$$

The *cost of a tangible capital asset*, such as *property, plant, and equipment*, is the purchase price plus taxes plus purchase commissions, and all other *necessary* costs incurred to ready the asset for its intended use. In Chapter 6, we applied this

EXHIBIT 10–1 Capital Assets and Their Related Expenses

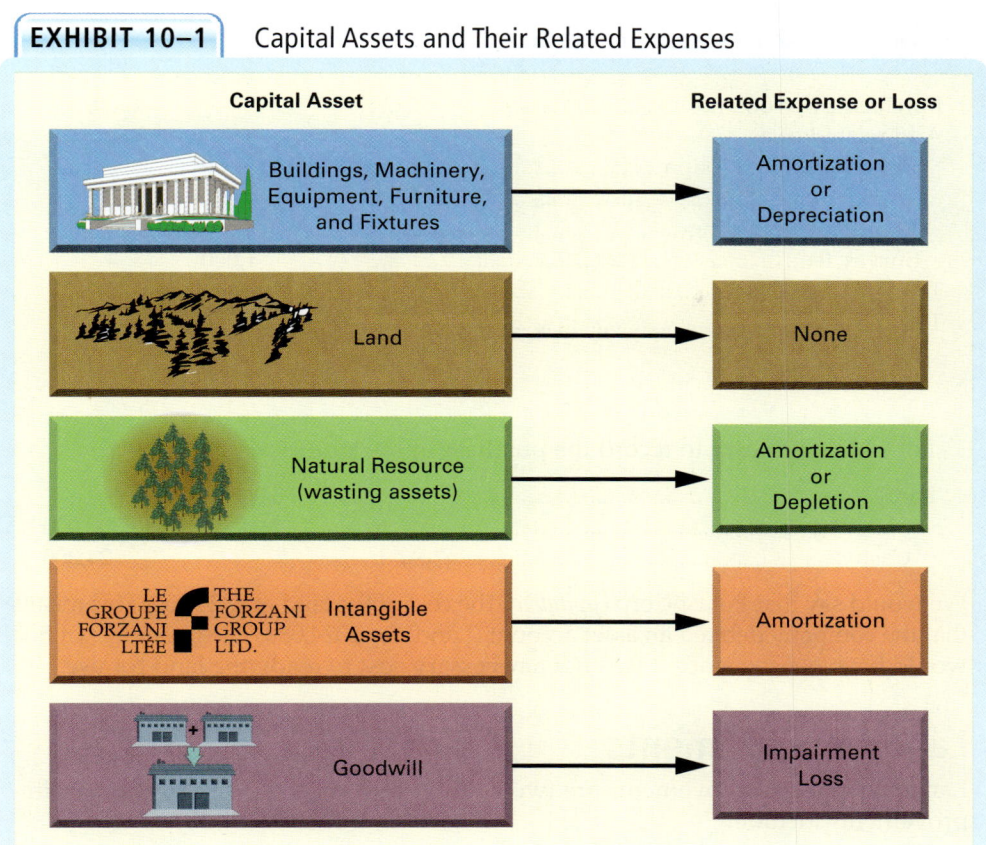

principle to determine the cost of inventory. These costs vary, so we discuss each asset individually.

Land

The cost of land includes the following costs paid by the purchaser:

- purchase price
- brokerage commission
- survey and legal fees
- any property taxes in arrears
- cost for grading and clearing the land, and for demolishing or removing any unwanted buildings.

The cost of land is not amortized.

The cost of land does *not* include the cost of

- fencing
- paving
- sprinkler systems
- lighting

These separate capital assets—called *land improvements*—are subject to amortization.

Suppose the Potash Corporation of Saskatchewan Inc. (PotashCorp) signs a $300,000 note payable to purchase 100 hectares of land. The company also pays $10,000 in brokerage commission, $8,000 in transfer taxes, $5,000 for removal of an old building, a tree removal fine of $200, and a $1,000 survey fee. What is the cost of this land? Exhibit 10–2 shows that all the *necessary* costs incurred to bring the land to its intended use are part of the land's cost.

KEY POINT

Land is not amortized because it does not wear out as do buildings and equipment.

LEARNING TIPS

The cost of an asset includes all costs *necessary* to ready the asset for its intended use; "cost" will even include amounts not yet paid in cash, such as a note payable on the asset.

EXHIBIT 10–2	Measuring the Cost of Land

Purchase price of land		$300,000
Add related costs:		
Brokerage commission	$10,000	
Transfer taxes..	8,000	
Removal of building..	5,000	
Survey fee..	1,000	
Total incidental costs		24,000
Total cost of land		$324,000

PotashCorp's entry to record the purchase of the land is:

Land	324,000	
Note Payable..		300,000
Cash		24,000

We would say that PotashCorp *capitalized* the cost of the land at $324,000. This means that the company debited an asset account (Land) for $324,000. The tree-removal fine would be expensed since it was not a necessary cost to ready the land for use.

Land Improvements

Land and Land Improvements are two entirely separate asset accounts. Land improvements include

- lighting
- signs
- fences
- paving
- sprinkler systems
- landscaping.

These costs are debited to the Land Improvements account and then amortized over their useful lives. It could be argued that decorative items such as trees and shrubs should be classified as land, since they would not decline in value. The accountant would need to use professional judgement to determine the proper classification.

Suppose PotashCorp spent $26,000 for the construction of fences around the land it had purchased above. The entry to record the expenditure is:

Land Improvements	26,000	
Cash		26,000

The fences are a land improvement, and their cost will be amortized over the useful life of the fences.

Buildings

The cost of constructing a building includes

- architectural fees
- building permits
- contractors' charges
- payments for materials, labour, and overhead.

The time to complete a new building can be many months, even years, and the separate expenditures can be numerous. If the company constructs its own assets, the cost of the building may include the cost of interest on money borrowed to finance the construction.

When an existing building is purchased, its cost includes all the usual items (but not GST), plus all the costs to repair and renovate the building for its intended use.

Machinery and Equipment

The cost of machinery and equipment includes

- purchase price (less any discounts)
- transportation charges
- insurance while in transit
- provincial sales tax (PST)
- purchase commission
- installation costs
- cost of testing the asset before it is used.

After the asset is set up, we cease capitalizing these costs to the Machinery and Equipment account. Thereafter, insurance, taxes, and maintenance costs are recorded as expenses.

There are many different types of equipment. WestJet has baggage-handling equipment and planes, Kinko's has copy equipment, and Purolator has delivery trucks.

The goods and services tax (GST) paid on the purchase of an asset is recoverable if the acquired asset is used to earn income. Therefore, it would not be part of the capitalized cost of the asset. For example, a computer purchased for $2,000 in Ontario would incur PST of 8 percent ($160.00) and GST of 6% ($120.00) for a total cost of $2,280.00. Assuming the computer was to be used to earn revenue, the cost of the asset would be $2,160.00, not $2,280.00, since the GST would be recovered from Canada Revenue Agency (CRA).

Furniture and Fixtures

Furniture and fixtures include desks, chairs, filing cabinets, and display racks. The cost of furniture and fixtures includes the basic cost of the asset (less any discounts), plus all other necessary costs to ready the asset for use. As was indicated above for machinery and equipment, GST is recoverable from CRA. All companies have furniture and fixtures, but they are most important to service organizations and retail businesses.

Leasehold Improvements

Leasehold improvements are similar to land improvements. *Leasehold improvements* are alterations to assets the company is leasing. For example, suppose TELUS Communications Inc., the telephone company, leases some of its vehicles. The company also customizes some of these vehicles to meet its special needs. For example, TELUS may paint its logo on a rental truck and install special racks on the truck. These improvements are assets of TELUS even though the company does not own the truck. The cost of improvements to leased assets appears on the company's balance sheet as *leasehold improvements*. The cost of leasehold improvements should be amortized over the term of the lease including the renewal option or the useful life of the leased asset, whichever is shorter.

THINKING IT OVER

Which of the following would you include in the cost of machinery:
(1) installation charges;
(2) testing of the machine;
(3) repair to machinery necessitated by installer's error;
(4) first-year maintenance cost?

A: Include 1 and 2, but not 3 or 4.

Construction in Progress and Capital Leases

Construction in Progress *Construction in progress* is an asset, such as a warehouse, that the company is constructing for its own use. Suppose, on the balance sheet date, the construction is incomplete and the building is not ready for use. The construction costs would still be shown as assets because the company expects the building, when completed, to render future benefits for the company.

Capital Leases A *capital lease* is an arrangement where a capital asset is acquired by making regular periodic payments that are required by the lease contract. Companies report assets leased through capital leases on the balance sheet the same way as purchased assets. Why? Because their lease payments secure the use of the asset over the term of the lease. For example, WestJet has long-term capital leases running until 2010.

A capital lease is different from an operating lease, which is an ordinary rental agreement, such as an apartment lease or the rental of a Budget automobile or a photocopier. The lessee (the renter) records operating lease payments as Rent Expense or Lease Expense.

Capitalizing the Cost of Interest

IPSCO Inc. constructs some of its capital assets itself and contracts with others to construct other capital assets. Often the construction is financed with borrowed money, on which IPSCO Inc. must pay interest. The *CICA Handbook* Section 3061, "Property, Plant and Equipment," permits a company to include interest costs up to the date the asset goes into service as part of the cost of the asset. The practice of including interest as part of an asset's cost is called *capitalizing interest*. To **capitalize a cost** means to debit an asset (versus an expense) account.

Capitalizing interest cost is an exception to the normal practice of recording interest as an expense. Ordinarily, a company that borrows money records interest expense. But on assets that the business builds for its own use, or has built, the company should, if it chooses, capitalize some of its interest cost. The reason is this: Suppose IPSCO Inc. contracts Argo Construction Co. to build a building for it. The price of the building will include Argo's interest cost that was incurred to finance the construction. Since self-constructed assets and assets that are paid for during construction should be treated as equivalent assets, it makes sense to capitalize any interest incurred to finance the construction.

A Lump-Sum (or Basket) Purchase of Assets

A company may pay a single price for several assets purchased as a group—a "basket purchase." For example, Halifax–Dartmouth Bridge Commission may pay one price for land and an office building. But for accounting purposes, Halifax–Dartmouth Bridge Commission must identify the cost of each asset as shown in the diagram at left. The total cost (100%) is divided among the assets according to their relative sales values. This allocation technique is called the *relative-sales-value method*.

Suppose High Liner Foods Incorporated, the seafood and pasta company located in Nova Scotia, purchases land and a building in Lunenberg to be used as a warehouse. The combined purchase price of the land and building is $270,000. An appraisal indicates that the land's market (sales) value is $100,000 and the building's market (sales) value is $200,000.

First, calculate the ratio of each asset's market value to the total market value of both assets combined. Total appraised value is $100,000 + $200,000 = $300,000. Thus, the land, valued at $100,000, is $1/_3$, or 33 percent, of the total market value. The building's appraised value is $2/_3$, or 67 percent of the total. The cost of each asset is determined as follows:

Total price of
land and a building

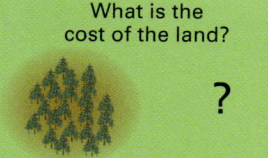

+

$270,000

What is the
cost of the land?

?

What is the
cost of the building?

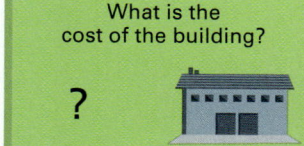

?

Asset	Market (Sales) Value	Percentage of Total Value		Total Purchase Price		Cost of Each Asset
Land	$100,000	$100,000 ÷ $300,000 = $1/3$	×	$270,000	=	$ 90,000
Building	$200,000	$200,000 ÷ $300,000 = $2/3$	×	$270,000	=	$180,000
Total	$300,000					$270,000

KEY POINT

It does not matter what the seller claims each asset is worth or what the book value is on the seller's books. The market (sales) value is determined by appraisal or some other objective method.

Suppose High Liner pays cash. The entry to record the purchase of the land and building is

Land	90,000	
Building	180,000	
Cash		270,000

STOP AND THINK

How would Tim Hortons divide a $120,000 lump-sum purchase price for land, building, and equipment with estimated market values of $60,000, $94,000, and $6,000, respectively? Round decimals to two places.

Answer:

Asset	Market (Sales) Value	Percentage of Total Value						Total Purchase Price		Cost of Each Asset
Land	$ 60,000	$60,000/$160,000	=	37.50%	×	$120,000	=	$ 45,000
Building	94,000	$94,000/$160,000	=	58.75%	×	120,000	=	70,500
Equipment....	6,000	$ 6,000/$160,000	=	3.75%	×	120,000	=	4,500
Total..............	$160,000			100.00%				$120,000

Betterments versus Repairs

When a company spends money on a capital asset it already owns, it must decide whether to debit an asset account for *betterments* or an expense account for *repairs*. Examples of these expenditures range from replacing the windshield on an Airways Limo Co. automobile in Toronto to adding an extension to a building at Big Rock Brewery in Alberta.

REAL WORLD EXAMPLE

Without the relative-sales-value method of allocating costs for tax purposes, the tendency would be to record higher estimates of the cost of equipment (which is amortized the fastest) and lower estimates of the cost of land (which is not amortized) resulting in the greatest amortization expense and the lowest income taxes early in the life of the assets. Just the opposite reasoning might apply for financial reporting purposes.

LEARNING TIPS

A capital expenditure causes the asset's cost to increase, which necessitates a revision of amortization.

Betterments are debited to an asset account because they

- Increase the capacity or efficiency of the asset, or
- Extend its useful life.

For example, the cost of a major overhaul that extends an Airways Limo automobile's useful life is a betterment. The amount of the expenditure, said to be *capitalized*, is a debit to the asset account Automobile.

Repairs, such as maintenance expenses and truck-repair expenses, do not extend the asset's capacity or efficiency but merely maintain the asset in working order. These expenses are matched against revenue. Examples include the following costs incurred after a period of use: repainting a Big Rock Brewery truck, repairing a dented fender, and replacing tires. These costs are debited to Repair Expense.

The distinction between betterments and repairs requires judgement. Does the cost extend the life of the asset (a betterment), or does it only maintain the asset in good order (a repair)? The other factor to consider is the materiality principle. Most companies have a minimum dollar limit for betterments. For example, a $400 betterment to a truck would be expensed if the company had a $500 minimum dollar limit for betterments.

Exhibit 10–3 illustrates the distinction between betterments (capital expenditures) and repairs (expenses) for several delivery truck expenditures.

EXHIBIT 10–3   Delivery Truck Expenditures—Betterment or Repair?

Betterment: Debit an Asset Account	Repair: Debit Repair and Maintenance Expense
Betterments 　Major engine overhaul 　Modification of truck for new use 　Addition to storage capacity of truck	**Repairs** 　Repair of transmission or other mechanism 　Oil change, lubrication, and so on 　Replacement tires or windshield 　Paint job

Treating a betterment as a repair, or vice versa, creates an accounting error. Suppose a company incurs the cost of a betterment to enhance the service potential of equipment and expenses this cost. This is an accounting error because the cost should have been debited to an asset. This error

• Overstates expenses

• Understates net income.

On the balance sheet, the equipment account is understated.

Capitalizing an expense creates the opposite error. Expenses are understated and net income is overstated. And the balance sheet overstates assets.

Measuring Capital Asset Amortization

As we have seen previously, **amortization**, defined in Section 3061 of the *CICA Handbook*, is the allocation of a capital asset's cost less salvage value or residual value to expense over its useful life. Another term used in the United States to describe the allocation of the cost when referring to capital assets such as property, plant, and equipment is *depreciation*. Amortization matches the asset's cost (expense) against the revenue earned by the asset (see Chapter 3, page 104, for a discussion of the matching principle). Exhibit 10–4 shows this process for the purchase of a Boeing 757 jet by Air Canada. The primary purpose of amortization accounting is to measure income. Of less importance is the need to account for the asset's decline in usefulness.

EXHIBIT 10–4   Amortization and the Matching of Expense to Revenue

Annual revenue, $10 million

Annual amortization expense, $2 million

Suppose AirCanada buys a Boeing 757 jet. Air Canada believes it will get ten years of service from the plane. Using the straight-line amortization method, Air Canada expenses one-tenth of the asset's cost in each of its ten years of use.

Let's contrast what amortization *is* with what it *is not*.

1. *Amortization is not a process of valuation.* Businesses do not record amortization based on the market (sales) value of their capital assets; they use their actual cost.

2. *Amortization does not mean that the business sets aside cash to replace assets as they become fully amortized.* Amortization has nothing to do with establishing a cash fund for the replacement of assets.

Causes of Amortization

All assets except land wear out. For some tangible capital assets, physical *wear and tear* creates the need to amortize their value. For example, physical factors wear out the jets that Air Canada, WestJet, and CanJet fly. The same is true of Zellers' store fixtures.

Assets such as computers and software, and airplanes may become *obsolete* before they wear out. An asset is obsolete when another asset can do the job more efficiently. Thus an asset's useful life may be shorter than its physical life. Accountants usually amortize computers over a short period of time—perhaps two to four years—even though they know the computers can be used much longer. In all cases, the asset's cost is amortized over its expected useful life.

Measuring Amortization

Amortization for a capital asset is based on three factors about the asset:

1. Cost
2. Estimated useful life
3. Estimated residual value

The asset's cost is known. The other two factors must be estimated.

Estimated useful life is the length of the service period expected from the asset. Useful life may be expressed in years, units of output, kilometres, or other measures. For example, a building's useful life is stated in years, a bookbinding machine's in the number of books the machine can bind, and a delivery truck's in kilometres.

Estimated residual value—also called **salvage value**—is the asset's expected cash value at the end of its useful life. **Scrap value** is the asset's value at the end of its physical life. For example, a business may believe that a machine's useful life (and physical life) will be seven years. After that time, the company expects to sell the machine as scrap metal. The expected cash receipt is the machine's residual value. Estimated residual value is *not* amortized, because the business expects to receive this amount when the machine is sold. If there is no residual value, then the company amortizes the full cost of the asset. Cost minus residual value is called **amortizable cost**.

Of the factors entering the computation of amortization, only one factor is known—cost. The other two factors—useful life and residual value—must be estimated. Amortization, then, is an estimated amount.

Amortization Methods

Three methods are used widely in Canada for computing amortization:

- straight-line
- units-of-production
- declining-balance

KEY POINT

While the exact cost of the asset is known, the useful life and residual value must be estimated. It is important that these estimates be as accurate as possible, because they have an impact on the amount of net income in each period that the asset is used.

KEY POINT

Note that the residual value is the portion of the asset's cost that will *not* be consumed or used; therefore it should *not* be amortized.

KEY POINT

The total amount of amortization recorded for an asset cannot exceed its amortizable cost. An asset can be used after it is fully amortized.

Objective 2
Calculate and account for amortization

KEY POINT

It is impossible to quantify the exact amount of the useful life of an asset that has been used up during the period, but there is no doubt that a portion of the asset has been consumed. An estimate of the amount must be made using one of the amortization methods. Without this expense, there would be no *matching* of the cost of the asset with the revenues generated during the time the asset is used.

The declining-balance method is one of two *accelerated* amortization methods, so-called because they expense greater amounts of amortization near the start of a capital asset's life and lesser amounts towards the end. The other accelerated method is sum-of-the-year's digits; it is little used in Canada and will not be discussed in this text. The three methods listed allocate different amounts of amortization expense to each period, but they all result in the same total amortization over the life of the asset. Exhibit 10–5 presents the data we will use to illustrate amortization for a Canadian Tire delivery truck. We cover the three most widely used methods.

EXHIBIT 10–5 Data for Recording Amortization for a Truck

Data Item	Amount
Cost of truck	$55,000
Estimated residual value	5,000
Amortizable cost	$50,000
Estimated useful life	
Years	5 years
Units of production	400,000 units (kilometres)

Straight-Line Method The **straight-line method** allocates an equal amount of amortization to each year of asset use. Amortizable cost is divided by useful life in years to determine annual amortization. The equation for straight-line amortization, applied to the Canadian Tire delivery truck data from Exhibit 10–5, is

LEARNING TIPS

The formula for the straight-line rate is: 1/useful life. If an asset has a 5-year useful life, then 1/5 of the asset is amortized each year. The straight-line rate is 1/5, or 20%.

$$\textbf{Straight-line amortization} = \frac{\textbf{Cost} - \textbf{Residual value}}{\textbf{Useful life in years}}$$

$$= \frac{\$55{,}000 - \$5{,}000}{5}$$

$$= \$10{,}000 \text{ per year}$$

The entry to record each year's amortization is

Amortization Expense	10,000	
Accumulated Amortization—Delivery Truck		10,000

Assume that this truck was purchased on January 1, 2007, and the business's fiscal year ends on December 31. A *straight-line amortization schedule* is presented in Exhibit 10–6. The final column of Exhibit 10–6 shows the asset's *book value*, which is cost less accumulated amortization. We introduced book value in Chapter 3.

EXHIBIT 10–6 Straight-Line Amortization for a Truck

		Amortization for the Year							
Date	Asset Cost	*Amortization Rate*		*Amortizable Cost*		*Amortization Amount*	Accumulated Amortization	Asset Book Value
1-1-2007	$55,000							$55,000
31-12-2007		1/5	×	$50,000	=	$10,000	$10,000	45,000
31-12-2008		1/5	×	50,000	=	10,000	20,000	35,000
31-12-2009		1/5	×	50,000	=	10,000	30,000	25,000
31-12-2010		1/5	×	50,000	=	10,000	40,000	15,000
31-12-2011		1/5	×	50,000	=	10,000	50,000	5,000

As an asset is used, accumulated amortization increases and the asset's book value decreases. See the Accumulated Amortization and the Asset Book Value columns in Exhibit 10–6. An asset's final book value is its *residual value* ($5,000 in Exhibit 10–6). At the end of its useful life, the asset is said to be *fully amortized*.

STOP AND THINK

1. An asset that cost $10,000 and has a useful life of four years and a residual value of $2,000 was purchased on January 1. What was the straight-line amortization for the first year? For the second year? For the fourth year?

2. What are some advantages of using the straight-line method?

Answers:

1.

$$\text{Amortization} = \frac{\text{Cost} - \text{Residual value}}{\text{Useful life, in years}} = \frac{\$10,000 - \$2,000}{4 \text{ years}} = \$2,000 \text{ per year}$$

2. It is easy to calculate, and it smoothes net income over the life of the asset because amortization is constant from year to year.

Units-of-Production (UOP) Method   The **units-of-production method** allocates a fixed amount of amortization to each unit of output produced by the asset. The equation for the units-of-production method, applied to the Exhibit 10–5 data, is

$$\frac{\text{Units-of-production amortization}}{\text{per unit of output}} = \frac{\text{Cost} - \text{Residual Value}}{\text{Useful life, in units of production}}$$

$$= \frac{\$55,000 - \$5,000}{400,000 \text{ kilometres}}$$

$$= \$0.125 \text{ per kilometre}$$

This truck is driven 90,000 kilometres the first year, 120,000 the second, 100,000 the third, 60,000 the fourth, and 30,000 the fifth. The amount of units-of-production (UOP) amortization per period varies with the number of units the asset produces. Exhibit 10–7 shows the UOP amortization schedule for this asset.

EXHIBIT 10–7   Units-of-Production Amortization for a Truck

		Amortization for the Year				
Date	Asset Cost	Amortization Per Unit	Number of Units	Amortization Amount	Accumulated Amortization	Asset Book Value
1-1-2007	$55,000					$55,000
31-12-2007		$0.125 ×	90,000 =	$11,250	$11,250	43,750
31-12-2008		0.125 ×	120,000 =	15,000	26,250	28,750
31-12-2009		0.125 ×	100,000 =	12,500	38,750	16,250
31-12-2010		0.125 ×	60,000 =	7,500	46,250	8,750
31-12-2011		0.125 ×	30,000 =	3,750	50,000	5,000

Double-Declining-Balance (DDB) Method The **double-declining-balance (DDB) method** involves computing annual amortization by multiplying the asset's book value by a constant percentage, which is two times (double) the straight-line amortization rate. DDB rates are computed as follows:

1. Compute the straight-line amortization rate per year. For example, the truck—100% ÷ 5 years = 20% per year.

2. Multiply the straight-line rate by 2. For the truck example, the DDB rate is 20% × 2 = 40%. To do the calculation in one step, compute 2 ÷ Useful life in years, express the result as a fraction or a percent, and multiply by the book value at the beginning of the period.

3. Compute the year's DDB amortization. Multiply the asset's book value (cost less accumulated amortization) at the beginning of the year by the DDB rate. Ignore residual value except for the last year. The first year's amortization for the truck in Exhibit 10–5 is

$$\substack{\text{Double-declining-balance} \\ \text{amortization for the first year}} = \substack{\text{Asset book value} \\ \text{at the beginning} \\ \text{of the period}} \times \substack{\text{Double-declining-} \\ \text{balance rate}}$$

$$= \qquad \$55,000 \qquad \times \qquad 0.40$$

$$= \$22,000$$

The same approach is used to compute DDB amortization for all later years, except for the final year.

The final year's amortization is the amount needed to reduce the asset's book value to its residual value. In the DDB amortization schedule in Exhibit 10–8, the fifth and final year's amortization is $2,128—the $7,128 book value less the $5,000 residual value.

The DDB method differs from the other methods in two ways:

1. Residual value is ignored initially. In the first year, amortization is calculated on the asset's full cost.

2. Final-year amortization is the amount needed to bring the asset's book value to the residual value. It is a "plug" figure.

KEY POINT

With declining-balance amortization, the asset's book value will rarely equal its residual value in the final year. Amortization expense in the final year is a "plug" figure, the amount that will reduce the asset's book value to the residual value.

EXHIBIT 10–8 | Double-Declining-Balance Amortization for a Truck

		Amortization for the Year				Asset
Date	Asset Cost	Double-Declining-Balance Rate	Asset Book Value	Amortization Amount	Accumulated Amortization	Book Value
1-1-2007	$55,000					$55,000
31-12-2007		0.40 ×	$55,000 =	$22,000	$22,000	33,000
31-12-2008		0.40 ×	33,000 =	13,200	35,200	19,800
31-12-2009		0.40 ×	19,800 =	7,920	43,120	11,880
31-12-2010		0.40 ×	11,880 =	4,752	47,872	7,128
31-12-2011				2,128*	50,000	5,000

*Amortization in 2011 is the amount needed to reduce asset's book value to the residual value of $5,000 ($7,128 − $5,000 = $2,128).

STOP AND THINK

What is the DDB amortization for each year for the asset in the Stop & Think on page 491?

Answer:

$$\text{DDB rate} = \frac{100}{4} \times 2 = 50\%, \text{ or } \frac{2}{4} = 50\%$$

Yr. 1: $5,000 ($10,000 × 50%)
Yr. 2: $2,500 [($10,000 − $5,000 = $5,000); $5,000 × 50%]
Yr. 3: $500 [($5,000 − $2,500 = $2,500); $2,500 − $2,000*]
Yr. 4: $0*

*Asset cost is not amortized below residual value.

LEARNING TIPS

Students sometimes confuse the double-declining-balance formula with other methods. Rather than use amortizable cost (as other methods do), the formula for double-declining balance is *book value* × double-declining-balance rate. (The book value in the first year is its original cost.)

KEY POINT

The double-declining-balance method is an accelerated amortization method. An accelerated method expenses more asset cost in the early years of an asset's life than in the later years. This method assumes that an asset is more useful (productive) in its early years and therefore should be amortized more then.

Comparing Amortization Methods

Let's compare the three methods we've just discussed. Annual amounts vary by method but the total is $50,000 for all methods.

	Amount of Amortization per Year		
Year	Straight-Line	Units-of- Production	Double-Declining-Balance
2007	$10,000	$11,250	$22,000
2008	10,000	15,000	13,200
2009	10,000	12,500	7,920
2010	10,000	7,500	4,752
2011	10,000	3,750	2,128
Total	$50,000	$50,000	$50,000

Which method is best? That depends on the asset. A business should match an asset's expense against the revenue that the asset produces.

Straight-line method For a capital asset that generates revenue fairly evenly over time, the straight-line method follows the matching principle. During each period the asset is used, an equal amount of amortization is recored.

Units-of-production method The units-of production method best fits an asset that wears out because of physical use, rather than obsolescence. Amortization is recorded only when the asset is used, and more use leads to greater amortization.

Double-declining-balance method The double-declining-balance or accelerated method works best for assets that produce more revenue in their early years. The greater expense recorded in the early periods matches best against those periods' greater revenue.

Comparisons Exhibit 10–9 graphs the relationship between annual amortization amounts for the three methods.

EXHIBIT 10–9   Amortization Patterns for the Various Methods

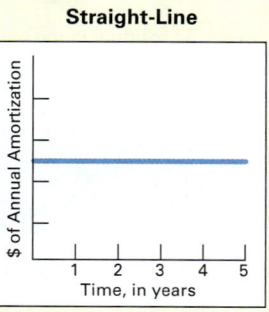
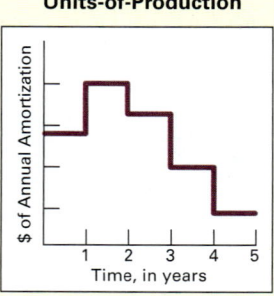
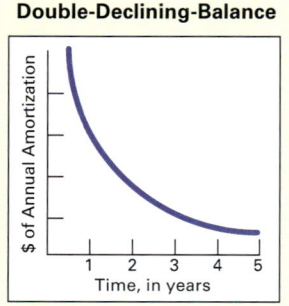

- The graph of straight-line amortization is flat because annual amortization is the same amount in each period.
- Units-of-production amortization follows no particular pattern because annual amortization varies depending on the use of the asset.
- DDB amortization is greatest in the first year and less in the later years.

A recent survey indicated that for companies using a single amortization method, 94 percent use straight-line. For companies using more than one method, the most popular combination was the straight-line and units-of-production methods, used by 43 percent of companies.[2] For example, ATCO Ltd., the conglomerate based in Calgary, uses straight-line, while WestJet uses straight-line for most capital assets and units of production for its aircraft.

STOP AND THINK

On January 1, 2007, Armstrong Marketing Co. purchased, for $15,000, equipment that had an expected 4-year life and $3,000 residual value. Through an accounting error, Armstrong expensed the entire cost of the equipment at the time of purchase. What is the effect (overstated, understated, or correctly stated) on (1) total assets, and (2) net income in 2007 to 2010?

Answer: Total assets will be understated each year. Net income will be understated in 2007 by $15,000 and net income will be overstated each year by the amount of the amortization that should have been recorded [($15,000–$3,000) ÷ 4] = $3,000.

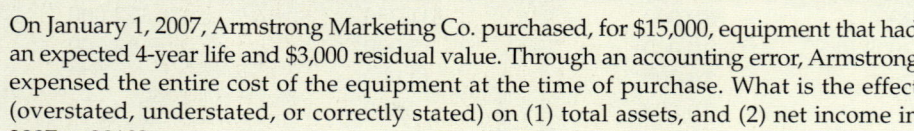

	Total Assets	Net Income		Total Assets	Net Income
2007	$12,000 U	$12,000 U	2009	$ 6,000 U	$ 3,000 O
2008	$ 9,000 U	$ 3,000 O	2010	$ 3,000 U	$ 3,000 O

[2] Byrd, C., I. Chen, and J. Smith, *Financial Reporting in Canada, 2004,* Thirtieth edition. (Toronto: Canadian Institute of Chartered Accountants, 2004), online edition, Chapter 25—Property, Plant and Equipment—Analysis and Discussion.

Mid-Chapter Summary Problem for Your Review

Ventura Industrial Products purchased equipment on January 2, 2007, for $44,000. The expected life of the equipment is ten years or 100,000 units of production, and its residual value is $4,000. Using three amortization methods, the annual amortization expense and total accumulated amortization at the end of 2007 and 2008 are:

	Method A		Method B		Method C	
Year	Annual Amortization Expense	Accumulated Amortization	Annual Amortization Expense	Accumulated Amortization	Annual Amortization Expense	Accumulated Amortization
2007	$4,000	$4,000	$8,800	$ 8,800	$1,200	$1,200
2008	4,000	8,000	7,040	15,840	5,600	6,800

Required

1. Identify the amortization method used in each instance, and show the equation and computation for each. (Round off to the nearest dollar.)

2. Assume continued use of the same method through the year 2009. Determine the annual amortization expense, accumulated amortization, and book value of the equipment for 2007 through 2009 under each method, assuming 12,000 units of production in 2009.

Name: Ventura Industrial Products
Industry: Industrial products producer
Accounting Period: Years ended December 31, 2007, 2008, and 2009

Solution

Requirement 1

One approach is to look for patterns in the annual amortization expenses for each method, then check your guesses by calculating the expenses using the data given. Equal annual expenses indicate the straight-line method. A random pattern indicates the units-of-production method. Declining annual expenses indicate the double-declining-balance method.

Calculating the number of units for 2007 and 2008 is not necessary, but it helps you prepare for the calculation you'll make in Requirement 2.

Method A: Straight-line method

Amortizable cost = $40,000 ($44,000 − $4,000)
Each year: $40,000 ÷ 10 years = $4,000

Method B: Double-declining-balance method

$$\text{Rate} = \frac{100\%}{10 \text{ years}} \times 2 = 10\%;\ 10\% \times 2 = 20\%$$

2007: 0.20 × $44,000 = $8,800
2008: 0.20 × ($44,000 − $8,800) = $7,040

Method C: Units-of-production method

$$\text{Amortization per unit} = \frac{\$44,000 - \$4,000}{100,000 \text{ units}} = \$0.40$$

2007: $0.40 × 3,000 units = $1,200
    (since $1,200 ÷ $0.40 = 3,000 units)
2008: $0.40 × 14,000 units = $5,600
    (since $5,600 ÷ $0.40 = 14,000 units)

Use the amortization rates calculated in Requirement 1 for the 2009 computations.

Requirement 2

Year	Method A Straight-Line			Method B Double-Declining-Balance			Method C Units-of-Production		
	Annual Amortization Expense	Accumulated Amortization	Book Value	Annual Amortization Expense	Accumulated Amortization	Book Value	Annual Amortization Expense	Accumulated Amortization	Book Value
Start			$44,000			$44,000			$44,000
2007	$4,000	$ 4,000	40,000	$8,800	$ 8,800	35,200	$1,200	$ 1,200	42,800
2008	4,000	8,000	36,000	7,040	15,840	28,160	5,600	6,800	37,200
2009	4,000	12,000	32,000	5,632	21,472	22,528	4,800	11,600	32,400

Computations for 2009

Straight-line:	$40,000 \div 10 \text{ years} = \$4,000$
Double-declining-balance:	$0.20 \times \$28,160 = \$5,632$
Units-of-production:	$\$0.40 \times 12,000 \text{ units} = \$4,800$

Other Issues in Accounting for Capital Assets

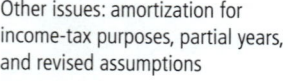

Objective 3

Other issues: amortization for income-tax purposes, partial years, and revised assumptions

Amortization for accounting and income-tax purposes differs (discussed briefly below). Also, companies have gains and losses when they sell capital assets, such as property, plant, and equipment. This section covers these topics.

The Relationship between Amortization and Income Taxes

Most companies use the straight-line method for reporting capital asset values and amortization expense to their owners and creditors on their financial statements. But businesses must often keep a separate set of records for calculating the amortization expense they claim on their tax returns because Canada Revenue Agency (CRA) specifies the maximum amortization taxpayers can deduct for income-tax purposes. This amount is often different from amortization expense reported on the income statement. Amortization for income-tax purposes is discussed in more detail in the Chapter 10 Appendix beginning on page 510.

Amortization for Partial Years

Companies purchase capital assets whenever they need them—such as on February 8 or August 17. They do not wait until the beginning of a year or a month. Therefore, companies develop policies to compute amortization for partial years. Suppose Falconbridge Limited, the mining company, purchases a building in Timmins, Ontario, as a maintenance shop on April 1, 2008, for $500,000. The building's estimated life is 20 years and its estimated residual value is $80,000. Falconbridge

Limited's fiscal year ends on December 31. How does the company compute amortization for the year ended December 31?

Many companies compute partial-year amortization by first calculating a full year's amortization. They then multiply full-year amortization by the fraction of the year during which they used the asset. In this case, Falconbridge needs to record nine months of amortization, for April to December. Assuming the straight-line method, the 2008 amortization for the maintenance shop is $15,750, computed as follows:

$$\textbf{Full-year amortization:} \quad \frac{\$500,000 - \$80,000}{20 \text{ years}} = \$21,000$$

$$\textbf{Partial-year amortization: } \$21,000 \times 9/12 = \$15,750$$

Another policy

- records a full month's amortization on an asset bought on or before the 15th of the month.
- records no amortization on assets purchased after the 15th of the month.

If Falconbridge purchased the building above on August 17, then it would record no amortization for August. In this case, the year's amortization for four months would be $7,000 ($21,000 \times \frac{4}{12}$).

Partial-year amortization is computed under the double-declining-balance and units-of-production amortization methods in the same way—by applying the appropriate percentage of the year during which the asset is used.

Most companies use computerized systems to account for capital assets, which will automatically calculate the amortization expense for each period.

Change in the Useful Life of an Amortizable Asset

Estimating the useful life of each capital asset poses an accounting challenge. As previously discussed, a business must estimate the useful life of a capital asset to compute amortization on that asset. This prediction is the most difficult part of accounting for amortization. As the asset is used, the business may change the asset's estimated useful life, based on experience and new information. Such a change is called a change in accounting estimate. Empire Company Limited, the parent company of Sobeys Inc., IGA Stores, and Price Chopper, included the following note in its April 30, 2001, annual report:

> **Note 1. Accounting Policies**
> **Depreciation**
> ". . . During the year the Company changed the estimated useful lives of its rental properties based on a review of its properties. This change in accounting estimate has been applied prospectively [applied to the current and future periods]. Prior to 2001, estimated lives ranged from 20 to 50 years from the date of acquisition.

The April 30, 2003, annual report indicates that rental properties were amortized over 20 to 40 years. When a company makes an accounting change, generally accepted accounting principles require the business to report the nature, reason, and effect of the accounting change. The Empire Company Limited example above reports this information.

Accounting changes like these are very rare despite the fact that no business has perfect foresight. To *record* a change in accounting estimate, the asset's remaining

In 1988, ABC Co. purchased for $600,000 a building that had an estimated residual value of $100,000 and a life of 40 years. In 2008, a $200,000 addition to the building increased its residual value by $50,000. The accumulated amortization on the building is $250,000. Calculate straight-line amortization expense for 2008.

A: Calculate book value:

Cost (new)	$800,000*
Acc. Amort.	250,000
Revised book value	$550,000

Revised straight-line amortization:

$$= \frac{\$550,000 - \$150,000}{20}$$

$$= \$20,000 \text{ per year}$$

*$600,000 + $200,000

amortizable book value is spread over its adjusted, or new, remaining useful life. The change is accounted for prospectively.

Assume that a Big Rock Brewery Income Trust machine cost $40,000, and the company originally believed the asset had a 16-year useful life with no residual value. Using the straight-line method, the company would record $2,500 amortization each year ($40,000 ÷ 16 years = $2,500). Suppose Big Rock Brewery used the asset for four years. Accumulated amortization reached $10,000 ($2,500 × 4 years = $10,000), leaving a book value of $30,000 ($40,000 − $10,000). From its experience with the asset during the first four years, management believes the asset will remain useful for the next 20 years. At the start of Year 5, the company would compute a revised annual amortization amount and record it as follows:

Asset's Remaining Amortizable Book Value	÷	(New) Estimated Useful Life Remaining	=	(New) Annual Amortization Amount
$30,000	÷	20 years	=	$1,500

The yearly amortization entry based on new estimated useful life is

Amortization Expense—Machine	1,500	
Accumulated Amortization—Machine		1,500

The equation for revised straight-line amortization is

$$\text{Revised Straight-line Amortization} = \frac{\text{Cost} - \text{Accumulated Amortization} - \text{New Residual Value}}{\text{Estimated Remaining Useful Life in Years}}$$

"Cost" in the equation is the original cost recorded in the general ledger plus any additions to the asset's cost, such as building an addition to add more space to an existing warehouse.

Companies use this equation when changes in the useful life of an asset are made partway through the year. Suppose, in our Big Rock Brewery example, the company used the machine for four-and-a-half years and then realized the machine will remain useful for 24 years in total. The revised straight-line amortization per year for the next 19.5 years (24 years − 4.5 years) is calculated as

$$\text{Revised Straight-line Amortization} = \frac{\$40,000 - (4.5 \times \$2,500) - \$0}{19.5 \text{ years}}$$

$$= \frac{\$28,750}{19.5}$$

$$= \$1,474$$

Since amortization is an estimate, always round amortization calculations to the neaest whole dollar.

Using Fully Amortized Assets

A *fully amortized asset* is one that has reached the end of its *estimated* useful life. No more amortization is recorded for the asset. If the asset is no longer useful, it is disposed of. But the asset may still be useful, and the company may continue using it. The asset account and its accumulated amortization remain on the books, but no additional amortization is recorded.

Disposing of a Tangible Capital Asset (Property, Plant, and Equipment)

Eventually, a capital asset no longer serves its purpose. The asset may be worn out, obsolete, or for some other reason, no longer useful to the business. The owner may sell the asset or exchange it. If the asset cannot be sold or exchanged, then it is junked. In all cases, the business should bring amortization up to date and then remove the asset from the books.

To record the disposal of a tangible capital asset

- Credit the asset account
- Debit its accumulated amortization.

Suppose a business is disposing of a machine and the final year's amortization expense has just been recorded. The cost was $6,000, and there is no residual value. The machine's accumulated amortization thus totals $6,000. Assume this asset cannot be sold or exchanged, so it is junked. The entry to record its disposal is

Accumulated Amortization—Machinery.........................	6,000	
Machinery		6,000
To dispose of a fully amortized machine.		

Now both accounts have a zero balance, as shown in the T-accounts below:

Machinery		Accumulated Amortization—Machinery	
6,000	6,000 ← → 6,000	6,000	

If assets are junked before being fully amortized, the company records a loss equal to the asset's book value. Suppose Zellers' store fixtures that cost $4,000 are junked at a loss. Accumulated amortization is $3,000 and book value is therefore $1,000. Disposal of these store fixtures generates a loss, as follows:

Accumulated Amortization—Store Fixtures	3,000	
Loss on Disposal of Property, Plant, and Equipment....	1,000	
Store Fixtures		4,000
To dispose of store fixtures.		

All losses, including this Loss on Disposal of Property, Plant and Equipment, decrease net income. Along with expenses, losses are reported on the income statement.

Objective

Account for the disposal of a tangible capital asset

When an asset is disposed of partway through the year, a partial year's amortization must be recorded to update accumulated amortization. Then record the gain or loss on disposal, and remove the asset from the books.

Selling a Tangible Capital Asset

Suppose Placer Dome Inc., the gold-mining company, sells surplus office furniture on September 30, 2008, for $5,000 cash. The furniture cost $10,000 when purchased on January 1, 2005, and has been amortized on a straight-line basis with a ten-year useful life and no residual value. Prior to recording the sale of the furniture, Placer Dome accountants must update its amortization. Since Placer Dome uses the calendar year as its accounting period, partial amortization must be recorded for nine months from January 1, 2008, to the sale date of September 30. The straight-line amortization entry at September 30, 2008, is

Sept. 30	Amortization Expense—Furniture....................	750	
	Accumulated Amortization—Furniture.......		750
	To update amortization ($10,000 ÷ 10 years × $\%_{12}$).		

Now, after this entry is posted, the Furniture and the Accumulated Amortization—Furniture accounts appear as follows:

Furniture	Accumulated Amortization—Furniture
Jan. 1, 2005 10,000	Dec. 31, 2005 1,000
	Dec. 31, 2006 1,000
	Dec. 31, 2007 1,000
	Sept. 30, 2008 750
	Balance 3,750

Book value = $6,250

Suppose Placer Dome sells the office furniture for $5,000 cash. The loss on the sale is $1,250, computed as follows:

Cash received from selling the asset		$5,000
Book value of asset sold:		
Cost..	$10,000	
Accumulated amortization up to date of sale..................	3,750	6,250
Gain (loss) on sale of the asset...		($1,250)

Placer Dome's entry to record the sale of the furniture for $5,000 cash is

Sept. 30	Cash	5,000	
	Loss on Disposal of Property, Plant, and Equipment	1,250	
	Accumulated Amortization—Furniture...........	3,750	
	Furniture...		10,000
	To dispose of furniture.		

When recording the sale of a capital asset, Placer Dome must

- Remove the balances in the asset account (Furniture, in this case) and its related accumulated amortization account
- Record a gain or a loss if the cash received differs from the asset's book value.

In our example, cash of $5,000 is less than the book value of $6,250. The result is a loss of $1,250.

If the sale price had been $7,000, Placer Dome would have had a gain of $750 (Cash, $7,000 − asset book value, $6,250). The entry to record this gain would be

Sept. 30	Cash	7,000	
	Accumulated Amortization—Furniture...........	3,750	
	Furniture...		10,000
	Gain on Disposal of Property, Plant, and Equipment		750
	To dispose of furniture.		

LEARNING TIPS

When an asset is sold, a gain or loss on the sale is determined by comparing the proceeds from the sale to the asset's book value:
- Proceeds > Book value = Gain
- Proceeds < Book value = Loss

A gain is recorded when an asset is sold for more than book value. A loss is recorded when the sale price is less than book value. Gains increase net income and losses decrease net income. All gains and losses are reported on the income statement in the "other gains and losses" section.

Exchanging Tangible Capital Assets

Businesses often exchange old tangible capital assets (property, plant and equipment) for newer, more efficient assets. The most common exchange transaction is a trade-in.

Section 3831 of the *CICA Handbook*, "Non-monetary Transactions," guides the accounting treatment of tangible capital-asset exchanges because property, plant, and equipment are defined as non-monetary assets. The first thing to determine in any exchange transaction is whether the transaction has commercial substance. **Commercial substance** exists when the entity's future cash flows from the new asset received will differ in risk, timing, or amount from the cash flows from the old asset given up in the exchange. In other words, if the economic conditions of the company receiving the new asset change, the exchange transaction has commercial substance.

If an exchange transaction has commercial substance, then the new asset is recorded at its fair market value. The old asset is valued at its net book value plus any cash paid as part of the trade-in. A gain or loss is recorded for the old asset in the same way as when an asset is sold for cash.

Suppose Horton Hardware owns a Ford Econoline van that it purchased for $32,000 on January 2, 2001. The van was expected to last eight years and was amortized on a straight-line basis. On January 2, 2006, Horton Hardware exchanged this van for a pick-up truck that had a fair market value of $43,000. Horton Hardware received a trade-in allowance of $8,000 for the van and paid the seller $35,000 cash. Horton Hardware will receive better gas mileage with the new truck and will be able to save delivery expenses by delivering more bulky items with the new truck. Therefore, *this exchange of assets has commercial substance*. The entry to record this exchange would be:

Truck	43,000	
Loss on exchange of assets	4,000	
Accumulated Amortization—Van (5 × $4,000)	20,000	
Cash		35,000
Van		32,000

To record exchange of the van and cash for a new light-duty truck.

THINKING IT OVER

Why is the trade-in allowance usually different from the book value?

A: The book value depends on the asset's historical cost and on the amortization method used. The trade-in allowance is based on the market value of the asset being traded in (or may be an adjustment to the selling price).

If an exchange transaction does not have commercial substance, then the new asset is recorded at the book value of the old asset. No gain or loss is reported for the old asset. Since most entities agree to an exchange of non-monetary assets only if it creates an economic improvement and, thus, has commercial substance, an exchange of non-monetary assets without commercial substance is expected to be rare, and will be discussed no further.

Exhibit 10–10 summarizes the accounting treatment of non-monetary-asset exchange transactions.

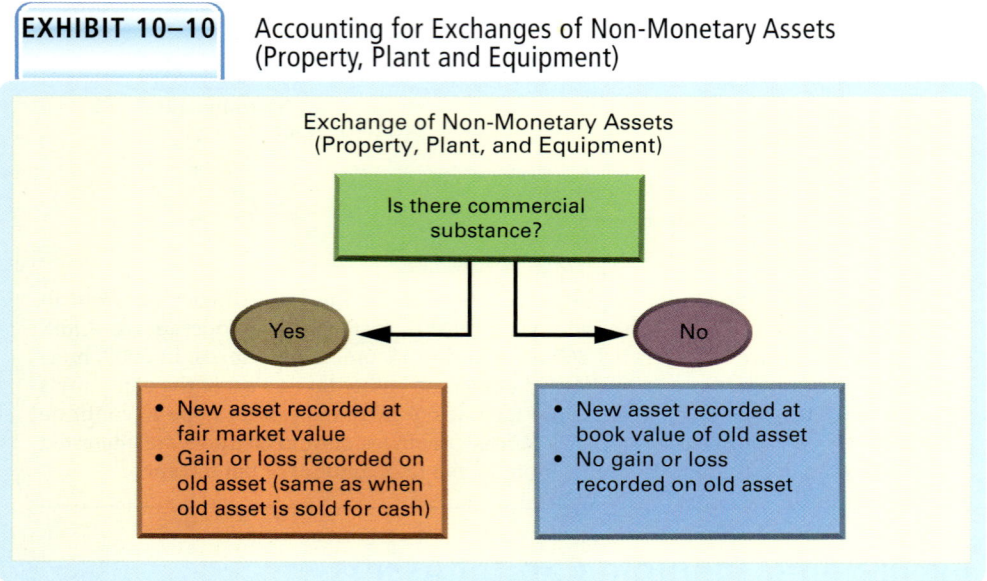

EXHIBIT 10–10 Accounting for Exchanges of Non-Monetary Assets (Property, Plant and Equipment)

Internal Control of Tangible Capital Assets (Property, Plant, and Equipment)

Internal control of tangible capital assets (property, plant, and equipment) includes safeguarding them and having an adequate accounting system. Recall from Chapter 8 the importance of a strong system of internal controls within a business. To see the need for controlling capital assets, consider the following situation. The home office and top managers of Petrol Mfg. Ltd. are in Calgary. The company manufactures gas pumps in Michigan, then sells them in Europe. Top managers and owners of the company rarely see the manufacturing facility and therefore cannot control their capital assets by on-the-spot management. What features does their internal control system need?

Safeguarding capital assets (property, plant, and equipment) includes:

1. Assigning responsibility for custody of the assets.

2. Separating custody of assets from accounting for the assets. (This separation of duties is a cornerstone of internal control in almost every area.)

3. Setting up security measures—for instance, guards and restricted access to property, plant, and equipment—to prevent theft.

4. Protecting capital assets from the elements (rain, snow, and so on).

5. Having adequate insurance against fire, storm, and other casualty losses.

6. Training operating personnel in the proper use of the assets.

7. Checking capital assets regularly for existence and condition.

8. Keeping a regular maintenance schedule.

Accounting for Natural Resources (Wasting Assets)

Objective 5

Account for natural resources

Natural resources are tangible capital assets that are often called *wasting assets* because they are used up in the process of production. Examples include iron ore, coal, oil, gas, and timber. Natural resources are like inventories in the ground (coal) or on top of the ground (timber). Natural resources are expensed through amortization. Some companies use the word **depletion** to describe amortization of natural resources. **Amortization expense**, or *depletion*, is that portion of the cost of natural resources that is used up in a particular period. Amortization expense for natural resources is computed by the *units-of-production* formula:

$$\frac{\text{Amortization}}{\text{expense}} = \frac{\text{Cost} - \text{Residual value}}{\text{Estimated total units of natural resource}} \times \frac{\text{Number of}}{\text{units removed}}$$

An oil well may cost $100,000 and contain an estimated 10,000 barrels of oil. (Natural resources usually have no residual value.) The amortization rate would be $10 per barrel ($100,000 ÷ 10,000 barrels). If 3,000 barrels are extracted during the first year, amortization expense is $30,000 (3,000 barrels × $10 per barrel). The amortization entry for the year is

Amortization Expense...	30,000	
Accumulated Amortization—Oil..		30,000

If 4,500 barrels are removed the next year, amortization is $45,000 (4,500 barrels × $10 per barrel).

Accumulated Amortization for natural resources is a contra account similar to Accumulated Amortization for property, plant, and equipment. Natural resource assets can be reported on the balance sheet as is shown for oil in the following example.

Property, plant, and equipment:		
Land		$120,000
Buildings..	$800,000	
Equipment...	160,000	
	960,000	
Less: Accumulated amortization	410,000	
		550,000
Oil and gas properties:		
Oil...	**$340,000**	
Less: Accumulated amortization	**90,000**	
Net oil and gas properties		250,000
Property, plant, and equipment, net		$920,000

STOP AND THINK

Suppose West Fraser Timber Co. Ltd. purchases, for $500,000, land that contains an estimated 500,000 fbm (foot-board measure) of timber. The land can be sold for $100,000 after the timber has been cut. If West Fraser harvests 200,000 fbm in the year of purchase, how much amortization should be recorded?

Answer:

$$\frac{\text{Cost} - \text{Residual value}}{\text{Estimated total units}} \times \text{Number of units produced}$$

$$= \frac{(\$500,000 - \$100,000)}{500,000 \text{ fbm}} \times 200,000 \text{ fbm}$$

$$= \$0.80/\text{fbm} \times 200,000 \text{ fbm}$$

$$= \$160,000$$

Future Removal and Site Restoration Costs

There is increasing concern by individuals and governments about the environment. Often, in the past, a company exploiting natural resources, such as a mining company, would simply abandon the site once the ore body was mined completely. Now, there is legislation in most jurisdictions requiring a natural resource company to remove buildings, equipment, and waste, and to restore the site once a location is to be dismantled and abandoned.

The *CICA Handbook* refers to future removal and site restoration costs as an "asset retirement obligation," which is estimated at the time the asset is acquired or the obligation becomes known. The liability (a credit) for the asset retirement obligation is recorded at its fair value, typically calculated as the present value of the future cash flows required to retire the obligation. The same amount is recorded as an asset retirement cost (a debit) and added to the carrying amount of its related asset (such as a factory). The asset retirement obligation is then amortized along with its related asset. Over its life, the liability is increased to reflect the passage of time and adjusted when estimates of future costs of retirement change. Companies must disclose a description of the liability, any assets legally restricted to pay the liability, and the assumptions for the calculation of the liability.

Accounting for Intangible Capital Assets and Goodwill

Objective 6

Account for intangible capital assets and goodwill

As we saw earlier in this chapter, **intangible assets** have no physical form. Instead, these assets convey special rights from ownership of patents, copyrights, trademarks, franchises, leaseholds, and from goodwill.

In our technology-driven economy, intangibles are very important. Consider the online auctioneer eBay. The company has no physical products or equipment, but it helps people buy and sell everything from toys to bathroom tiles. Each month eBay serves millions of customers. In a sense, eBay is a company of intangibles.

The intellectual capital of eBay, Research In Motion, or Open Text is difficult to measure, but when one company buys another, we get a glimpse of the value of the acquired intellectual capital. Intangibles can account for most of a company's market value, so companies must value their intangibles just as they do their physical and financial assets.

A patent is an intangible asset that protects a process or formula. The acquisition cost of a patent is debited to Patents, an asset account. The intangible is expensed as it expires through amortization. Amortization applies to intangibles in the same way as it applies to property, plant, and equipment, and natural resources.

Amortization is computed over the lesser of the asset's legal life or estimated useful life. Obsolescence often shortens an intangible asset's useful life. Amortization expense for intangibles can be written off directly against the intangible asset account with *no accumulated amortization account*. The residual value of most intangibles is zero.

Some intangibles have indefinite lives. For these intangibles, the company records no systematic amortization in each period. Instead, it accounts for any decrease in the value of the intangible, as we shall see for goodwill.

Specific Intangibles

Patents Patents are federal government grants conveying an exclusive right for 20 years to produce and sell an invention. The invention may be a product or a process. Patented products include Bombardier Ski-doos and the Research In Motion

BlackBerry. Like any other asset, a patent may be purchased. Suppose Nortel pays $200,000 to acquire a patent, and Nortel believes the expected useful life of the patent is five years. Amortization expense is $40,000 per year ($200,000 ÷ 5 years). The company's acquisition and amortization entries for this patent are:

Jan.	1	Patent..	200,000	
		Cash		200,000
		To acquire a patent.		
Dec.	31	Amortization Expense—Patent	40,000	
		Patent...		40,000
		To amortize the cost of a patent ($200,000 ÷ 5).		

At the end of the first year, Nortel would report the patent at $160,000 ($200,000 minus the first year's amortization of $40,000).

Copyrights Copyrights are exclusive rights to reproduce and sell software, a book, musical composition, film, or other work of art. Issued by the federal government, copyrights extend 50 years beyond the author's life. A company may pay a large sum to purchase an existing copyright from the owner. For example, the publisher McClelland & Stewart Ltd. may pay the author of a popular novel tens of thousands of dollars or more for the book's copyright. The useful life of a copyright for a popular book may be two or three years; on the other hand, some copyrights, especially of musical compositions, such as works by the Beatles, seem to be popular over several decades.

Trademarks and Brand Names Trademarks and brand names (or trade names) are distinctive identifications of products or services. For example, The Sports Network has its distinctive logo of the yellow letters TSN on a black background shaped like a television screen; Apple Computer has the multi-colored apple with a bite out of it; and the Edmonton Oilers and Toronto Blue Jays have insignia that identify their respective teams. Molson Canadian, Swiss Chalet chicken, WestJet, and Roots are everyday trade names. Advertising slogans such as Speedy Muffler's "At Speedy you're a somebody," are also legally protected. The cost of a trademark or trade name is amortized over its useful life.

Franchises and Licences Franchises and licences are privileges granted by a private business or a government to sell a product or service in accordance with specified conditions. The Vancouver Canucks hockey organization is a franchise granted to its owners by the National Hockey League. Tim Hortons and Re/Max Ltd. are well-known franchises. The acquisition cost of a franchise or licence is amortized over its useful life.

Leaseholds A leasehold is a right arising from a prepayment that a lessee (renter) makes to secure the use of an asset from a lessor (landlord). For example, most malls lease the space to the mall stores and shops that you visit. Often, leases require the lessee to make this prepayment in addition to monthly rental payments. The prepayment is a debit to an intangible asset account entitled Leaseholds. This amount is amortized over the life of the lease by debiting Rent Expense and crediting Leaseholds.

Sometimes lessees modify or improve the leased asset. For example, a lessee may construct a fence on leased land. The lessee debits the cost of the fence to a separate intangible asset account, Leasehold Improvements, and amortizes its cost over the lesser of the term of the lease and of its useful life.

Goodwill Goodwill is truly a unique asset. *Goodwill* in accounting is a more limited term than in everyday use, as in "goodwill among men." In accounting, goodwill is the excess of the cost to purchase a company over the market value of its net assets (assets minus liabilities). Suppose James Richardson International acquires Manitoba Express Ltd. at a cost of $10 million. The market value of Manitoba

THINKING IT OVER

Why might a business have goodwill? Why could a business earn more than a normal rate of return on its assets? Why might an acquiring company pay an amount greater than the market value of net assets acquired when purchasing a going business?

A: Good customer relations, good location of the business, efficient operations, monopoly in the marketplace, strong sources of financing, and so on. A business could earn more than a normal rate of return on its assets because of these factors. Thus, a purchaser will pay more than the market value of net assets for a business that has these factors.

Express's assets is $9 million, and its liabilities total $1 million. In this case, James Richardson International paid $2 million for goodwill, computed as follows:

Purchase price paid for Manitoba Express Ltd.		$10 million
Sum of the market value of Manitoba Express's assets.....	$9 million	
Less: Manitoba Express's liabilities......................................	1 million	
Market value of Manitoba Express's net assets..................		8 million
Excess is called *goodwill*..		$ 2 million

James Richardson International's entry to record the acquisition of Manitoba Express Ltd., including its goodwill, would be

Assets (Cash, Receivables, Inventories, Capital Assets, all at market value)	9,000,000	
Goodwill..	2,000,000	
Liabilities		1,000,000
Cash..		10,000,000
Purchased Manitoba Express Ltd.		

Goodwill has the following special features:

1. Goodwill is recorded, at its cost, only by the company that purchases another company. A company's favourable location, superior product, or outstanding reputation may create goodwill for a company, but it is never recorded by that entity. Instead, goodwill is recorded *only* by the acquiring entity when it buys another company. A purchase transaction provides objective evidence of the value of the goodwill.

2. Goodwill has an indefinite life, so it is not amortized like other intangibles. According to generally accepted accounting principles (GAAP), the purchaser must assess the goodwill every year and, if its value is impaired (if the fair value falls below the carrying value in the accounting records), the goodwill must be written down to reflect the impairment. The write-down amount is accounted for as a loss in the year of the write-down. For example, suppose James Richardson International's goodwill—purchased above—is worth only $1,500,000 at the end of the first year. In that case, James Richardson International would make this entry:

Loss on Goodwill	500,000	
Goodwill		500,000
Recorded loss on goodwill ($2,000,000 − $1,500,000).		

James Richardson International would then report this goodwill at its current value of $1,500,000.

International Accounting for Research and Development Costs Accounting for research and development (R&D) costs is one of the most difficult issues the accounting profession has faced. R&D is the lifeblood of companies such as Bombardier, Research in Motion, Open Text, and Nortel Networks because it is vital to the development of new products and processes. The cost of R&D activities is one of these companies' most valuable (intangible) assets.

Canada requires *development costs* meeting certain criteria to be capitalized, while other countries require such costs to be expensed in the year incurred. Canada and most other countries require *research costs* to be expensed as incurred.

Some critics argue that R&D costs represent future benefits and should be capitalized; others agree with the present accounting standards, and still others think all R&D costs should be expensed.

STOP AND THINK

How could companies around the world be placed on the same accounting basis?

Answer: If all companies worldwide followed the same accounting rules, they would be reporting income and other amounts computed similarly. But this is not the case. A company must follow the accounting rules of its own nation, and there are differences, as with development costs. This is why international investors keep abreast of accounting methods used in different nations—much the same as a Canadian investor cares whether a company uses FIFO or average cost for inventories. An international body, the International Accounting Standards Board (IASB), sets accounting standards, called *International Accounting Standards* or IAS. The Canadian Institute of Chartered Accountants, through its Liaison, Patricia O'Malley, FCA, is a strong supporter of international accounting standards, and the CICA's Accounting Standards Board (ACSB) is working to harmonize Canadian standards with the IASB. It is working with those bodies and other accounting bodies around the world to harmonize accounting standards worldwide.

Ethical Issues: Tangible and Intangible Capital Assets

The main ethical issue in accounting for tangible and intangible capital assets is whether to capitalize or expense a particular cost. In this area, companies have split personalities. On the one hand, they want to save on taxes. This motivates companies to expense as many costs as possible to decrease taxable income. But they also want their financial statements to look as good as possible, with high net income and high reported amounts for assets.

In most cases, a cost that is capitalized or expensed for tax purposes must be treated the same way for accounting purposes in the financial statements. What, then, is the ethical path? Accountants should follow the general guidelines for capitalizing a cost:

Capitalize all costs that provide a future benefit for the business, and expense all other costs.

Many companies have gotten into trouble by capitalizing costs that really should have been expensed. They made their financial statements look better than the facts warranted. WorldCom committed this type of accounting fraud, and its former top executives are now in prison as a result. There are few cases of companies getting into trouble by following the general guidelines, or even by erring on the side of expensing questionable costs. This is another example of accounting conservatism. We discussed accounting conservatism in Chapter 6, page 301.

STOP AND THINK

1. Suppose Hi Value Stores was having a bad year—net income below expectations and lower than last year's income. For amortization purposes Hi Value Stores decided to extend the estimated useful lives of its amortizable assets. This decision was *not* based on any belief that the actual useful life was longer than originally thought. How would this accounting change affect Hi Value Stores' (a) amortization expense, (b) net income, and (c) owner's equity?

Answer: An accounting change that lengthens the estimated useful lives of amortizable assets (a) decreases amortization expense, and (b) and (c) increases net income and

(continued on page 508)

owner's equity. This decision is unethical because it was made for the sole purpose of increasing net income, not because of a real change in the assets' useful lives.

2. Suppose that the Hi Value Stores' change in accounting estimate turned a loss year into a profitable year. Without the change, the company would have reported a net loss for the year. But the change enabled the company to report positive net income. Under GAAP, Hi Value Stores' annual report must disclose the change in accounting estimate. Would users of the financial statements, such as the bank, evaluate Hi Value Stores as better or worse in response to this disclosure?

Answer: Users' reactions are not always predictable. There is evidence, however, that businesses cannot fool users. If users have enough information—such as the knowledge of a change in accounting estimate disclosed in the annual report—they can process the information correctly. In this case, analysts would *probably* subtract from Hi Value Stores' reported net income the amount caused by the change in accounting estimate. Users could then use the resulting net *loss* figure to evaluate Hi Value Stores' lack of progress during the year. Users would probably view Hi Value Stores less favourably for having made this change in accounting estimate. For this reason, and because the ethics behind such a change are questionable, many owners and managers would not engage in this type of income manipulation.

As we conclude this chapter, we return to our opening questions: What are capital assets, and why are they important? Should you capitalize or expense costs associated with a new asset and with an existing asset? What is amortization, and how can amortization expense be calculated? How is amortization reported on the income statement and the balance sheet? Can a company use different amortization methods for accounting and income-tax purposes? These questions were answered throughout this chapter. And the Decision Guidelines end this chapter by applying the answers to decisions a franchise owner must make.

DECISION GUIDELINES — Accounting for Capital Assets and Related Expenses

Suppose you buy a GoodLife Fitness Club franchise and invest in fitness equipment. You have some decisions to make about how to account for the franchise and the equipment. The Decision Guidelines will help you maximize your cash flow and do the accounting properly. Remember that there can be exceptions to these guidelines if amounts are immaterial.

Decision	Guidelines
Capitalize or expense a cost?	General rule: Capitalize all costs that provide *future benefit*. Expense all costs that provide *no future benefit*.
Capitalize or expense: • Cost associated with a new asset? • Cost associated with an existing asset?	Capitalize all costs that bring the asset to its intended use. Capitalize only those costs that add to the asset's usefulness or its useful life. Expense all other costs as maintenance or repairs.
• Interest cost incurred to finance an asset's construction?	Capitalize interest cost only on assets constructed by the business for its own use. Expense all other interest costs.
Which amortization method to use: • For financial reporting? • For income tax?	Use the method that best matches amortization expense against the revenues produced by the asset. Use the maximum capital cost allowance rates allowed by Canada Revenue Agency to produce the greatest deductions from taxable income (see Chapter 10 Appendix). A company can use different amortization methods for financial reporting and for income tax purposes. In Canada, this practice is considered both legal and ethical.

Problem 1

The following figures appear in Solution, Requirement 2, on page 496.

	Method B Double-Declining-Balance		
Year	Annual Amortization Expense	Accumulated Amortization	Book Value
Start			$44,000
2007	$8,800	$ 8,800	35,200
2008	7,040	15,840	28,160
2009	5,632	21,472	22,528

Name: Ventura Industrial Products
Industry: Industrial products producer
Accounting Period: Asset sale on July 2, 2009

Ventura Industrial Products purchased this equipment on January 2, 2007. Management has amortized the equipment by using the double-declining-balance method. On July 2, 2009, Ventura sold the equipment for $25,000 cash.

Required

Record Ventura Industrial Products' amortization for 2009 using the double-declining-balance method, and the sale of the equipment on July 2, 2009.

Problem 2

Meben Logistics purchased a building at a cost of $500,000 on January 2, 2004. Meben has amortized the building by using the straight-line method, a 35-year life, and a residual value of $150,000. On January 2, 2008, the business changed the useful life of the building from 35 years to 25 years. The fiscal year of Meben Logistics ends on December 31.

Required Name: Meben Logistics
Industry: Not stated
Accounting Period: Revised amortization in 2008

Required

Record amortization for 2008 assuming no change in the building's residual value.

Solution

Problem 1

Amortization expense must first be recorded for the portion of the year that the asset was used before it was sold. Since the asset was sold during 2009, use 2008's book value in the amortization-expense calculation.

If Cash > Book value, then a gain on disposal.

If Cash < Book value, then a loss on disposal.

2009				
July	2	Amortization Expense—Equipment		
		($28,160 \times 0.20 \times \frac{1}{2})$	2,816	
		Accumulated Amortization—Equipment..		2,816
		To record amortization expense for the period January 1, 2009, to June 30, 2009.		
July	2	Cash	25,000	
		Accumulated Amortization—Equipment[*]	18,656	
		Loss on Sale of Equipment	344	
		Equipment		44,000
		To record sale of equipment.		

[*]$8,800 + $7,040 + $2,816 = $18,656.

Problem 2

The equation for revised straight-line amortization is

$$\text{Revised Straight-line Amortization} = \frac{\text{Cost} - \text{Accumulated Amortization} - \text{New Residual Value}}{\text{Estimated Remaining Useful Life in Years}}$$

where

Cost = $500,000 (given)

Accumulated Amortization = [($500,000 − $150,000) ÷ 35 years] × 4 years
= $40,000

New Residual Value = $150,000 (the same as old residual value)

Estimated Remaining Useful Life in Years = 25 − 4 = 21 years

Therefore,

$$\text{Revised Straight-line Amortization} = \frac{\$500,000 - \$40,000 - \$150,000}{21 \text{ years}} = \$14,762 \text{ per year, rounded}$$

2008			
Dec. 31	Amortization Expense—Building...................	14,762	
	Accumulated Amortization—Building......		14,762
	To record annual amortization for 2008.		

MyAccountingLab Go to MyAccountingLab at www.myaccountinglab.ca. You can practise this chapter's exercises and problems as often as you want. The guided solutions help you find an answer, step by step. There's a personalized study plan, too!

Chapter 10 Appendix

Explain capital cost allowance and amortization for income-tax purposes

 7

Capital Cost Allowance

Canada Revenue Agency (CRA) allows corporations as well as individuals with business or professional income to compute deductions from income to recognize the consumption or use of capital assets. The deductions are called **capital cost allowance (CCA)**, the term CRA uses to describe amortization for tax purposes. CRA specifies the *maximum* rates allowed for each asset class, called *capital cost allowance rates*. A taxpayer may claim from zero to the maximum capital cost allowance allowed in a year. Most taxpayers claim the maximum CCA since this provides the largest deduction from taxable income as quickly as possible. Claiming the maximum CCA reduces taxable income and thus tax payable, leaving more cash available for investment or other business uses.

Some typical CRA rates and classes are:

	Rate	Class
Automobiles	30%	10
Brick, concrete, or stone buildings bought after 1987	4%	1
Computer software	100%	12
Office furniture and fixtures	20%	8
Computers	30%	10

CRA allows the taxpayer to claim only 50 percent of the normal CCA rate in the year of acquisition. However, there are some exceptions and Class 12 is one of them. Class 12 assets have a full 100 percent capital cost allowance rate in the year of acquisition.

The CCA rate is applied to the balance in the asset class at the end of the year (cost minus accumulated CCA claimed to date) in the same manner as with the double-declining-balance method discussed on pages 492 to 493.

To illustrate, during the year beginning January 2, 2007, Doug Copely, the entrepreneur from Chapter 1, bought a computer and an accounting software package to help him account for his business income. The computer cost $2,200 and the software cost $300. Doug decided to amortize the computer and the software on a straight-line basis over five years, and expects the computer and software to have no value at the end of five years. These assumptions lead to an amortization expense of $440 per year ($2,200 ÷ 5 years) for the computer and an amortization expense of $60 per year ($300 ÷ 5 years) for the software.

For income-tax purposes, the computer is considered to be a Class 10 asset. The capital cost allowance rate for Class 10 assets is 30 percent. The software is considered to be a Class 12 asset. The CCA rate for Class 12 assets is 100 percent. Remember that for most asset classes, a taxpayer can claim only 50 percent of normal CCA in the year of acquisition, which in Doug's case is the year 2007. In 2007, Doug could claim up to the maximum capital cost allowance of $330 ([$2,200 × 30%] × 50%) for the computer. However, he can claim up to the maximum capital cost allowance of $300 for the software in 2007. These are the only capital assets in these classes.

In 2008, Doug would apply the Class 10 rate of 30 percent to the cost of the computer remaining after the 2007 CCA is deducted. In 2008, he could claim up to the maximum CCA of $561 ([$2,200 − $330] × 30%) for the computer. Following the same process in 2009, Doug could claim up to the maximum capital cost allowance of $393 ([$2,200 − $330 − $561] × 30%) for the computer. The table below shows the maximum CCA Doug could deduct from his business income for the first six years:

	2007	2008	2009	2010	2011	2012
Computer	$330	$561	$393	$275	$192	$135
Software	$300	0	0	0	0	0

Notice that in 2012, the sixth year that Doug owned the computer, he is able to deduct CCA for income tax purposes. However, for accounting purposes, the computer would be fully amortized at the end of 2011, the fifth year, since Doug decided to amortize the computer on a straight-line basis over five years. This example shows that amortization expense deducted from income on the income statement often differs from the capital cost allowance claimed by a taxpayer on the tax return.

CRA will allow a company to use any amortization method it chooses as long as the amount of capital cost allowance claimed for tax purposes does not exceed the maximum amount allowed by CRA. For tax purposes, most companies select the maximum amount allowed by CRA, which results in accelerated amortization of an item. Accelerated amortization minimizes taxable income and income tax payments in the early years of the asset's life, thereby maximizing the business's cash at the earliest possible time. Straight-line amortization spreads amortization evenly over the life of the asset, which would *not* minimize income tax in the same way. Capital cost allowance and amortization issues are quite complicated. These issues are studied more fully in advanced accounting courses and tax courses.

Summary

1. **Measure the cost of a tangible capital asset.** *Tangible capital assets*, such as property, plant, and equipment, are long-lived assets that the business uses in its operations. The cost of a tangible capital asset is the purchase price plus applicable taxes (but not GST), purchase commissions, and all other necessary amounts incurred to acquire the asset and to prepare it for its intended use.

2. **Calculate and account for amortization.** The process of allocating a capital asset's cost to expense over the period the asset is used is called *amortization*. Three common methods businesses use to account for the amortization of property, plant, and equipment are *straight-line*, *units-of-production*, and *declining-balance*. All these methods require accountants to estimate the asset's useful life and residual value.

3. **Other issues: Amortization for income-tax purposes, partial years, and revised assumptions.** Amortization for financial statement purposes and income-tax purposes often differ. This is both legal and ethical. When assets are purchased or sold during the year, calculate partial-year amortization. When significant changes occur to an asset's cost, residual value, or useful life, annual amortization expense must be revised for all future years to reflect the changes.

4. **Account for the disposal of a tangible capital asset.** Before disposing of, selling, or trading in a tangible capital asset, the business updates the asset's amortization. Disposal is then recorded by removing the book balances from both the asset account and its related accumulated amortization account. Sales often result in a gain or a loss, which is reported on the income statement. Disposal may or may not result in a reported gain or loss, depending on the circumstances.

5. **Account for natural resources.** The cost of natural resources (wasting assets), a special category of long-lived assets, is expensed through amortization. Amortization of natural resources is computed on a units-of-production basis.

6. **Account for intangible capital assets and goodwill.** *Intangible capital assets* are assets that have no physical form. They give their owners a special right to current and expected future benefits. The major types of intangible assets are patents, copyrights, trademarks, franchises and licences, leaseholds, and goodwill. Amortization of these intangibles is computed on a straight-line basis over the lesser of the legal life and useful life. Goodwill is not amortized, but its carrying value is assessed annually and written down if its market value is less than its carrying value.

7. **Explain capital cost allowance and amortization for income-tax purposes.** Canada Revenue Agency allows companies and individuals to claim capital cost allowance (amortization) against taxable income but sets maximum rates that may be claimed for each class of capital assets. Many companies use the maximum rates allowed for tax purposes but lower rates (for example, straight-line) for income statement purposes.

Self-Study Questions

Test your understanding of the chapter by marking the correct answer for each of the following questions:

1. Which of the following payments is not included in the cost of land? *(p. 483)*
   a. Removal of old building
   b. Legal fees
   c. Property taxes in arrears paid at acquisition
   d. Cost of fencing and lighting

2. Roche Products paid $120,000 for two machines valued at $90,000 and $60,000. Roche will record these machines at costs of *(p. 487)*
   a. $90,000 and $60,000
   b. $60,000 each
   c. $72,000 and $48,000
   d. $70,000 and $50,000

3. Which of the following items is a repair? *(pp. 487–488)*
   a. New brakes for delivery truck
   b. Paving of a company parking lot
   c. Cost of a new engine for a truck
   d. Building permit paid to construct an addition to an existing building

4. Which of the following definitions fits amortization? *(p. 488)*

   a. Allocation of the asset's market value to expense over its useful life
   b. Allocation of the asset's cost to expense over its useful life
   c. Decreases in the asset's market value over its useful life
   d. Increases in the fund set aside to replace the asset when it is worn out

5. Which amortization method's amounts are not computed based on time? *(pp. 490–493)*
   a. Straight-line
   b. Units-of-production
   c. Double-declining balance
   d. All are based on time

6. Which amortization method gives the greatest amount of expense in the early years of using the asset? *(pp. 492–493)*
   a. Straight-line
   b. Units-of-production
   c. Double-declining balance
   d. All are equal

7. A company paid $450,000 for a building and was amortizing it by the straight-line method over a 40-year life with estimated residual value of $50,000. After ten years, it became evident that the building's *remaining* useful

life would be 40 years. Amortization for the eleventh year is (pp. 497–498)

a. $7,500   c. $10,000

b. $8,750   d. $12,500

8. Labrador Stores scrapped an automobile that cost $14,000 and had a book value of $1,100. The entry to record this disposal is (p. 499)

a. Loss on Disposal of Automobile ...   1,100
       Automobile   1,100

b. Accumulated Amortization   14,000
       Automobile   14,000

c. Accumulated Amortization   12,900
       Automobile   12,900

d. Accumulated Amortization   12,900
       Loss on Disposal of Automobile ..   1,100
       Automobile   14,000

9. Amortization of a natural resource is computed in the same manner as which amortization method? (pp. 503–504)

a. Straight-line

b. Units-of-production

c. Declining-balance

10. Lacy Company paid $550,000 to acquire Gentech Systems. Gentech's assets had a market value of $900,000 and its liabilities were $400,000. In recording the acquisition, Lacy will record goodwill of (pp. 505–506)

a. $50,000

b. $500,000

c. $550,000

d. $0

Answers to the Self-Study Questions follow the Similar Accounting Terms.

Accounting Vocabulary

Amortizable cost   (p. 489)
Amortization   (p. 488)
Amortization expense   (p. 503)
Betterment   (p. 487)
Brand name   (p. 505)
Capital asset   (p. 481)
Capital cost allowance (CCA)   (p. 510)
Capitalize (a cost)   (p. 486)
Commercial substance   (p. 501)
Copyright   (p. 505)
Depletion   (p. 503)
Double-declining-balance (DDB) method   (p. 492)
Estimated residual value   (p. 489)
Estimated useful life   (p. 489)

Franchise   (p. 505)
Goodwill   (p. 505)
Intangible asset   (pp. 481, 504)
Leasehold   (p. 505)
Licence   (p. 505)
Patent   (p. 504)
Repair   (p. 487)
Salvage value   (p. 489)
Scrap value   (p. 489)
Straight-line method   (p. 490)
Trademark   (p. 505)
Trade name   (p. 505)
Units-of-production method   (p. 491)

Similar Accounting Terms

Amortization	Depreciation (for assets such as property, plant, and equipment); Depletion (for natural resources)
Capital assets	Property, plant, and equipment; Long-lived assets; Long-term assets
Natural resources	Wasting assets
Trade name	Brand name
Residual value	Salvage value; Scrap value

Answers to Self-Study Questions

1. d
2. c [($90,000/($90,000 + $60,000)) × $120,000 = $72,000; ($60,000/($90,000 + $60,000)) × $120,000 = $48,000]
3. a   4. b   5. b   6. c
7. a Amortizable cost = $450,000 − $50,000 = $400,000
       $400,000 ÷ 40 years = $10,000 per year
       $400,000 − ($10,000 × 10 years) = $300,000
       $300,000 ÷ 40 years = $7,500 per year
8. d   9. b
10. a [$550,000 − ($900,000 − $400,000) = $50,000]

Questions

1. Describe how to measure the cost of a tangible capital asset. Would an ordinary cost of repairing the asset after it is placed in service be included in the asset's cost?

2. Suppose land with a building on it is purchased for $525,000. How do you account for the $55,000 cost of removing this unwanted building?

3. When assets are purchased as a group for a single price and no individual asset cost is given, how is each asset's cost determined?

4. Distinguish a betterment from a repair. Why are they treated differently for accounting purposes?

5. Define amortization. What are common misconceptions about amortization?

6. To what types of long-lived assets does amortization expense apply?

7. Which amortization method does each of the graphs at the bottom of the page characterize: straight-line, units-of-production, or double-declining-balance?

8. When is it appropriate to capitalize interest? Prepare the journal entry for $25,000 interest cost during construction of a building.

9. Explain the concept of accelerated amortization. Which of the three amortization methods results in the most amortization in the first year of the asset's life?

10. The level of business activity fluctuates widely for Milton Schoolbus Co., reaching its slowest time in June through August each year. At other times, business is brisk. What amortization method is most appropriate for the company's fleet of school buses?

11. Felix Data Centre uses the most advanced computers available to keep a competitive edge over other service centres. To maintain this advantage, the company usually replaces its computers before they are worn out. Describe the major factors affecting the useful life of a tangible capital asset, and indicate which seems more relevant to this company's computers.

12. Which amortization method does not consider estimated residual value in computing amortization during the early years of the asset's life?

13. Describe how to compute amortization for less than a full year, and how to account for amortization for less than a full month.

14. Hudson Company paid $12,000 for office furniture. The company expected it to remain in service for six years and to have a $1,500 residual value. After two years' use, company accountants believe the furniture will last for the next seven years. How much amortization will Hudson record for each of these last seven years, assuming straight-line amortization and no change in the estimated residual value?

15. When a company sells a capital asset before the year's end, what must it record before accounting for the sale?

16. Describe how to determine whether a company experiences a gain or a loss when an old capital asset is exchanged for a new capital asset. Which accounting section of the *CICA Handbook* underlies your answer?

17. What expense applies to natural resources? By which amortization method is this expense computed?

18. How do intangible capital assets differ from most other assets? Why are they assets at all? What expense applies to intangible assets?

19. Why is the cost of patents and other intangible assets often expensed over a shorter period than the legal life of the asset?

20. Your company has just purchased another company for $500,000. The market value of the other company's net assets is $350,000. What is the $150,000 excess called? What type of asset is it? How is goodwill amortized under GAAP?

21. Bombardier Inc. is recognized as a world leader in the manufacture and sale of transportation systems and industrial products. The company's success has created vast amounts of business goodwill. Would you expect to see this goodwill reported on Bombardier Inc. financial statements? Why, or why not?

*22. What is capital cost allowance?

*23. Does amortization affect income taxes? How does amortization affect cash provided by operations?

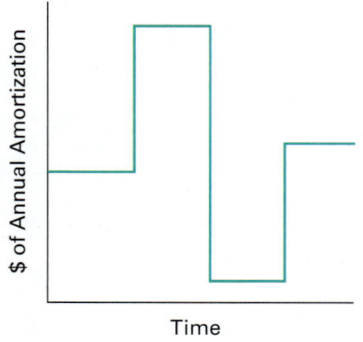

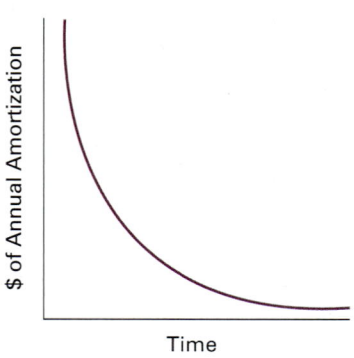

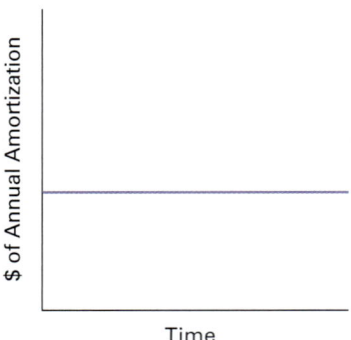

*This Question covers Chapter 10 Appendix topics.

Starters

Starter 10–1 This chapter lists the costs included for the acquisition of land. First is the purchase price of the land, which is obviously included in the cost of the land. The reasons for including the other costs are not so obvious. For example, the removal of a building looks more like an expense. State why the costs listed are included as part of the cost of the land. After the land is ready for use, will these costs be capitalized or expensed?

Measuring the cost of a tangible capital asset

Starter 10–2 Suppose you make a lump-sum purchase of land, building and equipment. At the time of your purchase, the land has a current market value of $80,000, the building's market value is $60,000, and the equipment's market value is $20,000. Journalize the lump-sum purchase of the three assets for a total cost of $120,000. You sign a note payable for this amount.

Lump sum purchase of assets

Land: $60,000

Starter 10–3 JetQuick Airways repaired one of its Boeing 767 aircraft at a cost of $800,000, which JetQuick paid in cash. JetQuick erroneously capitalized this cost as part of the cost of the plane. How will this accounting error affect JetQuick's net income? Ignore amortization.

Capitalizing vesus expensing capital-asset costs

Starter 10–4 At the beginning of the year, JetQuick Airways purchased a used Boeing jet at a cost of $42,000,000. JetQuick expects the plane to remain useful for five years (6,000,000 miles) and to have a residual value of $6,000,000. JetQuick expects the plane to be flown 750,000 miles the first year.

Computing amortization by three methods—first year only

2. Book value $34,800,000

1. Compute JetQuick's first-year amortization on the jet using the following methods:
   a. Straight-line
   b. Units-of-production
   c. Double-declining-balance

2. Show the jet's book value at the end of the first year under the straight-line method.

Starter 10–5 At the beginning of 2007, JetQuick Airways purchased a used Boeing aircraft at a cost of $42,000,000. JetQuick expects the plane to remain useful for five years (6,000,000 miles) and to have a residual value of $6,000,000. JetQuick expects the plane to be flown 750,000 miles the first year and 500,000 miles the second year. Compute second-year amortization on the plane using the following methods:

Computing amortization by three methods—second year

c. $10,080,000

a. Straight-line
b. Units-of-production
c. Double-declining-balance

Starter 10–6 On March 31, 2008, JetQuick Airways purchased a used Boeing jet at a cost of $42,000,000. JetQuick expects to fly the plane for five years and to have a residual value of $6,000,000. Compute JetQuick's amortization on the plane for the year ended December 31, 2008, using the straight-line method.

Partial-year amortization

Starter 10–7 Assume the Bonneville baseball club paid $50,000 for a hot dog stand with a ten-year useful life and no residual value. After using the hot dog stand for four years, the club determines that the asset will remain useful for only two more years. Record amortization on the hot dog stand for year 5 by the straight-line method.

Computing and recording amortization after a change in useful life

Starter 10–8 Return to the Canadian Tire delivery truck in Exhibit 10–6 on page 490. Suppose Canadian Tire sold the truck on December 31, 2009, for $28,000 cash, after using the truck for three full years. Amortization for 2009 has already been recorded. Make the journal entry to record Canadian Tire's sale of the truck under straight-line amortization.

Recording a gain or loss on disposal

Gain on sale $3,000

Starter 10–9 In 2005, Global Travel purchased a Dell computer for $3,000, debiting Computer Equipment. During 2005 and 2006, Global recorded amortization of $2,200 on the computer. In January 2007, Global traded in the computer for a new one with a fair market value of $3,100, paying $2,500 cash. This exchange transaction has commerial substance. Journalize Global Travel's exchange of computers.

Exchanging tangible capital assets

Loss on exchange $200

Accounting for the amortization
of natural resources

2. Amortization expense
$6.0 billion

Starter 10–10 Chevron, the giant oil company, holds huge reserves of oil and gas assets. Assume that at the end of 2006, Chevron's cost of oil and gas assets totaled approximately $18 billion, representing 2.4 billion barrels of oil and gas reserves in the ground.

1. Which amortization method does Chevron use to compute its annual amortization expense for the oil and gas removed from the ground?

2. Suppose Chevron removed 0.8 billion barrels of oil during 2007. Record Chevron's amortization expense for 2007.

Accounting for goodwill

Goodwill $500,000

Starter 10–11 Media-related companies have little in the way of tangible capital assets. Instead, their main asset is goodwill. When one media company buys another, goodwill is often the most costly asset acquired. Media Watch paid $700,000 to acquire *The Thrifty Nickel*, a weekly advertising paper. At the time of the acquisition, *The Thrifty Nickel's* balance sheet reported total assets of $1,200,000 and liabilities of $600,000. The fair market value of *The Thrifty Nickel's* assets was $800,000.

1. How much goodwill did Media Watch purchase as part of the acquisition of *The Thrifty Nickel?*

2. Journalize Media Watch's acquisition of *The Thrifty Nickel*.

Accounting for patents and
research and development cost

Net income $200,000

Starter 10–12 This exercise summarizes the accounting for patents and research costs.
Questor Applications paid $800,000 in research costs for a new software program. Questor also paid $500,000 to acquire a patent on other software. After readying the software for production, Questor's sales revenue for the first year totaled $1,700,000. Cost of goods sold was $200,000, and selling expenses were $400,000. All these transactions occurred during 2008. Questor expects the patent to have a useful life of five years. Prepare Questor Applications' income statement for the year ended December 31, 2008, complete with a heading.

Selecting the best amortization
method for income-tax purposes

2. Extra tax reduction
$3,300,000

*****Starter 10–13** This exercise uses the JetQuick Airways data from Starter 10–4. JetQuick is comparing the capital cost allowance (CCA) method used for income tax purposes with the straight-line amortization method.

1. Does CCA (at a rate of 25%) or the straight-line method offer the tax advantage for the first year? Describe the nature of the tax advantage.

2. How much extra amortization will JetQuick be able to deduct for income-tax purposes for the first year using CCA rates as compared with using the straight-line method? Assume the CCA rate is 25% and ignore the half-year rule.

Exercises

Determining the cost of property,
plant, and equipment

Exercise 10–1

The law firm of Marshall & Wilson purchased land, paying $95,000 cash as a down payment and signing a $155,000 note payable for the balance. In addition, the company paid property tax in arrears of $2,750, a legal fee of $1,500, and a $19,500 charge for levelling the land and removing an unwanted building. The company constructed an office building on the land at a cost of $750,000. It also paid $20,000 for a fence around the boundary of the property, $8,500 for the company sign near the entrance to the property, and $11,800 for special lighting of the grounds. Determine the cost of the company's land, land improvements, and building.

Allocating cost to assets
acquired in a lump-sum purchase

Truck 1: $17,280

Exercise 10–2

Lalonde Trucking bought three used trucks for $48,000. An independent appraisal of the trucks produced the following figures:

Truck No.	Appraised Value
1	$18,000
2	17,000
3	15,000

---

*This Starter covers Chapter 10 Appendix topics.

Lalonde Trucking paid 25 percent in cash and signed a note for the remainder. Record the purchase in the general journal, identifying each truck's individual cost in a separate Truck account.

Exercise 10–3

Measuring the cost of an asset; distinguishing betterments from repairs

Classify each of the following expenditures as 1. a cost/betterment, 2. a repair (expense) related to a machine used to earn revenue, or 3. other: (a) purchase price; (b) sales tax paid on the purchase price; (c) transportation and insurance while the machine is in transport from seller to buyer; (d) installation; (e) training of personnel for initial operation of the machine; (f) special reinforcement to the machine platform; (g) income tax paid on income earned from the sale of products manufactured by the machine; (h) major overhaul to extend useful life by three years; (i) ordinary recurring repairs to keep the machine in good working order; (j) lubrication before the machine is placed in service; (k) periodic lubrication after the machine is placed in service; and (l) goods and services tax on the purchase price.

Exercise 10–4

Capitalizing versus expensing; measuring the effect of an error

Zabba Shoes is a family-owned retail shoe operation with stores in Owen Sound and Thornbury. Assume that early in year 1, Zabba Shoes purchased computerized point-of-sale and operating systems costing $100,000. Bob Zabba expects this equipment will support the inventory and accounting requirements for four years. Because of technology obsolescence, no residual value is anticipated. Through error, Zabba Shoes accidentally expensed the entire cost of the equipment at the time of the purchase. Zabba Shoes' accounting policy for equipment amortization is the straight-line amortization method. The company is operated as a sole proprietorship, so it pays no corporate income tax.

Required

Compute the overstatement or understatement in these items immediately after purchasing the equipment.

1. Equipment
2. Net income

Exercise 10–5

Explaining the concept of amortization

Ron Zander has just slept through the class in which Professor Larston explained the concept of amortization. Because the next test is scheduled for Wednesday, Zander telephones Nancy Wu to get her notes from the lecture. Wu's notes are concise: "Amortization—Sounds like Greek to me." Zander next tries Sally Nadeau, who says she thinks amortization is what happens when an asset wears out. Barry Orwell is confident that amortization is the process of building up a cash fund to replace an asset at the end of its useful life. Explain the concept of amortization for Ron Zander. Evaluate the explanations of Nadeau and Orwell. Be specific.

Exercise 10–6

 Excel Spreadsheet Template

Determining amortization amounts by three methods

1. Amortization expense in 2008: Straight-line $32,000; UOP $30,720; DDB $7,111

Tarot Machine & Dye bought a machine on January 2, 2006, for $100,000. The machine was expected to remain in service for three years and produce 2,000,000 parts. At the end of its useful life, company officials estimated that the machine's residual value would be $4,000. The machine produced 700,000 parts in the first year, 660,000 in the second year, and 650,000 in the third year.

Required

1. Prepare a schedule of *amortization expense* per year for the machine using the straight-line, units-of-production, and double-declining-balance amortization methods.

2. Which method tracks the wear and tear on the machine most closely? Why?

3. After one year under the double-declining-balance method, the company switched to the straight-line method. Prepare a schedule of amortization expense for this situation, showing all calculations.

Changing a capital asset's useful life

Amortization for Year 20 $7,750

Exercise 10–7

Vachon Marketing Services purchased a building for $425,000 and amortized it on a straight-line basis over a 50-year period. The estimated residual value was $37,500. After using the building for 20 years, the company realized that wear and tear on the building would force the company to replace it before 50 years. Starting with the 21st year, the company began amortizing the building over a revised *total* life of 35 years, increasing the estimated residual value to $67,500. Record amortization expense on the building for years 20 and 21.

Analyzing the effect of a sale of a capital asset; double-declining-balance amortization

Gain on sale $6,598

Exercise 10–8

On January 2, 2007, Baldwin Gifts purchased store fixtures for $43,000 cash, expecting the fixtures to remain in service for seven years. Baldwin Gifts has amortized the fixtures on a double-declining-balance basis with an estimated residual value of $2,000. On October 31, 2008, Baldwin Gifts sold the fixtures for $30,000 cash. Record both the amortization expense on the fixtures for 2007 and 2008, and the sale of the fixtures on October 31, 2008. Baldwin Gifts' year end is December 31. Round all calculations to the nearest dollar.

Measuring a capital asset's cost, using units-of-production amortization, and trading in a used asset

Loss on exchange of trucks $14,467

Exercise 10–9

Robertson Distribution, based in Brampton, Ontario, is a large warehousing and distribution company that operates throughout Eastern Canada. Robertson Distribution uses the units-of-production method to amortize its trucks because its managers believe units-of-production amortization best measures the wear and tear on the trucks. Robertson Distribution trades in used trucks often to keep driver morale high and to maximize fuel efficiency. Consider these facts about one Mack truck in the company's fleet:

When acquired in 2004, the tractor/trailer rig cost $385,000 and was expected to remain in service for eight years, or 1,500,000 kilometres. Estimated residual value was $75,000. The truck was driven 150,000 kilometres in 2004, 195,000 kilometres in 2005, and 235,000 kilometres in 2006. After 100,000 kilometres in 2007, the company traded in the Mack truck for a Freightliner rig with a fair market value of $250,000. Robertson Distribution paid cash of $20,000. This trade-in will bring in significantly more income to Robertson by reducing operating cost. Determine Robertson Distribution's cost of the new truck. Prepare the journal entry to record the trade-in.

Recording natural resources and amortization

(3) Amortization expense $182,605

Exercise 10–10

Lakefield Mining Ltd. paid $870,000 for the right to extract ore from a 300,000-tonne mineral deposit. In addition to the purchase price, the company also paid a $1,000 filing fee, a $2,500 licence fee to the province of Quebec, and $55,000 for a geological survey. Because Lakefield Mining Ltd. purchased the rights to the minerals only, the company expected the asset to have zero residual value when fully depleted. During the first year of production, the company removed 59,000 tonnes of ore. Make general journal entries to record (1) purchase of the mineral rights (debit Mineral Asset), (2) payment of fees and other costs, and (3) amortization for first-year production.

Recording intangibles, amortization, and a change in the asset's useful life

2. Amortization for Year 3 $87,500

Exercise 10–11

1. Curzon Company manufactures flat screen monitors for the graphics industry and has recently purchased for $175,000 a patent for the design of a new monitor. Although it gives legal protection for 20 years, the patent is expected to provide Curzon Company with a competitive advantage for only four years. Assuming the straight-line method of amortization, use general journal entries to record (1) the purchase of the patent, and (2) amortization for year 1.

2. After using the patent for two years, Curzon Company learns at an industry trade show that another company is designing a more effective monitor. Based on this new information, Curzon Company decides to amortize the remaining cost of the patent over the current year, giving the patent a total useful life of three years. Record amortization for year 3.

Exercise 10–12

Thomson Industries acquired companies with assets with a market value of $145 million and liabilities of $50 million. Thompson paid $277 million for these acquisitions during the year ended December 31, 2007.

Measuring goodwill

2. Goodwill $182 million

Required

1. How would a value be assigned to the net assets acquired?
2. What value would be assigned to goodwill?
3. Will the goodwill be amortized? If so, by how much?

Exercise 10–13

The financial statements of Mallard Transportation for the year ended December 31, 2007, reported the following details of acquisitions (adapted):

Accounting for goodwill

1. Goodwill $24,450

Assets:	In thousands
Cash	$ 1,700
Current assets	4,200
Property, Plant, and Equipment	36,000
Intangibles	350
	$42,250
Liabilities:	
Long-term debt	$ 8,200

Mallard Transportation paid $58,500 cash for the acquisitions.

Required

1. How much goodwill did Mallard Transportation purchase as part of the 2007 acquisitions?
2. Prepare the Mallard Transportation Inc. summary journal entry to record the acquisition for 2007.
3. Assume that, in 2008, the annual review of goodwill identified a 15-percent impairment of the goodwill acquired in 2007. Prepare the journal entry required to record this impairment.

Exercise 10–14

In 2006, Caledan Electronics purchased Raytheon Radio Inc., paying $1.5 million in a note payable. The market value of Raytheon Radio Inc.'s assets was $2.6 million, and Raytheon Radio Ltd. had liabilities of $1.5 million.

Computing and recording goodwill

1. Goodwill $400,000

Required

1. Compute the cost of the goodwill purchased by Caledan Electronics.
2. Record the purchase by Caledan Electronics.
3. At 2006 year end, the annual review of goodwill value indicated no impairment of goodwill. Record the entry Caledan will make for goodwill for 2006.
4. At 2008 year end, the annual review of goodwill value indicated a 10-percent impairment of the Raytheon Radio goodwill. Record the entry for the goodwill loss for 2008.

*Exercise 10–15

In 2007, Maxwell Inc. paid $125,000 for equipment that is expected to have a five-year life. In this industry, the residual value is estimated to be five percent of the asset's cost. Maxwell Inc. plans to use straight-line amortization for accounting purposes. Discuss which amortization method Maxwell Inc. should use for income-tax purposes. Should the same method be used for reporting on the financial statements?

Selecting the amortization method for income tax purposes
7

---

*This Exercise covers Chapter 10 Appendix topics.

Challenge Exercises

Reconstructing transactions from the financial statements

1. $118 thousand

Exercise 10–16

Lenny's Furniture Limited's 2008 financial statements reported these amounts (in thousands of dollars):

| | December 31 | | | |
| | 2008 | | 2007 | |
Properties	Cost	Accumulated Amortization	Cost	Accumulated Amortization
Land	$ 41,378	—	$ 35,073	—
Buildings	116,832	$ 51,566	105,325	$ 46,981
Equipment	17,940	11,712	16,575	10,678
Vehicles	13,994	11,533	13,513	10,680
Computer hardware and software	6,869	4,335	5,885	3,614
Leasehold improvements	26,178	7,461	21,081	6,220
	$223,191	$ 86,607	$197,452	$ 78,173
Net book value		$136,584		$119,279

In the 2008 annual report, Lenny's Furniture Limited reported amortization expense in 2008 of $8,552,000. In addition, the company reported it had disposed of certain capital assets and acquired others. The gain on disposal of capital assets was $56,000.

Required

1. What was the accumulated amortization of the assets disposed of during 2008?
2. Assume that Lenny's Furniture Limited acquired assets costing $27,681,000 during 2008. What was the cost price of the assets sold during the year?
3. Write the journal entry to record the disposal of the assets during the year.

Beyond the Numbers

Beyond the Numbers 10–1

The following questions are unrelated except that they apply to capital assets:

1. Charlotte Quick, the owner of Quick Secretarial Services, regularly debits the cost of repairs and maintenance of capital assets to Plant and Equipment. Why would she do that, since she knows she is violating GAAP?
2. It has been suggested that, since many intangible assets have no value except to the company that owns them, they should be valued at $1.00 or zero on the balance sheet. Many accountants disagree with this view. Which view do you support? Why?
3. Marv Brown, the owner of Lakeshore Motors, regularly buys capital assets (property, plant, and equipment) and debits the cost to Repairs and Maintenance Expense. Why would he do that, since he knows this action violates GAAP?

Ethical Issue

Newport Group Developers purchased land and a building for a lump sum of $3.5 million. To get the maximum tax deduction, Newport's owner allocated 85 percent of the purchase price to the building and only 15 percent to the land. A more realistic allocation would have been 75 percent to the building and 25 percent to the land.

Required

1. Explain the tax advantage of allocating too much to the building and too little to the land.
2. Was Newport Group Developers' allocation ethical? If so, state why. If not, why not? Identify who was harmed.

Problems (Group A)

Problem 10–1A

Bodnar Landscaping incurred the following costs in acquiring land and a building, making land improvements, and constructing and furnishing an office building for its own use.

a. Purchase price of 2 hectares of land, including an old building that will be used as a shed for storage of landscaping and maintenance equipment (land appraised market value is $650,000; building appraised market value is $150,000) $575,000

b. Real estate taxes in arrears on the land to be paid by Bodnar Landscaping 3,000

c. Additional dirt and earth moving 2,995

d. Legal fees on the land acquisition 2,225

e. Fence around the boundary of the land 35,000

f. Building permit for the office building 500

g. Architect fee for the design of the office building 40,000

h. Company signs near front and rear approaches to the company property 9,500

i. Renovation of the storage building 80,000

j. Concrete, wood, steel girders, and other materials used in the construction of the office building 335,000

k. Masonry, carpentry, roofing, and other labour to construct the office building 275,000

l. Parking lots and concrete walks on the property 15,775

m. Lights for the parking lot, walkways, and company signs 10,350

n. Supervisory salary of construction supervisor (90 percent to office building and 10 percent to shed renovation) 50,000

o. Office furniture for the office building 67,500

p. Transportation of furniture from seller to the office building 1,000

q. Flowers and plants 1,750

Bodnar Landscaping amortizes buildings over 40 years, land improvements over 20 years, and furniture over six years, all on a straight-line basis with zero residual value.

Required

1. Set up columns for Land, Land Improvements, Office Building, Maintenance Shed, and Furniture. Show how to account for each of Bodnar's costs by listing the cost under the correct account. Determine the total cost of each asset.

2. Assuming that all construction was complete and the assets were placed in service on February 25, record amortization for the year ended December 31. Round figures to the nearest dollar.

Identifying the elements of a capital asset's cost

2. Amortization expense: Land improvements $3,016 Office building $14,490

Problem 10–2A

Rogers Research surveys Canadian opinions. The company's balance sheet reports the following assets under Property, Plant, and Equipment: Land, Buildings, Office Furniture, Communication Equipment, and Televideo Equipment. The company has a separate accumulated amortization account for each of these assets except land. Assume that the company completed the following transactions during 2007:

Feb. 2   Traded in communication equipment with a book value of $13,000 (cost of $101,000) for similar new equipment with a fair market value of $98,000. The seller gave Rogers a trade-in allowance of $18,000 on the old equipment, and the company paid the remainder in cash. This transaction meets the criteria for commercial substance.

Recording capital asset transactions; exchanges; changes in useful life

Dec. 31, 2007, Amortization expense—Buildings $700,000

July	19	Sold a building that had cost $525,000 and had accumulated amortization of $370,666 through December 31, 2006. Amortization is computed on a straight-line basis. The building has a 30-year useful life and a residual value of $45,000. Rogers received $75,000 cash and a $650,000 note receivable.
Oct.	21	Purchased used communication and televideo equipment from the A.C. Neilsen Company of Canada Ltd. Total cost was $100,000 paid in cash. An independent appraisal valued the communication equipment at $85,000 and the televideo equipment at $40,000.
Dec.	31	Recorded amortization as follows:

Equipment is amortized by the double-declining-balance method over a six-year life. Record amortization on the equipment purchased on February 2 and on October 21 separately.

Amortization on buildings is computed by the straight-line method. The company had assigned buildings an estimated useful life of 30 years and a residual value that is 30 percent of cost. After using the buildings for 10 years, the company has come to believe that their *total* useful life will be 20 years. Residual value remains unchanged. The buildings cost $15,000,000.

Required   Record the transactions in the journal of Rogers Research.

Explaining the concept of amortization

Problem 10–3A

The board of directors of Little People Nursery School is having its regular quarterly meeting. Accounting policies are on the agenda, and amortization is being discussed. A new board member, a personal trainer, has some strong opinions about two aspects of amortization policy. Marcia Goldblatt argues that amortization must be coupled with a fund to replace company assets. Otherwise, she argues, there is no substance to amortization. She also challenges the five-year estimated life over which Little People Nursery School is amortizing the centre's computers. She notes that the computers will last much longer and should be amortized over at least 10 years.

Required   Write a paragraph or two to explain the concept of amortization to Ms. Goldblatt and to answer her arguments.

Computing amortization by three methods

1. Book value, Dec. 31, 2009:
   Straight-line $47,375;
   UOP $45,467; DDB $17,500

Problem 10–4A

On January 5, 2007, Bassegio Construction purchased a used crane at a total cost of $125,000. Before placing the crane in service, the company spent $5,250 painting it, $2,000 replacing tires, and $4,750 overhauling the engine. Carlo Bassegio, the owner, estimates that the crane will remain in service for four years and have a residual value of $17,500. The crane's annual usage is expected to be 2,400 hours in each of the first three years and 2,200 hours in the fourth year. In trying to decide which amortization method to use, Mary Sharp, the accountant, requests an amortization schedule for each of the following generally accepted amortization methods: straight-line, units-of-production, and double-declining-balance.

Required

1. Assuming Bassegio Construction amortizes this crane individually, prepare an amortization schedule for each of the three amortization methods listed, showing asset cost, amortization expense, accumulated amortization, and asset book value. Assume a December 31 year end.

2. Bassegio Construction prepares for its bankers financial statements using the amortization method that maximizes reported income in the early years of asset use. Identify the amortization method that meets the company's objective.

Journalizing capital asset transactions: asset exchanges, betterments versus repairs

Dec. 31, 2007 Amortization expense $5,000

Problem 10–5A

Assume that Clark Warehousing completed the following transactions:

2006		
Mar.	3	Paid $10,000 cash for a used forklift.
	5	Paid $3,000 to have the forklift engine overhauled.

Mar.	7	Paid $1,300 to have the forklift modified for specialized moving of auto parts.
Nov.	3	Paid $1,588 for transmission repair and oil change after the forklift was put into use.
Dec.	31	Used the double-declining-balance method to record amortization on the forklift. (Assume a three-year life.)

2007

Feb.	13	Replaced the forklift's broken fork for $400 cash, the deductible on Clark Warehousing's insurance.
July	20	Traded in the forklift for a new forklift costing $30,000. The dealer granted a $6,000 allowance on the old forklift, and Clark Warehousing paid the balance in cash. Recorded 2007 amortization for the year to date and then recorded the exchange of forklifts. This transaction has commercial substance.
Dec.	31	Used the double-declining-balance method to record amortization on the new forklift. (Assume a five-year life.)

Required   Record the transactions in the general journal, indicating whether each transaction amount should be capitalized as an asset or expensed. Round all calculations to the nearest dollar.

Problem 10–6A

Part 1   Petral Canada Limited sells refined petroleum products. The company's balance sheet includes reserves of oil assets.

Suppose Petral paid $10 million cash for an oil lease that contained an estimated reserve of 1,990,000 barrels of oil. Assume that the company paid $375,000 for additional geological tests of the property and $115,000 to prepare the surface for drilling. Prior to production, the company signed an $80,000 note payable to have a building constructed on the property. Because the building provides on-site headquarters for the drilling effort and will be abandoned when the oil is depleted, its cost is debited to the Oil Properties account and included in amortization charges. During the first year of production, Petral removed 125,000 barrels of oil, which it sold on credit for $46 per barrel.

Required   Make general journal entries to record all transactions related to the oil and gas property, including amortization and sale of the first-year production.

Part 2   Maple Canada provides telephone service to most of Canada. Assume that Maple Canada purchased another company, which carried these figures:

Book value of assets	$1,280,000
Market value of assets	1,500,000
Liabilities	450,000

Required

1. Make the general journal entry to record Maple Canada's purchase of the other company for $1,350,000 cash.
2. How should Maple Canada account for goodwill at year end and in the future? Explain in detail.

Part 3   Suppose Research in Motion Limited (RIM) purchased a patent for $1,000,000. Before using the patent, RIM incurred an additional cost of $125,000 for a lawsuit to defend the company's right to purchase it. Even though the patent gives RIM legal protection for 20 years, company management has decided to amortize its cost over a seven-year period because of the industry's fast-changing technologies.

Required   Make general journal entries to record the patent transactions, including straight-line amortization for one year.

Recording intangibles and the related expenses

Amortization expense $663,945

1. Goodwill $300,000

Amortization expense $160,714

Identifying the elements of property, plant, and equipment's cost; accounting for amortization by two methods; accounting for disposal of property, plant, and equipment; distinguishing betterments from repairs

2. Total Property, plant and equipment $656,286

Problem 10–7A

Potter Toy Co. has a fiscal year ending August 31. The company completed the following capital asset transactions:

2007

Feb. 2 Paid $700,000 plus $40,000 in legal fees (pertaining to all assets purchased) to purchase the following assets from a competitor who was going out of business:

Asset	Appraised Value	Estimated Useful Life	Estimated Residual Value
Land	$300,000	—	—
Buildings	200,000	8 years	$20,000
Equipment................	100,000	3 years	8,000

Potter Toy Co. plans to use the straight-line amortization method for the building and for the equipment.

June 2 Purchased a delivery truck with a list price of $30,000 for $27,000 cash. The truck is expected to be used for three years and driven a total of 300,000 kilometres; it is then expected to be sold for $2,500. It will be amortized using the units-of-production method.

**   3** Paid $3,000 to paint the truck with the company's colours and logo.

Aug. 31 Recorded amortization on the assets. The truck had been driven 20,000 kilometres since it was purchased.

2008

Jan. 4 Potter Toy Co. paid $9,000 to Lawson Services Ltd. for work done on the equipment. The job consisted of annual maintenance ($1,000) and the addition of automatic controls ($8,000), which will increase the expected useful life of the equipment to a total of five years and increase its expected residual value by $1,000.

Aug. 25 Sold the truck for $18,000. The truck had an odometer reading of 140,000 kilometres.

Aug. 31 Recorded amortization on the assets.

Required

1. Record the above transactions of Potter Toy Co. Round all amounts to the nearest dollar.
2. Show the balance sheet presentation of the assets at August 31, 2008.

Accounting for natural resources, intangible assets, and related expenses

3. Total capital assets $5,925,500

Problem 10–8A

On October 2, 2008, Nunavut Mines Inc. acquired Resolute Exploration Ltd. for $5,500,000. At the time of the acquisition, Resolute's balance sheet contained the following items, which were transferred to Nunavut Mines Inc.:

- Mining Equipment: original cost of $11,000,000 and a present market value of $750,000. The equipment is expected to last another 10 years and have a residual value of $15,000 at that time.

- Mineral Rights: the rights to mine property by Grise Fiord. The mineral rights originally cost Resolute $1,500,000 but now have an appraised market value of $4,200,000. The mine is expected to produce 75,000,000 tonnes of ore over the next 10 years.

- Leasehold: the rights to rent office space in a nearby town for $5,500 per month for the next 12 years. The leasehold has a market value today of $60,000 because of high rental rates in the area.

- Mortgage Payable: a $700,000 mortgage is outstanding on the mining equipment with interest at current rates.

Required

1. Journalize the purchase of Resolute Exploration Ltd. by Nunavut Mines Inc.
2. Journalize the adjusting entries required for the year ending September 30, 2009, to amortize the cost of the assets, assuming 3,500,000 tonnes of ore were taken out of the mine. Use the most appropriate methods and time frames from the data given.

3. Show how the assets would appear in the capital assets section of Nunavut Mines Inc.'s balance sheet as of September 30, 2009.

Problems (Group B)

Problem 10–1B

Identifying the elements of a capital asset's cost

2. Amortization:
Land improvements $4,289
Office building $39,458

The owner of Big Heart Movers incurred the following costs in acquiring land, making land improvements, and constructing and furnishing the company's office building in the year ended December 31, 2008.

a. Purchase price of four hectares of land, including an old building that will be used for a garage (land appraised market value is $700,000; building appraised market value is $90,000)	$ 650,000
b. Additional dirt and earth moving	13,000
c. Fence around the boundary of the land	25,000
d. Legal fee for title search on the land	1,000
e. Real estate taxes in arrears on the land to be paid by Big Heart Movers	9,600
f. Company signs at front of the company property	6,000
g. Building permit for the office building	1,000
h. Architect fee for the design of the office building	59,500
i. Masonry, carpentry, roofing, and other labour to construct office building	1,622,000
j. Concrete, wood, steel girders, and other materials used in the construction of the office building	590,000
k. Renovation of the garage	62,000
l. Flowers and plants	15,000
m. Parking lot and concrete walks on the property	46,900
n. Lights for the parking lot, walkways, and company signs	17,400
o. Supervisory salary of construction supervisor (95 percent to office building and 5 percent to garage renovation)	100,000
p. Office furniture for the office building	170,000
q. Transportation and installation of office furniture	3,900

Big Heart Movers amortizes buildings over 35 years, land improvements over 15 years, and furniture over five years, all on a straight-line basis with zero residual value.

Required

1. Set up columns for Land, Land Improvements, Office Building, Garage Building, and Furniture. Show how to account for each of Big Heart Movers' costs by listing the cost under the correct account. Determine the total cost of each asset.

2. Assuming that all construction was complete and the assets were placed in service on June 10, record amortization for the year ending December 31, 2008. Round off figures to the nearest dollar.

Problem 10–2B

Recording capital asset transactions; exchanges; changes in useful life

Amortization expense
Motor carrier equipment
at Dec. 31, 2008 $75,625

Sanga Freight provides general freight service in Canada. The business's balance sheet includes the following assets under Property, Plant, and Equipment: Land, Buildings, and Motor Carrier Equipment. Sanga Freight has a separate accumulated amortization account for each of these assets except land.

Assume that Sanga Freight completed the following transactions during 2008:

Feb. 6 Traded in motor-carrier equipment with a book value of $43,000 (cost of $140,000) for similar new equipment with a fair market value of $165,000. Sanga Freight received a trade-in allowance of $60,000 on the old equipment and paid the remainder in cash. This transaction met the criteria for commercial substance.

June 3 Sold a building that had cost $625,000 and had accumulated amortization of $295,350 through December 31, 2007. Amortization is computed on a straight-line basis. The building has a 35-year useful life and a residual value of $75,000. Sanga Freight received $150,000 cash and a $500,000 note receivable.

Sept. 25 Purchased land and a building for a single price of $395,000. An independent appraisal valued the land at $130,000 and the building at $285,000.

Dec. 31 Recorded amortization as follows:

Motor-carrier equipment has an expected useful life of four years and an estimated residual value of 6 percent of cost. Amortization is computed using the double-declining-balance method.

Amortization on buildings is computed by the straight-line method. The company had assigned to its older buildings, which cost $3,900,000, an estimated useful life of 30 years with a residual value equal to 30 percent of the asset cost. However, the owner of Sanga Freight has come to believe that the buildings will remain useful for a total of 35 years. Residual value remains unchanged. The company has used all its buildings, except for the one purchased on September 25, for ten years. The new building carries a 35-year useful life and a residual value equal to 30 percent of its cost. Make separate entries for amortization on the building acquired on September 25 and the other buildings purchased in earlier years.

Required Record the transactions in Sanga Freight's general journal.

Explaining the concept of amortization

②

Problem 10–3B

The board of directors of Smythe Properties Ltd. is reviewing the 2008 annual report. A new board member, a dermatologist with little business experience, questions the company accountant about the amortization amounts. The dermatologist wonders why amortization expense has decreased from $250,000 in 2006, to $230,000 in 2007, and to $215,000 in 2008. He states that he could understand the decreasing annual amounts if the company had been disposing of properties each year, but that has not occurred. Further, he notes that growth in the city is increasing the values of company properties. Why is the company recording amortization when the property values are increasing?

Required Write a paragraph or two to explain the concept of amortization to the dermatologist and to answer his questions.

Excel Spreadsheet Template

Computing amortization by three methods

1. Book value Dec. 31, 2009:
   Straight-line $69,500;
   UOP $54,625; DDB $31,000

Problem 10–4B

On January 5, 2007, Nerdis Inc. paid $219,000 for equipment used in manufacturing computer equipment. In addition to the basic purchase price, the business paid $1,100 transportation charges, $300 insurance for the goods in transit, $17,600 provincial sales tax, and $10,000 for a special platform on which to place the equipment in the plant. Nerdis Inc.'s owner estimates that the equipment will remain in service for four years and have a residual value of $10,000. The equipment will produce 75,000 units in the first year, with annual production decreasing by 10,000 units during each of the next three years (that is, 65,000 units in year 2, 55,000 units in year 3, and so on). In trying to decide which amortization method to use, owner Deborah Balfour has requested an amortization schedule for each of three generally accepted amortization methods: straight-line, units-of-production, and double-declining-balance.

Required

1. For each of the generally accepted amortization methods listed above, prepare an amortization schedule showing asset cost, amortization expense, accumulated amortization, and asset book value. Assume a December 31 year end.

2. Nerdis Inc. prepares financial statements for its creditors using the amortization method that maximizes reported income in the early years of asset use. Identify the amortization method that meets the business's objective.

Problem 10–5B

Assume that Executive Limousines completed the following transactions:

2008
Jan. 5 Paid $25,000 cash for a used limousine.
      6 Paid $1,200 to have the engine overhauled.
      9 Paid $2,500 to have the company logo put on the limousine.
June 15 Paid $150 for a minor tune-up after limousine was put into use.
Dec. 31 Recorded amortization on the limousine by the double-declining-balance method. (Assume a four-year life.)

2009
Mar. 9 Traded in the limousine for a new limousine costing $50,000. The dealer granted a $15,000 allowance on the old limousine, and the company paid the balance in cash. Recorded year 2009 amortization for the year to date and then recorded the exchange of the limousines. This transaction has commercial substance.
Aug. 9 Repaired the new limousine's damaged fender for $3,500 cash.
Dec. 31 Recorded amortization on the new limousine by the double-declining-balance method. (Assume a four-year life and a residual value of $10,000.)

Required Record the transactions in the general journal, indicating whether each transaction amount should be capitalized as an asset or expensed. Round all calculations to the nearest dollar.

Journalizing capital asset transactions; betterments versus repairs

Dec. 31, 2009 Amortization expense $20,833

Problem 10–6B

Part 1 Norcan Inc. is a global producer and marketer of rolled aluminum products.

Suppose Norcan Inc. paid $2.2 million cash for a lease giving the firm the right to work a mine that contained an estimated 400,000 tonnes of bauxite. Assume that the company paid $15,000 to remove unwanted buildings from the land and $65,000 to prepare the surface for mining. Further assume that Norcan Inc. signed a $70,000 note payable to a landscaping company to return the land surface to its original condition after the lease ends. During the first year, Norcan Inc. removed 37,000 tonnes of bauxite, which it sold on account for $20 per tonne.

Required Make general journal entries to record all transactions related to the bauxite, including amortization and sale of the first-year production.

Accounting for natural resources, intangibles, and the related expenses

1. Amortization expense $217,315

Part 2 The Roasted Bean Ltd. operates franchised coffee shops. Assume that The Roasted Bean Ltd. purchased another company, which carried these figures:

Book value of assets	$2.4 million
Market value of assets	3.6 million
Liabilities	1.8 million

1. Goodwill $400,000

Required

1. Make the general journal entry to record The Roasted Bean Ltd.'s purchase of the other company for $2.2 million cash.
2. How should The Roasted Bean Ltd. account for goodwill at year end and in the future? Explain in detail.

Part 3 Suppose Sarah Belyea purchased a Roasted Bean franchise licence for $225,000. In addition to the basic purchase price, Belyea also paid a lawyer $7,500 for assistance with the negotiations. Belyea believes the appropriate amortization period for the cost of the franchise licence is 10 years.

Amortization expense $23,250

Required Make general journal entries to record the franchise transactions, including straight-line amortization for one year.

Identifying the elements of
property, plant, and equipment's
cost; accounting for amortization
by two methods; accounting for
disposal of property, plant, and
equipment; distinguishing
betterments from repairs

2. Total Property, plant and
equipment $793,536

Problem 10–7B

Noran TV Station's year end is June 30. The company completed the following capital asset transactions:

2007

Apr. 1   Paid $750,000 plus $75,000 in legal fees (pertaining to all assets purchased) to purchase the following assets from a competitor who was going out of business:

Asset	Appraised Value	Estimated Useful Life	Estimated Residual Value
Land	$340,000	—	—
Buildings	296,000	30 years	$60,000
Equipment	212,000	5 years	20,000

Noran TV Station plans to use the straight-line amortization method for the building and for the equipment.

May 1   Purchased a mobile broadcast unit truck with a list price of $150,000 for $130,000 cash. The truck is expected to be used for four years and driven a total of 300,000 kilometres; it is then expected to be sold for $30,000. It will be amortized using the units-of-production method.

3   Paid $11,000 to paint the truck with the station's colours and logo.

June 30   Recorded amortization on the assets. The mobile unit had been driven 12,500 kilometres since it was purchased.

Dec. 30   Noran TV Station paid $21,100 to Maxwell Auto for work done on the equipment. The job consisted of annual maintenance ($1,100) and the addition of automatic controls ($20,000), which will increase the expected useful life of the equipment by one year (making a total of six years) and increase its expected residual value by $10,000.

2008

June 1   Sold the mobile unit truck for $100,000. The unit had an odometer reading of 82,000 kilometres.

30   Recorded amortization on the assets.

Required

1. Record the above transactions of Noran TV Station. Round all amounts to the nearest dollar.

2. Show the balance sheet presentation of the assets at June 30, 2008.

Accounting for property, plant
and equipment, and amortization;
accounting for natural resources
and amortization; accounting for
intangible assets and
amortization

3. Total capital assets
$2,039,791

Problem 10–8B

On January 4, 2008, Silco Mines Ltd. acquired Maple Mines Inc. for $1,875,000. At the time of the acquisition, Maple Mines Inc.'s balance sheet contained the following items, which were transferred to Silco Mines Ltd.:

• Mining Equipment: original cost of $750,000 and a present market value of $500,000. The equipment is expected to last another eight years and have a residual value of $22,500 at that time.

• Mineral Rights: the rights to mine property by Long Lac. The mineral rights originally cost Maple Mines Inc. $1,250,000 but now have an appraised market value of $1,625,000. The mine is expected to produce 30,000,000 tonnes of ore over the next 12 years.

• Leasehold: the rights to rent office space in a nearby town for $2,375 per month for the next eight years. The leasehold has a market value today of $12,500 because of high rental rates in the area.

• Mortgage Payable: a $375,000 mortgage is outstanding on the mining equipment with interest at current rates.

Required

1. Journalize the purchase of Maple Mines Inc. by Silco Mines Ltd.

2. Journalize the adjusting entries required for the year ending December 31, 2008, to amortize the cost of the assets—assuming 2,750,000 tonnes of ore were taken out of the mine. Use the most appropriate methods and time frames from the data given.

3. Show how the assets would appear on Silco Mines Ltd.'s balance sheet as of December 31, 2008.

Challenge Problems

Problem 10–1C

Understanding amortization and betterments and repairs

The owner of newly formed Georgian Bay Air Taxi, a friend of your family, knows you are taking an accounting course and asks for some advice. Mr. Lind tells you that he is pretty good at running the company but doesn't understand accounting. Specifically, he has two concerns:

1. The company has just paid $1,000,000 for two used float planes. His accountants tell him that he should use accelerated amortization for his financial statements but he understands that straight-line amortization will result in lower charges to expense in the early years. He wants to use straight-line amortization.

2. A friend told him that Georgian Bay Air Taxi should capitalize all repairs to the planes and "spread the cost out over the life of the planes." He wonders if there is anything wrong with this advice.

Required Respond to Mr. Lind's questions using your understanding of amortization, and betterments and repairs.

Problem 10–2C

Accounting for natural resources

Zadok Mining Corp. is a new company that has been formed to mine for nickel in Northern Ontario. The ore body is estimated to contain 100,000,000 kilograms of pure nickel for which the world price is $14,400 per tonne. The costs of mine development are estimated to be $80,000,000.

Required Calculate the costs that would be charged against the nickel production in the form of amortization on a per-1,000-kilogram basis. Estimate any costs you think should also be included. Do not include the costs to mine and refine the ore, or shipping and selling costs.

Extending Your Knowledge

Decision Problem

Measuring profitability based on different inventory and amortization methods

1. Net income:
Louie Associates $152,000
Chan Co. $72,000

Suppose you are considering investing in two businesses, Louie Associates and Chan Co. The two companies are virtually identical, and both began operations at the beginning of 2008. During the year, each company purchased inventory as follows:

Jan.	10	12,000	units at $ 7	=	$ 84,000
Mar.	11	5,000	units at	9	=	45,000
July	9	10,000	units at	10	=	100,000
Oct.	12	12,000	units at	11	=	132,000
Totals		39,000				$361,000

During 2008, both companies sold 30,000 units of inventory.

In early January 2008, both companies purchased equipment costing $200,000 that had a five-year estimated useful life and a $20,000 residual value. Louie Associates uses the first-in, first-out (FIFO) method for its inventory and straight-line amortization for its equipment. Chan Co. uses last-in, first-out (LIFO) and double-declining-balance amortization. Both companies' trial balances at December 31, 2008 included the following:

Sales revenue	$560,000
Operating expenses	110,000

Required

1 Prepare both companies' income statements.

2. Write an investment newsletter to address the following questions for your clients: Which company appears to be more profitable? Which company will have more cash to invest in promising projects? Which company would you prefer to invest in? Why?

Financial Statement Cases

Financial Statement Case 1

Property, plant, and equipment, and intangible assets

2. Depreciation expense for 2005 $25,436,000

Refer to CHUM Limited's financial statements in Appendix A and answer the following questions.

1. With respect to broadcasting operations, which amortization method does CHUM Limited use for the purpose of reporting to shareholders and creditors in the financial statements? What rates are used? Where did you find your answer?

2. What was the total amount of depreciation expense for fiscal 2005? (CHUM Limited uses the term *depreciation* instead of *amortization*.)

3. CHUM Limited indicates one amount for depreciation on the income statement, yet the change in accumulated depreciation from fiscal 2004 to 2005 in Note 5 of the Notes to Consolidated Financial Statements is a lesser amount. What is the amount of the difference? What could be the reason(s) for this difference?

4. CHUM Limited classifies one type of asset as both a current asset and as a long-term asset. Why?

5. Does CHUM Limited capitalize interest costs? If so, how much was capitalized in fiscal 2005?

6. In Note 1, "Summary of Significant Accounting Policies" in the notes to the financial statements, there is the subsection "Impairment of Long-Lived Assets." Explain the meaning of this section, and give an example of when it is used.

Financial Statement Case 2

Property, plant, and equipment, and intangible assets

2. Amortization expense $3,857,000

Refer to Sun-Rype Products Ltd.'s financial statements in Appendix B and answer the following questions.

1. With respect to manufacturing operations, which amortization method does Sun-Rype Products Ltd. use for the purpose of reporting to shareholders and creditors in the financial statements? What rates are used, and where did you find your answer?

2. What was the total amount of amortization expense for 2005?

3. Sun-Rype Products Ltd. shows one amount for amortization on the income statement, yet the change in accumulated amortization from 2004 to 2005 in Note 4 of the notes to the financial statements is a lesser amount. What is the amount of the difference, and what could be the reason(s) for this difference?

4. Does Sun-Rype Products Ltd. capitalize interest costs? If so, how much was capitalized in 2005?

5. In Note 1 (g), "Significant Accounting Policies" in the notes to the financial statements, there is the subsection "Impairment of Long-Lived Assets." Explain the meaning of this section, and give an example of when it is used.

Current Liabilities and Payroll

Learning Objectives

1. Account for current liabilities of known amount

2. Account for current liabilities that must be estimated

3. Compute payroll amounts

4. Record basic payroll transactions

5. Use a payroll system and implement internal controls

6. Report current liabilities on the balance sheet

Computers, cameras, and automobiles are guaranteed against defects. Many other new products are too. When you buy a new car, the manufacturer agrees to repair it if something goes wrong. Do you ever consider this guarantee when you buy a product? That may motivate you to select a Honda over a Chevrolet. If not, you should consider the product guarantee because it can vary from company to company and repairs can be expensive.

Product guarantees are called warranties, and warranties are an important liability of companies such as Bombardier Recreational Products Inc., General Motors, and Nortel Networks. Warranties pose an accounting challenge because companies such as Bombardier Recreational Products don't know which vehicle might have to be repaired. If this type of information could be known in advance, companies such as Bombardier might question whether or not to sell these products. But it's almost certain that companies will have unforeseen problems with some of their new products, so companies like Bombardier and General Motors record a warranty liability based on estimates.

In this chapter we will see how companies account for their product warranties. We will also learn about the other current liabilities, such as accounts payable and payroll liabilities.

What are current liabilities of known amount and current liabilities of unknown amount, and why are they important?

How should you account for potential liabilities?

What is the ethical and legal challenge in accounting for current and potential liabilities?

What are the key elements of a payroll system?

What is an employer's total payroll expense?

How do you report payroll amounts in the financial statements?

These questions and others will be answered throughout this chapter. And the Decision Guidelines at the mid-point and end of this chapter will provide the answers in a useful summary.

Current liabilities are obligations due within one year or within the company's operating cycle if it is longer than one year. Obligations due beyond that period of time are *long-term liabilities.* We discussed current liabilities and long-term liabilities in Chapter 4, pages 170 and 171.

Current Liabilities of Known Amount

Objective ❶

Account for current liabilities of known amount

The amounts of most current liabilities are known. A few current liabilities must be estimated. Let's begin with current liabilities of known amount.

Accounts Payable

Amounts owed for products or services that are purchased on account are *accounts payable.* We have seen many accounts payable examples in previous chapters. For example, most businesses purchase inventories and office supplies on account. Collicutt Energy Services Ltd., a Red Deer, Alberta-based company engaged in natural-gas service and the fabrication of compression and power-generation equipment, reported accounts payable and accrued liabilities of almost $14 million at March 1, 2006 (see Exhibit 11–1).

EXHIBIT 11–1	How Collicutt Energy Services Ltd. Reports Its Current Liabilities

COLLICUTT ENERGY SERVICES LTD.
Balance Sheet (partial, adapted)
March 1, 2006

Liabilities	(In thousands)
Current	
Operating loan	$ 9,879
Accounts payable and accrued liabilities	13,690
Income taxes payable	669
Deferred revenue	14,643
Current portion of long-term debt	1,539
Other	8,127
	$48,547

One of Collicutt's common transactions is the credit purchase of its inventory. Collicutt's accounts payable and perpetual inventory systems are integrated. After the order is placed and the goods are received, clerks enter inventory and accounts payable data into the system. Collicutt Energy Services Ltd. records the purchase of inventory on account as follows (amount assumed):

Nov. 22	Inventory	600	
	Accounts Payable		600
	Purchase on account.		

The purchase increases both Inventory and Accounts Payable. Then, to pay the liability, Collicutt debits Accounts Payable and credits Cash, as follows:

Dec. 5	Accounts Payable	600	
	Cash		600
	Paid on account.		

Short-Term Notes Payable

Short-term notes payable are a common form of financing. For example, Home Supply Ltd. discloses in its December 31, 2008, annual report that it owes $24,744 in short-term borrowings. Short-term notes payable are promissory notes that must be paid within one year. The following entries are typical for a short-term note payable that Home Supply Ltd. might have issued in 2007 to purchase inventory:

2007

Oct. 31	Inventory...	16,000	
	Note Payable, Short-Term.....................................		16,000
	Purchase of inventory by issuing a one-year 10 percent note payable.		

At year end, it is necessary to accrue interest expense for 61 days.

2007

Dec. 31	Interest Expense	267	
	Interest Payable		267
	Accrued interest expense at year end ($16,000 \times 0.10 \times {}^{61}/_{365}$).		

The balance sheet at December 31, 2007, will report the Note Payable of $16,000 and the related Interest Payable of $267 as current liabilities. The income statement for 2007 will report interest expense of $267. Both the balance sheet and income statement are as follows:

HOME SUPPLY LTD. Balance Sheet December 31, 2007			
Assets		**Liabilities**	
		Current liabilities:	
Various	$XXX	Note payable, short-term...	$16,000
		Interest payable.................	267

HOME SUPPLY LTD. Income Statement For the Year Ended December 31, 2007	
Revenues:..........................	$XXX
Expenses:	
Interest expense	$267

KEY POINT

The interest on a note is separate from the principal. The accrued interest should be credited to Interest Payable—*not* to Note Payable.

The following entry records payment of the note at maturity:

2008			
Oct. 31	Note Payable, Short-Term..	16,000	
	Interest Payable	267	
	Interest Expense	1,333	
	Cash		17,600

Paid a note payable and interest at maturity.
Interest expense is $1,332.60 ($16,000 × 0.10 × $^{304}/_{365}$).
Cash paid is $17,600 [$16,000 + ($16,000 × 0.10)].

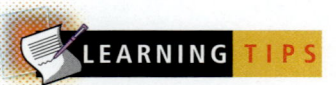
Interest expense of $267 was correctly allocated to the year ended December 31, 2007. Home Supply Ltd.'s interest expense will be $1,333 for 2008. At maturity, Home Supply Ltd. will pay a full year's interest, allocated as shown in this diagram.

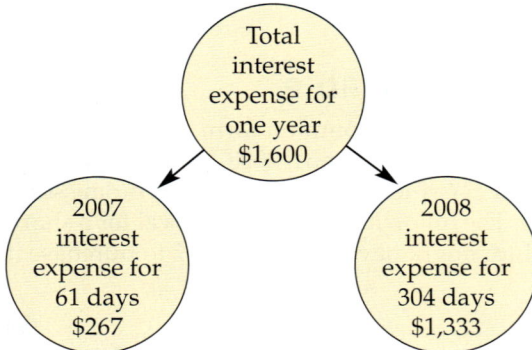

Short-Term Bank Loans and Operating Lines of Credit

Short-term banks loans are very similar to short-term notes payable. They are arranged with a bank or other financial institution, and are for a fixed time period at an interest rate negotiated between the bank and the borrower. If the bank loan is for less than one year or less than the company's operating cycle, it is considered short-term. Interest expense is recorded separate from the loan, and interest expense on a bank loan is accrued at the end of the year in the same way as for a note payable.

Many companies, and many people as well, arrange an operating **line of credit** with a financial institution to have cash available in case of a temporary cash shortfall. A line of credit is like a bank loan that is negotiated once, then drawn upon when needed. Interest is payable monthly only on the amount of the line of credit actually used—if the line of credit is not used, no interest is payable. Interest paid on a line of credit is recorded as interest expense. While most lines of credit are payable on demand (the bank can demand immediate repayment at any time), banks rarely demand repayment without warning. Typically, the amount of the principal to be repaid each month is flexible, with a minimum repayment required every month.

Many lines of credit are *secured*, meaning assets are pledged as security in case the borrower cannot repay the loan. Unsecured lines of credit do not have assets pledged as security. However, they often charge a higher rate of interest than secured lines of credit. CHUM Limited has an unsecured revolving credit facility for $500,000, which is similar to a line of credit.

Goods and Services Tax and Sales Tax Payable

There are two basic consumption taxes levied on purchases in Canada that are visible to the consumer: the goods and services tax (GST) levied by the federal government and the provincial sales taxes (PST) levied by all the provinces except Alberta; there are, at present, no sales taxes in the Yukon, Nunavut, or the Northwest Territories. The goods and services tax was introduced in Chapter 5, page 226. There are also excise or luxury taxes, which are a form of sales tax levied by the federal and provincial governments on products such as cigarettes, gasoline, jewellery, and alcoholic beverages; these taxes are hidden in that they are collected by the manufacturer. The focus of discussion in this section will be on the consumption or visible taxes; the goods and services tax and provincial sales taxes will be discussed in turn below. In order to simplify the discussion, the material concerning calculation and payment of the GST will exclude the PST and the material concerning calculation and payment of the PST will generally exclude the GST. Nova Scotia, New Brunswick, and Newfoundland and Labrador have harmonized the GST with their PST. Quebec has partially harmonized its sales tax (QST), and Prince Edward Island has also partly harmonized its sales tax (PST) with the GST. The Harmonized Sales Tax (HST) will be described below.

Goods and Services Tax In 1991, the federal government, through Canada Revenue Agency (CRA), implemented a goods and services tax (GST) that is collected from the ultimate consumer and includes most goods and services consumed in Canada. The tax and its application may be covered in an introductory tax course and is beyond the scope of this text; the ensuing discussion deals primarily with basic facts about the tax and how to account for it.

There are three categories of goods and services with respect to the GST:

1. Zero-rated supplies such as basic groceries, prescription drugs, goods and services exported from Canada to nonresidents, and medical devices;
2. Exempt supplies such as educational services, health care services, and financial services; and
3. Taxable supplies, which basically includes everything that is not zero-rated or exempt.

At the time of writing this text, the GST rate is 6 percent. The tax is collected by the individual or entity (called the *registrant*) supplying the taxable good or service (called *taxable supplies*) to the final consumer. The GST is remitted to the Receiver General. Suppliers of taxable goods and services have to pay tax on their purchases. However, they are able to deduct the amount of GST paid (called an *input tax credit*) from the GST they have collected from their sales of goods and services in calculating the amount due to the federal government. The GST Return and the net tax must be remitted to the Receiver General quarterly for most registrants and monthly for larger registrants.

For example, Mary Janicek, who lives in Whitehorse in the Yukon (no provincial tax), purchased a power lawn mower on July 2, 2006, with the intention of earning money by cutting grass during the summer.[1] The lawn mower cost $250; the GST was $15. Because Mary is planning to use the mower exclusively to cut grass for a fee, she could recover the $15. However, assuming she were a registrant, she would have to charge all her customers the 6 percent GST on her lawn-mowing services and remit it to the government. During the three-month first quarter, Mary earned revenue of $2,000.00, related GST of $120, and thus collected $2,120. She spent $106.00—$100.00 plus GST of $6—on gasoline for the mower. Her input tax credit

---

[1] If your business earns less than $30,000 per year, it does not have to be registered for GST purposes. In reality, Mary Janicek's business would be below the minimum threshold of $30,000, so Mary is unlikely to be a registrant. The scenario is illustrative. A business is only required to become a GST registrant if taxable revenues exceed $30,000 for the last four consecutive quarters.

of $21 included the $15 GST on the lawn mower and $6 GST on gasoline for the mower. The entries to record these transactions would be

2006

July 2	Equipment..	250	
	GST Recoverable	15	
	Cash..		265
	To record purchase of power mower.		
July–Sept.	Supplies Expense	100	
	GST Recoverable	6	
	Cash..		106
	To record purchase of gasoline for power mower.		
July–Sept.	Cash...	2,120	
	Lawn-Mowing Revenue...		2,000
	GST Payable...		120
	To record revenue from mowing lawns.		

Mary would be required to remit $99 ($120 − $15 − $6) as her first quarterly payment. Since Mary would be recovering the GST paid on the purchase of the mower and gasoline of $21 ($15 + $6), she would credit the recovery to the GST Recoverable account, to bring its balance to zero. The entry would be as follows:

Oct. 31	GST Payable...	120	
	Cash		99
	GST Recoverable		21
	To record payment of GST payable net of input tax credits to Receiver General.		

In the Mary Janicek example, we used two accounts—GST Recoverable (a receivable) and GST Payable—to illustrate input tax credits and GST collections to be remitted to the Receiver General. Some registrants use only one account—GST Payable—to record input tax credits *and* GST collections. When the GST Return is sent to the Receiver General, the final account balance in the GST Payable account is remitted if the balance is a credit, or a refund is requested if the balance is a debit. However, since CRA wants a report of both amounts, we will continue to use the two-account approach to illustrate input tax credits and GST collections.

Because they collect the GST for the federal government, the registrants owe the Receiver General the net tax collected; the account Goods and Services Tax Payable is a current liability. Most companies include GST owing with Accounts Payable and Accrued Liabilities, and GST recoverable as a current asset on their balance sheets. One can be netted against the other on the balance sheet.

Provincial Sales Tax As was mentioned above, all the provinces except Alberta (as well as the Yukon, Nunavut, and the Northwest Territories) levy a sales tax on sales to the final consumers of products; sales tax is not levied on sales to wholesalers or retailers. The final sellers charge their customers the sales tax in addition to the price of the item sold. The following provincial sales tax rates were in effect at the time of writing:

British Columbia	7%	
Saskatchewan	7%	
Manitoba	7%	
Ontario	8%	
Quebec	7.5%	(QST based on price including GST)
Prince Edward Island	10%	(PST based on price including GST)
New Brunswick	14%	(blended with GST)
Nova Scotia	14%	(blended with GST)
Newfoundland and Labrador	14%	(blended with GST)

As this list shows, four provinces charge PST and GST separately on the purchase price of a taxable good or service. Two provinces charge PST on the sum of the purchase price and the GST. Three provinces charge a combined GST and PST rate of 14 percent on the purchase price. This 14 percent rate is known as *Harmonized Sales Tax* (*HST*). By harmonizing their PST with the GST, New Brunswick, Nova Scotia, and Newfoundland and Labrador have reduced the cost of collecting and administering consumption taxes.

Consider a taxable item that costs $100 before tax. Ontario charges PST and GST separately; a taxable sale of $100.00 would have GST of $6.00 (0.06 × $100.00) and PST of $8.00 (0.08 × $100.00). Prince Edward Island charges PST on GST; a taxable sale of $100.00 would have GST of $6.00 (0.06 × $100.00) and PST of $10.60 [0.10 × ($100.00 + $6.00)]. Nova Scotia has harmonized the PST and the GST; a taxable sale of $100.00 would have PST and GST of $14.00 (0.14 × $100.00).

Consider Super Stereo Products, an electronics superstore located in Ottawa. Super Stereo does not pay provincial sales tax on its purchase of a TV set from Panasonic because it is inventory for resale, but you, as a consumer, would have to pay the province of Ontario's 8 percent provincial sales tax to Super Stereo when you buy a Panasonic TV from the store. Super Stereo pays the sales tax it collected from you to the provincial government. Panasonic, the manufacturer, would not have a sales tax liability at its year end, but Super Stereo probably would. (For purposes of the discussion of sales tax, we will ignore the GST.)

Suppose one Saturday's sales at the Super Stereo store totalled $20,000. The business would have collected an additional 8 percent in sales tax, which would equal $1,600 ($20,000 × 0.08). The business would record that day's sales as follows:

Cash	21,600	
Sales Revenue		20,000
Sales Tax Payable		1,600
To record cash sales of $20,000 and the related sales tax of 8 percent.		

Because the retailers owe to the province the sales tax collected, the account Sales Tax Payable is a current liability. Most companies include sales tax payable with Accounts Payable and Accrued Liabilities on their balance sheets.

Companies forward the collected sales tax to the taxing authority at regular intervals (typically monthly for large companies and quarterly for small companies), at which time they debit Sales Tax Payable and credit Cash. Observe that Sales Tax Payable does not correspond to any sales tax expense that the business is incurring. Nor does this liability arise from the purchase of any asset. Rather, it is the cash that the business is collecting on behalf of the government.

Current Portion of Long-Term Debt

Some long-term notes payable and bonds payable are paid in instalments, which means that equal portions of the principal are repaid at specific time intervals. The **current portion of long-term debt** is the amount of the principal that is payable within one year—a current liability. The remaining portion of the long-term debt is a long-term liability.

To illustrate, suppose Home Supply Ltd. borrowed $100,000 on January 1, 2007. This loan is to be repaid in instalments of $10,000 per year for 10 years on December 30 each year. On December 30, 2007, the first principal repayment of $10,000 is made (ignore interest), leaving a balance of $90,000. The December 31, 2007, balance sheet reports the $10,000 portion due to be repaid on December 30, 2008, as a current liability called "current portion of long-term debt" and reports the remaining $80,000 portion as long-term debt. On December 31, 2007, the company may make an adjusting entry to shift the current instalment of the long-term debt to a current liability amount as follows:

2007			
Dec. 31	Long-Term Debt	10,000	
	Current Portion of Long-Term Debt		10,000
	To transfer the portion of long-term debt due in 2008 to the current liability account.		

LEARNING TIPS

A current liability is due within one year, or within the company's operating cycle if it is longer than one year. The portion of a long-term debt payable within the year is classified as a current liability. The interest payable is classified separately from the principal.

Collicutt Energy Services Ltd.'s balance sheet (Exhibit 11–1, page 532) reports Current Portion of Long-Term Debt of $1,539 thousand as a current liability. On its full balance sheet, Collicutt reports long-term debt immediately after total current liabilities. *Long-term debt* refers to the notes, mortgages, and bonds payable that are payable later than one year beyond the balance sheet date.

The liabilities for the current portion of long-term debt do *not* include any accrued interest payable. The account, Current Portion of Long-Term Debt, represents only the appropriate portion of the *principal amount owed.* Interest Payable is a separate account for a different liability—the interest that must be paid. Collicutt Energy Services Ltd. includes interest payable under the current liability caption Accounts Payable and Accrued Liabilities.

STOP AND THINK

Suppose that Collicutt Energy Services Ltd. reported its full liability as long-term. Identify two ratios that would have been distorted by this accounting error. State whether the ratio values would be overstated or understated and whether they would report an overly positive or negative view of the company.

Answer: Reporting a liability as long-term could mislead external users because it understates current liabilities and has these effects:

Ratio	Overstated or Understated	View of the Company
Current ratio	Overstated	Overly positive
Acid-test ratio	Overstated	Overly positive

This example shows that accounting includes both *recording* transactions and *reporting* the information. Reporting is every bit as important as recording.

Accrued Expenses (Accrued Liabilities)

An **accrued expense** is an expense that has not yet been paid. An accrued expense creates a liability. This explains why accrued expenses are also called **accrued liabilities.** Accrued expenses typically occur with the passage of time, such as interest payable on long-term debt. We introduced accrued expenses in Chapter 3, page 111.

Like most other companies, Collicutt Energy Services Ltd. has salaries payable, other payroll liabilities, interest payable, and property taxes payable. We illustrated the accounting for interest payable on pages 533 and 534. The next section, plus the second half of this chapter, covers accounting for payroll liabilities.

Payroll Liabilities

Payroll, also called **employee compensation,** is a major expense of many businesses. For service organizations—such as public accounting firms and real-estate brokers—payroll is *the* major expense. Payroll expense for salaries and wages usually causes an accrued liability at year end. We show how to account for payroll expense in the second half of this chapter.

Unearned Revenues

Unearned revenues are also called *deferred revenues* and *revenues collected in advance.* As we saw in Chapter 3, page 114, an unearned revenue is a liability because it represents an obligation to provide a good or service. Each account title indicates that the business has received cash from its customers before it has earned the revenue. The company has an obligation to provide goods or services to the customer. Exhibit 11–1 shows Collicutt Energy Services Ltd. has received cash from customers for future services of $14,643,000 at March 1, 2006. Let's consider another example.

Canadian Business may be purchased every two weeks or by means of a subscription. When subscribers pay in advance to have *Canadian Business* delivered to their home or business, Rogers Publishing incurs a liability to provide future service. The liability account is called Unearned Subscription Revenue (which could also be titled Unearned Subscription Income or Deferred Subscription Income).

Assume that Rogers Publishing charges $39.95 for Bob Bish's one-year subscription to *Canadian Business*. Rogers Publishing's entries would be

2008			
July 2	Cash	39.95	
	Unearned Subscription Revenue		39.95
	To record receipt of cash at the start of a one-year subscription.		

After receiving the cash on July 2, 2008, Rogers Publishing owes its customer magazines that Rogers Publishing will provide over the next 12 months. Rogers Publishing's liability is:

Unearned Subscription Revenue

	39.95

During 2008, Rogers Publishing delivers one-half of the magazines and earns $19.98 ($39.95 × $\frac{1}{2}$) of the subscription revenue. At December 31, 2008, Rogers Publishing makes the following adjusting entry to decrease (debit) the liability Unearned Subscription Revenue and increase (credit) Subscription Revenue:

2008			
Dec. 31	Unearned Subscription Revenue	19.98	
	Subscription Revenue		19.98
	Earned revenue that was collected in advance ($39.95 × $\frac{1}{2}$).		

After posting, Rogers Publishing still owes the subscriber $19.97 for unearned revenue. Rogers Publishing has earned $19.98 of the revenue, as follows:

Unearned Subscription Revenue					Subscription Revenue		
Dec. 31	19.98	July 2	39.95			Dec. 31	19.98
		Bal.	19.97				

Customer Deposits Payable

Some companies require cash deposits from customers as security on borrowed assets. These amounts are called Customer Deposits Payable because the company must refund the cash to the customer under certain conditions. For example, telephone companies may demand a cash deposit from a customer before installing a telephone. Utility companies and businesses that lend tools and appliances commonly demand a deposit as protection against damage and theft. Certain manufacturers of products sold through individual dealers, such as Avon or Mary Kay, require deposits from the dealers who sell their products; the deposit is usually equal to the cost of the sample kit provided to the dealer. Companies whose products are sold in returnable containers collect deposits on those containers. Because the deposit is returned to the customer, the amount collected represents a liability.

Current Liabilities That Must Be Estimated

Objective 2

Account for current liabilities that must be estimated

A business may know that a liability exists but not know the exact amount. It cannot simply ignore the liability. This liability must be reported on the balance sheet.

Estimated current liabilities vary among companies. A prime example is Estimated Warranty Payable, which is common for companies such as Bombardier Recreational Products Inc. and Nortel Networks.

Estimated Warranty Payable

Many companies guarantee their products against defects under *warranty* agreements. Ninety-day warranties and one-year warranties are common.

The matching principle leads us to record the *warranty expense* in the same period we record the revenue. The expense occurs when you make a sale, not when you pay the warranty claim. For a review of the matching principle, see Chapter 3, page 104. At the time of the sale, the company does not know the exact amount of warranty expense, but the business must estimate its warranty expense and the related liability.

Assume that Collicutt Energy Services Ltd. made sales in 2006 of $80 million that are subject to warranty. In Note 2, "Significant Accounting Policies," Collicutt indicates that the company provides warranty coverage for its products for one year from date of sale. Assume that, in the past, the warranty provision and actual warranty cost was 1 percent of fabricating sales. Further, assume the company believes that 0.9 percent of the value of products sold in 2006 is the appropriate estimate of the cost of warranty work to be performed in the future. The company would record the sales of $80 million and the warranty expense of $720,000 ($80,000,000 × 0.009) in the same period as follows:

2006			
Various dates	Accounts Receivable	80,000,000	
	Sales Revenue (fabricating)		80,000,000
	Sales on account.		
Dec. 31	Warranty Expense	720,000	
	Estimated Warranty Payable		720,000
	To accrue warranty expense.		

Assume that the costs paid to repair defective merchandise total $700,000. If Collicutt repairs the defective products, Collicutt makes this journal entry:

2006–2007			
Various dates	Estimated Warranty Payable..............................	700,000	
	Cash		700,000
	To pay *repair* costs for defective products sold under warranty.		

LEARNING TIPS

A warrantied product may be sold in one year but repaired in another year. The dilemma in accounting is when the repair should be expensed—in the year the product is sold or in the year the product is repaired? The matching principle requires matching the warranty expense with the revenue from the sale in the year of the sale.

Collicutt Energy Services Ltd.'s expense on the income statement is the estimated amount of $720,000, not the $700,000 actually paid. After paying these warranty claims, Collicutt Energy Services Ltd.'s liability account would have a credit balance of $20,000.

Estimated Warranty Payable		
700,000		720,000
	Bal.	20,000

STOP AND THINK

Maxim Limited, a new company, made sales of $400,000. The company estimated warranty repairs at 5 percent of the sales. Maxim's actual warranty payments were $19,000. Record sales, warranty expense, and warranty payments. How much is Maxim's estimated warranty payable at the end of the period?

Answer:

Accounts Receivable	400,000	
Sales Revenue		400,000
Warranty Expense ($400,000 × 0.05)	20,000	
Estimated Warranty Payable		20,000
Estimated Warranty Payable	19,000	
Cash		19,000

Estimated Warranty Payable

19,000		20,000
	Bal.	1,000

Estimated Vacation Pay Liability

All companies are required by law to grant paid vacations to their employees. The employees receive this benefit when they take their vacation, but they earn the compensation by working the other days of the year. The law requires most employers to provide a minimum number of weeks holiday per year (usually two, but sometimes more, based on the number of years worked). To match expense with revenue properly, the company accrues the vacation pay expense and liability for each of the 50 work weeks of the year. Then, the company records payment during the two-week vacation period. Employee turnover, terminations, and ineligibility (for example, no vacation allowed until one full year has been worked) force companies to estimate the vacation pay liability and accrue vacation expense incurred.

Suppose a company's January payroll is $100,000 and vacation pay adds 4 percent, or $4,000 (with the 4 percent calculated as two weeks of annual vacation divided by 50 work weeks each year). Experience indicates that only 90 percent of the available vacations will be taken. Therefore, the January vacation pay estimate is $3,600 ($4,000 × 0.90). In January, the company records the vacation pay accrual as follows:

Jan. 31	Vacation Pay Expense	3,600	
	Estimated Vacation Pay Liability		3,600

Each month thereafter, the company makes a similar entry.

If an employee takes a two-week vacation in August, his or her $2,000 monthly salary is recorded as follows:

Aug. 31	Estimated Vacation Pay Liability	2,000	
	Various Withholding Accounts and Wages Payable[2]		2,000

Income Tax Payable (for a Corporation)

Corporations pay income tax in the same way as individual taxpayers do. Corporations file their income tax returns with Canada Revenue Agency (CRA) and their provincial governments after the end of the fiscal year, so they must estimate their income tax payable for reporting on the balance sheet. During the year, corporations make monthly tax payments to the governments, based on their

---

[2] The various payroll accounts are discussed later in the chapter.

estimated tax for the year. A corporation with a December 31 year end would record the payment of $100,000 of income tax expense for September as follows:

Sept. 30	Income Tax Expense	100,000	
	Cash		100,000
	To pay monthly income tax instalment.		

Assume at December 31, the corporation calculates actual tax expense for the year to be $1,240,000. Accordingly, the corporation pays the monthly instalment of $100,000 on December 30, and accrues the additional $40,000 at December 31. The entries are

Dec. 30	Income Tax Expense	100,000	
	Cash		100,000
	To pay monthly income tax.		
Dec. 31	Income Tax Expense	40,000	
	Income Tax Payable		40,000
	To accrue income tax at year end.		

The corporation will pay off this tax liability during the next year when it files its tax returns with Canada Revenue Agency and its provincial government, so Income Tax Payable is a current liability.

Contingent Liabilities

A *contingent liability* is not an actual liability. Instead, it is a potential liability that depends on a *future* event arising out of past events. For example, Packenham town council may sue North Ontario Electric Supply Ltd., the company that installed new street lights in Packenham, claiming that the electrical wiring is faulty. The past transaction is the street-light installation. The future event is the court case that will decide the suit. North Ontario Electric Supply Ltd. thus faces a contingent liability, which may or may not become an actual obligation.

It would be misleading for North Ontario Electric Supply Ltd. to withhold knowledge of the lawsuit from its creditors or from anyone considering investing in the business. The *disclosure principle* of accounting (see Chapter 6, page 300) requires a company to report any information deemed relevant to outsiders of the business. The goal is to give people relevant, reliable information for decision making.

The *CICA Handbook* requires *contingent losses* generally to be accrued or disclosed in the financial statements but bars *contingent gains* from being recognized *until* they are realized. This approach follows the principle of conservatism. The accounting profession divides contingent liabilities into three categories. Each category indicates a likelihood that a contingency will cause a loss and become an actual liability. The three categories of contingent liabilities, along with how to report them, are shown in Exhibit 11–2.

Sometimes the contingent liability has a definite amount. Sometimes the amount that will have to be paid, if the contingent liability becomes an actual liability, is not known at the balance sheet date. For example, companies face lawsuits, which may cause possible future obligations of amounts to be determined by the courts. In another case, Canada Revenue Agency (CRA) may have indicated to the entity that a reassessment of its income and taxes has been made or is forthcoming but the company may not know the amount of its liability at the financial statement date.

Sun-Rype Products Ltd. reported the following in Note 11(d) in the Notes to the Financial Statements for the year ended December 31, 2005:

11. (d) In January 2005, the Consumers' Association of Canada filed a class action lawsuit against a number of parties in the beverage industry, in-

EXHIBIT 11–2 | Contingent Liabilities: Three Categories

Level of Uncertainty*	How to Report the Contingency
Likely	Amount can be reasonably estimated: Accrue an expense (loss) and report an actual liability.
	Amount cannot be reasonably estimated: Disclose in the notes.
Unlikely	If loss would be significant, note disclosure is suggested.
Not determinable	Note disclosure is required.

*Determined by management. Management also determines the appropriate disclosure.

cluding Sun-Rype, other manufacturers, retailers and Encorp Pacific (Canada), the administrator of the beverage container deposit and recycling fee system in British Columbia ("BC"). The claim alleges the illegal use of consumer deposits collected under BC's beverage container stewardship program regulations. In January 2006, the defendants, including Sun-Rype, filed an application to strike the claim summarily as lacking sufficient merit to warrant certification of the class. Due to the early stages of this claim, the amount and likelihood of loss, if any, is not determinable. As a result, no provision for any loss has been recorded in these financial statements.

Since the Sun-Rype contingency is "not determinable," disclosure was provided in Note 11(d) and no liability was recorded or reported on the balance sheet.

Ethical Issues in Accounting for Current and Contingent Liabilities

Accounting for current liabilities poses an ethical challenge. Businesses want to look as successful as possible. A company likes to report a high level of net income on the income statement because that makes the company look successful. High asset values and low liabilities make the company look safe to lenders and help the company borrow at lower interest rates.

Owners and managers may be tempted to overlook some expenses and liabilities at the end of the period. For example, a company can fail to accrue warranty expense or employee vacation pay. This will cause total expenses to be understated and net income to be overstated on the income statement.

Contingent liabilities also pose an ethical challenge. Because contingencies are not real liabilities, they are easy to overlook. But a contingent liability can be very important. A business with a contingent liability walks a tightrope between (1) disclosing enough information to enable outsiders to evaluate the company realistically, and (2) not giving away too much information, which could harm the company. Ethical business owners and managers do not play games with their accounting. Falsifying financial statements can ruin one's reputation. It can also lead to a prison term.

At this half-way point of the chapter, review what you have learned by studying the following Decision Guidelines.

Decision	Guidelines
What are the two main issues in accounting for current liabilities?	• *Recording* the liability and the asset acquired or the expense incurred • *Reporting* the liability on the balance sheet
What are the two basic categories of current liabilities?	• Current liabilities of *known amount:* Accounts payable — Accrued expenses (accrued liabilities) Short-term notes payable — Payroll liabilities Sales tax payable — Salary, wages, commission, and bonus payable GST payable Current portion of long-term debt — Unearned revenues • Current liabilities that *must be estimated:* Estimated warranty payable Estimated vacation pay liability Income tax payable (for a corporation)
How to account for contingent (potential) liabilities?	• If it is likely and the amount can be reasonably estimated: Accrue an expense (loss) and report a liability • If it is likely but the amount cannot be reasonably estimated: Note disclosure • If it is unlikely but the loss would be significant: Note disclosure • If it is not determinable: Note disclosure
What is the ethical and legal challenge in accounting for current and contingent liabilities?	• Ensure that the balance sheet (and the related notes) reports the *full amount* of *all* the business's current and contingent liabilities

Mid-Chapter Summary Problem for Your Review

Name: Harvey's restaurant
Industry: Food services
Accounting Period:
Assumed after July 1, 2006

Name: Snippy Hair Salons
Industry: Hair salon services
Accounting Period: Years ended December 31, 2006 and 2007

Answer each question separately:

1. Suppose a Harvey's restaurant in Charlottetown, Prince Edward Island, made cash sales of $4,000 subject to the 6 percent GST and 10 percent provincial sales tax. Record the sales and the related consumption taxes (P.E.I. charges PST on GST). Also record payment of the sales tax to the provincial government and the GST to the Receiver General (assume input tax credits amount to $109.00).

2. At December 31, 2006, Snippy Hair Salons reported a 6 percent long-term debt payable as follows:

Current Liabilities (in part)	
Portion of long-term debt due within one year	$10,000
Interest payable*	6,300
Long-Term Debt (in part)	
Long-term debt	$200,000

*Calculated as $210,000 \times 0.06 \times {}^{6}/_{12}$

Snippy Hair Salons pays interest on June 30 each year. Show how Snippy Hair Salons would report its liabilities on the year-end balance sheet one year later—December 31, 2007. The current maturity of the long-term debt is $10,000 each year until the liability is paid off.

3. How does a contingent liability differ from an actual liability?

Solution

Since PEI charges PST on GST:
Step 1. Calculate GST on the sales.
Step 2. Calculate PST on the sales + GST.
Step 3. Add sales, GST, and PST to find total cash received.

After the company collects GST and PST from customers, it owes those amounts to the governments.

Separate journal entries are required for GST and PST because cheques are sent to two different governments.

1.
Cash..	4,664	
Sales Revenue		4,000
GST Payable		240
Sales Tax Payable		424

To record cash sales and related GST and provincial sales tax.
Cash is $4,664 [($4,000 × 1.06) × 1.10].
GST Payable is $240 ($4,000 × 0.06).
Sales Tax Payable is $424 ($4,240 × 0.10).

GST Payable...	240	
Cash...		131
GST Recoverable..		109

To pay GST to the Receiver General, net of the input tax credit.

Sales Tax Payable...	424	
Cash...		424

To pay sales tax to the provincial government.

2. Snippy Hair Salons' balance sheet at December 31, 2007, would be as follows:

Total long-term debt at Dec. 31, 2007 is $200,000:
$10,000 current portion from 2006 + ($200,000 long-term portion from 2006 − $10,000 repayment during 2007)

Current liabilities include the amount due to be paid within one year from the balance-sheet date:
• Principal repayment ($10,000)
• Accrued interest payment

Long-term debt is the amount due to be paid after one year from the balance-sheet date.

Current Liabilities (in part)	
Portion of long-term debt due within one year	$10,000
Interest payable*	6,000
Long-Term Debt (in part)	
Long-term debt	$190,000

*Calculated as $200,000 × 0.06 × $^6/_{12}$

3. A contingent liability differs from an *actual* liability since it is a *potential* liability, which may or may not become an actual liability. It arises out of a past transaction and depends on a future event to determine if it will become an actual liability.

Refer to Exhibit 11–2 on page 543 for the categories and accounting treatment of contingent liabilities.

Accounting for Payroll

Objective 3
Compute payroll amounts

Labour costs are so important that most businesses develop a special payroll system. This section covers the basics of accounting for payroll.

There are numerous ways to express an employee's gross pay:

- *Salary* is pay stated at an annual, monthly, or weekly rate, such as $48,000 per year, $4,000 per month, or $1,000 per week.
- *Wages* are pay amounts stated at an hourly rate, such as $10 per hour.
- *Commission* is pay stated as a percentage of a sale amount, such as a 5 percent commission on a sale. A realtor thus earns $5,000 on a $100,000 sale of real estate.
- *Piecework* is pay based on the number of pieces produced by the employee, such as number of trees planted or shirts sewn.
- *Bonus* is pay over and above base salary (wage or commission). A bonus is usually paid for exceptional performance—in a single amount after year end.
- *Benefits* are extra compensation items that aren't paid directly to the employee. Benefits could include health, life, and disability insurance. The employer pays the insurance company, which then provides coverage for the employee. Another type of benefit sets aside money for the employee for his or her retirement.

Businesses pay employees at a base rate for a set period—called *straight time*. For additional hours—called *overtime*—the employee may get a higher rate of pay.

Lucy Childres is an accountant for MicroAge Electronics Inc. Lucy earns $700 per week for straight time (35 hours), so her hourly pay rate is $20 ($700 ÷ 35). The company pays *time and a half* for overtime. That rate is 150 percent (1.5 times) the straight-time rate. Thus Lucy earns $30.00 for each hour of overtime ($20.00 × 1.5 = $30.00). For working 37 hours during a week, she earns $760, computed as follows:

Straight-time pay for 35 hours	$700
Overtime pay for 2 overtime hours (2 × $30.00)	60
Total pay	$760

Gross Pay and Net Pay

Two pay amounts are important for accounting purposes:

- **Gross pay** is the total amount of salary, wages, commission, piecework, and bonus earned by the employee during a pay period. Gross pay is the amount before income taxes or any other deductions. Gross pay is the employer's expense. In the preceding illustration, Lucy Childres's gross pay was $760.
- **Net pay,** also called *take-home pay,* is the amount the employee keeps. Net pay equals gross pay minus all deductions. The employer writes a paycheque to each employee or makes an electronic funds transfer (EFT) to each employee's bank account for his or her net pay.

The federal government and most provincial governments require by law that employers act as collection agents for employee's income taxes, which are deducted from employee paycheques. Insurance companies, labour unions, charitable organizations such as the United Way, and other organizations may also take portions of employees' pay. Amounts withheld from an employee's paycheque are called *deductions.* Exhibit 11–3 illustrates gross and net pay.

In addition to employee income taxes, Canada (or Quebec) Pension Plan contributions, and Employment Insurance premiums that employers must withhold from pay, employers themselves must pay some payroll expenses, such as the employer's share of Canada (or Quebec) Pension Plan and Employment Insurance. Many

EXHIBIT 11–3 Gross Pay and Net Pay

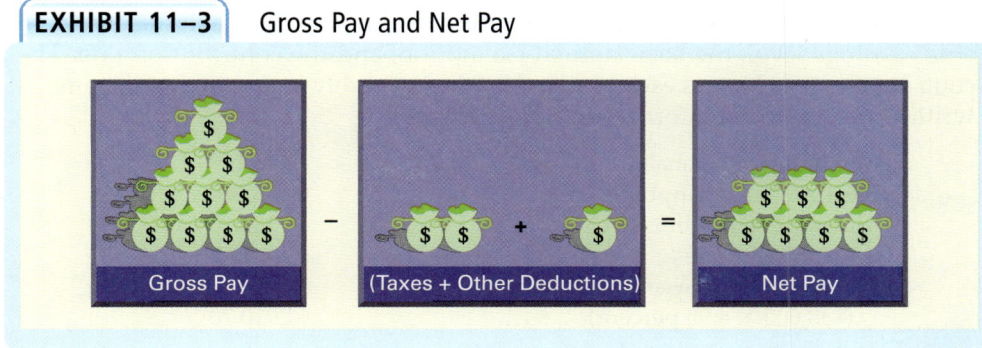

companies also pay employee *fringe benefits,* such as medical and life insurance premiums and pension plan payments.

Payroll Deductions

Payroll deductions create the difference between gross pay and net pay. They are *withheld* from employees' pay and fall into two categories:

- *Required* (or *statutory) deductions,* which include employee income tax, Employment Insurance, and Canada Pension Plan or Quebec Pension Plan deductions.
- *Optional deductions,* which include union dues (which may be automatic deductions for all unionized employees), insurance premiums, charitable contributions, and other amounts that are withheld at the employee's request.

After being withheld, payroll deductions become the liability of the employer, who assumes responsibility for paying the outside party. For example, the employer pays the government the employee income tax withheld and pays the union the employee union dues withheld.

Required Payroll Deductions

Employee's Withheld Income Tax Payable The law requires employers to withhold income tax from their employees' salaries and wages. The amount of income tax deducted from gross pay is called **withheld income tax.** For most employees, this deduction is the largest. The amount withheld depends on the employee's gross pay and on the number of non-refundable tax credits the employee claims. Each employee files a Personal Tax Credits Return (Form TD1), which is used by employers to determine how much income tax to withhold from an employee's gross pay.

The employer sends its employees' withheld income tax to the government. The amount of the income tax withheld by the employer determines how often the employer submits tax payments. Most employers must remit the taxes to the government at least monthly; larger employers must remit two or four times a month, depending on the total amounts withheld. Every business must account for payroll taxes on a calendar-year basis regardless of its fiscal year.

The employer accumulates taxes withheld in the Employees' Income Tax Payable account. The word *payable* indicates that the account is a liability of the employer, even though the employees are the people taxed. The payable is eliminated when the employer pays the withheld taxes to the government.

Employee's Withheld Canada (or Quebec) Pension Plan Contributions Payable
The **Canada** (or **Quebec**) **Pension Plan** (CPP or QPP) provides retirement, disability, and death benefits to employees who are covered by it. Employers are required to deduct premiums from each employee required to make a contribution (basically all employees between 18 and 70 years of age). The federal government, through

the Canada Revenue Agency (CRA), determines annually the maximum pensionable earnings level, the basic annual exemption, and the contribution rate. The contribution rate changes each year and has been steadily increasing. At the time of writing, the following information was applicable:

Maximum pensionable earnings	$42,100
Basic annual exemption	3,500
Maximum contributory earnings	38,600
Contribution rate	4.95%
Maximum employee contribution	
($38,600 × 4.95 percent)	$1,910.70

CRA provides tables that the employer uses to calculate the amount to deduct from each employee's pay each pay period; the tables take into account the basic exemption of $3,500 of income but also assume that the employee will be working for twelve months. For example, if your total employment income was earned when you worked for two months during the summer and earned $2,500 per month, the withholding would be $109.31 each month, the normal deduction for an employee earning $2,500 per month. However, based on your total income of $5,000 (2 × $2,500) and the basic exemption of $3,500, CPP is $74.25 [($5,000 − $3,500) × 0.0495] and your overpayment of $144.37 ($109.31 + $109.31 − $74.25) will be recovered when you file your income tax return.

Once the employee reaches the maximum contribution of $1,910.70, the employer stops deducting for that year. Some employees may have had more than one employer in a year; for example, you may have had a job for the summer and now have a part-time job while you are back at school. CRA requires each employer to deduct Canada Pension Plan contributions; however, you recover the overpayment when you file your income tax return for the year. The employers do not recover any overpayment.

The employer must remit the Canada Pension Plan contributions withheld and the employer's share, discussed below, every month to CRA. Larger employers must remit two or four times a month, depending on the amounts withheld.

Employee's Withheld Employment Insurance (EI) Premiums Payable
The Employment Insurance Act requires employers to deduct **Employment Insurance** premiums from each employee each time that employee is paid. The purpose of the Employment Insurance Fund is to provide assistance to contributors to the fund who cannot work for a variety of reasons. The most common reason is that the employee has been laid off; another reason is maternity leave.

The federal government, through CRA, establishes annually the maximum annual insurable earnings level and the Employment Insurance premium rate. The rate has been decreasing in recent years because the employment insurance fund has a surplus. At the time of writing, the following information was applicable:

Maximum insurable earnings	$39,000
Premium rate	1.87%
Maximum employee contribution	
($39,000 × 1.87 percent)	$729.30

CRA provides tables that the employer uses to calculate the amount to deduct from each employee's gross pay each pay period. For example, if you earned $2,000 per month, $37.40 ($2,000 × 1.87 percent) per month would be deducted for Employment Insurance.

As with the Canada Pension Plan, CRA requires every employer to deduct Employment Insurance premiums from every eligible employee. Overpayments may be recovered when the employee files his or her income tax return.

The employer must remit the Employment Insurance premiums withheld and the employer's share, discussed below, to CRA every month. Larger employers must remit two or four times a month depending on the amounts withheld.

KEY POINT

Divide the annual exemption of $3,500 by the number of pay periods in a year to ensure the correct amount of CPP exemption is calculated. For weekly pays, divide by 52; for two-week pay periods, divide by 26.

Optional Payroll Deductions

As a convenience to their employees, many companies make payroll deductions and disburse cash according to employee instructions. Union dues (which may not be optional), insurance payments, registered pension plan payments, payroll savings plans, and donations to charities such as the United Way are examples. The account Employees' Union Dues Payable holds employee deductions for union membership.

Employer Payroll Costs

Employers bear expenses for at least three payroll costs: (1) Canada Pension Plan contributions, (2) Employment Insurance Plan premiums, and (3) Workers' Compensation Plan premiums. Some provinces also levy a health tax on employers. Most employers must remit both employee and employer shares monthly. Larger employers must remit twice or four times monthly depending on the size of their payroll. Workers' Compensation payments are remitted quarterly.

Employer Canada Pension Plan Contributions In addition to being responsible for deducting and remitting the employee contribution to the Canada Pension Plan, the employer must also pay into the program. The employer must match exactly the employee's contribution. Every employer must do so whether or not the employee also contributes elsewhere. Unlike the employee, the employer may not obtain a refund for overpayment.

Employer Employment Insurance Premiums The employer calculates the employee's premium and remits it together with the employer's share, which is generally 1.4 times the employee's premium, to CRA. The maximum dollar amount of the employer's contribution would be 1.4 times the maximum employee's contribution of $729.30, which amounts to $1,021.02. Almost all employers and employees are covered by this program, unless someone is self-employed.

Workers' Compensation Premiums Unlike the previous two programs, which are administered by the federal government, the **Workers' Compensation** plan is administered provincially. The purpose of the program is to provide financial support for workers injured on the job. The cost of the coverage is borne by the employer; the employee does not pay a premium to the fund.

In Manitoba, for example, almost all employees are covered by the program. There are over 70 different categories that the Workers' Compensation Board uses to determine the cost of coverage. The category a group of workers is assigned to is based on the risk of injury to workers in that group, which is based on that group's and similar groups' experience. The employer pays a premium equal to the rate assessed times the employer's gross payroll.

Provincial Payroll Taxes Certain provinces levy taxes on employers to pay for provincial health care while others levy a combined health care and post-secondary education tax to pay for provincial health care and post-secondary education.

Payroll Withholding Tables

We have discussed the tables that employers use in calculating the withholdings that must be made from employees' wages for income taxes, Canada (or Quebec) Pension Plan contributions, and Employment Insurance premiums. Exhibit 11–4 provides illustrations of all four tables for a resident of Saskatchewan for 2006. Suppose an employee, Roberta Dean, is paid a salary of $2,000 twice a month (semi-monthly). Roberta is single and so her TD1 form for both federal and provincial taxes indicates a claim code of 1. From Panel A of Exhibit 11–4, you can see that Roberta will have $266.05 deducted for federal income taxes, and from Panel B, you can see that she will have $176.70 deducted for Saskatchewan income taxes. Panel C indicates that Roberta would have $91.74 deducted from each pay for Canada Pension Plan (CPP),

EXHIBIT 11–4 Payroll Withholding Tables

Panel A

Saskatchewan
Federal Tax Deductions
Effective July 1, 2006
Semi-Monthly: 24 Pay Periods Per Year

Pay	Federal claim codes										
	0	**1**	**2**	**3**	**4**	**5**	**6**	**7**	**8**	**9**	**10**
From Less than	*Deduct from each pay*										
1958 – 1976	313.90	258.15	252.15	240.25	228.30	216.40	204.45	192.50	180.60	168.65	156.75
1976 – 1994	317.90	262.10	256.10	244.20	232.25	220.35	208.40	196.50	184.55	172.60	160.70
1994 – 2012	321.85	266.05	260.10	248.15	236.20	224.30	212.35	200.45	188.50	176.60	164.65
2012 – 2030	325.80	270.00	264.05	252.10	240.20	228.25	216.35	204.40	192.45	180.55	168.60
2030 – 2048	329.75	273.95	268.00	256.05	244.15	232.20	220.30	208.35	196.45	184.50	172.55

Panel B

Saskatchewan
Provincial Tax Deductions
Effective July 1, 2006
Semi-Monthly: 24 Pay Periods Per Year

Pay	Federal claim codes										
	0	**1**	**2**	**3**	**4**	**5**	**6**	**7**	**8**	**9**	**10**
From Less than	*Deduct from each pay*										
1951 – 1969	211.35	172.00	168.05	160.20	152.30	144.45	136.55	128.70	120.80	112.95	105.05
1969 – 1987	213.70	174.35	170.40	162.55	154.65	146.80	138.90	131.05	123.15	115.30	107.40
1987 – 2005	216.05	176.70	172.75	164.85	157.00	149.10	141.25	133.35	125.50	117.60	109.75
2005 – 2023	218.40	179.00	175.10	167.20	159.35	151.45	143.60	135.70	127.85	119.95	112.10
2023 – 2049	221.25	181.90	177.95	170.05	162.20	154.30	146.45	138.55	130.70	122.80	114.95

Panel C

Canada Pension Plan Contributions

Semi-Monthly (24 pay periods per year)

Pay		CPP
From	**To**	
1964.22 – 1974.21		90.26
1974.22 – 1984.21		90.75
1984.22 – 1994.21		91.25
1994.22 – 2004.21		91.74
2004.22 – 2014.21		92.24
2014.22 – 2024.21		92.73
2024.22 – 2034.21		93.23
2034.22 – 2044.21		93.72
2044.22 – 2054.21		94.22

Panel D

Employment Insurance Premiums

Semi-Monthly (24 pay periods per year)

Insurable Earnings		EI
From	**To**	**Premium**
1997.60 – 1998.12		37.36
1998.13 – 1998.66		37.37
1998.67 – 1999.19		37.38
1999.20 – 1999.73		37.39
1999.74 – 2000.26		37.40
2000.27 – 2000.80		37.41
2000.81 – 2001.33		37.42
2001.34 – 2001.87		37.43
2001.88 – 2002.40		37.44

and Panel D shows that $37.40 would be deducted for Employment Insurance (EI). Roberta Dean's employer would keep track, as we will demonstrate later in the chapter, of Dean's Canada Pension Plan and Employment Insurance deductions and, when they reached the maximums of $1,910.70 and $729.30 respectively, would stop deducting premiums from Dean's pay. The employer's share would be $91.74 for Canada Pension Plan (matches employee's share), while the employer's share for Employment Insurance would be $52.36 (1.4 times employee share).

Exhibit 11–5 shows Roberta Dean's disbursement of payroll costs by her Saskatchewan employer company, assuming she pays $20.00 of union dues each pay period.

EXHIBIT 11–5 Disbursement of Roberta Dean's Payroll Costs by an Employer Company (Saskatchewan)

Employer Company disburses $2,159.10

| Net Pay to Employee $1,408.11 | Employee Withheld Income Tax to Federal Government $266.05 | Employee Withheld Income Tax to Provincial Government $176.70 | Employee Canada Pension Plan to Government $91.74 | Employee Employment Insurance to Government $37.40 | Employee union dues to Labour Union $20.00 | Employer share of CPP and EI to Government $144.10 | Employer cost of Workers' Compensation $15.00 |

Roberta Dean's Gross Pay
$2,000.00

Payroll Entries

The journal entries in this section show an employer's entries to record a monthly payroll of $60,000 (all amounts are assumed for illustration only).

The first journal entry records the employer's salary expense, which is the gross salary of all employees ($60,000) for a month. The employer acts as a collection agent for CRA (income tax and Canada Pension), the provincial government (income tax), the Employment Insurance Commission, and the union, withholding the employees' contributions from their gross pay. The remaining amount is the employees' net (take-home) pay of $46,278.

Salary Expense (or Wages or Commission Expense)	60,000	
Employee (federal and provincial) Income Tax Payable		8,100
Canada Pension Plan Payable		2,970
Employment Insurance Payable		1,120
Employee Union Dues Payable		1,532
Salaries Payable (net pay)		46,278

To record salary expense and employee withholdings.

The second journal entry represents the employer's share of Canada Pension Plan and Employment Insurance. Remember, the employer's share is 1.0 times and 1.4 times the employee's share respectively for these two deductions.

Employee Benefits Expense	4,538	
Canada Pension Plan Payable		2,970
Employment Insurance Payable		1,568

To record employer's share of Canada Pension Plan (1.0 × $2,970) and Employment Insurance (1.4 × $1,120).

Objective 4
Record basic payroll transactions

KEY POINT

Payroll liabilities are accrued liabilities. These liabilities are to various entities.

To the employee: For net wages, salaries, and bonuses

To the government: For income tax withheld, Employment Insurance, and Canada Pension

To outside providers of benefits: For insurance premiums, union dues, payroll savings plans

The third journal entry records employee benefits paid by the employer. This company has a dental benefits plan for its employees for which it pays the premiums.

Employee Dental Benefits Expense	1,092	
Employee Benefits Payable		1,092
To record employee benefits payable by employer.		

In this example, the total payroll expense for the month is made up of base salary ($60,000) plus the employer's share of Canada Pension Plan and Employment Insurance ($4,538) plus fringe benefits ($1,092) for a total of $65,630. There would also be Workers' Compensation, which, you will recall, is paid completely by the employer, and other costs depending on the province in which the company operates.

A company's payments to people who are not employees—outsiders called independent contractors—are *not* company payroll expenses. Consider two technical writers, Fermi and Scott. Fermi is the company's technical writer. Scott is a contractor hired to help Fermi during the busy season. Fermi is an employee of the company, and his compensation is a debit to Salary Expense. Scott, however, performs writing services for many clients, and the company debits Contract Labour when it pays him. Any payment for services performed by a person outside the company is a debit to an expense account other than payroll.

STOP AND THINK

Record the payroll, payroll deductions, and employer payroll costs, given the following information about an Ontario company:

Gross pay	$190,000
Employee withheld income tax	22,800
Employee withheld Canada Pension Plan	9,300
Employee withheld Employment Insurance	3,500
Union dues	2,945
Employer cost for Canada Pension Plan	1.0 × employee amount
Employer cost for Employment Insurance	1.4 × employee amount
Pension plan paid by employer only	1.0% of gross pay

Answer: *Payroll entry:*

Salary expense	190,000	
Employee Income Tax Payable		22,800
Canada Pension Plan (CPP) Payable		9,300
Employment Insurance (EI) Payable		3,500
Union Dues Payable		2,945
Salaries Payable		151,455

Employer payroll cost entry:

Employee Benefits Expense	14,200	
Canada Pension Plan (CPP) Payable		9,300
Employment Insurance (EI) Payable		4,900

Fringe benefits:

Pension Expense	1,900	
Employment Benefits Payable		1,900

The Payroll System

Objective 5

Use a payroll system and implement internal controls

Good business requires paying employees accurately and on time. A payroll system accomplishes these goals. The components of the payroll system are:

- A payroll register
- Payroll cheques
- Employee earnings records

Payroll Register

Each pay period, the company organizes payroll data in a special journal called the *payroll register*. The payroll register is like a cash payments journal and serves as a cheque register for recording payroll cheques. We introduced the cash payments journal in Chapter 7, page 347.

Exhibit 11–6 is a payroll register for Red Deer Provisioners. The payroll register has columns for each employee's gross pay, deductions, and net pay. This record gives the employer the information needed to record salary expense for the pay period as follows:

2006			
Dec. 31	Office Salaries Expense	4,464.00	
	Sales Salaries Expense	9,190.00	
	Employee Income Tax Payable		3,208.19
	Canada Pension Plan Payable		402.70
	Employment Insurance Payable		302.12
	United Way Payable		155.00
	Salaries Payable		9,585.99
	To record payroll expenses for the week ended December 31, 2006.		
2006			
Dec. 31	Employee Benefits Expense	825.67	
	Canada Pension Plan Payable		402.70
	Employment Insurance Payable ($302.12 × 1.4)		422.97
	To record the cost of employer's portion of payroll expenses for the week ended December 31, 2006.		

Payroll Cheques

Most companies pay employees by cheque or by electronic funds transfer (EFT). A *payroll cheque* has an attachment, or stub, that details the employee's gross pay, payroll deductions, and net pay. These amounts come from the payroll register, like that in Exhibit 11–6. Exhibit 11–7 (on page 555) shows payroll cheque number 1622, issued to C.L. Drumm for net pay of $397.12 earned during the week ended December 31, 2006. To enhance your ability to use payroll data, trace all amounts on the cheque attachment to the payroll register in Exhibit 11–6.

Increasingly, companies are paying employees by electronic funds transfer. The employee can authorize the company to make all deposits directly to her or his bank. With no cheque to write and deliver to the employee, the company saves time and money. As evidence of the deposit, most companies issue to employees either a paper or an electronic pay summary slip showing the data for that pay period (similar to the cheque-stub data above) plus year-to-date data.

Recording Cash Payments for Payroll

Most employers must record at least three cash payments: for payments of net pay to employees, for payments of payroll withholdings to the government, and for payments to third parties for employee fringe benefits.

Net Pay to Employees When the employer pays employees, the company debits Salaries Payable and credits Cash. Using the data in Exhibit 11–6, the company would make the following entry to record the cash payment (column (j)) for the December 31, 2006, weekly payroll:

2006			
Dec. 31	Salaries Payable	9,585.99	
	Cash		9,585.99

EXHIBIT 11–6 Payroll Register for Red Deer Provisioners

Week ended December 31, 2006

		a	b	c	d	e	f	g	h	i	j	k	l	m
		Gross Pay			**Deductions**						**Net Pay**		**Account Debited**	
Employee Name	Hours	Straight time	Overtime	Total	Federal Income Tax	Prov. Inc. Tax (Alberta)	Canada Pension Plan	Employ-ment Insurance	Red Deer United Way	Total	(c−h) Amount	Cheque No.	Office Salaries Expense	Sales Salaries Expense
Chen, W.L.*	40	500.00		500.00	45.50	18.15	21.42	9.35	2.00	96.42	403.58	1621	500.00	
Drumm, C.L.	46	400.00	90.00	490.00	43.75	17.05	20.92	9.16	2.00	92.88	397.12	1622		490.00
Elias, M.	41	560.00	21.00	581.00	57.35	25.65	25.43	10.47		118.90	462.10	1623	581.00	
Vokovich, E.A.**	40	1,360.00		1,360.00	217.75	101.80			15.00	334.55	1,025.45	1641		1,360.00
Total		12,940.00	714.00	13,654.00	2,186.15	1,022.04	402.70	302.12	155.00	4,068.01	9,585.99		4,464.00	9,190.00

*W.L. Chen earned gross pay of $500. His net pay was $403.58, paid with cheque number 1621. Chen is an office worker, so his salary is debited to Office Salaries Expense.

**E.A. Vokovich has exceeded maximum pensionable earnings of $42,100 and so has had the Canada Pension Plan maximum, $1,910.70, already deducted. Vokovich has also exceeded the maximum insurable Employment Insurance earnings of $39,000 and so has already had the maximum, $729.30, deducted.

EXHIBIT 11–7   Payroll Cheque

Red Deer Provisioners										1622
Payroll Account										
Red Deer, Alberta										

January 2, 2007

Pay to the
Order of _____ C.L. Drumm _____ $ | 397.12

Three hundred ninety-seven ------------------------- 12/100 Dollars

The Bank of Nova Scotia
Red Deer
Alberta T4P 3L9

Anna Figaro
Treasurer

⑈111900031⑈ 0787⑈500004 54⑈

Pay			Deductions							Net Pay	Cheque No.
Straight-time	Over-time	Gross	Federal Income Tax	Prov. Income Tax	C.P.P.	Employ-ment Ins.	United Way	Total			
400.00	90.00	490.00	43.75	17.05	20.92	9.16	2.00	92.88		397.12	1622

Payroll Withholdings to the Government and Other Organizations The employer must send income taxes withheld from employees' pay and the employee deductions and employer's share of Canada (or Quebec) Pension Plan contributions and Employment Insurance premiums to Canada Revenue Agency (CRA). The payment for a given month is due on or before the 15th day of the following month. In addition, the employer has to remit any withholdings for union dues, charitable donations, etc.; the payment would probably be made in the following month.

Assume federal income tax of $7,972.80, Province of Alberta income tax of $2,967.40, Canada Pension Plan contributions of $1,645.02, Employment Insurance premiums of $1,197.02, and United Way contributions of $465.00 were deducted in calculating the net pay for the employees of Red Deer Provisioners for the four weeks ended December 3, 10, 17, and 24, 2006. Based on those amounts and columns (d) through (j) in Exhibit 11–6, the business would record payments to CRA and Red Deer United Way for the month of December 2006 as follows:

2007
Jan. 10   Employee Income Tax Payable
               ($7,972.80 + $2,186.15 + $2,967.40 + $1,022.04) 14,148.39
          Canada Pension Plan Payable
               ($1,645.02 + $402.70 + $1,645.02 + $402.70) 4,095.44
          Employment Insurance Payable
               [$1,197.02 + $302.12 + 1.4 × ($1,197.02 + $302.12)] 3,597.94
                    Cash 21,841.77
          To record payment to CRA for December 2006
          withholdings.

2007
Jan. 10   United Way Payable 620.00
                    Cash 620.00
          To record payment to United Way for December 2006
          withholdings ($465.00 + $155.00).

Payments to Third Parties for Fringe Benefits The employer sometimes pays for employees' dental benefits coverage and for a company pension plan. Assuming the total cash payment for these benefits is $1,927.14 and the payment is made to one company, this entry would be

2007			
Jan. 10	Employee Benefits Payable—Dental Plan	600.14	
	Employee Benefits Payable—Pension Plan	1,327.00	
	Cash		1,927.14
	To record payment for employee dental benefits coverage and company pension plan.		

Earnings Record

The employer must file Summary of Remuneration Paid returns with Canada Revenue Agency (CRA) and must provide the employee with a Statement of Remuneration Paid, Form T4, by February 28 of the following year. Therefore, employers maintain an earnings record for each employee. (These earnings records are also used for Employment Insurance claims.) Exhibit 11–8 is a five-week excerpt from the earnings record of employee J.C. Jenkins.

The employee earnings record is not a journal or a ledger, and it is not required by law. It is an accounting tool—like the work sheet—that the employer uses to prepare payroll withholdings reports. The information provided on the earnings record with respect to year-to-date earnings also indicates when an employee has earned $42,100, the point at which the employer can stop withholding Canada Pension Plan contributions. The same is true for Employment Insurance deductions: the employer stops withholding Employment Insurance contributions after the employee has earned $39,000. There is no maximum income tax deduction.

Exhibit 11–9 is the Statement of Remuneration Paid, Form T4, for employee J.C. Jenkins. The employer prepares this form for each employee and a form called a T4 Summary—Summary of Remuneration Paid, which summarizes the information on all the T4s issued by the employer for that year. The employer sends the T4 Summary and one copy of each T4 to CRA by February 28 each year. CRA uses the documents to ensure that the employer has correctly paid to the government all amounts withheld on its behalf from employees, together with the employer's share. The employee gets two copies of the T4; one copy must be filed with the employee's income tax return, while the second copy is for the employee's records.

CRA matches the income on the T4 filed by the employer against the income reported on the employee's income tax return, filed by the employee, to ensure that the employee properly reported his or her income from employment.

Employers and employees can use the Internet to file T4 information for reporting as well as to file tax information.

EXHIBIT 11–8 Employee Earnings Record for 2006

Employee Name and Address:

Jenkins, J.C.
1400 Camousen Cres.
Victoria, BC V5J 5K9

Social Insurance No.: 978-010-789
Marital Status: Married
Net Claims Code: 4
Pay Rate: $700 per week; overtime $26.25 per hour.
Job Title: Salesperson

Week Ended	Hours	Gross Pay				Deductions						Net Pay	
		Straight time	Overtime	Total	To Date	Federal Income Tax	Province of BC Income Tax	Canada Pension Plan	Employment Insurance	United Way	Total	Amount	Cheque No.
Jan. 4	40	700.00		700.00	700.00	61.05	25.30	31.32	13.09	2.00	132.76	567.24	403
Dec. 3	40	700.00		700.00	35,437.50	61.05	25.30	31.32	13.09	2.00	132.76	567.24	1525
Dec. 10	40	700.00		700.00	36,137.50	61.05	25.30	31.32	13.09	2.00	132.76	567.24	1548
Dec. 17	44	700.00	105.00	805.00	36,942.50	83.00	34.45	36.39	15.05	2.00	170.89	634.11	1574
Dec. 24	48	700.00	210.00	910.00	37,852.50	105.85	44.00	41.63	17.02	2.00	210.50	699.50	1598
Dec. 31	46	700.00	157.50	857.50	38,710.00	93.55	38.85	39.36	16.04	2.00	189.80	667.70	1632
Total		36,400.00	2,310.00	38,710.00	38,710.00	4,091.20	1,871.80	1,742.90	723.88	104.00	8,533.78	30,176.22	

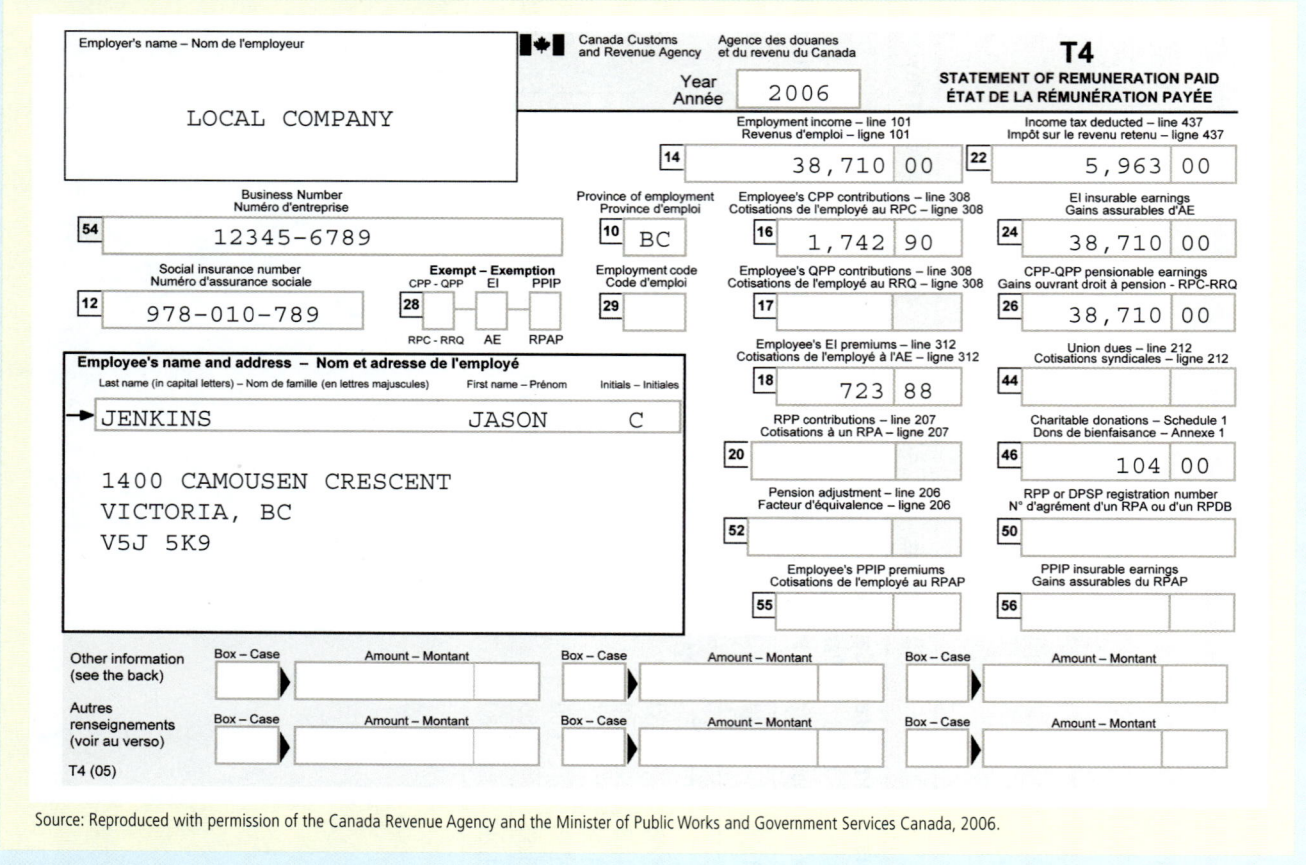

Source: Reproduced with permission of the Canada Revenue Agency and the Minister of Public Works and Government Services Canada, 2006.

Internal Control over Payroll

The internal controls over cash payments discussed in Chapter 8 also apply to payroll. There are two main types of controls for payroll: controls for efficiency and controls for safeguarding payroll disbursements.

Controls for Efficiency

Payroll transactions are ideally suited for computer processing. Employee payroll data can be stored in a file. The computer performs the calculations, prints the payroll register and the paycheques, and updates the employee earnings records electronically.

Payroll Systems and Internal Control

Companies use the payroll module of their accounting software to perform the detailed payroll calculations. This software is updated regularly by the software manufacturer to ensure that the tax tables and rates reflect the changes implemented by any of the laws relating to payroll deductions. At the end of the calendar year, this software can prepare employees' T4 slips.

The payroll software also interfaces with the banking system to instruct the bank to deposit the net pay into the employees' bank accounts by electronic funds transfers (EFT). This feature ensures that the appropriate employee is paid and that the payroll cheques are not lost. Not issuing paycheques also reduces administrative costs to the company.

Reconciling the bank account can be time consuming because of the large number of paycheques. There may be a large number of outstanding cheques for the bank reconciliation. To limit the number of outstanding cheques, some companies use two payroll bank accounts. They pay the payroll from one payroll account one month and from the other payroll account the next month. This way they can reconcile each account every other month, and that decreases accounting and auditing costs.

Other payroll controls for efficiency include following established policies for hiring and terminating employees, and complying with government regulations. Hiring and termination policies provide guidelines for keeping a qualified, diligent work force dedicated to achieving the business's goals. Complying with government regulations helps companies avoid paying fines and penalties.

Controls for Safeguarding Payroll Disbursements

Owners and managers of small businesses can monitor their payroll by personal contact with employees. Large corporations cannot do so. A particular risk is that a paycheque may be written to a fictitious person and cashed by a dishonest employee. To guard against this and other possible crimes, large businesses adopt strict internal control policies for payrolls.

The duties of hiring and terminating employees should be separated from payroll accounting and from distributing paycheques. Issuing paycheques only to employees with a photo ID ensures that only actual employees receive pay. Comparing the current employee list to a list of former employees ensures that terminated employees are not continuing to receive paycheques. A formal time-keeping system helps ensure that employees actually worked the number of hours claimed. Employees may punch time cards at the start and end of the work day to prove their attendance.

As we saw in Chapter 8, the foundation for good internal control is separation of duties. This is why companies have separate departments for the following payroll functions:

- hiring and terminating employees—Human Resources department
- maintaining employee earnings records—Payroll or Accounting department

> ### STOP AND THINK
>
> Centurion Homes of Calgary, Alberta, builds houses and has four construction crews. The supervisors hire—and terminate—workers and keep their hourly records. Each Friday morning the supervisors telephone their workers' hours to the home office, where accountants prepare the weekly paycheques. Around noon the supervisors pick up the paycheques. They return to the construction site and pay the workers at day's end. What is the internal control weakness in this situation? Propose a way to improve the internal controls.
>
> **Answer:** When the supervisors control most of the information used in the payroll system, they can forge the payroll records of fictitious employees and pocket their pay. To improve internal control, Centurion Homes could hire and terminate all workers through the home office. This would prove that all workers actually exist. Another way to improve the internal controls would be to have a home-office employee distribute paycheques on a surprise basis. Any remaining cheques would arouse suspicion. This system would probably prevent supervisors from cheating the company.

Reporting Payroll Expense and Liabilities

At the end of each period, a company reports all its current liabilities on the balance sheet. At December 31, 2005, Inco Limited had the current liabilities shown in Exhibit 11–10. Inco combines all payroll liabilities under a single heading, Accrued Payroll and Benefits.

Objective 6
Report current liabilities on the balance sheet

EXHIBIT 11–10 Inco Limited Balance Sheet at December 31, 2005 (Partial)

Current Liabilities	(U.S. $ in millions)
Long-term debt due within one year	$ 122
Accounts payable	253
Accrued payrolls and benefits	221
Other accrued liabilities	533
Income and mining taxes payable	36
Total current liabilities..	$1,165

As we conclude this chapter, we return to our opening questions: What are current liabilities of known amount and current liabilities of unknown amount, and why are they important? How should you account for potential liabilities? What is the ethical and legal challenge in accounting for current and potential liabilities? What are the key elements of a payroll system? What is an employer's total payroll expense? How do you report payroll amounts in the financial statements? These questions were answered throughout this chapter. And the Decision Guidelines in this chapter provide the answers in a useful summary.

DECISION GUIDELINES — Accounting for Payroll

Decision	Guidelines
What are the key elements of a payroll accounting system?	• Personal Tax Credits Return, Form TD1(E) • Payroll register • Payroll bank account and payroll cheques • Employee earnings record • Statement of Remuneration Paid, Form T4

What are the key terms in the payroll area?	*Gross pay* (Total amount earned by the employee)
	— *Payroll deductions:*
	  a. Withheld income tax
	  b. Withheld Canada (or Quebec) Pension Plan deductions— equal amount paid by employer
	  c. Withheld Employment Insurance deductions—employer pays 1.4 times employee deduction
	  d. Optional deductions (retirement savings plan, charitable contributions)
	= *Net (take-home) pay*

What is the employer's total payroll expense?	*Gross pay*
	+ *Employer's payroll expenses*
	  a. Canada (or Quebec) Pension Plan expense
	  b. Employment Insurance expense—employer pays 1.4 times amount employee pays
	+ *Fringe benefits for employees*
	  a. Insurance (dental, drug plan, and disability)
	  b. Employer's share of retirement savings plan (and other retirement benefits)
	  c. Workers' Compensation premiums
	  d. Club memberships and other benefits
	= *Employer's total payroll costs*

Where to report payroll amounts?	• Payroll expenses on the income statement • Payroll liabilities on the balance sheet

Summary Problem for Your Review

Best Threads, a clothing store in Moose Jaw, Saskatchewan, employs one salesperson, Sheila Kingsley. Her straight-time pay is $420 per week. She earns time and a half for hours worked in excess of 35 per week. For Kingsley's wage rate and "net claim code" on her Personal Tax Credits Return (TD1), the federal income tax withholding rate is approximately 11.5 percent, and the provincial rate is 7.7 percent. Canada Pension is 4.95 percent on income until the maximum total contribution of $1,910.70 is reached, while Employment Insurance premiums are 1.87 percent until the maximum total contribution of $729.30 is reached. In addition, Best Threads pays Kingsley's Blue Cross supplemental health insurance premiums of $31.42 a month and dental insurance premiums of $18.50 a month.

During the week ended February 28, 2006, Kingsley worked 48 hours.

Required

1. Compute Sheila Kingsley's gross pay and net pay for the week.
2. Record the following payroll entries that Best Threads would make:
   a. Expense for Kingsley's wages including overtime pay
   b. Cost of employer's share of Kingsley's withholdings (ignore the basic Canada Pension Plan exemption)
   c. Expense for fringe benefits
   d. Payment of cash to Kingsley
   e. Payment Best Threads must make to Canada Revenue Agency (CRA)
   f. Payment of fringe benefits for the month
3. How much total payroll expense did Best Threads incur for the week? How much cash did the business spend on its payroll?

Name: Best Threads
Industry: Clothing store in Saskatchewan
Accounting Period: Week ended February 28, 2006

Solution

Requirement 1

To compute gross pay, first separate hours worked into straight-time and overtime hours. Then multiply each by the appropriate hourly pay rate.

Gross pay:		
Straight-time pay for 35 hours		$420.00
Overtime pay		
Rate per hour ($420 ÷ 35 × 1.5)	$18.00	
Hours (48 − 35)	× 13	234.00
Total gross pay		$654.00

Compute the amount of each withholding, either using the information given or by consulting tax, CPP, and EI tables.

Gross pay − Total withholdings = Net pay

Net pay:		
Gross pay		$654.00
Less: Withheld federal income tax ($654 × 0.115)...............	$ 75.21	
Withheld provincial income tax ($654 × 0.077).........	50.36	
Withheld Canada Pension Plan ($654 × 0.0495)	32.37	
Withheld Employment Insurance ($654 × 0.0187) ...	12.23	170.17
Net pay...		$483.83

Requirement 2

<table>
<tr><td>a. Sales Salary Expense ....</td><td>654.00</td><td></td></tr>
<tr><td>   Employee Income Tax Payable ($75.21 + $50.36) ....</td><td></td><td>125.57</td></tr>
<tr><td>   Canada Pension Plan Payable..</td><td></td><td>32.37</td></tr>
<tr><td>   Employment Insurance Payable..</td><td></td><td>12.23</td></tr>
<tr><td>   Wages Payable...</td><td></td><td>483.83</td></tr>
<tr><td> To record expense for S. Kingsley's wages.</td><td></td><td></td></tr>
<tr><td>b. Employee Benefits Expense ($32.37 + $17.12) ....</td><td>49.49</td><td></td></tr>
<tr><td>   Canada Pension Plan Payable..</td><td></td><td>32.37</td></tr>
<tr><td>   Employment Insurance Payable..</td><td></td><td>17.12</td></tr>
<tr><td> To record cost of employer's portion of S. Kingsley's wages.</td><td></td><td></td></tr>
<tr><td>   CPP is $32.37 ($32.37 × 1).</td><td></td><td></td></tr>
<tr><td>   EI is $17.12 ($12.23 × 1.4).</td><td></td><td></td></tr>
<tr><td>c. Medical and Dental Expense ....</td><td>49.92</td><td></td></tr>
<tr><td>   Employee Benefits Payable ....</td><td></td><td>49.92</td></tr>
<tr><td> To record expense of fringe benefits ($31.42 + $18.50).</td><td></td><td></td></tr>
<tr><td>d. Wages Payable ....</td><td>483.83</td><td></td></tr>
<tr><td>   Cash ....</td><td></td><td>483.83</td></tr>
<tr><td> To record payment of wages to S. Kingsley.</td><td></td><td></td></tr>
<tr><td>e. Employee Income Tax Payable ....</td><td>125.57</td><td></td></tr>
<tr><td>   Canada Pension Plan Payable ($32.37 + $32.37) ....</td><td>64.74</td><td></td></tr>
<tr><td>   Employment Insurance Payable ($12.23 + $17.12)...............</td><td>29.35</td><td></td></tr>
<tr><td>   Cash ....</td><td></td><td>219.66</td></tr>
<tr><td> To record payment to CRA.</td><td></td><td></td></tr>
<tr><td>f. Employee Benefits Payable ....</td><td>49.92</td><td></td></tr>
<tr><td>   Cash ....</td><td></td><td>49.92</td></tr>
<tr><td> To record payment of monthly fringe benefits.</td><td></td><td></td></tr>
</table>

(Side notes)

This journal entry uses the gross pay, withholdings, and net pay amounts calculated in Requirement 1. "Wages Payable" is the amount of net pay.

Remember that the employer's EI expense is 1.4 times the employee's EI withholding.

This journal entry issues the paycheque or EFTs the funds to the employee's bank account.

Employers pay to CRA:
• federal and provincial taxes withheld from the employee
• EI premiums withheld from employee + paid by employer
• CPP (or QPP) withholdings from employee + paid by employer

Requirement 3

Best Threads incurred *total payroll expense* of $753.41 (gross salary of $654.00 + employer's cost of Canada Pension Plan of $32.37 + employer's cost of Employment Insurance of $17.12 + fringe benefits of $49.92). See entries a to c.

Best Threads paid cash of $753.41 on payroll (Kingsley's net pay of $483.83 + payment to CRA of $219.66 + fringe benefits of $49.92). See entries d to f.

(Side notes)

Total payroll expense = Gross salary + EI expense + CPP expense + fringe benefits

Total cash paid = Net pay + CRA payment + Fringe benefits payment (everyone who was sent a cheque)

Go to MyAccountingLab at www.myaccountinglab.ca. You can practise this chapter's exercises and problems as often as you want. The guided solutions help you find an answer, step by step. There's a personalized study plan, too!

Summary

1. **Account for current liabilities of known amount.** *Current liabilities* may be divided into those of *known amount* and those that must be *estimated.* Trade accounts payable, short-term notes payable, interest payable, GST payable, employee benefits payable, and unearned revenues are current liabilities of known amount.

2. **Account for current liabilities that must be estimated.** Current liabilities that must be estimated include warranties payable, vacation pay, and corporations' income tax payable.

   Contingent liabilities are not actual liabilities but potential liabilities that may arise in the future. Contingent liabilities, like current liabilities, may be of known amount or an indefinite amount. A business that faces a lawsuit not yet decided in court has a contingent liability of indefinite amount.

3. **Compute payroll amounts.** *Payroll* accounting handles the expenses and liabilities arising from compensating employees. Employers must withhold federal and provincial income taxes, Canada (or Quebec) Pension Plan contributions, and Employment Insurance premiums from employees' pay and send these *withholdings* together with the employer's share of the latter two to the appropriate government. In addition, many employers allow their employees to pay for insurance and union dues and to make gifts to charities through payroll deductions. An employee's net pay is the gross pay less all withholdings and optional deductions.

4. **Record basic payroll transactions.** An *employer's* payroll expenses include the employer's share of Canada (or Quebec) Pension Plan contributions and Employment Insurance premiums; employers also pay provincial health and post-secondary education taxes in those provinces that levy them and Workers' Compensation. Also, employers may provide their employees with fringe benefits, such as life insurance coverage and retirement pensions.

5. **Use a payroll system and implement internal controls.** A basic *payroll system* consists of a payroll register, a payroll bank account, payroll cheques or EFTs, and an earnings record for each employee. Good *internal controls* over payroll help the business to achieve efficiency and to safeguard the company's cash. The cornerstone of internal control is the separation of duties.

6. **Report current liabilities on the balance sheet.** The company reports on the balance sheet all current liabilities that it owes: current liabilities of known amount, including payroll liabilities; and current liabilities that must be estimated.

Self-Study Questions

Test your understanding of the chapter by marking the correct answer for each of the following questions:

1. A $10,000, 9 percent, one-year note payable was issued on July 31. The balance sheet at December 31 will report interest payable of (*pp. 533–534*)
   a. $0 because the interest is not due yet
   b. $522.74
   c. $377.26
   d. $900

2. Which of the following liabilities creates no expense for the company? (*p. 536*)
   a. Interest
   b. Sales tax
   c. Employment Insurance
   d. Warranty

3. Known liabilities of uncertain amounts should be (*p. 540*)
   a. Contingent liabilities
   b. Ignored. Record them when they are paid.
   c. Reported on the balance sheet
   d. Reported only in the notes to the financial statements

4. Suppose Canadian Tire estimates that warranty costs will equal 1 percent of tire sales. Assume that November tire sales totalled $900,000, and the company's outlay in replacement tires and cash to satisfy warranty claims was $7,400. How much warranty expense should the November income statement report? (*p. 540*)

   a. $1,600
   b. $7,400
   c. $9,000
   d. $16,400

5. Nu Systems Company is a defendant in a lawsuit that claims damages of $55,000. On the balance sheet date, it appears unlikely that the court will render a judgment against the company. How should Nu Systems Company report this event in its financial statements? (*p. 542*)
   a. Omit mention because no judgment has been rendered
   b. Disclose the contingent liability in a note
   c. Report the loss on the income statement and the liability on the balance sheet.
   d. Both b and c

6. Emilie Frontenac's weekly pay for 40 hours is $400, plus time and a half for overtime. The federal tax rate, based on her income level and deductions, is 10.5 percent, the provincial rate is 8.8 percent, the Quebec Pension Plan rate is 4.95 percent on her weekly earnings, and the Employment Insurance rate is 1.87 percent on her weekly earnings. What is Emilie's take-home pay for a week in which she works 50 hours? (*pp. 551–552*)
   a. $426.34
   b. $460.97
   c. $428.42
   d. $406.34

7. Which of the following represents a cost to the employer? (*p. 549*)
   a. Withheld income tax
   b. Canada Pension Plan
   c. Employment Insurance
   d. Both b and c

8. The main reason for using a separate payroll bank account is to (*p. 558*)
   a. Safeguard cash by preventing the writing of payroll cheques to fictitious employees
   b. Safeguard cash by limiting paycheques to amounts based on time cards
   c. Increase efficiency by isolating payroll disbursements for analysis and control
   d. All of the above

9. The best step to ensure good internal controls in the payroll area is (*pp. 558–559*)
   a. Using a payroll bank account
   b. Separating payroll duties
   c. Using a payroll register
   d. Using time cards

10. Which of the following items is reported as a current liability on the balance sheet? (*p. 560*)
    a. Short-term notes payable
    b. Estimated warranties
    c. Payroll withholdings
    d. All of the above

Answers to the Self-Study Questions follow the Similar Accounting Terms.

Accounting Vocabulary

Accrued expense   (*p. 538*)
Accrued liability   (*p. 538*)
Canada (or Quebec) Pension Plan   (*p. 547*)
Current portion of long-term debt   (*p. 537*)
Employee compensation   (*p. 538*)
Employment Insurance   (*p. 548*)
Gross pay   (*p. 546*)

Line of credit   (*p. 534*)
Net pay   (*p. 546*)
Payroll   (*p. 538*)
Short-term note payable   (*p. 533*)
Withheld income tax   (*p. 547*)
Workers' Compensation   (*p. 549*)

Similar Accounting Terms

Current portion of long-term debt	Current maturity
Unearned revenues	Deferred revenues; Revenues collected in advance; Customer prepayments
Payroll register	Payroll journal; Payroll record

Answers to Self-Study Questions

1. c $10,000 \times 0.09 \times {}^{153}/_{365} = \$377.26$
2. b
3. c
4. c $900,000 \times 0.01 = \$9,000$
5. b
6. d Overtime pay: $400 \div 40 = \$10$; $10 \times 1.5 = \$15$ per hour; 15 per hour $\times 10$ hours $= \$150$
   Gross pay $= \$400 + \$150 = \$550$
   Deductions $= (\$550 \times 0.105) + (\$550 \times 0.088) + (\$550 \times 0.0495) + (\$550 \times 0.0187)$
   $= \$57.75 + \$48.40 + \$27.23 + \$10.28 = \$143.66$
   Take-home pay $= \$550.00 - \$143.66 = \$406.34$
7. d
8. c
9. b
10. d

Assignment Material

Questions

1. What distinguishes a current liability from a long-term liability? What distinguishes a contingent liability from an actual liability?

2. A company purchases a machine by signing a $50,000, 4-percent, one-year note payable on June 30. Interest is to be paid at maturity. What two current liabilities related to this purchase does the company report on its December 31 balance sheet? What is the amount of each current liability?

3. Explain how GST that is paid by consumers is a liability of the store that sold the merchandise. To whom is it paid?

4. What is meant by the term *current portion of long-term debt,* and how is this item reported in the financial statements?

5. Why is an accrued expense a liability?

6. Describe the similarities and differences between an account payable and a short-term note payable.

7. At the beginning of the school term, what type of account is the tuition that your college or university collects from students? What type of account is the tuition at the end of the school term?

8. Why is a customer deposit a liability? Give an example.

9. Murray Company warrants its products against defects for two years from date of sale. During the current year, the company made sales of $1,000,000. Management estimated warranty costs on those sales would total $30,000 over the two-year warranty period. Ultimately, the company paid $35,000 cash on warranties. What is the company's warranty expense for the year? What accounting principle governs this answer?

10. Identify one contingent liability of a definite amount and one contingent liability of an indefinite amount.

11. What are the two basic categories of current liabilities? Give an example of each.

12. Why is payroll expense relatively more important to a service business such as a public accounting firm than it is to a merchandising company such as Zellers?

13. Two persons are studying Beauregarde Company's manufacturing process. One person is Beauregarde Company's factory supervisor, and the other person is an outside consultant who is an expert in the industry. Which person's salary is the payroll expense of Beauregarde Company? Identify the expense account that Beauregarde Company would debit to record the pay of each person.

14. What are two elements of an employer's payroll expense in addition to salaries, wages, commissions, and overtime pay?

15. What determines the amount of income tax that is withheld from employee paycheques?

16. What is the Canada (or Quebec) Pension Plan? Who pays it? What are the funds used for?

17. Identify three required deductions and two optional deductions from employee paycheques.

18. Identify the employee benefit expenses an employer pays.

19. Who pays Employment Insurance premiums? What are these funds used for?

20. Briefly describe a basic payroll accounting system's components and their functions.

21. How much Employment Insurance has been withheld from the pay of an employee who has earned $52,288 during the current year? What is the employer's Employment Insurance expense for this employee?

22. Briefly describe the two principal types of internal controls over payroll.

23. Why do some companies use two special payroll bank accounts?

24. Identify three internal controls designed to safeguard payroll cash.

Starters

Starter 11–1 On June 30, 2007, Cimmeron Corp. purchased $16,000 of inventory on a one-year, 10% note payable. Journalize the company's (a) accrual of interest expense on December 31, 2007 and (b) payment of the note plus interest on June 30, 2008.

Accounting for a note payable

(b) Credit Cash for $17,600

Starter 11–2 Refer to the data in Starter 11–1. Show what Cimmeron Corp. reports for the note payable and related interest payable on its balance sheet at December 31, 2007, and on its income statement for the year ended on that date.

Reporting a short-term note payable and the related interest

Interest expense $800

Accounting for warranty expense
and warranty payable

2. Estimated Warranty Payable
bal. $5,000

Starter 11–3 Arctic Corporation guarantees its snowmobiles for three years. Company experience indicates that warranty costs will be 5% of sales.

Assume that an Arctic dealer made sales totaling $600,000 during January 2007, its first month of operations. The company received cash for 30% of the sales and notes receivable for the remainder. Warranty payments totaled $25,000 during 2007.

1. Record the sales, warranty expense, and warranty payments for Arctic Corporation.

2. Post to the Estimated Warranty Payable T-account. At the end of 2007, what is the estimated warranty payable balance for Arctic Corporation?

Applying GAAP; reporting
warranties in the
financial statements

Starter 11–4 Refer to the data given in Starter 11–3.

What amount of warranty expense will Arctic Corporation report during 2007? Does the warranty expense for the year equal the year's cash payments for warranties? Which accounting principle addresses this situation?

Interpreting an actual company's
contingent liabilities

Starter 11–5 Harley-Davidson, Inc., the motorcycle manufacturer, used to include the following note (adapted) in its annual report:

Notes to Consolidated Financial Statements

7 (in Part): Commitments and Contingencies (Adapted)

The Company self-insures its product liability losses in the United States up to $3 million.

Catastrophic coverage is maintained for individual claims in excess of $3 million up to $25 million.

---

1. Why are these *contingent* (versus real) liabilities?

2. How can a contingent liability become a real liability for Harley-Davidson? What are the limits to the company's product liabilities in the United States?

Starter 11–6 begins a sequence of exercises that ends with Starter 11–8.

Computing an employee's
total pay

2. Net pay $731.98

Starter 11–6 Grant Teiman is paid $640 for a 40-hour work week and time-and-a-half for hours worked above 40.

1. Compute Teiman's gross pay for working 50 hours during the first week of February.

2. Teiman is single, and his income tax withholding is 10% of total pay. His only payroll deductions are taxes withheld, CPP of 4.95% and EI of 1.87%. Compute Teiman's net pay for the week.

Computing the payroll expense
of an employer

Total expense $1,007.60

Starter 11–7 Return to the Grant Teiman payroll situation in Starter 11–6. Teiman's employer, Jones Golf Corp., pays all the standard payroll expenses plus benefits for employee pensions (5% of gross pay), BC health Insurance ($60 per employee per month), and disability insurance ($8 per employee per month).

Compute Jones Golf Corp.'s total expense of employing Grant Tieman for the 50 hours that he worked during the first week of February. Carry amounts to the nearest cent.

Making payroll entries

a. Salary Payable $731.98

Starter 11–8 After solving Starters 11–6 and 11–7, journalize for Jones Golf Corp. the following expenses related to the employment of Grant Teiman:

a. Salary expense

b. Benefits

c. Employer payroll expenses

Carry all amounts to the nearest cent.

Computing payroll amounts

Net pay $2,980

Starter 11–9 Suppose you work for an accounting firm all year and earn a monthly salary of $4,000. There is no overtime pay. Your withheld deductions consume 20% of gross pay. In addition to payroll deductions, you elect to contribute 4% monthly to your pension plan. Your employer also deducts $60 monthly for your payment of the health insurance premium.

Compute your net pay for November.

Starter 11–10 Refer to the payroll information in Starters 11–6 and 11–7.

1. How much was the company's total salary expense for the week for Grant Teiman?
2. How much cash did Grant Teiman take home for his work?
3. How much did the *employee* pay this week for
   a. Income tax?
   b. CPP and EI?
4. How much expense did the *employer* have this week for
   a. CPP and EI?
   b. Benefits?

Using a payroll system

1. Total salary expense $1,007.60

Starter 11–11 What are some of the important elements of good internal control to safeguard payroll disbursements?

Internal controls over payroll disbursements

Exercises

Exercise 11–1

Record the following note payable transactions of Braidon Company in the company's general journal. Explanations are not required.

2008
June	1	Purchased delivery truck costing $86,000 by issuing a one-year, 4-percent note payable.
Dec.	31	Accrued interest on the note payable.

2009
June	1	Paid the note payable at maturity.

Recording note payable transactions

June 1, 2009 Credit Cash $89,440

Exercise 11–2

Make general journal entries to record the following transactions of Lavine Products for a two-month period. Explanations are not required.

June	30	Recorded cash sales of $115,000 for the month, plus provincial sales tax of 8 percent collected on behalf of the province of Ontario and goods and services tax of 6 percent. Record the two taxes in separate accounts.
July	6	Sent June provincial and goods and services taxes to appropriate authorities (Minister of Finance for PST and Receiver General for GST). Assume no GST input tax credits.

Recording sales tax and GST

June 30 Debit Cash $131,100

Exercise 11–3

Suppose Mars Technologies borrowed $2,000,000 on December 31, 2005, by issuing 5 percent long-term debt that must be paid in four equal annual instalments plus interest each January 2, commencing in 2007.

Required   Insert the appropriate amounts in the following excerpts from the company's partial balance sheet to show how Mars Technologies should report its current and long-term liabilities for this debt.

Reporting current and long-term liabilities

2006: Current portion of long-term debt $500,000; Interest payable $100,000

	December 31,			
	2006	2007	2008	2009
Current liabilities:				
Current portion of long-term debt........	$ _____	$ _____	$ _____	$ _____
Interest payable	$ _____	$ _____	$ _____	$ _____
Long-term liabilities:				
Long-term debt..	$ _____	$ _____	$ _____	$ _____

Exercise 11–4

Assume Jasper Electronics completed these selected transactions during December 2006:

1. Music For You Inc., a chain of music stores, ordered $105,000 worth of CD players. With its order, Music For You Inc. sent a cheque for $105,000. Jasper Electronics will ship the goods on January 3, 2007.

Reporting current and long-term liabilities

Total current liabilities $719,995

2. The December payroll of $600,000 is subject to employee withheld income tax of 16 percent, Canada Pension Plan expenses of 4.95 percent for the employee and 4.95 percent for the employer, Employment Insurance deductions of 1.87 percent for the employee and 1.4 times the employee rate of 1.87 percent for the employer. On December 31, Jasper Electronics pays employees but accrues all tax amounts.

3. Sales of $30,000,000 are subject to estimated warranty cost of 1.4 percent. This was the first year the company provided a warranty, and no warranty claims have been recorded or paid.

4. On December 2, Jasper Electronics signed a $50,000 note payable that requires annual payments of $12,500 plus 4 percent interest on the unpaid balance each December 2.

Required Report these items on Jasper Electronics' balance sheet at December 31, 2006.

Recording current liabilities

Exercise 11–5

The management of Marquis Marketing Services examines the following company accounting records at August 29, immediately before the end of the year, August 31:

Total current assets	$ 325,000
Property, plant, and equipment	1,079,500
	$1,404,500
Total current liabilities	$ 192,500
Long-term liabilities	247,500
Owner's equity	964,500
	$1,404,500

Marquis's banking agreement with The Royal Bank requires the company to keep a current ratio of 2.25 or better. How much in current liabilities should Marquis pay off within the next two days in order to comply with its borrowing agreements?

Accounting for unearned revenue

1. (2) January 31, 2008
Debit Retainer Fees $5,000

Exercise 11–6

The law firm Garner & Brown received from a large corporate client an annual retainer fee of $60,000 on January 2, 2008. The fee is based on anticipated monthly services of $5,000.

Required

1. Using the account title Retainer Fees for unearned revenue, journalize (1) Garner & Brown's receipt of retainer fees, and (2) the provision of services in the month of January 2008.

2. Post the journal entries in Requirement 1 to the unearned revenue account (Retainer Fees) T-account. What is the value of services to be provided to the client in the remaining 11 months?

Accounting for unearned revenue

2. Unearned subscription
revenue $75.00

Exercise 11–7

Assume *The Globe and Mail* completed the following transactions for one subscriber during 2007:

Oct.	1	Sold a six-month subscription, collecting cash of $150 plus sales tax of 7 percent and 6 percent GST.
Nov.	15	Remitted (paid) the sales tax to the Province of British Columbia and the GST to the Receiver General.
Dec.	31	Made the necessary adjustment at year end to record the amount of subscription revenue earned during the year.

Required

1. Using *The Globe and Mail* (assumed) account title Unearned Subscription Revenue, journalize the transactions above.

2. Post the entries to the Unearned Subscription Revenue T-account. How much does *The Globe and Mail* owe the subscriber at December 31, 2007?

Accounting for warranty expense
and the related liability

2. Estimated Warranty Payable
bal. $8,830

Exercise 11–8

The accounting records of Kenroy Industries included the following at December 31, 2008:

Estimated Warranty Payable

	Jan. 1, 2008	12,400

In the past, Kenroy Industries' warranty expense has been 2 percent of sales. During 2008, Kenroy Industries made sales of $519,000 and paid $13,950 to satisfy warranty claims.

Required

1. Record Kenroy Industries' warranty expense and warranty payments during 2008. Explanations are not required.
2. What balance of Estimated Warranty Payable will Kenroy Industries report on its balance sheet at December 31, 2008?

Exercise 11–9

Windsor Security Systems is a defendant in lawsuits brought against the monitoring service of its installed systems. Damages of $500,000 are claimed against Windsor Security Systems but the company denies the charges and is vigorously defending itself. In a recent newspaper interview, the president of the company stated that he could not predict the outcome of the lawsuits. Nevertheless, he said management does not believe that any actual liabilities resulting from the lawsuits will significantly affect the company's financial position.

Required   Describe what, if any, disclosure Windsor Security Systems should provide of this contingent liability. Total liabilities are $2.0 million. If you believe note disclosure is required, write the note to describe the contingency.

Exercise 11–10

Refer to the Windsor Security Systems situation in the preceding exercise. Suppose that Windsor Security Systems' lawyers advise that preliminary judgment of $150,000 has been rendered against the company. The company will appeal the decision.

Required   Describe how to report this situation in the Windsor Security Systems financial statements. Journalize any entry required under GAAP. Explanations are not required.

Exercise 11–11

Carolin Baker is a clerk in the shoe department of The Bay in Winnipeg. She earns a base monthly salary of $1,875 plus a 7 percent commission on her sales. Through payroll deductions, Carolin donates $15 per month to a charitable organization and pays dental insurance premiums of $39.15. Compute Carolin's gross pay and net pay for December, assuming her sales for the month are $50,000. The income tax rate on her earnings is 30 percent, the Canada Pension Plan contribution is 4.95 percent (account for the $3,500 basic annual exemption), and the Employment Insurance Plan premium rate is 1.87 percent. Carolin has not yet reached the CPP or EI maximum earning levels.

Exercise 11–12

Jason Chan works for a Bob's Burgers takeout for straight-time earnings of $10.50 per hour, with time and a half for hours in excess of 35 per week. Jason's payroll deductions include income tax of 16 percent, Canada Pension Plan of 4.95 percent on earnings (account for the $3,500 basic annual exemption) and Employment Insurance of 1.87 percent on earnings. In addition, he contributes $2.50 per week to the United Way. Assume Jason worked 40 hours during the week. He has not yet reached the CPP or EI maximum earning levels.

Required

1. Compute Chan's gross pay and net pay for the week.
2. Make a general journal entry to record the restaurant's wage expense for Jason's work, including his payroll deductions and the employer payroll costs. Round all amounts to the nearest cent. An explanation is not required.

Exercise 11–13

Maple Leaf Manufacturing incurred salary expense of $95,000 for September. The company's payroll expense includes Canada Pension of 4.95 percent and Employment Insurance of 1.4 times the employee payment, which is 1.87 percent of earnings. Also, the company provides

Reporting a contingent liability

Accruing a contingency

Computing net pay

Net pay $3,356.22

Excel Spreadsheet Template

Computing and recording gross pay and net pay

1. Net pay $345.25

Recording a payroll

Employee Benefits Expense (CPP + EI) $7,189.60

the following fringe benefits for employees: dental insurance (cost to the company of $5,723.09), life insurance (cost to the company of $461.09), and pension benefits through a private plan (cost to the company of $1,945.60). Record Maple Leaf Manufacturing's payroll expenses for Canada Pension Plan and Employment Insurance and employee fringe benefits. Ignore the CPP basic exemption.

Using a payroll system to compute total payroll expense

Total payroll expense $43,821.83

Exercise 11–14

Study the Employee Earnings Record for J.C. Jenkins in Exhibit 11–8, page 557. In addition to the amounts shown in the exhibit, the employer also paid all employee benefits plus (a) an amount equal to 5 percent of gross pay into Jenkins' pension retirement account, and (b) dental insurance for Jenkins at a cost of $35 per month. Compute the employer's total payroll expense for employee J.C. Jenkins during 2006. Carry all amounts to the nearest cent.

Challenge Exercises

Accounting for and reporting current liabilities

1. Current ratio:
2007 1.24
2006 0.85

Exercise 11–15

Suppose the balance sheets of a corporation for two years reported these figures:

	Billions	
	2007	**2006**
Total current assets	$ 7.25	$ 6.46
Capital assets	22.37	20.48
	$29.62	$26.94
Total current liabilities	5.83	7.56
Long-term liabilities	14.96	11.66
Shareholders' equity	8.83	7.72
	$29.62	$26.94

The notes to the 2007 financial statements report that during 2007, because of some refinancing arrangements, the corporation was able to reclassify $3.5 billion from current liabilities to long-term liabilities.

Required

1. Compute the corporation's current ratio at the end of each year. Describe the trend that you observe.

2. Suppose that the corporation had not refinanced and not been able to reclassify the $3.5 billion of current liabilities as long-term during 2007. Recompute the current ratio for 2007 to include the 3.5 billion. Why do you think the corporation tried to reclassify the liabilities as long-term?

Analyzing current liability accounts

1. Payment of notes payable $27.5 mil.

Exercise 11–16

Jericho Company recently reported notes payable and accrued payrolls and benefits as follows:

	December 31,	
	2008	**2007**
	(in millions of dollars)	
Current liabilities (partial):		
Notes payable	$ 13	$ 39
Accrued payrolls and benefits	135	149

Assume that during 2008, Jericho Company borrowed $1.5 million on notes payable. Also assume that Jericho paid $125 million for employee compensation and benefits during 2008.

Required

1. Compute Jericho Company's payment of notes payable during 2008.
2. Compute Jericho Company's employee compensation expense for 2008.

Beyond the Numbers

Beyond the Numbers 11–1

Suppose a large manufacturing company is the defendant in numerous lawsuits claiming unfair trade practices. The company has strong incentives not to disclose these contingent liabilities. However, generally accepted accounting principles require companies to report their contingent liabilities.

Required

1. Why would a company prefer not to disclose its contingent liabilities?
2. Describe how a bank could be harmed if a company seeking a loan did not disclose its contingent liabilities.
3. What is the ethical tightrope that companies must walk when they report their contingent liabilities?

Beyond the Numbers 11–2

The following questions are not related.

a. A warranty is like a contingent liability in that the amount to be paid is not known at year end. Why are warranties payable shown as a current liability, whereas contingent liabilities are reported in the notes to the financial statements?
b. A friend comments that he thought that liabilities represented amounts owed by a company. He asks why unearned revenues are shown as a current liability. How would you respond?
c. Auditors have procedures for determining whether they have discovered all of a company's contingent liabilities. These procedures differ from the procedures used for determining that accounts payable are stated correctly. How would an auditor identify a client's contingent liabilities?

Ethical Issue

Many companies, such as Campeau Corporation, borrowed heavily during the 1970s and 1980s to exploit the advantage of financing operations with debt. At first, the companies were able to earn operating income much higher than their interest expense and were therefore quite profitable. However, when the business cycle turned down, their debt burdens pushed the companies to the brink of bankruptcy. Operating income was less than interest expense.

Required Is it unethical for managers to commit a company to a high level of debt? Or is it just risky? Who could be hurt by a company's taking on too much debt? Discuss.

Problems (Group A)

Problem 11–1A

The following selected transactions of Town Choppers, a Saskatchewan company, occurred during 2007 and 2008. The company's year end is December 31.

Journalizing liability-related transactions

2007
Jan.	3	Purchased a machine at a cost of $175,000 plus 6 percent GST, signing a 3 percent, six-month note payable for that amount.
	29	Recorded the month's sales of $785,000 (excludes PST and GST), 80 percent on credit and 20 percent for cash. Sales amounts are subject to 7 percent provincial sales tax plus 6 percent GST.
Feb.	5	Paid January's provincial sales tax and GST to the appropriate authorities.
	28	Borrowed $1,500,000 on a 5 percent note payable that calls for annual instalment payments of $150,000 principal plus interest.

July	3	Paid the six-month, 3 percent note at maturity.
Nov.	30	Purchased inventory for $75,000 plus GST, signing a six-month, 3 percent note payable.
Dec.	31	Accrued warranty expense, which is estimated at 1 percent of annual sales of $4,000,000.
	31	Accrued interest on all outstanding notes payable. Make a separate interest accrual entry for each note payable.
2008		
Feb.	28	Paid the first instalment and interest for one year on the long-term note payable.
May	31	Paid off the 3 percent note plus interest at maturity.

Required   Record the transactions in the company's general journal. Explanations are not required.

Identifying contingent liabilities

Problem 11–2A

Morgan Motors is the Morgan dealer located in Victoria, British Columbia, and the only dealer in Western Canada. The dealership repairs and restores Morgan vintage cars. Hal Irwin, the general manager, is considering changing insurance companies because of a disagreement with Bart LeMesure, agent for the Dominion of Canada Insurance Company. Dominion is doubling Morgan Motors' liability insurance cost for the next year. In discussing insurance coverage with you, a trusted business associate, LeMesure brings up the subject of contingent liabilities.

Required   Write a memorandum to inform Morgan Motors of specific contingent liabilities arising from the business. In your discussion, define a contingent liability.

Computing and
recording payroll amounts

b. Total employee earnings
$25,542

Problem 11–3A

The partial monthly records of Westwood Golf Shop show the following figures:

Employee Earnings

Regular employee earnings...	$19,947	
Overtime pay	a	
Total employee earnings	b	

Employment Insurance	$	478
Medical insurance		541
Total deductions		7,947
Net pay		17,595

Deductions and Net Pay

Withheld income tax	6,379
Canada Pension Plan	c

Accounts Debited

Salaries Expense	d
Wages Expense	6,938
Sales Commission Expense....	1,681

Required

1. Determine missing amounts a, b, c, and d.
2. Prepare the general journal entry to record Westwood Golf Shop's payroll for the month. Credit Payroll Payable for net pay. No explanation is required.

Excel Spreadsheet Template

Computing and recording
payroll amounts

1. Net pay $70,762.00

Problem 11–4A

Assume that Shetal Patel is a Vice-President in Edco Capital's leasing operations. During 2006 she worked for the company all year at a $7,500 monthly salary. She also earned a year-end bonus equal to 20 percent of her salary.

Shetal's federal income tax withheld during 2006 was $2,398 per month. Also, there was a one-time federal withholding tax of $4,712 on her bonus cheque. She paid $356.85 per month into the Canada Pension Plan until she had paid the maximum of $1,910.70. In addition, Shetal paid $157.50 per month Employment Insurance through her employer until the maximum of $729.30 had been reached. She had authorized Edco Capital to make the following payroll deductions: life insurance of $55 per month; United Way of $37.50 per month.

Edco Capital incurred Canada Pension Plan expense equal to the amount deducted from Shetal's pay and Employment Insurance expense equal to 1.4 times the amount Shetal paid. In addition, Edco Capital paid dental and drug insurance of $38 per month and pension benefits of 6 percent of her base salary.

Required

1. Compute Shetal Patel's gross pay, payroll deductions, and net pay for the full year 2006. Round all amounts to the nearest cent.

2. Compute Edco Capital's total 2006 payroll expense for Shetal.

3. Prepare Edco Capital's general journal entries (explanations are not required) to record its expense for

   a. Shetal's total earnings for the year, her payroll deductions, and her net pay. Debit Salary Expense and Bonus Expense as appropriate for salary and employee benefit expense. Credit liability accounts for the payroll deductions and Cash for net pay.

   b. Employer payroll expenses for Shetal. Credit the appropriate liability accounts.

   c. Fringe benefits provided to Shetal. Credit Health Insurance Payable and Company Pension Payable.

Problem 11–5A

The general ledger of Shell Storage Units at June 30, 2007, the end of the company's fiscal year, includes the following account balances before adjusting entries.

Notes payable, short-term	$ 40,000	Employee insurance	
Accounts payable	471,240	benefits payable	_____
Current portion of		Estimated vacation	
long-term debt payable	_____	pay liability	$ 24,720
Interest payable	_____	Sales tax and GST payable	11,944
Salaries payable	_____	Unearned rent revenue............	30,000
Employee income tax		Long-term debt payable	500,000
payable..................................	_____		
Employer payroll costs			
payable..................................	_____		

The additional data needed to develop the adjusting entries at June 30 are as follows:

a. The $40,000 short-term note payable was issued on February 28. It matures six months from date of issuance and bears interest at 4.5 percent.

b. The long-term debt is payable in annual instalments of $100,000 with the next instalment due on August 31. On that date, Shell Storage Units will also pay one year's interest at 5 percent. Interest was last paid on August 31 of the preceding year.

c. Gross salaries for the last payroll of the fiscal year were $12,655. Of this amount, employee payroll withholdings payable were $2,730, and salary payable was $9,925.

d. Employer payroll expense payable was $1,639, and Shell Storage's liability for employee health insurance was $1,982.

e. Shell Storage estimates that vacation pay expense is 4 percent of gross salaries of $295,000 after adjustment for the last payroll of the fiscal year.

f. On March 1, the company collected one year's rent of $30,000 in advance.

g. At June 30, Shell Storage is the defendant in a $275,000 lawsuit, which the company expects to win. However, the outcome is uncertain.

Required

1. Open T-accounts for the listed accounts, inserting their unadjusted June 30, 2007 balances.

2. Post the June 30, 2007, adjusting entries to the T-accounts opened.

3. Prepare the liability section of Shell Storage Units' balance sheet at June 30, 2007.

Journalizing, posting, and reporting liabilities

3. Total liabilities $1,117,413

Excel Spreadsheet Template

Using payroll register; recording a payroll

1. Total net pay $2,395.55

Problem 11–6A

The payroll records of Nova Video Productions Inc. provide the following information for the weekly pay period ended September 21.

Employee	Hours Worked	Hourly Earnings Rate	Income Tax	Canada Pension Plan	Employ- ment Insurance	United Way	Year-to-date Earnings at the End of the Previous Week
Molly Dodge	43	$30	$374.10	$ 0	$ 0	$25	$47,200
Tally Lafarge	40	13	67.60	22.41	9.72	2	19,760
George White	49	10	63.70	20.92	10.00	2	20,250
Luigi Pogge	42	20	252.00	0	0	5	43,050

Tally Lafarge and George White work in the office, and Molly Dodge and Luigi Pogge work in sales. All employees are paid time and a half for hours worked in excess of 40 hours per week. Show computations.

Required

1. Enter the appropriate information in a payroll register similar to Exhibit 11–6. 554

2. Record the payroll information in the general journal, crediting net pay to Cash.

3. The employer's payroll costs include matching each employee's Canada Pension Plan contribution (employee rate 4.95 percent; maximum $1,910.70) and paying 1.4 times the employee's Employment Insurance premium (employee rate 1.87 percent; maximum $729.30). Record the employer's payroll costs in the general journal.

4. Why was there no deduction of Canada Pension Plan or Employment Insurance for Dodge and Pogge?

Reporting current liabilities

6

Problem 11–7A

Following are five pertinent facts about events during the current year at Coastal Fisheries, a Prince Edward Island fisheries supply company:

a. Sales of $911,000 were covered by Coastal Fisheries' product warranty. At January 1, the estimated warranty payable was $14,600. During the year Coastal recorded warranty expense of 2 percent of sales and paid warranty claims of $25,600.

b. On August 31, Coastal Fisheries signed a six-month, 4.5 percent note payable to purchase supplies costing $45,000. The note requires payment of principal and interest at maturity.

c. On November 30, Coastal Fisheries received rent of $18,000 in advance from a subtenant in their building. This rent will be earned evenly over three months.

d. December sales totalled $80,000 and Coastal Fisheries collected provincial sales tax of 10 percent plus goods and services tax of 6 percent on these sales. These taxes will be sent to the appropriate authorities early in January.*

e. Coastal Fisheries owes $150,000 on a long-term note payable. At December 31, $40,000 of this principal plus 5 percent accrued interest since September 30 are payable within one year.

*Note: Prince Edward Island bases PST on price including GST.

Required

For each item, indicate the account and the related amount to be reported as a *current* liability on Coastal Fisheries' December 31 (year-end) balance sheet.

Accounting for current liabilities; making basic payroll entries; reporting current liabilities

2. Total current liabilities $2,811,624.40

Problem 11–8A

Saywells Marine of St. John's, Newfoundland, operates a marine supply company with the following information available:

• 14 percent HST is applicable to all purchases and sales (assumed for this Problem).

• Payroll costs—the employer's share of Canada Pension and Employment Insurance are 1.0 times and 1.4 times the employees' share, respectively. The company pays Workers' Compensation of 3 percent and estimates vacation pay at 4 percent of all earnings.

The company prepares quarterly financial statements and had the following transactions for April, May, and June of 2006:

Apr. 30   Recorded the month's purchases of inventory, $775,000 (not including the HST). All purchases are on credit. The company uses the periodic inventory system.

30   Recorded the month's sales of $1,415,000 (not including the HST), of which 80 percent were on credit.

30   Recorded and paid the payroll for the month. Gross earnings were $295,000, with deductions of:
- Employee income taxes equal to 22 percent of gross earnings
- Canada Pension Plan deductions equal to 4.95 percent* of gross earnings (employees' share)
- Employment Insurance deductions equal to 1.87 percent of gross earnings (employees' share)
- Union dues deduction equal to $5,250.

May 2   Borrowed $250,000 from the bank by signing a 6 percent, 30-day note payable with the principal and interest payable on the maturity date.

7   Paid the HST for the month of April.

15   Sent cheques for all payroll deductions and contributions, including the employer's share, to the appropriate authorities.

31   Recorded the month's purchases of inventory, $600,000 (not including the HST). All purchases are on credit.

31   Recorded the month's sales of $1,450,000 (not including the HST), of which 75 percent were on credit.

31   Recorded and paid the payroll for the month. Gross earnings were $315,000, with deductions of:
- Employee income taxes equal to 22 percent of gross earnings
- Canada Pension Plan deductions equal to 4.95 percent* of gross earnings (employees' share)
- Employment Insurance deductions equal to 1.87 percent of gross earnings (employees' share)
- Union dues deduction equal to $5,420.

June 1   Paid the note payable from May 2.

7   Paid the HST for the month of May.

16   Sent cheques for all payroll deductions and contributions, including the employer's share, to the appropriate authorities.

30   Recorded the month's purchases of $850,000 (not including the HST). All purchases are on credit.

30   Recorded the month's sales of $1,500,000 (not including the HST), of which 85 percent were on credit.

30   Recorded and paid the payroll for the month. Gross earnings were $355,000, with deductions of:
- Employee income taxes equal to 22 percent of gross earnings
- Canada Pension Plan deductions equal to 4.95 percent* of gross earnings (employees' share)
- Employment Insurance deductions equal to 1.87 percent of gross earnings (employees' share)
- Union dues deduction equal to $5,697.

*For purposes of this calculation, ignore the basic exemption of $3,500.

Required

1. Journalize all of the transactions, and any adjustments that would be required on June 30, 2006 (the end of the first quarter). Use days, not months, to calculate interest amounts.

2. Show the current liability section of the balance sheet as of June 30, 2006. Assume there are nil balances in all accounts at April 1, 2006.

Accounting for current liabilities,
accounting for contingent
liabilities, reporting
current liabilities

2. Total current liabilities
$30,820

Problem 11–9A

Eastern Explorations produces and sells customized mining equipment in New Brunswick. The company offers a 60-day, all parts and labour—and an extra 90-day, parts-only—warranty on all of its products. The company had the following transactions in 2007:

Jan. 31   Sales for the month totalled $80,000 (not including HST), of which 90 percent were on credit. The company collects 14 percent HST on all sales and estimates its warranty costs at 3 percent of sales.

31   Based on last year's property tax assessment, estimated that the property taxes for the year would be $60,000 (3 percent of last year's $2,000,000 assessed value). Recorded the estimated property taxes for the month; credit Estimated Property Taxes Payable.

Feb. 4   Completed repair work for a customer. The parts ($500) and labour ($850) were all covered under the warranty.

7   Sent a cheque for the appropriate HST for the month of January (the company had paid $3,700 of HST on purchases in January).

28   Recorded the estimated property taxes for the month of February.

28   Sales for the month totalled $92,000 (not including HST), of which 85 percent were on credit. The company estimates its warranty costs at 3 percent of sales.

Mar. 7   Sent a cheque for the appropriate HST for the month of February (the company had paid $4,750 of HST on purchases in February).

8   Eastern Explorations Company received notice that it was being sued by a customer for an accident resulting from the failure of its product. The company's lawyer was reluctant to estimate the likely outcome of the lawsuit, but another customer indicated that a similar case had resulted in a $250,000 settlement.

15   Completed repair work for a customer. The parts ($2,500) and labour ($1,200) were all covered under the warranty.

21   Completed repair work for a customer. The parts ($750) were covered by the warranty, but the labour ($1,100) was not. Payment from the customer is due for the labour in 30 days.

31   Sales for the month totalled $88,000 (not including HST), of which 88 percent was on credit. The company estimates its warranty costs at 3 percent of sales.

31   Received the property tax assessment for 2007. It showed the assessed value of the property to be $2,200,000 and a tax rate of 3 percent of the assessed value. The company made the appropriate adjustment and used the Property Taxes Payable account.

Required

1. Journalize the above transactions.

2. Show the appropriate financial statement presentation for all liabilities.

Problems (Group B)

Problem 11–1B

The following transactions of Prairie Technology of Edmonton, Alberta, occurred during 2006 and 2007. The company's year end is December 31.

2006

Mar. 3   Purchased a machine for $66,000, signing a six-month, 4.5 percent note payable.

31   Recorded the month's sales of $134,500, one-quarter for cash, and three-quarters on credit. All sales amounts are subject to the 6 percent goods and services tax, to be calculated on the sales of $134,500.

Apr. 7   Paid March's goods and services tax to the Receiver General.

May 31   Borrowed $75,000 with a 5 percent note payable that calls for annual instalment payments of $15,000 principal plus interest.

Sept. 3 Paid the six-month, 4.5 percent note at maturity.
      30 Purchased inventory at a cost of $25,000, signing a 4 percent, six-month note payable for that amount.
Dec. 31   Accrued warranty expense, which is estimated at 1.5 percent of annual sales of $1,445,000.
      31 Accrued interest on all outstanding notes payable. Make a separate interest accrual entry for each note payable.

2007
Mar. 31   Paid off the 4 percent inventory note, plus interest, at maturity.
May 31   Paid the first instalment and interest for one year on the long-term note payable.

Required Record the transactions in the company's general journal. Explanations are not required.

Problem 11–2B

Identifying contingent liabilities

Sylvia Lemieux provides skating lessons for children ages 8 through 15. Most students are beginners. Sylvia rents ice time from the local arena. Because this is a new business venture, Sylvia wants to save money and does not want to purchase insurance. She seeks your advice about her business exposure to liabilities.

Required Write a memorandum to inform Sylvia Lemieux of specific contingent liabilities that could arise from the business. It will be necessary to define a contingent liability because she is a professional skater, not a businessperson. Propose a way for Sylvia to limit her exposure to these possible liabilities.

Problem 11–3B

Computing and reporting payroll amounts

1. b. $93,381

The partial monthly records of Parasol Products show the following figures:

Employee Earnings		Dental and	
Regular earnings	a	drug insurance.....................	$ 778
Overtime pay	$6,997	Total deductions	c
Total employee earnings	b	Net pay	70,405
Deductions and Net Pay		**Accounts Debited**	
Withheld income tax...............	15,852	Salaries Expense	33,234
Canada Pension Plan	4,600	Wages Expense	d
Employment Insurance	1,746	Sales Commission Expense....	29,678

Required

1. Determine missing amounts a, b, c, and d.
2. Prepare the general journal entry to record Parasol Products' payroll for the month. Credit Payroll Payable for net pay. No explanation is required.

Problem 11–4B

Excel Spreadsheet Template

Computing and recording payroll amounts

1. Net pay $64,139.53

Assume that Marcy St. Laurent is a marketing director in Metro Mobility's head office in Montreal. During 2006, she worked for the company all year at a $6,500.00 monthly salary. She also earned a year-end bonus equal to 20 percent of her salary.

St. Laurent's monthly income tax withholding for 2006 was $1,762.28. Also, she paid a one-time withholding tax of $4,095.11 on her bonus cheque. She paid $307.31 per month towards the Quebec Pension Plan until the maximum ($1,910.70) had been withheld. In addition, St. Laurent's employer deducted $136.50 per month for Employment Insurance until the maximum ($729.30) had been withheld. St. Laurent authorized the following deductions: 1.5 percent per month of her monthly pay to Metro's charitable donation fund and $34.00 per month for life insurance.

Metro Mobility incurred Quebec Pension Plan expense equal to the amount deducted from St. Laurent's pay. Employment Insurance cost the company 1.4 times the amount deducted from St. Laurent's pay. In addition, the company provided St. Laurent with the following fringe benefits: dental and drug insurance at a cost of $65 per month, and pension benefits to be paid to St. Laurent upon retirement. The pension contribution is based on her income and was $5,350.00 in 2006.

Required

1. Compute St. Laurent's gross pay, payroll deductions, and net pay for the full year 2006. Round all amounts to the nearest cent.
2. Compute Metro Mobility's total 2006 payroll cost for St. Laurent.
3. Prepare Metro Mobility's summary general journal entries (explanations are not required) to record its expense for
   a. St. Laurent's total earnings for the year, her payroll deductions and her net pay. Debit Salary Expense and Executive Bonus Compensation as appropriate for sales and employee benefit expense. Credit liability accounts for the payroll deductions and Cash for net pay.
   b. Employer payroll expenses for St. Laurent. Credit the appropriate liability accounts.
   c. Fringe benefits provided to St. Laurent. Credit Health Insurance Payable and Company Pension Payable.

Journalizing, posting, and reporting liabilities

3. Total liabilities $791,314

Problem 11–5B

Mills Hardware's general ledger at June 30, 2007, the end of the company's fiscal year, includes the following account balances before adjusting entries. Parentheses indicate a debit balance.

Note payable, short-term	$ 74,000	Employee Insurance benefits payable	_____
Accounts payable	335,680		
Current portion of long-term debt payable	_____	Estimated vacation pay liability	$ 7,896
Interest payable	_____	GST payable	4,900
Salaries payable	_____	Property tax payable	7,284
Employee taxes payable	_____	Unearned service revenue	27,000
Employer payroll payable	_____	Long-term debt payable	300,000

The additional data needed to develop the adjusting entries at June 30 are as follows:

a. The $74,000 short-term note payable was issued on July 31, 2006, matures one year from date of issuance, and bears interest at 6 percent.

b. The long-term debt is payable in annual instalments of $60,000, with the next instalment due February 28, 2008. On that date, Mills Hardware will also pay one year's interest at 5.5 percent. Interest was last paid on February 28, 2007.

c. Gross salaries for the last payroll of the fiscal year were $21,446. Of this amount, employee withholdings were $4,756, and salaries payable was $16,690.

d. Employer payroll costs were $2,788, and Mills Hardware's liability for employee life insurance was $150.

e. Mills Hardware estimates that vacation pay is 4 percent of gross salaries of $240,000 after adjustment for the last payroll of the fiscal year.

f. On March 1, 2007, the company collected one year's service contract revenue of $27,000 in advance.

g. At June 30, 2007, Mills Hardware is the defendant in a $100,000 small claims lawsuit, which the store expects to win. However, the outcome is uncertain.

Required

1. Open T-accounts for the listed accounts, inserting their unadjusted June 30, 2007 balances.
2. Post the June 30, 2007 adjusting entries to the accounts opened.
3. Prepare the liability section of Mills Hardware's balance sheet at June 30, 2007. Show total current liabilities and total liabilities.
4. Is there a contingent liability? If yes, write the note to describe it and indicate where it should appear.

Problem 11–6B

Excel Spreadsheet Template

Using a payroll register; recording a payroll

1. Total net pay $2,249.50

Assume that payroll records of a branch of Indigo Books provided the following information for the weekly pay period ended December 18, 2006:

Employee	Hours Worked	40-Hour Weekly Earnings	Income Tax	Canada Pension Plan	Employment Insurance	United Way	Year-to-date Earnings at the End of the Previous Week
Lucy Bourdon	45	$440	$ 62.85	$15.22	$ 9.77	$ 8	$19,130.00
Maura Wells	50	500	73.25	21.37	12.86	8	28,400.00
Carl Boyd	49	850	184.10	0.00	0.00	20	43,440.00
Maurice Lamont	40	380	42.60	10.25	7.11	2	8,966.00

Lucy Bourdon and Maurice Lamont work in the office, and Maura Wells and Carl Boyd are sales staff. All employees are paid time and a half for hours worked in excess of 40 hours per week. Show computations. Explanations are not required for journal entries.

Required

1. Enter the appropriate information in a payroll register similar to Exhibit 11–6.

2. Record the payroll information in the general journal, crediting net pay to Cash.

3. The employer's payroll costs are calculated by matching the employee's Canada Pension Plan contribution (employee rate 4.95 percent; maximum $1,910.70) and paying 1.4 times the employee's Employment Insurance premium (employee rate 1.87 percent; maximum $729.30). Record the employer's payroll costs in the general journal.

4. Why is no Canada Pension Plan or Employment Insurance deducted for Boyd?

Problem 11–7B

Reporting current liabilities

Following are six pertinent facts about events during the year at Hudson Farm Equipment Manufacturing, a Manitoba company:

a. On June 30, Hudson Farm Equipment Manufacturing signed a nine-month, 5 percent note payable to purchase a machine costing $120,000. The note requires payment of principal and interest at maturity.

b. Sales of $2,103,000 were covered by Hudson Farm Equipment's product warranty. At January 1, estimated warranty payable was $29,300. During the year, Hudson Farm Equipment recorded warranty expense of 4 percent of sales and paid warranty claims of $55,700.

c. On November 15, Hudson Farm Equipment received $10,000 on deposit for a tractor. The tractor will be delivered in March of next year.

d. December sales totalled $323,000 and Hudson Farm Equipment collected GST of 6 percent on these sales. This amount will be sent to the appropriate authority early in January.

e. Hudson Farm Equipment owes $200,000 on a long-term note payable. At December 31, 3 percent interest for the year plus $40,000 of this principal are payable within one year.

Required For each item, indicate the account and the related amount to be reported as a *current* liability on Hudson Farm Equipment Manufacturing's December 31 (year-end) balance sheet.

Problem 11–8B

Accounting for current liabilities; making basic payroll entries; reporting current liabilities
1 2 4 6
2. Total current liabilities $1,169,325

Headly Mountain, an Alberta company, is a ski resort with the following information available:

- Goods and Services Tax: 6 percent GST is applicable to all purchases and sales (assumed for this Problem).

- Employer Payroll Costs: the employer's share of Canada Pension and Employment Insurance is 1.0 times and 1.4 times the employees' share respectively. The company pays Workers' Compensation of 3 percent and estimates vacation pay at 4 percent of all earnings.

The company prepares quarterly financial statements and had the following transactions for the first three months of 2006:

Jan. 31   Recorded the month's purchases, $312,000 (not including the GST). All purchases are on credit.

Jan. 31   Recorded the month's sales of $429,000 (not including the GST), of which 85 percent were on credit.

31   Recorded and paid the payroll for the month. Gross earnings were $95,000, with deductions of:
- Employee income taxes equal to 17 percent of gross earnings
- Canada Pension Plan deductions equal to 4.95 percent* of gross earnings (employees' share)
- Employment Insurance deductions equal to 1.87 percent of gross earnings (employees' share)
- Union dues deduction equal to $1,560.

Feb. 3   Borrowed $50,000 from the bank by signing a 3 percent, 30-day note payable with the principal and interest payable on the maturity date.

7   Paid the GST for the month of January.

15   Sent cheques for all payroll deductions and contributions, including the employer's share, to the appropriate authorities.

28   Recorded the month's purchases, $349,000 (not including the GST). All purchases are on credit.

28   Recorded the month's sales of $550,000 (not including the GST), of which 75 percent were on credit.

28   Recorded and paid the payroll for the month. Gross earnings were $115,000, with deductions of:
- Employee income taxes equal to 17 percent of gross earnings
- Canada Pension Plan deductions equal to 4.95 percent* of gross earnings (employees' share)
- Employment Insurance deductions equal to 1.87 percent of gross earnings (employees' share)
- Union dues deduction equal to $1,872.

Mar. 4   Paid the note payable from February 3.

7   Paid the GST for the month of February.

15   Sent cheques for all payroll deductions and contributions, including the employer's share, to the appropriate authorities.

31   Recorded the month's purchases, $365,000 (not including the GST). All purchases are on credit.

31   Recorded the month's sales of $625,000 (not including the GST), of which 80 percent were on credit.

31   Recorded and paid the payroll for the month. Gross earnings were $145,000, with deductions of:
- Employee income taxes equal to 17 percent of gross earnings
- Canada Pension Plan deductions equal to 4.95 percent* of gross earnings (employees' share)
- Employment Insurance deductions equal to 1.87 percent of gross earnings (employees' share)
- Union dues deduction equal to $2,100.

*For purposes of this calculation, ignore the basic exemption of $3,500.

Required

1. Journalize all of the transactions, and any adjustments that would be required on March 31, 2006 (the end of the first quarter). Round all amounts to the nearest whole dollar. Use days, not months, to calculate interest amounts.

2. Show the current liability section of the balance sheet as of March 31, 2006. Assume there are nil balances in all accounts at January 1, 2006.

Accounting for current liabilities; accounting for contingent liabilities; reporting current liabilities

2. Total current liabilities $66,550

Problem 11–9B

Sinclair Technologies produces and sells customized network systems in Nova Scotia. The company offers a 60-day, all software and labour—and an extra 90-day, parts-only—warranty on all of its products. The company had the following transactions in 2007:

Jan. 31   Sales for the month totalled $350,000 (not including HST), of which 95 percent were on credit. The company collects 14 percent HST on all sales and estimates its warranty costs at 2 percent of sales.

31   Based on last year's property tax assessment, estimated that the property taxes for the year would be $38,000 (2 percent of last year's $1,900,000

assessed value). Recorded the estimated property taxes for the month; credit Estimated Property Taxes Payable. (Round amount.)

Feb. 4   Completed repair work for a customer. The software ($3,000) and labour ($3,250) were all covered under the warranty.

7   Remitted the appropriate HST for the month of January (the company had paid $15,610 HST on purchases in January).

28   Recorded the estimated property taxes for the month of February.

28   Sales for the month totalled $325,000 (not including HST), of which 90 percent were on credit. The company estimates its warranty costs at 2 percent of sales.

Mar. 7   Remitted the appropriate HST for the month of February (the company had paid $18,648 HST on purchases in February).

8   Sinclair Technologies received notice that it was being sued by a customer for an error resulting from the failure of its product. The company's lawyer was reluctant to estimate the likely outcome of the lawsuit, but another customer indicated that a similar case had resulted in a $100,000 settlement.

15   Completed repair work for a customer. The software ($3,500) and labour ($2,750) were all covered under the warranty.

21   Completed repair work for a customer. The software ($1,500) was covered by the warranty, but the labour ($1,650) was not. Payment for the labour is due from the customer in 30 days.

31   Sales for the month totalled $315,000 (not including HST), of which 95 percent was on credit. The company estimates its warranty costs will increase to 4 percent of sales.

31   Received the property tax assessment for 2006. It showed the assessed value of the property to be $2,300,000 and a tax rate of 1.8 percent of the assessed value. The company made the appropriate adjustment and used the Property Taxes Payable account.

Required

1. Journalize the above transactions.
2. Show the appropriate financial statement presentation for all liabilities.

Challenge Problems

Problem 11–1C

Public accounting firms acting as auditors of companies are very careful to ensure that all of the company's accounts payable are recorded in the proper period. In other words, they want to ensure that all payables relating to the year under review are recorded as a liability at year end.

Verifying the completeness of liabilities

Required   Explain why you think auditors are so concerned that all payables owing at year end be properly recorded in the right accounting period.

Problem 11–2C

There is no consensus on the proper amount for airlines to record with respect to frequent-flier expense. Two alternative scenarios are presented below:

a. The person claiming a ticket under the frequent-flier program would use a seat that otherwise would be empty.

b. The person claiming a ticket under the frequent-flier program would use a seat that otherwise would be used by a full-fare-paying passenger.

Accounting for estimated liabilities

Required

1. Recommend to an airline how much it should record as a liability under each of the scenarios. Which amount would you suggest the airline record since it doesn't know which will occur?

2. Write a response to the person who states that, since it is not known if the frequent-flier miles will be used, the liability is contingent and need not be expensed until the passenger actually uses the frequent-flier miles. This person suggests that because the liability is contingent, not actual, it should be disclosed in the notes.

Extending Your Knowledge

Decision Problem

Identifying internal control weaknesses and their solution

Schneider Construction is a large road-building business in Ontario. The owner is Neil Schneider, who oversees all company operations. He employs 15 work crews, each made up of 6 to 10 members. Construction supervisors, who report directly to Schneider, lead the crews. Most supervisors are long-time employees, so Schneider trusts them to a great degree. The company's office staff consists of an accountant and an office manager.

Because crew needs may vary in the construction industry, supervisors hire and terminate their own crew members. Supervisors notify the office of all personnel changes. Also, supervisors forward to the office the employee TD1 forms, which the crew members fill out to claim tax-withholding exemptions. Each Thursday the supervisors submit weekly time sheets for their crews, and the accountant prepares the payroll. At noon on Friday the supervisors come to the office to get paycheques for distribution to the workers at 5 p.m.

Schneider Construction's accountant prepares the payroll, including the payroll cheques, which are written on a single payroll bank account. Neil Schneider signs all payroll cheques after matching the employee name to the time sheets submitted by the supervisor. Often the construction workers wait several days to cash their paycheques. To verify that each construction worker is a bona fide employee, the accountant matches the employee's endorsement signature on the back of the cancelled payroll cheque with the signature on that employee's TD1 form. Delays occur in completing this task as well as reconciling the payroll bank account.

Required

1. List one *efficiency* weakness in Schneider Construction's payroll accounting system. How can the business correct this weakness?
2. Identify one way that a supervisor can defraud Schneider Construction under the present system.
3. Discuss a control feature Schneider Construction can use to *safeguard* against the frauds you identified in Requirement 2.

Financial Statement Cases

Current and contingent liabilities

Financial Statement Case 1

Details about a company's current and contingent liabilities appear in a number of places in the annual report. Use the CHUM Limited financial statements in Appendix A to answer the following questions.

1. Give the breakdown of CHUM Limited's current liabilities at August 31, 2005.
2. How is the current portion of long-term debt calculated?
3. How much was CHUM Limited's bank and other indebtedness at August 31, 2005? When is the long-term debt due? Where did you find the details related to CHUM's bank indebtedness?
4. Does CHUM Limited have any commitments coming due in the fiscal year ending in 2006? If so, where did you find information about them? Why are commitments not shown on the balance sheet as a liability?
5. Does CHUM Limited have any contingent liabilities at August 31, 2005? How do you know?

Current and contingent liabilities

Financial Statement Case 2

Details about a company's current and contingent liabilities appear in a number of places in the annual report. Use the Sun-Rype Products Ltd. financial statements in Appendix B to answer the following questions.

1. Give the breakdown of Sun-Rype's current liabilities at December 31, 2005.
2. In general, how is the current portion of long-term debt calculated?

3. How much was Sun-Rype's bank and other indebtedness at December 31, 2005? What is the account Long-Term Obligations, and where did you find this information?

4. Does Sun-Rype have any commitments coming due in 2006? If so, where did you find information about them? Why are commitments not shown on the balance sheet as a liability?

5. Does Sun-Rype Products Ltd. have any contingent liabilities at December 31, 2005? How do you know?

Comprehensive Problem for Part 2

Comparing Two Businesses

Suppose you are ready to invest in a small resort property. Two locations look promising: Sanibel Resort in Victoria, British Columbia, and Hyde Park Resort in Nova Scotia. Each place has its appeal, but Sanibel Resort wins out. The main allure is that the price is better. The property owners provide the following data:

	Sanibel Resort	Hyde Park Resort
Cash	$ 36,500	$ 68,300
Accounts receivable	21,900	19,600
Inventory	79,400	73,200
Land	289,500	716,000
Buildings	1,920,000	2,097,200
Accumulated amortization—buildings	(127,543)	(880,200)
Furniture and fixtures	803,000	998,300
Accumulated amortization—furniture and fixtures	(241,000)	(572,800)
Total assets	$2,781,757	$2,519,600
Total liabilities	$1,203,000	$1,079,100
Owner's equity	1,578,757	1,440,500
Total liabilities and owner's equity	$2,781,757	$2,519,600

Income statements for the last three years report total net income of $568,200 for Sanibel Resort and $302,800 for Hyde Park Resort.

Inventories Sanibel Resort uses the FIFO inventory method, and Hyde Park Resort uses the weighted-average method. If Sanibel Resort had used weighted-average, its reported inventory would have been $7,500 lower. If Hyde Park Resort had used FIFO, its reported inventory would have been $6,400 higher. Three years ago there was little difference between weighted-average and FIFO amounts for Sanibel, and weighted-average and FIFO amounts for Hyde Park.

Property, Plant, and Equipment Sanibel Resort uses the straight-line amortization method and an estimated useful life of 35 years for buildings and seven years for furniture and fixtures. Estimated residual values are $432,000 for buildings, and $0 for furniture and fixtures. Sanibel Resort's buildings and furniture and fixtures are three years old.

Hyde Park Resort uses the double-declining-balance method and amortizes buildings over 35 years with an estimated residual value of $490,000. The furniture and fixtures, now two years old, are being amortized over seven years with an estimated residual value of $90,900.

Accounts Receivable Sanibel Resort uses the direct write-off method for uncollectibles. Hyde Park Resort uses the allowance method. The Sanibel Resort owner estimates that $2,150 of the company's receivables are doubtful. Prior to the current year, uncollectibles were insignificant. Hyde Park Resort's receivables are already reported at net realizable value.

Required

1. To compare the two resorts, convert Sanibel Resort's net income to the accounting methods and the estimated useful lives used by Hyde Park Resort.

2. Compare the two resorts' net income after you have revised Sanibel Resort's figures. Which resort looked better at the outset? Which resort looks better when they are placed on equal footing?

WORMBOY: WHIZ KID TURNS GARBAGE INTO GOLD

Tom Szaky, the son of two Toronto doctors, had a bright future ahead of him. Enrolled at Princeton, this whiz kid could have been set for life. But a visit to a friend's apartment changed his path. In his friend's kitchen sat a square plastic container filled with dirt and worms, which his friend used as a composter for the garbage. The worm poo created by this process enriched the soil and was, apparently, terrific plant food. Seeing the potential for gold in worm poo, Tom Szaky became WormBoy, dropped out of Princeton, and set up a basement office across from the school to create Terracycle Plant Food.

Tom had the perfect eco-friendly product. The worms turned garbage into plant fertilizer, which was then mixed with water, pumped into recycled plastic pop bottles, and packaged into recycled cardboard boxes for shipping.

Initially, Tom was able to raise over US $1 million from investors that believed in Tom and the product. To keep costs down, student volunteers and dedicated friends were used to fill various positions within the company. The volunteers gained work experience, were provided with a place to stay, and were given future stock options. However, despite being CEO of his company, Tom felt like an overworked babysitter at times. Even with the volunteers, bills and expenses were still $50,000 per month, and Tom needed to raise more money to stay afloat. After three years, almost all of the initial $1 million was spent and Terracycle Plant Food was only sold on the Internet and in a few specialty stores.

A big break came when the QVC shopping network agreed to provide 15 minutes on the air. Tom presented an new untested product called plant jelly. Later tests provided that the jelly worked, and a Trenton warehouse was purchased for production to fulfill potential orders. Tom made a presentation to three venture capitalists to try to raise financing of $1 million that was needed right away and $4.5 million that would be needed to cover the next three years. Wal-Mart Canada's $300,000 order for the spring was welcome news for the whiz kid who had just turned 23 years old.

CASE QUESTIONS

1. Tom's bills and expenses were $50,000 per month despite using volunteer labour. List some of the items that would be included in those bills and expenses.
2. What were the problems Tom faced by using volunteers and friends?
3. Why did Tom decide to use a new, untested product on the QVC shopping channel?
4. Tom made a presentation to three venture capitalists with the hope of raising money to fund the next three years. Describe what venture capitalists do. What would Tom have included in his presentation?
5. Do you think Tom will be successful? Why, or why not?

Sources: CBC *Venture*, "The Big Adventures of WormBoy" Parts 1 and 2 (2005).

Appendix A

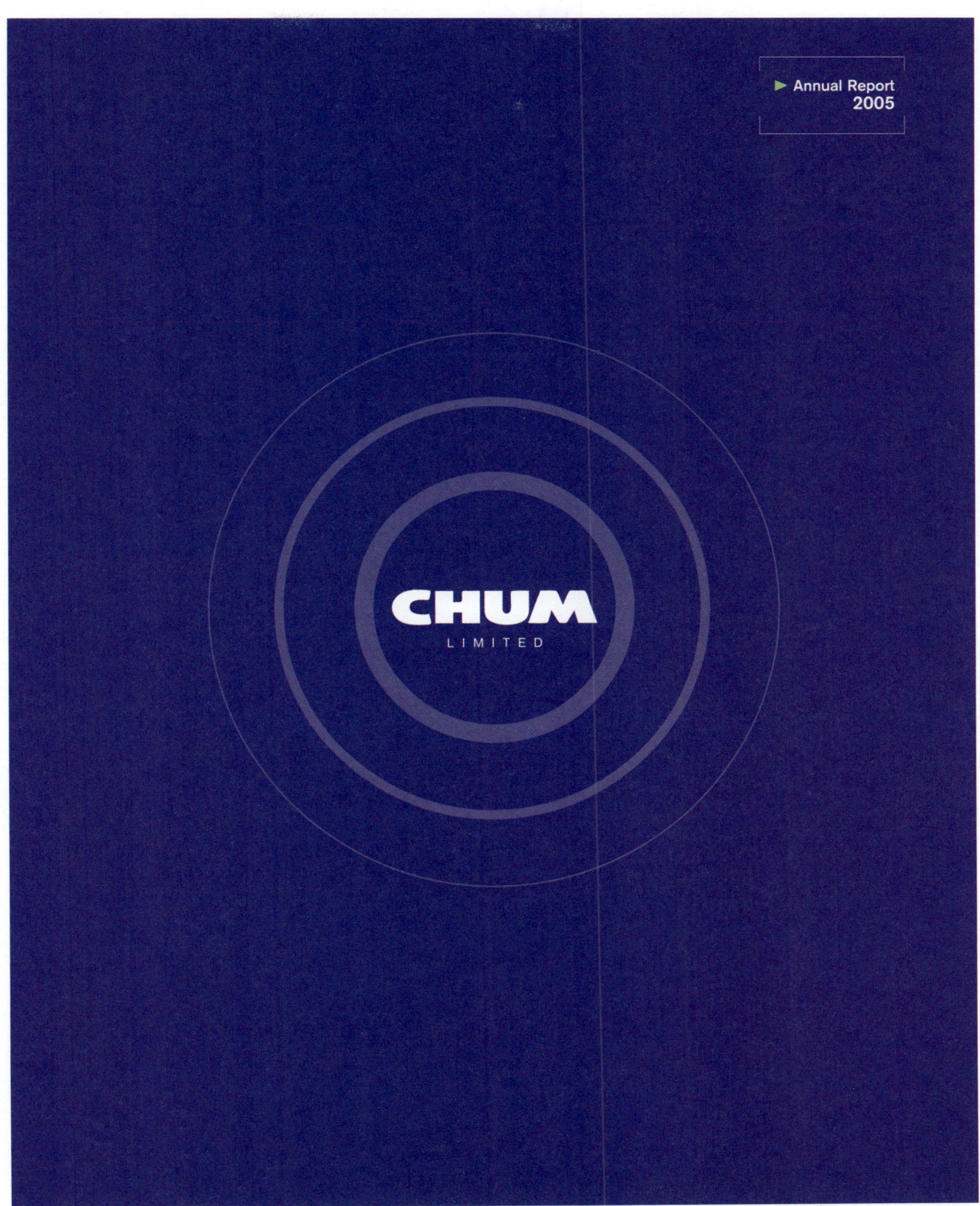

Management's
Report

The consolidated financial statements and other information contained in this annual report are the responsibility of the management of CHUM Limited.

These consolidated financial statements have been prepared in accordance with Canadian generally accepted accounting principles and include certain estimates that reflect management's best judgments. Financial and other information contained elsewhere is consistent with these consolidated financial statements.

Management maintains a system of internal controls designed to provide reasonable assurance that the consolidated financial statements accurately and reliably reflect the Company's operating results and that assets are adequately accounted for and safeguarded.

The consolidated financial statements have been reviewed by the Audit Committee and, together with the other information in this annual report, have been approved by the Board of Directors. PricewaterhouseCoopers LLP, an independent firm of chartered accountants, has audited the consolidated financial statements and provided a professional opinion (see Auditors' Report).

October 28, 2005

Jay Switzer
President and Chief Executive Officer
CHUM Limited

Alan Mayne
Chief Financial Officer
CHUM Limited

Auditors' Report

To the Shareholders of CHUM Limited

We have audited the consolidated balance sheets of **CHUM Limited** as at August 31, 2005 and 2004 and the consolidated statements of earnings, retained earnings and cash flows for the years then ended. These consolidated financial statements are the responsibility of the company's management. Our responsibility is to express an opinion on these financial statements based on our audits.

We conducted our audits in accordance with Canadian generally accepted auditing standards. Those standards require that we plan and perform an audit to obtain reasonable assurance whether the financial statements are free of material misstatement. An audit includes examining, on a test basis, evidence supporting the amounts and disclosures in the financial statements. An audit also includes assessing the accounting principles used and significant estimates made by management, as well as evaluating the overall financial statement presentation.

In our opinion, these consolidated financial statements present fairly, in all material respects, the financial position of the company as at August 31, 2005 and 2004 and the results of its operations and its cash flows for the years then ended in accordance with Canadian generally accepted accounting principles.

PricewaterhouseCoopers LLP

Chartered Accountants
Toronto, Ontario
October 27, 2005

As at August 31, (in thousands of dollars)	2005	2004
		(Restated – note 14)
ASSETS		
Current assets		
Cash	$ –	$ 17,910
Accounts receivable	128,791	95,302
Program rights (note 3)	68,921	70,978
Prepaid expenses and other assets	7,823	8,058
	205,535	192,248
Program rights (note 3)	109,241	100,339
Investments and other assets (note 4)	12,554	29,371
Property, plant and equipment (note 5)	202,623	182,547
Broadcast licences	256,879	87,109
Goodwill	216,929	124,809
	$1,003,761	$ 716,423
LIABILITIES		
Current liabilities		
Accounts payable and accrued liabilities	$ 64,959	$ 51,354
Current portion of long-term debt (note 7)	1,791	210
Income taxes payable	4,831	5,578
Program rights payable	72,007	57,426
	143,588	114,568
Program rights payable	19,932	24,162
Long-term debt (note 7)	319,563	131,561
Future income taxes (note 11)	35,494	19,184
Non-controlling interest	377	3,697
	518,954	293,172
SHAREHOLDERS' EQUITY		
Capital stock (note 9)	147,514	124,242
Retained earnings	337,293	299,009
	484,807	423,251
	$1,003,761	$ 716,423

Approved by the Board of Directors

Director   Director

Consolidated
Statements
of Earnings

For the years ended August 31, (in thousands of dollars, except per share amounts)	2005	2004
Revenue – less agency commissions	$ **628,392**	$ 560,792
Operations expenses	**511,939**	468,143
	116,453	92,649
Expenses		
Depreciation	**25,436**	23,895
Interest	**13,059**	6,964
Interest and other income	**(977)**	(641)
Asset writedowns (notes 3 and 4)	**9,347**	–
	46,865	30,218
Earnings before income taxes and non-controlling interest	**69,588**	62,431
Provision for income taxes (note 11)	**28,007**	23,777
Earnings before non-controlling interest	**41,581**	38,654
Non-controlling interest in earnings of subsidiaries	**216**	1,622
Net earnings for the year	$ **41,365**	$ 37,032
Net earnings per Non-voting Class B Share and per Common Share (note 9(b))	$ **1.49**	$ 1.35

Consolidated
Statements of
Retained Earnings

For the years ended August 31, (in thousands of dollars, except per share amounts)	2005	2004
Retained earnings – Beginning of year	$ **299,009**	$ 264,998
Net earnings for the year	**41,365**	37,032
	340,374	302,030
Deduct		
Dividends paid ($0.04 per share, regular and $0.07 per share, special)		
Non-voting Class B Shares	**2,339**	2,279
Common Shares	**742**	742
	3,081	3,021
Retained earnings – End of year	$ **337,293**	$ 299,009

For the years ended August 31,
(in thousands of dollars)

	2005	2004
CASH PROVIDED BY (USED IN)		
Operating activities		
Net earnings for the year	$ 41,365	$ 37,032
Items not affecting cash		
Depreciation	25,436	23,895
Non-controlling interest in earnings of subsidiaries	216	1,622
Future income taxes	10,458	(348)
Asset writedowns	9,347	–
Other	608	–
	87,430	62,201
Changes in non-cash balances related to operations		
(Increase) decrease in accounts receivable	(12,098)	6,075
Decrease (increase) in program rights	7,595	(6,774)
Decrease in prepaid expenses and other current assets	751	2,627
(Increase) decrease in other assets	(1,844)	360
Decrease in accounts payable and accrued liabilities	(13,882)	(3,933)
Decrease in income taxes payable	(1,426)	(8,935)
Decrease in program rights payable	(4,064)	(10,746)
	(24,968)	(21,326)
	62,462	40,875
Investing activities		
Additions to property, plant and equipment – net	(27,846)	(20,385)
Acquisitions – net of cash acquired	(223,628)	(430)
Increase in investments and other assets	(2,686)	(10,469)
Increase in deposits	–	(15,500)
	(254,160)	(46,784)
Financing activities		
Dividends paid	(3,081)	(3,021)
Financing costs paid	(2,421)	(210)
Long-term debt repayments	(56,873)	(139,266)
Increase in long-term debt	237,000	144,864
Dividends paid to non-controlling interest	(1,200)	–
Receipt of capital from non-controlling interest	363	–
	173,788	2,367
Change in cash during the year	(17,910)	(3,542)
Cash – Beginning of year	17,910	21,452
Cash – End of year	$ –	$ 17,910
Supplementary information		
Income taxes paid	20,657	33,061
Interest paid	$ 11,060	$ 8,838

August 31, 2005 and 2004 (in thousands of dollars)

1. SUMMARY OF SIGNIFICANT ACCOUNTING POLICIES

Basis of presentation

The consolidated financial statements present the operations of the company, its subsidiaries and its 50% interest in MusiquePlus Inc. and Sun Radio Limited accounted for on a proportionate consolidation basis. All other investments are carried at cost.

Use of estimates

The preparation of financial statements in accordance with Canadian generally accepted accounting principles requires management to make estimates and assumptions that affect the reported amounts of assets and liabilities and disclosures of contingent assets and liabilities at the date of the financial statements and the reported amounts of revenues and expenses during the reporting period. Actual results could be different from these estimates.

Significant estimates have been made with respect to the carrying values of goodwill, intangibles and program rights.

Revenue recognition

Revenue earned from sales of airtime is recognized in the accounts when the advertisement is aired. Revenues are recorded net of agency commissions as these charges are paid directly to the agency by the advertiser.

Revenue earned from television subscriber fees is recognized in accordance with distribution agreements in the period broadcasts are made available.

Program rights

Program right assets representing the right to broadcast feature films and television programs and related liabilities are recorded when the program cost is reasonably determinable, the licence period has begun and the program material is available for telecast or resale. Such costs are allocated between current and non-current assets using management's estimate of usage or recovery in the next fiscal year. Program rights are reported at the lower of net amortized cost and net realizable value.

The costs of broadcast rights are amortized over the period of the rights contract on the basis of usage. Where the initial airing generates more benefit to the television channel than later airings, an accelerated method of amortization is used. The amortization rates range from 35% to 100% on the first airing. If each airing is expected to generate similar benefit, the straight-line method of amortization is used based on the expected number of airings during the rights period.

Liabilities for program rights are payable in instalments in accordance with the licence agreements or on the basis of usage of the program material. The liability is segregated between current and non-current using payment terms and management's estimate of usage in the next fiscal year.

Program rights include investment in films for which the company has produced or acquired distribution rights. Costs include all production costs which are expected to be recovered from exploitation, exhibition or licensing and are capitalized and amortized using the individual film forecast method. Advances or contributions received from third parties to assist in development are deducted from these costs.

The valuation of investments in films is reviewed on a title-by-title basis. When circumstances indicate that the fair value, as determined by management's estimate of discounted future cash flows, is less than unamortized cost, a writedown of the unamortized cost to fair value is recorded.

Depreciation

Depreciation is provided on a declining balance basis using the following rates: buildings – 4% to 5%; broadcasting equipment – 20% to 30%; and other – 8% to 30%. Leasehold improvements are amortized on a straight-line basis over the term of the lease plus one renewal period.

Impairment of long-lived assets

Impairment of long-lived assets is recognized when an adverse event or change in circumstances causes the asset's carrying value to exceed the total undiscounted cash flow expected from its use and eventual disposition. The impairment loss is calculated by deducting fair value of the asset from its carrying value.

Start-up costs

Start-up costs for the preparation of new applications to the CRTC are expensed. Start-up costs for licences of successful applications, which are awarded by the CRTC, are capitalized from the date they are awarded to the date revenue is generated for the service. Start-up costs are amortized over a period that reflects their expected future benefit, not exceeding five years.

Goodwill and broadcast licences

Goodwill and broadcast licences with indefinite lives are not subject to amortization and are tested annually for impairment or more frequently when circumstances indicate an impairment may have occurred. The fair values of goodwill and broadcast licences are compared to the carrying values and an impairment loss recognized for the excess.

Income taxes

The company accounts for income taxes under the asset and liability method. Under this method, future income tax assets and liabilities are recognized for future income tax consequences attributable to the differences between financial statement carrying values and income tax bases of assets and liabilities. Future income tax assets and liabilities are measured using the substantively enacted income tax rates relating to the period in which they are expected to be settled. The effects of changes in substantively enacted income tax rates on future income tax assets and liabilities are recognized in income in the period the income tax rate is substantively enacted.

Post-employment benefits

The cost of providing benefits through defined benefit pensions is actuarially determined and recognized in earnings using the projected benefits method pro-rated on service. Differences arising from plan amendments, changes in assumptions and experience gains and losses are recognized in earnings over the expected average remaining service life of employees. The cost of providing benefits through defined contribution pension plans is charged to earnings when contributions become payable.

Actuarial gains and losses that fall outside a corridor defined as the greater of (a) 10% of the accrued benefit obligation and (b) 10% of the fair market value of the plan assets at the beginning of the year are amortized over the average remaining service period of active employees on a straight-line basis.

The expected return on plan assets is based on the fair value of plan assets.

Financing costs

Debt issue costs are capitalized and amortized over the term of the related credit facility.

2. ACCOUNTING CHANGES

Variable interest entities

During 2005, the company adopted Accounting Guideline 15 (AcG-15), "Consolidation of Variable Interest Entities" (VIEs). AcG-15 provides criteria for the identification of VIEs and further criteria for determining what entity, if any, should consolidate them. AcG-15 defines a VIE as an entity that either does not have sufficient equity at risk to finance its activities without subordinated financial support or where the equity investors lack the characteristic of a controlling financial interest. VIEs are subject to consolidation by a company if that company is deemed the primary beneficiary of the VIE. The primary beneficiary is the party that is either exposed to a majority of the expected losses from the VIE's activities or is entitled to receive a majority of the VIE's residual returns or both. The company has variable interests in certain production entities through its loans and advances repayable from future distribution revenues. The company has determined it is not the primary beneficiary of the VIEs identified; therefore, the new standard has no impact on the company's financial position or results of operations.

3. PROGRAM RIGHTS

(in thousands of dollars)	Current	2005 Long-term	Current	2004 Long-term
Broadcast rights, net of accumulated amortization	$ 63,539	$ 109,241	$ 70,978	$ 95,918
Prepaid rights	4,242	–	–	–
Investment in film	1,140	–	–	4,421
	$ 68,921	$ 109,241	$ 70,978	$ 100,339

The company expects that 40% of the unamortized cost of program rights will be amortized during the year ending August 31, 2006. The company expects that over 95% of the unamortized cost of program rights will be amortized during the five-year period ending August 31, 2010.

The company has entered into various agreements for the right to broadcast certain feature films and syndicated television programs in the future. These agreements, which range in term from one to five years, generally commit the company to acquire specific programs or films or certain levels of future productions. The acquisition of these additional broadcast rights is contingent on the actual production and/or the airing of the programs or films. See note 8 for commitments arising from these agreements.

During the year, the investment in a film was written down by $3,221, based on an assessment of the film's future revenue projections and recoverability of the advance. The charge is included in asset writedowns in the consolidated statements of earnings.

4. INVESTMENTS AND OTHER ASSETS

(in thousands of dollars)	2005	2004
Deposits	$ –	$ 15,500
Loans receivable	4,220	8,631
Investments – at cost	70	627
Deferred financing costs, net of accumulated amortization	2,333	321
Accrued pension benefit asset (note 10)	3,891	1,657
Other	2,040	2,635
	$ 12,554	$ 29,371

As at August 31, 2004, the deposit of $15,000 related to the acquisition of CMI. The remaining deposit of $500 related to the acquisition of the broadcasting assets of Seacoast. These have been included in the purchase price allocations completed in fiscal 2005 (note 6).

Loans receivable bear interest at the bank's prime rate plus 1% and are unsecured. The loans are repayable from the international distribution receipts from three third party productions commissioned by the company. During the year, the carrying value of a loan of $5,626 was determined to be impaired based on an assessment of the underlying production and written off to asset writedowns in the consolidated statements of earnings.

5. PROPERTY, PLANT AND EQUIPMENT

(in thousands of dollars)	2005	2004
Cost		
Land	$ 22,573	$ 21,741
Buildings	117,155	108,306
Broadcasting equipment	208,633	184,813
Other	80,412	71,436
	428,773	386,296
Accumulated depreciation		
Buildings	30,046	26,377
Broadcasting equipment	139,395	127,532
Other	56,709	49,840
	226,150	203,749
	$ 202,623	$ 182,547

6. SIGNIFICANT BUSINESS TRANSACTIONS

a)   Effective February 15, 2005, the company purchased all of the shares held by the minority shareholders (representing 40% of the total outstanding shares) of LTA. The purchase price was approximately $32,000, payable as $8,000 in cash and the issuance of 659,827 Non-voting, Class B Shares. These shares were valued at the weighted average closing price of such shares on the Toronto Stock Exchange for the five trading days prior to the closing date. The purchase price was determined by the vendors and purchaser based on an independent valuation. The vendors included individuals who are directors and/or officers of LTA, CHUM Limited and certain other subsidiaries of the company.

The transaction resulted in an increase of broadcast licence of $26,301, goodwill of $6,339, future income tax liabilities of $4,734 and a decrease in non-controlling interest of $3,389.

b)   On December 1, 2004, the company acquired 100% of the outstanding common shares of CMI. The results of CMI's operations have been included in the consolidated financial statements beginning on December 1, 2004. CMI operated conventional television stations in Ontario, Alberta and Manitoba, including Toronto 1 and specialty services across Canada. The aggregate purchase price was a cash consideration of $265,000, subject to a working capital adjustment, on a debt-free basis. The purchase price includes $16,117 that was paid in cash in the previous year and included in investments and other assets. In addition, the company has incurred a cost of $2,757 to the year-end in respect of termination payments for certain employees of the acquired business.

On December 2, 2004, the company sold Toronto 1 to the TVA Group Inc. and Sun Media Corporation, both subsidiaries of Quebecor Media Inc. for the price of $46,000 (less a preliminary working capital adjustment of $3,500) on a debt-free basis. As part of the transaction, the company obtained Sun Media Corporation's 29.9% ownership interest in southern Ontario cable news channel CP24, valued at $8,000, increasing the company's ownership of the channel to 100%.

c)   On September 30, 2004, the company purchased from Seacoast, the broadcasting assets of Victoria, B.C. radio stations, CFAX-AM and CHBE-FM, for $9,336. The purchase price includes $670 that was paid in cash in the previous year and included in investments and other assets.

The following table summarizes the assets and liabilities assumed for the CMI and Seacoast transactions at the dates of the acquisitions.

(in thousands of dollars)	Craig Media Inc.*	Seacoast
Current assets	$ 37,673	$ 558
Property, plant and equipment	16,708	311
Future income tax assets	19,843	–
Broadcast licences	127,000	8,467
Goodwill	86,131	–
	287,355	9,336
Current liabilities⁽ⁱ⁾	39,374	–
Long-term debt	1,737	–
Future income tax liabilities	23,052	–
Non-controlling interest	430	–
	64,593	–
Net assets acquired	$ 222,762	$ 9,336
Consideration		
Cash	$ 259,822	$ 8,734
Mortgages assumed	2,949	–
Acquisition costs paid	3,594	202
Acquisition costs accrued	–	400
Proceeds received on sale of Toronto 1	(43,603)	–
	$ 222,762	$ 9,336

* CMI's acquisition after the disposal of Toronto 1 operations for proceeds of $34,549 cash and outstanding non-controlling interest in CP24.

(i) Includes assumed liabilities relating to licence termination payments in the amount of $10,300 paid to MTV Networks International.

d) Effective June 15, 2004, the company purchased the assets of Kamco Music and Soundsystems Ltd., a Muzak franchise, for $430 cash and $193 payable by October 15, 2004 and $192 payable by February 15, 2005. Assets and liabilities assumed were property, plant and equipment of $83, inventory of $63, liabilities of $17 and an intangible of $686. The intangible relates to contractual customer relationships and is being amortized over a period of 17 years.

7. LONG-TERM DEBT

(in thousands of dollars)	2005	2004
Mortgage at 9.35%, maturing in 2006	$ 1,697	$ 1,907
Mortgage at 6.99%, maturing in 2008	1,760	–
Revolving credit facility	307,897	–
Revolving operating facility	–	15,560
Revolving term loan facility	–	104,304
Preferred shares at 10.00%, redeemable in 2009	10,000	10,000
	321,354	131,771
Less: Current portion	1,791	210
	$ 319,563	$ 131,561

On December 1, 2004, the company signed an agreement for a new five-year syndicated, revolving credit facility for an amount of $500,000. The facility is unsecured and bears interest based on several reference rates plus applicable margins based on certain ratios maintained by the company. The effective interest rate for the year ended August 31, 2005 is 4.2%. For the year ended August 31, 2004, the effective rates for the comparable facilities were 6.0% and 4.6% for the operating and term loan facilities, respectively. The new facility has a term to November 2009, unless extended in accordance with the agreement. This credit facility includes certain covenants requiring the company to maintain certain financial ratios.

Principal payments of the long-term debt, based on terms existing as at August 31, 2005 over the next five years are:

Year ending August 31, (in thousands of dollars)	
2006	$ 1,791
2007	100
2008	1,566
2009	10,000
2010	307,897

The preferred shares have been treated as debt for accounting purposes, as they bear a fixed rate of return and are retractable at the option of the holder. The preferred shares are classified as long-term debt on the consolidated balance sheets and dividends are classified as interest expense in the consolidated statements of earnings.

8. COMMITMENTS

Program rights

As at August 31, 2005, the company reported program rights payable for the years ending August 31, 2005 to 2010 totalling $91,939, of which, approximately $72,007 is payable over the next 12 months. In addition, commitments for the purchase of program rights have been concluded where the program material has not yet been made available for telecast. Estimated future commitments total $76,892, of which, approximately $62,727 is due over the next 12 months.

Leases

The company is committed under operating leases for rental of properties, broadcasting facilities and other equipment.

Future minimum payments are as follows:

Year ending August 31, (in thousands of dollars)	
2006	$ 9,005
2007	8,070
2008	6,498
2009	4,988
2010	2,394
2011 and subsequent years	11,373
	$ 42,328

9. CAPITAL STOCK

(in thousands of dollars)	2005	2004
Non-voting Class B Shares		
Authorized		
Unlimited number of Non-voting Class B Shares		
Issued		
21,378,929 (2004 – 20,719,102) shares	$ 145,424	$ 122,152
Common Shares		
Authorized		
Unlimited number of Common Shares		
Issued		
6,748,030 shares	2,090	2,090
	$ 147,514	$ 124,242

a) The holders of the Non-voting Class B Shares are entitled to receive, if, as and when declared by the Board of Directors, annual non-cumulative dividends at the rate of 4¢ per share. No dividends shall be declared on the Common Shares in any year until dividends of 4¢ per share have been paid on the Non-voting Class B Shares. In any year, when such dividends have been paid on both the Non-voting Class B and Common Shares, any further dividends shall be paid equally on the Non-voting Class B and Common Shares.

The Non-voting Class B and Common shareholders are entitled to share equally in any distribution of the company's assets on winding up.

b) Net earnings per Non-voting Class B Share and per Common Share have been calculated on the basis of the weighted average number of shares outstanding during the year of 27,825,066 (2004 – 27,467,132) shares.

c) The company issued 659,827 Non-voting Class B Shares on February 15, 2005 as consideration for the acquisition of the non-controlling interest in LTA (note 6(a)).

d) The company's common shares and Non-voting Class B Shares were split on a two for one basis effective January 9, 2004. The earnings per share and issued share information for all years presented have been restated to reflect this subdivision.

10. POST-EMPLOYMENT BENEFITS

The company has a defined benefit pension plan available to all full-time employees of CHUM Limited and defined contribution pension plans available to all full-time employees of CHUM Television Vancouver Inc. and former subsidiaries of CMI. Contributions to the defined contribution pension plan were $428 (2004 – $425). The change in the funded status of the company's defined benefit pension plan was as follows:

(in thousands of dollars)	2005	2004
Change in benefit obligation		
Balance – Beginning of year	$ 44,976	$ 38,486
Current service cost	4,264	4,117
Interest cost	3,260	2,841
Benefits paid	(1,872)	(1,045)
Actuarial losses	11,175	577
Balance – End of year	$ 61,803	$ 44,976
Change in plan assets		
Market value – Beginning of year	$ 40,323	$ 32,791
Actual return on plan assets	6,878	2,916
Employer's contributions	5,369	4,221
Employees' contributions	1,256	1,440
Benefits paid	(1,872)	(1,045)
Market value – End of year	$ 51,954	$ 40,323

	2005	2004
Plan assets – End of year consist of		
Equity securities	59%	61%
Debt securities	37%	35%
Real estate	4%	4%
	100%	100%

(in thousands of dollars)	2005	2004
Funded status – plan surplus (deficit)		
Deficit – End of year	$ (9,850)	$ (4,653)
Unamortized net actuarial loss	16,496	9,277
Unamortized transitional asset	(2,755)	(2,967)
Accrued pension benefit asset – End of year	$ 3,891	$ 1,657
Elements of defined benefit costs recognized in the year		
Current service cost – net of employees' contributions	$ 3,008	$ 2,677
Interest cost	3,261	2,841
Actual return on plan assets	(6,878)	(2,916)
Actuarial losses	11,175	577
Elements of defined benefit costs before adjustments to recognize the long-term nature of employee future benefit costs	10,566	3,179
Adjustments to recognize the long-term nature of employee future benefit costs		
Difference between expected return and actual return on plan assets for the year	3,675	284
Difference between actuarial gain recognized for the year and actual actuarial gain on accrued benefit obligation for the year	(10,894)	(256)
Amortization of the transitional obligation	(212)	(212)
	(7,431)	(184)
Defined benefit costs recognized	$ 3,135	$ 2,995

Assumptions

The significant actuarial assumptions used are as follows (weighted average):

	2005	2004
Accrued benefit obligation as at August 31		
Discount rate	5.50%	6.75%
Rate of compensation increase	4.00%	5.50%
Benefit costs for year ended August 31		
Discount rate	6.75%	6.75%
Expected long-term rate of return on plan assets	7.50%	7.50%
Rate of compensation increase	5.50%	5.50%

The measurement date is August 31, 2005. The last actuarial valuation of the defined benefit pension plan was performed on January 1, 2005. The next actuarial valuation of the defined benefit pension plan will be required as at January 1, 2006.

11. INCOME TAXES

The differences between the effective income tax rate reflected in the provision for income taxes and the Canadian statutory income tax rate are as follows:

	2005	2004
Corporate statutory rate of income taxes	35.8%	36.3%
Adjusted for the effect of		
Non-deductible preferred share dividends	0.5%	0.6%
Large corporations tax	0.9%	0.1%
Writeoff of loans	3.4%	–
Other	(0.4%)	1.1%
	40.2%	38.1%

The provision for income taxes comprises:

(in thousands of dollars)	2005	2004
Current	$ 17,549	$ 24,125
Future	10,458	(348)
	$ 28,007	$ 23,777

Future income tax liabilities and assets consist of the following:

(in thousands of dollars)	2005	2004
Liabilities		
Start-up costs	$ 398	$ 1,293
Broadcast licence	42,470	14,876
Goodwill	4,702	7,024
Property, plant and equipment	–	840
Other	1,482	840
	49,052	24,873
Assets		
Property, plant and equipment	41	–
Income tax losses available for carry-forward	7,853	1,938
Capital stock	674	1,356
Other	4,990	2,395
	13,558	5,689
	$ 35,494	$ 19,184

As at August 31, 2005, the company has non-capital loss carry-forwards for income tax purposes of $21,900. These losses expire from 2009 to 2015. In addition, the company has capital loss carry-forwards of $6,617. No benefit has been recognized in respect of capital loss carry-forwards.

12. SEGMENTED INFORMATION

The company's principal business activities are carried out through three reportable segments: television, radio and other. Television consists of the company's Ontario, Manitoba, Alberta and British Columbia television stations and specialty channels. Radio consists of AM and FM stations across the country. Other consists of the company's background music network and head office function.

Information on the operating groups is as follows:

(in thousands of dollars)	Television	Radio	Other	2005 Total
Revenues	$ 482,628	$ 134,479	$ 11,285	$ 628,392
Earnings (loss) before income taxes and non-controlling interest	60,635	39,979	(31,026)	69,588
Goodwill	155,438	55,855	5,636	216,929
Total assets	852,380	139,523	11,858	1,003,761
Capital expenditures	22,422	4,520	904	27,846
Depreciation	20,753	3,655	1,028	25,436

	Television	Radio	Other	2004 Total
Revenues	$ 426,987	$ 122,818	$ 10,987	$ 560,792
Earnings (loss) before income taxes and non-controlling interest	49,267	33,639	(20,475)	62,431
Goodwill	63,318	55,854	5,637	124,809
Total assets	559,302	142,962	14,159	716,423
Capital expenditures	17,023	2,709	653	20,385
Depreciation	18,764	3,408	1,723	23,895

13. FINANCIAL INSTRUMENTS

Fair values of financial instruments

The fair values of financial instruments included in current assets and liabilities, which include cash, accounts receivable, accounts payable and accrued liabilities and program rights payable, approximate their carrying values due to their short-term nature.

The fair values of loans receivable and investments included in investments and other assets are not readily determinable, as there are no fixed terms of repayment or market values.

The fair value of long-term debt approximates its carrying value, as interest charges under the credit facilities are based on current Canadian bank prime and bankers' acceptance rates.

The fair value of program rights payable approximates its carrying value.

Credit risk

The company is exposed to credit risk, primarily in relation to accounts receivable and loans receivable. Exposure to credit risk arises due to the concentration of individual balances with large advertising agencies or broadcasting distribution undertakings. The company performs regular credit assessments of its customers and provides allowances for potentially uncollectible accounts receivable.

Interest rate risk

The company is exposed to interest rate risk arising from fluctuations in interest rates on its drawings under its revolving credit facilities. The company has not entered into interest rate conversion agreements.

14. PRIOR YEAR'S CONSOLIDATED FINANCIAL STATEMENTS

Certain comparative figures for the year ended August 31, 2004 have been reclassified to conform to the 2005 basis of presentation.

The company restated its balances for goodwill and future income tax liabilities to reflect a change in the interpretation of the income tax treatment of the broadcasting licence acquired on the acquisition of CHUM Television Vancouver Inc. in October 2001. These balances were each reduced by $14,049.

Appendix B

SUN-RYPE
2005 Annual Report

Real Fruit Goodness.

Auditor's Report

To the Shareholders of Sun-Rype Products Ltd.

We have audited the balance sheets of Sun-Rype Products Ltd. as at December 31, 2005 and 2004, and the statements of earnings and retained earnings and cash flows for the years then ended. These financial statements are the responsibility of the Company's management. Our responsibility is to express an opinion on these financial statements based on our audits.

We conducted our audits in accordance with Canadian generally accepted auditing standards. Those standards require that we plan and perform an audit to obtain reasonable assurance whether the financial statements are free of material misstatement. An audit includes examining, on a test basis, evidence supporting the amounts and disclosures in the financial statements. An audit also includes assessing the accounting principles used and significant estimates made by management, as well as evaluating the overall financial statement presentation.

In our opinion, these financial statements present fairly, in all material respects, the financial position of the Company as at December 31, 2005 and 2004, and the results of its operations and cash flows for the years then ended in accordance with Canadian generally accepted accounting principles.

Deloitte & Touche LLP

Chartered Accountants
Vancouver, British Columbia
March 2, 2006

14 | 15

Balance Sheets

As at December 31 (in thousands of dollars)

	2005	2004
Assets		
Current assets		
Cash and cash equivalents	$ 19,965	$ 9,140
Accounts receivable (note 2)	11,868	12,194
Inventories (note 3)	13,331	14,546
Prepaid expenses	515	469
Future income taxes (note 9)	262	281
	45,941	36,630
Property, plant and equipment (note 4)	22,312	23,999
Deferred expenses	–	41
	$ 68,253	$ 60,670
Liabilities and Shareholders' Equity		
Current liabilities		
Promissory note (note 6)	$ 675	$ 675
Accounts payable and accrued liabilities	16,211	14,826
Income taxes payable	919	99
	17,805	15,600
Long-term obligations	430	184
Future income taxes (note 9)	1,735	1,828
	19,970	17,612
Shareholders' equity		
Share capital and contributed surplus (note 7)	18,698	18,698
Retained earnings	29,585	24,360
	48,283	43,058
	$ 68,253	$ 60,670

Commitments, guarantees and contingencies (note 11)

Approved by the Board of Directors

D. Selman, Director   **J. Alfonso**, Director

See accompanying notes to these financial statements.

Sun-Rype Products Ltd.

Statements of Earnings & Retained Earnings

For the years ended December 31 (in thousands of dollars except per share amounts)

	2005	2004
Net sales (note 14)	$ 125,411	$ 115,214
Cost of sales	80,618	75,973
Gross profit	44,793	39,241
Selling, general & administrative expenses	30,770	27,539
Amortization	3,898	3,358
Interest expense	39	86
Loss (gain) on capital dispositions	60	(691)
	34,767	30,292
Earnings before income taxes	10,026	8,949
Income taxes (note 9)	3,502	3,098
Net earnings	6,524	5,851
Retained earnings, beginning of year	24,360	19,483
Dividends paid	(1,299)	(974)
Retained earnings, end of year	$ 29,585	$ 24,360
Earnings per share (note 12)		
Basic	$ 0.60	$ 0.54
Diluted	0.60	0.54

See accompanying notes to these financial statements.

Sun-Rype Products Ltd.

Statements of Cash Flows

For the years ended December 31 (in thousands of dollars)

Cash provided by (used in):	2005	2004
Operating activities		
Net earnings	$ 6,524	$ 5,851
Non-cash items:		
Amortization of property, plant and equipment	3,857	3,346
Amortization of deferred expenses	41	12
Loss (gain) on capital dispositions	60	(691)
Future income taxes (note 9)	(74)	349
Employee future benefits and other	246	124
	10,654	8,991
Changes in non-cash working capital items (note 10)	3,700	(3,241)
	14,354	5,750
Financing activities		
Capital lease payment	–	(12)
Long-term obligations repaid	–	(586)
Dividends paid	(1,299)	(974)
Shares purchased and cancelled	–	(281)
Proceeds from issue of shares	–	182
	(1,299)	(1,671)
Investing activities		
Proceeds on capital dispositions	187	974
Expenditures for property, plant and equipment	(2,417)	(4,508)
	(2,230)	(3,534)
Increase in cash position	10,825	545
Cash and cash equivalents, beginning of year	9,140	8,595
Cash and cash equivalents, end of year	$ 19,965	$ 9,140
Supplemental information on cash flows		
Interest paid	$ 39	$ 37
Income taxes paid	2,947	3,244

See accompanying notes to these financial statements.

Notes to the Financial Statements

For the years ended December 31, 2005 and 2004

1. Significant Accounting Policies

(a) Basis of presentation

The financial statements have been prepared in accordance with Canadian generally accepted accounting principles ("Canadian GAAP").

(b) Measurement uncertainty

The presentation of financial statements in conformity with Canadian GAAP requires management to make estimates and assumptions that affect the reported amounts of assets and liabilities at the date of the financial statements and the reported amounts of revenues and expenses disclosed during reporting periods. Significant areas that involve estimates include provisions for uncollectible accounts receivable, the amortization rate and estimated useful life of property, plant and equipment, provisions for sales returns and allowances, and provisions for obsolete inventory. The actual amounts could differ from those estimates.

(c) Foreign currency translation

Transactions denominated in foreign currencies are translated into Canadian dollars at the exchange rate prevailing at the time of the transactions. At the balance sheet date, monetary assets and liabilities denominated in a foreign currency are translated at the period end rate of exchange. Exchange gains and losses arising on translation or settlement of foreign currency-denominated monetary items are included in the determination of net income for the current period.

(d) Cash and cash equivalents

Cash and cash equivalents include cash and short-term deposits in high quality, low risk money market instruments, which are cashable on demand 90 days or less from the date of issue.

(e) Inventories

Raw materials and supplies are recorded at the lower of cost, determined on a weighted average basis, and replacement cost.

Finished goods are recorded at the lower of cost and net realizable value. Finished goods include the cost of direct labour, direct materials and variable overheads related to production, applied at a standard rate, which approximates actual costs. Fixed overhead costs related to production are considered a period cost and, as such, are not included as a component of inventory but are expensed in the period they are incurred.

(f) Property, plant and equipment

Property, plant and equipment are recorded at cost, net of investment tax credits. The Company uses the straight-line method of providing amortization over the estimated lives of the property, plant and equipment as follows:

Buildings	15–40 years
Equipment	
Processing	5–25 years
Other	3–12 years

(g) Impairment of long-lived assets

The Company regularly compares the carrying value of long-lived assets to the estimated undiscounted future cash flows that may be generated from future use and eventual disposition of those assets. The Company records an impairment loss in the period when it is determined that the carrying amount of the asset exceeds the undiscounted estimate of future cash flows from the asset. The impairment loss is measured as the difference between the carrying amount and estimated fair value of the asset.

(h) Marketing and product launch costs

The Company records new product marketing and launch costs as an expense when incurred.

(i) Asset retirement obligations

The Company recognizes legal obligations associated with the retirement of property, plant and equipment that result from its acquisition, construction or normal operations. These obligations are recorded at fair value and subsequently adjusted for the accretion of discount and any changes in the underlying cash flows. The asset retirement cost is capitalized as part of the cost of the related asset, then amortized to earnings over the remaining life of the asset. The Company has determined that it has no material asset retirement obligations at December 31, 2005.

(j) Income taxes

The Company uses the liability method of accounting for income taxes. Under this method, temporary differences arising from the tax basis of an asset or liability and the corresponding carrying amount on the balance sheet are used to calculate future income tax assets or liabilities. Future income tax assets or liabilities are calculated using tax rates anticipated to be in effect in the periods that the temporary differences are expected to reverse. The effect of a change in income tax rates on future income tax assets and liabilities is recognized in income in the period the change occurs.

(k) Revenue recognition

Sales are recognized upon the transfer of risk and title to finished goods to customers, which typically occurs upon shipment and when collectibility of proceeds is reasonably assured. The Company deducts from gross sales all payments to customers related to pricing discounts, returns and allowances, certain sales and marketing discounts, promotion funds, co-operative advertising, coupons and product listing fees.

(l) Stock-based compensation plans

The Company has stock-based compensation plans, which are described more fully in note 7. Contributions by the Company to the employees' share purchase plan, which is available to all permanent full- and part-time employees, are recorded as a compensation expense. Shares are purchased on the employees' behalf by the Company's plan administrator.

The Company records stock-based compensation and other stock-based payments to employees and third parties as a stock-based compensation expense in the statement of earnings. The compensation expense is measured using a fair-value based method. As no stock options or stock-based payments were issued to employees or others during the years ended December 31, 2005 and 2004, the application of this accounting policy had no material impact on the results of operations and financial position of the Company or the related financial statement disclosure.

(m) Foreign exchange forward contracts

The Company periodically enters into foreign exchange forward contracts to manage foreign exchange risk associated with anticipated future purchases denominated in foreign currencies. Realized and unrealized gains and losses resulting from changes in the market value of these contracts are recorded as other investment income each period unless they meet specified criteria to qualify as hedging instruments under Canadian GAAP. If these contracts meet the criteria for hedging instruments, any unrealized gains or losses are deferred and recognized in earnings when the related hedge transaction occurs.

2. **Accounts Receivable** (in thousands of dollars)

	2005	2004
Trade	$ 10,964	$ 11,479
Other	904	715
Total	$ 11,868	$ 12,194

3. **Inventories** (in thousands of dollars)

	2005	2004
Parts	$ 1,899	$ 1,656
Raw materials and supplies	6,158	6,610
Finished goods	5,274	6,280
Total	$ 13,331	$ 14,546

4. **Property, Plant and Equipment** (tabular dollar amounts in thousands)

	2005			2004		
	Cost	Accumulated Amortization	Net Book Value	Cost	Accumulated Amortization	Net Book Value
Land	$ 170	$ –	$ 170	$ 179	$ –	$ 179
Buildings	16,475	11,487	4,988	16,085	10,796	5,289
Processing equipment	38,659	24,038	14,621	39,606	23,296	16,310
Other equipment	7,850	5,317	2,533	6,412	4,191	2,221
Total	$ 63,154	$ 40,842	$ 22,312	$ 62,282	$ 38,283	$ 23,999

5. **Bank Indebtedness**

The Company maintains a $15.0 million standby operating line of credit with a Canadian bank, which bears interest at the bank's prime lending rate (December 31, 2005 – 5.00%). This facility is secured by a general assignment of accounts receivable, inventories and demand debentures creating a fixed and floating charge over all Company assets. At December 31, 2005, no balances were outstanding under this operating line of credit.

20 | 21

6. Promissory Note

The promissory note, due on demand in the amount of $675,000 (2004 – $675,000), is secured by a letter of credit and bears interest at the bank prime rate plus $\frac{1}{4}$%.

7. Share Capital and Contributed Surplus

Authorized

100,000,000 – Common shares fully participating and without par value ("Common shares").

Authorized preference shares were cancelled in 2005. There were no preference shares issued and outstanding at the time of the cancellation.

Issued and fully paid capital (tabular dollar amounts in thousands)

	2005		2004	
	Shares	$	Shares	$
Common shares				
Opening balance	10,827,600	$17,756	10,796,900	$17,619
Issued for cash	–	–	57,500	182
Repurchased and cancelled	–	–	(26,800)	(45)
Closing balance	10,827,600	17,756	10,827,600	17,756
Contributed Surplus				
Opening balance		942		1,178
Excess of cost over book value on				
repurchased and cancelled shares		–		(236)
Closing balance		942		942
Total		$18,698		$18,698

Employee share purchase plan

The Company has an employee share purchase plan ("ESPP") enabling all permanent full- and part-time employees to acquire Common shares through payroll deductions with financial assistance provided by the Company. On September 27, 2005, the Company amended its ESPP whereby the 400,000 Company treasury shares reserved for issuance under the ESPP were cancelled. It was resolved that Company shares purchased in the future under the ESPP would continue to be either through a member firm of the Toronto Stock Exchange or from such other source as may be determined by the board of directors. Eligible employees may contribute monthly an amount, which shall not exceed 7% of salary, and the Company has agreed to contribute 35% of the amount contributed by each eligible employee. All funds and equity shares held by the administrator pursuant to the ESPP are held for the account of the individual eligible employee.

Normal course issuer bid transactions

During 2004, the Company maintained a normal course issuer bid ("NCIB") allowing shares to be repurchased for cancellation. In 2004, under the NCIB the Company purchased 26,800 shares for cancellation at an average price of $10.48 per share for a total consideration of $281,000. The excess purchase cost over book value of approximately $236,000 was applied to contributed surplus. There were no shares repurchased under the NCIB in 2005. The Company did not renew the NCIB when it expired on March 23, 2005.

Stock option transactions

The Company had a stock option plan that provided options to purchase Common shares of the Company for its employees, officers and directors. The options granted pursuant to this plan were exercisable at a price equal to or greater than the fair market value of the Common shares at the time the options were granted. During 2004, the remaining 57,500 stock options that were originally granted under this plan were exercised at a weighted average price of $3.16. No share options were issued in 2005 and there were none outstanding at December 31, 2005.

Shares reserved for future issuance

On September 27, 2005, the Company cancelled the remaining shares reserved for issuance (400,000 Common shares) under the ESPP. The Company has no shares reserved for future issuance in Treasury.

8. Post-employment Benefits (tabular dollar amounts in thousands)

The Company maintains a defined contribution (money purchase) pension plan for substantially all of its salaried employees. Pension costs charged to earnings for the defined contribution plan were $296,000 in 2005 (2004 – $287,000).

Under the terms of certain employment agreements with selected senior officers, the Company provides for compensation to be paid to the individuals at the date they cease their employment. These obligations, including any past service costs resulting from amendment to the compensation arrangements, are accrued on a straight-line basis over the expected average remaining service period of the employee. Details of the total post-employment benefit expense charged to earnings and the related long-term obligation for accrued benefits are as follows:

	2005	2004
Compensation expense	$ 246	$ 113
Accrued benefit obligation at December 31	430	184

At December 31, 2005, the estimated amount payable on settlement of this benefit obligation was $466,300 (2004 – $356,000).

9. Income Taxes (tabular dollar amounts in thousands)

Differences between the statutory income tax rate applicable to the Company and the Company's effective income tax rate applied to net earnings consist of the following:

	2005		2004	
Income tax provision at the combined basic Canadian federal and provincial rate	$ 3,501	34.9 %	$ 3,179	35.5%
Adjustment in income tax rate resulting from:				
Non-deductible expenses	37	0.4	56	0.6
Other	(36)	(0.4)	(137)	(1.5)
Effective income tax provision	$ 3,502	34.9%	$ 3,098	34.6%

The income tax provision consists of the following:

	2005	2004
Current tax expense	$ 3,576	$ 2,749
Future income tax expense	(74)	349
Total income tax provision	$ 3,502	$ 3,098

Significant components of future income tax assets and liabilities include:

	2005	2004
Accrued liabilities	$ 385	$ 368
Losses and other deductions	20	27
Future income tax assets	405	395
Property, plant and equipment	(1,869)	(1,923)
Other	(9)	(19)
Future income tax liabilities	(1,878)	(1,942)
Net future income tax liability	$ (1,473)	$ (1,547)

The net future income tax liability is reported as follows:

	2005	2004
Future income tax benefit (current)	$ 262	$ 281
Future income tax liabilities	(1,735)	(1,828)
Net future income tax liability	$ (1,473)	$ (1,547)

10. Changes in Non-cash Working Capital Items (in thousands of dollars)

	2005	2004
Accounts receivable	$ 326	$ (1,935)
Inventories	1,215	(1,275)
Prepaid expenses	(46)	(53)
Accounts payable and accrued liabilities	1,385	569
Income taxes	820	(547)
Total	$ 3,700	$ (3,241)

11. Commitments, Guarantees and Contingencies

(a) The Company has entered into operating lease and rental commitments for certain processing and office equipment and office space for the next five years as follows:

2006	$	444,425
2007		398,782
2008		150,844
2009		83,781
2010		55,043

(b) Under the terms of a processing and filling systems agreement, the Company is committed to purchasing a minimum number of units of beverage packaging material annually until 2009, or it would be liable for an annual penalty of $775,000. Management estimates that penalties would only be payable in the event of a dramatic decline in market demand.

(c) In the normal course of business the Company enters into commitments to purchase certain minimum quantities of energy and raw materials including fruit juice purées and concentrates, primarily in US dollars. At December 31, 2005, the Company had commitments to purchase approximately $3.7 million of these materials within the next year (2004 – $4.1 million).

(d) In January 2005, the Consumers' Association of Canada filed a class action lawsuit against a number of parties in the beverage industry, including Sun-Rype, other manufacturers, retailers and Encorp Pacific (Canada), the administrator of the beverage container deposit and recycling fee system in British Columbia ("BC"). The claim alleges the illegal use of consumer deposits collected under BC's beverage container stewardship program regulations. In January 2006, the defendants, including Sun-Rype, filed an application to strike the claim summarily as lacking sufficient merit to warrant certification of the class. Due to the early stages of this claim, the amount and likelihood of loss, if any, is not determinable. As a result, no provision for any loss has been recorded in these financial statements.

12. Earnings per Share

Basic earnings per share are computed using the weighted average number of Common shares outstanding during the period. The weighted average number of Common shares outstanding in 2005, on a non-diluted basis, was 10,827,600 (2004 – 10,817,203). Diluted earnings per share are calculated using the treasury stock method with the effect that the diluted average number of Common shares outstanding in 2005 was 10,827,600 shares (2004 – 10,834,835 shares).

13. Financial Instruments and Credit Risk

The Company's financial instruments include accounts receivable, a promissory note payable, accounts payable and long-term obligations for which the carrying values approximate fair values. Other instruments are instruments that may be settled by the delivery of non-financial assets, such as a commodity futures contract.

Credit risk is the risk of loss from non-performance of suppliers, customers or financial counter parties to a contract. The Company maintains credit policies that include a review of a counter party's financial condition, measurement of credit exposure and monitoring of concentration of exposure to any one customer or counter party. The Company's customers consist mainly of grocery stores, mass merchandisers and club stores across Canada. The Company's ten largest customers comprise approximately 84% of sales activity (2004 – 83%). At December 31, 2005, 87% (2004 – 84%) of accounts receivable were attributable to these customers.

24 | 25

The Company is exposed to foreign currency risk as certain of its raw material inputs are purchased in US dollars. In 2006, these purchases are estimated to be approximately US$29 million (2005 – US$26.6 million).

The Company periodically enters into foreign exchange forward purchase contracts to manage foreign exchange risk associated with anticipated future purchases and contractual commitments denominated in foreign currencies. As at December 31, 2005 and 2004, the Company had no financial or other instruments outstanding that related to hedging or forward purchase foreign exchange contracts.

14. **Segmented Information** (in millions of dollars)

The Company operates in the food and beverage industry in Canada and has only one industry segment.

Details of net sales by significant product lines are as follows:

	2005	2004
Beverage	$ 90.7	$ 83.8
Food	34.7	31.4
Total	$ 125.4	$ 115.2

15. **Comparative Figures**

Certain of the comparative figures have been reclassified in the financial statements to conform to the classifications used in 2005.

16. **Related Parties**

In the normal course of business, the Company sells beverage and food products to a major food retailer in western Canada that is controlled by a major shareholder that holds approximately 30% of the outstanding Common shares of Sun-Rype Products Ltd. Sales to this retailer are less than 10% of the Company's total sales.

17. **Subsequent Events**

On February 15, 2006, the Company declared a quarterly dividend of $0.03 per Common share, for a total of approximately $325,000, payable March 15, 2006, to shareholders of record at the close of business on February 28, 2006.

On March 2, 2006, the Company declared a special dividend of $1.50 per Common share, for a total of approximately $16 million, payable March 31, 2006, to shareholders of record at the close of business on March 15, 2006.

The Company has committed to purchase US$3.6 million using foreign exchange forward contracts and to use call and put options to purchase an additional US$18 million at market rates with a maximum price of $1.17 and a minimum price of $1.1056.

Appendix C

Summary of Generally Accepted Accounting Principles (GAAP)

Every technical area has professional associations and regulatory bodies that govern the practice of the profession. Accounting is no exception. In Canada, the Canadian Institute of Chartered Accountants (CICA) has the responsibility for issuing accounting standards that form the basis of generally accepted accounting principles (GAAP). The authority for setting GAAP was delegated to the CICA by the federal and provincial governments and the Canadian Securities Administrators in the 1970s.

The CICA's pronouncements, called *Recommendations*, are collected in Volume I of the *CICA Handbook*. The Recommendations specify how to account for particular business transactions and must be followed, except in those rare cases where a particular Recommendation or Recommendations would not lead to fair presentation. In those cases, the accountant should, using professional judgment, select the appropriate accounting principles. An accountant who determines that the *CICA Handbook* is not appropriate and selects some other basis of accounting must be prepared to defend that decision.

Each new Recommendation issued by the CICA becomes part of GAAP, the "accounting law of the land." In the same way that our laws draw authority from their acceptance by the people, GAAP depends on general acceptance by the business community. Throughout this book, we refer to GAAP as the proper way to do financial accounting.

The Objective of Financial Reporting

The basic objective of financial reporting is to provide information that is useful in making investment and lending decisions. Accounting information can be useful in decision making only if it is *understandable, relevant, reliable* and *comparable*.

Accounting information must be *understandable* to users if they are to be able to use it. *Relevant* information is useful in making predictions and for evaluating past performance—that is, the information has feedback value. For example, Canadian Tire Corporation, Limited's disclosure of the profitability of each of its lines of business is relevant for investor evaluations of the company. To be relevant, information must be timely. *Reliable* information is free from significant error—that is, it has validity. Also, it is free from the bias of a particular viewpoint—that is, it is verifiable and neutral. *Comparable* information can be compared from period to period to help investors and creditors assess the entity's progress through time. These characteristics combine to shape the assumptions and principles that comprise GAAP. Exhibit C-1 on the next page summarizes the assumptions, principles and constraints that accounting has developed to provide useful information for decision making.

Assumptions, Principles, and Financial Statements	Quick Summary	Text Reference
Assumptions		
Economic-entity assumption	Accounting draws a boundary around each organization to be accounted for.	Chapter 1
Going-concern assumption	Accountants assume the business will continue operating for the foreseeable future.	Chapter 1
Stable-monetary-unit assumption	Accounting information is expressed primarily in monetary terms.	Chapter 1
Cost/benefit constraint	The benefits of the information produced should exceed the costs of producing the information.	Chapter 1
Materiality constraint	Accountants consider the materiality of an amount when making disclosure decisions.	Chapters 1 and 6
Principles and Characteristics		
Reliability (objectivity) characteristic	Accounting records and statements are based on the most reliable data available	Chapter 1
Cost principle	Assets and services, revenues and expenses are recorded at their actual historical cost.	Chapter 1
Time period principle	Ensures that accounting information is reported at regular intervals.	Chapter 3
Revenue-recognition principle	Tells accountants when to record revenue (only after it has been earned) and the amount of revenue to record (the cash value of what has been received).	Chapter 3
Matching principle	Directs accountants to (1) identify all expenses incurred during the period, (2) measure the expenses, and (3) match the expenses against the revenues earned during the period. The goal is to measure net income.	Chapter 3
Consistency (comparability) characteristic	Businesses should use the same accounting methods from period to period.	Chapter 6
Full-disclosure principle	A company's financial statements should report enough information for outsiders to make informed decisions about the company.	Chapter 6
Financial Statements		
Balance sheet	Assets = Liabilities + Owners' Equity at a point in time (for proprietorships and partnerships). Assets = Liabilities + Shareholders' Equity at a point in time (for corporations).	Chapters 1 and 13
Income statement	Revenues and gains − Expenses and losses = Net income or net loss for the period	Chapters 1 and 14
Cash flow statement	Cash receipts − Cash payments = Increase or decrease in cash during the period, grouped under operating, investing, and financing activities	Chapters 1 and 17
Statement of owner's equity	Beginning owner's equity + Net income (or − Net loss) − Withdrawals = Ending owner's equity	Chapter 1
Statement of retained earnings	Beginning retained earnings + Net income (or − Net loss) − Dividends = Ending retained earnings	Chapter 14

Appendix D

Typical Charts of Accounts for Different Types of Businesses (For Businesses Discussed in Chapters 1–12).

SERVICE PROPRIETORSHIP

ASSETS

Cash
Accounts Receivable
Allowance for
  Doubtful Accounts
Notes Receivable,
  Short-Term
GST Recoverable
Interest Receivable
Supplies
Prepaid Rent
Prepaid Insurance
Notes Receivable,
  Long-Term
Land
Furniture
Accumulated
  Amortization—
  Furniture
Equipment
Accumulated
  Amortization—
  Equipment
Building
Accumulated
  Amortization—
  Building

LIABILITIES

Accounts Payable
Notes Payable, Short-Term
Salaries Payable
Wages Payable
Goods and Services Tax
  Payable
Employee Income Tax
  Payable
Employment Insurance
  Payable
Canada Pension Plan
  Payable
Quebec Pension Plan
  Payable
Employee Benefits Payable
Interest Payable
Unearned Service Revenue
Notes Payable, Long-Term

OWNER'S EQUITY

Owner, Capital
Owner, Withdrawals

Revenues and Gains

Service Revenue
Interest Revenue
Gain on Sale of Land
  (or Furniture,
  Equipment, or Building)

Expenses and Losses

Salaries Expense
Wages Expense
Employee Benefits
  Expense
Insurance Expense for
  Employees
Rent Expense
Insurance Expense
Supplies Expense
Bad-Debt Expense
Amortization Expense—
  Furniture
Amortization Expense—
  Equipment
Amortization Expense—
  Building
Property Tax Expense
Interest Expense
Miscellaneous Expense
Loss on Sale (or Exchange)
  of Land (Furniture,
  Equipment, or Buildings)

SERVICE PARTNERSHIP

Same as Service Proprietorship, except for Owners' Equity:

OWNERS' EQUITY

Partner 1, Capital
Partner 2, Capital
Partner N, Capital
Partner 1, Withdrawals
Partner 2, Withdrawals
Partner N, Withdrawals

(For Businesses Discussed in Chapters 13–26)

MERCHANDISING CORPORATION

ASSETS	LIABILITIES	SHAREHOLDERS' EQUITY

ASSETS

Cash
Held-for-Trading
   Investments
Fair-Value Valuation
   Allowance
Available-for-Sale
   Investments—Shares
Accounts Receivable
Allowance for Doubtful
   Accounts
Notes Receivable,
   Short-Term
Goods and Services Tax
   Recoverable
Interest Receivable
Inventory
Supplies
Prepaid Rent
Prepaid Insurance
Notes Receivable,
   Long-Term
Available-for-Sale
   Investments—Shares
Available-for-Sale
   Investments—Bonds
Investment Subject to
   Significant Influence
Held-to-Maturity
   Investments
Other Receivables,
   Long-Term
Land
Land Improvements
Accumulated
   Amortization—Land
   Improvements
Furniture and Fixtures
Accumulated
   Amortization—
   Furniture and Fixtures
Equipment
Accumulated
   Amortization—
   Equipment
Buildings
Accumulated
   Amortization—Buildings
Organization Cost
Franchises
Patents
Leaseholds
Goodwill

LIABILITIES

Accounts Payable
Notes Payable, Short-Term
Current Portion of
   Bonds Payable
Salaries Payable
Wages Payable
Goods and Services Tax
   Payable
Employee Income Tax
   Payable
Employment Insurance
   Payable
Canada Pension Plan
   Payable
Quebec Pension Plan
   Payable
Employee Benefits
   Payable
Interest Payable
Income Tax Payable
Unearned Service
   Revenue
Notes Payable, Long-Term
Bonds Payable
Lease Liability

Non-Controlling Interest

SHAREHOLDERS' EQUITY

Common Shares
Retained Earnings
Dividends

Revenues and Gains

Sales Revenue
Interest Revenue
Dividend Revenue
Equity-Method
   Investment Revenue
Gain on Sale of
   Investments
Unrealized Gain on Held-
   for-Trading Investments
Gain on Sale of Land
   (Furniture and Fixtures,
   Equipment, or Building)
Discontinued
   Operations—Gain
Extraordinary Gains

Expenses and Losses

Cost of Goods Sold
Salaries Expense
Wages Expense
Commission Expense
Payroll Benefits Expense
Insurance Expense for
   Employees
Rent Expense
Insurance Expense
Supplies Expense
Bad-Debt Expense
Amortization Expense—
   Land Improvements
Amortization Expense—
   Furniture and Fixtures
Amortization Expense—
   Equipment
Amortization Expense—
   Buildings
Incorporation Expense
Amortization Expense—
   Franchises
Amortization Expense—
   Leaseholds
Income Tax Expense
Loss on Writedown of
   Goodwill
Loss on Sale of
   Investments
Unrealized Loss on Held-
   for-Trading Investments
Loss on Sale (or Exchange)
   of Land (or Furniture
   and Fixtures,
   Equipment, or
   Buildings)
Discontinued
   Operations—Loss
Extraordinary Losses

MANUFACTURING CORPORATION

Same as Merchandising Corporation, except for Assets and Certain Expenses:

ASSETS	EXPENSES (CONTRA EXPENSES IF CREDIT BALANCE)

ASSETS

Inventories:
   Materials Inventory
   Work in Progress Inventory
   Finished Goods Inventory
Factory Wages
Factory Overhead

EXPENSES (CONTRA EXPENSES IF CREDIT BALANCE)

Overhead Production Volume Variance
Direct Materials Price Variance
Direct Materials Efficiency Variance
Direct Labour Price Variance
Direct Labour Efficiency Variance
Overhead Flexible Budget Variance

Glossary

Account The detailed record of the changes that have occurred in a particular asset, liability, or item of owner's equity during a period (p. 49).

Account payable A liability that is backed by the general reputation and credit standing of the debtor (p. 15).

Account receivable An asset, a promise to receive cash from customers to whom the business has sold goods or services (p. 16).

Accounting The system that measures business activities, processes that information into reports and financial statements, and communicates the findings to decision makers (p. 2).

Accounting cycle Process by which accountants produce an entity's financial statements for a specific period (p. 157).

Accounting equation The most basic tool of accounting: Assets = Liabilities + Owner's Equity (proprietorship) or Assets = Liabilities + Shareholders' Equity (corporation) (p. 12).

Accounting information system The combination of personnel, records, and procedures that a business uses to meet its need for financial data (p. 330).

Accrual-basis accounting Accounting that recognizes (records) the impact of a business event as it occurs, regardless of whether the transaction affected cash (p. 101).

Accrued expense An expense that has been incurred but not yet paid in cash (pp. 111, 538).

Accrued liability Another name for an accrued expense (p. 538).

Accrued revenue A revenue that has been earned but not yet received in cash (p. 113).

Accumulated amortization The cumulative sum of all amortization expense from the date of acquiring a capital asset (p. 110).

Acid-test ratio Ratio of the sum of cash plus short-term investments plus net current receivables to current liabilities. Tells whether the entity could pay all its current liabilities if they came due immediately. Also called the quick ratio (p. 453).

Adjusted trial balance A list of all the ledger accounts with their adjusted balances (p. 118).

Adjusting entry Entry made at the end of the period to assign revenues to the period in which they are earned and expenses to the period in which they are incurred. Adjusting entries help measure the period's income and bring the related

asset and liability accounts to correct balances for the financial statements (p. 106).

Aging-of-accounts-receivable method A way to estimate bad debts by analyzing individual accounts receivable according to the length of time they have been due (p. 441).

Allowance for Doubtful Accounts A contra account, related to accounts receivable, that holds the estimated amount of collection losses. Also called allowance for uncollectible accounts (p. 439).

Allowance for Uncollectible Accounts Another name for allowance for doubtful accounts (p. 439).

Allowance method A method of recording collection losses based on estimates made prior to determining that the business will not collect from specific customers (p. 439).

Amortizable cost The asset's cost minus its estimated residual value (p. 489).

Amortization The term the *CICA Handbook* uses to describe the systematic charging of the cost of a capital asset; it is often called depletion when applied to natural resources. The term is also used to describe the writing off to expense of capital assets (pp. 109, 488).

Amortization expense That portion of the cost of capital assets or natural resources used up in a particular period (p. 503).

Asset An economic resource a business owns that is expected to be of benefit in the future (p. 12).

Audit The examination of financial statements by outside accountants, the most significant service that public accountants perform. The conclusion of an audit is the accountant's professional opinion about the financial statements (p. 392).

Bad-debt expense Cost to the seller of extending credit. Arises from the failure to collect from credit customers. Also called doubtful-account expense or uncollectible-account expense (p. 439). (p. 439).

Balance sheet List of an entity's assets, liabilities and owner equity (proprietorship) or shareholder equity (corporation) as of a specific date. Also called the statement of financial position (p. 20).

Balance-sheet approach Another name for the aging-of-accounts-receivable method of estimating uncollectibles (p. 441).

Bank collection Collection of money by the bank on behalf of a depositor (p. 399).

Bank reconciliation Process of explaining the reasons for the difference between a depositor's records and the bank's records about the depositor's bank account (p. 397).

Bank statement Document for a particular bank account showing its beginning and ending balances and listing the month's transactions that affected the account (p. 395).

Batch processing Computerized accounting for similar transactions in a group or batch (p. 335).

Betterment Expenditure that increases the capacity or efficiency of an asset or extends its useful life. Capital expenditures are debited to an asset account (p. 487).

Brand name Distinctive identification of a product or service (p. 505).

Canada (or Quebec) Pension Plan All employees and self-employed persons in Canada (except in Quebec where the pension plan is the Quebec Pension Plan) between 18 and 70 years of age are required to contribute to the Canada Pension Plan administered by the Government of Canada (p. 547).

Capital Another name for the owner's equity of a business (p. 12).

Capital asset Long-lived tangible asset, like property, plant and equipment, natural resource, and intangible asset other than goodwill used in the operation of a business. Its value is in use (pp. 109, 170, 481).

Capital cost allowance Amortization allowed for income tax purposes by Canada Revenue Agency; the rates allowed are called capital cost allowance rates (p. 510).

Capitalize a cost To record a cost as part of an asset's cost, rather than as an expense (p. 486).

Carrying value of a capital asset The asset's cost less accumulated amortization (p. 110).

Cash-basis accounting Accounting that records only transactions in which cash is received or paid (p. 101).

Cash flow statement Reports cash receipts and cash payments classified according to the entity's major activities: operating, investing, and financing (p. 20).

Cash payments journal Special journal used to record cash payments by cheque (p. 347).

Cash receipts journal Special journal used to record cash receipts (p. 342).

Chart of accounts List of all the accounts and their account numbers in the ledger (p. 68).

Cheque Document that instructs the bank to pay the designated person or business the specified amount of money (p. 395).

Closing entries Entries that transfer the revenue, expense, and owner withdrawal balances from these respective accounts to the capital account (p. 165).

Closing the accounts Step in the accounting cycle at the end of the period that prepares the accounts for recording the transactions of the next period. Closing the accounts consists of journalizing and posting the closing entries to set the balances of the revenue, expense, and owner withdrawal accounts to zero (p. 163).

Collection period Another name for the days' sales in receivables (p. 454).

Commercial substance In an exchange of tangible capital assets, commercial substance exists when an entity's future cash flows from the new asset received will differ in risk, timing, or amount from the cash flows from the old asset given up. With commercial substance, the new asset is recorded at its fair market value, and a gain or loss on the exchange is recorded if applicable (p. 501).

Computer virus A malicious computer program that reproduces itself, gets included in program code without consent, and destroys program code (p. 394).

Conservatism Concept by which the least favourable figures are presented in the financial statements (p. 301).

Consistency characteristic A business must use the same accounting methods and procedures from period to period or disclose a change in method (p. 300).

Contra account An account that always has a companion account and whose normal balance is opposite that of the companion account (p. 110).

Control account An account whose balance equals the sum of the balances in a group of related accounts in a subsidiary ledger (p. 342).

Controller The chief accounting officer of a company (p. 391).

Copyright Exclusive right to reproduce and sell a book, musical composition, film, or other work of art. Issued by the federal government, copyrights extend 50 years beyond the author's life (p. 505).

Corporation A business owned by shareholders that begins when the federal government or provincial government approves its articles of incorporation. A corporation is a legal entity, an "artificial person," in the eyes of the law (p. 7).

Cost of goods sold The cost of the inventory that the business has sold to customers, the largest single expense of most merchandising businesses. Also called cost of sales (pp. 214, 245).

Cost of sales Another name for cost of goods sold (pp. 214, 245).

Cost principle States that assets and services are recorded at their purchase cost and that the accounting record of the asset continues to be based on cost rather than current market value (p. 11).

Credit The right side of an account (p. 53).

Credit memorandum (credit memo) The document issued by a seller for a credit to a customer's Account Receivable (p. 350).

Creditor The party to a credit transaction who sells a service or merchandise and obtains a receivable (pp. 436, 448).

Current asset An asset that is expected to be converted to cash, sold, or consumed during the next 12 months, or within the business's normal operating cycle if longer than a year (p. 170).

Current liability A debt due to be paid within one year or one of the entity's operating cycles if the cycle is longer than a year (p. 171).

Current portion of long-term debt Amount of the principal that is payable within one year (p. 537).

Current ratio Current assets divided by current liabilities. Measures the ability to pay current liabilities from current assets (p. 174).

Database Computerized storehouse of information that can be systematically assessed in a variety of report forms (p. 332).

Days' sales in receivables Ratio of average net accounts receivable to one day's sales. Indicates how many days' sales remain in Accounts Receivable awaiting collection (p. 454).

Debit The left side of an account (p. 53).

Debit memorandum (debit memo) The document issued by a buyer to reduce the buyer's Account Payable to a seller (p. 351).

Debt ratio Ratio of total liabilities to total assets. Gives the proportion of a company's assets that it has financed with debt (p. 175).

Debtor The party to a credit transaction who makes a purchase and creates a payable (pp. 436, 448).

Default on a note Failure of the maker of a note to pay at maturity. Also called dishonour of a note (p. 451).

Deferred revenue Another name for unearned revenue (p. 114).

Depletion Another word to describe the amortization of natural resources or wasting assets (p. 503).

Deposit in transit A deposit recorded by the company but not yet by its bank (p. 399).

Direct write-off method A method of accounting for bad debts by which the company waits until the credit department decides that a customer's account receivable is uncollectible and then debits Bad-Debt Expense and credits the customer's Account Receivable (p. 444).

Disclosure principle A business's financial statements must report enough information for outsiders to make knowledgeable decisions about the business (p. 300).

Discounting a note receivable Selling a note receivable before its maturity date (p. 457).

Dishonour of a note Failure of the maker of a note to pay a note receivable at maturity. Also called default on a note (p. 451).

Double-declining-balance method A type of amortization method that expenses a relatively larger amount of an asset's cost nearer the start of its useful life than does the straight-line method (p. 492).

Doubtful-account expense Another name for bad-debt expense (p. 439).

Due date The date on which the final payment of a note is due. Also called the maturity date (p. 448).

Electronic funds transfer (EFT) System that transfers cash by digital communication rather than paper documents (p. 395).

Employee compensation Payroll, a major expense of many businesses (p. 538).

Employment Insurance All employees and employers in Canada must contribute to the Employment Insurance Fund, which provides assistance to unemployed workers (p. 548).

Encryption The process of rearranging plain-text messages by some mathematical formula to achieve confidentiality (p. 394).

Enterprise resource planning (ERP) system Integrates all company data into a single data warehouse (p. 335).

Entity An organization or a section of an organization that, for accounting purposes, stands apart from other organizations and individuals as a separate economic unit. This is the most basic concept in accounting (p. 10).

Estimated residual value Expected cash value of an asset at the end of its useful life. Also called residual value, scrap value, and salvage value (p. 489).

Estimated useful life Length of the service that a business expects to get from an asset; may be expressed in years, units of output, kilometres, or other measures (p. 489).

Expense Decrease in owner's equity (proprietorship) or shareholders' equity (corporation) that occurs in the course of delivering goods or services to customers or clients (p. 13).

Financial accounting The branch of accounting that provides information to people outside the business (p. 4).

Financial statements Business documents that report financial information about an entity to persons and organizations outside the business (p. 2).

Firewall Barriers used to prevent entry into a computer network or a part of a network. Examples include passwords, personal identification numbers (PINs), and fingerprints (p. 394).

First-in, first-out (FIFO) inventory cost method Inventory costing method by which the first costs into inventory are the first costs out to cost of goods sold. Ending inventory is based on the costs of the most recent purchases (p. 291).

Franchise Privileges granted by a private business or a government to sell a product or service in accordance with specified conditions (p. 505).

General journal Journal used to record all transactions that do not fit one of the special journals (p. 338).

General ledger Ledger of accounts that are reported in the financial statements (p. 341).

Generally accepted accounting principles (GAAP) Accounting guidelines, formulated by the CICA's Accounting Standards Committee, that govern how businesses report their results in financial statements to the public (p. 8).

Going-concern assumption Accountants' assumption that the business will continue operating in the forseeable future (p. 11).

Goodwill Excess of the cost of an acquired company over the sum of the market values of its net assets (assets minus liabilities) (p. 505).

Gross margin Excess of sales revenue over cost of goods sold. Also called gross profit (p. 214).

Gross margin method A way to estimate inventory based on a rearrangement of the cost of goods sold model: Beginning inventory + Net purchases = Cost of goods available for sale. Cost of goods available for sale − Cost of goods sold = Ending inventory. Also called the gross profit method (p. 304).

Gross margin percentage Gross margin divided by net sales revenue. A measure of profitability (p. 237).

Gross pay Total amount of salary, wages, commissions, or any other employee compensation before taxes and other deductions are taken out (p. 546).

Gross profit Another name for gross margin (p. 214).

Gross profit method Another name for the gross margin method (p. 304).

Hardware Electronic equipment that includes computers, disk drives, monitors, printers, and the network that connects them (p. 331).

Imprest system A way to account for petty cash by maintaining a constant balance in the petty cash account, supported by the fund (cash plus disbursement tickets) totalling the same amount (p. 410).

Income from operations Another name for operating income (pp. 232, 250).

Income statement List of an entity's revenues, expenses, and net income or net loss for a specific period. Also called the statement of operations (p. 18).

Income-statement approach Another name for the percent-of-sales method of estimating uncollectibles (p. 440).

Income Summary A temporary "holding tank" account into which the revenues and expenses are transferred prior to their final transfer to the Capital account (p. 166).

Intangible asset An asset with no physical form, a special right to current and expected future benefits (pp. 481, 504).

Interest The revenue to the payee for loaning out the principal, and the expense to the maker for borrowing the principal (p. 448).

Interest period The period of time during which interest is to be computed, extending from the original date of the note to the maturity date (p. 448).

Interest rate The percentage rate that is multiplied by the principal amount to compute the amount of interest on a note (p. 448).

Internal control Organizational plan and all the related measures adopted by an entity to meet management's objectives of discharging statutory responsibilities, profitability, prevention and detection of fraud and error, safeguarding of assets, reliability of accounting records, and timely preparation of reliable financial information (p. 388).

Inventory All goods that a company owns and expects to sell in the normal course of operation (p. 213).

Inventory turnover Ratio of cost of goods sold to average inventory. Measures the number of times a company sells its average level of inventory during a year (p. 237).

Invoice A seller's request for cash from the purchaser (p. 218).

Journal The chronological accounting record of an entity's transactions (p. 49).

Last-in, first-out (LIFO) inventory cost method Inventory costing method by which the last costs into inventory are the first costs out to cost of goods sold. This

method leaves the oldest costs—those of beginning inventory and the earliest purchases of the period—in ending inventory (p. 292).

Leasehold Prepayment that a lessee (renter) makes to secure the use of an asset from a lessor (landlord) (p. 505).

Ledger The book of accounts (p. 50).

Liability An economic obligation (a debt) payable to an individual or an organization outside the business (p. 12).

Licence Privileges granted by a private business or a government to sell a product or service in accordance with special conditions (p. 505).

Limited–liability company (LLC) A form of proprietorship in which the company and not the proprietor is liability for the company's debts (p. 8).

Limited-liability partnership (LLP) A form of partnership in which each partner's personal liability for the business's debts is limited to a certain amount (p. 8).

Line of credit Similar to a bank loan, it is negotiated once, then drawn upon when needed. Interest is paid monthly only on the amount of the line of credit actually used (p. 534).

Liquidity Measure of how quickly an item may be converted to cash (p. 170).

Long-term asset An asset other than a current asset (p. 170).

Long-term liability A liability other than a current liability (p. 171).

Lower-of-cost-or-market (LCM) rule Requires that an asset be reported in the financial statements at the lower of its historical cost or its market value (current replacement cost for inventory) (p. 301).

Maker of a note The person or business that signs the note and promises to pay the amount required by the note agreement. The maker is the debtor (p. 448).

Management accounting The branch of accounting that generates information for internal decision makers of a business, such as top executives (p. 4).

Matching principle The basis for recording expenses. Directs accountants to identify all expenses incurred during the period, measure the expenses, and match them against the revenues earned during that same span of time (p. 104).

Materiality concept A company must perform strictly proper accounting only for items and transactions that are significant to the business's financial statements (p. 301).

Maturity date The date on which the final payment of a note is due. Also called the due date (p. 448).

Maturity value The sum of the principal and interest due at the maturity date of a note (p. 448).

Menu A list of options for choosing computer functions (p. 334).

Module Separate compatible units of an accounting package that are integrated to function together (p. 336).

Moving-weighted-average cost method A weighted-average cost method where unit cost is changed to reflect each new purchase of inventory (p. 294).

Multi-step income statement Format that contains subtotals to highlight significant relationships. In addition to net income, it also presents gross margin and income from operations (p. 236).

Net earnings Another name for net income or net profit (p. 18).

Net income Excess of total revenues over total expenses. Also called net earnings or net profit (p. 18).

Net loss Excess of total expenses over total revenues (p. 18).

Net pay Gross pay minus all deductions; the amount of employee compensation that the employee actually takes home (p. 546).

Net profit Another name for net income or net earnings (p. 18).

Net purchases Purchases less purchase discounts and purchase returns and allowances (p. 244).

Net sales Sales revenue less sales discounts and sales returns and allowances (p. 213).

Network The system of electronic linkages that allow different computers to share the same information (p. 331).

Nominal account Another name for a temporary account (p. 164).

Nonsufficient funds (NSF) cheque A "bounced" cheque, one for which the maker's bank account has insufficient money to pay the cheque (p. 400).

Normal balance The balance that appears on the side of an account—debit or credit—where we record increases (p. 58).

Note payable A liability evidenced by a written promise to make a future payment (p. 15).

Note receivable An asset evidenced by another party's written promise that entitles you to receive cash in the future (p. 50).

Note term Another name for the interest period of a note (p. 448).

Objectivity characteristic Another name for the reliability characteristic (p. 10).

Online processing Computerized processing of related functions, such as the recording and posting of transactions, on a continuous basis (p. 335).

Operating cycle The time span during which cash is paid for goods and services that are sold to customers who then pay the business in cash (p. 170).

Operating expense Expense, other than cost of goods sold, that is incurred in the entity's major line of business: rent, amortization, salaries, wages, utilities, property tax, and supplies expense (pp. 232, 278).

Operating income Gross margin minus operating expenses plus any other operating revenues. Also called income from operations (pp. 232, 250).

Other expense Expense that is outside the main operations of a business, such as a loss on the sale of capital assets (pp. 232, 250).

Other revenue Revenue that is outside the main operations of a business, such as a gain on the sale of capital assets (pp. 232, 250).

Outstanding cheque A cheque issued by the company and recorded on its books but not yet paid by its bank (p. 399).

Owner's equity In a proprietorship, the claim of an owner of a business to the assets of the business. Also called capital (p. 12).

Owner withdrawals Amounts removed from the business by an owner (p. 13).

Partnership An unincorporated business with two or more owners (p. 7).

Patent A federal government grant giving the holder the exclusive right for 20 years to produce and sell an invention (p. 504).

Payee of a note The person or business to whom the maker of a note promises future payment. The payee is the creditor (p. 448).

Payroll Employee compensation, a major expense of many businesses (p. 538).

Percent-of-sales method A method of estimating uncollectible receivables as a percent of the net credit sales (or net sales) (p. 440).

Periodic inventory system Type of inventory accounting system in which the business does not keep a continuous record of the inventory on hand. Instead, at the end of the period the business makes a physical count of the on-hand inventory and applies the appropriate unit costs to determine the cost of the ending inventory (p. 216).

Permanent account Another name for a real account—asset, liability, or owner's equity—that is not closed at the end of the period (p. 164).

Perpetual inventory system Type of accounting inventory system in which the business keeps a continuous record for each inventory item to show the inventory on hand at all times (p. 216).

Petty cash Fund containing a small amount of cash that is used to pay minor expenditures (p. 409).

Postclosing trial balance List of the ledger accounts and their balances at the end of the period after the journalizing and posting of the closing entries. The last step of the accounting cycle, the postclosing trial balance ensures that the ledger is in balance for the start of the next accounting period (p. 169).

Posting Transferring of amounts from the journal to the ledger (p. 57).

Prepaid expense A category of miscellaneous assets that typically expire or get used up in the near future. Examples include prepaid rent, prepaid insurance, and supplies (p. 107).

Principal The amount loaned out by the payee and borrowed by the maker of a note (p. 448).

Promissory note A written promise to pay a specified amount of money at a particular future date (p. 448).

Property, plant, and equipment Long-lived tangible capital assets, such as land, buildings, and equipment, used to operate a business (p. 170).

Proprietorship An unincorporated business with a single owner (p. 7).

Purchases journal Special journal used to record all purchases of inventory, supplies and other assets on account (p. 345).

Quick ratio Another name for the acid-test ratio (p. 453).

Real account Another name for a permanent account (p. 164).

Real-time processing Computerized processing of related functions, such as the recording and posting of transactions, on a continuous basis. Also called online processing (p. 335).

Receivable A monetary claim against a business or an individual, acquired mainly by selling goods and services and by lending money (p. 436).

Reliability characteristic Requires that accounting information be dependable (free from error and bias). Also called the objectivity characteristic (p. 10).

Repair Expenditure that merely maintains an asset in its existing condition or restores the asset to good working order. Repairs are expensed (matched against revenue) (p. 487).

Retail method A method of estimating ending inventory based on the total cost and total selling price of opening inventory and net purchases (p. 305).

Revenue Increase in owner's equity (proprietorship) or shareholders' equity (corporation) that is earned by delivering goods or services to customers or clients (p. 13).

Revenue-recognition principle The basis for recording revenues; tells accountants when to record revenue and the amount of revenue to record (p. 103).

Reversing entry An entry that switches the debit and the credit of a previous adjusting entry. The reversing entry is dated the first day of the period following the adjusting entry (p. 183).

Sales Another name for sales revenue (p. 213).

Sales discount Reduction in the amount receivable from a customer, offered by the seller as an incentive for the customer to pay promptly. A contra account to sales revenue (p. 225).

Sales journal Special journal used to record credit sales (p. 339).

Sales returns and allowances Decrease in the seller's receivable from a customer's return of merchandise or from granting the customer an allowance from the amount the customer owes the seller. A contra account to sales revenue (p. 225).

Sales revenue Amount that a merchandiser earns from selling inventory before subtracting expenses. Also called sales (p. 213).

Salvage value Another name for estimated residual value (p. 489).

Scrap value Another name for estimated residual value (p. 489).

Server The main computer in a network, where the program and data are stored (p. 331).

Shareholder A person who owns shares of stock in a corporation (p. 7).

Short-term note payable Note payable due within one year, a common form of financing (p. 533).

Single-step income statement Format that groups all revenues together and then lists and deducts all expenses together without drawing any subtotals (p. 236).

Software Set of programs or instructions that cause the computer to perform the work desired (p. 331).

Special journal An accounting journal designed to record one specific type of transaction (p. 338).

Specific identification method Another name for the specific-unit-cost method (p. 290).

Specific-unit-cost method Inventory cost method based on the specific cost of particular units of inventory (p. 290).

Spreadsheet A computer program that links data by means of formulas and functions; an electronic work sheet (p. 337).

Stable-monetary-unit assumption Accountants' basis for ignoring the effect of inflation and making no adjustments for the changing value of the dollar (p. 11).

Statement of earnings Another name for the income statement (p. 18).

Statement of financial position Another name for the balance sheet (p. 20).

Statement of operations Another name for the income statement. Also called the statement of earnings (p. 18).

Statement of owner's equity Summary of the changes in an entity's owner's equity during a specific period (p. 19).

Straight-line method Amortization method in which an equal amount of amortization expense is assigned to each year (or period) of asset use (p. 490).

Subsidiary ledger Book of accounts that provides supporting details on individual balances, the total of which appears in a general ledger account (p. 341).

Temporary account Another name for a nominal account. The revenue and expense accounts that relate to a particular accounting period and are closed at the end of the period are temporary accounts. For a proprietorship, the owner withdrawal account is also temporary (p. 164).

Time period Another name for the interest period (p. 448).

Time period principle Ensures that accounting information is reported at regular intervals (p. 105).

Trademarks and trade names Distinctive identifications of a product or service (p. 505).

Transaction An event that affects the financial position of a particular entity and may be reliably recorded (p. 13).

Treasurer The person in a company responsible for cash management (p. 391).

Trial balance A list of all the ledger accounts with their balances (p. 50).

Trojan A computer virus that does not reproduce but gets included into program code without consent and performs actions that can be destructive (p. 394).

Uncollectible-account expense Another name for bad-debt expense (p. 439).

Unearned revenue A liability created when a business collects cash from customers in advance of doing work for the customer. The obligation is to provide a product or a service in the future. Also called deferred revenue (p. 114).

Units-of-production (UOP) method Amortization method by which a fixed amount of amortization is assigned to each unit of output produced by the capital asset (p. 491).

Weighted-average cost method Inventory costing method based on the weighted-average cost of inventory during the period. Weighted-average cost is determined by dividing the cost of goods available for sale by the number of units available. Also called the average cost method (p. 300).

Withheld income tax Income tax deducted from employees' gross pay (p. 547).

Work sheet A columnar document designed to help move data from the trial balance to the financial statements (p. 158a).

Workers' Compensation A provincially administered plan that is funded by contributions by employers and that provides financial support for workers injured on the job (p. 549).

Index